African American National Biography

African American National Biography

SECOND EDITION

HENRY LOUIS GATES JR.
EVELYN BROOKS HIGGINBOTHAM

Editors in Chief

VOLUME 8: MCCROREY, MARY JACKSON – PATTERSON, GILBERT EARL

OXFORD
UNIVERSITY PRESS

OXFORD
UNIVERSITY PRESS

Oxford University Press is a department of the University of Oxford.
It furthers the University's objective of excellence in research, scholarship,
and education by publishing worldwide.

Oxford   New York
Auckland   Cape Town   Dar es Salaam   Hong Kong   Karachi
Kuala Lumpur   Madrid   Melbourne   Mexico City   Nairobi
New Delhi   Shanghai   Taipei   Toronto

With offices in
Argentina   Austria   Brazil   Chile   Czech Republic   France   Greece
Guatemala   Hungary   Italy   Japan   Poland   Portugal   Singapore
South Korea   Switzerland   Thailand   Turkey   Ukraine   Vietnam

Oxford is a registered trademark of Oxford University Press in the UK and certain other countries.

Published in the United States of America by
Oxford University Press
198 Madison Avenue, New York, NY 10016

Library of Congress Cataloging-in-Publication Data
African American national biography / editors in chief Henry Louis Gates Jr., Evelyn Brooks Higginbotham. – 2nd ed.
p. cm.
Includes bibliographical references and index.
ISBN 978-0-19-999036-8 (volume 1; hdbk.); ISBN 978-0-19-999037-5 (volume 2; hdbk.); ISBN 978-0-19-999038-2 (volume 3; hdbk.);
ISBN 978-0-19-999039-9 (volume 4; hdbk.); ISBN 978-0-19-999040-5 (volume 5; hdbk.); ISBN 978-0-19-999041-2 (volume 6; hdbk.);
ISBN 978-0-19-999042-9 (volume 7; hdbk.); ISBN 978-0-19-999043-6 (volume 8; hdbk.); ISBN 978-0-19-999044-3 (volume 9; hdbk.);
ISBN 978-0-19-999045-0 (volume 10; hdbk.); ISBN 978-0-19-999046-7 (volume 11; hdbk.); ISBN 978-0-19-999047-4 (volume 12;
hdbk.); ISBN 978-0-19-992077-8 (12-volume set; hdbk.).
1. African Americans – Biography – Encyclopedias.   2. African Americans – History – Encyclopedias.
I. Gates, Henry Louis.   II. Higginbotham, Evelyn Brooks, 1945-
E185.96.A4466 2012
920'.009296073 – dc23
[B]
2011043281

1 3 5 7 9 8 6 4 2
Printed in the United States of America
on acid-free paper

African American National Biography

McCrorey, Mary Jackson (1869–13 Jan. 1944), social welfare activist, was born Mary Catherine Jackson in Athens, Georgia, the youngest of eight children born to Alfred Jackson and his wife, Louise. Mary was the first of the Jackson children born in freedom; prior to Emancipation her parents had been the slaves of a professor at the University of Georgia in Athens. Little is known about her early life, but she graduated from Atlanta University around 1890 and later attended summer school at both Harvard University and the University of Chicago.

Jackson worked as a teacher in the Athens public school system from 1891 until 1895, when LUCY CRAFT LANEY appointed her as assistant principal of the Haines Institute in Augusta, Georgia. The institute, founded by Laney in 1883, was at that time one of the foremost black-run private colleges in the South and followed a traditional liberal arts curriculum. Jackson, who was for several years the most popular member of the Haines faculty, taught Greek until she left the institute in 1916 upon her marriage that September to Dr. Henry Lawrence McCrorey, a widower and the president of Biddle University (later Johnson C. Smith University) in Charlotte, North Carolina. Forty-seven years old at the time of her marriage, Mary Jackson McCrorey did not have any children of her own, but she helped to raise the four children from her husband's first marriage.

McCrorey performed secretarial duties at Johnson C. Smith University, but she increasingly focused her energies in Charlotte on establishing North Carolina's first African American branch of the Young Women's Christian Association (YWCA).

Lucy Laney encouraged McCrorey's interest in social welfare work at the Haines Institute, which in addition to its academic mission provided Augusta's black community with its first kindergarten. In common with other southern black progressive-era settlements such as LUGENIA BURNS HOPE's Neighborhood Union in Atlanta, the Haines Institute promoted hygiene and other public health programs to the growing number of working-class black migrants who began arriving from the countryside at the turn of the twentieth century. America's entry into World War I in 1917 accelerated this transition from farm to factory and exacerbated the problems of overcrowded housing, inadequate health care, crime, and prostitution in the black neighborhoods of several southern communities.

To address these social problems McCrorey established her YWCA branch in Charlotte in 1916. It was only the third black branch founded in the South, largely because of resistance by white southern YWCA leaders who believed that the institution should be the preserve of middle-class southern whites and rejected McCrorey's view of the YWCA as a haven for impoverished recent migrants. Moreover, national YWCA regulations limited McCrorey's freedom of maneuver. Although she chaired Charlotte's PHILLIS WHEATLEY Branch, McCrorey was forced to gain the approval of the three white members of a five-person board for all funding requests and in making all major decisions. A skillful diplomat, McCrorey was careful not to criticize her board's white leaders in public for fear of losing their financial support, and she forged a close relationship with Ida MacDonald Hook, Charlotte's preeminent white female reformer. Nor did McCrorey challenge the principle of segregated black and white YWCA branches. Along with fellow reformers Hope and CHARLOTTE HAWKINS BROWN, however, she did successfully lobby the YWCA's national organization to appoint Brown as its first African American board member in 1920.

McCrorey's YWCA work during World War I cemented her friendships with Brown and Hope and emboldened her in her relationships with southern white women reformers. She also became active in the Charlotte branch of the NAACP, one of several formed in North Carolina during the war, and invited W. E. B. DuBois there, a radical move given the organization's avowedly integrationist platform. Two years later, in July 1920, McCrorey urged delegates to the National Association of Colored Women (NACW) annual meeting in Tuskegee, Alabama, to abandon their organization's traditional emphasis on moral uplift. Instead, she urged the NACW to seek closer—and more equal—links with white feminists and other reformers. McCrorey also served on the board of the North Carolina chapter of a southern organization, the Commission on Interracial Cooperation (CIC), which was established that same year. Although the CIC marked something of an improvement in southern race relations, white members refused to endorse McCrorey's proposal that the organization issue a statement condemning lynching and supporting suffrage for all citizens, regardless of gender or race. Although Brown and Hope supported McCrorey, two of the leading black members of the CIC, MARGARET MURRAY WASHINGTON, widow of BOOKER T. WASHINGTON, and JENNIE DEE MOTON, wife of Washington's successor, ROBERT R. MOTON, greatly undermined McCrorey's position by siding with their white colleagues.

With the passage of the Nineteenth Amendment in August 1920, McCrorey was active in encouraging black women to vote for the first time. In spite of the state's racially discriminatory voting laws and strong resistance from white election officials, black women attempted to register throughout North Carolina. Their efforts were more successful in the white-majority cities of the urban piedmont, especially in McCrorey's Charlotte, where nearly two hundred black women registered, than in eastern North Carolina, where blacks formed a majority in many communities. In that region's largest city, Wilmington, only ten black women registered.

In spite of McCrorey's friendships with white suffragists, there were precious few examples of cooperation between black and white women's groups in North Carolina—or elsewhere in the South. The national leadership of the women's suffrage movement, notably Alice Paul, president of the National Women's Party, refused to investigate the widespread violations of the Fifteenth and Nineteenth amendments during that election. The 1920 elections nonetheless marked a significant advance in black political participation in North Carolina. The number of African Americans allowed to register and vote was small and remained small until after World War II. But it became clear in 1920 that the state's white political elite would at least tolerate modest electoral participation by educated, upper-middle-class blacks, including women like McCrorey and Charlotte Hawkins Brown.

McCrorey continued as chairperson of the Phillis Wheatley YWCA until 1924. Ma Mac, as her students affectionately called her, also taught English and psychology at Johnson C. Smith University for several years. In the 1930s she served on the state welfare and public charity board and was active on the executive committee of the Negro State Teachers Association, one of the most powerful black organizations in North Carolina. A lifelong Republican, McCrorey was appointed in 1931 as a delegate to President Herbert Hoover's Conference of Better Homes and Home Ownership. Six years later, in 1937 she became the first black woman to run for public office in North Carolina, but she lost in her bid for election to the Charlotte school board. In 1941 Benedict College in Columbia, South Carolina, honored McCrorey with an honorary doctorate in pedagogy. From 1922 until the time of her death she served as corresponding secretary of the International Council of Women of Darker Races and was also prominent in the home and foreign mission boards of the Presbyterian Church, USA.

Mary Jackson McCrorey died as a result of an accidental fire that destroyed her home, the president's residence on the Johnson C. Smith campus. She was survived by her husband, who was in Ohio on business at the time of the fire. Even after her death, however, McCrorey continued to influence the students at Johnson C. Smith and at other North Carolina colleges who were to be in the vanguard of the state's civil rights movement in the 1960s. Kat Crosby, a graduate of Johnson C. Smith in the 1960s and a leader of the effort to desegregate the Charlotte-Mecklenburg public schools in the 1970s, recalled that "the shadow of Ma Mac was on every door."

FURTHER READING

Information on Mary Jackson McCrorey can be found in the President H. L. McCrorey Collection at the Inez Moore Parker Archives and Research Center, James B. Duke Memorial Library, Johnson C. Smith University, Charlotte, North Carolina.

Gilmore, Glenda Elizabeth. *Gender and Jim Crow: Women and the Politics of White Supremacy in North Carolina, 1896–1920* (1996).

Gordon, Linda. "Black and White Visions of Welfare: Women's Welfare Activism, 1890–1945," *Journal of American History* 78.2 (Sept. 1991).

STEVEN J. NIVEN

McDaniel, Hattie (10 June 1895–26 Oct. 1952), film actress and singer, was born in Wichita, Kansas, the youngest daughter of Henry McDaniel, an itinerant preacher, carpenter, and entertainer, and Susan Holbert. The McDaniels moved to Denver, Colorado, in 1901, where Hattie enjoyed a more settled childhood than her seven older siblings had. Five other children had died in infancy. At home, at school, and at church, McDaniel sang spirituals and recited passages from the Bible. Usually she enchanted, though not always. She later recalled: "My mother would say, 'Hattie, I'll pay you to hush,' and she'd give me a dime. But in a few minutes I'd be singing and shouting again" (Jackson, 9). By 1910 McDaniel was already an accomplished singer and dancer, appearing in several minstrel shows in Denver. She later toured with her father and her brothers Sam and Otis in the Henry McDaniel Minstrel Show, a troupe popular throughout Colorado.

Around 1920 Henry's poor health and Otis's death forced McDaniel to find work as a cook, a clerk, and a laundress, though she longed to return to the stage. Her break came later that year, when she joined Professor GEORGE MORRISON and his Melody Hounds on a tour throughout the West and Mexico. McDaniel's well-received performances on that tour led to steady employment in the vaudeville circuits of the West and South for most of the 1920s. In 1925 she sang on the Denver radio station KOA, an appearance often credited as the first on radio by an African American. Although she could dance and displayed a keen talent for comedy, McDaniel rose to prominence as a blues singer, performing standards and recording some of her own compositions, including "Brown-Skin Baby Doll" and "Just One Sorrowing Heart."

McDaniel's singing career prospered until the Great Depression, when she was forced to find work as an attendant in the ladies' room of Club Madrid, a nightclub and casino near Milwaukee. Some of the customers, unaware of McDaniel's two decades in show business, urged the manager to let the singing washroom attendant perform with the house band; a rousing rendition of the "St. Louis Blues" earned her a standing ovation and more than ninety dollars in tips that night. McDaniel quickly became one of the hottest acts in Milwaukee, and the regulars at Club Madrid urged her to leave for Los Angeles and take her chances in the movies. The rags-to-riches scenario could have made a great Hollywood script, if only Hollywood wrote such scripts for blacks.

The "riches" part took a few years. McDaniel arrived in Los Angeles in 1931, not exactly an ingénue but still a relative unknown. With characteristic optimism, she made the most of her only connection, her brother Sam, who played the Doleful Deacon on the weekly KNX radio show *The Optimistic Do-Nut Hour*. Within a few weeks she was the star of the show and also wrote her own songs and gags. Despite her popularity, McDaniel received only five dollars per show. She earned the same amount for each movie in which she appeared as an extra or sang in the chorus. To augment her meager wages, she worked as a domestic, later joking that she had washed 3 million dishes on her way to stardom. By the mid-1930s McDaniel no longer needed to wash those dishes, as she had become that rarity in Hollywood: an actress with steady employment, and would ultimately appear in more than three hundred movies, most often as a maid. Her most notable performances came in John Ford's *Judge Priest* (1934) with Will Rogers and in James Whale's *Show Boat* (1936), where she played Queenie alongside PAUL ROBESON. McDaniel's most acclaimed role, as Mammy in David O. Selznick's *Gone with the Wind* (1939), also proved to be her most controversial. To be sure, the NAACP and the black press criticized the film's romanticized depiction of the antebellum South. Yet most commentators—black and white—credited McDaniel's performance as the feisty but loyal Mammy to Scarlett O'Hara as worthy of the Academy Award for Best Supporting Actress. McDaniel displayed her trademark flair for biting asides and broad comedy, but it was the melodramatic scene in which she mourned the death of Scarlett's child that clinched the Oscar. Accepting the award—the first ever won by an African American—a tearful McDaniel expressed

Hattie McDaniel, receiving the Academy Award from actress Fay Bainter (right) for the best performance by an actress in a supporting role in 1939 for her work as "Mammy" in the film version of *Gone With the Wind*, in Los Angeles, California, 29 February 1940. (AP Images.)

the hope that she would always be a credit to the motion picture industry and to her race.

During World War II, however, McDaniel found herself under fire from the NAACP's executive secretary, WALTER WHITE, for allegedly failing in that latter goal. At a time when the NAACP was spearheading a "Double V" campaign for victory against fascism abroad and racism at home, White criticized black actors for portraying the servile stereotypes of eye-rolling mammies and cringing Uncle Toms. As the most prominent black actress at that time, McDaniel became a lightning rod for these attacks, and she deeply resented what she saw as White's interference in her livelihood. She passionately believed that her skills as an actor glorified African American womanhood, and indeed, at her best, she portrayed servant characters with greater depth and complexity than White charged. Moreover, sexism as much as racism restricted her roles. The slim, glamorous LENA HORNE—the black

role model favored by Walter White—could insert a clause in her contract refusing to play maids; McDaniel had a clause in her contract forbidding her to lose weight.

The final years of McDaniel's life were not particularly happy. Although she appeared in several more movies, none brought her the acclaim of *Gone with the Wind*. She remained in the public eye, notably as the star of *Beulah*, a highly popular CBS radio show that ran from 1947 to 1951, in which she played a maid who did not speak in dialect. In 1951 a heart attack forced her to stop working on a television version of the show. McDaniel had suffered from diabetes and heart disease, and also from depression, for several years. An unsettled family life did not help. All four of her marriages were brief and often stormy, and her fervent desire for a child was never fulfilled; a well-publicized false pregnancy at the age of forty-nine made matters worse. At her lavish parties she remained the gregarious "Hi-Hat Hattie," but her friends noticed that she drank a little more, swore a little more, and on one occasion attempted suicide. Criticism from the NAACP still rankled, particularly because she had worked with the organization in 1945 to challenge successfully a restrictive covenant in her Los Angeles neighborhood. That court ruling helped the NAACP build its national campaign against restrictive covenants, which was finally endorsed by the U.S. Supreme Court in its 1948 *Shelley v. Kraemer* decision. In 1952 McDaniel was diagnosed with breast cancer; she died in the Motion Picture Country Home and Hospital in Woodland Hills, California.

It is not surprising that McDaniel's favorite poem was "We Wear the Mask," by PAUL LAURENCE DUNBAR. It stands as an appropriate tribute to a woman whose image received so much attention that the person behind the mask was often lost:We wear the mask that grins and lies, / It hides our cheeks and shades our eyes,— / This debt we pay to human guile; / With torn and bleeding hearts we smile, / And mouth with myriad subtleties.

FURTHER READING

McDaniel's most important papers are in the Margaret Herrick Library of the Academy of Motion Picture Arts and Sciences, Beverly Hills, California.

Bogle, Donald. *Toms, Coons, Mulattoes, Mammies and Bucks: An Interpretive History of Blacks in American Films* (1973).

Cripps, Thomas. *Slow Fade to Black: The Negro in American Film, 1900–1942* (1993).

Jackson, Carlton. *Hattie: The Life of Hattie McDaniel* (1990).

Watts, Jill. *"We Wear the Mask": The Life of Hattie McDaniel* (2004).

Obituaries: *New York Times*, 27 Oct. 1952; *Los Angeles Examiner*, 2 Nov. 1952.

STEVEN J. NIVEN

McDaniels, Darryl (31 May 1964–), rap music emcee pioneer, was born Darryl Matthew Lovelace to Berncenia Lovelace in Harlem, New York. He was adopted at three months old by Byford McDaniels, a station agent at the Metropolitan Transit Authority, and Bannah McDaniels, a nurse, who were already parents of one son, Alford. In 1970, at five years old, McDaniels and his family moved to the Hollis section of Queens, New York. For several years, he lived a fairly sheltered, comfortable life, attending Catholic St. Pascal Baylon Elementary School and spending his leisurely time hanging out with friends, playing basketball, and drinking.

In 1978 fourteen-year-old McDaniels became fascinated with hip-hop, after he and his brother Alford listened to a GRANDMASTER FLASH and the Furious Five mix tape. Influenced by what he had heard, McDaniels attempted to "scratch" a record with his mother's turntable. Noticing his brother's talent, Alford bought McDaniels DJ equipment to use in their home's basement and encouraged him to practice and sharpen his DJ skills. To create an image, McDaniels called himself Grandmaster Get High, the likely source of the name being his marijuana-smoking habit. McDaniels began making connections with others with the same interests, such as Joseph "Run" Simmons (REVEREND RUN), who learned his early skills as a DJ by emulating McDaniels. Grandmaster Get High became "Easy D," and after observing a freestyle battle between the Furious Five and the Cold Crush brothers, McDaniels became "DMcD." His new moniker came from how he signed his school assignments. It also stood for "Devastating Mic Controller." McDaniels later shortened his stage name to D.M.C.

After graduating from high school in 1982, McDaniels enrolled at St. John's University in New York. He remained in contact with Simmons, who attended LaGuardia Community College. Motivated by the possibility of recording an album, McDaniels formed a duo with Simmons and left college. Their duo, Runde-MC, was born. McDaniels attempted to find a company interested in recording and promoting them with the assistance of Simmons's older brother, the upstart impresario RUSSELL SIMMONS. In 1981 executives at Profile Records took notice, and renamed the group Run-D.M.C. DJ JAM MASTER JAY joined the group after his father's death in 1982 and the single "It's Like That/Sucka MCs" was released in early 1983. Profile released their album *Run-D.M.C.* in 1984. In 1985 the group became the first rappers to appear on the popular television show *American Bandstand*. The albums *King of Rock* (1985) and *Raising Hell* (1986) quickly followed and added to Run-D.M.C.'s success.

Raising Hell catapulted Run-D.M.C. into legendary status and proved a catalyst for the hip-hop genre. Perhaps what most distinguished *Raising Hell* from many of its rap contemporaries was its sampling of rock and roll music. The collaborative single "Walk this Way" with classic rock legends Aerosmith opened the door of universal acceptance for Run-D.M.C. It was the first rap album that reached the number-one spot on the R&B album charts. It also became the first rap album to sell over one million copies, becoming a platinum-selling record. McDaniels dubbed himself "King of Rock"

Darryl McDaniels, better known as D.M.C. of Run-D.M.C., performing at Guy's Bar in West Hollywood, California, 27 October 2005. (AP Images.)

after the 1985 album release. *Tougher than Leather*, the 1988 successor to *Raising Hell*, sold double platinum. By the late 1980s, however, the popularity of Run-D.M.C. began to wane. Scandal rocked the group, with Simmons being accused of rape by a female fan and McDaniels going on excessive drinking binges. McDaniels met the dancer Zuri Alston in 1991 and married her the following year. The two soon had a son, Darryl McDaniels Jr. The group released *Back from Hell* in 1990, which was a commercial flop. In the early and mid-1990s McDaniels experienced trouble with his vocal performance. In an attempt to keep up with the "gangster" era of rap music and rap's newer artists, Run-D.M.C. released *Down with the King* in 1993. It was one of the group's earliest attempts at collaborating with other mainstream rap artists. It reached gold and received better reviews than *Back from Hell*.

In 1994 McDaniels would pursue spirituality. He was ordained a deacon in the nondenominational Zoe Ministries in 1994. However, McDaniels continued to have trouble with his voice, and in 1996 doctors diagnosed the affliction as spasmodic dystonia. McDaniels had a rare case of the neurotic disorder, and immediately began botox treatments

for his vocal cords. McDaniels attributed the affliction to his excessive drinking and hard lyrical delivery. By 1997 McDaniels began a downward spiral of depression and alcoholism. In the midst of his depression, McDaniels heard a song by Sarah McLaughlin called "Angel." The song moved him, and McDaniels reevaluated both his career and his life. After beginning research about his childhood for his autobiography, *King of Rock: Respect, Responsibility, and My Life with Run-D.M.C.*, a thirty-five-year-old McDaniels discovered that he had been adopted. *Crown Royal* (2001), Run-D.M.C.'s last album, was released around the same time as McDaniels's autobiography and without major contribution from him. His creative influences leaned toward a softer sound because of his troubled voice and the spiritual rejuvenation happening in his life.

A year later, Run-D.M.C.'s DJ Jason "Jam Master Jay" Mizell was gunned down in his studio. Mizell's murder troubled McDaniels deeply because he had lost his dear childhood friend. After Mizell's death, the group officially disbanded in 2002. McDaniels continued to record, however, and in 2006 he released his first classic rock-influenced solo album, *Checks, Thugs, and Rock 'n' Roll*.

VH1 television producers traced McDaniels's search for his biological parents in the television documentary *DMC: My Adoption Journey*. The discovery of his own adopted roots encouraged McDaniels in 2006 to establish the Felix Organization and Camp Felix, a summer camp for adopted children. He was awarded the Congressional Angels in Adoption Award for his endeavors.

Run-D.M.C. provided the catalyst for hip-hop to be both a hybrid of popular culture and black culture at large. Because of their groundbreaking success with *Raising Hell* and comfort experimenting with other musical genres, Run-D.M.C. allowed hip-hop to flourish on a broader scale and to a wider audience. Because of their universal appeal and contributions to both hip-hop and music in general, Run-D.M.C. will be eligible for induction into the Rock and Roll Hall of Fame in 2008.

FURTHER READING

McDaniels, Darryl. *King of Rock: Respect, Responsibility, and My Life with Run-D.M.C.* (2001).

Ro, Ronin. *Raising Hell: The Reign, Ruin, and Redemption of Run-D.M.C. and Jam Master Jay* (2006).

REGINA N. BARNETT

McDonald, Gabrielle Kirk (12 Apr. 1942–), federal judge and international war crimes jurist, was born to James G. Kirk, a railroad dining car waiter, and Frances Retta English in St. Paul, Minnesota. Her father, who was later the director of the Community Development Corporation in St. Paul, and her mother divorced when Gabrielle was a young child, and she moved with her mother and brother, James, to New York City and later to Teaneck, New Jersey. Kirk's mother, an editor at Prentice Hall, was a forceful presence who resisted a New York landlord's attempt to evict the Kirk family from their home when he discovered that they were black; he had rented to the light-skinned Frances English believing that she was white. Determined from an early age to become a civil rights attorney, Kirk briefly attended Boston University and Hunter College in New York City before enrolling in Howard University's School of Law in Washington, D.C., in the early 1960s.

In 1966 Kirk received the Kappa Beta Pi Legal Sorority Award for Academic Excellence and an award for best oral argument and graduated first in her class at Howard law school, a distinction that she shares with THURGOOD MARSHALL, who was at that time solicitor general of the United States. In a tribute to Marshall in 1993 Kirk wrote that she

Gabrielle Kirk McDonald, federal judge and international war crimes jurist, in May 1998. (AP Images.)

had been driven by his vision of using the law as an instrument of liberation. She began her legal career as a staff attorney for the NAACP Legal Defense Fund (LDF), an organization shaped by Marshall's leadership in the 1940s and 1950s. By 1966, however, the passage of the 1964 Civil Rights Act had transformed the legal terrain upon which the LDF operated. It now focused on using Title VII of that act, which deals with employment discrimination, to assist African Americans seeking workplace fairness in large, unionized companies. Kirk led the LDF attorneys on several of these cases, notably a successful suit against Philip Morris, which, like other tobacco companies, had hired blacks for only the lowest-paying, most menial tasks. Kirk's victory in that 1967 case marked the first successful use of Title VII to improve equal employment opportunities.

After three years of working for the LDF, Kirk married the attorney Mark McDonald and with him founded McDonald and McDonald, a law firm in Houston, Texas, specializing in discrimination lawsuits against major Texas corporations. The couple had two children, Michael and Stacy, and later divorced. Even opposing corporate attorneys admitted that Gabrielle McDonald was one of the best trial lawyers in the South, particularly in 1976, when her firm won a settlement of $1.2 billion for 400 black workers at the Lone Star Steel Company. In addition to her work in private practice, McDonald also taught at the Thurgood Marshall School of Law at Texas Southern University in 1970 and from 1975 to 1977, and at the University of Texas at Austin in 1978. Recognizing her broad legal expertise, President Jimmy Carter appointed Gabrielle McDonald in

1979 to the U.S. District Court for the Southern District of Texas, the first federal judgeship awarded to an African American in that state.

As a federal judge, McDonald faced a vast caseload—nearly one thousand cases a year—focusing on a broad spectrum of constitutional matters. Her earliest rulings were broadly liberal, notably *Andrews v. Ballard* (1980), which overturned provisions of Texas law that had virtually outlawed acupuncture and other alternative medical practices in the state. McDonald's highest-profile case came in a 1981 dispute between white and Vietnamese shrimpers in the Gulf of Mexico. The Ku Klux Klan, supporting the white shrimpers, asked McDonald to recuse herself from the case, claiming that they could not receive a fair trial from a "Negress." Her family was also sent hate mail, including four one-way tickets to Africa. McDonald refused to remove herself from the case, however, and ultimately enjoined the Klan from intimidating the Vietnamese shrimpers. Commentators noted that her carefully worded injunction did not infringe upon the Klan's constitutional right to assemble.

Indeed, in her nine years on the federal bench, McDonald earned a reputation for fairness across the political spectrum. Conservatives praised her in 1986 when she upheld as constitutional a Houston ordinance that restricted the location of and signage used by topless bars. McDonald ruled that topless dancing "is not without its First Amendment right to freedom of expression" but also that the ordinance, which prohibited such bars from operating within 750 feet of a church, school, or day care center, did not restrict free speech, since it did not prevent them from operating elsewhere in the city. Such rulings did not endear her to some civil rights lawyers who viewed her jurisprudence as too cautious. By 1988 McDonald had begun to chafe at her ever-increasing caseload, and she stepped down from her lifetime judicial appointment. She worked for law firms in San Antonio and Austin until 1993, when a former LDF colleague at the U.S. State Department asked her to serve on the International Criminal Tribunal for the Former Yugoslavia (ICTY). Although she was surprised by the request, given her lack of experience in international law, she accepted, and the administration of President Bill Clinton submitted her name to the United Nations. In September 1993, after receiving the highest number of votes cast by the U.N. General Assembly for the tribunal's members, McDonald began to divide her time between Houston and the ICTY headquarters at The Hague in the Netherlands.

In May 1996 McDonald sat as one of three judges at the first war crimes proceedings since the Nuremberg trials after World War II. Exactly one year later, the panel sentenced Duško Tadić, a Bosnian Serb, to twenty years in prison for systematically raping, torturing, and murdering Muslims in a Serb-run prison camp in 1992. International commentators noted that, as the presiding judge, McDonald skillfully balanced her concern for the victims of the war crimes, especially rape victims, with scrupulous fairness and respect for the rights of the defendants.

The ICTY's findings in the Tadić case were significant in that they proved under international law the Serb policy of "ethnic cleansing" and set a precedent for further prosecutions. At the end of her tenure as president of the ICTY, McDonald praised the tribunal for melding different legal systems and traditions and for establishing clear international procedures for indictments and rules of evidence. She also argued that a permanent court with stronger backing from the United Nations would have brought war criminals to trial more quickly than had been the case in Serbia and in the similar tribunal dealing with atrocities in Rwanda. The establishment by the United Nations of an International Criminal Court (ICC) in 2002 appeared to have furthered McDonald's ideals, but the U.S. government declared its implacable opposition to such a court. Fearing, as President George W. Bush stated, that "our diplomats and our soldiers could be drug into this court," his administration joined Iraq, Israel, and North Korea in opposing a permanent organization to adjudicate war crimes.

After stepping down from the ICTY in 1999, McDonald accepted a position as a human rights adviser to Freeport-McMoRan Copper and Gold, Inc. This New Orleans–based company had come under attack from human rights organizations for dumping toxic waste from its copper and gold mines, the world's largest, in West Papua, Indonesia. By 2002 Freeport-McMoRan's more enlightened corporate policies had facilitated the passage of new legislation that ensured the indigenous population of West Papua a greater share of natural resource revenues. McDonald also participated in 2001 in an international mock tribunal that found the Japanese government guilty of creating, regulating, and maintaining a policy of sexual enslavement of "comfort women" for its troops in several Asian countries during World War II.

Several organizations have recognized McDonald's contributions to civil rights and human rights, among them the National Bar Association, an African American organization that gave her its RONALD BROWN International Law Award, and the American

Bar Association Commission on Women in the Profession, which chose her as its Woman Lawyer of Achievement in 2001. Perhaps the greatest testament to Gabrielle McDonald's commitment to human rights was given by Kofi Annan, secretary-general of the United Nations, who wrote:

> Perhaps more than any other single person, Judge McDonald helped bring us closer to a world which once seemed beyond attainment—a world in which those whose deeds offend the conscience of humankind will no longer go unpunished, in which human rights will be truly universal and in which the rule of law will finally prevail.

FURTHER READING

Felde, Kitty. "Profile of Gabrielle Kirk McDonald," *Human Rights Brief 7*, no. 3 (Spring 2000).

Horne, William. "Judging Tadić," *American Lawyer* (Sept. 1995).

May, Richard, et al. *Essays on ICTY Procedure and Evidence in Honour of Gabrielle Kirk McDonald* (2000).

STEVEN J. NIVEN

McDonald, Henry (31 Aug. 1890–12 June 1976), football player, was born in Port-au-Prince, Haiti. The names of his parents are unknown, and little is known about his early life except that he was brought to the United States when he was five years old after his natural parents agreed to his adoption by an American coconut and banana importer from Canandaigua, New York. "He was my father's boss," McDonald later explained, "and he just took a liking to me. My natural parents realized it was a great opportunity for me to go to America. I didn't see my mother again for over fifty-five years."

McDonald was raised in Canandaigua and attended Canandaigua Academy. After the family moved to Rochester, New York, McDonald became the first African American graduate of East High School, where he was a standout player in both baseball and football. In 1911 McDonald began playing professional football for the Oxford (New York) Pros, beginning a career that extended through 1920. McDonald was the third African American known to have played professional football. He was preceded by CHARLES W. FOLLIS, who played for the Shelby Athletic Club from 1902 to 1906, and by Charles "Doc" Baker, who played for the Akron Indians from 1906 to 1908 and in 1911.

In his first professional game, McDonald played halfback for the Oxford Pros against the Rochester Jeffersons, who promptly enticed him to play for them. He spent most of his career with the Jeffersons—later a charter member of the National Football League—occasionally playing for western New York All-Star teams; he concluded his playing career in 1920 with the All-Buffaloes team. A handsome, long-legged man, McDonald weighed only 145 pounds but possessed ample speed and was nicknamed "Motorcycle." "Most of the guys were bigger than me," he said, "but I was too quick for them to catch. I could run a hundred yards in ten point two seconds. The world record was ten flat in those days." Rochester owner and coach Leo Lyons agreed, stating that "you can't hit or hurt what you can't see. If you blinked your eyes, McDonald was on his way."

During his professional career McDonald had a difficult time making ends meet by playing football. He recalled that in all the years he played, "I never once took home more than fifteen dollars for one day of football." McDonald added that he "had to play two games to get that much." He often played a morning game in Rochester for the Jeffersons, then took a trolley to Canandaigua and played for the town team in the afternoon. In the summer McDonald supplemented his income by playing professional baseball for a number of different teams in the New York Negro leagues. In all, he played baseball for seven seasons. Despite his meager earnings McDonald gloried in being a halfback, because running backs were the star players and received the most money. McDonald recalled that the ball "was soft and shaped like a watermelon. We threw a couple of passes every game, but they were usually a last resort. The ball was made to be carried, not thrown all over the field." McDonald was one of the fine professional halfbacks of his era, noted for his long breakaway runs.

Like many early African American football players, McDonald tended to minimize the problems that he faced on the field because of his race. In a 1971 interview he recalled only one serious racial incident. During the 1917 season Coach Lyons recruited three college players to bolster the Jeffersons lineup for a game in Ohio against the Canton Bulldogs, who were led by Jim Thorpe. The trouble started when Canton's Earle "Greasy" Neale, a southern-born player, knocked McDonald out of bounds. Raising his fists Neale shouted at McDonald, "Black is black and white is white where I come from and the two don't mix." An accomplished boxer, McDonald stood ready to defend himself, but Thorpe intervened. According to McDonald, Thorpe "prevented a real donnybrook. He jumped between us and said, 'We're here to play football.' I never had any trouble after that. Thorpe's word was law on the field." Canton defeated the Rochester team that day by a score of 49 to 0.

After his retirement McDonald settled down in Geneva, New York. He was married to Paula (maiden name unknown), with whom he had three children. In 1973 he was among the thirty-eight original inductees into the National Black Sports Hall of Fame. McDonald died in Geneva.

FURTHER READING

Chalk, Ocania. *Pioneers of Black Sport: The Early Days of the Black Professional Athlete in Baseball, Basketball, Boxing, and Football* (1975).

Orr, Jack. *The Black Athlete: His Story in American History* (1969).

Obituary: *New York Times*, 15 June 1976.

This entry is taken from the *American National Biography* and is published here with the permission of the American Council of Learned Societies.

JOHN M. CARROLL

McDonald, William Madison (22 June 1866–5 July 1950), businessman and politician, was born in Kaufman County in the eastern part of Texas to George McDonald, a native Tennessean who had once (reportedly) been owned by the Confederate officer and founder of the Ku Klux Klan, Nathan Bedford Forrest. George was a farmer by trade. McDonald's mother, Flora Scott, was either a former slave or a freewoman, depending on the source. What appears certain is that she was from Alabama and died when McDonald was still very young. His father soon married a woman named Belle Crouch. Education in the family was a matter of great importance; McDonald was in fact named after William Shakespeare and the former U.S. president James Madison. He attended local schools and graduated from high school around 1884. As a young man, he took work from a local cattle rancher and lawyer named Z. T. Adams, who discussed the law with his young employee and took an active interest in his continued education. With Adams's help, McDonald applied to Nashville, Tennessee's Roger Williams University, an African American institution that was shuttered in 1929. There he studied in advance of what he expected to be a career as an educator.

The exact date of McDonald's graduation is not known. What is known is that following his stint at Roger Williams, he returned to Kaufman County, where he took a position as the principal of a black high school in the little town of Forney. During his time there, he met and married one of the school's

teachers, Alice Gibson. The couple would go on to have a son who died in childhood, and they never had other children. Increasingly, McDonald was turning his eye to state politics during a time when African American men were making amazing inroads in state and local office through the federal Reconstruction process. McDonald's moment came in 1892, when he was elected to the Texas state executive committee of the GOP. It was the beginning of a political career that would span more than three decades. McDonald used the avenues of black fraternal organizations and the suddenly discovered political clout of African Americans to fight the growing forces of white "redemption." With the death of NORRIS WRIGHT CUNEY in 1897, he was elected to lead the Texas Republican Party, the so-called Black and Tans: African Americans who made the GOP a force from the end of the nineteenth century through the early decades of the twentieth.

A year earlier, a newspaper reporter gave McDonald the nickname Gooseneck (owing, simply, to the fact that he had a rather long, thin neck), and it was by this name that he was known around the state for the rest of his life. In 1899 he was elevated to the status of grand secretary of the Prince Hall Free and Accepted Masons of Texas, a fraternal organization through which McDonald held considerable sway over other important politicians and business leaders in the state. Meanwhile, however, the "Lily White" faction was beginning to gain increasing power in Texas as the Reconstruction experiment began to fail. In 1906 he removed to Fort Worth, and there opened that city's first African American–owned bank, the Fraternal Bank and Trust Company. At the time, black banks were a virtual necessity, as many white banks refused to offer credit or loans to African American customers. McDonald's exalted status among numerous fraternal organizations made Fraternal Bank and Trust the natural choice among the black community, and McDonald's business was a huge success. He continued to dabble in state politics, but white control over the levers of power had now more or less been firmly reestablished. On the national level, he occasionally abandoned the Republican candidate in favor of the Democratic one, for example supporting Franklin Delano Roosevelt's bid for the presidency in 1928. He is sometimes cited as Texas's first black millionaire, though such a title is difficult to bestow accurately, and there are other claims to it.

With the waning of black influence on local and state party politics, McDonald concentrated more and more on his business affairs. He died on either the fourth or fifth of July and was buried in Fort Worth. He is remembered today in Texas as an early pioneer of black entrepreneurship and political influence in a time when African Americans were making forays into those arenas, only to see the backlash of white racism relegate them to smaller and more constrained roles.

FURTHER READING

Barr, Alwyn. *Black Texans: A History of African Americans in Texas, 1528–1995* (1996).

Beito, David T. *From Mutual Aid to the Welfare State: Fraternal Societies and Social Services, 1890–1967* (2000).

Foner, Eric. *Reconstruction: America's Unfinished Revolution, 1863–1877* (1988).

JASON PHILIP MILLER

McDowell, Mississippi Fred (12 Jan. 1904–3 July 1972), blues singer, songwriter, and guitarist, was born Fred McDowell in Rossville, Tennessee, the son of Jimmy McDowell and Ida Cureay, farmers. Little is known of his early life, primarily because of his own conflicting accounts. His earliest recollections, aside from those of farm life, focused on weekend parties and the guitar playing of his uncle and main inspiration, Gene Shields, who also may have helped raise young Fred after the death of his father. In a 1969 interview, McDowell recalled: "I was a little-bitty boy. My uncle, he played with a beef bone that come out of a steak. He reamed it out, took a file and smoothed it and wore it on this [little] finger here…. I said if I ever get grown I'm gonna learn to play a guitar. Boy it sound so good to me."

In his teens McDowell attended country dances, where he would sing rather than play guitar. He picked up pointers from local guitar players, but his own instrumental skill came slowly. It was never clear when McDowell became an accomplished guitarist, since he did not own a guitar early in life. McDowell left Rossville when he was around twenty-one years old to work at various jobs in and around Memphis. Working at a dairy in White Station, Tennessee, he finally acquired a guitar, supposedly a gift from a white man from Texas. Through the late 1920s and 1930s he played at dances and juke joints in the Mississippi Delta region.

In 1928 McDowell saw CHARLEY PATTON, perhaps the seminal figure in Delta blues, at a juke in Cleveland, Mississippi. Deeply impressed, McDowell added a number of Patton songs to his repertoire. During his Delta wanderings, he also ran across BUKKA WHITE, a bottleneck-style guitar player, who supposedly became belligerent after McDowell stole his crowd. By now an accomplished musician, McDowell could compete with other musicians at dances and in country jukes. He later claimed that he and Eli Green, a lifelong friend from whom he learned the song "When You Get Home Write Me a Few Lines," often played around Rosedale and Cleveland.

By his own account, McDowell moved to Mississippi for good sometime around 1940, after the death of his mother. Before she died, he supposedly promised her that he would give up blues, a promise that he claimed to have kept for six years. He settled in Como, in northern Mississippi hill country, just east of the Delta. In December 1940 he married Annie Mae Collins, with whom he had a son. McDowell worked a small cotton farm and began playing for local dances. He might have remained an obscure local performer except for a 1959 encounter with the folklorist Alan Lomax, who learned of McDowell from other local musicians while doing research in the area around Como and nearby Senatobia. Lomax spent a night recording McDowell in the summer of 1959, and those field recordings were later released in two of Lomax's documentary projects, the Southern Folk Heritage series for Atlantic Records and the Southern Journey series for Prestige International. The recordings brought McDowell little in the way of royalties but elicited interest among other folklorists and documentary record labels.

While continuing to work on his farm and at a local Stuckey's Candy outlet, McDowell recorded for Testament and Arhoolie, and in 1963 he made his festival debut at the University of Chicago Folk Festival, followed the next year by an appearance at the Newport Folk Festival. He was considered one of the purest "folk" discoveries of the folk-revival era, on a par with such rediscovered "bluesmen" as MISSISSIPPI JOHN HURT, Booker White, and Robert Wilkins—each of whom had recorded commercially before World War II. In 1965 McDowell toured California and then Europe with the American Folk Blues Festival. He continued to make what he referred to as "junkets" throughout the 1960s, working the festival and coffeehouse circuits and winning friends with his soft-spoken manner and willingness to share his musical ideas. Throughout the 1960s McDowell recorded extensively for both American and European labels, including Capitol, which produced his 1969 Grammy-nominated album *I Do Not Play No Rock and Roll*. McDowell also appeared in such films as *The Blues Makers* (1968) and *Fred McDowell* (1969).

A late-life switch to electric guitar in 1969 may have annoyed McDowell's folk following, but it won him new admirers among blues/rock fans and musicians. He influenced the British rocker Keith Richards and even toured briefly with the Rolling Stones, which had reprised his version of the traditional spiritual "You Got to Move." McDowell also played with the leading white blues musicians of the 1960s—Michael Bloomfield, Paul Butterfield, and Elvin Bishop—and worked with and enjoyed a close friendship with the guitarist and singer Bonnie Raitt, who recorded his "When You Get Home Write Me a Few Lines."

Despite his celebrity friends, McDowell's music changed very little, although his repertoire did expand. He remained a traditional artist who never forgot his country ties, recording for Arhoolie Records with his old partner Eli Green in 1966 and working with another down-home friend, the harmonica player Johnny Woods, at the Ann Arbor Blues Festival in 1969. Continuing to perform at festivals into the early 1970s, he returned to Como in 1971, suffering from stomach cancer. He died at Baptist Hospital in Memphis.

Along with the Texas guitarist MANCE LIPSCOMB, Mississippi Fred McDowell was widely considered to be the most important new rural blues discovery of the 1960s. His music seemed to be frozen in some earlier time, largely untouched by progressive changes in blues. His riff-driven instrumental style, in which complex, repeated melodic figures supported a bottleneck treble lead, paralleled the sound of Mississippi's hill-country fife-and-drum groups, combining the dual African traditions of complex rhythms and vocal tonality. As McDowell described the style, "I'm trying to make the guitar say what I say." Lionized by folk revival audiences and later by blues/rock fans, McDowell was a singular artist, one of the unmistakable voices of the blues tradition, remembered as both a gentleman and teacher and also an artist.

FURTHER READING

Cohn, Lawrence. *Nothing but the Blues: The Music and the Musicians* (1993).

Cook, Bruce. *Listen to the Blues* (1973).

Lomax, Alan. *The Land Where the Blues Began* (1993).

Pomposello, Tom. "Mississippi Fred McDowell," in Jas Obrecht, ed. *Blues Guitar: The Men Who Made the Music* (1990).

This entry is taken from the *American National Biography* and is published here with the permission of the American Council of Learned Societies.

BILL MCCULLOCH AND
BARRY LEE PEARSON

McElroy, Colleen J. (30 Oct. 1935–), poet and writer, was born in St. Louis, Missouri, to Ruth Celeste Rawls and Purcia Percell Rawls. McElroy's parents divorced three years later, in 1938, and McElroy and her mother moved in with her grandmother. Her mother's marriage to an army sergeant, Jesse Dalton Johnson, in 1943 marked a turning point in McElroy's creative development. As part of a military family, McElroy traveled a great deal. As her family moved from base to base, McElroy reportedly would use storytelling as a means to make friends. McElroy began college in 1953 at the University of Maryland and transferred to Harris Teachers College in 1956. She graduated in 1958 from Kansas State University with a B.S. in Speech Pathology. McElroy continued her studies at the University of Pittsburgh in the graduate program of neurological and language leaning patterns and returned to Kansas State University to complete her M.S. degree in Speech Pathology in 1963. As a speech pathologist McElroy specialized in working with people who had suffered neurological trauma.

In 1968, she married David F. McElroy, an author, and they had two children, Kevin and Vanessa, before they divorced. She then moved to Washington state, where she served as the director of speech and hearing services at Western Washington University in Bellingham. McElroy continued her education and training at the University of Washington, studying ethnolinguistic patterns of dialect difference and oral traditions. She received her Ph.D. in 1973 and joined the University of Washington faculty in the English Department. In 1983 McElroy became the first African American woman to hold a full professorship at the University of Washington–Seattle.

McElroy had been writing privately for years, but she did not begin to publish until she was in her thirties, in the late 1960s. It was around this time that she began to discover the works of poets like LANGSTON HUGHES and ANNE SPENCER. This helped McElroy to move beyond traditional Eurocentric models for her poetry. At first, she thought she was one of only a few African American writers, until she started to receive letters from other African American writers. One letter was from GWENDOLYN BROOKS. McElroy's poetry was against the black stereotypes written about by mainstream authors.

McElroy once compared writing poetry to dancing. McElroy used the music of language to express her ideas, thoughts, and feelings. For her, writing was a dance all its own, using different expressions as a way of saying the same thing. McElroy published her first book of poetry, *The Mules Done Long since Gone*, in 1973. *Music from Home: Selected Poems* (1976) was inspired by the beauty of the landscape of the Pacific Northwest, while her next publication, *Winters without Snow* (1979), detailed her divorce. With ISHMAEL REED, she co-wrote a "choreopoem," a collection of poems that are acted out, with the prose sung and accompanied by music. The piece, with themes centering on voodoo, was titled *The Wild Gardens of the Loup Garou* (1982).

Her *Queen of the Ebony Isles* (1984) was included in the Wesleyan University Press Poetry Series and was the winner of the Before Columbus Award in 1985. The book *Bone Flames* (1987) received the Washington State Governor's Award; *Follow the Drinking Gourd: A Play about Harriet Tubman* was written that same year. Additionally McElroy published two short-story collections: *Jesus and Fat Tuesday* (1987) and *Driving under the Cardboard Pines* (1990).

A Fulbright scholar, guest lecturer, speaker, and consultant, McElroy had an acclaimed career, receiving numerous awards for her writing. She received a National Endowment for the Arts fellowship for poetry; a Creative Writing Fellowship (1978); the *Callaloo* Creative Writing Award in Fiction, University of Kentucky (1981); Fulbright Creative Writing Residency, Yugoslavia (1987–1988); National Endowment for the Arts Creative Writing Fellowship for fiction (1991); and many more.

FURTHER READING

Margulis, Jennifer. "McElroy, Colleen," in *The Oxford Companion to African American Literature*, eds. William L. Andrews, Frances Smith Foster, and Trudier Harris (2001).

Sherman, Charlotte Watson. "Walking across the Floor: A Conversation with Colleen J. McElroy," *American Visions* (April–May 1995).

TERI B. WEIL

McFerren, Viola Harris (19 Oct. 1931–), civil rights activist and community leader, was born Viola Harris in Michigan City, Mississippi, the eleventh of Joseph Thomas Harris and Rose Etta (Webb) Harris's twelve children. Reared in the economically depressed cotton community of Benton County, Harris received her elementary education at the racially segregated one-room, one-teacher Moore's School, which had a student population of approximately sixty-five. Because Benton County provided no secondary education for its black citizens, Harris traveled across the state line to attend a segregated high school in Fayette County, Tennessee. She walked five miles a day to board a makeshift bus with no heat and traveled thirty-five miles one way to receive her secondary education. Although they were poor farmers, Harris's parents were involved in community activities and instilled these values in their daughter.

On 13 December 1950, shortly before her graduation from the Fayette County Training School in Somerville, Tennessee, Harris married John McFerren—whom she divorced 19 February 1980—and made the rural, poverty-stricken southwestern Tennessee county her home. John and Viola McFerren had five children.

After having moved to one of the country's most impoverished counties, McFerren became a registered cosmetologist. Like many of their ancestors, the McFerrens cultivated the land. For almost ten years they lived a modest, unobtrusive life rearing their children, farming, and trying to make a living. However, in 1959 the McFerrens took up the cause of black voter registration through direct nonviolent action protest. That year Viola McFerren's interest in the movement for civil rights spiked when her husband led Fayette County's voter registration drive. John and Viola McFerren's concern over black voting rights, which in theory were protected by the U.S. Constitution was ignited by the absence of African American jurors during the Burton Dodson trail. Dodson, an African American farmer in his seventies, was on trial for the alleged 1941 murder of a white man. Because African Americans were denied their participatory right in the electoral process, they were omitted from the pool of potential jurors. In response, John McFerren and others organized the Original Fayette County Civic and Welfare League in spring 1959. One of the organization's primary objectives was to set in motion a voter registration drive.

The following June and July the league successfully convinced a number of African Americans to register at the Fayette County courthouse in Somerville. However, when the Democratic primary was held in August, African Americans were prevented from voting. Consequently, league members filed a federal suit against the local Democratic Party. According to a statement by a U.S. justice department official, this was the first legal action filed against a party primary under the 1957 Civil Rights Act. Soon the attention of the entire nation was focused on Fayette County.

When McFerren's husband joined the voting rights movement, she attempted to dissuade him.

"I was just scared to death, and I did everything ... I could to discourage him.... But nothing stopped him," she recalled. "I decided I would just pray about the situation and just leave it completely up to our Eternal Father," she said. "Finally, all of that fear left. I didn't feel tired, worried, and dragged out.... I knew that regardless of what other people feel or say, that this struggle is right" (interview with the author, Jan. 2005).

Fayette County whites retaliated against African Americans who challenged white political and economic dominance. Scores of African Americans lost employment, credit, and insurance policies. Whites refused to let blacks purchase goods and services, and medical doctors refused to give them necessary medical care. The most egregious form of racial terror came without notice in the winter of 1960 when white property owners drove more than four hundred African American tenant families from their lands. However, Fayette County blacks remained undeterred. With the support of Shephard Towels, an African American property owner, they formed a makeshift commune known as Tent City, erecting surplus army tents as homeless families readied themselves to cope with the bitter cold and blustery winter weather. A second Tent City was erected east of Moscow in southern Fayette County on the farm of Gertrude Beasley. Families resided in both Tent City communities for a number of months, suffering unrelenting deprivation but refusing to yield to white supremacy.

McFerren worked tirelessly to serve the needs of the league's constituents and to tend to the organization's stated mission. "I could see all that what was happening to people, all of this wrongdoing that was being brought upon black folks.... I don't care what happens to me as long as I am trying to do what I feel is right and something that is necessary to be done," she said (interview with the author, Jan. 2005).

The U.S. justice department successfully litigated its case against Fayette County's landowners, who on 26 July 1962 were permanently enjoined "from engaging in any act ... for the purpose of interfering with the right of any person to register to vote and vote for candidates for public office" (Morris). Despite their victory, McFerren continued her crusade for African Americans in Fayette County.

A lifelong educational advocate, McFerren was instrumental in bringing the Head Start program to Fayette County. Although she intended the program to be for all of the county's children, regardless of race, the local board of education sanctioned Head Start only for African American children. She was in the forefront of bringing kindergarten and basic adult education programs to the county. In 1965 McFerren and her attorneys initiated a school desegregation lawsuit on behalf of her son, John McFerren Jr. Five years later she and others intervened in the federal court case filed by thirteen African American teachers who had been dismissed by the Fayette County board of education. A federal court ordered Fayette County schools to desegregate and mandated the board of education to maintain a ratio of 60 percent black and 40 percent white students. Blacks soon served on the board of education, and new school buildings were constructed.

Despite these achievements African Americans continued to experience racial discrimination nearly a decade after McFerren joined the movement. An unrelenting crusader, Viola McFerren helped organize a boycott against the county's white merchants. A charter member of the Fayette County Economic Development Commission, she assisted in securing employment and housing loans for African Americans in the county, and she was an active member of the county's reinstituted National Association for the Advancement of Colored People. McFerren also was executive director of the Commission on Aging from 1978 until 1995.

McFerren's courageous activism captured the attention of several United States presidents. Lyndon B. Johnson appointed her to the national advisory committee of the U.S. Office of Economic Opportunity in 1966. Later he invited her to the White House conference called To Fulfill These Rights. Richard M. Nixon awarded McFerren a certificate of commendation, and in 1989 George Herbert Walker Bush honored her as one of fifty West Tennessee volunteers. In 1992, for her role as a "fearless leader of voter register, desegregation and equal housing in Fayette County," she was given the Women of Achievement Award for Heroism (Smith). Ten years later the Fayette County Schools Alumni Association honored McFerren for her many years of community service, and later the New Sardis Baptist Church in Memphis, Tennessee, presented her with its 2005 Dr. MARTIN LUTHER KING JR. Award.

FURTHER READING

Hamburger, Robert. *Our Portion of Hell, Fayette County, Tennessee: An Oral Struggle for Civil Rights* (1973).

Morris, Jack. "U.S., Fayette Landowners End Suits," Memphis *Commercial Appeal*, 27 July 1962.

Smith, Laquita Bowen. "7 Women of Achievement," Memphis *Commercial Appeal*, 30 March 1992.

"Viola McFerren: Lending a Helping Hand," *The Fayette County Review*, 28 July 1983.

Wynn, Linda T. "Toward a Perfect Democracy: The Struggle of African Americans in Fayette County, Tennessee to Fulfill the Unfulfilled Right of the Franchise," *Tennessee Historical Quarterly* 55 (1996).

LINDA T. WYNN

McFerrin, Bobby (11 Mar. 1950–), scat singer and orchestra director, was born Robert McFerrin Jr. in New York City, the son of Robert McFerrin Sr., a baritone who was a contract singer with the Metropolitan Opera Company and who, according to his son's memory, sang in *Rigoletto*. Bobby's mother, Sara (whose maiden name is unknown), was also an opera singer who sang gospel music professionally in church choirs and taught singing. His younger sister Brenda also had singing talent. Proud of their son's musical precocity, the McFerrins enrolled Bobby at age six in the Juilliard School for a classical music education for gifted children. When Bobby was eight the family moved to Los Angeles, where McFerrin Sr. sang for the movie soundtrack of *Porgy and Bess* and found enough career opportunities to keep him on the West Coast. Bobby was the only one in the family who did not sing. Choosing piano and keyboards as his instruments, he studied composing and arranging at Sacramento State University, though as a young man he was so impressed with the film *The Ten Commandments* that he considered becoming an Episcopal priest.

After graduating from college, McFerrin toured the country, playing keyboards with the Ice Follies and then with groups that featured top-forty band hits for college dances. At a dance in Springfield, Illinois, he noticed a coed, Debbie Lynn Green, and during an intermission he introduced himself to her. Although she did not sing or play an instrument herself, she had an intense interest in music, and McFerrin was initially impressed that she subscribed to *Down Beat* magazine.

After attending a religious conference in the Midwest, McFerrin decided against becoming a priest, and he committed himself to a career in music. Auditioning for a gig in Salt Lake City, he was asked to sing as well as play keyboard. He learned a few songs and surprised himself by falling in love with singing. Thereafter he learned a new song every day. He and Debbie married, delighted that her mother as well as his parents accepted the interracial couple, though other relatives, including her father, did not.

The McFerrins began touring the country and then settled for a while in New Orleans, where McFerrin worked as a singer and his wife as a waitress. They decided to move to San Francisco and drove across the country in an old Ford, taking with them about a hundred dollars and their dogs, Charles and Ives, named after the composer Charles Ives, whom McFerrin revered. McFerrin was also influenced by the avant-garde pianist Keith Jarrett, who could walk onstage and improvise a concert, and by the elegant Broadway and Hollywood dancer Fred Astaire.

McFerrin performed as a popular singer in San Francisco, but he began to focus on improvising scat singing. He met Michele Hendricks, daughter of singer Jon Hendricks, formerly of the group Lambert, Hendricks, and Ross. Michele took McFerrin to meet her father, with whom McFerrin sang improvised scat. Soon McFerrin, thrilling Hendricks, joined the Hendricks Family Singers, but McFerrin stayed for only about a year and a half before deciding to return to San Francisco, where he worked as a singer and teacher. His wife gave birth to their son, Taylor John, in January 1981.

A young agent, Linda Goldstein, heard McFerrin in San Francisco, then again in New York. When he said that he would like to sing a cappella, she decided to commit herself to representing him. McFerrin became an exceptionally powerful and innovative scat singer and solo concert artist, able to interpret several instruments in one song, jumping around the octaves with lightning speed and the force of a tidal wave. Though the range of his voice is often stated to be four octaves, it can reach further than that at times. Many people tried to discourage McFerrin and Goldstein, with her firm Original Artists, from pursuing such a risky career move, but McFerrin persisted; years later he recalled, "I had prepared myself. I was ready for rejections." In 1981 and 1982 he appeared singing improvised scat in Carnegie Hall in the Kool Jazz Festival concerts, the second of which was called The Young Lions of Jazz. His first album, *Bobby McFerrin* (1982), for Elektra Musician, had a pop orientation.

Goldstein booked McFerrin on a tour of a cappella concerts in Europe, one of which she taped and presented to Bruce Lundvall, head of Blue Note Records in New York. He hesitated but finally decided to release it in 1984 under the title *The Voice*. Against the odds, it was quite successful; McFerrin's career was on its way.

When he won a *Down Beat* citation for the best male vocalist of 1985, McFerrin was not surprised. "When you know you're right, and it's the truth for you, then the angels in heaven come to you, and all the forces for good are on your side," he said (interview with the author). In May that year he and Debbie had their second son, Javon Chase. The family's shaky financial situation improved greatly.

Bobby McFerrin, performing on the Stravinski hall stage during "Jazz night" at the 35th Monteux Jazz Festival in Montreux, Switzerland, 17 July 2001. (AP Images.)

In 1986 McFerrin won a Grammy for his interpretation of THELONIOUS MONK's title tune for the movie 'Round Midnight, in which McFerrin sounds as eerie and arresting as a MILES DAVIS horn solo. When he won the Grammy, McFerrin sang a whimsical acceptance song, a scat masterpiece in which he sent his voice ricocheting around the registers. He had already won two Grammys, one for singing, one for arranging a version of DIZZY GILLESPIE's "A Night in Tunisia," but "'Round Midnight" alerted the public. Sales of his third album for Blue Note, *Spontaneous Inventions* (1986), jumped up. Also in the 1980s McFerrin did a popular voice-over for a Levi jeans advertisement and the soundtrack for Rudyard Kipling's story "The Elephant's Child," narrated by the actor Jack Nicholson on the Wyndham Hill label.

The best was yet to come. McFerrin's next album, *Simple Pleasures* (1988), contained his original song, "Don't Worry, Be Happy." This became an immense hit and made him an international superstar. When the song won him another Grammy, he took out a full-page newspaper ad to thank Linda Goldstein, who had produced the album. Years earlier she had borrowed money and even lived for a while with the lights shut off so that she could send his band to Europe.

In 1991 the McFerrins had a daughter, Madison. The following year McFerrin won his tenth Grammy, for a jazz album done with the pianist Chick Corea. In 1993 McFerrin did an on-camera, five-voice, a cappella version of Henry Mancini's "The Pink Panther Theme" that won him yet another Grammy nomination.

McFerrin joined the Saint Paul, Minnesota, Chamber Orchestra as creative chair, conducting for a subscription series, tours, and special concerts. He began recording for Sony Classical and in June 1995 released his first classical album, *Paper Music*, as conductor and singer with the Saint Paul orchestra. Then his album *Hush* with the cellist Yo-Yo Ma went gold in 1996. That same year McFerrin collaborated again with Corea, recording two Mozart piano concertos and a piano sonata on *The Mozart Sessions*.

Subsequently McFerrin began conducting such famed symphony orchestras as the New York Philharmonic, the Chicago Symphony, the Cleveland Symphony, the Los Angeles Philharmonic, and the London Philharmonic. In 2002 he was awarded the George Peabody Medal for Outstanding Contributions to Music in America. That same year he made his debut with the Vienna Philharmonic and toured with it in 2003, including a performance at the prestigious London Proms music festival. His tours with his jazz Voicestra have included surprise guests ranging from BO DIDDLEY to a ballerina.

McFerrin's innovative use of his voice broadened contemporary notions of scat in jazz and extended into the world of classical music, bringing his surprised and delighted fans along and inspiring German critics to dub him *Stimmwunder*, "Wonder Voice."

FURTHER READING

Ames, Katrine. "Roll over, Gustav Mahler," *Newsweek* (7 August 1995).

Franckling, Ken. "A Conversation with Magical Bobby McFerrin," *Jazz Times*, June 1987.

Gourse, Leslie. *Louis' Children: American Jazz Singers* (1984).

DISCOGRAPHY

McFerrin, Bobby. *Simple Pleasures* (Blue Note, 1988).

McFerrin, Bobby. *The Voice* (Blue Note, 1984).
McFerrin, Bobby, and Chick Corea. *Play* (Blue Note, 1990).

LESLIE GOURSE

McFerrin, Robert, Sr. (19 Mar. 1921–24 Nov. 2006), opera singer and educator, was born in Marianna, Arkansas, the son of Melvin McFerrin, a Baptist minister, and Mary McKinley McFerrin. McFerrin grew up in a musical family as his parents and siblings could sing and play various instruments. He moved with his family in 1926 to St. Louis, Missouri, where he was educated in the public school system. Wirt D. Walton, his music teacher at Sumner High School, encouraged him to pursue a career as a professional singer. Walton acted as both voice teacher and patron to McFerrin, giving him free lessons and assembling an interracial group of benefactors who established the Robert McFerrin Scholarship Fund to support McFerrin in his continuing vocal studies.

After a year in Tennessee at Fisk University, McFerrin moved to Chicago, where he studied with George Graham at Chicago Musical College, eventually receiving his B.A. in 1948. In Chicago, McFerrin began his professional career, appearing at the Chicago Musicland Festival in 1942 after winning a national voice competition sponsored by the *Chicago Tribune*. His early success was interrupted by his service in the U.S. Army from 1942 to 1946. A year after his discharge, McFerrin moved to New York, where he became a protégé of the African American composer and choral director Hall Johnson. The Russian conductor Boris Goldovsky noticed him and offered him a scholarship with Tanglewood's opera department, where he appeared in Christoph Willibald Gluck's *Iphigénie en Tauride* (Iphiginia in Tauris) and Giuseppi Verdi's *Rigoletto*. In 1949 he performed in Kurt Weil's *Lost in the Stars* and created the role of Popaloi in William Grant Still's *Troubled Island*. That same year he married fellow singer Sara Cooper, with whom he had two children, Brenda McFerrin, a recording artist, and Robert McFerrin Jr. better known as BOBBY MCFERRIN, a Grammy-winning vocalist. McFerrin's success continued in the early 1950s, when he appeared in the Broadway revival of *The Green Pastures* in 1951, toured extensively as a concert recitalist, and performed with various opera companies including the New England Opera Company and the impresario and choral director Mary Cardwell Dawson's National Negro Opera Company, which frequently cited McFerrin's accomplishments in their advertisements and fund-raising literature.

In 1953 McFerrin won the Metropolitan Opera Auditions of the Air, earning a full scholarship to the Katherine Turney Long School, which trained singers for the Metropolitan stage. McFerrin performed the role of Amonasro in Verdi's *Aida* with the Metropolitan Opera Company on 27 January 1955, just three weeks after MARIAN ANDERSON broke the color line at the Metropolitan with her performance as Ulrica in Verdi's *Un ballo in maschera* (A Masked Ball). With this performance of *Aida*, McFerrin became the first African American male to perform at the Metropolitan Opera and the first African American on the Metropolitan's permanent roster, a position he held until 1957. During his tenure with the Metropolitan he performed in ten operas including appearances as Valentin in Charles Gounod's *Faust* and the title role in Verdi's *Rigoletto*.

Uncertain of his ability to advance professionally and secure further lead roles with the Metropolitan Opera, McFerrin moved to Hollywood and in 1959 recorded the vocal track for Sidney Poitier's performance in Otto Preminger's 1959 film version of George Gershwin's *Porgy and Bess,* though he received no on-screen credit. McFerrin took a position as a teacher at Sacramento State College and remained in California until he and Sara divorced in 1973. He then returned to St. Louis, where he resided for the remainder of his life. McFerrin continued his career as an educator and recitalist, serving as an Artist-in-Residence at the University of Missouri, St. Louis, in the 1980s and receiving two honorary doctorates from St. Louis institutions, Stowe's Teacher's College in 1987 and the University of Missouri, St. Louis, in 1989.

Despite a stroke in 1989, which affected his speech but not his singing, he kept performing into the 1990s including occasional performances with his two children, both successful vocalists in their own right. McFerrin's son Bobby cites him as a chief musical influence. In 2003 McFerrin Sr. received a lifetime achievement award from Opera America. He died in St. Louis of a heart attack in 2006. Robert McFerrin's pivotal role in integrating the Metropolitan Opera Company and his subsequent artistic achievements and public service, as well as his influence on his son Bobby, made him one of the most important and influential African American opera singers of the twentieth century.

FURTHER READING
Cheatham, Wallace McLain. "Black Male Singers at the Metropolitan Opera," *The Black Perspective in Music* 16, no. 1 (Spring 1988): 3–20.

Southern, Eileen. *The Music of Black Americans* (1971, third edition 1997).

Obituaries: *New York Times*, 28 Nov. 2006; *Washington Post*, 29 Nov. 2006.

CHRISTOPHER J. WELLS

McGee, Charles Edward (7 Dec. 1919–), military pilot and veteran, was born in Cleveland, Ohio, to Lewis Allen McGee Sr., a World War I veteran, teacher, social worker, and African Methodist Episcopal minister, and Ruth Elizabeth Lewis. Ruth McGee died in 1921, leaving three small children. Almost constantly in search of work, Lewis McGee Sr., a graduate of Wilberforce College, moved his family at least nine times before Charles finished high school. Charles was introduced to the Boy Scouts of America as a youngster, and he thrived under the scouts' program rewarding loyalty, discipline, and service.

In spring 1938 McGee graduated ninth out of a class of 436 from DuSable High School in Chicago and took a job with the Civilian Conservation Corps in northern Illinois. He entered the University of Illinois at Champaign in 1940, studied engineering, enrolled in the ROTC, and pledged Alpha Phi Alpha fraternity. He worked in the steel mills of Gary, Indiana, during summers to earn money for tuition.

The Japanese attacked Pearl Harbor on McGee's twenty-second birthday, drawing the United States into World War II. McGee knew that he would soon be drafted, so he traveled to Chanute Field in nearby Rantoul, Illinois, and volunteered for the new Army Air Corps program to train African American military pilots. When he took the program's entrance exam, "There was a guy there who had never dealt with any blacks," McGee later remembered, "and he kept filling in the blanks wrong because he was writing [that I was] white." McGee was accepted into the program. He married Frances Edwina Brooks, a University of Illinois graduate cum laude, on 17 October 1942, and two days later he received his orders to report to Tuskegee Army Air Field.

McGee was initially assigned to the class of 43-G at Tuskegee, but he so excelled in the upper pre-flight portion of training that he was moved forward to the class of 43-F. He graduated in the June 1943 class of fighter pilots and was commissioned a second lieutenant in the Army Air Corps. McGee shipped overseas as a replacement pilot of the all-black 302d Fighter Squadron, 332d Fighter Group, in January 1944.

After three months of flying harbor and coastal patrol missions from Montecorvino and Capodichino, Italy, McGee and the pilots of the 332nd were transferred to an air base at Ramitelli on Italy's Adriatic coast and assigned to bomber protection. For the remainder of the war, these pilots, later known as the Tuskegee Airmen, flew missions escorting Allied bombers deep into Axis territory, and they famously claimed never to have lost a bomber under their protection to enemy fighters. McGee himself flew 136 missions in the war; then he returned to Tuskegee Army Flying School as an instructor pilot.

The Army Air Force closed the Tuskegee airfield in 1946, and McGee transferred to the nearly all-black Lockbourne Air Base outside of Columbus, Ohio. He served as assistant base operations officer at Lockbourne under the command of Colonel BENJAMIN O. DAVIS JR. until President Harry S. Truman's Executive Order 9981 of 1948 officially desegregated the armed forces.

Desegregation was a mixed blessing for McGee and other junior officers among the Tuskegee Airmen. They had created distinctively close bonds with one another during and after World War II, but with only one black unit in the entire air force, opportunities for promotion were limited. After the air force's nominal desegregation, moreover, it fell upon African Americans themselves to enforce Truman's integration edict at individual bases. That burden did have its lighter side; McGee later remembered with delight the time that he and DANIEL "CHAPPIE" JAMES (the man who became the nation's first African American four-star general) desegregated the swimming pool at the officers' club of Barksdale Air Force Base in Louisiana. McGee, seated in a lounge chair at poolside, watched as the facility's manager rushed in to remove them just as James, a giant of a man, completed a cannon ball from the diving board. The manager only got the words "You can't ..." out of his mouth before a prodigious splash drowned him out. "I don't know if they drained the pool later that day or what," McGee recalled.

McGee flew one hundred missions in the Korean War and became one of the first African Americans in the air force to command an integrated unit. He flew an additional 172 combat missions in the Vietnam War for a total of 408, the most combat missions flown by any U.S. pilot. McGee retired in 1973 as commanding officer of Richards-Gebaur Air Force Base near Kansas City, one of only three African Americans with a command wing assignment in the U.S. Air Force.

McGee earned a real estate broker's license and accepted a position with Interstate Securities Corporation, a nationwide holding company, in 1973; he later rose to the position of vice president for real estate. That job ended in 1978, and McGee took the opportunity to fulfill a lifelong dream: he resumed the studies that he had suspended in 1942 and earned a bachelor's degree from Columbia College in Missouri. McGee returned briefly to the workforce in 1980 as manager of the Kansas City Downtown Airport, but he retired for good in 1983. Frances, his wife of fifty-one years and the mother of their three children, Charlene Edwina McGee Smith, Yvonne Gay McGee, and Ronald Allen McGee, died in 1994.

McGee was among the veterans of the Tuskegee experience who began organizing in the early 1970s to ensure that their legacy was preserved and passed on to later generations of Americans. He chaired the committee that wrote the constitution and bylaws of a nonprofit organization, Tuskegee Airmen, Inc, dedicated to introducing young African Americans to careers in aviation and to educating Americans about the double victory of the Tuskegee Airmen in World War II. McGee served four terms as president of the organization, which in 2000 had approximately two thousand members, a scholarship fund with an endowment approaching two million dollars, and a national museum in Detroit, Michigan.

In a remarkable air force career, McGee earned the Legion of Merit with Oak Leaf Cluster, the Distinguished Flying Cross with two Oak Leaf Clusters, the Bronze Star, the Air Medal with twenty-five Oak Leaf Clusters, a Distinguished Unit Citation in World War II, and a Korean Presidential Unit Citation. He was proudest of his service with the Tuskegee Airmen. The Tuskegee Airmen proved "that a group of Americans, given an opportunity, were able to overcome myths that race or happenstance of birth are marks of capability or loyalty," McGee said in a 2001 oral history interview. "*All* Americans need to be given that opportunity, to bring their talents to bear for whatever we face in the future."

FURTHER READING

An oral history interview with McGee is housed in the archives of the National Park Service's Tuskegee Airmen Oral History Project in Tuskegee, Alabama.

McGee-Smith, Charlene E. *Tuskegee Airman: The Biography of Charles E. McGee, Air Force Combat Record Holder* (1999).

Sadler, Stanley J. *Segregated Skies: All-Black Combat Squadrons of World War II* (1992).

Scott, Lawrence P., and William M. Womack Sr. *Double V: The Civil Rights Struggle of the Tuskegee Airmen* (1992).

J. TODD MOYE

McGee, Henry Wadsworth (7 Feb. 1910–18 Mar. 2000), postmaster, labor organizer, civil rights advocate, and community leader, was born in Hillsboro, Texas, the eleventh of twelve children of William Henry McGee and Mary Washington. The occupations of his parents are unknown. After his mother died in 1914, Henry moved to Chicago where he lived with his older brother, the Reverend Ford W. McGee—a future bishop of a South Side Holiness Church—for three years before returning to Hillsboro to rejoin his family. Then, Henry returned home to rejoin his father in Texas before the family relocated to Kansas City, Missouri.

After graduating from high school, Henry returned in 1927 to Chicago, where he attended Crane Junior College by day and worked the night shift as a substitute mail clerk in the Chicago Post Office. After earning an associate's degree in 1929, McGee had aspirations to continue his education, but, like countless other young people during the Depression, he was forced to temporarily suspend his post-secondary ambitions and spend much of his time toiling as a temporary substitute mail carrier at the post office. Of his decision, McGee remarked in an interview, "the post office was one of the few places a young Negro could get employment" (*Chicago Courier*, 2 June 1973). However, his ambitions of securing a stable livelihood were greatly frustrated by the intermittent work hours offered by the Chicago Post Office at the time. The work was such that McGee elected to leave the post office for a position as an insurance salesman in 1931, the same year he married Attye Belle Truesdale, who later became an educator in the Chicago public school system and mother of their three children.

When the Chicago Post Office introduced a forty-hour workweek and increased its hiring of African Americans in 1935, McGee elected to return there as a full-time clerk, bidding farewell to a promising career as an insurance adjuster. Upon pushing his way through the double doors of the huge Chicago main office building, McGee discovered that many of his professional battles were just beginning. McGee's workday experiences, like those of countless other black postal service workers of this era, were dogged by racism, bigotry, and discrimination at every turn. Of the travails that he and his contemporaries faced in the post office at the time, McGee later recounted in 1961, "if a Negro was on a clerical list and it was the policy of the office in question not to hire Negroes as clerks, he was offered a position as carrier or in some cases as a laborer; if he refused to accept what was offered him, he was simply dropped from the rolls" (McGee, "The Chicago Post Office," 9).

At the same time, McGee and his contemporaries were galvanized by the independent black unionist strategies advanced by A. PHILIP RANDOLPH, the head of the Brotherhood of the Sleeping Car Porters union and the leader of the March on Washington Movement. By 1940, McGee had applied his skills to the organized labor movement, joining the Chicago branch of the National Alliance of Postal Employees (NAPE) (later the National Alliance of Postal and Federal Employees, a trade union organization formed to combat discrimination against African American postal employees in the workplace. Throughout the period, he waged a campaign to obtain equal access to supervisory positions for African Americans in the postal service. In early 1942, McGee, along with several other Chicago branch officials, filed a legal brief with the city's Fair Employment Practices Committee (FEPC) chronicling the discriminatory employment and promotion policies practiced by the postal department. Their efforts produced short-lived victories when, in April of that year, McGee, members of NAPE, and the FEPC field director participated in a series of hearings with Postmaster General Ernest J. Kruetgen to discuss the matter. The meeting yielded mixed results; while branch officials noted that some progress had been made in the areas of job assignment, it would take nearly five years before significant changes in promotion and upgrade policies toward African American postal employees would be made. McGee's commitment to mailroom equality placed him at odds with post office administrators and caused more than a few of his coworkers to remark, "Mac's gone too far this time. He's going to get kicked out of the post office" (McGee Papers, Chicago Historical Society, 2). McGee's tireless efforts to advance the cause of his postal comrades earned him the praise and admiration of NAPE's rank and file, and he was elected as the Chicago branch president in 1944.

Neither post office politics nor independent black unionism satisfied McGee's thirst for activism during the period. From 1946 to 1961, he threw himself into local civil rights and civic causes, becoming president of the Chicago chapter of the National Association for the Advancement of Colored People and holding memberships in the Community Fund of Chicago, the Joint Negro Appeal, and the Hyde Park Co-Operative Society. He also completed his long-delayed formal education, earning a B.S. in Personnel Management from the Illinois Institute of Technology in 1949 and a master's degree in Political Science from the University of Chicago in 1961.

After holding a series of administrative posts in the field of operations and personnel in the Chicago Post Office, McGee's career took an unprecedented turn when he was cited by the Regional Postmaster General as the most "Outstanding Federal Supervisor" among the 65,000 postal employees in the area (*Negro Heritage*, 26 Sept. 1966). The increasing respect that McGee demanded and received became readily apparent for all to see in 1966 when he was tapped by Illinois Senator Paul H. Douglas to become the acting postmaster of Chicago. Not long afterward, the U.S. Senate approved the appointment, and McGee became the first African American in a major metropolitan area to attain the position. As an innovator, McGee designed a string of training programs aimed at upgrading employee skills and implemented massive campaigns that emphasized the importance of using zip codes during the crush of the holiday season.

After enjoying a long and successful career, he retired from the U.S. Postal Service in 1973 and served on the Chicago Board of Education before retreating from public view (*New York Times*, 29 Mar. 2000). Following the death of his wife in 1993, McGee relocated to Corpus Christi, Texas. Late in 1999, at the age of eighty-nine, McGee was diagnosed with cancer. After waging a bitter fight against the disease, he died in March 2000, leaving behind his children and a host of grandchildren, along with a rich heritage of civil rights activism and community involvement. Public recognition of his steadfast service to the U.S. Postal Service and the Chicago community gained its fullest expression later that year when Congress passed a resolution renaming Hyde Park Post Office in Chicago in his honor. U.S. Representative BOBBY L. RUSH commented, "the legacy that Henry L. McGee leaves behind is both inspirational and impressive and renaming that post office after him is a fitting tribute" (*Chicago Defender*, 11 Oct. 2000).

FURTHER READING

Henry W. McGee's works, correspondence, and other primary material are housed in the Chicago Historical Society in Chicago, Illinois.

Bates, Beth T. *Pullman Porters and the Rise of Protest Politics in Black America, 1925–1945* (2001).

Drake, St. Clair, and Horace R. Cayton. *Black Metropolis: A Study of Negro Life in a Northern City* (1945).

Reed, Christopher R. *The Chicago's NAACP and the Rise of Black Professional Leadership, 1910–1966* (1997).

Obituary: *New York Times*, 29 Mar. 2000.

ROBERT F. JEFFERSON

McGhee, Brownie (30 Nov. 1915–23 Feb. 1996), blues musician, was born Walter Brown McGhee in Knoxville, Tennessee, the son of George "Duff" McGhee, a farmer and itinerant mill worker, and Zella Henley. Even as a child, he was called "Brownie." His family was musically active. Brownie's father was a guitarist and singer. One of Brownie's uncles, John Evans, was a fiddler and gave him his first instrument—a homemade banjo fashioned from an empty can of marshmallows. Through his mother, Brownie was exposed to the music of Jimmie Rodgers, a white country singer, as well as BESSIE SMITH and LONNIE JOHNSON, the great African American blues recording artists. As a child, Brownie contracted polio, which stunted the growth of his right leg and left him physically deformed. He therefore devoted much time to music. He played in church, acquiring some skill on the piano and organ, and with his father sang in a gospel quartet called the Golden Voices. He also toured with carnivals, medicine shows, and a group known as the Rabbit Foot Minstrels. His brother, GRANVILLE "STICK" (or "Sticks") McGhee, played guitar as well, and the two of them played together on occasion. (Granville received his nickname because he was often seen pushing Brownie around town in a homemade cart that had a tree branch for a handle.) Brownie left high school to play his guitar and work and busk around various towns in the South. In 1937 he underwent an operation to help correct his limp. Taking advantage of his increased mobility, he spent even more time traveling and playing music.

Sometime around 1939 Brownie was traveling in North Carolina with the harmonica player Jordan Webb, busking for small change and trying to avoid the police. In Durham, McGhee and Webb were introduced to J. B. Long, a white record store manager who managed blues singer BLIND BOY FULLER. Long arranged for Brownie to record in Chicago, and in August 1940 McGhee recorded his first sides for Okeh records with Jordan Webb on harmonica. Fuller's health was failing, and Long was perhaps grooming Brownie, among others, to fill his shoes. Fuller died in February 1941, leaving Long without a "star" recording act. Long procured Fuller's steel-bodied National guitar for Brownie's next recordings, made under the pseudonym "Blind Boy Fuller #2." Despite this deceit and exploitation, Brownie continued his association with Long and Okeh records and in the fall of 1941 recorded with the harmonica player SONNY TERRY.

In 1942 McGhee and Terry made their way to New York City and participated in that city's burgeoning folk music revival, working mostly as a duo. Brownie, young and handsome, provided a contrast with his older partner, who was noticeably blind and wore spectacles. Their earthy and exuberant country blues struck a chord with the middle- and working-class patrons of the folk clubs. McGhee and Terry befriended the more popular blues singer Huddie Ledbetter, known as LEAD BELLY, and often shared the bill with him. Fewer records were made during the war, so these concerts helped Brownie and the other musical transplants from the South earn at least a meager living. Beginning around 1945 Brownie ran the House of Blues, a school in Harlem for aspiring blues singers and guitarists. McGhee also worked for a seller of voodoo charms sometime during this period, though what exactly he did is unknown.

After World War II the recording industry picked up, and Brownie's career took off. His ongoing collaboration with Sonny Terry in the acoustic blues format was becoming popular with the mostly white, educated, and liberal (in those days "leftist") fans of American roots music. In 1948 he recorded with a rhythm and blues combo and scored a hit with "Robbie Doby Boogie." The following year he wrote the sequel to this tune, "New Baseball Boogie." These tunes were tributes to the great African American ball players Robbie Doby and JACKIE ROBINSON. His work in this vein was popular, especially with African Americans. Consequently, McGhee was one of the few black artists of the pre–civil rights era to reach both a white and a black audience.

In 1950 McGhee married Ruth Dantzler; they had six children. Having to provide for a large family may have been some of the incentive that kept McGhee so busy during the 1950s. Fortunately, his versatility extended beyond the role of music performer. In 1955 he and Terry appeared in Tennessee Williams's Broadway play *Cat on a Hot Tin Roof*. His associations with this landmark play continued through 1958, as he was part of the touring company that went on the road that year. He also appeared in LANGSTON HUGHES's *Simply Heavenly*, an off-Broadway musical revue that ran for several months at the Playhouse Theater during the summer of 1957.

During the 1950s the winds of change were beginning to affect the buying trends of music fans. McGhee continued to perform with his rhythm and blues combo as well as with Sonny Terry in a more or less traditional blues setting. However, their records for the Old Town label in 1956–1957 did poorly. In 1958 Terry and McGhee signed with the Folkways record label, which promoted them as authentic representatives of the Piedmont style of country blues.

McGhee and Terry worked steadily through the 1960s. Ironically, they played for mostly white audiences at folk festivals and coffeehouses throughout North America and Europe. An accurate description of their sound was offered by the noted Philadelphia folk music disc jockey Gene Shay in his liner notes to *Brownie McGhee and Sonny Terry at the Second Fret* (1962). Shay wrote of "Sonny's falsetto squeals and vocalized harmonica" and noted that "Brownie's guitar supplies strong rhythmic chording and single line improvisation." A few of McGhee's best recordings from this period are *Hometown Blues* with Terry and the 1976 release *Blues Is Truth* with Sugar Blue on harmonica and his brother Stick on guitar. Although McGhee pursued a few projects without Terry, the bulk of his work from the early sixties until their split in 1976 was as a member of the duo.

McGhee was one of the few blues musicians successful enough to retire somewhat comfortably. He made his home in Oakland, California. During the 1980s he made an appearance on the television sitcom *Family Ties* and started the Blues Is Truth Foundation. He passed away after succumbing to cancer in Oakland.

McGhee sang in a warm and articulate vocal style not typical of blues singers in general. His guitar playing was clean and inventive. He worked tirelessly for decades, leaving behind an extraordinary recorded legacy. The foundation he started is testament to his dedication to the African American art form known as the blues.

FURTHER READING

Charters, Samuel Barclay. *The Country Blues* (1959; rev. ed. 1975).
Cohn, Lawrence, et al. *Nothing but the Blues* (1993).
Oliver, Paul. *The Story of the Blues* (1969).
Obituaries: *San Francisco Chronicle*, 19 Feb. 1996; Philadelphia *Inquirer*, 20 Feb. 1996.

This entry is taken from the *American National Biography* and is published here with the permission of the American Council of Learned Societies.

CHARLES MESSINGER

McGhee, Frederick Lamar (1861–9 Sept. 1912), lawyer and black activist, was born in Aberdeen, Mississippi, the son of Abraham McGhee and Sarah Walker, slaves. Although Frederick's father, a blacksmith, was not allowed a formal education, he learned to read and write, later becoming a Baptist preacher. Abraham McGhee also made certain that his children were literate, teaching each of them how to read and write. Such skills served young Frederick well when his parents died in 1873. Having moved with his family to Knoxville, Tennessee, soon after his parents were freed, Frederick McGhee remained there, studying at Knoxville College under the tutelage of Presbyterian missionaries. Without completing his undergraduate studies, he soon ventured to Chicago, working as a waiter for a time and then studying law with Edward H. Morris, a prominent local lawyer.

By 1885 McGhee was admitted to the Illinois bar, and in 1886 he married Mattie B. Crane. The couple had one daughter. For the next three years McGhee engaged in private practice in Chicago, still working closely with Morris, who by then had become an Illinois state legislator and one of McGhee's partners. Despite his apparent success in Chicago, McGhee moved his family to St. Paul, Minnesota, in 1889. There he made a name for himself as one of the most highly skilled criminal lawyers of the old Northwest.

Although McGhee eventually became known for his efforts to end racial discrimination, his initial success as a litigator was a testament more to his eloquence and mental acuity than to any personal ambitions that he might have had to test the boundaries of racial equality. The first African American admitted to the bar in Minnesota, McGhee quickly attracted a biracial clientele by establishing a reputation as a tough criminal lawyer whose presence could be felt in the courtroom. Despite his success as a trial lawyer, he was no stranger to discrimination. One writer commented, "He knew by bitter experience how his own dark face had served as an excuse for discouraging him and discriminating unfairly against him" (*Crisis*, Nov. 1912). Although McGhee achieved such accolades as being the first black man allowed to argue cases before the Minnesota Supreme Court, he still resented any sort of racial slight, and by the early 1900s he became interested in the national discussion concerning race.

In 1898 McGhee responded to a formal call issued by Bishop ALEXANDER WALTERS of the African Methodist Episcopal (AME) Church to revive the defunct Afro-American League. That organization was founded in 1890 upon the views of T. THOMAS FORTUNE that agitation and perhaps even revolution were necessary if African Americans were to achieve racial equality. The meeting convened eight years later as the Afro-American Council, and though its precepts remained unchanged, its resolutions quickly acquired a conciliatory nature under the leadership of BOOKER T. WASHINGTON. Although, like Fortune, Washington advocated both solidarity and self-help, Washington vocalized his disapproval only when he felt that it would be effective, believing that agitation alone could not bring about justice. McGhee, like many other northern lawyers, differed from his southern counterparts. He depended on whites as well as blacks for his living, interacted daily with his white clientele, and established himself firmly in the upper echelon of St. Paul society. Therefore McGhee was an improbable ally for Washington and his principles of economic chauvinism and industrial education. McGhee wavered on the issue of social equality, stating as late as 1904 that, though he would not abide racial discrimination, he did not believe in absolute social equality.

McGhee acted as head of the council's legal department, served as program chairman for the 1902 St. Paul meeting, and in 1903 was elected financial secretary. He became disillusioned with Washington's tendency to placate whites in order to win marginal battles, and by 1903 McGhee was urging the Afro-American Council to use more aggressive tactics. Although McGhee, a well-known Catholic layman, never completely sided with the Tuskegeean in the national debate, Washington persuaded him in 1904 to approach the Catholic hierarchy in hopes of enlisting the church's explicit opposition to disfranchisement of black voters in Maryland.

McGhee helped initiate the Niagara Movement, an attempt by more radical blacks to oppose directly and openly the conservative actions and views of Washington. Writing for the *Voice of the Negro* in September 1905, W. E. B. DuBois went so far as to give McGhee full credit for creating the more radical entity, stating, "The honor of founding the organization belongs to F. L. McGhee, who first suggested it." McGhee served the new organization loyally, helping it to take legal action against the Pullman Company for discrimination in 1907. Although the Niagara Movement ultimately failed, McGhee, DuBois, and others did finally see the gradual decline of Washington's influence, especially when the Tuskegeean lost control of the Afro-American Council in 1907. The Niagara Movement's decline was evidence that neither militant nor conservative blacks were representative of the race as a whole. According to the author August Meier, without the help of a small number of white progressives, the Niagara Movement alone would not have been able to oust Washington or his influential allies, considering the fundamental characteristics of race relations in the United States at the turn of the century.

McGhee was a lifelong Democrat during a period when Republicans continued to experience the residual loyalty of many African Americans. Though he supported Theodore Roosevelt for president in 1904, within Minnesota he continued to vote the Democratic ticket because he believed that the Democrats were better to African Americans there. Furthermore, he rejected Republican imperialism, particularly the violent attempts to crush Filipino independence. In 1900 McGhee wrote of "the number of women and children killed in attacks upon villages defended by men armed with bamboo spears, this with the profoundly and oft-repeated assertion, of late so prevalent, that the proud Anglo-Saxon, the Republican party, by divine foreordination, is destined to rule earth's inferior races"—adding, "Is it to be wondered then that so little value is placed upon the life, liberty, freedom and rights of the American Negro? Is he not also one of the inferior races which Divine Providence has commissioned the Republican party to care for?" (Katz, 424).

By 1910 the National Association for the Advancement of Colored People (NAACP), which became the most powerful force for African Americans in the United States, had organized and held its first meeting, a tangible sign that Washington's influence was by this time negligible. Although the Niagara Movement did not actually merge with the new organization, most of its members soon joined forces with it, including McGhee, who helped organize the St. Paul chapter. McGhee died of pleurisy shortly after the NAACP's formation and was never able to experience the organization's eventual triumphs.

A tireless opponent of discrimination in the United States, McGhee, according to an obituary in the *Crisis*, "stood like a wall against the encroachment of color caste in the Northwest and his influence and his purse were ever ready to help." Despite his loyalty to African Americans and their particular circumstances, McGhee's attentions were never completely self absorbed. Throughout his life and career he remained acutely aware of the oppression of other races, particularly those overseas, remarking that because blacks had experienced oppression firsthand, they "should be the loudest in the protestations against the oppression of others" (Katz, 324).

FURTHER READING
Katz, William Loren. *The Black West* (1987).
Meier, August. *Negro Thought in America, 1880–1915* (1963).
Spangler, Earl. *The Negro in Minnesota* (1961).
Obituary: *The Crisis* (Nov. 1912).

This entry is taken from the *American National Biography* and is published here with the permission of the American Council of Learned Societies.

DONNA GREAR PARKER

McGhee, Howard B. "Maggie" (6 Mar. 1918–17 July 1987), jazz trumpeter, arranger, and composer, known as "Maggie" in the jazz community, was born in Tulsa, Oklahoma. His parents' names are unknown. His father, seeking factory work, moved the family to Detroit when McGhee was an infant, but his mother died soon thereafter, and Howard was raised by his grandmother in Bristow and Sapulpa, Oklahoma. His father returned from Detroit but died when McGhee was about five years old. After moving with his grandmother to Boley, Oklahoma, McGhee attended a boys' school, where he learned to play a scale on trumpet; then, to his disappointment, he was started on clarinet, so as not to be ahead of the rest of the class. McGhee lost an eye in a childhood accident and thereafter always wore dark glasses. Perhaps the fashion among beboppers of the 1940s for wearing dark shades in dingy nightclubs has in McGhee's experience a practical origin independent of the sartorial preferences of DIZZY GILLESPIE and THELONIOUS MONK. McGhee's first job in music was playing trumpet in a carnival band in Muskogee, Oklahoma, at about age thirteen or fourteen. He was still in school but spent the summer traveling with the carnival. He joined a quartet in a restaurant in Oklahoma City, where he developed his endurance as a trumpeter, but when he traveled to California to join Gene Coy's band it was as a tenor saxophonist. He switched permanently to trumpet to play with Art Bronson's jump band in 1935, at age sixteen. Bronson's men ridiculed McGhee for his intense admiration and excessive imitation of LOUIS ARMSTRONG, and he left after three months.

McGhee continued playing in obscure territory bands from 1936 to 1940, when he returned to Detroit to lead his own group. He joined LIONEL HAMPTON's big band in September 1941, but he quit soon after when he discovered that he could make the same wages in Detroit and not have to travel. The following year, though, he joined ANDY KIRK's big band in St. Louis. While with Kirk in New York, McGhee participated in jam sessions at Minton's Playhouse and Monroe's Uptown House. He met Gillespie at Minton's in July and thereby became involved in the emerging bop style. McGhee had begun writing arrangements for Kirk, and that same month, July 1942, he was featured on Kirk's recording of "McGhee Special," which McGhee had composed for his own band in 1940. Like many African American musicians, McGhee disliked traveling in the South and quit in August when Kirk announced his next tour.

Late in August 1942 McGhee became one of four African American instrumentalists to join the big band of the saxophonist Charlie Barnet, for whom he also supplied arrangements. As a freelancer in New York after August 1943, McGhee served as a substitute in COUNT BASIE's big band late in the year. He recorded with Kirk again in December. During his last tenure with Kirk, from February to 28 June 1944, McGhee tutored his section mate FATS NAVARRO in how to produce high notes on the trumpet. McGhee then went into another racially integrated endeavor, joining the saxophonist Georgie Auld's big band on 30 June as the featured trumpet soloist, as a regular member of the trumpet section, and as an arranger. He substituted in BILLY ECKSTINE's bop big band during this period and also wrote arrangements for Eckstine and Woody Herman.

In December 1944 McGhee joined tenor saxophonist COLEMAN HAWKINS's five-piece group, including the bassist OSCAR PETTIFORD, the pianist Sir Charles Thompson, and the drummer DENZIL BEST, at the Three Deuces in New York. McGhee traveled with Hawkins to California, where he participated in Jazz at the Philharmonic concerts. According to McGhee, at one of these concerts the producer Norman Granz made a recording of "How High the Moon" without telling the band; the successful disc brought McGhee celebrity but little money. Meanwhile, he worked as Hawkins's sideman in Los Angeles from February to mid-April 1945, when he quit in a dispute over money.

McGhee stayed in California for two years, initially coleading a group with Teddy Edwards from 1945 to early 1946 and then leading on his own. He participated in the chaotic and controversial Dial recording session of 29 July 1946, preceding the alto saxophonist CHARLIE PARKER's admittance to Camarillo Hospital. Three of the four resulting titles, including "Be-bop," were originally issued under McGhee's name. He led his own session for Dial on 18 October and then joined a recovered Parker on 26 February 1947 for celebrated versions of "Relaxin' at Camarillo," "Carvin' the Bird," "Cheers," and "Stupendous," the last three titles featuring themes composed by McGhee. In April he was also captured on record as a soloist in "Groovin'

High" at the producer Gene Norman's Just Jazz concert, a rival to Jazz at the Philharmonic.

Back in New York, McGhee appeared with Jazz at the Philharmonic at Carnegie Hall late in 1947 and toured with this assemblage of all-stars. He also toured and recorded with his own groups, his recordings including a session of 3 December 1947 with the saxophonist James Moody, the vibraphonist MILT JACKSON, the pianist Hank Jones, the bassist Ray Brown, and the drummer J. C. HEARD as his sidemen. In Chicago he recorded a further session featuring Jackson in February 1948. In May of that year McGhee took his own group, including the saxophonist JIMMY HEATH and the bassist Percy Heath, to the Paris Jazz Festival; they recorded on 14 May under the drummer KENNY CLARKE's leadership. In New York, with Jackson playing vibraphone and piano, McGhee recorded a marvelous session with Navarro, the two trumpets exchanging closely matched improvised bop phrases on "Boperation" and "Double Talk" (October 1948). McGhee was a member of the singer and percussionist MACHITO's Afro-Cuban group in the spring of 1949. The saxophonist Brew Moore and McGhee are the jazz soloists on "Cubop City," which Machito recorded in April. In 1949 McGhee was selected best trumpeter of the year in the annual *Down Beat* poll.

McGhee's attempt to found a big band in 1950, at exactly the time when many famous leaders were splitting their bands up, was a financial disaster. As a member of Pettiford's group he embarked on a USO tour of the United States, Japan, Korea, the Philippines, Guam, and Okinawa from late 1951 to early 1952. By this time, if not some years earlier, McGhee was addicted to heroin. He occasionally played with Parker in Boston during the early 1950s, and he led a fine recording session with the pianist HORACE SILVER and the guitarist Tal Farlow among his sidemen in June 1953, but he was largely inactive from 1952 through 1959. Arrested for possession of narcotics in 1958, he served about six months at the Tombs and on Rikers Island in New York City. After McGhee's release from jail, Woody Herman gave him a job in 1960. He began recording again, including the albums *Together Again!* with Teddy Edwards in May 1961 and *Maggie's Back in Town* with the pianist PHINEAS NEWBORN JR. in June. McGhee worked in Moody's band in Los Angeles in 1961 and late that year briefly joined DUKE ELLINGTON. McGhee received critical acclaim for his performances at the Newport Jazz Festival in July 1963.

From the mid-1960s into the 1970s McGhee led a big band in New York, largely for musical

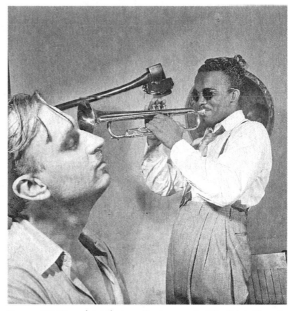

Howard McGhee (right) plays the trumpet while Brick Fleagle listens, New York City, c. September 1947. (© William P. Gottlieb; www.jazzphotos.com.)

satisfaction rather than for making money. During this period he often worked with the singer Joe Carroll. The Reverend John Gensel, the "jazz pastor," had helped McGhee secure a police cabaret card so that he could work in New York again after the narcotics conviction. Subsequently McGhee often donated his musical services to Gensel's church. He may be seen in the documentary film biography of Gensel, *Shepherd of the Night Flock*, made between 1972 and 1977. As the festival circuit blossomed in the 1970s, McGhee toured widely, including a visit to Europe with a group that included the trombonist J. J. JOHNSON and the alto saxophonist SONNY STITT. In the mid-1980s McGhee continued his activities with Gensel in the Jazz Vespers series at St. Peter's Lutheran Church. He died in New York City. He was survived by his wife, Tina, and their four children; Tina's maiden name and the marriage date are unknown.

McGhee was one of the few trumpeters of the mid- to late 1940s who could play bop well, meeting the technical demands that the style's melodies posed for a brass player and inventing creative lines in the process. Gillespie and Navarro set the standard in this regard; McGhee and Kenny Dorham were not far behind. In fact, distinguishing between Navarro's and McGhee's dovetailing and brilliant melodies on the two takes of "Double Talk" (1948) is almost certainly a matter for the jazz expert, not the general listener. Indeed, on liner notes to the first twelve-inch LP reissue of this session, even the bop expert Leonard Feather appears to have confused the two, stating that Navarro played the first two 32-bar choruses before initiating a series of trades back and forth (8 bars each; later 16, then 8, then 16 each), when in fact it sounds as though Navarro played 32 bars and McGhee the next 32 before Navarro began the quicker trading. This observation is not a criticism of Feather but rather testifies to how completely McGhee had absorbed the difficult bop melodic style, considerably removed from his upbringing in the tunefulness of the swing era.

FURTHER READING

An interview by Ira Gitler (16 and 23 Nov. and 1 and 6 Dec. 1982) is among the oral histories at the Institute of Jazz Studies, Newark, New Jersey.

Boenzli, Richard E. *Discography of Howard McGhee* (1961).

Hoefer, George. "The Early Career of Howard McGhee," *Down Beat* 30 (15 Aug. 1963): 33–34.

Schuller, Gunther. *The Swing Era: The Development of Jazz, 1930–1945* (1989).

Obituary: *New York Times*, 18 July 1987.

This entry is taken from the *American National Biography* and is published here with the permission of the American Council of Learned Societies.

BARRY KERNFELD

McGinty, Doris Evans (2 Aug. 1925–5 Apr. 2005), college professor, musicologist, pianist, and writer, was born Doris Valean Evans in Washington, D.C., the second daughter of Vallean Richardson Evans and Charlie Evans. Her mother worked for the federal government, and her father was a tailor. McGinty, encouraged by her pianist mother to pursue music, began the study of piano at age seven. At age twelve she gave her first public recital. She continued the study of piano with Andres Wheatley in the Junior Preparatory Department at Howard University and played for Sunday school at the District's Metropolitan African Methodist Episcopal Church. Among her treasured mementoes were the dress and shoes she wore to the historic 1939 MARIAN ANDERSON command performance at Washington's Lincoln Memorial.

Two baccalaureate degrees, in music education and German, were completed at Howard University in 1945 and 1946, respectively. McGinty then went to Radcliffe College in Cambridge, Massachusetts.

The only African American in her class, she earned an M.A. degree in Music in 1947 and then returned to Washington, D.C., to accept an assistant professorship in Music History at Howard. After teaching at Howard for a few years, McGinty took a study leave in 1951 and entered England's Oxford University as a Fulbright fellow. Along with the renewal of her Fulbright, the next year she received a General Education Board grant, awarded by the Rockefeller Foundation. In 1954 she made history by becoming the first American woman to earn a doctorate in musicology at Oxford. McGinty's brilliance and scholarship were praised by John Westrup and Egon Wellesz, her Oxford professors and two of the world's foremost musicologists.

At Oxford she had concentrated in opera and medieval music; her dissertation (never published) was titled "Music in the Middle Ages." However, after her return to the Howard academic community in 1954, she felt a compelling need to research and document the musical culture of black America. Howard University in the 1950s and 1960s was the right place and time for such research. It was a major academic community within black America, with a long history of African American intellectuals, trailblazers, and activists on the faculty. The District of Columbia and Howard had for decades been a hotbed of broad-based musical activity for black Americans. Moreover, this was a period when the civil rights movement was beginning to make powerful statements to the nation. Black college and university students on both African American and white campuses were beginning to demand that courses in "black music" be made a part of the curriculum.

Thus, with the exception of a summer appointment as a visiting professor at Texas Southern University in 1956 and an appointment as a Phelps-Stokes Caribbean exchange scholar in 1974, Howard University remained her academic home, where, until she retired from teaching and became professor emerita in 1991, she influenced, shaped, and propelled several generations of students. Her writing and research was international in scope. She was published in *Musik in Geschichte und Gegenwart* and *Schulfunk Westdeutscher Rundfunk*. She contributed to *The New Grove Dictionary of American Music, Dictionary of Negro Biography, The Black Perspective in Music*, and *Black Music Research Journal* and remained the preeminent scholar of the black music experience in the District of Columbia. McGinty was married on 6 September 1956, to Milton Oliver McGinty, a real estate businessman. The couple had three children: Derek Gordon McGinty, Dana Winston McGinty, and Lisa Megan McGinty.

McGinty's crowning achievement was *A Documentary History of the National Association of Negro Musicians*, published in 2004 by the Center for Black Music Research. Located at Columbia College in Chicago, the Center for Black Music Research is a conglomerate whose mission is the collection, documentation, and publication of data about the black experience in music. The book began as a project with EILEEN SOUTHERN, who, like McGinty, was a mainstream musicologist and had had the field of black music thrust upon her by the social unrest and growing political awareness of the 1960s and the struggles of the civil rights movement. McGinty and Southern, both towering figures in the field of musicology, were brought together for the National Association of Negro Musicians (NANM) history project by Willis Patterson, then-president of the association and a University of Michigan School of Music associate dean. Southern's illness and subsequent death on 13 October 2002, however, left McGinty with the gargantuan task of bringing the project to completion. Through primary and secondary documents, the book presents the history of the National Association of Negro Musicians, and is significant because it speaks to the contributions of black cultural organization to American history.

The District of Columbia's musical elite was at the forefront of early involvement to establish a national organization of Negro musicians. McGinty built upon data known from her years of involvement with studying black music in the District. One of the persons that McGinty had studied was HARRIET GIBBS MARSHALL (1869–1941), founder in 1903 of the District's Washington Conservatory of Music. Marshall was probably the first person to suggest that black classical musicians come together in a national organization. Henry Lee Grant, also of the District of Columbia, was the NANM's first president (1919–1922). At the 2004 National Association of Negro Musicians convention in Detroit, the year before her death, McGinty was recognized for her scholarship and involvement in making the book a reality.

FURTHER READING
As of 2007, McGinty's papers remained with her family. The expectation is that they will eventually be housed at Howard University.
"A Celebration of the Life of Doris Evans McGinty." Order of Service, Howard University (2005).

Notable Black American Women, book 2 (1996).
Southern, Eileen, ed. *Biographical Dictionary of Afro-American and African Musicians* (1982).
Obituary: *Washington Post*, 8 Apr. 2005.

WALLACE MCCLAIN CHEATHAM

McGirt, James Ephraim (1874–13 June 1930), poet, short-story writer, magazine publisher, and entrepreneur, was one of Madison and Ellen Townsend McGirt's four children. Born in Robeson County, North Carolina, he spent his childhood on the family farm and attended Whitun Normal School, a private school for blacks in nearby Lumberton.

While McGirt was still young, his family moved first to another farm in Robeson County and then to Greensboro, North Carolina. There McGirt's father drove a wagon and his mother was a launderer. Young McGirt took part-time jobs while completing his secondary education. In 1892 he entered Greensboro's Bennett College and graduated three years later with a bachelor's degree.

While in Greensboro McGirt began writing poetry and published his first book, *Avenging the Maine, a Drunken A. B., and Other Poems* (1899). McGirt's apologetic preface explains that he wrote the poems when his "body was almost exhausted from manual labor" (3). The themes in *Avenging the Maine* and in McGirt's subsequent books are typical of the black poetry of the day. Seeking acceptance into mainstream America, black poets wrote patriotic verse, often in reference to the recent Spanish-American War. Thirty-three blacks had died in the sinking of the *Maine*, and African American troops had fought in the war, including at San Juan Hill. For many blacks these soldiers represented their race. McGirt wrote in his poems of black troops who "fought like demons" (9) and of an African American soldier who presented the flag that he had defended to Uncle Sam, who, according to the poem, "knows no color" (23). To appeal to diverse readers, McGirt and other black poets also wrote on subjects common to poets of all races, such as nature, virtue, and disappointment in love. The last subject may have been particularly relevant to McGirt, who, like his siblings, never married. McGirt also wrote in dialect, as did his black and white contemporaries, though such poems constitute only a small part of his work.

McGirt published a second edition of *Avenging the Maine* (1900) with seventeen additional poems. The following year a third edition appeared as well as another collection called *Some Simple Songs and a Few More Ambitious Attempts*. In the new book he again begins on an apologetic note but declares that this book is a "great improvement" over the last one (5). Actually, fifteen of the twenty-one poems in the new volume had been in various editions of *Avenging the Maine.*

Soon after publication of *Avenging the Maine,* McGirt left Greensboro and moved north. His travels are difficult to trace, but by 1903 he was in Philadelphia. In August he began publishing *McGirt's Magazine,* an illustrated monthly containing poetry, fiction, and nonfiction. The number of African American periodicals had grown rapidly since Reconstruction, encouraging and publicizing black achievement. McGirt declared that his purpose in publishing a magazine was to enable black and white readers to "know great men of our race and what they are doing and saying" (Parker, 330).

While publishing the magazine, McGirt released another book of poetry, *For Your Sweet Sake* (1905), and a volume of short stories, *The Triumphs of Ephraim* (1907). Most of the forty-four poems in *For Your Sweet Sake* had been published previously. *The Triumphs of Ephraim* contains eight stories with a recurring theme of racial tension. In addition to his books, McGirt's writing appeared regularly in his magazine. One of his most interesting contributions was a serial, a mainstay of popular magazines at that time, called "Black Hand." The central character is a white bigot who, as a result of a brain injury sustained in a railroad accident, becomes black and has to contend with the oppression that he has helped foster, including rejection by his friends and fiancée.

The great debate of the day in African American periodicals was over the conflicting views of BOOKER T. WASHINGTON, who advocated gradualism and self-improvement, and W. E. B. DuBois, who called for racial equality. While *McGirt's Magazine* extolled black economic success and the value of higher education, the publication's editorial stance was closest to the views of DuBois. McGirt was a strong and vocal advocate for civil rights and the power of the black vote. His magazine was the official organ for the Constitutional Brotherhood of America, an organization promoting black suffrage, of which McGirt was secretary-treasurer. At McGirt's urging, DuBois submitted an article for the magazine called "The Training of Negroes for Social Power," and DuBois recommended *McGirt's Magazine* in his publication, *Horizon.*

McGirt's Magazine enjoyed sufficient success that in 1905 McGirt was able to found McGirt Publishing Company and move to a larger facility.

Prosperity was fleeting, however. Though *McGirt's Magazine* occasionally published notable writers, such as DuBois and PAUL LAURENCE DUNBAR, the overall quality of the content could not match that of the competition. While the peak circulation of *McGirt's Magazine* reached 1,500, the readership of the most popular black magazines of the period, *Voice of the Negro* and *Colored American Magazine,* was ten times greater. In 1909 McGirt retrenched and published his magazine as a quarterly. At year's end, he stopped publication altogether.

With the magazine's demise McGirt returned to Greensboro. There he cared for his aging parents and operated several businesses. He and his sister, Mary, built the Star Hair Grower Manufacturing Company into an international concern, selling hair grower, toiletries, and other products in the United States and abroad. McGirt also became a realtor. He bought property around the city, including a ten-room house where he, his sister, and parents lived. During the 1920s he operated People's Drug Store on East Market Street, in the heart of Greensboro's black business district. A prolonged illness in the late 1920s forced McGirt to reduce his business activities. When he died in Greensboro, *Greensboro Daily News* described him as "one of the best known Negro citizens" of the city (14 June 1930, 4).

Though his writing is largely forgotten, McGirt can be remembered as being representative of African American leaders born in the generation after slavery. He seized the opportunities denied his ancestors to seek personal success, while working for civil rights and promoting black achievement to cultivate respect for his race.

FURTHER READING
Daniel, Walter C. *Black Journals of the United States* (1982).
Parker, John W. "James Ephraim McGirt: Poet of 'Hope Deferred,'" *North Carolina Historical Review* 31 (July 1954).

LANG BARADELL

McGruder, Aaron (13 Jan. 1975–), cartoonist, was born Aaron Vincent McGruder in Chicago, the son of Bill McGruder, an employee with the National Safety Transportation Board, and Elaine (maiden name not known), a homemaker. When McGruder was six years old the family moved to the planned community of Columbia, Maryland. Created by the Rouse Company in the late 1960s, Columbia was envisioned as an integrationist, post–civil rights utopia. The young McGruder attended a Jesuit

Aaron McGruder, creator of *The Boondocks* comic strip, at work in his studio in Columbia, Maryland, 21 June 1999. (AP Images.)

school outside of Columbia from seventh to ninth grade. It was, as he said in a *New Yorker* profile, "a very strict, very, very white Jesuit school." As oppressive as the atmosphere was, it was while at this school that McGruder discovered the humor of Monty Python. When he transferred to public school in the tenth grade, he found himself mostly in the company of other black students. He became a fan of *Star Wars*, kung fu movies, and hip-hop, especially the politically conscious music of Public Enemy and KRS-ONE.

McGruder entered the University of Maryland in 1993, where he concentrated in African American studies with a focus on social and cultural analysis. In 1996 he was invited to join the independent student newspaper, the *Diamondback*. It was here that he introduced his cartoon strip, *The Boondocks*, its name a sardonic reference to the suburbs. Upon

McGruder's graduation in 1997, *The Boondocks* was published in the national hip-hop magazine the *Source*, where it ran until being pulled in 1999 following legal and contractual disagreements.

But McGruder was already moving on to wider exposure. In 1998 the Universal Press Syndicate, which published Garry Trudeau's *Doonesbury*, launched *The Boondocks* in 160 newspapers. It was the largest opening of a strip in the syndicate's history. By 2000 the strip was appearing in 250 newspapers and continued to grow to 300. Its success would have been notable no matter what, but in the context of cartoons and race, it was remarkable. In 2000 McGruder was one of only nine African American cartoonists with syndicated strips. Among these mostly bland and cautious strips, *The Boondocks* was distinguished by its forthright handling of racial and political matters.

In the comic strip's early period, roughly from 1998 to 2001, *The Boondocks* followed the daily adventures of brothers Huey and Riley Freeman, black grade-schoolers who have recently made the move to the suburbs outside Chicago, and their grandfather, whom they live with. McGruder has said that the three represent different facets of African American manhood: Huey, the angry, Afro-coiffed black nationalist socialist; Riley, the younger brother who aspires to be a "thug"; and Granddad, who is a cranky skeptic and pragmatist. Huey's best friend Michael Caesar, a young dreadlocked DJ from Brooklyn, provides a balance to Huey's harsh and sometimes paranoid rants. Then there are the little girls in the strip: Cindy, a little white girl who has never known any black people (other than what sees on *Yo MTV Raps!*), and Jazmine DuBois, the biracial daughter of a black lawyer and his white wife. This diverse cast of characters allowed McGruder to explore the nuances of race, race relations, education, the suburbs, popular culture, politics, and class in the United States in the late twentieth and early twenty-first century. The strip was funny but edgy, and its success led to the publication of two collections of *Boondocks* cartoons, *Because I Know You Don't Read the Newspapers* (2000) and *Fresh for '01—You Suckas* (2001).

After three years of producing daily comics, McGruder admitted that deadline pressures and impending burnout was pushing him to drop the strip. But when the terrorist events of 11 September 2001 occurred, *The Boondocks* turned more political and in many ways more focused. The strip's political humor became more streamlined and the artwork less detailed. In 2003 McGruder published

A Right to Be Hostile: The Boondocks Treasury. His 2004 collaboration with the filmmaker Reginald Hudlin and fellow cartoonist Kyle Baker, *Birth of a Nation*, was a graphic novel satirizing the administration of George W. Bush, among other targets.

FURTHER READING

McGrath, Ben. "The Radical," *New Yorker* (19–26 Apr. 2004).

CHARLES PETE BANNER-HALEY

McGuire, George Alexander (26 Mar. 1866–10 Nov. 1934), bishop and founder of the African Orthodox Church, was born in Sweets, Antigua, British West Indies, the son of Edward Henry McGuire and Mary Elizabeth (maiden name unknown). He graduated from the Antigua branch of Mico College for Teachers in 1886. Baptized in his father's Anglican church, he was educated in the Moravian tradition of his mother, graduating in 1888 from the Moravian seminary at Nisky, St. Thomas, in the Danish West Indies. Thereafter he pastored a Moravian congregation at Frederiksted, St. Croix. He married Ada Roberts in 1892; they had one daughter.

McGuire immigrated to the United States in 1894. The following year he was confirmed in the Protestant Episcopal Church. He studied for the Episcopal ministry under a fellow West Indian, Henry L. Phillips of Philadelphia, Pennsylvania. McGuire found himself in a church that desired to minister to African Americans but was generally unwilling to accept any blacks as equal to whites. McGuire's talent and Phillips's mentorship allowed him to advance swiftly through the offices open to him. Ordained deacon in 1896 and priest the next year, he pastored a succession of black congregations, including St. Andrew's, Cincinnati (1897–1899); St. Philip's, Richmond (1899–1901); and St. Thomas's, Philadelphia (1901–1904).

In 1905 McGuire accepted the appointment of Bishop William Montgomery Brown as archdeacon for colored work in the Diocese of Arkansas. This was the highest position open to a black man serving the church within the United States. The denomination's national General Convention, however, was considering two proposals for allowing blacks to serve as domestic bishops: the first would place black bishops in charge of all-black missionary districts independent of local dioceses; and the second would allow dioceses to elect suffragan bishops who would work under the supervision of the diocesan bishop. Soon after McGuire's arrival, Brown proposed a third plan: black Episcopalians should be separated into an independent denomination. In 1906 McGuire seems to have preferred the missionary plan; later, under his own initiative, he attempted to enact Brown's plan.

Racial conflicts in the Arkansas diocese led McGuire to accept an invitation to return to the North in 1909 to pastor St. Bartholomew's, a young congregation of West Indians in Cambridge, Massachusetts. Under McGuire's leadership the church grew dramatically, but again he was frustrated by the racism of the Episcopal Church, evident in the diocese's refusal to grant the congregation voting rights. In 1911 he moved to New York to become field secretary of the American Church Institute for Negroes. Two years later he accepted a call to serve as rector of St. Paul's Church, Falmouth, in his native Antigua.

While in the Islands McGuire encountered the ideas of racial independence and nationalism advocated by MARCUS GARVEY. These resonated with McGuire's experience of whites' inability to treat blacks as equals within the church. He returned to New York in 1919 to support Garvey's newly formed Universal Negro Improvement Association (UNIA) and African Communities League. McGuire soon established his own congregation, the Church of the Good Shepherd, which affiliated briefly with the Reformed Episcopal Church but soon united with a few other congregations to form the Independent Episcopal Church.

In August 1920 the first International Convention of the Negro Peoples of the World elected McGuire chaplain-general of the UNIA and "titular Archbishop of Ethiopia." McGuire strengthened the work of local UNIA chaplains and, according to the UNIA's *Negro World*, sought to create a church "big enough for all Negroes to enter, retaining their own worship" (2 Apr. 1921). McGuire linked Christianity and racial independence in *The Universal Negro Catechism* (1921) and *The Universal Negro Ritual* (1921), which he composed for the UNIA. The catechism taught that if one "had to think or speak of the color of God" it should be described "as black since we are created in His image and likeness." The infant baptism rite charged the baptized to "fight manfully ... for the freedom of his race, and the redemption of Africa unto his life's end."

The formality of the rituals did not appeal to many Protestant supporters of the UNIA, nor did McGuire's ordination of a UNIA leader as a presbyter of the church. Within a year the *Negro World* was at pains to stress, "We favor all churches, but adopt none as a UNIA Church" (16 July 1921).

Although Garvey desired to unite blacks into "a great Christian confraternity," he did not want the church and hierarchy that McGuire sought to create. After a brief period of estrangement, McGuire resumed a prominent role in the UNIA, presiding over the movement's "canonization" of Jesus as the "Black Man of Sorrows" in 1924.

Unable to establish a church linked to the UNIA, McGuire sought to provide an independent black church for Anglo-Catholics. Elected bishop of the Independent Episcopal Church in September 1921, he insisted that the church be renamed the African Orthodox Church (AOC) to emphasize its racial leadership. He maintained that his new church was "neither schismatic nor heretical," but a legitimate national or racial "branch" of the one Holy Catholic Church.

When trying to form a church linked to the UNIA, McGuire had been willing to forgo apostolic succession, but he believed this was essential to authenticate the claims of the AOC. Refused consecration by Episcopal, Catholic, and Russian Orthodox bishops, he finally received it from Joseph René Vilatte of the Old Catholic Church of America. Having an autonomous church headed by a black bishop in apostolic succession was a great source of pride for McGuire and his followers, but the questionable authenticity of Vilatte's consecrations haunted their relations with other churches.

McGuire crafted a liturgy for his church based largely on the Book of Common Prayer and Anglo-Catholic practices, but also incorporating a few elements from Eastern Orthodoxy. The liturgy included prayers for the race and the redemption of Africa, though less pronounced than those in *The Universal Negro Ritual*. McGuire also founded Endich Theological Seminary in 1923 and edited the church's monthly *Negro Churchman* from 1923 to 1931. By the mid-1920s church membership numbered twelve thousand, with congregations in the northeastern United States, Nova Scotia, and the Caribbean. In 1927 McGuire was raised to the rank of patriarch and expanded the church to South Africa by receiving a few congregations and consecrating their leader, Daniel William Alexander, as bishop. McGuire died in New York City as head of a slowly expanding church.

McGuire broke new ground in extending the autonomy enjoyed by many black Protestants to black Anglo-Catholics. He was among the most important religious leaders in Garvey's movement and a talented member of the corps of West Indian clergy serving the Episcopal Church in the United States. The churches led by Alexander in Africa proved to be an enduring and significant presence on that continent. Yet in the United States the AOC became a small, though enduring, community of less than six thousand people. As a black church leader who boasted of a claim to apostolic succession that few recognized, McGuire remained a marginal figure in both the church and predominantly Protestant black America.

FURTHER READING
McGuire, George Alexander. *The Universal Negro Catechism* (1921).
McGuire, George Alexander. *The Universal Negro Ritual* (1921).
Burkett, Randall K. *Black Redemption: Churchmen Speak for the Garvey Movement* (1978).
Burkett, Randall K. *Garveyism as a Religious Movement: The Institutionalization of Black Civil Religion* (1978).
Farajajé-Jones, Elias. *In Search of Zion: The Spiritual Significance of Africa in Black Religious Movements* (1990).
Lewis, Harold T. *Yet with a Steady Beat: The African American Struggle for Recognition in the Episcopal Church* (1996).
This entry is taken from the *American National Biography* and is published here with the permission of the American Council of Learned Societies.

DAVID R. BAINS

McGuire-Duvall, Edith (3 June 1944–), track and field athlete, was born Edith McGuire in Rockdale, Georgia, one of four children of Alberta, a domestic worker, and Clifford McGuire, a railroad worker. As a child, McGuire first participated in track and field at her elementary school during its May Day celebration. She next attended Samuel Howard Archer High School and was coached by Georgia Sports Hall-of-Fame member Marian Morgan and Olympian Mildred McDaniel Gold. As a high school student athlete McGuire excelled in the classroom and was selected to the honor roll. She also participated in cheerleading, basketball, and track and field. At the age of 15, McGuire defeated top-ranked local sprinter Fronnie Tucker, and Morgan recommended she attend Coach ED TEMPLE's summer camp at Texas Southern University. In the summer of 1960, between her junior and senior years of high school, McGuire attended Coach Temple's track-and field camp, which she credits for much of her athletic development. Coach Temple allowed her to watch film to supplement her skills as well as attend both the Amateur Athletic Union (AAU) national meet in Texas and the Olympic Trials. McGuire was impressed by the success of the TSU women's track-and-field team, known as the "Tigerbelles," and she pledged to join them after graduation.

After winning the AAU junior division sprints in both the 50-meter and 100-meter dashes, McGuire entered TSU in 1961 on a work-aid scholarship. That same year McGuire represented the United States on an international tour in meets against Russia, Poland, Germany, and England. In 1962 she placed third in the 100-meter dash and was a member of the first place 4 × 100-meter relay team in a dual meet with the USSR in Stanford, California. The Pan-American Games were held in Sao Paulo, Brazil, the following year, and McGuire again was first in the 100 meters and a member of the 4 × 100-meter relay team. Also in 1963 McGuire won the 100-yard dash and the long jump at the AAU Indoor Championships in Columbus, Ohio, and surpassed her second place finish the previous year by winning the 100-meter dash in 1963 in San Diego, California.

By the end of 1963 McGuire was America's premier female sprinter. In 1964 she won the 100-meter dash at the AAU Outdoor Championships in Hanford, California, and became the first woman to win the 100-meter and 200-meter dashes and be a member of the victorious 4 × 100-meter relay team in a United States versus USSR track-and-field meet. McGuire's success brought increased pressure, as her teammates nicknamed her "Top Cat." As a student at TSU, McGuire attempted to live a normal life. Along with other teammates, including U.S. Track-and-Field Hall of Famers WILMA RUDOLPH and WYOMIA TYUS, McGuire joined the Delta Sigma Theta sorority. She could not, however, escape lofty expectations, as *Stars and Stripes* labeled her the number-one woman to beat heading into the 1964 Olympic Games in Tokyo, Japan. Coach Temple believed McGuire would be the "next Wilma Rudolph" and similarly win gold medals in the 100-meter, 200-meter, and 400-meter relay events, respectively.

McGuire had a successful start at the Tokyo Olympics and won her first two heats in the 100-meter dash. Heading into the final, all the media and public attention remained on her. Little did she know that teammate and freshman Tyus would shock the world and win the gold medal. Temple, serving as the U.S. women's track-and-field coach, reminded McGuire that it is better to lose to a Tigerbelle than to anyone else, as she recomposed herself for the 200-meter final. McGuire rekindled her winning ways by taking the gold medal in the 200-meter dash. She also anchored the 400-meter relay team, which won a silver medal.

McGuire ended an impressive year by being one of ten finalists for the James E. Sullivan Award, presented to the most outstanding amateur athlete of the year in the United States. She capped off her career by setting a new meet record in the National AAU Outdoor Championships in the 220-yard dash in Columbus, Ohio, and was named to the AAU All-American team in 1961, 1963, 1964, 1965, and 1966. In 1965 Atlanta, Georgia, mayor Ivan Allen Jr. proclaimed 29 January as "Edith McGuire Day" in appreciation of her accomplishments in track and field.

McGuire graduated from TSU with a B.S. in Elementary Education in 1966. After graduation, she returned to the Atlanta area to become a teacher, and in 1967 she married Charles Duvall. By 1977 and for the next 27 years, the Duvalls owned and operated five McDonald's restaurants and also started community-service athletic programs for children. In the 1990s the Duvalls collaborated with the Oakland Police Department and that city's school system to start Hoop It Up for Education, a community enrichment program that stressed education as a necessity for athletic youths.

McGuire's track-and-field accomplishments were cemented by her induction into various sports Halls of Fame, including the Tennessee Sports Hall of Fame in 1975 and the U.S. Track-and-Field Hall of Fame in 1979. She also was a 1991 recipient of the National Collegiate Athletic Association Silver Anniversary Award, an honor for former athletes who went on to distinguished careers outside of athletics.

FURTHER READING
Lewis, Dwight. *A Will to Win* (1983).
Molzahn, Arlene Bourgeois. *Top 10 American Women Sprinters* (1998).
Plowden, Martha Ward. *Olympic Black Women* (1996).
Temple, Ed, and B'Lou Carter. *Only the Pure in Heart Survive* (1980).

JAMAL RATCHFORD

McJunkin, George (1851–21 Jan. 1922), renaissance man of diverse interests who spent most of his life as a cowboy and foreman on New Mexico horse and cattle ranches; amateur natural historian, geologist, astronomer, and archaeologist; and self-taught violinist and surveyor, discovered what was later identified as North America's first Paleo-Indian site, in Wild Horse Arroyo near Folsom, New Mexico. This discovery pushed back the date of known human settlement on the continent from 3,000 years to over 10,000 years.

McJunkin was born in 1851 on a ranch near Midway, Texas, where the laws of that time defined him as the property of persons unknown. The names of his parents have never been established, and even the origin of his surname is disputed; accounts that he worked for a Jack McJunkin in Texas (whether before or after emancipation is not clear), point to John Sanders McJunkin of Midway. In 1910 he informed a U.S. census taker that his father was born in Illinois and his mother in Mississippi, which suggests that his father may have been a free man from birth, but there are no contemporary records. The father had his own blacksmith shop before George was born.

Whether his father was born free or purchased his freedom, he accumulated money to purchase his wife, and son George, when emancipation was officially proclaimed in Texas in 1865. Freed at age fourteen, George assisted his father for three years in blacksmith work; at age seventeen George slipped away in the night and struck out on his own, finding his first job as assistant cook on a trail drive. It is a common but disputed tale that he rode off on one of his former owner's mules, and returned it later after earning enough money to acquire his own horse.

What is known about McJunkin's life derives primarily from recollections of people who had known him personally, collected thirty to forty years after he died. He had gotten some practice, with the help of Mexican *vaqueros*, learning riding and lariat skills, as well as Spanish, which helped him obtain his first jobs. He learned to read and write, although it is unlikely he had any opportunity to attend school. He participated in two trail drives of cattle from Texas to the railroad terminus at Dodge City, Kansas. One of his early employers, Gideon Roberds, hired McJunkin around 1868 to help get a herd of horses from Texas via New Mexico to Colorado; he may have remained there until 1874. McJunkin is said to have taught Roberds's sons to ride horses, in exchange for reading lessons.

He was a trail driver for John McCandless, rough herding steers from the Bell Ranch in New Mexico, which opened in 1881. (Some sources refer to an earlier ranch on the Canadian River, in Texas.) One of McJunkin's better known employers was Dr. Thomas E. Owen, who settled in 1885 on the Pitchfork Ranch near Perico, in the Cimmaron Valley of New Mexico. After working for Owen as a trail boss, McJunkin became foreman of the Crowfoot Ranch, near Ragtown, owned by William H. (Bill) Jack, where he remained for most of his adult life. He also managed the nearby Oak Grove ranch near Silver City for several years.

At Crowfoot, McJunkin built saddle, tool, and hay sheds; a chicken house; and barns—showing that carpentry was another of his many skills—and added a wing to the ranch house for himself. He was expert at gentling, training, and gelding horses. He collected bones, stone projectile points (spear or arrow heads), and other artifacts, while building up a collection of books on anthropology, geology, astronomy, and surveying. One of his most cherished possessions was a telescope given to him by a retired military officer. He obtained a surveyor's transit—some accounts say it was purchased for him by Antine Meloche of TO Ranch. Equipped with this tool, and widely recognized as a fair man, McJunkin was called on to settle disputes between ranchers over land and property lines.

Ivan Shoemaker, who worked for McJunkin as a young man, recalled an incident when hands from a number of outfits came to help with branding at a wealthy ranch employing several black servants. Called in for lunch, the hands asked, "Where's George?" When the mistress of the house replied, "He'll eat in the kitchen with the other darkies," they got up from the table, and rode away. When George and some coworkers had been at the bar of the Eklund Hotel in Clayton, and decided to go to the dining room for lunch, the manager informed them, "It is our policy not to serve Negroes here." Gay Mellon, generally remembered as a calm and respectful man, pulled out his long-barreled Colt revolver, announcing "Your policy has just been changed." They were all seated. (Hewett, p. 23).

McJunkin never married. New Mexico territory in 1900 had 1,610 people described as "colored," only 587 of whom were female. The prejudices of that time would not have accepted any man considered "colored" marrying any woman of a different complexion. He was often referred to as "Nigger George," even by men who worked with him and respected his skills.

Inspecting fences south of Folsom, New Mexico, 29 August 1908, after intense flooding, McJunkin observed a large bone in the side of an eroded gully. The site became known as the Great Bone Pit, but its significance was not recognized until after McJunkin's death at the age of seventy-one. He had often described the site to Carl Schwachheim, a Raton blacksmith, who also collected artifacts, and later to Fred Howarth, employed by a Raton bank. Neither found time to go look at the site, although both were impressed by the bones that McJunkin showed them.

In 1926, four years after McJunkin's death, excavation by Harold Cook, Marie Wormington, and Jesse D. Figgins, from the Colorado Museum of Natural History, revealed twenty-three remains of bison, and nineteen stone projectile points, with a distinct style later named Folsom Points, including one spear-point embedded in a bison rib-cage, which established that humans had hunted in North American during the Pleistocene era. Carbon 14 tests, developed in the 1950s, would eventually date the points to around 9,000 B.C., a little more recent than the points found in 1932–1934 near Clovis, New Mexico.

Late in life, McJunkin accumulated the money to build his own house in Folsom, but never had time to move in. Bill Jack had died, and McJunkin was supervising the operation until Mrs. Jack could find a buyer. He continued working under the new owner, Lud Shoemaker. He rented out the house to cover his costs, then lost all his most cherished books and tools when lightning caused a fire in the shack where he lived on the ranch. Too ill to live in the house, he spent his last days in a back room at the Folsom Hotel.

FURTHER READING

Agogino, George. "The Search for Answers at Wild Horse Arroyo: The McJunkin Controversy." *New Mexico Magazine*, May–June 1971, 41–44.

Folsom, Franklin. *Black Cowboy: The Life and Legend of George McJunkin* (1992).

Hewett, Jaxon. "The Bookish Black at Wild Horse Arroyo: How the Folsom Man Came to Light." *New Mexico Magazine*, Jan–Feb 1971, 20–24.

CHARLES ROSENBERG

McKaine, Osceola (18 Dec. 1892–17 Nov. 1955), soldier, journalist, businessman, and political activist, was born Osceola Enoch McKain in Sumter, South Carolina, to Selena Durant McKain. His father's name is not recorded. Selena Durant McKain was only sixteen when she gave birth to Osceola, whom she named after a Seminole Indian warrior from the 1830s. By the time that Ossie, as he was known in the family, was six, his mother was working as a self-employed laundress in Sumter and had married George Abraham, a waiter and janitor. The couple raised four sons and two daughters in addition to Osceola, but Abraham never formally adopted him. Osceola also retained his mother's surname, adding an extra "e" for a touch of individuality, just as his mother had changed her name from McCain to McKain.

From an early age Osceola worked. Along with his siblings he helped his mother make her laundry deliveries, assisted his stepfather in his janitorial duties, and joined his grandfather McCain, a drayman, on his rounds. He was also devout, joining Sumter's Mt. Pisgah African Methodist Episcopal (AME) Church at the age of twelve, as well as attending several revival meetings. His later skills as a political orator were probably honed at these summer revivals. Although educational provision for African Americans in Sumter was poor, Selena Abraham provided Osceola with extra instruction at home, which was augmented by frequent visits to a neighbor, Miss Jeanette, who had an extensive library.

McKaine had a passion for education, but he also knew that there were few opportunities for a young man of his talents in Sumter. After graduating from the city's Lincoln High School in 1908, he found work as a stevedore on a freighter bound from Savannah, Georgia, to the West Indies. When the ship docked a year later in Boston, he decided to stay, graduated in 1910 from Sumner High School, and briefly attended Boston College. Still restless, he enlisted in the Twenty-fourth Infantry, an all-black U.S. Army regiment, in October 1914 and served at the regimental headquarters in Manila in the Philippines, at Fort Russell, Wyoming, and in the Mexican Punitive Expedition. Promoted to the rank of first lieutenant in 1917, McKaine was assigned to the famed Buffalo Soldiers of the 367th Infantry Regiment just before American entry into World War I.

A month before setting sail for France in June 1918, McKaine penned "A Negro's Faith in American Justice," an article for the *Southern Workman*, in which he sounded a patriotic and optimistic note about the U.S. involvement in a war that President Woodrow Wilson claimed would make the world "safe for democracy." "I am eager for the fray," McKaine wrote. "Death does not matter, for it will mean life for thousands of my countrymen, and for my race, for right must triumph." Like other African Americans at the time, notably W. E. B. DuBois, McKaine enthusiastically endorsed black participation in the war effort, believing that "the free allied nations of the world will not condone America's past treatment of her colored citizens in the future" ("Negro's Faith," 591–592).

It soon became apparent, however, that the regiment's senior white officers expected African Americans to be treated exactly as in the Jim Crow South. Fraternization between black troops and French and Belgian civilians, especially women, was prohibited, and military intelligence routinely intercepted and censored letters from black soldiers complaining about discrimination. These senior officers also discredited the contributions of African American soldiers, and especially junior black officers like McKaine, whom they feared might lead a racial revolt in the United States when the war was over. There were, however, many instances of bravery and initiative by black soldiers on the battlefield, notably on 9 November 1918, two days before the armistice, when the Buffalo Soldiers played a central role in the long-awaited, bloody, and decisive assault on the German fortress at Metz. In his *Official History of the American Negro in the War* (1919), EMMETT JAY SCOTT recorded that the Buffaloes "established and maintained a perfect liaison" and that "their Supply Department under that efficient supply officer, Lieutenant McKaine, coordinated perfectly with the line advancing to Metz."

Shortly after the armistice McKaine wrote a second article for a national newsweekly, the *Independent*, which struck a less optimistic note than the *Southern Workman* article had a year earlier. In "With the Buffaloes in France" he revealed how the black forces in France had to fight not only against the Germans in the trenches facing them but also against "their traditional oppressors and enemies in the rear," namely, their white superior officers. McKaine was much more positive, however, about relationships on the battlefield itself, where black and white soldiers "sang together, played together, and fought together to make the world safe for democracy."

McKaine hoped that such unity would continue when the American forces returned home, but by the spring of 1919 the military high command had placed severe restrictions on the movements of black soldiers who remained in Europe. Some officers feared that black soldiers might ally with radical elements in the French and British forces, while others feared that they would smuggle weapons into the United States. To combat these restrictions—which forbade black soldiers from leaving their billets or talking with female civilians—McKaine and other black officers then stationed at Brest in France formed a civil rights organization for black veterans, the League for Democracy (LFD).

When McKaine returned to the United States in April 1919, he moved to Harlem and became the LFD's field secretary and most impressive orator. He spoke out against the wave of lynchings and race riots that had greeted returning black soldiers and demanded that the War Department maintain a black officer corps in peacetime. The large crowds of veterans who flocked to LFD rallies in New York and Washington, D.C., brought McKaine to the attention of military intelligence and others in the War Department, who saw him as a dangerous radical. By the early 1920s, however, high unemployment, the chilling effect of the red scare on progressive politics, and the rival attractions of MARCUS GARVEY's movement had taken their toll on the LFD. Its membership declined significantly from its 1919 peak, and the LFD's newspaper, the *Commoner*, which McKaine had edited, folded. McKaine's marriage in 1922 to a showgirl was also short-lived.

In 1924, exhausted by six years of fighting racism in America, McKaine returned to Europe, where he traveled extensively before opening a nightclub in Ghent, Belgium, in 1928. With performances by many of the entertainers he had known in Harlem, Mac's Place became one of the most popular clubs in the city. When Nazi Germany invaded and occupied Belgium in 1940, however, McKaine left his nightclub in the hands of a partner and, at the age of forty-eight, returned to Sumter, South Carolina.

McKaine's cosmopolitan air, stylish suits, and French-inflected speech soon made an impression on Sumter. He began a series of articles about his foreign travels for a black newspaper, the *Columbia Palmetto Leader*, and also wrote a piece for that city's leading white paper, the *State*, that lauded the improvement in Sumter's race relations since he had left the town thirty years earlier. McKaine was adamant, however, that Sumter—and the rest of the South—still had far to go to achieve full equality between the races. As secretary of the Sumter branch of the NAACP he worked with MODJESKA SIMKINS on a statewide campaign to equalize teachers' salaries, and as the associate editor on JOHN MCCRAY's *Lighthouse and Informer* he helped to energize black political activism throughout the state during World War II.

In 1944 McKaine was elected secretary of a new political organization led by McCray, the Progressive Democratic Party (PDP), which launched a major voter registration campaign among African Americans. That year McKaine also became the first African American to run as a Democrat in South Carolina for the U.S. Senate when he challenged Olin Johnston. The official tally recorded that McKaine received only 3,200 votes, though the true number may have been as high as ten thousand. Either way, the PDP knew that it could not win, but McKaine's campaign proved a useful recruiting tool for the civil rights cause in South Carolina.

McKaine traveled widely through the South during the war years and in 1946 began working with the Southern Conference on Human Welfare (SCHW), a left-leaning and interracial organization. Appropriately, given his earlier efforts for the LFD, he began his first tour as field secretary for the SCHW by leading a parade of one hundred African American veterans of World War II in a rally for voting rights in Birmingham, Alabama. McKaine earned a reputation for his skillful oratory and for his tireless and meticulous planning of voter registration and electoral campaigns. The success of these registration drives was often spectacular. In 1946 McKaine's leadership helped to add tens of thousands of blacks to the voting rolls throughout the South. For McKaine, voting was the key to defeating Jim Crow. Moreover, he insisted, increasing black political strength in the South would help white southern liberals to "be more vocal, more consistent, and more steadfast in their efforts to bring democracy to Dixie" (quoted in Sullivan, 202).

McKaine's positive views of the Soviet Union did not sit well with several of his fellow South Carolina activists, notably John McCray. McKaine's relationship with McCray also soured over what McKaine viewed as McCray's dictatorial leadership of the PDP. Exhausted by his efforts for the SCHW, McKaine returned to Belgium in December 1946 to check on his business interests there. He kept in touch with developments in South Carolina and wrote articles on European affairs for several black newspapers, but he remained in Ghent until his death from an acute digestive hemorrhage on 17 November 1955. His body was returned to Sumter, South Carolina, and on 3 December 1955, Lieutenant Osceola McKaine was buried with full military honors. A racially integrated honor guard attended the funeral, a fitting tribute to a man who had begun his public career by challenging segregation and discrimination in the military.

FURTHER READING

Egerton, John. *Speak Now against the Day: The Generation before the Civil Rights Movement in the South* (1994).

Richards, Miles S. "Osceola E. McKaine and the Struggle for Black Civil Rights: 1917–1946," Ph.D. diss., University of South Carolina (1994).

Sullivan, Patricia. *Days of Hope: Race and Democracy in the New Deal Era* (1996).

STEVEN J. NIVEN

McKane, Alice Woodby (1865–1945), physician and educator, was born Alice Woodby in Bridgewater, Pennsylvania, the daughter of Charles Woodby and Elizabeth B. Frazier. As a child Alice suffered from the loss of her sight and remained blind for three years. After recovering she attended public schools in Bridgewater, less than thirty miles from Pittsburgh.

From 1884 to 1886 Woodby attended Hampton Institute in Virginia. Although she never graduated, Woodby fully embraced the Hampton principles of "education for life" and "learning by doing." In an 1897 letter to the *Southern Workman* she explained her decision to leave Hampton: "Students were sent out to teach one year before graduating. Not wishing to become a teacher, I thought it best not to begin, for fear the temptation to continue might thwart my plans for obtaining my profession."

Woodby entered the Institute for Colored Youth (ICY) in Philadelphia, Pennsylvania, in 1886. The ICY was one of the most prestigious nineteenth-century African American academic institutions. The school was led by FANNY JACKSON COPPIN, the first black woman to head an institution of higher learning in the nation, and was located in the heart of Philadelphia's African American community, near the historic Mother Bethel African Methodist Episcopal (AME) Church. While attending classes Woodby also worked as Coppin's private secretary.

After graduation Woodby entered the Woman's Medical College of Pennsylvania in October 1889. She completed her studies at the first medical college for the exclusive purpose of training women to be physicians and received her medical degree in May 1892. She relocated to Augusta, Georgia, to establish a practice and to teach at the Haines Institute. Woodby privately taught classes on nursing, while teaching chemistry and physiology and serving as the resident physician at the institute. The school was founded on the principle that educated women were a prerequisite for the advancement of the black race. The Haines Institute was chartered by the state of Georgia as a normal and industrial school in 1888. LUCY CRAFT LANEY, whose formal training included summer programs at the Hampton Institute, was the school's founder.

Less than a year after earning her medical degree, Woodby married Cornelius McKane on 2 February 1893. Grandson of a Liberian king, Cornelius was born in Demerara, British Guiana (Guyana). He was a civil rights activist, clergyman, teacher, scholar, and practicing physician in Savannah, Georgia. Alice McKane and her husband founded the first training school for black nurses, in southeast Georgia, with the first graduates finishing in 1895. The school doubled as a much-needed free clinic, providing free treatment to local citizens. Of the venture McKane wrote that "the training of women of my race as nurses was still of the greatest interest to me for many reasons, so I begged my husband to assist me to start such work…. He consented, and together we started work in our office. Few understood that our motives were to try to do good" (*Southern Workman*, 1897). Although local black churches provided some support for the medical facility, funding was insufficient, and the school became Charity Hospital in 1901.

Around 1894 the McKanes traveled to Liberia and set up a hospital in Monrovia. While in Liberia, Alice McKane worked as a medical examiner for the U.S. government, overseeing the health of Civil War veterans living in the country. She was also the co-organizer and head of the department of diseases of women at the first hospital in Monrovia. African fever forced the couple to leave the country, but they returned to the United States determined to open a hospital for African Americans in their hometown of Savannah, Georgia.

In June 1896 they established the McKane Hospital, after a small group of African Americans received a state charter to operate the McKane Hospital for Women and Children and Training School for Nurses. The five-room wooden building was the first hospital in Savannah to train African American doctors and nurses. Local white doctors helped with donations of their time and money.

Seeking better educational opportunities for their children—Cornelius Jr., born in 1897, Alice Fanny, born the following year, and William Francis, born in 1902—the McKanes moved to Boston in 1909. Both of the McKanes passed the Massachusetts state medical board exam within their first two weeks in Boston, and they quickly established a private practice. Alice McKane focused primarily on the care of women. In addition to her practice McKane lectured nurses at Plymouth Hospital and was active in the St. Martin's Day Nursery Association.

Active in Massachusetts politics, McKane was part of the women's suffrage movement and served as an elected delegate to the Republican Massachusetts state convention. She was also director of the South End Cooperative Bank of Boston. Additional civic duties led her to memberships in Boston's Business and Professional Women's Republican Club, the NAACP, and the National Equal Rights League. McKane was a contributor to numerous religious magazines and journals. She published two books, the *Fraternal Sick Book* in 1913, which dealt with the art of healing, and *Clover Leaves* in 1914, a volume of poetry. She was also a member of the League of Colored Poets of the World. McKane died of arteriosclerosis.

FURTHER READING

Bailey, Brooke. *The Remarkable Lives of 1000 Women Healers and Scientists* (1994).
Southern Workman (Aug. 1898, Mar. 1911, Aug. 1927).

KAREN JEAN HUNT

McKay, Claude (15 Sept. 1890–22 May 1948), poet, novelist, and journalist, was born Festus Claudius McKay in Sunny Ville, Clarendon Parish, Jamaica, the son of Thomas Francis McKay and Hannah Ann Elizabeth Edwards, farmers. The youngest of eleven children, McKay was sent at an early age to live with his oldest brother, a schoolteacher, so that he could be given the best education available. An avid reader, McKay began to write poetry at the age of ten. In 1906 he decided to enter a trade school, but when the school was destroyed by an earthquake he became apprenticed to a carriage- and cabinet-maker; a brief period in the constabulary followed. In 1907 McKay came to the attention of Walter Jekyll, an English gentleman residing in Jamaica who became his mentor, encouraging him to write dialect verse. Jekyll later set some of McKay's verse to music. By the time he immigrated to the United States in 1912, McKay had established himself as a poet, publishing two volumes of dialect verse, *Songs of Jamaica* (1912) and *Constab Ballads* (1912).

Having heard favorable reports of the work of BOOKER T. WASHINGTON, McKay enrolled at Tuskegee Institute in Alabama with the intention of studying agronomy; it was here that he first encountered the harsh realities of American racism, which would form the basis for much of his subsequent writing. He soon left Tuskegee for Kansas State College in Manhattan, Kansas. In 1914 a financial gift from Jekyll enabled him to move to New York, where he invested in a restaurant and married his childhood sweetheart, Eulalie Imelda Lewars. Neither venture lasted a year, and Lewars returned to Jamaica to give birth to their daughter. McKay was forced to take a series of menial jobs. He was finally able to publish two poems, "Invocation" and "The Harlem Dancer," under a pseudonym in 1917. McKay's talent as a lyric poet earned him recognition, particularly from Frank Harris, editor of *Pearson's* magazine, and Max Eastman, editor of the *Liberator*, a socialist journal; both became instrumental in McKay's early career.

As a socialist, McKay eventually became an editor at the *Liberator*, in addition to writing various articles for a number of left-wing publications. During the period of racial violence against blacks known as the Red Summer of 1919, McKay wrote one of his best-known poems, the sonnet "If We Must Die," an anthem of resistance later quoted by Winston Churchill during World War II. "Baptism," "The White House," and "The Lynching," all sonnets, also exemplify some of McKay's finest protest poetry. The generation of poets who formed the core of the Harlem Renaissance, including LANGSTON HUGHES and COUNTÉE CULLEN, identified McKay as a leading inspirational force, even though he did not write modern verse. His innovation lay in the directness with which he spoke of racial issues and his choice of the working class, rather than the middle class, as his focus.

McKay resided in England from 1919 through 1921, then returned to the United States. While in England, he was employed by the British socialist journal *Workers' Dreadnought*, and published a book of verse, *Spring in New Hampshire*, which was released in an expanded version in the United States in 1922. The same year, *Harlem Shadows*, perhaps his most significant poetry collection, appeared. McKay then began a twelve-year sojourn through Europe, the Soviet Union, and Africa, a period marked by poverty and illness. While in the Soviet Union he compiled his journalistic essays into a book, *The Negroes in America*, which was not published in the United States until 1979. For a time he was buoyed by the success of his first published novel, *Home to Harlem* (1928), which was critically acclaimed but engendered controversy for its frank portrayal of the underside of Harlem life.

His next novel, *Banjo: A Story without a Plot* (1929), followed the exploits of an expatriate African American musician in Marseille, a locale McKay knew well. This novel and McKay's presence in France influenced Léopold Sédar Senghor, Aimé Césaire, and other pioneers of the Negritude literary movement that took hold in French West Africa and the West Indies. *Banjo* did not sell well. Neither did *Gingertown* (1932), a short story collection, or *Banana Bottom* (1933). Often identified as McKay's finest novel, *Banana Bottom* tells the story of Bita Plant, who returns to Jamaica after being educated in England and struggles to form an identity that reconciles the aesthetic values imposed upon her with her appreciation for her native roots.

McKay had moved to Morocco in 1930, but his financial situation forced him to return to the United States in 1934. He gained acceptance to the Federal Writers' Project in 1936 and completed his autobiography, *A Long Way from Home*, in 1937. Although no longer sympathetic toward communism, he remained a socialist, publishing essays and articles in the *Nation*, the *New Leader*, and the *New York Amsterdam News*. In 1940 McKay produced a nonfiction work, *Harlem: Negro Metropolis*, which gained little attention but has remained an important historical source. Never able to regain the stature he had achieved during the 1920s, McKay blamed his chronic financial difficulties on his race and his failure to obtain academic credentials and associations.

McKay never returned to the homeland he left in 1912. He became a U.S. citizen in 1940. High blood pressure and heart disease led to a steady physical decline, and in a move that surprised his friends, McKay abandoned his lifelong agnosticism and embraced Catholicism. In 1944 he left New York for Chicago, where he worked for the Catholic Youth Organization. He eventually succumbed to congestive heart failure in Chicago. His second autobiography, *My Green Hills of Jamaica*, was published posthumously in 1979.

Assessments of McKay's lasting influence vary. To McKay's contemporaries, such as JAMES WELDON JOHNSON, "Claude McKay's poetry was one of the great forces in bringing about what is often called the 'Negro Literary Renaissance.'" While his novels and autobiographies have found an increasing audience in recent years, modern critics appear to concur with ARTHUR P. DAVIS that McKay's greatest literary contributions are found among his early sonnets and lyrics. McKay ended *A Long Way from Home* with this assessment of himself: "I have nothing to give but my singing. All my life I have been a troubadour wanderer, nourishing myself mainly on the poetry of existence. And all I offer here is the distilled poetry of my experience."

FURTHER READING
The bulk of McKay's papers is located in the James
    Weldon Johnson Collection at Yale University.

Bronz, Stephen H. *Roots of Negro Racial Consciousness: The 1920s, Three Harlem Renaissance Authors* (1964).

Cooper, Wayne F. *Claude McKay: Rebel Sojourner in the Harlem Renaissance, a Biography* (1987).

Cooper, Wayne F., ed. *The Passion of Claude McKay* (1973).

Gayle, Addison. *Claude McKay: The Black Poet at War* (1972).

Giles, James R. *Claude McKay* (1976).

Tillary, Tyrone. *Claude McKay: A Black Poet's Struggle for Identity* (1992).

Obituary: *New York Times*, 24 May 1948.

This entry is taken from the *American National Biography* and is published here with the permission of the American Council of Learned Societies.

FREDA SCOTT GILES

McKay, Nellie Y. (12 May 1930–22 Jan. 2006), scholar, teacher, editor, and author, was born Nellie Yvonne Reynolds in New York City, the daughter of Harry, a taxi driver, and Nellie Reynolds, a homemaker. Graduating cum laude from Queens College in 1969 with a B.A. in English, McKay was accepted into the Ph.D. program at Harvard University for British and American Literature.

McKay was part of the first cohort of African American graduate students determined to include the literatures, histories, and religions of African Americans in their research and study. However, McKay often reminisced about Harvard not having any black literature class and how her graduate colleagues taught one another. Not only did they have to teach one another but they also had to create their own bibliographies and share the few extant copies of the books. McKay dedicated her life to filling this void.

In 1973 she began teaching at Simmons College. By 1977, the year she completed her Ph.D., she had also earned tenure, perhaps becoming the first woman of African descent to do so at Simmons.

A year later, in 1978, McKay accepted the challenge of creating a viable literature component in the fledgling department of Afro-American studies at the University of Wisconsin (UW) at Madison. Five students enrolled for the first class. Two years later, she had designed five African American literature courses that enrolled hundreds of students. Under her leadership, the Afro-American studies department at UW Madison became a model for its intensive yet broad curricula, high-quality scholarship, racially integrated faculty and students, and university-wide collaborations. McKay was also the central figure in the establishing of black women's studies as a presence in academic and intellectual life.

As a scholar, McKay was astonishing. In 1984 she published *Jean Toomer, Artist: A Study of His Literary Life and Work, 1894–1936*, a work that combined close textual analysis with illuminating biographical and social context. Eminent scholars such as Thadious Davis and HENRY LOUIS GATES JR. called McKay's study brilliant and a foundational text for study of Toomer, of the Harlem Renaissance, and American literature of the 1920s and 1930s generally. McKay's specialty, however, was producing accurate and insightful editions and anthologies of African American literature that could be used as textbooks as well as for scholarly reference. She was among the first to recognize the importance of TONI MORRISON as an artist, and her three edited collections *Critical Essays on Toni Morrison* (1988), *Approaches to Teaching the Novels of Toni Morrison* (1997), and *Beloved: A Casebook* (1999) were instrumental in establishing Morrison as one of the most taught and most written about authors in the United States. McKay authored and edited nearly a dozen books and more than sixty articles and essays on topics that ranged from the eighteenth-century poetry of PHILLIS WHEATLEY to twentieth-century controversies such as the U.S. Senate confirmation hearings on the U.S. Supreme Court nomination of CLARENCE THOMAS.

Probably her most enduring legacy came from her coediting of the *Norton Anthology of African American Literature*, the first of the prestigious Norton Anthologies to become a bestseller in the trade market. Norton's original marketing survey had predicted a breakeven point if the anthology sold 30,000 copies in two years. But the volume sold 30,000 copies in its first six weeks. Moreover, the sales were not in the college textbook market for which it was intended. Appearing just before Christmas, the hardback volumes were snatched up for presents and pleasure reading. Reportedly Hillary Clinton bought a copy for Bill, and a Green Bay Packer football player carried the book with him throughout the 1996–1997 season and spoke passionately about its usefulness in the midst of routine sports interviews.

The *Norton Anthology of African American Literature* illustrated McKay's steadfast commitment to scholarly collaboration and was acknowledged as an academic tour de force for bringing eleven of the best scholars of African American literature together to compile and publish what many deemed the canon of African American literature. McKay's vision, her extensive knowledge of the discipline, and her diplomatic and strategic skills in collaboration and mediation were essential to that pathbreaking project. Many considered McKay the glue that held the entire enterprise together.

McKay worked assiduously to ensure that African American studies was as intellectually rigorous and as accessible as possible. She received grants from places such as the Ford Foundation to research models for African American studies programs nationally, and she presided over the MidWest Consortium of Afro-American Studies. But her influence and her interest were not confined to Afro-American studies nor was her collaboration bound within the walls of academe. McKay participated in countless conferences, worked on numerous committees, and spoke at prisons, community centers, churches, and sorority teas. She recorded more than fifty hours of interviews and lectures for public radio in Wisconsin. She served on advisory and editorial boards, including the Feminist Press, *African American Review*, and *American Literary History*. For years, she was a consultant to the annual ZORA NEALE HURSTON festival sponsored by Hurston's home town of Eatonton, Florida, and to the Women in Religion Program at Harvard Divinity School. McKay was elected to the executive board of the 20,000-member Modern Language Association and was the first African American woman nominated for its presidency. She was the keynote speaker at the 1998 founding conference in Heidelberg, Germany, of MELUS-Europe (Multi-Ethnic Literature of the United States) (later Multi-Ethnic Studies of Europe and America) and accepted invitations to lecture at sites as diverse as Auburn University in Alabama and the University of Zimbabwe in Harare. In 2001 McKay was inducted into the Wisconsin Academy of Sciences, Arts and Letters, and in 2002 the University of Michigan awarded her an Honorary Doctorate of Humane Letters.

However, McKay's forte was teaching. She never forgot the difficulties she and her cohort had in learning about African American culture, and she worked to create institutions and curricula to ensure that never again would anyone thirst for such knowledge. Her numerous teaching awards included being named in 1988 the Teacher of the Year for the entire University of Wisconsin system. McKay was renowned for her accessibility to students not only in her large classes and not only to the more than fifty Wisconsin graduates upon whose master and Ph.D. committees she served but also to students and faculty around the world, who wrote her, visited her, and implored her for counsel and recommendations. When she died of cancer in a hospice in Fitchburg, Wisconsin, she held an endowed chair as the Evjue Professor of American and African American Literature. On 1 April 2006 the University of Wisconsin hosted an international symposium in her memory. Participants agreed that she refused to posture as an academic superstar. But she chose instead to act as a conduit for the merging communities of teachers, scholars, readers, and writers who will shape public intellectuals for years to come.

FURTHER READING
McKay, Nellie Y. "A Troubled Peace: Black Women in the Halls of the White Academy, *Black Women in the Academy: Promises and Perils*, ed. Lois Benjamin (1997).
Benjamin, Shanna Greene. "Breaking the Whole Thing Open: An Interview with Nellie Y. McKay," *PMLA* 121.5 (Oct. 2006).
Hall, Donald E. "A Changing Profession …, " *Professions: Conversations on the Future of Literary and Cultural Studies* (2001).
"Nellie McKay–A Memorial," *African American Review* 40.1 (Spring 2006).
Obituaries: *New York Times*, 28 Jan. 2006.

FRANCES SMITH FOSTER

McKegney, Tony (15 Feb. 1953–), hockey player, was born in Montreal, Quebec, to a Nigerian father, who returned to Nigeria shortly after Tony's birth, and a Canadian mother who put him up for adoption. Larry McKegney, a chemist, and Cathy McKegney, both white, adopted one-year-old Tony, one of five children they adopted, and raised him in Sarnia, Ontario. Even though he was the only African American in his neighborhood, and one of only twenty in a town of 50,000, he felt accepted.

A gifted athlete, McKegney played football, baseball, basketball, and hockey. He knew early that hockey was his future, and like most Canadian boys, dreamed of a career in the National Hockey League (NHL). To help develop his and his brothers' skills, his father built a skating rink in their backyard. He played junior hockey in Sarnia, becoming the star of the Sarnia Blackhawks, before moving up to major juniors in 1974. He played for the Kingston Canadians of the Ontario Junior Hockey League (OJHL), scoring 152 goals in four seasons. With the majority of NHL players coming from the OJHL, his success there propelled him onto the NHL's radar.

Though there were few blacks playing hockey, his race was never a factor playing in Canada. He recalled, in an interview with *Ebony* in 1989, that his status as a hockey player was first and foremost, and his race was merely a footnote. Racial politics and hockey collided when McKegney turned professional in 1978. The Birmingham (Alabama) Bulls of the World Hockey Association (WHA) offered McKegney a two-year, $150,000 contract with a $75,000 signing bonus. He thought the WHA was a good stepping-stone to the NHL, and he had a friend from juniors, Ken Linesman, on the team. While aware of racial problems in the South, McKegney did not view his situation as a racial issue, but a hockey issue, and he hoped his play on the ice would speak for him. When he signed, Bulls fans were vocal with their disgust at McKegney and threatened to cancel their season tickets. Bulls owner John F. Bassett Jr. caved to the pressure and declared the contract null and void. While McKegney could have fought the decision, he decided not to do so. He considered the week of his WHA signing the worst of his life. Putting the incident behind him, McKegney entered the NHL draft in 1978 and was taken with the thirty-second pick by the Buffalo Sabres. He

became only the fourth black (following WILLIE O'REE, Mike Marson, and Bill Riley) and second McKegney in the NHL (his brother Ian played for the Chicago Blackhawks). McKegney was touted as a big, physical (six feet, 200 pounds) winger with a deft scoring touch, particularly with his ability to shoot the puck in the tiniest amount of space. He was not known for his skating, which was described at times as odd, but he was deceptively quick. He started the 1978–1979 season with Buffalo's minor league team, the Hershey (Pennsylvania) Bears. In twenty-four games he scored twenty-one goals, earning a promotion to the NHL. He completed five seasons with Buffalo, including two seasons scoring more than thirty goals. He said that when the team traveled they were often mistaken for a baseball or football team because few believed blacks played hockey.

Following the 1982–1983 season, Buffalo traded McKegney to the Quebec Nordiques, the first of many trades that brought McKegney to seven teams over the next eight seasons. After a little more than one season in Quebec, McKegney played for the Minnesota North Stars (1984–1986), New York Rangers (1986–1987), St. Louis Blues (1987–1989), Detroit Red Wings (1989), Quebec (1989–1991), and Chicago Blackhawks (1991), all via trades. He

Tony McKegney, of the St. Louis Blues, trying to cut off Detroit Red Wings' Steve Ciasson (3) during a game at the Joe Louis Arena in Detroit, Michigan, 20 December 1998. (AP Images.)

had his best season with St. Louis in 1987, tallying forty goals and thirty-eight assists for seventy-eight points, the first black to score forty goals. That season also marked the one racial incident McKegney experienced on the ice, when Detroit forward Joey Kacur called McKegney a "nigger" and McKegney retaliated by swinging his stick. After the league investigated, Kacur was fined $10,000 and suspended for one game. While trash talk on the ice was common, the league hoped Kacur's punishment would serve notice that racial epitaphs were forbidden. McKegney and Kacur put the incident behind them and became good friends when Tony joined the Red Wings in 1989.

McKegney's short stay in Chicago in 1991 would be his last NHL stop. Over his thirteen NHL seasons, McKegney amassed impressive statistics, including 912 career games, 320 goals, 319 assists, and eight twenty-goal seasons. His many trades earned him the nickname "suitcase Tony" and the reputation of being a streaky goal scorer who started strong and faded after a season or two. McKegney viewed his trades as positives, saying it was not a matter of one team not wanting him as much as another team did want him. Sportswriters, and even his mother, wondered if his race played any role in the trades, but Tony never dwelled on it. The only time he felt race might have been a factor was his trade from Buffalo to Quebec. Before the trade, an assistant coach asked him if he would start dating black women. At the time, Tony was dating a white woman named Susan, whom he later married, and they had two children.

McKegney played two more seasons of professional hockey, competing for HC Varese of the Italian League in 1991 and the San Diego Gulls of the International Hockey League in 1992, before ending his playing career. He settled in Amherst, New York, before moving to Michigan in 2000. He worked for Dome Consultants, Inc., a company that constructed sports domes and family entertainment centers. While he may not be considered a hockey star, McKegney was the first black player to reach prominence in the NHL and carve out a successful professional hockey career. He became a role model for blacks to follow into the NHL, such as the 2002 Most Valuable Player Jarome Iginla, though he had no role models himself.

FURTHER READING

Harris, Cecil. *Breaking the Ice: The Black Experience in Professional Hockey* (2003).

"Soul on Ice: Blacks in the NHL," *Ebony* (Feb. 1989).

MICHAEL C. MILLER

McKenzie, Vashti Murphy (30 May 1947–), community leader and African Methodist Episcopal (AME) bishop, was born to Edward Smith, a high school teacher and track coach, and the former Ida Murphy, a journalist and newspaper manager. The Smiths had three children. The young Vashti and her parents attended St. James Episcopal Church, where she sang in the junior choir. She grew up in a middle-class environment and was educated in local public schools. Her maternal great-grandfather founded one of the most prominent black newspapers on the East Coast, the *Afro-American*, and the Afro-American Newspaper Company. Her grandmother Vashti Turley Murphy was one of the founders of Delta Sigma Theta Sorority, a predominantly black collegiate female organization that was established in 1913. Murphy attended Morgan State University, where she met Stanley McKenzie, a professional basketball player with the Baltimore Bullets. They dated, and when Stan joined the Phoenix Suns he asked Murphy to marry him. She agreed, and they moved to Phoenix, Arizona. This union produced three children.

In Phoenix McKenzie took a reporting job with the *Arizona Republic* and worked as a model. In 1974 her husband retired from professional basketball, and they returned to Baltimore. She completed college, earning a B.A. in Journalism from the University of Maryland in College Park. Afterward she took several positions in the media business, working for the Afro-American Newspaper Company that published the *Baltimore Afro-American* and the *Washington Afro-American*, and hosted a television show for WJZ, which later promoted her to vice president of programming. McKenzie also worked as a disc jockey for a local gospel radio station, WYCB, and was later promoted to program manager.

In Baltimore McKenzie joined Bethel AME Church, then pastored by Bishop John R. Bryant. RICHARD ALLEN, a former slave, chartered the AME Church as a denomination in 1816. This was the earliest denomination founded by blacks in America. Soon McKenzie felt a call for the ministry, but because the AME required a seminary degree from its ministers she first went to secure the master of divinity from the Howard University School of Divinity and the doctor of ministry degree from United Theological Seminary in Dayton, Ohio.

After graduating from Howard, McKenzie was ordained as a deacon and assigned to a seven-member congregation in Chesapeake City, Maryland. After a year she was made elder and assigned to Oak Street AME Church in Baltimore. In 1990 she was sent as the first woman pastor to Payne Memorial AME Church, Baltimore, a community filled with drug dealers and poorly kept buildings. At first the new pastor met resistance even from female members, but she eventually grew Payne Memorial from 330 to 1,700 members.

Assigned to a growing congregation, McKenzie ultimately found a path to the bishopric since, historically, only pastors of large churches had reached the AME episcopate. At Payne Memorial, McKenzie revealed herself to be a holistic leader in the AME tradition, concerned with both the spiritual and material needs of her constituency and community. As a woman leader the young elder saw herself as a path breaker for others. In July 1996 she released *Not Without a Struggle*, a strong challenge to sexism within the AME Church. The AME Church was deemed sexist because it allowed women to pastor but did not appoint them as bishops, the rulers of the denomination. With *Not Without a Struggle* McKenzie intentionally opened her well-managed campaign for the episcopate while developing her pastorate.

Like many progressive black ministers McKenzie turned her local church into a community organization. She opened the Human Economic Development Center, an organization that provided job training, day care services, and education programs for youths and adults. She partnered with other churches, banks, and community leaders to form the Collective Banking Group (CBG) of which she was founding president. Through this program black leaders encouraged African Americans to open accounts in CBG banks that were in turn required to invest in black communities. This effort created more financial opportunity for minorities than were typically made available by conventional lending agencies. By 2000 forty local churches had completed construction projects, and sixty businesses were able to open or expand. Taking advantage of the charitable choice provision of the 1996 Welfare Law, Pastor McKenzie pioneered Payne Memorial Outreach, a nonprofit, faith-based organization. She secured a $1.5 million contract from the state of Maryland and succeeded in getting six hundred people off public assistance. McKenzie also saved a public school from closing and initiated twenty-five ministries, including twelve community service programs.

As McKenzie became an accomplished pastor she readied herself for the 2000 episcopal elections. Having grown up in an environment in which women were expected to be leaders—several female members of the Murphy clan had served as publishers of the *Afro-American Newspapers*—she stood her ground despite criticisms from both men and women and pressed forward in her quest for more recognition in the AME Church. Delta Sigma Theta, which she served as national chaplain, donated nearly fifty thousand dollars to her campaign, and other women supporters raised money for her. She also received support from Bishop John Bryant and her local bishop, Rev. Vinton R. Anderson. Female ministerial support from her local conference also shaped the 2000 elections because one-third of the Baltimore Conference ministers was female. All these factors led to Rev. McKenzie's election as the first female bishop of the AME Church on 11 July 2000.

Her designated episcopal area of supervision was the Eighteenth Episcopal District that included Lesotho, Mozambique, Swaziland, and Botswana. This formed five districts with two hundred churches and twenty thousand members. Bishop McKenzie moved to Lesotho and committed herself to improving the AME Church in Africa. She completed construction of twelve church buildings, opened computer labs in two church schools, built children's homes for thirty AIDS orphans, and planted thirty-seven churches. Bishop McKenzie's African tenure ended in 2004, when she was reassigned to the Thirteenth Episcopal District that covered Tennessee and Kentucky. Elected president of the AME Council of Bishops in 2004, McKenzie also became the titular head of the AME Church. As a result of her pioneer work two other female ministers, Carolyn Tyler-Guidry and Sarah Frances Davis, were elected bishops in 2004 in the AME Church. Presiding over an American district, Bishop McKenzie focused on economic development, financial management, and better health care. She served on the board of trustees of Wilberforce University and was the recipient of honorary doctorates from Goucher College, Howard University, Wilberforce, and Morgan State University. She also wrote several motivational books for African American women and was a sought-after speaker for women's groups.

FURTHER READING

"AME Church Elects More Women Bishops," *Christian Century*, 27 July 2004.

"Black Churches Push Collective Banking," *Washington Times*, 5 Aug. 2000.

Goodstein, Laurie. "After 213 years, A.M.E. Church Elects First Woman as a Bishop," *New York Times*, 12 July 2000.

Hine, Darlene Clark. *Black Women in America* (2005).

Murphy, Caryle. "Pioneer of the Spirit: The First Female AME Bishop Has Flung Open the Doors of the Church," *Washington Post*, 1 Aug. 2000.

DAVID MICHEL

McKinlay, Whitefield (15 Sept. 1852–14 Dec. 1941), businessman, was born in Charleston, South Carolina, the son of George McKinlay and Mary E. Weston. His father, a free black man, had purchased a house on Meeting Street in Charleston in 1848; his grandfather, Anthony Weston, was a well-known mixed-race millwright and slave owner in antebellum South Carolina. After the Civil War McKinlay studied at Avery Institute in Charleston, and in 1874 he enrolled at the University of South Carolina, where he remained for three years, until blacks were excluded after the Democrats came to power. After teaching school in South Carolina, he matriculated at Iowa College in Grinnell, Iowa, where he remained until 1881. By the age of twenty-nine, McKinlay could boast of a very strong education.

Although the profession of teaching was open to a person of his talents, McKinlay moved to Washington, D.C., and found a job in the Government Printing Office. In 1887 he married Kate Wheeler; the couple had two children. That same year he entered the real estate and loan business in the nation's capital. His clients included both whites and blacks, but he built up his business by catering principally to well-to-do blacks, either as a broker for the purchase of their homes or as the manager of their real estate investments. Among his elite black customers were the lawyer, editor, and civil rights leader ARCHIBALD GRIMKÉ; the physician, medical educator, and hospital administrator CHARLES BURLEIGH PURVIS; the Memphis real estate executive, banker, investor, and philanthropist Robert Reed Church; and the District of Columbia lawyer, Harvard graduate, and municipal court judge Robert Herberton Terrell. McKinlay had a keen eye for realty investment and a penchant for detail. He charged modest fees for his work (usually 5 percent), and he usually managed his investors' property profitably. Estimates of his net worth vary, but by the early twentieth century he was one of the wealthiest blacks in the United States, probably worth two hundred thousand dollars.

McKinlay's education, wealth, success, location, and dealings with upper-class blacks made him a natural to serve in some political capacity, but he accepted only two political appointments. In 1907 he agreed to serve on a commission on housing for the poor in the District of Columbia, and he accepted an assignment as collector of the Port of Georgetown, District of Columbia (1910–1913), both presidential appointments. McKinlay's most important political role was as a friend, adviser, and confidant of BOOKER T. WASHINGTON, who stayed in McKinlay's home during his visits to the nation's capital. McKinlay advised his friend Washington on who his supporters were in the District of Columbia and on the activities of his enemies. McKinlay gained audiences with presidents at Washington's behest, and he drove Washington to the White House in his buggy for Washington's famous 1901 supper with Theodore Roosevelt and returned for him afterward.

McKinlay made a strong plea two years later for the appointment of WILLIAM DEMOS CRUM, a politically active and socially prominent physician, as collector for the Port of Charleston. He wrote Roosevelt, "If the southern opponents of the Negro succeed in defeating this appointment it will establish a precedent which will make it almost impossible for you or any other President to appoint, for years to come, a colored man to any office in the southern states." During a bitter and divisive fight, Roosevelt gave Crum an interim appointment until the Senate finally confirmed him as collector in 1905. In 1912 McKinlay was among the first to protest against segregation of federal employees in government offices, a trend that became more pronounced during Woodrow Wilson's first administration.

During the 1920s and 1930s, while maintaining his activities as a real estate agent and lessor of District properties, McKinlay became, according to the historian CARTER G. WOODSON, "a faithful coworker of the Association for the Study of Negro Life and History." Along with Woodson, McKinlay sought to save primary source records concerning blacks, and he turned over to the association all of his own remarkable correspondence with distinguished persons of both races, including members of the cabinet and presidents of the United States. He also made available his large correspondence with Booker T. Washington. McKinlay continued his work in realty until he became enfeebled. He died in Washington, D.C.

FURTHER READING

Gatewood, Willard B. *Aristocrats of Color: The Black Elite, 1880–1920* (1990).

Obituary: *Journal of Negro History* 27 (Jan. 1942): 129–130.

This entry is taken from the *American National Biography* and is published here with the permission of the American Council of Learned Societies.

LOREN SCHWENINGER

McKinney, Cynthia (17 Mar. 1955–), state legislator and member of Congress, was born in Atlanta, Georgia, the daughter of Leola McKinney, a nurse, and James ("Billy") McKinney, a police officer and state legislator. A Roman Catholic and educated at Catholic schools, she graduated from Saint Joseph High School in 1973 and earned a bachelor of arts degree in International Relations from the University of Southern California in 1978.

McKinney's political ambitions reflected a family tradition. In 1948 Billy McKinney was among the first black police officers in Atlanta and worked to eliminate racial segregation. In 1973 he ran as a Democrat for the Georgia state legislature and won; routinely reelected, he served twenty years in office. Cynthia McKinney accompanied him to demonstrations in her youth and learned firsthand the importance of activism. In 1979, alongside her father, she encountered Ku Klux Klan members mocking a rally to protest the rape conviction of a mentally impaired black man; as she said, "prior to that day, everything was theory" but at the rally "I saw fact" and "knew that politics was going to be something I would do" (*Washington Post*, 5 July 1995).

McKinney pursued a Ph.D. in International Studies, earning an M.A. in Law and Diplomacy from the Fletcher School of Law and Diplomacy at Tufts University in Medford, Massachusetts, in 1986. She married Coy Grandison, a Jamaican politician, and moved to Jamaica in the 1980s; they had a son, Coy McKinney Grandison, and divorced in 1990. In 1986 her father, Billy McKinney, startled his fellow state representative and fellow Democrat Barbara Couch by entering his daughter as a write-in challenger to Couch. McKinney took 20 percent of the vote. Convinced that she could win if she campaigned seriously, McKinney ran again in 1988 and won.

During her two terms in the Georgia legislature, McKinney supported creation of the Eleventh Congressional District with a strong African American majority. Running in 1992 on the Democratic ticket to represent that district in the U.S. House of Representatives, McKinney won and became the first black woman from Georgia to enter Congress. She won reelection in 1994, but in 1995, the Supreme Court ruled in *Miller v. Johnson* that the Eleventh District's borders had been wrongly drawn to ensure a black majority. McKinney denounced the decision as racially discriminatory but ran successfully from the new Fourth District in the subsequent election in 1996, and was re-elected in 1998 and 2000.

McKinney's oratorical skills and vibrant personality, alongside her strong opposition to all forms of discrimination and social inequity, drew national attention to her status as a progressive member of Congress. She became well known to allies on the left and critics on the right. In the House, McKinney occasionally broke with Democratic Party leaders over international issues like trade restrictions (she voted against the North American Free Trade Agreement) or the primacy of human rights in diplomacy (she sponsored an unsuccessful bill to ban arms sales to countries with poor human rights records). With the Democratic Party seeking a centrist identity under President Bill Clinton from 1993–2001, McKinney's unwillingness to mimic the party's rightward shift drew attention. Right-wing political pundits targeted McKinney as pushy and radical. Not to be intimidated, McKinney refused to mute her criticisms of policies that she felt favored the affluent or powerful sectors of society.

After the terrorist attacks of 11 September 2001, McKinney questioned the lack of national preparedness and whether President George W. Bush had ties to corporations that would profit from Middle East conflict. While such questions would eventually become more commonplace, Bush supporters castigated McKinney. Moderate Democrats gave her little support. In the 2002 Democratic primary, she lost to Denise Majette, a black DeKalb County judge who then won the November election.

Out of office, McKinney held an appointment at Cornell University (she had taught at Agnes Scott College in Decatur, Georgia, and at Clark Atlanta University in Atlanta while in the Georgia legislature) and traveled widely to address international issues. She criticized the U.S. invasion of Iraq in 2003 and spoke of returning to Congress. When Denise Majette ran for the Senate in 2004, McKinney entered the race to replace her and narrowly won her sixth term in the House.

Returning to Congress in 2005, McKinney noted that the 9/11 Commission Report, a bipartisan analysis of the factors that contributed to the success of the 9/11 attacks, mirrored some concerns that she had voiced in 2001 and 2002. Many were surprised when she so quickly resumed criticism of the Bush administration, arguing that her loss in 2002 had reflected voters' hesitance to support challenges to the president. But McKinney continued such challenges, castigating federal inaction in response to Hurricane Katrina in 2005 and disputing the validity of the war in Iraq. In 2005 she received a nomination for the Nobel Peace Prize.

In March 2006 McKinney avoided a metal detector in a Congressional building and a Capitol Police officer pursued her for identification (Congress members with ID pins may bypass security). Annoyed, McKinney may have struck the officer. This altercation became a major media controversy. McKinney noted that officers routinely identified Congress members by sight rather than through ID pins. However, already a favorite target of conservative pundits, McKinney faced a barrage of hostile barbs and even possible assault charges. Charges were not filed and McKinney expressed regrets over the incident, but the media coverage enhanced the notion that she lacked self-control.

In the July 2006 Democratic Party primary in Georgia, McKinney edged out challenger Hank Johnson but did not gain the necessary 50 percent of the total vote to avoid a runoff. Johnson won the resulting August runoff and the November election. McKinney used her remaining months in office to introduce a bill to impeach George W. Bush, a proposal not supported by mainstream Democrats and seen as a symbolic statement on McKinney's part.

Not known for success in forging the compromises that usually push bills through Congress, McKinney's strongest attributes included the courage to criticize popular political leaders and a commitment to speak up for people on the social and economic margins. In the words of political scientist Charles Bullock, McKinney stood as a "symbolic representative" with speaking "truth to power" as "her theme" (*Los Angeles Times*, 8 Aug. 2006). In her political career through 2006, Cynthia McKinney's political positions were unaltered by the opprobrium that accompanied her efforts to challenge both national and international balances of power.

FURTHER READING

Jarvie, Jenny. "Congresswoman Is in Unforeseen Struggle for Seat; 'Backbone in Politics' Is the Slogan of Georgia's Combative McKinney," *Los Angeles Times*, 8 August 2006.

Jones, Ricky L. "'Black Hawk' Down: Cynthia McKinney, America's War on Terror, and the Rise of Bushism," *The Black Scholar* 32 (Fall 2002).

Masters, Kim. "The Woman in the Hot Seat," *Washington Post*, 5 July 1995.

Nichols, John. "Cynthia McKinney," *Progressive* (July 1996).

BETH KRAIG

McKinney, Ernest Rice (7 Dec. 1886–30 Jan. 1984), labor organizer and socialist, was born in Malden, West Virginia, in the home of his maternal grandfather, a coal miner and Baptist preacher. He and three younger sisters were born to Janie Rice McKinney, a graduate of the Hampton Institute in Hampton, Virginia, and William Tecumseh McKinney, a teacher who later became principal of the Negro school in Huntington, West Virginia, and then, as a loyal Republican, was awarded a post in the Treasury Department in Washington, D.C.

To provide the children a superior education, the family relocated to Oberlin, Ohio, where between 1910 and 1913 McKinney attended the Academy, a preparatory school run by Oberlin College. In 1911 he helped found the Oberlin chapter of the National Association for the Advancement of Colored People (NAACP) after a visit from W. E. B. DuBois. After encountering a member of the Socialist Party in a Cleveland bookstore, McKinney began reading socialist texts and voted for Socialist Eugene V. Debs in the presidential election of 1912. Although he completed some college-level courses, McKinney did not graduate from the Oberlin Academy. Instead he took a social welfare job in Denver, Colorado, for two years.

McKinney resided briefly in Pittsburgh, Pennsylvania, before serving in the army in World War I in France. He returned to Pittsburgh after the war, where he participated in the 1919 steel strike, joined the Communist Party in 1920, and served as Western Pennsylvania secretary of the NAACP from 1920 to 1922. In this same period he contributed to A. PHILIP RANDOLPH and CHANDLER OWEN's *Messenger* and edited the *Pittsburgh American*, a Negro paper that ultimately failed to obtain adequate advertising and circulation. In 1925 McKinney became a regular columnist for the *Pittsburgh Courier*, then the most prominent black newspaper in the country. He wrote as something of a black H. L. Mencken, a freethinker contemptuous of religious fundamentalism and fears of radicalism. McKinney's columns made him a notable black writer in the Jazz Age of the late 1920s.

By 1926 McKinney had quit the Communist Party for reasons that are not clear. Thereafter, he was devoted to the anti-Stalinist left, a current of radicalism that opposed capitalism as an exploitative class system but also faulted the Communist Party for slavish adherence to Soviet foreign policy. By 1929 McKinney was associated with the Conference for Progressive Labor Action (CPLA), an independent radical group established by A. J. Muste. As the Great Depression hit its depths, McKinney became an organizer of the CPLA-organized Unemployed Leagues, which fought for better relief for unemployed workers by direct action and political mobilization. By 1933 McKinney was the executive secretary of the Unemployed Citizens' League of Allegheny County, and he was elected vice president of the National Unemployed Leagues (NUL) the following year. Throughout 1935 he edited the NUL newspaper *Mass Action*.

McKinney was a partisan throughout this period, writing for *Labor Action*, the paper put out by Muste's followers, and serving on the national leadership body of the American Workers Party (AWP), a revolutionary socialist organization that replaced the CPLA in 1933. In 1934 the AWP merged with the American followers of Leon Trotsky, the Communist League of America, to form a new party, the Workers Party of the United States, again with McKinney in the elected national leadership. This party, in turn, merged with the more moderate Socialist Party in 1936, a merger that McKinney opposed but to which he acquiesced. When that merge took place, the Unemployed Leagues merged into the Socialist-led Workers Alliance of America. McKinney was required to find other fields of employment, so he became an organizer for the Steel Workers Organizing Committee (SWOC) in 1936 and 1937. Stationed in Youngstown, Ohio, he traveled to steel mills in Pennsylvania, West Virginia, and Ohio, primarily organizing black workers.

When the Trotskyists split with the Socialist Party in 1937 to form their own organization, the Socialist Workers Party (SWP) in 1938, McKinney became SWP branch organizer in Newark, New Jersey. When the SWP sundered in 1940, McKinney went with the large dissenting minority led by Max Shachtman, which held that the Soviet Union was an exploitative class society. This group established a new Workers Party in 1940, for which McKinney became the primary labor official and a close political associate of Shachtman's.

Between 1940 and 1942 McKinney traveled for the Workers Party to Buffalo, New York, where he worked organizing blacks to advance their interests through the steel and auto unions, and southeast Missouri, where he organized black and white sharecroppers to strike for better conditions. From then until 1949 McKinney served as a Workers Party functionary in New York City, sitting on the party's top leadership bodies, running symbolically for public office, and writing for its press, *Labor Action* and the *New International*. During this period he was married to Kate Leonard, a white Vermont-born schoolteacher, with whom he had a daughter, Phyllis. Throughout his life McKinney was a consistent advocate for race-blind integration. As a Marxist he believed the vehicle for attaining racial equality was the trade union movement. In the Workers Party this often pitted him against C. L. R. JAMES, whose advocacy of independent black self-organization McKinney derided as separatism that merely reinforced Jim Crow.

After 1949 McKinney, increasingly irascible, withdrew from radical politics. He was soured by developments in the Workers Party, including its decision to rename itself the Independent Socialist League. Returning to intellectual pursuits in arduous research at the New York Public Library, he self-published a bibliography on the subject of cybernetics in 1954. After a long period of withdrawal McKinney returned to political activity in the 1960s and 1970s as an organizer for the AFL-CIO's A. Philip Randolph Institute, traveling to campuses to speak against Black Power and separate ethnic studies programs. Viewed by young black militants as a reactionary, McKinney at age ninety-one told the *New York Times*, "I remain a Marxist and a Leninist in the theoretical sense" (29 Jan. 1977). He died at age ninety-seven.

FURTHER READING

An oral history, "The Reminiscences of Ernest Rice McKinney" (1962), has been transcribed by the Oral History Research Office at Columbia University in New York.

Cline, Francis X. "Decades of a Black Man," *New York Times*, 29 Jan. 1977.

Obituary: *New York Times*, 1 Feb. 1984.

CHRISTOPHER PHELPS

McKinney, Nina Mae (12 June 1912?–3 May 1967), actress, singer, and dancer, was born Nannie Mayme McKinney in Lancaster, South Carolina. Her father Hal McKinney was a postal worker; not much is known about her mother, Georgia Crawford McKinney. McKinney's early life is also a mystery, including her birth year, which has been listed as both 1912 and 1913. When McKinney was a child, her parents moved to New York, and she was raised by either her grandmother or a great aunt in

South Carolina. Other sources suggest that she was raised in Philadelphia.

McKinney's parents sent for her when she was twelve or thirteen years old. She fell in love with New York and immediately began looking for venues in which to express her natural showmanship. At the age of seventeen, she won a part in the chorus of the musical revue *Blackbirds of 1928*. During this time she took on the stage name "Nina Mae McKinney."

After the film director King Vidor saw her perform in *Blackbirds*, he cast her in the leading role of Chick for the first all-black musical, *Hallelujah*, produced by MGM studios. The role proved important for African American women in film because it was the first time a black woman appeared in a leading role and was portrayed as a beautiful seductress rather than as an asexual mammy. It unfortunately also helped support the stereotypes of the overly sexual African American woman.

Historians also differ concerning Vidor's choice of McKinney for the role. In her essay on McKinney in *Notable Black American Women*, Nagueyalti Warren writes that actress "Honey" Brown was Vidor's original choice for the role he chose McKinney to replace her (Warren, 707). DONALD BOGLE in *Toms, Coons, Mulattoes, Mammies & Bucks* states Vidor's first choice was singer and dancer ETHEL WATERS (Bogle, 31). In fact, both sources are correct: Waters was Vidor's first choice, however, he next considered Brown, another actress from *Blackbirds of 1928*. After seeing McKinney's *Blackbirds'* performance, Vidor had both Brown and McKinney go through a round of auditions resulting in McKinney winning the historic role.

Hallelujah, set in the rural South, showcased every conceivable stereotype of African Americans under the guise of revealing true African American folk culture. Featuring songs written by Irving Berlin and W. C. HANDY and performed by the Dixie Jubilee Choir, the story focused on a southern Christian family whose older son, played by DANIEL L. HAYNES, loses his way in the arms of a beautiful, seductive cabaret singer but ultimately repents of his sins and finds redemption.

Before LENA HORNE, FREDI WASHINGTON, and DOROTHY DANDRIDGE, there was McKinney. Young, beautiful, and light-skinned, McKinney physically fit the "mulatto" stereotype. Her performance in *Hallelujah* included singing Berlin's "Swanee Shuffle" and Handy's "St. Louis Blues." McKinney was a self-taught dancer and singer, and her hands-on-hips-swinging dance that accompanied her rendition of "Swanee Shuffle" became a show business legend. She received such rave reviews that MGM signed her to a five-year contract.

Throughout that contract McKinney had only minor roles in two movies: *Safe in Hell* (1931) and *Reckless* (1935). Actually McKinney did not appear in the latter; instead, her voice was dubbed in for a song "sung" by Jean Harlow (considered to be one of many white actresses who imitated McKinney's movements and gestures). Although Hollywood was not comfortable promoting an African American woman as a leading lady, McKinney continued to act in non-Hollywood and independently produced black films such as *Gang Smashers* (1938), with Mantan Moreland, *The Devil's Daughter* (1939), and *Straight to Heaven* (1939) among others. Even so she never achieved the stardom she deserved.

Using her triple threat skills as an actress-dancer-singer, McKinney worked in Europe, where she found her talents to be more appreciated than in the States. Labeled the "Black Garbo," McKinney toured cabarets and clubs in Paris, London, Greece, Dublin, and Budapest with her accompanist Garland Wilson. While in England, she met and co-starred with PAUL ROBESON in *Sanders of the River* (1935). Some of her other films include *Pie, Pie Blackbird* (1932), with ragtime pianist and composer EUBIE BLAKE, *Dark Waters* (1944), *Night Train to Memphis* (1946), and *Danger Street* (1947).

In 1940 McKinney married jazz musician Jimmy Monroe and went on a national tour with her own jazz band. It was not until 1949 that McKinney appeared in her second major film, Elia Kazan's *Pinky*, about a light-skinned African American woman who has been passing as white. In the historic and controversial movie McKinney had a supporting role as a hardened, razor-carrying woman who threatens the lead character. Fame still eluded her, and she returned to live and work in Greece, where she was known as the "Queen of the Night."

During her film, stage, and musical career, McKinney appeared in more than twenty productions. Considered by fans and scholars to be Hollywood's first black goddess, McKinney returned to the United States in the 1960s. She died of a heart attack, virtually unknown, in New York City. In 1978 her legacy was revived, however, when she was inducted into the Black Filmmakers Hall of Fame.

FURTHER READING

Bogle, Donald. *Toms, Coons, Mulattoes, Mammies & Bucks: An Interpretive History of Blacks in American Films* (1991).

Chilton, John. *Who's Who of Jazz: Storyville to Swing Street* (1979).

Warren, Nagueyalti. "Nina McKinney," *Notable Black American Women*, ed. Jessie Carney Smith (1992).

JONETTE O'KELLEY MILLER

McKinney, Roscoe Lewis (8 Feb. 1900–30 Sept. 1978), educator and anatomist, was born in Washington, D.C., the son of Lewis Bradner McKinney, an employee of the U.S. Printing Office, and Blanche Elaine Hunt. McKinney attended Dunbar High School, the all-black grammar school on M Street in Washington. Dunbar's faculty, composed of highly motivated African American scholars, inspired generations of black youth to strive for academic excellence. McKinney himself recalled the atmosphere of "hopeful purpose and tremendous encouragement" that pervaded the school.

After graduating in 1917, McKinney enrolled at Bates College in Lewiston, Maine. Unlike many other white colleges at the time, Bates admitted African American students. Some of McKinney's Dunbar teachers were Bates graduates; BENJAMIN E. MAYS, later the president of Morehouse College in Atlanta, was a year ahead of McKinney at Bates, and other blacks were to follow. Nevertheless, McKinney found race to be an issue in at least one Bates program. Following his induction into the Army Reserve Training-Corps, the commanding officer made it clear that he was personally opposed to the participation of African American students, even though he tolerated the participation as required by college policy. Other aspects of campus life, both social and academic, proceeded more smoothly. McKinney joined several clubs, including the Young Men's Christian Association, the Outing Club, and the Forum, and he competed on the varsity track team. Ranked near the top of his class, McKinney earned an award for "declamations," was elected to Phi Beta Kappa, and graduated with a bachelor of science degree in 1921.

At Bates, McKinney developed an interest in biology that carried over into his future academic career. One of his professors told him about the work of the eminent African American zoologist ERNEST EVERETT JUST, whom McKinney came to revere as a role model. This same professor encouraged McKinney's budding interest in cellular research, especially the relation of the cell to extracellular products and connective tissues. Yet as McKinney approached graduation, he did not seriously consider a career in research or academics. Rather, he was hoping to study medicine and establish himself in practice in the Washington, D.C., area. "Who is the fellow," a contributor to his class yearbook wondered, "that we see over in the zoology laboratory six or eight hours a day, noting a few fine points in the embryological development of the chick or preparing slides for [the professor]? We all shall watch with interest and admiration his work at Harvard Medic for the next four years, and we know he will make some Doctor."

For unknown reasons, McKinney never attended medical school. Instead, he accepted an instructorship in zoology at Morehouse College in 1921. Two years later he joined the faculty of the zoology department at Howard University as an instructor under Just. Also in 1923 he began studies toward a doctorate in anatomy. Each summer he attended the University of Chicago, taking courses and working on various projects in tissue culture under Alexander A. Maximow, the eminent Russian histologist. When Maximow died in 1928, McKinney continued his studies at Chicago under William Bloom, and he worked with Bloom to complete Maximow's histology textbook. This work, *A Textbook of Histology*, went into several editions and became a standard reference source for medical students. McKinney's contribution, acknowledged in Bloom's preface, included preparation of the figures and the manuscript for publication. The text appeared in 1930, the same year that McKinney received his Ph.D. in Anatomy. His thesis, a study of fibers in tissue culture, was published in 1929 in a major German scientific journal.

McKinney was among the earliest African Americans to earn a Ph.D. in Anatomy. He returned to Howard University in 1930 and joined the anatomy department in the School of Medicine, where he was-soon joined by two other African American anatomists, WILLIAM MONTAGUE COBB and Moses Wharton Young, as part of a larger campaign to upgrade the institution's medical teaching and research programs. McKinney served as professor and department head from 1930 to 1947 and as vice dean of the school from 1944 to 1946. He maintained an active research program despite a heavy administrative and teaching load.

In 1952, on the recommendation of the National Advisory Cancer Council, McKinney was awarded a grant by the National Institutes of Health for "An *In Vitro* Study of the Development of Intercellular Fibers in Tissue Culture of Normal and Cancer Cells." Although he did not publish widely, he worked on several projects in tissue culture, microcinematography, radioactive isotopes in cells and tissues, and the origin and development of connective tissue. McKinney and Just collaborated occasionally, for example, on skin-graft experiments with lower amphibious animals such as tadpoles and frogs. Editions of *Gray's Anatomy* included slides of tissue stains made by McKinney. His doctoral thesis was cited in the medical and scientific literature eleven times between 1955 and 1989.

Along with his departmental colleagues Cobb and Young, McKinney played a role in pressuring scientific associations on key civil rights issues. In 1950, for example, all three (plus two other members of the Howard anatomy department) boycotted the New Orleans meeting of the American Association of Anatomists to protest a decision to house all nonwhite participants at a remote site where they would "feel comfortable." A similar protest was organized a year later by members of the mathematics department at Fisk University with regard to arrangements for a Nashville meeting of the Mathematical Association of America. Though a few professional groups, such as the American Anthropological Association, the Association of American Medical Colleges, the American Psychological Association, and the American Association of Physical Anthropologists, had established antisegregationist policies by 1950, in particular by refusing to have meetings in southern cities with segregated facilities and accommodations, several years elapsed before most other professional groups followed suit.

McKinney retired from Howard with emeritus rank in 1968 but was quickly reappointed to the active faculty, serving as professor of anatomy in the 1968–1969 academic year and again from 1971 to 1976. His career also took him overseas. He served for two years as professor of microscopic anatomy at the Royal Iraq Medical College in Baghdad—first as a Fulbright fellow, from 1955 to 1956, and then on the invitation of the Iraqi government, from 1956 to 1957; he taught, under the auspices of the U.S. State Department, at Osmania Medical College, Hyderabad, India, from 1960 to 1962; and he was a consultant in anatomy to the medical faculty at the University of Saigon, Vietnam, from 1969 to 1971. The U.S. ambassador to Iraq wrote that McKinney "made a most favorable impression here during his two years' stay ... not only in academic circles where his professional competence was readily recognized, but also among a wide circle of Iraqis."

McKinney was a member of the American Association for the Advancement of Science, the American Association of Anatomists, and the Tissue Culture Association. He had married Ethel Berena James in 1937, and they had four children. He died in Washington, D.C.

FURTHER READING

A biographical file made up of newspaper obituaries and a program for McKinney's memorial service is preserved at the Moorland-Spingarn Research Center, Howard University.

Obituary: *Journal of the National Medical Association* 71 (May 1979).

This entry is taken from the *American National Biography* and is published here with the permission of the American Council of Learned Societies.

KENNETH R. MANNING

McKinney Steward, Susan Maria Smith. *See* Steward, Susan Maria Smith McKinney.

McKinney, William (Bill) (17 Sept. 1895–14 Oct. 1969), jazz drummer and bandleader, was born in Cynthia, Kentucky. As a teenager, he began playing drums. McKinney later served in the U.S. Army during World War I and picked up the drumsticks again after being demobilized in 1919. He toured with the Sells-Floto Circus Band, but then settled in Springfield, Ohio, where he found work with O'Neill's Orchestra led by the saxophonist Don O'Neill.

Springfield in the 1920s was a thriving city of fifty thousand people and only a few bands. Sensing a good opportunity, McKinney joined the pianist Todd Rhodes and the saxophonist/clarinetist Milton Senior in forming the Synco Trio in about 1921. Senior served as the musical director, responsible for rehearsals. When another musician joined, it became the Synco Quartet, then the Synco Quintet, and, eventually, the Synco Jazz Band. By 1924 the band was known as both McKinney's Synco and the Synco Jazz Band. The group consisted of Senior, Rhodes, McKinney, Wesley Stewart, Claude Jones, and Dave Wilborn.

In 1923 McKinney gave up the drums to concentrate on managing the band. The switch met with approval from the band members, who noted that McKinney had a stiff, military-style of drumming that did not suit jazz arrangements. In his new position, McKinney rarely interfered with rehearsals and seldom offered advice on the band's musical performances. An introverted loner who fronted the band in its early days, he rarely joined in the banter and backstage joking that the other musicians enjoyed. As a result, according to Wilborn, the band had no rapport with McKinney and did not respect him. Additionally, audiences were not especially comfortable with McKinney since he displayed no showmanship to win a crowd. However, McKinney was a superb manager who consistently found well-paying gigs for the jazzmen.

McKinney's Syncos played regularly at the Arcadia Ballroom in Detroit. The management of the Arcadia, the National Amusement Corporation, wanted the band to play at its Graystone club, the leading jazz venue in Detroit in autumn 1927. However, the company did not want to use McKinney's Syncos on the bill, arguing that the name was uninviting. One of the company's employees, a white man named Charlie Stanton, suggested McKinney's Cotton Pickers. The African American musicians immediately objected because of the dubious connotations of the name. In the face of the determination of the venue management, however, they reluctantly agreed to promote themselves as a southern band under a new name that would be temporary. Meanwhile, McKinney hired the alto saxophonist DON REDMAN to enhance the band's lineup and turned over conducting duties to the new addition. At this point, the band consisted of Redman, Rhodes, Senior, Wilborn, Jones, George Thomas, Leonard Bailey, John Nesbitt, Gus McLung, Cuba Austin, and Ralph Escudero. With this lineup, the band became famous as McKinney's Cotton Pickers. In 1928 they made their debut at New York City's famous Roseland Ballroom. The show proved so successful that the Cotton Pickers had an extended booking and received offers to play at leading ballrooms around the nation.

In 1931 the group escaped Depression-hit Detroit with several months in California, where many nightclubs were mushrooming. The long residency and discontent over McKinney's frugal management style eventually prompted the band's breakup.

McKinney created another group with the same name but different musicians. The second version of the Cotton Pickers, formed in late summer of 1931, consisted of REX STEWART, Roscoe "Red" Simmons, JOE SMITH, Ed Cuffee, Quentin Jackson, Cuba Austin, Jimmy Dudley, Dave Wilborn, Billy Taylor, Todd Rhodes, ADOLPHUS "DOC" CHEATHAM, Elmer Williams, and Bennett "Benny" Carter. The Graystone in Detroit served as home, but the band continued to tour extensively. The Cotton Pickers stopped recording in 1932 when their contract with Victor was not renewed. Since published accounts of bands generally focused on recording activities, national reports on the band virtually ceased, and

many fans in both America and Europe thought that the musicians had gone their separate ways. McKinney was not a strong enough manager to revive the waning spirits of the musicians, and the group fell apart in 1934. McKinney formed a third Cotton Pickers late that same year, and this version played only in Detroit.

When musicians and musicologists recall the great black jazz bands of the 1920s, 1930s, and 1940s, McKinney's Cotton Pickers is usually mentioned. The group's contemporaries, including FLETCHER HENDERSON and DUKE ELLINGTON, drew their band members from among the ranks of musicians living in New York City. McKinney's Cotton Pickers was different, the only African American territory band (a band that works mainly in its home state and adjoining states) to achieve national fame during the 1920s. Additionally, in comparison to the other major groups of the era, McKinney's band had a small output. The Cotton Pickers recorded about seventy songs for Victor Records, with McKinney apparently responsible for part-authorship of only the band's 1930 recording, "Cotton Picker's Scat." A versatile band, the Cotton Pickers played dance music, ballads, and waltzes. Typical of 1920s era groups, the band's repertoire included many specialty numbers that featured comedy routines and jokey vocals. The Cotton Pickers was also one of the earliest African American groups to be played on national radio.

In 1937 McKinney decided to become a nightclub owner. He opened the Cozy Corner Café in Detroit, but the venture was short-lived. During the spring of 1939 he l ed a band at the Harlem Casino in Pittsburgh, then played dates at the Club Plantation in Detroit, before spending the summer season at the Ocean Beach Pier in Jackson, Michigan. He spent the 1940 summer season with a band at the Crystal Ballroom in Crystal, Michigan. McKinney's last important bookings outside Michigan occurred in 1941 in Chicago and South Carolina.

Despite twenty years of leading a band, McKinney had little money. During World War II he worked at the River Rouge plant of Ford Motors. He then became a bellhop at a Detroit hotel. In the 1950s his health began to fail. After a series of heart attacks, he returned to the town of his birth, which was where he died.

FURTHER READING

Chilton, John. *McKinney's Music: A Bio-Discography of McKinney's Cotton Pickers* (1978).

CARYN NEUMANN

McKissack, Pat (9 Aug. 1944–), children's book editor and author, was born Patricia Carwell in Smyrna, Tennessee, to Robert Carwell and Erma Carwell (her mother's maiden name is unknown), both of whom were civil servants. At the age of three, Patricia and her family moved north to St. Louis, Missouri. Several years later, following her parents' divorce, Patricia, her mother, and her siblings moved back to Nashville, Tennessee. By age twelve, Patricia had developed a love for reading and would often spend countless hours memorizing a good story. It was during this time she would meet and become lifelong friends with her future husband, Fredrick McKissack. During these formative years, Patricia loved to listen to family elders weave tales of the old days, recite poems, read Bible stories, and make up spine-tingling ghost tales on the porch before dusk. The love of these tales fed her desire to learn how to read and write stories of her own.

McKissack entered Tennessee State University in Nashville. In 1964, armed with a B.A. in English, she became a certified English teacher. That same year, Patricia bumped into her old friend Fredrick McKissack. On their second date, Fredrick proposed, and four months later they were married. Following the wedding, the couple moved to St. Louis so that she could further her education and he could start his own engineering firm. While she was studying for her master's degree at Webster University, McKissack taught junior and senior high school English. The McKissacks established themselves in the community and soon developed friendly relations with their neighbors. This not only endeared the family to the community but allowed their neighbors to trust and value their friendship while providing support to their newly opened general contracting firm. McKissack gave birth to three children, Fredrick Lemuel, and twins, Robert and John. McKissack matured into a sophisticated writer by spending hours in the public library and honing her craft in classes at Webster University and professional workshops.

In 1975 McKissack graduated from Webster University with an M.A. in Early Childhood Literature and Media Programming and became a children's book editor for Concordia Publishing, developing their children's product line, which released ten to fifteen books per year. In 1981 she decided to work part time and write seriously in order to publish work of her own. After beginning as a teacher and editor, in 1981 McKissack became a full-time writer. That year her first book, *Martin Luther King: A Man to Remember*, was published by Children's Press. A year later, the McKissacks decided to coauthor children's and young adult books written for and about African Americans.

Community service was at the core of all McKissack's writing. Her books made history come alive for children and informed a wide audience of the important global contributions made by African Americans. She wrote or cowrote over one hundred books and showed her commitment to the community by providing workshops, conferences, and continually sharing words of wisdom for aspiring authors. McKissack continued to receive honors as well. Alpha Kappa Alpha Sorority, Inc., established the Patricia McKissack reading program to honor its alumni and promote reading to students in elementary school. She devoted countless hours to public readings at St. Louis-area libraries and was a member of many civic organizations. Later in her career McKissack received a Newbery Award for *The Dark-Thirty: Southern Tales of the Supernatural*, the Caldecott Honor Medal for *Mirandy and Brother Wind*, and two National Association for the Advancement of Colored People Awards for *Sojourner Truth: Ain't I A Woman* and *Let My People Go: Old Testament Bible Stories*. She also received the Boston Globe/Horn Book Award for nonfiction, four Coretta Scott King Awards for Text, the Regina Medal for Lifetime Achievement in Children's Books by the Catholic's Librarians Association, the 2005 Alumni of the Year at Webster University, and an honorary doctorate from the University of Missouri at St. Louis.

FURTHER READING
Harris, Violet. "African American Children's Literature: The First One Hundred Years," *Journal of Negro Education* (1990).
Sims Bishop, Rudine. "Profile: A Conversation with Patricia McKissack," *Language Arts* (Jan. 1992).
MONIQUE MILES BRUNER

McKissick, Floyd Bixler (3 Mar. 1922–28 Apr. 1991), civil rights lawyer and activist, was born in Asheville, North Carolina, the son of Ernest McKissick, a hotel bellman, and Magnolia Esther Thompson, a seamstress. When Floyd was four years old, an angry bus driver ordered him to the rear of the bus after he had wandered into the white section to join some white children who were watching the driver. That incident revealed to him that black children did not have the same freedom and opportunity in North Carolina as white children did. Black children attended segregated schools with inferior facilities, sat in the back of the bus, and could not sit down and eat at lunch counters. They received harsh treatment from city employees like bus drivers and police officers. They did not have public skating rinks or swimming pools, and they could not use the public library. As a result of his awareness, McKissick decided early in life that he would study law to fight for equal rights for black Americans. In fall 1939 he began a prelaw course at Morehouse College in Atlanta, Georgia, working his way through the year as a dining hall waiter. At Morehouse he became the personal waiter for the black political activist, sociologist, and historian W. E. B. DuBois. DuBois's belief that blacks must demand absolute equality without compromise, and his opinion that educated black people had an obligation to improve the condition of the race, had an influence on the young college student. McKissick left Morehouse in February 1942, after the United States entered World War II. In that same year he married his childhood sweetheart, Evelyn Williams; they would have three daughters and one son. McKissick joined the U.S. Army and

was eventually assigned to a field artillery unit. He taught in army literacy programs in the United States for two years before he was shipped overseas. Eventually he served in battle in Europe, where he earned a Purple Heart.

Eager to continue his education, McKissick applied to the segregated University of North Carolina after his discharge from the army in 1945. His application was not even acknowledged. Unwilling to concede defeat, he got a job as a waiter to earn enough money to reenter college. He began his long career as a civil rights activist in 1947 when he joined BAYARD RUSTIN on the Journey of Reconciliation. The journey, a bus trip, was organized by the Congress of Racial Equality (CORE) to test a recent Supreme Court decision requiring the integration of interstate travel. The objectives of CORE, an interracial organization founded in Chicago, Illinois, in 1942, were to draw attention to and take direct action against racial discrimination in public facilities.

In the late 1940s McKissick returned to Morehouse and again applied to the all-white law school at the University of North Carolina. When he was rejected, THURGOOD MARSHALL

Floyd Bixler McKissick (right) at a news conference in Memphis, Tennessee, with (from left) Stokely Carmichael and Martin Luther King Jr., in the wake of the shotgun attack on James Meredith near Hernando, Mississippi, on 7 June 1966. (AP Images.)

and the National Association for the Advancement of Colored People (NAACP) filed a suit on his behalf. While he waited for the case to be decided, McKissick attended the all-black law school at North Carolina College. In 1951 he won his suit and became the first African American to earn the LLB degree at the University of North Carolina, although all of his course work already had been completed at North Carolina College.

McKissick passed the North Carolina bar exam in 1952 and began a general law practice in Durham, North Carolina. In 1958 he filed his first civil rights case, a suit on behalf of his eldest daughter to integrate a public school in Durham. Active in Durham's black community, he joined the Durham Business and Professional Chain (a black businessmen's organization), became an adviser to the state's NAACP youth groups, and became the director of Durham's CORE chapter.

Because of his role as adviser to the NAACP youth groups in North Carolina, McKissick was contacted by the students who began the sit-in at the Woolworth's lunch counter in Greensboro, North Carolina, in February 1960. That sit-in marked the beginning of a great increase in the demand by blacks for equal rights. McKissick helped the students expand the sit-ins to other towns, and he led workshops on nonviolence for sit-in participants. During the first half of the 1960s McKissick represented many of the demonstrators who were arrested in direct action campaigns against segregated facilities in the South. He often served as a negotiator between the demonstrators and the local authorities, seeking to secure integrated facilities and fair employment policies.

From 1963 to 1966 McKissick served as the national chairman of CORE's board, the group responsible for determining policy at the national level. In 1966 he replaced JAMES FARMER as the director of the national office, assuming responsibility for implementing CORE's policies. After JAMES MEREDITH, the first black man admitted to the University of Mississippi, was shot, McKissick joined the Reverend MARTIN LUTHER KING JR. and STOKELY CARMICHAEL, president of the Student Nonviolent Coordinating Committee (SNCC), to complete Meredith's March against Fear in 1966. McKissick supported Carmichael's effort to change the emphasis of the march to voter registration and the achievement of black power. During the period that McKissick led CORE, it became an all-black organization that was more militant in its demands for black political and economic power. As the

decade became more violent, McKissick and CORE moved away from nonviolence as a philosophy and advocated self-defense.

In 1968 McKissick resigned as national director of CORE to pursue his dream of building a black community that would ultimately become economically and politically self-sufficient. Soul City, North Carolina, located about fifty miles from Durham, began with a grant from the U.S. Department of Housing and Urban Development. McKissick hoped that black-owned businesses would be attracted to the area once housing and a community infrastructure were in place. However, his plans for Soul City never materialized, partly because federal money for the project ceased. In 1979 the Department of Housing and Urban Development foreclosed on Soul City although McKissick and others continued to live there.

In 1969 McKissick published *Three-Fifths of a Man*, his analysis of the race problem in the United States. McKissick believed the problem was primarily economic and that a redistribution of the nation's wealth was needed to enable black people to share in the nation's prosperity. In the book, McKissick expressed his belief that the Declaration of Independence and the U.S. Constitution already contained all the tools necessary to solve the nation's racial problems; they only had to be enforced. McKissick continued to practice law in Durham until June 1990, when he was appointed by North Carolina governor James G. Martin as a judge in the state's Ninth Judicial District. McKissick died in Soul City.

As the national leader of CORE from 1963 to 1968, McKissick helped determine the direction of the 1960s civil rights movement. As a result of this movement, Congress passed extensive civil rights legislation in 1964 and 1965. These laws instituted profound changes in American society.

FURTHER READING

McKissick's papers are located at the Hayti Heritage Center in Durham, North Carolina.

Farmer, James. *Lay Bare the Heart: An Autobiography of the Civil Rights Movement* (1985).

Meier, August, and Elliott Rudwick. *CORE: A Study in the Civil Rights Movement, 1942–1968* (1973).

Obituaries: *New York Times, Raleigh News and Observer,* and *Washington Post,* 30 Apr. 1991.

This entry is taken from the *American National Biography* and is published here with the permission of the American Council of Learned Societies.

JENIFER W. GILBERT

McKoy, Millie and Christine McKoy (11 July 1851–8 and 9 Oct. 1912), also known as "Millie-Christine," entertainers, were conjoined twins born to an enslaved couple named Jacob and Monemia, who were owned by Jabez McKay, a Columbus County, North Carolina, blacksmith. The twins quickly became a local sensation in the wake of the success of the original "Siamese Twins," Chang and Eng Bunker (conjoined twins made famous by showman and entrepreneur P. T. Barnum) and the growth of the national circus movement. Before the McKoy twins were a year old, McKay and his partner John C. Pervis arranged for them to be exhibited throughout the area; soon after, their career was taken over by a manager named Brower, and they were sold to North Carolina businessman Joseph Pearson Smith. By this point, though, Brower, who was in possession of the young girls, had been swindled and the girls were stolen away to Philadelphia, Pennsylvania, where, in 1854, they were exhibited in a small "museum" run by a Colonel Wood.

By August of 1854, they were in New York City at P. T. Barnum's famous American Museum. Barnum, riding the wave of the popularity of General Tom Thumb (the three-foot-tall Charles Sherwood Stratton), promoted them actively but briefly. Under unclear circumstances, the twins were taken to Canada and then Britain by promoters William Thompson and "Professor" William Millar. Thompson and Millar set a pattern that lasted for the next several years: the twins were examined by prominent doctors from a given city and then, once the doctors had pronounced that they were indeed "genuine," the McKoys were publicized with broadsides that often included racist caricatures and then exhibited to the paying public as curiosities. Millar eventually "stole" the twins from Thompson, and the press coverage that followed nationalized their fame.

Eventually Millar went to the United States and teamed with Joseph Pearson Smith. Millar and Smith went back Britain early in 1857, and in a massive court battle widely covered in the British press took possession of the twins. Like most machinations of the McKoys' various owners, this was simply another move to profit from young children, but it did at least return them to their mother, Monemia, whom Smith brought to Britain with him. By this point, the British public was charmed by the twins, who had begun singing during exhibits, and flocked to see the "African Twins," now exhibited with Monemia. Soon, though, Smith separated from Millar and took both the twins and their mother back to North Carolina. Smith's wife, Mary, seems to have cared for the twins and taught them how to read and write (even though such was illegal) and, perhaps for more mercenary reasons, to sing and dance.

By the beginning of 1858, the McKoys were once again out on exhibit—this time in New Orleans. From there, it was on to St. Louis to start a tour of towns on the Mississippi and Missouri rivers before moving to the Smiths' new home in Spartanburg, South Carolina. Further musical training for the twins—including piano lessons by Mary Smith—followed before another tour on the eve of the Civil War.

Smith died in 1862; Millie and Christine McKoy were described in an estate inventory as "a great natural curiosity" and valued at $25,000—over a third of the estate that also included a fine piano forte valued at $500. Smith's finances forced his widow to sell off much of her property, but she kept her slaves throughout the war. In one of the myriad arrangements set up between former slaves and owners after Emancipation, the McKoys decided to return to exhibiting themselves, for the first time taking a share of the monies but also, in an arrangement that continued for some time, giving some to Mary Smith.

The twins also gained some control over the conditions of their exhibitions and specifically ruled out many of the intrusive "medical exams" by town doctors that had prefaced showings. This tour, which opened in Raleigh and moved to Baltimore, Washington, and then Philadelphia, eventually led to truly national exposure through coverage in *Frank Leslie's Illustrated Newspaper* and to another stay with Barnum's American Museum in New York. But this was only the entrée to a tour with Chang and Eng Bunker at the end of 1868, a promotional autobiography (*History and Medical Description of the Two-Headed Girl*), and successful tours of New England and the South. In 1871, Barnum arranged another British tour.

The McKoys captivated British audiences; by now, though barely twenty, they were seasoned performers, skilled at playing to the crowd. They sang, danced, and worked closely with their fellow Barnum troupe members; when Anna Swan and Captain Bates were united in the so-called "Giants' Wedding," they were part of the wedding party. On 24 June 1871 Millie and Christine gave a command performance for Queen Victoria, who rewarded them with diamond-studded hair clips, which they wore in performance for years after. The event led to further performances for British nobility and, beginning in late 1872, a European tour; the McKoys did not return to the United States until October 1878. They began touring again almost immediately—this time heading as far west as California and as far south as Cuba. In the 1880s, more and more of the McKoys' touring took place in circuses—especially the Great Inter-Ocean Show; 1884 saw another European tour before they rejoined P. T. Barnum for his "Nine Jumbo Shows United."

During this time, the McKoy family built a significant homestead in Columbus County—with patriarch Jacob and matriarch Monemia at the head and Millie and Christine as the prime earners. This home became not only a stopping point between tours but, more and more, a haven. Ties with the white Smith family continued to be close. In early 1891, Jacob McKoy passed away. The twins gradually slowed their touring and focused more energy on family and community—funding a local black school at Welches Creek that they had founded in 1880 and giving funds to several black colleges. When a fire burned their home down in 1909, they never fully recovered. A lifetime of hard touring combined with tuberculosis weakened them—especially Millie, who died a day before her sister.

Millie and Christine McKoy endured a childhood full of exploitation to survive and even thrive as they negotiated not only nineteenth-century stereotypes about race but also stereotypes about "freaks."

FURTHER READING

Illinois State University's Milner Library has a significant collection of photographs of Millie and Christine McKoy.

Description and Songs of Miss Millie-Christine, the Two-Headed Nightingale (1882).

History and Medical Description [of Millie-Christine] (1869).

Martell, Joanne. *Millie-Christine: Fearfully and Wonderfully Made* (2000).

Pancoast, William H. "The Carolina Twins" in *Photographic Review of Medicine and Surgery* (1870–1871).

ERIC GARDNER

McLaurin, George W. (16 Sept. 1887–4 Sept. 1968), educator and civil rights pioneer, is a person about whom. Little is known prior to his residence in Oklahoma City, Oklahoma, in 1942. He earned a bachelor's degree from Langston University and in 1943, a master's degree in Education from the University of Kansas. Throughout his career McLaurin taught education courses at Langston University, Oklahoma's segregated institution of higher education for African Americans. McLaurin and his wife, Peninah, placed a high value on education. Peninah also graduated from Langston, taught there, and operated a bookstore out of their home. In 1923 she applied for admission for a graduate degree at the University of Oklahoma and was rejected because of her race. However, Peninah and all three of their children, Dunbar, J. C., and Phyllis, completed master's degrees. McLaurin's sons, Dunbar and J. C., completed doctorates after their military service during World War II. By 1948 they were recognized in The the *Daily Oklahoman* newspaper as one of the most highly educated families in the state.

Throughout its history Oklahoma had been a racial and cultural crossroads. At the time of statehood in 1907 it contained more than fifty all-black communities composed of former Indian Nation slaves, post- Civil War black migrants, and descendants of the Buffalo Soldiers. The National Association for the Advancement of Colored People (NAACP) found the presence of a significant unified black population in Oklahoma fertile ground for test cases to overturn segregation. ROSCOE DUNJEE, the editor of the *Black Dispatch* newspaper, and the Oklahoma NAACP endorsed numerous cases, most notably, *Guinn v. Oklahoma* (1915), which declared the "grandfather clause" unconstitutional.

In 1945 THURGOOD MARSHALL, attorney for the NAACP Legal Defense Fund, attended the Oklahoma state convention and outlined a plan to end segregated higher education. Marshall, attorney CHARLES HAMILTON HOUSTON, and Tulsa attorney Amos T. Hall were seeking an honor graduate to apply to the University of Oklahoma (OU) Law School. While African Americans could receive undergraduate degrees at Langston, any graduate or professional training had to be taken out of state. A token state stipend reflected Oklahoma's attempt to provide for "separate, but equal" education. Langston graduate, ADA LOIS SIPUEL FISHER, accepted the challenge and applied to OU in January 1946. The *Sipuel v. Board of Regents of the University of Oklahoma* case, decided in by the U.S. Supreme Court in 1947, provided only an incomplete resolution. The Supreme Court ruled that OU must either admit Sipuel or create an equal law school education for blacks in Oklahoma. The state regents for higher education proposed a makeshift "law school" consisting of a room in the state capitol building and Sipuel its only student. Sipuel and her attorneys refused the makeshift "law school" the state regents for higher education proposed, and another round of litigation moved forward to demand her admission to OU. As long as Sipuel's appeals remained in the courts, the state's black and white press focused on her battle. This atmosphere of debate established the context for the emergence of McLaurin into national civil rights history. McLaurin, along with six other black Oklahomans, immediately applied for graduate school admission at the University of Oklahoma in January 1948. Most were seeking master's degrees, but McLaurin applied for a Ph.D. in School Administration. On the advice of state Attorney General Mac Williamson, the university rejected all seven on the basis of Oklahoma's segregation laws. The state regents created a commission composed of its chancellor, Dr. M. A. Nash, and six deans, three each from OU and Oklahoma A&M

College, to study the issue. The commission reported that the expense of creating multiple graduate programs and recruiting qualified black faculty made the continuation of segregated universities irresponsible. Although there were several qualified candidates among the OU applicants, Marshall specifically chose McLaurin for the test case because of his age. Student rallies in support of the admission of black students and demonstrations opposed to integration were nearly equal in size. The opposition, however, voiced a perennial concern about cross-race dating and eventual marriage. At sixty-one years old, the married McLaurin suggested no likelihood of either of these eventualities. Because the Sipuel case and other similar cases faced such lengthy appeal appeals processes, Marshall decided on a new approach. He pursued McLaurin's challenge directly through a three-judge District Court of Appeals. This court heard cases when federal, state, or municipal laws conflicted with the Constitution. The appeal of a decision by the District Court of Appeals went directly to the

George W. McLaurin attends class apart from the other students at the University of Oklahoma, after the school was forced to admit him following a Supreme Court ruling, 1948. (Library of Congress.)

U.S. Supreme Court. Marshall and Hall represented McLaurin and all other African Americans before federal judges, Edgar S. Vaught, Alfred P. Murrah, and Bower Broaddus in August 1948. The following month the court applied the Sipuel Supreme Court ruling, ordering Oklahoma to provide McLaurin with the education he sought. When the governor made promises of eventual resolution, Marshall went back to court demanding McLaurin's immediate enrollment.

On 13 October 1948 McLaurin became the first African American to gain admission to the University of Oklahoma. The state legislature and the OU regents, however, modified the rules to admit African Americans only with the most extreme form allowable under segregation. McLaurin sat alone in an alcove adjacent to the classroom during instruction. He ate alone at a separate, roped off, table in the cafeteria, studied alone at a separate table in the library, and had the use of a single campus restroom. While McLaurin's treatment appeared to offer an equal education and contained no threats to his safety, it inflicted daily humiliations that affected his ability to continue his study successfully. Twenty-five additional black students joined McLaurin in 1949, all pursuing their goals under these circumstances. Their isolation was compounded by the fact that Norman, Oklahoma, had long been a segregated community where African Americans were not allowed to live. Black students were forced to commute each day in order to attend the school. Over time OU lessened the racial divide by allowing black students to sit in the same classroom in rows marked "Reserved for Colored." Supportive white students eventually tore these signs down. Marshall appealed to the three-judge District Court for an injunction against these distinctions on the basis that they impaired McLaurin's ability to study and to relate to his professors and classmates. McLaurin testified that the conditions were personally humiliating, but the court rejected his argument. This decision sent the case to the U.S. Supreme Court, and on 5 June 1950 Chief Justice Fred Vinson announced a unanimous decision. The Court ruled that the restrictions imposed on McLaurin denied him the Fourteenth Amendment right to equal protection under the laws, and, further, that he must receive the same treatment as students of other races. McLaurin withdrew from OU after two semesters and retired from public life. After the death of his wife in 1966, he moved to Los Angeles, California, to live with his son, J. C. McLaurin. When he died at

age eighty-one, the Oklahoma NAACP petitioned Governor Dewey Bartlett to request that McLaurin's body be returned to Oklahoma City for burial. Overshadowed in his lifetime by the coverage of Sipuel's struggle, the quiet McLaurin initiated the civil rights case that would have consequences far greater for Oklahoma and for the United States. By 1950, ninety-six African Americans had attended the University of Oklahoma, and segregated higher education had ended in the state. In addition, through the McLaurin case Marshall established the legal precedent that equal conditions of education as well as equal admission affected black equality. McLaurin's case paved the way for *Brown v. Board of Education* and the end of legally sanctioned segregation in American life. McLaurin's case planted the legal precedent that the conditions of education affected black equality. Without McLaurin the *Brown v. Board of Education* decision would have taken much longer to justify.

FURTHER READING
Fisher, Ada Lois Sipuel, with Danney Goble. *A Matter of Black and White, The Autobiography of Ada Lois Sipuel Fisher* (1996).
Hubbell, John T. "The Desegregation of the University of Oklahoma, 1946–1950," *Journal of Negro History* 57 (Oct. 1972).
Kluger, Richard. *Simple Justice: The History of Brown v. Board of Education and Black America's Struggle for Equality* (2004).
Patterson, Zella J. Black, with Lynette L. Wert. *Langston University, A History*, vol. II (1993).

LINDA W. REESE

McLean, Jackie (17 May 1932–31 Mar. 2006), alto saxophonist, composer, and teacher, was born John Lenwood McLean Jr. in Harlem, New York, to John Lenwood McLean Sr., a jazz guitarist who died when Jackie was seven. Raised by his doting mother, whose name is unknown, Jackie McLean grew up in Harlem's Sugar Hill district, a community teeming with musical talent. In this neighborhood he met and worked with BUD POWELL, THELONIOUS MONK, and SONNY ROLLINS, musicians who served as his early mentors and later became jazz greats. At the age of fifteen McLean began playing alto saxophone. The bebop pianist and composer Bud Powell gave McLean music lessons, teaching him chord changes and the important lesson of how to keep and extend rhythmic time. McLean later described Powell as "my inspiration." In 1948 Powell introduced McLean to the jazz giant and fellow alto saxophonist CHARLIE PARKER, who quickly became a major influence on McLean as the precocious sixteen-year-old searched to find his own sound in the maelstrom of revolutionary jazz styles emerging in the mid- and late 1940s.

In 1951 the nineteen-year-old McLean made his public debut at the famous midtown New York jazz club Birdland (named after Parker), where he was introduced by his mentor Powell. During that year McLean made his recording debut with his neighborhood friend, the twenty-year-old tenor saxophonist Sonny Rollins and the twenty-five-year-old trumpeter MILES DAVIS. The record, entitled *Dig!*, on the Prestige record label quickly became an early classic in the bebop tradition. After a few years on the road honing his skills, McLean emerged as a leading new force on his instrument. By 1955 he was playing in many major bands of the period, including those of the composer and bassist CHARLES MINGUS. During an intense two-year apprenticeship with Mingus's innovative and musically challenging Jazz Workshop ensemble, McLean began a stint as a member of the drummer ART BLAKEY's Jazz Messengers in 1956. McLean also asserted himself as a leader of his own group, recording albums for the Prestige and New Jazz labels, including the 1956 releases *Lights Out!* and *McLean's Scene* and 1957's *Strange Blues*. By 1960 McLean had become one of the premier young musicians of the hard bop style.

This early success in his creative work came at a great personal cost as McLean became addicted to heroin in the late 1950s. From 1959 to 1963 McLean found a form of psychological therapy and eventually physical rehabilitation by performing in the popular Off-Broadway production of *The Connection*, a play about the underground drug world featuring both professional actors and musicians in the drug addict and pusher roles. McLean and others also played the production's soundtrack. His work as both actor and musician was critically lauded in the long-running play, which had a positive influence on McLean's own successful attempt to wean himself off drugs, and he finally kicked the habit altogether in 1963. During this period he began a long and successful association with the independent jazz record label Blue Note, recording his first album, *Jackie's Bag*, in 1959. He quickly followed this album with *Vertigo* and *New Soil*, both released in the same year. Creatively this was a pivotal turning point in McLean's career as he made an artistic transition from the hard bop foundations of the recent past to the aesthetically dynamic and controversial decade of what was called free jazz in the 1960s.

During the 1960s McLean played a leading and crucial role in bridging the gap between the older musicians from the bebop and hard bop revolution and the emerging younger generation of avantgarde experimentalists who further extended the boundaries of the music with free jazz. McLean eventually recorded twenty-one albums for Blue Note before ending his association with the label in 1967. He then began a decade-long affiliation with the European label Steeplechase, which was based in Denmark, where he continued to record for an appreciative international audience, including two albums with his early saxophone idol, DEXTER GORDON.

McLean's other great interest was teaching. In 1968 he began a professional association with the Hartt School of Music at the University of Hartford in Connecticut, teaching and advising music students in jazz improvisation, harmony, orchestration, composition, arranging, and saxophone technique. He became less active as a player in the 1970s as he dedicated himself to teaching. McLean and his wife, Dollie (maiden name unknown), with whom he had four children, founded the Artists Collective in 1970, teaching music, dance, drama, and martial arts to Hartford's black youth. The program developed into one of the most acclaimed and nationally renowned music and arts educational programs in the United States. As McLean explained in 2002, "We're trying to keep the community clean and keep the kids inspired to go out and make something of themselves, whether it's a doctor or a musician. We offer them the arts as a means to study and something they'd really enjoy doing on another level" (*Down Beat*, June 2002, 26).

In the 1980s McLean returned to playing live, sometimes appearing onstage with his son Rene as a part of his sextet. In 1988 he recorded his first release in nine years. He became more active as a player, recording several albums for various American and European labels before returning to Blue Note in 1996 with *Hat Trick*. This critically and commercially successful recording was followed by a number of other successful recordings. In 2001 McLean was honored with a Beacon of Jazz Award from the New School University's jazz and contemporary music program. The following year McLean was recognized as a Jazz Master by the National Endowment for the Arts, and he was inducted into the *Down Beat* Jazz Education Hall of Fame.

FURTHER READING

Giddins, Gary. *Riding on a Blue Note: Jazz and American Pop* (1981).

Gioia, Ted. *The History of Jazz* (1987).

Rosenthal, David. *Hard Bop: Jazz and Black Music, 1955–1965* (1992).

KOFI NATAMBU

McLendon, Johnny (5 Apr. 1915–8 Oct. 1999), basketball coach, was born John B. McLendon Jr. in Hiawatha, Kansas. McLendon obtained a piecemeal education, steadily taking advantage of each opportunity that he was offered. He graduated from Sumner High School in Kansas City, Kansas, in 1932 and entered Kansas City Junior College. He finished his B.S. in Physical Education at the University of Kansas in 1936 and earned a master's degree from the University of Iowa in 1937. One of McLendon's professors in the physical education program at Kansas was Dr. James Naismith, who had invented the game of basketball in 1891, while he was a student at the International YMCA Training School (now Springfield College), in Springfield, Massachusetts.

In his undergraduate years, McLendon took a couple of high school coaching jobs in Lawrence and Topeka. Following his graduate studies, he was hired as an assistant basketball coach at the North Carolina College for Negroes (NCCN) in Durham (now North Carolina Central University). He ascended to head coach in 1940 and immediately began churning out successful teams that played a revolutionary style of basketball.

Since basketball was mostly played in a slow, painstaking manner, it had traditionally been considered a game destined to be dominated by taller, bigger teams. Players moved among one another in proximity, attempting to displace opponents physically through a process called "screening." This style emphasized patience on offense and rigid defensive fundamentals, both of which capitalized on the assets of bigger players while virtually eliminating their primary liabilities, slowness, and premature fatigue.

McLendon saw a way to physically and mentally exhaust his opponents, no matter their size. To accomplish this, he did more than any coach in history to hone the fundamentals of the "fast break," a single type of play that became synonymous with his overall basketball philosophy. In the older style of basketball, a fast break was an unplanned, opportunistic play that occurred when a player exploited a brief advantage by stealing the ball and running

faster than everyone else. McLendon's genius was to see the potential of the fast break in the routine and inevitable moments of a game—a loose ball, a rebound, a blocked shot—and to give each player a specific role in the action of the play. His fast breaks required that players maintain maximum spacing over the entire court, which allowed for greater creativity and adaptation than did traditional offensive plays designed for the half-court. McLendon's fast break demanded a frantic defensive intensity and superior physical conditioning and often resulted in victories of forty points or more. This new style collided with traditional basketball as the jazz of MILES DAVIS did with the more formal ragtime of SCOTT JOPLIN: whereas the older school was fixed in its precision, the newer one was thrilling and unpredictable in its improvisational creativity.

McLendon also devised a way to apply fastbreak principles to a half-court offense, namely, by putting one player in each corner of the court and allowing the fifth to roam in the middle. This extremely effective offense came to be known as "Four Corners"; when the University of North Carolina's coach Dean Smith adopted it at Chapel Hill in the mid-1960s, he was popularly credited as its inventor. Using the fast break and Four Corners to near perfection, NCCN compiled a record of 239-68 between 1940 and 1952. With two other coaches from the Central Intercollegiate Athletic Association for historically black colleges and universities, McLendon founded the CIAA tournament in 1946 and, in 1950, the Tournament of the Carolinas. McLendon's teams proceeded to win eight titles between the two tournaments.

McLendon's tenure at NCCN, and later at Hampton Institute and the Tennessee Agricultural and Industrial State Normal School (now Tennessee State University), resulted in a catalog of firsts. In 1943 he coached the first black player to be signed by an NBA team, NCCN's Harold Hunter, who played for the Washington Caps. He also cofounded the National Athletic Steering Committee, a precursor to the Black Coaches Association, which worked toward desegregating college basketball. McLendon's efforts paid dividends in the late 1950s, when black colleges were allowed to compete for a single spot in the National Association of Intercollegiate Athletics Tournament. From 1957 to 1959 McLendon led Tennessee A & I through both tournaments for three straight years, becoming the first black basketball coach to win a national title and the first college coach to win three consecutively. The team's first national title came almost a full decade before Texas Western's all-black team defeated Adolph Rupp's all-white Kentucky squad in the 1966 NCAA championship, the game commonly cited as the first national championship for an African American team.

McLendon's success in the college ranks led to his appointment as head coach of the National Industrial Basketball League's (NIBL) Cleveland Pipers in 1959. In an exhibition game the following year, he directed his amateur Pipers to an unprecedented victory over a U.S. Olympic team that included the future NBA stars Jerry West and OSCAR ROBERTSON. When the NIBL became the professional American Basketball League (ABL) in 1961, McLendon consequently became the first black coach of a team in a professional basketball league. The Pipers won the ABL championship that season, but in 1962 the team's owner, George Steinbrenner (later the owner of the New York Yankees), withheld players' paychecks because of their supposedly lackadaisical play. McLendon resigned, protesting that he could not "stand by and see a good group of young athletes intimidated" (Ashe, 56).

McLendon returned to college ball at Kentucky State, where he coached from 1963 to 1966, and he wrote two books on fast-break basketball. His final college coaching position marked a long-awaited breakthrough, when he became the first black coach at a predominantly white institution, Cleveland State University. He held the post until 1969, when he returned to the professional ranks for one season as head coach of the fledgling American Basketball Association's Denver Rockets (now the NBA's Denver Nuggets).

One of the most telling moments in McLendon's career remained secret for more than fifty years. While he was at North Carolina College in 1944, McLendon coached his team in the first integrated college basketball game in the country, against an all-white intramural team from the neighboring Duke University Medical School. The game did not achieve public notice until the historian Scott Ellsworth interviewed Coach McLendon in 1995 and published his findings in a *New York Times Magazine* article the following year. According to Ellsworth, "The Secret Game" was held on a Sunday morning, 12 March 1944, in the NCCN gymnasium. They played on Sunday morning, knowing that many Durham residents, both black and white, would be in church, and they played at NCCN because it was less difficult, logistically, than sneaking the NCCN players onto Duke's campus.

The medical school team boasted at least five players who had experience in some of the most competitive undergraduate programs around the country; it was rumored to be the best team at Duke—indeed, possibly in Durham. But McLendon's 1944 Eagles, despite having only seven players, had posted a 19-1 record. Somehow a hypothetical question arose among Durham's students and in some of the town's barbershops: If the two teams ever played each other, who would win? The teams eventually became intrigued with the question themselves, but when they finally took the court together—with one referee and a scorekeeper, to make it official—they realized how dangerous their participation in such a game in the segregated South could potentially be.

Both teams struggled to find their rhythm early, but when NCCN's furious defense and explosive fast break finally erupted, they ran away with the game. The NCCN guard Aubrey Stanley, just sixteen years old, remembered that it suddenly occurred to him that Duke's players "weren't supermen. They were just men. And we could beat them" (Ellsworth). By halftime word had leaked on the NCCN campus, and students were climbing outside the gymnasium to peer through the windows. They witnessed seven of their classmates soundly defeat Duke, 88-44.

As Ellsworth writes, the next thing they saw was even more shocking: the two teams traded players and played a second game—with two integrated teams. The score was not recorded, but McLendon later described the experience of watching two communities and two distinctive basketball styles coalesce for the first time: "That was the way basketball's supposed to be" (Ellsworth).

McLendon and his wife, Joanna, had four children. He was inducted into the James Naismith Basketball Hall of Fame in 1978. His career college coaching record was 523-165; his professional record was 108-71. Before his death in 1999 in Cleveland, Ohio, the National Association of Collegiate Directors of Athletics endowed a scholarship in his name for minority students who intended to pursue graduate studies in athletic administration. McLendon regarded this scholarship among his highest achievements.

FURTHER READING
McLendon, John B., Jr. *Fast Break Basketball: Fundamentals and Fine Points* (1965).
Ashe, Arthur. *A Hard Road to Glory: A History of the African American Athlete Since 1946* (1988).

Ellsworth, Scott. "Jim Crow Loses: The Secret Game," *New York Times Magazine* (31 Mar. 1996). Available at http://www.nccu.edu/campus/athletics/jmsecret.html.

DAVID F. SMYDRA JR.

McLin, Lena (5 Sept. 1929–), composer, pianist, and educator, was born Lena Johnson in Atlanta, Georgia, the daughter of Bernice Dorsey Johnson, a church music director, and Benjamin J. Johnson, a pastor. Her childhood was much involved in the music and religion of the Baptist church. Her parent's church, Greater Mount Calvary Baptist Church in Atlanta, was the venue for her first musical performances. She spent a great amount of time there and became rooted in the various styles of the black sacred music. In her home, music also remained central. Her mother was her first piano teacher and was strict in developing McLin's musicianship. In addition to having young McLin assist in directing the choir at church, playing for service, and writing music for worship, she exposed her to performances and recordings of the western European art music tradition by regularly taking her to operas and symphony orchestra concerts. Her parents' religious leadership and musicianship were the foundations for her career. McLin, resentful of the restrictions of the Jim Crow South, also developed a keen social and political consciousness that inspired her to create opportunities for African Americans throughout her life. One of her childhood friends was MARTIN LUTHER KING JR. From 1933 to 1943 McLin occasionally lived with her uncle THOMAS A. DORSEY, the father of gospel music, in Chicago. The time spent with Dorsey proved to have significant influence on McLin's music. She accompanied the gospel singer MAHALIA JACKSON and heard her own grandmother, a former slave who lived with her uncle, sing spirituals daily. Though it was not apparent to McLin at the time, her grandmother's spirituals would be the source of many of her own compositions. While living in Chicago, McLin played piano at Pilgrim Baptist Church, where Dorsey was music director. Though she spent significant time in Chicago, McLin graduated from Atlanta's Booker T. Washington High School in 1947 and then went to Spelman College, where she earned a BM in Piano and Violin Performance in 1951. While at Spelman, McLin studied with the piano professor Florence Brinkman, and Leonora Brown and Willis Laurence James taught her music theory and composition. Also in 1951 She married

Nathaniel, and they subsequently had a son and a daughter.

After college McLin returned to Chicago, where she was awarded a scholarship to continue music study at the American Conservatory of Music. She studied music theory, composition, and counterpoint with Stella Roberts and piano with Howard Hanks, earning an MM degree in 1954. McLin's return to Chicago included a return to Dorsey's Pilgrim Baptist Church. She served as the choir accompanist from 1952 until 1953. Determined to gain a broader musical aptitude, McLin continued her studies at Chicago's Roosevelt University, where she studied electronic music and voice with Thelma Waide Brown, a colleague of the contralto MARIAN ANDERSON.

Concerned about the limited performance opportunities for African American singers due to racial segregation, McLin founded and operated the McLin Opera Company from 1957 until 1968. She also founded a gospel ensemble, the McLin Singers, in the late 1960s. McLin wrote the music curriculum for the Chicago Public School system and taught for over thirty-five years. She began her teaching in 1959 at Julius H. Jess Upper Grade Center, taught at Hubbard High School in 1960, John Marshall Harlan High School from 1963 to 1968, and at Kenwood Academy where she was the head of the music department from 1969 until 1991. She extended her curriculum development beyond the Chicago Public School System producing a film, *The Origin of the Spiritual* (1972), writing a textbook, *Pulse: A History of Music* (1977), and serving as an adviser to the Music Educators National Conference on rock music. A regular choral clinician at universities around the country, McLin was also a consultant for Westminster Choir College in Princeton, New Jersey, and a regular conductor for the National Convention of Gospel Choirs and Choruses and the Music Educators National Conference. She influenced hundreds of critically acclaimed performing artists, including the opera singers Mark Rucker and Nicole Heaston, the Tony Award winner Mandy Patinkin, the rhythm and blues artist Robert "R" Kelly, and the jazz artists Kim English and Maggie Brown.

Her mother's musical influence, as well as her father's religious leadership, remained constant in her life. In 1982 she founded and pastored the Holy Vessel Christian Center. As trained by her mother, McLin continued to compose music for worship for her church. For seven years she composed new music for every Sunday of the year.

Her compositions, numbering over four hundred, included such secular genres as rock, symphonic music, and opera. Her two most popular compositions were musical portraits of Martin Luther King Jr., titled "Free at Last" (1973), and of the poet GWENDOLYN BROOKS, "Gwendolyn Brooks: A Musical Portrait" (1972). Both convey powerful messages about racism in the United States. She also composed a rock opera titled *Comment*, masses, and works for solo chamber ensembles, choral groups, and solo voice.

McLin's awards include an outstanding composer award from the Critics Association (1971), a teacher of the year award in Chicago (1972), and honorary doctorates from her alma mater Spelman College and Virginia Union University (1975). Like many groundbreaking artists, the Reverend Dr. Lena Johnson McLin unapologetically navigated through a wide range of musical styles, but not without a consciousness of musical politics. In a time when gospel music was not taken as seriously as classical music, McLin found a place for both styles in her musicianship. Throughout her life she valued the development of new musical styles that encouraged many of her young students. Her many compositions in their many diverse styles demonstrated her capacity as a master of multiple musical traditions. With music and religion framing her life, she was a testament to the importance of a wide musical palate, artistic integrity, and to the gifts of pioneering black female composers.

FURTHER READING

Green, Mildred Denby. *Black Women Composers: A Genesis* (1983).

Kahlil, Timothy. *International Dictionary of Black Composers* (1999).

MARTI K. NEWLAND

McMahon, Ezra. *See* Ezra.

McMillan, Terry (18 Oct. 1951–), poet, novelist, and screenplay writer, was born in Port Huron, Michigan, the oldest of the five children of Edward Lewis McMillan, a sanitation worker, and Madeline Washington (Tillman) McMillan, a factory and domestic worker. The family struggled financially but Madeline instilled a strong sense of responsibility in her young children. Terry McMillan took her first paying job at sixteen, shelving books at the local library for $1.25 an hour. As a child the only book in her home had been the Bible, but McMillan quickly became fascinated by the literary world, especially African American fiction.

As soon as she finished high school, McMillan moved to Los Angeles, where she worked as a typist during the day and attended evening classes at Los Angeles City College. She later transferred to the University of California at Berkeley where she earned a B.A. in Journalism, wrote for the student newspaper, and studied under ISHMAEL REED. She published her first short story, "The End," in 1976, when she was twenty-five years old. In 1979 McMillan moved to New York City to pursue a master's degree in film studies at Columbia University.

To support herself and her son Solomon, who was born in 1983, McMillan worked as a word processor for a high-profile law firm in New York City, but she really wanted to be a writer. She had been writing poetry and short fiction since her workshops with Reed. Determined to finish her first novel, *Mama*, she applied for residencies at Yaddo and the Macdowell Colony. She also joined

Terry L. McMillan at a signing for her book *The Interruption of Everything* in New York City, 20 July 2005. (AP Images.)

the Harlem Writers Guild, where she forged new friendships and made important connections with other writers.

Balancing full-time work, single parenthood, and a burgeoning writing career could have been daunting, but McMillan was strong willed and determined to have a successful, fulfilling life and to provide for her son as best she could. In 1987 *Mama* was published by Houghton Mifflin, whose policy was to spend little money on first-time writers. McMillan refused to let her book suffer the usual fate of the first novel, sending out nearly 3,000 letters to universities and bookstores across the country. She set up her own book tour and *Mama*'s first printing was sold out before its publication date.

In the next two years she became an associate professor at the University of Arizona and published her second book, *Disappearing Acts*. The novel, published by Viking, received mostly excellent reviews and sold more than 100,000 copies in paperback. It also provoked a defamation lawsuit from Leonard Welch, Solomon's father, who claimed that Franklin, one of the main characters in the book, was modeled after him. The $4.75 million lawsuit was unsuccessful, however, and McMillan soon returned to her writing.

In 1990 McMillan edited *Breaking Ice*, an anthology of contemporary African American writing, which she hoped would inspire other young African Americans to become writers. *Waiting to Exhale*, published in 1992, sold four million copies and spawned a highly successful black "chick flick" in Hollywood's movie of the same name four years later. McMillan had begun a national revolution, lending a voice to the often-overlooked world of successful black women. McMillan was credited with opening the world of contemporary fiction to African American writers, especially women. Many prominent black women writers were writing about the past; McMillan saw that African American women also wanted books that related directly to their own lives, and she set out to fill that void. Until her unabashed success, much of the publishing industry believed that African American women did not read. McMillan proved them wrong with her fresh, racy novels, which strongly resonated with the real lives of her readers. Though she was criticized for ignoring the issue of race and writing for a white audience, McMillan considered herself part of the new black aesthetic. When McMillan lost her mother and her best friend within two years, she put her writing career on hold. After wandering emotionally for over a year, she took a spontaneous trip to Jamaica, where she met her future husband and the inspiration for her next best-selling book. *How Stella Got Her Groove Back*, her most autobiographical novel, was published in 1996 and led to a multimillion-dollar movie deal. Closely involved with the making of her movies, McMillan served as executive producer and co-writer of both *How Stella Got Her Groove Back* and *Waiting to Exhale*.

In 1998 she married Jonathan Plummer, and soon settled in Danville, California, with her new husband and her son. Another novel, *A Day Late and a Dollar Short*, was published in 2001. The book focused on relationships within a dysfunctional family, as did her 2005 novel *The Interruption of Everything*. Also in 2005, McMillan divorced Plummer after a nine-month, acrimonious court battle after Plummer announced he was gay.

FURTHER READING
Patrick, Diane. *Terry McMillan: The Unauthorized Biography* (1999).
Richards, Paulette. *Terry McMillan: A Critical Companion* (1999).

JESSICA SMEDLEY

McNair, Barbara (4 Mar. 1934–4 Feb. 2007), singer, nightclub entertainer, and actress, was born Barbara Joan McNair in Chicago, Illinois, and raised from the age of three in Racine, Wisconsin. McNair's father, a foundry worker, and her mother, a housekeeper at an institution for mentally disabled children, recognized her vocal musical gifts early on. After discussions with McNair's teachers, her parents decided that she should receive formal training in music. McNair went on to study at the Racine Conservatory of Music and Chicago's American Conservatory of Music, and later majored in music at the University of California, Los Angeles, where she studied for one year before deciding to move to New York City in the early 1950s.

Once she arrived in New York, McNair secured a secretarial job at the National Federation of Settlements to support herself while she went to open auditions at various nightclubs in the city. Even after she was hired by Max Gordon to sing at the Village Vanguard, however, McNair kept her secretarial job during the day. Her Village Vanguard performances helped her to secure an agent and a weeklong appearance on *Arthur Godfrey's Talent Scouts* competition, which she won with her rendition of the song "Lullaby of Broadway."

A subsequent engagement at the Purple Onion in 1957 marked a turning point in McNair's career.

She became known as a headliner and quit her secretarial job. She was quickly booked at major venues across the country, such as the Persian Room in New York City's Plaza Hotel, the Ambassador Hotel and the Coconut Grove in Los Angeles, and numerous Las Vegas hotels and clubs. McNair enjoyed career-enhancing media attention when the famed radio news commentator and newspaper journalist Walter Winchell saw her perform in Las Vegas and began to mention her in his column. These mentions by Winchell, however brief, were significant. Since the end of World War I, nightclubs had become a central part of American culture, yet the Las Vegas nightclub culture was notoriously racist, barring blacks from hotels, casinos, and clubs even if they were headlining performers who brought in revenue for these venues. Winchell was well connected with legitimate as well as alleged "underworld" figures that monopolized the Las Vegas nightclub business. For him to positively promote McNair in his coverage meant a level of acceptance for her that could ameliorate the questionable and outright hostile treatment other black performers such as NAT KING COLE had endured in the city. McNair's Las Vegas performances also brought her to the attention of Coral Records, and

Barbara McNair, singer and actress, photographed in 1963. (AP Images.)

in 1958 the company offered her a recording contract. McNair's hit record "Bobby" was actually the B side of her debut single "Till There Was You." As her national reputation grew, her career expanded onto Broadway. In 1958 she made her stage debut as Marge in the original musical comedy *The Body Beautiful*. She received critical acclaim for her performance, although the production was short-lived, running from 23 January to 12 March of that year.

Additionally, McNair hosted her own local television show, *Schaefer Circle*, in New York in 1958. Her increased popularity led to guest appearances on numerous national television variety shows, including multiple appearances on *Toast of the Town* and *The Bell Telephone Hour* in the late 1950s, and on *The Dean Martin Show* in the mid-1960s. From 1961 to 1964 McNair toured frequently with Nat King Cole in his stage show *I'm with You*. She also performed with Cole at Los Angeles's Greek Theatre in *The Merry World of Nat King Cole*.

McNair replaced DIAHANN CARROLL in the role of Barbara Woodruff for the national tour of the Richard Rodgers hit musical *No Strings*, which ran on Broadway from 15 March 1962 to 3 August 1963. That same year she also made her feature film debut in *Spencer's Mountain*, starring Henry Fonda and Maureen O'Hara. She continued to record for the Signature, Roulette, and Warner Bros. record labels, and she eventually signed with Motown Records in 1965. Motown's agenda was to groom and popularize glamorous black performers who could attract not only a core black audience but also a significant white audience who would find their polish more palatable than the raucous performances of many of the day's black rock and roll acts. McNair embodied the Motown image made familiar by groups like the Temptations and the Supremes, with their elegant attire, precise choreography, and smooth harmonies, and her 1965 debut single for the label, "You're Gonna Love My Baby," was one of her biggest hits.

McNair made her next feature film appearance in 1968, opposite Raymond St. Jacques in *If He Hollers, Let Him Go*, an adaptation of a CHESTER HIMES novel. Her nude scenes in the film made news. *Change of Habit* followed in 1969, in which McNair was cast as Sister Irene opposite Mary Tyler Moore and Elvis Presley in his last film appearance.

Also in 1969 McNair became one of few women and only the second black performer after Nat King Cole and his 1956 NBC television variety series *The Nat King Cole Show* to host her own musical variety show for national television. *The Barbara*

McNair Show was produced by Motown Television Productions and aired from 1969 to 1971. McNair hosted such diverse guests as ETHEL WATERS, Bobby Sherman, LIONEL HAMPTON, B. B. KING, Bob Hope, Sonny and Cher, and the EDWIN HAWKINS Singers.

McNair's film career hit a particular high point in 1970 when she was cast as Valerie Tibbs, the wife of Lieutenant Virgil Tibbs, opposite Academy Award winner SIDNEY POITIER in *They Call Me MISTER Tibbs!*, the sequel to *In the Heat of the Night*. She reprised the role in 1971 in the third and final film of the series, titled *The Organization*.

Also in 1971 the International Society of Cosmetologists voted McNair one of "The World's Ten Most Beautiful Women," making her the first black woman to be so acknowledged. That recognition inspired McNair to coauthor *The Complete Book of Beauty for the Black Woman* (1972) with Stephen Lewis. On her official Web site, www.barbaramcnair.com, McNair wrote that, "When I learned that I was the first Black woman to be named … I was glad to see that in the eyes of the beauty establishment, the Black woman had at last come into her own."

McNair experienced personal difficulties during the early and mid-1970s. In 1972 she and her third husband, Richard Manzie, were charged with heroin possession. Eventually cleared of the charges, McNair would later face loss when, in 1976, Manzie was shot and killed.

Through the late 1970s and into the 1980s McNair made several film and television appearances, including a recurring role on the daytime series *General Hospital* in 1984. She also appeared in the 1990 television movie *Fatal Charm* and the 1996 feature film *Neon Signs*.

Since the days of her USO tours to Vietnam with Bob Hope, McNair participated in civic and charitable activity. She attended the Lift Ev'ry Voice fund-raiser in 2004 to benefit the Democratic presidential candidate Senator John Kerry, sponsored by African American Women for Peace and Justice, California Women for Kerry, and African Americans for Kerry. On 19 February 2005 McNair introduced new songs from her latest, independent CD, *Here's to Life!*, in a one-night-only performance of her one-woman cabaret show at the Ruth B. Shannon Center for the Performing Arts in Whittier, California. She donated a portion of the proceeds of that evening's CD sales to the Sri Lanka tsunami relief effort.

Regarding her feelings about performing new music cabaret-style at age seventy, McNair told the *Whittier Daily News* in a 15 February 2005 staff report posted on www.whittierdailynews. com, "I get to sing songs that are special to me, knowing I am being listened to, understood, and appreciated."

McNair succumbed to throat cancer on 4 February 2007, in Los Angeles, California. She was survived by her sister, Jacqueline Gaither, and her fourth husband, Charles Blecka.

FURTHER READING

McNair, Barbara, and Stephen Lewis. *The Complete Book of Beauty for the Black Woman* (1972).
Obituary: *New York Times*, 6 Feb. 2007.

SHARON D. JOHNSON

McNair, Denise (17 Nov. 1951–15 Sept. 1963), schoolgirl and terrorist bombing victim, was born Carol Denise McNair in Birmingham, Alabama, the first child of Christopher McNair, a freelance photographer, and Maxine Pippen McNair, a schoolteacher. Denise, or "Niecie" as her friends called her, enjoyed a relatively comfortable, somewhat sheltered upbringing as part of Birmingham's small but growing African American middle class. Chris McNair's photography business prospered, and teachers like Maxine Pippen McNair had long been the backbone of the city's tight-knit black bourgeoisie. Denise's parents, both graduates of the Tuskegee Institute, believed strongly in the importance of education and encouraged their daughter's early interest in poetry, music, and dance. Active in the Brownies, a dedicated student of the piano, and a keen softball player, Denise emerged as one of the most popular children in her neighborhood and at Birmingham's Center Street Elementary School. Absorbing at an early age her parents' ideal of service to the community, Niecie encouraged her friends to join her in performing skits and dances to raise money for muscular dystrophy. Church was also important in Denise's short life. While her father attended a Lutheran congregation, she followed her mother into Sixteenth Street Baptist Church, Birmingham's elite black congregation, where Maxine McNair's father, F.L. Pippen, the owner of a dry cleaning store, was deacon.

Indeed, Denise McNair's childhood in many respects typified the devout, prosperous optimism of America in the Eisenhower and Kennedy years. It also reflected the underside of the American dream in her hometown of Birmingham, at that time the nation's most racially divided city. "Bombingham," as it was known, was rocked by more than fifty dynamite explosions between 1947 and 1963, nearly all of them in African American neighborhoods or at black churches or businesses. Although many in Birmingham knew the Ku Klux Klan members responsible for the bombing campaign and other incidents of racial violence, no one had ever been convicted, largely because of the efforts of the city's all-powerful public safety commissioner, Eugene "Bull" Connor, himself a Klansman. In the summer of 1963 Connor earned the praise of his fellow Klansmen and the opprobrium of much of the rest of the world by turning his billy-club-wielding, all-white police force and its dogs and high-pressure water cannon on thousands of children and teenagers who had joined the direct-action desegregation protests launched by Birmingham's FRED SHUTTLESWORTH and supported by MARTIN LUTHER KING JR.

The McNairs supported the goals of the civil rights movement, but like many other parents they struggled both to explain the harsh reality of racial discrimination to their daughter and to shelter her from the most flagrant racial abuses in Alabama, whose governor, George Wallace, stood as the embodiment of southern white resistance to racial change. Chris McNair later recalled his shame and discomfort at having to tell his hungry daughter that he could not purchase a sandwich for her at a segregated lunch counter. Although she was still only eleven years old in 1963, Denise may have already absorbed the lesson of the hundreds of Birmingham schoolchildren, some only a few years older than herself, who braved water cannon and tear gas that summer to express their desire for freedom and an end to second-class citizenship. When she found that her reading books at school featured only white characters, Denise offered her own civil rights protest by writing and illustrating an integrated alternative, "The Boy Who Wanted a Pet," about a group of black and white children and a chicken.

On Sunday, 15 September 1963, before they left for services at Sixteenth Street Baptist, Denise and her mother discussed a group of youngsters who had begun marching together to church. Denise wanted to join them, but her mother responded firmly that she was too young. At around 10 A.M.,

Mr. and Mrs. Christopher McNair hold a picture of their eleven-year-old daughter Denise in Birmingham, Alabama, as they tell a newsman about the bombing of the Sixteenth Street Baptist Church, 16 September 1963. One day earlier, Denise and three other girls died in the blast while attending Sunday school. (AP Images.)

Denise left her Sunday school service, where the lesson had been "The Love That Forgives," and made her way to the basement ladies' lounge. There she and fellow choristers CYNTHIA WESLEY, CAROLE ROBERTSON, and ADDIE MAE COLLINS prepared for the main 11 A.M. church service. At around 10:22 A.M. a massive explosion ripped through the church, killing the four girls instantly and injuring at least twenty others, including Collins's sister Sarah. The blast was caused by the detonation of a bundle of dynamite that had been placed on the northeast side of the church several hours earlier by white supremacists. The church had probably been targeted for its role in supporting the recent civil rights protests and for its reputation as the church of Birmingham's black middle class. Among the first to arrive on the scene to search through the rubble was Deacon Pippen, who helped remove large concrete blocks from the mangled bodies of the girls and who first recognized his granddaughter among the four bodies. After telling his own daughter that her only child had perished in the blast, the normally staid Deacon Pippen screamed in anguish, "I'd like to blow the whole town up," referring to the Birmingham of Bull Connor, the wealthy white big business "mules" who controlled the city, and the working-class Klansmen whose defiance of civil rights had created a hateful racial climate (McWhorter, 526). Deacon Pippen's fury was shared by many African Americans in Birmingham and by millions of others who were stunned that opponents of the civil rights movement would target a Sunday church service with a bomb, fully aware that children would be among the four hundred congregants in attendance. Like other civil rights leaders, CORETTA SCOTT KING viewed the bombing as a racist response to the optimism of her husband's "I Have a Dream" speech at the March on Washington just three weeks earlier. With the brutal deaths of four innocent girls, Scott King recalled, "you realized how intense the opposition was, and that it would take a lot more than what was being done to change the situation" (Hampton, 174). Although Klansman Robert Chambliss was immediately identified as the likely perpetrator of the blast, obstruction by local authorities and the FBI delayed the prosecution of the case, and he was not tried until 1977, when he was finally convicted of the first-degree murder of Denise.

Like her three friends, Denise would never grow to adulthood or fulfill her undoubted promise. Family friends believed that she could have been a teacher, or that she may have achieved her childhood dream of becoming a pediatrician. Indeed, the passage of the 1964 Civil Rights Act and the 1965 Voting Rights Act vastly expanded the opportunities available to young African American women like Denise. She might even have followed a path as noteworthy as that of her family friend and kindergarten classmate, CONDOLEEZZA RICE.

FURTHER READING

Hampton, Henry, and Steve Frayer. *Voices of Freedom* (1990).

McWhorter, Diane. *Carry Me Home: Birmingham, Alabama: The Climactic Battle of the Civil Rights Revolution* (2001).

Mendelsohn, Jack. *The Martyrs: Sixteen Who Gave Their Lives for Racial Justice* (1966).

STEVEN J. NIVEN

McNair, Ronald Erwin (21 Oct. 1950–28 Jan. 1986), physicist, astronaut, and victim of the *Challenger* Space Shuttle disaster, was born in Lake City, South Carolina, the second of three children of Pearl McNair, an educator, and Carl McNair, a mechanic. Ronald McNair and his brothers, Carl Jr. and Eric, were raised to place great emphasis on education and achievement.

During the 1950s and 1960s, segregation dictated all social practices in Lake City, South Carolina. McNair, though, did not allow the world around him to define his path. At age three, he began reading his mother's classroom books. At age nine, after exhausting his collection at home, McNair staged a "sit-in" at the whites-only library, refusing to leave until he was able to check out a book. Among his schoolmates, McNair was deemed the hardest worker and the smartest; anything less than a perfect score on exams only fueled his drive for success. McNair was also successful outside of the classroom; during his high school days, he excelled in football, baseball, and track, and was a proficient saxophonist. McNair received a music scholarship to North Carolina Agricultural and Technical University (NCA&T) in 1967.

While at NCA&T McNair was drawn to physics as a field of study and decided to change majors after taking a few classes. He soon discovered that the rigors of the science curriculum exceeded his secondary education training. McNair worked hard to overcome his deficiencies and continued to display his well-rounded personality by participating in campus activities and even learning karate; eventually obtaining a fifth-degree black belt. In 1969 McNair was afforded an opportunity to study at the Massachusetts Institute of Technology (MIT). The experience of living in Boston while studying at one of the most prestigious technological schools in the country opened McNair's eyes to a world he hardly knew. When he graduated from NCA&T in 1971 with a degree in physics, McNair returned to MIT to do his graduate work.

Despite the help of a fellowship to fund his matriculation at MIT, McNair ran into more than a few obstacles on his way to earning a P.hD. . Just as in his undergraduate experience, he encountered troubles adjusting to the advanced classes at MIT. However, he applied the same diligent work ethic to rise to the top of his class. At one point he lost a notebook containing two years of his thesis research. Instead of feeling sorry for himself, he put in extra time to make up the research in only a few months.

He continued to balance his school life in Boston with a vibrant personal life, which included teaching karate, playing saxophone to make a little money, and regularly attending church. At one particular church dinner, McNair met Cheryl Moore, a schoolteacher from New York. The two would marry on 27 June 1976, shortly after McNair's graduation from MIT. That same year, he obtained his first job with the Hughes Research Laboratories in Malibu, California, working in advance laser research. Within a short amount of time, McNair became both a family man and one of the nation's experts in laser physics.

In 1977 McNair began his relationship with the National Aeronautics and Space Administration (NASA). At the time, NASA was expanding opportunities to minorities and people who did not have pilot or military experience, and in 1978 McNair received news that his application had been accepted. Perhaps it was fitting that McNair would end up in the space program since he became interested in space travel after hearing about the *Sputnik* launch in 1957. After advanced training in flight, earth and physical sciences, and space simulators, in 1979 McNair became a mission specialist astronaut for NASA.

McNair saw a few significant firsts after he entered the space program: the first woman in space, Sally Ride in 1983 and the first African American in space, GUION BLUFORD in 1983. During that same time, McNair became a father to son Reginald in 1982, and his daughter Joy would follow in 1984. That year, McNair would make his first journey into space. As part of a six-member crew, the STS-11 flight accomplished liftoff from Kennedy Space Center on the morning of 3 February 1984. During the mission,

McNair was responsible for numerous tasks including experiments on acoustic levitation and chemical separation in space. He also operated the mechanical arm for the first Manned Maneuvering Unit, designed to assist repairs outside of the shuttle. McNair, who brought his trusted saxophone on board the shuttle, became the first person to play the sax in space. The shuttle landed at Kennedy Space Center on 10 February 1984.

After returning from space, McNair became a popular public figure, lecturing at MIT, speaking in the Massachusetts State Legislature, sharing his story with schoolchildren, and visiting Lake City as an honored son of the community. In 1985 McNair was chosen for another mission on the *Challenger* shuttle. This launch would be historic because the crew included the first private citizen to venture to space, a schoolteacher named Christa McAuliffe. But the flight became infamous under the most tragic circumstances.

Mission 51L aboard the *Challenger* was originally scheduled for launch in July of 1985, but various mechanical issues during retrials pushed the flight back to January of 1986. A few nights before the actual liftoff, a severe artic weather front gripped the east coast of the country; not even Florida's usual tropical climate was spared from the cold and ice storms. NASA crews worked overtime to thaw out the ship for the flight. The crew boarded the cabin on 28 January and began countdown to liftoff. As engines propelled the shuttle from the launch pad, it took less than a minute for complications to take place. Fire erupted from the rockets and the shuttle exploded 73 seconds into its flight, scattering debris and smoke across the Florida morning sky. All seven crewmembers including McNair, age thirty-five, died in the crash.

In December 1986, MIT rededicated the building for its Center for Space Research after Ronald Erwin McNair. In the years after his passing, many scholarships and awards have been named in his honor. Among the most significant of these is Ronald E. McNair Postbaccalaureate Achievement Program, a federal program designed to motivate and support students from disadvantaged backgrounds, which operates in 200 colleges across America.

FURTHER READING

Naden, Corinne. *Ronald McNair* (1991).
Phelps, J. Alfred. *They Had a Dream: The Story of African American Astronauts* (1994).

JOHN BRYAN GARTRELL

McNair, Steve (14 Feb. 1973–4 July 2009), professional athlete, NFL quarterback, was born in Mount Olive, Mississippi, one of five sons to Selma and Lucille. His father abandoned the family when Steve was very young, and his mother worked a factory job to make ends meet. His older brother Fred was a gifted athlete and passed his love of sports to his younger sibling. McNair attended Mount Olive High School, where he participated in nearly every available team sport. In 1989 he led the school's football team to a state title as quarterback. He graduated in 1990.

Shortly thereafter, McNair found himself faced with a number of significant career decisions. He was drafted by baseball's Seattle Mariners, but decided instead to play football. He was courted by a number of major programs and was widely considered a likely Heisman Trophy hopeful, but they all wanted the physically large McNair—at 6 feet 2 inches and 230 pounds—to play defense, and McNair had his heart set on the quarterback spot. Ultimately, he chose that position and proximity to home over the glamour of the big programs and elected to attend tiny Alcorn State, an HBCU and Division I-AA Southwestern Athletic Conference school in Lorman, Mississippi. His career there was the stuff of college sports lore. In his first year, McNair set nine team records and threw for an amazing 3,541 yards. A year later, his team led all schools in total offense with 405.7 yards per game. Under center, McNair was a defensive coordinator's nightmare. He earned the nickname Air McNair for his rocket arm, but his ability (and quick willingness) to tuck the ball and scramble made him a double threat on the field. He was tempted to join the NFL draft as a junior but remained in school at the urging of his family and completed his bachelor's degree in Recreation. During that senior campaign, McNair racked up amazing numbers: 53 touchdowns with only 17 interceptions, and nearly 6,000 yards total offense (passing and rushing). He was named All-American, won the Walter Payton Award (given to the most outstanding offensive player in college football), and finished third in Heisman Trophy voting.

In 1995 McNair was taken in the third round of the NFL draft by the Houston Oilers, though he saw little action until the 1997 season. That year, the team relocated to Tennessee, playing at the Liberty Bowl in Memphis while their permanent home in Nashville was under construction. It was the second of three straight 8–8 seasons, though the team was beginning to develop into an offensive powerhouse with McNair as one of its key pieces. In 1997—his first year as a starter—he set a franchise record for fewest interceptions (13) and led his team

in rushing touchdowns. His rushing yards (674) were the third highest for any quarterback in NFL history. That same year, McNair married Mechelle Cartwright. They had four sons.

In 1998 the Oilers moved to Nashville. While McNair showed flashes of brilliance, the team again finished a disappointing .500, despite nabbing second place in the AFC Central division. Still, expectations for a breakout year were high. Supporting McNair were Jeff Fisher, quickly regarded as one of the best game-day coaches in the league; the franchise's star running back Eddie George; and a defense that was showing signs of becoming a dominant force.

That breakout year came in the following season, 1999. The Oilers changed their name to the Tennessee Titans and inaugurated their new home—currently known as LP Field—on Nashville's east side. Though sidelined for part of the season with a back injury and surgery, McNair returned to lead the Titans to a 13–3 season and a spot in the post-season. After beating the Buffalo Bills in a wildcard game in Nashville featuring what would become one of the most famous football plays in the history of the game—the so-called Music City Miracle—the Titans advanced past the Indianapolis Colts and the seemingly dominant Jacksonville Jaguars (whom they had to face in Florida) to win a spot against the St. Louis Rams in the Super Bowl.

Like the Music City Miracle game, Super Bowl XXXIV is widely considered an NFL classic. The offensive powerhouse Rams led the more defensively minded Titans by 9–0 at the half, but quickly scored in the third quarter to extend their lead to 16–0. McNair's response was brilliant. He threw, scrambled, and made plays, engineering sixteen unanswered points to tie the game. After the Rams scored another long touchdown, McNair again drove his team downfield, and again he was brilliant. The penultimate play in the game, one that saw McNair slip away from what appeared to be a sure sack and find his receiver downfield, is widely regarded as among the best of his professional career and emblematic of his toughness and style of play. With only seconds in the fourth quarter left, a pass to Titans wide receiver Kevin Dyson would have tied the game, but the play came up short when Dyson was tackled by Rams linebacker Mike Jones a yard from the goal line. Despite the loss, McNair had become an NFL star. The Titans signed him to a $47 million contract in 2001.

In that season, McNair had his best season yet. He threw for 3,350 yards and 21 touchdowns and earned a quarterback rating of 90.2, all career bests. He was named to the Pro Bowl, but nagging injuries kept him from playing. Injuries, in fact, were becoming more of an issue, and the list of ailments that McNair had suffered was growing. His tenacity and toughness were by now the stuff of NFL legend, but increasingly McNair's availability on Sunday morning was the subject of constant speculation from Monday to Saturday night. In 2002, he again led the Titans deep into the playoffs, but lost in the conference championship game to the Oakland Raiders.

In May 2003 McNair was arrested in Nashville for driving under the influence, a charge made worse when the arresting officer found a loaded handgun in McNair's vehicle. The gun was registered but—according to Tennessee law—McNair's state of intoxication invalidated his permit. The charges were eventually dropped, but McNair's reputation for maturity and discipline took a hit. Despite these troubles, McNair finished the 2003 campaign with the best numbers of his storied career. He threw for 3,215 yards, 24 touchdowns, and only 7 interceptions. His quarterback rating was a league-leading 100.4. The Titans finished the season at 12–4 but again fell short of a second Super Bowl appearance. Nevertheless, McNair was named league MVP, though he shared the honor with the Indianapolis Colts' Peyton Manning.

After two injury-plagued seasons, the Titans dealt McNair to their longtime rivals the Baltimore Ravens in 2006. The end of his career in Nashville was overshadowed by what many observers considered McNair's poor treatment at the hands of the Titans, including reports that McNair was asked to leave the Titans training facility. Despite predictions that he would not last the season, McNair started every game, and led the team to an AFC North title; the Ravens, however, fell to the Colts in the first round of the playoffs. McNair was sidelined for much of 2007 with multiple injuries, and in 2008, after thirteen seasons, he announced his retirement.

In 2009 McNair and a young woman, 20-year-old Sahel Kazemi, were arrested for DUI. Kazemi was behind the wheel and McNair was subsequently released and posted her bail. Two days later, on 4 July, McNair's body was found in a Nashville apartment leased to him. Kazemi was there, too, both dead by gunshot wound. The police investigation came back with a determination of murder-suicide. McNair had apparently been dating Kazemi for some time. Following the investigation, the police held that Kazemi had shot McNair while he slept on a living room sofa, then lay down beside him

and shot herself. She may have feared that McNair was prepared to break off their relationship, though this is limited to speculation.

McNair was buried in Prentiss, Mississippi. The following season, the Titans wore his number 9 on their uniforms in commemoration of their fallen leader.

FURTHER READING

Stewart, Mark. *Steve McNair: Running and Gunning* (2001).
Obituary: Associated Press. "Steve McNair." http://www.legacy.com/obituaries/ tennessean/obituary.aspx?n=steve-mcnair&pid=129304792

JASON PHILIP MILLER

McNairy, Francine (13 Nov. 1946–), college president, educator, social worker, and mentor, was born in Pittsburgh, Pennsylvania, the daughter of Francis E. McNairy, a steel mill worker and Baptist deacon with only an eighth-grade education, and Gladys McNairy. McNairy's mother, who cared for nine foster children in addition to her own family, became deeply involved with Pittsburgh's public schools to ensure that her daughter and other African American students would get the best education possible. A graduate of a business career school, Duff's Business College, Gladys McNairy was unable to get a job matching her qualifications because of racism. However, she rose from being a maid at the local department store, Kaufmann's, to becoming a trustee of the University of Pittsburgh, a member of the Pennsylvania State Board of Education, and one of the few black women named a Distinguished Daughter of Pennsylvania. In 1971 she became the first black female president of the Pittsburgh City School Board.

As a young girl Francine McNairy lived in the small neighborhood of Sugar Top in Pittsburgh's Hill District, a mostly black community. In the 1950s, among those leafy, cobblestone streets was a tight-knit community that valued religion, order, and education. McNairy played the violin and participated in a youth group that her mother advised at the Central Baptist Church. For the most part, Sugar Top was a wonderland that cocooned the children from the harshness of racism.

At nearby Schenley High School, McNairy was active in the orchestra, majorettes, Honor Society, and Future Teachers of America. She graduated in 1964 and entered the University of Pittsburgh, a predominantly white institution with few faculty members of color. McNairy sat in large lecture classes, where few whites wanted to sit beside her and white professors often ignored her raised hand. Socially McNairy made her way: she joined a sorority, Iota Chapter of Alpha Kappa Alpha, and sang with the Heinz Chapel Choir. A stint with Urban Youth Action, a career-prep program for inner-city high school students, deepened her community involvement and motivated her to improve her grades in college.

In 1968 she graduated with a B.A. in Sociology, then enrolled in Pitt's Graduate School of Social Work. After earning an MSW in 1970 she worked for three years as a social worker, two years with Allegheny County Child Welfare Services, later called Allegheny County Children and Youth Services, and one year with Community Action Regional Training. A few years later McNairy continued her studies at the University of Pittsburgh, earning a Ph.D. in Speech/Communication in 1978, and later she attended the Institute for Educational Management at Harvard University.

In 1973 McNairy's life took a dramatic turn. The big-city girl headed into the rural green pastures of western Pennsylvania to begin a career as a counselor at Clarion University. McNairy flourished at Clarion, growing in her self-confidence and in the recruitment and retention programming she developed to assist students of color. Her efforts broke down barriers and became models for other schools within the Pennsylvania State System of Higher Education, a group of fourteen mostly rural campuses struggling to increase minority-student enrollment. By 1980 she had been promoted to associate professor, and two years later she was named coordinator of academic development and retention; in 1983 she became dean of academic support services and assistant to the vice president for academic affairs. Along the way she cofounded the Minority Recognition Dinner and a program called Project Flourish that facilitated faculty and student development. Ultimately these programs strengthened the retention of all students, particularly students of color. Her relationships with students deepened, too. "I tried to be real with them," she said. "I was not born a doctor or a president. They needed to know how I stumbled and how someone helped me," McNairy told the Clarion Alumni Association when it honored her with a Distinguished Service Award in 2004. She was so committed to her students that she would often ferry them home to Pittsburgh when she came for visits and then take them back to campus. This occurred so often that she became known as the "McNairy shuttle."

McNairy moved in 1988 to West Chester University in eastern Pennsylvania as associate vice president for academic affairs. While in that position she spent four months as interim director of social equity and assistant to the vice chancellor of academic and student affairs in the office of the chancellor of the State System of Higher Education for Pennsylvania.

In 1994 McNairy found her way to Millersville University, a 250-acre campus in Lancaster County, Pennsylvania, where minorities represented about 10 percent of the student body of eight thousand. Single and without children, McNairy embraced the students at Millersville, many who came to know her personally. She devoted her energy to making a difference. She served as provost (the university's second in command) and vice president of academic affairs, and in 1997 she briefly served as acting vice president. During her time as provost McNairy developed five new master's degree programs and five new minors for the university. She also coordinated the school's online courses with two other universities and helped to found sister-school collaborations with universities in London, Spain, Chile, and Germany. As she had done at Clarion, she recruited academically talented and financially challenged minorities to campus and provided them with support networks to enhance their chances for graduation.

In April 2004 McNairy was inaugurated as president of Millersville University, becoming the first African American and the first female to head the former teachers' college. In Millersville, McNairy also joined the boards of the Lancaster Chamber of Commerce and the Lancaster General Medical Group and was a member of the State Board of Education.

FURTHER READING

Downey, Dennis B. *We Sing to Thee: A History of Millersville University* (2004).

Dyer, Ervin. "College Chief in the Hope Business," *Pittsburgh Post-Gazette*, 29 Feb. 2004.

Dyer, Ervin. "On the Right Path: Millersville President's Personal Commitment to Minority Student Recruitment, Retention Brings Her to Historic Post," *Black Issues in Higher Education* (25 Mar. 2004).

ERVIN DYER

McNatt, Rosemary Bray (1955–   ), writer, minister, journalist, and editor, Rosemary McNatt was born in Chicago, Illinois, to Nehemiah Bray, a laborer, and Mary Love Bray, a service industry worker. In her critically acclaimed memoir, *Unafraid of the Dark* (1998), McNatt wrote about her experiences growing up as the oldest of four children born in a family aided by welfare.

Both of her parents had received little formal education; her father hauled junk, worked as a butcher, or peddled food from a lunch wagon. Mary Love Bray worked in Chicago's service industry. McNatt's mother reserved some of the family's welfare money to send McNatt and her siblings to Catholic school. In sixth grade, a teacher noticed her promise, and she went on to attend Chicago's prestigious and highly selective Francis W. Parker School from 1967 to 1972. McNatt won a scholarship to Yale University in 1972. She graduated from Yale with a B.A. in English in 1976.

McNatt worked first at a small newspaper in Connecticut and went on to hold editorial positions at *Essence*, the *Wall Street Journal, Ms.*, and the *New York Times Book Review*. An essay she wrote about growing up on welfare at the *New York Times* was later expanded to a better-known book-length memoir, *Unafraid of the Dark*. The memoir resonated with many readers because it was written during a heated national discussion around welfare reform in the 1990s. Bray wrote the book in part to counter stereotypes about welfare and the recipients of what was then called Aid to Families with Dependent Children. "I have written this book, in part, to show the good that could happen—that did happen—under the welfare system of the 1960s," she wrote.

For over twenty years, McNatt was a widely anthologized writer whose work appeared in mainstream publications and academic journals. She published *Martin Luther King*, a biography of the famous civil rights leader with illustrations by Malcah Zeldis, for juveniles in 1995. She and Zeldis also published another juvenile biography, *Nelson Mandela*, in 1999. In 2002 Bray published a book of prayers for black children, *Beloved One: The Black Child's Book of Prayers*.

After the publication of her memoir, Bray answered the call to ordained ministry by studying at the Drew Theological School, a seminary in Madison, New Jersey. She was ordained as a Unitarian Universalist minister in 2000. She spent time living in New Jersey and New York City with her husband, Robert McNatt, and their two sons, Allen and Daniel. In 2002 the Reverend Rosemary Bray McNatt was appointed minister of The Fourth Universalist Society in the City of New York, a 170-year-old Unitarian Universalist congregation on the Upper West Side of Manhattan.

In the twenty-first century, she contributed to *UU World*, a magazine affiliated with the church, and founded the Unitarian Universalist Trauma Response Ministry, created to provide culturally sensitive liberal religious responses to mass disaster and other significant trauma. The group was founded after McNatt's experiences on 11 September 2001, when her church was used as a refuge from the chaotic and tragic events of that day. Her work has reached an even broader audience on the Web site Beliefnet.com; her blog, RevRose.com; and through other new social media forms. In 2010 McNatt's Facebook page highlighted her fervent support for a range of progressive causes ranging from the National Equality March, a pro–gay rights organization, to the group Telling Dick Cheney to Shut the Hell Up. That same year her Twitter page provided a succinct summary of Rosemary Bray McNatt's career and philosophy: "Don't want much: just hope to change the world."

FURTHER READING
Bray, Rosemary L. *Unafraid of the Dark: A Memoir* (1998).
Jones, Nancy Palmer, and Unitarian Universalist Association. *Soul Work: Anti-Racist Theories in Dialogue* (2002).
Morrison-Reed, Mark D., and Jacqui James, eds. *Been in the Storm So Long: A Meditation Manual* (1991).
JOSHUNDA SANDERS

McNeely, Cecil James (Big Jay) (29 Apr. 1927–), saxophonist and vocalist, was born Cecil James McNeely in Los Angeles, California. His musical knowledge was abetted by frequent instruction, both with private tutors and within the local school system. While matriculating at Thomas Jefferson High School, he studied with Samuel R. Browne, known to his students as Count Browne. Over the years, this influential individual trained such noted jazz musicians as DEXTER KEITH GORDON, Chico Hamilton, Buddy Collette, and Art Farmer before their careers took off. McNeely initially studied the alto saxophone, lent to him by his brother while he served in the military, but switched permanently to tenor while still in high school. He began performing locally as a teenager, along with two notable musicians, the saxophonist SONNY CRISS and the pianist HAMPTON HAWES.

Many historians connect the origins of the honking school with ILLINOIS JACQUET, both his solo on the 1942 LIONEL LEO HAMPTON release "Flying Home" and his own 1944 live recording at the 2 July Jazz at the Philharmonic concert known as "Blues." Other performers latched onto the bandwagon before McNeely took off, including Lynn Hope ("Blow Wynn Blow," 1948), Wild Bill Moore ("We're Gonna Rock," 1947), and Hal Singer ("Cornbread," 1948). Like them, McNeely followed the bridge Jacquet had constructed between jazz and the musical precursors of rock and roll.

McNeely first attracted attention at the amateur nights held at the Barrelhouse, a club in Watts owned by the bandleader and recording artist Johnny Otis and his partner Bardu Ali. He recorded his first sides with Otis's orchestra on the Excelsior label in 1948, but then signed with Savoy Records, owned by Herman Lubinsky, and was supervised by the noted A&R man Ralph Bass. His sessions for Savoy included "Deacon's Hop" (1949), which rose to number 1 on the *Billboard* race charts. The success of this material attracted the interest of Leon Rene, African American owner of the Excelsior label and writer of such hits as "When It's Sleepy Time Down South" and "When the Swallows Come Back to Capistrano." McNeely released half a dozen singles on the label in 1949.

The major event that catapulted McNeely into the entertainment limelight was the 10 July 1949 5th Annual Cavalcade of Jazz. Hampton was the headliner, but McNeely's set electrified the crowd. Hampton invited McNeely back on stage for the climax of the show, "Flying Home," and his solo clinched the public's conviction that here was a new star. McNeely did not just play. He accompanied his notes with remarkable gymnastic skills. The concert was held on a baseball field, and the saxophonist not only led the Hampton ensemble into the stands and among the audience but also lay on his back and crawled between the bases without stopping the music for a moment.

Other recordings followed, issued by the Aladdin (1950) and Imperial labels (1950–1951). In 1952 McNeely signed with the Cincinnati-based King Records, and his material on their subsidiary Federal line was once again supervised by the A&R man Ralph Bass. His visibility in the public media took off after an appearance at the Olympic Auditorium in October of 1951 was photographed by Bob Willoughby. The shots of wide-eyed and open-mouthed white teenagers taking in his act retain the kind of electricity that, a few years later, would typify the public reception of rock and roll.

Other black saxophonists took up the honking cause, such as Chuck Higgins ("Pachuko Hop," 1952) and Joe Houston ("All Night Long," 1954). However, the ascendance of both rock and roll and rhythm and blues eroded the interest in instrumental material. Increasingly, the saxophone became subsumed within the accompaniment to singers, and the kind of volatile playing that permeated the honking style appeared only as an interruption to a song. Ever alert to commercial necessities, McNeely acceded to the demands of the marketplace and released one of his most successful discs, "There Is Something on Your Mind" on the Swingin' label in 1958. The compelling lyrics along with McNeely's soloing were a winning combination. The single stayed on the *Billboard* R&B charts for nearly half a year, rising as high as number 5. A cover version by the New Orleans vocalist Bobby Marchan on the New York-based Fire label itself became a best-seller.

Success, however, proved short-lived. Though McNeely released a live recording on the Warner Brothers label, *Live at Cisco's*, in 1964, his heyday had ended. Though he played local gigs and did some studio work, McNeely gave most of his time to the Jehovah's Witness church and his day job in the post office. However, in 1983, he left his day job following a successful R&B reunion show at the Hollywood Palladium. His career was resurrected, and McNeely indicated he had lost none of his technique or his audacity.

McNeely continued to perform and record well into his seventies. He released two albums on his own Big J label in 1988 and 1992. In June 2000 *Smithsonian* magazine featured his saxophone on the cover, and in 2001, he received a Pioneer Award from the R&B Foundation. He performed as part of the ceremony and, typical of him, brought down the house.

FURTHER READING
Dawson, Jim. *Nervous Man Nervous. Big Jay McNeely and the Rise of the Honking Tenor Sax* (1994).
DAVID SANJEK

McNeil, Claudia (13 Aug. 1917–25 Nov. 1993), actress, was born in Baltimore, Maryland, the daughter of Marvin Spencer McNeil and Annie Mae (Anderson) McNeil, of whom little is known. Although she was identified as an African American performer, McNeil was half Native American, as her mother was Apache.

When McNeil was quite young, her family moved to New York City, where her mother owned and operated a small grocery store. McNeil's father left the family after the move to the North, and Claudia was reared primarily by her mother. In 1929, at the age of twelve, McNeil began working as a volunteer for the Heckscher Foundation for Children, a charitable organization founded in 1921 to promote the welfare of children, particularly those in New York City. Two members of the foundation, a married couple named the Toppers, took an interest in McNeil. McNeil's relationship with her mother was often quite difficult, and it was agreed that the Toppers could legally adopt the girl and rear her as their own daughter. Although the Toppers were Jewish and McNeil became fluent in Yiddish, she had been brought up as a Catholic.

McNeil had been performing in public from age eleven, and when she turned twenty, she decided to pursue a career as a professional singer. Perhaps to ensure that she always had a profession, she also became a licensed librarian. McNeil performed in several vaudeville theaters in New York City and surrounding areas, but her breakthrough performance took place at the Black Cat club in Greenwich Village. Still in her early twenties McNeil was

Claudia McNeil as Mamie in *Simply Heavenly* by Langston Hughes, 10 June 1957. (Library of Congress/Carl Van Vechten.)

booked as a regular at the Black Cat and paid $13.50 per week, a good sum when Americans were still struggling with the Great Depression. For more than fifteen years McNeil was a fixture in New York City nightclubs and also made frequent appearances performing live on the radio. In 1951 she toured South America as part of the KATHERINE DUNHAM Dance Company, America's first African American modern dance troupe. McNeil was a featured singer on the tour.

During the 1930s McNeil married and divorced, although the name of her husband and the exact dates of the marriage have been lost. She had one son, who was killed during the Korean War. A second marriage also ended in a divorce.

In 1953 McNeil began an acting career, reportedly on the advice of ETHEL WATERS. Undertaking an acting career at age thirty-six would be challenging for almost any performer but would have been particularly difficult for an African American woman in the 1950s, when film and television roles were relatively scarce. McNeil's career developed slowly therefore; she made her first stage appearance as an understudy in the original Broadway production of Arthur Miller's *The Crucible*, which ran from January to July 1953. In 1957 she appeared in her first Broadway musical comedy, *Simply Heavenly*, in which she portrayed Mamie. The play's book and lyrics were written by LANGSTON HUGHES, who auditioned McNeil himself. In 1958 McNeil performed for a brief run—ten days—as Mary in the Broadway production of Sherwood Anderson's *Winesburg, Ohio*.

McNeil firmly established her stage credentials when she appeared in the Broadway production of LORRAINE HANSBERRY's *A Raisin in the Sun*. While the play is considered today to be a classic and a landmark in African American theater, it was a risky venture at the time, having experienced a disappointing preview despite a successful tour with a cast that included McNeil, SIDNEY POITIER, and RUBY DEE. On opening night, however, the play received positive reviews and an enthusiastic audience response. McNeil portrayed Lena Younger from March 1959 to June 1960.

McNeil's stage career declined somewhat in the 1960s, as she was never able to repeat the success she had had with *A Raisin in the Sun*. Her conflicts with Josh Logan, who directed her in the play *Tiger, Tiger Burning Bright* from December 1962 to January 1963, were well documented. Her Yiddish skills were put to good use in Carl Reiner's *Something Different* from November 1967 to February 1968.

McNeil's last Broadway play, *The Wrong Way Light Bulb*, lasted for only seven performances in 1969, although she followed it with a successful revival of JAMES BALDWIN's *The Amen Corner* in London in 1970.

In 1959 McNeil had launched her film career with a small role in the motion picture *The Last Angry Man*, which she often named as a favorite among her own films. More notably, she appeared in the film production of *A Raisin in the Sun* in 1961, again re-creating her stage role as Lena Younger. McNeil received a Golden Globe nomination for Best Actress in a Drama for her performance in the film. The actress's other films included *There Was a Crooked Man* in 1970 and *Black Girl* in 1972. The latter film was particularly noteworthy: based on J. E. Franklin's play of the same title and directed by OSSIE DAVIS, the film was a sympathetic look at the life of a young African American woman growing up in the ghetto, and it-joined *Sounder* as one of the 1970s films that attempted to counter the "blaxploitation" movies of the period with more complex cinematic works. Many of McNeil's acting appearances in the 1960s and 1970s were on television. With the medium attempting to provide more relevant programming during this period, roles for African American performers had increased. McNeil appeared on some topical dramatic programs such as *The Nurses* (1963) and *The Mod Squad* (1972) and was even a mystery guest on the game show *What's My Line* in 1962. Her most significant television appearances were in *Roots: The Next Generations*, the sequel to ALEX HALEY's *Roots*, in 1979 and on the television special *To Be Young, Gifted, and Black* (1972), which was based in part on works by Lorraine Hansberry.

Health problems forced McNeil to retire from acting in 1983. Her last professional work was to record material for a book on tape, *Great American Women's Speeches*, in 1995. McNeil died at the Actors' Fund Nursing Home in Englewood, New Jersey.

FURTHER READING

Bogle, Donald. *Brown Sugar: Eighty Years of America's Black Female Superstars* (1980).

Obituaries: *New York Times*, 29 Nov. 1993; *Jet*, 20 Dec. 1993.

RANDALL CLARK

McNeill, Robert H. (1917–27 May 2005), photographer, was born in Washington, D.C., into a middle-class family. His father was a physician, and his mother was an educator. In the 1930s he attended Dunbar High School, where his classmates included future photographers Harrison Allen and brothers Bobby and GEORGE SCURLOCK, sons of prominent African American photographer ADDISON SCURLOCK. Allen recalled that on several occasions the boys walked from school to Scurlock's photography studio at Ninth and U Streets to watch him work. This sparked their interest in pursuing photography, first as a hobby, then as a career. The Scurlocks later took over their father's studio, and Allen became a photographer for the Department of Labor.

McNeill entered Howard University as a premed student but kept up his skills by photographing campus events, particularly celebrity visitors to the university. When Olympic track star JESSE OWENS made a campus visit, McNeill snapped a picture of him standing with university president MORDECAI JOHNSON, surrounded by hundreds of students. McNeill sold the photograph to fourteen black newspapers on the East Coast. Through this experience, McNeill saw the importance of photography to the African American press: Images of the lives and accomplishments of black people were central to the newspapers' uplift mission, and by producing them, black photographers could earn a steady living.

In 1936 McNeill went to New York and enrolled in the New York Institute of Photography. During the 1930s, photography-driven magazines had become increasingly important and popular. Like the mainstream publications *Life* and *Look*, African American publications of this type employed many photographers to illustrate their reports on black communities around the country. Dutton Ferguson, editor of *Flash!* magazine, asked McNeill, still a student, to photograph the Bronx Slave Market, an open-air space on Walton Avenue where women gathered and potential employers often hired them for day labor. Ferguson gave McNeill a three-page spread to document a day in the lives of these women. *Flash!* published thirteen of McNeill's photographs of not only women waiting for work opportunities but also employed women working—scrubbing floors and cooking meals for the meager wages of 20 to 30 cents an hour. Subsequently, McNeill became a regular feature photographer for *Flash!* and for the Washington, D.C., office of Otto McClarrin's *NewsPic* magazine.

In 1940 McNeill was invited to participate in a Federal Writers' Project study under the guidance of writer STERLING BROWN. Led by scientist Roscoe

Lewis, McNeill and other members of the all-black staff traveled to Virginia to collect information for *The Negro in Virginia*. McNeill's role was to photograph African American life, work, and leisure in the aftermath of the Great Depression. Despite the initial reluctance of many subjects to be photographed, they were ultimately casual and relaxed in front of McNeill's camera. The result was a body of work that illustrated McNeill's growing mastery of photography and his skills in the darkroom. One photograph, entitled *Spring Planting*, portrays a farmer riding on his plow, and by using the darkroom technique of burning the corners of the print on each side of the farmer's head, McNeill drew the viewer's eye to the man's countenance. Although other photos may have adequately documented farm laborers, *Spring Planting* compelled its audience to recognize the farmer's humanity. At the completion of *The Negro in Virginia* project, McNeill returned home and launched the McNeill News Service.

McNeill ran his studio in the back of the first floor of his family's home in Washington, D.C.'s prominent Shaw neighborhood, while his father used the front for his medical practice. The basement served as his darkroom. His former classmate Allen became his technician. McNeill and Allen operated the business together until World War II, when both were called to service in 1942 within days of each other.

When they returned, Allen took a job with the Library of Congress, and McNeill returned to photography. He and fellow photographer Larry Grymes started Gem Photography in a studio located at Thirteenth and U Streets and continued to supply the black press with candid photographs of businesses, social functions, and local and national celebrities. But business was slow, and in 1950 McNeill closed down his studio and accepted work as a government photographer, first for the Naval Gun Factory and later the Pentagon, the Naval Ordnance Laboratory, and finally the State Department in 1956, where he remained as chief of the photography branch until his retirement in 1978.

When he was not photographing heads of state, McNeill gave back to the photographic community. He remained active as a member of the FotoCraft Camera Club, which had been organized around 1938. FotoCraft was an offshoot of the photography program offered by the Twelfth Street YMCA, the first Y founded for African Americans. As a professional photographer, he frequently returned to conduct Fotocraft workshops on photography and darkroom work for aspiring photographers and hobbyists. He also juried some of the member shows.

Held in high esteem by his peers, McNeill saw his work exhibited in local, national, and international venues. McNeill's studio was one of four photo studios featured in *Visual Journal: Harlem and D.C. in the Thirties and Forties*, developed by the Smithsonian's Center for African American History and Culture in 1996. The exhibit and publication of the same title featured the work of GORDON PARKS and MORGAN and MARVIN SMITH in New York and the Scurlock Studio and McNeill in Washington, D.C. In 1998 the Exposure Group African American Photographers Association honored him with their Maurice Sorrell Lifetime Achievement Award. He died in 2005 at the age of eighty-eight.

FURTHER READING

Natanson, Nicholas. *The Black Image in the New Deal: The Politics of FSA Photography* (1992).

Natanson, Nicholas. "From Sophie's Alley to the White House: Rediscovering the Visions of Pioneering Black Government Photographers," in *Federal Records and African American History* (summer 1997).

Willis, Deborah, and Jane Lusaka. *Visual Journal: Harlem and D.C. in the Thirties and Forties* (1996).

DONNA M. WELLS

McPhatter, Clyde (15 Nov. 1931–13 June 1972), rhythm and blues singer, was born in Durham, North Carolina, to George McPhatter, a preacher, and Beulah Newton McPhatter, an organist and choir director. While his birth date has also been given as 15 November 1932, 1933, and 1934, Social Security records indicate 1931. At age five, Clyde Lensey McPhatter began singing with his siblings in the choir of Mount Calvary Baptist Church, where his father preached and his mother was organist and choir director.

In the 1940s, his family moved to New York, where his father preached at Mount Lebanon Church in Harlem. McPhatter attended Chelsea Vocational School, worked in a food market, and toured in a gospel sextet, the Mount Lebanon Singers, whose members included author JAMES BALDWIN's brothers David and Wilmer Baldwin.

Despite his conservative parents' objections, McPhatter competed in the Apollo Theater's Amateur Night. One of the spectators that evening was Juilliard School–trained Billy Ward, and he recruited McPhatter to sing high tenor in a doo-wop quartet he was forming, Billy Ward's Dominoes. On 14 November 1950, the group released its debut single "Do Something for Me" (the first release on the Federal label, a subsidiary of King), and it climbed to number six on *Billboard*'s rhythm and blues chart. The Dominoes' fourth single represented its most controversial and well-known release, the sexually swaggering "Sixty Minute Man" (with bass Bill Brown singing lead). The song made number one on the R&B chart in 1951, and also became one of the first doo-wop singles to break the pop charts. Subsequent hits included "That's What You're Doing to Me" and "Have Mercy Baby" (both 1952), which blended gospel vocal styles with sensual secular music, establishing a precedent for later artists such as RAY CHARLES and SAM COOKE. Besides risqué jump blues and doo-wop, the Dominoes also recorded standards such as "Over the Rainbow."

McPhatter was sometimes introduced to audiences as Billy Ward's brother, Clyde Ward. Ward's original notion was that McPhatter refused to adhere to Ward's direction that he should sing smoothly like Bill Kenny of the Ink Spots, but McPhatter developed his own melodic style, one that emphasized a youthful exuberance to which teenagers could relate. As such, it became a successful template for the doo-wop vocalizing that dominated its outgrowth, rhythm and blues field in the early 1950s. Unhappy with Ward's strict regimen and a low salary with no royalties from record sales, however, McPhatter he left the group, but not until he literally had trained his successor, JACKIE WILSON.

In 1953, he signed with Atlantic Records and formed the Drifters (including Andrew and Gerhart Thrasher from the gospel-singing Thrasher Wonders) to be his backup singers. McPhatter co-owned the group's name with businessman George Treadwell (husband of jazz great SARAH VAUGHAN). Its-first release, "Money Honey," was credited to "Clyde McPhatter and the Drifters" and skyrocketed to made number one on *Billboard*'s rhythm and blues chart. With their suggestive lyrics and McPhatter's androgynous-sounding squeals of ecstasy, the next two releases, in 1954, "Honey Love" and "Such a Night," sold well but did not get extensive airplay because they were banned on many radio stations. Recorded in New York on 2 February 1954, their intricately arranged black doo-wop version of Irving Berlin's classic "White Christmas," based on a 1948 adaptation by the Ravens, remained a holiday mainstay on

rhythm and blues radio. Despite his upbringing and his music's gospel roots, McPhatter rarely recorded sacred songs, once remarking that to him, "Religion was nothing but another word for discipline."

Drafted into the U.S. Army in May 1954, McPhatter was stationed at Fort Dix, New Jersey, and on Grand Island, Buffalo, New York. He obtained leave to make recordings during his nearly two-year military hitch. Prior to his discharge from the army in April 1956, he began recording solo and sold his rights to the Drifters' name to Treadwell (who over the years hired other singers, including the Five Crowns with BEN E. KING, to assume the Drifters' name and fulfill the group's contracts). McPhatter's melodramatic ballad "Treasure of Love" (1956) achieved his ambition to penetrate the mainstream market as NAT KING COLE had, reaching number sixteen on *Billboard*'s pop chart. Subsequent hits on Atlantic included "Without Love" and "Just to Hold My Hand" (both 1957) and his final number one R&B single, "A Lover's Question" (1958). He lip-synched two songs in the teen exploitation 1957 musical *Mister Rock and Roll* (1957).

Hoping to move further into mainstream pop music, he signed with MGM Records in 1959, but after an unfruitful year left for Mercury records in 1960. Late that year in Atlanta, he walked beside the Reverend MARTIN LUTHER KING SR. at the latter's first picket-line demonstration. In 1962, his childless nine-year marriage to Nora Thompson ended in divorce, and the teen-oriented "Lover Please" made number seven on the pop charts. His final pop hit, a cover of "Little Bitty Pretty One," also appeared in 1962. Although his music was generally apolitical, his 1964 concept album *Songs of the Big City* viewed life in New York City through the eyes of its underclass.

Leaving Mercury after his last R&B hit, "Crying Won't Help You Now" (1965), he recorded unsuccessfully for Amy Records (1965–1967) and later moved to England. His private life suddenly became public after police arrested him for "loitering with intent." Charges eventually were dropped. Returning to the United States, he attempted a comeback on the Decca label.

Unhappy about his declining career, issues related to his lack of a high school diploma, his bisexuality, and the waning of his handsome features and the diminishing of his voice's upper range, pushed McPhatter to a psychological brink. He sank into alcoholism and was unreliable on stage. He died of heart failure while sleeping in a New York hotel room after a night of drinking.

Following his death, the process he had begun to adopt his uncle's grandson, Patrick McPhatter, was completed by his widow, Lena Rackley McPhatter, whom he had wed in 1965. In the 2000s, his friend and occasional duet partner RUTH BROWN's son Ronald (born Ronald Brown in 1954) performed as Ronnie McPhatter, son of Clyde McPhatter.

A member of the Rock and Roll Hall of Fame since 1987, McPhatter was honored with a twenty-nine-cent postage stamp in June 1993.

FURTHER READING

Escott, Colin. "The Joint Is on Fire," *All Roots Lead to Rock* (1999).

Duckett, Alfred. "McPhatter Tunes Something New, Something Blue for Platter Fans," *Chicago Defender*, 15 May 1954.

Gillett, Charlie. *The Sound of the City* (1970).

DISCOGRAPHY

Billy Ward and the Dominoes (King/Federal).

Clyde McPhatter: The Forgotten Angel (R&B Records).

Rockin' & Driftin': The Drifters Box Set (Rhino Records).

The Dominoes Featuring Clyde McPhatter (King/Federal).

BRUCE SYLVESTER

McPhatter, Thomas Hayswood (8 Oct. 1923–1 May 2009), U.S. Marine Corps sergeant, U.S. Navy captain, World War II and Vietnam veteran, Montford Point marine, and Iwo Jima survivor, was born in Lumberton, North Carolina, the eleventh and last child and only son of Elizabeth Morrissey and Thomas Matthew McPhatter, a master barber. During the Depression his family lost everything they had in the bank and they struggled for food and clothing. On 19 May 1941 he graduated from high school, registered for the draft, and enrolled at Johnson C. Smith University in Charlotte, North Carolina, intending to study history. His parents could not afford to pay his tuition so he worked summers and during the school year.

When the Japanese bombed Pearl Harbor in 1941 McPhatter did not want to go to war. He was exempted as an only son and had a deferment as a pre-theological student; because he also worked in a shipyard he had a defense deferment as well. As the war continued the classrooms emptied and student unrest was brewing over a lack of student government and no inclusion of students on the discipline committee. In 1942 President Franklin Delano Roosevelt established a presidential directive allowing African Americans to enlist in the U.S. Marine Corps, but they were not permitted to train with their white counterparts; instead, they trained at the all-black Montford Point at Camp Lejeune, North Carolina.

Frustrated and unable to pay his tuition, McPhatter applied to the merchant marine but was rejected because he was a minor. He decided to join the military and chose the Marine Corps. Several of his classmates had joined and he thought it was daring and different. He was reclassified to 1-A and enlisted. Approximately twenty thousand African American marines, including McPhatter, received basic training at Montford Point between 1942 and 1948. After eleven weeks he graduated from boot camp and was set to be assigned to the chapel, but instead asked to join the Eighth Marine Ammunition Company of the Third Marine Division with his buddies. He went to ammunition technician school and became a squad leader before returning to his platoon. He was promoted to the rank of sergeant just before he was deployed to Pearl Harbor.

Black marines of World War II did not have the same designation as their white counterparts; they were designated USMC (SS) Selective Service, which meant they were on trial. The poor treatment and segregation of the black marines disturbed McPhatter. Every black company had a white captain, but they rarely saw them, except during inspections. White noncommissioned officers were granted privileges their black counterparts did not receive. While stationed in Hawaii, McPhatter wrote his mother to ask her to contact the NAACP and tell it of the poor treatment of black marines, but the mail was censored and his commanding officer threatened to charge him with insubordination.

Not long after that there was a mini-riot. Frustrated black marines were firing live ammo and shooting on the concrete floor; they opened up fire hydrants and set fires in the trash, setting off alarms. As a result they were taken out at daybreak and marched and drilled all day. The regiment commander then told them that since they wanted to raise hell he would send them to war. Shortly thereafter, McPhatter's unit was sent to Iwo Jima. He arrived at the island on 7 June 1944, the day after the D-day invasion in France. When his company went in, there were bloated bodies bobbing in the water and on the beach of black volcanic sand. McPhatter's job was to bring the ammunition from ship to shore and get it to the troops that were on the front lines. He fused the rockets, mortars, and all the heavy projectiles and got them to the marines. He was on Iwo Jima for two months. About seventy thousand marines fought and close to seven thousand died. Over seven hundred who served were African Americans, according to the Montford Point Marine Association.

After his service on Iwo Jima, McPhatter was sent back to Hawaii to prepare for the invasion of Japan. His ship was about two days away from Japan when the Japanese surrendered. When he returned to Montford Point after the war he had done enough to be promoted but he did not want to stay in the marines.

On Iwo Jima, while under attack, he made a promise to God that if he lived he would devote his life to him in the service, which he did. He went back to Johnson C. Smith University and graduated in 1948, and in 1951 received an M.A. in Divinity. He married Genevieve Redona Bryant in 1949, and they had six children. They divorced in 1978.

From 1951 until 1959 McPhatter was the pastor of St. Paul Presbyterian Church in Kansas City, Missouri, and was on President Eisenhower's Minority Affairs Advisory committee. He also was moderator of the Presbytery for Greater Kansas City, vice president of the Council of Churches for that region, and active in the civil rights movement where he worked to integrate the public tennis courts and led the march for the integration of a local high school in Kansas City, Missouri. He served as vice president of the Missouri State Conference of the NAACP. As a member of the San Diego Park Board, he fought for parks, pools, and open space for the disenfranchised black communities. He also led many voter registration drives.

McPhatter entered the Naval Reserves as a chaplain in 1953. In 1959 he moved his family to San Diego and went on active duty as a U.S. Navy chaplain. He served at the Great Lakes Naval Training Center in Illinois, in Okinawa and Vietnam, and on bases in California. He went back into the reserves in 1969 because of unsatisfactory fitness reports, but believed he was labeled a troublemaker because he spoke out against racial inequality. While he was on inactive duty from 1969 to 1979 he was temporarily called back to duty several times to help quell race riots and general racial disturbances. He fought to get back on active duty and in 1979 he was called back.

He married Gilda Jean Johnson in 1980; they divorced in 1981. That same year he was promoted to captain and retired from the navy in 1983. He then did volunteer work for the NAACP, preached, and was awarded an honorary doctor of divinity degree

from Interdenominational Theological Center in Atlanta, Georgia. He wrote articles for local and national newspapers, including the *Kansas City Star, Okinawan Morning Star*, and *Charlotte Observer*. In 1993 he wrote and self-published his autobiography, *Caught in the Middle: A Dichotomy of an African American Man*. McPhatter delivered the invocation at the fiftieth anniversary of Iwo Jima in Washington, D.C., and at the VJ Day fiftieth anniversary ceremony at Fort Myer, Virginia. He was also featured at events at the Smithsonian Institution in Washington, D.C., and at the National Constitution Center in Philadelphia. He married Suzanne Louise MacRenato in 2003.

McPhatter died in Chula Vista, California.

FURTHER READING
Latty, Yvonne. *We Were There: Voices of African American Veterans from World War II to the War in Iraq* (2004).

YVONNE LATTY

McPherson, Christopher (1763?–1817), clerk, storekeeper, and millenarian prophet, was born in Louisa County, Virginia, and was the property of David Ross of Richmond until Ross emancipated him in 1792. Much of what is known of McPherson's life is chronicled in the posthumously published *A Short History of the Life of Christopher McPherson, alias Pherson, Son of Christ, King of Kings and Lord of Lords* (1855), written by McPherson around 1811. According to McPherson's account, while a slave of Ross he was given an elementary education and became a capable bookkeeper, gaining skills that he briefly used to clerk for one of the commissary generals in the Continental Army during the siege of Yorktown in 1781. Upon his emancipation, McPherson remained in Ross's employ until 1799, when his conversion to Christianity led him to believe that he was a divinely commissioned millenarian prophet. That transformation precipitated a falling-out with Ross. McPherson married a free black woman, Polly Burgess, in 1800 and then embarked on a doomed career as an entrepreneurial businessman, investing the money he made in spreading his apocalyptic messages. As did other ambitious free blacks in the South, McPherson struggled against the pervasive prejudice that hindered his ability to realize his dreams. That he appeared to be a mentally unbalanced religious fanatic made his later life all the more difficult.

McPherson glosses over the details of his life before his conversion in the *Short History*, except to note his service to the revolutionary cause. He dates his conversion to 15 February 1799, which was accompanied by dreams and visions that convinced him "that these United States were the new Zion," and that his true identity was as Pherson, the Son of Christ, an "appointed messenger to the world" of Christ's imminent return (McPherson, 5). His new-found commission clearly interfered with his work for Ross, who dismissed him, precipitating a law-suit by McPherson against the Ross family. The suit came to nothing, a pattern that would be repeated throughout the rest of his life. Harkening to what he believed to be commands from the Holy Spirit, McPherson "cried aloud through the streets of Richmond, Williamsburg, Norfolk and Portsmouth, of the approach of Christ's Millennium," and wrote letters to Presidents John Adams, Thomas Jefferson, James Madison and to members of Congress "advising of this event" and demanding an audience (McPherson, 5). Such demands were ignored, as was his visit to Philadelphia in order to convey his message in person to the president and the Senate. Undaunted in his divine mission, over the next ten years McPherson continued to draft letters and petitions to federal and state gov-ernment officials, as well as to "the King of Great Britain, Napoleon Bonaparte, the Pope of Rome, and to other potentates, &c.," attempting to con-vince someone of his divinity and the imminence of the Millennium, as well as becoming an advocate for the rights of free blacks in Virginia (McPherson, 8). In the latter capacity he attempted to procure from the legislature a new cemetery for blacks, "as the old one, in every respect, was perfectly unfit for the purpose," and to have a law preventing blacks from hiring carriages rescinded. These and other petitions were likewise ignored. Enraged at these personal slights, McPherson began to seek justice through the newspapers and the courts, for which he and his wife began to suffer many hardships at the hands of local authorities (McPherson, 6).

To finance his religious mission, McPherson worked as a merchant and importer/exporter, though he was apparently not very successful. He applied several times for a loan from the Bank of Virginia, but in spite of claiming "several good endorsers," he was repeatedly denied. In early 1811 he established a night school for free, black men, for which he was hauled into court for being a public nuisance. A postponement of the case gave him time to advertise for the establishment of a "seminary of learning of the arts and sciences, and of the living languages," but this too came to nothing (McPherson, 6). An argument between McPherson and his wife that April brought out a neighbor who called the constabulary. Authorities jailed the McPhersons for disturbing the peace. This and the nuisance case came to trial together in May, and McPherson was acquitted, though not compensated for any damages. While walking through Richmond loudly proclaiming his apoc-alyptic message, he was arrested and sent to the hospital in Williamsburg, where he was treated for mental illness. He was later released upon being found no harm to himself or others, and he went on with his prophetic activities, which included posting broadsides throughout the Richmond area. While staying aboard a packet boat for lack of proper lodging, McPherson claimed to have been physically attacked by one William Parish, whom McPherson attempted to sue for $1,000. This began a round of attempted litigations against real and perceived assailants for enormous sums totaling tens of millions of dollars, none of which the courts would hear. McPherson chalked this up to racism, concluding that "under existing circumstances, in the State of Virginia, a man of colour at present, had but a slender chance of success in going to law with weighty officers of the land" (McPherson, 7). While racism certainly cannot be discounted as a factor in the issue, the frivolous nature of the suits provided ample justification for their rejection.

McPherson spent the remainder of his life ada-mantly convinced of his divinity, proclaiming the coming of Christ's Kingdom. In spite of his hard-ships, he never lost his belief that the "United States of Columbia," was "the new Jerusalem of the Lord God," and that the American people were "the apple of his [God's] eye" (McPherson, 28). However strange his personality and tragic his career, McPherson is representative of the mil-lenarian orientation of American society during the Jeffersonian period that witnessed the Second Great Awakening, as well as of the difficulties rou-tinely experienced by free blacks in the slavehold-ing states who strove to improve their lives and strengthen their communities.

FURTHER READING
McPherson, Christopher. *A Short History of the Life of Christopher McPherson, alias Pherson, Son of Christ, King of Kings and Lord of Lords* (1855).
Berkeley, Edmund, Jr. "Prophet without Honor: Christopher McPherson, Free Person of Color," *Virginia Magazine of History and Biography* 77 (1969).

Sheldon, Marianne Buroff. "Black-White Relations in Richmond, Virginia, 1782–1820," *The Journal of Southern History* 45 (1979).

JOHN HOWARD SMITH

McPherson, James Alan (16 Sept. 1943–), short story writer and essayist, was born in Savannah, Georgia, to James Allen McPherson, a master electrician, and Mable Smalls McPherson, a domestic servant.

McPherson grew up attending segregated public schools and sometimes played hooky from school to read at the "colored" branch of the local Carnegie library. As a teenager, he worked as a dining car waiter on passenger trains—an exclusively African American profession that figures prominently in some of his work. "The well-known short story, 'A Solo Song: For Doc' (from his first collection, 1969's *Hue and Cry*), for example, is a character study of two railroad waiters of different generations. McPherson continued to work on the trains of the Great Northern Railroad while attending Morris Brown College, a private, predominately African American institution in Georgia" (in "James Alan McPherson," *Contemporary Black Biography*, no. 70 [2009].). He was able to attend college because of the National Defense Student Loan Program.

At Morris Brown, McPherson said, he had some great teachers who loved literature and passed that love onto him. He graduated from the school with a bachelor's of art in 1965. While supporting himself and working as a janitor, he earned a law degree at Harvard Law School three years later. In a law school class, he wrote, he became intrigued by the Fourteenth Amendment. After reading a brief of the lawyer-novelist Albion W. Tourgeé in *Plessy v. Ferguson*, McPherson's imagination was taken with his thoughts. "What he (Tourgeé) was proposing in 1896, I think, was that each United States citizen would attempt to approximate the ideals of the nation, be on at least conversant terms with all its diversity, carry the mainstream of the culture inside himself .... As an American, by trying to wear these clothes he would be a synthesis of high and low, black and white, city and country, provincial and universal. If he could live with these contradictions, he would be simply a representative American." (http://www.iowalum.com/pulitzerPrize/mcpherson.html).

McPherson earned his law degree in 1968. That same year, he submitted a short story, "Gold Coast," to the *Atlantic Monthly*, which was based in Cambridge, Massachusetts, home to Harvard and MIT. Ed Weeks, an editor there, published McPherson's first story and was instrumental in the publication of McPherson's first collection of stories. Editors at the magazine have continued to publish his short stories for decades. "I believe that if one can experience diversity, touch a variety of its people, laugh at its craziness, distill wisdom from its tragedies, and attempt to synthesize all this inside oneself without going crazy, one will have earned the right to call oneself 'citizen of the United States,'" (http://www.theatlantic.com/past/docs/unbound/mcpherso/jambio.htm).

He was an instructor at the University of Iowa between 1968 and 1969, and he earned his master's in fine arts there in 1969 from the Writers Workshop. He also attended the Yale University Law School in New Haven, Connecticut. He became a contributing editor at the *Atlantic Monthly* in 1969.

He taught at other schools in the 1970s, and worked as a lecturer at University of California Santa Cruz as an English lecturer between 1969 and 1976. He was married in 1973 and later divorced. McPherson has a daughter, Rachel Alice. He worked as an associate professor at Morgan State University and University of Virginia.

His work includes the short story collections *Hue and Cry* (1969), *Elbow Room* (1977)—both of which explore the ironies McPherson felt Tourgee wrote about—and the essay collections *Crabcakes* (1998) and *A Region Not Home: Reflections from Exile* (1999). He offered an uncommon perspective with his stories: "McPherson's stories actually tend to reflect the dilemma confronting the black intellectual in America: on the one hand attracted by much that the white society has to offer, such as quality education, on the other hand embittered by that same society's racist record.... His approach avoids the fiery bitterness of Eldridge Cleaver or James Baldwin, but McPherson is sensitive to the bigotry and injustice which permeate American life" (Blicksilver, Edith. "The Image of Women in Selected Short Stories." *CLA Journal* 22, no. 4 [June 1979], pp. 390–401.). There was a long pause between books, because of his divorce and depression.

Ralph Ellison provided a blurb for *Hue and Cry* and called McPherson "a writer of insight, sympathy and humor and one of the most gifted young Americans I've had the privilege to read" (in "James Alan McPherson," *Contemporary Black Biography*, no. 70 [2009].). The book led to the first of McPherson's many literature awards, a 1970 Academy Award for Literature from the National

Institute of Arts and Letters (which is now called the American Academy of Arts and Letters.) It was not, however, without its detractors. One reviewer wrote that McPherson's work lacked characterization. "In fiction, good characterization is a necessity and McPherson's people are like figures snatched from some dour and lascivious comic strip" (Sullivan, Walter. "Review: 'Where Have All the Flowers Gone?' The Short Story in Search of Itself." *Sewanee Review* 78, no. 3 [Summer, 1970]: 531–542).

McPherson earned a fellowship from the Guggenheim Foundation in 1972. He was awarded the Pulitzer Prize for fiction in 1978 for *Elbow Room*. One reviewer described the work: "A fine control of language and story, a depth in his characters, humane values, these are a few of the virtues James Alan McPherson displays in this fine collection of stories." (Macauley, Robie, "White and Black and Everything Else." *New York Times Book Review*, 25 Sept. 1977, p. 31). He earned a MacArthur "genius grant" in 1981 and was inducted into the American Academy of Arts and Sciences in 1995. He served as guest editor for the literary journal *Ploughshares* in 1985 and 1990.

McPherson has been a full professor of English at the University of Iowa since 1981. He coedited *Fathering Daughters: Reflections by Men* (1998) with DeWitt Henry.

FURTHER READING
Beavers, Herman. *Wrestling Angels into Song: The Fictions of Ernest J. Gaines and James Alan McPherson* (1995).
Schafer, William J. "James A. McPherson: Overview." *Contemporary Novelists.* Edited by Susan Windisch Brown. 6th ed. (1996).
Wooton, Carol. "Wrestling Angels into Song: The Fictions of Ernest J. Gaines and James Alan McPherson." *CRITIQUE: Studies in Contemporary Fiction* 37, no. 4 (1996): 314ff.

JOSHUNDA SANDERS

McQueen, Butterfly (8 Jan. 1911–22 Dec. 1995), stage and screen actor, was born Thelma McQueen in Tampa, Florida, the only child of a stevedore and a domestic worker. McQueen moved to Augusta, Georgia, at the age of five after her parents separated, and in her early teens joined her mother in New York. After graduating high school McQueen enrolled in nursing school but soon abandoned her plans after a teacher suggested she pursue an acting career. While studying dance and auditioning for roles, she joined Venezuela Jones's Harlem-based Youth Theatre Group. It was while appearing in the "Butterfly Ballet" in the Group's 1935 production of *A Midsummer Night's Dream* that she earned the nickname "Butterfly."

In 1937 the director George Abbot cast her in the Broadway production *Brown Sugar*, which garnered her positive reviews during its brief run. She continued to work with Abbot and appeared in subsequent productions, including *Brother Rat* and the long-running comedy *What a Life!*, where she came to the attention of the film producer David O. Selznick, who later asked McQueen to audition for the role of Prissy in the film *Gone with the Wind*. McQueen, who was initially excited that she had won the part, came to dislike her character and frequently objected to demeaning treatment on- and off-screen. She refused to do a scene in which she was to appear in a stereotypical pose of eating watermelon and spitting out seeds, and told producers that Rhett Butler's description of Prissy as a "simple-minded darkie" in another scene was unnecessary. In an early take of the infamous birthing scene, where Scarlett actually finds out Prissy does not know a thing about birthing babies, McQueen objected to the intensity of Vivien Leigh's slap and refused to resume shooting until Leigh formally apologized. She also joined her black cast-mates in voicing objections to other indignities on the production, including segregated restrooms and transportation arrangements.

McQueen's performance in *Gone with the Wind* brought her fame and positive reviews, but it was also the source of criticism from those who found her hysterical antics and childlike persona demeaning. Prissy, as originally written, represented a stereotypical characterization of African Americans as foolish and slow-witted; however, McQueen's performance in the role accomplished something more than mere comic relief. Her screen persona— a high-pitched quavering voice and a dazed and confused stare were her artistic tools—gave the appearance that she was in a world of her own making. She could be incoherent, and somewhat mysterious, projecting a fragility that spoke of something deeper within. The film historian Donald Bogle described her performance as a form of artistic mayhem that blended a unique combination of the comic and the pathetic and flowed naturally with the rest of the film (90).

Gone with the Wind was a Hollywood success that brought fame and recognition to its leading and supporting players. McQueen, like her other

African American co-stars, HATTIE MCDANIEL and Oscar Polk, hoped to capitalize on this success but met only with frustration and disappointment. The roles Hollywood offered black performers continued to be domestic servants or helpmates whose sole purpose was to provide a comic or musical interlude or serve the plot's white characters. McQueen did appear in a select number of films including *The Women* (1939), *Affectionately Yours* (1941), the all-black musical *Cabin in the Sky* (1943), *I Dood It!* (1943), *Flame of the Barbary Coast* (1945), *Mildred Pierce* (1945), *Duel in the Sun* (1946), and the all-black independent slapstick comedy *Killer Diller* (1948). However by the late 1940s, she had grown tired of playing racial stereotypes, explaining, "I didn't mind playing a maid the first time, because I thought that was how you got into the business. But after I did the same thing over and over, I resented it. I didn't mind being funny, but I didn't like being stupid." McQueen was vocal about her resentment over the roles that were offered, and essentially gave up on a Hollywood film career. She continued to stay in the public eye for a time

and appeared as Mary Livingstone's maid on the Jack Benny radio show, and as a regular on the radio program, *Beulah*. In 1950 she signed on to do the television version of *Beulah*, the first television show to feature an African American actress. McQueen brought her unique, comic sensibilities to the role of Oriole, the best friend of the title character, working alongside the legendary ETHEL WATERS, and later her *Gone with the Wind* co-star Hattie McDaniel.

In 1951 McQueen returned to New York to produce her own one-woman show at Carnegie Hall. Having spent most of her money in that production she eventually took on a variety of clerical, sales, and domestic jobs to support herself. She managed to continue acting in the 1950s and 1960s in the occasional stage and television production. Her appearances included *The World's My Oyster* (1956); a televised version of *The Green Pastures* (1957); *School for Wives* (1960), and *The Athenian Touch* (1964). Nevertheless, finding consistent work remained a struggle and she decided to move back to her hometown of Augusta, Georgia, to see if she

Butterfly McQueen, in a scene from the re-release of the 1939 classic *Gone With the Wind*, with Vivien Leigh (left). (AP Images.)

could find more opportunities. While in Georgia, McQueen gave music lessons, opened a restaurant, and hosted her own radio show. Still, those ventures did not generate enough income and she returned to Harlem a year later. It was at this time that McQueen dedicated herself to service in the black community. During the late 1960s and 1970s she became a familiar face at the Mount Morris Park Recreation Center where she worked as a receptionist and taught children tap dancing and ballet. She continued to act sporadically, appearing in *Curley McDimple* in 1968 and hosting her own musical revue, *Butterfly McQueen and Friends* in 1969. Later that same year she reunited with the director George Abbot and gave a powerful performance in *Three Men on a Horse*.

McQueen resumed film work in 1974 in *Amazing Grace*. During this time she also earned a bachelor's degree in political science from City College in New York City. A number of television projects came her way in the late 1970s: *The Seven Wishes of Joanna Peabody* (1978) for which she won a Golden Globe and Emmy award; *Seven Wishes of a Rich Kid* (1979); *The Adventures of Huckleberry Finn* (1986); and *Polly* (1989). Her last film role was as Ma Kennywick in *The Mosquito Coast* in 1986, and her last television appearance was in 1989 in the television movie, *Polly*.

In 1989 McQueen was the guest of honor at the 50th Anniversary celebration of *Gone with the Wind*. Given the fact that, fifty years earlier, she and her other African American co-stars were not permitted to attend the film's premiere because it was held in a whites-only theater, her career had indeed come full circle.

Butterfly McQueen died at the age of eighty-four, after suffering critical burns in a fire that destroyed her home near Augusta, Georgia. Her screen immortality may reside with *Gone with the Wind* but it is in her perseverance and her ability to imaginatively change any role she was given to create a character which was uniquely her own that her true legacy lies.

FURTHER READING

Bogle, Donald. *Toms, Coons, Mammies & Bucks: An Interpretive History of Blacks in American Film* (2003).

Cripps, Thomas. *Slow Fade to Black: The Negro in American Film, 1900–1942* (1997).

Harris, Art. "The Reluctant Butterfly. McQueen Recalling Her Pioneering Role in GWTW," *New York Times*, 13 Mar. 1989.

Watkins, Mel. *On the Real Side: A History of African American Comedy* (1994).

Obituary: *New York Times*, 23 Dec. 1995.

DWANDALYN R. REECE

McRae, Carmen (8 Apr. 1920–10 Nov. 1994), jazz and popular singer, was born in New York City, the daughter of Osmond (or Oscar) McRae, the manager of a health club, and Evadne (maiden name unknown), both immigrants from the West Indies. During her lifetime McRae's birth year was widely reported to be 1922, but according to obituaries she was actually born in 1920.

McRae took classical piano lessons for five years but practiced pop tunes whenever her parents were out of earshot. She attended Julia Richman High School in Manhattan. At age seventeen she won an amateur contest as a singer at the Apollo Theater in Harlem. The pianist and songwriter Irene Kitchings, then the wife of the jazz pianist TEDDY WILSON, helped McRae begin her career. McRae idolized BILLIE HOLIDAY, who in 1939 recorded McRae's song "Dream of Life." McRae in turn imitated Holiday closely in performances at the start of her career, during which time, at her parents' insistence, she also took secretarial courses and did clerical work.

After spending two years as a government employee in Washington, D.C., McRae returned to New York City in 1943. She resumed singing at night while continuing her clerical work. In 1944 she married the jazz drummer KENNY CLARKE; they had no children. During that year she sang briefly as a substitute in the big bands of Benny Carter, EARL HINES, and COUNT BASIE. As Carmen Clarke, she joined Mercer Ellington's big band in 1946 and in that same year completed her first recording. Ellington's group disbanded after an engagement in Chicago in 1948. McRae separated from Clarke and took a seventeen-week job as a self-accompanied singer and pianist in a Chicago club. She performed in Chicago for three and a half years, during which time the influence of Holiday gave way to that of SARAH VAUGHAN, and McRae's own style began to emerge.

McRae returned to New York to record with the jazz accordionist Mat Mathews and then took a job at Minton's Playhouse in Harlem, initially as the intermission pianist and then as a member of the clarinetist Tony Scott's group. By 1953 she was working as a singer and only occasionally playing piano. She recorded her first album in 1954 and the following year finally gained widespread recognition for her album *By Special Request*, which included versions of "Suppertime," "Yardbird Suite," and "You Took Advantage of Me." A career of extensive touring began with stands at the Black Hawk in Los Angeles, the Rainbow Grill in New York, and the Colonial in Toronto. In 1956 she divorced Clarke and married the bassist Ike Isaacs; they had no children. For two years he led her accompanying trio. The couple separated in 1958 and later divorced.

Among McRae's albums were *After Glow* (1957), *Something to Swing About* (1959), and *Lover Man* (1961), the last a collection of tunes associated with Holiday but executed in McRae's own style and with the accompaniment of the forcefully energetic tenor saxophonist EDDIE "LOCKJAW" DAVIS, in contrast to Holiday's association with LESTER YOUNG's understated tenor sax. In 1962 she recorded a version of the pianist Dave Brubeck's instrumental hit "Take Five," with lyrics added by Brubeck's wife, Iola, and that June she performed with Brubeck at a New York Daily News Jazz Concert in Madison Square Garden.

McRae traveled internationally over the next two decades and continued to make fine albums, including *The Great American Songbook* (1971), *Live at Bubba's* (1981), and most notably, *Carmen Sings Monk* (1988). This last collection grew out of concerts at the Great American Music Hall in San Francisco, where she performed a number of the pianist THELONIOUS MONK's instrumental compositions set to lyrics (and retitled for reasons of copyright).

McRae suffered from asthma, which led to respiratory failure after a show at the Blue Note nightclub in New York in May 1991; she was bedridden thereafter. She suffered a stroke in October 1994 and died the following month at her home in Beverly Hills, California.

McRae was a strong, forthrightly honest, and sometimes intimidating woman whose outlook was encapsulated by the subtitle of the writer James T. Jones's article: "Cut the Crap." She had an actress's commanding stage presence and sensitivity to the enunciation and meaning of lyrics and a jazz instrumentalist's talent for phrasing. Her cutting, mocking vocal timbre was inimitable, conveying a sound that was, as the writer Jack Batten described it, "lazy, sexy, kind of autumnal and a little bittersweet." Perhaps owing to these qualities and a corresponding absence of sentimentality, McRae never achieved the same kind of widespread fame as Sarah Vaughan or ELLA FITZGERALD. Her voice simply was not suited to sweet ballads, and indeed it was near the end of her career when she discovered that Monk's angular melodies were the perfect musical match for her singing. These performances are arguably her finest work.

FURTHER READING

Giddins, Gary. *Rhythm-a-ning: Jazz Tradition and Innovation in the '80s* (1985).

Gleason, Ralph J. *Celebrating the Duke, and Louis, Bessie, Billie, Bird, Carmen, Miles, Dizzy, and Other Heroes* (1975).

Gourse, Leslie. *Carmen McRae: Miss Jazz* (2001).

Gourse, Leslie. *Louis' Children: American Jazz Singers* (1984).

Obituaries: *New York Times* and *Pittsburgh Post-Gazette*, 12 Nov. 1994.

This entry is taken from the *American National Biography* and is published here with the permission of the American Council of Learned Societies.

BARRY KERNFELD

McShann, Jay (12 Jan. 1916–7 Dec. 2006), pianist and bandleader, was born James Columbus McShann in Muskogee, Oklahoma. McShann grew up in a religious family. His father worked as a deliveryman for a furniture store and his mother was a homemaker. As a child McShann taught himself the rudiments of music on the family piano. He began his professional career during the early 1930s with Al Denny's big band in Tulsa, Oklahoma, and Eddie Hill and His Bostonians, a leading "territorial" band. The bands that barnstormed across the Southwest were known as territorial bands, after the vast territories they toured in the western United States. After the Bostonians disbanded in fall 1936 he was traveling through Kansas City, Missouri, and a friend invited him to stay. A wide-open town known as the "Paris of the Plains," Kansas City sported hundreds of clubs.

McShann found steady work with the drummer Elmer Hopkins at the Monroe Inn, located in the northeast section of town. After hours, McShann explored the nightlife on Twelfth Street, a bustling strip of saloons and gambling houses stretching a mile east of downtown. While strolling down Twelfth Street one night, McShann heard music coming from inside a club and the player turned out to be the young alto saxophonist CHARLIE PARKER. McShann and Parker met and agreed to get together in the future, setting the stage for their later association.

Following a summer engagement in 1937 with the trumpeter Dee Stewart's band, McShann formed a duo and opened at Wolf's Buffet at Eighteenth and Vine, the business and social hub of Kansas City's African American community. In May 1938 McShann formed a small ensemble and launched a long-term engagement at Martin's on the Plaza, located in the upscale Country Club Plaza shopping district. In January 1940 the McShann band opened at the Century Room, a medium-size ballroom in midtown. Charlie Parker joined the band in March, when McShann expanded the band to full size. Already a masterful soloist, Parker led the reed section. After an engagement at the Pla-Mor, an entertainment complex in midtown, the band toured the Midwest, playing one-night stands, but stopping long enough in November 1940 for McShann to marry Isabelle Williams.

The McShann band recorded for the Decca label in Dallas on 30 April 1941 and featured a modern hard-swinging style, but the producer of the session, Dave Kapp, wanted to record blues and boogie-woogie. Kapp kept requesting blues and boogie tunes while recording the band without their knowledge. "Confessin' the Blues," featuring the vocalist Walter Brown, became an overnight sensation, establishing the band nationally. Brown's lazy vocal style and McShann's understated blues piano created a nationwide demand for McShann's band and inspired a number of small ensembles, leading to the development of rhythm and blues. The flip side, "Hootie Blues," featured a twelve-bar solo by Charlie Parker that first introduced his genius to a national audience. After wrapping up the recording session the band returned to Kansas City for a summer engagement at Fairyland Park, a popular amusement park on the southeastern edge of the city. In late September 1941 the McShann band embarked on a tour of one-night stands leading to New York.

During the band's trip east the Japanese bombed Pearl Harbor, bringing the United States into World War II. McShann managed to get to New York ahead of the shockwaves of war by signing with the Moe Gale Agency, a booking firm that operated the Savoy Ballroom in Harlem. The band made its debut at the Savoy 13 February 1942 in a musical battle against the wildly popular LUCKY MILLINDER band. A little intimidated by the Millinder band, McShann held his players back until the final set. At midnight McShann unleashed his band. Thereafter, McShann frequently played the Savoy between tours of the South. In December 1942 Parker left the band for the EARL FATHA HINES band.

The war took its toll on McShann's group and on the entertainment industry in general. Ballrooms and theaters across the country closed. The government rationed rubber and gasoline, making touring difficult, particularly for African American bands that traveled great distances between one-night stands. The draft decimated the ranks of the big bands. On 21 May 1944, while McShann was in Kansas City for an engagement at the Municipal Auditorium, he was inducted into the armed forces, bringing his band to an end.

After his discharge from service in October 1944, McShann returned to Kansas City and recorded with a group that featured WALTER PAGE on bass and JULIA LEE on vocals for the Capitol label. He then headed back to New York and formed a new big band. After a brief stint at the Downbeat Club on Fifty-second Street, McShann led his big band to the West Coast. Unable to sustain this large group, McShann disbanded and formed a small ensemble. He moved easily into the thriving West Coast rhythm and blues circuit, recording for a number of small labels. Jimmy Witherspoon, a husky vocalist, joined the band in Vallejo, California. During the next few years the two recorded a number of hit records, including "Ain't Nobody's Business."

In 1951 McShann settled down in Kansas City to raise his family. Working out of the musical mainstream, McShann recorded sporadically and worked mostly in the Midwest through the 1950s and 1960s. Beginning in the late 1960s he toured Europe extensively. He resumed recording in the mid-1970s, producing a string of critically acclaimed records. In 1979 McShann was featured prominently in the documentary *The Last of the Blue Devils*. Clint Eastwood featured McShann in his 2003 documentary *Piano Blues*.

As a bandleader McShann influenced the course of American music. A liberal leader, McShann gave Charlie Parker the support and musical latitude that led to the development of bebop. "Confessin' the Blues" and his other small group recordings for Decca sparked the development of rhythm and blues in the post–World War II period. Refusing to rest on his laurels, McShann remained active for the rest of his career, touring the world from his base in Kansas City, where his career had started and where he died.

FURTHER READING

The Kenneth J. LaBudde Department of Special Collections and the Marr Sound Archives in the Miller Nichols Library at the University of

Missouri–Kansas City hold interviews, recordings, contracts, photos and other material chronicling McShann's career.

Driggs, Frank, and Chuck Haddix. *Kansas City Jazz: From Ragtime to Bebop—a History* (2005).

Haddix, Chuck. "Still Confessin' the Blues," *Down Beat* (May 2001).

DISCOGRAPHY

Blues from Kansas City (GRP 614).

Goin' to Kansas City (Stony Plain Records 1286).

Man from Muskogee (Sackville 3005).

Paris Blues (Music Masters 5052).

CHUCK HADDIX

McTell, Blind Willie (5 May 1898?–19 Aug. 1959), blues artist, was born Willie Samuel McTell near Thomson, Georgia, the son of Minnie Watkins and Eddie McTell. Probably blind from birth, he was one of two children. His birth date remains obscure; some sources report 5 May 1901, but in a 1940 recorded interview the folklorist John Lomax announced him to be forty-two years old. Both of his parents played guitar, as did an uncle. McTell told Lomax that he took up music when he was "quite a child," learning mainly from his mother after the family had moved to Statesboro, Georgia, the place he later referred to as his real home. Allegedly he ran away from home as a teenager to work in various traveling shows, although what he

Blind Willie McTell, with his 12-string guitar in Atlanta, Georgia, November 1940. (Library of Congress.)

did in the shows remains unclear (he told Lomax he quit the guitar for eight years, then returned to playing). According to McTell, he attended several schools for the blind: the state school in Macon from 1922 to 1925, then a school in New York City, and finally a school in Michigan, where he learned to read Braille. He then returned to Georgia and resumed the life of an itinerant musician. Ranging as far afield as Miami and Nashville, he often teamed up with other street musicians, chief among them the legendary BLIND WILLIE JOHNSON, a religious singer and bottleneck slide guitar virtuoso from Texas. According to McTell, he and Johnson were great pals, traveling together "from Maine to the Mobile Bay." Johnson's music clearly influenced McTell's style and repertoire.

On 18 October 1927 McTell began a productive recording career. His initial session for RCA Victor in Atlanta resulted in four sides. They were artistic successes and did well enough commercially to earn McTell a return session a year later, at which he recorded his best-known composition, "Statesboro Blues." On all the Victor sides he was identified as Blind Willie McTell. Over the next five years he recorded for Columbia as "Blind Sammie," for Okeh as "Georgia Bill," and for Victor again as "Hot Shot Willie." In 1933 he did four Vocalion sessions with fellow Atlanta street musicians Buddy Moss and Curley Weaver.

Throughout his recording career, McTell continued to ply his trade on the streets of Atlanta, playing house parties or other informal street corner venues. As the pianist Piano Red recalled, McTell, Moss, and Weaver "walked the streets with their guitars on their backs. And during the day they would have them daytime parties, house to house, where they had that white lightning ... and they made a little money doing that. They'd try this side of town this morning, the other side the next morning. They go in a different territory every day. Just start walking. People call them with their guitars, say, 'How about playing us a number?' About twenty or thirty minutes, they'd have a house full or a porch full."

In 1934 McTell married Ruthy Kate Williams. The following year the couple recorded blues and religious pieces for Decca, accompanied by Curley Weaver. Continuing as a street singer, McTell ranged as far as Tennessee, Alabama, and North Carolina; he toured Georgia and Kentucky with a medicine show and was involved in one unproductive Vocalion session. In October 1940 McTell had a chance encounter in Atlanta with Lomax, who arranged a documentary recording session for the Library of Congress. The session, conducted on 5 November 1940 in Lomax's hotel room, showed the breadth of McTell's repertoire and included spoken interview material. Lomax, who paid McTell a dollar and cab fare for the session, wrote in his field notes how easily McTell got around the city, finding his way by memory. He also reported that McTell followed tourists to resorts in Florida and the Georgia Sea Islands, going wherever the money went.

Traveling as far as New York City, McTell continued as a street performer, gradually leaning further and further toward religious music. After a nine-year break in recording—indicative of the public's loss of appetite for old-style music—McTell returned to the studio in 1949 and 1950 to record blues and religious songs for two labels, Atlantic and Regal. In both cases, the recordings had more documentary value than popular appeal.

By this time McTell had curtailed his traveling, staying closer to home in Atlanta or Macon. He played religious music with a second guitarist, Little Willie, and played on several religious radio programs. His final 1956 recording session, an informal affair in the back of an Atlanta record store run by Ed Rhodes, was captured on tape and stored away.

While McTell left an extensive recorded legacy spanning some four decades, he was never a best-selling blues artist. He spent most of his life traveling the country, playing to diverse audiences, surviving on tips and handouts. He was, however, a fine musician with a remarkably extensive and eclectic repertoire that included ballads, ragtime, pop, novelty tunes, and even pseudo-country tunes as well as some of the finest religious music ever recorded.

According to his wife, McTell devoted himself exclusively to religious songs soon after the 1956 session and became active as a preacher. At this time his health was declining, and he suffered several strokes. In 1959 he entered Milledgeville State Hospital, where he died of a cerebral hemorrhage. He was buried near Jones Grove Church in Thomson.

A master of the twelve-string guitar and the major exemplar of the East Coast/Atlanta sound, McTell was perhaps more appreciated after his death. His "Statesboro Blues" became a blues revival standard after its rerelease in 1959 and went on to become a rock classic in the repertoires of artists ranging from TAJ MAHAL to the Allman Brothers. The tape of his 1956 session in Rhodes's record store was retrieved from storage and issued as part of the Prestige Bluesville series in 1961. McTell was elected to the Blues Foundation Hall of Fame in 1981.

FURTHER READING

Bastin, Bruce. *Red River Blues: The Blues Tradition in the Southeast* (1986).

Charters, Samuel. *The Blues Makers* (1991).

Harris, Sheldon. *Blues Who's Who: A Biographical Dictionary of Blues Singers* (1979; repr. 1981).

This entry is taken from the *American National Biography* and is published here with the permission of the American Council of Learned Societies.

BARRY PEARSON AND
BILL MCCULLOCH

McWhorter, John (1965–), linguist and scholar, was born John Hamilton McWhorter V in Philadelphia, Pennsylvania. His father was John McWhorter IV, a university administrator. His mother was a college professor, and so McWhorter's world was one of learning and educational attainment. He attended Friends Select School, a small Quaker K-12 school in Philadelphia, and was a precocious student who often felt himself more intelligent than his teachers and who reportedly began teaching himself Hebrew when he was still just a young child.

McWhorter's academic skill led him to be invited to attend the Bard College at Simon's Rock, a preparatory college for especially gifted young people in Great Barrington, Massachusetts. He was

John McWhorter, cultural commentator and academic. (Courtesy of the Manhattan Institute for Policy Research.)

in the tenth grade when he enrolled, and he graduated with honors and an associate's degree. He then matriculated at Rutgers, from which he graduated in 1985 with a B.A. in French and Romance Languages. He removed to New York University in New York and took a master's degree in American Studies, with a special interest not only in language but also in culture and music. His thesis was "Scott Joplin and the Operatic Form in Pre–World War I America." In 1993 he earned a Ph.D. in linguistics from Stanford University.

The following years saw a rapid flowering of McWhorter's early promise. In 1993 he found a home at Berkeley as a postdoc but remained only until 1994, when he relocated to Cornell University in Ithaca, New York. Unhappy there, he returned to Berkeley a year later. There he undertook the intense focus on creole and pidgin—specifically, their origins and early formative periods—that would inform much of his important early work. In 1999 Berkeley awarded him tenure.

Throughout his career, McWhorter sought to balance what he saw as the necessity of academic rigor with the need for accessibility to his work by a broader, nonspecialized public. As such, he appeared not only at academic conferences and published in academic journals but he took part also in more popular forums, like National Public Radio's (NPR) *Fresh Air* program as well as Fox News Network's *The O'Reilly Factor*, and the *Today Show*, among too many others to name. A self-described centrist, many of whose opinions lean toward the politically conservative, McWhorter courted controversy with views that often seemed to blame African Americans for their relatively poor showing in academics. His 2000 *Losing the Race: Self-Sabotage in Black America* argued that certain aspects of African American culture led young blacks to devalue the importance of intellectual and scholarly achievement. Much of his work focused on African Americans and their use of language, both in the popular and public sense, as a means of building and perpetuating a black identity.

In 2003 McWhorter left Berkeley to take a spot at the conservative Manhattan Institute, a New York–based think tank and public policy workshop. In 2008 he signed on as a lecturer in the Slavic Languages Department at New York's Columbia University. McWhorter's publications are too numerous to do justice to in this space. Among them are *Towards a Model of New Creole Genesis* (1997), *The Missing Spanish Creoles: Recovering the Birth of Plantation Creole Languages* (2000), *Spreading the Word: Languages and Dialects in America* (2000),

The Power of Babel: A Natural History of Language (2002), *Language Interrupted: Signs of Non-Native Acquisition in Standard Language Grammars* (2007), and *Our Magnificent Bastard Tongue: The Untold Story of English* (2008). Since 2001 he has published articles in the *City Journal*—on topics as diverse as the legacy of SAMMY DAVIS JR. to what he called "the reparations racket"—and was a columnist for the *New York Sun*. His work has also appeared in the *Washington Post*, the *Wall Street Journal*, the *New York Times*, and the *Los Angeles Times*. Among his various awards and accolades, he was awarded the Presidential Fellowship by the University of California, Berkeley, in 1998 and the Patricia Roberts Harris Fellowship by Stanford from 1988 to 1992.

FURTHER READING

Lanehart, Sonja, ed. *Sociocultural and Historical Contexts of African American English* (2001).

Wolfram, Walt, and Erik R. Thomas. *The Development of African American English* (2002).

JASON PHILIP MILLER

McWorter, Frank. *See* Free Frank (Frank McWorter).

Meachum, John Berry (1790?–1854), craftsman, minister, and businessman, was born a slave in Virginia. The names of his father, a Baptist preacher, and his mother are unknown. A skilled carpenter and cooper, Meachum was allowed to save some of his earnings, and eventually he bought his freedom. Moving to Louisville, Kentucky, he married a slave, Mary, and then purchased her out of bondage; they had an unknown number of children. About 1815 he moved with his wife to St. Louis, reportedly with only three dollars in his pocket. There Meachum used his carpentry skills to find a job as a cooper. He established his own cooper's shop a few years later and began buying St. Louis real estate.

During the 1830s, in order to help fellow African Americans become free, Meachum started buying slaves, training them in barrel making and letting them earn money to pay him back for their liberty. By 1846 he had emancipated "twenty colored friends that I bought." Except for one, who was an alcoholic, they were all successful, as Meachum boasts in *An Address to All the Colored Citizens of the United States* (1846). In fact, one former slave not only acquired his own freedom, but purchased his wife, built a home for his family, and became a highly proficient blacksmith.

Meachum's *Address* does not include all the facts, however. In 1834 Julia Logan petitioned the Circuit Court of St. Louis, claiming that she was entitled to her freedom but that she was being "held as a Slave by Berry Meachum a man of color in Saint Louis and [was] bound and imprisoned in his house." Logan feared that she would soon be sold "to some distant place." In 1836 the case went to the Missouri Supreme Court, which ruled against Meachum.

By 1850 Meachum owned two brick homes in St. Louis and an Illinois farm. According to the census that year, his eight thousand dollars in real estate holdings made him the third-richest free African American in Missouri. Yet Meachum conducted himself modestly, even with this sizable wealth. An 1854 inventory of Meachum's estate listed a few basic chairs, a carpet worth seven dollars, and about forty books, valued at eight dollars. The 1850 census showed twelve people living at his home, including his wife, their two grandchildren, various other adults and children, and two African American coopers who appeared to be working to reimburse Meachum for buying their liberty.

Meachum also organized and maintained two schools for African American youth, one even after a state law had been passed that prohibited the teaching of black children. When the Englishman whom he hired to teach at the school was arrested, Meachum got him out of jail and later reopened the school secretly on one of the steamboats that he built and owned.

As the son of a Baptist preacher, Meachum followed his father's lead. He joined the St. Louis Mission Church about 1816 and became its pastor about 1828, when it became an independent black church, called the First African Baptist Church. By the late 1830s his congregation included two hundred slaves and twenty free blacks. Meachum's style as a preacher was so energetic and enthusiastic that in 1846 a small group led by John R. Anderson, a former slave described as "quiet" with "reserved power," left the church. Even the name of Meachum's steamboat—*Temperance*—reflected his concerns as a minister and as a leader in his community. Meachum died in St. Louis.

FURTHER READING

Bellamy, Donnie. "Free Blacks in Antebellum Missouri, 1820–1860," *Missouri Historical Review* 67 (Jan. 1973).

Sobel, Mechal. *Trabelin' On: The Slave Journey to an Afro-Baptist Faith* (1979; repr. 1988).

This entry is taken from the *American National Biography* and is published here with the permission of the American Council of Learned Societies.

LOREN SCHWENINGER

Meadows, Lucile Smallwood (23 May 1918–17 Apr. 1997), educator and state legislator, was born in Glen Ferris, West Virginia, the only child of Solomon and Luvenia Galloway Smallwood. The Smallwoods had moved from North Carolina during the early 1900s and settled in Fayette County in southeastern West Virginia. They later relocated to Glen Ferris in Raleigh County. Growing up in Glen Ferris during the Jim Crow era, Meadows experienced racial discrimination firsthand. She attended a poorly equipped, two-room elementary school for black children. Although a high school was only two miles from her parents' home, she had to travel twenty-five miles to attend Simmons High School for blacks.

After high school Meadows enrolled in West Virginia State College, where she earned a B.A. in Education in 1939. Her first teaching assignment came in 1941 at Summerlee Elementary School in Fayette County. She recalled that often black schools were one-room structures with no running water and where teachers taught in half-day shifts. Because of insufficient funding from the state, black teachers and parents often raised the money needed to purchase necessary school supplies. In 1944 she married Reginald Clinton Meadows on 12 July 1944 in Richmond, Virginia. He worked in the metallurgical division of the Union Carbide Corporation in Alloy, West Virginia. They had one daughter and made their home in Glen Ferris until 1948, when they moved to the town of Fayetteville. Meadows taught in the Fayette County school system until 1956, when she became principal of Harlem Heights Elementary, where she remained until the school was closed in 1966. The school was closed when authorities deemed its facilities and playground inadequate for use. Harlem Heights was the last African American school in Fayette County to be closed.

Although happy with the 1954 Supreme Court decision in *Brown v. Board of Education*, Meadows maintained that the decision brought with it both gains and losses for blacks. While integration meant better school facilities for blacks, she lamented the decision's unintended consequences: an overemphasis on sports and a de-emphasis on education, as teachers were encouraged not to assign homework on nights with sporting events. African Americans lost the closeness that existed among parents, teachers, and students, and they lost role models and a major institution in the black community when black teachers and principals retired or were not rehired. As happened throughout the South, blacks hoped that desegregation would break down racial barriers, but white school authorities devised their own plans, which included closing black schools. Although Meadows lost her principal's position, she was transferred to Fayetteville Elementary School. Arguing that ignorance was a major obstacle to better race relations and that schools could do much to lessen the problem through classroom teaching, she continued to incorporate African American history in her lessons with the idea of removing misconceptions about blacks.

The West Virginia State Teachers' Association merged with the West Virginia Education Association (WVEA) in 1954, but blacks had no significant roles in the new organization until after the 1960s. With a resolve to champion the rights of African Americans, women, and teachers, Meadows helped to create the WVEA's Human Relations Committee and in 1973 organized the black members into a black caucus for the purpose of pushing for more minority representation on committees, programs, and staff. When the WVEA established a political action committee, Meadows became a charter member. In 1975 she became a member of the National Education Association's (NEA) Congressional Contact Team, a group made up of two educators from every congressional district in the country to serve as contact persons to their national congress members, informing them of important educational issues. She was appointed to the Governor's State Advisory Council on Vocational Education in 1977, and U.S. senator Robert Byrd appointed her to an advisory task force on education in 1982.

As an ardent supporter of MARTIN LUTHER KING JR., Meadows initiated a campaign in her town of Fayetteville to name the street she lived on as King Avenue, and she openly advocated the passage of legislation that would establish 15 January as a state holiday in honor of King. As chairperson of the Fayette County Black Caucus, she wrote letters to members of the state legislature and the U.S. Congress requesting their support for the holiday. When the King bill became law, Meadows also organized annual King luncheons, honoring his memory in Fayetteville.

Meadows's activism led her to contact state and national leaders to express her concerns over education and civil rights issues. She also wrote for local newspapers and helped organize local political functions. Because she had the ability to bring together a large voting bloc, state dignitaries, including Robert Byrd, John D. (Jay) Rockefeller IV, Robert Wise, and Nick Rahall, were usually present at the annual King luncheons. Meadows was a hands-on activist. She was actively involved in the gubernatorial campaigns of Jay Rockefeller during the 1970s and Gaston Caperton during the 1980s. Both men expressed appreciation for her input and advice, and both depended on her for voter turnout during their campaigns. When Rockefeller set his sights on the U.S. Senate in 1984, Meadows again rallied to support him. After winning the governorship in 1988, Caperton appointed her to the King Holiday Commission Board the following year. Meadows also served as secretary of the West Virginia State Democratic Executive Committee, president of the Fayette County Democratic Women's Club, and as state director of the Federation of Democratic Women for District Two.

Her efforts did not go unnoticed. In 1982 she was presented with the WVEA's Mary L. Williams Memorial Award for her contributions in human relations. She received the State Martin Luther King Holiday Commission Living the Dream Award in 1987 for her work in promoting equality between the races. For her efforts in working to bridge the gap between different ethnic groups by pushing to eliminate discrimination, she was presented with the NEA's H. Council Trenholm Award. In 1991 she was named Fayetteville's Distinguished Citizen and presented with the NEA's Mary Hatwood Futrell Award for her leadership in advancing the rights of women.

Even at age seventy-two, Meadows remained committed to public service. When a vacancy occurred in the West Virginia House of Delegates, she was one of the top three candidates recommended to Governor Caperton by the Fayette County Democratic Executive Committee. The governor appointed Meadows to the post, making her the first African American woman from Fayette County to serve in the state legislature. As a freshman delegate Meadows introduced a bill to raise the state's minimum wage, which was passed by the senate and enacted into law after minor changes. Although no longer legal, the state's constitution still contained references to "negro schools" being separated from white public schools. Meadows introduced a bill that resulted in the removal of these obsolete references. Near the end of her term

Meadows won approval of her resolution to rename the Cotton Hill Bridge, which spans the New River near Fayetteville, in honor of Charles C. Rogers, an African American Fayetteville native who had been awarded the Congressional Medal of Honor for bravery during the Vietnam War.

Very little has been written about the role of African American women in West Virginia or Appalachian history. Lucile Meadows saw herself as an agent of change and successfully recruited many in the state, from average citizens to state leaders, to support her causes. Although she had planned to run for election at the end of her appointed term in the House of Delegates, poor health prevented it. She eventually moved to Greensboro, North Carolina, to be with her daughter and her family, where she remained until her death in 1997.

FURTHER READING

Lucile Meadows's papers are the sole possession of her daughter, who resides in Greensboro, North Carolina.

Cecelski, David S. *Along Freedom Road: Hyde County, North Carolina, and the Fate of Black Schools in the South* (1994).

Rice, Otis K., and Stephen W. Brown. *West Virginia: A History* (1993).

Williams, John Alexander. *West Virginia: A History* (2001).

Obituary: *Beckley Register-Herald*, 19 Apr. 1997.

M. LOIS LUCAS

Mease, Quentin Ronald "Quent" (25 Oct. 1908–24 Feb. 2009), community and civil rights activist, was born the youngest of five children of Charles Henry and Cornelia Tate Mease in Buxton, Iowa, a coal-mining town called a "Black Utopia." At different times Charles was a coal miner, union organizer, and justice of the peace. Cornelia was a seamstress and came from a long line of freeborn persons of color.

For the first twelve years of his life, Mease lived in Buxton, where he spent many hours at the YMCA that was the town's center of activity. The Buxton YMCA was established by the Consolidated Coal Company in an attempt to prevent its workers from joining unions. Considered "welfare capitalists," the company executives hoped the Y would improve the lives of its workers and families and thus make unions less attractive.

In 1918 Mease's father died, and his mother moved the family to Des Moines, Iowa. Mease completed his public education at the early age of sixteen because he had been skipped several school grades in both Buxton and Des Moines. After graduating from West High School, he entered Des Moines University, a local Baptist institution. When he was nineteen years old and attending Des Moines University, Mease was asked to serve as temporary executive secretary at the Crocker Street Branch of the YMCA. However, the position lasted twenty-one years, ending in 1942 when Mease was drafted into the military. In the meantime he earned a liberal arts degree from Des Moines University.

Military service for Mease began at Dale Mabry Field, which was located outside Tallahassee, Florida. His train trip to Tallahassee was his first taste of southern-style Jim Crow. In Indiana he had to change from an integrated train car to an all-black one to continue the ride farther south to Florida. During this period in history, all branches of the military were segregated, as was his unit of the U.S. Air Corps (later the Air Force). His prior work with the YMCA, his college degree, and his involvement in many community services made him a good choice for promotion in his unit. Within six months he had been promoted to sergeant major with a tech-sergeant rating. Later Mease enrolled in Officers' Candidate School (OCS) and was commissioned as second lieutenant. He served in the air force Quartermasters Corps and was stationed in the Pacific theater from 1942 until June 1946. He ended his active military career with the rank of captain and his reserve career with the rank of major. Without plans for the future Mease was encouraged by Bob Lindberg, the general secretary of the Des Moines YMCA, to attend George Williams College (later Aurora University) in Chicago. The college was noted for preparing students for careers at YMCAs. While working toward his degree, Mease again became a YMCA employee working at the Wabash Branch as assistant program secretary. His affiliations with Chicago organizations such as the Interracial Commission, the NAACP, the Chamber of Commerce, and the YMCA ignited his interest in challenging racial barriers. In 1948 he received a master's of science degree in group work administration.

Mease accepted a job offer from the YMCA in Houston, Texas, that presented the biggest challenge of his career—to start a building program. When he arrived in Houston in 1948 most of the city's public facilities were legally segregated. The Colored Branch of the YMCA—later renamed the Bagby Street Branch—was in a run-down rented facility. Mease soon discovered that while funds had been raised in 1939 for two YMCAs—one for whites and one for blacks—only the white facility had been built.

In 1950 he married Jewell Chenault, who was from San Antonio, Texas. She worked in a beauty school as an electrologist, a hair removal expert. The beauty school was located in the Pilgrim Building where Mease shared an office with his friend, James "Jim" H. Jemison, who was an influential black businessman in Houston. Jemison had introduced Chenault to Mease.

By 1951 the building program remained stalled. Mease threatened the Metropolitan YMCA Board that he would establish the Bagley Branch as an independent entity if a new building was not constructed. The Metropolitan Board reluctantly agreed to appoint a steering committee to investigate the matter, and eventually a Capital Fund Campaign was launched. By 1955 the newly named South Central YMCA had been built.

Under Mease's leadership the South Central YMCA became a major gathering place for the black community. Because of his ability to foster collaborations, many community and civic organizations were established at the South Central YMCA. The connections and communication networks he established would become essential in nurturing community activism in Houston in the 1960s and 1970s.

During the late 1950s Houston officials became interested in attracting a major league sport team, but the city's hot, sultry weather made the plan seem fruitless. However, Judge Roy Hofheinz conceived an idea to build a state-of-the art, dome-shaped building that would protect fans and players from the extreme weather. Since public funds would be required for such an undertaking Mease saw an opportunity to negotiate for an integrated facility. He indicated to Hofheinz and his business partner, R. E. "Bob" Smith, that the black community would support public funding for the stadium only if it were racially integrated. Promising the support of the Houston Business and Professional Men's Club—a kind of Black Chamber of Commerce, which he had previously organized—Mease persuaded the National League of Major League Baseball and club owners to integrate the stadium in return for the African American community's endorsement of the bond referendum needed to finance the proposed stadium. These stipulations having been agreed to, the bond referendum for the Astrodome passed.

While student sits-ins were taking place in other cities during the 1960s Mease challenged

Eldrewey Stearns, a Texas Southern law student and part-time YMCA worker, to desegregate public facilities in Houston using sit-ins and other public demonstration tactics that were being used elsewhere. Sterns accepted the challenge and started the Progressive Youth Association (PYA), a sit-in movement. Unbeknownst to the students and the general public, Mease and others were involved in behind-the-scenes conferences. Mease's plan was to get the message to the city's white business owners that Houston could avoid civil disturbances such as those that had occurred in Watts, Chicago, Detroit, and Washington, D.C., if they would voluntarily open their facilities to blacks. The message was carried to business owners by Jesse Jones, the largest property owner in Houston and later his nephew, John T. Jones Jr. In 1962 John Jones desegregated Houston's downtown convention hotels. Several more behind-the-scenes conferences were held, and afterward restaurants began serving blacks. Theaters followed, and department stores began hiring blacks. After each public facility declared its intention to integrate, testers were sent to see if blacks would be refused service. There were no incidents of denials, and facilities in Houston quietly integrated without newspaper involvement, fanfare, riots, and demonstrations.

By 1967 many urban areas were experiencing civil unrest. Though federal legislation to end segregation had passed, in many cities de facto segregation was alive and well. To head off such problems in Houston, Mease advised that not only the social conditions but also the economic conditions of blacks should be addressed. Although theaters, hotels, and other public facilities had been desegregated, most Houston blacks lacked the financial means to frequent these establishments or to improve their housing conditions. Mease stressed that Houston was the only large city that did not have a National Urban League to address the economic needs of its black community, since city leaders had opposed its establishment. In July 1968, however, the Houston Urban League was chartered, due largely to the efforts of Quentin Mease, who became its first board president.

For twenty-five years Mease served as executive secretary of the Houston YMCA. In 1967 he created the Black Achievers Program to provide role models for youth, a program that later became a nationwide YMCA program.

Mease's wife, Jewell, died in 1978 while visiting Barbara, their daughter, in Oakland, California.

Mease served on many boards, including those of the Baylor College of Medicine and Texas Medical Center, but of special note was his position as chairman of the Harris County Hospital District, where he was also the first African American named to the public hospital system. In 1983, after he had served as chairman for more than nineteen years and as a member for twenty-five years, the board named its new facility in his honor, the Quentin R. Mease Community Hospital.

Quentin Mease was a master negotiator who, according to a May 2004 article in the *Houston Forward Times*, "symbolizes civic, economic and business progress ... and continues to be a pillar of the community." He died in Houston, Texas, at the age of 100.

FURTHER READING

Mease, Quentin R. *On Equal Footing: A Memoir* (2001).

Gray, Lisa. "Playing Hardball: Quentin Mease's Drive to Desegregate the Dome Gave Rise to a New Black Power in Houston," *Houston Press*, 7 June 2001.

Houston Defender News Service. "The Beginning of a Community Institution," *Houston Defender*, 2–8 Sept. 1990.

Schwieder, Dorothy, Joseph Hraba, and Elmer Schwieder. *Buxton: A Black Utopia in the Heartland* (2003).

YVONNE JACKSON EDWARDS

Mebane, George Allen (4 July 1850–1935?), teacher, school administrator, businessman, journalist, public official, and state legislator, was born a slave at the Hermitage, a large plantation on the Chowan River in Bertie County, North Carolina. He was the son of Allen Mebane and an unnamed mother.

George Mebane's education before the Civil War was limited by circumstance; later he attended the public schools in two Pennsylvania towns, Prentissvale and Eldred, for at least a year or more.

After much of northeastern North Carolina was occupied by Union forces in early 1862, Mebane served as a mess boy or waiter for Company A, 85th Regiment of New York State Volunteers, which was stationed at Roanoke Island. After much of the regiment surrendered to Confederate forces at Plymouth in April 1864, Mebane and his family fled North Carolina for McKean County, Pennsylvania, on the New York border, where they remained until after the war.

After his brief interlude in the North, Mebane moved back to Windsor, North Carolina, where he obtained a teacher's certificate in 1871 and became a teacher in the public schools of predominantly black Bertie County. For more than a decade, he taught in schools across eastern North Carolina, while also pursuing a career as a journalist and holding public office.

Like many youthful colleagues in Bertie and other counties of the "Black Second" congressional district, Mebane quickly became active in Republican Party circles. In 1876, he was nominated by his party to run for the state senate seat from the 3rd District (Bertie and Northampton Counties) and won that election by a margin of 2,161 votes over his Democratic opponent. One of five African Americans elected to the senate in the 1876 General Assembly, he served on the committee on education.

Mebane was married on 11 February 1877 to Jennie Mills Sanderlin, daughter of Robert Sanderlin of Windsor. The couple had as many as 12 children, of whom only the two oldest sons, George E. and H. A. W. Mebane, are listed by name.

Mebane stepped down at the end of his first term, accepting an appointment as a census enumerator in Bertie County for the 1880 federal census. In 1882, he returned briefly to statewide politics, nominated by Republicans for his old senate seat, amassing a majority of 1,200 votes over his Democratic opponent. One of twenty African Americans to serve in the 1883 General Assembly, he was named to the Committee on Corporations and took a more assertive role in his second term, first proposing an unsuccessful Sunday prohibition bill. Reacting to a bill aimed at restricting legal relationships between white women and African American men, Mebane proposed an ironic counterpart: a bill outlawing any cohabitation between white men and African American women. His bill died in committee.

In some ways Mebane's aggressive outspokenness reflected his maturing outlook, as well as his new private career. By 1880, he had become coeditor, with Ezekiel Ezra Smith of Goldsboro, of a weekly newspaper called the *Carolina Enterprise*, aimed at African American readers in the state's eastern counties with emphatic, sometimes controversial, stands on racial issues of the day. In about 1883, the struggling newspaper moved to Raleigh to merge with JOHN H. WILLIAMSON's *Banner*, organ of the North Carolina Industrial Association. The new *Banner Enterprise*, edited by Mebane, Smith, and Williamson, proved an unwieldy triumvirate and closed soon after Williamson left to establish the more successful *Gazette*.

Mebane returned to Bertie County, where he operated a general provisions store in Windsor and was soon elected register of deeds. In his spare time, he began to pursue an ambitious project, one aimed at profiling more than 200 of the state's prominent African American businessmen and politicians between 1860 and 1885, along with historical sketches of educational and charitable institutions benefiting his race. The proposed 300-page book would have included responses to a detailed questionnaire, asking each man to describe his background, education, and accomplishments. Lack of sufficient subscribers may have doomed the volume, which was apparently never published but gained a second life, of sorts, in Robert C. Kenzer's 1997 scholarly study, *Enterprising Southerners*, which was inspired by a copy of the questionnaire found among papers at Duke University.

Mebane's personal, political ambitions resurfaced in 1888, when he emerged as one of two top Republican contenders for the "Black Second" congressional nomination. At thirty-eight, the former legislator had a substantial following in Bertie and other counties, and a badly split convention produced disputed nominations for both Mebane and a newcomer, Vance County's HENRY PLUMMER CHEATHAM. Observers feared that the split in GOP ranks might simply re-elect the incumbent Democrat Furnifold Simmons, who had defeated JAMES O'HARA two years earlier in a three-way race, despite the Republicans' overwhelming numerical advantage.

Mebane gained indelible notoriety for his sudden withdrawal in late September, just weeks before the final ballot, in a widely rumored exchange for substantial political payoffs from influence peddlers in both parties—one to stay in the race, the other to get out of it. With Mebane out of the race, Cheatham managed to win a narrow victory over Simmons and served until 1893.

Whatever the truth behind the rumors, Mebane was publicly disgraced by the episode, and never again sought political office. He remained active in education, however, and served as an incorporator of the normal school for African American teachers established in Elizabeth City in 1891 by the state legislature. In the mid-1890s, he moved to Pasquotank County to serve as financial agent and superintendent of the new school, which eventually became Elizabeth City State University.

In 1900, Mebane published an article in a national publication, *The Arena*, titled "Have We An American Race Question? The Negro Vindicated," and defending the progress of the race using data from the 1890 federal census. That same year, he also compiled and edited a brief pamphlet on behalf of the National Afro-American Council. *"The Negro Problem" as Seen and Discussed by Southern White Men in Conference at Montgomery, Alabama, with Criticisms by the Northern Press* included a range of articles and newspaper editorials on the national race conference and its participants.

Few details are available about Mebane's activities after 1900, but federal censuses from 1910 to 1930 list him as a laborer in Durham, North Carolina, living with his wife and grandchildren. He is believed to have died there about 1935.

FURTHER READING

Anderson, Eric. *Race and Politics in North Carolina, 1872–1901: The Black Second* (1981).

Kenzer, Robert C. *Enterprising Southerners: Black Economic Success in North Carolina, 1865–1915* (1997).

BENJAMIN R. JUSTESEN

Mebane, Mary Elizabeth (26 June 1933–5 Mar. 1992), writer and educator, was born in Durham County, North Carolina. Her father, Samuel Nathaniel Mebane, was a farmer and laborer; her mother, Carrie Brandon Mebane, was employed at the Liggett & Myers tobacco factory. Mary Mebane, the second of the Mebanes' three surviving children, grew up in the rural Wildwood area of Durham County with her parents and two brothers.

Mebane, who always excelled in academics, attended North Carolina College (now North Carolina Central University), a historically black college in the city of Durham. She graduated summa cum laude with a bachelor's degree in Music and English in 1955, then taught in segregated public schools in rural North Carolina and in the city of Durham. Angered by the lack of resources and emotional support available to her students, she quickly became bored and frustrated with teaching poor black children in small towns: "I talked about nouns and verbs to people who had been in the fields yesterday and would be in the fields tomorrow, and who would be in the fields the rest of their lives" (Mebane, *Mary, Wayfarer*, 19). Mebane decided to enroll in the graduate program at the University of North Carolina at Chapel Hill. After receiving her M.A. in English in 1961 she returned to teaching, first as an instructor and later as an assistant professor at her alma mater, North Carolina College. She eventually returned to the University of North

Carolina and completed a Ph.D. in English in 1973 with a dissertation on family dynamics in the works of CHARLES W. CHESNUTT and RICHARD WRIGHT. During her years of doctoral study, Mebane was also an associate professor of English at South Carolina State College in Orangeburg. In 1974 she became associate professor of English at the University of South Carolina at Columbia, a post she left in 1977, disappointed by and dissatisfied with the slow progress of her career in the English department. In 1980 she took a position as a lecturer in English and creative writing at the University of Wisconsin–Milwaukee, a position she held until 1983.

In 1981 she published *Mary*, an autobiographical account of her childhood and adolescence in Durham County. Mebane's raw, highly personal stories and vivid descriptions of the people and places of her southern childhood earned *Mary* many admirers. *Mary* openly discusses her stormy and distant relationship with her mother, whom she felt "had no warmth, no love, no human feeling for me" (*Mary*, 23). Mebane was highly interested in the position of the intellectual in African American folk communities, especially the female intellectual. She uses the struggles between the grade school–educated tobacco factory worker and her imaginative, bookish daughter as an example of the conflict between the undereducated, hardworking poor black community and its intellectually inclined offspring. Mary and her mother (called "Nonnie" in the autobiographies) are perpetually unable to understand and connect to one another. Each woman is defensive about her own way of life, recognizing both its fragility and its value, and often seems to want to reach out to the other—but always holds back, uncertain of how to approach or respond.

Mebane chafed under the assumption that she was to take on the same kinds of tedious menial labor African American women had borne the brunt of since slavery, accept a life of poverty or near-poverty, and place marriage and childbearing at the center of her life. She found these paths restrictive and felt that they fed the racist system out of which they came. She declared: "Black women like me have scrubbed a hundred billion miles of tiled corridors and washed an equal number of dishes. I wasn't going to do that" (*Mary*, 99). Her mother, who had accepted a carefully regulated, unchanging life as a factory worker, is unable to understand why her daughter is so opposed to the kind of life she leads. The tension between young Mary and her mother is replayed in her interactions with other members of the

community, who also find her strange and incomprehensible. Communication quickly breaks down as it becomes apparent that she is following a different path. Again and again Mary finds herself alienated from her family, neighbors, and classmates because of her interests and aspirations.

Mebane's story continued with the publication of *Mary, Wayfarer* in 1983. *Mary, Wayfarer* takes the reader through the early years of Mebane's career, following her from college graduation to her experience as a college professor in South Carolina. She writes of the difficulties of teaching in segregated schools; having come from the same culture, she simultaneously understands and rails against the psychology of her young students. Mebane carefully explains to readers who may not fully understand the effects of forced segregation and the racial oppression of the 1950s how these pupils, many of them very talented, were burdened at early ages with such heavy responsibilities, so little parental supervision, and such a crushing, subconscious awareness that they were considered the underclass that they have little hope left for their futures. Despite her efforts to encourage her students and to serve as a role model, they do not aspire to lead lives different from those of their parents—lives too often marked, in Mebane's eyes, by poverty, conformity, and silent, passive acceptance of disparity.

Mary, Wayfarer is also notable for Mebane's explicit, relentless attack on class and color lines as well as gender bias within black communities, as she recounts her experiences as a dark-skinned woman attempting to make a career in academia. She finds that her aspirations are most often challenged by other African Americans in shaky and indefinable terms that she feels stem from their own prejudices about class status or skin color. She strongly refutes the idea that all racism and oppression African Americans experience is external and roundly criticizes both the black upper classes as well as the poor for contributing to the situation. Mebane's second installment of her autobiography also recounts her experiences as an observer of and occasional participant in the civil rights movement in South Carolina and her encounters with the activist MALCOLM X and the authors JAMES BALDWIN and RALPH ELLISON.

Both of Mebane's autobiographies were well received by critics and audiences. In *Mary, Wayfarer* she recounts being pleasantly surprised by the many letters she received from readers of *Mary* all over the world; she was shocked to discover that this highly personal account of a rural southern black female growing up in the middle of the twentieth century had touched so many diverse lives. The acclaim she received for her first book led to her being presented with a Distinguished Alumnus Award from the University of North Carolina in 1982. *Mary, Wayfarer* received a similarly enthusiastic response, and she was awarded a fellowship from the National Endowment of the Arts in 1983 to work on another book.

In the 1970s and 1980s Mebane frequently wrote articles for national publications, including several pieces that appeared in the *New York Times* under the pseudonym "Liza." These articles often expressed a deep concern for the largely invisible members of the black underclass. Harrison Salisbury, the Op-Ed page editor of the *Times* from 1971 to 1975, became her mentor, and she dedicated both of her published books to him.

Very little is known about Mebane's life after the publication of *Mary, Wayfarer*. Her lectureship at the University of Wisconsin ended in 1983. It appears that she remained in Milwaukee for the last nine years of her life, but it is unclear what she did for financial support during this time. The profound loneliness and social discomfort she confesses in her autobiographies seemed to plague her throughout her life; she was tormented by an inability to develop and sustain personal relationships. She never married or had children. She died in poverty, ill and alone, in a nursing home in Milwaukee in 1992. Many former friends and colleagues were not even aware of her death until several months after the fact—no obituary was published either in Milwaukee or in her hometown of Durham, North Carolina. She was buried in Milwaukee by the county.

Despite the resistance and alienation Mary E. Mebane often felt from the black community, she retained a great interest in and respect for African American culture, especially black folk culture. She once declared: "[T]he black folk are the most creative, viable people that America can produce. They just don't know it" (*Contemporary Authors*, 272). Her academic projects focused on black literature at a time when the field of black studies was in the primary stages of its disciplinary and curricular development and the pursuit of such interests was rare and difficult. Her autobiographies, while perhaps occasionally appearing harsh or bitter, reveal a woman deeply interested in understanding the world that created her and communicating its often overlooked and underappreciated complexities to her readers.

FURTHER READING
Mary E. Mebane's personal papers and manuscripts from the publication of *Mary, Wayfarer* are located in the Southern Historical Collection of the Louis Wilson Library, University of North Carolina at Chapel Hill.

Mebane, Mary E. *Mary* (1981).

Mebane, Mary E. *Mary, Wayfarer* (1983).

Holladay, Hilary. "A Native Daughter's Troubled Journey," *Independent Weekly* (Durham, N.C.), 28 Apr. 1993.

"Mebane, Mary E(lizabeth)," in *Contemporary Authors New Revision Series*, vol. 30 (1990).

Salisbury, Harrison E. "Travels through America," *Esquire* (Feb. 1976).

KRISTINA D. BOBO

Meek, Carrie Mae Pittman (29 Apr. 1926–), the granddaughter of slaves who became the first African American elected to Congress from Florida since Reconstruction, grew up as one of twelve children born to the sharecropper William Pittman and the domestic worker Carrie Pittman in Tallahassee, Florida. Meek grew up in the shadow of the Capitol in a neighborhood called the Bottom and attended Primitive Baptist churches. A gifted track and field athlete, she graduated with a bachelor's degree in biology and physical education from Florida A&M University in 1946. Unable to attend graduate school in Florida because African Americans were not permitted to do so, she went to the University of Michigan and earned a master's degree in public health and physical education in 1948. Meek returned to her home state to work as a physical education instructor at Miami-Dade Community College. She would ultimately spend more than forty years at the school as both a teacher and administrator. Meek married Harold H. Meek, but the couple later divorced after producing three children.

A liberal Democrat and an especially skilled orator, Meek has been quoted as saying that the last Republican who did something for African Americans was Abraham Lincoln. She spent much of her political career working for racial equity. Elected to the Florida House of Representatives in 1978 to replace the deceased pioneer black legislator Gwen Cherry, she represented the heavily Democratic district in northern Miami-Dade County. She served until 1982, when she joined Arnett Girardeau in becoming the first African Americans elected to the upper chamber since Reconstruction. Meek also became the first African

American woman in the Florida Senate. During her tenure, Meek sponsored legislation creating the Florida Commission on the Status of Women. She also promoted a change in policy toward Haitian refugees, the creation of affordable health care, and the improvement of child protection programs. Many of her efforts focused on providing help to poor people. Meek gained the respect of her colleagues as a consensus builder and was consistently rated among Florida's most effective senators.

Elected to the U.S. House of Representatives in 1992 at the age of 66, Meek joined the 103rd Congress as the delegate from Florida's 17th Congressional District. ALCEE L. HASTINGS and CORRINE BROWN stood alongside Meek in becoming the first black Floridians elected to Congress since JOSIAH T. WALLS in the 1870s. Meek, a freshman member of the Congressional Black Caucus in 1993, took an active role in the struggle to restore democracy to Haiti by urging President Bill Clinton to order an invasion of the country to oust its military regime and give power back to exiled President Jean-Bertrand Aristide. She was also a strong critic of Fidel Castro of Cuba, like most Florida legislators. Meek supported gun control, abortion rights, and health care reform. As a freshman, she managed the unusual step of gaining membership on the powerful House Appropriation Committee, which funds all executive branch programs and independent agencies. Meek also served on the Subcommittee on Treasury, Postal Service, and General Government as well as the Subcommittee on Veteran's Affairs, Housing and Urban Development, and Independent Agencies. Meek, once regarded as the most powerful African American politician in Florida, is credited with passing legislation to protect the victims of stalkers, increasing the availability of affordable housing, and providing funds for education. Meek ran unopposed in 1992, 1994, and 1998. In 1996, she won reelection with 89 percent of the vote and, four years later, won against a write-in candidate.

In 2000 Meek opposed Governor Jeb Bush's One Florida plan that ended affirmative action in university admissions and state contracting. Later that year, she helped bring national attention to charges that the rights of black voters in Florida were violated during the 2000 presidential election. She publicly observed that voters in her district, about 60 percent black at the time, had their rights trampled because of inadequate ballot instructions and other roadblocks that prevented them from casting ballots.

Largely as a result of health issues, Meek announced in July 2002 that she would not seek a sixth term in Congress. KENDRICK MEEK, her youngest child and a Florida state legislator, won election to succeed his mother. Upon retiring, Meek devoted herself to the Carrie Meek Foundation, a nonprofit organization that aims to improve the quality of life and to build a stronger community in the inner-city neighborhoods of Miami-Dade County. Meek resides in Liberty City, a historically black section of Miami.

FURTHER READING

Gill, LaVerne McCain. *African American Women in Congress: Forming and Transforming History* (1997).

CARYN E. NEUMANN

Meek, Kendrick B. (6 Sept. 1966–), congressman, was born Kendrick Brett Meek in Miami, Florida, one of three children and the only son of Carrie Pittman Meek, a member of Congress. Carrie Pittman Meek and Kendrick's father divorced; the first name of Meek's father is unknown. After completing high school, Meek attended Florida A&M University in Tallahassee. In college, Meek demonstrated a keen interest in politics and public affairs by founding the Florida A&M University's Democratic Club. Meek, within a year, was elected president of Florida's College Young Democrats. The future congressman was also a standout football player. He graduated with a B.S. in Criminal Justice in 1989. After being introduced by a judge with whom he was acquainted, Meek courted and married Leslie Dixon of Brooklyn, New York, in 1991. The couple has two children, Lauren and Kendrick Jr.

After his successful performance in college, Meek used his degree to secure a position as a Florida State Trooper with the Florida Highway Patrol. His hard work earned him the position of captain, a first for an African American in the state of Florida. During his time in law enforcement, Meek became acquainted with several powerful people. Two in particular, Lt. Governor Buddy MacKay and Governor Lawton Chiles, whom he served as a member of the traveling security detail, provided a tutorial in state government. Meek's enthusiasm for law enforcement was tempered by the fact that he had no authority to write the laws he was enforcing. He resigned from the Florida Highway Patrol in 1994 and ran for a seat in the Florida House of Representatives. He defeated his Republican opponent and served in the chamber from 1995 to 1999. Eager to have a larger political role, Meek ran for the Florida Senate in 1998. His victory allowed him to serve, with distinction, from 1999 to 2003. Meek also drew attention for staging a sit-in at the office of Governor Jeb Bush because of his plans to end affirmative action in contracts and education.

When Congressman Meek's mother decided to retire from the House in 2002, Meek jumped at the chance to replace her. Meek was easily elected in 2002 to represent Miami and was reelected in 2004, 2006, and 2008. In 2008 Meek supported then Senator Hillary Rodham Clinton in the Democratic primaries. In Congress, Meek has served on the important Ways and Means committee, the Congressional Black Caucus, as a member of the NATO Parliamentary Assembly, and the Democratic Steering and Policy Committee. Meek has been active in promoting education, relief for Haitians in the wake of the 2010 earthquake, affordable housing, job creation, immigration, and public transportation. Meek's career in politics has been center-left and progressive compared to more conservative black politicians such as Harold Ford Jr.

Congressman Meek has been lauded by his fellow members in the Democratic Caucus and by newspapers in Florida, and is generally considered to be a rising star in the Democratic Party. In the wake of the election of BARACK OBAMA to the U.S. Senate and later the presidency, Meek, like Artur Davis in Alabama and Harold Ford Jr. in Tennessee, has sought statewide office. In 2009 Meek announced his intention to run for the Democratic nomination for the United States Senate. In 2010 Meek won the Democratic party's nomination for the U.S. Senate, which made him the first African American nominee for a statewide political office in Florida. In the general election, Meek came in third with 20 percent of the vote, behind Charlie Crist, the former Republican governor, running as an independent, and the official GOP Candidate, Marco Rubio. Meek had decided not to seek another term in the House, in order to run for Senate, and so left the House, officially, in January 2011.

FURTHER READING

Cave, Damien. "Democrat Seeks Part of Spotlight in Florida Senate Race," *New York Times*, 25 Feb. 2010.
McCutheon, Chuck, and Christina L. Lyons. *CQ's Politics in America 2010: The 111th Congress* (2009).
U.S. Congress, House, Committee on House Administration of The U.S. House of Representatives. *Black Americans in Congress, 1870–2007* (2008).

DARYL A. CARTER

Meeks, Gregory (25 Sept. 1953–), political activist, New York legislator, and congressman, was born in New York City, the oldest of four children. The Meeks family lived in public housing in East Harlem, but his parents were hard working and kept the family tight-knit. Meeks's father, James, worked several jobs to help cover household expenses and his mother focused on raising the children, tutoring and encouraging them to excel in school. When Meeks and his siblings were older, his mother would return to school to earn her college diploma. When he was a young man, Meeks's parents tried to instill in him a sense of pride and duty to his community. His mother was active in the neighborhood watch and his father worked with neighborhood youths. He was also exposed to many different cultures. One of his father's many jobs was porter at the Shubert Theatre on Broadway where Meeks attended virtually every performance. Meeks attended Julia Richman High School, where he was active in student government and was a member of the football team, which his father coached. After graduating in 1971 he enrolled at Adelphi University in Garden City, New York, where Meeks became a student activist during the turbulent era of the civil rights and Black Power movements. He

Gregory Meeks, speaking during the Hip-Hop Summit on Financial Empowerment at the Hammerstein Ballroom in New York City, 22 April 2006. (AP Images.)

fought to increase the number of minority students on campus, chaired the Black Student Union, and served as a student representative on the university admissions committee. Through his involvement, the numbers of minority students increased substantially. After graduating in 1975 with a B.A. in History, Meeks enrolled at Howard University Law School, earning his law degree in 1978.

After law school, Meeks joined the Queens County District Attorney's Office as an assistant district attorney. In 1982 he was promoted to work as an assistant to the Special Narcotics Office for New York City, an office created to tackle the city's heroin epidemic. A year later, he joined the State Investigations Commission, investigating organized crime and corruption. In 1984 he was appointed supervising judge of New York State Worker's Compensation Board. During the 1980s Meeks was active in his Queens community, becoming involved in numerous neighborhood organizations and working closely with local politicians, and helping on the New York presidential primary campaigns for JESSE L. JACKSON. In 1991 he decided to enter a crowded field for a seat on the city council. Although he lost, he proved to be an attractive candidate. In 1992 Meeks was elected to a seat on the New York State Assembly.

In the early 1990s the issue of police brutality grabbed the national spotlight. In Los Angeles, the beating of RODNEY KING by police officers sparked one of the city's worst riots. In New York, Meeks joined many of the city's black leaders in condemning the actions of police who abused their power. In 1997 New York Representative FLOYD FLAKE decided to retire from the United States Congress; Meeks was his choice to replace him. Meeks had made a name for himself in the assembly working on labor and transportation issues and displayed a talent for developing political relationships. Meeks's public profile rose considerably with his condemnation of police officers involved in the torture and sodomy of Abner Louima, a Haitian immigrant. With the support of Rev. Flake, REV. AL SHARPTON, and other black leaders, Meeks was elected to Congress in a special election. Upon entering Congress in 1998, Meeks joined members from the Congressional Black Caucus (CBC) in speaking out against the lack of minority employees in Congress. He led a campaign to increase the hiring of minority clerks in the Supreme Court. In Congress, Meeks focused the majority of his energies on economic development in his home district. Many parts of Queens struggled with persistent poverty and economic blight. Meeks was central in the expansion of air carriers to John F. Kennedy International Airport, which provided access for low cost carriers to serve smaller markets. He also played a role in the extension of the Air Tram system, providing a connection to business in several areas of Queens.

In 2000 the issue of police brutality would again grab the headlines. Amadou Diallo, an unarmed African immigrant, was killed by police officers in a hail of bullets. Meeks used his influence in Congress to encourage action by the Justice Department. During this time Meeks also advocated for a national moratorium on the death penalty, in order to give prisoners an opportunity to explore the possibility of DNA evidence. Meeks was not afraid to take unpopular positions. Against the urgings of many Democrats and labor unions, Meeks was a decisive vote in giving China permanent trade status He also lobbied for normalizing relations with Cuba, moving the nation from a policy of isolation to one of engagement. Meeks believed both actions would benefit the U.S. economy.

In the aftermath of Hurricane Katrina in 2005, Meeks stood with members of the CBC in denouncing the government response and demanding that efforts be made to make the gulf region high priority for relief and reconstruction. He was outspoken in his displeasure with President George W. Bush's administration, channeling the frustrations of the majority of his constituents. Meeks, who was reelected in 2008 and 2010, faced an ethics probe in July 2011. The investigation by the House ethics committee was related to his initial non-disclosure of a $40,000 loan he received in 2007 from a Queens real estate broker with a track record of fraud and predatory lending. Meeks and his wife Simone-Marie have three daughters, Ebony, Aja, and Nia-Aiyana.

MICHAELJULIUS IDANI

Melvin, Chasity (1976–) professional women's basketball player, was born in Roseboro, North Carolina, the second oldest of five children of Jimmy Melvin a minister, and Janet Melvin. Chasity grew up in a small-town community surrounded by family and friends. To stay entertained, Melvin and her siblings along with their cousins would play basketball on the dirt-court and outdoor basketball goal their father had purchased for them. Melvin fell in love with the game of basketball and began playing organized basketball in the seventh grade.

She led her teams to back-to-back championships in both the seventh grade and eighth grade.

Melvin attended Lakewood High School in Roseboro. She excelled in every sport that she played including volleyball, softball, track and field, and basketball. Basketball, however remained Melvin's first love and she led her team each year to the regional playoffs, including winning the 1A State Championship game along with her sisters, Danielle and Jimmelle Melvin in 1994. Chasity scored over two thousand points in her high school career and received numerous MVP awards and Player of the Year honors.

After graduating high school in 1994, Melvin signed a four-year athletic scholarship with the University of North Carolina State in Raleigh, North Carolina. She played all four years for the legendary basketball coach Kay Yow, made the ACC (Atlantic Coast Conference) All-Rookie team and led her team to the NCAA Final Four in 1998 in Kansas City, Missouri, during her senior season. During the Final Four, Melvin set a NCAA semifinal record in points with thirty-seven. Melvin was also chosen as a Kodak All-American during her senior year.

Upon graduating with her B.S. degree in Mass Communications in May 1998, Melvin was selected as the second pick to play for the Philadelphia Rage, of the women's American Basketball League. After one season, she was drafted as the eleventh pick in the WNBA (Women's National Basketball Association) in 1999 and subsequently played for several teams including Cleveland Rockers (1999–2003), Chicago Sky (2007–2009), and Washington Mystics (2004–2007, 2009–). As a WNBA center and forward Melvin has led her teams to several playoff spots (2000, 2001, 2003, 2004, 2006, 2009) as well as receiving the honor of being a WNBA All-Star in 2001.

Along with Melvin's national professional experience in the WNBA, Melvin has enjoyed a prominent international professional career as a women's basketball player. Melvin has played in several countries including Spain, Israel, Italy, Russia, Poland, China, South Korea, and Turkey. Her international career includes several League Championships and many tournament victories.

Melvin played twelve seasons in the WNBA. In 2011 the Washington Mystics waived her contract.

FURTHER READING

Zonars, Stephanie. *Leader of the Pack* (2009).

DANIELLE D. MELVIN

Melvin, Harold (25 June 1939–24 Mar. 1997) singer and leader of Harold Melvin and the Blue Notes, was born in Philadelphia, Pennsylvania. There is no available information on his parents. Melvin taught himself to play piano in his youth, and as a teenager joined the Charlemagnes, a street-corner harmony group that formed during the early years of the doo-wop phenomena. Melvin changed the group's name to the Blue Notes in 1954 and took on a multifaceted leadership role within the renamed group; at one time Melvin acted as lead singer, songwriter, arranger, and choreographer. Chart success eluded the group during their early tenure on Josie, Dot, and other R&B labels, though they did score minor hits like 1960's "My Hero," their first charting record, and 1965's "Get Out (And Let Me Cry)." In 1963 Melvin weathered a split with original member Bernard Williams, who formed the Original Blue Notes as rival to Melvin's ensemble. Despite internal tension, personnel changes, and middling commercial success, the Melvin-led Blue Notes continued recording throughout the 1960s, with John Atkins as its lead singer.

It was at the dawn of the new decade, however, that the group's fortunes turned significantly upward. In 1970 Atkins left the Blue Notes, and Melvin promoted TEDDY PENDERGRASS—hired as a drummer after the Blue Notes toured with his previous band, the Cadillacs—to lead singer. Pendergrass' powerful voice, soaked in the tortured transcendence of gospel, propelled Melvin and the Blue Notes to a 1972 recording deal with Philly International, an upstart R&B label run by producers and songwriters Kenny Gamble and LEON HUFF, who sought to transplant the Motown formula into the talent-rich Philadelphia scene. The Blue Notes became one of Philly International's first and most consistent hit groups, beginning a run of success on both R&B and Pop Charts with 1972's "I Miss You (Part 1)." It was with second single "If You Don't Know Me by Now," though, that the Blue Notes' established themselves. A sweeping ballad with echoes of soul, doo-wop, pop, and gospel traditions, Pendergrass's aching vocal, with gospel moans and R&B cries, proved a perfect match for the Blue Notes' insistent backing and the textured Gamble-Huff production. The song—written, as were most of their Philly International hits, by Gamble and Huff—topped the R&B charts for two weeks and crossed over to number three Pop, the only time they achieved such significant crossover success.

For the next five years, Melvin and the Blue Notes were a cornerstone of Philly International.

Bridging soul, pop, and funk, Blue Notes tracks paved the way for disco: the pulsating "The Love I Lost," from 1973, is often referenced as one of the first disco tracks, and "Don't Leave Me This Way," an extended groove sung with bluesy intensity by Pendergrass, later became a huge disco hit for Thelma Houston, though the Blue Notes themselves never released it as a single. The Blue Notes also recorded "Wake Up Everybody," an assertive call-to-arms that sounded a celebratory note of Black Power action while warning against the rising antipathy and frustration that lay ahead in the Reagan era. Without doubt, social and political awareness and responsibility represented a central element to the label's philosophy; Gamble and Huff—who wrote "Wake Up Everybody"—crafted a number of anthems and cautionary tales that captured the conflicting energies in African American communities during the 1970s. Combining serious, even grave, thematic material with the bright, buoyant music of the "Philadelphia sound" made for compelling (and effective) musical alchemy. Though certainly not the label's only, or necessarily

biggest, stars, Melvin and the Blue Notes—led by Pendergrass—played a major role in Philly International's success. By 1976 increasing pressure on Pendergrass to parlay his Blue Notes success into an assuredly prosperous solo career led to his departure from the group. Indeed, Pendergrass's sexy persona and riveting performances brought him tremendous success as a solo artist for the next several years, until a 1982 car crash left Pendergrass paralyzed, and—to a great extent—brought his career to a halt. Melvin and the Blue Notes continued to record, replacing Pendergrass with similar-sounding David Ebo, as well as female singer Sharon Paige, but the lightning captured by Pendergrass's tenure had escaped from the bottle; the group soon left Philadelphia International. Signing with ABC Records, the group recorded a major hit, "Reaching for the World" in 1977, and they had a few more successful outings on the R&B charts until 1980, when Paige—following two other members—left the group. Melvin once again regrouped, taking his new ensemble to Source, an MCA subsidiary, this time with Gil Saunders as

Harold Melvin (center) with the Blue Notes, in an undated photograph. (AP Images.)

lead singer. Despite a brief 1984 comeback, when their most recent album made a minor splash in the UK, Melvin and the Blue Notes—along with many of their "Philadelphia sound" contemporaries— were no longer a relevant commercial force by the mid-1980s. Melvin continued playing shows with various Blue Notes line-ups into the 1990s, but he suffered a stroke in 1996 that left him incapacitated, and ultimately killed him in 1997. He left behind his wife, Ovelia (nee McDaniels), and five children.

Despite Melvin's early death, the legacy of the Blue Notes remained strong. Beyond the continued popularity of Blue Notes songs on oldies and R&B radio, Blue Notes material was widely covered by a variety of artists. The British "blue-eyed soul" group Simply Red returned "If You Don't Know Me by Now" to the top of the American charts in 1989. In 2004 Wyclef Jean organized an all-star group of pop, R&B, and hip-hop artists to record a version of "Wake Up, Everybody" to raise awareness for voter registration. These, and other, covers of Melvin and the Blue Notes suggested that the group, and its leader, maintained a place within the consciousness of modern listeners as one of the most important and successful contributors to the wildly successful "Philadelphia sound," a musical style that greatly influenced the course of American popular music.

FURTHER READING

Huey, Steve. "Harold Melvin and the Blue Notes," in *All Music Guide*, eds. Vladimir Bogdanov et al. (2001).

Jackson, John. *A House on Fire: The Rise and Fall of Philadelphia Soul* (2004).

Pendergrass, Teddy, and Patricia Romanowski. *Truly Blessed* (1998).

CHARLES L. HUGHES

Memphis Minnie (3 June 1896 or 1897–6 Aug. 1973), blues singer, guitarist, and songwriter, was born Lizzie Douglas in Algiers, Louisiana, the oldest of thirteen children born to Abe Douglas and Gertrude Wells, sharecroppers. "Kid," as everyone knew her, moved with her family to the northwest Mississippi community of Walls around 1904. She got her first guitar as a Christmas present in 1905, and from an early age she frequently ran away to nearby Memphis and Beale Street to play music. Her early influences are not well known, but she probably learned some technique from Memphis musicians active at that time, including Frank Stokes, FURRY LEWIS, and Robert Wilkins; "but before long, Minnie herself was the reigning blues queen of

Memphis, and there was little she could learn from the competition" (Garon and Garon, 19).

For about six years Douglas worked the area around the Bedford Plantation near Lake Cormorant, Mississippi, regularly playing with the guitarist Willie Brown and sometimes joined by the guitarist Willie Moore as a trio. It is apparent from the recollections of those who heard them that Douglas was the lead vocalist and guitarist. During World War I Douglas toured with a Ringling Brothers show that she joined in Clarksdale, Mississippi. Sometime in the 1920s she met her first husband, the versatile musician Joe McCoy, and they became a musical team. McCoy and his brother Charlie (who later recorded with Douglas) were part of an influential group of musicians in the Jackson/Crystal Springs area that included the Mississippi Sheiks (the Chatman brothers and Walter Vinson), TOMMY JOHNSON and his brothers, and Houston Stackhouse. McCoy recorded under many pseudonyms and with a great variety of musicians, including jug and jazz bands.

Douglas and McCoy were discovered by a Columbia Records talent scout while playing in a Beale Street barbershop. In June 1929 the duo traveled to New York for their first recording session. They recorded six songs (three vocals by McCoy, two by Douglas, and one with both), all of which were released; one song, Douglas's composition and vocal "Bumble Bee," was released by Columbia only after several later versions had been hits for the Vocalion label. Douglas's early recordings with Joe McCoy demonstrate a similarity to, and possible influence from, the intricate guitar interplay evident in the recordings of the Beale Street Sheiks (Frank Stokes and Dan Sane). The records were released as by "Kansas City Joe and Memphis Minnie," apparently a marketing ploy of the record company. McCoy discontinued use of the Kansas City moniker after parting with Douglas in 1935; Douglas became Memphis Minnie and used that name for the rest of her life. Along with TAMPA RED, Minnie and McCoy were among the first African American musicians to adopt the new and louder National steel guitars.

The duo next recorded in February 1930, for Vocalion in Memphis. After that was a session for Victor in May, including backing by the Memphis Jug Band and most likely Minnie singing harmony on BUKKA WHITE's gospel record. In June 1930 the duo traveled to Chicago and recorded again for Vocalion, the label that was Minnie's primary recording outlet for the rest of the decade, though

Minnie's 1930s records also appeared on the Okeh, Decca, and Bluebird labels. The Victor sides were issued by McCoy and Johnson, and the Vocalion sides were typically issued as either by Memphis Minnie or by Memphis Minnie and Kansas City Joe. During the 1930s Minnie's accompanists on record included Jed Davenport's Jug Band, Tampa Red and Georgia Tom (who later became the gospel legend THOMAS A. DORSEY), Bumble Bee Slim, Black Bob, Casey Bill Weldon—who some have claimed to have been Minnie's first husband—and her second husband, Ernest "Little Son Joe" Lawlars, with whom she began recording in 1939. On several of these 1930s recordings Minnie played mandolin rather than guitar (it has been written that she also knew how to play banjo, but her biographers the Garons found no evidence of this). Minnie's early lyrics frequently emphasized rural themes and farm life.

Minnie and McCoy's intricately picked guitar duets—where McCoy supplied the underlying rhythm through elaborate bass runs supporting Minnie's dexterous lead guitar—were discontinued in favor of a performance style in which the guitar played "a more supporting role." "This was a music styled for the tough joints on Chicago's South Side, and not for the country suppers and fish fries Minnie played for in the South" (Garon and Garon, 43). Working for the Lester Melrose–controlled blues recording industry of the 1930s and 1940s, Minnie, like BIG BILL BROONZY (in his autobiography he described a guitar battle in which Minnie beat him), was an important innovator, changing guitar playing styles, adding jazz musicians to her sidemen, doing songs in a variety of popular styles, and by 1941 adopting the electric guitar. Minnie was a leader in the evolution of the blues from the styles prevalent in the 1920s to the blues of the 1950s. Unlike Broonzy, who in later years played folk blues for white audiences, Minnie continued to play for her core African American audience.

Much of the blues recorded under Melrose's direction has been characterized as monotonously similar, but that cannot be said of Minnie, who continued to renew herself and her music by frequent trips down South. She heard the ensemble sound and the new ways of playing guitar on the Helena, Arkansas, radio station KFFA's *King Biscuit Show*, and she may even have gotten the idea of playing electric guitar from JOE WILLIE WILKINS and ROBERT JR. LOCKWOOD, the radio program's guitarists.

Another southern influence on Minnie's music was her partnering with Ernest "Little Son Joe" Lawlars (according to the Garons, the spelling "Lawlers," which is frequently used, including on the program for Minnie's funeral, is incorrect). Lawlars was a skillful guitarist and washboard player who accompanied Minnie on record and in person for the rest of their lives. He had previously recorded for ARC in Jackson, Mississippi, in 1935, but no records were issued; his first known records are from his 1939 recording session with Minnie in Chicago.

In the early 1940s the pair produced some of Minnie's biggest hits, including "Me and My Chauffeur Blues" (to the tune of SONNY BOY WILLIAMSON's popular 1937 recording, "Good Morning, School Girl"), "Can't Afford to Lose My Man," "Looking the World Over," "In My Girlish Days," "Nothing in Rambling," and Lawlars's "Black Rat Swing" (sung by Lawlars and released as by "Mr. Memphis Minnie"). In August 1942 the American Federation of Musicians initiated a ban on new recording that lasted for three years.

From 1940 up to her 1949 Regal session, all of Minnie's records were released by Columbia/Okeh. For Minnie this was a period of less frequent recording, characterized by her experimenting with newly popular rhythm and blues and pop styles. The 1949 Regal session marked the end of Minnie's work for major national labels and marked her continuing adaptation to the new, harder, electric sound of postwar Delta blues.

Minnie worked with and mentored some of the younger musicians who helped create the 1950s Chicago blues sound, including the harmonica player Billy Boy Arnold and the guitarists JIMMY ROGERS and Homesick James Williamson. For Regal, Minnie was accompanied by a small ensemble that included the pianist Sunnyland Slim, an important player in the new blues sound of 1950s Chicago. At her next session in 1952, for the Chess Records subsidiary Checker, she recorded four first-rate postwar blues (including a remake of "Me and My Chauffeur"), featuring the harmonica great LITTLE WALTER JACOBS. On 5 October 1953 Minnie and Lawlars, in the company of the pianist LITTLE BROTHER MONTGOMERY, recorded nine songs for Chicago's JOB label—her finest in the new, bolder style of the 1950s.

In 1958, in declining health, Minnie and Lawlars returned permanently to Memphis, where they continued to play with and teach younger musicians. They recorded last in Memphis in 1959 for Audiodisc, but these recordings have not been released. Lawlars died in 1961, and Minnie soon suffered a second stroke that left her wheelchair-bound and unable to perform. Incapacitated, Minnie lived first with her youngest sibling, Daisy Johnson, before moving into Jell Nursing Home in north Memphis. Minnie died on 6 August 1973 and was buried in New Hope Cemetery in Walls.

Physically quite attractive, Minnie was tough enough to hold her own in a male-dominated profession and to face the frequent dangers of the streets, bars, taverns, and life on the road. More than 180 of Minnie's recordings were issued in her lifetime, and many performers have covered them, from MUDDY WATERS and CLIFTON CHENIER to Bob Wills and Moon Mulligan, and from Led Zeppelin to Jefferson Airplane. Her influence on several generations of blues musicians is remarkable. In 1973 Minnie was voted the top female vocalist in *Blues Unlimited*'s readers' poll. She was in the first group of artists inducted into the W. C. Handy Awards Hall of Fame in 1980.

FURTHER READING
Broonzy, William. *Big Bill Blues* (1964).
Garon, Paul, and Beth Garon. *Woman with Guitar: Memphis Minnie's Blues* (1992).
LaVere, Steve. "Memphis Minnie," *Living Blues* (1973).
Obsequies of the Late Mrs. Minnie Lawlers, Mt. Vernon Baptist Church, 9 Aug. 1973.

DISCOGRAPHY
Dixon, Robert M. W., John Godrich, and Howard W. Rye. *Blues and Gospel Records, 1890–1943* (1997).
Fancourt, Les, and Bob McGrath. *The Blues Discography: 1943–1970* (2006).

FRED J. HAY

Memphis Slim (3 Sept. 1915–24 Feb. 1988), blues singer and pianist, was born John Len Chatman in Memphis, Tennessee, the son of Peter Chatman, a roadhouse proprietor and musician who played piano and guitar, and Ella Kennedy, who died when her son was only two. Raised by his father, the younger Chatman learned piano by age seven, became a competent blues player at thirteen, and began playing on Beale Street in Memphis while still in his teens. He attended Lester High School, playing bass in the school band, but his main teachers were the itinerant boogie and blues pianists who came to Memphis, particularly ROOSEVELT SYKES, whose style Chatman clearly emulated early in his career. Sometime around 1931 Chatman succeeded Sykes as house pianist at the Midway Cafe in South Memphis, earning "a dollar and a half a night and two pints of whiskey." As Chatman later recalled,

the clubs in Memphis, particularly the clubs run by gangsters, operated with little regard for Prohibition and gambling laws, but they did provide steady employment for blues piano players.

According to another Memphis piano player, Booker T. Laury, a crackdown in 1935 forced many musicians, including Chatman, to look for work across the state line in West Memphis, Arkansas. Chatman already had tested his skills as a musician and gambler in Arkansas, working jooks and levee camps and, by his own account, teaming up briefly with blues guitarist ROBERT JOHNSON in Marianna and Marked Tree.

In the late 1930s Chatman joined the migration of southern blues musicians to Chicago, and by 1939 he was firmly established among the city's fraternity of blues players. Blues producer Lester Melrose, who brokered Chicago blues talent through the 1940s, set up Chatman's initial recording date with the Okeh label. Accompanied by a "washboard band," he recorded six songs on 6 August 1940 using his father's name, Peter Chatman. Several months later he was back in the studio, recording seven sides, including his first hit, "Beer Drinking Woman," for RCA Victor's Bluebird label. These were the first sides released as Memphis Slim, the professional name Chatman retained for the next forty-eight years.

In Chicago, Memphis Slim came under the patronage of the guitarist and recording star BIG BILL BROONZY. After the 1942 death of Broonzy's pianist, Joshua Altheimer, he joined Broonzy's group, which held court at Ruby Lee Gatewood's tavern on the South Side. With Broonzy's encouragement, Memphis Slim began to develop a style more in tune with changing African American musical tastes, and eventually he put together his own band, the House Rockers. After World War II he returned to the studio with the House Rockers, recording for two small, independent labels: Hy-Tone in 1946 and Miracle in 1947. The band included two saxophones, bass, and drums and later a third saxophone and a guitar. The bassist on the 1947 session was WILLIE DIXON, a songwriter, vocalist, and blues hustler who stayed with the band for three years, producing hits such as "Rocking the Joint" in a postwar, jump-blues format.

In 1947 Memphis Slim, Broonzy, and another former bandmate from Ruby's tavern, the harmonica player JOHN LEE "SONNY BOY" WILLIAMSON, participated in folk-song collector Alan Lomax's Music at Midnight concert series in New York. The trio also went into the studio with Lomax and recorded what

Lomax later titled *Blues in the Mississippi Night*, an informal mix of conversation, music, and stories about the living conditions they faced as black men in the South. During the session, Slim talked about working the levee camps in Arkansas, mixing blues with a discussion of the conditions in which blues developed. Although Slim included similar ruminations in performances years later, he and his fellow artists were afraid their off-the-cuff comments would be too controversial in 1947, so they were given pseudonyms—Slim's being "Leroy."

From 1949 until well into the late 1950s, Memphis Slim continued as a major rhythm and blues figure, touring with the House Rockers and jumping from label to label—King, Peacock, Chess, Mercury, Money, Premium, and United.

In 1959 Memphis Slim branched out into the more lucrative "folk blues" market, playing primarily to white audiences. He played the Newport Folk Festival to a standing ovation, did a show at Carnegie Hall in New York with MUDDY WATERS, began to work upscale nightclubs—the Gate of Horn in Chicago, for one—and hit the coffeehouse circuit. He continued to record rhythm and blues with his band for the independent VeeJay label in Chicago while also cutting albums for Folkways in New York, working solo or as a duo with longtime sidekick Willie Dixon. He even recorded with the folk icon Pete Seeger.

In 1960 and 1961, on tours with Dixon, Memphis Slim got his first exposure to the European market. By 1962 he had married Christine Freys, the daughter of a French club owner (he was previously married in the United States to Doris Owens), and had settled permanently in Paris, taking a job as house pianist at a Left Bank jazz club, Les Trois Mailletz. He quickly became a celebrity in France, appearing frequently on television, touring the continent, and returning occasionally to the United States. He developed a one-man show, the *Story of the Blues*, which wove together his music and his early recollections; he also worked as an actor and musician in three films. According to Memphis Slim, he moved to France because he could make a better living as a musician there. Indeed he clearly enjoyed the trappings of success, with an elegant wardrobe, a Paris apartment, and a Rolls-Royce automobile.

Although he was slowed by heart problems in the 1980s, Memphis Slim returned to the United States in 1983 to perform with B. B. KING and Bobby Blue Bland at a Smithsonian Institution program celebrating the Memphis blues tradition. He died in Paris, survived by his wife and six children. A funeral, attended by dignitaries and music celebrities, was held in Memphis, where flags flew at half-staff, and he was buried in Galilee Memorial Gardens next to his father.

Memphis Slim wrote three hundred songs and recorded almost five hundred during his career. His own compositions included his theme song "Every Day I Have the Blues," a hit for the COUNT BASIE vocalist JOE WILLIAMS in 1955 and, later, B. B. King; it remained a standard among later blues artists.

He worked with a veritable blues who's who: Big Bill Broonzy, Buster Brown, LOWELL FULSON, BUDDY GUY, Robert Johnson, LITTLE WALTER JACOBS, Muddy Waters, JUNIOR WELLS, and both Sonny Boy Williamsons, No. 1 and No. 2 (SONNY BOY WILLIAMSON). He figured prominently in major blues transitions, first when he merged Beale Street and Arkansas barrelhouse blues with the prewar ensemble sound in Chicago and later when he helped reshape the prewar sound into the jump-blues and rhythm and blues styles that emerged in the 1950s. Later still, he shifted from rhythm and blues star to become a thoughtful interpreter of the blues for the folk-revival audience. And finally, Memphis Slim became the most successful expatriate blues ambassador ever, bringing his musical stylings to appreciative audiences throughout Europe. Late in his career, he was honored in the U.S. Senate as an "ambassador-at-large of good will" and was named commander of arts and letters by the French government. In 1989 he was inducted into the Blues Foundation Hall of Fame in Memphis.

FURTHER READING

Charters, Samuel. *The Legacy of the Blues: A Glimpse into the Art and the Lives of Twelve Great Bluesmen* (1977).
Cook, Bruce. *Listen to the Blues* (1973).
Obituary: *Living Blues* 80 (May–June 1988): 31–32.

DISCOGRAPHY

Leadbitter, Mike, et al. *Blues Records 1943–1970*, vol. 2, *The Bible of the Blues*, L–Z (1994).
Memphis Slim: You Got to Help Me Some (Blues Encore CD 52013 AAD).
This entry is taken from the *American National Biography* and is published here with the permission of the American Council of Learned Societies.

BILL MCCULLOCH AND
BARRY LEE PEARSON

Menard, John Willis (3 Apr. 1838–8 Oct. 1893), politician, poet, journalist, and activist, was born in rural Kalkaska, Illinois, to French Creole parents who had traveled up the Mississippi River to escape oppression in Louisiana. Only scattered details about Menard's early life in Illinois remain. He likely spent part of his youth working on area farms before attending an abolitionist preparatory school in Sparta, Illinois. He also attended Iberia College (later Ohio Central College) in his early twenties, though he did not complete a degree there, presumably because of financial setbacks.

In 1859 Menard spoke to a crowd gathered at the Illinois state fairgrounds to celebrate the abolition of slavery in the West Indies. The *Illinois State Journal*'s laudatory coverage of the speech points to Menard's budding career in social activism. A year later, in response to growing racial discrimination in the Illinois legislature, Menard published "An Address to the Free Colored People of Illinois," a text modeled on the Declaration of Independence. In this address, his first publication, Menard implored black Americans to "Awake!—from your long sleep of inactivity and death—from darkness to light— from the state of nominal 'chattels' to that of men of stability, of firmness and confirmed virtue." He indicts northern and southern whites alike in his condemnation of American slavery, the "monster" that "civilization and Christianity" hoped would perish long before. However, Menard continues, "He still lives … He is dressed in the cloak of the slaveholders; he is fed and petted by the dough-faces of the North."

By 1862 Menard had moved to Washington, D.C. According to the first edition of his book of poems, *Lays in Summer Lands* (1879), Menard became the first African American to hold a clerkship in the federal government when he accepted a post in the Bureau of Immigration, Interior Department. As part of his position the U.S. government sent him to Belize (at the time, British Honduras) to examine the country's potential for African American colonization, a plan that Menard endorsed.

Menard also traveled to Jamaica, where he met and married his wife, Elizabeth (maiden name unknown). They had three children, Willis Jr., Mary Jeanette, and Alice. While in Jamaica, Menard founded the Workingmen's Literary Society of St. David and wrote letters that were published in two Jamaican newspapers, *Watchman* and *Sentinel*. Menard's liberal politics, as expressed in these controversial letters, earned him scorn and suspicion among the island's planter class. His outspokenness, his position as leader and founder of the Workingmen's Literary Society, and his friendship with the politician Samuel Clark all proved dangerous for Menard after the outbreak of the Morant Bay Rebellion in 1865. Jamaican authorities led by the British governor Edward Eyre accused Menard of sedition and of working in complicity with the rebels and deported him.

Upon his return to America, Menard was appointed inspector of customs in New Orleans. His family relocated to New Orleans, his parents' birthplace, which was under martial law. Though tensions were high, Menard was protected by federal forces and performed well his tasks as inspector and later as commissioner of streets. He became active in the Republican Party and is said to have aided in the ratification process for the Reconstruction-mandated Louisiana state constitution. While in New Orleans he published and edited the *New Orleans Free South*, which later became the *New Orleans Radical Standard*.

In 1868 Menard was nominated to run for the U.S. House of Representatives from Louisiana's Second Congressional District to complete the late James Mann's unfinished term. Easily defeating his white opponent, Caleb S. Hunt, by a margin of more than two thousand votes, Menard became the nation's first African American elected to the U.S. House. However, Congress denied Menard his seat when his opponent contested the election. Menard pled his case before the House in the first-ever address given by an African American before Congress. His speech was praised by the northern media, but neither the plea nor the press was enough to convince the House that the time had come to admit an African American to Congress. Though neither Menard nor Hunt was given the seat, the government paid them half the wages that each would have earned had he been seated.

It is thus not surprising that in 1871 Menard chose to leave New Orleans to seek better opportunities in Jacksonville, Florida. There he purchased land, published the *Florida Sun*, remained active in the Republican Party, and reentered politics, receiving appointments for postal clerk and deputy collector of internal revenue in Jacksonville and running successfully in 1873 for a seat in the state legislature. Two later attempts to win a seat in the U.S. Congress as a representative from Florida were unsuccessful. Most notably, an 1874 race for the seat held by JOSIAH WALLS, Florida's first black congressman, led to a bitter feud during which Walls and a third candidate, John R. Scott, launched a smear campaign based on ambiguous charges of impropriety filed against Menard by a New Orleans woman shortly before Menard left Louisiana. Menard denied the claims, noting that the woman sought only to blackmail him and that the charges had been resolved in the Louisiana courts. Nevertheless Menard left the race.

In 1874 he was named a justice of the peace in Duval County, and in 1876 he was elected a delegate to the Republican National Convention in Cincinnati. Growing disillusionment with the carpetbaggers in Florida after the elections of 1869 and 1874 led Menard to question publicly the Republican Party's dedication to African Americans. His disaffection caused him to run unsuccessfully as an independent in the 1876 congressional elections. In 1877 Florida's Democratic governor reappointed Menard a justice of the peace.

Meanwhile Menard turned his attention overseas and sought to become a diplomat in South America, but he failed to win a nomination. He secured a position as a customs inspector, this time in Key West, Florida, where he later served as editor of the *Florida News* (also known as the *Island City News*) and gained a reputation as a courageous journalist willing to engage controversial issues.

Eclipsed by his political achievements, Menard's literary career has been largely forgotten. In 1879 Menard compiled years of writings, some of which had appeared earlier in newspapers, and published a collection of poetry entitled *Lays in Summer Lands*. Most of the poems are set in Florida, though a few treat topics such as Menard's Illinois youth, Caribbean culture, and the political landscape of Washington, D.C. "To Lincoln" and "Stanzas on Cuba" testify to Menard's political and social convictions, while "The Wife's Invocation" and "In Mama's Bed" speak of more intimate relationships. Though modern critics debate the aesthetic value of Menard's verse, *Lays in Summer Lands* met with considerable acclaim from both black and white critics in Florida.

While living in Jacksonville, Menard befriended the poets DANIEL A. PAYNE, who spent his winters in the town, and Thomas M. D. Ward. The publication of *Lays in Summer Lands* marked the beginning of a poetic boom for black Americans in Florida, a boom that continued for generations. Menard's work is thought to have been an inspiration for the likes of T.-THOMAS FORTUNE. Menard also influenced the young JAMES WELDON JOHNSON, whose family had once lived in Jacksonville and socialized with the Menards.

In 1884, when the Democrat Grover Cleveland won the presidential election, Menard left the customs position that he felt he would inevitably lose and returned to Jacksonville. There he published the relocated *Florida News* as the *Southern Leader*, an influential, civil rights–oriented black newspaper with a strong editorial voice. In 1889, however, after again trying unsuccessfully to secure a foreign post, he moved to Washington, D.C., to work as a clerk in the census office. He also helped organize the Southern States Colored Republican Organization and set the groundwork for a new monthly magazine, the *National Afro-American*. But his failing health prevented the magazine's launch.

Menard died in Washington, D.C. His obituary notice celebrated the wide range of his political, social, and literary contributions. The sentiments of these final memorials are best summarized in the praise of Frederick G. Barbadoes, a prominent antislavery and civil rights leader, who wrote in his preface to the first edition of *Lays in Summer Lands* that for Menard's "brave and determined efforts to prove the ability of his race, he deserves their approval, and that of every true lover of justice and equality."

FURTHER READING

Beaty, Bess. "John Willis Menard: A Progressive Black in Post–Civil War Florida," *Florida Historical Quarterly* 59 (Oct. 1980).

Heuman, Gad. *The Killing Time: The Morant Bay Rebellion in Jamaica* (1994).

Menard, John Willis. *Lays in Summer Lands*, eds. Larry Eugene Rivers, Richard Mathews, and Canter Brown Jr. (1879, 2002).

Sherman, Joan R., ed. *African-American Poetry of the Nineteenth Century: An Anthology* (1992).

JENNIFER LARSON

Mendez, José (1888–6 Nov. 1928), baseball player, was born José de la Caridad Mendez in Cárdenas, Cuba. The names of his parents are unknown. Mendez developed his physique by chopping sugarcane as a boy. At age twenty he startled the baseball world by pitching what was almost a no-hitter against the touring Cincinnati Reds. A scratch single in the ninth spoiled the bid. Two weeks later, playing with one of Cuba's two leading professional teams, Mendez pitched sixteen more shutout innings against the Reds.

Cuban fans hailed him as *el Diamante Negro* (the Black Diamond), and newspapers in the United States began calling him "the black Mathewson," after the New York Giants star Christy Mathewson. Old-timers said that Mendez's fastball "looked like a pea" and that his curveball "looked like it was falling off a pool table." After his showing against the Reds, Mendez sailed to Key West, Florida, with a Cuban squad and pitched what may have been the first integrated baseball game in the southern United States—a no-hitter against a local club.

In the winter of 1908–1909 in the Cuban professional league, Mendez won fifteen games and lost six. Barnstorming in the United States with a Cuban professional team the following summer, he was credited with forty-four wins and two losses, presumably against semiprofessional opponents. That autumn Mendez was back in Havana as the two top Cuban teams, the Havana Reds and the Almendares Blues, won eight of the twelve games against the American League champion Detroit Tigers. Ty Cobb did not play in the series, but the following winter the Tigers brought Cobb along. He had one hit and struck out once facing Mendez, who lost the game 6 to 3. Over the winter Mendez's record with Almendares was 11 and 2.

When the New York Giants' manager John McGraw's National League champions arrived in Havana in 1911, the American players spent their World Series money nightclubbing and lost their first two games. "I didn't come down here to let a lot of coffee-colored Cubans show me up," McGraw thundered, and the next day Mathewson beat Mendez, 4 to 0. However, the following week Mendez and another Cuban pitcher, Eustaquio Pedroso, combined to defeat Mathewson 7 to 4. Mendez's totals against major leaguers came to eight victories—including one against the Philadelphia Athletics' Hall of Fame pitcher Eddie Plank—and eight defeats.

McGraw was much impressed by the dark-skinned Cuban pitcher, declaring that "José Mendez is better than any pitcher except Mordecai Brown and Christy Mathewson—and sometimes I think he's better than Matty." McGraw said that he would have paid fifty thousand dollars for Mendez, "if only he were white." Although McGraw, in his wife's words, "bemoaned the failure of baseball, himself included, to cast aside custom or unwritten law … and sign a player on ability alone, regardless of race or color," he would not violate existing racial taboos and "thus settled for players who were undeniably Cuban." The first light-skinned Cubans soon appeared on U.S. major league teams, but Mendez was left to a career of barnstorming.

From 1912 until 1915 Mendez's Cuban league win-loss record was 9-5, 1-4, 10-0, and 2-0. He spent summers traveling by bus through the U.S. prairie states with the All Nations team out of Kansas City—a team that included American blacks, Cubans, Asians, and even one woman. They barnstormed through small midwestern towns, offering a baseball game in the afternoon and a dance band at night. Mendez played pitcher, shortstop, and cornet. One of his best games took place in Chicago in 1912 when he dueled the great black pitcher RUBE FOSTER to a twelve-inning 2 to 2 tie.

In 1916 Mendez was warmly received on arriving in San Juan, Puerto Rico. He entertained guests with his guitar each evening while coaching baseball by day. He is given much credit for spreading the popularity of baseball to Puerto Rico and from there to other Caribbean nations.

In 1920, when Rube Foster formed the first successful black league in the United States, the Negro National League, Mendez joined the Kansas City Monarchs, owned by former All Nations owner J. L. Wilkinson. Mendez was the manager, the team's shortstop, and occasionally a pitcher. He played nine games at shortstop in 1920, batting .061, but he hit .284 the following season. No records have been found for 1922, but in the Monarchs' pennant-winning season of 1923, Mendez's pitching record was 8 and 1. Monarchs pitcher Chet Brewer recalled Mendez as "a good teacher, a man of very high character, and a very neat dresser. Just an all-round class guy."

As the manager, Mendez led the Monarchs to two more pennants, in 1924 and 1925. The 1924 team faced the Philadelphia Hilldales in the first modern black World Series. The series went ten games, including one tie, and Mendez put himself in to pitch the final game. "Gray, gaunt, and grim," as one newspaper described him, he pitched eight shutout innings, and the game went into the ninth tied 0–0 before the Monarchs won.

No records for Mendez's next few years have been located. He died in Havana, probably in 1927, from tuberculosis. His family asked for government financial help to pay for the funeral.

A striking commentary on how white Americans' prejudice hobbled Mendez's career was provided in 1923 when another great Cuban pitcher, the light-skinned Dolf Luque, returned home in triumph after leading the National League with twenty-seven victories for the Cincinnati Reds. Luque was given a parade, a new car, and more. Spotting Mendez on the sidelines, Luque went over and embraced him. "You should have gotten this car," he said. "You're a better pitcher than I am. This parade should have been for you."

FURTHER READING
Holway, John B. *Blackball Stars: Negro League Pioneers* (1988).

This entry is taken from the *American National Biography* and is published here with the permission of the American Council of Learned Societies.

JOHN B. HOLWAY

Menéndez, Francisco (c. 1709–177?), Spanish militia captain, corsair, and founder of the first free black town in what became the United States, was born in "Guinea" (a name used by Europeans and Americans for the slave-trading coast of West Africa) to unknown parents. Menéndez's birth date and birth name are also unknown, but when he was baptized a Catholic he took the name of his Spanish godfather, the royal accountant in St. Augustine, and Menéndez's former owner.

Enslaved as a young man, Menéndez was transported to South Carolina by British traders to work alongside large numbers of Africans already herding cattle, cutting timber, and producing naval stores, indigo, and, later, rice. Soon Carolina was said to be "more like a Negro country" (Wood, 132), and planters began to fear retaliation from the slaves who now outnumbered them. Slave revolts rocked Carolina periodically in the first decades of the eighteenth century.

Then in 1715 the Yamasee Indian war erupted in Carolina, and Menéndez and other enslaved Africans saw their chance to escape bondage. Fleeing their masters, they joined the Yamasee to fight English colonists who were exploiting both groups. Had reinforcements not arrived from other English colonies, they might have succeeded in driving the English from Carolina. The Yamasee chief Jorge (George) testified in 1738 that Menéndez and three other escaped slaves fought with his forces for several years before they were ultimately defeated and fled south across the international border to Spanish Florida.

Spanish officials had recorded the arrival of escaped slaves from Carolina as early as 1687 when eight men and two women from Carolina requested Catholic baptism in St. Augustine for themselves and a nursing child. Other runaways soon followed, and Florida's governor, Manuel de Montiano, asked for royal guidance. Spain's state religion, Roman Catholicism, encouraged the conversion of other races to the "True Faith," and in 1693 King Philip II issued a decree "giving liberty to all ... the men as well as the women ... so that by their example and by my liberality others will do the same" (Landers, 25). The initiative and determination of those enslaved Africans changed Spanish

policy and shaped the geopolitics of the Southeast and the Caribbean for years to come. Because of them Menéndez and his followers would become free. Although Spaniards also held slaves, Spanish law more so than English law recognized slaves as human beings with souls and legal personalities; under English law slaves were considered chattel or property, on par with a cow or a piece of furniture, with no legal personality or voice. Enslaved persons living in Spanish colonies could buy their freedom or win it by meritorious acts, such as military service and, in some cases, religious conversion. Moreover, Spain and England were locked in a cycle of territorial and religious warfare, and St. Augustine suffered frequent attacks from English colonists to the north. In an effort to fulfill his Christian obligation to grant religious sanctuary, while also fortifying his northern border, in 1738 Florida's governor freed Menéndez and others who had escaped from the English and authorized them to establish the first free black town in what is today the United States, Gracia Real de Santa Teresa de Mose. The site where Mose stood has been designated a National Historic Landmark, and a museum now interprets this story for local schoolchildren and visitors.

Menéndez and the other new homesteaders of Mose wrote to express their gratitude to the king of Spain and vowed to be "the most cruel enemies of the English," and to risk their lives and spill their "last drop of blood in defense of the Great crown of Spain and the Holy Faith" (Landers, 30). The black homesteaders included skilled craftsmen who soon built a fort, a church, and homes for a population of almost one hundred people. They planted crops on the periphery of their new town and fished and gathered oysters from the nearby creek. A Catholic priest assigned to Mose instructed the newcomers in the tenets of the faith, and once they were examined, he baptized them all. The new Spanish subjects then ratified their marriages in the Catholic faith. Menéndez and his wife, Ana María de Escovar, were married on 28 December 1739, and their entry in the parish registry states that they were both Mandingas who had once belonged to the royal accountant named Francisco Menéndez. A census taken of Mose in 1759 lists Menéndez's age as fifty-five and Ana María's as thirty-nine, although these are rough estimates only.

Less than two years after the town was built, however, England declared war on Spain, and in 1740 Governor James Oglethorpe of Georgia led a major invasion of Florida and occupied Mose. Its residents were forced to take refuge in St. Augustine. Seven ships of the royal navy sailed up from Jamaica to join the assault. Menéndez led many sallies against the invaders, and his troops eventually helped retake Mose. The Spanish governor recognized the black troops' bravery in reports to the king, noting especially that of Menéndez. Menéndez, who was literate in Spanish (and probably also in Arabic), wrote the king two letters recounting his military services and asking for appropriate compensation. Hoping to get to Spain to seek his reward in person, Menéndez became a corsair who harried British ships and settlements along the Atlantic coast. On one voyage Menéndez was captured by Englishmen who tortured him in retaliation for "Bloody Mose" (Landers, 37). His captors sold Menéndez into slavery in the Bahamas, but by 1759 the indomitable captain had regained his freedom and the leadership of Mose. In 1762 Spain finally ceded Florida to England in a peace treaty, and Menéndez, his wife, their four children, and the rest of the Mose residents joined other Floridians evacuating to Cuba. The Spanish Crown gave each refugee new lands, food, tools, and an African slave, and Menéndez and other black Floridians helped establish a new town called San Agustín de la Nueva Florida in Matanzas Province. Harsh conditions on the Cuban frontier eventually drove Menéndez and his family back to Havana, where they received a subsidy from the Spanish government and where Menéndez ended his days. The African-born Menéndez spent more than fifty years of his long life fighting for freedom and more than forty years serving the Crown of Spain that freed him.

FURTHER READING

Deagan, Kathleen, and Darcie MacMahon. *Fort Mose: Colonial America's Black Fortress of Freedom* (1995).

Landers, Jane. *Black Society in Spanish Florida* (1999).

Wood, Peter H. *Black Majority: Negroes in Colonial South Carolina from 1670 through the Stono Rebellion* (1996).

JANE G. LANDERS

Mercer, Mabel (3 Feb. 1900–20 Apr. 1984), cabaret and concert singer, was born Mabel Alice Wadham in Burton upon Trent, Staffordshire, England, the daughter of Benjamin Mercer, an African American tumbler or acrobat, and Emily Mame Wadham, an English-Welsh music hall entertainer. Mabel's parents were unmarried, and Mabel was reared by her maternal grandparents in north Wales in a family of singers, dancers, and painters. Her mother, before going on a world tour, put Mabel on an empty music hall stage and, after climbing to the balcony, yelled, "All right, sing! And I want to understand every word!" Mabel experienced the first of lifelong stage fright, but her mother heard every word (Balliett, 60). At age seven Mabel was placed in a Catholic convent school in Manchester, where she—because she had golden skin, frizzy black hair, and her mother's blue eyes—was ridiculed and called a golliwog. To make matters worse she was a "gammy," who crossed herself with her left hand. Mabel responded by becoming the traditional "seven-year-old Catholic for life" who never missed a day at Mass. She left school at age fourteen, and when she learned her father's name, she took Mercer as her surname and began a long but unsuccessful search for him.

As a music hall singer and dancer, she was generally fired as soon as the manager noticed her hair. Mercer was rescued by an aunt who, with her husband and sons, had a traveling vaudeville troupe in the Midlands. To accommodate her hair they became the Five Romanys, a gypsy song and dance group. During World War I, Mercer and a Cockney girl named Kay sang and danced in France, Belgium, and the Netherlands, wherever they could find engagements. As one of the Chocolate Kiddies, Mercer wore an enormous blond beehive wig. When Mercer first met black entertainers from America, the girl who had thought that she was the only "colored" person on the planet was transported. In a revue called *Coloured Society*, she performed minstrel acts mixed with Italian opera, ballads, and spirituals. Mercer starred as the soprano in *Lucia* and was inspired to take concert singing lessons. When the flu pandemic of 1918 swept Europe, the teenager, wearing white tie and tails and a monocle, replaced the ailing orchestra director.

Though Mercer sang in both the London and the Paris choruses of Lew Leslie's *Blackbirds of 1926*, recognition as a soloist began at clubs in Paris, where American jazz was the rage. Soft-voiced and shy, she sang with a small megaphone in a pure soprano as she moved from table to table, enchanting the international set at BRICKTOP's famous cafe with her humor and charm. Her devoted fans included Edward, Prince of Wales; Marlene Dietrich, who arranged the recording of an early Mercer song, "You'd Better Go Now"; and the American expatriates Ernest Hemingway, Gertrude Stein, and F. Scott Fitzgerald. Mercer performed the sassy compositions of Cole Porter and met the jazz pioneers DUKE ELLINGTON and LOUIS ARMSTRONG and the singer-actor PAUL ROBESON. Songs were composed especially for her. Mercer could belt out "Black Minnie Sings the Blues" and "Mandy," or reduce grown men to tears with ballads by Jerome Kern, Oscar Hammerstein and Richard Rodgers, and Lorenz Hart. Her style, enunciation, and phrasing introduced a new style of singing popular songs. The nonjudgmental depths of her understanding won her a devoted following, especially among homosexuals.

World War II forced Mercer to flee to New York in 1938. Her mother, now residing in upstate New York and fearing reprisals from white neighbors, pretended to be her daughter's aunt. To Mercer's keen disappointment they seldom met. Mercer lived in Harlem and opened at Le Ruban Bleu at 4 East Fifty-sixth Street. When a tonsillectomy changed her voice to a husky mezzo-soprano, she rose to fame. During an unprecedented seven years at Tony's, a small New York nightclub, the "*doyenne* of American popular singing" introduced a vast range of ballads, poetry, and show tunes, all while seated with great dignity in a high-backed chair.

"What a lesson to watch that entrance," said BOBBY SHORT, one of Mercer's many disciples. "A monarch adored by and adoring all her subjects.... She developed enormous style such as I had never heard. It was a wonderfully warm, entertaining, informing presence. I often saw Sinatra and BILLIE HOLIDAY and LENA HORNE and even Edith Piaf in her audience." Frank Sinatra himself said, "Her gift with a song is enough to make other vocalists seek a different occupation." To Leonard Bernstein she was "the eternal guardian of elegance in popular music" (William Livingstone, "The Singer's Singer," *Stereo Review*, Feb. 1975). Metropolitan opera star Eileen Farrell considered Mercer the best teacher that she ever had, despite the cabaret singer never teaching a lesson in her life. Margaret Whiting remembered, "One night Peggy Lee, Duke Ellington, Frank Sinatra, and I were there at the same time and we all agreed that we sat at her feet.... When she would start to talk about lyrics, she would say, 'Just mean them.' I think Mabel had the most respect of anyone in entertainment. She was very special and beloved."

Mercer engaged in a "paper marriage" in 1940 to the young African American singer Kelsey Pharr II, who predeceased her in 1960. She became a U.S. citizen in 1952.

Mercer sang the French street song "Tu reviendras" to open the Pulitzer Prize–winning opera *The Consul*, by Gian Carlo Menotti, which won the New York Drama Critics Award for 1950. However, like most of the great stars of the golden age of cabaret—the 1940s and 1950s—Mercer found herself, with the closing of nightclubs during the next three decades, with fewer and fewer singing engagements. She bought a farm near Chatham, New York, and moved there in the late 1950s, living happily with her dogs and cats but returning to New York City for occasional appearances. As she grew older, she suffered financial hardship. Among her close friends were the prolific composer Alec Wilder and her manager and lover, Harry Beard.

Despite her failing voice, Mercer was rediscovered and made more famous in her seventies by the young agent Donald F. Smith. After Beard's death in 1981, Smith revived "Mabel Mercer Madness." She sang to sell-out audiences at the Playboy Clubs in London and Chicago, as well as touring in Los Angeles and San Francisco. Her seventy-fifth birthday was celebrated at an enormous party at the St. Regis Hotel in New York, where a plaque marked the Mabel Mercer Room. Atlantic Records reissued many of her recordings as "A Tribute to Mabel Mercer on the Occasion of Her 75th Birthday." She appeared twice in concert with her friend and disciple Eileen Farrell in the Kool Jazz Festival and at Alice Tully Hall, both in New York City. Mercer was the first distinguished recipient of *Stereo Review*'s Mabel Mercer Award; President Ronald Reagan honored her with the Presidential Medal of Freedom in 1983.

Mercer died in Pittsfield, Massachusetts, and was buried beside Harry Beard. Her fame continued to grow after her death. The Mabel Mercer Foundation, a nonprofit corporation organized by Smith and others, launched annual weeklong Cabaret Conventions at Town Hall, New York City, in 1986. These soon burgeoned into other cabaret events, spreading to San Francisco and elsewhere. Mercer's posthumous influence led to cabaret contagion in the 1990s and created new venues for gifted vocalists and for the classic American popular song.

FURTHER READING

Mercer's papers are at the Schomburg Center for Research in Black Culture, New York Public Library.

Balliett, Whitney. *Alec Wilder and His Friends* (1974).

Cheney, Margaret. *Midnight at Mabel's: The Mabel Mercer Story* (2000).

Haskins, James. *Mabel Mercer: A Life* (1987).

This entry is taken from the *American National Biography* and is published here with the permission of the American Council of Learned Societies.

MARGARET CHENEY

Meredith, James Howard (25 June 1933–), civil rights activist, was born J. H. Meredith near Kosciusko, Mississippi, the son of Moses "Cap" Meredith, a farmer, and Roxie Smith Meredith, a school cafeteria worker. J.H. adopted the names James Howard when he entered the U.S. Air Force in 1951; until then he went by the initials given to him by a father who did not want neighboring whites to call his son by his first name only. Indeed, the stubborn—some might say, reckless—courage that James Meredith displayed in integrating the University of Mississippi owed much to the example of his father, who refused to display the deference expected of blacks in Jim Crow Mississippi. Cap Meredith viewed his eighty-five-acre homestead as a sovereign state and ruled it like a patriarch. He restricted his children's contacts with outsiders, black or white, and prohibited them from ever entering a white family's home by the back door or from working in service to whites. The Merediths

also instilled in their children a passionate belief in the power of education; all ten completed high school, and seven attended college, a remarkable feat in the segregated, desperately poor Mississippi hill country of the 1940s.

On graduating from high school in 1951, Meredith joined the air force, serving first in Kansas and then Japan as a clerk-typist, rising in rank to staff sergeant. After his military service, he hoped to return to Mississippi to study law and to carry out what he described in his autobiography as a "divine responsibility" to end white supremacy in his home state (21). In the meantime, he took classes at the University of Kansas, Washburn University in Topeka, Kansas, the U.S. Armed Forces Institute, and the University of Maryland's Far Eastern Division in Japan. He also maintained a keen interest in the emerging civil rights movement, though he drew greater inspiration from DAISY BATES's efforts to integrate the schools in Little Rock, Arkansas, than from the nonviolent philosophy espoused by MARTIN LUTHER KING JR. during the 1955 bus boycott in Montgomery, Alabama.

Meredith later recalled that he found the concept of nonviolence "crazy," at least when applied

James Meredith, walking to class accompanied by U.S. marshals, 1 October 1962. (Library of Congress.)

to Mississippi (Doyle, 20). He believed that blacks could secure full citizenship rights only if they were supported by the full force of the U.S. military, as had been the case at Little Rock when President Dwight D. Eisenhower sent in the 101st Airborne Division to escort nine black students into Central High School. Meredith viewed his goal of ending white supremacy as a "war," but after receiving an honorable discharge from the air force in 1960, he kept his powder dry for a time, returning home to study history and political science at Jackson State College, a black institution.

The student sit-in movement that began in Greensboro, North Carolina, in early 1960 had not yet spread to Mississippi, but Meredith joined a secret society on the Jackson State campus that distributed antisegregation pamphlets and debated the possibility of active opposition to Jim Crow. In January 1961, however, having decided that it was time to move beyond debate, he applied for admission to the all-white University of Mississippi. MEDGAR EVERS, the field secretary of the Mississippi NAACP, offered his assistance and persuaded the national NAACP Legal Defense Fund (LDF) to provide Meredith with the legal expertise needed to overcome the university's inevitable opposition. Meredith proved to be exactly the kind of determined plaintiff needed to win such a case, although his "Messiah complex" and self-righteousness often exasperated the LDF's CONSTANCE BAKER MOTLEY (Doyle, 32). Such tenacity paid off, however, in June 1962, when Judge John Minor Wisdom of the Fifth Circuit Court of Appeals condemned the University of Mississippi's "carefully calculated campaign of delay, harassment, and masterly inactivity" and ordered Meredith's immediate admission. Only a "man with a mission and a nervous stomach," Wisdom concluded, could have broken the color line at Ole Miss (Doyle, 33).

Yet Wisdom's ruling neither completed Meredith's mission nor settled the applicant's stomach, because Mississippi's governor, Ross Barnett, vowed to defy what he called the "unlawful dictates" of the federal government and even traveled to the Oxford campus to personally—and theatrically—block Meredith's admission. Barnett's flagrant defiance of federal authority climaxed in his inflammatory speech before an Ole Miss football game on 29 September 1962, one day before Meredith's scheduled arrival on campus. One spectator later recalled that the students "were being whipped into a fever-pitch of emotion by their own leaders … it was just like the Nazis had done" (Dittmer, 140). What the crowd did not know was that Barnett, for all of his outward bravado, was secretly negotiating with Attorney General Robert Kennedy to allow Meredith's admission. The next day, one hour after marshals escorted Meredith into his dormitory, thousands of white students, townspeople, and segregationists from out of town began an armed riot that left two men dead, injured 168 marshals, and left the bucolic, magnolia-lined campus looking more like a war zone. Federal authorities later confiscated scores of guns and other weapons from fraternity houses such as Sigma Nu, although that fraternity's president, Trent Lott—who was later the majority reader of the U.S. Senate—reportedly ordered his brothers away from the riot for their safety. Although President John F. Kennedy made a nationally televised appeal for calm, peace was restored only when he ordered in twenty-three thousand combat troops. One day later, under heavy military escort, James Meredith became the first African American to register at Ole Miss.

After graduating nine months later, Meredith studied at Ibadan University in Nigeria and began work toward a law degree at Columbia University in New York. In 1966, however, he set out on what appeared to be another iconoclastic mission: a "walk against fear" from Memphis, Tennessee, to Jackson, Mississippi, aimed at persuading blacks in his home state that, following the passage of the 1965 federal Voting Rights Act, it was now safe to register to vote. Meredith's march attracted the attention of only a few reporters until he was shot three times as he crossed the Mississippi border; fortunately, his assailant had been armed only with buckshot, but Meredith was hospitalized with some eighty pellets embedded in his body.

Images of the shooting brought the leading lights of the civil rights movement to Mississippi to continue Meredith's march. They succeeded in adding thousands of new black voters to the electoral register. Meredith rejoined the final leg of the march from Tougaloo College to Jackson, where fifteen thousand people gathered to hear King declare Meredith's walk against fear "the greatest demonstration for freedom ever held in Mississippi" (Dittmer, 402). The march also exposed fissures in the civil rights movement as younger activists, such as the Student Nonviolent Coordinating Committee's STOKELY CARMICHAEL, responded to violent intimidation by state troopers by advocating a more aggressive philosophy of "black power," much to the consternation of King and others still committed to nonviolence.

After publishing a well-received autobiography, *Three Years in Mississippi* (1966), and receiving a law degree from Columbia in 1968, Meredith faded from public view. He taught briefly at the University of Cincinnati in Ohio, ran several unsuccessful campaigns for Congress; and managed a nightclub and a car rental business. Many who had lauded his courage at Ole Miss were incredulous, however, in 1989, when he took a position as a special assistant to Jesse Helms, the far-right-wing senator from North Carolina. They were horrified, too, two years later, when Meredith advocated support for David Duke, a former—though unrepentant—Louisiana Klansman running for the U.S. Senate. Following the death in 1979 of June Wiggins, his first wife and the mother of his three sons, Meredith married Judy Allsobrook, a journalist, and adopted her son and daughter.

Defeating white supremacy in Mississippi was no easy task. It would take men and women as obdurately defiant as James Meredith, Medgar Evers, and FANNIE LOU HAMER to overcome the will of a white majority determined to keep blacks as second-class citizens. Though many commentators viewed Meredith's rightward shift in the 1980s as strange—or even heretical—his seemingly erratic career makes more sense if he is viewed, rather, as an iconoclast. Neither consistency nor propriety mattered much to Meredith, but nobody could accuse him of lacking determination. As Medgar Evers once noted, James Meredith had "more guts than any man I know," but he also found him to be "the hardest headed son-of-a-gun I ever met" (Doyle, 32).

FURTHER READING

James Meredith's papers are housed in the Department of Archives and Special Collections, J. D. Williams Library, University of Mississippi, Oxford, Mississippi.

Meredith, James. *Three Years in Mississippi* (1966).

Dittmer, John. *Local People: The Struggle for Civil Rights in Mississippi* (1994).

Doyle, William. *An American Insurrection: The Battle of Oxford, Mississippi, 1962* (2001).

STEVEN J. NIVEN

Meriwether, Louise (8 May 1923–), writer, author, and social activist, was born Louise Marion Jenkins in Haverstraw, New York, the third child and only daughter among five children of Marion Lloyd Jenkins, a bricklayer and house painter, and Julia Jenkins, a domestic worker. Meriwether's parents were from South Carolina and, typical of many black families, migrated north in search of increased opportunity. From Haverstraw, the family moved to Brooklyn and finally settled in Harlem. During the Great Depression and owing to an inability to find legitimate work to support his family, Marion Jenkins became a numbers runner. Louise Meriwether later acknowledged that she grew up under "mean circumstances," with the family eventually entering the welfare roles. She spent her formative years in Harlem, attending P.S. 81 and graduating from Central Commercial High School located in Manhattan in 1940. During World War II she worked as a file clerk for the Navy Department in Washington, D.C. In 1944 she returned to New York and worked as a secretary during the day and studied English at New York University by night, graduating with a B.A. in 1949. Eventually she married Angelo Meriwether, a Columbia University graduate student who became a teacher. When he obtained a teaching position in St. Paul, Minnesota, the couple moved there and eventually relocated to Los Angeles. Her marriage to Meriwether ended in divorce although she retained his name. A brief second marriage to Earl Howe, a bus driver, ended in divorce as well. No children were born from either union.

Meriwether was always determined to become a writer. She became a reporter for the *Los Angeles Sentinel*, where she remained from 1962 to 1964, and then enrolled full-time in the graduate school at the University of California (UCLA), graduating with an M.A. in Journalism in 1965. From 1965 to 1967 she became a story analyst for Universal Studios, the first black to be hired in that position. Committed to writing, Meriwether published book reviews and news articles for the *Los Angeles Times* and *Los Angeles Sentinel*. She also contributed articles to predominantly black publications, such as *Negro Digest*, where she wrote "James Baldwin: The Fiery Voice of the Negro Revolt" (Aug. 1963) and "An American Dilemma, The Negro: Half a Man in a White World" (Oct. 1965), a call to African Americans to demand their civil rights. Meriwether then put her commitment to-civil rights into action by becoming a Congress of-Racial Equality (CORE) worker in Bogalusa, Louisiana, during the summer of 1965. There she carried guns in her oversized purse for a black radical group, the Deacons for Defense and Justice, who offered protection to black citizens against intimidation from the Klu Klux Klan.

In 1967 Meriwether became a full-time staff member for the Watts Writers' Workshop, where she gained more success as a writer after the *Antioch Review* solicited works from the group for publication. Her *Antioch Review* contributions, including, in 1967, a chapter from her unpublished novel, *Daddy Was a Number Runner*, and the short story "A Happening in Barbados" (1968), brought her to the attention of the editor Bill Gross at Prentice-Hall. Admiring her writing, he requested a copy of *Daddy Was a Number Runner*. The press eventually published the manuscript in 1970, becoming the first novel to be published out of the Watts Writers' Workshop.

It took Meriwether approximately three years to complete writing *Daddy Was a Number Runner*, delayed by a nine-month hiatus to oppose the Hollywood film adaptation of William Styron's controversial novel *The Confessions of* NAT TURNER (1967). David L. Wolper, A Twentieth Century–Fox producer, had bought the film rights and teamed with the director Norman Jewison to bring the novel to the big screen. Meriwether and other black intellectuals were outraged by Styron's negative, emasculating depiction of Nat Turner and determined to stop the production of the movie. In particular, she joined with Vantile Whitfield, founder of the Performing Arts Society of Los Angeles, to organize the Black Anti-Defamation Association (BADA). Although Styron bitterly complained that Hollywood surrendered to the whims of black militants like Meriwether, the organized effort to halt the film's production created meaningful dialogue on the accurate images of historical black figures.

Daddy Was a Number Runner brought Meriwether much acclaim. The story highlights the maturation of twelve-year-old protagonist, Francie Coffin, and the debilitating poverty she and her family, neighbors, and community suffered in Harlem during the Great Depression. Partially autobiographical, the novel gave a realistic account of the devastating effects poverty, racism, and oppression had on a black community. Impressed by the work, JAMES BALDWIN wrote its foreword and the book received positive reviews in the *New York Times Book Review* and in the *New Yorker*.

Before the publication of *Daddy Was a Number Runner*, Meriwether moved back to New York, in 1969, to continue her writing. She was awarded two grants, from the National Endowment for the Arts and the New York Foundation for the Arts. Disturbed by the distorted view of black heroes in children's historical literature, Meriwether wrote to correct this oversight. In three consecutive years she wrote books for children based on the lives of famous black figures: *The Freedom Ship of* ROBERT SMALLS (1971), *The Heart Man: Dr.* DANIEL HALE WILLIAMS (1972), and *Don't Ride the Bus on Monday: The* ROSA PARKS *Story* (1973). Meriwether wrote a fictional short story in *Black Review* (1972) called "That Girl from Creektown" based on her CORE activities.

After the publication of "Creektown," Meriwether returned to social activism. Concerned with black Americans' violating the boycott of the Organization of African Unity (OAU) by visiting South Africa, Meriwether formed the Committee of Concerned Blacks. She teamed with JOHN HENRIK CLARKE, who had edited a book that critically examined Styron's *Confessions of Nat Turner*, and collaboratively wrote and distributed a pamphlet called *Black Americans Stay out of South Africa*, and spoke on radio and at the United Nations to gain support for the anti-apartheid effort. The campaign successfully persuaded some prominent black Americans, notably MUHAMMAD ALI, from traveling to the embattled country.

Meriwether spent several years teaching the fiction writing workshop at the Frederick Douglass Creative Arts Center and the Harlem Writers Guild in New York, and writing courses at Sarah Lawrence College. She traveled to Charleston and the Sea Islands to conduct historical research for her next novel, *Fragments of the Ark* (1994), a fictionalized account of the Robert Smalls story. She wrote a third novel, *Shadow Dancing* (2000), a contemporary love story, and in all of her novels she sought to portray black people positively and honestly.

Although not as well known or prolific as some of her contemporaries, Meriwether played a pivotal role in adding to the literary discourse of black female writers. She successfully merged her writing and social activism to become a powerful voice to advocate for black concerns in the United States.

FURTHER READING

Noble, Jeanne. *Beautiful, Also, Are the Souls of My Black Sisters: A History of the Black Woman in America* (1978).

Schraufnagel, Noel. *From Apology to Protest: The Black American Novel* (1973).

Walker, Melissa. *Down from the Mountaintop: Black Women's Novels in the Wake of the Civil Rights Movement, 1966–1989* (1991).

Washington, Mary Helen. *Black-Eyed Susans: Classic Stories by and about Black Women* (1975).

ALEXIS D. MCCOY

Merrick, John (7 Sept. 1859–6 Aug. 1919), insurance company founder and entrepreneur, was born a slave in Sampson County, North Carolina. Merrick never knew his father, but his mother, Martha, was a strong presence in his life. Little is known of Merrick's early years, except that, to help support his mother and brother, he began working in a brickyard in Chapel Hill when he was twelve. In 1877 he moved with his family to Raleigh, where he worked as a helper on the crew that constructed the original buildings on the campus of Shaw University. Merrick could have remained in the construction trade—he advanced to brick mason, a highly skilled and relatively well-paid occupation—but he had far greater aspirations. Merrick's first goal was to open his own barbershop, one of the few business opportunities open to black southerners at that time. So he soon quit being a brick mason and took a menial job as a bootblack in a barbershop, in the process learning the barbering trade. After becoming a barber in Raleigh, Merrick began to attract as his customers several of the area's most prestigious men, among them the tobacco magnates Washington Duke and Julian S. Carr, who convinced him and another barber in the shop, John Wright, to move to the nearby tobacco town of Durham and open a decent barbershop there.

Durham was a quintessential "New South" city. Created in the wake of burgeoning industrialization in the region, Durham was a frontier of sorts, undeveloped and open, one of the few places in the South where African Americans had a chance of achieving success on their own terms. Merrick and Wright opened a shop in Durham in 1880 and ran it together until 1892, when Wright sold out to Merrick. Soon after arriving, Merrick began to branch out, purchasing in 1881 the first of many lots in Hayti, the developing African American section of town, where he himself lived. Merrick constructed small rental houses on these lots, eventually becoming one of Hayti's largest landholders. In the late 1890s he expanded his barbering business—at one time owning as many as nine shops—and also developed a broadly advertised cure for dandruff.

Merrick's most significant involvement during his early years in Durham was his purchase, along with several others, of the Royal Knights of King David, a black fraternal order, in 1883. An important feature of the Royal Knights, as with other fraternal orders of the era, was the provision of insurance plans to its members. Merrick came to realize, however, that the meager death benefits

offered by the Royal Knights were not enough to provide adequate coverage for African Americans. As a result, in conjunction with several other prominent blacks in Durham and Raleigh, Merrick founded the North Carolina Mutual and Provident Insurance Company in Durham in 1898. The firm began operations in April 1899 but almost failed after six months, primarily from lack of adequate attention by the founders. At that point Merrick and AARON MCDUFFIE MOORE, Durham's first black physician, bought out the other investors and reorganized the firm as the North Carolina Mutual Insurance Company. They also hired CHARLES CLINTON SPAULDING, a relative of Moore's, to take over full-time management of the concern. Although Merrick was not the firm's operating manager, he was the primary figurehead during its first two decades. Initially, North Carolina Mutual only underwrote industrial insurance, but the firm soon expanded into industrial straight life and, later, into other policies. Income, which was just $840 in the company's first year, had surged to about $1.7 million by 1919, the year of Merrick's death.

North Carolina Mutual was only one of Merrick's many business enterprises in Durham. He was vice president of the Mechanics and Farmers Bank, organized in 1907. A vitally important element in the development of local capitalist ventures by African Americans, Mechanics and Farmers Bank helped Durham become what the sociologist E. FRANKLIN FRAZIER called the "capital of the black middle class." By the early 1920s, when the bank had more than $600,000 in deposits and assets of $800,000, it had become a crucial source of capital for blacks who wanted to purchase homes and start small businesses. In 1910, when BOOKER T. WASHINGTON visited Durham, he described it as the most progressive city in the South and praised Merrick for his incomparable leadership in the black business community.

Merrick's real estate purchases led him to join with Moore and Spaulding in organizing the Merrick-Moore-Spaulding Land Company to own and manage properties owned by Merrick and by North Carolina Mutual. In 1906 North Carolina Mutual established its own newspaper, the *Durham Negro Observer*. Its more successful successor, the *North Carolina Mutual*, was for decades the city's only African American newspaper. In 1908 Merrick and several others started the Bull City Drug Company to operate drugstores in Hayti. One of Merrick's most important, though short-lived, ventures was the Durham Textile Mill, established in

1914 to manufacture socks. The mill was historically significant because it attempted to show, contrary to white southern myth, that African Americans could profitably be employed as textile workers.

At Merrick's death, from cancer, he was survived by his wife, Martha Hunter, and four of their five children. His son Edward later served for many years as treasurer of North Carolina Mutual, which eventually became the largest black business enterprise in America (until after World War II) and which still operates in virtually every state. It was John Merrick's organizational ability, his contacts with the white community, and his status in the broader African American community that did much to make the venture the success it became. His influence with wealthy whites was well known. It was Merrick who persuaded the Duke family to provide funds for the establishment of the private Lincoln Hospital in 1901. Indeed, Merrick's greatest talent was perhaps his ability to push for greater economic and social opportunities for blacks while adapting those efforts to the realities of the time. In seeking white investment for various black business concerns, he never put the independence of those ventures in jeopardy.

FURTHER READING

Andrews, Robert McCants. *John Merrick: A Biographical Sketch* (1920).
Kennedy, William J. *The North Carolina Mutual Story* (1970).
Weare, Walter B. *Black Business in the New South: A Social History of the North Carolina Mutual Insurance Company* (1973).

This entry is taken from the *American National Biography* and is published here with the permission of the American Council of Learned Societies.

JOHN N. INGHAM

Merriweather, "Big Maceo" (31 Mar. 1905–23 Feb. 1953), blues piano player whose style influenced practically every post–World War II blues pianist of note, was born Major Merriweather, on his family's farm near Atlanta, Georgia. He was one of eleven children. Major was nicknamed "Big Maceo" as an adult, because of his large stature. He stood well over six-feet tall and weighed more than 250 pounds. Around the age of fourteen, he developed an interest in the piano. He taught himself to play and soon began performing at cafes, rent parties, and fish fries throughout the Atlanta area.

In 1924, when Merriweather was nineteen, his family joined the great migration of people leaving the South for Detroit in search of better economic opportunities. Merriweather secured a job with the Ford Motor Company, but still played at house parties and clubs when his schedule allowed. It was at one of these house parties that he met his wife, Hattie Spruel. Hattie hired him to play for a few of her parties. Believing in her husband's talent, she began promoting him around town. When the two moved to Chicago, Illinois, in 1941, she managed to score a meeting between Merriweather and the renowned Chicago guitarists TAMPA RED and "BIG BILL" BROONZY. Red and Broonzy had both moved from the South to Chicago in the 1920s in pursuit of individual musical aspirations. Like Merriweather, they both developed their craft playing at rent parties and other small, social gatherings. Tampa Red caught his big break when he was asked to accompany the legendary MA RAINEY on a recording in 1928. He also collaborated with THOMAS A. DORSEY, known at that time as "Georgia Tom," as the "Hokum Boys," who recorded over eighty sides in a bawdy, humorous style known as "hokum." Dorsey would later leave the blues behind and go on to become one of the most famous gospel recording artists in the world.

Red and Broonzy were very impressed with Big Maceo and introduced him to Lester Melrose, who had produced Tampa Red and Thomas A. Dorsey's 1929 hit, "It's Tight Like That." Melrose had also enjoyed success with Broonzy. Within a few weeks of meeting Melrose, Big Maceo was in the studio recording for the RCA Victor Bluebird label. In his very first session, Big Maceo recorded fourteen tracks—six of his own and eight more as an accompanist to Tampa Red. That session produced his first hit record, "Worried Life Blues," which would become the most important recording of his career. Big Maceo and Tampa Red went on to record a number of songs together for Bluebird, creating a unique, new sound that became known as the "The Bluebird Beat." Big Maceo developed his style listening to players such as ROOSEVELT SYKES, ALBERT AMMONS, and MEADE "LUX" LEWIS, prominent contemporaries of Maceo on the Chicago blues scene. It was LEROY CARR's laid-back vocal style, however, that Maceo patterned his own vocals after. Big Maceo took the sounds of the barrelhouse and boogie that his contemporaries had become known for and added heavier bass patterns, creating his own sound that would prove to be quite popular. With this style, he produced a string of hits that included "Chicago Breakdown," "Texas Stomp," and "Detroit Jump."

Big Maceo's career was, unfortunately, cut short after he suffered a stroke in 1946 that left him paralyzed on his right side. He attempted to record a few more times, despite his handicap, pairing with up-and-coming pianists such as Eddie Boyd and Johnny Jones to play the right side of the piano during recording sessions. OTIS SPANN would sometimes fill in for him at gigs whenever he was unable to perform. All three of these musicians went on to become headliners on the Chicago Blues scene, having learned at the side of Big Maceo Merriweather.

After suffering a second stroke in 1949, Maceo retired from playing. Four short years later, he suffered a fatal heart attack in Chicago. Although his career was brief, his influence on the urban blues genre is unquestionable. "Worried Life Blues," his first record, has become a blues standard and has been covered or performed by everyone from CHUCK BERRY to Eric Clapton. It was among the first batch of songs inducted into the Blues Hall of Fame.

FURTHER READING

Keil, Charles. *Urban Blues* (1992).

Johnson, Greg. "Big Maceo Merriweather." *Blues Notes*, Jan. 2000.

Rowe, Mike. *Chicago Blues: The City and Music* (1981).

KAHLIL GROSS

Metcalfe, Ralph Harold (30 May 1910–10 Oct. 1978), track-and-field athlete and U.S. congressman, was born in Atlanta, Georgia, the son of Clarence Metcalfe, a stockyard worker, and Marie Attaway, a seamstress. He moved to Chicago, Illinois, in 1917, grew up in a slum area on the South Side, and attended Tilden Technical High School. Metcalfe won the 1929 interscholastic track-and-field sprint championship and, as a member of the Chase Athletic Club, captured the 1930 Amateur Athletic Union (AAU) junior 100-yard title in 9.7 seconds.

A 5-foot 11-inch, 180-pound speedster, Metcalfe attended Marquette University, breezing through the 1932 track-and-field season undefeated in both the 100-meter and 200-meter dashes and taking both events at the NCAA and AAU championships. That same year Metcalfe dethroned Eddie Tolan as the dominant American sprinter. On 11 June he tied Tolan's world mark in the 100-yard dash and shattered the world record in the 220-yard dash. At the Olympic trials Metcalfe bested Tolan in both the 100-meter and 200-meter dashes.

During the 1932 Los Angeles, California, Summer Olympic Games, however, Tolan edged Metcalfe in the 100-meter dash in 10.3 seconds in one of the closest races in Olympic history. Tolan's time broke both Olympic and world records. Although favored to take the gold medal, Metcalfe false started and did not respond quickly to the second shot of the starter's pistol. Tolan led the race until Metcalfe pulled even at 80 meters. Several hours later, seven judges viewed a film of the race and determined that Tolan crossed the finish line two inches ahead of silver medalist Metcalfe. Metcalfe won the bronze medal in the 200-meter, trailing Tolan's record-breaking 21.2 seconds by 0.3 of a second. Metcalfe may have been deprived of a gold medal because his lane was inadvertently two meters longer than it should have been. He did not protest the results, however, because other African Americans had garnered the gold and silver medals. Following Tolan's departure, Metcalfe dominated the sprints from 1933 to 1936. Noted for his strong

Ralph Metcalfe, on the track in Milwaukee, Wisconsin, in an undated photograph. (AP Images.)

finishes, Metcalfe tied the world 100-meter record three times officially and the world 200-meter mark once. His victories included the 100-yard and 220-yard dashes at the 1933 and 1934 NCAA championships, the 100-meter dash at the 1933 and 1934 AAU championships, and the 200-meter dash at the 1933, 1934, 1935, and 1936 AAU championships. In 1936 he repeatedly defeated JESSE OWENS in 100-yard dash competition until one week before the U.S. Olympic trials. Metcalfe may have been a better sprinter than Owens, capturing two more NCAA crowns and five more AAU titles.

The politically charged 1936 Berlin, Germany, Summer Olympic games showcased Adolf Hitler's Nazi dictatorship and belief in the supremacy of the "Aryan" race. Hitler boasted publicly that his athletes would prevail and scorned what Nazi newspapers termed "America's black auxiliaries." America's black athletes, however, quickly demolished Hitler's supremacist propaganda. Owens earned a gold medal with a 10.3-second time in the 100-meter dash, edging Metcalfe by one second. The 400-meter relay team, consisting of Owens, Metcalfe, Foy Draper, and Frank Wykoff, romped to a gold medal by 15 yards. The quartet covered the 400-meter distance in 39.8 seconds, setting a world record that endured for 20 years. This historic race marked Metcalfe's final track-and-field competition.

Metcalfe earned a PhB (an undergraduate degree) from Marquette University in 1936 and an M.A. in Physical Education from the University of Southern California in 1939. From 1936 to 1942 he taught physical education and political science and coached track and field at all-black Xavier University in New Orleans. Metcalfe served in the U.S. Army as a first lieutenant from 1943 to 1945, receiving the Legion of Merit for directing the physical training of troops.

After moving to Chicago in 1945, Metcalfe operated an insurance agency. He directed the Department of Civil Rights for the Chicago Commission on Human Relations from 1945 to 1949 and headed the Illinois State Athletic Commission from 1949 to 1952. Metcalfe married Madalynne Fay Young in 1947; they had one child.

Metcalfe joined the Chicago Democratic Party organization as an assistant precinct captain in 1949 and controlled patronage as Third Ward committeeman from 1953 to 1972. He served on the Chicago City Council from 1955 to 1971, becoming president pro tempore in 1969. Metcalfe, a close ally of Mayor Richard Daley from 1955 to 1972, advanced rapidly because of his loyalty to the political machine and

his popularity as a former sports hero. He chaired the powerful Building and Zoning Committee.

In 1970 WILLIAM LEVI DAWSON (1886–1970), political boss of the South Side ghetto in the overwhelmingly black First Congressional District, retired from the U.S. House of Representatives after serving fourteen terms. Metcalfe was elected to Dawson's seat in 1970 after defeating Alderman A. A. "Sammy" Rayner in a spirited Democratic Party primary. He was reelected to the House in 1972, 1974, and 1976 and won the 1978 Democratic primary, but he died a few weeks before the general election.

Metcalfe fought discrimination in transportation and consumer affairs while serving on the House Committee on Interstate and Foreign Commerce and its subcommittees on Transportation and Commerce and Consumer Protection and Commerce. He insisted that the administration of federal programs remain equitable for all Americans. Metcalfe wrote comprehensive antidiscrimination provisions in the Railroad Revitalization and Regulatory Reform Act, added two anti-redlining amendments to the no-fault auto accident insurance legislation, and helped defeat the Waxman amendment, which would have prohibited special programs for minorities in medical schools.

Housing and employment issues particularly interested Metcalfe. He insisted that homeowners be compensated for deficient appraisals and helped secure a $22 million Housing and Urban Development grant for the huge Robert Taylor housing project in his congressional district. Metcalfe protested discrimination in the treatment of minority prisoners and deplored widespread unemployment among black people, urging adoption of the Humphrey-Hawkins bill of 1978.

Metcalfe also belonged to the House Committee on Merchant Marine and Fisheries and chaired its Subcommittee on the Panama Canal. Besides wholeheartedly supporting the Panama Canal treaties in 1977, he diligently sought to protect human rights, improve housing conditions, and expand educational and job opportunities of Panamanians.

Metcalfe served as secretary of the Democratic Study Group, as vice chairman of its task force on crime and drug abuse, and as a member of the Democratic Steering and Policy Committee. He authored the Amateur Sports Bill of 1978, which provided federal funds to sponsor American Olympic athletes.

In 1971 Metcalfe joined the Congressional Black Caucus, comprising all thirteen African American members of the House of Representatives. The group, which monitored federal enforcement of civil rights laws, consisted of Democrats representing poor, urban, predominantly black congressional districts. He and LOUIS STOKES of Ohio co-chaired the Health Brain Trust.

Low-income and middle-class constituents provided the core of Metcalfe's support within his congressional district. The poor were attracted by his control of patronage jobs, while the middle class liked his law-and-order stance against South Side youth gangs. Metcalfe represented his constituents in a methodical, reserved style, mastering political detail and working deliberately.

Black militants, meanwhile, opposed Metcalfe until 1972, when he broke with Mayor Daley and spoke out against alleged police brutality toward black Chicagoans. The Afro-American Patrolmen's League charged that the Chicago Police Department had verbally and physically abused South Side residents. Metcalfe arranged extensive negotiations with the police superintendent James Conlisk on ways of increasing confidence among blacks in the police department and enlisting black community support for work against street crime. Mayor Daley, however, abruptly terminated the talks and made only minor changes.

Metcalfe also opposed Mayor Daley's attempt to renominate Edward Hanrahan as state's attorney for Cook County in 1972 and declared that it would be impossible for him to deliver the Third Ward. According to Metcalfe, Hanrahan had supervised a 1969 raid fatal to two Black Panther Party officials and had tried to frame the raid's survivors for attempted murder. Hanrahan won reelection despite being indicted for obstruction of justice.

Metcalfe continued to criticize the Chicago police, exploiting the law-enforcement issue among South Side blacks. Daley, fearing that Metcalfe might use Chicago's African Americans, one-third of the city's population, as a base to capture the entire party organization, unsuccessfully ran formidable opponents against Metcalfe in subsequent Democratic congressional primaries. Metcalfe retaliated by supporting an unsuccessful liberal challenger to Daley in the 1975 Democratic mayoral primary.

In 1973 Metcalfe arranged a panel of concerned Chicago citizens to help protect South Side residents from alleged mistreatment by police. The same year he sponsored congressional legislation to make municipal corporations legally and financially responsible for damages assessed against an individual police officer. Metcalfe's measure encouraged cities to improve selection, training, and supervision of police officers. He also served as a director of the National Council to Control Handguns.

Metcalfe participated in several civil rights and athletic organizations. His civil rights activities included work with the National Association for the Advancement of Colored People, the Urban League, the Joint Negro Appeal, the Mahalia Jackson Scholarship Fund, and the Dr. Martin Luther King Urban Progress Center. He cochaired the organizing committee for the 1959 Pan American Games at Chicago, was elected to the U.S. Olympic Committee in 1969, and served on the President's Commission on Olympic Sports from 1975 to 1977. His Ralph H. Metcalfe Foundation promoted athletic, health, and educational programs for ghetto youth and support for needy Chicago families.

Metcalfe held enormous athletic and political significance for African Americans. He, along with Eddie Tolan, began a long period of dominance by African American sprinters in track and field. Metcalfe was elected to the Helms Athletic Foundation Hall of Fame, Black Athletes Hall of Fame, U.S. Track and Field Hall of Fame, National Track and Field Hall of Fame, and Wisconsin Hall of Fame. His political independence of the Daley machine paved the way for the rise of HAROLD WASHINGTON as the first black mayor of Chicago. Metcalfe died at his Chicago apartment.

FURTHER READING
Ashe, Arthur R., Jr. *A Hard Road to Glory* (1993).
Cornfield, Michael. *Ralph H. Metcalfe: Democratic Representative from Illinois* (1972).
Porter, David L., ed. *Biographical Dictionary of American Sports: Outdoor Sports* (1988).
Obituaries: *Chicago Tribune* and *Chicago Sun-Times*, 11 Oct. 1978.
This entry is taken from the *American National Biography* and is published here with the permission of the American Council of Learned Societies.

DAVID L. PORTER

Metoyer, Augustin (22 Jan. 1768–19 Dec. 1856), slave, wealthy landowner, and community leader, was born Nicholas Augustin Metoyer in Natchitoches, in the Spanish colony of Louisiana. His mother was MARIE-THÉRÈSE COINCOIN, a slave and later a free woman and successful agriculturalist, and his father was Claude Thomas Pierre Metoyer, a wealthy French merchant and planter with whom his mother had a nineteen-year liaison. Marie-Thérèse was enslaved when Augustin and his twin sister Marie Susanne were born, and he was subsequently bought by his father on 31 May 1776 from Madame de St Denis, along with three of his siblings, for 1,300 livres. He grew up as the oldest male child in a wealthy household, where, in an unusual situation, an enslaved woman and a white man cohabited almost completely openly. Although Pierre Metoyer never explicitly acknowledged his children with Marie-Thérèse as his own, most of them took his name, and even before they were emancipated, they were treated as free in the Natchitoches community. Pierre Metoyer was a well respected member of the Natchitoches community, and it seems that Augustin Metoyer inherited many of his father's characteristics. In 1777, when still a boy, he acted as a godfather at a baptism, and he would serve this role for many dozens of free people of color over the decades.

When Pierre and Marie-Thérèse separated in 1786, Augustin Metoyer was still owned by his father, and he probably continued to live and work with him. On 1 August 1792 at age twenty-four, Metoyer was freed, and shortly after, on 22 August, he married Marie Agnes Poissot, another free person of color, who was the daughter of a slave and a prominent local white planter. The couple was extremely prolific. Their first child, Marie Modeste, was born about 1793, and over the following fifteen years they had eight more children: Jean Baptiste Augustin, Jean Baptiste "Maxille", Marie Louise, Auguste Augustin, Marie Pompose, Joseph Augustin, Marie Suzanne, and Francois Gassion.

In 1795, Metoyer was granted his first tract of land on the Cane River, south of Natchitoches. Two years later, he bought his first slave, a young man of about twenty years. In 1800, he began to buy and liberate family members: Rose, the daughter of his brother LOUIS METOYER, then a year later, Marie Perine, who then married his brother Pierre. Metoyer continued to buy and liberate slaves with family connections, and to offer loans to others to purchase their family members, for the rest of his life. Over the next ten years Metoyer accumulated land through astute deals with his neighbors, and at the same time he purchased slaves to work on these plantations. In 1809 he bought eight enslaved Africans, a man, five boys, and two girls, all for $3,500, and a year later he owned seventeen slaves. Through buying more slaves, and through his own slaves bearing children, by 1820 this figure had risen to twenty-five slaves. In 1813, he bought a whole family—Ned and Ginnee, with their

children Mina, Jack, and Ketty. We know many of the names of Metoyer's slaves at this time, because as a Catholic, he encouraged his slaves and those of his neighbors to be baptized at his house. Buying and emancipating family members while continuing to buy and keep slaves was not seen as contradictory at this time in Louisiana for free blacks. As the key means of developing a labor force and accumulating wealth, buying slaves was necessary to create financial and social stability.

Metoyer's land purchases put him in an excellent position to profit from the cotton boom of the 1830s. He became one of the wealthiest men in the area, and his fortune, combined with that of his family, made the Metoyers one of the wealthiest families of African descent at that time in the United States. The small house built on his original land grant was joined by a more impressive mansion, and on the rest of his land Metoyer built two cotton gins, a grist mill, and twenty-two slave cabins. At the beginning of the nineteenth century, the community of free people of color living along the Cane River was a considerable distance from the nearest church in Natchitoches. To remedy this, Metoyer established a church specifically for his neighbors, but he also welcomed white Catholics who found the journey to Natchitoches too long. St. Augustine's Church was recognized in 1829, and in 1856 it was finally given its own parish. The current building was raised in 1916 and stands on Metoyer's original land grant on the Cane River.

Like many of his generation—including some prominent white planters—Metoyer was illiterate for much of his life, but he brought tutors from New Orleans to teach his family. At some point quite late in his life he learned to write, as evidenced by a note written and signed in his hand to a slave for payment for chickens. Metoyer had a very strong sense of justice, and throughout his life he was never afraid to defend his rights, often in court, against more powerful and wealthy white men. In 1807 Metoyer made a deposition about his rights in relation to a white man named Jacques Paillette, making it clear that he would defend them in the courts if necessary. The nature of this dispute is not stated. Many years later in 1835 Metoyer went to court with Francois Roubieu (a local white merchant) over a boundary dispute and won.

Metoyer and his family were always distant from the white community, but this was a respectful separation won and maintained through his sage handling of his business and personal life. A mark of his status at this time is the large portrait that he commissioned in 1836 from the New Orleans artist J. Feuille. Metoyer stares directly at the viewer, with his right hand gesturing to the church that bears his name in the background. This church became the home of the portrait. In 1840 Metoyer's wife died, and he effectively retired, dividing his land between his children. At this date his estate was worth $140,958. For the final sixteen years of his life he was a retiring yet patriarchal figure on the Cane River. He was known as Grandpère Augustin, and tradition recounts the awe in which he was held by residents of the area. He died in December 1856, and he is buried alongside his wife under an imposing tombstone directly behind St. Augustine's Church. His many descendants, later known as the Cane River Creoles, modeled themselves on his example of Catholicism, wisdom, and the importance of family values. His legacy is one of great achievement for a former slave who became not only extremely wealthy but also highly respected by all who knew him.

FURTHER READING

Surviving materials related to Metoyer and his family are in the Natchitoches Parish Courthouse, Natchitoches, and the Cammie G. Henry Research Center, Northwestern State University, Natchitoches.

Mills, Gary B. *The Forgotten People: Cane River's Creoles of Color* (1977).

Mills, Gary B. "A Portrait of Achievement: Nicholas Augustin Metoyer," *Red River Valley Historical Review* 2 (Fall 1975).

FIONA J. L. HANDLEY

Metoyer, Louis (c. 1770–11 Mar. 1832), slave, wealthy landowner, and community leader was born in Natchitoches, in the Spanish colony of Louisiana. His mother was MARIE-THÉRÈSE COINCOIN, a slave who became a free woman and a successful agriculturalist, and his father was Claude Thomas Pierre Metoyer, a wealthy French merchant and planter with whom his mother had a nineteen-year liaison. Marie-Thérèse was enslaved when Louis was born, and he was subsequently bought by his father on 31 May 1776 from Madame de St Denis along with three of his siblings, for 1,300 livres. Louis Metoyer's upbringing was unusual for its day. His parents shared a household in a scarcely disguised fashion, and unlike most other mixed-race families in the Louisianan upper classes, there was no white family to compete for the financial and emotional affection of the father. Pierre Metoyer reunited his children with Marie-Thérèse under one roof, and as one of the richest merchants and planters in the area, his children in some respects had an advantaged upbringing. Although he never explicitly acknowledged his children with Marie-Thérèse as his own, they all took his name, and even before they were emancipated, they were treated as free in the Natchitoches community.

By the time Marie-Thérèse and Pierre separated in 1786, Louis Metoyer was sixteen years old and was probably involved in many aspects of his father's work on the plantation. He petitioned the Spanish government for land in his own name on the Cane River, south of Natchitoches, in 1795, and he gained it in 1796. What makes the success of the claim unusual is that Metoyer was still legally a slave at this time. His claim to the land was later challenged in the courts by the previous occupier (though surprisingly, not on the grounds of Metoyer's former slave status), a case that Metoyer won in 1818. Metoyer was finally liberated by his father on 28 May 1802, although Pierre Metoyer backdated his liberation to 1 January 1801. By this point Metoyer had fathered five children, Catiche (who was bought and liberated by his mother), Rose, (who was bought and freed by his brother AUGUSTIN METOYER), Therese, Antoine, and Jean Baptiste Louis. On 9 February 1801, soon after his liberation, Metoyer married the mother of Jean Baptiste Louis, Marie-Thérèse Le Comte. Marie-Thérèse was half French and half Native American—her mother was an enslaved Kiowa Apache, described at that time as being of the "Cancey" nation. They had no children after their marriage, but they settled the land on the Cane River that Louis had been granted. When Louis claimed the land, it was unimproved and covered in thick cane beds backing into cypress forest. Clearing it was a huge challenge, and in 1802 Louis bought his first slave, George, aged thirty-five. This was a typical first purchase for a young man on a budget, for George, although still strong, would be past his peak and thus relatively cheap. Over the following years he bought other slaves including Marie, Jasmin, and three African boys. He also bought and freed two slaves, Baba and Françoise who at age forty-five and fifty-five were considered elderly as they would have been past their most productive for agricultural work. Although no ties to the Metoyer family are apparent, Metoyer promised that he and his heirs would protect them for life.

In the 1810 census, Metoyer is recorded as owning fifteen slaves, and by this time he was already acquiring land in the surrounding area. These purchases, along with his stable and efficient plantation economy, made it possible for him to take advantage of the rapid changes in agricultural production that took place in the following twenty years. During this period, agriculture began to focus on cotton, instead of maize and tobacco. As the size of Metoyer's land holdings increased, so did his slave holdings, both through purchases and through the births of children to his slaves. Many births are recorded in the Catholic Church records because Metoyer encouraged his slaves to be baptized by the local priest. Metoyer's faith was also manifested in the support he gave to his brother Augustin in founding St. Augustine's Church, which was created to serve the needs of the growing population of free people of color and their white Catholic neighbors.

Metoyer had initially built a house on the south side of his original land grant, but by about 1815 he had built a new structure, north of the river that divided his land grant. This timber-framed building became known as Yucca House. Archaeological excavations show that this house was a typical example of a home on a reasonably well-off plantation in the area, with glass windowpanes, imported English ceramics, and evidence that the occupiers had kept some precious ceramics from the 1780s. Metoyer, and indeed the rest of his family, were becoming increasingly wealthy; in 1820 he owned twenty-two slaves, and ten years later this had more than doubled to fifty-four slaves, making him one of the most important slave owners in the area. By the 1830s, Metoyer's increasing wealth permitted him to begin building a much larger brick plantation mansion near Yucca on the same plot of land, now known as Melrose Plantation. When he died on 11 March 1832, this house remained incomplete.

As one of the wealthiest men in the parish, and the son of one of the most powerful, Metoyer was an influential and well respected member of the Cane River community of free people of color. The descendants of this community survived as the Cane River Creoles, and Melrose, the house that Metoyer started to build, became the central location for the interpretation of their history. Melrose Plantation became one of the few plantation homes in existence that took the story of people of African descent as a key storyline, and it therefore played a national role in celebrating the contribution of this community.

FURTHER READING

Surviving materials related to Metoyer and his family are in the Natchitoches Parish Courthouse, Natchitoches, and the Cammie G. Henry Research Center, Northwestern State University, Natchitoches.

Gould, P., R. Seale, R. Deblieux, and H. M. Guidry. *Natchitoches and Louisiana's Timeless Cane River* (2002).

MacDonald, K. C., D. W. Morgan, F. Handley, A. L. Lee, and E. Morley. "The Archaeology of Local Myths and Heritage Tourism: The Case of Cane River's Melrose Plantation," *The Future of the Past: Papers in Honour of Peter Ucko*, ed. R. Layton Shennan and P. Stone (2006).

Mills, Gary B. *The Forgotten People: Cane River's Creoles of Color* (1977).

FIONA J. L. HANDLEY

Mfume, Kweisi (24 Oct. 1948–) television and radio host, U.S. congressman, and president and chief executive officer of the NAACP, was born Frizzell Gray, the first of four children of Mary Elizabeth Willis in Turners Station, Maryland. His mother worked at several occupations, including as an elevator operator and as a domestic, while Clifton Gray, his stepfather, was employed as a truck driver. Gray was raised believing that he shared the father of his three sisters; only later did he learn that he was not Clifton Gray's biological son. Gray spent his early childhood in Turners Station, a small rural black community thirteen miles south of Baltimore City, wedged between predominantly white Dundalk and Sparrows Point, home to Bethlehem Steel, the largest employer in the area. Founded in the late 1880s by an African American doctor, Turners Station was isolated on the western shore of the Chesapeake Bay. In the early 1940s the town had one doctor and one elementary school; older students had to commute to continue their education.

While Gray's youth was filled with typical rural pursuits, such as baseball, fishing, and crabbing, he also had to contend with an abusive stepfather and the limitations of segregation. As it did for many young African Americans of his generation, the civil rights movement politicized him, fostering the sense that he was a representative of his race and that his victories, whether on the baseball field or in the classroom, reflected back on his community. A distant descendant of Maryland slaves, Gray was aware of not only his family's experiences but also the history of the larger African American community. The contributions of leaders such as WILLIAM MONROE TROTTER and W. E. B. DUBOIS were well known in the Gray household and provided a foundation for his sense of history, racial consciousness, and community responsibility.

Gray's parents separated in late 1959, and by March 1960 his mother had moved the children to Baltimore's West Side, an urban center rich in politics and culture. Nationally recognized African American leaders, such as the civil rights attorney THURGOOD MARSHALL, and political families like the Mitchells of the NAACP and the Murphys of the Baltimore *Afro American*, had started their careers there. West Baltimore was also made famous by Pennsylvania Avenue, home of the Royal Theater and the New Albert Hall, which featured the best-known African American entertainers, including ELLA FITZGERALD, DUKE ELLINGTON, and BILLIE HOLIDAY, who spent her formative years in Baltimore.

Gray's adolescent experiences were shaped by the two worlds of west Baltimore. He attended school, sold copies of the Baltimore *Afro American* newspaper, owned by the Murphy family and led by CARL MURPHY, a longtime civil rights activist, who served as president and editor. Gray also played the French horn in the Falcon Drum and Bugle Corps. At the same time the world of the streets drew him away from respectable pursuits and introduced him to a demimonde of prostitution, gambling, and crime. By his own accounts he had thirteen brushes with the law, but most were not serious enough to land him in jail.

Gray's childhood ended abruptly with the death of his mother in April 1964. He discovered then that his biological father was Rufus "Rip" Tate, and not Clifton Gray, as he had always believed.

Kweisi Mfume, national president of the NAACP, voicing his organization's opposition to the presence of the Confederate flag on the Statehouse grounds in Columbia, South Carolina, 19 April 2002. (AP Images.)

Gray promised his mother on her deathbed that he would care for his younger sisters. In 1965 he left school, armed with only a tenth-grade education, working three poorly paying jobs, eventually moving into the more lucrative world of numbers running. It was on the streets in 1968 that he had his first brush with local politics, volunteering in the campaign of PARREN MITCHELL during his first run for Congress. Mitchell, the brother of CLARENCE MITCHELL JR., the head of the Washington, D.C., branch of the NAACP, would be one of the founding members of the Congressional Black Caucus, pioneering the road that Gray would follow.

In the early 1970s Gray began to abandon the world of the streets. He completed his GED and met Linda Shields, whom he married in 1972. He enrolled in the Community College of Baltimore, where he quickly developed into a skillful activist and organizer in the emerging black student movement. Gray cofounded the Black Student Union, served as the editor of the school newspaper, and led the protest and sit-in movement for a black studies program. He also led a student boycott of Gulf Oil because of its investments in South Africa. Gray merged his political activism with a budding career in radio broadcasting. For a short time he worked as an on-air host at WEBB, a radio station owned by the legendary entertainer JAMES BROWN. Gray's Sunday show featured music inspired by the civil rights and Black Power movements, speeches by MALCOLM X, and an open dialogue with his African American audience on racial justice. In many ways, Gray's programming choices were emblematic of the new generation of civil rights activists' merging of political and cultural traditions to promote a new and more radical political action. Gray changed his name to Kweisi Mfume, which he interprets as "conquering son of kings," a reflection of his new consciousness. His career as a student activist laid the foundation for his continuing crusade for racial justice, both nationally and internationally. After graduating from the Community College of-Baltimore, Mfume continued his education and political development at Morgan State University, a historically black institution, combining his interest in communications and politics. He was one of the founding members of Morgan's radio station, WEAA, and, after graduating magna cum laude from the university in 1976, he worked as its program director, using his own show as a format to discuss issues affecting the African American community. His marriage ended in part because of his political activities while in college, but Mfume's passion for activism was undiminished.

In 1979 Mfume ran as a Democrat for a seat on the Baltimore City Council, challenging politicians who ignored problems in the African American community and the iron-fisted governing style of Mayor William Donald Schaffer. In his grassroots campaign, he drew support from childhood and college friends and sought advice from well-known black business people and politicians, including VERDA F. WELCOME, the first African American woman elected to the state legislature in Maryland's history. Mfume displayed his trademark tenacity during this hard-fought campaign. Initially declared the loser by fewer than fifty votes, Mfume demanded a recount and was declared the winner by three votes. He served for seven years on the council, while continuing to host a talk show on WEAA. In 1984 he completed an M.A. degree in Liberal Arts at Johns Hopkins University, with a concentration in International Studies. As a member of the city council, Mfume promoted diversity in municipal agencies, increased opportunities for minority-owned businesses, fostered improvements in public safety, and cosponsored legislation that led to the divestment of city investments in South Africa.

Mfume's desire to effect change on both national and international levels inspired him to run for U.S. Congress in 1986, when Parren Mitchell announced his retirement. Although he faced vigorous opposition, Mfume was elected to the One Hundredth Congress by an overwhelming majority. Mfume joined a new generation of African American political officials who came of age during the civil rights movement, including FLOYD FLAKE of New York, JOHN LEWIS of-Georgia, and MICHAEL ALPHONSO (MIKE) ESPY of Mississippi, each in their first term in the House of Representatives.

Mfume served Maryland's Seventh Congressional District for ten years. He was instrumental in passing legislation for civil rights, fair housing, and the Americans with Disabilities Act. He continued working in broadcasting, hosting an award-winning Baltimore television talk show, *The Bottom Line*, for seven years. In 1993 he was elected chairman of the twenty-two-year-old Congressional Black Caucus (CBC), where he called attention to discrimination in corporate America, established a dialogue with the NAACP and the Urban League, and created a strong working relationship between the CBC and the Congressional Hispanic Caucus. In addition, Mfume was seated on the Banking and Financial Services, Ethics, and Small Business committees. During his third term he served on the Joint Economic Committee of the House and Senate, which he later chaired.

As part of a U.S. delegation, Mfume traveled to South Africa in 1994 to witness Nelson Mandela's inauguration. His numerous appearances on political programs hosted by the major television networks increased his national prominence. Respected as a politician who excelled at building interracial and intraracial bridges, and for representing all Americans, he also challenged the nation's leaders when he believed that they had failed the country. Mfume criticized President Ronald Reagan's unwillingness to impose sanctions on apartheid South Africa, opposed President George H. W. Bush's 1991 war in Kuwait and Iraq, and chided President Bill Clinton for his tardiness in addressing human rights violations in Haiti in the 1990s.

In February 1996 Mfume formally announced that he would leave Congress to serve as the president and CEO of the NAACP. The nation's oldest civil rights organization was at that time still reeling from financial problems, including a $3.2 million debt and the stormy two-year tenure of BENJAMIN CHAVIS as president. Mfume's skills as a legislator, his status as an elected official, and his ability to cross both race and class lines propelled the civil rights organization in a new direction. Along with civil rights, his vision for a revitalized NAACP addressed issues such as health care, economic and educational growth, political mobilization, and youth programs. As the head of the NAACP, Mfume launched a variety of campaigns, from increasing the numbers of people of color on television to increasing the participation of African Americans in local and national elections.

In 2004 Mfume parted company with the NAACP to prepare a run for the United States Senate. He launched his campaign to replace the Maryland senator Paul Sarbanes in March 2005. After a closely fought campaign for the Democratic nomination, Mfume lost out to Ben Cardin. His success in Baltimore, where Mfume gathered twice the number of votes as Cardin, sparked speculation he would run for mayor in 2007, but he eventually chose not to do so. In 2010, in the lead up to the passage of Health Care reform in the 111th Congress, Mfume was appointed President of the National Medical Association, representing 30,000 African-American physicians and their patients. He stepped down from that position in 2011.

FURTHER READING

Mfume, Kweisi. *No Free Ride: From the Mean Streets to the Mainstream* (1996).

Holmes, Steven. "The N.A.A.C.P.'s New Hope: Kweisi Mfume," *New York Times*, 11 Dec. 1995.

McConnell, Roland C., ed. *Three Hundred and Fifty Years: A Chronology of the Afro-American in Maryland, 1634–1984* (1985).

Snipe, Tracy D. "The Role of African American Males in Politics and Government," *Annals of the American Academy of Political and Social Science* 569 (2000): 10–28.

Swain, Carol. *Black Fences, Black Interests: The Representation of African Americans in Congress* (1995).

PRUDENCE D. CUMBERBATCH

Michaux, Lewis H. (4 Aug. 1885?–25 Aug. 1976), bookseller and black nationalist, was born in Newport News, Virginia, the son of Henry Michaux and Blanche Pollard. Some uncertainty about his birth date exists because his death certificate from the New York Vital Records Department lists it as 23 August 1884. Before coming to New York, Michaux worked variously as a pea picker, window washer, and deacon in the Philadelphia, church of his brother, LIGHTFOOT SOLOMON MICHAUX. According to Edith Glover, his secretary when he was a deacon, Michaux started selling books in Philadelphia with an inventory of five. When he founded his bookstore in 1932 in Harlem, he still had only a few books with him, including *Up from Slavery*, plus a bust of its author, BOOKER T. WASHINGTON. Michaux initially sold books from a wagon, then moved to a store on Seventh Avenue (later renamed Adam Clayton Powell Jr. Boulevard), at first sleeping at the back of the store.

Michaux quickly realized the necessity for a bookstore in Harlem. "You couldn't find 15 to 20 books by black people," he said (*New York Times*, 27 Aug. 1976). When the bookstore first opened, Michaux's daily receipts were often less than a dollar; when he retired, the daily receipts totaled up to $1,500 per day, and the National Memorial African Bookstore had become a Harlem landmark.

Michaux called his bookstore, which became the largest in Harlem, the "House of Common Sense and the Home of Proper Propaganda" and installed a sign over it reading, "Knowledge is power; you need it every hour. Read a book."

Michaux's bookstore attracted customers and visitors from all over the world, including his fellow black nationalist MALCOLM X, Kwame

Nkrumah (later the first president of Ghana), W. E. B. DuBois, Langston Hughes, Joe Louis, Eartha Kitt, and Louis Armstrong. The store became a landmark for black scholars and for anyone who was interested in literature by or about African Americans, Africans, Caribbeans, and South Americans. Michaux almost single-handedly operated his bookstore for forty-four years and increased his inventory to two hundred thousand volumes, making the store the largest in the nation devoted entirely to subjects concerning blacks and Africa. Professor John Henrik Clarke of Hunter College called the bookstore an "intellectual haven." Michaux influenced and advised many people of all ages, white and black. He encouraged average customers to begin home libraries and invited those who could not afford to buy books to sit down and read them without charge. "The ambition of our people was to make ends meet," he once said in response to the difficulty in getting Harlemites to read (*New York Times*, 31 Aug. 1976). This aspect of African American life, it was recalled at his eulogy, led Michaux to observe, "The way to hide something from the black man is to put it in a book."

In 1968 Michaux's store was moved from Adam Clayton Powell Jr. Boulevard to West 125th Street to accommodate the State Harlem Office Building, despite strong protests by Michaux and the community. In 1974 the store was closed after additional conflict with state authorities over its location.

Active in the black nationalism movement in Harlem from the 1930s to the 1960s, Michaux served as leader of the African Nationalists in America, backed Marcus Garvey's back-to-Africa movement, picketed in Harlem to promote black business, and protested the United Nations' actions in the Republic of the Congo (now Zaire) in the period 1960–1964. He also sat on the advisory board of the *Liberator* (established in 1961), a magazine that published the early work of many now-famous black authors and critics, including Amiri Baraka (LeRoi Jones), James Baldwin, Ishmael Reed, Ossie Sykes, Clebert Ford, and Hughes. Michaux deplored the term "Negro." He felt that it was a derogatory term used for slaves and that it denied African Americans their heritage. He preferred to use "black man." In addition, despite both his brother's career as an evangelist and his own upbringing, Michaux shunned the church, claiming that it robbed him of his individuality and saying, "No white God answers no black prayers. The only lord I know is the landlord, and I don't have to pray for him, he comes every month for the rent" (*New York Times*, 27 Aug. 1976).

Michaux was married to Bettie Kennedy and had one son. The first of three annual Lewis H. Michaux Book Fairs was held in May 1976, just three months before his death in the Bronx. In 1978 Ishmael Reed and Toni Morrison were the first recipients of the Lewis H. Michaux Awards, sponsored by the Studio Museum in Harlem.

Practical, outspoken, and self-reliant, Michaux was known as the world's greatest seller of books. His bookstore in Harlem came to symbolize the quest for knowledge that animated so many of the black nationalist movements of the twentieth century.

FURTHER READING

The Schomburg Center for Research in Black Culture of the New York Public Library holds an extensive collection of taped interviews, photographs, and published articles on Michaux.

Obituary: *New York Times*, 27 Aug. 1976.

This entry is taken from the *American National Biography* and is published here with the permission of the American Council of Learned Societies.

BARBARA KRALEY YOUEL

Michaux, Lightfoot Solomon (7 Nov. 1884–20 Oct. 1968), radio evangelist, was born in Newport News, Virginia, the son of John Michaux, a fish peddler and grocer, and May Blanche. Lightfoot, whose ancestry was African, Indian, and French Jewish, spent his formative years in Newport News among Jewish and white gentile merchants on Jefferson Avenue, the main commercial street where the Michauxs lived in quarters above the family's store. He attended the Twenty-second Street School, quitting after the fourth grade to become a seafood peddler. Impressed with the town's commercial atmosphere, he aspired to be a successful businessman. While engaged in one business venture, he met Mary Eliza Pauline, an orphan of mixed race. They married in 1906; the couple had no children of their own but helped raise Michaux's two young sisters.

During World War I, Michaux obtained government contracts to furnish food to defense establishments. With the profits from his enterprises he moved his business to Hopewell, Virginia, in 1917. Finding no churches in that wartime boomtown, he and his wife joined with a Filipino evangelist to found a church there. Michaux's wife subsequently convinced him to accept the call to preach, and in 1918 he was licensed and ordained in the Church of Christ (Holiness) U.S.A. He returned to Newport News in 1919, went into business with his father, and launched a tent revival. The first 150 of Michaux's converts formed a congregation within the Church of Christ denomination. In 1921 the Michaux congregation seceded from the Church of Christ to establish an independent church, calling it the Church of God. This church, along with its other related operations, was incorporated under an umbrella grouping known as the Gospel Spreading Tabernacle Association. In 1922 Michaux and several of his members were arrested for singing on the streets of Newport News during early-morning hours while inviting townsfolk to join the church. When Michaux was fined, he unsuccessfully appealed to the Virginia Supreme Court, contending that his actions were based on a directive from God. In 1924 he began to establish branch churches in cities along the East Coast as he followed members who had migrated north to find jobs during the postwar recession.

Michaux began his radio ministry in 1929 at station WJSV in Washington, D.C., and became famous as a radio evangelist. The broadcast moved to the Columbia Broadcasting System (CBS) in 1932, the eve of radio's golden era. As a result of the radio program's syncopated signature song, "Happy Am I," Michaux became known from coast to coast and overseas as the "'Happy Am I' Preacher." His aphorisms and fundamentalist-like sermons of hope and good neighborliness caught the attention of millions. His wife, an exhorter and the premier broadcast soloist, was a regular on the radio program. Michaux's radio program was so popular that American and foreign dignitaries flocked to his live, theatrically staged radio broadcasts. The British Broadcasting Corporation contracted with him for two broadcasts in the British Empire, in 1936 and 1938. Booking agents and moviemakers offered him contracts. In 1942 he collaborated with Jack Goldberg to make one commercial film, *We've Come a Long, Long Way*.

During the Great Depression, Michaux used his radio pulpit to offer free housing and employment services to the black and white indigent, and he invited the hungry to sell copies of the church's *Happy News* paper in exchange for meals in the Happy News Cafe. After President Herbert Hoover evicted the Bonus Army (fifteen thousand unemployed World War I veterans and their families who converged on the capital in 1932 to demand immediate payment of bonuses that were not due until 1945) for which Michaux had been holding worship services, Michaux used his radio pulpit to campaign for Franklin Delano Roosevelt in 1932, 1936, and 1940. For this reason, observers credit Michaux with influencing the first African Americans to leave the Republican Party and enter the Democratic fold in 1932. Political observers were baffled therefore when, in 1952, Michaux campaigned as vigorously for the Republican candidate Dwight Eisenhower as he had for Roosevelt and Harry Truman.

Crowds attended Michaux's annual baptisms, which he moved from the Potomac River bank in 1938 and held in Griffith Stadium until 1961. These patriotically festooned stadium services were full of pageantry, fireworks, and enthralling precision drills and choral singing from the 156-voice Cross Choir. Vocal renditions were supported by the syncopated instrumentation of the church band, while hundreds were baptized annually in a canvas-covered tank at center field. About Michaux and his baptismal services, Bill Sunday quipped that "any man who had to hire a national baseball park, seating 35,000 to hold ... meetings is the man to preach the gospel."

One reporter observed that Michaux should "not be passed off as just another gospel spreader ... but should be regarded as a shrewd businessman." He had made lucrative deals in real estate, such as the 1934 purchase of 1,800 acres of land along the beachfront in Jamestown, Virginia, where he intended to develop a National Memorial to the Progress of the Colored Race of America. His plans for selling investment shares fell through when lawsuits that alleged mismanagement of monies were filed against him. Around 1940 he purchased the old Benning Race Track in Washington and received $3.5 million from the Reconstruction Finance Corporation to construct Mayfair Mansions, a 594-unit housing development, which was completed in 1946. Despite allegations on Capitol Hill in the 1950s of favoritism from federal lending agencies, in 1964 he acquired $6 million in FHA loans to build Paradise Manor, a 617-apartment complex adjacent to Mayfair Mansions. These successes were due in part to his friendship with prominent Washingtonians, some of whom were honorary members of the "Radio Church."

While Michaux initially espoused race consciousness and proclaimed the brotherhood of all races, he became increasingly conservative in his later years. In the 1960s he criticized the civil rights and black nationalist movements and alleged that the activities of ELIJAH MUHAMMAD and MARTIN LUTHER KING JR. were contributing to racial polarization.

Because of his successful radio ministry in the nation's capital, Michaux had moved the church's headquarters there in 1929 and had renamed and reincorporated it several times. During the forty-nine years of his career he established seven churches and several branches and attracted a membership that numbered in the thousands. He amassed and bequeathed to the church an estate, consisting of temples, apartment dwellings, cafes, tracts of land, and private residences in several cities, that was estimated to be in excess of $20 million in 1968. When Michaux died in Washington, D.C., his radio program was estimated to be the longest continuous broadcast in radio annals.

Continuing to operate under the name Church of God, the institution founded by Michaux had three thousand members and eleven churches by the mid-1990s. Michaux's most significant contribution was in religious broadcasting, where he pioneered in the use of electronic and print media for worldwide evangelism.

FURTHER READING

The bulk of material on Michaux is located in the Church of God's headquarters in Washington, D.C. Additional correspondence is located in the Franklin D. Roosevelt, Harry Truman, and Dwight D. Eisenhower papers and in Department of Interior Correspondence in the National Archives. Sound recordings from Michaux's radio ministry are at the Library of Congress.

Lark, Pauline, ed. *Sparks from the Anvil of Elder Michaux* (1950).

Webb, Lillian Ashcraft. *About My Father's Business: The Life of Elder Michaux* (1981).

Obituaries: *New York Times* and *Washington Post*, 21 Oct. 1968.

This entry is taken from the *American National Biography* and is published here with the permission of the American Council of Learned Societies.

LILLIAN ASHCRAFT-EASON

Micheaux, Oscar (2 Jan. 1884–1 Apr. 1951), filmmaker, writer, and entrepreneur, was born on a farm near Metropolis, Illinois, the fifth of eleven children of the former slaves Calvin Swan Micheaux and Belle Willingham. After leaving home at age sixteen and working in several southern Illinois towns, he moved to Chicago and opened a shoe-shine stand in a white barbershop. Contacts he made there led to a job as a Pullman porter. Train porters were assigned to passengers for the length of their travel, and Micheaux took full advantage of the opportunity to mingle with wealthy whites and watch while they conducted business.

Micheaux fell in love with the Northwest and Great Plains while working the Chicago-to-Portland run, and in 1905 he used his savings to purchase land in southern South Dakota, on the newly opened Rosebud Sioux Indian reservation. By age twenty-five he had amassed five hundred acres and began publishing articles in the *Chicago Defender* with titles like "Colored Americans Too Slow to Take Advantage of Great Land Opportunities Given Free by the Government," urging African Americans to follow in his footsteps and take up homesteading. Micheaux's homespun "Go west, young black man" philosophy combined elements of Frederick Jackson Turner's "frontier thesis," principles of American exceptionalism and individualism, and

Oscar Micheaux, filmmaker, writer, and entrepreneur, in an undated photograph. (AP Images.)

BOOKER T. WASHINGTON's belief in racial uplift through self-reliance, "brains, property, and character." His confidence in the curative power of the western frontier and the successful pioneer formed the foundation of Micheaux's future efforts and attitudes.

In 1910 Micheaux married Orlean McCracken, the daughter of a Chicago minister who became the model for the villainous clergyman later depicted in Micheaux's films. Unhappy with pioneer life, she left the marriage within a year. Micheaux's bad luck continued with foreclosures of his land in 1912, 1913, and 1914. Looking for a new source of income, he wrote *The Conquest: The Story of a Negro Pioneer*, a thinly veiled autobiographical novel about the experiences of Oscar Devereaux, a lone African American homesteader in South Dakota. Micheaux, who had begun marketing the book even before its completion in 1913, sold copies door-to-door throughout the Great Plains and South. Sales were good, and he formed his own company, the Western Book Supply Company, through which he published and distributed two more semiautobiographical novels: *The Forged Note: A Romance of the Darker Races* (1915) and *The Homesteader* (1917). In 1918 the Lincoln Motion Pictures Company, which had been established three years earlier by the African American brothers Nobel and George Johnson, approached Micheaux about filming *The Homesteader*. After the brothers refused to let him direct the picture, Micheaux decided to make the film himself. He renamed his business the Micheaux Book and Film Company and raised fifteen thousand dollars by convincing small investors of the market potential for black films. *The Homesteader* (1919), an eight-reel silent film melodrama of love, murder, suicide, and passing, was the longest African American feature film produced by that date. Micheaux used photos of himself and ad copy that spoke directly to issues of race, "Every Race man and woman should cast aside their skepticism regarding the Negro's ability as a motion picture star, and go." His second film, *Within Our Gates* (1920), included a graphic scene of the lynching of an African American sharecropper, prompting consternation from both blacks and whites. He followed with *The Brute* (1920), starring the black boxer SAM LANGFORD, and the controversial film *The Symbol of the Unconquered* (1920), featuring a hero who strikes oil in the West and fights the Ku Klux Klan.

Micheaux produced an average of two pictures a year throughout the 1920s, including *The Gunsaulus Mystery* (1921), a reworking of the events surrounding the 1913 lynching of the Jewish Atlantan Leo Frank; *The Virgin of the Seminole* (1922), whose young black protagonist becomes a Canadian Mountie and successful ranchero; and *Deceit* (1923), the story of a black filmmaker, Alfred DuBois, who clashes with censors. Micheaux gave PAUL ROBESON his first screen role in *Body and Soul* (1925) and became the first black filmmaker to use African American source material with *The House behind the Cedars* (1924), based on CHARLES W. CHESNUTT's 1900 novel of the same name. The filmmaker also adapted several plays by the African American sailor HENRY FRANCIS DOWNING as well as the 1922 novel *Birthright* by the white southerner T. S. Stribling.

With more than twenty films in distribution, Micheaux filed for bankruptcy in 1928. Undeterred, he reemerged a year later as Micheaux Pictures, this time with backing from whites. By 1931, when he released *The Exile*, the first all-sound film made by an African American filmmaker, most black moviemakers were closing up shop. The advent of sound and Hollywood's foray into black-cast films were severely challenging the commercial viability of race movies. Micheaux responded by recycling material and themes and by remaking a half dozen of his silent films into "talkies." With a nod to Hollywood, he produced the musicals *The Darktown Revue* (1931) and *Swing!* (1938), and he introduced musical sequences and nightclub settings into his melodramas, suspense films, and gangster movies.

Micheaux suspended film production during World War II and returned to writing. Of the four novels he published in quick succession, *The Wind from Nowhere* (1944), proved the most successful, and he used the proceeds to make America's last race film, *The Betrayal* (1948). Although it was promoted as the "Greatest Negro photoplay of all time," audiences' apathy and poor critical reception doomed the picture and, with it, the last vestiges of race films.

While only thirteen of his films survive, Micheaux produced at least thirty-eight and perhaps as many as fifty films, making him the most prolific African American filmmaker. Working on the margins of a new medium, he told stories from a black perspective, populated by black characters. Micheaux, who entered the film business with little education and no contacts, succeeded by sheer entrepreneurial skill, creative vision, and salesmanship. He parlayed door-to-door sales into a grassroots promotional machine that both maximized the opportunities offered by established urban movie theaters catering to black audiences and introduced distribution and exhibition routes into underserved areas. Sweeping into town in a chauffeur-driven car, wearing a long fur coat and a wide-brimmed hat, Micheaux created a mystique around himself and a hunger for his films. He made extensive use of the African American press and built a following for his stars, in part through a star system modeled after white Hollywood, promoting LORENZO TUCKER as the "black Valentino," Slick Chester as the "colored Cagney," and Bee Freeman as the "sepia Mae West."

Courting controversy, Micheaux introduced into his films such explosive subjects as rape, church corruption, racial violence, and miscegenation. Protests were customary, and censor boards routinely rejected or severely edited the films. In a typical ruling, Virginia's censor board rejected *Son of Satan* (1924), claiming: "It touches unpleasantly on miscegenation. Furthermore, many of its scenes and sub-titles will prove irritating if not hurtful alike to quadroons, octoroons, half-breeds and those of pure African descent.... there is the intermingling of the two races which would prove offensive to Southern ideas ... [and the riot scenes] smack far too much of realism and race hatred" (Bowser, *Oscar Micheaux and His Circle*, 252). Micheaux turned protestations into promotion, advertising "banned" films and "uncensored" versions and aggressively selling his films' racial themes, which he often tied to current events of significance to African Americans. Advertisements for *The Homesteader* called the film "a powerful drama ... into which has been deftly woven the most subtle of all America's problems—THE RACE QUESTION," while ads for *The Dungeon* (1922) linked the film to the federal anti-lynching bill, known as the Dyer Bill. Several years later, promotion for *The House behind the Cedars* remarked on its parallel to the 1925 Leonard "Kip" Rhinelander case, in which a man sued for annulment after discovering that his wife was black.

Limited resources necessarily compromised quality, and the production values of Micheaux's films were poor. Crews were often hired by the day, with multiple camera operators working on the same film. Mixing professionals with amateurs was common. Action was generally filmed in one take, without benefit of rehearsal, and limited to one set, filmed on borrowed locations. To meet hurried production schedules, Micheaux edited his films based on the footage available, sometimes reediting, retitling, and rereleasing existing films. As Thomas Cripps explains, "It was as though [PAUL LAURENCE] DUNBAR or LANGSTON HUGHES published their first drafts without benefit of editing, their flair and genius muffled in casual first strikes" (183). A few contemporary scholars have disagreed, arguing instead that Micheaux was a maverick aesthetic stylist who intentionally eschewed what is now called Classic Hollywood Style.

Criticisms of Micheaux and his films from African Americans in general and the black press in particular began in the 1920s and became increasingly common by the 1930s. These voices decried what they perceived as Micheaux's preference for light-skinned actors, his "negative" depictions of African Americans, and the poor quality of his productions. Threats of protest and boycott often hung over the release of his films. A black critic voiced the concern of many when he took the filmmaker to task for his "intraracial color fetishism" where "all the noble characters are high yellow; all the ignoble ones are black" (*New York Amsterdam News*, 1930). Occasionally, censure came from outside the black community. Upon the release of *God's Stepchildren* (1938), the Young Communist League charged that the film "slandered Negroes, holding them up to ridicule" and set "light-skinned Negroes against their darker brothers" (Cripps, 342).

Micheaux died in 1951 in Charlotte, North Carolina, while on a promotional tour. He was survived by his wife of twenty-five years, Alice B. Russell, an actress who had appeared in and produced a number of his films. Despite, and perhaps owing to, the fact that audiences continue to argue about Micheaux's depictions of African Americans and African American life, his work remains powerfully relevant. An alternative to popular media images of African Americans, Micheaux's films offered unusually complex, sophisticated, and varied representations.

FURTHER READING

Bowser, Pearl, Jane Gaines, and Charles Musser, eds. *Oscar Micheaux and His Circle: African American Filmmaking and Race Cinema of the Silent Era* (2001).

Bowser, Pearl, and Louis Spence. *Writing Himself into History: Oscar Micheaux, His Silent Films, and His Audiences* (2000).

Cripps, Thomas. *Slow Fade to Black: The Negro in American Film, 1900–1942* (1977, 1993).

LISA E. RIVO

Mickens, Ronald Elbert (7 Feb. 1943–), mathematician, theoretical physicist, and university professor, was born in Petersburg, Virginia, the son of Joseph Percivall Mickens, a carpenter, and Daisy Brown Williamson, a house wife. His twin brothers Calvin and Carroll were born a year later on 13 February 1944. As a child, Mickens's interest in mathematics and science was sparked by his maternal grandfather who taught him to read and write, and discussed the nature of science. As a consequence, in high school, he enrolled in all of the available courses in these areas. After graduation from Peabody High School, in 1960, he entered Fisk University where in 1964 he completed a B.A. in Physics with a minor in mathematics. Mickens continued his education at Vanderbilt University and earned a doctoral degree in Theoretical Physics in August 1968. From 1968 to 1970 he continued his research in high-energy physics by becoming a National Science Foundation Postdoctoral Fellow at the Center for Theoretical Physics at the Massachusetts Institute of Technology (MIT).

In 1970 Mickens returned to Fisk University as an assistant professor in the Department of Physics. Based on his outstanding research and excellent teaching abilities, he was promoted to full professor in 1977. In June 1970 he was a visiting scientist at the Los Alamos Scientific Laboratory. He also spent parts of summers carrying out research in theoretical particle physics at the Stanford Linear Accelerator Center (1971, 1972, 1977), Lawrence Berkeley Laboratory (1974), and Les Houches Summer Institute of Theoretical Physics (1975) in Les Houches, France. During Mickens's tenure at Fisk University, he held visiting research positions at Morehouse College from 1978 to 1979; Vanderbilt University from 1980 to 1982; and the Joint Institute for Laboratory Astrophysics in Boulder, Colorado, from 1981 to 1982. In 1982 he accepted the position of Professor of Physics at Atlanta University (later Clark Atlanta University) and was named the Fuller E. Callaway Distinguished Professor in 1985.

Mickens's research covered a broad range of issues in theoretical elementary particle physics, chemical kinetics, nonlinear oscillations, numerical integration of differential equations, difference equations, and the history of science. From 1964 to 1979 he engaged in a study using mathematics from complex function theory to construct and analyze what occurs when two elementary particles collide with very high energies. He then applied these techniques to derive a number of results relating to chemical reaction rates. For example, he showed that the chemical equilibrium constant could be determined from the principles of scattering theory and that the general behavior of the temperature dependence of three-body association reactions could be understood within this framework.

In 1977, while he was at Fisk, Mickens taught an undergraduate course on nonlinear oscillations. Finding that no appropriate text was available, he wrote and published his first book, *Introduction to Nonlinear Oscillations*, in 1981. During the writing of this volume, he acquired an interest in the general subject of nonlinear oscillations, and it led to several dozen publications on topics ranging from the construction of new procedures for calculating approximations to the solutions of nonlinear oscillatory differential equations to the creation of new methods for obtaining numerical solutions. Several of his analytical approximation methods have been extended by himself and other researchers. In particular, he created procedures to obtain solutions to these types of differential equations for which none of the standard methods can be applied.

In 1977, Mickens married Maria Kelker. She was a 1975 graduate of Fisk University and had a Ph.D. degree in Political Science from Atlanta University (1981). They had two children, James and Leah.

During the decade and a half after 1990, Mickens created a new subfield on the numerical integration of ordinary and partial differential equations. This methodology differs from the standard rules normally used for this task. His schemes modify the usual definition of the discrete derivative and also extend the representation of the various terms appearing in the differential equations. These discrete nonstandard finite difference methods are increasingly being used for numerical work by researchers in the natural, engineering, and mathematical sciences. In 1994 he published a summary of this work in *Finite Difference Models of Differential Equations*. This was followed by two edited volumes illustrating their broad applicability to equations modeling important phenomena in science and technology, *Applications of Nonstandard Finite Difference Schemes* (2000) and *Advances in the Applications of Nonstandard Finite Difference Schemes* (2005).

Mickens developed a passion for the history of science during high school. His scholarship in the area includes a number of biographical essays on several distinguished African American scientists. Mickens published more than 265 abstracts, 280 peer-reviewed papers, seventy-five general and scholarly papers, six books, and nine edited volumes. His presentations included invited talks at a broad range of universities and both national and international conferences and workshops. He was also active in several scientific organizations, including the American Association for the Advancement of Science; the American Physical Society, for which he was an elected fellow (1999); the Society for Industrial and Applied Mathematics; and the American Mathematical Society. In 1994 and 1998, respectively, he began service as a member of the editorial boards of the *Journal of Difference Equations and Applications* and the *International Journal of Evolution Equations.*

Mickens was also an elected fellow of Phi Beta Kappa (Fisk University, 1964). For graduate studies at Vanderbilt University, he received both the Woodrow Wilson Fellowship (1964–1965) and a Danforth Foundation Fellowship (1965–1968). His postdoctoral research at MIT (1968–1970) was supported by the award of a National Science Foundation Postdoctoral Fellowship. In addition to many honors and awards, during 1984–1985 he was a United Negro College Fund Distinguished Faculty Fellow at Atlanta University and was given the National Association of Mathematicians Distinguished Service Award in 1996. His abilities as teacher, researcher, and presenter of scientific concepts to the public were recognized by his selection to be an American Physical Society Centennial Speaker (1998–1999) in celebration of the 100th anniversary of the founding of the organization. Further, he was a Distinguished National Lecturer for Sigma Xi, the Scientific Research Society (2000–2002), and was the first recipient of the Annual Aldridge-McMillian Achievement Award at Clark Atlanta University for "Overall Achievement in Teaching, Scholarship, and Service" (2000). On the occasion of his sixtieth birthday, two special issues of the *Journal of Difference Equations and Applications* were dedicated to him (both 2003).

His research and scholarship have been supported by a variety of government agencies and private foundations, including the Army Research Office, National Science Foundation, NASA, Department of Energy, and Alfred P. Sloan and Ford Foundations. Mickens had a distinguished career in applied mathematics and mathematical physics for nearly four decades. His research and scholarly activities in nonlinear oscillations, difference equations, scattering theory, numerical analysis of differential equations, and the history of African Americans in science was recognized nationally and internationally by researchers and scholars in the relevant areas.

FURTHER READING

Kessler, James H., J. S. Kidd, Renee A. Kidd, and Katherine A. Morin, eds. *Distinguished African American Scientists of the 20th Century* (1996).

Krapp, Kristine, ed. *Notable Black American Scientists* (1999).

Oyedeji, 'Kale. "Career of Professor Ronald E. Mickens," *Journal of Difference Equations and Applications* 9 (2003).

Spangenburg, Ray, and Kit Moser, eds. *African Americans in Science, Math and Invention* (2003).

'KALE OYEDEJI

Middleton-Hairston, Jeanne (8 Dec. 1949–), professor, author, community activist, and National Director of the Children's Defense Fund Freedom Schools, was the last child and only daughter born to Chaplain Colonel Richard T. Middleton Jr., a colonel in the U.S. Army and rector, and Johnie Beadle Middleton, an elementary school teacher.

Jeanne's early youth was spent in several U.S. Army military bases across the country where she experienced President Harry Truman's commitment to racial integration at these bases. These early experiences with children of different racial, ethnic, and religious backgrounds would stand her in good stead as a lifelong educator and civil rights activist. She was an exceptionally bright student, and the love of learning was instilled in her very early by both her parents and grandparents, whom she admired and respected throughout their lifetimes.

When her father retired from the military, the family returned to their familial roots in segregationist Jackson, Mississippi. It was during the Civil Rights era of Mississippi's history that Jeanne's commitment to the educational advancement of her people was firmly established. Experiencing overt racism and segregated schooling, she became committed to integrating educational institutions. As part of this deliberate commitment, Jeanne became one of the first African American undergraduates admitted to Millsaps College in Jackson, a national liberal arts college founded in 1891 by a former Confederate major, Reuben Millsaps. Jeanne withstood persistent racism within this formerly segregationist educational institution and found considerable support to continue her mission to graduate from Millsaps College. She discovered several key Millsaps faculty mentors on her path to the B.A. in Political Science, including early civil rights professors Robert Bergmark, Howard Bavendar, John Quincy Adams, T. W. Lewis, Francis Coker, and Charles Sallis. At the urging of philosophy professor Robert Bergmark, Jeanne applied for and received the prestigious Danforth Fellowship for graduate study in the United States. After acceptance from several distinguished graduate schools, Jeanne enrolled at Harvard's Graduate School of Education in the fall of 1971. During her graduate years there, which included master and doctoral studies in educational administration, planning, and social policy research, Jeanne met and was supported by Harvard professors such as GENEVA SMITHERMAN (author of the best-selling book *Talking and Testifying* [1990]), Sara Lawrence Lightfoot (a longtime family friend), Charles V. Willie (her dissertation adviser), and DERRICK ALBERT BELL JR. For the first time in her post-secondary school studies, the impact of being mentored by these pioneering African American academic giants was tremendous. It was also during her study at the Harvard Center for Law and Education that Jeanne became involved as a researcher for several key federal law cases and, later in 1979, became an expert witness in the Federal District Court Case of *Loewen v. Turnipseed*. Also, before she embarked upon her dissertation research, Jeanne was asked by Professors Charles Sallis and Jim Loewen (author of *Lies My Teacher Told Me* [1996]) to co-author a book on Mississippi history entitled *Mississippi: Conflict and Change*, published in 1974 by Pantheon Press in New York City. This award-winning book was recognized as a groundbreaking model for state history texts in its discussion of issues of race, class, culture, and gender.

Jeanne returned to her native state after her doctoral studies at Harvard, with renewed vigor to her earlier commitment. Following a year as a research assistant and Title I project evaluator for the Office of Research and Evaluation for the Jackson Public Schools, she was offered and accepted a tenure-track position at her alma mater, Millsaps College, in 1978. Jeanne became their first full-time African American professor. As she worked diligently toward national accreditation of the teacher education program there, she also became the first African American to be awarded tenure and became full professor, chair of the Education Department, and division chair of the Social and Behavioral Sciences by 1990. She instituted several well-known academic and professional programs and curricula including new undergraduate courses in Educational Theory, Policy, and Practice and the Evolution of Slavery in the United States, the Millsaps College Principals' Institute, and was director of the Ford Teaching Fellows Program.

In 1982 she married David Forsythe, a native of Guyana, and together they had two daughters. Their marriage dissolved in 1997. Four years later, Jeanne married James M. Hairston Jr. and they went on to have one son.

In 2003, after Jeanne and her husband moved to Washington, D.C., she accepted the position of national director of Freedom Schools for the Children's Defense Fund. A longtime admirer of CDF's founder, lawyer, and child advocate MARIAN WRIGHT EDELMAN, the role had Jeanne lead the successful summer literacy enrichment program that arose from the Civil Rights Movement's Mississippi Summer Project of 1964 to provide quality educational opportunities for children and families in communities where there otherwise would be none. For Jeanne, this brought her life back to full circle as much of her commitment to civil rights for blacks was formed in educational circles, coordinating a national program that capitalizes on her background in literacy, cultural heritage, parental involvement, servant-leadership, and social action.

FURTHER READING

Loewen, J., C. Sallis, J. Middleton. *Mississippi: Conflict and Change* (1974).

Titcomb, C., W. Sollars, T. Underwood, eds. *Blacks at Harvard: A Documentary History of African American Experiences at Harvard and Radcliffe* (1993).

LOUIS B. GALLIEN JR.

Mifflin, James (1839–?), Civil War sailor and Medal of Honor winner, was born a slave in Richmond, Virginia. Although nothing is known for certain of his life before the Civil War, it is likely that once the war began Mifflin escaped from his master and made his way to Union forces in Virginia. One of thousands of such slaves who were termed "contrabands" (as opposed to the more legally ambiguous terms "freeman" or "runaway slave") by Union Army officials, Mifflin was among a large number of such men who would subsequently enlist in the Union Navy. Mifflin, who stood only five feet four inches, was twenty-five years old when he joined the navy in New York on 1 April 1864. He was first rated a landsman, which was an entry level position for a recruit with no sea experience, and he served on shore at the Brooklyn Navy Yard. While Mifflin may have received some training in his first month of duty, it is more likely that he was a servant to yard officers, or perhaps worked in the navy yard helping to prepare the newly recommissioned USS *Brooklyn*, a 2,500-ton, wooden sloop-of-war, for sea duty. On 10 May 1864 the *Brooklyn* headed out to sea for duty with Admiral David Farragut's Western Gulf Blockade Squadron off Mobile, Alabama; that same day, Mifflin joined the crew, possibly as a last-minute replacement. Mifflin was listed as a cook, a possible indicator of either prior experience or newly attained skills. Soon thereafter, he was assigned as an engineer's cook as part of the commissary crew devoted to the *Brooklyn*'s engineering officers and their mess department.

Mifflin was one of about eighteen thousand African Americans who served in the navy during the Civil War, comprising 20 percent of its manpower. Most African Americans served in lower-level commissary or steward positions; but some, such as JOACHIM PEASE and ROBERT SMALLS, served in more skilled positions, such as able-bodied seamen or pilots. No matter what their rating, the service of these men was vital to the Union cause. Because there were few epic sea battles during the Civil War, those men who fought in the Union Navy were often relegated to the back pages of history, perhaps none more so than African Americans. However, black sailors were vital to the war effort, and such men as Mifflin and AARON ANDERSON fought bravely and were recognized for their heroic contributions.

Once at sea on the *Brooklyn* in May 1864, Mifflin most likely had to adjust to his new environment. Perhaps he battled seasickness in his first days on the open ocean (most sailors did), and certainly he had to get used to his new quarters deep within the ship near the engine room. Diminutive in stature, Mifflin probably had few problems in adapting to the confined spaces, and his new job in the navy was certainly more rewarding than the work he performed as a slave. In fact, contraband slaves, accustomed to discipline and hard work, as a rule proved to be excellent sailors and served in racially mixed crews. The navy, unlike the army, did not form segregated units.

Commanded by Captain James Alden, the *Brooklyn* and its crew arrived off Mobile Bay on 31 May 1864. The ship spent the next two months patrolling the waters of the Gulf Coast and saw little action. This relatively placid situation would change, however, in August 1864, when Admiral Farragut finally had all the ships he needed (as well as coordinated ground forces) to attack Mobile, Alabama, the only port on the Gulf Coast still in Confederate hands. On the morning of 5 August

1864, Farragut and his forces moved in for the attack, the admiral himself was near the head of his column in his flagship *Hartford* and gave the battle cry "Damn the torpedoes, full speed ahead!" Having to pass close by the Confederate-occupied Fort Morgan, which guarded the approaches to the bay, the *Brooklyn*, with Mifflin aboard serving as an ammunition passer, steamed in company with the Union monitor *Tecumseh* under the guns of the fort. Suddenly, disaster struck; while steaming to engage the Confederate ram *Tennessee*, the *Tecumseh* struck a mine (in those days called "torpedoes") and veered out of control, quickly sinking with ninety-three of its crew. In grave danger from the mines, the *Brooklyn* was forced to reverse and steer clear of the mines while still within close range of Fort Morgan's guns. The ship took a terrific pounding and suffered fifty-four killed and forty-three wounded. The battle station of Engineer's Cook Mifflin was twice hit by enemy fire, but Mifflin remained at his post and continued to carry powder throughout the battle.

Three hours after the battle began, Union forces secured the victory, as Fort Gaines and Fort Morgan finally surrendered on 7 and 23 August, respectively. The last Confederate blockade-running port on the Gulf Coast was now in Union hands and effectively closed. Indicative of the overall contribution of black sailors to this victory were the three men who were awarded the Medal of Honor for their heroism and devotion to duty under fire at Mobile Bay—Mifflin on the *Brooklyn* and WILSON BROWN and JOHN LAWSON on the *Hartford*. Following the Battle of Mobile Bay, Mifflin remained on the *Brooklyn* while the ship was stationed off Mobile Bay and subsequently departed for duty off Hampton Roads, Virginia, with the North Atlantic Blockade Squadron on 6 September 1864. In September of that same year, Mifflin briefly served on the *Ossipee*, a 1,240-ton sloop of war that also participated in the Battle of Mobile Bay. Then he returned to the *Brooklyn* for a time until mustering out of the navy. He most likely continued on the *Brooklyn* during its subsequent action in covering the landing of troops in the capture of Fort Fisher, North Carolina, and stayed onboard until the vessel was decommissioned in New York on 31 January 1865. Following his naval service, nothing further is known of Mifflin. However, his status as a Medal of Honor recipient ensured that his heroism will be remembered. An artist's conception of Mifflin was featured on a U.S. Navy poster issued during America's Bicentennial in 1976.

FURTHER READING

Reidy, Joseph P. "Black Men in Navy Blue during the Civil War," *Prologue* (Fall 2001).

U.S. Navy. *Medal of Honor, 1861–1949: The Navy* (1950).

GLENN ALLEN KNOBLOCK

Milai, A. Sam (23 Mar. 1908–30 Apr. 1970), editorial cartoonist and illustrator, was born Ahmed Samuel Milai in Washington, D.C.

During the 1930s Milai served as illustrator of JOEL AUGUSTUS ROGERS's black history comic titled *Your History*. Rogers's comic brought to readers of the black press information about the remarkable achievements of individuals throughout the African diaspora, which was conspicuously absent from elementary school history books across America. The fully illustrated *Your History* comic was presented in a style similar to that of the popular *Ripley's Believe it or Not!* feature. Although Milai worked in association with the *Pittsburgh Courier*, *Your History* also appeared in a number of other black press publications nationally.

On 31 July 1937 the *Pittsburgh Courier* debuted Milai's comic domestic family strip titled *Bucky*. This weekly comic strip centered on an adolescent boy and his interaction with his parents, schoolmates, and the obligatory assortment of tough guys and bullies. Over the comic's thirteen-year run, Bucky aged (slowly) to become a young man poised to enter high school. However, he could also inexplicably become younger again, possibly because of the reprinting of older comics. On 31 July 1950 the weekly *Bucky* strip was replaced by a new color comic feature illustrated by Milai. The new comic character was introduced in the final *Bucky* strip by the giant hand of the cartoonist speaking directly to the character. The new comic strip character, named Don Powers, was intended to be Bucky's older cousin. Despite an original impression that the comic strip *Bucky* was only taking a brief vacation, it did not return for any length of time to the *Pittsburgh Courier*.

For five years *Don Powers* was part of a new full-color comic section in the magazine section of the *Pittsburgh Courier*. Don was an all-American athlete, who played several different sports as well as acted as a goodwill representative for his nation around the world. Using good sportsmanship and personal integrity, the clean-cut Don Powers was able to solve mysteries and thwart mobsters and foreign agents alike. The comic ran in color from 1950 until mid-1955 when all the cartoons changed to a black-and-white format, possibly because the Smith—Mann Syndicate could not generate enough advertisement revenue to defray for the cost of the four color format. Unfortunately, the first year of the *Pittsburgh Courier* color comics was not recorded on microfilm and the years that were microfilmed were poorly photographed in black and white, so the images are muddy and nearly unreadable. Still a few bound records of the pages in color can be found in a small number of university libraries.

On 11 April 1942, between the run of *Bucky* and the start of *Don Powers*, Milai illustrated the detective strip titled *Society Sue*. The comic was credited to Bobby Thomas, but the strips were clearly signed by Milai.

Carrying on in the tradition of Rogers's *Your History* feature from the 1930s, Sam Milai created a beautifully illustrated feature titled *Facts About the Negro* during the 1960s that also highlighted little known or often ignored historic, social, educational, and scientific accomplishments achieved by people of African descent.

In 1966 *The Pittsburgh Courier* was taken over by *Chicago Defender* publisher, John H. H. Sengstacke, and the name was changed to the *New Pittsburgh Courier*. Milai drew political cartoons that appeared in the *New Pittsburgh Courier*, apparently taking over that position form the long-time cartoonist, Wilbert T. Holloway. Milai's views, as expressed through his editorial cartoons, were firmly from a centrist point of view. In his cartoons he was as opposed to the motives and radical actions of dashiki-wearing, black power extremists, as he was to club-toting, cross-burning white supremacists. While favoring the Lyndon B. Johnson administration, Milai opposed his successor, Richard M. Nixon. Although Milai supported the civil rights movement, he did not appear to be especially impressed with Dr. MARTIN LUTHER KING JR.'s call for civil disobedience nor did he shy away from criticizing the black leadership and organizations of the day.

Sam Milai shared his political knowledge and experiences as a cartoonist through his position as a part-time instructor at the Ivey School of Professional Art in Pittsburgh from 1964 until 1967 and then as a professor at the Pittsburgh Art Institute beginning in 1968. During his three-decade career with the *Pittsburgh Courier*, Milai was the winner of the National Newspaper Publishers Association Russwurm trophy for best cartoon on eight different occasions.

Sadly, much of Milai's original illustrations were never returned to him by the newspapers that published them over the decades, and cartoons created later were destroyed in a fire. The surviving collection of cartoons, tear sheets, papers, and photographs from the 1960s was donated by a family member to the Cartoon Research Library at Ohio State University in Columbus, Ohio, where they were exhibited for the first time from 22 September until 31 December 2008.

FURTHER READING

An online version of the Ohio State University exhibit can be viewed at any time by visiting http://library.osu.edu/sites/exhibits/sammilai/intro.html.

Jackson, Tim. *A Salute to Pioneering Cartoonists of Color*, http://web.mac.com/tim_jackson.

Obituary: *Jet*, 11 June 1970.

TIM JACKSON

Milburn, Amos (1 Apr. 1927–3 Jan. 1980), pianist and singer, was born in Houston, Texas, one of thirteen children of Amos Milburn Sr., a laborer for a general contractor, and Amelia, a homemaker. Milburn exhibited a precocious musical talent and began to play piano at the age of five. Eager to serve in the military, Milburn lied about his age and entered the U.S. Navy when only fifteen years old. He served in the Pacific Theater and was wounded in engagements at Guadalcanal and the Philippines. In his off-hours, he played at military clubs, and when he returned home to Houston at the age of eighteen, he possessed sufficient skill and organizational wherewithal to form a band.

In 1946, during a performance in San Antonio, Lola Anne Cullum, the wife of a Houston dentist, approached Milburn and solicited him for her booking and management agency. She recorded some work by Milburn and sent the material to the Los Angeles-based Aladdin Records, owned by Eddie, Lou, and Ira Mesner (the other Houston-based artist Cullum successfully submitted to Aladdin was LIGHTNIN' HOPKINS). Aladdin had recently opened its doors, one of the many independent recording companies that emerged in the wake of World War II. Their most successful releases include ILLINOIS JACQUET's "Flying Home" (1945), HELEN HUMES's "Be-Babu-Leba" (1945), Shirley & Lee's "Let the Good Times Roll" (1957), and Thurston Harris's "Little Bitty Pretty One" (1957). In the late 1950s, the label succumbed to the hegemony of rock and roll, and the Messners sold it to Lou Chudd, the owner of Imperial Records (later owned by the Universal Music Group).

The Messners signed Milburn, and he moved to Los Angeles. His third release, a cover of Don Raye's 1940 hit "Down the Road Apiece," made some waves, but it was his 1948 single "Chicken Shack Boogie" that established his reputation, reaching number one on the *Billboard* R&B charts. So successful was the record and so identified was Milburn with it that he named his band the Aladdin Chicken Shackers. Also of note, the record was arranged and featured tenor saxophone solos by Maxwell Davis, one of the most prolific and influential individuals in the African American music community of Los Angeles during the period. He was replaced in the Chicken Shackers by Don Wilkerson, who after a five-year residence with Milburn joined RAY CHARLES's orchestra and performed a number of indelible solos for him.

Between 1948 and 1954, Milburn released an extraordinary succession of nineteen Top 10 hits on the *Billboard* R&B charts. The insouciant groove and celebratory tone remained a mainstay, along with the frequent affirmations of alcohol, as heard in "Bad Bad Whiskey" (1950), "Just One More Drink" (1951), "Let Me Go Home, Whiskey" (1943), "One Scotch, One Bourbon, One Beer" (1953), "Vicious, Vicious Vodka" (1954), and "Juice, Juice" (1956).

In 1952, Milburn unexpectedly broke up the Chicken Shackers and played as a solo act for the next three years. In 1957 he returned to his native Houston and reformed his band, but the audience for his material had withered. The sale of the Aladdin label led to his being signed by the Cincinnati-based King Records, though his releases for it did not duplicate his earlier success. He was signed by BERRY GORDY's Motown label in 1962 and released one single and an album, *Blues Boss*, which featured a young STEVIE WONDER. Once again, however, his career stalled, and he returned to Houston.

A stroke in 1969 incapacitated Milburn, yet in 1972 he recorded some final sides for Johnny Otis, although he was so debilitated that Otis reportedly had to play the left-hand parts for him. A second stroke rendered him an invalid, and shortly before his death in 1980, a leg was amputated.

Milburn's catalog has sometimes been associated with the unfortunately designed "cocktail blues" of the 1940s, a languid, piano-focused, less emotionally demonstrative subspecies of the genre. Some commentators berate the material as lacking in the fervent emotionalism of the repertoire associated with the Mississippi Delta. That position, however, overlooks a number of important factors. First, it denies that one can hear elements of this performance style in the work of influential 1930s pianist LEROY CARR, best known for his duets with guitarist Scrapper Blackwell and the classic song "How Long Blues."

Also, such a point of view overlooks the demonstrable skill of Milburn's instrumental abilities and vocal stylings, which demonstrate a beguiling extroversion and epitomize a certain kind of hard living, devil-may-care persona that makes up in raucousness what it may lack in reflection. In addition, Milburn's influence on his contemporaries was considerable, as illustrated by the material recorded by other contemporaneous R&B keyboard players, such as Floyd Dixon or Little Willie Littlefield, and by the later styles of some of the emerging pianists of rock and roll, such as LITTLE RICHARD and Jerry Lee Lewis.

FURTHER READING

Oliver, Paul, ed. *Blackwell Guide to Recorded Blues* (1991).

Shaw, Arnold. *Honkers and Shouters. The Golden Years of Rhythm & Blues* (1978).

Tosches, Nick. *Unsung Heroes of Rock 'n' Roll. The Birth of Rock in the Wild Years Before Elvis* (1991).

DAVID SANJEK

Milburn, Rodney "Hot Rod" (18 Mar. 1950–11 Nov. 1997), track-and-field athlete, was born in Opelousas, Louisiana, the youngest of seven children. His mother, Mary Tyler Milburn, and father, Rodney Milburn Sr., raised their children in a four-room, rural home, and as a young boy Rodney often escaped to the countryside, where he chased galloping horses through the bayou with his cousins.

At J.S. Clark High School, Milburn's speed and agility soon became obvious to his coach, Claude Paxton. The segregated school had few resources for its athletes, however. Lighting was virtually non-existent at night, and the hurdles were homemade affairs cobbled together with scrap wood. But Milburn was dedicated, even mowing the track's grass himself. His coach, "Pax" as he was called, became like a father figure to Milburn and devised a unique training philosophy known as the "dime technique" encouraging the athlete to sail over hurdles leaving no more than the space of one undisturbed dime.

Recruited by Southern University, Rodney trained with 1968 Olympic gold medalist Willie Davenport (then a graduate student at the college), bringing "Pax" with him. He worked hard, maybe even too much, as he told reporters in 1970. But his efforts paid off in 1971 when, at age twenty-one, he broke the oldest world record in track and field—running a 120-yard high hurdle race in thirteen seconds flat. He was nearly undefeated all year, winning twenty-seven consecutive races and being named Track & Field News' World Athlete of the Year.

Ironically, Milburn almost did not make it to the 1972 Olympic Games in Munich. After hitting two hurdles in the qualifying trials, he barely squeezed into third place. Once at the games however, he was back at the height of his power. Not only did he win the gold medal but he also set a new world record in the 110-meter hurdle, at 13.24 seconds.

It was a "grand excitement, a grand feeling," he later told reporters. "I knew I probably would never feel like that again." He was right. Upon returning home that September, Milburn quickly learned that a gold medal did not equal a paycheck. Nor did being an Olympic champion qualify him for corporate sponsorships in an era when amateurs were not allowed to receive payments. Though he would remain a world record holder for the next five years, Milburn returned to Opelousas, at twenty-two, to little fanfare.

Both the Olympic games of 1968 and 1972 were known, in part, for the famous protests of African American athletes. Milburn did not participate in any such acts, however, and when asked for his thoughts about them, he refused to comment. Often described by peers and sportswriters of the day as soft-spoken and humble, Milburn was intent on simply offering his best performance without distraction.

This did not mean that he was without opinions however. Clearly, he was frustrated by the lack of equal compensation and opportunities afforded to black athletes, including himself, and expressed his disillusionment and anger to reporters at the Olympic trials in Eugene, Oregon. "Track is nothing but hassles. You run for your country and what do you get? Nobody says, 'Thanks, Rod.' They don't care. We have to pay our own way to this meet. Man, look at all the people in the stands. Where's all the money going? This is it for me. Hassles, hassles, hassles. I'm getting out of track after the Olympics. I'm going to play football." Later, he would repeat the sentiment, saying you just "can't run around a track and make a living."

Although he had an opportunity to go professional in 1972, he believed, rightfully, that such a move was "too risky" and instead, that year, was drafted as a wide receiver for the Los Angeles Rams. There are conflicting reports about why he did not ultimately stay. Some say that he did not make the cut. But according to most reports, including that of his sister Lillie Lazard, Milburn left because the team failed to recognize his talent and did not offer him an equitable contract.

And so, during the Christmas holidays of 1972, the Olympic medalist with the quiet gentle smile worked as a salesman in a local department store. In 1973, he fathered a daughter, Nichelle. In 1974, as Milburn completed the final requirements for his degree and financial pressures mounted, he reversed his earlier decision and joined the International Track Association, a newly formed professional circuit, just before the birth of his son Rodney III in 1975. During this time, Milburn may have also attempted to offer financial support to two daughters from previous relationships: Latina Vanwright, who was born in 1965 when Rodney was fifteen, and Detra Cole, whose birth date is unclear.

Milburn did well on the pro-circuit, but the fledgling organization folded within two years, and in yet another twist of bad luck Milburn now no longer qualified for the 1976 Olympics since he had given up his amateur status. He was not reinstated until 1979, at age thirty. But by that time there were plenty of younger stars waiting to take his place, such as RENALDO NEHEMIAH, twenty, who had broken Milburn's world record and defeated him in their first meeting.

Placing fourth in the national championships, Milburn did not qualify for the 1980 Moscow Olympics. Even if he had, he would not have attended owing to the United States-led boycott. In 1982, Milburn remarried after meeting Betty Comeaux at an alumni gathering. Although he continued to train, and tried to remain optimistic, he was simply not able to repeat his earlier success. In 1983 Milburn happily accepted a coaching position at his alma mater and Betty gave birth to a daughter, Falecia Milburn, that same year. A son, Russell Pierre, was born in 1986.

In 1987 Milburn was stunned when he was fired in a staff overhaul by Southern's new athletic director. The loss was devastating, according to Milburn's cousin Jonah Kay Milburn, who said that although Rodney was not one to talk about his troubles, he never got over it. He had done his best, said Milburn, but one reporter described him as "dazed." In 1988 Milburn took a job at the Georgia Pacific paper plant in Baton Rouge, where he would remain an exemplary employee for nine years. He never gave up his love of track and often returned to Southern—impeccably dressed and even offering his coaching services for free. But his induction into the National Track and Field Hall of Fame in 1993, at age forty-three, must have been a bittersweet victory. Despite his many accomplishments, Milburn had not been able to earn a living doing what he loved most. He proudly carried the Olympic torch in 1996, at age forty-six, but not even that thrill could change the fact that he was now a forgotten hero.

In 1995 tragedy struck three times. His father, Rodney Milburn Sr., died, as did his beloved coach, "Pax." And Betty, his wife of thirteen years left him, filing for divorce and seeking legal custody of the couple's two young children. In April 1996 Milburn's twenty-one-year-old son Rodney III (who had previously been arrested for driving under the influence), was sentenced on first degree robbery charges.

The following year, Milburn stayed at the home of his cousin, Jonah Kay, for six months, as he attempted to recover from his emotional losses while digging himself out of a financial hole of past-due federal taxes, legal fees from his divorce, and child support payments. Not wanting to overstay his welcome, however, he left for the Bishop Ott Shelter in New Orleans in early November. After just two nights, Milburn was asked to leave because working the night shift (his hours were from 6 p.m. to 6 A.M.) was against shelter rules.

On 11 November 1997, Milburn sold his blood for cab fare to work. Looking thinner than usual, he had also sold blood the previous week, and possibly the week before that. His last paycheck had been garnished for back taxes, he told his cousin Jonah, and he had only taken home $36. But his deepest sorrow was reserved for his eldest son Rodney III's imprisonment. Milburn attended church services that evening before heading to work. At about 10:45 p.m. his badly burned body was found floating face-down at the bottom of a rail car filled with sodium chlorate solution and scalding hot water. His death, at age forty-seven, was ruled an accident.

FURTHER READING

The Opelousas Museum and Interpretive Center houses a permanent exhibition, Reaching for the Gold: The Rod Milburn Story, which contains several photos, medals, and various memorabilia. The whereabouts of many of Milburn's personal belongings and awards, however, including his Olympic Gold Medal, are unknown.

Ashe, Arthur R., Jr. *A Hard Road to Glory: A History of the African-American Athlete since 1946* (1988).

Gildea, William. "Blacks Find Olympic Gold No Ticket to Better Things," *Washington Post*, 28 Mar. 1973.

Obituaries: *The* (Baton Rouge, Louisiana) *Advocate*, 16 Nov. 1997; *Associated Press*, 21 Dec. 1997.

KRISTAL BRENT ZOOK

Miles, John "Mule" (11 Aug. 1922–), Tuskegee aircraft mechanic and Negro League baseball player, was born in San Antonio, Texas. His parents' names are unknown, as are details of his childhood. He was nicknamed "Sonny Boy" in high school, where he played baseball and graduated in 1940. He went on to play basketball while a student at St. Phillips Junior College in San Antonio.

Miles left home for Tuskegee, Alabama, in 1943. He attended Tuskegee Institute and was trained as a civilian aircraft sheet-metal worker. Miles would later say about his time at Tuskegee: "As soon as I heard about Tuskegee I knew it was what I wanted to do. I really wanted to learn a trade and work with my hands. It sounded like a once-in-a-lifetime opportunity so I jumped on the chance" (Maurice, 1). At the time Tuskegee Institute was part of a new experiment by the army air corps in training black pilots and ground crew. His time as both a student and employee there was an exciting period in Miles's life, but it could also be trying. Miles recalled that "Tuskegee was hard work" and also stated that "we dealt with protestors outside the base everyday … there were a lot of angry people who were against Tuskegee … but we went on with life just the same" (Maurice, 1). Miles worked at Tuskegee from 1943 to 1945, servicing all kinds of military aircraft flown by the Tuskegee Airmen. In 1945 he returned to his native state, where he was employed as a civil service aircraft mechanic at Kelly Field Air Force Base in his hometown of San Antonio. While Miles would work at Kelly Field for thirty years to earn a living, he would also rediscover the passion of his life: baseball.

Miles first returned to the game while employed at Kelly Field. He joined the base team, the Brown Bombers, playing third base or outfield, and was an immediate success. An imposing six feet three inches in height, Miles soon came to the attention of a Negro League scout for the Chicago American Giants and in 1946 was signed on the spot for three hundred dollars a month, a good wage but not on the level of the superstars of the Negro Leagues. Miles would later recall that "I loved to play ball and that was my ambition … when I had a chance to go professional, I had no doubt in my mind about making it" (Kelley, 208). While Miles's wife, Bernice, was skeptical about his chances of making the Chicago American Giants, she had no trouble with his pursuit of the dream, even though he had to take a leave of absence from his job.

Miles made his Negro League debut with the Chicago American Giants in 1946. A right-handed batter that played the outfield, he batted somewhere between .250 and .270. As was typical of the Negro Leagues, statistics for individual players have often been lost or were never kept. Because of this, official statistics for his career are lacking. The year 1947 was when Miles's star shone most brightly and when he earned a place in the historic lore of the Negro Leagues. It was also a year that changed the face of America's favorite pastime forever.

The 1947 debut of JACKIE ROBINSON in a Brooklyn Dodgers uniform forever broke the color line in baseball. Prior to this time African Americans could only play in the Negro Leagues; Major League Baseball was an all-white institution. No matter how high the talent level of white baseball, the talent found in the Negro Leagues at this time was, by many accounts, at least equal to, if not greater than, that in the Major Leagues. The Negro League and its players were often vastly more entertaining to watch; such talented and flamboyant Negro League players like JOSH GIBSON and SATCHEL PAIGE were the stars of the day, and their exploits on the baseball diamond were followed by African Americans nationwide, as well as many whites. This was also the year that Miles came into his own as a hitter in the Negro Leagues. Now more experienced, and perhaps inspired by Robinson's feat in breaking the color barrier, Miles became an accomplished hitter. While playing outfield and third base, he hit twenty-seven home runs to tie the Negro League's all-time season record for home runs set by WILLIE WELLS in 1926. (There is some dispute as to this year; some sources place Wells's accomplishment in 1929.) But the season highlight for Miles was his feat of hitting eleven homers in eleven consecutive games, the all-time record as of 2007 for all of baseball, black or white. Miles's power was so great that his manager, "Candy" Jim Taylor, told him, "Miles, you hit as hard as a mule kicks" (Kelley, 206), and from that day on he was known as "Mule" Miles. Indeed, all of 1947 was a dream season for Miles; in one game against the Memphis Red Sox he hit two home runs, one off Dan Bankhead, the other off Lefty Mathis; in New Haven, Connecticut, during an exhibition game against a white team, Miles hit a home run that broke a scoreless tie and won the game. Despite his accomplishments, however, Miles has never gained the full recognition he deserves because of the lack of records for the Negro Leagues.

Miles would play two more years with Chicago, but he never again hit at the same level. Perhaps he simply tried too hard to hit home runs and lost his stroke. Lyman Bostock Sr., his teammate on the Chicago American Giants, would later state that manager Jim Taylor once told Miles to "stop lookin' at that goddamn fence! Every time you look at the fence you hit the ball two hops to the pitcher" (Kelley, 66). At this time the Negro Leagues were fading fast because of the ever-increasing numbers of players going to the Major Leagues. With his wife pregnant with twins and a job waiting at home, Miles left the Negro Leagues at age twenty-seven. He played baseball for several more years close to home, with the Laredo Apaches in the Gulf Coast League as its only black player in 1950 and for a local team in San Antonio in 1951. He hung up his cleats for good in 1952.

Though his career was short and his achievements largely undocumented, John "Mule" Miles is representative of the men of the Negro Leagues whose accomplishments in a time of racial inequality have often gone unnoticed. Following his retirement, Miles remained in San Antonio and was active in his community working with local youths and acting as a nationwide ambassador helping to keep alive the history of the Negro Leagues.

FURTHER READING

Holway, John, ed. *Black Diamonds: Life in the Negro Leagues from the Men Who Lived It* (1989).

Kelley, Brent. *Voices from the Negro Leagues* (1998).

Maurice, Lindsey. "Tuskegee Airman Visits Former Unit at Randolph," *Air Force Link* (22 Feb. 2006). Available online at http://www.af.mil/news/story.asp?id=123016505

GLENN ALLEN KNOBLOCK

Miles, Lizzie (31 Mar. 1895–17 Mar. 1963), blues singer, was born Elizabeth Mary Landreaux Miles in New Orleans, Louisiana, the daughter of J.-C. Miles, whose occupation is unknown. Her mother was a singer, whose name is unknown (Landreaux, presumably). Lizzie's stepbrothers were the trumpeter Herb Morand, who at some point during the 1920s played in New York in a band accompanying Lizzie, and the drummer Maurice Morand. Lizzie first sang in church at age five. She also sang in school before dropping out to perform at parties and dances. From 1909 to 1911 she sang with the cornetist KING OLIVER, the trombonist KID ORY, the trumpeter BUNK JOHNSON, and the violinist ARMAND JOHN PIRON at numerous venues in New Orleans. Around this time she married; no other details are known. Her second marriage was to August Pajaud; again, details are unknown.

Miles toured southern theaters as a member of the Benbow Stock Company. She rode elephants and other animals while traveling with the Jones Brothers and Wilson Circus, which billed her as "Queen Elleezzee," and the Cole Brothers Circus. She then toured with the Alabama Minstrels and the Rabbit Foot Minstrels. She sang with the pianist Manuel Manetta in New Orleans in 1917, and around this time she began working as a song plugger for the composer and publisher CLARENCE WILLIAMS. The sequence of these activities is unclear, as are reports of a serious illness, perhaps a heart attack, in 1918 or 1919, when she was with the pianist George Thomas's band at the Pythian Temple Roof Garden in New Orleans. Evidently Miles had to stop singing for some time.

In 1921 Miles was in Chicago, where she continued to promote Williams's songs. She sang with Oliver at the Dreamland Ballroom, as well as in bands led by FREDDIE KEPPARD, CARROLL DICKERSON, WILBUR SWEATMAN, Charlie Elgar, and Glover Compton. Late that year she moved to New York City, where in February 1922 she made her first recordings, "Muscle Shoals Blues" and "She Walked Right Up and Took My Man Away." While in New York she recorded regularly into 1923; she sang with Piron's orchestra at the Cotton Club that same year, and in 1924 she sang with SAM WOODING's orchestra at the Nest Club. She performed in Paris at the nightclub Chez Mitchell, where she was billed as *La rose noire*, and she toured Europe into 1925, at which time she returned to New Orleans to perform with the New Orleans Creole Jazz Band.

While singing in New York clubs from 1926 to 1931, Miles resumed recording. Her work included a session accompanied by Oliver's trio in 1928, "I Hate a Man like You" and "Don't Tell Me Nothin' 'bout My Man" with the pianist JELLY ROLL MORTON late in 1929, and "My Man o' War" and "Electrician Blues" with the pianist Harry Brooks early in 1930. Early in the 1930s she appeared in two little-known films, *The Stardust Ring* and *Tick Tack Toe*, but from 1931 she was mainly inactive, initially because of a serious lung illness and then because of her determination to stick to a religious resolution that if she recovered from her illness—she did—she would cease touring in stage shows.

In 1935 Miles resumed regular nightclub work, performing with the drummer PAUL BARBARIN at the Strollers Club in New York. She sang with

FATS WALLER in New York in 1938 and then began working in Chicago, where the following year she recorded "Stranger Blues" and "Twenty Grand Blues." Miles performed in Chicago until 1942 and then left music for the remainder of the decade.

Ending her retirement in 1950, Miles performed with the band of the clarinetist GEORGE LEWIS at the Hangover Club in San Francisco from 1953 to 1954; at the Blue Note Club in Chicago in 1954; with the band of the trumpeter Bob Scobey in the San Francisco Bay Area, the Los Angeles area, and Las Vegas from 1955 to 1957; with the band of the clarinetist Joe Darensbourg in San Francisco in 1958; and at the Monterey Jazz Festivals of 1958 and 1959. She also worked regularly in New Orleans, including residencies at the Parisian Room and with the band of the drummer Freddie Kohlman at the Mardi Gras Lounge (both perhaps before the engagement in San Francisco, although the chronology is unclear), as well as in 1958 with Barbarin on a riverboat.

During the final segment of her career Miles recorded two titles at a session with the trumpeter Sharkey Bonano in 1952, several tracks on the album *George Lewis Live at the Hangover Club* (1953–1954), and her own albums *Moans and Blues*, *Hot Songs My Mother Taught Me* (both c. 1954), *Torchy Lullabies My Mother Sang Me* (c. 1955), and *Music from Bourbon Street*, with Scobey's band (1956). She also appeared on Paul Gregory's network television show and in 1957 sang on a Voice of America broadcast.

Miles retired to New Orleans in 1959 and became active with the Sisters of Holy Family Chapel and Jesuit Church. She died in New Orleans.

Miles sang in English, in Louisiana Creole patois (known as "gombo French"), and in a Creole that is closer to Parisian French. Like other classic female blues and vaudeville singers, Miles often performed sexy lyrics replete with double entendres of the sort popularized during the latter half of the 1920s. Miles occasionally pushed what was, in her lifetime, the boundary of propriety, passing from the risqué into obscenity, but compared to many twenty-first century lyrics, hers are not shocking.

A characteristically cynical Darensbourg remembered Miles thus:

> She was a typical New Orleans broad, just as evil as hell. What's that song? *Go to church all day Sunday and barrel-house all day Monday.* That was Lizzie. She was supposed to be a great

church broad, went to church almost every day, yet she had a young-assed pimp on the side, taking all her money (151).

Interviewer Berta Wood painted a much brighter portrait, recalling Miles's "zest and seemingly boundless energy" and that she was "a virtuoso conversationalist." Wood continued:

> She skims, dips, wheels about, breaks up with laughter and darts off again with such rapidity that it would take an ambidextrous shorthand writer to come out about even with her.... Her incredible mental agility and powerful spirit are the natural manifestations of a woman who does her own thinking.

FURTHER READING

Dahl, Linda. *Stormy Weather: The Music and Lives of a Century of Jazzwomen* (1984).

Darensbourg, Joe. *Telling It Like It Is*, ed. Peter Vacher (1987).

Stewart-Baxter, Derrick. *Ma Rainey and the Classic Blues Singers* (1970).

Wood, Berta. "Lizzie Miles from New Orleans," *Jazz Journal* (June 1957).

This entry is taken from the *American National Biography* and is published here with the permission of the American Council of Learned Societies.

BARRY KERNFELD

Miley, Bubber (3 Apr. 1903–20 May 1932), jazz trumpeter and composer, was born James Wesley Miley in Aiken, South Carolina, the son of Valentine Miley, an amateur guitarist. Nothing is known of his mother, but his three sisters sang professionally as the South Carolina Trio. In 1909 the family moved to the San Juan Hill section of Manhattan, where at age fourteen Miley began studying trombone and cornet in school.

In 1918 he enlisted in the navy and after eighteen months of duty started playing locally with the Carolina Five and in Harlem with the pianist Willie Gant. In late 1921 Miley replaced Johnny Dunn, then New York's leading trumpeter, in the vaudevillian blues singer MAMIE SMITH's Jazz Hounds and did much traveling and some recording with her popular act. At this time Miley was playing in the stiff, ragtime-based style common to early New York jazzmen. While on tour with Smith in mid-1922 he heard the cornetist KING OLIVER's Creole Jazz Band at the Lincoln Gardens in Chicago. Deeply impressed with both the rhythmic drive of authentic New

Orleans jazz and Oliver's use of blues inflections and the "wa-wa" plunger mute, Miley quickly began to incorporate these elements into his own playing.

In December 1922 he left the Jazz Hounds and played at O'Connor's in Harlem and Reisenweber's in Manhattan before going on tour with *The Sunny South* revue. Following his childhood friend, the trombonist Charlie Irvis, in September 1923 Miley joined ELMER SNOWDEN's Washingtonians at the Hollywood Club in Times Square, but the following February Snowden was ousted from the band, and its leadership was turned over to the group's pianist, DUKE ELLINGTON. In spring 1924 Ellington added the New Orleans clarinetist and soprano saxist SIDNEY BECHET to the band. However, because of his temperamental nature, frequent lateness, and ongoing friction with Miley and Irvis, Bechet was fired in the late summer, but he had wielded a powerful stylistic influence on both Miley and Ellington during his brief stay. In addition to their gigs at the Hollywood Club—remodeled and reopened as the Club Kentucky or, more popularly, the Kentucky Club—the Washingtonians also played in Harlem and at venues throughout New England.

Between 1923 and 1928 Miley also freelanced as an accompanist on many blues record dates, as well as recording with the Kansas City Five, the Texas Blues Destroyers, and CLARENCE WILLIAMS. Although few of the singers or other musicians involved in the earlier New York sessions were experienced in southern blues expression, by 1924 Miley had already succeeded in adapting Oliver's blues inflections, plunger mute facility, and rhythmic swing to the staccato attack and double-timed triplets that were his legacy from Dunn. By this time he had also contributed an element of his own to this synthesis, the pronounced guttural rasp known as "growling," a timbral effect that quickly distinguished him from his colleagues. Miley first recorded with the Washingtonians in November 1924 and again in June 1926, but the results are, with the exception of a fairly competent solo on "Animal Crackers," largely unimpressive, primarily because of Ellington's own band style, one still rooted in the rigid, unswinging, bouncy syncopations of white dance bands. Ellington did, however, continue to assimilate the lessons learned from Bechet's earlier example, and he recognized Miley as his most promising jazz soloist and a valuable source of melodic ideas and orchestral color.

After November 1926 the band's musical identity started to develop at a fairly rapid pace, largely because of Miley but also because of some important changes and additions in personnel. The trombonist JOE "TRICKY SAM" NANTON, a ready student of Miley's plunger-muted growling, had replaced Irvis in late June, while the addition in mid-1927 of the alto and baritone saxophonist HARRY CARNEY and the bassist WELLMAN BRAUD and in 1928 of the clarinetist BARNEY BIGARD and the alto saxophonist JOHNNY HODGES provided the final touches to Ellington's first stylistically integrated orchestra. Especially important was the presence of the New Orleanians Bigard and Braud, for their grounding in blues and swinging rhythm set off the necessary sparks missing from the previous lineups, while Hodges, already a confirmed disciple of Bechet's, lent a grandeur and majesty to the band's sound.

Through the combination of these unique soloists, Miley's guiding hand, and the fortuitous circumstance of the band's employment, which necessitated a steady flow of "primitivistic" music, the Ellington "jungle style" was born. Growling brass, wailing clarinets, ominously moaning saxophones, dissonant blues sonorities, and "savage" tom-tom rhythms were the basic ingredients of the style, but rather than being mere formulaic effects, they provided a colorful foundation for the melodic ideas of both Miley and the other soloists. As a major voice in shaping this revolutionary orchestral timbre, Miley was responsible either in part or in whole for the composition of "East St. Louis Toodle-Oo," "Black and Tan Fantasy," "Creole Love Call," "The Blues I Love to Sing," "Blue Bubbles," "Goin' to Town," "Doin' the Voom Voom," and perhaps several more as well. Miley's horn is prominent throughout most of Ellington's recordings through January 1929 and can also be heard in stylistically definitive solos in "Immigration Blues," "New Orleans Low-Down," "Song of the Cotton Field," "Red Hot Band," "Take It Easy," "Jubilee Stomp," "Got Everything but You," "Yellow Dog Blues," and "The Mooche."

The Ellington band played at the Kentucky Club and other venues for more than four years before entering the Cotton Club in December 1927, where they continued to present a Harlem Renaissance view of African mystique for their wealthy, all-white clientele. Like many of the sidemen, Miley was a heavy drinker, but even in this carefree, hedonistic company he stood out for his lack of professional responsibility. Like Bechet before him, he often showed up late for work, and on two occasions in 1927 he failed to appear at all for scheduled record dates. Worst of all, he was frequently absent when important club owners and bookers came to hear the band, a behavior that so tried the patience of Ellington and his manager, Irving Mills, that in January 1929 Miley was fired. His replacement was COOTIE WILLIAMS, a highly flexible disciple of LOUIS ARMSTRONG who soon learned the now-essential growl technique directly from Nanton.

Miley freelanced for a while in New York and in May 1929 went to Paris with NOBLE SISSLE, in whose orchestra he narrowly escaped another encounter with the bellicose Bechet by virtue of Bechet's incarceration some months before. After two weeks with Sissle, Miley returned to New York, where he worked with ZUTTY SINGLETON's band at the Lafayette Theatre and with Allie Ross at Connie's Inn. In January 1930 the society bandleader Leo Reisman hired Miley as a featured "hot" soloist for both records and theater performances, but for the theater performances Miley was required to play behind a screen or in the guise of a special act so as not to outrage the public with the sight of a racially mixed orchestra. In 1931, though, he was asked to play onstage while accompanying the dancer Roger Pryor Dodge in Billy Rose's *Sweet and Low*.

The records that Miley made in 1930 do not always present him in ideal settings, but his solos on King Oliver's "St. James Infirmary" and JELLY ROLL MORTON's "Little Lawrence" and "Pontchatrain" from January and March 1930 are undoubtedly among his best. Apart from his work with Ellington, perhaps the most notable session of Miley's career was with Bix Beiderbecke, Joe Venuti, and Bud Freeman on a Hoagy Carmichael date in May. He also appeared on several sides with Reisman between January 1930 and June 1931, of which "What Is This Thing Called Love?" "Puttin' On the Ritz," "Happy Feet," and "Take It from Me" warrant attention. However, the six titles from his own Mileage Makers dates between May and September yield only "I Lost My Gal from Memphis," "Without You, Emaline," and "Chinnin' and Chattin' with May" as performances worth hearing. With Irving Mills's backing, in late 1931 Miley formed his own band for a *Harlem Scandals* revue at the Lincoln Theatre in Philadelphia and the Lafayette Theatre in Harlem. But he became ill during the Philadelphia run and was feeling even worse on returning home. In January 1932 he was diagnosed with tuberculosis and, weighing only seventy-six pounds, was admitted to Bellevue Hospital and then transferred to Welfare Island (later Roosevelt Island) in New York City, where he died.

Although he possessed neither the soaring passion, creativity, swing, or emotional depth of Louis Armstrong, nor the lyrical beauty, harmonic adventurousness, or stylistic self-reliance of Bix Beiderbecke, Miley nevertheless emerged as one of the three most influential trumpeters of the 1920s. As the first to develop and master a style almost wholly based on plunger-muted growl effects, his influence, both direct and indirect, can be heard in the playing of such other trumpet stylists as SIDNEY DE PARIS, REX STEWART, Bobby Stark, Ed Allen, Henry Goodwin, Cootie Williams, RAY NANCE, HOT LIPS PAGE, and Max Kaminsky, as well as all of the trombonists who based their plunger growl techniques on what Tricky Sam Nanton had learned from Miley.

FURTHER READING

Charters, Samuel B., and Leonard Kunstadt. *Jazz: A History of the New York Scene* (1962).
Dance, Stanley. *The World of Duke Ellington* (1970).
Schuller, Gunther. *Early Jazz: Its Roots and Musical Development* (1968).
Tucker, Mark. *Ellington: The Early Years* (1991).
Tucker, Mark, ed. *The Duke Ellington Reader* (1993).

DISCOGRAPHY

Rust, Brian. *Jazz Records, 1897–1942*, 4th ed. (1978).
This entry is taken from the *American National Biography* and is published here with the permission of the American Council of Learned Societies.

JACK SOHMER

Miller, Bebe (20 Sept. 1950–), dancer, choreographer, and director, was born Beryl Miller in Brooklyn, New York, to Hazel Carter Miller, an elementary school nurse. Miller and her mother relocated to Queens in the early 1960s. Her introduction to dance began under the tutelage of Murray Louis at the Henry Street Settlement on the Lower East Side of Manhattan. She was exposed to dancers such as Louis, as well as others who studied under and collaborated with the innovative choreographer Alwin Nikolais. With Louis, Miller became familiar with the concepts of composition and improvisation. When she was twelve years old Miller studied ballet. She felt quite isolated during the study of this particular dance form and refers to the experience as "disastrous," explaining that it discouraged her from rigorously studying dance until her college years (discussion with author, 10 Dec. 2006).

In 1967 Miller left New York to attend Earlham College in Richmond, Indiana. She spent one term involved in off-campus study, immersing herself in Balkan folk dance. At this time she also had the opportunity to take a master class in Cincinnati, Ohio, with the choreographer Merce Cunningham. Cunningham's class was a particularly significant experience, as it helped to rekindle her desire to dance. In 1971 she graduated from Earlham College with a B.A. in Fine Arts.

Following her graduation Miller returned to New York to pursue a career in dance. Two years later she was accepted into the master's program in dance at the Ohio State University in Columbus, where she formally trained as a dancer and choreographer. Her studies offered intense technical and theoretical training, and introduced her to visiting dancers and choreographers with whom she would work in the future, among them Lynn Dally and Nina Wiener. In 1975 Miller completed her M.A. in Dance, with an emphasis in performance and choreography.

Between 1976 and 1982 Miller danced with Nina Wiener and Dancers. Wiener's company provided her an opportunity to develop her impassioned style. This was her first experience as a long-term member of a dance company.

In 1984 Miller formed the Bebe Miller Company (BMC), which focused on cross-disciplinary exploration as it created new performance works. Miller's desire to find a "physical language for the human condition" continued to influence the direction of her work. She worked with the composers Don Byron, Fred Frith, and Robin Holcomb; the visual artists Caroline Beasley-Baker, Robert Kushner, and Christian Marclay; and the writers and directors Holly Anderson, Ain Gordon, and Talvin Wilks. Although Miller occasionally created work outside of it, the BMC continued to be her primary company.

Miller used the term "director" as well as "choreographer" when she created dances. She often allowed herself to step outside of the work, which put a tremendous amount of trust in her collaborators. In addition to her artistic collaborators, she engaged in a literal dialogue with her audience following performances, discussions that included topics such as the creation of dance, the importance of community, and the work of African American artists.

Miller's choreography was performed internationally. She created pieces for the Boston Ballet, ALVIN AILEY Repertory Ensemble, the PACT Dance Company of Johannesburg, South Africa, and Phoenix Dance of Great Britain, among others. Her work was presented at the Walker Arts Center in Minneapolis and the Joyce Theater in New York City. In addition, she received commissions or co-commissions for her work at Jacob's Pillow Dance Festival, the Danspace Project, and Dance Theater Workshop. At the last she developed a piece called *The Hendrix Project*, using JIMI HENDRIX's "Red House" for the score.

Miller became a full-time professor of dance at Ohio State University in 2000. In addition to teaching, she experimented with Ohio State's Motion Capture Lab, part of the Advanced Computing Center for the Arts and Design, or ACCAD. The Bessie Award–winning *Landing/Place* (2006) was developed with ACCAD technology, which includes real-time manipulated video as well as animation.

In 2004 Miller restructured BMC, which had functioned for twenty years as a traditional touring dance company. The new format, called a "virtual dance company," comprised members who were located throughout the United States. Miller continued to develop new work within the context of long-term dance residencies that included rehearsals as well as community-based activities. The outreach component was pivotal to Miller's work. In addition to the virtual company work development, Miller made use of digital media such as DVDs, CD-ROMs, and a Web site that she referred to as "process-bulletins" through which collaborators were able to communicate with each other in a virtual residency. The virtual residency media was shared with the public. Not only did Miller document the actual choreography event but she also allowed the public to view the process of development, including the innovative technological experimentations. In addition to her own dance documentation, she collaborated with other colleagues at Ohio State to develop a software template called DanceCODES.

Miller received numerous awards and grants. She received four Bessie awards, established in 1983 to honor outstanding creative work in the dance field: for *Gypsy Pie* (1985); *Two*, with collaborator Ralph Lemon (1986); *Verge* (2001); and *Landing/Place* (2006). She was awarded a John Simon Guggenheim Foundation Fellowship, an American Choreographer Award, Artist's Fellowship from the New York Foundation for the Arts and Ohio Council in 1988, funding from the National Endowment for the Arts, and a Rockefeller MAP Grant for *Verge*.

In addition to experimenting with the technological innovation of a virtual company, she continued to research how diverse populations and audiences perceive her projects, then incorporating this component into the research and development of her new work.

DONNY LEVIT

Miller, Cheryl (3 Jan. 1964–), basketball player, coach, and sportscaster, was born Cheryl Deanne Miller in Riverside, California, the third of five children of Saul Miller, a computer technician and musician, and Carrie Turner Miller, a registered nurse. At age seven Miller began to learn the game of basketball by competing against her two older brothers on the court her father had built in the family's backyard. She continued to hone her basketball skills playing one-on-one with her younger brother Reggie, who would go on to become a college and NBA star. Miller graduated from Riverside Polytechnic High School in 1982 and went on to receive a B.A. in Communications from the University of Southern California (USC) in 1986.

Miller's intense preparation as a youngster served her well as she earned varsity letters in each of her four years of competition while in high school. Her athletic achievements as a high school basketball player reflect individual greatness and the impact a single player can have on a program. At the conclusion of her high school career, Miller averaged nearly 33 points and 15 rebounds per game, and in her senior season she scored an astounding 105

Cheryl Miller, after leading the U.S. Women's basketball team to a victory over South Korea to win the gold medal at the Summer Olympics in Los Angeles, California, 8 August 1984. (AP Images.)

points in a single contest. An unselfish player, she also contributed 368 assists while leading Riverside High School to a number of team honors, including the California Interscholastic Federation statewide championship in 1982. Riverside's overall record during Miller's tenure was a remarkable 132-4. She was named a *Parade* All-American for four straight years, becoming the first male or female athlete to earn that honor. In addition, Miller was named *Street and Smith's* High School Player of the Year in 1981 and 1982.

Miller's accolades and the unprecedented public response to her high school career reflected the massive rise in the popularity of girls' and women's basketball in the late 1970s and the early 1980s. Between 1972 and 1981 the number of girls participating in high school basketball increased from 400,000 to 4.5 million. This increase can be attributed, at least in part, to congressional passage of Title IX of the Omnibus Education Act of 1972 on 23 June 1972. As an extension of the Civil Rights Act of 1964, Title IX prohibited sex discrimination in any educational program receiving federal financial assistance. As a result, resources poured into girls' and women's sports, including basketball, in an effort to create more equitable athletic opportunities based upon sex. Miller's athletic career, including her move to the college ranks, was shaped by these revolutionary changes taking place in the landscape of women's sports. Hoping to consolidate and advance those changes, Miller joined with the volleyball legend FLO HYMAN on Capitol Hill in 1985 to testify in support of strengthening Title IX.

Miller's basketball talents, along with her strong academic skills, attracted the attention of colleges as early as her junior high school days, though she ultimately chose nearby USC from the more than 250 college basketball programs that tried to recruit her. Such frenzied interest in one of the nation's best female basketball prospects reflected the growth of the women's college game and would not have been a likely scenario just a decade earlier. In the fall of 1982 Miller, at six feet three inches tall, joined a host of other very talented USC players, including Paula and Pam McGee, Paula Longo, and Cynthia Cooper, under the direction of Coach Linda Sharp. Expectations were high, and the USC squad did not disappoint themselves or their fans. During Miller's first year USC finished with thirty-one of thirty-three wins for the season and their first national championship. By the end of her sophomore year the team had earned its second national title.

Miller's individual athletic accomplishments while at USC are impressive. She finished her college career averaging more than 23 points per game, an average of 12 rebounds per contest, and 700 steals in the 128 games in which she was a participant. During the four years Miller played for USC the team won 112 games against only 20 losses. Miller won many national collegiate honors, including in 1985 and 1986 the Broderick Cup, given to the nation's best female player. *Sports Illustrated* named Miller the best basketball player, male or female, in the nation in 1986. Miller was also a four-time All-American and a three-time Naismith Player of the Year, and in 1986 she won the prestigious Wade Trophy, given by the National Association for Girls and Women in Sports for excellence in academics and community service as well as basketball prowess. In March 1986 USC retired her jersey number 31, the first time the institution had bestowed such an honor on an athlete. In 1995 Miller was inducted into the Naismith Memorial Basketball Hall of Fame, and in 1999 she was an inductee of the inaugural class of the Women's Basketball Hall of Fame in Knoxville, Tennessee.

Had Miller graduated from college in the mid-1990s instead of the mid-1980s, professional basketball opportunities in the United States would have awaited her, with the emergence of the American Basketball League and the Women's National Basketball League. However, the Women's Professional Basketball League collapsed in the early 1980s after only three years in existence, forcing the best American women's basketball players to travel to Europe if they desired to play professionally after college. For Miller this was not an option, as she wanted to remain close to her family in Southern California.

Miller's collegiate basketball successes did provide her with the chance to represent the United States in international competition. She played on the U.S. team in the Pan American Games in 1983 and 1986, winning the gold medal in 1983. Miller also helped the United States win the gold medals at the Los Angeles Olympics and at the 1986 Goodwill Games in Moscow, after which she said, "This is even better than the Olympics in '84.... This is beating the Russians in Russia, I've waited a long time for this." Whether playing before a national or an international audience, Miller's play embodied intense emotion and a flamboyant style, drawing critics and fans alike. While even her critics were quick to underscore Miller's great athleticism, some, including fellow basketball star Ann

Meyers, believed Miller's showboating on the court detracted from her overall potential contributions to the game. Unfortunately, Miller suffered knee injuries in 1987 and 1988 that brought her competitive playing days to an end.

Capitalizing on the academic skills learned at USC, Miller became a television sportscaster, working first for ABC's *Wide World of Sports* before becoming a sideline reporter and studio analyst for TNT and TBS. In 1996 she became the first female analyst for a nationally televised basketball game. In addition to her broadcasting career, Miller also tried her hand at being a coach. In 1993 she accepted the head women's basketball coaching position at her alma mater, USC. However, her hiring was not without controversy. Miller replaced Marianne Stanley, who was not retained by USC after she demanded a salary commensurate with that of the Trojans' men's coach, George Raveling. Some USC players, including the star, Lisa Leslie, voiced their support of Stanley and opposed her dismissal. Furthermore, several college coaches turned down employment offers from USC to express their solidarity with Stanley. Despite that uneasy baptism as coach of the Women of Troy, Miller persevered, guiding her team to the NCAA women's basketball play-offs in 1993–1994 and 1994–1995 seasons. In the fall of 1995 she resigned her position at USC to move back into broadcasting, leaving the team with an impressive record of forty-four wins and fourteen losses.

The formation of the Women's National Basketball Association in 1997 enabled Miller to return to the court as head coach of the Phoenix Mercury. In four seasons with Phoenix, Miller directed her team to seventy wins against fifty-two losses, including play-off appearances in three of those years. As a player in the 1980s and a coach in the 1990s Cheryl Miller's emotion, skill, and passion helped to transform competitive women's basketball from a slower, more deliberate passing game to a fast-paced, high-energy game enjoyed by players and spectators alike.

More than simply serving as a role model for elite female basketball players, Cheryl Miller also has given young girls across the country a strong, confident image to emulate. Moreover, her dedication to the sport and her superior athleticism brought the game to a national stage in the 1980s. Miller's efforts secured an even brighter future for young girls whose desire is to play basketball, from backyard pickup games to professional contests, in the United States.

FURTHER READING

Freeman, Patricia. "The Magic of Cheryl Miller," *Women's Sports and Fitness* (Feb. 1986).

Kirkpatrick, Curry. "Lights! Camera! Cheryl!," *Sports Illustrated* (20 Nov. 1985).

RITA LIBERTI

Miller, Dorie (12 Oct. 1919–24 Nov. 1943), war hero, was born Doris Miller in Waco, Texas, the son of Conery Miller and Henrietta (maiden name unknown), sharecroppers. Miller attended Waco's segregated Moore High School and became the school's two-hundred-pound star fullback. As the third of four sons in a family engaged in subsistence farming, however, he was forced to drop out of school to find work. In September 1939 he joined the navy as a mess attendant.

The navy was then rigidly segregated. Except for a small group of black sailors in the general service, survivors of the mostly integrated pre–World War I fleet, blacks were restricted to the steward's branch, where they wore distinctive uniforms and insignia. Even chief stewards could not exercise authority over men with lower ratings in the general service. Stewards manned the officers' mess, maintained the officers' billets aboard ship, and in some instances, took care of the quarters of high officials

Dorie Miller, receiving the Navy Cross at Pearl Harbor, 27 May 1942. (Library of Congress.)

ashore. Despite the fact that their enlistment contracts restricted their training and duties, stewards, like everyone aboard ship, were assigned battle stations, including positions at the guns and on the bridge. Miller received the standard eight-week training course given mess attendants at the Naval Receiving Station, Norfolk, Virginia, and, after a brief stint on an ammunition ship, was assigned to the battleship *West Virginia*. In the early hours of 7 December 1941, the *West Virginia* was at its berth in Pearl Harbor, Hawaii, and Miller was going about his daily chore of collecting officers' laundry when the call to battle stations sounded. Miller arrived at his station in the antiaircraft battery magazine amidships to find it aflame, a victim of the initial Japanese torpedo attack. Hurrying topside, he followed his supervisory officer to the bridge, where, despite enemy strafing and in the face of a serious fire, the powerful young sailor carried the ship's mortally wounded captain to a safer place.

The officer then loaded the two fifty-millimeter bridge guns and ordered the untrained Miller to man one of them. Asked later about his subsequent actions, Miller said: "It wasn't hard. I just pulled the trigger and she worked fine. I'd watched others use those guns. I guess I fired her for about fifteen minutes. I think I got one of those Jap planes. They were diving pretty close to us." In fact, Miller continued firing at the enemy planes until ordered to abandon the burning bridge.

In the confused aftermath of Pearl Harbor, Miller's feat, although noted in naval dispatches, went unheralded. Rumors continued to circulate, however, and on 14 March 1942 the *Pittsburgh Courier*, a widely read black newspaper, broke the story, demanding official public recognition of Miller's heroism. Secretary of the Navy Frank Knox, an ardent defender of the navy's racial exclusion policy, reacted belatedly by writing Miller a letter of commendation, but this only fueled the growing demand for public honors. Edgar Brown, representing the National Negro Council, urged congressmen to pass a bill introduced by Senator James M. Mead of New York and others to award Miller the Medal of Honor, and Wendell Willkie, the Republican leader, called on President Franklin D. Roosevelt to intervene.

Knox argued that his letter of commendation and Miller's anticipated promotion to mess attendant, first class, provided sufficient recognition, but the president, no doubt reacting to widespread charges of racism in the navy, overruled Knox. In an extraordinary move, Roosevelt personally ordered Miller awarded the Navy Cross. On 27 May 1942 the commander of the Pacific fleet, Admiral Chester W. Nimitz, bestowed the navy's second-highest award on Miller with due ceremony.

Despite Knox's intransigence, the position of blacks in the navy had changed considerably by mid-1942. Forced to open its general service to African Americans and now dependent exclusively on the selective service with its 10 percent black quota for manpower, the navy witnessed a dramatic increase in the number of black sailors in all jobs and ratings. The Bureau of Naval Personnel faced the daunting task of training and assigning thousands of black members while maintaining their morale in a segregated environment. Civil rights spokespeople deftly connected recognition of Miller's heroism to the growing aspirations of the new black sailors and the black public at large, and the bureau readily endorsed the *Courier*'s suggestion that Miller come home to speak to the young black draftees.

Miller, the high school dropout, proved surprisingly effective at his public affairs assignments, speaking before large audiences throughout the United States. In due course, however, he was promoted to petty officer rank (cook, third class) in the general service and was reassigned to sea. He returned to the fleet in time to participate in the battle for Tarawa, but on 24 November 1943 he was among the 644 men lost when the escort carrier *Liscome Bay* sank during the battle for Makin.

Almost thirty years after Miller's death a more racially enlightened navy, desiring to honor the exploits of its minority heroes, named the Service School Command barracks at Great Lakes Naval Station, Illinois, in Miller's honor, and in June 1973 his mother christened the USS *Miller*, a Knox-class destroyer escort. But again, such honors were not without controversy, because they followed closely another effort to use the memory of Miller's experience to advance the general civil rights agenda. The navy opposed an effort, this time led by Senator Edward M. Kennedy among others, to award Miller the Medal of Honor posthumously. The chief of naval operations, Admiral Elmo M. Zumwalt, himself an ardent champion of minority rights in the navy, rejected the demand on the grounds that, in the absence of new evidence, the Navy Cross had been the appropriate award and that naming a ship and barracks in Miller's honor constituted sufficient recognition. In the late 1980s Representative Joe DioGuardi of New York, chagrined that no black serviceman was awarded the Medal of Honor

in either world war, again nominated Miller for the nation's highest decoration as representative of all the black heroes of World War II, but to no avail. In 1997 President Bill Clinton bestowed the Medal of Honor upon seven black World War II veterans, but Miller was not among them.

FURTHER READING

Foner, Jack D. *Blacks and the Military in American History* (1974).
MacGregor, Morris J., Jr. *Integration of the Armed Forces, 1940–1965* (1981).
This entry is taken from the *American National Biography* and is published here with the permission of the American Council of Learned Societies.

MORRIS J. MACGREGOR

Miller, Gertrude C. Hood (1867?–16 June 1939), educator, textile mill supervisor, dressmaker, was born Gertrude C. Hood in North Carolina, the eldest daughter of four children to Sophia J. Nugent, of Washington, D.C., and JAMES WALKER HOOD of Pennsylvania. Miller's father was a prominent bishop and educator in the African Methodist Episcopal Zion (AMEZ) Church. Gertrude Hood Miller, also known as "Gertie," spent her life in Fayetteville, North Carolina. Miller's mother, Sophia Nugent died in 1875. Two years after her mother's death, James Walker Hood married Keziah "Katie" Price McCoy of Wilmington, North Carolina. The couple went on to have more children, making Hood the eldest of eleven children (Martin, p. 41) Shortly after her birth, Miller's father moved the family to his new post with the Evans AMEZ Church in Fayetteville, North Carolina. HENRY EVANS, an African American pastor, built the church in 1796, and it became the first and longest-running African American institution in the city. With support and influence of her parents and church family, Gertrude Miller invested her life to the uplift of her race through work within the AMEZ denomination's educational system and in the development of the one of the first all-black operated textile mills in the South.

Miller spent her early years between in Raleigh and Fayetteville, North Carolina. According to the 1880 census, she received her early education at Fayetteville's Howard School, the second-oldest black institution in North Carolina, now the home of Fayetteville State University. The school specialized in teacher training and instruction. After her education concluded at Howard, Miller attended

Livingstone College in Salisbury, North Carolina. Livingstone, founded in 1880, was an AMEZ coeducational institution founded and staffed by both male and female faculty. Later, Hood became a member of the faculty and more than likely taught dressmaking, a skill she would use in her next endeavor in her role as a supervisor in the Ashley & Bailey Silk Mill of Fayetteville, North Carolina.

In 1901 Miller entered the national spotlight as a symbol of the power of education in the economic development of the African American community. BOOKER T. WASHINGTON specifically mentioned Hood's work in the North Carolina textile factory in an article he authored for *Gunton's Magazine*, a prominent periodical during this period. Washington described the accomplishments of African Americans in industry including Hood's work as a supervisor of the winding and doubling department, where she supervised African American children between the ages of twelve and eighteen.

The Ashley & Bailey Company gained national attention due to its unique place in African American and labor history. The company, based in Paterson, New Jersey, regularly employed African Americans in all capacities in their northern plants: an unusual practice in this period. Textile mills across the country regularly employed native white and immigrant labor, but rarely hired African Americans outside of custodial work in the mills. The mill decided to enter into the Southern labor market and opened up the Fayetteville plant with four hundred employees, all of whom were black.

When the mill hired Hood, they chose her because of her education, experience, and standing in the community as a respectable woman and daughter of a nationally recognized race-leader. These high qualifications were not the standard set for white workers, but were deemed necessary for African Americans. Miller symbolized the best and the brightest. The black community, the mill, and Hood argued against the belief that blacks were incapable of performing the complicated and intricate work of silk weaving. Her position and national recognition paved the way for other African American women to participate in North Carolina's growing textile industry and served as inspiration for similar enterprises across the South in the same period. The silk mill was staffed primarily with women and children, and the company opened a mill school for its employees to continue their education. The company became the largest employer of African Americans in the area for fourteen years until its close in 1913 due to financial issues found across all of its plants.

Miller's work in the community did not end with her managerial work at the mill. She continued to serve the community through her work in the Evans church and in major functions of the denomination. On 16 May 1916 she addressed a conference of the all-male clergy of the African American Methodist Church to deliver her father's posthumous report on the work he had completed in the four years preceding his death. By 1930, she married Cicero Miller, a drug store clerk and tinner. Miller lived within Fayetteville the majority of her remaining years and died in New York at the home of her niece.

FURTHER READING
A research file on Gertrude C. Hood Miller is housed in the Cumberland Public Library, Fayetteville, North Carolina.

Billie, Annette C. *The History of Evans Metropolitan African Methodist Episcopal Zion Church: A Chronicle of Events* (2006).

Martin, Sandy Dwayne. *For God and Race: The Religious and Political Leadership of AMEZ Bishop James Walker Hood* (1999).

Silva, Kathryn M. *"Six Days Thou Shalt Labor: African Americans in the Southern Textile Industry, 1895–1929* (2010).

KATHRYN M. SILVA

Miller, Kelly (18 July 1863–29 Dec. 1939), educator and essayist, was born in Winnsboro, South Carolina, the son of Kelly Miller, a free black who served in the Confederate army, and Elizabeth Roberts, a slave. The sixth of ten children, Miller received his early education in one of the local primary schools established during Reconstruction and later attended the Fairfield Institute in Winnsboro from 1878 to 1880. Awarded a scholarship to Howard University, he completed the preparatory department's three-year curriculum in Latin, Greek, and mathematics in two years (1880–1882), then attended the college department at Howard University from 1882 to 1886.

After his graduation from Howard, Miller studied advanced mathematics (1886–1887) with Captain Edgar Frisby, an English mathematician at the U.S. Naval Observatory. Frisby's chief at the observatory, Simon Newcomb, who was also a professor of mathematics at Johns Hopkins University, recommended Miller for admission. The first black student admitted to Johns Hopkins, Miller studied mathematics, physics, and astronomy there from

1887 to 1889 but did not graduate because he ran out of funds. After teaching mathematics briefly at the M Street High School in Washington, D.C. (1889–1890), he was appointed to the faculty of Howard University in 1890. Five years later Miller added sociology to Howard's curriculum because he thought that the new discipline was important for developing objective analyses of the racial system in the United States. From 1895 to 1907 Miller was professor of mathematics and sociology, but he taught sociology exclusively after that, serving from 1915 to 1925 as head of the new sociology department. In 1894 Miller had married Annie May Butler, a teacher at the Baltimore Normal School; the couple had five children.

Noted for his brilliant mind, Miller rapidly became a major figure in the life of Howard University. In 1907 he was appointed dean of the College of Arts and Sciences. During his twelve-year deanship, the college grew dramatically, as the old classical curriculum was modernized and new courses in the natural sciences and the social sciences were added. Miller's recruiting tours through the South and Mid-Atlantic states were so successful that the enrollment increased from seventy-five undergraduates in 1907 to 243 undergraduates in 1911.

Although Miller was a leader at Howard for most of his tenure there, his national importance derived from his intellectual leadership during the conflict between the "accommodationism" of BOOKER T. WASHINGTON and the "radicalism" of the nascent civil rights movement led by W. E. B. DuBois. Critical of Washington's famous Cotton States Exposition Address (1895) in 1896, Miller later praised Washington's emphasis on self-help and initiative. Miller remained an opponent of the exaggerated claims made on behalf of industrial education and became one of the most effective advocates of higher education for black Americans when it was attacked as inappropriate for a people whose social role was increasingly limited by statute and custom to agriculture, some skilled trades, unskilled labor, and domestic service.

In the *Educational Review, Dial, Education,* the *Journal of Social Science,* and other leading journals, Miller argued that blacks required wise leadership in the difficult political and social circumstances following the defeat of Reconstruction, and only higher education could provide such leaders. Moreover, the race required physicians, lawyers, clergymen, teachers, and other professionals whose existence was dependent on higher education. Excluded from most white colleges, black Americans would have to secure higher education in their own institutions, Miller argued, and some of them, like Howard, Fisk, and Atlanta universities, would emphasize liberal education and the professions rather than the trades and manual arts (industrial education) stressed at Hampton and Tuskegee institutes. In the debate between the advocates of collegiate and industrial education, Miller maintained that the whole matter was one of "ratio and proportion," not "fundamental controversy." Recognized as one of the most influential black educators in the nation because of his extensive writing and his leadership at Howard, Miller was sought out by both camps in the controversy but was trusted by neither because of his refusal to dogmatically support either of the rival systems.

Miller's reputation as a "philosopher of the race question" was based on his brilliant articles, published anonymously at first, on "radicals" and "conservatives" in the *Boston Transcript* (18 and 19 Sept. 1903). With some alterations, these articles later became the lead essay in his book *Race Adjustment* (1908). Miller's essays insisted on the right of black Americans to protest against the injustices that had multiplied with the rise of the white supremacy movement in the South, as the DuBois "radicals" did, but he also advocated racial solidarity, thrift, and institution building as emphasized by the followers of Washington. Characteristically, Miller had two reputations as a public policy analyst, first as a compromiser between black radicals and conservatives, and second as a race spokesman during the prolonged crisis of disenfranchisement and the denial of civil rights by white supremacists and their elected representatives in Congress. *The Disgrace of Democracy: An Open Letter to President Woodrow Wilson*, a pamphlet published in August 1917, was Miller's most popular effort. Responding to recent race riots in Memphis and East St. Louis, Miller argued that a "democracy of race or class is no democracy at all." Writing to Wilson, he said: "It is but hollow mockery of the Negro when he is beaten and bruised in all parts of the nation and flees to the national government for asylum, to be denied relief on the basis of doubtful jurisdiction. The black man asks for protection and is given a theory of government." More than 250,000 copies of the pamphlet were sold, and military authorities banned it at army posts.

Although Miller was best known as a controversialist, he also made important but frequently overlooked contributions to the discipline of sociology. His earliest contribution was his analysis of Frederick L. Hoffman's *Race Traits and Tendencies of the American Negro*, published by the American Economic Association in 1896. Hoffman attempted to demonstrate that the social disorganization of black Americans (weak community institutions and family structure) was caused by an alleged genetic inferiority and that their correspondingly high mortality rate would result in their disappearance as an element of the American population. Miller's refutation of Hoffman's claims, *A Review of Hoffman's "Race Traits and Tendencies of the American Negro,"* published by the American Negro Academy in 1897, was based on a technical analysis of census data.

Perhaps Miller's most lasting contribution to scholarship was his pioneering advocacy of the systematic study of black people. In 1901 he proposed to the Howard board of trustees that the university financially support the publications of the American Negro Academy, whose goals were to promote literature, science, art, higher education, and scholarly works by blacks, and to defend them against "vicious assaults." Although the board declined, it permitted the academy to meet on the campus. Convinced that Howard should use its prestige and location in Washington to become a national center for black studies, Miller planned a "Negro-Americana Museum and Library." In 1914 he persuaded JESSE E. MOORLAND, a Howard alumnus and Young Men's Christian Association official, to donate to Howard his large private library on blacks in Africa and in the United States as the foundation for the proposed center. This became the Moorland Foundation (reorganized in 1973 as the Moorland-Spingarn Research Center), a research library, archives, and museum that has been vital to the emergence of sound scholarship in this field.

The years after World War I were difficult ones for Miller. J. Stanley Durkee, the last of Howard's white presidents, was appointed in 1918 and set out to curtail the baronial power of the deans by building a new central administration. Miller, a conspicuously powerful dean, was demoted in 1919 to dean of a new junior college, which was later abolished in 1925. A leader in the movement to have a black president of Howard, Miller was a perennial favorite of the alumni but was never selected. Although Miller's influence at Howard declined significantly by the late 1920s through his retirement in 1934, his stature as a commentator on race relations and politics remained high. He had become alarmed by the vast social changes stimulated by World War

I and was seen as increasingly conservative. He opposed the widespread abandonment of farming by black Americans and warned that the mass migration to cities would be socially and culturally destructive. At a time when many younger blacks regarded labor unions as progressive forces, Miller was skeptical of them, citing their history of persistent racial discrimination. He remained an old-fashioned American patriot despite the nation's many disappointing failures to extend democracy to black Americans. As a weekly columnist in the black press, Miller published his views in more than one hundred newspapers. By 1923 it was estimated that his columns reached a half million readers. Miller died at his home on the campus of Howard University.

FURTHER READING
A limited collection of Miller's papers, including an incomplete autobiography and a scrapbook, is at the Moorland-Spingarn Research Center at Howard University.
Eisenberg, Bernard. "The Negro Leader as a Marginal Man," *Journal of Negro History* 45 (July 1960).
Holmes, D. O. W. "Kelly Miller," *Phylon* (Second Quarter, 1945).
Meier, August. "The Racial and Educational Philosophy of Kelly Miller, 1895–1915," *Journal of Negro Education* (July 1960).
Obituary: Woodson, Carter G., *Journal of Negro History* (Jan. 1940).
This entry is taken from the *American National Biography* and is published here with the permission of the American Council of Learned Societies.

MICHAEL R. WINSTON

Miller, Loren (20 Jan. 1903–14 July 1967), judge, newspaper owner, and civil rights activist was born in Pender, Nebraska, to John Bird Miller and Nora Herbaugh. His father was born a slave, and his mother was a school teacher. Miller has been recognized for his significant gains in spearheading court cases which resulted in equal opportunity and fair housing for all Americans.

Miller graduated from high school in Highland, Kansas. He studied at the University of Kansas in Lawrence, Kansas, as well as Howard University in Washington, D.C., where he majored in journalism. He obtained his bachelor of laws degree from Washburn University in Topeka, Kansas, in 1928, and graduated from the University of Southern California Law School as well (Flamming, 2005,

p. 302). Miller was admitted to the Kansas bar, and the California bar in 1933.

In Los Angeles he met notable poet LANGSTON HUGHES who noticed some of his articles, and was instrumental in getting him hired as a writer for the National Association for the Advancement of Colored People's (NAACP) *Crisis* magazine (Smith, 2006, p. 242). *The Crisis* editor W. E. B. DuBois would become his mentor.

He wrote for the *California News* in Los Angeles from 1929 to 1933 and for the weekly *California Eagle* in the early 1930s. In 1933 Miller married Juanita Ellsworth, a social worker. This union produced two sons, Loren, Jr. and Edward. Loren, Jr. followed in his father's footsteps as a judge as well.

In 1943 Miller worked as a reporter for the *Los Angeles Sentinel*. He also continued to make notable achievements in the legal field. One of his key motivating factors may have been that his white mother could not continue teaching school in his hometown simply because she was married to Miller's black father (p. 242).

Miller made significant strides against racial discrimination in housing. Some of the highlights in his law career include winning *Fairchild v. Rainers* in 1944 for a Pasadena, California, family. In 1945 he represented black entertainers HATTIE McDANIEL, LOUISE BEAVERS, and ETHEL WATERS who sought to move into the Sugar Hill Los Angeles residential area. The residents were determined to block their entry into the neighborhood. Miller based his position on the California State Constitution and the Fourteenth Amendment. Superior Judge Thurmond Clarke threw the case out of court in Miller's favor.

By 1947 he had represented more than one hundred plaintiffs in their struggle for fair housing policies. That year he partnered with future first black Supreme Court Justice THURGOOD MARSHALL on *Shelley v. Kraemer* 334 U.S. 1 (1948), which originated in Missouri, and won in 1948 at the United States Supreme Court.

This case entailed construction worker J. D. Shelley and his munitions plant worker wife, Ethel Lee, who sought to buy a house in a predominantly white neighborhood in St. Louis. Louis and Fern Kraemer, who lived ten blocks away on the same street, sued the Shelleys to bar their entry into the residential area. The trial judge determined that the case was unlawful since nine residents had not signed the racial covenant. An appeals judge reversed this decision in 1946 (Tushnet, 1994, p. 89).

The Supreme Court finally heard the case in conjunction with a similar one from Michigan. Miller and Marshall cited that Louisville's 1917 *Buchanan v. Warley* (No. 33) case precedent showed that racial covenants in housing impaired the civil rights guaranteed under the 1866 Civil Rights Act (p. 90). Loren was distinguished as the first U.S. lawyer to win against racial covenants with Federal Housing Authority (FHA) or Veterans Administration (VA) financing.

He bought the *California Eagle* newspaper in 1951 from Charlotta Bass to continue espousing his ideologies of racial equality. During this time he also wrote for *The Nation, Law in Transition, The New Masses*, and *American Mercury* magazine. In 1953 Miller won *Barrows v. Jackson* which disallowed damage awards for racial covenant violations using the *Shelley v. Kraemer* precedent. Miller also assisted in preparing some of the legal briefs that Marshall used in 1954 to win the landmark *Brown v. Board of Education of Topeka, Kansas* case which desegregated public school systems (Smith, p. 275).

His affiliations included board member of the American Civil Liberties Union (ACLU), and co-chair of the West Coast legal committee of the NAACP. He was also vice president of the NAACP, and on the civil rights committee of the State Bar of California.

Governor Edmund G. Brown appointed Miller California Superior Court Justice of the County of Los Angeles in 1964. He sold the *California Eagle* on 7 July 1964 to accept the judgeship. He served in this position until his death on 14 July 1967. He passed away at Temple Hospital in Los Angeles from emphysema complicated by pneumonia. The year before his death, Loren wrote *The Petitioners: The Story of the Supreme Court of the U.S. and the Negro* (1966).

In 1968 the Loren Miller Bar Association began in Seattle, Washington, as an affiliate of the National Bar Association. The same year South Central Los Angeles named an elementary school after him. A Los Angeles recreation center also bears his name. The State Bar of California started the Loren Miller Legal Services Award in 1977 on its fiftieth anniversary.

From 1975 to 1997 Miller's son Loren, Jr. served the Los Angeles County bench, and continues to sit by assignment. Miller's granddaughter Robin Miller Sloan was appointed to the Los Angeles Superior Court in 2003. They are the first linear third generation judges in the history of the California court system.

FURTHER READING

Caughey, LaRee, and John. *Los Angeles: Biography of a City* (1976).

Flamming, Douglas. *Bound for Freedom: Black Los Angeles in Jim Crow America* (2005).

Horne, Gerald. *Fire This Time: The Watts Uprising and the 1960s* (1995).

Miller, Loren. "Covenants in the Bear Flag State," *The Crisis* 53 (May 1946).

Miller, Loren. *The Petitioners: The Story of the Supreme Court of the US and the Negro* (1966).

Miller, Loren. "A Right Secured," *The Nation* (29 May 1948).

Sides, Josh. *L.A. City Limits: African American Los Angeles from the Great Depression to the Present* (2003).

Smith, R. J. *The Great Black Way: Los Angeles' Central Avenue in the 1940's and the Lost African-American Renaissance* (2006).

Tushnet, Mark V. *Making Civil Rights Law: Thurgood Marshall and the Supreme Court, 1936–1961* (1994).

"Victory on Sugar Hill," *Time* (17 December 1945).

Watts, Jill. *Hattie McDaniel: Black Ambition, White Hollywood* (2005).

MELINDA BOND SHREVE

Miller, May (26 Jan. 1899–8 Feb. 1995, poet, playwright, and teacher was born May Miller in Washington, D.C., the daughter of Annie May Butler and KELLY MILLER, the dean of the College of Arts and Sciences at Howard University. Little is known about the background of Miller's mother, but her father was popular among black intellectuals. The Miller home on the campus was often visited by such luminaries as the writer PAUL LAURENCE DUNBAR, who once lived with the family; BOOKER T. WASHINGTON, the founder of the Tuskegee Institute; and the writer and activist W.E.B. DuBOIS, a cofounder of the National Association for the Advancement of Colored People. Miller lived in a community of college-educated blacks who worked as artists and musicians. Following the opening of the Howard Theatre in 1910, the neighborhood of Seventh and T was filled with restaurants, row houses, nightclubs, and after-hours social clubs.

Miller's father encouraged her writing career by teaching her poetry. He often quoted bits of poetry to his children, leaving them to wonder if the lines were real or something he made up on his own. Presumably, the family's large collection of books also influenced young Miller. The collection included, among others, *Oak and Ivy*, Dunbar's first volume of poetry. She began writing on her own and

her first poem was published in the *Washington Post* when she was fourteen and her first play, *Pandora's Box*, was published in 1914. Miller graduated from the M Street School, a predecessor to Paul Laurence Dunbar High School, where the prominent black dramatist MARY BURRILL and the poet and playwright ANGELINA WELD GRIMKÉ were among her teachers. She studied drama at Howard, where she directed, acted, and produced plays. In 1920 Miller graduated first in her class and earned the Howard University Drama Award for her play, *Within the Shadows*.

The Harlem Renaissance, a period during which black literature and art flourished in this community, was at its peak in the 1920s. Miller often traveled between Harlem and Washington, meeting poets like LANGSTON HUGHES and COUNTÉE CULLEN at literary gatherings. In 1925 her play *The Bog Guide* was published, followed by *Scratches* in 1929, *Stragglers in the Dust*, and *Nails and Thorns* in 1933. *The Bog Guide* and a later play, *The Cuss'd Thing*, both won prizes in the Opportunity Contest. She managed to balance her writing with her work at Baltimore's FREDERICK DOUGLASS High School, where she taught English, speech, and drama. At one point in Baltimore, Miller became acquainted with the young ZORA NEALE HURSTON, whom she encouraged to attend Howard University. In 1935 four of Miller's plays were published in the anthology *Negro History in Thirteen Plays*, which she edited with Willis Richardson. It included her plays *Harriet Tubman* and *Sojourner Truth*. Miller also did postgraduate study in literature at American University and Columbia University. She was a lecturer and poet in residence at Monmouth College in Monmouth, Illinois, in 1963, the University of Wisconsin-Milwaukee in 1972, and the Phillips Exeter Academy in Exeter, New Hampshire, from 1973 to 1976. She married John "Bud" Sullivan in 1940 and added Sullivan to her name.

Heart ailments caused Miller to retire from teaching in 1945, which left her more time to write poetry. She published several volumes of verse, including *Into the Clearing* (1959), *Poems* (1962), *Lyrics of Three Women: Katie Lyle, Maude Rubin and May Miller* (1964), and *Not that Far* (1973). In the 1960s Miller became an arts coordinator for the Washington, D.C., public schools and served on the Folger Library advisory committee. Meanwhile, the modern civil rights movement was well under way. The NAACP and the Student Nonviolent Coordinating Committee (SNCC) staged sit ins and protests at establishments that refused to serve blacks. Miller purposely kept her distance from the racial upheaval in the country and was criticized for not being more outspoken on the issue of civil rights by other writers at the time.

Miller continued to live around Washington, often reading her poems at community gatherings and telling stories about growing up in the city. She never shied away from public appearances, and in 1976 she read her poetry at the inauguration of President Jimmy Carter. She often appeared on panel discussions and was mentioned in at least one documentary, *7th and T*, which aired in May 1987, to talk about her old neighborhood, which began a downward spiral after the 1968 riots.

A resurgence of interest in Miller's work took place in the late 1980s. Miller published more of her poetry in *The Ransomed Wait* (1983), which addressed the 1963 Birmingham bombing in a poem called "Blazing Accusation." She wrote: "Beyond allotted time and self, the four of them will go down red gullies of guilt and alleys of dark memories through snagging fields of scarecrows and up an unforgetting hill to blazon accusation of an age." In 1986 she received an award from the Institute for the Preservation and Study of African American Writing. Her last work, *Collected Poems of May Miller*, was published in 1989. Miller died from pneumonia at her home in Washington, D.C., in 1995; her husband had died in 1982. Her work never gained her celebrity status, but Miller did not seem to be bothered by that fact. She once said, "If out of silence I can fill that silence with a word that will conjure up an image, then I have succeeded."

FURTHER READING

Koolish, Lynda. "Miller, May," in *The Concise Oxford Companion to African American Literature*, eds. William L. Andrews, Frances Smith Foster, and Trudier Harris (2001).

Obituary: *Washington Post*, 10 Feb. 1995.

SHANTEÉ WOODARDS

Miller, Robert (fl. 1740s), King George's War soldier, was most likely born in Hampton, New Hampshire, the son of Neb Miller, a slave of Colonel Christopher Toppan. Whether Robert Miller was born free is unknown, but if he was a slave, he was freed at an early age; by August 1738 he was living with his wife, name unknown, in a locale called Murray's Row in nearby Hampton Falls, New Hampshire. Described as "mulattoes," Miller and his wife were warned to "Depart forthwith out of this Parish of-hampton fals (*sic*)" on 10 November 1738 (Knoblock, 149).

This "warning out" procedure was a widespread custom in New England, where town officials were suspicious of most newcomers and fearful that those without a visible means of support would become a financial burden on the town. While such warnings were issued to those of all races as a matter of law, in many cases they were a distinct signal to people of color that their presence in town was undesirable. No matter what the intended message may have been, Miller would stay in Hampton Falls and rear a family as well as serve his colony.

Miller's military service commenced in early 1745, when he served in the Hampton Falls company of Captain Edward Williams at the siege of the French fortress at Louisburg on Cape Breton Island, Canada, during King George's War. Also known as the War of Jenkins's Ear, King George's War (1740–1747) set the English against the Spanish and the French in the Caribbean and the North American mainland. Miller and the men from his town served under the colony of Massachusetts, which raised and organized a force of nearly 4,000 men under the command of William Pepperell. The force landed on Cape Breton Island on 30 April 1745 and, though little fighting of consequence actually occurred, the fort capitulated on 17 June. While many men were lost owing to illness and disease, Miller was one of the relatively few casualties suffered as a result of gunfire, having his "arm shot off" during "the Unfortunate Attack of the Island battery in the Siege of Louisbourgh [*sic*]" (Knoblock, 150). Despite his wounds, Miller survived to return to Hampton Falls. Though the number of black soldiers who served in King George's War is unknown, Miller was not alone; Cuff Manis of Moulton's Regiment was employed in late 1745 repairing the fort at Louisburg, while Peter, "Major Greenleaf's Negro," was employed in a "gard" unit within New Hampshire for Rochester and Barrington (Knoblock, 314). The service of these men and likely a number of others from Massachusetts, though not yet fully examined and documented, is another example of the gradually increasing role that blacks like Miller, BARZILLAI LEW, and CASTOR DICKINSON would play in manning colonial regiments during times of war, and one that would gain an even greater importance in the American Revolution three decades later.

Crippled for life, Miller petitioned the government of New Hampshire in July 1747 for monetary assistance because he was "Incapable of Labouring for the Support of himself & a Large family" (Knoblock, 314). Miller had previously been denied assistance from Massachusetts because of his New

Hampshire residency. The results of Miller's request are unknown, but clearly he was not entirely incapacitated; on 3 January 1753 Miller was charged by Meshach Weare, the Justice of the Peace for Hampton Falls, "that he had the Carnal Knowledge ... at several times" of Katharine Bryan, "Singlewoman," and "that she is now with Child and that the said Robert did beget the same on her body" (Knoblock, 150). Miller was forced to pay fifty pounds and provide two sureties in the amount of twenty-five dollars each and appear in court the following March, as well as be on good behavior. While no details regarding Bryan are known, nor the final outcome of this case, the record of this charge against Miller is unusual in several aspects; not only does it provide a small glimpse into the personal life of a black man in colonial New England, and the attendant consequences of violating its social mores, but the actual court summons document itself also serves as a birth certificate of sorts for his son, Robert Miller Jr., born later in 1753. For those citizens of color born well before the American Revolution and, indeed, for long after, records of any kind regarding births and parental identification are largely absent and even "negative" documents such as that for Miller are valuable.

After 1753 Miller disappears from the records, though he likely continued to live in Hampton Falls, New Hampshire, and it seems likely that he was supported in his old age by his children. Interestingly, two sons, Robert Miller Jr. and Jonathan Miller, would serve as soldiers in the American Revolution, their desire to fight no doubt fueled in part by the tales of their father's military service years before. Robert Miller Jr. enlisted for service in Poor's Second New Hampshire Regiment under Captain Winthrop, following the Lexington Alarm, on 29 May 1775. However, Miller's service was conditional, contingent on "if the committee accept him" (Knoblock, 150). The younger Robert Miller was indeed accepted as a soldier and would serve in the American Revolution for nearly five consecutive years, seeing action at New York City, Fort Ticonderoga, Saratoga, and Monmouth.

Miller's other known son, Jonathan Miller, was born sometime around 1755 and enlisted with his brother in the same regiment in 1775, but served for only six months. He would later serve for several enlistment periods in local militia units and Scammell's Third New Hampshire Regiment and, like his brother, saw heavy action at Fort Ticonderoga, Saratoga, and Monmouth. Late in the war, perhaps in ill health, Miller hired a substitute

to serve his final six months of garrison duty at Newburgh, New York. His occupation listed as that of a fisherman, Jonathan Miller occasionally ran afoul of the law and continued in Hampton Falls for an undetermined amount of time. Like his brother, nothing is known of Jonathan Miller's life after the war.

FURTHER READING

Knoblock, Glenn A. *"Strong and Brave Fellows":*
New Hampshire's Black Soldiers and Sailors of the
American Revolution, 1775–1784 (2003).

GLENN ALLEN KNOBLOCK

Miller, Thomas Ezekiel (17 June 1849–8 Apr. 1938), political leader and educator, was born in Ferrebeeville, South Carolina, the son of Richard Miller and Mary Ferrebee, occupations unknown. Miller's race was a source of periodic concern and speculation. Although he always considered himself to be black, Miller's very fair complexion led to allegations during his political career that he was white, the abandoned child of an unmarried white couple.

Miller moved to Charleston with his parents in the early 1850s, where he attended schools for free black children. His mother died when he was nine. As a youngster he distributed the *Charleston Mercury* to local hotels, and during the Civil War he worked aboard South Carolina Railroad trains delivering newspapers between Charleston and Savannah, Georgia. When the Confederate government seized the railroads, Miller found himself in the service and in the uniform of the Confederacy. Union forces captured him as they advanced into South Carolina in January 1865 and confined him for two weeks in a Union stockade.

Following the war Miller accompanied Union troops to Long Island, New York, and then pursued his education in Hudson, New York, south of Albany. After graduation from Pennsylvania's Lincoln University in 1872, he returned to South Carolina and enrolled at South Carolina College (now the University of South Carolina), where he took at least one law course. He read law with both the state solicitor P. L. Wiggins and the state supreme court chief justice Franklin J. Moses Sr., and he was admitted to the South Carolina bar in 1875, moving to the city of Beaufort to set up practice. Miller had married Anna M. Hume, probably in 1874; they had nine children, seven of whom survived him.

Miller spent most of the next two decades active in politics and the Republican Party. He was elected to the Beaufort County School Commission in 1872, and he represented Beaufort in the state house of representatives from 1874 to 1880. Elected to the state senate in 1880, Miller resigned two years later. He lost a bid for a seat in the U.S. House of Representatives in 1886, but in 1888 he challenged William Elliott's election to the U.S. House, and following a protracted House investigation Miller was seated. He represented South Carolina's Seventh District from September 1890 to March 1891. In reaction to white southern Democratic attacks on the Lodge Federal Elections bill (also known as the "Force Bill"), a proposal created to protect the voting rights of southern black men, Miller passionately defended the progress made by blacks since emancipation. He also condemned white landowners for exploiting black farmers, charging that they negotiated unfair contracts and often paid blacks in worthless scrip. Miller defeated Elliott again in the 1890 congressional election but lost the subsequent challenge in the South Carolina Supreme Court when the justices ruled that though Miller's ballots were printed on the required white paper, it was "white paper of a distinctly yellow tinge." The 1892 congressional election went to the black candidate George W. Murray when Miller's too-light coloring became an issue in the campaign. Miller returned to the South Carolina House in 1894 to serve until 1896. When not in public office, Miller returned to his position as an attorney on the payroll of the Beaufort merchant D. H. Wall, an association that he maintained for fifty years, until Wall's death in 1935.

Miller was one of six black men elected to the 1895 state constitutional convention called expressly for the purpose of disenfranchising black voters. Tenaciously and eloquently he defended black voting rights, rejecting claims that black political leaders had proven more corrupt and dishonest than white politicians. He challenged the convention's presiding officer, U.S. senator Benjamin R. Tillman, to recognize the contributions and sacrifices made by black Americans to the nation:

> Mr. President, this country and its institutions are as much the common birthright and heritage of the American negro as it is the possession of you and yours. We have fought in every Indian war, in every foreign war, in every domestic struggle by the side of the white soldiers from Boston commons and Lake Erie to the Mississippi Valley and the banks of the Rio Grande.

He tried to reassure whites by insisting that black people neither sought political control nor opposed segregation: "The negroes do not want to dominate. They do not want and would not have social equality, but they do want to cast a ballot for the men who make their laws and administer the laws. Is there anything new in this plaintive appeal to the nation[?]" He concluded by "pleading for justice to a people whose rights are about to be taken away with one fell swoop." Most of the 154 white delegates were unmoved. Urged on by Tillman, they fabricated an array of disenfranchisement measures—the principal one of which required potential voters to demonstrate an understanding of the state constitution—that would allow election officials to exclude black voters at will. Miller and the other five black delegates refused to sign the new constitution.

Miller was more successful in demanding the establishment of a black college. Beginning in 1872 most of South Carolina's federal land-grant funds were appropriated to State A&M College, an institution operated by Claflin University in Orangeburg. Claflin, a Methodist school for freedmen that opened in 1869, was run by northern white teachers and administrators. Miller and other black leaders wanted the land-grant monies allocated to an autonomous black institution. Miller convinced Tillman and his lieutenants to support legislation creating the Colored Normal, Industrial, Agricultural, and Mechanical College of South Carolina (now South Carolina State University) by severing State A&M College's ties with Claflin. By law, the awkwardly named new institution could admit and employ only blacks. Miller later exclaimed, "Thank God the College is in the hands of Negroes."

Four days after the legislation creating the college passed, Miller resigned his house seat, and a few weeks later Governor John Gary Evans and the all-white board of trustees selected Miller as the institution's first president. The new college became a training school modeled after Hampton Institute and BOOKER T. WASHINGTON's Tuskegee Institute. Opened in 1896, it did not grant four-year bachelor's degrees until 1925. In an 1897 speech Miller explained the purpose of the new institution: "The work of our college is along the industrial line. We are making educated and worthy school teachers, educated and reliable mechanics, educated, reliable and frugal farmers."

In 1910 Miller publicly opposed the election as governor of Coleman Blease, a demagogue devoted to white supremacy. Following Blease's victory, the new governor demanded and received

Miller's resignation as president of the college. Miller moved to Charleston, where he retired but remained active in community affairs. He enthusiastically supported U.S. entry into World War I and offered to help recruit thirty thousand black men. When an all-white state committee on civic preparedness decided to appoint a black subcommittee to aid the war effort, Miller agreed to serve on it. He was a prominent figure in the successful effort in 1919 to replace white teachers with black teachers in Charleston's black public schools. In 1923 Miller moved to Philadelphia, Pennsylvania, but he returned in 1934 to Charleston, where he died. The inscription on his tombstone reads, "Not having loved the white man less, but having felt the Negro needed me more."

FURTHER READING

Drago, Edmund L. *Initiative, Paternalism, and Race Relations: Charleston's Avery Normal Institute* (1990).

Holt, Thomas. *Black over White: Negro Political Leadership in South Carolina during Reconstruction* (1977).

Newby, I. A. *Black Carolinians: A History of Blacks in South Carolina from 1895 to 1968* (1973).

Tindall, George B. *South Carolina Negroes, 1877–1900* (1952).

Obituaries: *Charleston News & Observer*, 9 Apr. 1938; *Journal of Negro History*, July 1938.

This entry is taken from the *American National Biography* and is published here with the permission of the American Council of Learned Societies.

WILLIAM C. HINE

Millinder, Lucky (8 Aug. 1900–28 Sept. 1966), bandleader and composer, was born Lucius Venable Millinder in Anniston, Alabama. The identity and circumstances of his parents are unknown. He was raised in Chicago, Illinois, where he attended Wendell Phillips High School.

As Lucius Venable he began to work as a master of ceremonies and danced in nightclubs, including one run by Al Capone's brother Ralph in Cicero, Illinois. He became a bandleader in 1931, touring the RKO theater circuit. Early in 1932 he took over the little-known Doc Crawford band, and later that year he moved to New York.

Millinder appeared in the film short *Scandals of 1933*. In 1933 the promoter Irving Mills began grooming Millinder to take over the Mills Blue Rhythm Band by making him the frontman for the Congo Knights, a ten-piece band. Millinder and the band members worked locally and then played on the French Riviera from July to October 1933, at which time the group was billed as Lucky Millinder and His Orchestra. Millinder split the group up when they returned to New York.

Late that year or early in 1934 Millinder took over the Mills Blue Rhythm Band. Its members included the trumpeter HENRY "RED" ALLEN, the trombonist J. C. HIGGINBOTHAM, the clarinetist BUSTER BAILEY, and a rhythm section of Edgar Hayes (pianist and arranger), Lawrence Lucie (guitar), Elmer James (bass), and O'Neill Spencer (drums). In 1935 they recorded "Spitfire" and the band's best-known piece, "Ride, Red, Ride," composed by Millinder and Mills and featuring Allen, whose showy trumpeting is encouraged by Millinder's speech-song. Alto saxophonist Tab Smith joined in the fall of 1935. One year later the pianist Billy Kyle joined; the bassist JOHN KIRBY is also believed to have become a band member at this time, though discographies list Hayes Alvis as the group's bassist.

From 1936 onward the group's recordings were sometimes issued under the name Lucky Millinder with the Mills Blue Rhythm Band, and from 1937 the group performed as Lucky Millinder and His Orchestra. Among Millinder's sidemen from this period were the trumpeters Harry "Sweets" Edison and CHARLIE SHAVERS, the trombonist WILBUR DE PARIS, the guitarist DANNY BARKER, Tab Smith, and Bitty Kyle. "Jammin' for the Jackpot," recorded in 1937, was notable for a couple of melodic snippets that soon after formed the core of COUNT BASIE's masterpiece "Jumpin' at the Woodside," but otherwise this piece was the work of a well-accomplished but not especially memorable big band of the swing era. They split up in 1938.

In late May 1938 Millinder took over Bill Doggett's big band, with Doggett remaining as pianist. They toured until January 1939, when Millinder went bankrupt. He appeared in the film *Paradise in Harlem* (1939), featuring the singer and actress MAMIE SMITH, and in the film short *Readin', 'Ritin' and Rhythm*, including performances by the trumpeter FRANKIE NEWTON and the tenor saxophonist DON BYAS.

In September 1940 Millinder formed a long-lived and significant big band that initially worked regularly at the Savoy Ballroom in Harlem. Early on, the band featured the singer and guitarist SISTER ROSETTA THARPE. Having already recorded blues and gospel pieces on her own, Tharpe made several sensational recordings of blues and secularized gospel themes (gospel music with secular lyrics substituted for the original religious texts) for Millinder, including "Trouble in Mind," "Rock, Daniel," "Shout,

Sister, Shout" (composed by Doggett and Millinder), and "Rock Me" (all from 1941). That same year she appeared with the band in three "soundies" (film shorts for jukeboxes): *The Lonesome Road*, *Shout, Sister, Shout*, and *Four or Five Times*. As a response to the orchestra's "Big Fat Mama" and to the soundie *I Want a Big Fat Mama* (also from 1941), Tharpe recorded Millinder's song "I Want a Tall, Skinny Papa" in February 1942, at which time she had a change of heart and abandoned the group to devote herself exclusively to religious music.

Millinder's recordings of "Apollo Jump," from September 1941, and "Savoy," from February 1942 (the latter not to be confused with "Stompin' at the Savoy," popularized by Benny Goodman), are bouncy instrumental performances anticipating his later involvement in rhythm and blues. Millinder claimed credit as composer for both titles ("Savoy" again with Doggett), as well as for "Mason Flyer" (with Tab Smith) and "Little John Special," this last recording featuring the trumpeter DIZZY GILLESPIE, who joined in 1942. During this period the trumpeter Freddie Webster played alongside Gillespie. The rhythm section comprised Doggett, who was replaced by the pianist Clyde Hart at some point in 1942; the guitarist Trevor Bacon, who in July 1942 sang on another incipient rhythm and blues hit, "When the Lights Go on Again"; the bassist George Duvivier; and the drummer Panama Francis. The tenor saxophonist David A. Young told the writer Dempsey J. Travis that while touring as accompanists to the Ink Spots, Millinder's sixteen-piece band also included THELONIOUS MONK on piano. Nevertheless, in a battle of the bands at the Savoy in April 1942, Millinder's orchestra was outplayed by JAY MCSHANN's big band, featuring the alto saxophonist CHARLIE PARKER.

Further soundies include two from around 1942 featuring Mamie Smith, *Harlem Serenade* and *Because I Love You*, and *Hello Bill* from around 1943. In October 1943 the group recorded "Shipyard Social Function." In May 1944 the singer WYNONIE HARRIS was featured in "Hurry, Hurry!" and in an irreverent account of a drunken preacher, "Who Threw the Whiskey in the Well?" These two recordings moved Millinder more firmly into the rhythm and blues camp, but apart from the tenor saxophonist Bull Moose Jackson, featured from 1945 to 1947, Millinder's most distinguished sidemen during this period were associated mainly with jazz: the saxophonists Lucky Thompson, EDDIE "LOCKJAW" DAVIS, Frank Wess, and PAUL QUINICHETTE; the pianists Ellis Larkins and Sir

Charles Thompson; the bassist Al McKibbon; and the drummer Panama Francis.

Around 1946 the band made another soundie, *I Want a Man*, followed by *Let It Roll* in 1947. The next year Millinder was featured in the film *Boarding House Blues* and on NBC radio's *Swingtime at the Savoy*, an African American variety show. In June 1952 the big band accompanied Harris on "Night Train" in a raucous vocal rendition of the tenor saxophonist JIMMY FORREST's instrumental rhythm and blues hit. At this point Millinder split the band up.

Millinder became a disc jockey, hosting the *Harlem Amateur Hour*, a late-night show broadcast from the Apollo Theater on station WJZ. He also worked as a liquor salesman, a publicist, and a fortune teller, while reconstituting a big band for specific occasions. Millinder died in New York City. He was survived by his wife, Vivian Brewington, and their two children.

Millinder was an acrobatic showman and an exceptional big band conductor. As Francis recalled for the writer Stanley Dance, "He couldn't read a note. But if you gave him a bunch of guys who could read, in one week's time he'd have them sounding like a band that had been organized for a year. He could remember everything in an arrangement after it was run down once. He was a genius in that way." Gillespie added:

> He was the greatest conductor I'd ever seen. He had the biggest ears of anybody. He didn't know anything about music, and all he could do was rely on his memory—but his memory was astounding. He knew arrangements. He knew what everybody was playing all the time—the whole band—and if you missed something, he'd look at you.

FURTHER READING
Dance, Stanley. *The World of Swing* (1974; repr. 1979).
McCarthy, Albert. *Big Band Jazz* (1974).
Schuller, Gunther. *The Swing Era: The Development of Jazz, 1930–1945* (1989).
Shaw, Arnold. *Honkers and Shouters: The Golden Years of Rhythm and Blues* (1978).
Whitburn, Joel. "Lucky Millinder and the Mills Blue Rhythm Band," *Record Research*, no. 88 (June 1968).
Obituaries: *New York Times*, 30 Sept. 1966; *Down Beat*, 3 Nov. 1966.

DISCOGRAPHY
Discography of Lucky Millinder (1962).
This entry is taken from the *American National Biography* and is published here with the permission of the American Council of Learned Societies.

BARRY KERNFELD

Mills, David (20 Nov. 1961–30 Mar. 2010), journalist, writer, and television producer was born in Washington, DC. His family moved to Lanham, Maryland, when his childhood home in Northeast Washington was destroyed by fire. He had two sisters and a brother. The professions and names of his parents are unknown.

One of his sisters, Gloria Johnson, told the *Washington Post* that Mills "had a knack for writing that was noticed very early … [she] recalled that when Mills, then 10, and her son, then 5, played with G.I. Joe toys, Mills wrote their dialogue on 3-by-5 cards" (De Moraes and Trescott).

Mills went on to earn a four-year scholarship to the University of Maryland, College Park, where he met his future collaborator and producer of the popular HBO series, *The Wire*, David Simon. Mills and Simon met at the student newspaper, the *Diamondback*. When Mills graduated from college, he went to work at the *Wall Street Journal* in Chicago, where he stayed for a year. He then returned to Washington, DC, where his writing at the *Washington Times* caught the eye of *Post* editors.

His May 1989 interview with Richard Griffin, better known as Professor Griff, who was the "minister of information" for the rap group Public Enemy at the time, led to Griff's being ousted from the group. The article included quotes from Griff saying, among other things, that "'Jews have a grip on America' and that they 'have a history of killing black men.'… Further, Griff told writer David Mills that Jews are responsible for 'the majority of wickedness that goes on across the globe'" (Baker).

Mills was hired in 1990 as a staff writer for the *Post*'s Style section, according to the newspaper. As a light-skinned black man who also blogged as Undercover Black Man (undercoverblackman.blogspot.com), he was known for writing about race with skill, humor, and insight. He updated the blog with interviews from his newspaper days in the 1980s with everyone from OPRAH WINFREY to ELDRIDGE CLEAVER. A popular recurring feature was "Misidentified Black Person," in which Mills reprimanded TV and newspaper out-

David Mills, one of the writers of *NYPD Blue*, poses on one of Twentieth Century Fox's New York street facades, on Dec. 26, 1995 in Los Angeles. (AP Images.)

lets for, in his words, being unable to regularly "tell black people apart."

He made headlines again when he interviewed the rapper Sistah Souljah after the 1992 Los Angeles riots, when then-presidential-candidate Bill Clinton quoted her incendiary comments from her interview with Mills: "I mean, if black people kill black people every day, why not have a week and kill white people?"

That year, Simon asked Mills to help him write an episode of the television drama, *Homicide: Life on the Street*, an adaptation of Simon's 1991 book on the topic. After that episode aired in 1994, Mills left the *Post* to work in Hollywood.

"Mills stood out, colleagues said, for his commitment to provocative stories about race and rap music …. He wasn't afraid to tell his bosses how the paper should cover minority issues and culture. 'He liked being a rebel in the newsroom. He embodied that style,' former *Post* executive editor Leonard Downie Jr. said" (De Moraes and Trescott).

Mills won Emmy Awards for his work as a television writer who delved into racial tensions and relationships for television dramas like *Homicide* and *The Wire*. He won two Emmys for his work with David Simon and Ed Burns on *The Corner*, a series about a year in the ghettoes of Baltimore: Outstanding Mini-Series and Outstanding Writing for a Mini-Series. He also wrote and produced several other critically acclaimed shows that didn't have predominantly black casts like *NYPD Blue*, *Picket Fences*, *ER*, and *Kingpin*, a series about Latin American drug trafficking that was canceled by NBC after six episodes in 2003.

"I don't know anything about Mexican culture …. But I know about the human condition …. The breakthrough here is, this is a story about the condition of a man's soul …. Often in TV, to get that deeply in the psyche of a character, that character is white. It's pretty rare that a nonwhite character [gets that kind of attention]" (Wiltz).

He was on the set of *Treme* a show based in New Orleans that he was working on with Simon when he died from a brain aneurysm at forty-eight years of age.

FURTHER READING

Baker, Greg. "The Education of Professor Griff." *Miami New Times*, 11 July 1990.

Obituary: "David Mills, 48, journalist, Emmy-winning TV writer." *Washington Post*, 1 Apr. 2010.

Wiltz, Teresa. "We Lost Our Undercover Black Man." *The Root*, 1 Apr. 2010.

Weber, Bruce. "David Mills, Television Writer and Producer, Dies at 48." *New York Times*, 2 Apr. 2010.

JOSHUNDA SANDERS

Mills, Florence (25 Jan. 1895–1 Nov. 1927), entertainer, was born Florence Winfree in Washington, D.C., the daughter of John Winfree, a carpenter, and Nellie Simons, who did laundry. Educated locally, by age five Mills was winning contests in cakewalking and buck dancing. Her first professional engagement came as Baby Florence Mills in the second company (1902) of the BERT WILLIAMS–GEORGE WILLIAM WALKER *Sons of Ham*, singing a song she had learned from its originator, AIDA OVERTON WALKER, titled "Miss Hannah from Savannah," the tale of a high-class African American who had come north.

Mills served a lengthy apprenticeship before becoming an "overnight" sensation in *The Plantation Revue* in 1922. After several years in vaudeville with the Bonita Company as a "pick" (i.e., a pickaninny), she and her sisters, Olivia and Maude, became the vaudeville Mills Sisters. When this act broke up, Mills joined others until 1914, when she began to sing in Chicago nightclubs. The jazzman Mezz Mezzrow recalled her "grace and … dignified, relaxed attitude. Florence, petite and demure, just stood at ease and sang like a humming bird" (*Really the Blues*, 22).

At the Panama Club Mills formed the singing Panama Trio with Ada Smith—later known as BRICKTOP, a favorite of American expatriates in Paris—and Cora Green; the trio toured the Pantages vaudeville circuit, where in 1916 Mills joined the Tennessee Ten. After four seasons with the group as the female singer-dancer in a trio with U. S. "SLOW KID" THOMPSON and Fredi Johnson, Mills married Thompson. The year of their marriage is not firmly established, and they had no children. (She may have had an earlier marriage, in 1912, to James Randolph.) Mills and Thompson were recruited into *Shuffle Along*, the 1921 black musical comedy by NOBLE SISSLE and EUBIE BLAKE that began a decade-long Broadway vogue for shows featuring African American performers. *Shuffle Along* lured predominantly white audiences farther "uptown" than before to the Sixty-third Street Theatre and ran for a year and a half before enjoying a two-year road tour.

Shuffle Along coincided with the general post–World War I upsurge in theatrical, musical, and literary achievement by African Americans that became known as the Harlem Renaissance. Even the poet CLAUDE MCKAY, who characterized Harlem as "the glorified servant quarters of a vast estate" in *Harlem: Negro Metropolis*, expressed the hope that *Shuffle Along* might help black performers break through the "screen of sneering bigotry" to express their authentic "warmth, color and laughter."

Replacing *Shuffle Along*'s original female star, Gertrude Saunders, Mills soon stopped the show singing "I'm Craving for That Kind of Love" with her particular blend of ethereality and sensuality. Shortly her picture appeared on the sheet music of the show's hit, "I'm Just Wild about Harry." The white entrepreneur Lew Leslie hired Mills to star in his 1922 black revue at the Plantation Club at Fiftieth and Broadway. Adding a few acts, he then moved the entire show into the Forty-eighth Street Theatre.

Sometimes dressed in feathers and sometimes in male evening clothes, Mills created a sensation, particularly by her spontaneous dancing. She said: "I just go crazy when the music starts, and I like to give the audience all it craves. I make up the dances to the songs beforehand, but then something happens like one of the orchestra talking to me and I answer back and watch the audience." The musical historian Allen Woll quoted an uncredited critic: "In that season not to have seen and heard Florence Mills was to be quite out of the know on Broadway" (*Black Musical Theatre from "Coontown" to "Dreamgirls,"* 96).

Leslie took the Plantation Revue to London in 1923 as the second (and most effective) half of an Anglo-American revue, *From Dover Street to Dixie*; Mills sang "I'm a Little Blackbird Looking for a Bluebird," a poignant piece that wrung audiences dry. The impresario Charles B. Cochran wrote of the tension on its opening night, partly due to the recent failure of another black American revue. Upon Mills's appearance, he told his companion: "She owns the house—no audience in the world can resist that.... [She] controlled the emotions of the audience as only a true artist can ... there was a heart-throb in her bird-like voice ... her thin, lithe arms and legs were animated with a dancing delirium. It was all natural art" (*Secrets of a Showman*, 97–98).

After further European touring with *Dixie*, Leslie brought an enhanced version, built around Mills, to the Shubert Organization's Broadhurst Theatre in the heart of Times Square as *Dixie to Broadway*, and Mills was also added to the *Greenwich Village Follies of 1923*. JAMES WELDON JOHNSON wrote in *Black Manhattan* that *Dixie to Broadway* "broke away entirely from the established tradition of Negro musical comedies" in starring one woman. Writing in the *New York World* (23 Nov. 1924), Lester Walton said that "the long cherished dream ... to see a colored musical comedy successfully playing in the very heart of Broadway" had become a reality. *Dixie to Broadway*, like other African American shows of the era, however, was produced by whites, who made most of the money. Still, Mills was quoted as saying that attitudes toward "colored people" were gradually changing; she saw a great future for "high browns."

After *Dixie to Broadway*, Mills settled in Harlem amid leaders of the Renaissance such as Johnson, LANGSTON HUGHES, COUNTÉE CULLEN, ZORA NEALE HURSTON, JEAN TOOMER, WALTER WHITE, and the actor CHARLES GILPIN. In 1925 Mills turned down an offer to star in a revue at the Folies Bergère in Paris; after ETHEL WATERS also declined, JOSEPHINE BAKER took the job and became famous. The artist Miguel Covarrubias caricatured Mills, and in 1926 the classical composer WILLIAM GRANT STILL wrote a jazz piece for her. Likewise, the choreographer BUDDY BRADLEY wrote that the prima ballerina Alicia Markova reminded him of Mills. The theater historian Loften Mitchell wrote that in the Harlem of the 1920s her name "was on the lips of everyone in the community. People sat in parlors, on stoops, or stood in hallways, trying to find words that might describe her" (*Black Drama*, 78).

Leslie's next show, *Blackbirds*, named for Mills's trademark song, was built around Mills. After six weeks early in 1926 at the Alhambra Theater in Harlem, it opened in Paris, where it ran for six months, moved to London, and continued until August 1927. With slick bobbed hair and soft eyes, she was, Cochran wrote, the only performer he had ever seen who could count on an ovation upon entry and before doing a number. The Prince of Wales confessed to seeing *Blackbirds* twenty-two times. In London there were Florence Mills dolls, and the most fashionable shade for clothing was the "Florence Mills shade." The black British jazz musician Spike Hughes, however, questioned her authenticity: whites who thought she epitomized "Negroes" also thought the for-whites-only shows at the Cotton Club in Harlem were authentic. Comparing her unfavorably with BESSIE SMITH, who sang mainly for black audiences, Hughes said he could not tell from her singing whether she was black or white, British or American.

Mills returned to New York in late September 1927, and huge crowds turned out in Harlem to greet her. The 14 October 1927 edition of the *Inter State Tatler* called on her "to give the people the one great gift within her power ... a national, or if you please, a race drama.... Miss Mills can do more than anyone else to satisfy the latent, unexpressed hunger for race drama."

Mills was twice operated on for appendicitis in late October 1927 and died in New York City of peritonitis and paralyticileus resulting from the appendicitis. Tributes came from London, where the composer Constant Lambert wrote an "Elegiac Blues" for her, and Paris, where, according to the *New York Times* correspondent, she was lauded as greatest of all. More than 75,000 mourners viewed her body before her funeral, which was attended by 5,000 people in a church meant for 2,000, while thousands waited outside. The jazz composer ANDY RAZAF contributed a poem beginning "All the World is Lonely / For a Little Blackbird" and ending "Sadness rules the hour / Left us only in tears." A chorus of 500 sang to the accompaniment of a 200-piece orchestra. An estimated 150,000 watched the funeral procession. Johnson wrote: "An airplane ... released a flock of blackbirds.... They fluttered overhead a few seconds and then flew away" (*Black Manhattan*, 201).

FURTHER READING

Materials concerning Florence Mills are at the Billy Rose Theatre Collection of the New York Public Library for the Performing Arts, Lincoln Center.

Clarke, John Henrik, ed. *Harlem USA* (1964).

Lewis, David Levering. *When Harlem Was in Vogue* (1997).

Sampson, Henry T. *Black in Blackface: A Source Book on Early Black Musical Shows* (1980).

Shapiro, Nat, and Nat Hentoff. *Hear Me Talkin' to Ya* (1955).

Obituary: *New York Times*, 2 Nov. 1927.

This entry is taken from the *American National Biography* and is published here with the permission of the American Council of Learned Societies.

JAMES ROSS MOORE

Mills, Harry and Herbert Mills (19 Aug. 1913–28 June 1982) and (2 Apr. 1912–12 Apr. 1989), singers, were born in Piqua, Ohio, the sons of John Hutchinson Mills, a barber, and Eathel Harrington. Harry and Herbert Mills, with their younger brother Donald, had a fifty-seven-year career in which they made 2,246 records and helped to found modern-day black harmony singing. With an older brother, John Jr., the boys began singing in the choir of the Cyrene African Methodist Episcopal (AME) Church in Piqua. They also sang Sundays at the Park Avenue Baptist Church in the same city.

After their lessons at the Spring Street grammar school they would gather in front of their father's barbershop on Public Square and begin singing to draw a crowd. Sometimes they sang at the corner of Greene and Main or at the Hardin Road monument, where passersby threw coins at their feet. To improve business John Jr. began accompanying the four-part harmony with a ukulele and then a guitar. The boys practiced imitating orchestras that they heard on the radio. On summer nights they could hear the Roof Garden Orchestra at the local Knights of Columbus hall and would practice every note. John, originally the bass, became the tuba part. Harry, at baritone, was first trumpet. Herbert did the second trumpet and Donald the trombone. At house parties, lawn fetes, music halls, and supper clubs each brother would double as the saxophone or clarinet part when needed.

The brothers' big break came in 1925. After playing May's Opera House in Piqua between silent film features, they accompanied the Harold Greenameyer Band to Cincinnati for an audition with radio station WLW. The band was not hired, but the Mills Brothers were. The station kept them so busy that they moved to Cincinnati and took a tutor. For Sohio Motor Oil they were billed as the Steamboat Four. For Tasty Yeast they became the Tasty Yeast Jesters. At other times they were billed as Four Boys and a Guitar, and on Sundays they were billed as the Mills Brothers.

In 1929 friends at WLW arranged an audition for the Mills Brothers at CBS radio in New York City. After the broadcasting executive William S. Paley heard the performance in his office on a speaker phone, he put the brothers on CBS radio that very night. When the Mills Brothers signed a three-year contract the next day, they became the first African Americans to have a network show on radio. The exposure won them a national following and a recording contract. "Tiger Rag," which the Mills Brothers had first recorded in Indianapolis while imitating the Roof Garden Orchestra, was rerecorded for Brunswick Records and became a number one seller. Other hits quickly followed: their theme song "Goodbye Blues," "You're Nobody's Sweetheart Now," "Ole Rockin' Chair," "Lazy River," "How'm I Doin'," "Paradise," "Oh, I Heard," and "Sweet Lucy Brown."

The brothers' popularity brought sponsorship from the largest advertisers in early radio, including Standard Oil, Procter & Gamble, Crisco, and Crosley Radio. They began appearing in films. Their first, *The Big Broadcast* (1932), was an all-star radio revue that included Bing Crosby, CAB CALLOWAY, and the Boswell Sisters. They shared the bill at New York's Paramount Theatre with Crosby, Kate Smith, and George Burns and Gracie Allen. By 1934 the Mills Brothers were in Hollywood, starring with Crosby for Woodbury Soap and recording their classics "Lazy Bones," "Sweet Sue," "Lulu's Back in Town," "Bye-Bye Blackbird," "We're in the Money," "Sleepy Head," and "Shoe Shine Boy." Film appearances included *Twenty Million Sweethearts* (1934) and *Broadway Gondolier* (1935), both for Warner Brothers.

The Mills Brothers were the first African Americans to give a command performance for British royalty, playing at the Palladium before King George V and Queen Mary. While performing at the Regal Theatre, John Jr. became ill with pneumonia. He never recovered, and he died in 1936. The group had lost its leader and considered breaking up. Then their father, John Sr., joined his sons in the quartet, imitating the tuba and singing bass as his son had.

The group's greatest success was still ahead of them. "Lazy River" was rerecorded and quickly surpassed 1931 sales. It was followed by "Someday You'll Want Me to Want You," "Swing Is the Thing," "'Long about Mid-night," "Organ Grinders Swing," and "The Song Is Ended." They honored their idol, DUKE ELLINGTON, with a swinging version of his "Caravan," and then they produced a series of classic recordings: "South of the Border," which they performed during a tour of South America, along with "Ain't Misbehavin'," "It Don't Mean a Thing (If It Ain't Got That Swing)," "Jeepers Creepers," "Three Little Fishes," "If You Can't Sing It, You'll Have to Swing It," and "Basin Street Blues." But this served only as prelude to a string of successes rarely matched in recording history. In 1943 Donald Mills chose "Paper Doll" as the B side of "I'll Be Around." Recorded in fifteen minutes, it sold 6 million copies and became the group's biggest hit.

In their twenty-four-year association with Decca, the Mills Brothers continued their enduring barbershop harmonies with a flurry of top ten hits that included "You Always Hurt the One You Love," "Till Then," "Across the Alley from the Alamo," and "Someday." Film appearances included *Reveille with Beverly* (1939), which helped launch Frank Sinatra, and *Chatterbox* (1943). The rise of rock and roll did little to diminish the brothers' success. "Glow Worm," their first recording with an orchestra, rose to number two on the pop charts in 1952. Soon "Opus One," an updated version of the Tommy Dorsey hit, was keeping it company, along with "You're Nobody 'til Somebody Loves You," "Yellow Bird," "Standing on the Corner," and "If I Had My Way."

In 1954 John Sr., then seventy-two, reluctantly stopped touring with the group. As a trio in the 1960s the Mills Brothers recorded for Dot Records and were frequent guests on *The Jack Benny Show*, *the Perry Como Show*, *The Tonight Show*, and *Hollywood Palace*. They played at theaters and clubs, touring forty weeks a year. They were financially independent but sang, according to Harry, "because we love singing and love an audience." Harry and his wife, Ruth (they had no children), and Donald were neighbors in Los Angeles. Herbert lived with his wife, Dorothy, in Las Vegas; they had one child. "Cab Driver," recorded in 1968, was their last great hit. Harry explained five decades of success by saying, "Maybe people want to hear plain, simple songs and easy harmony." By this time Harry, a diabetic, was losing his sight. After the death of Harry's wife in 1974, Donald's son, John, became Harry's valet and helped his uncle onstage.

The brothers celebrated their fiftieth anniversary in show business in 1975 with a nostalgic tribute hosted by Bing Crosby at the Dorothy Chandler Pavilion in Los Angeles. A 1981 historical tribute to harmony groups in New York's Savoy Theatre opened with the Temptations doing a medley of Mills Brothers hits. The evening underscored the significance of the Mills Brothers in the development of the doo-wop style of rock and roll.

The death of Harry Mills in West Los Angeles, California, ended a musical partnership that had been as long and as successful as that of any group in the country's history. Herbert Mills died in Las Vegas, Nevada. Even into the 1990s Donald and his son, John, continued to perform under the name the Mills Brothers. They were in Piqua, Ohio, on 3 June 1990 when the town unveiled a monument to their favorite sons on the public square where they had first sung. The plaque reads, "The Mills Brothers ... America's greatest singing group ... and musical ambassadors to the world."

FURTHER READING

Barlow, William, and Cheryl Finley. *From Swing to Soul: An Illustrated History of African-American Popular Music from 1930 to 1960* (1994).

Ewen, David. *All the Years of American Popular Music* (1977).

Hennessey, Thomas J. *From Jazz to Swing: African-American Jazz Musicians and Their Music, 1890–1935* (1994).

Robinson, Louie. "The Eternal Mills Brothers," *Ebony* (Sept. 1979).

This entry is taken from the *American National Biography* and is published here with the permission of the American Council of Learned Societies.

BRUCE J. EVENSEN

Mills, Stephanie (22 Mar. 1957–), singer and actress, was born in Brooklyn, New York, the second youngest of six children to parents about whom little is known. As a child, she began singing in the choir of Cornerstone Baptist Church in Brooklyn. A natural performer who was the center of attention at home, Mills auditioned and earned the part of Pansie in the short-lived musical *Maggie Flynn*. She participated in and won six consecutive Amateur Hour competitions at the Apollo Theater, and subsequently was invited to open for the Isley Brothers as a teenager in the early 1970s. A hard-working, talented performer, Mills participated in the Negro Ensemble Company Workshop in 1966, and eventually studied at Julliard. Mills soon won her first recording contract, which produced the 1974 MCA single, "I Knew It Was Love," and although it did not produce a high-selling album, it did position her for the role that made both her and Judy Garland famous.

In 1974 Mills was cast as Dorothy in the Broadway musical *The Wiz*. Based on *The Wizard of Oz* but set with an all-black cast, the show ran for five years and played in venues such as Carnegie Hall, the Metropolitan Opera House, and Madison Square Garden. Her signature songs, "Ease on Down the Road" and "When I Think of Home" became types of modern anthems, and her performances were as mesmerizing during the run of the show as Garland's singing had been in *The Wizard of Oz*. The musical became one of Broadway's longest-running and her popularity increased. She received a Tony Award for the role. During this time, she also signed with Motown under the urging of Jermaine Jackson and the Jackson 5, however, the business relationship ended in 1976. After the musical's run closed in January 1979, Mills continued touring, but on the concert circuit as an opener for the O'Jays, TEDDY PENDERGRASS, and the Commodores.

After her release from Motown, she signed with Twentieth Century Records in 1979, and her new company released her next three albums. She scored Top 10 hits with "What Cha Gonna Do with My

Lovin'," "Sweet Sensation," and "Never Knew Love Like This Before," and won a Grammy Award in 1980 for Best Female R&B Vocal and an American Music Award in 1981 in the same category.

Although critics attributed the Broadway success of *The Wiz* to Mills and her portrayal of the naïve Dorothy, when the musical was taped for the big screen, she was not selected for the title role. Instead she watched as one of her idols, DIANA ROSS, took the lead. Mills's personal achievements, including her influence on music and performance, were not affected by her not receiving the movie role, and, perhaps, that snub may have helped her career instead.

Her personal life mirrored her professional one with the same peaks and valleys. She was married and divorced two times; one of them being Jeffrey Daniel, a singer with the group Shalimar (1980–1981). Mills left Twentieth Century Records and joined Casablanca in 1981, but a lull in her popularity followed as she produced only one Top 10

Stephanie Mills, arriving at a benefit at the Museum of Natural History in New York City, 15 October 2003. [AP Images.]

single in her next four albums. In 1984 she had the opportunity to return to her role as Dorothy when *The Wiz* was revived. In the midst of experiencing an upswing in her career, she uncovered that some of her handlers had stolen millions of dollars from her and she filed a lawsuit against the parties. She endured rough financial times, and it appeared that she would lose her estate, a twenty-seven room home in Mount Vernon, but the New York Housing Assistance Corporation provided a loan that helped her avoid the tragedy.

Mills remarried in 1992 for the third time, Michael Saunders, a Charlotte radio station programmer, and stated in *Jet* magazine that she made the decision to remove herself from the hectic life of stardom. She took residence in North Carolina and gave birth to her son, Farad, in February 2001. She continued to volunteer her talent to raise funds for worthy causes, such as Hale House in New York, a home for children born to drug-addicted mothers.

FURTHER READING

"Bringing Up Baby: Stephanie Mills in the Family Spotlight," *Washington Post*, 19 May 1980.

Campbell, Bebe Moore. "A Sassy New Stephanie," *Essence* (Jan. 1988).

Norment, Lynn. "The New Stephanie Mills," *Ebony* (Dec. 1992).

Smith, Jessie Carney, ed. *Notable Black American Women*, book 2 (1996).

Who's Who among Black Americans, 1993–1994 (1994).

Who's Who in Entertainment, 1992–1993 (1993).

SIBYL COLLINS WILSON

Milton, Little (7 Sept. 1934–4 Aug. 2005), singer, songwriter, and blues musician, was born James Milton Campbell Jr. in the Delta town of Inverness, Mississippi. He was one of the thirteen children of Milton and Pearl Campbell and was raised in Greenville, Mississippi. His parents were sharecroppers and his father also earned a living as a blues musician playing with local bands. Milton grew up listening to Memphis radio stations, which played country music from Nashville's Grand Ole Opry, as well as gospel and blues music. He became interested in playing the guitar and nailed wires to the side of his house for practice. Milton worked picking cotton and performing odd jobs in the community to earn money for a real guitar. When he was twelve he had saved enough money and ordered a Roy Rogers-style guitar for over $14. Though Milton's mother protested the cost of the instrument, "Big" Milton allowed his son to keep

the guitar. Milton taught himself to play the guitar by watching and listening to blues artists at picnics and house parties. He began performing as a teenager and became known as Little Milton because of his age and the notoriety of his father, "Big" Milton. Milton played small venues throughout the South and wherever else he could, including street corners. His stage presence was playful and spirited; ultimately bringing him to the attention of the band leader IKE TURNER.

Milton moved to East St. Louis, Missouri, at the behest of Turner, and together they became very popular on the club circuit in Missouri and across the river in Illinois, often working up to twenty gigs a week. In addition, Turner introduced Milton to Sam Phillips at Sun Records. In the Memphis studio he recorded his first single, "Beggin' My Baby"; however, the rising white Sun artist Elvis Presley was given priority, and Milton faded into the background by 1954. He formed his own band and in 1957 recorded one single for the small label Meteor before moving to St. Louis, Missouri, in 1958. Milton befriended DJ Bob Lyons, and together they formed

Little Milton, blues and R&B recording artist, pictured in an undated file photo. (AP Images.)

the label Bobbin Records and recorded several titles including his first successful hit, "I'm a Lonely Man," which sold sixty thousand copies. Milton became respected for his business acumen and brought the artists ALBERT KING and Fontella Bass to the label as an A&R. In 1962 he joined Chess Records in Chicago, Illinois, as an artist on the Checkers label. Milton gained notoriety at Checkers, and his 1965 hit recording, "We're Gonna Make It" climbed the R&B charts to number one, becoming an anthem of the civil rights movement along the way. Through 1969, when the label folded, he achieved several Top Ten R&B singles, including "Grits Ain't Groceries," "Baby I Love You," "If Walls Could Talk," "Feel So Bad," and "Who's Cheating Who?" In 1969 Milton joined Stax Records, based in Memphis, where his style evolved with highlighted vocals and a studio sound expanded to include larger horn and string sections. He recorded several hits, including "Walkin' the back Streets and Cryin'" and "That's What Love Will Make You Do." As an artist for Stax he participated in a major California concert for black unity and appeared in the subsequent documentary film entitled, "Wattstax," in 1973. The label went bankrupt in 1975, and eight years later in 1983 he recorded his first and only album with a major label, "Age Ain't Nothin but a Number," on the MCA imprint Mobile Fidelity Records. The following year in 1984, Milton returned to his home state, Mississippi, where he signed with the Jackson-based Malaco Records, a label committed to the preservation of Southern soul and blues music. He remained with the label for thirty years and enjoyed many successes. Milton recorded the blues music anthem, "The Blues Is Alright," and fourteen hit albums with *Cheatin Habit*, and *Little Milton's Greatest Hits* among them.

Throughout Little Milton's career he was recognized as an artist and awarded many honors. He was inducted into the Blues Hall of Fame in 1988 and the same year earned the W.C. Handy Blues Award for Entertainer of the Year. In 1999 his former label, Malaco, released an album entitled *Welcome to Little Milton*, a collection of duets featuring artists such as Delbert McClinton and Lucinda Williams, which was nominated for the distinguished Grammy Award.

In April 2005 Milton headlined a Memphis Blues festival in London, England, and the following month released his final album, *Think of Me*, in May on the Telarc imprint. Three months later on 4 August 2005, Little Milton died from complications following a stroke. He was married to Pam Campbell, and together they had four children.

FURTHER READING
Cohn, Lawrence. *Nothing but the Blues* (1999).
Gioia, Ted. *Delta Blues: The Life and Times of the Mississippi Masters Who Revolutionized American Music* (2009).
Sonnier, Austin Jr. *A Guide to the Blues* (1990).
Palmer, Robert. *Deep Blues: A Musical and Cultural History of the Mississippi Delta* (1982).
SAFIYA DALILAH HOSKINS

Milton, Roy (31 July 1907–18 Sept. 1983), rhythm and blues musician, was born in Wynnewood, Oklahoma. He spent his early years on an Indian reservation in Oklahoma because his mother was part Native American. The family later moved to Tulsa. Milton began his musical career as a singer with Ernie Fields's Tulsa jazz band, the Royal Entertainers, in the late 1920s and began doubling on drums after the band's regular drummer was arrested.

The Great Depression struck African Americans especially hard, with one out of every two blacks out of a job by 1933. In Oklahoma the Dust Bowl aggravated the Depression by shriveling up the plants that farmers and sharecroppers tried to grow. About 1 million "Okies" were driven off their land by the dry weather. In 1933 or 1934 Milton joined the other Okies fleeing to California in the hope of a greener future. Los Angeles offered more opportunities, and Milton took advantage of them. He formed a band, the Solid Senders, sometime in the late 1930s, and the group appeared regularly at Los Angeles' top night spots, typically playing for hours and declining to advertise itself as a blues band, perhaps in an effort to avoid stereotyping. The band played a style of blues known as "jump blues" because it made listeners get up and dance. Milton handled the drums and most of the singing duties, along the way earning the admiration of his peers.

Milton is credited as one of the pioneers of rhythm and blues, although he never garnered the public attention that many early blues pioneers received. He had an energetic, boogie-woogie style with an up-tempo rhythm and a repeated melody that aimed to get the audience jumping and dancing. By 1945 Milton's band was thriving. The group played in three movies in the 1940s with the singer June Richmond, but these have apparently not been preserved.

Milton grabbed the opportunity to sign with Juke Box Records (later Specialty Records). The label, run by Art Rupe, produced "R. M. Blues" in 1946.

The song—which featured Milton's vocals, a steady backbeat, and a large dose of swing—became both one of Milton's biggest hits and one of Specialty's largest sellers. Milton stayed with Specialty Records until 1954. His band scored nineteen top ten rhythm and blues hits for the label including "Milton's Boogie," "True Blues," "Hop, Skip, and Jump," "Information Blues," "Best Wishes," and a cover of Louis Prima's "Oh Babe." While Milton did most of the singing on the records, the Solid Sender pianist Camille Howard contributed to a few of the pieces, including the 1947 hit "Thrill Me." Howard would later branch off from the Solid Senders to have a successful solo career.

In 1954 Milton left Specialty for Dootone Records. He had a best-selling instrumental, "Succotash," for this label. He subsequently recorded with the record labels Hamp-Tone, King, Warwick, and Kent. With Warwick, Milton had a minor rhythm and blues hit in 1961's "Red Light," but he never managed to duplicate the commercial or critical success that he had enjoyed with Specialty. By the early 1960s rock and roll had taken most of rhythm and blues' audience. Milton became a figure from yesteryear. A love of music kept him playing, and he had a minor comeback in 1970 at the Monterey Jazz Festival, when he joined Johnny Otis's All-Star Band, to the delight of the crowd. In the 1970s, as part of the movement to acknowledge the heroes of the African American past, Milton began to receive long-overdue credit for his pioneering efforts with the blues. His records, long out of print, were made available for a new audience. The first batch of Milton songs to be reissued appeared in 1978 on the album *Roy Milton and His Solid Senders*. In 1985 "R. M. Blues" was re-released on the album of the same name and *Groovy Blues, Vol. 2* appeared in 1992. Two years later, in 1994, *Blowin' with Roy* came out, to be followed by *Rhythm and Blues from California, 1945–1949* in 2000 and *Instant Groove* in 2004.

A steady, somewhat low-key personality made Milton popular among his peers. However, as often happened with underappreciated African American entertainers, much of his life is lost from the historical record. Any surviving family is unknown.

FURTHER READING
Black Music Research Journal 9.1 (Spring 1989): 19–33.
Obrecht, Jas, ed. *Rollin' and Tumblin': The Postwar Blues Guitarists* (2000).
Otis, Johnny. *Upside Your Head!: Rhythm and Blues on Central Avenue* (1993).
Sonnier, Austin, Jr. *A Guide to the Blues: History, Who's Who, Research Sources* (1994).

CARYN E. NEUMANN

Ming, William Robert "Bob," Jr. (7 May 1911–30 June 1973), lawyer and civil rights activist, was born in Chicago, Illinois, to William Ming Sr., a South Side municipal worker, and Annie Ming (maiden name unknown). While growing up in Chicago he worked as a grocery clerk and on wrecking crews. It was the latter position that allowed him to finance his University of Chicago education. An academic standout, he was the first African American member of the University of Chicago Law Review. Ming was also published in the Law Review's inaugural issue. He graduated Order of the Coif in 1933.

In 1941 at the age of thirty, Ming married Irvena, an attendance officer for the Chicago public school system. The couple resided in the Hyde Park neighborhood in Chicago. Two years later he enlisted in the U.S. Army during World War II. The army granted Ming a leave of absence to argue an election-law case before the United States Supreme Court. He left the military with a captain's rank and joined the University of Chicago as the institution's first African American law professor, where he taught civil procedure. This was the first faculty appointment for any African American at a major American law school. His tenure lasted from 1947 to 1953.

Simultaneous to his academic career and private law firm practice, Ming was an active member of the National Association for the Advancement of Colored People. While serving on the organization's legal committee, he urged the Department of Justice to investigate violent crimes with racial undertones, such as the 1940 firebombing of a black family's home in Northwest Chicago. Ming's passion for civil rights and his sharp legal mind placed him at the center of a number of landmark cases. Those cases included *Shelley v. Kramer*, a 1948 case in which the Supreme Court declared unconstitutional state judicial enforcement of racially restrictive covenants. He also worked on the 1950 case *Sweatt v. Painter*, which challenged separate but equal facilities for black professionals and graduate students in state universities.

The most famous case on which Ming worked was *Brown v. Board of Education*, which led to the 1954 Supreme Court ruling that public school segregation was wrongfully separate and unequal. He worked closely with other legal team members, including future Supreme Court Justice THURGOOD

MARSHALL. The team members regarded Ming as outspoken and favoring bold policies. Marshall often served as the mediator between the various personalities. As one observer recalled, "For all the dogmatism of his style, Ming's mind was supple and his position on the cases fluid, and Marshall knew how to get the most out of him" (*The Civil Rights Era: A Look Back by Those Who Lived and Litigated Through It*, p. 1424).

In 1960 Ming agreed to serve as counsel to MARTIN LUTHER KING JR. in Montgomery, Alabama. King faced charges of perjury connected to tax evasion in completing his Alabama state taxes in 1956 and 1958. It was the first time such an indictment was obtained against an individual in the state's history. The state alleged that King's income during an earlier tax year was $16,162 as opposed to the $9,150 claimed by King. Ming countered that fraudulent means were used to by the state to derive the $16,162 figure. At the time of the alleged misconduct, King's ministries were already relocated from the Dexter Street Church in Montgomery to his father's church in Atlanta, Georgia. The indictment alleged that King diverted money raised for the Southern Christian Leadership Conference (SCLC) for his own personal use while failing to report the funds as income. Because the SCLC was King's primary tool for advancing desegregation efforts, it was clear that the charges were an attempt to thwart the organization and its leader. However, in defending King against the charges, Ming chose to deviate from the easy, most obvious reason for the inappropriateness of the charges. Instead, he told jurors, "If you want the government of this state to set your tax rate based on all of the money that goes through your bank account, then you fine this man and enjoy it" (*Brown v. Board of Education: A Moot Court Argument*, p. 1374).

On 28 May 1960 the all-white jury deliberated for only a few hours before returning with a not guilty verdict. Ensuring that the jury had as many businessmen on it as possible proved to be the winning strategy.

The trial remained a memorable experience for King. It illuminated the central role attorneys played in the civil rights struggle. King recalled in his autobiography, "I am frank to confess that on this occasion I learned that truth and conviction in the hands of a skillful advocate could make what started out as a bigoted, prejudiced jury, choose the path of justice. I cannot help but wish in my heart that the same kind of skill and devotion which Bill Ming and Hubert Delaney accorded to me could

be available to thousands of civil rights workers, to thousands of ordinary Negroes, who are every day facing prejudiced courtrooms" (King, p. 135).

Commenting further on Ming's skillful advocacy, King reflected, "Defeat seemed certain, and we in the freedom struggle braced ourselves for the inevitable. There were two men among us who persevered with the conviction that it was possible, in this context, to marshal facts and law and thus win vindication. These men were our lawyers—Negro lawyers from the North: William Ming of Chicago and HUBERT [T.] DELANEY from New York" (King, p. 135). The King family would long feel a sense of gratitude and loyalty to Ming long after the trial. When Ming would later face legal problems of his own, MARTIN LUTHER KING SR. was one of his staunchest supporters.

Ming became the subject of an Internal Revenue Service (IRS) investigation after failing to file taxes from 1963 to 1966. The IRS filed criminal charges and U.S. District Judge Julius J. Hoffman presided over the case. Hoffman was well known for his caustic courtroom demeanor. His acerbic nature was perhaps most famously displayed when he oversaw the trial of the "Chicago Seven," a case stemming from the arrest of protestors during the 1968 Democratic Convention. Hoffman's harshest ruling during the case occurring when he ordered Defendant and Black Panther leader, BOBBY SEALE, to be gagged and shackled in the courtroom. Drawing Hoffman as the judge in his tax evasion trial did not bode well for Ming.

Ming was found guilty of four counts tax evasion and sentenced to four months for each count running consecutively. When a January 1973 petition for clemency to President Richard Nixon proved unsuccessful, Ming reported to a Sandstone, Minnesota, federal prison. After complaining of dizziness, Ming fell in a prison shower and hit his head. As his health diminished, his friends rallied for his release. Martin Luther King Sr.—still grateful for Ming's assistance to his son—wrote an impassioned plea to the U.S. Parole Board asking for Ming's release. His 23 March 1973 letter stated, "In the days when my son Martin Luther King, Jr. lived and was struggling in what proved to be his destined way to bring full freedom to black citizens in their own country, Bob Ming came to the legal assistance of Martin, RALPH D. ABERNATHY and others who worked with them … [a]nd but for the legal brilliance, fearlessness and dedication of Bob Ming, the struggle may well have died aborning" (McLehatton, p. 1).

The Parole Board allowed the ailing Ming to return home where he died on 30 June 1973.

FURTHER READING

McLehatton, Jim. "Standing on 'the Shoulders of Bob Ming.'" *The Washington Times*, 7 December 2008.

Symposium: The Civil Rights Era—A Look Back by Those Who Lived and Litigated Through It (2003).

King, Martin Luther, Jr. *The Autobiography of Martin Luther King, Jr.* (1998).

Brown v. Board of Education: A Moot Court Argument (2003).

JOCELYN L. WOMACK

Mingus, Charles, Jr. (22 Apr. 1922–5 Jan. 1979), bassist and composer, was born in Nogales, Arizona, the youngest of three children and the only son of Charles Mingus Sr., a retired U.S. Army staff sergeant and postal worker from North Carolina, and Harriett Sophia Phillips, from Texas. Seeking medical treatment for Harriett, the family moved to the Watts community of Los Angeles in October 1922. Shortly after the move, Harriett Mingus died from chronic myocarditis, an inflammation of the heart muscles associated with alcohol consumption. Mingus Sr. married again, to Mamie Carson, whose son, Odell Carson, took Mingus as his surname. All the children were encouraged to take music lessons. Mingus's sisters, Grace and Vivian, learned the violin and piano; Odell took up the guitar; and Mingus began on the trombone, then moved to cello, piano, and bass. Mingus studied bass with the former New York Philharmonic bassist H. Rheinschagen and the jazz bassist Red Callender, and their influences led Mingus to take pride in technical perfection and improvisation in his bass playing and composing. He was further influenced by the music he heard with his stepmother in her Pentecostal church.

After high school Mingus directed all his energies toward becoming a professional musician, although he made ends meet by working at the post office. At the onset of World War II, several of Mingus's friends enlisted, but Mingus himself failed a preliminary medical examination, disqualifying him from service. During the 1940s Mingus worked as a sideman for a number of jazz luminaries, including LOUIS ARMSTRONG, KID ORY, DINAH WASHINGTON, BILLIE HOLIDAY, and LIONEL HAMPTON. While with Hampton, he recorded his first composition, "Mingus Fingers." In 1944 Mingus married Canilla Jeanne Gross; they had two children before divorcing in 1947. The 1950s was a decade of change and transition for Mingus. He had grown up in Los Angeles, playing in the black district of Central Avenue with visiting musicians and musicians who had been childhood friends, including Britt Woodman and Buddy Collette, who were actively involved in the 1953 amalgamation of the Los Angeles segregated locals of the American Federation of Musicians. The popularity of jazz in the 1950s provided Mingus with ample opportunities for work both as a sideman and as a bandleader. He seized these opportunities, moving from Los Angeles to New York City, the recording center of the music business. His bands played in New York nightclubs and also traveled across the United States and in Europe. In 1950, just before moving to New York, Mingus married his second wife, Celia Nielson, with whom he had a son, Dorian.

Mingus's skill as a bassist combined virtuosity with improvisation. Unlike the earlier generation of bassists, whose role was simply to keep the rhythm section in time, Mingus and others of his cohort, like OSCAR PETTIFORD, envisaged the bass as a solo instrument. JIMMY BLANTON, who played with DUKE ELLINGTON in the early 1940s, was widely regarded as pioneering this new direction. One of Mingus's most famous solos is the introduction to his composition "Haitian Fight Song," on *The Clown* album (1957). As well as a soloist, Mingus also defined himself as a composer and found Ellington a major influence. He experimented stylistically with his compositions to challenge prevailing ideas that jazz was primarily an improvised music. As with his performance style, Mingus's compositions were an attempt to integrate collective improvisation techniques with a written score. His compositions were also marked by blues chords, gospel influences, an attention to individual musician's styles, polyrhythms, and modal sections. Mingus usually recorded his own compositions. He also wrote extended-form pieces such as *Cumbia and Jazz Fusion* (1977) and *The Black Saint and the Sinner Lady* (1963).

Mingus struggled with a question that many other artists have attempted to resolve—how to control their music both artistically and financially. With his wife, Celia, and the drummer MAX ROACH, in 1952 Charles Mingus established an independent record label called Debut (now distributed through Fantasy Records). Over the course of its five-year life, the company released at least twenty-seven albums by musicians (including Mingus) as diverse as the pianists HAZEL SCOTT, Bill Evans, Paul Bley, and John Dennis; the drummers ART BLAKEY,

Arthur Taylor, and Max Roach; the bassists Oscar Pettiford and Percy Heath; the trumpeters MILES DAVIS, Kenny Dorham, and THAD JONES; the trombonists Kai Winding, J. J. JOHNSON, and Jimmy Knepper; and the saxophonists John La Porta and JIMMY HEATH. Running an independent label was a tricky and exhausting enterprise, and Mingus, Roach, and Celia were responsible for the artistic and creative aspects of the business as well as its management, production, and distribution. As a consequence, Debut, like other independents, suffered from a financial instability that resulted in its eventual demise. After a brief attempt at reconciliation, Mingus and Celia divorced in 1958, shortly after the dissolution of Debut.

The social and political climate of the civil rights movement and the cold war encouraged Mingus to express an explicitly political voice in his compositions, indicating his belief that music should speak to the times and that it could be a protest against social injustice. Among these compositions are *Fables of Faubus* (1958), an indictment of Arkansas governor Orval Faubus's stance on school integration; *Prayer for Passive Resistance* (1958); *Oh Lord, Don't Drop That Atomic Bomb on Me* (1961); and *Remember Rockefeller at Attica* (1974), a response to New York governor Nelson Rockefeller's treatment of prisoners during the 1971 Attica uprising.

In 1960 Mingus married for the third time, to Judy Starkey, with whom he had two children. The couple divorced in 1970. Mingus recorded with a variety of artists in the 1960s, including Ellington, ERIC DOLPHY, Toshiko Akiyoshi, and LANGSTON HUGHES, and for labels such as Impulse!, Atlantic, Candid, and Columbia. Still trying to make his music a profitable enterprise, in 1964 Mingus established the Jazz Workshop Inc., a publishing and mail-order company from which fans could purchase copies of his live albums *Town Hall Concert* (1962), *Mingus at Monterey* (1964) *My Favorite Quintet* (1965), and *Music Written for Monterey, Not Heard, Played in Its Entirety at UCLA* (1965). In the late 1960s Mingus experienced a fallow creative period and disappeared from the jazz scene. Although sometimes performing in local New York nightclubs, he did not record, and it is unclear whether he attempted much composition.

In the 1970s Mingus experienced a creative rebirth, releasing some of his most exciting music, including the widely acclaimed double album *Changes* (1974). ALVIN AILEY used Mingus's compositions for a ballet, *The Mingus Dances*, performed by New York's City Center Joffrey Ballet

in 1971. His autobiography, *Beneath the Underdog* (1971), on which Mingus had been working sporadically for more than a decade, was at last published. The reviews were mixed, many critics seeking a more straightforward autobiography than the fictionalized self-analysis that was *Beneath the Underdog*. The work explored Mingus's childhood, his romances, and his music, but in a way that challenged deeply set ideas about what to expect in a musician's memoir. Rather than report the facts of his career, Mingus took a more courageous step and tried to "reveal the truth" of himself in words as he had long done in music. Now considered a classic of jazz autobiography, *Beneath the Underdog* continues to challenge ideas about how musicians create and think about the world in which they live.

Mingus and his longtime companion and business partner, Sue Graham Ungaro, married in 1975. In her memoir *Tonight at Noon*, Sue Mingus recounts the story of their relationship and the impact the physical paralysis of amyotrophic lateral sclerosis (ALS) had on Mingus during the last several years of his life. As Mingus struggled with the debilitating paralysis, he continued to compose by singing into a tape recorder. He and Joni Mitchell collaborated on her *Mingus* album (1979), for which she wrote lyrics to his compositions.

Charles Mingus died in Cuernavaca, Mexico, where he and his wife had gone in search of treatment for his ALS. Mingus's ashes were scattered over the Ganges River in India by his wife.

On 3 June 1989 Mingus's two-hour magnum opus, *Epitaph*, premiered at Lincoln Center in New York under the baton of conductor Gunther Schuller. Throughout his life, Mingus hinted that he was working on such a project. Although he had recorded portions of the score on earlier albums, it was not until his death that the various parts of the piece were put together and performed.

FURTHER READING

Charles Mingus's papers are housed in the Music Division at the Library of Congress in Washington, D.C.

Mingus, Charles. *Beneath the Underdog* (1971).

Coleman, Janet, and Al Young. *Mingus/Mingus* (1989).

Collette, Buddy, with Steven Isoardi. *Jazz Generations* (2000).

Mingus, Sue Graham. *Tonight at Noon* (2002).

Priestley, Brian. *Charles Mingus: A Critical Biography* (1982).

Santoro, Gene. *Myself When I Am Real: The Life and Music of Charles Mingus* (2000).

DISCOGRAPHY

Charles Mingus: The Complete Debut Recordings
(Debut 12-DCD-4402-2).

*Charles Mingus: Passions of a Man, the Complete
Atlantic Recordings, 1956–1961* (Atlantic R2 72871).

NICHOLE T. RUSTIN

Minkins, Shadrach (1812?–13 Dec. 1875), runaway slave arrested under the 1850 Fugitive Slave Law, was born to David Minkins and a woman whose name is unknown, both of them slaves. The place of Shadrach's birth remains unknown, as do details of his childhood. No record of his birth exists, but according to Gary Collison, in 1861 Minkins claimed that he was forty-seven years old, making his year of birth 1814. Earlier court records filed by Minkins's Norfolk owner give his age as twenty-seven, which puts his year of birth at about 1822. The handwritten burial record notes his age as sixty-three at the time of his death, which puts the date at 1812.

As a youth Shadrach Minkins was called Sherwood. Thomas Glenn, the owner of the Eagle tavern and hotel in Norfolk, Virginia, apparently owned Minkins's father and mother and so probably owned Minkins, too. When Glenn died in 1832, followed by his wife, Ann, in 1836, the estate was dissolved, and the proceeds were divided among the five Glenn children. Until the Glenn children came of age the Norfolk businessman Elijah P. Goodridge managed the assets. Minkins and the other Glenn slaves were hired out. Minkins worked for Richard S. Hutchings and Company, which included a grocery and liquor store.

When Hutchings died, his wife, Martha, purchased Minkins and operated the business. When Hutchings and Company closed down in 1849, John A. Higgins, a commission agent, purchased Minkins. Months later he was sold to John Debree, a purser in the U.S. Navy whose wife, Mary, was Higgins's daughter. At this point Minkins's name was changed from Sherwood to Shadrach, and he became a house servant. Shortly thereafter in May 1850 Minkins fled to Boston, where he went by the name Frederick Wilkins or Frederick Jenkins. William H. Parks, a commission merchant who had formerly lived in Norfolk and worked in the counting room at Martha Hutchings's store, initially helped Minkins find work. Soon afterward he found steady employment as a waiter at the well-regarded Cornhill Coffee House. Four months later the passage of the 1850 Fugitive Slave Law changed Minkins's life dramatically.

A component of the Compromise of 1850, the Fugitive Slave Law gave owners of runaway slaves the full backing of the federal government in recovering their property. It supplanted the vague 1793 slave law under which owners had to recapture fugitives without assistance from state or federal law enforcement. As specified by the 1850 Fugitive Slave Law, a slave owner or representative needed only to convince a federal commissioner of his or her rights to the property in order to reclaim a slave. That effectively meant that fugitive slaves were not safe anywhere—not even in northern free states—unless they were beyond the reach of the slave owner. In addition, the 1850 law provided that bystanders had to assist in the capture or recovery of fugitives or face fines and imprisonment. In response, antislavery forces formed vigilance committees to protect fugitives from recapture.

On 12 February 1859 John Caphart (or Capehart), a Norfolk constable, arrived in Boston bearing legal papers and power of attorney on behalf of Minkins's owner, John Debree. Three days later federal authorities in Boston issued a warrant for Minkins. Minkins was arrested at the Cornhill Coffee House and taken to the courthouse. As news of the arrest spread, lawyers, including Robert Morris, Richard Henry Dana Jr., and Ellis Gray Loring, were appointed by the Boston Vigilance Committee to defend Minkins. When a three-day recess was granted to the defense attorneys, Dana and others began to prepare a writ of habeas corpus. If the strategy worked, Minkins would be brought before a Massachusetts judge who could order his release based on unlawful restraint, since Massachusetts was not a slave state.

Although it is not altogether clear what happened next, the courtroom was stormed and a frightened Minkins was literally carried off by a group of black rescuers, followed by a jubilant crowd. It is believed that he was then taken to the house of the Reverend Joseph C. Lovejoy, the brother of the martyred antislavery editor Elijah Lovejoy, who had been murdered when a mob attacked his printing press in Alton, Illinois, in 1837. Minkins traveled to Cambridge and then to Concord, Massachusetts. Following the northern route of the eastern corridor of the Underground Railroad, he crossed into Quebec Province (or Canada East). Six days after his rescue he reached Montreal.

During the mid-1850s Minkins operated several restaurants in Old Montreal. By 1853 he had married a young Irish woman named Mary (maiden name unknown), who gave birth to a daughter,

Eda, in 1853 or 1854. Two years later a son, William, was born. Both children died from childhood diseases. By 1859 Minkins was operating a barbershop in a community of free blacks in Montreal. The couple had another daughter, Mary, in 1858 and a son, Jacob, in 1860; both survived. Having settled in Montreal's black community, Minkins and other fugitives remained in Canada after the Emancipation Proclamation was issued. Minkins died of natural causes in December 1875, when his age was noted as sixty-three. He was buried in an unmarked grave in the Protestant cemetery on Mount Royal.

The Shadrach Minkins case was one of four famous Boston fugitive slave cases that tested the 1850 Fugitive Slave Law. The first involved the noted fugitives WILLIAM AND ELLEN CRAFT, who escaped from Georgia in 1848 by disguising themselves as a sickly plantation owner (Ellen) who was accompanied by an attentive servant (William). Well known in antislavery circles, they became an early test case when Bostonians refused to assist in their recapture. After hiding in various places in Boston, the Crafts were spirited away to England in order to avoid capture. After the Minkins case, other slave owners who came to Boston were more successful. In 1851 Thomas Sims, a fugitive slave from Georgia, was arrested in Boston and returned to his owner. In 1854 ANTHONY BURNS was returned to slavery despite an abolitionist attack on the Boston courthouse.

The Minkins case tested not only the authority of the 1850 Fugitive Slave Law but also the resolve of the northern antislavery movement itself. Equally important, it illuminated the vital role played by blacks in the resettlement of fugitives and their active resistance to the Fugitive Slave Law.

FURTHER READING

Collison, Gary. *Shadrach Minkins: From Fugitive Slave to Citizen* (1997).

Harding, Vincent. *There Is a River: The Black Struggle for Freedom in America* (1981).

JAYNE R. BEILKE

Minor, Jane (1792?–1858?), a nurse, was born into slavery and given the name Jensey (also spelled "Gensey" in the public record) Snow. She later took the name Jane Minor after being manumitted by her Petersburg, Virginia, slaveowner Benjamin Harrison May and becoming married to Lewis Minor. She demonstrated extraordinary nursing skill, courage, and generosity, first in attending to the sick during a fever epidemic (which prompted May's decision to free her), then in using the money she earned subsequently to purchase and free over a dozen other slaves, and in creating a hospital in Petersburg. She also became the mother-in-law of JOSEPH JENKINS ROBERTS, a former resident of Petersburg, the African American who became the first president of Liberia.

As the historian Todd L. Savitt notes, health care in the antebellum South consisted of a varied landscape of sometimes competing, sometimes complementary, models and methods of care. Trained allopathic physicians were called in when home remedies or other treatments did not suffice, often in extremis, because their fees could be discouraging or prohibitive. Folk remedies might be the first line of treatment, but Virginians were also inclined to Thomsonian, homeopathic, and hydropathic treatments, which were sometimes more successful than the interventions of physicians because they did less harm than medical doctors' treatments that employed purging, bleeding, and unwitting poisoning (like the use of calomel with mercury). Thomsonians favored herbal and vegetable tonics; homeopaths, the use in minute amounts of substances that in larger amounts produced the same symptoms as the disease; hydropaths, the use of water therapy. African American health practitioners ran a similar spectrum from the spiritual (root doctors and conjurers), viewing disease as the product of a curse, to the empiric, familiar with root and herbal medicines. Although trusted African Americans were typically allowed to look after the physical health of slaves, they were also sometimes called to the bedside of white patients, particularly in cases of epidemic or of maternity, labor, and childbirth. In this context, Jensey Snow (as she was known at the time) distinguished herself for both skill and courage during the fever epidemic of 1824.

In freeing Snow, Benjamin Harrison May noted her "several acts of extraordinary merit performed … during the last year, in nursing, and at the imminent risk of her own health and safety, exercising the most unexampled patience and attention in watching over the sick beds of several individuals of this town" (quoted in Pierson, p. 113), and further expressed the hope that she would "continue, whenever occasion shall require to perform similar acts equally meritorious & praiseworthy" (quoted in Savitt, p. 180). Indeed, her meritorious work continued with her founding of a hospital in Petersburg that was still in operation more than three decades later, according to Savitt, based on references to the hospital in the local newspaper, the *Daily Express*. That Minor was permitted to continue living and working in Petersburg is also remarkable, testifying to her contribution to the town's well-being. As the historian Marie Tyler-McGraw notes, after the GABRIEL slave rebellion conspiracy in Richmond in 1800, white citizens of Petersburg became anxious about the already large free-black population of the town, and successfully petitioned the Virginia General Assembly in 1806 to enact legislation requiring banishment from the state within one year after manumission; this virtually ended private emancipations for over a decade; the practice resumed later in much reduced numbers.

Remaining in Petersburg, Minor worked diligently and saved her earnings from her nursing work, which she applied to the manumission of at least fifteen others, women and children, according to a study by the Virginia State College history professor, LUTHER P. JACKSON, in the 1930s. In one instance this required Minor's expense of $1,500, a considerable sum, to David May for the freedom of a mother and five children. Minor's manumission paid to the Hill sisters of a "mulatto slave woman slave named Phebe who has resided in Petersburg for some years past & who has been employed generally in nursing sick people & leeching etc. in said town" ("Manumission," p. 536) hints at a more extensive network of African American woman healers. As the historian Suzanne Lebsock observes, among free women of color, nurses occupied a status between midwife and folk healer, with very few nurses, cuppers (using heated glass cups to draw blood to the skin), and leechers (using leeches to draw blood) rising out of poverty in order to acquire taxable property. Their invisibility and obscurity (very few even advertised in the newspapers, and those only rarely) was the product of their constrained social and economic status, which renders Minor's accomplishment even more remarkable.

In 1826 Snow married a freed laborer in Petersburg, Lewis Minor, and changed her name to Jane Minor. Her daughter, Sarah Minor, married Joseph Jenkins Roberts, and died in Liberia. From the most unpromising circumstances at the beginning of her life, Jane Minor distinguished herself as a skilled health care provider and a generous and courageous citizen, whose work made a substantial contribution to the well-being of black and white people in Petersburg in the decades before the Civil War.

FURTHER READING

Davis, Veronica A. "Jane Minor." *Inspiring African American Women of Virginia* (2005).

Jackson, Luther P. "Manumission in Certain Virginia Cities." *Journal of Negro History* 15, no. 3 (July 1930): 278–314.

Lebsock, Suzanne. *The Free Women of Petersburg: Status and Culture in a Southern Town, 1784–1860* (1984).

"Manumission Papers of Free People of Color of Petersburg, Virginia, Deeds of Emancipation of Negroes Freeing Negroes." *Journal of Negro History* 13, no. 4 (Oct. 1928): 534–538.

Piersen, William D. *Black Legacy: America's Hidden Heritage* (1993).

Savitt, Todd L. *Medicine and Slavery: The Diseases and Health Care of Blacks in Antebellum Virginia* (1978).

Tyler-McGraw, Marie. *Slavery and the Underground Railroad at the Eppes Plantations* (2005).

THOMAS LAWRENCE LONG

Mitchell, Abbie (25 Sept. 1884–16 Mar. 1960), singer, actress, and teacher, was born in New York City to an African American mother and German Jewish father. Her mother died during childbirth, and Mitchell moved to Baltimore, Maryland, with her maternal aunts, Alice and Josephine, and maternal grandmother. She attended St. Elizabeth's Convent, moving back to New York with her aunt Josephine when she was twelve to study music, a musical education that continued throughout her young adulthood. Her coaches included HARRY BURLEIGH, Emilia Serrano, and Jean de Retzke.

Mitchell began her fifty-year career in the theater in 1898, singing in *Clorindy, or the Origin of the Cakewalk*, composed by WILL MARION COOK and with lyrics by PAUL LAURENCE DUNBAR. This production marked the beginning of Mitchell's lifelong professional and personal relationship with Cook, whom she married in 1900 (Carter, 55). The couple had two children, Marion Abigail and Will Mercer, who became an ambassador and Howard University professor. The couple divorced in 1908, and according to the *New York Age*, Mitchell then married William Phillips, a Chicago Railroad employee, in 1910. According to the Chicago *Bee*, she married Leslie Tompkins, an art student, in 1926. Mitchell's unpublished memoir, however, mentions neither of these men, and her obituary identifies her as the "widow" of Cook, who died in 1944.

In addition to Cook, Mitchell collaborated with BERT WILLIAMS, GEORGE WALKER and AIDA OVERTON WALKER, J. ROSAMOND JOHNSON,

Robert Cole, Sissieretta Jones ("Black Patti"), and other notable entertainers in concert tours (with Black Patti's Troubadours and the Nashville, later Memphis, Students) and musical comedies such as *Jes Lak White Folks* and *The Policy Players* (1899), *The Casino Girl* and *Sons of Ham* (1900), *Uncle Eph's Christmas* and *The Cannibal King* (1901), *Wild Rose* (1902), *In Dahomey* (1903), *The Southerners* (1904), *Abyssinia* and *My Friend from Georgia* (1906), *The Man from 'Bam* (1907), *Bandana Land* and *Panama* (1908), *The Red Moon* (1909), *The Traitor* (1913), *Darkydom* (1915), *Darktown Follies* (1916), and *Harlem Rounders* (1925). In these works, which played in New York City, Chicago, various European capitals, and other venues, Mitchell scored personal triumphs with her renditions of musical numbers like "Brown Skin Baby Mine," "Mandy Lou," and "Red, Red Rose." She was equally admired for her classical repertoire, which featured German lieder, Puccini, Gounod, and Verdi. She was the first black woman to do a single vaudeville turn at New York's Majestic Theater, in May 1910.

In 1914 Mitchell made her nonmusical debut in *The Gentleman Burglar* at the Howard Theatre in Washington, D.C. From 1916 to 1929 she became one of the leading performers, in musical and nonmusical works, of the famed Lafayette Players in Harlem. Her Lafayette credits include *Within the Law*, *Madame X*, *A Fool There Was*, *Madame Sherry*, *45 Minutes from Broadway*, *Faust*, *The Eternal Magdalene*, *Resurrection*, *Paid in Full*, *Charlie's Aunt*, *Damaged Goods*, *The Great Divide*, and *The Chocolate Soldier*. In the early 1920s Mitchell also toured the United States and Europe as a concert singer, including another collaboration with Cook as singer and bookwriter for the concert series Negro Nuances. From 1924 to 1927 she appeared as a prima donna at the Club Alabam' in midtown Manhattan, singing semi-classics and popular ballads.

In 1926 Mitchell broke into the New York theater mainstream with her appearance in the Pulitzer Prize–winning *In Abraham's Bosom*, also featuring Rose McClendon. Mitchell developed a rewarding professional relationship with the director Jasper Deeter, later appearing regularly at his Hedgerow Theatre in Pennsylvania. In 1927 Mitchell appeared on Broadway in *Coquette* (with Helen Hayes), *House of Shadows*, and a revival of *In Abraham's Bosom*. From 1929 to 1931 she was featured as the "Studebaker Songbird" on the Studebaker Radio show. As an established dramatic and musical star Mitchell coached the

aspiring performers Etta Moten, Adelaide Hall, Fredi Washington, and Butterfly McQueen, and from 1931 to 1934 she was head of the voice department of Tuskegee Institute. Also in 1934 she returned to the stage as Binnie in the Theatre Union's *Stevedore* (replacing Georgette Harvey), appearing later in *Cavalleria Rusticana* with Todd Duncan. In 1935 Mitchell created the role of Clara in George Gershwin's opera *Porgy and Bess*. In 1938 she became one of several outstanding actresses to star as Cora in Langston Hughes's *Mulatto*. From 1939 until 1940 Mitchell appeared with Tallulah Bankhead in *The Little Foxes*. In the summer of 1943 Mitchell was a guest artist and teacher at Atlanta University.

In Broadway productions like *Coquette* and *The Little Foxes*, Mitchell played servants, usually darkening her naturally light complexion to do so. Despite the recognition she received for imbuing such limiting roles with dignity and strength, Mitchell remained frustrated by the lack of opportunities afforded black actresses, and so throughout the 1940s she tried to create more meaningful roles for herself, organizing the Abbie Mitchell Players and presenting her own one-woman show, Harriet Tubman, in 1944. In 1943 Mitchell directed and starred in a revival of *The Eternal Magdalene* for the Ira Aldridge Players and performed Granny in *White Dresses* for the Harlem Boys' Club. In 1943 and 1944 Mitchell directed Allan R. Kenward's *Cry Havoc*, a drama of heroic nurses on Bataan, first for her own company, then for the Frederick Douglass Players. In 1945 Mitchell performed in *Arsenic and Old Lace* at the McKinley Square Theater, a production that included the young Ruby Dee as Elaine and Avon Long as Mortimer. The following year she returned to Broadway as Cora in *On Whitman Avenue*, a play exploring race relations and produced by Canada Lee. In 1947 Mitchell performed the role of Lina in *The Skull beneath the Skin* at the Westport Country Playhouse.

In addition to her stage work and concert appearances Mitchell appeared in at least five films, all by black film companies: *Uncle Remus' First Visit to New York* (1914), *The Scapegoat* (1917), *Eyes of Youth* (1920), *A Night in Dixie* (1926), and *Junction 88* (1947). She was also active in the Negro Actors Guild from 1937 until the 1950s, serving as executive secretary in 1946.

Battling failing health and fading vision Mitchell continued to teach at her studio in Harlem throughout the 1950s. According to the actress Rosetta LeNoire, Mitchell was widely recognized as the "grande dame of drama," and everyone sought her coaching. (Tanner, 126). At Mitchell's memorial service in 1960 the era's leading black performers, including EUBIE BLAKE, Helen Dowdy, and Leigh Whipper, honored the "Great Lady of the Negro Theater" by singing the songs that made her famous.

FURTHER READING

Correspondence and unpublished memoirs by Mitchell and Will Marion Cook can be found in the Mercer Cook Papers, Moorland-Spingarn Collection, Howard University. Clippings files on Mitchell as well as individual productions in which she appeared can be found in the Billy Rose Theatre Collection, New York Library of the Performing Arts and the Negro Actors Guild file, Actors' clipping files, and Black Theatre Scrapbook, Schomburg Center for Research in Black Culture, New York Public Library.

Carter, Marva Griffin. "The Life and Music of Will Marion Cook," Ph.D. diss., University of Illinois (1988).

Fletcher, Tom. *The Tom Fletcher Story: One Hundred Years of the Negro in Show Business* (1954).

Isaacs, Edith J. R. *The Negro in the American Theatre* (1947).

Sampson, Henry T. *The Ghost Walks: A Chronological History of Blacks in Show Business, 1865–1910* (1988).

Tanner, Jo A. *Dusky Maidens: The Odyssey of the Early Black Dramatic Actress* (1993).

Thompson, Mary Francesca. "The Lafayette Players: 1915–1932," Ph.D. diss., University of Michigan (1972).

Obituaries: *New York Times*, 20 Mar. 1960; *New York Amsterdam News*, 26 Mar. 1960.

CHERYL BLACK

Mitchell, Arthur (27 Mar. 1934–), dancer, educator, choreographer, and artistic director, was born Arthur Adams Mitchell Jr. in Harlem, New York, the second of six children of Arthur Adams Mitchell and Willie Mae Hearns, who were both from Savannah, Georgia. Mitchell's father, a riveter by trade, also worked as a building superintendent to secure a rent-free apartment for his family. The Mitchells moved several times before Arthur Sr. found a suitable situation where he could earn extra money by working at carpentry, plumbing, and automobile repair.

Aware of his family's financial difficulties, the younger Mitchell worked delivering newspapers and shining shoes to supplement the family income. By

Arthur Mitchell, photographed by Carl Van Vechten, 20 December 1955. (Library of Congress/Carl Van Vechten.)

the age of twelve he was working in a butcher shop and was employed there until he became a dance instructor. Mitchell's early creative outlets were varied. He sang in the neighborhood Police Athletic League's Glee Club and the Convent Avenue Baptist Church Choir. At the age of ten he began studying tap dance at the Police Athletic League. Mitchell notes that he later auditioned for the New York City School for the Performing Arts "using a routine an old vaudeville man, Tom Nip, taught me: Steppin' Out With My Baby." Despite his lack of formal dance training, Mitchell was accepted into the dance program in 1949. Although in his first year a teacher suggested he give up dance, Mitchell's resolve was so strong that he redoubled his efforts to prepare his body, overextending himself and tearing his stomach muscles in the process.

Mitchell was encouraged to specialize in modern dance, since there were professional opportunities for black dancers in that style. His professional career as a dancer and choreographer began during his junior and senior years when he was one of two current students to join the alumni in the Repertory Dance Company of the High School of Performing Arts. His first choreographed piece, *Primitive Study*, presented in Altoona, Pennsylvania, was well received. He was cast in several works, performing with the modern dancers Sophie Maslow, Anna Sokolow and the New Dance Group, Donald McKayle, John Butler, and LOUIS JOHNSON. In 1952, his senior year, Mitchell performed in Gertrude Stein's *Four Saints in Three Acts* in Paris and later on Broadway. He became the first male dancer ever to receive the coveted Dance Award at graduation. Throughout his dance training, Mitchell continued to provide financial support to his family. When he was only fifteen, his father became ill and was unable to work, so Mitchell stayed on at the butcher shop and worked at other odd jobs, even as he maintained a demanding training and performance schedule. Upon graduation from high school, Mitchell turned down a scholarship to Bennington College, where he would have continued to study modern dance, and accepted a scholarship to the School of American Ballet (SAB), the official school of the New York City Ballet (NYCB). Mitchell also received a scholarship to study ballet at the Katherine Dunham School of Cultural Arts. Here he was introduced to the ballet master Karel Shook as well as many of the most accomplished black dancers of the time, including ALVIN AILEY, KATHERINE DUNHAM, Donald McKayle, and TALLEY BEATTY. Both Mitchell and Ailey were taking classes with Shook while they were dancing in the Broadway production of *House of Flowers*. Beatty not only danced with Dunham at this time, but had also studied at the SAB a few years before Mitchell.

In the 1950s there were few black ballet dancers, and most were in all-black dance companies. The scholarship to SAB represented both an opportunity and a challenge to Mitchell, an already accomplished modern dancer. He now had the opportunity to broaden his professional repertoire and the chance to enter the professional ballet arena, still largely closed to black dancers. Studying under George Balanchine and Karel Shook, Mitchell quickly transformed himself from a modern dancer to a ballet dancer. He progressed through the School of American Ballet curriculum in the requisite three years, although he did not initially train as a ballet dancer. A large part of this success was due to Mitchell's rigorous training schedule and his determination to succeed in an arena where very few black dancers were allowed.

Shook, who became both teacher and mentor, gave Mitchell private lessons in addition to his regular classes at both schools. These lessons not only deepened Mitchell's ballet training, but also served as the basis for a lasting collaboration between the two. When the Dunham School closed in 1954, Shook opened the Studio of Dance Arts and hired Mitchell as a dance instructor. Mitchell could finally use dance to support his vision as a performing artist and to support his family.

Mitchell continued his ballet training and performed with a variety of choreographers and Broadway producers—both black and white—during the early 1950s, including McKayle, Johnson, William Dollar, Guy Lombardo, Truman Capote, and Harold Arlen, to gain exposure and stage experience. In 1955, after finishing his three years at the School of American Ballet, Mitchell joined the John Butler Dance Theatre. In August 1955 he was invited to become a permanent member of the NYCB, becoming the first black dancer to serve as a permanent member of a major ballet company in the United States.

Mitchell's passion and dedication to ballet, combined with the focus on talent of NYCB cofounder and choreographer George Balanchine, earned him a place in the company. Although hired as a member of the corps de ballet, in his first week with the company he debuted in *Western Symphony*, substituting for Jacques D'Amboise. This performance, and the critical acclaim it garnered, led to more opportunities for featured performances and to roles that were created especially for him. Balanchine's first modern ballet, *Agon*, included a pas de deux, danced with Diana Adams, created for Mitchell, and in 1962 Balanchine created the role of Puck in *A Midsummer Night's Dream* for him. Mitchell danced in almost all the ballets of the company during his long and distinguished fifteen-year career. He also taught at the School for American Ballet.

Although his principal activity was with the NYCB, Mitchell organized other dance projects, resulting in two appearances at the Festival of Two Worlds held in Spoleto, Italy, in 1960 and 1961. In 1966 Mitchell participated in a cultural exchange program with the Brazilian government, where he established the National Ballet of Brazil, serving as choreographer and director. He also appeared on Broadway in *House of Flowers* (along with Alvin Ailey and Donald McKayle), *Carmen Jones, Kiss Me Kate, Shinbone Alley, Noël Coward's Sweet Potato*, and *Arabian Nights*.

The assassination of MARTIN LUTHER KING JR. in 1968 was a turning point in Mitchell's career. He learned of this tragedy on his way to Brazil to work with the National Ballet and resolved to put his energies into a project in the United States rather than continue to work overseas. Upon his return from Brazil, Mitchell began to teach ballet to black children in a converted garage. In 1968 Mitchell organized the Dance Department of the Harlem School of the Arts, founded by Dorothy Maynor, and invited Shook to join him. The relationship between Mitchell and Maynor became strained, and the collaboration ended in 1969.

Mitchell and Shook, with funding from Mrs. Alva B. Gimbel and the Ford Foundation, founded the Dance Theatre of Harlem (DTH) to provide classical ballet training to black students in that same year. In its first year, the school went from thirty pupils to four hundred, and soon developed a company to showcase the students' talents. Two years after its founding, DTH was invited to perform *Concerto for Jazz Band and Orchestra* with the New York City Ballet (NYCB), with DTH dancing the jazz portion and NYCB dancing the classical portion. Both companies closed the piece with classical ballet, a temporarily integrated ballet collaboration that was the first of its kind. Mitchell developed DTH into a world-renowned institution, beginning with its first New York City season in 1974 and a season at Covent Garden in London in 1981. In 1992 DTH became the first American company to dance in South Africa in thirty years.

Arthur Mitchell has earned numerous awards and honors, including Living Landmark status by the New York Landmark Conservancy, the MacArthur Foundation Genius Fellowship, the School of American Ballet Lifetime Achievement Award, the Award for Distinguished Service to the Arts from the American Academy of Arts and Letters, the NAACP Hall of Fame Image Award, and the PAUL ROBESON Leadership Award. Other awards of distinction include the induction of DTH into the Kirov Ballet Museum, the John F. Kennedy Center for the Performing Arts Award for Excellence, and the Barnard College Medal of Distinction. He also received honorary doctorates from the North Carolina School of the Arts, Harvard, Yale, Princeton, the Juilliard School, and Williams College.

FURTHER READING

Long, Richard A. *The Black Tradition in American Dance* (1989).

Thorpe, Edward. *Black Dance* (1990).

C. DALE GADSDEN

Mitchell, Arthur Wergs (22 Dec. 1883–9 May 1968), U.S. representative, was born in Chambers County, Alabama, the son of Taylor Mitchell and Alma (whose maiden name is unknown), farmers and former slaves. At the age of fourteen, Arthur ran away from home, traveled sixty-six miles to BOOKER T. WASHINGTON's Tuskegee Institute, and paid his way through college as a farmhand and office boy for Washington. He came to revere Washington as a father, and the Tuskegean's philosophy of free enterprise and political moderation would profoundly shape Mitchell's future career. Mitchell then earned a teacher's certification from Snow Hill Normal and Industrial Institution in Alabama and taught in rural schools until 1908, when he founded Armstrong Agricultural College in West Butler, Alabama. In 1904 Mitchell married Eula King; they had one child before she died in 1909. In 1911 he married Annie Harris; they had no children.

Following service in the army during World War I, Mitchell, like many black Alabamians, migrated north, yet unlike many of his fellow migrants, he prospered. He began a successful real estate business in Washington, D.C., and studied law at Harvard and Columbia. He was admitted to the bar in 1927.

Increasingly Mitchell's interests turned to politics. In 1928 he campaigned for Republican candidates, including Chicago's OSCAR DE PRIEST, the first African American elected to Congress since 1898. Settling in Chicago, Mitchell hoped to carve out his own political career but found his ambitions thwarted by De Priest's GOP machine. The Depression opened up new possibilities for ambitious politicians, however, and Mitchell bolted to the Democrats in 1932, winning party backing to contest Illinois's First Congressional District, De Priest's seat, two years later. In a tight race, two-thirds of the black voters cast their ballots for the more race-conscious De Priest, but Mitchell won massive support in white wards loyal to the New Deal and defeated the Republican by three thousand votes. Although Mitchell owed his margin of victory to whites, his triumph integrated the Democratic congressional caucus and gave legitimacy to his party's effort to woo African Americans. For the next fifty-eight years all blacks elected to the House would be Democrats.

Mitchell's freshman term was shaped by a conflict of loyalties to his party and to his race. Believing that good relations with southern Democrats might soften their racial prejudices, he constantly reminded colleagues of his love for his native

Alabama, a strategy that won plaudits from moderate southerners but left conservatives unmoved. When Mitchell, the first African American to speak from the floor at a Democratic convention, rose to second Franklin D. Roosevelt's renomination in 1936, Senator "Cotton Ed" Smith of South Carolina stomped out of the hall, protesting it "humiliated the South."

To black critics like WALTER WHITE of the National Association for the Advancement of Colored People NAACP, Mitchell put party before the interests of 12 million African Americans. White particularly resented Mitchell's ties to Hatton Sumners of Texas, chairman of the House Judiciary Committee and chief foe of the 1937 Gavagan antilynching bill. Sumners believed that the NAACP would not "have the nerve to oppose" Congress's sole black member and persuaded Mitchell to introduce a rival, much weaker bill. When the House refused to consider his proposal, Mitchell duly backed the Gavagan measure, but the episode further strained his relationship with civil rights activists.

Mitchell's record in Congress was modest but more consequential than his critics allowed. He exposed racial discrimination in the civil service, nominated black cadets to West Point and Annapolis, and while many others remained silent, condemned anti-Semitism in Germany. Above all, he pledged unswerving loyalty to Roosevelt's New Deal. When northern Republicans attacked Jim Crowism in New Deal agencies, Mitchell retorted that blacks should have no quarrel with policies that provided relief, jobs, and housing for Americans of all races. Increasing numbers of blacks voted for Mitchell and his party after 1936, appearing to vindicate his emphasis on class issues.

Mitchell made a more lasting contribution to civil rights in the courts. Traveling from Chicago to Hot Springs, Arkansas, in April 1937, the congressman purchased a ticket guaranteeing first-class Pullman service. When the train crossed the Arkansas border, however, a conductor ordered him to a second-class coach reserved for blacks. That Mitchell was a member of Congress, the conductor remarked, "didn't make a damn bit of difference ..., that as long as [Mitchell] was a nigger [he] couldn't ride in that car." Fearing a violent confrontation, Mitchell duly moved but later filed suit with the Interstate Commerce Commission (ICC) against the Chicago, Rock Island and Pacific Railway. When the ICC and a federal district court dismissed his claim, he took the case to the Supreme Court and won a unanimous ruling. The railroad, Chief Justice Charles Evans Hughes concluded, had violated Mitchell's

"fundamental right of equality of treatment" (*Mitchell v. United States*, 1941). Although *Mitchell* prompted southern rail lines to integrate first-class carriages, second-class rail travel remained segregated until 1956. The case was nonetheless significant in setting a precedent for postwar challenges to Jim Crow transit. The solicitor general's brief supporting Mitchell also foreshadowed growing support for civil rights in the executive branch.

In his final two terms in Congress, Mitchell pledged blacks' loyalty to the United States against enemies at home and abroad. Blacks, he claimed, would be the last Americans to succumb to communism and among the first to give their lives in a war against fascism. Yet if blacks were good enough to die for their country, he reminded Congress after Pearl Harbor, they should also be given the "opportunity to-live for [their] country without any type of racial discrimination."

Mitchell retired from Congress in 1942 and settled in Petersburg, Virginia. His second wife died in 1947, and Mitchell married Clara Smith one year later. They had no children. By the 1960s he had devoted his energies to farming. He kept his own counsel on the new generation of civil rights leaders but noted that the moderate, interracial Southern Regional Council offered the best hope for change in the South.

Born in the year that the civil rights cases symbolized the end of the first Reconstruction, Mitchell died in Petersburg just as the assassination of MARTIN LUTHER KING JR. signaled the end of the second. In breaking the color line among congressional Democrats and in challenging segregated transportation, Mitchell played a singular role in bridging the two eras.

FURTHER READING
Mitchell's personal and congressional papers are in the Chicago Historical Society.
Weiss, Nancy J. *Farewell to the Party of Lincoln* (1983).
Zangrando, Robert L. *The NAACP Crusade against Lynching, 1909–1950* (1980).
Obituary: *New York Times*, 10 May 1968.
This entry is taken from the *American National Biography* and is published here with the permission of the American Council of Learned Societies.

STEVEN J. NIVEN

Mitchell, Bert Norman (12 Apr. 1938–), founder of the largest African American-owned certified public accounting firm, was born in Jamaica, West Indies, to Joseph Benjamin, a farmer with a third-grade education, and Edith Maud McCourty, a dressmaker. Mitchell grew up in a rural area in the town of Porus, the oldest of seven children and was the first person in his family to go to high school. He attended Kingston Technical High School and then moved to the United States in 1958 with his family, settling in the Bronx. Mitchell found a job in an ink factory and soon, through a black employment agency, he found a bookkeeping position for the Teamsters union downtown near city hall. He wanted to further his education, so he planned to attend the City College of New York (CCNY) and take engineering courses at night while working. His employer, however, did not want him to leave work early to make classes at the uptown campus of City College and pointed out that there was a closer CCNY at 23rd and Lexington.

To appease his employers, Mitchell went to register at CCNY-Baruch and found that this branch of the university was a business school and, therefore, did not offer any engineering courses. Undeterred, he registered for an accounting class. He enjoyed the subject and graduated in 1963 as one of the top students in his class. He had learned at Baruch that the most prestigious start to an accounting career was to work for one of the "Big Eight"—one of the eight largest public accounting firms—and to earn a certified public accountant (CPA) license. Unfortunately, at the time that Mitchell graduated from Baruch, these firms did not hire African Americans. He walked from the southern tip of Manhattan all the way to 53rd Street, applying at every major public accounting firm along the way. He dropped off dozens of resumes, all with the same result: no job offer. Some potential employers told him that while they did not object to hiring him, they did not believe that their clients would tolerate having an African American looking over their accounting records.

Finally, on 53rd Street, this top student was offered a position with J. K. Lasser & Company, a large firm, though not one of the Big Eight, becoming the first African American the firm had ever hired. Mitchell passed the CPA examination on his first attempt—typically only 15 to 25 percent of examinees do so—and was on his way to completing the remaining requirement to earn a CPA license—working for a certified public accounting firm for three years. At J. K. Lasser he enjoyed his work and was promoted quickly. He was popular with the firm's clients, but frequently when he showed up as the leader of the audit team, the client would look past Mitchell and greet one of his white, male staff members, assuming that he, not Mitchell, was the supervisor.

While a student, Mitchell married Carole Harleston on 19 August 1961; she became a social worker and a homemaker for their three children. Mitchell graduated during a decade of enormous change for African Americans. Because of the civil rights movement, the Civil Rights Act of 1964, and lawsuits detailing discrimination against African American applicants for professional positions, major corporations began hiring black professionals. In contrast to when he wore out a pair of shoes looking for a job, when Mitchell completed his apprenticeship requirement in 1966, the young CPA found himself with several employment options. He turned down a job at IBM and accepted a position as assistant controller with the Ford Foundation, where he developed an accounting system for its international operations and traveled around the world to ensure that it was functioning properly. He also wrote articles about accounting and continued to go to school at night, finishing a master's in Business Administration at Baruch in 1968.

While working at the Ford Foundation, he won his employer's approval to sponsor a study of African Americans in the public accounting profession. Mitchell attempted to identify all the African American CPAs in the United States, traveling to cities such as Chicago and Los Angeles to meet with other black CPAs and to discuss their experiences. The results of his landmark study were published in the profession's leading journal, the *Journal of Accountancy*, in 1969. His finding that there were fewer than 150 black CPAs in the United States—about 1 in 1,000 CPAs—illuminated the fact that African Americans represented a smaller percentage of CPAs than they did in any other profession. His article led to many changes at the American Institute of Certified Public Accountants (AICPA), including the adoption of a nondiscrimination code and the institution of a scholarship program for minority students. It also established a minority recruitment committee, and Mitchell served as a charter member.

Like many other young black CPAs at the time, Mitchell soon decided that he would like to work for a black-owned organization, and in 1969 he joined Lucas, Tucker & Co., one of the few black-owned CPA firms in the United States, as a partner. In 1973 he started his own firm and was joined in 1974 by a friend from the AICPA committee, Robert Titus; the firm became Mitchell & Titus. Mitchell started his own firm for the ability to both exert his vision and leadership and establish not simply a financially successful firm but also one that made a difference to others and treated its employees fairly. The firm was successful immediately; many of its clients were government agencies or not-for-profit organizations that had mushroomed in size under President Lyndon Johnson's Great Society programs. In addition to tending to his rapidly growing firm, Mitchell spent considerable energy encouraging young African Americans to join the accounting profession.

Many state and local governments, including New York State and New York City, developed programs in the 1970s to promote opportunities for African Americans in business. Through city and state requirements for minority involvement in government contracts, Mitchell & Titus conducted joint-venture audits with major public accounting firms—the very firms that had not wanted to hire him only a few years earlier. As a direct consequence of the mid-1970s fiscal crisis in New York City, in 1978 the city had its first external audit of its finances. Mitchell's firm worked with a Big-Eight firm on this audit. Although opportunities grew dramatically from when he was a student, Mitchell remained concerned about the paucity of African American participation in the public accounting profession and was particularly appalled by the decline in African American representation in the major firms that occurred in the 1980s. In addition to the overall decline in representation, African Americans were not being promoted to manager and partner positions as rapidly as Mitchell had expected. He spoke of the "dismal pace of upward mobility" and attributed the decline to the lack of enforcement—particularly by the Ronald Reagan Administration—of the equal employment programs that had been instituted in the 1970s. In addition, many black-owned firms went out of business in the 1980s as the Reagan Administration successfully challenged many government set-a-side programs.

Despite the lack of support in the political environment, Mitchell & Titus continued to grow rapidly. By 2005 it had 150 employees in its offices in New York, Washington, D.C., Philadelphia, Baltimore, and Rutherford, New Jersey. Clients of the firm included Dance Theatre of Harlem, Revlon, *Black Enterprise* Magazine, the District of Columbia, Time, Inc., the National Urban League, Pepsico, Philip Morris, Bristol-Myers Squibb, Comcast, the National Association for the Advancement of Colored People's Legal Defense Fund, Viacom, Verizon, Chase Manhattan Bank, United Technologies, the State of New York, the City of New York, and the U.S. Department of Housing and Urban Development. Mitchell & Titus became a member firm of Ernst & Young Global Limited in 2006. Mitchell achieved many firsts, but acknowledged the mixed feelings he had about those achievements, "There are two sides to being 'first black.' On one hand, you feel you're accomplishing something; on the other, you feel too little has been done if you're first at this late date" (Wollman, 8). He was the first black person to serve on the Board of Directors of the AICPA. He was the first black chairman of the New York State Board of Public Accountancy, which sets accounting regulations for the state. When he assumed the role of president of the New York State Society of CPAs in 1987, he became the first African American in the United States to be president of a state professional society of CPAs.

Mitchell published over fifty articles on business and accounting, including follow-ups to his 1969 pathbreaking study on African American CPAs in 1976 and 1990. He was awarded honorary doctorates from Baruch, Western New England College, the State University of New York, and the University of the West Indies. He received alumni awards from Baruch, City College, and Harvard Business School, from whose Owner-President Management program he graduated. Other awards included the Marcus Garvey Award for Excellence from the Jamaican-American Council and the Minority Business Person of the Year from the U.S. Small Business Administration. He was profiled in *Black Enterprise*, *Fortune*, and *New York Times*. He cofounded the National Association of Minority CPA firms and was chairman of the board of the Association of Black CPA firms. Mitchell also served on many boards of directors, including the Dance Theater of Harlem, the Greater New York Fund United Way, One Hundred Black Men, Ariel Mutual Funds, BJ's Wholesale Club, Pepsi-Cola Ethnic Advisory Board, the Rouse Company, Harvard Business School, and the Baruch College Fund. His daughter Tracey became a partner in Mitchell & Titus in 2002. Tracey passed away as the result of a stroke on 14 September 2005.

FURTHER READING

Hammond, Theresa. *A White-Collar Profession: African American Certified Public Accountants since 1921* (2002).

Mitchell, Bert. "The Black Minority in the CPA Profession: A Case for Affirmative Action," Abraham J. Briloff Lecture Series on Accounting and Society (1987, 1988, 1989).

Wollman, Jane. "The Two Sides of Being 'The First Black,'" *Newsday Magazine*, 15 Apr. 1990.

THERESA A. HAMMOND

Mitchell, Blue (13 Mar. 1930–21 May 1979), jazz musician, was born Richard Allen Mitchell in Miami, Florida. The names of his parents are unknown. He began his musical career by studying the trumpet in high school and was touring by the time he was twenty-one. Mitchell's early career was with rhythm and blues groups. From 1951 to 1955 he performed with bands led by Paul Williams, EARL BOSTIC, and Chuck Willis.

Mitchell's trumpet style—characterized by blues elements, occasional punctuated high notes, and a soulful sound—was enhanced by his knowledge of jazz, especially chord changes. It was his knowledge of and familiarity with bebop concepts that led CANNONBALL ADDERLEY, a fellow Floridian, to arrange a recording date for Mitchell with Riverside in 1959 in New York City. Two albums, *Big Six* and *Blue Soul*, were produced with Mitchell as leader.

Mitchell became an exponent of a new trumpet aesthetic. Whereas the bebop and hard-bop eras produced trumpeters who emphasized technique, endurance, high notes, and a strong adherence to the contrafact, trumpeters like Mitchell, MILES DAVIS, and Lonnie Hillyer adopted a less technical and more subtle approach. Mitchell was not as technically proficient as either CLIFFORD BROWN or DIZZY GILLESPIE, and rather than projecting loudly he would use a quieter dynamic to stress emotion and feeling in his music, thereby crafting his own musical identity. Examples of his style can be heard on his recordings with the jazz pianist HORACE SILVER in compositions like "Finger Poppin'," "Cookin' at the Continental," "Come on Home," and "Mellow D" from *Finger Poppin'* (1959) and "Me and My Baby," "Nica's Dream," and "Horace-Scope" from *Horace-Scope* (1960), as well as in his work on *Doin' the Thing* (1961). Mitchell had been hired by Silver in 1958 and remained with the group, which included Junior Cook, Gene Taylor, and Ray Brook, until 1963.

After Silver split up the quintet Mitchell formed his own group with Cook and Taylor. At the piano was Chick Corea and Al Foster was on drums; they were later replaced by Harold Mabern (piano) and BILLY HIGGINS (drums). Although Mitchell played an electric repertoire with Silver, both his group and Silver's became known as "funky style" bands that retained a conventional tunefulness in contrast to the dissonant, "outside" sounds prevailing in free jazz. Their style was permeated with blues and gospel elements featuring inside solos, a complementary, often repetitious rhythmic feel, repetitious melodies, and a trumpet-tenor front line harmonized in fourths.

After limited success as a bandleader, Mitchell resumed his career as a sideman. Between 1967 and 1978 he performed with a diverse group of musicians. He toured with the rhythm and blues singer RAY CHARLES and with the blues singer and guitarist John Mayall, recording *Jazz Blues Fusion* in 1971. From 1974 until his death he worked with Louis Bellson, Tony Bennett, the Bill Berry Big Band, Harold Land, and LENA HORNE and Bill Holman. From 1975 to 1977 he also recorded several jazz fusion albums, and he recorded *Mapanzi* (1977) with Land.

Mitchell was diagnosed with cancer in October 1978 and was thereafter unable to perform. He died in Los Angeles and was honored with memorial services in Los Angeles, New York, and Miami. He and his wife, Thelma (maiden name unknown), evidently did not have children. Mitchell left a legacy of having developed his own sound and aesthetic, fitting any jazz or jazz-related situation.

FURTHER READING

Gardner, Mark. "Blue Mitchell on Blue Note," *Jazz Festival* 23, no. 2 (1979).
Kernfeld, Barry. "Blue Mitchell," in *The New Grove Dictionary of Jazz* (1988).
Obituary: *Down Beat*, 12 July 1979.

This entry is taken from the *American National Biography* and is published here with the permission of the American Council of Learned Societies.

EDDIE S. MEADOWS

Mitchell, Bobby (6 June 1935–), pro football player and team executive, was born Robert Cornelius Mitchell in Hot Springs, Arkansas. His extraordinary talent in sports was revealed during his time as a student at Langston High School. He played basketball, football, and baseball and was a member of the school's track team. He was so skilled in baseball that he was offered a contract by the St. Louis Cardinals, but he turned it down to pursue an education. He was offered a number of scholarships from major universities and chose to attend the University of Illinois, where he played football and was on the school's track team. His success in track was overshadowed by his achievements in football. He set a world record that lasted for 6 days with a time of 7.7 seconds in the 70-yard indoor low hurdles. He ran the 100-yard dash in 9.7 seconds and broad jumped 24 feet, 3 inches, and in his sophomore year he led the University of Illinois to the Big Ten Championship in track. A star halfback, Mitchell ran sixty-four yards for a touchdown against Michigan the first time he was given the ball. In that game against Michigan, Mitchell gained 173 yards on just 10 carries. That year he averaged a record 8.6 yards per rush.

After graduating from Illinois in 1958, Mitchell married his college sweetheart, Gwen Morrow. They had two children, Terri and Robert C. Later that year Mitchell was selected in the seventh round of the National Football League draft by the Cleveland Browns. He was paired with JIM BROWN in the Browns backfield even though he lobbied to play wide receiver. In his four years with the Cleveland Browns, Mitchell ran for 2,297 yards and gained 1,463 yards receiving. He also returned punts and kickoffs and amassed 607 yards on punt returns and 1,550 yards on kickoff returns. He scored a total of thirty-eight touchdowns.

In 1962 Mitchell was traded to the Washington Redskins. At the time the Redskins were the last National Football League team to be segregated. The team had moved from Griffith Stadium to D.C. Stadium, a government-owned venue. Secretary of the Interior Stewart Udall demanded that the Redskins conform to the law that prohibited discrimination in federal facilities. The owner of the Redskins, George Preston Marshall, was given the choice of integrating the team or moving. So the team made the trade for Mitchell, another black halfback was selected in the draft, and two other black players were added to the team's roster for the 1962 season. When Mitchell joined the Redskins, he was immediately switched from running back to flanker. The Redskins quarterback at the time was Norman Snead, and Mitchell became a favorite target for Snead. In 1962 Mitchell caught 72 passes for 1,384 yards and 11 touchdowns. In 1963 he caught 69 passes for 1,436 yards and 7 touchdowns. After the 1963 season the Redskins traded Snead to the Philadelphia Eagles for Sonny Jurgensen. Jurgensen and Mitchell went on to tear up the league. In 1964 Mitchell caught 60 passes for 904 yards, in 1965 he caught 60 passes for 867 yards, in 1966 he caught 58 passes for 905 yards, and in 1966 he caught 60 passes for 905 yards. In 1963 he teamed with George Izo for a 99-yard touchdown reception, a league record.

Mitchell retired as an active player just prior to the 1969 season. During his career he was among the leagues top ten in rushing touchdowns in 1960

Bobby Mitchell (right and above) of the Washington Redskins making a leaping catch during a game against the St. Louis Cardinals in St. Louis, Missouri, 14 October 1962. (AP Images.)

and 1961, receptions in 1960 through 1967, receiving yards in 1962 through 1967, receiving touchdowns in 1960 through 1966, and yards from scrimmage from 1960 through 1963. He garnered 14,078 combined net yards in his career, scored 91 touchdowns, caught 521 passes, and had 8 kickoff returns for touchdowns. He was selected to the All-NFL team three times and played in four Pro Bowls. He was elected to the Pro Football Hall of Fame in 1983, and he was also elected as one of the seventy greatest Redskins.

After his retirement in 1969, Mitchell joined the Redskins front office as a scout and later served the club as assistant general manager. He was instrumental in building the Redskins Super Bowl teams.

FURTHER READING

Attner, Paul, and Ken Denlinger. *Redskin Country: From Baugh to the Super Bowl* (1983).
Tandler, Rich. *The Redskins from A to Z*, vol. 1, *The Games* (2002).
Whittingham, Richard. *Hail Redskins: A Celebration of the Greatest Players, Teams, and Coaches* (2001).

ROBERT JANIS

Mitchell, Charles Lewis (10 Nov. 1829–13 Apr. 1912), Massachusetts legislator, and civil rights and women's rights champion, was born in Hartford, Connecticut, the son of William Mitchell and Clara (Green) Mitchell, of whom nothing is known. It is probable that he had a brother, William. Other than the fact that he trained and worked as a printer, little is known of Mitchell's early life. When the Civil War broke out, Mitchell joined the Fifty-fifth Massachusetts Regiment at the age of thirty-three. Little is known of his military service, but he apparently lost a foot in the Battle of Honey Hill, South Carolina, in November 1864. He was one of the few African Americans commissioned as an officer at the close of the war. Unfortunately for Mitchell—and for GEORGE E. STEPHENS in the Fifty-fourth as well—while the Commonwealth of Massachusetts recognized his promotion, the U. S. War Department did not. He was, however, always known as Lieutenant Mitchell after the war and was allowed to participate in the regiment's Massachusetts Officers' Association.

Charles Lewis Mitchell was the first African American legislator in Massachusetts. The results of his election were published on 6 November 1866 by the City of Boston. In 1867 he represented Suffolk District 6 and lived at 13 Anderson Street, located in a fashionable section of Boston, and occupied Seat #159 in the legislature. In 1867 the area later known as Beacon Hill was in fact a thriving black community and the home of notables such as Sarah Roberts and her father BENJAMIN ROBERTS, who in 1849 had sued the city of Boston in an effort to desegregate the public schools. Mitchell's occupation was listed as junior printer and he rented from Mark R. DeMortie, a wealthy black Republican operative who had been the sutler—a private supplier of goods—for the famed black Civil War unit, the Fifty-fourth Massachusetts Regiment.

Although it appears that he was only in the House of Representatives for one year, Mitchell did make history in that he was the first African American in the Massachusetts legislature to run for the seat of speaker of the house. He failed to get elected, however, garnering only one vote out of 228 cast.

Despite failing in his bid for a leadership position Mitchell did vote his conscience for important civil rights legislation that reached the House. For example, on 13 March 1867, the House voted on a report from the Committee on Federal Relations to ratify an amendment to the United States Constitution. The Committee recommended the following language: "That the legislature of Massachusetts earnestly requests congress to propose to the states an amendment to the federal constitution prohibiting the disfranchisement of any citizen on account of color."

The amendment was rejected, 14 to 130.

In the same year, a petition was brought by Representative Mehitable Haskell to amend the state constitution to provide the vote to women in the Commonwealth. The petition was defeated with a vote of 44 to 97, with Mitchell supporting the measure.

After leaving the legislature Mitchell continued in his profession as a printer and remained in Suffolk County. By 1895 Mitchell was working as the statistical clerk for the United States Custom House in Boston and owned a home valued at $4,700. Sometime before 1906 he moved to 24 Sherman Street in the Roxbury section of Boston and purchased a home on one of the largest lots in the neighborhood. While the 1870 Census did not list a wife or family, by the 1910 Census he had moved from Ward 6, where he served as representative, to Ward 21 in Suffolk County, and Nellie B. was listed as his wife; her background and maiden name are unknown. By 1915 the city of Boston listed the property in his wife's name. According to his death certificate Mitchell died of apoplexy with the contributing illness of endocarditis and was buried in Dover, New Hampshire.

FURTHER READING

Atlas of the City of Boston (1895).

Journal of the House of Representatives of the Commonwealth of Massachusetts, Archives Division.

Manual for the Use of the General Court (1867).

Massachusetts Death Records, #3769, Vol. 11.

Returns of Voters Given in the Several Wards, 6 Nov. 1866.

Street Book, 1866, Ward 6, Book A, assessing Department, City of Boston Archives, Boston.

United States Federal Census (1850, 1870).

ROBERT JOHNSON JR.

Mitchell, Clarence Maurice, Jr. (8 Mar. 1911–18 Mar. 1984), civil rights lobbyist, was born in Baltimore, Maryland, the son of Clarence Maurice Mitchell, a waiter, and Elsie Davis. He attended St. Katherine's Episcopal Church and later became a member of the Sharp Street Memorial Methodist Church. From Douglass High School in Baltimore, he entered Lincoln University in Pennsylvania in 1928 and graduated in 1932 with a B.A. In 1938 Mitchell married Juanita Elizabeth Jackson, daughter of Keiffer Bowen Jackson and LILLIE MAE JACKSON of Baltimore; they had four children. President of the Baltimore branch of the due NAACP and the Maryland State Conference of NAACP Branches, Lillie Jackson spearheaded the freedom movement in the state and became a celebrated historical figure. From 1933 to 1936 Mitchell was a reporter for the *Baltimore Afro American*. He left for a year of graduate study at the Atlanta School of Social Work as a National Urban League fellow. After completing the program in 1937, he served for six months as director of the Maryland office of the Division of Negro Affairs of the National Youth Administration, developing training and jobs program for blacks. In November 1937 he became executive secretary of the Urban League office in St. Paul, Minnesota, where his primary concerns were breaking down racial barriers in housing and fighting employment discrimination. He was especially effective in attacking closed-shop agreements in union contracts that barred blacks from jobs.

In 1941 Mitchell assumed a new job as field employment assistant under ROBERT C. WEAVER, who headed the Negro Employment and Training Branch in the labor division of the Office of Production Management in Washington. Soon afterward he was named assistant director of the department. In January 1943 Mitchell was appointed associate director of the division of field operations for the Fair Employment Practice Committee (FEPC) and in 1945 director of field operations. In 1946, after Congress had discontinued the agency, WALTER WHITE, executive secretary of the NAACP, hired him as labor secretary in the organization's Washington bureau to carry on the FEPC's work. Four years later Mitchell became director of the bureau.

One of Mitchell's early accomplishments was helping to secure passage in Congress of an amendment to the Railway Labor Act through his vigorous lobbying efforts. This act prohibited both unions and railroads from dismissing workers who refused to join Jim Crow unions and locals. He prepared another provision, which Congressman ADAM CLAYTON POWELL JR. of Harlem successfully

Clarence Maurice Mitchell Jr., standing behind a lectern in church, c. 1955. (Library of Congress.)

introduced in 1955 as an amendment to the National Reserve Training Act. The amendment blocked adoption of a proposal to give the Department of Defense authority to transfer draftees to segregated units in the National Guard. Mitchell also authored a provision to bar discrimination in federally funded education programs that became known as the "Powell Amendment" because the Harlem congressman introduced it in the House in the 1950s repeatedly without success. Nevertheless, Mitchell helped persuade President Dwight D. Eisenhower to implement through executive action a policy barring discrimination in the spending of federal funds. His other early accomplishments included lobbying the Eisenhower administration to bar segregation at military facilities and, ultimately, to complete the desegregation of all branches of the armed services in 1954. Crucial aspects of Mitchell's strategy included persuading Eisenhower to publicly commit himself to ending such discrimination and exposing administration officials who contravened the president's expressed views that such practices were wrong and harmful to the services.

Mitchell was the principal force in the struggle for the passage of the 1957 Civil Rights Act. His strategy included winning the support of Attorney General Herbert Brownell for a broad civil rights bill and organizing bipartisan coalitions in the House and Senate that included powerful conservatives like California Republicans Congressman Thomas Kuchel and Senator William F. Knowland. Of the act, Mitchell said: "In due time, this legislation will make the Congress itself a more realistic reflection of the American scene because it will guarantee that future southern delegations in the nation's highest legislative body will include qualified colored men and women. After the stern restraint of a Federal injunction has been applied, those who use force, economic pressure and deception to keep voting lists lily white will realize that the ballot is for all without regard to race."

Even though the 1957 act was primarily an inadequate voting rights law, it created the Civil Rights Division of the Justice Department and the U.S. Civil Rights Commission, both of which became important instruments in the struggles to pass and enforce subsequent laws. In an effort to strengthen the 1957 act, Mitchell lobbied for passage of the 1960 Civil Rights Act, although it was a weak amendment of the 1957 law. Persevering, he spearheaded the struggle for passage of the omnibus 1964 Civil Rights Act. Acknowledging his vision, ROY WILKINS, executive director of the NAACP,

said: "Clarence Mitchell was the man in charge of this operation. He perfected and directed flawlessly a wonderful group of representatives of church, labor and all facets of the community to make this possible." As with the previous acts, this coalition of groups worked with the NAACP through the Leadership Conference on Civil Rights, which Mitchell served as legislative chairman. The following year, Mitchell utilized the same strategy to win passage of the 1965 Voting Rights Act.

Of all the civil rights leaders and activists at a White House meeting on 18 March 1966, Mitchell was the only one who supported President Lyndon B. Johnson's decision to seek a fair housing law in Congress. Johnson did not want to deal with the problem piecemeal. The other leaders, however, suspicious of Johnson's intentions and fearing that Congress would not pass the law, wanted the president to issue an executive order barring discrimination in housing. Mitchell was opposed, and he convinced them that a law was permanent whereas an executive order lasted only as long as a presidential administration. His vision and determination paid off when on 10 April Congress passed the 1968 Fair Housing Act. The next day President Johnson signed the measure into law. This success finally won Miller the recognition from the civil rights community he deserved as one of the most skillful and effective lobbyists in the nation's history. Among other things, the *Washington Post* (28 Apr. 1968) noted that the *Congressional Quarterly* (26 Apr. 1968, 931–34) had documented extensively his role in passing the law.

The next phase of Mitchell's work involved providing for the enforcement of laws for which he fought so hard and seeking adoption of strengthening provisions. Those efforts included lobbying for passage of extensions of the 1965 Voting Rights Act in 1970 and 1975.

The central thrust of Mitchell's life's work, as he himself said, was "to make the Constitution a meaningful document for all people. I began this job by, first, trying to make the executive branch of government work properly. We needed not only just laws but also right national policies. Second, we had to get Congress to enact laws for the protection of our rights. Third, we had to make sure that the laws were enforced. Without enforcement, it would not have been worth getting the laws in the first place." He said he felt "privileged to live in a time when we have gotten all three branches of our national government to work for civil rights."

Among his awards were the NAACP's Spingarn Medal, which he received in 1969, and the Medal of Freedom, which President Jimmy Carter presented to him in 1980. Mitchell died at his home in Baltimore.

FURTHER READING

The personal papers of Clarence Mitchell Jr. are in the Manuscript Division of the Library of Congress. Oral histories of both Mitchell and his wife, Juanita Mitchell, are at the Maryland Historical Society. Other materials are in the Civil Rights Documentation Project of the Ralph J. Bunche Oral History Collection located in the Manuscript Department of the Moorland-Spingarn Research Center at Howard University.

Watson, Denton L. *Lion in the Lobby* (1990).

Obituaries: *New York Times* and *Baltimore Sun*, 20 Mar. 1984.

This entry is taken from the *American National Biography* and is published here with the permission of the American Council of Learned Societies.

DENTON L. WATSON

Mitchell, Elvis (1956?–), film critic, author, and producer, was born and raised in Detroit, Michigan. He was one of nine children born to his parents. His father, Lou Mitchell, worked two blue-collar jobs at a laundry and a dairy farm to support the family. Despite the fact that he dropped out for a time, Mitchell graduated from Wayne State University, where he majored in English. While he was in college, he started his career reading his movie reviews on Detroit public radio. But it was his people-savvy that began his career in journalism. He found out where the prominent film critic Pauline Kael was about to conduct a television interview and ended up accompanying her to the interview, thus gaining a powerful mentor who would go on to recommend him for a job at the *Detroit Free Press*.

He didn't get that job, but he went on to work for a suburban Detroit paper and freelanced for a variety of publications from the *Village Voice* to *Spin* before he moved to a full-time job with the *Fort Worth Star-Telegram* in 1997. Two years later, he was hired by the *New York Times*. "Part of my job is about stirring up trouble—to get people to think about what they're seeing" Mitchell told Ryan Underwood in *Fast Company*, a business and technology magazine. In addition to his unique, stream-of-consciousness writing style, Mitchell acquired what one reporter called a "dude about town" persona and he was well-known for never

doing only one job at a time. In 1992, when he was recruited to a development job at Paramount Pictures by his friend Brandon Tartikoff, he was also reviewing movies on National Public Radio's *Weekend Edition* and was fired six months later when Paramount realized there was a conflict of interest, according to a *New York* magazine profile written by Carl Swanson in April 2010. He tried to write screenplays in the mid-nineties, including a movie about Bob Marley, and was reportedly consistently considered for jobs in the industry he was covering, including being in the running at Sony Pictures and to be the head of Warner Independent Films, Swanson wrote. He denied both stories. He also freelanced for the *Village Voice* and worked for the Independent Film Channel, sometimes in overlapping jobs.

Swanson referred to Mitchell as "bigger than life, or at least bigger than most print journalists, a road show of pop-culture exuberance who makes the rounds of TV shows, film festivals, and lecture appointments, hobnobbing with stars and industry figures." Mitchell surprised his coworkers at the *Times* and other newspapers by always seeming to work multiple jobs at once. He worked not only as a writer, but he also was the host of a public radio show called *The Treatment* and hosted the cable show *TCM Presents: Elvis Mitchell Under the Influence*. He also worked as a host for *Independent Focus* on the Independent Film Channel.

Swanson's profile suggested that Mitchell's many jobs played a partial role in his departure from the *New York Times* in 2005. Before he left, he taught as a visiting lecturer at the Harvard University Department of African and African American Studies and taught two classes while working full-time for the *Times*. HENRY LOUIS GATES told Swanson that Mitchell is "certainly the most powerful black film critic in history, full stop," and that it was a great day for the race when he got the *New York Times* job. His fame and influence as a critic, however, has been beset somewhat by gossip items about his work life, and sometimes, his finances. Between 2007 and 2009, the Internal Revenue Service filed three liens against him totaling close to $500,000. The *Detroit News* reported that Mitchell told U.S. border guards who stopped him at the Detroit-Windsor Tunnel and found $12,000 in cash inside a cigar box, that "he's just afraid of banks." But he ended up forfeiting more than $6,000 of the cash because it's illegal to carry more than $10,000 in cash across the border.

Elvis Mitchell, left, and photographer Timothy Greenfield-Sanders attend the HBO premiere of *The Black List: Volume 2* at The Apollo Theater, in New York, on Feb. 24, 2009. (AP Images.)

In 2008 he began working with the author Timothy Greenfield-Sanders on *The Black List*, a project intended to "track the black experience in America and by doing so, to exhibit the wealth and variety in it." The two interviewed twenty-five prominent African Americans from all walks of life, from FAYE WATTLETON, the former president of Planned Parenthood, to Zane, the erotica writer. The end result was an 87-minute HBO documentary, a reference-sized coffee table book, and an audiobook—all well received and critically acclaimed.

FURTHER READING

Mitchell, Elvis, and Timothy Greenfield-Sanders. *The Black List* (2008).

Underwood, Ryan. "Fast Talk: I Want That Job." *Fast Company*, 31 Jan. 2003. http://www.fastcompany.com/magazine/67/fasttalk.html

Snell, Robert. "Critic Gets 2 Thumbs Down from IRS." *Detroit Free Press.* Thursday, 24 Sept. 2009. http://community.detnews.com/apps/blogs/taxingdetroitblog/index.php?blogid=165

Swanson, Carl. "Elvis and His *Times*." *New York*, April 2010. http://nymag.com/nymetro/news/media/columns/media/n_1335/

JOSHUNDA SANDERS

Mitchell, George (8 Mar. 1899–27 May 1972), jazz trumpeter and cornetist, was born in Louisville, Kentucky. His widowed mother, whose name is unknown, worked as a maid. Nothing is known of his father. When Mitchell was about twelve years old he became interested in music through a friend, Leonard Fields, who had a cornet (or, by another account, an alto horn). Mitchell began taking lessons from Fields's father, a member of the Louisville Musical Club Brass Band, the leading African American ensemble in the city. A year later his mother bought him a trumpet. By 1912 or 1913 Mitchell was a member of the congregational marching brass band of St. Augustine Church, and soon thereafter he joined the Louisville Music Club Brass Band, playing concert band music and ragtime. He learned to improvise while working with this ensemble and with dance and theater orchestras drawn from within the club's ranks and led by Wilbur Winstead and the trombonist John Emory. At some point he acquired the nickname "Little Mitch" because of his hunched back and small frame.

Mitchell toured the South from 1917 to 1918 with the Rabbit Foot Minstrel Show. Back home he rejoined Winstead and Emory; a photo from July 1919 shows Mitchell on stage at the Hawaiian Gardens in Louisville as a member of Emory's eight-piece dance band. Late that year a job in Chicago with John Wickliffe's band fell through, and instead Mitchell joined the pit band for Irving Miller's *Brown Skin Models* revue at the Grand Theater. He also worked at the Club Alvadere for eight months while taking every opportunity to hear the great New Orleans musicians resident in Chicago, especially the cornetist KING OLIVER.

Mitchell worked with the pianist Tony Jackson and the drummer Tubby Hall in a band at the Deluxe Cafe from late 1920 into 1921. With Hall he toured Canadian theaters in Clarence Miller's band from 1921 into 1922, when they were stranded in Hamilton, Ontario. He performed in Detroit, briefly returned to Louisville, and then joined Doc Holley's band at the Castle Ice Garden in Milwaukee.

Early in 1923 Mitchell settled in Chicago, where he first joined Wickliffe's band. In late summer he joined the band of the violinist CARROLL DICKERSON at the Sunset Cafe, and early in 1924 they were at the Mahjong Club. In late summer 1924 Mitchell was with Doc Cook's orchestra at Harmon's Dreamland Ballroom, and concurrently he worked with the clarinetist Jimmie Noone, replacing FREDDIE KEPPARD, at the Paradise Gardens. At this time Mitchell switched permanently from the trumpet to a hybrid trumpet-cornet, which offers something of the more compact tubing shape and darker sound that distinguishes a cornet from a trumpet. Mitchell left Cook in 1925 and became a member of the band of the pianist LIL ARMSTRONG at the Dreamland Café until spring 1926. Armstrong's husband, LOUIS ARMSTRONG, often sat in, replacing Mitchell. Mitchell also worked during 1926 with Vernon Roulette's band, and until at least 1927 he continued doubling after hours at Paradise Gardens, where earnings from tips exceeded his nightly wages elsewhere. He became a member of DAVE PEYTON's orchestra in spring 1927, and he doubled with the band of the saxophonist Verona Biggs until he once again replaced Keppard in Cook's orchestra, then at the White City Ballroom. He stayed with Cook for two years.

In these same years, Mitchell became a distinguished recording artist. On 10 March 1926 he entered the studio with the band of the pianist LUIS RUSSELL, soloing and leading the ensemble in "Sweet Mumtaz" and "29th and Dearborn," and accompanying the blues singer ADA BROWN on "Tia Juana Man." For contractual reasons Mitchell rather than Louis Armstrong recorded with Lil Armstrong in the New Orleans Wanderers and New Orleans Bootblacks sessions of July 1926, including "Papa Dip" and "Perdido Street Blues."

Between September 1926 and June 1927 Mitchell was the trumpeter-cornetist in the pianist and composer JELLY ROLL MORTON's Red Hot Peppers, playing on some of the most significant jazz recordings ever made. Mitchell can be heard on titles familiar to any fan of early jazz, including "Black Bottom Stomp," "Smoke-House Blues," "The Chant," "Sidewalk Blues," "Dead Man Blues," "Grandpa's Spells," "Original Jelly-Roll Blues," "Doctor Jazz," "Wild Man Blues," "Beale Street Blues," and "The Pearls." Following in a tradition established by Oliver and Armstrong, Mitchell was paired with the trumpeter Natty Dominique in October 1927 for recordings by the clarinetist JOHNNY DODDS's Black Bottom Stompers, including "Come On and Stomp, Stomp, Stomp" and "Joe Turner Blues." Mitchell's last recording of any consequence was "Let's Sow a Wild Oat," made at a session with Noone in December 1928. He may also be the unidentified brassman on a session from February 1929 directed by Oliver.

Mitchell joined EARL HINES's big band at the Grand Terrace from summer or autumn 1929 to spring 1930. He was fired for alleged incompetence, rehired in summer 1930, and then fired again the following spring, for reasons unknown, though it seems likely that Mitchell's ragtime-based style had become too old-fashioned for Hines. Mitchell worked for the little-known banjoist Jack Ellis that summer. Thereafter he had difficulty securing work in music, and he became a clerk in a financial firm in Chicago. After performing with the little-known Freddie Williams Gold Coast Orchestra in 1934, with a Works Progress Administration concert orchestra in around 1935, and with Charles Elgar's Federal Concert Orchestra in 1936, Mitchell abandoned music. He retired from his clerkship in the early 1960s and died a decade later in Chicago.

Mitchell was not a dominating, showy trumpeter-cornetist. Often using mutes for discreet timbral effects, he led ensembles and played polite, precise, lyrical melodies in a manner that conveyed a lilting sense of swing and a rhythmic punch, despite its delicacy. Mitchell was a player perfectly suited to Morton's conception of a New Orleans jazz in which composed themes within intricate instrumental structures carry more weight than improvisation and personal glory.

FURTHER READING

Chilton, John. *Who's Who of Jazz: Storyville to Swing Street*, 4th ed. (1985).

Erskine, Gilbert M. "Little Mitch," *Down Beat* (7 Nov. 1963).

Schuller, Gunther. *Early Jazz: Its Roots and Musical Development* (1968).

Obituary: *Down Beat*, 21 Dec. 1972.

This entry is taken from the *American National Biography* and is published here with the permission of the American Council of Learned Societies.

BARRY KERNFELD

Mitchell, John, Jr. (11 July 1863–3 Dec. 1929), newspaper editor and banker, was born near Richmond, Virginia, on the estate of James Lyons, where his parents, John Mitchell and Rebecca (maiden name unknown), were house slaves. After gaining their freedom, the Mitchells were employed by Lyons as servants in his mansion in the city, where their son performed various chores and became a keen observer of the rituals of polite society practiced there. Mitchell's mother exerted a decisive influence on him during his formative years: she instilled in him a fierce sense of racial pride, instructed him in the ways of gentlemanly conduct, and insisted on his regular attendance at the First African Baptist Church, where he was baptized at the age of fourteen. Over the objections of her white employer, Rebecca Mitchell arranged for her son's education, first in a private school and later in public schools. An intensely competitive student with considerable artistic ability, Mitchell regularly won medals for superior performance, graduating at the head of his class at the Richmond Normal and High School in 1881.

Failure to obtain an apprenticeship in architecture prompted Mitchell to seek employment as a teacher. In 1883, after teaching for two years in Fredericksburg, Virginia, he returned to Richmond, where he had secured a post in the city's public schools. A conspicuous figure in the social, cultural, and religious life of Richmond's black community, he also served as a correspondent for the *New York Globe*, a leading black newspaper. For several years, beginning in 1883, he contributed a weekly column to the *Globe* on events in black Richmond under the pen name "More." A strikingly handsome, courtly man, always fashionably attired, Mitchell never lacked for female companionship. Although he carried on a courtship over several decades with Marietta Chiles, a normal school classmate, he remained a bachelor. An intensely private man, he impressed many as a lonely, solitary figure.

When, after only a year, Mitchell lost his teaching job in Richmond because of political changes in the city, he embarked on a career in journalism as editor of the *Richmond Planet*, a black weekly founded in 1883. Assuming direction of the virtually bankrupt newspaper with the help of friends in December 1884, Mitchell remained its editor for the next forty-five years. In time he modernized the newspaper's equipment, enlivened its pages with his own artwork, increased its circulation, and ultimately transformed the Planet Publishing Company into a modestly profitable enterprise. Active in the Colored Press Association by the mid-1880s, he served as its president from 1890 to 1894. Despite a succession of legal battles that challenged his ownership of the *Planet*, Mitchell managed to retain control and to pursue his intensely personal style of journalism.

The *Planet* was in many respects a model weekly paper, but its principal distinction lay in Mitchell's pithy and fiery editorials. Known as "the fighting editor," Mitchell continually protested all forms of racial discrimination and ridiculed the pretensions and hypocrisies of white prejudice. As the racial climate deteriorated in the late nineteenth century, he advised blacks to arm themselves in self-defense on the grounds that quiet submission to white oppression only increased assaults on their dignity. Described as "courageous almost to a fault," the *Planet*'s editor on one occasion wrote that the South needed "Jim Crow beds" far more than it needed "Jim Crow cars" and advocated legislation to penalize white men who kept black mistresses. Oblivious to threats on his life, Mitchell, on another occasion, armed himself and personally went into the countryside to investigate a lynching.

In addition to gaining recognition as a crusading editor who boldly defended the civil rights of African Americans, Mitchell also achieved considerable prominence in Virginia's Republican Party. Chosen as a delegate to the party's national convention in 1888 and as an alternate delegate four years later, he served as a member of the Richmond City

Council from the predominantly black Jackson Ward between 1888 and 1896. Convinced that the repeated use of fraud and racism by Democrats and the spread of lily-whitism among Republicans precluded any chance of blacks and poor whites uniting politically, Mitchell sought to enlist the support of upper-class, conservative whites. But his efforts were futile, as evidenced by his losing a bid to regain his seat on the city council in 1900 and the disenfranchisement of Virginia blacks two years later.

Although Mitchell moderated the militancy of his rhetoric late in the 1890s, he was still capable of wielding a pen "dipped in vitriol." As an opponent of imperialism, for example, he denounced the Spanish-American War as "a war of conquest" that would subject the dark-skinned inhabitants of Cuba and the Philippines to the horrors of racism rampant in the South. After the turn of the century Mitchell moved closer to, but never fully embraced, the accommodationist philosophy of BOOKER T. WASHINGTON. Differences in their styles and tactics were abundantly evident in Mitchell's outspoken condemnation of disenfranchisement in 1902, his leadership of a boycott to protest Richmond's segregated streetcars two years later, his vocal opposition to the city's successful effort to legalize residential segregation in 1911, and his futile campaign for governor of Virginia on a "lily-black" ticket in 1921.

When disenfranchisement effectively ended his political career, Mitchell turned to economic development as a means of assisting blacks in their struggle for first-class citizenship. In 1902 he founded the Mechanics Savings Bank, which grew rapidly—in part because of funds deposited by the Virginia chapter of the Knights of Pythias that he headed. As the founder and president of what was publicized as a showpiece of black enterprise, Mitchell won the support and admiration of much of the white business community and for many years was the only African American member of the American Bankers Association. When the bank failed in 1922, he was indicted for mismanagement. Although he was not convicted of the charge, depositors blamed him for their misfortune. Unable to regain the respect he had so long enjoyed among African Americans, Mitchell died a poor man seven years after the bank's failure and was buried in Richmond's Evergreen Cemetery.

FURTHER READING

Alexander, Ann Field. *Race Man: The Rise and Fall of the "Fighting Editor," John Mitchell Jr.* (2002).
Penn, I. Garland. *The Afro-American Press and Its Editors* (1891).
Simmons, William J. *Men of Mark: Eminent, Progressive and Rising* (1970).
Suggs, Henry Lewis, ed. *The Black Press in the South, 1865–1979* (1983, 1996).
This entry is taken from the *American National Biography* and is published here with the permission of the American Council of Learned Societies.

WILLARD B. GATEWOOD

Mitchell, Joseph E. (1876–17 Dec. 1952), newspaper publisher, editor, community leader, and entrepreneur, was born Joseph Everett Mitchell in Coosa County, Alabama, one of eight children of Henry Mitchell, a farmer and sawmill owner, and his wife, Cassana. In 1898 Mitchell left Alabama for work in Atlanta, Georgia, but when President William McKinley called for volunteers for the Spanish American War, he enlisted and became a member of the Twenty-fourth Infantry Regiment, one of the six African American regiments in the U.S. Army. The regiment served in the Philippine Islands from 1899 until August 1902, during the Philippine Insurrection. After his honorable discharge Mitchell returned to Alabama to marry Mattie Elizabeth Thomas on 20 January 1901 at Cottage Grove, Alabama. On 2 June 1940, two years after Mattie's death, he married Edwina Wright, daughter of RICHARD ROBERT WRIGHT SR., thirty-year president of Georgia State College, founder of the Citizens and Southern Bank of Philadelphia, Pennsylvania, and advocate for National Freedom Day. Edwina's brother, Bishop Richard Robert Wright Jr. of the African Methodist Episcopal (AME) Church, performed the ceremony.

Upon his return to Coosa County Mitchell was arrested for having breached a southern social taboo—before his departure to Atlanta, he had fought and defeated a local white youth. When the sheriff got Mitchell's side of the story, he offered some sage advice—leave the South. Shortly thereafter Mitchell and Mattie moved to St. Louis, Missouri, in hope of finding opportunity as the midwestern city prepared for the 1904 World's Fair. In St. Louis Mitchell became an entrepreneur and community leader. By 1905 he was the general manager of the Western Union Relief Association, a beneficial insurance organization created to care for its members during illness and death and to protect the widows and orphans of deceased members. As general manager Mitchell created a small trade paper for the membership. When the insurance company failed, Mitchell chose to continue publishing the newspaper with his brother William, who had also relocated to St. Louis, and two other investors. Called the St. Louis Argus Publishing Company, the business published the St. Louis *Argus* newspaper and engaged in job printing. Mitchell, his brother William, Benjamin W. James, and Lewis E. Hawkins incorporated the company in the state of Missouri on 27 March 1916, four years after they began publishing the newspaper. The St. Louis *Argus* was recognized nationally as an influential voice in the African American community, and Mitchell was among the forty editors and opinion makers invited to Washington in June 1918 for a three-day conference coordinated by George Creel, director of the Committee on Public Information during World War I. An *Argus* editorial on 13 May 1918 entitled "Why Not Now" probably brought Mitchell to the attention of the national government. In it he argued that black men should not wait until the end of the war to ask for justice but that "now is the time to protest; now is the time to complain; now is the time to contend of legal rights that are being denied us; and now is the time to let the world know that we are not satisfied." Although Mitchell reported the outcome of the conference positively, others in attendance, notably A.-PHILIP RANDOLPH, viewed it as an attempt to mute the voice of the black press.

In 1921 Mitchell purchased a double lot of land on Market Street in downtown St. Louis and constructed the three-story St. Louis Argus building. Mitchell was an adherent of BOOKER T. WASHINGTON's philosophy of self-help and business development, though not of accommodation. He actively encouraged the formation of the Negro Business League in St. Louis and was responsible for the development of two other businesses, the People's Finance Corporation and the St. Louis Underwriters' Corporation.

A Republican before 1936, Mitchell helped found the Citizens' Liberty League, a political action group dedicated to getting African Americans elected to political office in St. Louis on the Republican ticket. Although Mitchell never ran for political office, he used his money, influence, and the *Argus* to support black candidates. In 1920 he was instrumental in getting Walthall Moore elected as Missouri's first black state representative. Politically, Mitchell was moderate. He editorialized against the actions of southern politicians such as Cole Blease, Theodore Bilbo, and Gene Talmadge, but for St. Louis, Mitchell chose cooperation rather than agitation. He insisted that issues that affected the citizens of St. Louis be handled by committees whose membership reflected the whole of St.-Louis. In regard to African American activism, Mitchell was conservative. During the 1920s he called for railroad workers to reject the leadership of A. Philip Randolph and unionization. Although he later worked with Randolph in the March on Washington movement, he never backed down from this earlier stance. Mitchell's ability to work with people despite his personal beliefs made him the ideal branch president in 1932 to help the St. Louis branch of the NAACP transition from the defensive-minded leaders of the 1920s to the more aggressive, legal-minded, and trained leadership that characterized the local and national organizations after 1930.

As a member of the black press, Mitchell was an active member of the National Negro Press Association (NNPA) and longtime chairman of its executive committee. In 1923, when he was elected to the position, Mitchell was described as a "live wire in the newspaper fraternity and the *Argus* one of the leading journals published" by African Americans (J. E. Mitchell, "Newspaper Man High Honored," *Argus*, 5 Oct. 1923, p. 1). Mitchell pushed for more national advertisers in black newspapers. When the National Newspaper Publishers Association supplanted the National Negro Press Association, Mitchell eventually became a member of its board of directors. In 1945 Mitchell became the first African American newspaper publisher to meet with President Harry Truman in the White House. They had a relationship that dated to Truman's time as U.S. senator for Missouri. Mitchell reportedly told Truman that "as president he was in a position to do big things for the Negro."

J. E. Mitchell died in St. Louis, Missouri, after a long illness. He was eulogized by former president Truman, several Missouri governors, and politicians at every level and by black leaders of the day as a man who had made a difference. At the time of his death he had led the St. Louis Argus Publishing Company for four decades and supported black social and political activism in Missouri for half a century.

FURTHER READING

The microfilmed issues of the St. Louis *Argus* newspaper are in Newspaper Library of the Missouri State Historical Society, Columbia, Missouri. Mitchell's papers are housed in the university archives, Inman Page Library, Lincoln University in Jefferson City, Missouri.

Greene, Lorenzo, Gary Kremer, and Antonio Holland. *Missouri's Black Heritage* (1993).

Kimbrough, Mary, and Margaret Dagen. *Victory without Violence: The First Ten Years of the St. Louis CORE* (2000).

Kirby, John B. *Black Americans in the Roosevelt Era: Liberalism and Race* (1980).

Kirkendall, Richard. *A History of Missouri, 1919–1953* (1986).

Lipsitz, George. *The Sidewalks of St. Louis: Places, People, and Politics of an American City* (1991).

Mitchell, Edwina W. *The Crusading Black Journalist: Joseph Everett Mitchell* (1972).

Primm, James Neal. *Lion of the Valley: St. Louis, Missouri, 1764–1980* (1998).

Suggs, Henry L. *The Black Press in the Middle West, 1865–1985* (1996).

Weiss, Nancy. *Farewell to the Party of Lincoln: Black Politics in the Age of FDR* (1983).

Wesley, Doris A. *Lift Every Voice and Sing: St. Louis African Americans in the Twentieth Century* (1999).

Wright, John A. *Discovering African American St. Louis: A Guide to Historical Sites* (1994).

DEBRA FOSTER GREENE

Mitchell, Juanita Jackson (2 Jan. 1913–7 July 1992), civil rights activist and lawyer, was born in Hot Springs, Arkansas, one of four children born to LILLIE MAE CARROLL JACKSON, a schoolteacher and civil rights icon, and Keiffer Jackson, a traveling salesman for religiously themed films. Because of the peripatetic nature of her father's work, Mitchell traveled the country during much of her childhood. Eventually, the family resettled in Baltimore, Maryland, where Mitchell attended public schools, including Frederick Douglass High School. She was a fine student, and when she graduated in 1927 she did so at the top of her class. She matriculated to Baltimore's Morgan State College but later transferred to the University of Pennsylvania in Philadelphia, where she attended the normal school and graduated in 1931. Continuing on at the school, she took a Master's in Sociology in 1935.

As a young activist, Mitchell relied on her mother as a role model, and the economic catastrophe of the Great Depression and the poverty that it left in its wake as a call to action. She became active in Baltimore, acting as one of the cofounders of the City-Wide Young People's Forum of Baltimore and serving as its first president. Meantime, she worked as a teacher in the city's public schools. In 1935 she was approached by WALTER WHITE, then executive secretary of the National Association for the Advancement of Colored People (NAACP), who asked Mitchell to help create and take charge of the of the organization's first national youth program. Mitchell accepted, and for the next three years she threw herself into the task of broadening, restructuring, and reviving the NAACP's young activist infrastructure. Mitchell also wrote the program's constitution and increased its effectiveness by focusing its efforts in areas of most need, including education and employment.

On 7 September 1938 Mitchell married CLARENCE MITCHELL JR., who was also involved in the NAACP youth effort and who would go on to become one of his generation's most famous and effective civil rights leaders. The couple would go on to have four children. In 1942 she opened a voter registration drive that culminated in a march on the state capitol, but she soon found herself wanting to do more for the cause of legal equality. Five years later, in 1947, she entered the University of Maryland Law School and emerged three years later with her J.D., becoming the first black woman to earn that degree at the school. She began a private practice and set to work challenging segregation in her home city and state. In 1950 she filed a lawsuit with THURGOOD MARSHALL to challenge the segregation of Maryland's public facilities—for example, parks and swimming pools. The case eventually reached the U.S. Supreme Court and Mitchell was victorious. Other cases followed. Throughout the early 1950s Mitchell pursued a goal of school desegregation for Baltimore, which she hoped would become the first Southern city to finally dispel "separate but equal" following *Brown v. Board of Education* (1954). In 1955 she helped to achieve that remarkable goal—herself litigating a number of key lawsuits that led directly to the end of segregation at several Baltimore public schools—and the city education system was in fact desegregated. Meanwhile, Mitchell kept up her efforts on behalf of voter registration and fairness in elections.

Mitchell pressed on with her campaign against segregation in Maryland. In 1960 a dozen students took part in a sit-in at a Baltimore lunch counter. They were refused service and subsequently arrested and charged with trespass (the penalty was a $10 fine). The case, *Robert Mack Bell v. Maryland*, was eventually heard by the U.S. Supreme Court, which issued a determination in 1964 voiding the trespassing convictions and holding that, though the restaurant was a private business, the city of Baltimore had violated the plaintiffs' civil rights by denying them equal access to a place of public accommodation. She was also the key litigator in the so-called Veney Raids case (1966), helping to end the police practice of mass searches of private homes without search warrants.

Meanwhile, Mitchell remained active with her local NAACP branch. She eventually rose to the directorship of the Baltimore branch, and throughout the decade of the 1970s was director of all state branches. Both presidents John F. Kennedy and Lyndon Baines Johnson appointed her to presidential commissions. In 1986 she was inducted into the Maryland Women's Hall of Fame and in 1990 was made an honorary member of the Maryland Women's Bar Association, the only such honorary membership the group had ever bestowed.

Mitchell died of heart failure after years of declining health, having led a full and remarkable life of courage and commitment to the principle of equal justice and fair treatment for all citizens.

FURTHER READING

Collier-Thomas, Bettye, and V. P. Franklin, eds. *Sisters in the Struggle: African American Women in the Civil Rights–Black Power Movement* (2001).

Smith, C. Fraser. *Here Lies Jim Crow: Civil Rights in Maryland* (2008).

Obituary: *New York Times*, 9 July 1992.

JASON PHILIP MILLER

Mitchell, Littleton Purnell (26 Nov. 1918–6 July 2009), teacher and civil rights activist, was born in Milford, Delaware. The son of Littleton V. Mitchell and Helen A. Mitchell, he was one of four children born to the couple. From a young age Mitchell remembered regularly having to "outrun the white boys' stones," and he chafed at the racist mores and inequalities that marked his small community in southern Delaware (interview with the author, 15 Aug. 2003). He attended Milford Colored School and then Howard High School in Wilmington in 1939. After graduation he briefly attended West Chester College in Pennsylvania before joining the U.S. Army, serving from February 1942 to February 1946. Mitchell was stationed in Tuskegee, Alabama, during World War II and served as an instructor for the Tuskegee Airmen. He married Jane Evelyn Watson in the first year of his service, and the couple had one child, Philip. Even though Delaware was a segregated state at the time, the harshness of Alabama's brand of Jim Crow and the violence and deprivations imposed on black citizens there left a deep impression on him. When Mitchell returned to Delaware in 1946 he continued his education at West Chester College, graduating in 1948.

After graduation Mitchell became a teacher at the Governor Bacon Health Center in Delaware City until he retired in 1983, becoming the first black teacher to teach white students at the facility.

His civil rights career began as a young man when, as he recalled, his mother purchased for him a membership in the NAACP. He stayed active in the local branch before serving as the president of the Delaware State Conference from 1961 to 1991. Under Mitchell's leadership the NAACP continued after World War II as one of the most prominent civil rights organizations in the state. The organization was active in a multitude of civil rights efforts that had state and national import. Mitchell would frequently visit migrant labor camps throughout the agricultural regions of the state and report on the deplorable and exploitative conditions of the workers. The NAACP membership spearheaded sit-in campaigns at restaurants throughout the state and worked to integrate downstate hospitals. The NAACP was particularly active in lobbying for the passage of fair-housing legislation in the mid-1960s. Mitchell also admonished state officials to take stronger condemnatory stands against the activities in Delaware of hate groups such as the Ku Klux Klan, and he pressured the state police to integrate their force and make police more accountable for their actions. Additionally, he took up national issues when he urged the tristate director of the NAACP to begin a letter-writing campaign to Secretary of Defense Robert C. McNamara to take disciplinary measures against members of the armed forces who displayed the Confederate flag.

Mitchell's efforts to desegregate Delaware's public schools and ensure equitable educational opportunities for all students exemplified the NAACP's evolving civil rights strategy. Throughout the southern part of the state Mitchell worked closely with the attorney and civil rights stalwart LOUIS REDDING in his litigation campaign to desegregate public schools in the decades following *Brown v. Board of Education* (1954). In the Wilmington metropolitan area Mitchell led the opposition to the public funding of parochial schools, which, he charged, contributed to the segregation of public schools in the early 1970s. And under his leadership the NAACP lobbied state officials to take substantive steps to integrate Wilmington-area schools even before the litigation campaign to integrate metropolitan-area schools gained momentum in 1971.

On a national level Mitchell helped organize the participation of the Delaware chapter of the NAACP in a Boston rally commemorating the twenty-first anniversary of *Brown* in May 1975 in order to bring attention to the lack of integration in northern schools and to highlight the failure of the nation to live up to the Supreme Court's "all deliberate speed" edict. He was particularly critical of those who opposed busing as a means of furthering desegregation in the Wilmington metropolitan area. "For more than fifty years," he asserted on the eve of the Boston rally, "the busing of school children has been a commonplace adjunct to American educational facilities. Only in the context of school desegregation has busing become an issue of emotion and controversy" (*News Journal*, 12 May 1975).

Throughout the years of Mitchell's presidency the work of the NAACP continued even after de jure forms of discrimination had been removed. The organization's unwavering support of desegregation often brought it into conflict with black administrators and teachers who were concerned about job losses in integrated school systems. As Delaware closed black schools throughout the 1960s—eventually phasing out all-black districts in 1967—many of the teachers' concerns came to fruition as the percentage of black teachers in integrated districts declined. The NAACP responded by supporting their claims of employment discrimination, and Mitchell worked with school officials to ensure that black teachers were retained, hired, and promoted in an equitable manner. The NAACP also advocated on behalf of black students in integrated school settings, and Mitchell was adamant that in academic and disciplinary matters school staffs treat black students in an equitable manner.

Mitchell continued to be a source of great insight into the state of Delaware's political economy and was widely recognized for civil rights work. He was appointed to the *Brown v. Board of Education* Fiftieth Anniversary Commission, established by the U.S. Department of Education to coordinate commemorative exercises. And he was awarded numerous awards, including the Gerald E. Kandler Memorial Award from the American Civil Liberties Union, the Joseph P. Del Tufo Award for Distinguished Service from the Delaware Humanities Council, the Delaware State Bar Liberty Bell Award, the Most Worshipful Prince Hall Grand Lodge of Delaware Award, the Delaware State Police United Troopers Alliance Award, the Delaware Credit Union League Volunteer of the Year Award, and the Delaware Alliance Credit Union Volunteer Leadership Award for his contributions to freedom and democracy in the state.

Mitchell died in Newark, Delaware, in 2009.

FURTHER READING

The most detailed considerations of Mitchell's work during his tenure as the president of the state conference of the NAACP are contained in the *News Journal* (previously called the *Morning News* and the *Journal Every Evening*), the newspapers of record in Wilmington, Delaware. Further information is available from the National Association for the Advancement of Colored People Collection at the Library of Congress, Washington, D.C.

Jacobs, Sidney. "Interview with Littleton Mitchell," in *A History of African Americans of Delaware and Maryland's Eastern Shore*, ed. Carole Marks (1998).

Nutter, Jeanne. *A Separate Place: The Schools P. S. Du Pont Built* (film; 2003).

BRETT GADSDEN

Mitchell, Matt (9 Feb. 1905–7 Oct. 1960), railroad fireman and union activist, was born Matt Meacham in the township of Springfield, Greene County, Alabama, the fifth of seven children of Anthony Meacham, an ex-slave and farmer, and Hazel Cooks, also a farmer. Almost five years old when the Emancipation Proclamation was signed in 1863, Anthony became a sharecropper in Greene County, but relocated, following a racially motivated financial dispute with the landowner, to nearby Pickens County about 1915. A defining moment in Meacham's life, it influenced his decision to confront the pervasive racism in the railroad industry in the 1940s.

Meacham's odyssey began at seventeen in July 1922. Like thousands of poorly educated yet ambitious rural Alabama black youths in the 1920s, he migrated to the thriving small city of Tuscaloosa, seeking a better life and in the process assumed a new surname, Mitchell. Hired as a coal heaver on the coal chute by the Gulf, Mobile and Northern Railroad, later the Gulf, Mobile and Ohio (GM&O), in March 1925, he became what was equivalent to a part-time fireman. The last black fireman hired in the Montgomery-Tuscaloosa District between 1925 and 1951, he was placed on the extra board, an arrangement that allowed aspiring full-time firemen to gain experience. In 1926, he married Lorean Stockstill and by 1936, they had three children. Becoming full-time in 1937, in railroad jargon, he was assigned to the "Pool Service." It was a year of celebration and sadness, due to Lorean's death. He married Ruth Works in 1938, and by the end of 1943, his family had grown by three.

Four years later, in July 1947, when the GM&O became 100 percent dieselized in his district, he was seemingly arbitrarily reassigned to the extra board, with a pay reduction, and elevated white firemen junior in seniority to the Pool Service. A white fireman similarly treated would have filed a grievance with the Brotherhood of Locomotive Firemen and Enginemen (BLFE), the certified bargaining agent that, pursuant to the 1926 Railway Labor Act, as amended in 1934, was obligated to represent all firemen without distinction. This was a conundrum for the BLFE because it barred black membership and had conspired with the GM&O to cause Mitchell's unlawful reassignment, a decision traceable to 1924.

Through pacts and secret understandings and agreements, the railroads and BLFE had agreed to remove black firemen by limiting their access to particular runs, establishing a quota system, and restricting or denying them employment as a company dieselized. Supposedly the final solution was a win-win for both parties because it insured the company-backed purging of the expensive practice of featherbedding coupled with BLFE's plan to get rid of all black firemen. Classified as "promotables," whites were assumed to be literate and could pass written tests qualifying them to become enginemen on diesels. Blacks, classified as "unpromotables, were assumed to be illiterate, could not pass the same tests, and consequently would be fired as coal engines were retired. At long last, a lone white man would operate the diesel engine. The plan, however, backfired.

The conspirators had arrogantly ignored Mitchell's seniority, BLFE's legal obligation to represent him, and more egregiously, U.S. Supreme Court decisions upholding the constitutionality of his seniority rights and right to be represented under the Railway Labor Act in cases such as *Steele v. Louisville & Nashville Railroad Co.* (1944), *Tunstall v. Brotherhood of Locomotive Firemen and Enginemen* (1944), and *Graham v. Brotherhood* (1949). Considered a non-person by the BLFE, yet physically threatened by some of its members, undeterred, Mitchell chose the most effective option in seeking relief: adjudication in the federal courts.

For this assistance he turned to the Provisional Committee to Organize Colored Locomotive Firemen, created in 1941 by the Brotherhood of Sleeping Car Porters' (BSCP) president A. PHILIP RANDOLPH and chief field organizer B. F. McLaurin, among others, to spearhead a unified national effort to protect the seniority rights of rapidly disappearing black firemen. Mitchell had joined perhaps as early as 1944, recruited new members, and served as vice president of his district in 1949. Under provisions of the Railway Labor Act, in what developed into a class action suit, they demanded recognition of their seniority rights that would result in a return to the positions from which they had been removed, as well as back pay.

In 1949 early case preparations were hosted by Mitchell in his Tuscaloosa home in precautionary predawn meetings to discourage violent reactions from disgruntled white BLFE members or their surrogates. Participants in Tuscaloosa, Birmingham, and Washington, D.C., included a nephew, Banks Sanders; a friend, R. B. Winston; Mitchell's spouse, Ruth; the primary attorneys, Jerome Cooper and Hugo Black Jr., the son of U.S. Supreme Court Justice Hugo Black Sr.; the Americans for Democratic Action cofounder, committee attorney, and a key adviser, Joseph Rauh Jr.; as well as McLaurin and fellow lead litigants, James Harris and George Sams. On 23 January 1950, *Mitchell et. al. v. Gulf, Mobile and Ohio R. Co. et al.* was filed in the United States District Court for the Northern District of Alabama, Western Division. That Court ruled in their favor on 2 May 1950, and the Court of Appeals, Fifth Circuit, heard BLFE, the only party to appeal, rejecting its plea on 11 July 1951.

One of the key cases adjudicated in the Federal courts in the 1940s and 1950s aimed at eliminating discrimination against black firemen, it helped to set the stage for broader legal challenges to the racial status quo during the turbulent 1950s and 1960s. The monetary settlement was minimal. More importantly, the concept of seniority was restored in principle and in fact, underscored by the ruling's applicability to all areas where the BLFE and railroads conducted business. Mitchell was lauded by Randolph and McLaurin for his leadership role in the conflict and refusing to retreat when his adversaries threatened his life.

Mitchell died of lung cancer in a Tuscaloosa hospital in 1960. By then his family included five additional children. In 1958 he reclaimed Meacham as his family name.

FURTHER READING

Information in Mitchell can be found in the papers of the Brotherhood of Sleeping Car Porters and A. Philip Randolph, Library of Congress.

Arnesen, Eric. *Brotherhoods of Color: Black Railroad Workers and the Struggle for Equality* (2002).

Eberlein, E. Larry. "Judicial Regulation of the Railway Brotherhoods' Discriminatory Practices." *Wisconsin Law Review* (1953).

"Race Firemen Win Damages: Court Order Nixes Railmen's Jim Crow." *Pittsburgh Courier*, 13 May 1950.

CARL E. MEACHAM

Mitchell, Parren (29 Apr. 1922–28 May 2007), U.S. congressman, was born Parren James Mitchell, the ninth child of Clarence Maurice Mitchell, a waiter, and Elsie Davis in Baltimore, Maryland. The Mitchells lived in a cramped, two-story row house on one of the "alley" streets of Old West Baltimore, and the family could be considered poor. Parren attended segregated Garnet Elementary School, BOOKER T. WASHINGTON Junior High School, and FREDERICK DOUGLASS High School, from which he graduated in 1940. In 1942 he joined the army and was immediately shipped overseas where he served in the Ninety-Second Infantry Division as a commissioned officer and company commander. Mitchell was awarded the Purple Heart in 1944 after being wounded during fighting in Italy.

After being honorably discharged from the army in 1946, Mitchell returned to Baltimore to attend Morgan State College. There he earned a B.A. in Sociology and graduated with honors in 1950. Immediately upon graduating from Morgan, Mitchell petitioned the Circuit Court of Baltimore City for a writ of mandamus ordering that he be admitted to the then-segregated University of Maryland graduate school. He was represented in this suit by the National Association for the Advancement of Colored People (NAACP) Legal Defense Fund Chief Counsel THURGOOD MARSHALL, a close family friend, and his sister-in-law, Juanita Jackson Mitchell, counsel to the Maryland NAACP. Since the mid-1930s, the NAACP had been systematically attacking the legal concept of "separate but equal" by challenging the constitutionality of segregated graduate school programs. The NAACP's first case in this effort was won against the University of Maryland School of Law in *University v. Murray, 169 Md. 478* (1936). After a brief lull in the litigation during World War II, the NAACP scored two huge victories before the Supreme Court in *Sweatt v. Painter* (1950) and *McLaurin v. Oklahoma* (1950), desegregating the University of Texas Law School and the University of Oklahoma graduate school respectively. A lesser-known victory for the NAACP that summer came when the Circuit Court of Baltimore City ruled in Mitchell's favor. He entered the graduate school that

fall, making him the first African American to do postgraduate work at the University of Maryland, College Park campus. Mitchell graduated in 1952 with an M.A. in Sociology. Upon completion of his degree, Mitchell returned to Morgan State to become a professor of sociology and assistant director of the Urban Studies Institute. From his perch at Morgan, Mitchell involved himself in the liberal reform bureaucracy of the 1950s and 1960s. His choice of career overlapped with that of his by-then famous family. In the preceding decades, the Mitchell family had emerged as the most prominent civil rights family in the state. CLARENCE MITCHELL JR., Parren's older brother, was the director of the Washington bureau of the NAACP; Juanita was the first black woman to attend the University of Maryland School of Law and the first black woman admitted to the Maryland bar; Juanita's mother, Dr. LILLIE MAY CARROLL JACKSON, was the president of the Maryland NAACP; and in 1962 Parren's nephew, Clarence Mitchell III, would leave the Student Nonviolent Coordinating Committee to become

Parren Mitchell, talking to reporters after a meeting with President Carter at the White House, 31 August 1977. (AP Images.)

the youngest state legislator in Maryland history. From 1954 to 1957 Parren worked as the supervisor of probation work for the Supreme Bench of Baltimore City. In 1963 he became executive director of the Maryland Human Relations Commission. In this position Mitchell was pivotal in advocating for passage of and implementing the Maryland Public Accommodations Law of 1964. In 1965 Mitchell left the Human Relation Commission to become executive director of the Baltimore Community Action Agency (CAA), a War on Poverty program, a federal program that funded state and local anti-poverty offices and programs. He would hold this position for three years. While at the CAA, Mitchell worked to organize the black communities that would be crucial to his election to the U.S. House of Representatives in 1970.

In 1968 Mitchell challenged the incumbent congressman Samuel Friedel (D) for the seat from Maryland's Seventh District, which included much of West Baltimore and a substantial slice of surrounding Baltimore County. The controlling vote in the district had been Jewish since World War II and Friedel had held his seat since 1952. By 1968, however, Jewish out-migration to the county and black migration to the center city had made the district 40 percent Jewish, 40 percent black, and 20 percent non-Jewish whites. In the 1968 Democratic primary, Mitchell lost to Friedel in a three-way race by only 5,000 votes. Following the campaign, Mitchell took a position as president of Baltimore Neighborhoods, Inc., biding his time until the next congressional election. In 1970 Mitchell again challenged Friedel. The primary election was a squeaker with each candidate claiming victory by a margin of only several hundred votes. Subsequent investigations by the U.S. Civil Rights Commission determined that members of the Baltimore City Board of Supervisors of Elections loyal to Friedel had engaged in a host of fraudulent activities that disfranchised several hundred black voters. After a number of recounts, Friedel conceded the election to Mitchell in early October. Although many of the districts' white Democratic voters defected to the Republican candidate Peter Parker in the general election, Mitchell was victorious in November. In 1971 the Maryland General Assembly altered the boundaries of the seventh district eliminating many of the suburban, Jewish precincts that had been loyal to Friedel and incorporating more of the urban, black precincts of the central city that had voted for Mitchell. With the new district encompassing about 80 percent of the majority black city, the Seventh District became the base of black political power in Maryland.

Mitchell would serve in the 92nd and the seven succeeding Congresses (January 1971 to January 1987). During his sixteen years in the House of Representatives, he followed a simple credo: "I am elected from a mixed district, part white, part black; I will serve all of the people. But I will give my priority to black people and the poor because they need more" (Rovetch, 102). Seeking to fulfill this mandate, Mitchell focused his energies on minority business development. He attached an amendment to the Public Works Bill of 1976 that compelled state, county, and municipal governments seeking federal grants to allocate 10 percent of each grant they received to minority firms as contractors, subcontractors, or suppliers. The Mitchell amendment created the basic framework for the federal minority set-aside program. Two years later President Jimmy Carter signed Public Law 95-907, a measure authored by Mitchell that required prime contractors with federal agencies to set specific goals for awarding contracts to minority subcontractors. In 1981 Mitchell increased the scope of the set aside program yet again by attaching an amendment to the Surface Transportation Act that required the federal government to set aside 10 percent of its business for minority contractors. Since 1976 Mitchell's "set aside" provisions have channeled billions of federal dollars into minority businesses. The set-aside model emerged as the primary affirmative action program targeting black businesses on the federal, state, and municipal levels.

Mitchell entered Congress at the high point of black nationalism and white reaction in post-World War II electoral politics. He was, therefore, at the center of attempts to organize "parallel institutions" for the black community. Soon after being sworn in, Mitchell worked with the twelve other African American members of Congress to found the Congressional Black Caucus (CBC). For the next sixteen years Mitchell was a leading member of the caucus, serving as its chairman from 1977 to 1978. In 1976 he was a founding member of the Congressional Black Caucus Minority Business Brainstrust. In 1980 Mitchell founded the Minority Business Enterprise Legal Defense and Education Fund, Inc. (MBELDEF), a legal defense and advocacy organization for minority businesses. Mitchell created the MBELDEF, he claimed, because, "In years past if everything else failed you could count on the Justice Department [to protect African Americans]. We can't do that anymore....

I recognized this when the Reagan Administration came in. I said we needed to set up our own justice department for minority businesses" ("'On My Own Terms,' An Interview with Parren Mitchell," *Point of View: A Publication of the Congressional Black Caucus Foundation*, Fall 1986).

In 1986 Mitchell announced his plans to retire from Congress and endorsed his nephew State Senator Clarence Mitchell III to succeed him. Later in the campaign season, Mitchell announced that he would seek the Democratic nomination for the lieutenant governorship, running alongside Maryland attorney general Steve Sachs. That September, Sachs and Mitchell failed to gain the Democratic nomination. Clarence Mitchell III, too, failed to gain the Democratic nomination, coming in third behind KWEISI MFUME in the Democratic primary. These defeats dramatically reduced the Mitchell family's strength in the seventh congressional district.

Mitchell, who never married, had no children. After suffering a series of strokes in the 1990s, he moved to an assisted living home. He died on 28 May 2007 at the Greater Baltimore Medical Center in Baltimore, Maryland.

FURTHER READING

Parren Mitchell's official papers are housed in the Morgan State University Library, Baltimore, Maryland. Many of his personal papers are held by Mitchell family historian Michael Mitchell in Baltimore, Maryland.

Clay, William L. *Just Permanent Interests: Black Americans in Congress, 1870–1992* (1993).

Kupferstein, Linda. *Parren J. Mitchell: Democratic Representative from Maryland* (1972).

Rovetch Emily, ed. *Like It Is: Arthur E. Thomas Interviews Leaders of Black America* (1970).

GEORGE DEREK MUSGROVE

Mitchell, Walter M. (28 Dec. 1893–3 Oct. 1983) minister, carpenter, and civil rights activist, was born Walter Melvin Mitchell, the eldest child of Minnie Mitchell, a homemaker, and an unknown father, in rural Greene County, Georgia. Mitchell was told by relatives that his father was Fate Buice, the son of a white planter in the community where his mother lived. Although Buice never openly acknowledged Mitchell as his son, he maintained contact with Mitchell over the years. In the mid-1920's Buice traveled nearly a hundred miles from Greene County to Augusta, Georgia, to hear Mitchell preach at the historic African American Springfield Baptist Church. Mitchell's early life was greatly influenced by his grandfather, Pano Mitchell, who maintained a strong affinity for the land and his African heritage. Mitchell and his five sisters and brothers attended the local school through the sixth grade, the highest grade available for African Americans in that rural area during the 1890s and the early 1900s. Later he completed high school at the Union Baptist Institute in Athens, Georgia. While in Athens, after he became a minister, Mitchell completed four years of extension class training for ministers provided by Morehouse College.

During the early 1900s, as the South moved from post-Reconstruction to the so-called Progressive South era, the specter of Jim Crow and racial inequality still reigned. Within the social and economic context of this era, Mitchell began his young adult life. After his grandfather died in 1906, the thirteen-year-old Mitchell, as his mother's eldest son, became the chief farmer for the family for more than two years. At age sixteen he moved to live with an uncle who was a skilled carpenter and brick mason. While living with his uncle, Mitchell learned the carpentry and masonry skills that he would use later in his career. In 1910 he married Lula Willis; they would have five children.

Many young African Americans of this period migrated to northern cities in search of economic opportunities and to escape the cyclic oppression of sharecropping in the rural South and sometimes to escape potential or real physical danger. Mitchell moved to Evanston, Illinois, where he worked in construction for four years. He did not send for his family to join him in Evanston, for he believed the harsh winters would be difficult for his young family to endure.

Mitchell returned to Greene County in 1918 and began sharecropping near Penfield, Georgia. He soon received the call to become a minister and in 1921 was licensed to preach at the Boswell Chapel Baptist Church. In 1922 he was ordained a minister and became pastor of the Flat Rock Baptist Church, the oldest African American church in Greene County. Mitchell's wife, Lula, died in 1924. In 1928 he married Gertrude Harris; they had two children. This marriage ended in divorce in 1936.

As the Great Depression overtook the nation in the 1930s, Mitchell's life began a new chapter with the opportunity to focus his previous training and skills on ministry. After serving several churches in middle Georgia from 1922 to 1935, in 1936 he became pastor of the Corinth Baptist Church in Social Circle, Georgia. During that time he met Hazeltine

Jones, a registered nurse and public schoolteacher; they were married in 1937 and Mitchell moved to Madison, Georgia, where his wife lived. They had one child, a daughter. Over the next twenty years the couple often worked as a team in rural ministry, Mitchell as pastor and his wife as teacher in the local community.

As the nation made the transition from the Depression era to the wartime economy of the early 1940s, Mitchell looked for ways to help improve the economic status of the people in the communities where he served as pastor. During that time he enrolled in the Rural Pastor's Institute at Fort Valley State College near Macon, Georgia. This institute was sponsored by the Home Mission Council of the National Council of Churches.

After the training he received at the institute, Mitchell returned to Madison and began reading the *Farm Bulletin* and other farm-related publications. He contacted farm agents and others that might have useful information for the farmers who attended local churches. Mitchell became known as the "farmer preacher." At first he worked with the farm agents to improve farming practices and living conditions. Later Mitchell's attention turned to encouraging his members to move from sharecropping to home ownership. It is likely that less than 20 percent of the African American farmers in that area owned their own farms. Mitchell told the farmers about the Farmers Home Administration (FmHA) and helped the men secure loans to purchase their own farms. During this time Mitchell supplemented his pastor's salary by working as a carpenter and builder. He built houses for church members in Madison and constructed the agricultural building at the school for African American students. In addition to the carpentry and building for which he received pay, he also remodeled churches and built rural schoolhouses without compensation.

After World War II, Mitchell's attention turned to the "separate but equal" laws of the state of Georgia, particularly as related to public school education. Separate but equal laws were enacted following the U.S. Supreme Court's 1896 *Plessy v. Ferguson* decision that institutionalized racial segregation. While services were rigidly maintained as separate, they were rarely equal in quality. To combat racial segregation and discrimination, Mitchell founded and was elected the first chairman of the Morgan County Civic League. This organization's first project was a voter registration drive. By the late 1940s eight hundred of the three thousand eligible African Americans in Morgan County had registered to vote, a significant increase. The Civic League also worked to change the inequities in educational opportunities in the county. Through petitions to the Morgan County Board of Education, the Civic League obtained the same monthly pay for African American teachers as received by white teachers. Bus transportation was provided for the first time for African American students in rural areas to attend the only high school for them in the county.

A major concern for Mitchell and the Civic League was obtaining "equal" school facilities for African American students. In the late 1940s the Morgan County Board of Education had constructed a well-equipped modern brick high school for white students. At that time African American students, both elementary and high school, attended school in an eight-room, poorly maintained frame building constructed in the early 1900s. On 13 January 1949 the Civic League presented a petition to the board of education to obtain "equal school facilities for Negro students." Eventually a fifteen-room brick high school was constructed; however, it was not an "equal facility" as compared with the white high school. The building did not have a science laboratory, gymnasium, auditorium, or cafeteria. The county had constructed a new building but one that was still very much separate and unequal.

Mitchell met with the Civic League to discuss the inequalities between the black and white school buildings and recommended a follow-up petition to the school board to upgrade the facilities of the new school. The members were reluctant to petition the all-white board again, so Mitchell went alone. A board member asked about the absence of the other Civic League members. After this, a new level of racial tension began for the minister; Mitchell's life was threatened and at least one attempt was made to kill him. These events occurred a few years after the 1946 lynching of four African Americans at Moore's Bridge in adjacent Walton County, Georgia.

Mitchell soon moved his family to Atlanta for their safety. In Atlanta he continued to pastor and serve as moderator of the Madison Missionary Baptist Association for several years. As moderator, he emphasized youth training and education. In the 1950s the association established a scholarship fund to pay tuition for college students. In 1977 Mitchell received the Annual Freedom Fund Award from the Madison Branch of the NAACP. The award ceremony was attended by the white mayor and the integrated board of education as well as other civic leaders, both black and white.

This event represented the culmination of a life of service to the people of middle Georgia.

Mitchell died in Atlanta in 1983 after several months of declining health. In 1989 the Morgan County NAACP dedicated the Afro-American Cultural Program to the memory of the Reverend Walter M. Mitchell in recognition of his untiring work for equal justice for all.

FURTHER READING

Andrews, Raymond. "Black Boy and Man in the Small-Town South," in *The Prevailing South: Life and Politics in a Changing Culture*, ed. Dudley Clendinen (1988).

Camp, Lynn Robinson. *Black American Series: Morgan County, Georgia* (2004).

Camp, Lynn Robinson, and Jennifer E. Cheeks-Collins. *Black American Series: Walton County, Georgia* (2003).

Felton, Ralph A. "W. M. Mitchell," in *Go Down, Moses: A Study of 21 Successful Negro Rural Pastors* (1952).

ROSALYN MITCHELL PATTERSON

Mitchell-Bateman, Mildred (1922–), psychiatrist, administrator, and physician, was born Mildred Mitchell in Brunswick, Georgia, the daughter of a minister and registered nurse. At the age of 12, she volunteered for the Red Cross to care for those injured in a tornado that swept through her hometown of Cordele, Georgia. This experience as well as her love for science and her need to help people, greatly influenced her decision to pursue medicine. She attended Barber-Scotia College in Concord, North Carolina, from 1937 to 1939 and graduated from Johnson C. Smith University, in Charlotte, North Carolina, in 1941. She received her medical degree from Women's Medical College of Pennsylvania in 1946, completed her internship, and then became a general practitioner. She was recruited as a staff physician while completing her internship at Lakin State Hospital, a facility in West Virginia for mentally ill African Americans. Her experience at Lakin brought to her attention the chronic deficiencies in mental health care and laid the groundwork for her to become an advocate for the mentally ill. On 25 December 1947 she married William L. Bateman of Parkersburg, who worked as a therapist at the hospital.

After a year at Lakin, Mitchell-Bateman returned to Philadelphia to start her own private practice in 1948 and then received further training in psychiatry at the Menninger School of Psychiatry in Topeka, Kansas, in 1952. Three years later, in 1955, she returned to Lakin as the hospital's clinical director, and in 1958 she was promoted to superintendent of the hospital. In 1960, she was named supervisor of professional services for the West Virginia Department of Mental Health. In this capacity, she developed a working relationship with the state's various psychiatric facilities. In July 1962, the department's director, Charles A. Zeller, died, and Mitchell-Bateman was named acting director. In December, Governor Wallace "Wally" Barron named her director, and she remained in that position for the next fifteen years, becoming the first African American woman to reach such a high level in West Virginia state government. During Mitchell-Bateman's tenure as director of the state's Department of Mental Health, she had four convictions that shaped the way she practiced community medicine. First, she believed that patients had to be treated and rehabilitated to the best of their ability. Second, with adequate care, a patient who may seem to be totally disabled may be able to improve. She became famous for her statement, "No one has the right to decide that patients aren't going to get any better" (www.wvculture.org/HiStory/bateman.html). Third, she maintained that the Department of Mental Health should promote prevention of mental disability, in addition to treating the mentally disabled. She developed a program titled Breaking the Disability Cycle, which used federal funds to develop community mental health centers. Fourth, she firmly believed that a mentally disabled patient should not only be treated with dignity, but also be in a setting that allows the patient as much respect as possible in the home community. She made this possible by reorganizing mental health services to permit patients from the same neighborhood to be treated at the same mental health center.

In 1965, she led the state's implementation of Volunteers in Service to America, which allowed the average person to become involved providing supportive services for the mentally ill. In 1973, she became the first African American to serve as vice president of the American Psychiatric Association. In 1977 she became one of four psychiatrists on the President's Commission on Mental Health, which oversaw implementation of the Mental Health Systems Act passed in 1980, allowed the federal government to have more control over health policy while reducing the amount it was paid for treatment. The same year, Mitchell-Bateman became the first chair of the Psychiatric Department at Marshall University's new Medical School in Huntington, West Virginia. In 1985, she was appointed as associate clinical director of Huntington State Hospital. She worked for the accreditation of Huntington State Hospital, and when Dr. Roy Edwards retired,

Mitchell-Bateman succeeded him as clinical director at Huntington in 1996. As commissioner of mental health, she had been unsuccessful at affiliating the medical school with one of the state institutions; however, as clinical director of the hospital, she was able to establish a relationship with Huntington. On 2 October 1999, the hundredth anniversary of Huntington Hospital, Governor Cecil Underwood read a proclamation changing the hospital's name to the Mildred Mitchell-Bateman Hospital. "When I first came to the Huntington Hospital, it was so overcrowded patients had to walk across beds to get to a door," Mitchell-Bateman recalled. "And if a person was committed to a mental hospital he or she was committed for life. One of the things I'm proudest of is that the hospital named for me has changed so much. It is fully accredited now and medical students can do their internships there" (www.nlm.nih.gov/locallegends/Biographies/Mitchell_Bateman_Mildred.html). Although she retired in February 2000, Mitchell-Bateman continued to see patients part time at the Marshall University's psychiatric outpatient clinic and remained involved in teaching medical students. She believed that no matter what one's position is in the health field, the health-care worker and health-care community must be the focus of decisions affecting delivery of services to patients and the community at large.

Mitchell-Bateman was nominated as a "Local Legend" by Representative Shelley Moore Capito in 2005. The "Local Legends" project is a companion to the National Library of Medicine exhibition "Changing the Face of Medicine: Celebrating America's Women Physicians." Mitchell-Bateman also received awards from the National Medical Association Section on Psychiatry and Neurology (1974), the E. Y. Williams Distinguished Clinical Scholar's Award (1995), and the Wyeth-Ayerst Physician Award for community work (1996). She was the recipient of a Lifetime Achievement Award from the American Psychiatric Association (2000) and the Governor's Award for Civil Rights Contributions from West Virginia's Governor Joe Manchin III (2004). She received several honorary doctorate degrees from Johnson C. Smith University (1963), West Virginia State College (1969), Alderson-Broadus College (1970), Bethany College (1971), and West Virginia Wesleyan College (1972).

FURTHER READING

"Mildred Mitchell-Bateman," in *West Virginia Archives and History*. Available at www.wvculture.org/HiStory/bateman.html.

"Mildred Mitchell-Bateman, M.D.," in *Local Legends*,-Available at www.nlm.nih.gov/locallegends/Biographies/Mitchell_Bateman_Mildred.html.

Spurlock, Jeanne. *Black Psychiatrists and American Psychiatry* (1999).

WILNISE JASMIN

Mix, Sarah Ann Freeman (5 May 1832–14 Apr. 1884), first African American female faith healing evangelist, was born Sarah Ann Freeman, one of thirteen children, in Torrington, Connecticut, the daughter of Datus and Lois Freeman. Little is known about her parents except that Mix was "born of a consumptive family," and tuberculosis deeply affected her life, eventually taking both her father and mother's lives (Mix, 8). Both her parents were "professing Christians," and Mix attended Sabbath school, where she was taught to "fear evil and to choose the good" (Mix, 201). These teachings left a deep impression on Mix, and throughout her life she tried to be a Christian in spirit and action. How many years Mix attended day school is unknown. She experienced a stark realization when a younger brother, with whom she attended school, suddenly sickened and died the next day, apparently from poison. With his sudden death she realized the depth of human vulnerability, including her own. She wrote, "The thought came to me, 'what if it had been you' and again the same old convictions would come up in my mind, 'you are so wicked.'" Although "after a while these convictions wore away," all her life Mix had periods of deep concern about her sinfulness and weakness of faith (Mix, 202).

After her father died of tuberculosis the family moved to New Haven, Connecticut, where Mix was converted during a revival at Bethel African Methodist Episcopal (AME) Church. There she also came into contact with the growing Holiness movement, an evangelical faction within Methodist churches that taught that God could forgive sin and free or "sanctify" a person from sinning again in either thought, word, or deed. In the nineteenth century thousands of people, like Mix, stepped to altars, confessed their sins, and received God's forgiveness and sanctification in an intense, emotionally charged ceremony.

When her mother died from tuberculosis some three years later Mix moved to New York City and worked in service. She contracted tuberculosis and went to live with a sister in rural Goshen, Connecticut. Although she would have reoccurring bouts of tuberculosis and ill health throughout her life, living in the countryside improved her health. There she met and married Edward Mix on 9 March 1856. She wrote that they both "wandered from God," but eventually the couple became Seventh Day Adventists (Mix, 207). It was a time of both joy and sorrow for the Mixes. From 1856 through 1870 the Mixes had seven children, but all had died by August 1873. The children's deaths left Mix "alone and brokenhearted we have nothing left but tears … all died of lung disease" (Mix, 9). This great tragedy caused her to think that perhaps "God wanted me to do something more for him that I had ever done" (Mix, 207). But she continued to experience periods of what she calls "Doubting Castle," until one night, after praying for God's guidance, she experienced a vision, a revelation, and "I was so filled with the glory of God! I shouted and praised God until I awoke my husband…. The Lord opened the way and I obeyed, and He has blessed the labors" (Mix, 209). The way that opened for Mix was a faith healing ministry.

On 19 December 1877, when Mix was forty-five, she experienced healing of her physical afflictions through prayer and the laying on of hands, or faith healing. Ethan Otis Allen, a Methodist layman and one of the founders of the faith healing movement, healed Mix. The faith healing movement, or divine healing, grew out of the Holiness movement. Just as Holiness advocates believed in spiritual healing that would result in human perfection, the faith healing movement believed in both physical and spiritual healing through prayer, confession, and the laying on of hands. Allen and his followers quoted James 5: 14–16 and Mark 16:17–18 as the foundations of their belief. After her divine healing Mix and her husband became assistants to Allen and traveled throughout New England with him, healing the sick. Allen believed Mix had the "gift of healing" and encouraged her ministry. After two years assisting Allen, Mix, and Edward began their own faith healing ministry.

One of the first people to contact Sarah Mix directly and ask for healing was Carrie Judd (Montgomery). Judd describes suffering "with blood consumption" (quoted in Mix, 36). Having heard about "Mrs. Mix," she wrote to Mix asking for help. Mix's brief reply entreated Judd to "pray for yourself, and pray believing and than *act faith* [*sic*]" (quoted in Mix, 39). Simultaneous praying by Mix's prayer group in Connecticut and Judd's family in upstate New York apparently healed Judd, who later became one of the nation's leading white faith healers. Testimony of Mix's healings continued to appear in newspapers and spread by word-of-mouth. Reports of her ministry noted that she was a person of color, but her race did not prevent white people, such as Judd, from asking her to heal them. The Mixes published a monthly of testimonials entitled "Victory through Faith" and in 1882 gathered some sixty letters, written from 1879 to 1882, testifying of her healing powers into a book, *Faith, Cures, and Answers to Prayer*. The book also includes letters from several ministers of white established churches who witnessed Sarah Mix's faith healings.

Mix died seven years after beginning her faith healing ministry. "Symptoms of consumption" had reoccurred, and she died of tuberculosis at fifty-two years of age (*Victory through Faith* 2.5 [1884]: 39). An obituary in the *Torrington Register* attests to her national fame as a faith healer in stating that "probably no one person who has ever lived in Torrington, except John Brown was ever known over so large a territory as Mrs. Edward Mix."

FURTHER READING

The papers of Sarah Ann Freeman Mix and newspaper articles, including accounts of her ministry, the *Torrington Register* obituary, and a twenty-four-page autobiography, *The Life of Mrs. Edward Mix*, by Sarah Ann Freeman Mix are at the Torrington, Connecticut, Historical Society.

Mix, Sarah. *Faith Cures, and Answers to Prayers*, ed. and introduced by Rosemary D. Gooden (2002).

Skinner Keller, Rosemary, and Rosemary Radford Ruether, eds. *In Our Own Voices: Four Centuries of American Women's Religious Writing* (1995).

LINDA SPENCER

Mizell, Jason. *See* Jam Master Jay.

Mobley, Hank (7 July 1930–30 May 1986), jazz musician and composer, was born Henry Mobley in Eastman, Georgia; his parents (names unknown) moved to Elizabeth, New Jersey, in 1932. After his parents separated, Mobley's father moved to Philadelphia, Pennsylvania, and young Hank remained with his mother in New Jersey. An uncle, Danny Mobley, a pianist and bandleader, helped to inspire his musical endeavors and provided him with early instruction in jazz. Mobley learned to play alto saxophone on his own at age sixteen; he worked at a bowling alley to earn enough money to buy an instrument. According to the noted jazz critic and historian John Litweiler, it was a shop teacher who encouraged Mobley to abandon machinist training and devote himself to music.

The rhythm and blues bandleader Paul Gayten selected Mobley in 1949 for his orchestra. In addition to playing alto, tenor, and baritone saxophone, Mobley also wrote for the group. Around this time he also worked with the pianist Walter Davis Jr., playing tenor saxophone in a house band at a Newark club. Artists such as BILLIE HOLIDAY, BUD POWELL, MILES DAVIS, and MAX ROACH performed with the band during Mobley's stint in Newark. It was after Roach's 1951 performance that he hired Mobley as a sideman and brought him to New York, where Mobley achieved immediate success.

Mobley worked with Roach until 1953. During this period he came into contact with musicians such as CHARLIE PARKER, SONNY ROLLINS, JACKIE McLEAN, Kenny Dorham, and Gerry Mulligan, and his first song, "Mobleysation," was recorded by Roach. When Roach's group broke up in 1953, Mobley still had ample playing opportunities. In addition to freelance jobs, he worked with Gayten and, briefly, with DUKE ELLINGTON (substituting for Jimmy Hamilton). In the summer of 1953 Mobley worked alongside CLIFFORD BROWN in TAD DAMERON's band at the Club Harlem in Atlantic City. It was at this time that Mobley almost became a member of the renowned Brown-Roach Quintet, but Roach, who was in California, was unable to reach Mobley when the historic group was being organized. Later in 1953 Mobley joined DIZZY GILLESPIE's big band on the recording of two band dates and one sextet date. It was in Gillespie's band that he made the acquaintance of the pianist WYNTON KELLY and the trumpeter LEE MORGAN, future sidemen on Mobley's solo sessions for Blue Note.

Mobley began to emerge as one of several recognized successors to Charlie Parker (along with Sonny Rollins, SONNY STITT, JIMMY HEATH, and JOHN COLTRANE) in the hard-bop scene. Mobley considered Parker by far the most significant source of inspiration for his style; other musicians who influenced him included Bud Powell, LESTER YOUNG, DON BYAS, BEN WEBSTER, and DEXTER GORDON. A very consistent musician with a preference for the middle register, Mobley reached a maturity of style relatively early in his career. Aspects of his style—and traits that were very much in keeping with Parker's influence—included a remarkable mastery of formal structure, a subtle yet complex rhythmic juxtaposition, and a highly developed sense of organization within the framework of his solos. Mobley also had an uncanny knack for presenting original material at unexpected, yet highly effective, moments in his solos, an ability that altered the audience's sense of expectation. His overall musical expressivity was unparalleled.

Mobley joined the hard-bop pianist HORACE SILVER in late 1953, performing at Minton's Playhouse and recording with the Horace Silver Quintet, which included the drummer ART BLAKEY. Mobley remained with Silver for the next four years, recording several albums with him and forming a new group that included the trumpeter Kenny Dorham, Silver, Blakey, and the bassist Doug Watkins. Together they decided to establish a cooperative venture called the Jazz Messengers, in which any job that a member got was performed by all of the members of the group, with all proceeds to be divided equally. The first of its kind—later groups included the Modern Jazz Quartet, the Miles Davis Quintet, and the Brown-Roach Quintet—the Jazz Messengers established a structure for performing groups that soon became standard among jazz musicians. Mobley performed with the group until 1957; it was to be his crowning achievement in ensemble work.

During the period 1954–1956, Mobley also recorded a great deal of material for solo albums, much of which he composed. These albums are considered by many to contain the best playing of his career. The labels on which Mobley recorded these solo albums included Prestige, Savoy, and Blue Note, the last of which maintained a long-standing relationship with Mobley. From late 1956 to mid-1958 Mobley recorded ten solo albums and performed on twelve more. By this time, however, he was addicted to heroin, which significantly interfered with his playing; although he remained prolific, the quality of his playing generally was not as strong as it had been.

Mobley's career was interrupted in 1959 by a drug conviction and one-year prison term. Following his release in 1960, he returned to Art Blakey's Jazz Messengers, which at that time featured Lee Morgan. Later that year Mobley joined the Miles Davis Quintet, replacing Sonny Stitt. Present on such Davis sessions as *At Carnegie Hall*, *Someday My Prince Will Come*, and *In Person at the Blackhawk*, Mobley recorded with one of the legendary jazz rhythm sections (Wynton Kelly on piano, PAUL CHAMBERS on bass, and PHILLY JOE JONES, Jimmy Cobb, and Art Blakey on drums) as well as one of its greatest artists. Mobley also hired Miles Davis's rhythm section for a series of four solo albums—*Soul Station*, *Roll Call*, *Workout*, and *Another Workout*—also acknowledged to be some of Mobley's best work.

Mobley remained with Davis until 1961. Davis had almost finished his exploration of hard bop by the time Mobley joined the group, and it took little time for Davis to become bored with Mobley's playing. This, combined with the implicit comparisons that were constantly being made between Mobley and his tenor predecessors John Coltrane and Sonny Rollins, had a devastating effect on the sideman. Dejected and discouraged, Mobley returned to drugs and in 1964 was arrested and imprisoned a second time on narcotics charges. Once he was out of prison, Mobley formed another cooperative group with Lee Morgan. In addition, he worked with Kenny Dorham, wrote for Blakey, and freelanced. Mobley recorded eighteen dates for Blue Note from 1965 until 1968, when he was arrested a third time for drugs.

A tour of London in 1967, including a seven-week stay at Ronnie Scott's, was followed by a tour of Europe, which lasted until mid-1970. While in Europe, Mobley performed in Paris (where he wrote a score for a movie set during the French-Algerian War), Munich, and Rome, as well as throughout Poland, Hungary, and Yugoslavia. He led a sextet session (*The Flip*, 1969; Blue Note) and played sideman with ARCHIE SHEPP for a European label. Among the many musicians with whom Mobley performed are Ben Webster, KENNY CLARKE, ORNETTE COLEMAN, Johnny Griffin, Steve McCall, Don Byas, and Art Taylor.

Returning to the United States, where jazz was being overshadowed by rock and roll, depressed Mobley, who became addicted to alcohol. Nonetheless, by 1973 he had made twenty-three solo albums, participated as sideman on fifty-six others, and written eighty songs. A brief stay that year in Chicago led to dates with the pianist MUHAL RICHARD ABRAMS, the bassist Reggie Willis, the drummer Wilbur Campbell, and the late-bop trumpeter Frank Gordon. Mobley lived in Philadelphia for the remainder of his life but performed very little after 1975; he was hospitalized periodically in the mid-1970s with tuberculosis. He performed briefly in New York City in 1986 before dying later that year in Philadelphia after a bout with pneumonia.

FURTHER READING

Davis, Miles. *Miles: The Autobiography of Miles Davis, with Quincy Troupe* (1989).
Gelly, Dave. *Jazz Journal International* 39 (Sept. 1986): 23.
Litweiler, John. "Hank Mobley: The Integrity of the Artist—The Soul of the Man," *Down Beat* 40, no. 6 (1973): 14–15, 30.

This entry is taken from the *American National Biography* and is published here with the permission of the American Council of Learned Societies.

DAVID E. SPIES

Mobley, Mamie Till. *See* Till-Mobley, Mamie.

Mollison, Irvin C. (24 Dec. 1898–5 May 1962), civil rights attorney and federal judge, was born Irvin Charles Mollison in Vicksburg, Mississippi, the sixth of seven children born to WILLIS E. MOLLISON, an attorney and businessman, and Ida T. Welbourne, a teacher. Irvin's father had once served as school superintendent of Issaquena County and briefly as a state district attorney, but after the passage of a new Mississippi state constitution in 1890, he and other African Americans were effectively excluded from all state and local public offices. Willis Mollison's private legal practice and his involvement in several black-owned banks and businesses nonetheless ensured that his children were among the most economically fortunate African Americans in Mississippi. Both parents kept an extensive library and ensured that their four daughters and three sons were also among the best-read children in a state where educational and library resources were inadequate for whites and almost nonexistent for blacks. A biographical sketch of the Mollison family published in 1911 noted that at age twelve Irvin was "one of the best informed boys of his age in the State of Mississippi … an inveterate reader and an embryo walking encyclopedia of useful and valuable information" (Hamilton, 435). That same sketch noted that Irvin was "well on in the development of one of the brightest minds that will some future day grace the institutions of this country" (436).

Though those words proved to be prophetic, it became increasingly apparent to Irvin, and indeed to the entire Mollison family at this time, that such a bright future could not be secured in their native Mississippi. Between 1912 and 1915 Irvin attended Tougaloo College, a preparatory school established for blacks in 1869 by the American Missionary Association in Jackson, Mississippi. In 1916, however, Irvin transferred to Oberlin College, a liberal arts university in Ohio where his father had studied forty years earlier. After one year he transferred to the University of Chicago, entering as a sophomore. By that time his parents had also moved to Chicago so that his father could continue to practice law. The state of Mississippi had prohibited black lawyers from testifying in court in 1913.

Mollison graduated from Chicago with honors in 1920 and was also inducted into Phi Beta Kappa. Inspired by his father, who now had a flourishing law firm in the city, Mollison continued his studies at the University of Chicago Law School, receiving his J.D. from there in 1923. He was admitted to the Illinois bar that same year and began working in his father's law firm. A prominent figure in the NAACP and the Urban League, Mollison was elected secretary of the Cook County Bar Association for 1928 through 1930. A keen amateur historian, he paid tribute to his father and eleven other attorneys who practiced law in Mississippi in the nineteenth century in an article that appeared in the *Journal of Negro History* in 1930. That same year Mollison married Alice L. Rucker, the daughter of a wealthy Georgia businessman and Republican Party activist.

Mollison's legal career in Chicago coincided with the Great Migration, when hundreds of thousands of African Americans left the South in search of better job prospects and in the hope of securing the citizenship rights denied to them in their home states. In Chicago alone the black population increased from only forty-four thousand in 1910 to slightly less than a quarter of a million by 1930. The "Black Metropolis," as the sociologists St. Clair Drake and Horace Cayton nicknamed Chicago, certainly offered the new-migrants greater opportunities and rights than they had enjoyed in the Jim Crow South, but many also found that the city was not the promised land they had dreamed of.

Poverty drove many of the migrants into lives of petty and not so petty crime. While gangsters, both black and white, controlled Chicago's African American South Side, a predominantly white and often racist police force provided the migrants only limited protection. Increasingly, black Chicagoans turned to the city's growing cadre of black attorneys for assistance, most notably the law firm headed by Irvin C. Mollison, William L. Dawson, and Herman Moore. In addition to an extensive criminal caseload, Mollison, Dawson, and Moore worked on several civil rights cases. The most significant of these was *Hansberry et al. v. Lee* (1940), which Mollison argued before the U.S. Supreme Court. Mollison successfully persuaded the court to uphold the right of Carl Hansberry, a realtor (and father of the playwright Lorraine Hansberry), to purchase a property in the wealthy Hyde Park neighborhood in Chicago. A campaign of violence and intimidation and a racially restrictive housing covenant which stated that the property could not be sold to blacks had forced the Hansberrys

to vacate the house they had purchased in 1937. Mollison's victory in the case ensured that the Hansberrys could return to their home and opened up thirty blocks of South Side Chicago to black buyers. The case also helped lay the groundwork for the Supreme Court's ruling in *Shelley v. Kraemer* (1948), which declared all racially restrictive housing covenants unconstitutional and illegal.

Although he did not follow his partner Congressman William Dawson into active party politics, Mollison was active in Chicago civic affairs. In 1938 Mayor Edward Kelly appointed him to a seat on the board of directors of the Chicago Public Library, and that same year he was elected president of the Illinois Conference of the NAACP. In 1942 he was appointed secretary of the Provident Hospital Board, an institution that his wife served for many years in a volunteer capacity. From January 1944 to October 1945 Mollison served on the City of Chicago's board of education; he was as that time the only African American on that board.

In October 1945 President Harry Truman recognized Mollison's legal and civic work by nominating him as an associate justice on the U.S. Customs Court (later the U.S. Court of International Trade). The appointment made Mollison the first African American federal judge with lifetime tenure. In accepting, Mollison informed President Truman that he viewed the post as not just a personal honor but also a general recognition of the value and contributions of all black Americans. More specifically, Mollison's selection was the consequence of sustained lobbying efforts by William Dawson, his congressional colleague Adam Clayton Powell Jr., and others who urged Truman to make a high-profile appointment of an African American to a federal post and to take a more active stance in support of civil rights than his predecessor, Franklin D. Roosevelt, had done.

The Customs Court's presiding judge stated on the day of Mollison's swearing in that he had joined "the strangest court in the entire world" ("New Federal Judge Takes Office," *New York Times*, 4 Nov. 1945). Though that description was something of an exaggeration, it was certainly the case that Mollison had joined the least-known body of the federal judiciary. The judicial decisions that he wrote on matters of international and interstate trade rarely made national headlines, though they would have some effect on civil rights, including several that dealt with racially restrictive covenants. One of the few cases that made the national press involved a 1958 case in which Mollison found an attorney in contempt of court for refusing to submit a Treasury Department report of an investigation of foreign merchandise. Mollison's ruling was later reversed at the appellate level, which found that he had abused his discretion.

Although he devoted most of his time to his federal duties, Mollison remained active in civil rights affairs, though he was one of several prominent black Chicagoans publicly to resign as a director of the National Urban League to protest that organization's racial conservatism in 1954. Mollison received several national awards. In 1946 he was one of eighteen people, among them JACKIE ROBINSON, Frank Sinatra, ANNA HEDGEMAN, and HORACE MANN BOND, honored by the Schomburg Center for Research in Black Culture of the New York Public Library for strengthening race relations. In 1955 a Chicago public school was named in his honor. Although he moved his family home to New York City, where the Customs Court was located, Mollison continued to travel frequently to Chicago. While traveling by train to that city from New York on 5 May 1962, he suffered a massive heart attack and was found dead in his compartment upon arrival at Chicago's Grand Central Terminal.

Mollison's estate left several significant art pieces to the Schomburg Center in New York City and to the Clark Atlanta University Galleries, but his most enduring legacy remains his role in the campaign against racial discrimination in housing and his breakthrough appointment to the federal judiciary.

FURTHER READING

Grossman, James R. *Land of Hope: Chicago, Black Southerners, and the Great Migration* (1991).
Hamilton, Green P. *Beacon Lights of the Race* (1911).
Plotkin, Wendy. "Deeds of Mistrust: Race, Housing and Restrictive Covenants in Chicago, 1900–1953," Ph.D. diss., University of Illinois at Chicago (1999).
Obituary: *New York Times*, 6 May 1962.

STEVEN J. NIVEN

Mollison, Willis E. (15 Sept. 1859–June 1924), lawyer and fraternal leader, was born Willis Elbert Mollison to Robert Mollison and Martha Gibson, slaves, in Mayersville, the county seat of Issaquena County in the Mississippi Delta. According to the federal census taken when Mollison was in his first year, he was born in the second wealthiest county in the entire United States. Practically all of that wealth was divided among the county's 587 white citizens, whose total wealth averaged more than eighteen thousand dollars per white freeman. The primary source of their wealth was Issaquena County's 7,244 slaves, including young Willis, whom they owned and whom they had purchased primarily to pick cotton on what one contemporary observer called "the best land which our globe is able to produce." One estimate suggests that as much as 75 percent of the slave children born on Delta plantations at that time died before reaching infancy, in part because pregnant slave women continued to work right up to the time they gave birth. Cholera, typhoid, and other fevers common in the swampy lands of Issaquena accounted for the death of scores of slave children each year. Given the hand that fate had dealt him, Willis Mollison had beaten the odds simply by surviving the first three years of childhood.

Little is known about Mollison's childhood, other than that he began to learn to read at the age of four, around the time that he, like most slave children in Issaquena, began to labor in the cotton fields. Willis's precocious ability to read was unusual for a slave child in his community. Indeed, even after the end of slavery in 1865, when he was six, until 1870, when he was eleven, Willis Mollison was, according to one of his biographers, the only black child in Mayersville who could read and write. Encouraged by a northern white woman who took an interest in his education, he mastered Webster's blue-back spelling book and was often called upon by his neighbors to write letters for them and to give public readings from the Bible. Indeed, Mollison spent so much time reading and memorizing both testaments as a child that he quickly developed an aversion to the Bible, though he later recommitted to Christianity and became an active Episcopalian.

In 1876, at age seventeen, Mollison left Mayersville for Nashville, Tennessee, to further his education at Fisk University. He studied there for around ten months, eventually reaching the middle preparatory class, before traveling to Ohio, where he completed his formal education at Oberlin College, one of the few white colleges open to African Americans at that time. At Oberlin Mollison learned Greek, Latin, and German, but he ended his formal studies in 1879 to return home to Mayersville to assist his mother in running her farm. He later received a law degree from Campbell College in Jackson, Mississippi, in 1913. In October 1880, shortly after he returned to Mississippi, Mollison married Ida T. Welbourne, a teacher and Fisk graduate who was a native of Clinton, Mississippi, and the daughter of a former slave who had served in the Mississippi state legislature during Reconstruction. The couple had seven children.

In 1880, while still only twenty, Mollison ran his first political campaign, for the office of chancery clerk of Issaquena County. He lost, but he indicated his determination to continue in local politics by purchasing and editing a newspaper and by studying law with Judge Jeffords, a onetime Mississippi Supreme Court justice who ensured that Mollison received a rigorous training in Blackstone's *Commentaries* and other legal classics. Mollison was admitted to the Mississippi bar in 1881; he was only the second black Mississippi native to be admitted.

The politics of Issaquena County in the 1880s were in limbo. The more radical black Republicans had been driven from office in 1875 when white Democrats had launched a campaign of fraud, intimidation, and political violence to "redeem" their state from majority-black rule. Though Issaquena had voted Republican, the kidnapping and execution of NOAH B. PARKER, a former justice of the peace, and six other black men at Rolling Fork in December 1875 forced several black officeholders to resign and signaled the return of white supremacy in politics. Yet African Americans, who remained in the electoral as well as numerical majority in the county, continued to vote and to hold minor local offices, albeit that the holders of such positions depended upon the good graces of white sponsors. Ambitious but pragmatic, Mollison was willing to compromise with the Delta's fusion politics. He joined the Democratic Party and was appointed superintendent of the county's public schools in 1882. While continuing to hold that office, as well as publish his newspaper, he was elected clerk of Issaquena's chancery and circuit courts in 1883. Reelected to those offices in 1887, Mollison served until the end of his term in 1891.

In 1892 Mollison was appointed district attorney pro tempore in a case, *State v. John Brown*, when the county's regular district attorney was unavailable. Though his appointment was only temporary and lasted a year, Mollison was the first African American ever to hold such a post in Mississippi. He was also the last African American to hold such a post in the state until the 1970s. Following his stint as district attorney, Mollison dedicated himself full-time to his law practice, moving to Vicksburg, whence he built a large client base spread throughout nine Mississippi counties.

Nearly all of Mississippi's black lawyers at this time practiced in the Delta. Not surprisingly, given the importance of agriculture in the region and the fact that nearly all blacks were farm renters, sharecroppers, or owners, the preponderance of his cases involved matters of land law. He did, however, work in a number of criminal cases, usually in defense of black clients, though in the case of *State v. McGuire*, Mollison joined with a team of white lawyers in successfully defending a white client charged with murder. In another case, while he was defending a man accused of enticing black laborers away from a plantation—a crime rated almost as heinous as rape or murder by Delta planters—Mollison was amazed to hear the judge suddenly declare his client guilty and sentence him to thirty days in jail. The judge had acted quickly in order to prevent a white witness from striking Mollison with a club. Mollison was also successful in winning several cases on appeal in the Mississippi Supreme Court. In the most notable of these, *State v. Collins*, he reversed the conviction of one black man for killing another in a case where the district attorney had declared that the victim had been "a white man's nigger and these bad niggers like to kill that kind. The only way you can break up this pistol toting among niggers is to have a necktie party," that is, a lynching.

Mollison served as legal counsel for several black fraternal organizations of which he was an active member, including the Knights of Tabor and the Supreme Camp Colored Woodmen, and he represented several black-owned businesses, including some in which he controlled stock. Notable among these were the Delta Savings Bank, founded by WAYNE M. COX, and the Mound Bayou Oil Mill and Manufacturing Company, founded by Benjamin T. Green and ISAIAH T. MONTGOMERY, of which Mollison was also a director.

Mollison's specialty, though, was damage suits against the Illinois Central Railroad, whose branch line, the Yazoo and Mississippi Valley Railroad (Y&MV) ran through the Delta. At the turn of the twentieth century, small farmers and renters of both races, who were already suffering from a severe economic depression and a decline in cotton prices, resented the high tariffs that the railroad charged them for shipping cotton. Despite the lean economic times of the 1890s, the Y&MV continued to rack up massive profits. Any legal case involving the railroad thus offered juries, primarily composed of small farmers and renters—and by that time almost exclusively white—a rare opportunity to express their resentment at the large corporations that threatened their livelihoods. Thus on one occasion an all-white jury secured a judgment of five thousand dollars against the Y&MV on behalf of Mollison's black client, who had been struck on the head by a ticket-punching device wielded by a Y&MV employee.

The economic security that Mollison's legal work secured also provided him with relative political independence. Even though he had earlier secured election at the county level as a Democrat, in 1889 he ran, unsuccessfully, for the Republican nomination for secretary of state. Three years later, as committee secretary of the Mississippi Republican Party, Mollison attended the Republican National Convention and made a speech nominating James G. Blaine. In return for his services to the Republican Party, President William McKinley appointed Mollison as supervisor of the U.S. Census for Mississippi's Seventh District (covering mostly counties in the Delta) in 1900.

The MINNIE M. COX affair made clear three years later, however, that proximity to the national Republican Party was of little defense in the wake of the successful U.S. Senate campaign launched by the rabid segregationist James K. Vardaman. After Vardaman's election in 1904, it became increasingly difficult for black lawyers to practice in Mississippi's courts. The general respect that Mollison had enjoyed in his first days at the bar gave way to a situation in which an opposing lawyer personally excised all references in a stenographer's transcript to "Mister" Mollison. By 1913 most counties in Mississippi had prohibited the state's dwindling band of black lawyers from testifying in court. By that time the rapid decline in farm ownership among blacks had at any rate greatly reduced the potential number of clients for black lawyers. Any grievances held by sharecroppers were now to be decided by the powerful white men they rented from—or by the private justice of the lynch mob.

Around 1916 Mollison moved to Chicago and established a law practice that prospered as the result of the Great Migration north of thousands of black southerners, many of them from Mississippi, in the decade that followed. Significantly, Mollison was one of several Mississippi black businessmen who at the urging of white planters wrote newspaper articles dissuading his fellow blacks from migrating north. He was later joined in his legal practice in Chicago by his second-youngest child, IRVIN C. MOLLISON, and was elected president of the Cook County Black Bar Association in 1923. The civil rights work of the Mollisons achieved its greatest success fourteen years later in the victory against racially restrictive housing covenants in Chicago won by Carl A. Hansberry, father of the playwright LORRAINE HANSBERRY. The Hansberrys, like the Mollisons, had their roots in Issaquena County. Willis Mollison did not live to see that victory, however, having died at the age of sixty-five in Chicago in June 1924.

FURTHER READING
Cobb, James. *The Most Southern Place on Earth: The Mississippi Delta and the Roots of Southern Regional Identity* (1992).
Hamilton, Green P. *Beacon Lights of the Race* (1911).
Mollison, Irvin C. "The Black Lawyers of Mississippi," *Journal of Negro History* 15.1 (Jan. 1930).
Obituary: *Chicago Broad Ax*, 7–14 June 1924.

STEVEN J. NIVEN

Molyneaux, Tom (c. 1784–4 Aug. 1818), pugilist, first appeared on the London boxing scene in 1809. All that is known of his earlier life is that he was a freed slave, probably from Baltimore. He had come to Great Britain by way of working on the New York docks. No evidence supports the fanciful claims of the journalist Pierce Egan that he was descended from a warlike hero who had been the all-conquering pugilist of America.

Molyneaux appeared at BILL RICHMOND's Horse and Dolphin tavern in St. Martin's Lane. The tavern, next door to the Fives Court where sparring exhibitions took place, was a natural magnet for a big, tough, aspiring fighter. Richmond, himself an African American, was well established in the ring and had a high reputation among wealthy backers. He was so impressed by the newcomer that he set about promoting him with such success that after only two easily won fights—one a pickup match following a bullbait, and another against a hardy old London fighter, Tom Blake—Molyneaux was matched against Tom Cribb, the champion.

Richmond's training added some science to Molyneaux's original wild, rushing methods, while Cribb prepared little for the fight. When it took place, at Cropthorne, near East Grinstead in Sussex, on 18 December 1810, the champion was overweight and out of shape. The fight was the highlight of Molyneaux's career and was eventually to be the subject of some twentieth-century controversy over its fairness. The crowd, apart from Molyneaux's backers, were certainly on Cribb's side and showed it, but the contest's questionable events were not unusual by the undemanding standards of the day—the breaking of the ring by spectators when Molyneaux was gaining the upper hand and the delays by Cribb's seconds when their man needed a longer break to recover. In the end, Cribb did win, possibly after Molyneaux had fallen against one of the ring posts or had banged his head on the ground in a wrestling fall. The few eyewitness accounts vary, but none at the time alleged any unfairness. It was nearly twenty years later, when moral expectations about sport were beginning to be raised, that a reminiscing Pierce Egan, who almost certainly saw the fight, referred to a possible injustice toward Molyneaux. Molyneaux himself made no such accusations in his letter to Cribb (doubtless the literate Richmond's work) challenging him to a return match.

Cribb at once began preparing for this contest under the strict training regime of Captain Allardyce Barclay, who had just won national fame by covering one thousand miles in one thousand hours on foot. By contrast, Molyneaux went on a lucrative provincial tour with Richmond, intermittently exhibiting and sparring; took on a relatively meaningless fight with Rimmer, a rough and ready Lancastrian, in May 1811; and relished his fame and the chance to live the good life as he saw it. The outcome was defeat in the rematch, in September 1811, at Thistleton Gap, near Leicester, where Cribb was the fit man and Molyneaux the jaded fighter.

Molyneaux's career was now all anticlimax. An attempt by Richmond to rehabilitate his man in a match against Jack Carter ended with Carter's dubious surrender after he appeared to be winning throughout the fight. Carter and Molyneaux went on tour together, and Richmond broke with his now unmanageable countryman who was giving full rein to all his passions—for fine clothes, food, drink, and the indiscriminate company of women. There was one more fight in Scotland in 1813, against the young William Fuller who, by a fine irony, was in his turn to move to the United States and do much to promote the cause of boxing in North America. Molyneaux moved on to Ireland, where his damaging lifestyle took its final toll. He died in the arms of two other African Americans serving in the Seventy-seventh Regiment in the guardhouse of Galway Barracks, where he was taking refuge. It was a mere seven and a half years after his first famous battle with Tom Cribb.

The impact made by Molyneaux's achievements in his own country was minimal and scarcely noted in the press. However, his importance in the history of prizefighting was considerable. While he was by no means the first black fighter in the British ring, he made the path somewhat easier for the dozen or more black boxers who appeared during the next twenty years. His challenge, too, raised the issue of the nature of the "Championship," and the question, scarcely asked at the time, as to whether it was a solely British preserve. Finally, the sight of a white and a black fighter struggling against each other at the highest levels of sport had a significance that went beyond boxing and sport itself.

FURTHER READING

Anonymous. *Pancratia, or a History of Pugilism*, 2d ed. (1815).
Brailsford, Dennis. *Bareknuckles: A Social History of Prize-Fighting* (1988)
Egan, Pierce. *Boxiana* (5 vols., 1812–1829).
Gorn, Elliott J. *The Manly Art: Bare-Knuckle Prize Fighting in America* (1986).
This entry is taken from the *American National Biography* and is published here with the permission of the American Council of Learned Societies.

DENNIS BRAILSFORD

Mongoula, Nicolas (1720–2 May 1798), master mason, militia captain, and property owner in colonial Mobile, Alabama, was a prominent free black man whose last name meant "my friend" in Mobilian Jargon, a major Native American pidgin used throughout the region during his lifetime. His first name used the French spelling "Nicolas."

Born in roughly 1720 according to his burial record, the exact place and date of Mongoula's birth are unknown. Nor is much certain about his parentage. He was possibly one of two children named "Nicolas" born the same year to enslaved black mothers in Mobile, which is now a port city of Alabama but which in the colonial era changed hands among France, Great Britain, and Spain. Just as little is known of Nicolas Mongoula's early life; how he came to be identified—and to identify himself—with Mobilian Jargon remains unresolved.

This pidgin, also known as the Mobilian Trade Language, was used primarily by diverse Indian groups to communicate with one another, but Africans and Europeans also learned to use the language to communicate with the Native Americans in and around Mobile. In French Louisiana, Indian slavery and African slavery overlapped, especially in Mobile during the 1720s. Almost half of colonial Mobile's households owned slaves in this decade, and slave owners usually employed a combination of both Indian and African slaves. In daily contact, owing to shared labor and household arrangements,

Africans and Indians in Mobile formed sexual unions, intermarried, and often served as godparents for one another's children. Indian slavery was officially outlawed in the region following Mobile's incorporation into Spanish West Florida in 1780, but the social patterns formed during the early eighteenth century continued throughout the colonial period. Nicolas Mongoula's familiarity with Mobilian Jargon could be explained by his having spent his childhood or early adulthood in close proximity to enslaved Native Americans. We are left to speculate, however, as to how he received the name "my friend," and why he continued to use the name throughout his life.

As suggested by his roles as godfather, master mason, and militia captain, Mongoula attained a position of considerable responsibility among people of color in Spanish Mobile. Appearing at three Catholic baptisms in Mobile between 1764 and 1781, Mongoula served as godfather for an enslaved African man, and for two children born locally to enslaved black women. The women who appeared alongside Mongoula as godmothers were two enslaved black women, and one free *mulata*. One reason for Mongoula's popularity as a godfather was his social status as a free, black, property-owning artisan. Described in Spanish pay records as a "master mason," Mongoula may have built the house that he sold to a man named Hugh Krebs for thirty-six dollars in 1792. Located on Royal Street, the house appears eleven years later on an 1803 map of Mobile. A further indication of Mongoula's prominence, and his role as an authority figure, among people of color in Spanish Mobile was his status as captain of Mobile's *Pardo* militia. Like free black militia officers in Spanish cities all along the Gulf of Mexico, from Veracruz to Havana to New Orleans, Mongoula was commissioned by the Spanish government to lead a local militia composed of free people of color in the defense of Mobile, should the need arise.

Historical records uncovered thus far reveal few details concerning Mongoula's personal and family life. He married a free black woman named Francisco Mimi, a marriage fully recognized by Mobile's Catholic parish, though the actual date of the marriage is still unknown. The couple had two children, both described as "legitimate," named Santiago and Luisa. Employed as a carpenter in New Orleans in the 1790s, Santiago was also enrolled as a non-commissioned officer in New Orleans' free black militia. Little is known of Luisa except that she was unmarried and was still living in Mobile when her father was on his deathbed in 1798.

On 1 April 1798 Nicolas Mongoula dictated his last will and testament in Mobile. At seventy-eight years old, he had seen his city claimed by three different European empires, passing from French Louisiana, to British West Florida, to Spanish West Florida (Mobile would be claimed by the United States in 1813, only fifteen years after Mongoula's death). His wife, Francisca Mimy (as her name was variously spelled), was to assume control over all their possessions: a plot of land and a cabin in Mobile, ten or twelve head of cattle, and a concession of land by St. Stephens creek, where he and his family had grown rice, corn, and beans. Mongoula died one month later, receiving a Catholic burial with full rites in Mobile's parish church on 2 May 1798.

Known records mentioning Nicolas Mongoula offer no direct evidence that he interacted with Native Americans, but his name alone—"our friend"—remains an important clue. Furthermore, people described as "black" or "mulato" in colonial-era Spanish and French documents often had a Native American parent, or may have been familiar with indigenous practices in other ways. It remains a possibility that Mongoula might have had an Indian parent himself. Though we ultimately know little about his life, Mongoula nonetheless provides insight into relations between Africans, Indians, and people of color in the colonial Gulf South, particularly during the French period. His life also bears testimony that during the late eighteenth century, Mobile was much like other Spanish American societies, in which free men and women of African descent played significant and visible roles in their city's economy and defense.

FURTHER READING

Brown, Richmond F., ed. *Coastal Encounters: The Transformation of the Gulf South in the Eighteenth Century* (2007).

Drechsel, Emanuel J. *Mobilian Jargon: Linguistic and Sociohistorical Aspects of a Native American Pidgin* (1997).

Hanger, Kimberly S. *Bounded Lives, Bounded Places: Free Black Society in Colonial New Orleans, 1769–1803* (1997).

Landers, Jane. *Black Society in Spanish Florida* (1999).

Usner, Daniel H., Jr. *Indians, Settlers, & Slaves in a Frontier Exchange Economy: The Lower Mississippi Valley before 1783* (1992).

DAVID WHEAT

Monk, Thelonious (10 Oct. 1917–5 Feb. 1982), pianist, composer, and bandleader, was born Thelonious Sphere Monk (though his birth certificate reads

"Thelious Junior Monk") in Rocky Mount, North Carolina, the son of Thelonious Monk Sr., a laborer, and Barbara Batts, a maid. When Monk was three, the family moved to New York City, settling on the Upper West Side's San Juan Hill. He was surrounded by music as a youth. His father played music in the home, probably even the blues. Monk came to love the "Harlem stride" piano style, and it is likely, growing up in a West Indian neighborhood, that he heard Caribbean music and light opera. Scholars have heard echoes of all of these styles of music, especially blues and stride, in his playing. The Monk family did not initially provide for his musical education, though his sister, Marion, took piano lessons as part of the standard education of an upwardly mobile young woman. Her younger brother enjoyed watching these lessons and took in much of what she was taught. By the age of twelve, he had developed some piano technique, and Marion's teacher suggested that his talent should be cultivated.

Monk distinguished himself early on as a scholar as well, excelling particularly in mathematics and earning admission to the prestigious Stuyvesant High School. But because of an invisible race barrier at the school, he was not allowed to play in the band, and in his sophomore year he left school in order to play music full-time. Like many jazz

Thelonious Monk performs at Minton's Playhouse in New York City, c. September 1947. The pianist and composer had a formative effect on modern jazz. (© William P. Gottlieb; www.jazzphotos.com.)

musicians, Monk came of age musically in both the sacred and secular worlds of black vernacular music making. By his early teens he had played for "rent parties" and served as an organist at Union Baptist Church, but he became truly acquainted with the rigors of life as a professional musician working as an accompanist for a barnstorming evangelist from 1935 to 1937. There is no documentation of what Monk played for the preacher, but some things can be reasonably surmised. Playing for a preacher on a circuit of diverse African American audiences around the country would have required considerable flexibility in musical interaction and would certainly have been good training for the modern jazz performances Monk engaged in soon after. Upon returning to New York, Monk played sporadically in a number of clubs around the city, with his own quartet and as a sideman, until 1947, when he was hired for the house band at Minton's Playhouse. DIZZY GILLESPIE singled out Monk's role in the development of bebop's complex harmonic language in jam sessions at Minton's. Monk was already a prolific composer, and his songs "'Round Midnight," "Epistrophy," and "I Mean You" quickly became jazz standards. Monk's dramatic sense of style and self-presentation at the time may well also have had an impact on early boppers, who were becoming famous as much for their sartorial and linguistic style as for their music.

Monk's career appeared to be gaining steam, but it was surprisingly derailed in the mid-1940s, leaving him a marginal figure as other jazz modernists gained fame. Many explanations have been suggested, the most plausible being that although his musical ideas had contributed significantly to the bop style, he really did not play bebop himself. The few recordings made in situ at Minton's in the mid-1940s give the impression that Monk's playing at the time owed a great deal to pianists from an earlier generation and that while he was a very capable accompanist, he was not a virtuoso soloist, as were his contemporaries Gillespie, CHARLIE PARKER, and BUD POWELL.

In 1947 Monk married Nellie Smith. She was important to Monk in numerous ways, often earning the family living when Monk was unable to, but perhaps most significantly supporting him emotionally and physically during periods when he was under psychological strain. The home life that Thelonious and Nellie nurtured was remarkable in that it contradicts cherished stereotypes about jazz musicians. The two were devoted to each other and their two children, Thelonious Sphere III and

Barbara. Both Thelonious and Nellie were essentially homebodies, more interested in cultivating family life than being "on the scene." Leaving aside the irregularities of a musician's life and Monk's nonconformist style, their lives looked little like anything out of bohemian idylls of the jazz life.

Monk made his first recordings as a leader for the Blue Note label in 1947. These remain striking for the extent to which they present his musical conception in all its stark and complex beauty. They are remarkable especially for their distance from other jazz recordings from the time, for their sparse textures, for an idiosyncratic use of dissonance, and for the freshness of the musical signatures that would later become familiar. In 1951 Monk had a substantial setback both personally and professionally when he was convicted of possession of narcotics. Worse than his imprisonment was the loss of his cabaret card, a license to perform in New York City taverns and nightclubs. Whether Monk was framed on the narcotics charges, as has been suggested, the punitive withdrawal of his livelihood was clearly unjust—a glaring example of the ways in which New York police used the card system to punish arbitrarily.

Even though he could not appear live in New York's high-profile jazz venues, the period from 1952 began a slow process of Monk's emergence as a major public figure. In 1952 Monk signed with Prestige records, where he was unhappy despite the opportunity to record with such jazz greats as MILES DAVIS and SONNY ROLLINS. Three years later Monk's contract with Prestige was bought out by the new label Riverside Records, leading to what was perhaps the most fruitful recording period in his life. Monk's recordings with Riverside are unsurpassed, whether solo, with a trio, in quartet settings with leading tenor players of the day, including JOHN COLTRANE, Johnny Griffin, and CHARLIE ROUSE, or with larger ensembles.

With the help of his friend and sometime benefactor the Baroness Pannonica de Koenigswarter, Monk secured the return of his cabaret card in 1957. There followed a period of intense activity, including two extended engagements at the Five Spot, a Greenwich Village tavern that soon became a central spot in "hipster" culture. In 1962 he signed with Columbia Records, a major label with the ability to promote him quite broadly. Throughout the 1960s Monk appeared regularly in the United States and abroad, at nightclubs, concert halls, and jazz festivals with a fairly stable quartet, and in 1964 he became only the third jazz musician to have his portrait on the cover of *Time* magazine.

The 1960s were, nevertheless, a period of mixed fortunes for Monk. Even as audiences appeared to have caught up to his music at last, and as bookings became more regular and fees more lucrative, Monk went into a decline. The playing on his recordings for Columbia, though marked by occasional brilliance, became routine, often lacking the quality of discovery that had made his earlier work so compelling. More alarming was the deterioration in his mental health. Periods of dissociation were exacerbated by inept psychiatric care.

Monk's contract with Columbia ended in 1968, although he continued to perform regularly, albeit sporadically, until 1974 and recorded some of his finest trio and solo performances for the Black Lion label in 1971. By the end of 1972, however, he began to withdraw. He and his wife moved to the Baroness de Koenigswarter's residence in Weehawken, New Jersey, and by 1975 Monk had become almost totally reclusive. He described himself as simply being tired, and his illness was never satisfactorily diagnosed or treated.

Monk died from an aneurysm in Weehawken just as the jazz world was beginning to rediscover his music. While he had perhaps been something of a fad in the 1960s—lauded, but not quite understood—and had quickly fallen out of favor by the early 1970s, in the 1980s Monk's lasting place in the jazz canon was cemented. Starting in 1982 musicians began exploring his music in a series of tribute albums and concerts that has not abated to the present day. Along with DUKE ELLINGTON and a few others, Monk has become one of those overarching figures that jazz musicians from literally every style draw upon and learn from.

FURTHER READING
Fitterling, Thomas. *Thelonious Monk: His Life and Music* (1997).
Gourse, Leslie. *Straight, No Chaser: The Life and Genius of Thelonious Monk* (1997).
Kelley, Robin D. G. *Thelonious Monk: The Life and Times of an American Original* (2009).
Obituary: *New York Times*, 18 Feb. 1982.

DISCOGRAPHY
Sheridan, Chris. *Brilliant Corners: A Bio-discography of Thelonious Monk* (2001).

GABRIEL SOLIS

Monroe, Vernon Earl "The Pearl" (21 Nov. 1944–), professional basketball player, sports commentator, and businessman, was born in Philadelphia, Pennsylvania. Growing up in a tough neighborhood in South Philadelphia, Monroe loved to play soccer and baseball; but by the age of fourteen, he had reached six feet three inches and began drawing the attention of high school basketball coaches. He struggled at first, especially with his coordination and timing, but soon adjusted to the center position. Playing long hours on outdoor asphalt playgrounds, he developed what were known as "shake and bake" moves, which involved using small hesitation movements followed by launching in the air to avoid being blocked by defenders. This earned Monroe the street nickname of "Thomas Edison" as he continued to build a repertoire of "flukey-duke" shots, fakes, and spins to keep opposing players off balance in the rough world of street ball. "All my style came from the Philadelphia school yards," he said when asked about his mentors.

Monroe attended Philadelphia's John Bartram High School, playing basketball at the center position and averaging 21.7 points a game in his senior year. After graduating in 1963, he worked for a year in a factory and briefly attended Temple Prep School in Philadelphia. He then accepted a basketball scholarship to Winston-Salem State College in North Carolina, where he played under the leadership of Basketball Hall-of-Fame coach CLARENCE "BIG HOUSE" GAINES. At the all-black college, Gaines became a mentor to Monroe and reminded him about the difficulties posed by

Earl Monroe, of the Baltimore Bullets (left), relaxing with teammate Jack Martin in the dressing room at Madison Square Garden in New York City, 19 April 1971. (AP Images.)

white-dominated professional sports and the struggles with racism black professional athletes such as Cleo Hill had faced. At Winston-Salem, Monroe switched to guard and his game flourished, peaking with an average of 41.5 points per game in his senior year. He also broke the National Collegiate Athletic Association (NCAA) Division II record for the most points in a season (1,329) and played a leading role as the team won the NCAA Division II Championship in 1967.

After completing college in 1967, the Baltimore Bullets (later the Washington Wizards) selected him in the first round of the National Basketball Association (NBA) draft (he was the second overall pick that year). In his rookie year, Monroe established himself as a formidable player, running a high tempo fast break with star center WES UNSELD. When asked about his wild scoring maneuvers, he said, "The thing is, I don't know what I'm going to do with the ball, and if I don't know, I'm quite sure the guy guarding me doesn't know either." In 1967 Monroe was voted the NBA Rookie of the Year on the strength of his 25.8 points per game average. In 1971 the Bullets traded Monroe to the New York Knicks, where he joined forces with the flamboyant guard WALT FRAZIER, who had previously been an archrival of Monroe's. With a skilled backcourt, the Knicks became a dominating team, winning the NBA Championship title in 1973. Monroe's play was defined by a quick and stylish jump shot and the use of numerous agile head and body fakes. Often these skilled moves would leave opponents far enough behind him to allow for a simple lay-up to the hoop. Longtime Knicks star Bill Bradley once called Monroe the "ultimate playground player" in the *New York Post*. Sports critics weren't as receptive to this approach and criticized Monroe as lacking discipline and rudimentary skills, even calling him a show-off. Physical wear began to take its toll on Monroe when he was with the Knicks. Both knees were battered, and he experienced a chronic ankle problem. His play also changed over time, as he was often given the toughest one-on-one defensive assignment, freeing up Frazier to patrol the lanes and seek loose balls. Although his moves dazzled players and fans alike, Monroe played unselfishly, often making quick, last-minute assists to allow others to score. He was an NBA All-Star four times, played a career 926 games, scored 17,454 points (18.8 per game), and dished out 3,594 assists. He retired in 1980, and six years later the team retired his number fifteen jersey.

Following his retirement from basketball, Monroe tested his skills in the entertainment industry. He managed a few singing groups, launched Pretty Pearl Records, had a restaurant named after him, and worked as a television commentator. However, he always stayed close to the sport he loved; and in 1985 Monroe was chosen to be commissioner of the U.S. Basketball League. In 1990 he was enshrined in the Naismith Memorial Basketball Hall of Fame. Monroe stayed active in the New York and New Jersey area, serving as a commissioner of the New Jersey Urban Development Corporation. He also served on the President's Council on Physical Fitness and Health and as spokesperson for the American Heart Association. His awards include a Harlem Professionals Inspiration Award, YMCA Citizenship Award, and the Big Apple Sportsman of the Year Award.

FURTHER READING

Berkow, Ira. "Pearl Still Glitters," *New York Times*, 23 Apr. 1983.

Goldaper, Sam. "Monroe, Last of '73 Knicks Title Knicks to Be Elected to Hall of Fame," *New York Times*, 9 Feb. 1990.

Jackson, Robert Blake. *Earl the Pearl: The Story of Baltimore's Earl Monroe*. (1974).

Nelson, George. *Elevating the Game: Black Men and Basketball*. (1992).

"The Knicks Shoot Ahead," *Sports Illustrated* (16 Apr. 1973).

JAMES FARGO BALLIETT

Montana, Allison Marcel "Tootie" (16 Dec. 1922–27 June 2005), folk artist, community activist, and Mardi Gras Indian leader, was born in New Orleans, Louisiana, the son of Alfred Montana, "Big Chief" of the Yellow Pocahontas, a leading Mardi Gras Indian organization, and Alice Herrere Montana, both natives of New Orleans. When he was young, one of his cousins nicknamed him Tootie, and the name stuck. Masking as Mardi Gras Indians ran deep in the Montana family. Tootie was a third-generation black Indian leader. His great-uncle Becate Batiste was the legendary founding Big Chief of the Creole Wild West, the city's first and oldest masking Indian society; his father Alfred Montana was a famous leader of the Yellow Pocahontas, which was an offshoot of the Creole Wild West; but Tootie eventually surpassed both by far in terms of craftsmanship, influence, and fame.

The Mardi Gras Indian culture developed as an expression of black resistance against a white supremacist environment in New Orleans. When Reconstruction failed in 1877, whites-only secret societies or "Krewes" became the city's dominant Carnival organizations, replacing older, informal, racially integrated, Roman Catholic street processions. The Krewe of "Rex" ranked most prominently among these clubs celebrating the pomp of imagined former European monarchs. The "king" of Rex, always a member of the white elite, was annually appointed to "rule" over the reveling city for the duration of Mardi Gras. Rex's shiny costume bore shocking resemblance to the hooded gowns of the Ku Klux Klan. To protest these Jim Crow developments, African Americans created their own Carnival traditions, the "Zulus" and the Mardi Gras Indians. King Zulu mocks King Rex. Dressed in "black-face" in minstrel show fashion, wrapped in grass skirts, and with nappy wigs covering their heads, the Zulus poke fun at white stereotypes. Nevertheless, they conform to the regulations of the city. They have official routes and pay for police protection and parade permits, just like their white counterparts. In stark contrast, the grassroots movement of the Mardi Gras Indians defy white bureaucracy altogether. Reminiscent of the Native American chieftains who roamed freely the prairies of North America and resisted the "white man," and honoring their partial Native American ancestry, the Mardi Gras Indians march unannounced, spontaneously, following their own inspiration. Masking in Africanized versions of Native garbs, they parade proudly through the most economically deprived black neighborhoods to cheer up their people with their amazing colorful outfits and mesmerizing, trance-like chants, drumming, and dances.

Every year, early in the morning on Mardi Gras, the Indian chiefs come out together with their entourage—their "tribe"—consisting of a Spy Boy, who walks a block ahead of the group to scout out the neighborhood for rivals and the police, a Queen, a Flag Boy, a Medicine Man or Wild Man who march closely to the chief, and a chorus of drummers, singers, and dancers that will accompany him all day long. Supported by their families, relatives, and friends, a chief and his associates would spent a whole year sewing their stunning Indian suits made of canvas, cardboard, feathers, sequins, beads, rhinestones, and shells. Shining in bright colors, the suits are a veritable feast for the eyes. According to local tradition, surprisingly, these marvelous artworks are made for only one season. An active chief has to produce an entirely new suit every year, which requires enormous sacrifices of both time and money.

During World War II, Tootie Montana served in the shipyards of Richmond, Virginia, and Oakland, California. Upon returning to New Orleans in 1947, he managed to create an amazing new suit annually for more than five decades, and emerged thus as the undisputed master of the craft. Because of his unique three-dimensional innovations and his elaborate beadwork he stood out among other Mardi Gras Indians. But Big Chief Tootie Montana was not only the "the prettiest" of all the Indians but he was also deeply troubled by the violence that surrounded him as many internal battles between rival Mardi Gras Indian groups turned deadly and decided to make it his life's mission to change the game from battling with knives and guns to competitions of skill and craftsmanship. Because of his tireless efforts for peace in the community and for the artistic development of the Mardi Gras Indian tradition, he became known as the peaceful warrior and was eventually crowned as the first and only "Chief of Chiefs." Montana's Indian suits were spectacular and much-coveted art works and have been purchased by museums around the world, including the Smithsonian Institution in Washington, D.C.

Chief Tootie grew up in the Faubourg Treme neighborhood, steeped in New Orleans old Creole culture. He spoke French fluently and was a lifelong devout Roman Catholic. He was an active member of St. Augustine Church, the oldest African American Catholic congregation in the United States. Tootie was the proud husband of Joyce Frances Montana, who was his most faithful supporter and stood always by his side, and the dedicated father of eight children. By profession, Montana was a widely respected iron worker and plasterer.

Tootie Montana was struck by a fatal heart attack while addressing the New Orleans City Council. After speaking about his fifty-two year involvement with the Indians, he expressed his outrage over the recently escalating police repression against their traditions. With all his Indian chiefs gathered around him, his last words were a call for the end of such repression. The city celebrated the life of the much revered "Chief of Chiefs" with a grand memorial service followed by a colorful traditional Jazz funeral procession. Thousands, black and white, attended, including hundreds of Mardi Gras Indians clad in full regalia.

FURTHER READING

"Allison 'Tootie' Montana—'Tootie' Montana, 82, Mardi Gras Indian icon" in New Orleans *Times-Picayune*, 29 Jun. 2005.

Diallo, Marcel. "Chief's Greatest Triumph Comes after His Death," in *Chicken Bones: A Journal for Literary & Artistic African-American Themes* (2005–2007).

Elie, Lolis Eric. "Big Chief Gets Spirited Sendoff," (New Orleans) *Times-Picayune*, 11 July 2005.

Elie, Lolis Eric. "Chief Died Fighting Cultural War," (New Orleans) *Times-Picayune*, 29 June 2005.

Fagaly, William A. "He's the Prettiest: A Tribute to Big Chief Allison 'Tootie' Montana's 50 Years of Mardi Gras Indian Suiting," in exhibit catalog by the New Orleans Museum of Art (1997).

"Hail to the Big Chief," (New Orleans) *Times-Picayune*, 10 July 2005.

LaFrance, Siona. "Tootie's new suit," in New Orleans *Times-Picayune*, 21 Feb. 2004.

Perlstein, Michael, "Chief of chiefs dies at meeting—He was trying to get Indians, cops together" New Orleans *Times-Picayune*, 28 Jun 2005.

Pope, John, "No defibrillator was near when 'chief of chiefs' fell" New Orleans *Times-Picayune*, 29 Jun. 2005.

Reich, Howard, "Struggle to Reclaim Threads of Past," (New Orleans) *Tribune*, 26 Dec. 2006.

Smith, Michael P. *Mardi Gras Indians* (1994).

Ya Salaam, Kalamu. "New Orleans Mardi Gras Indians and Tootie Montana," in exhibit catalog by the New Orleans Museum of Art (1997).

INA J. FANDRICH

Montgomery, Benjamin Thornton (1819–12 May 1877), businessman, was born a slave in Loudoun County, Virginia. As the boyhood companion of his owner's son, Benjamin completed in the afternoon the lessons the young white boy learned from his tutor in the morning. In this manner he gained a basic education. In 1836 he was sold to a trader who transported him to Natchez, Mississippi, where he was purchased by Joseph Davis, elder brother of future Confederate president Jefferson Davis, and settled on Davis Bend below Vicksburg. Davis had determined to apply the reform principles of Robert Owen, who sought order and efficiency in the management of industrial labor, to the management of his plantations. This required a rational relationship between owner and worker that, in Davis's application, meant a relationship between master and slave based on kindness, not cruelty, and on wholesome living conditions, not squalor. Davis sought and gained the confidence of Montgomery in his reform endeavor and gave the young slave access to his library. Montgomery learned to survey the land, construct levees, and design architectural plans for the construction of plantation buildings. He also gained the mechanical skills necessary to operate the plantation's steam-powered cotton gin. As a slave on Davis Bend, Montgomery enjoyed significant privileges and emerged as the leading figure of the slave community.

On Christmas Eve 1840, Montgomery formed a conjugal union with Mary Lewis, the daughter of Virginia slaves who had been among the earliest settlers on Davis Bend. Marriage among slaves had no legal standing, but Montgomery worked successfully to establish a nuclear family. From his earnings, Montgomery paid Davis the equivalent of his wife's earnings to ensure that she would live and labor only in the Montgomery household. Four of their children lived to become adults, but slavery severely limited Montgomery's ability to maintain an independent household. When Davis and his wife, Eliza, wanted to take the Montgomerys' youngest son, ISAIAH THORNTON MONTGOMERY, into their house as a servant, the child's parents could only express their anguish. Davis, in his role as an Owenite manager, attempted to console the Montgomerys by promising to oversee the boy's education.

With the initial assistance of Davis, Montgomery became a successful merchant, importing manufactured goods from New Orleans and selling them to the slaves on Davis Bend in exchange for chickens and vegetables they raised on their garden plots. Davis subsidized Montgomery's first consignment from New Orleans in 1842, but thereafter Montgomery maintained his own account with his New Orleans suppliers. Montgomery's store also provided the white planters and their families with a convenient means of purchasing goods from distant points of manufacture. The produce that Montgomery acquired in this trade supplied the Mississippi River steamboats with fresh food. Montgomery's combined store and home were located near the Davis Bend steamboat landing, where he became a key figure in Davis's efforts to achieve, within a slave labor system, aspects of the Owenite ideal of harmonizing the moral virtues of agrarian life with the material benefits of industry.

The Civil War and, specifically, General Ulysses S. Grant's campaign against Vicksburg thoroughly disrupted life and labor on Davis Bend. Joseph Davis sought refuge for himself and his family in the interior of the state, but most of his slaves,

Montgomery included, did not follow. Freed under the terms of the Emancipation Proclamation on 1 January 1863, Montgomery resettled his family in Cincinnati in June 1863. Both of his sons briefly served with Admiral David D. Porter's Mississippi Squadron before joining their father in Cincinnati. After Vicksburg fell on 4 July 1863, Union forces commanded by Admiral Porter took control of Davis Bend. Almost completely surrounded by the Mississippi River, the bend was easily defended by gunboats. With a detachment of black soldiers guarding the neck of the bend, Porter reported in the fall of 1863 that about six hundred freedmen had returned to the bend and were preparing enthusiastically for the 1864 agricultural season.

In March 1864 President Abraham Lincoln placed freedmen affairs in the Mississippi Valley under the control of the army, whose Bureau of Negro Affairs appointed Colonel Samuel Thomas as superintendent for the bend. Federal authorities confiscated the Davis plantations as "abandoned lands," and Treasury Department agents leased much of the Davis plantation to white speculators. Nevertheless, under Thomas's direction 180 black lessees farmed an average of 30 acres each on the bend during the 1864 season and raised 130 bales of cotton despite an army worm infestation. When leases expired in November 1864, Thomas excluded white planters from the bend, declaring that the land was reserved for "military purposes" and that it would be devoted to the "colonization, residence and support of the Freedmen." In March 1865 Congress created the Freedmen's Bureau (officially the Bureau of Refugees, Freedmen, and Abandoned Lands), and Thomas became bureau commissioner for Mississippi. In the spring of 1865 the Montgomery family returned to Davis Bend. Montgomery became a central figure in a dispute between Thomas and Davis as Davis led his family's efforts to regain control of their antebellum plantations.

Early in October 1865 Davis, now eighty years old, moved to Vicksburg. Since his only remaining assets, the Davis Bend plantations, were a prime target for federal confiscation, Davis eagerly sought a business partnership with Montgomery. On 21 October Davis leased the Davis Bend land to Montgomery for the 1866 agricultural year. Thomas fought this effort to wrest the Davis plantations from bureau control and described Montgomery as a "shrewd and intelligent" agent serving the interests of his former master. In April 1866 President Andrew Johnson replaced Thomas as bureau commissioner.

In September the president pardoned Davis, and the Freedmen's Bureau settled its dispute with the Davis family by agreeing to pay Davis the income from the Montgomery lease while maintaining management of the estates until January 1867. Rather than resume direct control of the Davis Bend estates, Davis agreed to sell the land to "Montgomery & Sons" for three hundred thousand dollars over a period of ten years. With the approbation of the *New York Times* and the suspicion of whites in Vicksburg, the Davis Bend estates began production in 1867 entirely under black direction and control.

In partnership with Davis, Montgomery flourished as a merchant on the bend. Montgomery & Sons extended credit to 80 percent of the freedmen on the bend, accepting cotton in exchange for merchandise. Montgomery had become a prominent figure in Reconstruction-era Mississippi. In 1867 he became Mississippi's first black justice of the peace, and by 1872, despite serious financial difficulties, the Montgomerys were reportedly the wealthiest black family in the South.

Unfortunately for Montgomery & Sons, the spring of 1867 brought devastating floods that cut a channel across the narrow western neck of the peninsula, turning Davis Bend into the more isolated Davis Island. The 1867 and 1868 seasons put Montgomery & Sons—plantations and store—in debt, and although their fortunes improved somewhat over the next several years, the Montgomerys were never able to pay any of the principal of the debt they owed Davis.

Late in December 1874, while Montgomery was working with a crew to raze an old building, a wall collapsed. Montgomery sustained severe injuries from which he never fully recovered. His death, combined with repeated floods, poor crops, and declining cotton prices, made the economic status of the Montgomery firm increasingly unstable. In 1878 the Mississippi State Supreme Court awarded one of Joseph Davis's plantations to Jefferson Davis. In 1881 foreclosure proceedings forced the Montgomery family to sell all their mortgaged lands to Jefferson Davis and the heirs of Joseph Davis. In 1887 Isaiah Montgomery, already a prominent spokesman for black accommodation to segregation, relocated his family to seven hundred purchased acres in northern Mississippi, where he founded the new black town of Mound Bayou.

FURTHER READING

Approximately two hundred letters from Montgomery and his sons are in the Joseph E. Davis Family

Papers in the Mississippi Department of Archives and History, Jackson.
Foner, Eric. *Reconstruction: America's Unfinished Revolution, 1863–1877* (1988).
Hermann, Janet Sharp. *The Pursuit of a Dream* (1981).
Schweninger, Loren. *Black Property Owners in the South, 1790–1915* (1990).
Wharton, Vernon Lane. *The Negro in Mississippi, 1865–1890* (1947).
This entry is taken from the *American National Biography* and is published here with the permission of the American Council of Learned Societies.

LOUIS S. GERTEIS

Montgomery, Isaiah Thornton (21 May 1847–6 Mar. 1924), planter and founder of Mound Bayou, Mississippi, was born on the "Hurricane" plantation of Joseph Davis at Davis Bend, Mississippi, the son of BENJAMIN MONTGOMERY, the plantation business manager and later a planter and owner of a mercantile store, and Mary Lewis. As a result of his father's prominent position among the slaves, Montgomery was chosen at the age of nine or ten to serve as Davis's personal secretary and office attendant. Davis, the older brother of Confederate president Jefferson Davis, granted Montgomery full access to all the books, newspapers, and periodicals within his home, enabling Montgomery to continue the education begun first by his father and later continued by another slave. Following the Civil War, in November 1866, Davis sold his two plantations to the Montgomery family. During the next fifteen years, the Montgomerys struggled and ultimately failed to make the plantations profitable, yet they still succeeded in garnering numerous prizes for the quality of their cotton and consistently high ratings from national credit firms. The Montgomery family lost both plantations in 1881. In 1871 Montgomery married Martha Robb; they had twelve children, only four of whom survived to adulthood.

In 1877 Montgomery embarked on his most successful venture, the founding of the all-black town of Mound Bayou in the Yazoo-Mississippi Delta. The Louisville, New Orleans, and Texas Railroad, which actively sought farmers to settle the land alongside the newly laid tracks between New Orleans and Memphis, hired Montgomery as a land agent with the understanding that he would choose an area of land within the delta for exclusive purchase by blacks. Montgomery enlisted the support of family and friends, especially former residents of

Davis Bend, in purchasing the plots, and the group quickly cleared and settled the heavily overgrown land. During the early years, Montgomery and his cousin Benjamin Green, the town's generally acknowledged cofounder, established several joint ventures, including the town's first cotton gin, mercantile firm, and post office.

In 1890 Montgomery was the only African American delegate elected to the Mississippi constitutional convention. The convention delegates drafted a constitution that effectively disfranchised African American Mississippians. During the proceedings, Montgomery gave a speech supporting disfranchisement. He described his support as "a fearful sacrifice laid upon the burning altar of liberty." In an interview published in the *New York World* (3 Oct. 1890), he explained that the temporary disfranchisement of blacks would hopefully signal "the beginning of the end of the great race question," allowing political division along lines other than race. Montgomery mistakenly believed that as African Americans became better educated, white Mississippians would allow them to vote and integrated parties would be formed based on political beliefs, not race. Not surprisingly, most white leaders, including former president Grover Cleveland, applauded Montgomery's position, while most black leaders initially expressed surprise and then dismay. According to FREDERICK DOUGLASS: "We may denounce his policy, but must spare the man…. He has made peace with the lion by allowing himself to be swallowed." In many ways, Montgomery's stance foreshadowed BOOKER T. WASHINGTON's infamous Atlanta Compromise of 1895. Washington and Montgomery maintained a correspondence throughout their lives, and Washington often pointed to Mound Bayou as a model African American community. Later in his life, Montgomery privately lamented the impact of the disfranchisement proposals, expressing frustration with the racist application of the law. Publicly, he never rescinded his initial stance.

In 1898, following the incorporation of Mound Bayou, Montgomery was elected the town's first mayor. He held that office until 1902, when President Theodore Roosevelt, under guidance from Washington, appointed him as receiver of public monies in Jackson, Mississippi. The honor proved short-lived, however, as Montgomery was forced to resign in 1903 amid controversy over the alleged placement of five thousand dollars in government funds in his personal account. While he never held another elective or appointive office,

Montgomery maintained an active role in both Mississippi Republican Party and local politics throughout the remainder of his life.

Montgomery's political ambitions, however, remained secondary to his efforts on behalf of Mound Bayou. In a letter to the director of the U.S. Land Office in Mississippi upon acceptance of his position as receiver of public monies, Montgomery noted that in the previous fourteen years he had expended his "best energies" to ensure the "advancement materially, morally, and socially" of his community and thus he was "loath to turn aside for political preferment." During his lifetime, Montgomery had a hand in almost every project that concerned Mound Bayou. He played a key role in the founding and improvement of the town's educational institutions, joined with his son-in-law E. P. Booze to establish the Farmer's Cooperative Mercantile Company in 1909, and helped develop the Mound Bayou Oil Mill & Manufacturing Company between 1911 and 1913. Montgomery's importance to the town was suggested by CHARLES BANKS, a banker and community leader, who insisted in a letter to Washington's secretary that "no work or statement on Mound Bayou, however brief, should be without [Montgomery's] name." Montgomery died in Mound Bayou.

Montgomery's historical significance derives from his role as an African American accommodationist and entrepreneur. Through his 1890 address and his activities on behalf of Mound Bayou, he displayed a consistent belief that educational and economic advancement, not political activity, offered the best means for African Americans to improve their plight. He closely monitored his own actions and those of his fellow Mound Bayou citizens to ensure the continual support of the white community. As a result, he earned nearly universal acclaim from white Mississippians, and upon his death, local whites purchased a lavish headstone. In contrast, the reaction among the African American community was decidedly mixed and increasingly hostile after his death. The African American Mississippi politician SIDNEY REDMOND declared fifty years after Montgomery's speech that Montgomery would always be remembered as "the Judas of his people." Montgomery's actions, however, highlight the horrific conditions for African Americans in Mississippi at the turn of the century and demonstrate the pragmatic philosophy that was necessary for survival and limited success.

FURTHER READING

Montgomery's papers are scattered throughout several collections, including the Benjamin Montgomery Family Papers and the Booker T. Washington Papers at the Library of Congress. The Mississippi Department of Archives and History in Jackson contains a substantial collection of material on Mound Bayou.

Hamilton, Kenneth Marvin. *Black Towns and Profit: Promotion and Development in the Trans-Appalachian West, 1877–1915* (1991).

Hermann, Janet Sharp. "Isaiah T. Montgomery's Balancing Act," in *Black Leaders of the Nineteenth Century*, ed. Leon Litwack and August Meier (1988).

Hermann, Janet Sharp. *The Pursuit of a Dream* (1981).

McMillen, Neil R. *Dark Journey: Black Mississippians in the Age of Jim Crow* (1989).

Obituary: *Vicksburg Evening Post*, 24 Mar. 1985.

This entry is taken from the *American National Biography* and is published here with the permission of the American Council of Learned Societies.

DAVID MARK SILVER

Montgomery, Little Brother (18 Apr. 1906–6 Sept. 1985), blues and jazz pianist, singer, and bandleader, was born Eurreal Wilford Montgomery in Kentwood, Louisiana, the son of Harper Montgomery and Dicy Burton. His father led mule and horse teams, set railroad ties, hauled wood, farmed cucumbers, and had a log pond in which Montgomery himself assisted, riding logs to help chain them for the trip to the mill. Most significantly for Montgomery, his father also ran a barrelhouse—a southern saloon that often had a piano and a dance floor, where alcohol was served from barrels. Montgomery claimed that his father served no hard liquor, just food and soft drinks, and that patrons brought their own alcohol. In any event, there he had an opportunity to listen to many accomplished pianists, including the great JELLY ROLL MORTON and numerous now-forgotten players whom Montgomery recalled fondly. His father played cornet, his mother, organ, and his father's uncle Gonzy Montgomery was a multi-instrumentalist and bandleader who worked with ARMAND JOHN PIRON in New Orleans.

At age five Montgomery began to teach himself to play piano. From age ten he regularly visited an aunt in New Orleans and was able to hear music there. He attended Tangipahoa Parish Training School but ran away before finishing the seventh grade. During the early 1920s he traveled throughout Louisiana and Mississippi, playing in juke joints and barrelhouses as a soloist and occasionally as a member of jazz bands, including an affiliation with the clarinetist GEORGE LEWIS around 1921.

While in Ferriday, Louisiana, he and other pianists worked out a tune that came to be known as the "44 Blues." By one account, one of these pianists, Delco Robert Johnson (not to be confused with blues guitarist and singer ROBERT JOHNSON), was known as "Big Brother," and Montgomery, owing to his height, thus became "Little Brother" when they played together. Others claim that he received the nickname in infancy, as the sixth of ten children.

Montgomery worked with the cornetist Buddy Petit around 1925, and he toured logging camps with the blues singer and guitarist BIG JOE WILLIAMS (c. 1926) and the guitarist Danny Barker (c. 1927). In 1928 he left the South to tour with the New Orleans bandleader Clarence Desdune's band, dropping out when they reached Omaha, Nebraska, later that year. By 1929 he was in Chicago, where he played house parties. The pianist Bob Alexander, from whom Montgomery took some lessons, and Alexander's wife, Aletha Dickerson, were talent scouts for Paramount Records. In 1930 they hired Montgomery to accompany singer Irene Scruggs. In addition, he made several solo titles, including "No Special Rider Blues" and his best-known recording, "Vicksburg Blues," an elaboration of "44 Blues" (which had already been recorded by the pianist ROOSEVELT SYKES). Montgomery then toured with Dickerson, accompanying her on the Theater Owners' Booking Association circuit as far as Atlanta.

After recording "Frisco Hi-ball Blues" at the beginning of 1931, Montgomery came to Jackson, Mississippi, to organize an eight- to fourteen-piece southern and midwestern touring band, the Southland Troubadours. As a soloist he recorded "Something Keeps Aworryin' Me," "Farish Street Jive," "Crescent City Blues," and "Shreveport Blues" in New Orleans in 1936. He continued to lead the Southland Troubadours until the late 1930s. He then turned the group over to his sideman Doc Parmley and resumed working in Mississippi and Texas as soloist or in a duo with a drummer.

Montgomery settled in Chicago in 1942. He worked in a defense plant and resumed playing at house parties. In 1947 he recorded "*El Ritmo*" and "Long Time Ago," and the following year he toured briefly in the trombonist KID ORY's band and continued to work for various "race" labels. Over the next three decades Montgomery worked extensively in Chicago clubs as a bandleader and as a member of the reed player Franz Jackson's Original Jass All-Stars. He toured England in 1960, and, after recording the singer VICTORIA SPIVEY's album *The Queen and Her Knights* in 1965, he went to Europe in 1966 with the touring American Folk Blues Festival.

In 1967 Montgomery suffered a stroke that affected his left hand, but he kept playing and continued to appear at folk and blues festivals as a singer and pianist. He also led his own jazz band in Chicago clubs. Montgomery was married to Gladys Hawthorne (date unknown) and Janet A. Floberg (1967), and he had a son from one of the marriages; details of his marriages are unknown. Montgomery and his second wife, who often recorded as a duo, formed a record label, FM, in 1969, while continuing to record for many other labels as well. He toured Europe again in 1972 and recorded the unaccompanied album *Deep South Piano* in Copenhagen. He performed at the Berliner Jazztage in 1974 and at the New Orleans Jazz and Heritage Festival in 1976. Another fine solo album, *Tishomingo Blues*, dates from his last visit to England in 1980. He died in Chicago.

Montgomery was equally comfortable with earthy and heady material. Indeed, though he was much in demand as a blues soloist, he preferred to be associated with jazz bands, where the level of technical instrumental playing tended to be higher. "He is quick to tell you that most all the blues players break time, and that most of them couldn't tell one note from another any more than a pig knows when it's Sunday." Nonetheless, it was in this domain, the blues, that Montgomery left his most memorable recordings.

FURTHER READING

Taped interviews of Montgomery are held at the University of Chicago and Tulane University, the latter material dating from May 1958 and August 1960.

Heide, Karl Gert zur. *Deep South Piano: The Story of Little Brother Montgomery* (1970).

Hodes, Art, and Chadwick Hansen, eds. *Selections from the Gutter: Jazz Portraits from "The Jazz Record"* (1977).

Standish, Tony. "'Billed out and Bound to Go': The Story of Little Brother Montgomery," *Eureka* 1 (Sept.–Oct. 1960): 18–20.

Obituaries: *Chicago Tribune*, 9 Sept. 1985; *Footnote* 17 (Dec. 1985–Jan. 1986): 23–25.

DISCOGRAPHY

Staden, Dietrich von. "A Little Brother Montgomery Discography," *Storyville* 111 (Feb.–Mar. 1984): 94–99; 112 (Apr.–May 1984): 147–150; 113 (June–July 1984): 169–171; and 114 (Aug.–Sept. 1984): 206–211.

This entry is taken from the *American National Biography* and is published here with the permission of the American Council of Learned Societies.

BARRY KERNFELD

Montgomery, Ralph (1795?–July 1870), slave and civil rights litigant, was born Rafe Nelson in Virginia and renamed after his master in infancy; nothing is known about his parents. In 1834 Montgomery, then a slave in Marion County, Missouri, heard stories of fortunes to be made in the lead mines of Dubuque, a rough frontier village of about two thousand people located on the upper Mississippi River in the Iowa Territory. Montgomery's sister Tilda was already living in Dubuque, where she was one of seventy-two other African Americans and sixteen slaves recorded in the county in the 1840 census, although slavery was illegal in Iowa. Ralph and his master Jordan Montgomery drew up an agreement allowing him to work in the mines for five years, after which he would pay $550 for his freedom; he may have hoped to purchase his sister's freedom as well.

When the five-year period ended, Montgomery had barely earned enough money to buy his own food and clothes, and his master hired two agents to bring him back to Missouri so that he could be sold at market. With the help of a sheriff who had been told that he was a fugitive slave, Montgomery was seized at his lead mine and brought to the docks for transport downriver. Alexander Butterworth, a local farmer, city councilman, and friend of Montgomery's, overheard the commotion, got a local judge to issue a writ of habeas corpus preventing his removal, and then chased down the slave catchers just as they were about to board their boat. All the parties involved agreed to let the controversy be settled by the Iowa Supreme Court in what would be only the second case ever heard in its chambers.

In the 1839 case of *In re Ralph*, Montgomery was represented without charge by David Rorer, a native Virginian who had freed his own slaves years before and was responsible for giving Iowa its "Hawkeye" nickname. Rorer reminded the court that slavery was illegal in Iowa under the 1820 Missouri Compromise. Although other laws did require that fugitive slaves be returned to their master, he argued, Montgomery could not be considered a fugitive since he had left Missouri with the consent of his master, who had thus accidentally freed him by allowing him to enter a free state. Montgomery was liable for the $550, he conceded, but he could not be enslaved for non-payment of this debt. The very fact that his master had contracted with him, Rorer argued, indicated "a state of freedom on the part of the slave." If his master had not wanted Montgomery to become free, Rorer was in effect saying, he should not have treated Montgomery like a free man. Montgomery's master's lawyer countered that Montgomery's failure to pay his debt did in fact make him a fugitive slave and that the Missouri Compromise required his removal from Iowa in order for his master to maintain ownership.

Charles Mason, chief justice of the Iowa Supreme Court, was a staunch conservative and racist who would one day write that racial equality was no different than "social equality and fraternity with the chimpanzee, the gorilla and the whole monkey tribe" ("Negro Equality and Its Consequences," 1866). Nevertheless, on Independence Day 1839, Mason authored the unanimous opinion in Montgomery's favor, accepting every aspect of Rorer's argument. Any master who permitted his (or her) slaves to live in Iowa, Mason held, "cannot, afterwards, exercise any acts of ownership over him within this Territory.... The law does not take away his property in express terms, but declares it no longer to be property at all." The law extended "equal protection to men of all colors and conditions," he concluded, and Ralph Montgomery was a free man. The following year the former slave repaid Mason in his own way, showing up in the judge's garden one morning and explaining, "I want to work for you one day every spring to show that I never forget you" (Acton, 48).

Montgomery's master returned home empty-handed and never recovered financially. Montgomery, however, was even less successful. He struck a rich lode after returning to the lead mines but then lost all of his money either by gambling or by being swindled out of it, according to varying stories. In 1845 he was forced to take work as a gardener in order to pay his debts, while his spouse (remembered only as "Black Rafe's wife" in a white miner's diary) worked as a domestic. He eventually moved farther downriver to Muscatine, Iowa, spent his last years in a poorhouse, and in 1870 contracted a fatal case of smallpox while nursing a sick neighbor.

The case that won Ralph Montgomery his freedom took place fourteen years before the U.S. Supreme Court made a nearly opposite ruling in the DRED SCOTT decision. It was not indicative, however, of a general feeling of racial liberalism in Iowa or the larger Midwest. Many in Dubuque and elsewhere may have opposed slavery, but they did not want their territories settled by free blacks. Montgomery found assistance from influential whites in part because as a slave he posed less of a threat to the racial status quo. All black Iowans lived under territorial laws that banned them from voting, holding office, attending public school, serving in the state militia, or even settling in Iowa at all unless they could post a bond of five hundred dollars as a guarantee of their good behavior. Only months after the *In re Ralph* decision a prosperous black landowner in Dubuque whose wife had helped build the town's first church was lynched under the pretense of having stolen clothes from a white man. And yet Ralph Montgomery's actions are indicative of the agency shown by antebellum blacks who actively fought for their freedom and for their rights, especially those like ELIZABETH FREEMAN, HOMER PLESSY, FANNY LEIPER, ELIZABETH BUTCHER, and JAMES SOMMERSETT, who sought justice in the courts.

FURTHER READING
Acton, Richard, and Patricia Nassif Acton. *To Go Free: A Treasury of Iowa's Legal Heritage* (1995).

Dykstra, Robert R. *Bright Radical Star: Black Freedom and White Supremacy on the Hawkeye Frontier* (1993).

Stiles, Edward H. *Recollections and Sketches of Notable Lawyers and Public Men of Early Iowa* (1916).

Swisher, Jacob A. "The Case of Ralph," *Palimpsest 7* (1926).

DAVID BRODNAX SR.

Montgomery, Wes (6 Mar. 1923–15 June 1968), jazz and popular guitarist and bandleader, was born John Leslie Montgomery in Indianapolis, Indiana. After his parents (whose names are unknown) separated, the young Montgomery lived with his mother and stepfather, who both worked as laborers making sleeve fittings for pipes. He and his brothers then moved to Columbus, Ohio, to live with their father, a truck driver who delivered wholesale fruits and vegetables. Around 1935 Wes's older brother, the bassist Monk (William Howard) Montgomery, bought Wes a four-string tenor guitar.

Montgomery attended Champion High School. When he was seventeen the family moved back to Indianapolis, where he apprenticed as an arc welder.

After hearing a record featuring the electric guitarist CHARLIE CHRISTIAN, Montgomery bought a six-string electric guitar and began practicing incessantly. Self-taught, he never learned to read traditional music notation or even to read jazz chord symbols, and yet his ear, memory, and technique were so extraordinary that he was able to fit into any of the diverse musical situations that came his way. He had trouble playing with a guitar pick and thus inadvertently developed a beautifully rounded timbre by strumming the strings with the soft part of his right thumb. Somehow he managed to do this without restricting the speed and clarity of his playing.

In 1943 Montgomery married Serene (maiden name unknown), a dancer. They had seven children. Around this time he began working with some regularity as a musician, occasionally abandoning his various day jobs when an opportunity to tour arose. He was a laborer at Pope's Milk Company for several years until 15 May 1948, when the vibraphonist LIONEL HAMPTON heard him and immediately hired him for two years of touring. Montgomery recorded a few solos with Hampton, and he may be seen performing in the film short *Lionel Hampton and His Orchestra* (1949). But he grew tired of being apart from his family and returned home once again to take jobs outside of music.

In Indianapolis Montgomery worked in the pianist Eddie Higgins's quartet with the bassist Bob Cranshaw and the drummer Walter Perkins, and then in the trumpeter Roger Jones's quintet, which included the bassist Leroy Vinnegar. From 1955 to 1957 he was a member of the cooperative Montgomery-Johnson quintet, based at the Tropics Club; the quintet included Monk Montgomery and Monk and Wes's brother, the pianist and vibraphonist Charles F. "Buddy" Montgomery.

Wes Montgomery traveled to San Francisco to play briefly with Monk and Buddy's new group, the Mastersounds, at the Jazz Workshop, and he occasionally returned to the West to perform with his brothers. Their recordings include Wes's celebrated solo in "Falling in Love with Love" from the album *Montgomeryland* (1958–1959). During 1959, to support his family, Montgomery worked days as a welder while holding two nightclub jobs, activities that together allowed him perhaps an hour for sleep; his biographer Adrian Ingram speculates that this impossibly grueling schedule—to say nothing of Montgomery's chain smoking—may have contributed to his early heart disease.

In September 1959 the alto saxophonist CANNONBALL ADDERLEY heard Montgomery and was so impressed that he persuaded Orrin Keepnews of Riverside Records to offer Montgomery a contract. Keepnews brought Montgomery, the organist Melvin Rhyne, and the drummer Paul Parker to New York City for the guitarist's first album as a leader, *A Dynamic New Sound: The Wes Montgomery Trio* (1959). The trio then toured for four months.

In January 1960 Montgomery recorded perhaps his finest jazz album, *The Incredible Jazz Guitar of Wes Montgomery*. The Mastersounds split up, and a new Montgomery Brothers quintet formed that included Wes. He continued to make a number of jazz albums on his own, as well as with the tenor saxophonist Harold Land, with Adderley, with an all-star group headed by the vibraphonist MILT JACKSON, and with his brothers. Apart from Montgomery's own playing, these recordings are consistently pleasant but perhaps somewhat cautious and uninspired; this is particularly true of Montgomery's work with his brothers, who were greatly overmatched by Wes's talent, of which Montgomery himself seemed unaware. Ingram reports that in September 1961, while the tenor saxophonist JOHN COLTRANE was at San Francisco's Jazz Workshop and the Monterey Jazz Festival with the wind player ERIC DOLPHY, the pianist MCCOY TYNER, the bassist Reggie Workman, and the drummer ELVIN JONES, Coltrane asked Montgomery to play with the group. Coltrane was so impressed that he invited Montgomery to join permanently; however, Montgomery declined, feeling that he was not good enough, and instead resumed touring with his brothers.

The Montgomery Brothers split up in spring 1962 due to a lack of steady work, and Montgomery rejoined Rhyne's organ trio in Indianapolis. He left home for only a few days in June 1962 to visit Berkeley, California, where he performed and made the album *Full House* in the company of the tenor saxophonist Johnny Griffin and the rhythm section from the trumpeter MILES DAVIS's current band—the pianist WYNTON KELLY, the bassist PAUL CHAMBERS, and the drummer Jimmy Cobb. Late in 1963 the Rhyne trio split up.

In 1964 and 1965 Montgomery performed on a segment of the BBC television series *Jazz 625*. Late in 1964 he began recording for the Verve label. Under the guidance of the producer Creed Taylor, Montgomery turned from hard-bop groups to studio orchestras from 1965 onward, beginning with the album *Bumpin'* (May 1965). He continued to play hard bop in clubs, as documented on *Smokin' at the Half Note*, which was recorded live with Kelly,

Chambers, and Cobb between late spring and early autumn 1965. But *Goin' Out of My Head* (December 1965) won a Grammy Award for its title track, and from that point on Taylor's authorized mix of jazz standards and instrumental versions of pop hits moved increasingly toward the latter, as heard on *Tequila* (March 1966); *California Dreaming*, with its hit single "Bumpin' on Sunset" (September 1966); *A Day in the Life* (June 1967), which held the number one position on the *Billboard* magazine jazz charts for thirty-two weeks; and *Down Here on the Ground* (December 1967–January 1968). At the height of his commercial success Montgomery died of a heart attack in Indianapolis.

Translating into English an interview from the French magazine *Jazz Hot* (February 1979), Ingram quoted Griffin's description of Montgomery: "Wes was a marvellous person. He didn't drink, and was very difficult about what he ate.... He was the perfect father. He spoke slowly, ... never letting out a word he did not want, and all with great humour.... no drugs, no drink, only rarely jamming in the clubs, no women."

Given his gentle and responsible outlook, Montgomery in his final years found himself caught between a rock and a hard place, lambasted by jazz critics for selling out and disappointing live non-jazz-oriented audiences whenever he focused on improvising rather than on delivering literal versions of his greatest hits. In delivering literal versions of his greatest hits, Montgomery's role on record became increasingly restricted to rendering melodies in octaves, though it must never be forgotten that he, like LOUIS ARMSTRONG, had a rare ability to bring a special vitality to the task, as the writer Pete Welding explained in a March 1968 *Down Beat* review of the album *The Best of Wes Montgomery*: "It's a pleasure to hear him just state the melody: his sound and control are lovely, and his sense of time, of note placement is uncanny." By contrast the writer Gary Giddins took a harsh view of these activities. Given Montgomery's struggle to support his family, no one could possibly object to his having finally found commercial success, but Giddins rightly took Taylor to task for defining Montgomery's work in an ever-more-limited way, so that the greatest jazz guitarist after Charlie Christian was not afforded any further opportunity to record as a jazz guitarist.

In those contexts where his hands were not, in effect, tied to octaves, Montgomery's solos often followed a pattern of increasing fullness: a single-note line continued in parallel octaves and was brought to a climax with the melody fully harmonized in block chords. His perfect dexterity in executing the parallel octaves astonished listeners, but for Montgomery what was most impressive was not this subsequently widely imitated technical gimmick itself, but that it served to support an exquisite sense of melody and tone.

FURTHER READING

Some of Montgomery's papers and oral history interviews are at the Institute of Jazz Studies, Newark, New Jersey.

Ingram, Adrian. *Wes Montgomery* (1985; repr. 1993).

This entry is taken from the *American National Biography* and is published here with the permission of the American Council of Learned Societies.

BARRY KERNFELD

Montgomery, William Thornton (1 Feb. 1843–3 July 1909), slave, farmer, and merchant, was born at Davis Bend, Mississippi, to BENJAMIN T. MONTGOMERY and Mary Lewis, both slaves on the plantation of Joseph Davis, the elder brother of the future president of the Confederacy, Jefferson Davis. Thornton Montgomery, as he was generally known, was the eldest of the couple's four children who survived to adulthood. Little is known about his early life, other than that he grew up on the experimental plantation established by Joseph Davis at Davis Bend, modeled on the utopian communities of Robert Owen in New Lanark, Scotland, and New Harmony, Indiana.

Although all the African Americans at Davis Bend remained enslaved under Davis's plan, Benjamin Montgomery enjoyed a broader degree of autonomy than did most antebellum slaves. He also worked hard to ensure that his children benefited from his successful management of the Davis lands and from the thriving plantation store that he established in the 1850s. Income from his father's various enterprises ensured that Thornton was raised in a stable family, where his mother could devote her full energies to the needs of her own children rather than work in the fields or in the big house. She was able to do so because her husband purchased her time from Davis. Thornton's parents, both of whom were literate, also encouraged to him to read and write, and they probably arranged tutors for him, as they did for his younger brother, ISAIAH T. MONTGOMERY.

Although Davis Bend was little affected by the first year of the Civil War, by early 1863 the Union army had pushed deep into Mississippi, forcing

Joseph Davis to relocate his slaves to a plantation in the backcountry lands of Hinds County. Many of Davis's slaves took advantage of nearby Union forces and President Abraham Lincoln's Emancipation Proclamation to flee, among them Thornton Montgomery's father, mother, and siblings, who reached Cincinnati, Ohio, in June 1863. It is unclear why Thornton Montgomery remained with Davis in Hinds County rather than leave with his family, but he may have hoped to return to Davis Bend to work the land with other slaves who had become Union contrabands. In any case, Montgomery enlisted in the Union navy on 15 July 1863, eleven days after Vicksburg fell to Union forces, serving as an officer's steward on USS *Carondelet* for a year before joining his father and brothers, who were working at a canal-boat yard in Cincinnati.

With the war drawing to a close, Montgomery's father sent him back to the Davis plantations to investigate the business opportunities were the family to return there as freedmen. In February 1865 Montgomery began that process by establishing a company to purchase and distribute government rations to the former slaves on Davis's plantation, and he later reopened his father's store at Davis Bend. Following the formal surrender of the Confederacy he was joined there by the rest of his family, who invested their savings in the store and established the company of Montgomery & Sons. Business was brisk, bolstered by the large number of freedmen, many of them now wage earners, who frequented the Montgomery store. In November 1866 Montgomery & Sons' purchase of Joseph Davis's four thousand acres made the Montgomerys the wealthiest black family in the postwar South.

Like many young Mississippi planters before him, Thornton Montgomery then began looking to politics as a means of protecting his economic assets. In May 1867 he became the first African American appointed to federal political office in Mississippi history when General E. O. C. Ord appointed him as postmaster at Davis Bend, shortly before also appointing him as the community's constable and selecting Benjamin Montgomery as the state's first black justice of the peace. W. T. Montgomery also served as Warren County treasurer, but for the most part, business came before politics in the 1870s. While being groomed as his father's successor and managing the family plantation at Ursino, Mississippi, Thornton Montgomery attempted to improve his personal fortunes by opening a large general store in Vicksburg in 1874. Although the store was capitalized at one hundred thousand dollars and did well in its first year, it soon fell victim to the general economic uncertainty caused by the Panic of 1873. Matters were not helped by a series of floods and poor harvests and a sharp fall in the price of cotton, which limited the number of customers able to make cash purchases. A lengthy and expensive legal battle with Jefferson Davis and the death of Montgomery's father in 1877 hastened the decline of Montgomery & Sons, forcing the sale of the company to Jefferson Davis's family in 1881 for much less than its true value.

Disillusioned about the prospects for African Americans in both business and politics, Montgomery left Mississippi in the early 1880s, settling near Fargo in Dakota Territory. One of the only black farmers in a largely Scandinavian homesteading community, he prospered at first, increasing his holdings from 640 acres to more than one thousand acres by 1884, the year that he traveled as one of the Dakota Territory's representatives to the New Orleans Exposition. He also built a general store and a grain elevator, both of which led to the growth of a small community named Lithia and helped earn him a reputation as one of the most successful African American farmers in the Northwest.

Montgomery was less successful, however, in his efforts to persuade other Mississippi blacks to leave Jim Crow and cotton behind and move north to grow wheat. Montgomery himself hated Dakota's long, harsh winters, preferring to travel back to Vicksburg while leaving his property in the hands of managers. Sometime before 1900 he sold his Dakota land, returned to Mississippi, and invested some of his fortune in his brother Isaiah's effort to build an all-black colony at Mound Bayou. He also helped found the Mound Bayou Loan and Investment Company, served as a director and vice president of the Bank of Mound Bayou, and served as president of the Mound Bayou Business League. Less successful were his speculations in Canadian land and his investments in Midwest grain futures, which left William Thornton Montgomery in poverty at the time of his death in 1909.

FURTHER READING
Hermann, Janet Sharp. *The Pursuit of a Dream* (1999).
STEVEN J. NIVEN

Montjoy, Zilpah (1742?–1821), convert to Methodism and religious contemplative, was born probably in New York City, of unknown but most likely enslaved parents. All the details of Zilpah Montjoy's life are derived from Abigail Mott's 1826 *Narratives of Colored Americans*, a collection of biographical sketches of prominent and, in Mott's view, exemplary black Christians that includes RICHARD ALLEN, BENJAMIN BANNEKER, PAUL CUFFE, Gustavus Vassa (OLAUDAH EQUIANO), and PHILLIS WHEATLEY, as well as more obscure figures such as "Billy and Jenny," "Poor Pompey," and "Old Dinah." The circumstances surrounding Zilpah Montjoy's birth and parentage are unknown. According to her biographer, Montjoy spent her early life in domestic slavery in New York City, serving masters who invested nothing in her spiritual development beyond calling her by a name that had biblical origins. Montjoy was reportedly bound so tightly to her work that, throughout her youth, she remained ignorant of the fact that death was a universal human fate. The sermon for a young friend, whose funeral she was permitted to attend, brought this stark reality home. Through this loss of a peer, and the psychological discomfort that followed, Montjoy discovered Christianity. Later, she had a profound and direct conversion experience, during which, as Mott notes in *Narratives of Colored Americans*, "the Lord was pleased to reveal Himself, and impress on her untaught mind a belief in an omnipotent and omniscient Being, and that His law was written on the heart" (Mott, 161).

Montjoy's newfound interest in Christianity led her to Methodism. The choice was a natural one: Methodists had been actively seeking converts among America's enslaved and free people of color since at least the middle of the eighteenth century. RICHARD ALLEN, the founder and first bishop of the African Methodist Episcopal (AME) Church, described the denomination's attraction for new black Christians as "the plain and simple gospel [that] suits best for any people, for the unlearned can understand, and the learned are sure to understand" (Noll, 115).

But Montjoy's devotion to Methodism coincided with a particularly turbulent time in relations between black New Yorkers and their white coreligionists. She entered a white-dominated church that at once aggressively evangelized people of color yet eventually denied the converts full participation and equal recognition in its congregations. For years, African American Methodists of the late eighteenth and early nineteenth centuries were mistreated by many of their white coreligionists, relegated to race-specific sections of churches, and barred from church leadership.

Black New Yorkers eventually took matters into their own hands. In 1821, the same year Zilpah Montjoy died, they followed the trail blazed by Philadelphia's black Methodists under Allen's leadership several years before by breaking with the white church and forming AME congregations. One of these, Mother Zion, became the largest black congregation in antebellum New York City and attracted worshippers like SOJOURNER TRUTH and HARRIET TUBMAN.

According to Mott, Montjoy remained a slave for much of her adult life. She married, although nothing is known about her husband, and gave birth to two daughters. One daughter was sold away from her family, the other died as a young woman. Montjoy was widowed soon after. Eventually manumitted, she spent most of the later decades of her life living alone. Like other urban blacks who had outlived their usefulness to their masters, she had difficulty finding work. Devoted friends contributed to her well-being.

Illiterate for most of her life, Montjoy was sixty-eight before she learned to read. She received her education at a school at a Clarkson Association, one of several abolitionist and mutual aid societies for people of color that honored Thomas Clarkson, the British abolitionist and associate of William Wilberforce. Because of her age and poor eyesight, the teachers at the school tried to dissuade her from enrolling. She persevered, however, for the sole purpose of reading Scripture for herself. Her favorite passage became the Sermon on the Mount, which she referred to as "the blessed chapter" (Mott, 163). To Montjoy, education was a means to an end. Her religious engagements remained her first priority, though she could often be seen on city streets shuttling between church and school.

In her final years, Montjoy lived a solitary life of spiritual contemplation amid her diminishing physical capacity. A friend who came to visit bearing a gift of bread expressed her concern when she found the older woman unable to leave her home and without food of any kind. Montjoy attempted to assuage the friend's fears by stating, "I am never alone; my Master is with me. When I awake in the night season he talks with me. He has promised to take care of me, and He has done it; He has now sent me that loaf of bread" (Mott, 164).

Her profound conviction to her religious principles, and her personal drive to achieve the goals that would support them, "rendered her an object of peculiar interest to many of her acquaintances" (Mott, 160). Her ability to find the time, means, and resources to support her spiritual endeavors attests to both the commitment of New York's black

Christians despite limitations on their physical freedoms, as well as to the prevalence and importance of women in crafting devotional practices for black American Christians. But like New York's other black Christians, Zilpah Montjoy was, in her own way, determined to use available resources to take custody of her own spiritual welfare.

FURTHER READING

Burrows, Edwin G., and Mike Wallace. *Gotham: A History of New York City to 1898* (1999).

Hatch, Nathan O. *The Democratization of American Christianity* (1989).

Mott, Abigail Fields. *Narratives of Colored Americans* (1826).

Noll, Mark. *The Old Religion in a New World: The History of North American Christianity* (2002).

Porter, Dorothy. *Early Negro Writing* (1995).

LAURA M. CHMIELEWSKI

Moody, Anne E. (15 Sept. 1940–), writer and civil rights activist, was born Essie Mae Moody, in Wilkinson County, Mississippi, the eldest of nine children of Fred Moody and Elmire Williams Moody, both of whom worked in various capacities to support their families. After working on a plantation for several years, Moody's parents split up, and she and her siblings lived with their mother in the town of Centerville. Moody attended Willis High, Centerville's only school for African American children. She joined the junior high basketball team and became involved in church activities. To assist with the family's finances, eleven-year-old Moody got her first job sweeping porches for a neighboring elderly white woman, and she was paid seventy-five cents and two gallons of milk a week. Moody also made money collecting pecans, babysitting, and doing housework for white people in town. She was elected homecoming queen in the eighth grade. Moody earned *As* and *Bs* in school and graduated third in her eighth-grade class.

Because of the climate of Centerville during Moody's high school years, she was discouraged by her mother from talking openly about EMMETT TILL, the young African American man who was murdered in Money, Mississippi, for allegedly whistling at a white woman. Moody's mother told her, "You go on to work before you is late. And don't you let on like you know nothing about the boy being killed … Just do your work like you don't know nothing," (Moody, 130). Moody's mother and her teacher both encouraged her not to discuss other local racially based murders and harassments, the integration of public schools in the South, or the National Association for the Advancement of Colored People (NAACP) (Moody, 133–135). To ameliorate her frustration and anger, she focused on church, school, athletics, keeping house for a local white woman, and tutoring not only her siblings but also white adolescents in town.

In the summers Moody stayed with extended family in Baton Rouge and New Orleans and worked to earn money for school clothes and college. She worked as a waitress at a restaurant and made friends with her fellow employees—local drag queens and gay men. A fellow male employee named Lola gave Moody pointers on how to do her hair and dress to complement her body. Once back in Centerville, Moody's new look drew lascivious stares from men, including her basketball coach and her stepfather. After an argument with her stepfather over his staring at her in a way she found offensive, she moved in with her father in Woodville and completed her senior year at Johnson High School.

Moody graduated from high school in 1959 and two days later left for New Orleans to work until she saved enough for college. That summer she landed a basketball scholarship to Natchez Junior College in Mississippi. Because of her high grades and test scores, in 1961 she was given a full-tuition scholarship to Tougaloo Southern Christian College in Tougaloo, Mississippi. She graduated from Tougaloo with a B.S. in 1964. It was during her years there that Moody first became involved in the civil rights movement. Moody joined the NAACP chapter on campus, the Student Nonviolent Coordinating Committee (SNCC), and the Congress of Racial Equality (CORE). Once Moody became involved in the movement, however, her grades dropped and the money she had saved for school ran out. Moody canvassed, gave church speeches, and joined mass rallies, including one to protest the murder of civil rights activist MEDGAR EVERS. With fellow students Joan Trumpauer and Memphis Norman, Moody started the sit-in at Woolworth's lunch counter in Jackson, Mississippi, in 1963 in an attempt to integrate the establishment. As her activism escalated and Moody became more visible, her mother became increasingly concerned for her daughter's safety. She warned Moody to never come back to Wilkinson County or she would be killed; Moody heeded her mother's advice (Moody, 299).

Moody spent the summer of 1963 in Canton, Mississippi, working for CORE to register voters, with varying degrees of success, owing to the tactics, including rumors, threats, and shootings, adopted by whites to squelch activists' attempts to increase the number of African American voters. She also joined the March on Washington on 28 August 1963, where MARTIN LUTHER KING JR gave his "I have a dream" speech. But she felt dissatisfied with the urging of nonviolent activism. In her memoir she wrote: "I sat on the grass and listened to the speakers, to discover we had 'dreamers' instead of leaders leading us. Just about every one of them stood up there dreaming. Martin Luther King went on and on talking about his dream. I sat there thinking that in Canton we never had time to sleep, much less dream" (Moody, 325). As a result of the stress of her activism and the increasingly hostile threats to activists from whites outside the movement, Moody lost weight and had trouble sleeping. She was blacklisted by the Ku Klux Klan, her picture passed around in Klan leaflets. Moody returned to New Orleans and worked as a waitress, living with her sister to recuperate.

When Moody graduated in 1964 from Tougaloo, for the next year (1964–1965) she worked as a civil rights project coordinator at Cornell University. She then moved to New York City to work as a counselor for the New York City Poverty Program and to write her memoir, *Coming of Age in Mississippi*, which in 1969 was awarded the National Council of Christians and Jews Brotherhood Award and the National Library Association Best Book of the Year Award. Her short story "New Hope for the Seventies" won *Mademoiselle*'s silver medal (1970). At some point during those years she married Austin Stratus; the couple divorced on 9 March 1969. They had one child together, Sascha Moody. Moody was a writer-in-residence in Berlin, Germany, in 1972 and received a German Academic Service Grant for that same year. She later published a collection of short stories, *Mr. Death: Four Stories* (1975).

Moody's memoir *Coming of Age in Mississippi* provides readers with a detailed picture of the constraints that race, gender, and class put on those who attempted to challenge the hegemonic order of Mississippi during the civil rights movement.

FURTHER READING

Moody, Anne. *Coming of Age in Mississippi* (1968).
Anderson, Jace. "Re-Writing Race: Subverting Language in Anne Moody's *Coming of Age in Mississippi* and Alice Walker's *Meridian*," *A/B: Auto/Biography Studies* 8.1 (Spring 1993).
McKay, Nellie Y. "The Girls Who Became Women: Childhood Memories in the Autobiographies of Harriet Jacobs, Mary Church Terrell, and Anne Moody," *Tradition and the Talents of Women*. Florence Howe, ed. (1991).
Rishoi, Christy. "Hegemonic Inscription of the Body in *Coming of Age in Mississippi*," *From Girl to Woman: American Women's Coming-of-Age Narratives*. (2003).

LAURA MADELINE WISEMAN

Moody, Charles David (30 Aug. 1932–), educator and founder of the National Alliance of Black School Educators, was born in Baton Rouge, Louisiana, to James Nathaniel Moody and Rosetta Ella Hall. Moody's parents were both educators, his mother a teacher and his father a supervisor of rural, black schools for the Jeanes Fund. The Jeanes Fund was created by Anna T. Jeanes, a Quaker from Philadelphia, Pennsylvania, who used her wealth to provide educational assistance to black schools and students across the rural South. As the youngest of eight children Moody insisted upon coming out from underneath the shadow of his brothers and sisters. Instead of attending Southern University in his hometown of Baton Rouge, he ventured to Central State University in Wilberforce, Ohio—a place where he knew no one and no one knew him. There Moody's accomplishments or failures were his own, not measured against those of his siblings. While at Central State he joined the Reserve Officers' Training Corps (ROTC), in which he earned a salary of twenty-five dollars a month. Upon graduating from Central State with a B.S. in Biology in 1954, he was assigned to Fort Davis, Panama, where he served as a second lieutenant in the U.S. Army, becoming his company's first black officer. Before leaving for Fort Davis he married Christella Delois Parks in 1955; to their union three sons were born. A year after being discharged Moody began his postgraduate studies at the Chicago Teachers College (now Chicago State University), where he earned a master of science education degree in 1961.

As a teacher Moody labored diligently to educate children in the sciences and social studies in Posen-Robbins, Illinois. His efforts were rewarded when he was appointed assistant principal and chairman of the science department for School District 65 of Evanston, Illinois. Moody was appointed at a time when the Evanston school district was in the throes of desegregation. His involvement in the district's desegregation efforts would lead him to develop his equity-based model for desegregation. He believed that "desegregation is more than just a mixing of bodies. An institution's culture (process) is just as important as access [to it]" (Moody, 34). Moody conceived of four stages that an institution must undergo in order to become integrated: access, process, achievement, and transfer. Access is the first step toward integration. It refers to the opening of all-white schools to black students. Once there is access, an institution must then go through the process of changing its culture. This is accomplished by altering its policies and procedures so as to promote equity and fairness among its students, parents, and staff. A changed culture encourages student achievement. Scholastic achievement should then transfer into other areas such as additional educational opportunities and, eventually, employment. The work he did while in Evanston served as the catalyst for one of his greatest accomplishments: assisting with the integration of several midwestern school districts.

In 1968 Moody was offered and accepted the superintendency for School District 147 of Harvey, Illinois, and became its first black superintendent. Three years later he earned his Ph.D. in Educational Administration from Northwestern University. For his dissertation, "Black Superintendents in Public School Districts: Trends and Conditions," he conducted research on black superintendents across the country, aided by the renowned psychologist KENNETH B. CLARK. His research was a first in the area of black superintendency and sought to provide a network and system of support for the sixteen superintendents. This work led to the creation in 1970 of the National Alliance of Black School Superintendents, which in 1973 became the National Alliance of Black School Educators (NABSE). A nonprofit organization comprising teachers, administrators, and superintendents, by 2005 the NABSE had a membership of close to 7,000, with 125 affiliates in the United States, Canada, the Caribbean, and Europe. In its mission statement the organization described itself as "dedicated to improving both the educational experiences and accomplishments of African American youth through development and use of instructional and motivational methods that increase levels of inspiration, attendance and overall achievement."

Having actively participated in desegregation efforts in Evanston, Moody was prepared to accept the position of director of the Program for Educational Opportunity at the University of Michigan in 1970. Sixteen years after the landmark *Brown v. Board of Education* decision, school districts across the country were still wrestling with the issue of desegregation. Under his direction the Program for Educational Opportunity assisted school districts in Michigan, Ohio, Indiana, Illinois, Wisconsin, and Minnesota with the development of strategies for desegregation and equity. Moody served in various capacities at the university. He was a professor of education, chairman of the Division of Educational Specialists, and director of the Center for Sex Equity in Schools. In 1987 the University of Michigan's students of color marched on the president's office and waged a sit-in to demand an increase in the numbers of minority students in attendance at the university. They also called for the creation of programs aimed at ensuring the retention of students of color. The march and sit-in became known as the Black Action Movement III. The students' actions brought the Reverend JESSE JACKSON to the campus to help with the negotiations. Jackson called on Moody to participate in the discussions. Subsequently Moody was appointed vice provost for minority affairs, a position in which he developed programs that aimed to recruit and retain students and faculty of color. Under his guidance the enrollment of students of color increased by 8 percent and the number of faculty of color rose by 3 percent. Some of the important affirmative action programs set in motion by Moody and others would be challenged in the 2003 U.S. Supreme Court case of *Gratz v. Bollinger*, in which the Court ruled that the university's use of race in its undergraduate admissions policy violated the Equal Protection Clause. This Supreme Court decision would ultimately lead to a ballot initiative to amend the state constitution by prohibiting the use of race or gender in public education or in state government hiring practices and issuances of contracts.

While Moody was still serving as vice provost, the University of Michigan decided to confer an honorary degree upon Nelson Mandela. Moody led a delegation from the university to South Africa in 1991 to honor Mandela with the degree. Upon meeting Mandela, Moody remarked, "If he can be forgiving and exhibit such grace after what has happened to him, what complaint could I have" (Moody, 53). Moody was so affected and transformed by his South African experience that, upon his return to the University of Michigan, he began planting seeds of a transatlantic partnership between the university and South Africa. In 1993 he was appointed to his final position at the university, executive director of the South Africa Initiative Office. This position allowed him to develop and implement programs to improve the quality of life for black South Africans by effecting change in its educational institutions. He created a fund that awarded grants to University of Michigan students to travel to South Africa and partake in the transformation of that nation. Moody worked passionately and tirelessly to strengthen the South African educational infrastructure through the South Africa Initiative Office until his retirement in 1996.

FURTHER READING

Moody, Christella D. *Milestones: Reaching beyond the Breaks* (1992).

Smith, Willy DeMarcell, and Eva Wells Chunn, eds. *Black Education: A Quest for Equity and Excellence* (1989).

CHASITY BAILEY-FAKHOURY

Moon, Harold Warren (18 Nov. 1956–), professional football quarterback, was born in Los Angeles, California, the fourth of seven children (and only son) born to Harold Warren Moon, a janitor, and Pat Moon, a nurse. In 1963 the elder Harold Moon died suddenly of liver and heart ailments, leaving Pat to raise Warren and his six sisters. Warren played almost every sport growing up, but had decided by the age of fourteen that football offered his likeliest shot at a professional career. Thus he attended Los Angeles's Hamilton High School even though it was outside his school district, as much because of its reputation for football as for its academic strength. Moon was the varsity starting quarterback his junior and senior years at Hamilton, overcoming Los Angeles's rising gang culture (more than once, his life was threatened by gang members at rival high schools) and apparent racism (though a prolific passer on a successful team, he was passed over for most all-city honors). It was at Hamilton that he met his future wife, Felicia Hendricks. At the end of Moon's senior year, several Division I-A schools, most notably Arizona State and the University of Southern California, recruited him, but as a running back or defensive back—never as a quarterback.

Instead of making the position switch, Moon opted instead to attend West Los Angeles Junior College to hone his passing skills. In 1975, after only one season at West Los Angeles, he transferred to the University of Washington at Seattle, where the coaches promised him they would consider him at quarterback. Just as in high school, Moon had to endure numerous racial taunts, mostly owing to the fact that, as an untested sophomore, he unseated the senior incumbent for the starting quarterback position before the 1975 season began. Moon's first two seasons at Washington were solid if unspectacular, but his senior season (1977) was his breakout campaign. That year, he led the Huskies to the Rose Bowl, where they upset the heavily favored University of Michigan, and Moon was named Pac-8 Player of the Year.

Nevertheless, coming out of college, "the NFL basically rejected him as a quarterback" (*Sports Illustrated*, 27 Sept. 1993). The black quarterback was still a novelty act in the NFL of the late 1970s, and Moon was at somewhat of a disadvantage in 1978 in that there was already a "can't-miss" quarterback available in DOUG WILLIAMS of Grambling University (who in 1988 became the first black quarterback to start in a Super Bowl), and it seems as though there was a limit on the number of black quarterbacks that the NFL could accept at any one time. Moon found himself touted as a lower-round pick, if even that. Instead of trying his luck, Moon signed with the Edmonton Eskimos of the Canadian Football League (CFL).

Warren Moon of the Houston Oilers, throwing a pass during a game against the Cincinnati Bengals in Houston, Texas, 14 October 1990. (AP Images.)

Despite being one of the few black players in an overwhelmingly white city, Moon felt comfortable and accepted playing in Edmonton—not least because he married Felicia in 1981, who gave birth to their first son, Joshua, in 1982. He began to come into his own as a quarterback. Whether as a starter, or as half of a quarterback "platoon" with Tom Wilkinson, he threw for 144 touchdowns and over 21,000 yards while leading the Eskimos to an unprecedented five straight Grey Cup championships. After the 1983 CFL season, teams south of the border finally began to take notice of Moon's talents. This reappraisal was mainly the result of the bidding war that was taking place between the NFL and the upstart United States Football League (USFL). Four NFL and two USFL teams offered Moon a contract. In the end, he chose the Houston Oilers' offer of $6 million a year, which immediately made him the highest-paid player in pro football.

Moon's first few seasons with Houston were difficult. Whenever he threw an interception or an incompletion, he heard the old familiar boos and racially inflected heckles. Moon seemingly took it all in stride, just as he had at Washington. He never lashed out at fans; indeed, his most notable public response to such heckling, after a December 1991 game, took the form of a public apology from Moon for his lackluster performance. With time, Moon's stock began to rise in Houston. Neither very big nor exceptionally quick, he nonetheless gained a reputation as one of the NFL's most potent two-way threats—meaning he was adept both at throwing and running with the ball. Perhaps his best all-around season came in 1988, when he threw thirty-three touchdowns (compared with only thirteen interceptions) and rushed for 215 yards and two touchdowns. Such was his versatility that coach Jack Pardee installed a completely new offense to take advantage of it—called the "run and shoot."

Notwithstanding this statistical success, however, Moon was criticized during his days as an Oiler for his inability to lead his team to glory in the play-offs. Moon's Oiler teams were almost always competitive. However, they never managed to advance even as far as the conference championship game in any of his seasons with the team. The low point of this futility was in January 1993, when Moon led the Oilers to a 20-3 halftime lead against the Buffalo Bills (and set the AFC's postseason record for most completed passes with thirty-six), only to see the Bills come back to win 41-38 in the closing seconds of overtime.

After the 1993 season Moon was traded to the Minnesota Vikings for two future draft picks. At the age of thirty-eight, he adapted well to the situation in Minnesota, throwing for over 4,000 yards in two of his three seasons (and thirty-three touchdowns in a stellar 1995 campaign). However, the Vikings never advanced past the first round of the National Football Conference play-offs, and after the 1996 season Minnesota released Moon, opting for the much younger Brad Johnson as their quarterback. In a homecoming of sorts, Moon was picked up by the Seattle Seahawks, where he spent two seasons before again being released. The twilight of Moon's long and prolific career came with the Kansas City Chiefs, for whom he only played three games over two seasons. In 2000 Moon decided to retire after twenty-three seasons at the age of forty-four.

At his retirement Warren Moon ranked third all-time in NFL passing yardage and fifth in touchdowns thrown. However, his effect on the National Football League must be viewed in much wider terms than merely his career statistics, or the absence of his name from the Vince Lombardi Trophy. Along with Doug Williams and Randall Cunningham of the Philadelphia Eagles, Moon helped to transform the image of the successful black starting quarterback from a novelty to an accepted fact on the field and in the locker room. Moon's presence must be recognized, at least indirectly, as helping to create the situation where two black quarterbacks could start against each other in a conference championship game, as Michael Vick and Donovan McNabb did in 2005. Furthermore, by his tireless charity work through the Crescent Moon Foundation, which he cofounded in 1989 to help underprivileged youths, Moon served as a powerful example of an African American role model and community builder.

FURTHER READING
Montville, Leigh. "Father Moon," *Sports Illustrated* (27 Sept. 1993).
NFL Quarterback Club. *Warren Moon* (1999).

ANDREW JAMES KELLETT

Moon, Henry Lee (20 July 1901–7 June 1985), NAACP publicist, author, journalist, and editor of *The Crisis* was born in Pendleton, South Carolina, to William J. Moon and Georgia Bullock. Henry Lee Moon was raised in Cleveland. Much of his life became intertwined with the NAACP and its chief print organ, *The Crisis*, which began publication in 1910. Moon's connection to the NAACP dated back to June 1919, when, as a graduating high school senior he met the national leaders of the then decade-old organization when its national conference was hosted in his hometown of Cleveland. Among the luminaries he met were Mary White Ovington, W. E. B. DuBois, Joel Spingarn, WILLIAM PICKENS, JAMES WELDON JOHNSON, and Walter Frances. As his father was a founder of the Cleveland branch, Moon literally grew up with the group.

Educated at Howard University, he earned a master's degree from Ohio State University. Moon then served as Tuskegee University's public relations director before working as a journalist for New York's *Amsterdam News*.

In 1934, while an editor at the *Amsterdam News*, Moon received letters from a wide range of people, including Pan-Africanists such as George Padmore, who were critical of the immediate and future status of the movement. Over the next decade this correspondence detailed the contours of Padmore's Pan-African position and precipitated a call for a Fifth Pan-African Congress, to be held in Manchester, for which Moon requested DuBois serve as chairperson.

In 1938 Moon advised the federal housing authority on race relations. Six years later he became assistant to the director for the political action committee of the Congress of Industrial Organizations. During the pivotal period following the end of World War II, Moon's career was virtually inseparable from the history of the NAACP, the oldest American civil rights organization.

The 1930s marked a period during which Moon was employed in the Federal Writers' Project, working alongside TED POSTON, supervised by FWP Negro Affairs Director STERLING ALLEN BROWN. Moon subsequently became involved as a member of President Franklin Delano Roosevelt's "Black Cabinet," an unofficial advisory group of African American leaders and opinion shapers loosely organized around the National Youth Administration Negro Affairs director MARY MCCLEOD BETHUNE.

Following World War II, Moon's 1948 book, *Balance of Power: The Negro Vote*, called attention to a phenomenon previously overlooked by both major political parties: the potentially decisive voting strength of the African American electorate. Beginning with a historical survey tracing both the progress and problems following male black enfranchisement made possible by ratification of the Fifteenth Amendment in 1870, Moon systematically made the case for paying closer attention to the rise of African American influence in the polls, despite structural obstacles such as legal and customary discrimination. In the course of examining the status of black voters, Moon exploded stereotypes portraying African Americans as particularly venal, ignorant, illiterate, and thus corruptible, balancing myths with detailed exposition of the struggles facing blacks seeking to exercise their right to vote.

When the book appeared, Moon was NAACP Director of Public Relations, a post he held from 1948 to 1964. These years were among the most challenging faced by the organization since its inception in 1909 and were bracketed by the desegregation of the armed forces in 1948 and the passage of the Civil Rights Act of 1964. During these years Moon made the transition from being a journalist and a southern field CIO-PAC organizer to becoming the NAACP's most visible and influential spokesman.

As the battle to implement the momentous 1954 *Brown v. Board of Education* Supreme Court decision mounted, Moon was drawn into some of the most high-profile cases of this contentious era. Among his most difficult tasks were comforting family members and fielding public reaction to the murders of EMMETT LOUIS TILL in 1955 and the NAACP leader MEDGAR EVERS in 1963, among others.

Moon served as fourth editor of the NAACP print organ, *The Crisis*, from 1965 to 1974. As ex-NAACP Public Relations Director, Moon responded quickly to media missteps. In the 18 April 1969 issue of *Time*, for example, he responded to the magazine's assertion that the NAACP executive director ROY WILKINS, "ha[d] lost more ground than any other leader, with the decline of integration as the principal issue," Moon's vehement retort was precise: "Our membership figures, our incoming mail and the demand for his public appearance indicate no 'loss of ground' by our executive director. On the contrary, there has been ample evidence of his increase in stature. Integration remains a vital issue despite the loud and widely publicized demands of the black neo-segregationists."

In 1972 Moon paid homage to the contributions of W. E. B. DuBois, publishing a book-length study almost ten years after DuBois's death on the eve of the 1963 March on Washington. In *The Emerging Thought of W. E. B. DuBois*, Moon sought to capture the essence of the leader's outlook while still in its nascent stages. Moon's own relationship to the illustrious founder of the NAACP and *The Crisis* appeared in introductory and concluding sections. The concluding twelve pages reprise Moon's lifelong connection to DuBois in a section at once autobiographical and highly analytical.

Henry Lee Moon died in 1985 at eighty-four years of age. The NAACP archive's library now bears his name.

FURTHER READING

Moon, Henry Lee. *Balance of Power: The Negro Vote* (1948).

Moon, Henry Lee, Channing H. Tobias, Adam Clayton Powell, and Thomas L. Stokes. "The Passing of Walter Frances White," *Phylon* (1955).

Moon, Henry Lee. "Letters," *Time* (18 April 1969).

"The Future of Black Leadership," *Time* (4 April 1969).

Evers, Medgar Wiley. *The Autobiography of Medgar Evers: A Hero's Life and Legacy as Revealed Through His Writings, Letters and Speeches* (2005).

DAVID H. ANTHONY III

Mooney, Paul (4 Aug. 1941–), actor and comedian, was born Paul Gadney in Shreveport, Louisiana, to George Gadney and LaVoya Ealy. When he was seven, his family relocated to Oakland, California, and there Mooney spent the remainder of his childhood. His father was not a stable figure in his life, and soon disappeared altogether. Throughout his youth, Mooney was closest to his grandmother, Aimay Ealy. It was she who gave him the nickname "Mooney," though Mooney himself later claimed that she never bothered to explain what it meant. However, the name stuck, and, perhaps eager to relieve himself of his father's name, Mooney adopted it as his professional moniker. While in his teens, Mooney dropped out of school and left home to join the tiny Charles Gody Circus, working in various roles until he was promoted to ringmaster. According to Mooney himself, this made him the first black ringmaster in the history of the country, though whether this is fact or legend seems difficult to verify.

After his time in the circus, Mooney began to appear on various television programs, usually in uncredited background roles. His first such appearance was in 1971, when he played a soldier in the TV movie *Carter's Army*. He later showed up on *The Dating Game* and *Playboy after Dark*, in this latter appearing only as one of the show's numerous background stand-ins (the setting was a sophisticated cocktail party, with those in attendance listening in politely while the hosts interviewed their famous guests). He also did stand-up comedy, including at Ye Little Club in Hollywood, where he met the comedian Joan Rivers and other up-and-coming talents of the day. In 1969 he met RICHARD PRYOR, but their meeting was less than auspicious. Mooney was living with his half-sister, a model, at the time, and her Sunset Strip hotel room had become something of a flop for visiting performers. One day Pryor showed up and, apparently not realizing that the woman was Mooney's sister, propositioned the pair. Mooney ordered him out of the apartment. Despite this, the two would soon hatch an association that would become Mooney's big break and claim to fame.

By the early 1970s, Mooney was developing a reputation as both as a comedian to watch and as a controversial voice. With Jane Fonda and others, he toured with the anti-Vietnam Fuck the Army improv group. He again ran into Pryor, and this time the two hit it off and decided to try to work together. By 1972 the pair had been hired as writers for REDD FOXX's hit *Sanford and Son* television program. As Pryor's stand-up career began to take off, Mooney followed him as writer and, in many senses, the driving force behind Pryor's increasingly risky, sexually explicit, and controversial style of comedy. In 1975

Paul Mooney and *Apprentice 2* contestant Stacie Jones Upchurch arrive at Elton John's Dream Ticket DVD Launch Party at Caesar's Palace on October 24, 2004, in Las Vegas, Nevada. [AP Images.]

Pryor was famous enough to secure a spot on the National Broadcasting Company's (NBC) *Saturday Night Live*. Mooney wrote much of what has since come to be regarded as a classic performance. The experience, though, was perhaps somewhat less than glamorous, at least for Mooney, who was taken aback both by the drug use and mutual antagonism among the show's stars (Pryor and Chevy Chase, in particular, had a bad relationship) and by a virtual interrogation by the show's producers, who were mistrustful of a black comedy writer.

Nevertheless, the performance helped to launch Pryor's career, and with it Mooney's writing and performing, to a new level. In 1977 NBC gave Pryor his own television program, and Mooney again was responsible for cowriting many of the routines. He wrote material, too, for many of the program's visiting comedians, Robin Williams and Sandra Bernhard among them. Pryor and Mooney's comedy, however, was risky for the time, encompassing political and social topics and broaching racial subjects that in the pre-cable era were still almost unheard of on network television and that NBC considered unacceptably controversial. Pryor and Mooney found themselves at odds with the network executives, and the show was canceled after just four episodes.

Still, Mooney and Pryor were reaching a high point in their art. In 1976 Pryor released his classic *Bicentennial Nigger* album, recorded during gigs around Hollywood. The recording won a Grammy in 1977 for Best Comedy Album. The year 1982 saw the release of the Pryor concert film *Richard Pryor: Live on the Sunset Strip*, with Mooney again as cowriter. As always, the material was frank, risqué, and profane. Pryor talked about explicit sexual topics, racial prejudice, and his own drug use, including an infamous incident in which he set himself on fire while smoking cocaine. This story would play a key part in Pryor's 1988 semiautobiographical film *Jo Jo Dancer, Your Life Is Calling*. Mooney cowrote the screenplay.

Beyond his association with Pryor, Mooney himself acted in a number of films and television shows. He played the role of SAM COOKE in *The Buddy Holly Story* (1978). In 1981 he appeared in *Bustin' Loose* alongside Pryor and CICELY TYSON. In 2000 he played a part in SPIKE LEE's controversial take on Hollywood racism, *Bamboozled*. Mooney also appeared in a number of stand-up films and other comedy performances as himself, such as *Know Your History: Jesus Is Black; So Was Cleopatra* (2006) and *It's the End of the World* (2010). Among his other

writing duties, Mooney served as head writer for the first year of the Fox Network's groundbreaking black comedy show, *In Living Color* (1990). Among his creations was the bitter, often violent Homey the Clown, one of the show's most popular reoccurring characters. He also wrote for DAVE CHAPPELLE's highly rated (and abruptly abandoned) cable comedy program.

Mooney's career has at times proven controversial. In 2006 he was reportedly forced off of the stage at the Apollo Theater after making fun of the U.S. president George W. Bush and his mother, Barbara Bush. Reportedly this was done at the behest of executives with the Time Warner Group, though the corporation has denied being involved in the incident. Mooney has also had a troubled and quite public relationship with the word "nigger," a word that Pryor had famously disavowed following a trip to Africa, but which Mooney had continued to use in his routine. However, following an incident in which the (white) comedian Michael Richards used the word repeatedly on stage in Los Angeles in response to hecklers, Mooney swore never to use the word again in his routines.

FURTHER READING

Mooney, Paul, and Dave Chappelle. *Black Is the New White* (2010).

Rabin, Nathan. Interview: Paul Mooney (2007). The A.V. Club. http://www.avclub.com/articles/ paul-mooney,14071/

JASON PHILIP MILLER

Moore, Aaron McDuffie (6 Sept. 1863–29 Apr. 1923), physician, was born in Rosindale, Columbus County (later Bladen County), North Carolina, the son of Israel Moore, a free black farmer, and Eliza (maiden name unknown). Moore's family was of African American, Native American, and European descent and had owned land and farmed in the Columbus County area since the early nineteenth century. He worked on the family farm and attended the local public elementary schools available to African Americans between the harvesting and planting seasons. After completing the eighth grade he attended the Whitin Normal School in Lumberton, North Carolina, and then the normal school in Fayetteville, North Carolina. His schooling was interspersed with periods when he worked on his father's farm and taught in the county school.

In 1885 Moore enrolled in Shaw University, an African American institution located in Raleigh, North Carolina. He entered the university's Leonard

Medical School, which had opened in 1882, and completed the four-year curriculum in three years. In 1888 he took his examination for a North Carolina medical license along with thirty whites and nine other blacks. He passed his state examination, second in rank, and became the first African American physician to practice in Durham, North Carolina. In 1889 Moore married Cottie S. Dancy, daughter of John C. Dancy, one of North Carolina's leading early African American political figures. They had two children.

In 1888 Moore ran for county coroner but found whites so antagonistic to his campaign that he withdrew from the race and never again stood for elected office. Henceforth he directed his energies to his medical practice, various business and public enterprises for African American self-improvement, and his Baptist church.

In October 1898 Moore, JOHN MERRICK, a Durham barber and businessman, and five other black community leaders met in Moore's medical office for the purpose of establishing an insurance company. African American insurance companies were first organized in the American South in the mid-nineteenth century; white companies actively competed for African American business during the mid-to late nineteenth century. In 1881, after a study by the Prudential Insurance Company that argued that there was an excessive loss rate on policies for African Americans, white insurance companies reduced the size of policies they were willing to write for blacks and significantly increased the premiums. This provided the opportunity for African American companies to compete for business. Moore, Merrick, and their associates formed the North Carolina Mutual Life Insurance Company. Originally housed in Moore's medical office, the company benefited from his financial support and guidance. Moore served as its secretary-treasurer and medical director and, from 1919 to 1923, company president. Ultimately the company grew to become the largest African American financial institution in the United States.

Durham's Lincoln Hospital, also founded by Moore, was granted a charter in February 1901. The facility was erected with a gift of $85,550 from Washington Duke, a noted businessman and philanthropist whose name Duke University carries. It had at first been proposed to add an African American wing to the existing city hospital, but Moore opposed the idea, because he believed that adding a separate wing on a white hospital would not provide facilities for the practice of black physicians or for the

training of black nurses. Duke had in mind erecting a monument on the campus of Trinity College (now Duke University) to the memory of African American slaves for their loyalty during the Civil War. Moore, in cooperation with Dr. S. L. Warren and Merrick, convinced Duke that a hospital for the care of the descendants of the slaves would be more appropriate. The hospital opened as a 125-bed acute-care facility, with Moore as its superintendent. It served Durham's African American community until the 1960s, when it merged with the white community hospital, Watts Hospital, to form Durham County General Hospital.

In 1895 Moore helped launch the Bull City Drug Company, a pharmacy staffed by a black pharmacist and designed to serve Durham's African American community. In 1907 he helped found the Mechanics and Farmers Bank and served that institution as a member of its board of directors and as vice president. In 1913 he also helped establish the Durham Colored Library, which had begun with Moore's donations in the basement of the White Rock Baptist Church. Many people would not utilize a library located in the church, so Moore secured a building and enlisted city and county funds to support the facility and served as president of the library. Later in life Moore became deeply involved in the rural education movement for the black schoolchildren of North Carolina. In 1914 he personally paid the salary of North Carolina's first rural school inspector as an initial step in demonstrating the need for such a program. The inspector visited rural schools and recommended steps for improvement. Moore successfully petitioned for state funds to sustain the program and obtained a matching grant from the Rosenwald Foundation.

Moore was chairman of the Board of Trustees of Shaw University for ten years, a founder of the Durham Young Men's Christian Association, a trustee of the Colored Orphan Asylum, and chairman of the board of deacons, superintendent of the Sunday school, and member of the board of trustees of Durham's White Rock Baptist Church. He was president of the Baptist State Sunday School Convention and worked for the Lott Carey Foreign Mission Convention and used funds he raised in the United States to travel to Haiti (at his own expense), where he founded the Haitian White Rock Baptist Church. During World War I he accepted an appointment as special agent and supervisor of Negro economics in North Carolina. He was influential in securing jobs for African

Americans and assisting African American farmers. Moore died in Durham.

FURTHER READING
Weare, Walter B. *Black Business in the New South: A Social History of the North Carolina Mutual Life Insurance Company* (1973).
Obituary: *Journal of the National Medical Association* 16 (1924).

This entry is taken from the *American National Biography* and is published here with the permission of the American Council of Learned Societies.

EDWARD C. HALPERIN

Moore, Acel (5 Oct. 1940–), Pulitzer Prize–winning journalist and newspaper editor, was born in Philadelphia, Pennsylvania, the son of Jerry A. Moore, an electrician and stationary engineer at the Philadelphia Naval Shipyard and the Pyramid Tire Retreading Co., and homemaker Hura May Harrington. Moore grew up in West Philadelphia, where he attended Philadelphia's Overbrook High School and studied trumpet and French horn at the Settlement Music School. After graduating in 1958, he played jazz professionally for a year before enlisting in the U.S. Army, where he served as a medic. Returning to Philadelphia after being discharged from the Army in 1962, Moore applied for a job as a copy boy at the *Philadelphia Inquirer*—"Because I could type," he said (telephone interview with subject, April 2007).

When Moore began as a copy clerk, he was responsible for running copy to editors and reporters and was one of only three African Americans among the staff of three thousand employees at the paper. Moore apprenticed with seasoned reporters, practiced rewriting copy, and took night classes in journalism. He married Carolyn Weaver in 1964, and their son Acel Moore Jr. was born in 1967.

In 1968 Moore was promoted to a reporter position and assigned to the police beat in northwest Philadelphia. He then spent two years covering the Philadelphia juvenile court. He received a Scales of Justice Award from the Philadelphia Bar Association in 1970 for his series on the juvenile court system, and a Keystone Press Award. Promoted to general assignment reporter, Moore became known for his innovative profiles of people and community groups. Moore's efforts changed the way the paper covered African Americans, not limiting its coverage of them to the sports and entertainment fields.

In 1974 Moore and his wife divorced, and in 1975 he married Cheryl Rice. He moved into investigative reporting, breaking a story about white Philadelphia policeman shooting two unarmed teenagers in a middle-class black neighborhood. His biggest investigative story, however, concerned the abuse and beating deaths of more than thirty inmates at the Farview State Hospital for the Criminally Insane in Pennsylvania. The 1976 series of articles known as "The Farview Findings," earned Moore and co-author Wendell Rawls a Pulitzer Prize for local investigative specialized reporting in 1977. Moore was the first African American to win the Pulitzer for investigative reporting, and the third to win for journalism.

The road to the Pulitzer began in January of 1976 when Moore was asked to write a daily story about a note that came over the AP wire. A coroner in Delaware County, Pennsylvania, had asked to exhume the ten-year-old corpse of Robert "Stonewall" Jackson to determine the cause of death. Jackson, a man in his thirties, had died in 1966 of what was originally determined to be a heart attack. Jackson's mother became suspicious when the funeral director told her that her son's neck had been broken. Robert Jackson *had not* died of a heart attack, and his mother had spent years trying to get the media or the authorities to investigate. Moore interviewed Jackson's mother about her son's case and the story ran in the paper's Metro section on 30 January 1976.

The next day, Moore received a phone call from a man who claimed he had witnessed Jackson being beaten to death. The source, a former Farview inmate, was reluctant to come into the newsroom for an interview, so Moore met him in a seedy bar in North Philadelphia. The source laid out the brutal details of the beating death and the repeated atrocities at Farview. He described beatings, murders, human cockfights; he recalled that guards had also withheld medical care and forced prisoners to endure freezing ice baths in the wintertime.

The *Inquirer* editor Gene Roberts told Moore to run with the story, and assigned Wendell Rawls to work with him. The two did extensive research and talked to hundreds of people: former guards and prisoners, and social workers. "That story turned around the entire criminal justice system, how it deals with the mentally ill," Moore said in an interview. "Now, you have to have a psychiatrist determine you're insane, and your condition gets reviewed every 60 days…. Used to be, if you were in prison, you could be determined insane by a guard, and be sent to Farview, where you'd be beaten, kicked, given ice baths in the winter. You could be beaten to death, and they'd say it was a heart attack" (telephone interview with subject, April 2007). Shortly after the publication of "The Farview Findings," Pennsylvania state law changed so that prisoners could no longer be sent to places like Farview and forgotten about for years.

In 1979 Moore went to Harvard University on a Nieman Fellowship. Upon his return to the *Inquirer* in 1980, he was promoted to associate editor, thus becoming a member of the *Inquirer*'s editorial board. He wrote a regular column that covered issues of the day and urban personalities. Internally, he directed recruiting, training, and staff development, ensuring that staff members were trained in reporting issues of cultural and ethnic interest.

At the request of then-editor Gene Roberts, in 1983 Moore conducted a content analysis of the *Inquirer* and its coverage of African Americans. Talking with several hundred readers and analyzing what was covered and how, he documented a clear history of biased coverage of African Americans. "Our paper's representation shows ignorance, lack of knowledge, and racism," Moore told a shocked group of the paper's top editors (telephone interview with subject, April 2007). To reinforce his point, he had assembled a quiz made of photos of the most prominent African American leaders in the city. None of the editors could identify the leaders in the photos; and yet, as Moore pointed out, he would have been irresponsible as a reporter not to be able to visually identify the most prominent white leaders in the city. Moore's efforts proved effective, and resulted in substantive changes in the *Inquirer*'s coverage of African Americans. "When WILSON GOODE ran for mayor, he was covered more fairly and evenly than any other candidate ever," said Moore. Goode won the 1982 election and in 1983 became Philadelphia's first African American mayor.

In 1973, as part of his efforts to increase diversity in newsrooms in Philadelphia and across the nation, Moore founded the Association of Black Journalists in Philadelphia (ABJP) with about fourteen or fifteen members. In 1975 he became a founding member of NABJ, the National Association of Black Journalists.

Moore was responsible for training a substantial number of young journalists. He taught basic reporting at Temple University in Philadelphia, and was responsible for Temple hiring more African American journalism professors. In 1979 he began a training program at the *Inquirer* for copy editors that ran until 2005. Moore taught for several years at a Dow Jones summer reporting program for high school students. He initiated a similar five-week program at the *Inquirer*, as well as a career development workshop (now named after him) to bring local high school students to the *Inquirer* newsroom to learn to produce a newspaper. From 1980 to 1990 he served on the senior faculty at the University of California at Berkeley's Institute for Journalism Education, which prepared journalists of color for their first newspaper job. In its heyday, the program produced one-third of the country's journalists of color.

Divorced from Cheryl Rice in 1986, in 1988 Moore married fellow journalist Linda Wright. Their daughter Mariah was born in 1991. In 2006, after the *Inquirer* changed ownership, he decided to take advantage of an early retirement offer. After retirement, he remained a member of the editorial board of the *Inquirer*, retaining the title of associate editor emeritus.

FURTHER READING

Gregory, Kia. "Always Room for Moore," *Philadelphia Weekly* (Nov. 2005).

Dawkins, Wayne. *Black Journalists: The NABJ Story* (June 1997).

MEREDITH BROUSSARD

Moore, Amzie (23 Sept. 1911–1 Feb. 1982), civil rights activist, was born on the Wilkin plantation in Grenada County, Mississippi. He was the grandson of a former slave who had accumulated remarkable wealth and land that was eventually lost during the Great Depression. Moore worked alongside his family as a sharecropper when his mother died unexpectedly in 1925, leaving the fourteen-year-old on his own while his father took custody of his younger brother and sister. Amzie then traveled from the hill country of his birth to the Mississippi Delta to find work picking cotton in order to provide himself food and shelter and an education. Moore attended Stone Street High School in Greenwood, Mississippi, from 1926 to 1929, before settling in Cleveland to begin his lengthy career with the U.S. Post Office, a tenure that was interrupted in 1942 when he was drafted into the U.S. Army.

Like many African American veterans of World War II, Moore returned to the South four years later a changed man. He had joined the NAACP while in the Army, and his travels throughout the world had convinced him not only of the universality of human beings but also gave him an acute sense of the economic disparities and grossly unequal social conditions at home between blacks and whites.

A registered voter since 1936, Moore was involved briefly in the Black-and-Tans, the African American wing of the Republican Party in the South, whose roots reached back to the Reconstruction Era. In 1950 Moore was instrumental in the founding of the Mississippi Regional Council for Negro Leadership in Mound Bayou, a markedly successful all-black town in the Delta. The Council served to address economic as well as political issues, stressing the importance to African Americans of property rights as well as the right to vote and hold public office.

From its inception the council enlisted the help of a coalition of organizations, including the NAACP, to accomplish its goals. In 1952 THURGOOD MARSHALL addressed the council, further cementing Moore's ties with the venerated organization. Following the Supreme Court's 1954 *Brown v. Board of Education* school desegregation decision, and the subsequent creation of numerous White Citizens' Councils to resist the unanimous ruling, Moore faced increased pressure from community members to assume a greater leadership role. That year Moore had built a combination service station, beauty shop, and restaurant that defied the segregationist status quo by refusing to post a "Black Only" sign and by serving both blacks and whites.

His business success and courage in challenging Jim Crow reinforced his standing as a leader in the community, and in January 1955 he was entreated by the Cleveland branch of the NAACP to become its president and elected in absentia. Moore, with the help of NAACP Field Secretary MEDGAR EVERS, promptly built the chapter up to nearly five hundred members, a remarkable feat since the Citizens Councils encouraged whites to harass and fire from their jobs any African Americans who openly joined the NAACP. Moore himself was a prominent victim of the councils' economic reprisals, when a Cleveland bank called in the $6,000 mortgage for his home and businesses.

The year of Moore's election also saw the brutal, racially motivated murders of several African Americans, including the Reverend George Lee in Belzoni, the farmer Lamar Smith, and fourteen-year-old EMMETT TILL. The reaction of the NAACP, spurred by a noticeably more defiant black citizenry, included boycotts of white businesses that were countered by even more repressive measures by local Citizens' Councils. Moore and others nonetheless persisted, setting up a citizenship school and pursuing voter registration into the late 1950s with even greater vigor. This included a 1956 challenge to allow African Americans to vote in party primaries. Although the Supreme Court had invalidated the all-white primary in the 1940s, most African Americans in Mississippi and other Deep South states were kept from the polls by intimidation and other means.

In 1960, following the sit-in movement that began in North Carolina, and consequent formation of the Student Nonviolent Coordinating Committee (SNCC), ROBERT MOSES, a young teacher from New York, traveled south to Mississippi to meet with Moore at the behest of long-time NAACP activist, ELLA BAKER. Armed with a letter from Baker, Moses found Moore, then vice-president of the state's conference of NAACP branches, receptive to SNCC and its voter registration aims. Though Moore opposed many of the young organization's efforts at desegregation, notably the Freedom Rides of 1961, he was steadfastly dedicated to black voter registration and supported SNCC in this endeavor. Moore's willingness to collaborate with organizations outside of the NAACP was often met with disapproval from NAACP stalwarts. Nevertheless, Moore placed the primacy of the vote over organizational loyalty, and played a central role in helping out of state civil rights workers like Moses earn the trust of African Americans in the Delta.

In 1962, Moore played a central role in the formation of the Council of Federated Organizations (COFO), the organization that would consolidate a number of civil rights organizations seeking to secure equality for black Mississippians. These included SNCC, the NAACP, and the Congress of Racial Equality (CORE), and served as an umbrella for coordinating voter-registration drives in Mississippi. COFO sponsored the "Freedom Vote," a mock election, in 1963, demonstrating black citizens' willingness to take part in the political process. The following year Moore was also contacted by FANNIE LOU HAMER to help organize the Mississippi Freedom Democratic Party; and served by finding ways for blacks to pay their poll taxes and instructing them on how to interpret sections of the constitution—voting requirements that were left to the discretion of racist white election officials.

In 1964 Moore met with President Lyndon Johnson about the state of Mississippi's economy, and lobbied for funds to start a Head Start Program in Bolivar County. Upon retirement from the U.S. Post Office in 1968, Moore worked with the National

Council of Negro Women to develop low-income housing in Cleveland and other parts of the Delta. In the 1970s he played a central role in encouraging a Cleveland employer, Baxter Laboratories, to hire more African Americans and supported Jimmy Carter's presidential campaigns.

In the years following Moore's death in 1982, Delta citizens honored him in numerous ways. In 2001 the city of Cleveland renamed a major city park Amzie Moore Park, and in 2004 activists began raising funds for an Amzie Moore/Fannie Lou Hamer National Heritage Center and Civil Rights Museum near the park. Delta State University in Cleveland offered a Human Rights Fellowship in honor of Moore and fellow civil rights activist SAM BLOCK.

FURTHER READING

Dittmer, John. *Local People: The Struggle for Civil Rights in Mississippi* (1994).

Payne, Charles. *I've Got the Light of Freedom: The Organizing Tradition and the Mississippi Freedom Struggle* (1995).

TIFFANY T. HAMELIN

Moore, Archie (13 Dec. 1913?–9 Dec. 1998), boxer, was born Archibald Lee Wright, the son of Thomas Wright, a farm laborer and drifter, and Lorena Wright. He always insisted that he was born in 1916 in Collinsville, Illinois, but his mother told reporters that he was actually born in 1913 in Benoit, Mississippi. His father abandoned the family when Archie was an infant. Unable to provide for him and his older sister, his mother gave them into the care of an uncle and aunt, Cleveland and Willie Pearl Moore, who lived in St. Louis, Missouri. Archie later explained why he was given their surname: "It was less questions to be called Moore." He attended all-black schools in St. Louis, including Lincoln High School, although he never graduated. His uncle and aunt provided him with a stable upbringing, but after his uncle died in a freak accident around 1928, Moore began running with a street gang. One of his first thefts was a pair of oil lamps from his home, which he sold so that he would have money to buy boxing gloves. He later recalled of his stealing: "It was inevitable that I would be caught. I think I knew this even before I started, but somehow the urge to have a few cents in my pocket made me overlook this eventuality." After he was arrested for attempting to steal change from a motorman's box on a streetcar, he was sentenced to a three-year term at a reform school in

Boonville, Missouri. He was released early from the school for good behavior after serving twenty-two months.

Around 1933 Moore joined the Civilian Conservation Corps, working for the forestry division at a camp in Poplar Bluff, Missouri. Having determined to become a boxer, he decided to make his work at the camp a form of training. He later recalled that the other boys constantly kidded him about one daily exercise—standing upright in the bed of a truck as it drove along primitive forest roads, waiting until the last possible moment before ducking or weaving away from tree branches. The captain of the camp permitted him to organize a boxing team, which competed in Golden Gloves tournaments in southern Missouri and Illinois. Many of his fights occurred in a racially charged atmosphere; he later described one of them, against

> a white boxer named Bill Richardson in Poplar Bluff: I knocked him down with a volley of head punches about one minute into round one. His brother … was the referee. He was furious at me and told me to keep my punches up. Since I had been hitting Bill in the head I would have

Archie Moore, shown in an action pose in 1955. (AP Images.)

missed him altogether if I threw my punches any higher. But the referee said I had fouled him…. I got steamed at this and offered to fight [the referee], too. I resolved not to hit Bill any place but his head…. In the second round I dropped him with a left hook that spun his head like a top…. I heard a man at ringside say, "For two cents I'd shoot that nigger."

After the bout, the boxing team was followed back to camp by a line of cars loaded with angry "townies." They dispersed only when the camp captain threatened them with a submachine gun.

Moore first boxed professionally as a middleweight. Sources differ about the circumstances of his first professional fight, which occurred either in 1935 against "Piano Mover" Jones or in 1936 against "the Poco Kid," who was knocked out in the second round. In 1936 Moore appeared in 22 fights, winning all but 4 of them, 16 by knockout. In 1937 and 1938 he averaged one bout a month, winning 20 by knockout and losing only once. During these years he moved his base of operations from St. Louis to San Diego. He first gained prominence in 1938 when he twice fought Johnny Romero, a top-ranked middleweight contender. Romero beat Moore in a ten-round decision in the first match, but in the rematch Moore knocked Romero out in the eighth round. In 1940 Moore boxed in Australia, winning seven consecutive bouts, including two against Ron Richards, who at the time held the Australian light-heavyweight and heavyweight crowns. That year Moore married Mattie Chapman; they became estranged when he toured Australia without her and divorced soon after he returned to the United States. He had three more failed marriages during the 1940s and early 1950s, about which little is known; he had two children from these marriages. He later explained to the sportswriter Frank Deford about his difficulties with women: "You've got to marry [boxing]. And so I did. Boxing was my lover. It was my lady…. When you're married to a career, as I was, your wife must be cognizant of that."

When he returned from Australia, Moore was ranked fourth among the world's middleweights. His career almost ended in February 1941, however, when he spent five days in a coma after undergoing surgery for a perforated ulcer. During his recovery he suffered complications from peritonitis and pneumonia, and when he was released from the hospital his weight had dropped from 163 to 108 pounds. By January 1942 he had returned to the ring, winning five consecutive fights by knockout. That year he was ranked as the world's top middleweight contender. He won the California middleweight title in 1943 by defeating Jack Chase in a fifteen-round decision. In 1945 he moved from San Diego to Baltimore so he could fight on the East Coast. After knocking out Lloyd Marshall in a fight in June 1945, he became the top-ranked light-heavyweight contender. Over the next few years he lost three times to EZZARD CHARLES, a former heavyweight champion, but he defeated such well-regarded boxers as Harold Johnson and Jimmy Bivins. Although he continued to be highly ranked, for a number of reasons he was unable to get a shot at the title. Boxing historians have suggested that during these years there was an effort by promoters to "freeze out" black challengers from title bouts against white champions. In addition, the nation's boxing capital was New York City, and because of incompetent or crooked management, Moore was able to secure only two matches there between 1945 and 1953. Relegated to fighting in out-of-the-way places—such as Flint, Michigan; North Adams, Massachusetts; and Cordoba, Argentina—he was not considered a marketable boxer. In 1949 he attempted to end his relationship with one manager, Charley Johnston, but in retaliation Johnston influenced promoters to boycott Moore. He recalled bitterly that in 1950, when he was the top-ranked contender, "I fought only twice and made my living with my pool cue, hustling for small bets in neighborhood pool rooms in whatever town I was in."

Determined to gain a title bout against the light-heavyweight champion Joey Maxim, Moore mounted a letter-writing campaign to New York City newspapers. He wrote as many as thirty letters a night, winning the support of influential sportswriters, such as Red Smith at the *New York Herald Tribune*. Through the pressure of Moore's publicity efforts, he finally gained a match with Maxim, but only after guaranteeing him a $100,000 cut of the purse. On 17 December 1952, at the age of 39, he defeated Maxim in a fifteen-round unanimous decision. After the purse was divided, Moore was paid $800. He successfully defended his title against Maxim in June 1953 and in January 1954. In August 1954 he knocked out Harold Johnson in the fourteenth round to again retain his title. In 1955 he knocked out Bobo Olson, the middleweight champion, in three rounds. Moore next sought to fight the heavyweight champion, Rocky Marciano. He spent $50,000 on letter writing and advertising to prod Marciano into a bout; in a typical bit of showmanship, he put up "wanted" posters that offered a reward for the "capture and delivery" of the heavyweight champ to "sheriff Archie Moore." On 21 September 1955 the 41-year-old Moore met the 32-year-old Marciano.

In one of his greatest moments in the ring, Moore knocked Marciano down in the second round—only the second time in Marciano's career that he had gone down to the canvas. Marciano, however, came back to batter Moore for the next six rounds. At the end of the eighth round, the referee told Moore that he was stopping the fight, but Moore insisted that he would only go out on his back like a fallen champion. In the next round, Marciano knocked him out.

A right-hander at five feet eleven inches, Moore looked unimposing and somewhat flabby in the ring. *New Yorker* writer A. J. Liebling described his "commonplace body" and his "serene and scholarly aspect," comparing his features in repose to those of the actor Orson Welles. He was an analytical, careful counterfighter rather than an aggressive puncher, spending much of his time in a bout in what he called his "shell defense" to ward off blows, taking only one step for his opponent's every two, waiting for his opponent to leave himself exposed or to wear himself out. Possessing expert timing and reflexes, he reportedly could hit the light bag at a gymnasium eight hundred times in three minutes—an average of almost five times per second. He was nicknamed "the Mongoose" because of his ability to strike suddenly and then backpedal. Loquacious and funny, he was well liked by other boxers and sportswriters; Red Smith sometimes published entire letters from Moore in his column. As a champion he proved to be a good entertainer, dressing flamboyantly in a homburg and a midnight-blue tuxedo for one weigh-in and often wearing a yachting cap because "it lends the impression that you own a yacht." He also made much of his "secret" diet that he used to make weight for matches, which he claimed he had learned from watching the aborigines in Australia. "I never saw a fat aborigine," he noted. At his training camps he ate behind a screen, hidden from the prying eyes of reporters. A few years before his retirement, he revealed that the diet included drinking a cup of sauerkraut juice in the morning and chewing meat for its juices only, then spitting out the fiber.

In 1955 Moore married Joan Hardy, a model; they had five children and remained married for the rest of his life. In November 1956 he fought FLOYD PATTERSON for the heavyweight title following Marciano's retirement; Patterson knocked him out in the fifth round. In 1958 he defended his light-heavyweight title against Yvon Durelle in what boxing historians consider one of the most exciting fights of the 1950s. Durelle knocked Moore down three times in the first round and once more in round five, but Moore persevered and went on to knock Durelle out in the eleventh round. As a result of this fight, Moore was named Fighter of the Year by the Boxing Writers Association; his knockout of Durelle was the 127th of his career, setting the record for most knockouts by one fighter. In a rematch with Durelle in 1959, Moore won by a knockout in three rounds. He failed to defend his title in 1960 and 1961, and as a result his crown was stripped away by boxing's sanctioning boards in February 1962. Altogether he was light-heavyweight champion for nine successive years, longer than any other boxer. In 1962 he fought Cassius Clay (who later changed his name to MUHAMMAD ALI) and was knocked out in the fourth round; Moore thus became the only boxer to fight both Marciano and Ali. In his final professional fight, he knocked out Mike DiBiase in three rounds in March 1963, a few months before his fiftieth birthday. His career record for 231 professional bouts was 196 wins, 26 defeats, 8 draws, and one identified as "no contest." He won 143 fights by knockout and was knocked out only 8 times. In 1966 he was elected to the Boxing Hall of Fame.

Moore appeared as the slave Jim in Metro-Goldwyn-Mayer's *The Adventures of Huckleberry Finn* (1960), a film that received mixed reviews. He hoped to pursue an acting career following his retirement from boxing, and in subsequent years he won small roles in a few films, including *The Carpetbaggers* (1964), *The Fortune Cookie* (1966), and *Breakheart Pass* (1976). During the 1960s he founded an organization called Any Boy Can, which taught boxing to underprivileged youth in the San Diego area. In 1974 he helped train the heavyweight boxer GEORGE FOREMAN for his famous "Rumble in the Jungle" title bout in Zaire against Ali. In 1976 he served as an assistant coach for the Nigerian Olympic boxing team. Actively involved in efforts to teach children about the dangers of drug abuse, he worked during the 1980s as a youth boxing instructor for the federal Department of Housing and Urban Development, assigned largely to ghettos in San Diego and Los Angeles. "I try to pass on the arts I know: self-control, self-reliance, self-defense," he told a reporter. In the early 1990s he again worked as a trainer for George Foreman. He died in San Diego.

FURTHER READING
Moore, Archie. *The Archie Moore Story* (1960).
Deford, Frank. "The Ageless Warrior (Archie Moore)," *Sports Illustrated* (8 May 1989).
Obituary: *New York Times*, 10 Dec. 1998.

This entry is taken from the *American National Biography* and is published here with the permission of the American Council of Learned Societies.

THOMAS W. COLLINS JR.

Moore, Cecil Bassett (2 Apr. 1915–13 Feb. 1979), outspoken Philadelphia civil rights leader, attorney, and city councilman, was born in Yukon, West Virginia, to Alexander Moore, a physician, and Beulah Moore, a teacher whose maiden name is now unknown. A student during the Great Depression, he attended West Virginia State College from 1933 to 1934 and Bluefield State College from 1935 to 1939. He failed the final literature class needed to graduate from Bluefield State, but considered himself its alumnus ever after and took part in its alumni association.

After working in Athens, Georgia, as an insurance salesman, Moore enlisted in the Marine Corps in 1942. He saw combat against the Japanese during World War II in the Pacific. His time in the Marines imbued Moore with discipline, toughness, and command experience, emboldening him to insist on his rights.

In 1946 Moore married Theresa Wyche Lee, a Howard University graduate who later taught elementary school in Philadelphia, with whom he had three daughters, Cecily, Alexis, and Melba. In the postwar years while stationed until 1951 as a Marine sergeant at Fort Mifflin, and later as a whiskey salesman, Moore took night classes at Temple University's law school in Philadelphia. He graduated in 1953 and passed the bar in 1954, establishing a criminal defense practice serving North Central Philadelphia, a district then becoming overwhelmingly African American.

Moore's willingness to defend even those who could pay little or nothing, combined with his renowned courtroom prowess, made him one of the city's busiest lawyers. He ran for U.S. representative unsuccessfully as a Republican in 1958, but won election handily in 1962 as president of the Philadelphia chapter of the NAACP.

Moore's maverick NAACP leadership at the height of the civil rights movement transformed a cautiously reformist Philadelphia chapter into a bold, dynamic organization. Upon taking office in January 1963, Moore declared that "no longer will the plantation system of white men appointing our leaders exist in Philadelphia" (Countryman, 126). Within a few years, the chapter's membership increased from 7,000 to more than 30,000—Moore sometimes claimed 60,000—with the new ranks drawn primarily from the black working class.

Moore's first act was to criticize the Ford Foundation for not involving blacks in an impending study of North Philadelphia. When the foundation ignored him, he threatened a black boycott of Ford Motor Company. Judge RAYMOND PACE ALEXANDER and other prominent Philadelphia blacks issued a letter critical of Moore, stating that black involvement could be achieved "without bombast, silly threats, and other ineffective antics" (Early, 92–93). Moore promptly erected a sign denouncing his critics as "15 UNCLE TOMS AND AN AUNT DINAH" (*Time*, 11 Sept. 1964). When the Ford Foundation appointed black staff to its Philadelphia study, Moore claimed victory.

Moore's defiant style symbolized the new refusal of urban blacks in the 1960s to tolerate liberal paternalism or black leaders seen as beholden to the white-dominated power structure. He scorned "so-called Northern white liberals" and blasted "your so-called middle-class Negro" as "a 'professional Negro' who doesn't come into contact with the masses" (*Time*, 11 Sept. 1964). His audacity, humor, and utter disregard for Philadelphia's Democratic machine made Moore wildly popular with his base supporters. With more than a hint of the rascal about him, he loved cigars, bourbon, silk suits, and flamboyant language. His ego was legendary. "I'm the goddamn boss," he once said, and, replying to a critic who called him "the self-appointed savior of the Negro in Philadelphia," Moore retorted, "I'm not self-appointed. I was elected" (*Time*, 11 Sept. 1964). Moore resided in North Philadelphia long after other black professionals began to flee the inner city. "I run a grassroots group, not a cocktail-party, tea-sipping, fashion-show-attending group of exhibitionists," he said. "That's the difference. Those things divide the Negro, separate him into classes. I want nothing to divide the Negro; I want a one-class Negro community. I'd be lost if I had to move up to Mount Airy or one of those places where I'd have to be so damned respectable that I couldn't go out and stand on a street corner on Saturday night" (*Time*, 11 Sept. 1964).

Moore's appeals to cross-class racial solidarity, all-black mobilization, self-help, self-defense, and direct action lent him a militant, almost nationalist, charisma. His objective, however, was to break down obstacles to full participation in the wider society. He secured his position as the foremost civil rights leader in Philadelphia in 1963 by blocking the construction site of the Strawberry Mansion Junior High School in repudiation of all-white building trades unions. Moore's subsequent negotiations with the Trailways and Greyhound bus companies yielded agreements to hire blacks into previously white-exclusive job categories.

When massive rioting erupted in Philadelphia in August 1964, resulting in two deaths, 339 injuries, and millions of dollars in property damage, Moore discouraged the looting from a sound truck. Crowds resisted his advice, but he was credited with helping limit the violence and destruction to three days. Moore sought a constructive release for black anger. In 1964, after threatening demonstrations, Moore obtained a court order forbidding the Mummers, an annual New Year's Day parade, from appearing in blackface. His most spectacular campaign came in 1965 when he led a seven-month demonstration to change the charter of Girard College, a whites-only school for orphans located in the heart of North Philadelphia. The institution's high walls symbolized racial barriers. "It's a perpetual red flag. A boy wakes up every morning to see a reminder that he's inferior," said Moore (*Time*, 23 July 1965). In 1968 the U.S. Supreme Court compelled the integration of Girard College.

In 1965 Moore won reelection as NAACP chapter president by a 5-to-1 margin against moderate minister Rev. Henry Nichols. The national NAACP under ROY WILKINS, who had not escaped Moore's sharp tongue, responded by carving up the Philadelphia branch into five units. Moore charged that the national office was trying "to discredit and destroy militant, independent-thinking chapters" (Countryman, 230). He resisted his chapter's fragmentation for several years in court and by picketing the NAACP national convention, but lost out in 1967. That year Moore ran unsuccessfully for mayor as the candidate of the Political Freedom Rights Party. His wife died in 1970, and Moore was remarried to Helen Golden Boyer in 1972. He was elected city councilman in 1975 as a Democrat from the Fifth District, serving until his death from a cardiac arrest brought on by kidney failure.

Moore's name is now etched into the geography of Philadelphia. The Cecil B. Moore Homes, a low-income housing complex, was christened in 1985. In 1986 the city renamed part of Columbia Avenue in North Philadelphia as Cecil B. Moore Avenue. Denounced in his lifetime as arrogant, obstreperous, profane, and demagogic, Moore was often celebrated after his death. "Without his efforts," wrote the *Philadelphia Inquirer* editorial board member Claude Lewis in 1985, "chances are there would be no black mayor, no black president of City Council, no black superintendent of schools, no high-ranking black police officers, nor any of the other highly placed blacks in Philadelphia government today" (*Philadelphia Inquirer*, 23 Dec. 1985).

FURTHER READING

Countryman, Matthew J. *Up South: Civil Rights and Black Power in Philadelphia* (2006).

Early, Gerald L. *This Is Where I Came In: Black America in the 1960s* (2003).

Sugrue, Thomas. "Affirmative Action from Below: Civil Rights, the Building Trades, and the Politics of Racial Equality in the North, 1945–1969," *Journal of American History* (June 2004).

Obituaries: *Philadelphia Inquirer*, 13 Feb. 1979; *The New York Times*, 14 Feb. 1979.

CHRISTOPHER PHELPS

Moore, Charles (22 May 1928–23 Jan. 1986), dancer, choreographer, and teacher, was born in Cleveland, Ohio, to parents whose names and occupations are unknown. As a child he was a popular soprano soloist in churches and studied voice at the Karamu House, a local arts center devoted to celebrating the African American experience through the arts in a racially integrated environment. As he grew older Moore studied modern dance with Eleanor Frampton at the cultural center. He had the opportunity to see ASADATA DAFORA, the famed West African choreographer and dancer, perform the *Ostrich Dance* at Severance Hall. This event so moved Moore toward his future work in re-creating African dance that, as he explained in the 1984 documentary by Chris Hegedus and D. A. Pennebaker, *Dance Black America*, he "never forgot that first glimpse of Africa."

In 1948 Moore received a Charles Weidman dance scholarship and moved to New York City. There he learned ballet and modern and African dance from Weidman, PEARL PRIMUS, Dafora, and KATHERINE DUNHAM. He also studied with the Nigerian dancers M. Olatunji and S. Ilori and with the Ghanaian dancers Kobla Ladzekpo and A. Opoku. From 1952 to 1960 Moore was a member of Dunham's dance company. At the Dunham School of Dance and Theater he also met his future wife, the dancer and performer Ella Thompson. They married in 1960 and had one son. In 1959 Moore began teaching Dunham's technique in New York City at the Clark Center, the New Dance Group Studio, and Harlem Youth Activities (Har-You-Act). He later taught her technique at his own school.

He also taught dance at Hunter College, Medgar Evers College, City College, and the Hanson Place Methodist Church in Brooklyn.

Working with this group of celebrated instructors, performers, and choreographers of African and African-inspired dance fostered Moore's passion for creating, preserving, and performing the traditional dances of Africa. "There is a pride in these dances and every one of them has something in it that makes you feel gorgeous. And they're so important historically. Before Dafora, about all we knew of Africa was what we saw in the Tarzan movies," Moore explained to the dance critic Jennifer Dunning (*New York Times*, 29 Feb. 1996).

Moore became a well-respected performer and was featured in many dance companies, including those of Dunham, GEOFFREY HOLDER, Donald McKayle, Pearl Primus, TALLEY BEATTY, JEAN-LEON DESTINÉ, and ALVIN AILEY. He was known for fully embodying the roles given to him. He said of performing with Dunham, "When I danced her dance, *Shango*, I wasn't Charles Moore anymore, I was possessed. You had to be in order to do the dance" (*Dance Black America*). Moore also performed on Broadway in several productions, including the revival of *House of Flowers* in 1954–1955 and *Carmen Jones* in 1956, *Jamaica* from 1957 to 1959, *Kwamina* in 1961, *The Zulu and the Zayda* from 1965 to 1966, *Trumpets of the Lord* in 1969, and *Les Blancs* in 1970. In 1968–1969 he was in the New York City Opera production of *Bomarzo*. He also appeared on television with HARRY BELAFONTE, SAMMY DAVIS JR., Anne Bancroft, and Lauren Bacall.

In 1974 Moore and his wife founded the Charles Moore Center for Ethnic Studies in New York City under the parent company Dances and Drums of Africa, one of the oldest nonprofit African American arts organizations in Brooklyn. At that time he also established the Charles Moore Dance Theatre and the Charles Moore Youth Ensemble "to demonstrate the beauty and variety of African, Caribbean, and African American culture." The center educated children and adults in full programs of modern and African dance and percussion. Through diligent study and research, Moore used his company to carefully reconstruct many African dances that were considered lost. He creatively blended the techniques of his teachers with his own interpretations. His company specialized in authentic re-creations of African and Caribbean dances, revivals of works by great African choreographers, and original pieces created out of the spirit of African

and Caribbean traditional dances, "with respect for heritage and a boldness and jubilation that make tradition come alive." His company included master drummers, such as Chief Bey, as well as dancers. He often brought renowned African musicians and dancers to the United States to teach and perform. From 1974 to 1985 his company performed nationally and internationally.

One of Moore's most celebrated pieces was his interpretation and performance of Dafora's *Ostrich Dance* and *Awassa Astrige* (1932). Wearing a skirt of ostrich feathers, Moore strutted about the stage, torso undulating, the wide expanse of his arms rippling as his head jutted forward rhythmically. Each bit of arm was distinctly articulated. He held his head proudly, his eyes were alert, and his movement was constant, repetitive, and focused. Moore became an ostrich. "It's a tribute to Moore that his choreography has kept so close to some of the first African dances to be seen in this country" (Michael Robertson, "From Soho to Africa," *Dance Magazine*, Oct. 1976). *Dance Black America* includes Moore's performance of the *Ostrich Dance*, as well as his company's performance of Dunham's *Shango*.

Though Moore never went to Africa, his reconstructions of traditional African dances, such as *Bundao*, *Spear Dance*, *Sacred Forest*, and *African Congo*, were well respected and inspired a wealth of related dances in the repertoires of other African dance companies in the United States. At the time of his death in New York, Moore was working on *Traces: An American Suite*, an overview of American black dance encompassing slavery to the early 1940s. Jennifer Dunning wrote that *Traces* "ought to be required viewing for anyone who believes that multiculturalism and traditional black American arts are inseparable concepts" ("Moore Troupe Makes a Point on Popular Black Culture," *New York Times*, 6 Mar. 1993). *Traces* was completed under the care of his wife with additional choreography by Eleanor Harris and Pepsi Bethel.

After Moore's death, LOUIS JOHNSON created *Spirit: A Dance for Charles* to celebrate Moore's devotion to the power of African music and dance. Johnson's tribute is a testament to Moore's influential role in popularizing African dance with the American public.

FURTHER READING

DeFrantz, Thomas F., ed. *Dancing Many Drums: Excavations in African American Dance* (2002).
Emery, Lynne Fauley. *Black Dance from 1619 to Today*, 2d ed. (1988).

Long, Richard A. *The Black Tradition in American Dance* (1989).

Manning, Susan. *Modern Dance, Negro Dance: Race in Motion* (2004).

Obituary: *New York Times*, 25 Jan. 1986.

This entry is taken from the *American National Biography* and is published here with the permission of the American Council of Learned Societies.

JADA SHAPIRO

Moore, Dorothy Rudd (4 June 1940–), composer, singer, pianist, teacher, and poet, was born in New Castle, Delaware, the oldest of six children: five girls and one boy. Her father, James M. Rudd, was a-government worker in logistics and her mother, L. Rebecca Ryan Rudd, was a pianist and singer.

In 1963 Moore graduated magna cum laude from Howard University, where she studied composition with Mark Fax, piano with Thomas Kerr, and voice with Louise Burge. ADOLPHUS HAILSTORK, an internationally renowned composer and professor of composition, was one of her Howard classmates. Moore became fascinated with mathematical connections to music during her student days at Howard, where she delved into harmony, counterpoint, and the structural cohesiveness of Johann Sebastian Bach. A scholar of her art form, she also, early on, became a student of melodic shape and inventiveness. Moore viewed composing as being an organic process, the unfolding of ideas, each score a creative entity unto itself. Moore majored in music theory and composition, and minored in piano and voice. A Lucy Moten fellowship made it possible, after graduation, for Moore to study composition with Nadia Boulanger at the Conservatoire de Musique in Fontainebleau, France. When she returned to the United States, she studied composition privately, in New York, with the Columbia University professor Chou Wen Chung. She was married to the distinguished cellist, conductor, and composer, Kermit Moore in 1964.

Moore's compositional output was broad and comprehensive: instrumental solo works for cello, clarinet, piano, and violin; small instrumental ensembles; chamber orchestra; full orchestra; concert band; solo voice and voice with instrumental ensemble; choral music; and the opera, for which she wrote both libretto and music for FREDERICK DOUGLASS (commissioned by Opera Ebony and premiered by Opera Ebony in 1985). Commissions came from individual artists such as Richard Elias, Kermit Moore, and William Brown; and performing arts organizations such as the Reston Trio, Brooklyn Philharmonic, Boys Choir of Harlem, and Opera Ebony. Moore's scores, which began to be programmed in major settings while she was still a student at Howard, were performed throughout the United States, Europe, South America, and Asia. A number of her compositions were published and she had an impressive discography.

Moore received grants from the American Music Center (1972), New York State Council of the Arts (1985), and beginning in the 1970s Meet the Composer. She cofounded the Society of Black Composers (1968) with her husband. She served on numerous boards and panels, including the New York State Council of the Arts (1988–1990), the composers panel for the Illinois Arts Council (1987), the Wisconsin Arts Board (1991), and two National Endowment for the Arts boards: music recording, 1986–1988; and composer panel, 1988. Moore became a member of the New York Singing Teachers Association and New York Women Composers in 1972, and the American Composers Alliance and Broadcast Music Incorporated in 1973. In addition to teaching voice and sight singing in a New York studio, she served on the faculties of Harlem School of the Arts as a teacher of theory and piano (1965–1966) and on that of New York University (1969) and Bronx Community College (1971) as a professor of music history and appreciation.

Musicologists have found Moore's compositions to be involved, yet melodic; intense, but accessible; intellectual, but not beyond reach. Critics have said that her works show giftedness and creativity; original and intense lyricism through complex harmonic and contrapuntal texture.

From a grounding in childhood and high school, through a rich college experience, and development far beyond, Moore's life, like her philosophy of composition (a philosophy reborn, revisited, and revived, with, through, and within each compositional project), was an organically artistic and aesthetic experience. Her philosophy of composition kept her writing fresh and alive with possibility. Above all, Moore refused to let "composer" be defined for her by the "majority" community. She believed that African American composers should be accepted as organic craftspersons and not be expected to limit themselves to those genres that were identified as being stylistically black. Moore effectively acted upon her philosophy through her catalog of compositions. Her scores were the articulation of creative and intellectual ideas that went far beyond racial identity.

FURTHER READING

Cheatham, Wallace McClain. *Dialogues on Opera and the African American Experience* (1997).

Floyd, Samuel A., Jr., ed. *International Dictionary of Black Composers*, vol 2. (1999).

Walker-Hill, Helen. *From Spirituals to Symphonies African American Women Composers and Their Music* (2002).

Williams, Ora. *American Black Women in the Arts and Social Sciences* (1973).

WALLACE MCCLAIN CHEATHAM

Moore, Frederick Randolph (16 June 1857–1 Mar. 1943), journalist and politician, was born in Prince William County, Virginia, the son of Eugene Moore and Evelina Diggs, whose occupations are unknown. Having left Virginia in early childhood, Fred Moore grew up in Washington, D.C., where he attended public schools and sold newspapers to help support himself and his family. At age eighteen he began work as a messenger for the U.S. Treasury Department, and a few years later he was the personal messenger for the secretary of the treasury. He worked under six successive secretaries and traveled to Europe in 1887 with Secretary Daniel Manning. Also in 1887 Moore resigned from the Treasury Department and moved to New York City, where he became a clerk at the Western National Bank, which later merged with the National Bank of Commerce; he held the position of clerk for eighteen years.

Moore began his career as a journalist in New York City as general manager and then editor and publisher in 1904 of the *Colored American Magazine*. Originating in Boston in 1900, the magazine changed under Moore's editorship from a mainly literary magazine into one that stressed black economic advancement. Moore's purchase of the magazine and its removal to New York were aided by the secret financial support of the influential black educator BOOKER T. WASHINGTON. Washington wanted a publication that promoted his philosophy of black economic development, and he supported editors who accepted his conservative position on black political and civil rights. Washington also wanted to silence opponents like W. E. B. DuBois and WILLIAM MONROE TROTTER, who condemned him repeatedly for emphasizing vocational training rather than challenging lynching, disenfranchisement, and Jim Crow legislation. Moore shared Washington's belief in cultivating economic development in the black community as a means for gaining political equality. Black unity was key to Moore's political and economic philosophy. He believed that African Americans should own their own homes and businesses in their communities. Black success in this endeavor, Moore thought, would mean political and economic equality.

Consequently, as editor of the *Colored American Magazine*, Moore explained that the new focus of the periodical was to illustrate "the successes of our people as a whole and as individuals." In this way the editor hoped that the magazine would reach "the masses of the people," not merely "those who are highly educated and cultured." The *Colored American Magazine* became a didactic tool that encouraged African Americans to become entrepreneurs and, equally important, to patronize black businesses. The majority of black Americans needed, Moore argued, "information of the doings of the members of the race rather [than] the writing of dreamers or theorists." Yet Moore did not ignore political issues. He consistently published articles and wrote editorials that condemned disenfranchisement and lynching. At the same time, Washington's public policy of accommodationism and gradualism regarding southern black political and legal rights was promoted through articles by Washington and pro-Washington writers. Tuskegee Institute, Washington's agricultural and vocational training school in Alabama, received extensive coverage. Most important, there were no longer any attacks on Washington in the *Colored American Magazine*, as there had been before Moore became editor.

In 1907 Moore again advanced through Washington's clandestine maneuvering and financial support by becoming editor and publisher of the *New York Age*. Published under various names and editors this weekly newspaper had become the most prominent black paper in the country under the editorship of T. THOMAS FORTUNE. Fortune supported Washington's goals but not his accommodationist strategy or his loyalty to the Republican Party. Under Moore's editorship the *Age* became a much more partisan paper. However, even though he was a devoted Republican, Moore did not endorse Washington or Republican Party policies completely; in fact, he challenged them on the editorial pages of the *Age*, condemning Republican quiescence on lynching and disenfranchisement and criticizing white southern political inequities and brutality.

Moore redirected the *Age* toward his own interest in black business development, and he highlighted such activities. Numerous articles featured the successes of black businessmen and businesswomen, stressing not only their achievements but also a work ethic of industry, frugality, and sobriety. Moreover, Moore almost entirely ignored black radicals like DuBois, Trotter, and MARCUS GARVEY. And as he had done with the *Colored American Magazine*, which died under new editorship in 1909, Moore added special features and increased the circulation of the *Age* to about twenty-seven thousand in 1937.

After Washington's death in 1915 Moore was more outspoken in his support for southern black migration and political protest, two activities that Washington had decried. After a trip to the South Moore in 1917 urged southern blacks to agitate for fair treatment: "Now is the time for the Negroes of the South to speak out for their rights—not offensively but frankly." He began publishing speeches by liberals like ADAM CLAYTON POWELL SR., who called in 1917 for blacks to take advantage of the nation's need for manpower and wage a "bloodless war" for constitutional rights. By 1924 the *Age* focused extensively on Harlem, where Moore had moved, and it revealed his concern for social issues, including medical services for Harlem residents. In the 1920s and 1930s the *Age* supported boycotts of white Harlem merchants who refused to employ blacks in their stores, and advocated city government investment in the rehabilitation of substandard housing for the poor. Moore's last contributions to the *Age* were during the early years of U.S. involvement in World War II when he supported A. PHILIP RANDOLPH's March on Washington movement, which demanded fair employment practices in the defense industry. Still, Moore's firm belief in black economic development and black patronage of black business remained a prominent theme in the newspaper.

Moore's career in journalism coexisted with the development of his own business interests. Consistent with his philosophy of racial solidarity and black economic development, in 1893 he helped establish the Afro-American Investment and Building Company, which bought New Jersey and New York property and sold it to blacks at reasonable interest rates. By late 1904 Moore was owner of the Moore Publishing and Printing Company, which published both the *Colored American Magazine* and the *New York Age*. Moore noted with pride that the company was owned by blacks and "that all of the mechanical work of construction connected with publishing the magazine has been done by members of the race exclusively." Also in 1904 he was organizer and in the following year he was general secretary of the National Negro Business League, an organization that Washington created to promote black business. Moore was secretary and treasurer in 1904 of an investment company, the Afro American Realty Company, which purchased Harlem property to sell or rent to New York City blacks in need of decent housing. Although the company failed in 1908, Afro-American Realty played a significant role in creating a predominantly black Harlem community.

Moore was also a politician and community activist. Always a faithful Republican, he began his political career as district captain in his Brooklyn community. In 1904 he was appointed deputy collector of internal revenue but resigned within a few months to become an organizer of the National Negro Business League. Moore also acted as a delegate or alternate delegate to several Republican National Conventions and served on the National Negro Republican Committee from 1908 to 1920. Although he quit after three months and did not actually leave the United States, Moore was appointed minister of Liberia by President William Howard Taft in 1912. After moving to Harlem, Moore was elected to the New York City Board of Aldermen for the Nineteenth District in 1927, replacing a white incumbent. He was reelected to this position in 1929.

Moore's community activism is illustrated by the fact that until his death at age eighty-five he was president of the Parent Teacher Association of the local public school in his neighborhood. More important, Moore helped found the National Urban League in 1911. The Urban League grew out of several northern interracial urban service organizations established to help the great wave of black migrants from the South. Moore had served on the board of several of these groups and was founder and chairman of the New York Association for the Protection of Colored Women in 1905, an organization created to protect southern black women migrants from labor exploitation in the North. He was also active in the National League for the Protection of Colored Women, founded the following year.

Moore married Ida Lawrence, a native of Washington, D.C., in 1879. The Moores had eighteen children, six of whom lived to adulthood. Actively involved with the *Age* until 1942, Moore died in New York City.

FURTHER READING

Detweiler, Frederick. *The Negro Press in the United States* (1922; repr. 1968).

Meier, August. "Booker T. Washington and the Negro Press: With Special Reference to the *Colored American Magazine*," *Journal of Negro History* 38 (Jan. 1953).

Thornbrough, Emma L. "More Light on Booker T. Washington and the New York *Age*," *Journal of Negro History* 43 (Jan. 1958).

Wolseley, Roland. *The Black Press, U.S.A.* (1971).

This entry is taken from the *American National Biography* and is published here with the permission of the American Council of Learned Societies.

RITA ROBERTS

Moore, Gwen (18 Apr. 1951–) U.S. congresswoman, was born Gwendolynne Sophia Moore in Racine, Wisconsin, the eighth of nine children. Her father was a member of the United Auto Workers union, and her mother, Beatrice Dailey Lee, taught English in Milwaukee Public Schools. Moore served as student council president at Milwaukee's North Division High School, graduating in 1969. She earned a bachelor's degree in political science from Marquette University in 1978, having entered as an expectant single mother receiving Aid to Families with Dependent Children (AFDC).

Already on the board of Midtown Neighborhood Association, representing the inner city area where she grew up, Moore enlisted with Volunteers in Service to America (VISTA), leading development of Cream City Credit Union, for which she was awarded "VISTA Volunteer of the Decade" for 1976–1986. The first shareholders were recruited by a persistent door-to-door campaign to prove that Cream City could become a viable financial institution in the community. In the following years, she worked for Milwaukee Department of City Development, Wisconsin Department of Employment Relations, and Wisconsin Housing and Economic Development Authority.

Elected to the Wisconsin state assembly in 1988, she represented the most racially diverse district in the state, estimated to be fifty percent black, five percent Hispanic, four percent Asian, one percent Native American, and about forty percent white (*MJS*, 11 Aug. 1991). Moore remained active in street politics as well as the legislative arena, leading a rally in October 1990 protesting President George H. W. Bush's veto of the Civil Rights Act of 1990.

Moore chaired the assembly's Urban Infrastructure Committee.

Moore and other black assembly representatives opposed Governor Tommy Thompson's nomination of Sheboygan businessman Terry Kohler to the University of Wisconsin's board of regents, despite his endorsement by the black-oriented *Milwaukee Community Journal*. Moore was concerned that Kohler had not only referred to homosexuals as "queers" but also asserted that blacks in South Africa were in the "Stone Age," so that it would be disastrous to give them the right to vote. The *Community Journal* endorsed Kohler as "a political conservative whose agenda often coincides with that of a growing segment of the African-American community," citing his financial contributions to black colleges and support of a school choice voucher program (*MJS*, 11 June 1991).

Familiar with all of Milwaukee's traditional ethnic communities, Moore learned German, French, and Spanish, became conversant with the city's varied Slavic cultures, and also learned Hebrew from a niece who taught the language, while assisting the recently arrived Hmong community. After the 1990 census, Moore supported creation of black-influenced districts, but kept a wary eye on Republican interest in 90- percent black districts, which would reduce overall Democratic representation in the legislature. In 1992 she ran for the newly created 4th state senate district, carefully drawn as a minority influenced district with a 45 percent black voting-age population. Winning a Democratic primary against fellow representative Louis Fortis, Moore swept the general election, becoming the first black woman to serve in the state senate.

Moore was a persistent and detailed critic of Governor Tommy Thompson's W-2 program, variously referenced as "Wisconsin Works" or "Work not Welfare," which became a forerunner of the 1996 national compromise between Democratic President Bill Clinton and the Republican House Speaker Newt Gingrich on "ending welfare as we know it." Moore observed that with insufficient job openings to absorb those receiving welfare payments, dead-end jobs paying minimum wage would leave children in poverty: "McDonald's will not be able to absorb your entire 'Work not Welfare' proposal" (*MJS*, 2 Sept. 1993). As a member of the Legislative Working Group on Welfare Reform, she led efforts to include substantial educational, job training, and child-care programs in any efforts to move welfare recipients into the workforce (*MJS*, 18 Aug 1994), an idea patronizingly resisted by Thompson's administration as having "people go to graduate school on welfare" (*MJS*, 2 Sept. 1993).

In 1996 she was chosen as president pro tem of the senate, and served in that role through 1998. In 1997 she observed that when first elected, she had expected to be "making things happen, getting things done" and was amazed at the amount of time she had to spend "fighting dumb ideas, warding off the worst evils" (*MJS*, 27 July 1997). In 2000, Moore received a Harvard University Certificate for Senior Executives in State and Local Government.

In 2004 Moore entered the Democratic primary to succeed the retiring incumbent congressman Jerry Kleczka, and won 64 percent of the vote in a three-way race, taking first place in two-thirds of the wards in the city of Milwaukee, and second place in many others. During the primary campaign, while pundits advised that she needed to focus on voter turnout in predominantly black wards, Moore cheerfully observed "I don't see a racial divide—everybody's going to vote for me" (*MJS*, 25 Aug. 2004).

In the general election, she carried the Democratic-leaning district by the usual margin of 70 percent, winning the suburbs of Cudahy, St. Francis, South Milwaukee, West Milwaukee, and the older portions of West Allis, as well as the city of Milwaukee. Moore called on supporters to remain engaged "to preserve life, preserve resources and start focusing on a domestic agenda that's going to relieve us of a dearth of jobs, a lack of health care and a divestment in educational opportunities," while her Republican opponent, the attorney Gerald H. Boyle, said, "I think we healed a lot of wounds in this city" with an issue-oriented campaign. (*MJS*, 3 Nov. 2004).

Assigned in her freshman year to the House Financial Services Committee, and the Committee on Small Business, Moore continued to focus on the community and job development issues that dominated her legislative career. During her second term she was appointed to the Budget Committee. Moore emphasized support for working families, including legislation to increase the minimum wage, establish universal health care, and protect overtime pay, and to stimulate economic growth in the United States. She supported environmental protection, which she linked to economic issues on the grounds that impoverished citizens suffer the worst of toxic waste dumping.

Some years before corporate executive compensation became a hot-button public issue (in the wake of the 2008–2009 financial melt-down),

Moore cosponsored the Protection Against Executive Compensation Abuse Act in 2006. In her own district, she reported, Delphi corporation moved a bankruptcy court to cancel its contract with the United Auto Workers, while offering six hundred executives and managers $510 million in compensation, some labeled as "performance bonuses" (*Protecting Investors and Fostering Efficient Markets: A Review of the SEC Agenda*, 25 May 2006, House Financial Services Committee, Serial 109–97, 64).

In 2007 Moore received the Helen Way Klinger College of Arts and Sciences Distinguished Alumna Award from her alma mater, Marquette University. "Although God imbued me with the basic intelligence to succeed," she said in accepting the honor, "I don't know if my background would have enabled me to graduate had there not been an intervention on the part of the university in disrupting the sociological train wreck of a poor person."

A firm supporter of health care reform, Moore expressed reservations that the bill finally taking shape in early 2010 was insufficient, but voted for the Patient Protection and Affordable Care Act, telling reporters, "This is a tremendous, tremendous moment" when the final bill was passed and sent to President BARACK OBAMA for signature. Moore has three children and three grandchildren.

FURTHER READING

Information on Moore's political career can found in the pages of the *Milwaukee Journal-Sentinel* (*MJS*), 1991–2010.

Clarke, Robyn D. "Striving for More: Gwen Moore Worked her Way from Welfare to Washington." *Black Enterprise*, June 2005 vol. 35, 290–291.

Samuel, Terence. "Uphill Battle." *The Crisis*, March/April 2005, 22–27.

CHARLES ROSENBERG

Moore, Harry Tyson (18 Nov. 1905–25 Dec. 1951), civil rights martyr and educator, was born in Houston, Florida, the son of S. Johnny Moore, a farmer and store owner, and Rosalea A. Tyson, an insurance agent. Harry spent most of his early life in Suwannee County, attending school, performing chores on the farm, riding horses, and fishing. Living with aunts where he could obtain a better education, he received portions of his schooling in Daytona Beach and Jacksonville prior to attending and graduating in 1925 from high school at Florida Normal Institute in Live Oak (later Florida Memorial University in Miami). Later, while teaching in Brevard County, he received his AA (1936) and B.S. (1951) degrees from Bethune-Cookman College in Daytona Beach. Harry married Harriette V. Sims, a teacher, and the couple had two daughters, Annie Rosalea and Juanita Evangeline. The Moore family made its home in the small rural town of Mims, Florida.

Moore began his career in education in Brevard County—teaching at Cocoa Elementary School (1925–1927), serving as principal of Titusville Junior High (1927–1936), and principal and teacher at Mims Elementary School (1936–1946). In order to help improve condition at the schools in the county and in black society in general, he founded the Brevard County Branch of the NAACP in 1934, and served as its president. He also was active with the Florida State Teachers' Association, serving as regional president in 1937 when the organization led the fight for equalization of salaries for African American teachers in the state. In 1941 Moore became the founding president of the Florida Conference of NAACP Branches, a position he held until 1946, after which he served as executive secretary until 1951.

Moore campaigned tirelessly for equal educational opportunities, equal political participation, and the protections of due process of law for all Americans. He understood that to realize these rights would require the building and maintaining of a strong NAACP state conference. He traveled the dusty roads and highways of virtually every county seeking new members and additional funds. Under his leadership, the conference grew from nine branches in 1941 to fifty-six in 1946. In making his appeals, Moore reminded church congregations and those who attended mass meetings that there was a price to be paid for freedom, and those who wanted it should be willing to make the sacrifice.

For several years, Moore fought for the equalization of education, but he learned from long experience that there was no such thing as "separate, but equal" education. Following this realization, his primary goal became the elimination of the Jim Crow educational system. In addition to opposing vigorously "second class" school facilities for African Americans, he opposed "out of state tuition,"—whereby the state of Florida reimbursed students for first-class travel and for tuition for them to attend graduate or professional schools in other states—and the designation of the all-black Florida A&M College to university status, with substandard programs.

Perceiving the ballot as the most important vehicle for obtaining racial equality, in August 1944 Moore spearheaded the organizing of the Progressive Voters League (PVL) and became its executive secretary. Throughout its existence, the PVL registered thousands of new black voters in Florida, endorsed candidates favorable to the black community, and successfully thwarted legislators' attempts to disenfranchise African Americans. As voting participation of blacks increased, the racist tone of political campaigning decreased. White officer-seekers, valuing black voters, began to be less vocal in their use of racist slurs, and in some cases more generous in making limited political promises, for greater police protection and better garbage service, for example.

Moore's voice was heard loudly against lynching, mob action, and police brutality in Florida. At a time when many African Americans preferred to remain silent when abused, he complained to governors, the Justice Department, and to President Harry S. Truman. Moore openly deplored the complicity of law-enforcement in vicious racial crimes, and urged two Florida governors—Millard Caldwell and Fuller Warren—to suspend and punish the involved officials. Moore sought to obtain justice for the victims through the courts, and he fought vigorously to convince state and national legislators to pass anti-lynching laws.

Moore and his wife, Harriette, paid dearly for their courageous civil rights activities. In 1946 the Brevard County School Board refused to renew their teaching contracts. With her teaching career ended in her home county, Harriette accepted a teaching position in Palm Beach County, more than a hundred miles away. Deciding to devote full time to his civil rights efforts, Harry assumed employment as executive secretary of the Florida Conference of NAACP Branches. In November 1951 he suffered a major setback when the conference abolished his office, citing its financial situation as the major reason for its action. Moore, determined to continue his work, agreed to serve as state coordinator, without pay.

The most tragic sacrifice of Harry and Harriette Moore occurred on Christmas night 1951. After they returned from a family dinner at her mother's home, a bomb exploded under their bedroom, seriously injuring them. Harry Moore died en route to an all black hospital in a neighboring county, and Harriette Moore died nine days later. Although the FBI and state authorities investigated the bombing, no one was ever indicted. Five decades later, in response to calls for reopening the case, Florida's attorney general Charlie Crist launched a new investigation, and reported in 2006 that four Klansmen—all dead—were the culprits.

For his contribution to the civil rights cause, Harry T. Moore has been recognized in many ways. The NAACP honored him in 1952 by presenting him, posthumously, its Spingarn Medal, and the State of Florida named him one of its two Great Floridians for 2007. In Brevard County he and his wife have been honored in a variety of ways. The City of Titusville named its Social Service Center after him in 1985, and the Brevard County Community College of Cocoa established a multicultural center for the improvement of human relations in their names in 1995. Brevard County officials named its newly built justice center in Viera after the civil rights leaders in 2002, and two years later they, with the support of the state and local NAACP branches, erected and dedicated the Harry T. and Harriette V. Moore Cultural Complex in Mims.

Following the victorious *Sweat v. Painter* decision of the U.S. Supreme Court in 1950, the NAACP decided to seek the end of all segregated education, rather than equalizing it. On the state level, Moore embraced that position and sought to accomplish that goal in Florida. Even though he was assassinated prior to the *Brown v. Board of Education* decision of 1954, his work contributed to it. Likewise, several of his letters to members of Congress sought the adoption of legislation similar to some of the provisions of the 1964 Civil Rights Act and the 1965 Voting Rights Act.

FURTHER READING

Harry T. Moore's letters are housed in the NAACP files in the Manuscript Division of the Library of Congress.

Clark, James C. "Civil Rights Leaders Harry T. Moore and the Ku Klux Klan in Florida," *Florida Historical Quarterly*, 73 (Oct. 1994).

Emmons, Caroline S. "Somebody Has Got to Do That Work: Harry T. Moore and the Struggle for Black Voting Rights in Florida," *Journal of Negro History* 82 (Spring 1997).

Green, Ben. *Before His Time: The Untold Story of Harry T. Moore, America's First Civil Rights Martyr* (1999).

JAKE C. MILLER

Moore, John Jamison (c. 1814–9 Dec. 1893), minister and activist, was born in Berkley County, at that time a part of Virginia, later West Virginia, to Fannie Riedoubt, a free black woman who had been kidnapped into slavery, and an enslaved man surnamed Hodge. Sources vary as to his birthdate, citing from 1804 to 1818; Moore was one of the family's early owner's surnames. When Moore was six, his parents attempted to escape with their six children. They were captured, and four of the children were sold south. Moore, his brother William, and his parents finally escaped to Pennsylvania a few years later. Moore was bound out to an area farmer, in part because his parents' owner continued to pursue them. Moore did keep in contact with his parents, though, and as late as 1870 his mother was living with him.

Moore worked a variety of jobs and moved to Harrisburg as a teenager. He had learned to read and write while bound, and while in Harrisburg he hired tutors to help him learn Hebrew, Latin, and Greek. In 1835 he was licensed to preach and entered the Philadelphia Conference of the African Methodist Episcopal Zion (AMEZ) Church. He preached throughout Pennsylvania, Ohio, and Maryland, and he served as the conference's assistant secretary in 1843 and secretary from 1845 to 1851. At some point prior to 1850 he married a Pennsylvania-born free African American woman whose first name was Francis. They do not appear to have had children.

In 1852 the couple moved to California, where they settled in San Francisco. Moore quickly became a leading figure in the AMEZ Church's growth in northern California, worked actively in a range of civil rights battles (including those for equal education and black testimony rights), and in 1854 was engaged as the first teacher at an all-black school in San Francisco that was partially sponsored by St. Cyprian's AME Church. This work, like most of his activities in California, bridged the AME-AMEZ divide and placed him in close contact with figures such as pioneering California AME ministers THOMAS M. D. WARD and BARNEY FLETCHER. Moore also worked closely with JONAS H. TOWNSEND in founding the San Francisco-based *Mirror of the Times*.

Though Moore, like many blacks in northern California, briefly immigrated to British Columbia in the late 1850s, he returned to California, where he continued to work for church goals, for education, and for broader civil rights. He served as a trustee for the failed Livingston Institute, a proposed secondary school for blacks in northern California, and wrote regularly for the San Francisco *Elevator*, whose editor PHILIP BELL held him in great esteem.

Central to Moore's work in this period (and many of his *Elevator* pieces) was the fight for black suffrage. By the late 1860s Moore's San Francisco church had become a gem of AMEZ efforts in the West, his reputation as a "silver tongued" orator was well established, and his place as a key voice for blacks in California was clear.

The church hierarchy called Moore east in 1868, and he was ordained as a bishop on 29 May in Washington, D.C., alongside JERMAIN W. LOGUEN. He served as bishop for the rest of his life, including three years as the presiding bishop of the Philadelphia Conference, though the size, character, and location of his charges varied. In the mid-1870s he helped found the AMEZ newspaper *Our National Herald*. One AMEZ historian said that Moore was "not a great organizer" but "was truly a great preacher" (Hood, 177). Thus, Moore traveled widely—not only in the United States but also to Great Britain in 1879—advancing the AMEZ cause and continuing to fight for black civil rights and education. He remained a respected voice in the church hierarchy, and worked with AME Bishops like DANIEL A. PAYNE when the AME and the AMEZ churches were considering merger in the 1880s. For much of his last decade of life, he had charge of the AMEZ Church at Salisbury, North Carolina, and was Presiding Bishop of the Western and Central North Carolina Conference.

In these later years, though he continued to preach, he turned more and more to writing. He edited the *Sunday School Worker for Parents and Teachers* and wrote articles for the *Star of Zion* and the *AME Zion Quarterly*, as well as poetry. He is perhaps best known for his *History of the A. M. E. Zion Church in America*, which was published in York, Pennsylvania, in 1884. This massive compilation of information on the church, its members, and its clergy, remains a valuable and oft-cited source for AMEZ history. Moore died in Greensboro.

FURTHER READING

Hood, James Walker. *One Hundred Years of the African Methodist Episcopal Zion Church* (1895).

Lapp, Rudolph. *Blacks in Gold Rush California* (1977).

Obituary: *Washington Post*, 10 Dec. 1893.

ERIC GARDNER

Moore, Johnny "Dizzy" (5 Oct. 1938–16 Aug. 2008), aka "Dizzy" Johnny Moore, trumpeter, composer and arranger, was born John Arlington Moore in Kingston, Jamaica, and was raised by strict Seventh Day Adventist parents who did not consider music a favorable or viable career option. Forbidden to touch the piano they had in their home, the music-smitten Moore turned to fashioning rudimentary wind instruments out of papaya stalks and pumpkin vines. After discovering that a drumming friend learned to play at the Alpha Boys' School, a Catholic charitable institution for "wayward boys" run by the Irish Catholic Order of the Sisters of Mercy in St. Andrew, Moore set his mind on attending the school and started pretending to be out of control so his parents would eventually allow him to attend.

At Alpha Moore was taught electrical engineering and printing as well as music. In the music department, led by Sister Mary Ignatius Davies, for whom Moore would hold a soft spot in his heart the remainder of his life, he was taught to play the trumpet by band master Ruben Delgado and became close friends with trombonist Don Drummond and saxophonist Lester Sterling, with whom he would later go on to form the now legendary Skatalites band.

On leaving Alpha after graduating in 1955 Johnny joined the Jamaica Military Band. It was there he earned his moniker "Dizzy," because he was always playing the music of the likes of Dizzy Gillespie and Charlie Parker instead of the classical pieces by Bach or Beethoven favored by the military band. Moore was discharged after three years for "not [being] amenable to military discipline, though a good musician" (*Jamaica Observer* obituary, 17 August 2008).

Moore then started playing with the Mapletoft Poulle Orchestra, but soon was asked to leave when he refused to cut his locks because of the Rastafarian beliefs he had adopted. It was at this stage that Dizzy started spending a lot of his time on Wareika Hill in Rockfort, where the mystical drummer and band leader Oswald "Count Ossie" Williams, whose "Oh Carolina" is often regarded as the first ska song ever to have been recorded, had his camp. Another regular at the camp was saxophone player Tommy McCook. Together with McCook, his former Alpha schoolmates Don Drummond (trombone) and Lester Sterling (sax), and fellow musicians Jackie Mittoo (keyboards), Lloyd Knibb (drums), Lloyd Brevett (bass), Jerome "Jah Jerry" Haynes (guitar), and Roland Alphonso (sax), Moore became a regular session musician at Clement "Coxsone" Dodd's famous Studio One recording studio. It was this group of musicians that would eventually become The Skatalites.

Formed just after the launch of the Russian Sputnik satellite, the band got their name when McCook changed Knibb's suggestion The Satellites into The Skatalites. Although their golden moment only lasted for little over a year, in that short period of time The Skatalites had recorded dozens of tracks—ska evergreens like "Eastern Standard Time," "Confucius," and "Ringo"—for Dodd, and backed leading ska and reggae artists like Lord Creator, Lord Tanamo, Alton Ellis, The Maytals, Jackie Opel, Lee Perry, Delroy Wilson, and even the young Wailers (featuring Bob Marley, Peter Tosh, and Bunny Livingston, aka Bunny Wailer). In 1965 Drummond was imprisoned for the murder of his girlfriend. The Skatalites still soldiered on a few months, but eventually split up into Tommy McCook and the Supersonics and Ronald Alphonso and the Soul Vendors. The first mainly played for Arthur "Duke" Reid's Treasure Isle and the latter, whom Moore joined until he moved to the United States in the early 1970s, stayed on at Studio One.

During his stay in the United States Dizzy gradually became less active in the music business until he rejoined The Skatalites, who had reunited to perform at the 1983 Reggae Sunsplash festival. Moore would continue to have an on-and-off relationship with the band—in this period he also toured with Bunny Wailer for a while—until he finally left in 2002 to join the Jamaica All Stars. In this band, which mainly focused on Jamaica's musical past, playing old mento, calypso, and ska tunes, Johnny played alongside Justin Hinds (of Justin Hinds & The Dominoes), Noel "Skully" Simms (ska, rocksteady, and reggae percussionist and singer), and fellow Alpha Old Boy, Winston "Sparrow" Martin (as of 2009 the band master at Alpha Boys' School). After the demise of Justin Hinds, who succumbed to cancer in 2005, and because Dizzy had also been diagnosed with the disease, the band eventually stopped touring and recording.

At the end of his life Moore was awarded the Jamaican Order of Distinction in the Rank of Officer for his contribution to the music industry. One of his first instruments, a Bundy trumpet from 1958 he named Annaloria, is now housed at the Experience Music Project in Seattle.

Fighting an uphill battle with colon cancer Johnny "Dizzy" Moore passed away at age sixty-nine in his birthplace of Kingston.

Johnny "Dizzy" Moore talks about his days at the Alpha Boys School in Kingston, Jamaica at the Experience Music Project in Seattle on June 7, 2001. (AP Images.)

FURTHER READING

Chang, Kevin, and Wayne Chen. *Reggae Routes: the Story of Jamaican Music* (1998).

Obituary: *Jamaica Observer,* 17 August 2008.

DISCOGRAPHY:

Augustus Pablo. *Blowing with the Wind* (1991).

Bob Marley & The Wailers. *Simmer Down at Studio One, Vol. 1* (1994).

Bunny Wailer. *Liberation* (1989).

Delroy Wilson. *Greatest Hits* (1995).

Jamaica All Stars. *Back To Zion* (2003).

Jamaica All Stars. *Right Tracks* (2004).

Jamaica All Stars. *Jamaica All Stars* (2005).

Jamaica All Stars. *On the Footsteps of Jah* (2007).

Ken Boothe. *A Man and His Hits* (1999).

Lee "Scratch" Perry. *Chicken Scratch* (2008).

Lord Creator. *Greatest Hits* (1997).

The Melodians. *Swing & Dine* (2009).

The Skatalites. *Foundation Ska* (1996).

The Skatalites. *Stretching Out* (1998).

The Skatalites. *Rolling Steady* (2007).

Slim Smith. *Rain from the Skies* (1997).

Toots & the Maytals. *Ska Father* (1998).

TIM IANNA AND
KATRIEN VAN DER AA

Moore, Kevin (Keb' Mo') (3 Oct. 1951–), singer, musician, songwriter, and actor, was born in Los Angeles, California. Moore's parents came from Louisiana and Texas and brought with them a heritage of gospel and popular music. Kevin grew up in Los Angeles and began playing guitar at age 12 when his uncle gave him an instrument as a gift. He took French horn lessons throughout middle and high school. He also enjoyed visiting a neighborhood music store run by a father and son in Compton (located in south-central Los Angeles) where Moore took four years of guitar lessons and two more of conga instruction. Moore played rhythm guitar in a rock group during his years in high school. He was influenced by the guitarist and local resident TAJ MAHAL (HENRY ST. CLAIR FREDERICKS).

Mahal, along with L.A.'s Ryland Cooder, took traditional blues and added an unusual interpretative twist. Jazz, Caribbean, and folk music were all melded into traditional blues tunes in their unique and interesting arrangements and these tunes had a profound influence on Moore.

By the 1970s, Moore was working with a variety of bands and musical styles, while honing his skills on guitar and banjo. He worked as a backup singer and musician and made a living as a studio sideman.

His band Zulu was hired to play backup to Papa John Creach on a 1972 tour of the United States and he later played on three of Creach's solo albums as Almo Music company's in-house arranger. He also played in backup bands opening for Jefferson Starship, Loggins and Messina, and the Mahavishnu Orchestra. Moore gained experience in many diverse musical genres during this time, including a brief period of regular employment as a member of Top 40 cover bands. In 1980 he recorded his first solo album, under the name Kevin Moore, for Chocolate City, a division of Casablanca Records, but it did not sell well. The album, titled *Rainmaker*, had barely been released when Chocolate City Records closed its doors.

Moore continued as a sideman, joining the Rose Brothers Band and Whodunit Band, both in Los Angeles. The Whodunit Band was headed by Monk Higgins, a regular group at Marla's Memory Lane in L.A. in 1983. Higgins was the producer for the Bobby Blue Band group and played lead guitar in the Whodunits. Moore credited Higgins as one of his mentors in helping him to understand the nature of the music industry. He gained valuable experience from this engagement that he would use later in promoting his own recordings. Moore also gained a nickname during this period. The moniker Keb' Mo' was a takeoff on street slang for his given name Kevin Moore. It was given to Moore by Quentin Dennard, jazz drummer, when Moore played with him as a sideman. Moore claimed his music underwent a metamorphosis when he first heard the records of the bluesman BIG BILL BROONZY in 1989. Before that date, his music was more influenced by classic jazz. Moore credited the bluesman MISSISSIPPI FRED MCDOWELL with having an influence on his music, and he also discovered the richness of blues played on an acoustic guitar, rather than the solid-bodied guitars used by many modern players. Moore described himself not as a traditional bluesman, saying that instead that he interpreted blues, jazz, pop, and other musical genres.

In 1990 Moore's career took a new turn when he was hired as an actor to portray a blues guitarist in a Los Angeles Theater Center's production of *Rabbit Foot*, a role that required him to play blues and slide guitar on stage while in character. His acting career continued when he was hired as the understudy to Chick Streetman in *Spunk*, a play based on the writings of ZORA NEALE HURSTON, and he subsequently was cast as delta blues legend ROBERT JOHNSON in the 1998 docu-drama film *Can't You Hear the Wind Howl?* He continued to act over the next decade, appearing as a musician in the film *All the King's Men* and as The

Angel of Music on numerous episodes of the television series *Touched by an Angel*. His music was featured on the final show of the series *The West Wing* in 2006. Keb' Mo' released his first, self-titled album in 1994 for Okeh Records, with two songs co-written by his wife, Georgina Graper. It peaked at number four on Billboard's blues album charts and continued to sell strongly for seventy-two weeks. In 1995 the album won the W. C. HANDY Award for Country/Acoustic Blues Album of the Year. Mo's second album, *Just Like You* (1996), shared the charts for twenty-eight weeks with his first release and won the Grammy Award for Best Contemporary Blues Album. The album included covers of two Robert Johnson standards, "Last Fair Deal Gone Down" and "Come on in My Kitchen." Moore's selection of these songs was quite ambitious and daring, since re-recordings of Johnson's tunes would be evaluated carefully by reviewers and would make comparisons to Johnson inevitable. The album cover photos further invited comparison, featuring Mo' in poses similar to those seen in vintage images of Robert Johnson. Moore, however, won critical acclaim by interpreting the songs as his own, using jazz riffs and his own vocal phrasing.

Moore captured top honors as Acoustic Blues Artist of the Year for 1997 at the W. C. Handy

Keb' Mo', singer and guitarist, in a publicity photo from 1998. (AP Images.)

Awards ceremony. Mo' released ten albums as a headliner and was awarded Grammys for Best Contemporary Blues Album for *Slow Down* (1998) and *Keep It Simple* (2004). *The Door* (2000) was nominated for Grammy Awards, but did not win. *Big Wide Grin* (2001) was awarded a Grammy for Best Musical Album for Children and Moore's fourteen year old son, Kevin Jr., played harmonica on the award-winning CD. In 1998, during the height of his musical and acting careers, he was divorced. Moore, with members of The Dixie Chicks, co-wrote the country hit "I Hope" and earned another Grammy nomination in 2006. He co-produced his CD *Suitcase* for One Haven/Red Ink/ Epic Records in 2006.

Mo's music quickly found its way beyond the standard outlets for blues. His music was heard on AT&T commercials and in his original composition of the theme music for the 2005 *Martha Stewart Show*. He was also featured as a guest on the *Tonight Show* and was a frequent visitor to *The Rosie O'Donnell Show*. On the concert stage, Mo' opened for the headliners Celine Dion, Bonnie Raitt, and Jackson Browne. He was involved in benefit concerts to promote environmental awareness, in addition to working on behalf of social and political issues, including the 2004 Vote for Change tour. In 2003, he hosted a 13-hour series on the history of the blues for Public Radio International.

Moore's performances helped to introduce the blues to a new generation. Just as the guitarist Taj Mahal and the musicologist Ry Cooder recorded classic blues for motion picture soundtracks and television shows, Moore provided that same link for the young people of the 1990s and 2000s, his award-winning albums re-casting blues classics for a wider and younger audience. Moore was honored in 2007 when he was inducted into the Rock Walk in front of Hollywood nightclub The Music Box @ Fonda, a music star sidewalk modeled after the Hollywood Walk of Fame.

FURTHER READING

Aykroyd, Dan, and Ben Manilla. *Elwood's Blues: Interviews with the Blues Legends and Stars* (2004).

Moore, Allan, and Jonathan Cross. *The Cambridge Companion to Blues and Gospel Music* (2002).

Oakley, Giles. *The Devil's Music: A History of the Blues* (1997).

Tipaldi, Art. *Children of the Blues: 49 Musicians Shaping a New Blues Tradition* (2002).

PAMELA LEE GRAY

Moore, Lenny (25 Nov. 1933–), professional football player, was born in Reading, Pennsylvania, one of eight children of Virginia Moore and George Moore, a steel-mill worker. At Reading High School Moore starred in track, but football would become his main focus: Moore scored twenty-two touchdowns during his senior season in 1951, earning a scholarship to Pennsylvania State University. Penn State coach Rip Engle would not allow players to wear the low-cut shoes Moore had worn in high school. Uncomfortable with high-top shoes, Moore learned from teammate Bob Pollard that he could use tape to eliminate the tightness of the upper part of the shoe. Because of this white tape, Moore became known as "Spats."

Moore became the first Penn State running back to gain over one thousand yards in a season. After graduating in 1956, he was chosen by the Baltimore Colts in the first round of the 1956 National Football League (NFL) draft, despite worries that the six-foot-one-inch, 195-pound Moore might be too fragile. Joe Paterno, then an assistant coach at Penn State, assured the Colts that they would be making a great mistake by passing up Moore. His position was what was then called "flanker"—a player used as both a running back and a wide receiver. In his rookie season he ran for 649 yards and 8 touchdowns and caught 11 passes for 102 yards and another touchdown. As a runner, he averaged 7.5 yards per carry, leading the league in this category for the first of four times. He was named the NFL Rookie of the Year. Moore, along with quarterback Johnny Unitas, receiver Raymond Berry, and running back Alan Ameche, formed the National Football League's most potent offense. Moore tied Ameche's team record with a seventy-nine-yard touchdown run against the Green Bay Packers. After teammate Eugene "Big Daddy" Lipscomb nicknamed Moore "Sputnik," after the Soviet satellite, Unitas called him "Sput" for the rest of his career.

In 1957 the Colts had the talent to win the league championship. On the final day of the season, Moore caught an eighty-two-yard touchdown pass from Unitas to give Baltimore a 13–10 lead over the San Francisco 49ers with two minutes remaining— only to lose the game and thus a shot at the championship. In 1958, however, the Colts had their greatest season, with Moore running for 598 yards (a 7.3 per-game average), catching fifty passes for 938 yards, and scoring fourteen touchdowns. In the league championship game against the New York Giants, though injured and used mostly as a decoy,

Moore had five catches for ninety-nine yards as Baltimore won 23–17. As the Colts drove for the tie that sent the game into overtime, Moore caught an eleven-yard pass on third down to keep the drive going. He made a key block to allow Ameche to score the winning touchdown. The game was the first overtime contest in NFL history and is often called the greatest game ever played. The drama of the Colts' victory helped bring professional football to the forefront of the nation's popular consciousness.

Racism dogged many early black football players such as Moore. In a 2006 interview with *Sports Illustrated*, Moore remarked that that the Colts had only six or seven black players during the time he played and that they were often subjected to taunts by opponents, although in later years many of his opponents apologized for their behavior. Off the field, he found himself restricted to restaurants, nightclubs, and theaters on predominantly black Pennsylvania Avenue in Baltimore, with the rest of the city off limits to him despite his local fame. He found himself invited to cocktail parties at which no one would speak to him. On the road, Moore and his black teammates were often barred from

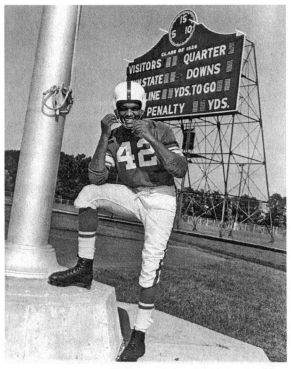

Lenny Moore, star halfback of the Pennsylvania State University football team, photographed in University Park, Pennsylvania, 2 September 1955. (AP Images.)

the hotels and restaurants frequented by the Colts' white players. He described the racism of the time in detail in his autobiography, *All Things Being Equal*, expressing bitterness over his white teammates' failure to protest the treatment of black players. Still, he believed that over time the Colts' success helped diminish racial prejudice in the city.

In 1962 Moore became a running back but was slowed by injuries. In 1962–1963 he played in only seventeen of twenty-eight games. He rebounded in 1964, running for 584 yards, catching twenty-one passes for 472 yards, and scoring a league-record twenty touchdowns. He set another record by scoring touchdowns in eighteen consecutive games from 1963 to 1965. During this period he scored nineteen rushing touchdowns, four receiving, and one on a fumble recovery. His record would be tied by LaDainian Tomlinson of the San Diego Chargers in 2005. Moore told *USA Today* that he was not aware of this record at the time because he believed that only his team's victories mattered, not individual statistics.

By the time of his retirement following the 1967 season, Moore had rushed for 5,174 yards for 4.8 yards per carry, caught 363 passes for 6,039 yards, and scored 113 touchdowns. He was named to All-Pro teams from 1958 to 1961 and again in 1964—he was selected to play in the Pro Bowl seven times during his career. Moore was inducted into the Pro Football Hall of Fame in 1975. He was elected to the Pennsylvania Hall of Fame in 1976. Moore credited the blocking of offensive lineman Jim Parker with much of his success, and the two remained close friends until Parker's death in 2005. Moore also praised Berry's intellectual approach to the game. Berry, who had chided Moore as a rookie for his weak work habits, eventually taught him the importance of varying his patterns on pass play and the necessity of watching films of his opponents.

Married to Edith Randolph and the father of Lenny, Jr., Leslie, Carol, Toni, and Terri, Moore joined the Maryland Department of Juvenile Services in 1984, working with troubled youth. He helped start Camp Concern, a program for intercity children, as a response to the 1968 riots sparked by the assassination of Dr. MARTIN LUTHER KING JR.

FURTHER READING

Moore, Lenny, and Jeffrey Jay Ellish. *All Things Being Equal* (2005).

Bagli, Vince, and Norman L. Macht. *Sundays at 2:00 with the Baltimore Colts* (1995).

Harrington, Denis J. *The Pro Football Hall of Fame: Players, Coaches, Team Owners and League Officials, 1963–1991* (1991).

MICHAEL ADAMS

Moore, Louis (or Lewis) Baxter (1 Sept. 1866–12 Dec. 1928), classicist, Congregationalist preacher, and the first African American to earn a Ph.D. at the University of Pennsylvania, was born in Huntsville, Alabama, the youngest child of Henry Moore and his second wife Rebecca (née Beasley). Louis would in his early years have witnessed the black community's enthusiasm toward such new freedoms as political participation. At the same time, he suffered the hardships besetting his family of twenty-eight in the transforming Deep South. Before Louis turned ten years old, his home state's race relations started slipping toward their "nadir." Alabama endured Ku Klux Klan terrorism and voter intimidation; a "Redeemer" government rose to power in 1874 as black workers and sharecroppers fell into economic dependency on their former owners; and in 1876, federal Reconstruction efforts were sacrificed to political deal-making, which further impeded blacks' access to polls and lecterns. Still, increasing numbers of African Americans came to consider education as one of their last viable ways up the social ladder and out of de facto reenslavement. Embracing academia, Louis Baxter Moore found his personal remedy to political and intellectual disfranchisement in the classical world of the ancient Greeks and Romans.

After attending elementary school in Huntsville, Moore enrolled at all-black Fisk University in Nashville, Tennessee, where he earned an A.B. degree in 1889. It was here that Louis—aside from taking his first tentative steps in the liberal arts—also asserted his foothold in another of his life's formative areas, as a preacher of the gospel. Moore's proselytizing in the greater Nashville area helped pay for his education and enabled him to join the accelerating migration of blacks out of the Jim Crow South. For the graduate work he pursued at Clark University summer school in Worcester, Massachusetts, and at the University of Pennsylvania, Fisk granted him a Master of Arts degree as late as 1893. At that time, the now twenty-seven-year-old had already lived in Philadelphia for four years. Here, Moore became secretary of the S. E. Branch YMCA and rubbed shoulders with at least one family of civil rights activists—on 19 November 1895 he married Sarah (or Sadie) Elizabeth Tanner, the daughter of the AME bishop BENJAMIN TUCKER TANNER and sister of HENRY OSSAWA TANNER, the prominent painter. That same year, Moore completed his doctoral work in Ancient Greek with minors in Latin and Philosophy at the University of Pennsylvania (though the degree was not conferred until the following year) and accepted a teaching position in Howard University's Preparatory Department.

Louis B. Moore's time in Philadelphia had thus led to precious successes at a time of an ever-worsening national race climate. Throughout the 1890s, hundreds of blacks—particularly in the South—fell victim to lynchings, and Moore earned his Doctor of Philosophy in 1896—the same year that the U.S. Supreme Court cemented segregation in its *Plessy v. Ferguson* decision. As such, his dissertation "The Stage in Sophocles' Plays" stands as a testimony to the abilities of a race then widely considered mentally inferior. Moore was merely the fifth African American Ph.D. and the first to receive this honor from Penn, one of the nation's oldest and most distinguished universities. This is even more exceptional considering that the few blacks who pursued degrees at "white" institutions usually came from the Northern states. Furthermore, the Greek and Latin classics of Moore's choice remained entrenched at the very core of the nation's nineteenth-century curriculum. While his dissertation has had no measurable impact on its field, it still tackles a playwright who has remained central to the Western canon for 2,400 years.

Upon the Moores' arrival in Washington, DC, Louis first taught Mathematics, English, and History for a year before he was made Professor of the Latin Language and Literature in Howard's College Department. Another two years on, in 1898, he became Professor of Latin and Pedagogy. In 1899, Moore's personal feats in the latter area led to the creation of the black flagship university's Department of Pedagogy, for which he was hand-picked as dean, and in 1900, Moore traveled the South in an attempt to recruit underrepresented students from the former Confederate States. Yet in 1901, the year that his department became the Teacher's College, Moore's stellar rise through Howard's ranks was offset by the death of his wife. Sarah's passing left Louis the sole guardian for their two children, Sarah and Tanner, at a time of increasing professional obligations (an influential Howard deanship was understood to come with a lifelong appointment and aspirations to the institution's presidency). Moore's numerous responsibilities may have contributed to his decision to marry Lavinia E. Waring on 17 June 1903. Another addition

to the family was a niece of Louis's first wife, SADIE TANNER MOSSELL (LATER: ALEXANDER), who boarded with the Moores while she attended Washington's segregated M Street High School. (In 1915, Sadie followed in her uncle's footsteps. Tracing his path back to Philadelphia, she enrolled at Penn and became one of the first African American women to earn a Ph.D. Later, she set additional records as the first black woman to graduate Penn law school and to pass the Pennsylvania Bar.)

In 1903, Moore was also ordained a Congregationalist preacher and came to shepherd the People's Congregational Church through the next seven years of the dawning twentieth century. In 1906, his wards financed a trip to Europe, during which Moore gained firsthand experience in educational systems that formed the basis of U.S. academe (England) or were the main model for its push toward modernization (Germany). The Prussians possibly appreciated that Reverend Moore—a portly, diplomatic man of partly Native American ancestry whose curly hair was parted at the center—wore a Kaiser-Wilhelm mustache and goatee.

Back at Howard, class redundancies had in the meantime led to competition between the College of Arts and Sciences and Moore's Teacher's College. In 1907, the two departments were temporarily merged into the College of Liberal Arts, though both deans—Moore and KELLY MILLER—retained their positions. In these years, Moore, Miller, and GEORGE WILLIAM COOK, a third powerful dean, acted as the school's "Triumvirate" (W. Dyson). Moore, in particular, would have appreciated this term's allusion to Roman Republican politics. Yet when Howard's chief administrator Wilbur Patterson Thirkield resigned in 1912, the triumvirs found themselves locked in a three-way tie for the position that ultimately thwarted each candidate's hope to become the institution's first black president.

From 1917 to 1922, Moore was the first black to serve on the Executive Committee of the American Missionary Association. As the United States entered World War I and the nation's black soldiers vainly hoped greater liberties would reward their patriotic commitment, Moore requested a leave of absence from Howard. The minister supported the war effort as a lecturer for the National Committee on the Churches and the Moral Aims of the War, which was based in New York City and advertised the War Department's goals of spreading democracy and establishing a League of Nations. He also served as regional director of education for the National Security League, a nationalistic advocacy group that pushed to militarize U.S. society while it sought to contain class struggles. When a generation of ambitious "New Negroes" returned home after the Versailles Peace, Dr. Moore retired from teaching. Rather than return to Howard, he resigned his professorship in 1920 and returned to Philadelphia.

L. B. Moore's career was a milestone in the history of black classicism. Relatively conservative and staunchly religious like many of his "colleagues," Moore had a less visible public persona than WILLIAM HENRY CROGMAN or DANIEL BARCLAY WILLIAMS. Yet within the "movement" spearheaded by WILLIAM S. SCARBOROUGH and capped by FRANK SNOWDEN, he was the first to complete a dissertation. He died in Philadelphia at age sixty-two while serving his third year as pastor of the Faith Presbyterian Church in Germantown.

FURTHER READING

Crogman, William H., J. W. Gibson, and J. L. Nichols. *Progress of a Race... or... The Remarkable Advancement of the American Negro: From the Bondage of Slavery, Ignorance and Poverty to the Freedom of Citizenship, Intelligence, Affluence, Honor and Trust* (1969).

Dyson, Walter. *Howard University—The Capstone of Negro Education: A History, 1867–1940* (1941).

Ronnick, Michele Valerie. "Early African-American Scholars in the Classics: A Photographic Essay," *Journal of Blacks in Higher Education*, 2004.

MATHIAS HANSES

Moore, Melba (29 Oct. 1945–), actor, musician, singer, educator and philanthropist, was born Melba Hill in Harlem, New York City, the only child to a single mother, the successful big band singer Bonnie Davis (née Melba Gertrude Smith). Moore's biological father, Teddy Hill, was a saxophonist who managed the Harlem jazz club, Minton's Playhouse. They separated before Moore was born.

Davis performed with bands associated with COUNT BASIE, DIZZY GILLESPIE, and DUKE ELLINGTON. On the road constantly, she left her daughter to the care of a grandmother and then hired a fulltime nanny named Lulubelle Hattie Mae Stetley Hawkins ("Mama Lu"). Moore endured a physically abusive childhood under Hawkins, a violent upbringing that she claimed helped her to develop a strong sense of self that would assist her in dealing with future hardships.

When Moore was nine, her mother married the keyboardist Clement Moorman and the family moved to New Jersey. Moorman had children from a former marriage, providing Moore with instant siblings, Clementine, Dennis, and Elliot Moorman. Moore also had a half-brother, Girard. Moore's stepfather was the guiding force that eased Moore's transformation from street-savvy wild child to culturally astute middle-class student. During the 1960s Davis and Moorman performed together in a popular jazz group, the Piccadilly Pipers and Bonnie Davis.

Moore attended Waverly Avenue Elementary and Cleveland Junior High schools in Newark. She pursued her musical passions while attending the High School for Performing Arts, studying voice and piano. Intrigued by both the technical and creative aspects of music, she decided to become a teacher.

Moore earned a bachelor's degree in music education from Montclair College and pursued a career in teaching. She excelled as an educator while working at a high school in Newark, but felt unsatisfied with her career and quickly resigned. She longed for the stage but needed to pay bills, so she took jobs singing in the Catskills, providing background vocals. Moore's big break came in 1968 when she auditioned for the musical *Hair*. The producers hired her and she performed several roles with the show for eighteen months, receiving critical acclaim, before securing the leading role of Sheila. Meanwhile, tensions grew between Moore and her husband, the manager George Brewington, who disapproved of the nudity required of Moore in the show. The marriage, the dates of which are unknown, produced no children and ended in divorce.

By the end of 1970 Moore had completed more than a dozen appearances on late night television shows, a small role in the movie *Cotton Comes to Harlem*, and the release of her first album, *Learning to Give*. The role of Luttibelle in the musical *Purlie* earned her a 1970 Tony Award for Best Supporting Actress in a musical, the New York Drama Critics Award, and the Drama Desk Award. Moore's star continued to rise, transforming her into a well known, respected entertainer.

The year 1970 also marked the beginning of a major personal association. Moore became involved in a serious relationship with the actor and singer Clifton Davis. In 1971 he wrote the song "Never Can Say Goodbye," which dramatized the love affair between him and Moore. The Jackson Five later recorded the song and it became an instant hit. In 1972 the couple took their relationship to a professional level by co-starring on television in *The Melba Moore-Clifton Davis Show*, produced by Viacom International for CBS. Designed as temporary programming to air during the five-week summer hiatus left by the vacationing *Carol Burnett Show*, it was a variety show with musical numbers and special guest appearances. Though the show received good reviews, it ended after the five weeks when the network declined to order more episodes. During this time, Moore and Davis parted ways, and she suffered financial losses at the hands of business managers. She also fell so seriously ill that she required hospitalization for over a year.

A partially recovered Moore emerged from the hospital under her mother's care. To maintain a public presence, she performed at various local venues, including the Apollo Theater in New York City. It was there that Moore met Charles Huggins, a restaurateur. They married in 1976, and later had a daughter named Charli. The couple formed Hush

Melba Moore, singer and actress, posing in January 1972. (AP Images.)

Productions, a multi-million-dollar entertainment production and management agency. Moore's reputation and success were instrumental in securing several acts for the company, including Freddie Jackson. Moore entrusted her husband with all of the financial affairs of the business and her career, while she recorded and performed.

Between 1975 and 1986 Moore released over a dozen singles, including the chart-topping hits "A Little Bit More," "Falling," and "Lift Every Voice and Sing." "Lift Every Voice and Sing," originally written by James Weldon Johnson, was popularized by Moore's rendition. On 18 April 1990, District of Columbia Congressman Walter Fauntroy read the words of the song into the United States Congressional Record as the African American national anthem. In 1986 Moore starred in her own show, *Melba*, a CBS network sitcom.

In 1993 Moore's personal tragedies returned. Her husband divorced her under bizarre circumstances. He apparently fraudulently used her signature on the divorce papers. She counter-sued, and retained full custody of their daughter. Financially, the news appeared grave. Her husband lost her money and she ended up devastated, destitute, and on welfare.

In 1996, however, Moore assumed the coveted role of Fantine in *Les Misérables*, resuming her place of honor on Broadway. In 1998 she began touring the country giving solo performances of her autobiographical musical, *Sweet Songs of the Soul*. It touched upon the triumphs and tragedies of her life, while at the same time showcasing her extraordinary talent. The show received rave reviews.

Moore's personal and professional pain did not inhibit her ability to care for others. She donated her time and voice to many causes including serving as the National Celebrity Spokesperson for the National Council of Negro Women. She was a staunch pro-life advocate and spoke publicly for related organizations. Additionally, she served as an advocate for children's rights through the Melba Moore Foundation for Abused & Neglected Children, raising thousands of dollars for programs nationwide.

FURTHER READING

"Melba Moore Bounces Back with One-Woman Show, 'Sweet Songs: A Journey in One Life,'" *Jet* (17 Aug. 1998).

Saline, Carol, and Sharon J. Wohlmuth. "Clementine and Melba: The Moorman Sisters," in *Sisters* (2004).

Shuler, Deadra. "Melba Moore: 'Here I Come … Get Ready!'" *Amsterdam News*, 23 Oct. 2003.

NANCY T. ROBINSON

Moore, Queen Mother (27 July 1898–2 May 1997), black nationalist, was born Audley Moore, the daughter of St. Cyr Moore and Ella Hunter, in New Iberia, Louisiana, a small town near New Orleans. As a young child, she heard stories about her maternal grandfather being lynched, her paternal grandmother being raped by a slave master, and her father being forcibly removed from his position as deputy sheriff by whites. Yet her family instilled in her a strong sense of racial pride and resistance.

By 1914, with only a fourth-grade education, Moore was obliged to take care of her younger sisters, Eloise and Lorita. They moved to New Orleans, where she worked as a domestic and hairdresser and learned firsthand the drudgery of the black urban, working-class life. Moore and her sisters moved to Anniston, Alabama, a highly segregated town, during World War I. Eloise Moore established a recreation center for black soldiers from the nearby Fort McClellan, since they were barred from military recreation halls and white-owned establishments in town.

They returned to New Orleans, where in 1919 Audley Moore heard the Jamaican black nationalist MARCUS GARVEY speak for the first time. She was instantly attracted to his message of racial pride, self-determination, Pan-African unity, and the glories of ancient Africa. As she recalled years later, "It was Garvey who brought the consciousness to me." She enthusiastically joined Garvey's Universal Negro Improvement Association. At the same time, she married Frank Warner, a working-class Haitian immigrant and Garveyite who had come to New Orleans in search of better opportunities. By 1923 the couple had moved to New York City to work for the Garvey movement.

By the end of the decade, Moore had organized Harlem tenants and campaigned for the Republican party. In 1930 she had a son. In late 1933 she took part in an exciting, massive, communist-led protest in Harlem demanding the freedom of the SCOTTSBORO BOYS, nine black adolescents falsely accused of and sentenced to death for raping two white women in Alabama. Impressed with the Communist Party's commitment to fighting for racial justice, she joined the communist-affiliated International Labor Defense and became a party member. Later in life she credited the party, noting, "I really learned to struggle in the Communist Party."

A powerful speaker and tireless organizer, Moore became a leading communist in Harlem during the 1930s and 1940s, organizing efforts around the Scottsboro Boys, the Italian invasion of Ethiopia, housing, unemployment, and unions. In 1943 she served as the campaign manager for BENJAMIN J. DAVIS JR., a communist who was elected to the New York City Council. She also joined the National Association of Colored Women and MARY MCLEOD BETHUNE's National Council of Negro Women. In the late 1940s she worked on the legal defense committee for CLAUDIA JONES, a high-ranking communist indicted by the government for subversion. Moore left the party in 1950, claiming it was no longer committed to fighting for racial equality.

After her resignation from the party, Moore gradually emerged as a radical black cultural nationalist, embracing all things African (real and imagined). She espoused the premise that black people themselves had to lead their own movements and that African Americans needed to, as she often put it, "denegroize" their minds of internalized racism. She also began wearing African clothes, which became her trademark.

With her sister Eloise, Moore founded the Universal Association of Ethiopian Women, an

Queen Mother Moore, outspoken civil rights leader and black nationalist, attends a tribute in her honor in New York City, 18 April 1996. Moore is seated on the left, with Winnie Madikizela-Mandela (right) and Kwame Toure (center), the activist formerly known as Stokely Carmichael. (AP Images.)

organization dedicated to welfare rights, antilynching, and prisoners' rights. Moore claimed that she and Eloise in the late 1950s schooled MALCOLM X on the importance of Africa to the black American struggle. In 1962 she founded the Reparations Committee of Descendants of U.S. Slaves, Inc., after discovering an obscure clause in a Methodist encyclopedia that stated "international law considers an enslaved people satisfied with their condition if the people do not demand recompense after 100 years have passed." Decades before the movement gained momentum, Moore vocally called for reparations from the federal government as compensation for slavery and discriminatory Jim Crow laws in the South. Moving to Philadelphia, Pennsylvania, in the early 1960s, she served as an elder mentor to the Revolutionary Action Movement, a black radical organization. She also became a follower of ROBERT FRANKLIN WILLIAMS, a black militant who advocated armed self-defense. Later in the decade she and Lorita started the Ethiopian Coptic Church of North and South America. In 1968 she was a cofounder of the Republic of New Afrika, an organization that called for the establishment of an independent black state in the American South.

In 1972 she took an extensive trip to Africa to attend the funeral of Kwame Nkrumah, the exiled Pan-Africanist founder of Ghana, in Guinea. She was invited to Ghana, where according to her own report the title "Queen Mother" was bestowed on her by Otumfuo Opoku Ware II, spiritual and cultural leader of the Asante people. She also traveled to Dar es Salaam, Tanzania, where she addressed the All-African Women's Conference. She traveled to Africa several more times in later years. Inspired by her travels, she founded the Queen Mother Moore Research Institute and the Eloise Moore College of African Studies and Vocational and Industrial School on a mountain in upstate New York they named Mount Addis Ababa. The two institutions, however, burned down in 1978. Critical of what she felt was persistent racism within the predominantly white feminist movement, she remained an advocate of black women's organizations.

During the 1980s Moore was a recipient of several awards, and she was one of fifty prominent African American women featured in Brian Lanker's critically acclaimed *I Dream a World: Portraits of Black Women Who Changed America* (1989). In 1994 she addressed a Detroit conference of the National Coalition of Blacks for Reparations, where she declared "Reparations. Reparations. Keep on. Keep on. We've got to win" (*New York Times*, 7 May 1997). She was one of four revered elder black women activists invited to address the 1995 Million Man March in Washington, D.C. Beloved by many for her passionate commitment to reparations and fighting against racism, her death marked the end of a long, extraordinary career of political activism merging black nationalism, Pan-Africanism, and communism.

FURTHER READING

Ahmad, Muhammad. "Queen Mother Moore," in *Encyclopedia of the American Left*, ed. Mari Jo Buhle, Paul Buhle, and Dan Georgakas (1998).

"The Black Scholar Interviews: Queen Mother Moore," *Black Scholar*, Mar.–Apr. 1973.

Hill, Ruth Edmonds, ed. *The Black Women Oral History Project*, vol. 8 (1991).

Obituary: *New York Times*, 7 May 1997.

This entry is taken from the *American National Biography* and is published here with the permission of the American Council of Learned Societies.

ERIK S. MCDUFFIE

Moore, Richard Benjamin (9 Aug. 1893–18 Aug. 1978), activist, communist, and Pan-Africanist, was born in Hastings, Christ Church, Barbados, the son of Josephine Thorn Moore and Richard Henry Moore, a building contractor. Moore's mother died when he was three, and his father married Elizabeth McLean. In 1902 Moore's father died and Moore lived with his stepmother while attending middle school. After graduating in 1905 he became an office clerk, a job he would hold at different firms until he emigrated. During this period he also converted to an evangelical Christian group led by a white American preacher.

In 1908 two of his elder sisters immigrated to New York City, and on 4 July 1909 Moore and his stepmother followed. Moore briefly secured an office assistant job at a Manhattan advertising firm until an infatuation with a white coworker caused a scandal and forced him to leave his job. He then found employment with a silk company, first as an elevator operator and later as head of the stock department. He would remain employed for this firm until 1923.

Like many Caribbean immigrants, Moore encountered racism in his new American home that was quite different from his experiences in Barbados. When he applied to take secretarial classes at a Midtown YMCA he was denied entrance. When he attempted to attend services hosted by the sister organization of the church he had joined in Barbados, he was again denied because of his race. At this time Moore was searching for answers and companionship. He helped formed a tennis club in 1911, eventually becoming its president and helping to establish the first tennis court in Harlem. Moore also became a partner in a Harlem printing company. At the same time he read widely about American history and racism, perhaps most importantly in the *Life and Times of* FREDERICK DOUGLASS (1881). Moore would eventually become an expert on Douglass, whose tenacity and dedication to black liberation he greatly admired.

Moore was greatly influenced by HUBERT H. HARRISON, one of the most eloquent Socialist speakers of the time, and one of the first black Socialists to attempt to analyze American race relations from a Socialist perspective. In 1918 Moore joined the 21st Assembly District Branch of the Socialist Party (SP). In some ways this was a strange decision, since the Socialist Party had been unable—or unwilling—to address the relationship between the systematic oppression of black people and capitalism in the United States. Even more left-wing Socialists tended to ignore the "Negro Question" altogether, reducing the oppression of black people to simply general economic oppression. However, despite the blind spot of the national SP, the Harlem Socialists had attracted an impressive cadre of black supporters, including A. PHILIP RANDOLPH and CHANDLER OWEN (who co-edited the *Messenger*), W. A. DOMINGO, Grace Campbell, OTTO HUISWOUD, and others. This amorphous group would form a core of black radicalism during the late teens and twenties, helping to contribute to the "New Negro" movement and, subsequently, the early black cadre of the Communist Party. Soon after joining the SP, Moore established himself as a capable Socialist orator.

The Harlem Socialists, who tended to remain aloof from the downtown SP headquarters, actively campaigned for votes in the 1918 and 1920 elections, and some, like Grace Campbell, stood for office themselves (as an immigrant, Moore was ineligible to vote or run for office). Largely because of this effort, the SP received some 25 percent of the black vote in the 1918 election. In March 1920 Moore, along with the former Garveyite W. A. Domingo, launched the *Emancipator*, an important black radical voice.

In November 1919 CYRIL V. BRIGGS, another Caribbean migrant and editor of the radical *Crusader*, launched a radical black nationalist organization, the African Blood Brotherhood (ABB), of which Moore and other black Socialists were early members. Amid the rising tide of racist attacks in the aftermath of the war, the ABB emphasized pan-Africanism, black nationalism, and sympathy to anti-colonial liberation movements, including, vaguely, the Bolsheviks. During this period Moore married Kathleen James, a Jamaican immigrant, on 24 June 1919; they had a daughter, Joyce Webster, in August 1920.

In the aftermath of the Bolshevik Revolution left-wing Socialists established the American Communist movement. Like their Socialist parents, the early Communists all but ignored black Americans; nonetheless, the Bolshevik Revolution, in its opposition to Great Russian chauvinism and colonialism, was tremendously popular among black socialists, especially those from the British colonies in the Caribbean. By the early 1920s the New York ABB had joined the Communist Party. Some time after this—the exact date is unclear—Moore himself joined the Communist Party.

Moore helped organize the "Negro Sanhedrin Conference," a meeting in February 1924 of several black organizations. In 1925 he became a leader of the American Negro Labor Congress (ANLC) and in 1927 he replaced LOVETT FORT-WHITEMAN as the national organizer and general secretary. In 1926 Moore was hired by the Party as a full-time functionary, which he remained until the 1940s. In 1927 Moore represented the ANLC (and, oddly, the New York branch of Garvey's organization) at the International Congress Against Colonial Oppression and Imperialism in Brussels, Belgium, and later toured France. The most successful result of the ANLC under Moore's watch, however, was the Harlem Tenants League, which was organized in early 1928 to protest poor conditions and high rents. Out of this work two important black leaders, GEORGE PADMORE and JAMES FORD, joined the party. During this time Moore was a regular spokesman for the party and ran for national and state office three times. During one of these campaigns he was arrested by the police. This political activity also took a toll on Moore's personal life; he separated from his wife, who died in 1946 of cancer.

In 1930 the Communist Party dissolved the ANLC and replaced it with the League of Struggle for Negro Rights, with Moore as general secretary and LANGSTON HUGHES as president. Moore's biggest role as a communist leader came in the

1930s when he became the vice president of the International Labor Defense (ILD). In 1931 Moore served as the "defense attorney" in the "trial" of August Yokinen, a Finnish American communist who was accused of white chauvinism. More importantly, later that year, Moore organized the ILD's protest campaign in defense of the SCOTTSBORO BOYS, nine black youths who were falsely accused of raping two white women in Alabama. This case highlighted the "legal lynching" that Jim Crow "justice" meant in the American South, and it earned the party respect as a militant fighter for black rights. Moore toured the country and wrote a pamphlet entitled *Mr. President: Free the Scottsboro Boys* (1934).

In the mid-1930s Moore had a falling-out with Ford and in 1934 resigned as head of the LSNR. He became the Boston representative of the ILD until 1936. In 1937 he returned to New York and increasingly immersed himself in black history, especially the life of Frederick Douglass. In the early 1940s he attempted to publish, for the first time in forty years, *The Life and Times of Frederick Douglass*. His relations with the Communist Party became more attenuated, and in 1942 the party expelled Moore for, among other things, supposed softness on black nationalism. After his expulsion Moore threw himself into studying black history and collecting and trading black art and literature. With partners, he opened the Frederick Douglass Book Center in Harlem (which remained open until 1968). In September 1950 he married Lodie Briggs, one of his partners and another expelled Communist. He lectured widely on black history and politics until 1976.

Moore organized the Committee to Tell the Truth About the Name "Negro," which advocated for using the term "Afro American" instead. In 1960 he published a small book, *The Name "Negro"—Its Origin and Evil Use*. Moore also maintained an interest in the Caribbean. During the Second World War, unlike the first, Moore and other former ABBers supported the British; nonetheless, Moore advocated self-determination for the British colonies in the Caribbean. In 1941 he founded the West Indian National Emergency Committee, and in 1942 the West Indian National Council. At the founding of the United Nations after the war he also advocated Caribbean independence.

Moore continued lecturing and collecting books for the next several decades. He also renewed his connections to Barbados. In November 1966 the Barbadian government invited Moore, his wife, and other expatriates to witness the turnover from Britain. He sold his immense library of 15,000 volumes, the product of a lifetime of collecting, to the University of the West Indies in Barbados. In the late 1970s Moore's health suffered, and he fell ill to cancer. He died in Barbados and was buried there.

FURTHER READING

Moore's papers are deposited at the Schomburg Center, New York Public Library.

James, Winston. *Holding Aloft the Banner of Ethiopia: Caribbean Radicalism in Early Twentieth Century America* (1998).

Naison, Mark. *Communists in Harlem During the Depression* (1984).

Solomon, Mark. *The Cry Was Unity: Communists and African Americans, 1917–1936* (1998).

Turner, W. Burghardt, and Joyce Moore Turner, eds. *Richard B. Moore, Caribbean Militant in Harlem: Collected Writings 1920–1972* (1988).

Obituary: *Amsterdam News*, 23 Sept. 1978.

J. A. ZUMOFF

Moore, Ruth Ella (19 May 1903–19 July 1994), microbiologist, was born in Columbus, Ohio, the youngest of William E. and Margaret Moore's three children. Moore's father worked as an electrician for a local manufacturing firm; all five members of the Moore family were listed as "mulattos" in the 1910 census. Ruth Moore completed her entire education within Columbus, enrolling at Ohio State University for her B.S. (1926), M.A. (1927), and Ph.D. (1933); the latter two degrees were awarded in the field of microbiology. She taught both hygiene and English at Tennessee State College, a historically black college, to support herself during graduate school (1927–1930).

Moore was not only the first African American woman to receive a Ph.D. in Microbiology but she was also the first African American woman to receive a Ph.D. in the Natural Sciences. Her dissertation focused on the bacteriology of *Mycobacterium tuberculosis*, the organism that causes tuberculosis in humans. Tuberculosis posed a major threat to public health before effective antibiotics were introduced against it in the 1940s; in 1900 nearly one out of every seven deaths in the United States was caused by tuberculosis. As one of the original disease-causing agents discovered by Robert Koch in the 1880s, the tubercle bacillus was an early target of public health initiatives aimed at limiting contagion. Massive health campaigns were aimed to identify and treat people who had been infected, as a small army of microbiologists and bacteriologists turned their attention to every aspect of the bacillus's structure and behavior. Because of bacteriology's close connection to food science and home economics, a significant number of these bacteria-hunters were women.

Upon completion of her Ph.D. in 1933, Moore was offered a position at Howard University College of Medicine as an instructor of bacteriology. She remained at Howard in a variety of teaching and administrative positions for the rest of her career. In 1939 she was named assistant professor of bacteriology; in 1948 she became acting head of Howard's department of bacteriology, preventive medicine, and public health. Moore served as chair of the bacteriology department from 1955 to 1960, at which point she became an associate professor until her retirement in 1973.

Moore arrived at Howard at a time when educational opportunities for African Americans who wished to study medicine were severely limited. In 1900, Howard was one of seven black medical colleges; by 1915, in the aftermath of reforms proposed by the American Medical Association's Flexner Report in 1910, only Howard and Meharry Medical College in Nashville, Tennessee, remained. With few exceptions, only Howard and Meharry educated black physicians in the United States until the 1960s. The university's affiliated teaching facility, the Freedman's Hospital, was similarly one of the only teaching hospitals that accepted African American interns and residents. Importantly for Moore, in 1941 the hospital opened a special facility dedicated to treating tuberculosis patients.

As the first woman to chair a medical department at Howard University, Moore opened the doors for a new generation of women entering medical school in the 1960s. While most African American women studying the health sciences until the 1970s planned on careers in nursing, at the beginning of the twenty-first century women made up almost 40 percent of medical students at Howard University. Moore led at a time when few women, black or white, were offered leadership positions within colleges and universities; her leadership at Howard is particularly notable given the company she kept. DR. CHARLES DREW, the inventor of the blood bank, served as the head of the department of surgery from 1941 until his death in 1950; the department of anatomy was chaired from 1947 to 1969 by DR. WILLIAM MONTAGUE COBB, a prominent civil rights leader who served as president of

the NAACP and the National Medical Association, the black medical society.

After her retirement in 1973, Moore remained active in the American Public Health Association, the American Association for the Advancement of Science, and the American Society of Microbiology. She was also a member of the National Council of Churches and the Augustana Lutheran Church in Washington, D.C. Moore died from heart failure at the National Lutheran Home for the Aged in Rockville, Maryland, at the age of ninety-one.

FURTHER READING
Bruno, Leonard C. "Ruth Moore, 1903–," in *Notable Twentieth-Century Scientists*, ed. Emily J. McMurray (1995).
Tomes, Nancy. *The Gospel of Germs: Men, Women, and the Microbe in American Life* (1998).
Obituary: *Washington Post*, 5 Aug. 1994.

AUDRA J. WOLFE

Moore, Undine (25 Aug. 1904–6 Feb. 1989), composer and teacher, was born Undine Smith in Jarrat, Virginia, the daughter of James William Smith, a brakeman for the railroad, and Hattie Turnbull. When Undine was four, her family moved to Petersburg, Virginia, but they returned to Jarrat every summer to visit family. Moore felt that her early years spent in Jarrat "among the rich musical culture endemic to 'Southside' Virginia" were the inspiration for quite a few of her later compositions. Instilling in their children the importance of education, the Smiths were supportive of Undine's early interest in music and were able, despite their limited financial resources, to provide their daughter with a Steinway piano. While in Petersburg, Undine began to study with Lillian Allen Darden and was able at age eight to provide accompaniment for a local high school graduation.

Moore continued her musical study at Fisk University in Nashville, Tennessee, particularly under the influence of the choral director JOHN W. WORK JR. and the keyboard instructor Alice Grass. Graduating at the top of her class, she received both a bachelor of arts degree and a bachelor of music degree (in Piano and Theory) in 1926 from Fisk. Many people thought that Moore would begin a career as a concert pianist, but she decided to pursue the profession of teaching. She received an M.A. from Columbia University Teachers College. She also attended the Juilliard School as Fisk's first scholarship recipient, later studying theory and composition at the Manhattan School of Music and at the Eastman School of Music in Rochester, New York.

For several years Moore taught in the school system of North Carolina before joining the faculty of Virginia State College (later University) in Petersburg. In a 1980 interview with *Black Creative Artists* Moore expressed dismay "that each generation appeared to know less and less about Black achievement." Using a grant from the National Endowment for the Humanities she cofounded with her colleague Altona Trent Johns the Black Music Center at Virginia State University, establishing a repository of African American music materials and a venue for the presentation of concerts and workshops. The idea behind the Black Music Center was to focus not only on classical music but also on what Moore and Johns felt was the "true Creative genius of the black people in the ditches and the sawmills." Because the project did not receive the support she felt it merited, Moore resigned from the university in 1972. Among her students during her long tenure in Petersburg were the jazz pianist Billy Taylor, the opera singer CAMILLA WILLIAMS, the conductor Leon Thompson, the gospel singer Robert Fryson, the music educators Michael V. W. Gordon and James Mumford, and the composer Phil Medley. At Virginia State University she met James Arthur Moore; they married and had one daughter.

Moore's best-known works are marked by an affinity with the tradition of the spirituals, although her early works—such as "Before I'd Be a Slave," for piano—illustrate a more venturesome vocabulary. She was most comfortable in the medium of keyboard and choral music, venturing into chamber music with "The Afro-American Suite," written for D.-Antoinette Handy's Trio Pro Viva ensemble (flute, violoncello, and piano), and with one large-scale work, "Scenes from the Life of a Martyr," an oratorio tribute to DR. MARTIN LUTHER KING JR. that was prepared with the assistance of Donald Raescher. This oratorio was nominated for a Pulitzer Prize.

Moore's deep appreciation of African American folklore, coupled with her devotion to classical European literature, is reflected in her music with texts by Sappho, William Blake, John Milton, and Michelangelo, as well as LANGSTON HUGHES. Moore was quite active in her retirement. She held residencies at Richmond's Virginia Union University and on three Minnesota campuses (Carleton College, St. Benedict College, and St. John's University).

Respected as a matriarch among African American composers, she secured frequent performances of her choral works, particularly on college campuses, where her dignified bearing and warm personality were greeted with enthusiasm.

FURTHER READING

de Lerma, Dominique-René. *The Black Composer: A Discography* (1996).
de Lerma, Dominique-René, ed. *Reflections on Afro-American Music* (1973).
This entry is taken from the *American National Biography* and is published here with the permission of the American Council of Learned Societies.

DOMINIQUE-RENÉ DE LERMA

Moore, Willie Hobbs (23 May 1934–14 Mar. 1994), physicist, engineer, and industrial manager, was born Willie Hobbs in Atlantic City, New Jersey, the daughter of William Hobbs, a plumber and small businessman, and Elizabeth Hobbs, a worker in a resort hotel. Because she was a straight-A high school student with a strong background in mathematics and science, a counselor suggested that she continue her education in engineering. Moore later credited her close-knit and supportive family with spurring her success, explaining that she and her sisters, Alice and Thelma, were "raised with the expectation that they would always do their best and they did" (Green, 4).

Hobbs attended the University of Michigan, Ann Arbor, earning a B.S. in 1958 and an M.S. in Electrical Engineering in 1961, after which she worked as a junior engineer at the Bendix Aerospace Systems Division in Ann Arbor from 1961 to 1962. This was followed by a year at the Barnes Engineering Company in Stamford, Connecticut, where she worked as an engineer on the problem of approximating the infrared radiation from the wake of space reentry vehicles and on the reduction and interpretation of the associated data. In August 1963 Hobbs married Sidney L. Moore, a psychologist who for forty years at the University of Michigan hospital taught adolescents with psychological problems. The couple had two children, Christopher in 1968 and Dorian in 1971.

Willie Moore returned to Ann Arbor in 1963 to accept a position as systems analyst at the Sensor Dynamics Incorporation, where she was responsible for the theoretical analysis of stress optical delay devices and for formal and informal presentations to company executives and visitors. Moore returned to the University of Michigan in 1965 as a research associate at the Institute of Science and Technology, where she was in charge of establishing valid empirical models for optical hypersonic wakes used in verifying existing flow field models. In 1966 she began doctoral work at the University of Michigan, earning her Ph.D. in Physics in 1972 and becoming the first African American woman to earn a Ph.D. in that field. Her doctoral research, "A Vibrational Analysis of Secondary Chlorides," was directed by the renowned spectroscopist Samuel Krimm and was centered on a theoretical study of the secondary chlorides for polyvinal-chloride polymers. During this period she was working as a system analyst, from 1967 to 1969 at KMS Industries and from 1969 at the Datamax Corporation, both in Ann Arbor.

After earning her P.hD. , Moore held the position of postdoctoral scholar in the department of physics and in the Macromolecular Research Center at the University of Michigan from 1972 to 1977. During this period she and her Ph.D. adviser, Samuel Krimm, and several other collaborators published more than thirteen papers on their research. Krimm remembers Moore as "an intelligent and creative person [who] always had a positive attitude and showed it in her approach to problems that arose in the research, moving purposefully to solve them." He believes that were "it not for financial considerations she would undoubtedly have progressed in the academic area" (letter from Samuel Krimm to Ronald E. Mickens, 1999).

In 1977 Moore accepted a position as an executive with the Ford Motor Company. After a series of increasing managerial responsibilities, she advanced to manager of corporate learning. A highlight of her career at Ford was the significant role she played in extending the use of Japanese-style manufacturing and engineering methods at the company in the 1980s. This effort was codified in a book written jointly with Yuin Wu, *Quality Engineering Products and Process Design Optimization* (1986), explaining the application of the "robust" methods of the Japanese engineering professor Genichi Taguchi.

Moore's career of more than three decades was recognized by a number of honors and awards. When she was an undergraduate, the chair of another academic program pointedly told her, "You don't belong here. Even if you manage to get through your program, there's no place for you in the professional world you seek." Moore's subsequent life, career, and achievements demonstrated this view to be false. Moore died in her Ann Arbor home after a long battle with cancer.

FURTHER READING
Green, Deborah M. "Failure Is Not an Option," *Michigan Engineer* (Winter 1994).
Wu, Yuin, and Willie Hobbs Moore. *Quality Engineering Products and Process Design Optimization* (1985).
Obituary: *Detroit News*, 16 Mar. 1994.

RONALD E. MICKENS

Moorhead, Scipio (fl. 1773), painter and poet, was an enslaved servant for the Reverend John Moorhead, a Presbyterian minister, and his wife, Sarah Moorhead, in Boston, Massachusetts. Limited information is available about Scipio Moorhead's place of birth or parents, but historically a large majority of the slaves in Massachusetts came from the West Indies or the Western coast of Africa.

As slavery in the United States became inextricably linked to the nation's economy, society, government, and identity, race assumed a larger role in becoming a determining factor regarding occupational opportunities. In terms of the fine arts, race determined who could be trained. There were few schools in the seventeenth and eighteenth centuries where blacks could receive specialized training or venues that would exhibit their work. The alternatives for many artists were at the hands of fellow slaves, freed blacks working as artisans or through their owners' families who provided knowledge, direction, and resources to cultivate their artistic talent. There is a matter of contention as to whether Moorhead's teacher was his owner's wife or his daughter.

Credited with being one of the first identifiable African American painters, Moorhead made an ink drawing on paper of PHILLIS WHEATLEY in 1773, his most famous and only documented work. In need of an image to verify her race and gender as the author of *Poems on Various Subjects, Religious and Moral* (1773) Wheatley commissioned Moorhead to render her likeness for the book of verse, the first book published by a black woman. As a friend during her childhood in Boston, Wheatley considered Moorhead a natural choice, as did her owners who were neighbors to the Moorheads and familiar with the Church of the Presbyterian Strangers where Reverend Moorhead officiated. Titled by art historians as *Portrait of Phillis Wheatley*, Moorhead's rendering of Wheatley presents the poet in profile as a thoughtful woman of letters.

Noted for its superior craftsmanship in the *Boston Gazette* the following year and regarded as an exact replica by Wheatley's grand niece, *Portrait*

Phillis Wheatley, half-length portrait engraved by Scipio Moorhead,1 September 1773. (Library of Congress.)

of Phillis Wheatley depicts the subject in a manner that not only comments on her studious nature and survives as Phillis Wheatley's only image but that also provides a visual accompaniment to what many scholars believe was a primary motivation for Wheatley's patrons and supporters—the furthering of the abolitionist movement. Wheatley is shown as a slender young woman wearing a modest, wide-collared dress, white ruffled cap, and necklace. Seated at a desk with assorted papers, an inkpot, and opened book neatly on top, Wheatley holds a pen and gazes thoughtfully as if contemplating her next words for a poem.

Poems on Various Subjects includes a verse dedicated to the artist, applauding two other paintings entitled *Aurora* and *Damon and Pythia* and commenting on Moorhead's talent in poetry. Wheatley's "To S.M., A Young African Painter on Seeing His Work," is the only documentation that exists acknowledging other work composed by Moorhead.

No signed works by Moorhead have been uncovered and little else is known about his personal and professional life outside the Wheatley portrait and her accompanying poem and family correspondences.

FURTHER READING
Patton, Sharon. *African-American Art* (1998).
Richmond, M.A. *Bid the Vassal Soar: Interpretative Essays on the Life and Poetry of Phillis Wheatley and George Moses Horton* (1974).

MAKEBA G. DIXON-HILL

Moorland, Jesse Edward (10 Sept. 1863–30 Apr. 1940), book collector and religious leader, was born in Coldwater, Ohio, the son of William Edward Mooreland (*sic*) and Nancy Jane Moore, farmers and members of a black family that had been free for several generations. Raised by his maternal grandparents because of his parents' early deaths, Moorland, an only child, attended Northwestern Normal University in Ada, Ohio, and the theological department of Howard University. In 1886 he married Lucy Corbin Woodson; they had no children. Moorland was ordained to the ministry in the Congregational Church in 1891 and became the organizing pastor of a church in South Boston, Virginia, as well as secretary of the Young Men's Christian Association (YMCA) in Washington, D.C. From 1893 to 1896 he was minister of Howard Chapel, Nashville, Tennessee, and then went to Mount Zion Congregational Church in Cleveland, Ohio.

A social gospel preacher who believed in working to uplift poor urban blacks and protect them from vice by providing a more wholesome environment, Moorland joined WILLIAM A. HUNTON in 1898 as a secretary for Negro work with the Colored Men's Department of the YMCA, the association having decided to form separate racial branches. Moorland's intent was to establish centers where athletics, Bible study, job training, and other positive activities would serve as alternatives to the social and economic disintegration and ethical demoralization of the growing black ghettos in major cities.

Given the absence of adequate facilities, Moorland began an ambitious fund-raising campaign for construction of the Twelfth Street YMCA in Washington in which he combined solicitation of African Americans on the basis of race pride and white philanthropists on the basis of paternalism. The formula was successful, and Moorland went to Chicago to raise money for a YMCA building there. He convinced Julius Rosenwald to give $25,000 to any black YMCA in any city that raised $75,000 independently. Over the years Moorland realized more than $2 million for construction, much of it from African Americans committed to social improvement and self-help.

Moorland served as a senior YMCA secretary from 1898 to 1923 and relocated to New York City along with his office in 1920. After his retirement in 1926, he took on the presidency of the National Health Circle for Colored People. At this stage of his life, however, he also became an influential member of the Howard University Board of Trustees, which he had joined in 1907, and he now devoted much of his time and energy to the university. Moorland was considered something of a statesman on the board, able to rise above the frequent frays and negotiate practical compromises. In fact, he usually sided with Howard's conservative white presidents, even the thoroughly unpopular J. Stanley Durkee, and represented them and their interests to the black faculty and alumni. During the stormy administration of MORDECAI W. JOHNSON, Howard's first black president, Moorland was chairman of the board's executive committee, where his gifts for conciliation and compromise were put not only to great use but also to the test.

Moorland is best remembered not for his service to church, YMCA, or university but for his extensive library devoted to black history and culture, especially the history of slavery. He inherited a book collection from his uncle, William C. Moore, and added to it over the years—books, pamphlets, engravings, documents, manuscripts, clippings, portraits—until he had amassed more than three thousand items. KELLY MILLER and ALAIN LOCKE of the Howard faculty had long hoped to establish an African American research collection—a "Negro Americana Museum and Library," as they said—in order to make Howard a center of black scholarship and even eventually establish a chair in the field. Influenced by Miller and by Howard's president Stephen M. Newman, "who unconsciously inspired me with the desire for historic research," Moorland in 1914 gave the university his library. It was then considered the largest and most comprehensive private collection of materials by and about people of African descent, and it was valued at between two thousand and three thousand dollars. The university established the Moorland Foundation, a Library of Negro Life, which was housed in a separate location in the new Carnegie library building.

Moorland was a Republican, a Mason, a member of Alpha Phi Alpha, and a trustee of the Frederick Douglass Home Association. He was also a member of the prestigious but ineffectual American Negro Academy and its executive committee. In 1919 he opposed the academy's invitation to A. PHILIP RANDOLPH to speak on "The New Radicalism and the Negro," but his was a lone voice of disapproval, and he reduced his participation in the academy as a result. Moorland was secretary-treasurer of the Association for the Study of Negro Life and History, but he had a falling out with its founder, the contentious CARTER G. WOODSON, who found him too accommodating to the white establishment. Moorland died in New York City.

Fair-complected enough to pass easily for white, Moorland consciously and intentionally devoted his life to what was then called racial uplift. His positive relationships with white philanthropists, however, influenced him to be something of a cautious mediator and broker between the races. His nonideological practicality kept him from taking unpopular positions, and his penchant for cooperation kept him from controversial views. Moorland's lasting contribution was the gift of his library to Howard. W. E. B. DuBois commented at the time, "I think you have a fine beginning in Negro Americana. I trust that the University will take immediate and thoughtful steps to make Howard University Library a great center in this line." The Moorland collection made Howard the first university research library committed to collecting materials on African Americans.

FURTHER READING

The Jesse Moorland Papers are in the Manuscript Division, Moorland-Spingarn Research Center, Howard University.

"The J. E. Moorland Foundation of the University Library," *Howard University Record* 10 (1916): 5–15.

Obituary: *Journal of Negro History* 25, no. 3 (July 1940): 401–3.

This entry is taken from the *American National Biography* and is published here with the permission of the American Council of Learned Societies.

RICHARD NEWMAN

Morel, Junius C. (c. 1806), activist, journalist, educator, was born in slavery at Pembroke Hall, South Carolina (or North Carolina), the son of a white planter and an enslaved African American mother. His father was probably Catholic and of French origin, since Morel (sometimes spelled Morell or Morrel) remembered that "I have been sprinkled and crossed and blessed, and my father had read prayers out of a large book in Latin and French, and kissed and caused me to kiss the pictures in the book." His mother may have been Native American as well as African American, since Morel listed his ethnicity in census records as either mulatto or, in 1870, as Indian. Morel remembered his father as "affectionate" and his mother as "dear," and he left his home and slavery with his father's blessing, sailing north to Philadelphia on the schooner *Olive Branch* of Shrewsbury, New Jersey.

There is conflicting evidence about Morel's date of birth. Census records suggest that he was born in 1819, 1815, 1812, or 1806, while other records suggest 1801. He may have worked on Philadelphia's defenses in 1814, and he most likely spent time as a sailor (Winch, 135). In 1829 he initiated his lifelong career as a journalist and reformer by becoming a subscription agent for SAMUEL CORNISH's paper the *Rights of All*. With John P. Thompson he planned to publish a newspaper, the *American*. The newspaper never appeared, but Morel was politically and publicly active in numerous other ways. Morel organized the Political Association in Philadelphia, a group that asserted the right of African Americans to vote. He also helped to organize the Library Company, became a member of the Young Men's Anti-Slavery Society, and beginning in 1830 was a prominent member of five of the first six black national conventions.

Although he condemned Philadelphia's leadership for its "criminal apathy and idiot coldness," his education and his commitment earned him the nickname of the "classic Morel," "our noble friend," and "my learned friend." The *Colored American*, which published many of Morel's articles, noted that "we have few among us, who know the condition and wants of our colored population, so well as brother Morel; and still fewer, who have made so many sacrifices and efforts in their behalf" (*Colored American*, 9 Dec. 1837; 3 May 1838; 13 July 1839; 31 Aug. 1839). Morel married Caroline Richards, a Christian abolitionist and Underground Railroad activist who died on 26 July 1838.

Morel moved to Harrisburg, Pennsylvania, in 1837 and then to Newark, New Jersey, before he settled in Weeksville, an independent African American community on the outskirts of Brooklyn, New York, in about 1847. By 1850 Morel was living near the school on "Morell's Lane" and actively promoting land sales to African Americans through advertisements in FREDERICK DOUGLASS's *North Star* (*North Star*, 25 Jan. 1850).

However, Morel was more than a real estate entrepreneur. During his years in Weeksville he worked as an educator, journalist, and activist. As an educator, Morel was principal of a school initially called Colored School No. 2 and later PS 68 and PS 83. "As a teacher of youth," said one man who visited his school, "Mr. Morrell has few equals, and still fewer superiors" (*Christian Recorder*, 26 Jan. 1867). As more European Americans began to move into Weeksville, this school changed from one with almost all African American students to one that included many European Americans. When debate arose about the employment of a white teacher, Emma Prime, in 1869, Morel found himself at odds with many longtime allies in Weeksville in defending Prime's employment. "He had been a teacher in the locality for over twenty years," Morel said. "Two generations of his pupils lived around him.... In his school at present there were forty white children. They had equal school facilities elsewhere, but they preferred to attend his school. While he said this he did not desire to be suspected of any lack of fidelity to his own people ... but he would bear true testimony if it cost him his place" (*Brooklyn Eagle*, 24 Feb. 1869). Morel's work laid the foundation for the Weeksville school to become what Carleton Mabee has identified as the nation's first public school in which African American teachers taught European American students on a regular basis, including regular supervision of practice teachers (Mabee, 221–225; Wellman, 89–97).

As a journalist Morel wrote prolifically for African American newspapers, beginning with the *Colored American* from 1837 to 1841. He became an agent for the *North Star* in 1851, wrote sporadically for *Frederick Douglass' Paper* in the 1850s, and then became a regular correspondent for the *Christian Recorder*, the African Methodist Episcopal (AME) Church newspaper, under the pen name "Junius." In 1853 "C.W." listed Junius C. Morel as one among several distinguished African American editors.

As an activist, Morel became a member of the Committee of Thirteen in New York City to promote African American rights and help people escape from slavery after passage of the Fugitive Slave Act in 1850. Speaking at a mass meeting held in Zion's Church New York City on 1 October 1850, Morel advised African Americans "to be prepared, but not to be the aggressors" and added the following:

I would not tell you what to do, but I will tell you what I will do. I am a freeman, and I care not for the constitution or the laws made by man. There is a law above them; and I tell you that before they drag me into Slavery they will have to take my life. The man that would cross the threshold of my door to drag me into Slavery, although I am not a fighting man, but when I am put to the wall I will use this right arm, and deal death and destruction around me. But, my friends, be not the aggressors—keep the peace; but always be prepared (*North Star*, 24 Oct. 1850).

He may have felt vulnerable to prosecution himself, for he listed his name in the 1850 federal manuscript census as Joseph Merrill and his birthplace as the West Indies.

Morel helped rejuvenate the national black convention movement in the 1850s. In 1853 he received more votes (346) than any other of the forty-six candidates for the New York State Convention of Colored People. He acted as a Brooklyn delegate to the National Council of the Colored People in 1855 and promoted the national convention held in Syracuse in 1864.

An issue Morel dealt with all his life was emigration. He opposed the European American–dominated African Colonization Society, describing Liberia as "a kind of Botany Bay for the United States" and expressing his "utter abhorrence of the Colonizationists and their designs." In 1863 he criticized President Lincoln's proposal to resettle African Americans in South America and the Caribbean. He defended the rights of African Americans to U.S. citizenship after the DRED SCOTT decision. At the same time, he endorsed African American emigration initiatives, beginning with Canadian emigration in 1830, settlement in Honduras in the 1860s, and the creation of new communities in the South and Southwest in the 1860s. His move to Weeksville, a community established in the 1830s by African American land developers (whose population was 82 percent black in 1850) fit his own interest in promoting communities under African American control. In the 1860s he became a supporter of the African Civilization Society, whose national headquarters moved to Weeksville, and during the Civil War Draft Riots of 1863, he helped create a safe haven in Weeksville. (Wellman, 39–46, 56–58, 76).

In about 1853 Morel married a woman named Sarah, born in New York County in 1835. They had a daughter, Alice, born in 1860. He purchased a house on the north side of Pacific Street in Weeksville in 1855. Census records suggest that this property was worth $2,000 in 1865 and $15,000 in 1870. Morel continued to live there until his death in 1874.

Underlying Morel's work was his large-spirited view of the world. Although he considered himself a Christian and as an adult became affiliated with the African Methodist Episcopal Church in Weeksville, Morel was never narrowly sectarian. He developed an acceptance of a variety of cultural traditions, reinforced by his early experience growing up with a French father and an African Indian mother and his travels abroad. In 1838 he noted that "in the course of a not uneventful life, it has been my case to have visited the four corners of the Globe, and consequently to have been brought into contact, more or less, with Christians, Mahomedans and Pagans." When he first arrived in Philadelphia, Morel stayed with a British family in which the husband was an Anglican and the wife was a Quaker. Both, wrote Junius, were "exemplary members of God's universal Church" (*Frederick Douglass' Paper*, 19 May 1854). He called himself "somewhat Quakerish in my notions," and he ended one article in 1838 with a benediction that suggested a guideline for his own life: "May we all be led to turn inward more frequently, and closely examine what manner of spirits we are" (*Colored American*, 3 May 1838, 22 Dec. 1838). Junius C. Morel's passionate, lifelong commitment to African American self-determination has been largely unrecognized by historians, primarily because many of his voluminous writings for African American newspapers appeared under the pen name "Junius." He left no known manuscript records.

FURTHER READING
Mabee, Carleton. *Black Education in New York State: From Colonial to Modern Times* (1979).
Ripley, C. Peter, ed. *The Black Abolitionist Papers*, vol. 4 (1991).
Wellman, Judith. "African American Life in Weeksville, New York, 1835–1910," Historic Context Statement Prepared to Support National Register Nomination for Society of Weeksville and Bedford Stuyvesant History (2004).
Winch, Julie, ed. *The Elite of Our People: Joseph Willson's Sketches of Black Upper-Class Life in Antebellum Philadelphia* (2000).

JUDITH WELLMAN

Moret, J. Adolph, Jr. (7 Apr. 1917–21 May 2006), instructor pilot for the Tuskegee Airmen, was born in New Orleans, Louisiana, to Adolph J. Moret Sr., a printer, and Georgianna Perez. Moret grew up in an integrated neighborhood in the Creole community in New Orleans's Seventh Ward, but he attended segregated schools and used segregated public transportation. He attended Sisters of the Blessed Sacrament and Xavier Prep Catholic schools in New Orleans. As a pole vaulter in high school, Moret won a bronze medal at the Tuskegee Ninth Relays at Tuskegee Institute in Alabama in 1935.

From 1935 to 1937 Moret attended Xavier University in New Orleans. After completing nearly two years of college, Moret found employment as a spotter at the Pinkerton Detective Agency, the leading agency at that time. His primary responsibility was to observe bus drivers to ensure that they placed fares in the designated receptacle. This was an uncommon position for an African American to hold, since all of the conductors were white. Moret worked in southern cities including New Orleans and Baton Rouge, Louisiana, and in Jackson, Mississippi. After he reported the impropriety of one conductor in particular not putting the fares in the designated receptacle in Jackson, Mississippi, the bus company managers advised him to leave town immediately. In fear for his life, he complied.

Because he had completed the required two years of college, Moret was eligible to enroll in the Civilian Pilot Training Program at West Virginia State College in the summer of 1940. The Civilian Pilot Training Program was authorized under the Civil Aeronautic Act of 1938 to provide aviation training to a targeted twenty-thousand college students throughout the nation to train civilian pilots with the additional purpose of preparing military pilots in the event of war. The Civilian Pilot Training Program at West Virginia State College began on 11 September 1939. After completing the training, Moret returned to New Orleans and secured work at the U.S. Postal Service as a mail handler because there were no opportunities for black pilots prior to World War II.

Moret married Eline in October 1941. Six weeks later the Japanese bombed Pearl Harbor, and the United States entered World War II. Moret learned of opportunities for instructor pilots at Tuskegee Institute and applied for a position. At Tuskegee, he received the additional training needed to obtain the required instructor's rating and commercial pilot's license.

In early 1942 Moret was one of four black pilots who had graduated from Tuskegee's instructor school to become the first black officers to offer primary flight instruction to black aviation cadets.

During the war, one of his duties was to verify the flying skills of pilots returning from overseas duty.

Moret was discharged from the military in 1946 and returned to his postal job in New Orleans. He and some fellow pilots purchased an airplane from CHARLES "CHIEF" ANDERSON, chief flight instructor at Tuskegee, and formed the Pelican Flying Club.

Because of the degrading racial segregation in New Orleans, Moret moved his family, including his wife and ten children, to Los Angeles, California. After the Watts Riots in 1965, Moret worked with some of the local youth, but he did not see conditions improving. Upon his retirement from the post office in 1972, he moved his family to Santa Rosa, California, and started a business building sheds.

In an interview on 22 January 2001, Moret fondly recalled his days as an instructor pilot for the famed Tuskegee Airmen: "The people at Tuskegee," he stated, "were probably the best of humanity."

LISA BRATTON

Morgan, Clement Garnett (1859–1 June 1929), attorney and civil rights leader, was born in Stafford County, Virginia, the son of slaves whose names are unknown. Emancipated during the Civil War, the family moved to Washington, D.C., where Morgan attended the well-regarded Preparatory High School for Colored Youth. He left school and worked briefly as a barber in Washington before moving to St. Louis, Missouri, where for four years he worked as a teacher.

In 1885 Morgan moved to Boston to attend the Boston Latin School. After graduating in 1886 he enrolled in Harvard College, where he and W. E. B. DuBois were then the only African American students. While at Harvard, Morgan supported himself by working as a barber and by giving readings and speeches at summer resorts. Sizable scholarships for academic excellence took care of most of his tuition costs. In 1889 he won the Boylston Prize for oratory (DuBois finished second). In his senior year Morgan was named class orator. After graduating from college in 1890 Morgan entered Harvard Law School, receiving his LLB in 1893. That year he passed the bar and established a law office in Cambridge.

In addition to his law practice Morgan developed a career in local electoral politics. Running as a Republican in 1895, he became the first African American elected from the predominantly white Ward Two to the Common Council of Cambridge.

In 1898, after serving the two-year term on the common council, he successfully ran for a two-year term as alderman. He then ran unsuccessfully for the state legislature in 1899, 1900, and 1908. In 1897 Morgan married Gertrude Wright.

In the late 1890s Morgan became part of the so-called Negro Radicals, a group of prominent African American intellectuals, attorneys, and activists that included BUTLER R. WILSON, ARCHIBALD HENRY GRIMKÉ, George Forbes, and most notably WILLIAM MONROE TROTTER. This group, which advocated agitation for full civil rights, led the opposition to BOOKER T. WASHINGTON's politics of accommodation. Morgan served as an attorney for Trotter when Trotter was charged with inciting what came to be known as the Boston Riot of 1903, during which several of the Radicals disrupted a speech being given by Washington.

In 1904 Morgan helped form the Committee of Twelve for the Advancement of the Interests of the Negro Race, a short-lived coalition of Radicals and followers of Washington that attempted to reconcile the two factions. In 1905, after the Committee of Twelve fell apart, Morgan joined the Niagara Movement, an organization founded by DuBois that split sharply from Washington in its forceful denunciations of Jim Crow laws and its militant advocacy for African American rights. Morgan was named as the head of the Massachusetts branch of the new organization.

Morgan soon became involved in factional disputes that ultimately led to the demise of the Niagara Movement. He feuded with Trotter over support for the Massachusetts governor Curtis Guild's reelection. In exchange for supporting Guild, Morgan had been nominated for the state legislature by the Republicans. Trotter opposed the governor on the grounds that Guild had approved giving state funds to Jamestown, Virginia, for the town's segregated tercentennial exposition. In 1907 Morgan excluded Trotter from the planning of a Niagara fund-raising event in Boston. The Niagara executive committee sided with Trotter and voted to remove Morgan from his position as president of the Massachusetts branch. DuBois then interceded and convinced the executive committee to retain Morgan. A subsequent split developed between DuBois and Trotter over another Boston event in which Morgan was involved, leading to the virtual disintegration of the Niagara Movement by 1909.

In 1910 Morgan and DuBois joined the newly formed National Association for the Advancement of Colored People (NAACP), and from 1912 to 1914 Morgan served on the executive committee of the organization's Boston branch. In the last years of his life he continued his law practice in Cambridge and remained active in local civil rights work. He was a leading organizer of the campaigns to stop the showing of the film *The Birth of a Nation* in Boston in 1915 and 1921. Morgan died in Cambridge.

FURTHER READING
Fox, Stephen R. *The Guardian of Boston: William Monroe trotter* (1970).
Lewis, David Levering. *W. E. B. DuBois: Biography of a Race, 1868–1919* (1993).
Rudwick, Elliott M. *W. E. B. DuBois: Propagandist of the Negro Protest* (1968).
Obituaries: *Boston Globe*, 3 June 1929; *New York Age*, 8 June 1929.

This entry is taken from the *American National Biography* and is published here with the permission of the American Council of Learned Societies.

THADDEUS RUSSELL

Morgan, Connie (17 Oct. 1935–14 Oct. 1996), baseball player, was born Constance Enola Morgan in Philadelphia, Pennsylvania, to parents whose name are unknown. She attended John Bartram High School and excelled in basketball, softball, and baseball, frequently playing on boys' teams. She also attended William Penn Business School.

Growing up in South Philadelphia, Connie Morgan rose to the top of the region's recreational sports. For the North Philly Honey Dippers women's baseball team, she played nearly every position, primarily catcher, every season from 1949 to 1954. In her final year she batted .368. She also played basketball in the winter for a well-known citywide team, the Rockettes. Fans regarded the team, known for playing a competitive and memorable brand of basketball, as the top squad in the state. One fan remembered, "Outside the city, they were mean! If they were here today, somebody would be making a film on them because that's how great they were" (*Philadelphia Tribune*, 25 Oct. 1996).

The decline of Negro League baseball in the early 1950s ironically opened doors for three women athletes—TONI STONE, Mamie "Peanut" Johnson, and Morgan—who were offered an unprecedented opportunity to play professional baseball. Negro League baseball clubs began to have difficulty attracting fans to their games after JACKIE ROBINSON integrated the Brooklyn

Dodgers in 1947, paving the way for a progression of African American baseball players into the major leagues. Owners of Negro League teams were looking for new ways to keep their fan base, and in 1953 Syd Pollack, owner of the Indianapolis Clowns, signed Toni Stone, the first woman ever to play professional baseball on a men's team. Stone, an accomplished athlete from Minneapolis, was contracted to play second base and took over for HANK AARON when he left the Clowns for the majors. Mamie "Peanut" Johnson, a right-handed pitcher from Washington, DC, was later signed as a pitcher for the Clowns. When Stone was traded in 1954 to the Kansas City Monarchs, Connie Morgan became the third woman to be signed to a Negro League contract, signing with the Clowns in 1954.

Morgan initiated the signing herself. Always an avid sports fan, she read a newspaper article about women playing for the Clowns and wrote owner Syd Pollack directly to ask for a tryout. When the Clowns came to Baltimore in 1954 to play an exhibition game with the Orioles, Pollack invited her to come down and show what she could do. "They thought I had a good arm," she recalled. "I tried out at third base but they thought it was too hot a corner for me, so they put me at second" (*Philadelphia Tribune*, 19 Oct. 1993). Pollack was impressed with Morgan's ability and signed the nineteen-year-old to a two-year contract.

Though many observers looked upon women playing professional baseball as nothing more than a publicity stunt, Morgan took her playing seriously and reported that she did not consider herself a gate attraction sideshow. The second baseman, five-feet-four inches tall and weighing one hundred and thirty-five pounds, hit around .300 for the Clowns, sharing second-base duties with Ray Neil and batting third in the lineup. The Clowns manager OSCAR MCKINLEY CHARLESTON later called her "one of the most sensational" female players he had ever seen (*Philadelphia Tribune*, 25 Oct. 1996). Ray Doswell, curator of the Negro Leagues Baseball Museum in Kansas City, remembered Morgan as simply a great athlete.

The highlight of Morgan's career came on 12 July 1954 when she returned to her hometown for a game with the Kansas City Monarchs in Philadelphia's Connie Mack Stadium. Life on the road traveling for long days from town to town in broken-down buses began to wear on Morgan. However, she had few complaints about being one of two women on an all-men's team. "They treated me well," she said

of her male teammates, "they treated me like a sister" (*Philadelphia Tribune*, 19 Oct. 1993). After two seasons Morgan retired from the game, confessing that she was homesick for Philadelphia.

Morgan returned home and worked in an office position for the AFL-CIO and later drove a bus for the Philadelphia schools. Morgan never married. In her later years she occasionally attended Negro League reunions, including one in Indianapolis where she had played so many games. She was inducted into the Pennsylvania Sports Hall of Fame in 1995. Morgan died in Philadelphia.

FURTHER READING

Berlage, Gai Ingham. *Women in Baseball: The Forgotten History* (1994).

Lanctot, Neil. *Negro League Baseball: The Rise and Ruin of a Black Institution* (2004).

MARTHA ACKMANN

Morgan, Frank (23 Dec. 1933–14 Dec. 2007), jazz alto saxophonist, was born in Minneapolis, the son of the jazz guitarist Stanley Morgan and Geraldine (maiden name unknown), a homemaker. Frank's father worked with such important early bebop musicians as HOWARD MCGHEE during the years around 1940. Morgan grew up primarily in Milwaukee, Wisconsin, and as a child began his musical studies on guitar. At the age of seven, while visiting Detroit with his parents, he was taken to see the big band of JAY ("HOOTIE") MCSHANN at the Paradise Theater. The McShann band included the young alto saxophonist CHARLIE PARKER, and when Parker soloed on "Hootie Blues" the young Morgan immediately wanted to take up the same instrument. His father took Frank backstage to meet Parker, the beginning of a long friendship. Parker decided Morgan should begin on the clarinet, a smaller instrument, but Morgan was allowed to begin study of the alto saxophone at the age of ten.

In 1947, the Morgan family moved to Los Angeles, where Frank became involved in the thriving Central Avenue jazz scene, just as bebop began to dominate as the common language of the younger jazz musicians. Musicians in Los Angeles included CHARLES MINGUS and saxophonist Buddy Collette. Morgan soon won a talent contest and appeared on his first recordings, including a solo spot, at the age of fifteen. His father prevented his leaving high school to join the DUKE ELLINGTON Orchestra, and a brief apprenticeship in the big band of Lionel Hampton was unsatisfying. By the early 1950s, Morgan was a busy professional musician, recording with the likes of KENNY CLARKE and Teddy Charles. His first recording as a leader, *Introducing Frank Morgan*, made in 1955, was well received.

However, by this time Morgan had become involved with drugs. Like many young musicians of his generation, his idolization of Charlie Parker led him to the erroneous conclusion that Parker's great musicianship was linked to his use of heroin. Although Parker tried to dissuade him, Morgan began using the drug at the age of seventeen. Morgan later remarked that his emotional growth stopped at that point and that he remained in a state of arrested development for decades thereafter.

To support his drug habit, Morgan turned to crime, particularly theft. He served the first of several long prison terms for drug possession beginning in 1955. Morgan found prison life congenial. He was treated as a celebrity by the other inmates, had a steady supply of heroin, and was able to practice daily and perform in prison. Other good jazz musicians were incarcerated alongside Morgan. During his residence in San Quentin Prison, the white alto saxophonist Art Pepper co-led a band with Morgan, and their combo became legendary for the high quality of its musicianship. Jazz fans repeatedly took the prison's "Warden's Tour" to hear this ensemble. For three decades, Morgan was unwilling or unable to achieve a cure for his addictions, and he was in prisons and Los Angeles jails repeatedly, on both drug charges and parole violations. He did not attempt a return to the jazz big time until 1985, and by then many jazz aficionados assumed he was dead.

Morgan's return to professional appearances and recording was a major jazz event of the mid-1980s. In 1985, he released *Easy Living*, his second recording as a leader (his first in thirty years) to great acclaim. However, he had once again violated the terms of his parole, requiring him to serve a final six-month jail sentence. Following his final incarceration, Morgan became highly prolific in the recording studio, releasing *Lament* in 1988, three albums as a leader in 1989, *Reflections, Yardbird Suite,* and *Mood Indigo,* and *A Lovesome Thing* in 1990. He also appeared on albums by other musicians, such as the Indian violinist L. Subramanian, during this period. An appearance at Cannes in 1990 with a fellow Parker protégé, the trumpeter Red Rodney, was released as a DVD, entitled *Tribute to Charlie Parker.* On his 1992 album *You Must Believe in Spring,* he recorded with a who's who of jazz pianists—Hank Jones, Barry Harris, Tommy Flanagan, Roland Hannah, and Kenny Barron.

Although he had now embarked on the career that had been for so long forestalled, Morgan was still plagued by drug cravings. Like many addicts, he turned to methadone in an effort to become clean once and for all. This drug also blunted his emotions, and he found it necessary to discontinue methadone treatment in 1993, after sixteen years. His final fourteen years of performance, post-methadone, found Morgan rising to greater heights as a performer than he had attained previously.

In 1998, Morgan suffered a serious stroke en route to a jazz festival, and it was feared he might never perform again. However, he made another remarkable recovery and was soon playing brilliantly. A late pinnacle of his recording career is the series of three live recordings made at the New York club The Jazz Standard in November 2003: *City Nights, Raising the Standard,* and *A Night in the Life.* Morgan's performances here, particularly of ballads, are models of jazz interpretation. Morgan lived in the Topanga area of Los Angeles for much of his later life but he died of cancer in Minneapolis, his home town, nine days short of his seventy-fourth birthday.

Morgan's tone color, predominantly sweet with sharper tones added for variety, was among his most distinctive musical assets. Long phrases of crystalline clarity were spiked with an occasional smoky note, and he occasionally uttered little strangled cries high in his instrument's range. Although he seldom indulged in feats of technical showmanship for their own sake, Morgan possessed a fine technique. He drew on flutter-tonguing at will, as heard on the song "Skylark" (on the album *Love, Lost & Found,* 1995). More than an energetic musical modernist, Morgan developed into one of the greatest performers of standards in the modern jazz pantheon. He was able to play long chains of rapid runs in the manner of his model, Charlie Parker. Although he never surpassed Parker in such pyrotechnics, he grew into one of the finest ballad players of his generation. His recordings of such standards as "It's Only a Paper Moon" and "All the Things You Are" (also on *Love, Lost & Found*) will help ensure that his music will remain of great value to music lovers for generations to come.

FURTHER READING
Davis, Francis. "West Coast Ghost," in *Outcats* (1990), 94–99.

Giddins, Gary. "The Wizard of Bop," in *Faces in the Crowd: Players and Writers* (1992), 135–140.

Sidran, Ben. "Frank Morgan," in *Talking Jazz* (1992; rev. ed. 1995).

Williams, K. Leander. "Coming Clean," in *Down Beat* (August 1994), 26–27.

ELLIOTT S. HURWITT

Morgan, Garrett Augustus (4 Mar. 1877?–27 July 1963), inventor and entrepreneur, was born in 1875 or 1877 in Paris, Kentucky, the seventh of eleven children to former slaves Elizabeth "Eliza" Reed, a woman of African and American Indian ancestry, and Sydney Morgan, a railroad worker of mixed race. Garrett left home for Cincinnati, Ohio, at age fourteen with only six years of education. After six years working as a handyman for a wealthy landowner, he moved to Cleveland, Ohio, where he remained until his death. Enchanted by all things mechanical, Garrett worked as a mechanic for several sewing machine shops and in 1901 sold his first invention, a sewing machine belt fastener.

Morgan opened his own sewing machine sales and repair shop in 1907. He soon earned enough money to buy a house and help support his mother, and in 1908 he married a seamstress, Mary Anne Hassek. The union lasted fifty-five years and produced three sons, John Pierpoint, Garrett Jr., and Cosmos Henry. (Morgan's first marriage in 1896 to Madge Nelson had ended in divorce after only two years.)

Morgan consistently improved the quality and sophistication of his company's sewing machines with innovations like his zigzag stitching attachment. In 1909 he expanded his business with the establishment of the Morgan Skirt Factory, a men's and women's clothes-manufacturing plant that eventually employed more than thirty workers. Morgan's next business enterprise resulted from a serendipitous discovery he made while experimenting with lubricants in an effort to reduce the damage done to wool fabrics by the fire-producing friction of fast-moving sewing machines. Coming across a concoction that appeared to straighten hair, he tested it on a neighbor's Airedale terrier and then on himself. In 1913 he formed the G. A. Morgan Hair Refining Company, offering hair-straightening cream and a complete line of hair products to an enthusiastic public.

In an effort to help firefighters, Morgan set out to create a reliable, portable, water-resistant protective mask that worked without impeding sight, hearing, or mobility. Through studying both the behavior of combustion and the activities of firefighters, Morgan learned that smoke and gases proved the most lethal dangers. By 1912 he had developed a "breathing device" that provided fifteen to twenty minutes of clean air and that could be put on or pulled off in a matter of seconds. Morgan patented his National Safety Hood in 1914 and established the National Safety Device Company to produce and sell it. After several months of unsuccessful attempts to enlist black investors, Morgan turned to financing from outside the African American community. To drum up business, he advertised in trade journals and with direct-mail pieces that included customer testimonials and newspaper accounts. Morgan traveled nationwide, demonstrating the mask at fairs and exhibitions. Elaborate publicity stunts included spending twenty minutes wearing the hood inside tents filled with toxic

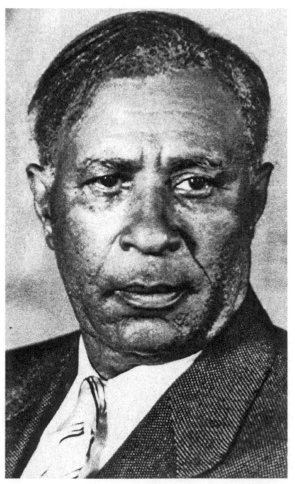

Garrett Augustus Morgan, inventor of the gas mask, photographed in Cleveland, Ohio, in 1945. (AP Images.)

fumes or mixtures of tar, sulfur, formaldehyde, and manure set on fire. For demonstrations in the South, Morgan employed white salesmen who pretended to be "Garrett Morgan" while he "played" an Indian assistant.

The Lake Erie crib disaster of July 1916 proved to be the defining moment for Morgan and his mask. Following an explosion in a tunnel under construction deep below Lake Erie, Morgan and his brother Frank donned his safety hoods and made four trips through smoke and toxic gases to rescue workers. Along with citations, including a gold medal from the city of Cleveland, came orders for Morgan Safety Hoods from fire and police departments and mining companies nationwide. Some orders, however, were rescinded after it was revealed that the mask's inventor was black. The dramatic tunnel rescues also led to a contract with the U.S. Navy to develop the hood for combat use. By World War I, Morgan had modified the mask to carry its own air supply, creating the first gas mask, which by 1917 was standard equipment for the U.S. Army.

Morgan began work on what would become his second major invention after witnessing a traffic accident between a horse carriage and a car. While the automobile had gained popularity after World War I, traffic rules and road behavior were evolving more slowly. After analyzing traffic patterns, Morgan invented the G. A. Morgan Safety System, the precursor of today's electric traffic signal. Advertised as "better protection for the pedestrian, school children, and R.R. crossings," Morgan's device—a tall pole with "stop" and "go" flaps raised and lowered by a crank at the base—established a new system of traffic control. The mechanism also introduced a neutral position, the forerunner of the "caution" or "yellow light." Morgan's invention was granted a patent in 1923, and patents in Canada and England followed. Concerned that the racism he would inevitably face in producing and marketing the device himself would limit the traffic signal's adoption, he sold the invention to the General Electric Company for forty thousand dollars.

Morgan was an active community and civic leader, serving as treasurer of the Cleveland Association of Colored Men and on the board of the Home for Aged Colored People. In 1920 he established, and through 1923 published, the *Cleveland Call*, a weekly African American newspaper today called the *Cleveland Call and Post*. In 1931 Morgan ran unsuccessfully for city council as an independent candidate, promising relief for the unemployed, better housing conditions, and improved policing and hospital access.

Early gas-mask testing had compromised Morgan's health, and in 1943 he was diagnosed with glaucoma. By the 1950s he was nearly blind. An inveterate innovator—smaller inventions included a women's hat fastener, a round belt sewing machine fastener, a friction drive clutch, and a curling comb—Morgan continued inventing even after he lost his sight. Several years before his death in 1963, he developed a pellet designed to extinguish a cigarette if the smoker fell asleep while smoking. Morgan received several awards, including a citation from the United States government for inventing the traffic signal, and an honorary membership in the International Association of Fire Engineers. In 1976 a public school in Harlem was named for him and in 1997 the U.S. Department of Transportation launched the Garrett A. Morgan Technology and Transportation Futures Program, which encourages students to pursue careers in engineering and transportation.

FURTHER READING

Morgan's papers are at the Western Reserve Historical Society in Cleveland, Ohio.

Brodie, James Michael. *Created Equal: The Lives and Ideas of Black American Innovators* (1993).

Jenkins, Edward Sidney. *To Fathom More: African American Scientists and Inventors* (1996).

LISA E. RIVO

Morgan, Joe (19 Sept. 1943–), baseball player and television analyst, was born in Bonham, Texas, the oldest of the six children of Leonard Morgan and Ollie-Mae Cook. Bonham was a small town of 7,500 when Joe was born and, as in many rural towns with clearly demarcated racial residences, this community conspired to shield its children from the social and psychological scars of segregation. Rather than remembering Bonham's segregation and discrimination, Joe would later recall his close-knit extended family who lived in Bonham until 1948. During this time Joe received his first exposure to organized baseball as the bat boy for a semi-professional team that included his father and several uncles.

Facing economic hardship in Bonham, the Morgan family, including aunts and uncles, moved to Oakland, California. There Joe's father and uncles found employment with the Pacific Tire and Rubber Company, and just as in Bonham the family attended school, church, and social functions together. Ironically, their move from the segregated South to the integrated North brought racial tensions into focus for the family when their white neighbors moved out and the neighborhood became all black. In Oakland, Joe, his father, and sister would attend the Pacific Coast League Oaks baseball games, which took place just a few blocks from their house. When Joe was thirteen he tried out for the local Babe Ruth League, made the team as a shortstop, and was an all-star for three consecutive seasons. Although he had played street games, and had practiced with his father for years, this was the first organized baseball team he had been on.

When Morgan was fifteen he entered Castlemont High School, where he continued to enjoy baseball success, making the varsity team his freshman year and helping it to the take the league championship game his senior year. Morgan was an excellent player who dreamed about playing professionally but was initially passed over by scouts as simply "a good little player" because of his 5'7" frame (Morgan, 28). Un-drafted, Morgan decided to attend Oakland City College as a

Joe Morgan of the Houston Astros, phographed in April 1971. (AP Images.)

business major. He played second base and helped Oakland City to a league championship, while leading the team in batting and base stealing and proving himself to be one of the top players in the league. For the first time in his career, major league scouts showed an interest in him, and he was drafted in the spring of 1963 by an expansion team, the Houston 45s.

Morgan signed with the 45s for a two-thousand dollar bonus and salary of five hundred dollars a month, below market value even by 1960s standards. It was through contracts such as these that baseball owners continued to enforce the racial divide in the post–JACKIE ROBINSON era. Owners also physically segregated players, making sure that the handful of African Americans who reported to camp were housed separately from white prospects. It was only on the baseball diamond that Morgan and other African Americans had an opportunity for equality.

Though he was at first not regarded as a top prospect, Morgan's success in the 45s' minor league camp surprised the entire organization. After the 1963 minor league spring training camp, Morgan received top ratings for arm strength, range, speed, and batting. Originally slated to play in Modesto, he was instead promoted to the Durham Bulls of the Carolina League. There Morgan was the only black player on the team and in his first game he was subjected to a steady diet of racial slurs for eight innings. In the ninth, Joe hit the game-winning home run. As his superior play continued, Morgan eventually became popular with the local fans and finished the season as one of the Bulls' most liked players. However before this happened Morgan came close to ending his baseball career during the Bulls' first road trip to Winston-Salem when he arrived at the stadium to find the colored seating section fenced in. Questioning the ethics of supporting such a system, he considered quitting the Bulls to return home; however, convinced that his teammates were not racists, he remained and continued to strive for the major leagues. Morgan was called up to the 45s near the end of the 1963 season, but returned to the minors for half of the 1964 season.

In 1965 Morgan's first full year in the major leagues, the 45s moved into their new stadium, the Astrodome, and were subsequently known as the Astros. Morgan immediately made headlines when he criticized the design of the new stadium. His criticism, that players could not see the ball against the glass roof, soon became apparent to all and the roof was painted white. Unfortunately, without sun the grass quickly died; and the management resorted to painting the field green until the next season when the first artificial playing surface (Astroturf) was developed to allow the revolutionary dome stadium to become functional.

From the outset of the season it was clear that Morgan was being groomed to become the Astros' starting second baseman. Nellie Fox, a veteran, whose job Morgan would soon take, took him under his wing and helped him learn how to turn a double play, a crucial skill for that position. Fox showed Morgan a film of Bill "No Touch" Mazeroski, a second baseman who turned the double play exceptionally well, and Morgan learned to emulate both his foot and glove work, even designing a small glove similar to Mazeroski's.

After a successful first season in which Morgan finished second in rookie of the year balloting, he went on to become the Houston Astros first All-Star in his second season. Following this season in which he hit .275, Morgan played only ten games in 1968 before a knee injury forced him to sit out the rest of the year. When he returned in 1969, the Astros had a new manager—Harry Walker. Walker regularly singled out African American players for criticism and created a poisonous atmosphere in the clubhouse. Morgan tried to stay out of the emotional melee but was unable to; after accusing Walker of not playing to win, Morgan knew that his days in Houston were numbered.

Morgan was traded at the conclusion of the 1971 season in a blockbuster nine player deal that sent star slugger Lee May to Houston and Morgan to the Reds. In Cincinnati Morgan became part of a team known as the Big Red Machine, which was anchored around Joe Morgan, Pete Rose, Tony Perez, and Johnnie Bench. The Reds, managed by the legendary Sparky Anderson, won two World Series Championships (1975 and 1976), six Western Division Titles, four National League Pennants, and more games than any other baseball team in the 1970s. In the 1975 World Series Morgan had the winning hits in games three and seven against the Boston Red Sox. He also won five consecutive Gold Glove awards at second base beginning in 1973. Morgan was named league MVP in both 1975 and 1976, batting over .320, scoring over 100 runs, and stealing at least sixty bases in each season. Unfortunately, when Tony Perez was traded before the 1977 season the Big Red Machine faltered. In 1979 Pete Rose left the team as a free agent and

Manager Sparky Anderson was fired. As the heart of the team broke up, Morgan decided that it was time for him to move on as well. When his contract expired in 1979 Morgan was signed by the Astros and returned to Houston.

The Astros sought veteran leadership when they acquired Morgan and were not disappointed as he was an integral part of directing the team to the National League Championship Series. Unfortunately, Morgan felt that the Astros spoiled their chance to appear in the World Series when he and Art Howe were pulled early from a game that the Astros lost in eleven innings. Because of differences with Astros management he decided not to return in 1981. Morgan spent the next spent two years with the San Francisco Giants almost leading them to a surprise pennant in 1982. Still a productive player, although never again at the levels he attained with the Reds, Morgan played with former Big Red Machine teammates Pete Rose and Tony Perez in 1983 for the Phillies. The Phillies went to the World Series but lost to Baltimore in five games. Morgan ended his playing career with Oakland in 1984. After retiring from baseball Morgan has worked for the Oakland Athletics, ABC and ESPN television, as a Coors distributor, a Wendy's franchise owner, and social activist supporting outreach and scholarship programs in and around the San Francisco Bay area.

Joe Morgan was a rare player, possessing both speed and power. Only 5'7", the 150-pound. "Little Joe" finished his career fifth all time in walks behind BARRY BONDS, RICKY HENDERSON, Babe Ruth, and Ted Williams. He was also the only second baseman to win consecutive MVP awards and was a key part of the Cincinnati Reds who were the first National League team to win back to back World Series titles since the 1921 and 1922 New York Giants. Morgan's accomplishments were recognized in 1990 when he was elected to the Baseball Hall of Fame and in 1998 when the Cincinnati Reds retired his number. Morgan's career as a player overlapped the struggle for civil rights, and his experiences as an underpaid player who was occasionally discriminated against also highlight the role of sports not only in defining athletic excellence but also in providing a common forum for social discourse.

FURTHER READING

Morgan, Joe. *Joe Morgan: A Life in Baseball* (1993).
Shiner, David. *Baseball's Greatest Players: The Saga Continues* (2001).

JACOB ANDREW FREEDMAN

Morgan, Lee (10 July 1938–19 Feb. 1972), jazz trumpeter and composer, was born in Philadelphia, Pennsylvania. Little is known about his parents, except that his father was a pianist for a local church choir. Morgan's older sister, Ernestine, was influential in his musical education. When he was in his early teens she took him to hear the alto saxophone legend CHARLIE PARKER and the bop pianist BUD POWELL at the Earle Theatre. She also gave Morgan his first trumpet when he was fourteen. With his parents' support Morgan amassed a substantial record collection, and many of his colleagues congregated at his home to listen to his library.

Philadelphia in the late 1940s and 1950s was a vital center for modern jazz. Morgan studied trumpet privately as well as at his high school, Mastbaum Tech, which was known for its depth of young jazz talent. Considered a prodigy, Morgan astonished local contemporaries. When he was fifteen Morgan began to perform professionally with his own group, which included at various times the pianist BOBBY TIMMONS, the drummers ALBERT "TOOTIE" HEATH and Lex Humphries, and the bassists Spanky DeBrest and Henry Grimes. In addition Morgan participated in many jazz workshops at the Music City instrument shop. It was through these sessions that he had the opportunity to play with such jazz legends as the trumpeters MILES DAVIS, Kenny Dorham, ROY ELDRIDGE, and DIZZY GILLESPIE; the saxophonists SONNY ROLLINS and SONNY STITT; the drummers ART BLAKEY, KENNY CLARKE, and MAX ROACH; and the pianist Bud Powell.

Morgan viewed the trumpeters FATS NAVARRO and CLIFFORD BROWN as the most direct influences on his personal style. His favorite trumpeters, in the order of his personal preference, were Navarro, Brown, Gillespie, Davis, and Dorham.

The year 1956 proved to be significant for Morgan. He performed with both Navarro and Brown in Philadelphia, and he first recorded as a leader for the Blue Note (*Lee Morgan Indeed*) and Savoy (*Introducing Lee Morgan*) jazz labels. Gillespie, another significant figure in Morgan's musical development, hired him for the trumpet section of his big band in the summer of 1956. Morgan toured and recorded with the band until its dissolution in January 1958. Several albums from 1957 that feature Morgan with Gillespie include *Birk's Works*, *Big Band Sound of Dizzy Gillespie*, and *Dizzy Gillespie at Newport*. The pianist WYNTON KELLY, a colleague of Morgan's in the Gillespie band of 1957, and HANK MOBLEY, who performed with Gillespie in 1953,

were also among the musicians with whom Morgan first recorded. In the liner notes to the 1960 album *LeeWay* the noted critic Nat Hentoff described the first time that he heard Morgan soloing with Gillespie in 1957 on the standard "Night in Tunisia": "a trumpet soared out of the band into a break that was so vividly brilliant and electrifying that all conversation in the room stopped."

Morgan performed often during 1957. His solo endeavors with Blue Note included *City Lights*, *Lee Morgan, Volume 3*, *Candy*, and *The Cooker*. Featured artists on these albums include the alto saxophonist GIGI GRYCE; the tenor saxophonist Benny Golson; the baritone saxophonist Pepper Adams; the pianists Kelly, SONNY CLARK, and Timmons; the bassists Victor Sproles, Doug Watkins, and PAUL CHAMBERS; and the drummers BILLY HIGGINS, Art Taylor, and PHILLY JOE JONES. As a sideman, Morgan, along with the trombonist CURTIS FULLER, the pianist Kenny Drew, Paul Chambers on bass, and Philly Joe Jones on drums, was featured on the tenor saxophonist JOHN COLTRANE's legendary 1957 album *Blue Train*. Another remarkable appearance in 1957 was on the tenor saxophonist Johnny Griffin's appropriately named *A Blowing Session*, which featured Griffin with both Coltrane and the tenor saxophonist Mobley, along with the rhythm section of Kelly, Chambers, and Blakey, all in a casual setting much in keeping with club-style jam sessions. Fellow Philadelphian, the jazz organist Jimmy Smith included Morgan on similarly oriented sessions for two albums in 1957 and 1958. *The Sermon* in 1957 included the trombonist Fuller, the alto saxophonist Lou Donaldson, the tenor saxophonist Tina Brooks, the guitarists Eddie McFadden and KENNY BURRELL, and the drummers Donald Bailey and Blakey. *House Party* in 1958 used mostly the same personnel, with the substitution of George Coleman on alto sax and the use of only Blakey on drums.

Griffin's and Smith's recordings highlighted some of Morgan's style from his early years, best described as effervescent, flashy, and even arrogant. Bending and smearing tones by means of a half-valve technique, precarious leaps in rhythmically unstable areas, and unexpected bold swooping passages musically depicted the raw feelings of maliciousness that were associated with the style later dubbed "hard bop."

This style reached a zenith during the late 1950s with Morgan's incorporation into the Jazz Messengers. Blakey invited Morgan in 1958 to join the recently formed cooperative venture that served as one of the most important crucibles for young jazz musicians over nearly four decades. Throughout Morgan's tenure with the group he performed with the tenor saxophonists Golson, Mobley, and WAYNE SHORTER, the pianist Timmons, the bassist Jymie Merritt, and Blakey. At the forefront of jazz during the late 1950s and early 1960s the Messengers were major sponsors of the hard bop and funky jazz movements. Morgan performed on club dates and recorded often, most significantly on the albums *Moanin'* (1958) and *A Night in Tunisia* (1960), the title track of which was a Gillespie standard. Morgan's association with the Jazz Messengers was perhaps one of the greatest achievements of his career.

Morgan's efforts as a leader from 1958 to 1961 included the 1958 album *Peckin' Time* and three albums in 1960, *Here's Lee Morgan*, *LeeWay*, and *Indestructable-Lee*. Notable sideman appearances included a series of recordings for Blue Note with Brooks (1958–1961); *Wrinkles*, a 1959 album led by Kelly that also included the tenor saxophonist Shorter, the bassist Chambers, and the drummers Jones and Jimmy Cobb; and the 1960 THAD JONES album *Minor Strain*.

The years 1958 to 1961 marked a transition for Morgan in which he tended toward greater critical selectivity of melodic and rhythmic material. This maturity was, in large part, from the influence of Blakey's Jazz Messengers. *Moanin'* reflected the beginning of this change, and with *A Night in Tunisia* Morgan had nearly attained his mature style, displaying a commanding sense of rhythmic, tonal, and formal mastery.

Morgan left the Jazz Messengers in 1961 and returned to his hometown for a year to bring an increasingly overwhelming drug addiction under control. While in Philadelphia he performed with the tenor saxophonist JIMMY HEATH but reduced his recording activity. Morgan appeared on Blakey's *The Freedom Rider* in 1961 and recorded *Take Twelve* in 1962, which featured the tenor saxophonist Clifford Jordan, the pianist Barry Harris, the bassist Bob Cranshaw, and the drummer Louis Haynes. In 1963 Morgan returned to New York City, and later that year he appeared as sideman on Mobley's *No Room for Squares* with the pianist ANDREW HILL, the bassist John Ore, and the drummer Jones. The album, which included modal, gospel-inflected blues, and ballad styles, marked Morgan's popular resurgence. Morgan's style achieved full maturity during this period, with a considerable emphasis upon melodic and rhythmic discrimination and a darkening of his tone to reflect a cynical, sardonic character, all of which is present in his later recordings.

Morgan returned to the forefront of jazz and popular music with a vengeance in 1964 with two landmark recordings: as a leader on his signature album *The Sidewinder*, which included original compositions by Morgan, and as a sideman on the trombonist and composer Graham Moncur III's *Evolution*. *The Sidewinder*, which featured the tenor saxophonist JOE HENDERSON, Harris, Cranshaw, and the drummer BILLY HIGGINS, became one of Blue Note's all-time best-sellers. It showed up on jukeboxes, was adopted as a television theme, made *Billboard*'s Top 200 LP list in 1964, and was even featured in a Chrysler television advertisement. This level of popularity was almost nonexistent in the jazz community at the time, since virtually no jazz albums produced the economic interest found in other segments of popular music. The title track's rhythmic vitality, danceable beat, and energetic playing by Henderson and Morgan made for a recording that became a time-honored standard. The popularity of this album caused Blue Note to delay the release of two sessions recorded at the same time, *Search for a New Land* and *Tom Cat*; the latter was released in 1980.

Within weeks of recording *The Sidewinder* Morgan participated in a memorable session for Moncur's *Evolution*. According to Morgan's brother James in the fall 1989 newsletter *Blue Notes*, Morgan considered the album *Evolution* a critical point in his style development. Moncur placed Morgan and Cranshaw alongside the team of the alto saxophonist JACKIE MCLEAN, the vibraphonist Bobby Hutcherson, and the extraordinary seventeen-year-old drummer TONY WILLIAMS. McLean and Morgan proved to be an ideal pairing for blend of sound. This album foreshadowed the gradual elimination of the stylistic barriers placed by hard bop's creators around its basic tenets—frenetic melodic activity and the malicious contempt of jazz within the context of bebop.

Additional albums led by Morgan in 1964 included the notable *Search for the New Land* with Shorter, the guitarist GRANT GREEN, the pianist HERBIE HANCOCK, the bassist Reggie Workman, and the drummer Higgins, and *Delightfulee Morgan* with Joe Henderson, the pianist MCCOY TYNER, Cranshaw, and Higgins. Morgan performed on Shorter's *Night Dreamer* alongside Tyner, Workman, and the drummer Elvin Jones.

Morgan continued to record for Blue Note as a leader throughout the mid- to late 1960s. Of his many recordings after 1964 of special note were *The Gigolo* and *The Rumproller*, both recorded in

1965, as well as *Cornbread* and *The Rajah*, both recorded in 1966. *The Rumproller*, although a fine album in its own right, failed to achieve the success of its conceptual predecessor *The Sidewinder*. Other albums of this period included *Tom Cat*, *Infinity*, and *The Cat* (all 1965), *Charisma* (1966), *The Procrastinator* (1967), and *Caramba* (1968). Morgan returned to the Jazz Messengers in 1965 and remained with the group for another year. During this time he recorded *Indestructible*, which featured the trombonist Fuller and on which pianist Timmons was replaced by Cedar Walton. As a sideman Morgan appeared with Mobley in 1965 on *Dippin'*, with McLean on *Consequence* (1965) and *Jacknife* (1966), with Joe Henderson on *Mode for Joe* (1966), and with the keyboardist Lonnie Smith on *Think* (1968).

The early 1970s saw Morgan active in a crusade for musicians' rights. A leader of the short-lived Jazz and People's Movement, he helped to combat perceived media ignorance and indifference toward jazz artists. As part of the group's efforts to gain regular access to television for jazz groups, it picketed and disrupted the talk shows of Johnny Carson, Merv Griffin, Dick Cavett, and David Frost.

Notable recordings by Morgan during the early 1970s included the 1970 performance *Live at the Lighthouse* with reedman Bennie Maupin, the pianist Harold Mabern, the bassist Merritt, and the drummer Mickey Roker, the 1971 release *Capra Beach*, and Morgan's last completed project for Blue Note, a 1972 two-record set completed six weeks before his death, simply titled *Lee Morgan*. Sidemen on this album included the saxophonist Billy Harper, Mabern, Merritt, Workman, and the drummer FREDDIE WAITS. On 19 February 1972 a quarrel erupted between Morgan and his longtime companion Helen More while Morgan performed with his quintet at the New York City nightclub Slugs. The argument escalated, and Morgan was shot through the heart at close range. He died instantly, and More was charged with the murder.

Morgan displayed explicit virtuosic command of chord changes with bold conviction. Morgan was a master of formal manipulation, and his intelligent phrasing often featured irregularities that supported his advanced harmonic and melodic delineation. Morgan's playing style came across as sassy and brash early in his career—half-valving, bending, and smearing were favorite techniques and epitomized the "badness" of hard-bop style. His extensive range and bold, clear sound, combined with great precision and accuracy in his solos, made an enormous influence upon subsequent jazz trumpeters. Morgan was widely perceived as the direct successor to Clifford Brown because of the remarkable similarity between Brown's and Morgan's trumpet styles. Many of Morgan's stylistic characteristics found their way into his numerous blues-based compositions, which became more modal in orientation in the latter half of the 1960s and early 1970s.

FURTHER READING

Arnaud, Gérald, and Jacques Chesnel. *Masters of Jazz* (1991).

Lyons, Len, and Don Perlo. *Jazz Portraits: The Lives and Music of the Jazz Masters* (1989).

Rosenthal, David. *Hard Bop: Jazz and Black Music 1955–1965* (1992).

Obituaries: *Down Beat* 39, no. 6 (1972); *Rolling Stone* (30 Mar. 1972).

DISCOGRAPHY

Piazza, Tom. *The Guide to Classic Recorded Jazz* (1995).

This entry is taken from the *American National Biography* and is published here with the permission of the American Council of Learned Societies.

DAVID E. SPIES

Morgan, Nathaniel (?–6 Sept. 1840), racial murder victim, was born between 1805 and 1815. The place of his birth and his parents' names are unknown. In fact nothing is known about Morgan's life until after he moved from Galena, Illinois, to Dubuque, Iowa Territory in 1833. At that time Dubuque was a violent frontier town where several thousand whites, most from Ireland or the American South, worked on the Mississippi River or in lead mines alongside several dozen free blacks and slaves.

In 1834 Morgan's wife Charlotte (maiden name unknown) was one of twelve charter members of the Iowa Territory's first church. Records show that several slaves also offered small donations to help build the edifice, which also served as a courthouse, schoolhouse, and town meeting hall. Despite being marginalized by a society that did not appreciate their presence, the Morgans and other black Iowans were determined to have a presence in Iowa's early community institutions.

Nathaniel worked as a cook and waiter in a hotel, and Charlotte was employed as the laundress. They saved enough money to purchase a house at a time when nearly all of Dubuque's African Americans boarded in hotels or with white families. In fact, another black townsperson rented a room from the Morgans. Although some whites claimed that

Morgan occasionally stole cigars, stockings, and other small goods from guests at the hotel where he worked, he was generally well respected. One account of his life and death, for example, declared that "no charge of felony or misdemeanor had ever been alleged against himself or household, and they pursued the even tenor of their way without the tinge of suspicion attaching that the lives they led were not free from guile" (*History of Dubuque County*, 1880, 395).

However, when a trunk of clothes came up missing from the hotel in early September 1840, Morgan immediately became a suspect. Led by the local militia commander, a group of white men—later characterized in the *Galena North Western Gazette & Advertiser* as Dubuque's "loafers" and "grog-bruisers"—dragged him from the hotel while he was serving dinner and demanded that he confess. Despite his protestations of innocence, the mob took him down to the riverbank and whipped him between thirty-nine and several hundred times (according to different accounts) until he told them where he had hidden the stolen clothes. However, when they arrived at the confessed hiding place, nothing was found; so they whipped Morgan thirty-nine more times until he explained that he had actually hidden the trunk in his home. Nothing was found there either, and the mob began whipping him again.

Now nearly dead, Morgan confessed that the trunk was really on the river bluff. It was clear by now that the frightened man had stolen nothing and was telling his captors whatever they wanted to hear, but they did not care. After threatening a white doctor who tried to intervene with the same treatment if he did not back off, the mob dragged Morgan into the woods for further beatings. When they returned, he was dead, his back and ribs had been violently broken. Although several abolitionist and mainstream newspaper editors from as far away as Chicago called for the lynchers to be punished for their deed, an all-white jury acquitted them, saying that there was no proof that they had intended to commit murder.

Charlotte Morgan lost her house and job and by 1850 was a live-in housekeeper for two immigrant miners. The incident was eventually forgotten by most, and those who remembered were largely indifferent toward Nathaniel Morgan and forgiving of his killers. White residents generally believed that Morgan had been murdered in a rash and exceptional outbreak of violence by a drunken rabble.

Morgan's death eliminated an African American community leader who by his economic success had posed a threat to the racial status quo. Most white midwesterners, immigrants from the East, South, and Europe, wanted to live in a new region free of both slaves and free blacks. Many believed that the newly opened western territories should be populated by free white laborers but showed little sympathy for the plight of slaves or free blacks. Iowans in particular had strong economic ties to the slave states, since most of their agricultural produce was shipped down the Mississippi for southern consumption. Dubuque's Irish population was often even more hostile to African Americans, with whom they competed for the lowest-paying jobs. Thus even if local whites opposed slavery, they did not want to live in multiracial societies where African Americans were equal partners in the economic, political, or social order. The very first territorial legislature had passed laws that banned African Americans from voting, holding office, serving in the state militia, attending public schools, or coming to Iowa at all without posting a bond of five hundred dollars.

Only a few months before the lynching, the newspaper editor James Clark stated that "it is true that a few of our population are willing to place themselves on an equal with the negro, but like visits from the angels, they are few and far between" (*Wisconsin Territorial Gazette*, 8 June 1839). Although rough frontier justice was the order of the day in Dubuque and its surrounding regions, Morgan was the only accused criminal during this period to be killed without some form of due process. Even suspected murderers were given legal counsel, and those found guilty were usually whipped, tarred and feathered, or driven out of town, but not executed.

It was within this context that Nathaniel Morgan, who had subtly opposed the prevalent racial dynamics by his financial success and independence, lost his life. His lynching was an exceptional incident that took place because of quite commonplace racial mores. Simply by trying to live a normal, middle-class life, Nathaniel and Charlotte Morgan posed an unacceptable challenge to the power structure of early antebellum midwestern society.

FURTHER READING

Dykstra, Robert R. *Bright Radical Star: Black Freedom and White Supremacy on the Hawkeye Frontier* (1993).

"Horrid Murder at Du Buque," *Galena (Illinois) North West Gazette & Advertiser*, 11 Sept. 1840.

Litwack, Leon. *North of Slavery: The Negro in the Free States, 1790–1860* (1961).

Pfeifer, Michael J. *Rough Justice: Lynching and American Society, 1874–1947* (2004).

DAVID BRODNAX SR.

Morgan, Norma (16 Jan. 1928–), painter and printmaker, was born Norma Gloria Morgan in New Haven, Connecticut, the only child of Ethel Morgan, a seamstress, fashion designer, singer, and poet. Norma began painting at age nine and completed a mural for her classroom at age thirteen. Morgan said that while she painted the mural, she listened to her teacher speak of history and mathematics; it was then she decided that art would be her career. The first African American artist Morgan came into contact with the artist and writer ELTON FAX while she was still a high school student in New Haven. After graduating from high school in New Haven, Morgan studied for a year at the Whitney School of Art in New Haven. In 1949 Morgan moved with her mother to New York City where Fax assisted the two in finding living accommodations and where Ethel started a new business as a dress designer.

In New York, Morgan enrolled at the Art Students League and took painter Julian Levi's morning class, and in the afternoon studied privately with the famed abstractionist Hans Hoffman. While she already knew how to paint, Morgan stated that Hoffman "taught me the relationship between color, one object to another" (Smith, p. 34). She also studied printmaking with Stanley Hayter at Atelier 17, his print studio in New York. Hayter later included Morgan's etching *Granite Tor* in his 1962 book, *About Prints*. She also studied painting at the Art Students League for two years and in 1951 received the John Hay Whitney Traveling Fellowship from the John Hay Whitney Foundation. Morgan traveled widely in England and Scotland, and was inspired by both the English and the Scottish countryside. Her love of English and Scottish landscapes would inform the content of her engravings and paintings, notably *Castle Maol, Isle of Skye*, and *Alf, Man of the Moors*. She also received two fellowships from the Tiffany Foundation, allowing her to continue her travels to Yorkshire and Southwest England as well as to the Netherlands.

Morgan returned to New York in 1953 and opened her first studio on West 63rd street, in rented rooms of a parish house. In 1961 she received the John and Anna Lee Stacy Foundation Fellowship and returned to England, where she remained until returning to New York in 1964. Morgan spent part of the 1960s abroad, but she supported the American civil rights movement by exhibiting in group shows that increased public awareness of the work of African American artists. During the summer of 1969 Morgan first discovered the artists' community of Woodstock, New York. Since then she has divided her time between her painting studio in Woodstock and her printmaking studio in Manhattan. During the early 1970s Morgan was commissioned by the New-York Historical Society to reproduce the naturalist artist John Ruthven's acrylic painting, *Carolina Paraquets;* the intricacy of the engraving took Morgan five months to produce the final image. Morgan's 1972 print *A Portrait of My Grandfather* became part of the permanent collection at Metropolitan Museum of Art in 1978 and in 2006 another print of the same work became part of the permanent collection of the Museum of American Art in New Britain, Connecticut. Morgan exhibited extensively during this period at institutions that include the Victoria Museum in Yorkshire, England, the Carnegie Institute, the Art Institute of Chicago, the Smithsonian Institution, the Pennsylvania Academy of the Fine Arts, and the National Gallery of Art.

Her work traveled for two years with the exhibition Contemporary American Graphics. The works in this exhibition were *An Old Barn, Salisbury, CT*, and *Alf, Man of the Moors*. She produced engravings of Sojourner Truth in 1998 and Harriet Tubman in 2002. They were included in several exhibitions as were the engravings *Fernworthy Stone Circle, Dartmoor*, 1986, and *Ethel: Mother of the Artist*, 1992. In 1998 she was awarded the International Biographical Centre's 20th Century Award for Achievement Medal of Honor acknowledging her contribution to the arts. In 2004 she was listed in American Biographical Institute's *Notable American Women* and in *Who's Who in American Art*, 2006.

Since the late 1990s Morgan has continued her labor-intensive work as a painter and printmaker, and has been rewarded with ongoing exhibitions that include the Hillwood Museum, Washington, D.C., Cinque Gallery, New York, the Portland Art Museum, Portland, Oregon, the James E. Lewis Museum of Art at Morgan State University, Baltimore, Maryland. Her work is in the permanent collections of many institutions, including the Library of Congress, the Schomberg Center for Research in Black Culture in New York City, the Art Institute of Chicago, the John Hay Whitney Foundation, the International Graphic Art Society, the Associated American Artists, Howard University

Museum, the Museum of Modern Art, the Glasgow Museum in Glasgow, Scotland, the Leeds Museum in Leeds, England, the Arts Council of Great Britain, the Montclair Museum in Montclair, New Jersey, the Museum of African and American Art, Washington, D.C. and the Victoria and Albert Museum, London.

FURTHER READING

Exler, E. "Norma Morgan-Romanticism and Printmaking." *Journal of the Print World* (n.d.)

Henkes, Robert. *The Art of Black American Women: Works of Twenty-four Artists of the Twentieth Century* (1993).

Smith, Sandra Lee. "Norma Morgan: A Matter of Balance." *Black American Literature Forum* 19 (Spring 1985).

CYNTHIA HAWKINS

Morgan, Raleigh, Jr. (12 Nov. 1916–29 Jan. 1998), linguist, diplomat, and educator, was born in Nashville, Tennessee, to Raleigh Morgan Sr., a porter at Union Station, and Adrien Louise Beasley Morgan. The eldest of three children, Raleigh Jr. lived with his extended family; his mother left the household when Morgan was four years old. In addition to his father (b. 1888), Morgan's nurturers were his grandfather Jackson (b. 1865), a business owner; his-grandmother Anna (b. 1868), a homemaker; his uncle John W. (b. 1890); and his aunts Elizabeth and Adrien (both b. 1895). His younger siblings were John Edward (b. 1918) and Helen A. (b. 1919).

Morgan took his first course in Latin at age twelve and began to study German and French at ages fourteen and fifteen respectively. He eventually became a contemporary Renaissance man, whose life unfolded in three phases: professor and teacher, American diplomat, and linguist and researcher. Through these interlocking roles he became an important contributor to the development of Romance linguistics and African French Creoles, and to the shaping of the African American image abroad.

As a child Morgan was encouraged to read by his family. By age twelve he had skipped three grades to become a high school freshman. When he began to study Latin he discovered his gift for language learning. Around 1931 Morgan's father moved his children to St. Louis, Missouri, where he found employment in a terra-cotta company. In 1932, at age fifteen, Morgan graduated from the prestigious Charles Sumner High School, then returned south to his grandparents to enter college at Fisk University in Nashville. There he was inspired by LORENZO DOW TURNER, one of his professors, who in 1932 began systematic fieldwork on the Sea Islands off the coast of Georgia and South Carolina through the Linguistic Atlas project, researching *Africanisms in the Gullah Dialect* (1949). Morgan completed a course on Gullah with Turner and an anthropology course on Chichewa with Mark Hanna Watkins, a specialist in the Bantu languages.

Completing his AB degree at Fisk in 1938, Morgan relocated to the University of Michigan at Ann Arbor on the advice of John Cotin, one of his French professors at Fisk and a Michigan graduate. Morgan accepted a teaching fellowship to work toward a master's degree in French with German as a cognate. After completing his master's in 1939 he returned to St. Louis to teach French at Sumner High School from 1940 to 1942. On Christmas Day 1941 Morgan married Virginia Carol Moss (1920–1993), an elementary school teacher. They became the parents of three daughters: Carol, Jill, and Phyllis Adrien.

In 1942 Morgan was drafted into the U.S. Army, where he served as a second lieutenant in the infantry. Stationed in Italy and France during much of the war, his direct exposure to native speakers of French further stimulated his interest in linguistics. "Linguistics gave me new perspectives on the role of language in society and culture," he explained. "This struck a responsive chord. No longer just a study of the French language to assimilate a foreign culture, but the role of French as a vehicle of communication worldwide, its structure and its linguistic history through time, the consequences of contact of this structure with completely different ones in the speech of bilinguals" (correspondence with the author, 28 June 1985).

At the end of World War II Morgan returned to the United States, settling in Arlington, Virginia, as a research specialist for the Army Security Agency (1946). By 1946, Morgan was eager to return to the classroom. Consequently he joined the faculty of North Carolina College (now North Carolina Central University) in Durham, where he served as head of the department of French (1946–1949). Encouraged by the administration of the college to pursue a P.hD., Morgan returned to the University of Michigan in 1949. He enrolled in Introduction to Linguistics with Charles Fries, who inspired him to focus on a linguistics P.hD. . The University of Michigan hosted the Summer Linguistic Institute for the years that Morgan was in residence. Through the institute his exposure to the discipline was further enhanced as he met and interacted with linguists from around the country.

After Morgan completed his course requirements for the P.hD. , he returned to his position at North Carolina College for five years (1951–1956). During the summer of 1951 he undertook fieldwork in St. Martin's Parish, Louisiana, in an attempt to construct a grammar of Louisiana Creole similar to Turner's *Africanisms*. However, he soon determined that such a project was not possible without immersion in the African languages that served as the substratum. Consequently Morgan selected another topic, completing the Ph.D. while teaching full-time. His dissertation was *A Lexical and Semantic Study of Old French 'jogleor' and Kindred Terms* (1952), published as a monograph in 1954. Morgan subsequently published five articles on the syntax, semantics, and folk literature of Louisiana Creole.

Morgan's career as a diplomat began in 1956 during President Dwight D. Eisenhower's administration, when he and his family moved to Cologne, Germany, and he became director of Amerika Haus, the American cultural center serving Düsseldorf and Cologne. His German was functional. The civil rights movement was under way in the United States, and the German press often contacted Morgan to explain America's relations with its citizens of African ancestry. His role was to enhance the image of the United States abroad. Satisfactory explanations challenged his rhetorical creativity and created in him the psychological dilemma of W. E. B. DuBois's "two warring souls," one committed to presenting the United States as an ideal democracy, the other to enlightening the world about the second-class citizenship imposed on black Americans (unpublished interview with the author, 28 May 1986).

As African nations began to mount active resistance to European colonialism, Morgan visited eight French-speaking African countries on a goodwill tour, lecturing in Benin, Mali, Chad, Togo, Cameroon, Ivory Coast, Algeria, and Zaire in 1956 under the auspices of the U.S. Department of State. He also participated in goodwill tours to several Caribbean countries, including Guadeloupe, Haiti, and Nicaragua. In 1957 Morgan transferred to the American Embassy in Bonn, Germany, where he served as deputy chief of cultural operations. Morgan's role in organizing cultural events removed him a few degrees from the eye of the storm. He remained until 1959, at which time Charles Ferguson, based at Harvard, having received $2 million from the Linguistic Society of America, wrote Morgan in Germany to offer him a position in the newly created Center for Applied Linguistics (CAL) in Washington, D.C. Morgan and his family returned to the United States, where he served as associate director of CAL from 1959 to 1961. There he initiated the newsletter *Linguistic Reporter*, pursued grants for CAL, and interacted with groups of educators who advocated that speakers of Black English be taught Metropolitan or "standard" English through a bilingual education or "English as a second language" approach.

Frank Snowden, dean of arts and sciences at Howard University, invited Morgan to Howard, where he served as professor of Romance languages and department chair from 1961 to 1965. In that capacity he diversified the Romance language faculty, with an emphasis on native speakers, and increased the level of technology by advocating for and overseeing a language laboratory. Soon Howard received a contract from the Peace Corps to train volunteers in carpentry to build a network of schools in Gabon. Morgan's responsibility was to prepare the volunteers in French, the language of the government of Gabon.

Consistently seeking opportunities to advance bilingualism, Morgan served as a lecturer for the National Defense Education Act, Summer Language Institute at Virginia State College in 1960 and 1961, and at Howard University in 1962, 1963, and 1965. He received two grants for his research from the American Council of Learned Societies (1953, 1955) and a Fulbright Fellowship to conduct research in Montpellier, France, on the roots of the French spoken in Quebec (1974).

By 1965 the University of Michigan had invited Morgan to return to teach Romance linguistics. There he remained until his retirement in 1987. Among his favorite courses was French in the New World, a comparative analysis of varieties in the Caribbean, Louisiana, and Quebec. His book *The Regional French of County Beauce, Quebec* appeared in 1975. Morgan published fifteen articles and a number of book reviews, many written in French.

Morgan's research places him as the sole African American Romance Creolist of the 1950s and 1960s. His particular interest was the syntax and semantics of African French Creoles in Louisiana and Guadeloupe and the French of Quebec. In his research he analyzed the ways in which Creole use expanded in the French-speaking Caribbean after World War II, in structure (pronominal system and morphosyntax) and in domains (newspapers, films, radio announcements, and children's books), a trend that he viewed as vital and positive.

Morgan was a member of a number of professional organizations, among them the Linguistic Society of-America, the International Linguistic Association, the Modern Language Association, the Society for Caribbean Linguistics, and the Société de Linguistique Romane. He gave willingly of his time, serving as a member of the Visiting Committee on Germanic Languages and Literature, Board of Overseers at Harvard (1972–1980); a consulting linguist for Modern Language Association Materials Development (1962); chair of the Michigan Council for the Humanities (1974–1977); vice chair of the Ann Arbor Historic District Commission (1977–1982); and consultant for the Project on French as a World Language (1978–1980). He retired from Michigan in 1987, with plans to complete a dictionary on Louisiana Creole, compile a book of its folktales, and complete other manuscripts from his various fieldwork experiences. The debilitating effects of diabetes, however, limited his options, and Morgan succumbed to the illness in January 1998.

FURTHER READING

Contemporary Authors (1979).

Unpublished interview with the author, Ann Arbor, Mich. (28 May 1986).

Who's Who among African Americans (2000).

Who's Who in America (1996).

Obituary: *University Record* (Ann Arbor, Mich.), 18 Feb. 1998.

MARGARET WADE-LEWIS

Morgan, Raphael (1869?–1916?), Greek Orthodox priest, was born Robert Josias Morgan in Kingston, Jamaica, the son of Robert Josias Morgan and Mariam Morgan. His father died six months after his birth. Morgan received his early education in Jamaica and spent time in Honduras, the United States, and Germany. As a young adult he served as a missionary in Sierra Leone for the Church of England. There he attended the Church Missionary Society Grammar School in Freetown. During this time, the Right Reverend Samuel David Ferguson, bishop of the Protestant Episcopal Church in Liberia, appointed Morgan as a lay-reader in the Anglican Church. From Sierra Leone, Morgan traveled to England for further study. According to some sources, he studied briefly at Saint Aidan's Theological College, Birkenhead, and King's College, University of London. However, the colleges themselves do not contain records of his attendance. After studying in England, by 1895 Morgan had moved to the United States.

Morgan began his ministry at the Protestant Episcopal Church's St. Matthew's parish in Wilmington, Delaware. In 1895 he was ordained a deacon by Bishop Leighton Coleman, a well-known opponent of racism. Despite his association with the Protestant Episcopal Church, Morgan maintained doubts concerning some teaching of the Anglican communion. After three years of struggling to discern which form of Christianity (Protestant, Roman Catholic, or Orthodox) must be the true form, he concluded that the Orthodox Church was the pillar and ground of truth. Morgan had met the local Greek Orthodox priest in Philadelphia, the Reverend Demetrios Petrides, and subsequently ventured on a trip to Russia, after which he published his reaction in the *Russian Orthodox Messenger* in 1904. In this open letter, Morgan expressed hope that the Anglican Church could unite with the Orthodox Churches, clearly moved by his experience in Russia. People of African descent were generally well-received within the Russian Empire, Morgan believed. Abram Hannibal had served under Emperor Peter the Great, and rose to lieutenant general in the Russian Army. Visiting artists, foreign service officials, and athletes, such as famous horse jockey JIMMY WINKFIELD, were likewise welcomed.

With his experience of Russia and Russian Orthodoxy fresh in his mind, Morgan returned to the United States and continued his spiritual quest. By 1907 he had decided to seek entry and ordination in the Greek Orthodox Church.

In July 1907 Morgan arrived in Constantinople (Istanbul) with two letters from Petrides. In the first letter, Petrides presented Morgan as a man who had become convinced of the truth of Orthodoxy after several years of intense study and as a person who was worthy of becoming an Orthodox priest. In the second, Petrides suggested that Morgan could remain in Philadelphia as an assistant priest. Ecumenical Patriarch Joachim III assigned Bishop Joachim of Pelagoneia the task of confirming what Petrides had written. Upon Joachim of Pelagoneia's positive appraisal of Morgan's intentions and understanding, he baptized Morgan, giving Morgan the name Raphael, and subsequently ordained him a deacon and then a priest. In October 1907 Morgan returned to Philadelphia to minister to the African American community in Philadelphia. Late in 1908 he even wrote to Patriarch Joachim III, recommending an Episcopalian minister, Reverend A. C. V. Cartier (sometimes listed in sources as A. V. C. Cartier), as a candidate for conversion and ordination, though nothing came of this recommendation. Raphael

Morgan's conversion to the Greek Orthodox Church made him the first African American Orthodox priest. Up to that point, the Greek Orthodox Church had concentrated on serving Greek immigrants, though the Russian Orthodox Church had been evangelizing in North America since 1794.

In 1913 Morgan returned to Jamaica, with the hopes of establishing a parish in his home country. Despite going on an extensive lecture circuit to speak in various parishes in Jamaica, Morgan came to believe that he could better fulfill his goal of establishing a black Orthodox community in Philadelphia, where he returned the following year. He began working among fellow Jamaicans, forming the Order of the Cross of Golgotha. In 1916 he wrote an open letter against MARCUS GARVEY, protesting Garvey's portrayal of the situation in Jamaica, governmental misrule, the social condition between blacks and whites, the minimum wage, and the prejudice of the Englishmen in Jamaica against blacks. Morgan enumerated several objections to Garvey's stated preference for the prejudice of the American whites over that of English whites. The letter was cosigned by several other Jamaicans, presumably members of the Order of the Cross of Golgotha.

Unfortunately, Morgan's trail runs cold after 1916. Although he was clearly making headway with his order and participated in Jamaican and African American events, nothing is known of him after 1916—perhaps the year of his death. Parish records for his Greek Orthodox community in Philadelphia are incomplete for this time period. Although it is almost certainly the case that it was Morgan who first introduced GEORGE ALEXANDER MCGUIRE (the founder of the African Orthodox Church) to the parish in Wilmington and possibly helped influence McGuire's own thinking regarding Orthodox Christianity, Morgan's work among Jamaicans in Philadelphia appears to have been transitory. Nevertheless, he did serve as an important precedent for current African American interest in Orthodoxy, especially that of Father Moses Berry, director of the-Ozarks African American Heritage Museum, who served as the priest to the Theotokos, the "Unexpected Joy," Orthodox Mission in Ash Grove, Missouri.

FURTHER READING

Blakely, Allison. "The Negro in Imperial Russia: A Preliminary Sketch," *Journal of Negro History* 61.4 (1976).

Manolis, Paul G. "The First African American Orthodox Priest," *Epiphany* 15.4 (1996).

Morgan, Raphael. "Letter Denouncing Marcus Garvey," in *The Marcus Garvey and Universal Negro Improvement Association Papers, vol. 1, 1826–August, 1919,* eds. Robert A. Hill and Carol A. Rudisell (1983).

Morgan, Raphael. "Letter of a Deacon of the Anglican Church in America, Mr. R.J. Morgan, addressed to the public," *Russian Orthodox American Messenger* (Oct.–Nov. English Supplement, 1904).

White, Gavin. "Patriarch McGuire and the Episcopal Church," *Historical Magazine of the Protestant Episcopal Church* 38.2 (1969).

OLIVER HERBEL

Morgan, Sam (18 Dec. 1887–25 Feb. 1936), cornetist and bandleader, was born in Bertrandville, Louisiana, the son of a railroad worker. The names of his parents are unknown. Although Morgan's year of birth has been given as 1895, his tombstone in Holt Cemetery offers exact dates, together with the inscription "age 48 years." His parents sang in a Baptist church, and his brothers Isaiah, also a cornetist, and Andrew, a clarinetist and saxophonist, played with Sam. His youngest brother, Albert, a string bassist, also played with Isaiah's group but had a separate, distinguished career in jazz.

After playing in brass bands in Plaquemines Parish, Louisiana, in 1915 Sam Morgan moved to New Orleans, where he led the Magnolia dance band and the Magnolia brass band while working as a track laborer for the Grand Island Railroad. He suffered a stroke in 1924. By autumn 1926 he was sufficiently recovered to join Isaiah's Young Morgan Band, founded in 1922. Sam Morgan took over its leadership because he was better known and had access to better jobs. The group, now known as Sam Morgan's Jazz Band, played primarily at dances in New Orleans. It included two cornetists (Sam and Isaiah), a trombonist (JIM ROBINSON), two reed players (including Andrew after 1925), a banjo player, a string bassist, and a drummer. Occasionally a pianist was added, notably for two recording sessions in 1927. That same year the band began broadcasting regularly from Meridian, Mississippi, on a radio show sponsored by Regal Beer. It toured occasionally at first, usually in the Deep South, but it also made a trip to Chicago in 1929. The band's regional touring became more frequent in the early 1930s as the Depression worsened. In 1932 while performing in Bay St. Louis, Mississippi, Sam suffered a second stroke. Isaiah reassumed the group's leadership until it split up in 1933. Sam played in a Works Progress Administration band in 1934, but ill health forced his retirement the following year. He died of pneumonia in New Orleans. It is not known if he ever married or had children.

Morgan's significance was threefold. In deference to the church, Sam Morgan's Jazz Band did not play hymns at dances, but at the request of its producers it recorded versions of "Sing On," "Down by the Riverside," and "Over in the Gloryland." These 1927 recordings anticipated by more than a decade a key component of the repertory of the New Orleans jazz revival, and more broadly they hinted at the intertwining secular and sacred roots of jazz. Further, Morgan's band's prominent use of saxophones rather than clarinets offered testimony against the stereotypical view of the role of the clarinet in the New Orleans jazz style; moreover, the saxophone is played in a manner more central to the jazz tradition than that of recordings by PAPA CELESTIN's Original Tuxedo Orchestra, which used the same instrumentation in the same year. Finally, Morgan's renditions of "Steppin' on the Gas" and "Bogalousa Strut" (also from these sessions of 1927) are believed to be among the best and most authentic documents of early jazz, exhibiting a devotion to collective improvisation and a wonderful rhythmic drive.

FURTHER READING

Charters, Samuel Barclay, IV. *Jazz: New Orleans, 1885–1963* (1963).

Schuller, Gunther. *Early Jazz: Its Roots and Musical Development* (1968).

This entry is taken from the *American National Biography* and is published here with the permission of the American Council of Learned Societies.

BARRY KERNFELD

Morganfield, McKinley. *See* Waters, Muddy.

Morial, Ernest Nathan "Dutch" (9 Oct. 1929–24 Dec. 1989), judge, politician, civil rights activist, was born in New Orleans, Louisiana, the youngest of six children of Leonic V. and Walter Etienne Morial, the latter a "black Creole" cigar maker. Morial attended public and private schools, graduating from Xavier University in 1951, and was the first African American graduate of Louisiana State University Law School in 1954. After serving two years in the army, he returned to his law partnership in New Orleans in 1956 and served as general counsel to the Standard Life Insurance Company from 1960 to 1967, and he was appointed assistant U.S. attorney for New Orleans from 1965 to 1967 before embarking on a career in electoral politics.

In the intervening years he lectured at Tulane University. Sybil Gayle Haydel, the daughter of a prominent New Orleans family, became his wife on 17 February 1955, and the couple had three daughters and two sons. A Roman Catholic, Morial belonged to several fraternal organizations including the Elks and the Knights of Columbus. *Ebony* included him in their list of one hundred most influential blacks in 1971, 1972, 1973, and 1978.

A stocky five-foot-eight-inch man who boxed in his youth, Morial came to represent a generation removed from, but strongly influenced by, the legatees of Reconstruction's struggles. It is no mere coincidence that his law partner and mentor was the much older A.P. Tureaud—a black Creole like Morial's father. The civil rights attorney had been a key player in the New Orleans political scene since the 1930s. Although both men were fair-complexioned enough to "pass," they clearly identified as black. Indeed, as president of the New Orleans chapter of the NAACP from 1962 to 1965, Morial was at the forefront of black protest and the dismantling of Jim Crow. Distinct from the new race consciousness of the 1960s, his career was largely a struggle against race privilege. In an interview Morial explained that his actions stemmed from his desire to promote a system that respected the moral and human rights of all people (Hirsch and Logsdon, 292).

Even in the context of a time when blacks across the country were making important inroads in attaining civil rights, Morial's accomplishments are impressive. The first black graduate of the Louisiana State University Law School, he went on to be Louisiana's first black representative to the state legislature in the modern era, the first black assistant U. S. attorney in New Orleans, the first black to serve as juvenile court judge, and the first black on the Fourth Circuit Court of Appeals. He was New Orleans's first black councilman (1967) and ultimately its first black mayor.

At the end of his first term on the city council representing the Twentieth District, he nearly captured a citywide race for councilman-at-large—losing by just over 3 percent at a time when blacks constituted only 30 percent of the electorate. His larger role that year was in helping Moon Landrieu capture the mayor's office with over 90 percent of the black vote and just a minority of the white vote. Landrieu had opposed segregationists but his support from the black community owed more to Morial's support and the strength of new black political organizations empowered by the 1965 Voting Rights Act and President Lyndon Johnson's urban programs, including Model Cities. However, that solidarity slowly unraveled over the next decade.

After losing the council race, Morial returned to his legislative seat. In 1970 the governor appointed him to the Orleans Parish Juvenile Court. He was then elected to the Fourth Circuit Court of Appeals in 1972. Throughout the Landrieu years, Morial served from the bench, insulated from the racially charged climate of urban politics. By the time he announced his 1977 candidacy for mayor, the city's black political organizations were divided. Nonetheless, his identification with civil rights and his general independence from the embattled factions helped him to grab 97 percent of the black vote; his long years of service, along with his manners and erudition helped him secure 20 percent of the white vote, enough to produce a six-thousand-vote victory (with 175,000 cast).

Less than six months after his victory, nearly forty of his opponents in the black political organization Community Organization for Urban Politics (COUP) were arrested in a police raid. The organization had been openly criticized for corrupt use of federal poverty funds. While COUP charged that the actions were politically motivated, the U.S. Conference of Mayors selected Morial's Office of Manpower and Economic Development as a national model for cleaning up a dire situation.

His first year as mayor included another controversy, one that well illustrates his political style and attitude. In advance of the annual Mardi Gras celebrations, police and sanitation workers believed they could force the city's hands. However, Morial refused to be manipulated, brought in the National Guard, and cancelled the celebration, costing the city an estimated $10 million in tourist income. National headlines included a picture of him standing with his arm inside his coat leading to characterizations of Morial as Napoleonic.

A fiscal conservative who preached the gospel of self-reliance during the early years of the "Reagan revolution," Morial joined progressive elements in the local business community. The *Wall Street Journal* portrayed him as the "black Calvin Coolidge." However, he committed the city to affirmative action in its hiring practices and increased the proportion of black city employees from 40 percent to 53 percent during his tenure as mayor, and he refused to tolerate old vestiges of white power. Such actions hurt his standing with the city's white voters. Conversely, his battles with black political organizations and insistence on cleaning up scandalous public programs hurt his position with some black voters. In the end, he ran into the practical limits of his office and was unable to overcome an inadequate tax base, a failing infrastructure, and federal dependency.

Despite a political style that seemed to alienate many, Morial was reelected in 1982. Then, despite two pleas to voters to alter the city charter, he was prohibited from seeking a third term. In his final months in City Hall, he sought a seat on the city council but withdrew after a poor showing in the primary. He considered running for mayor again in the election of 1990, but his sudden death before endorsing an opponent blocked both his aspiration to return to office and any opportunity to play kingmaker.

FURTHER READING

Hirsch, Arnold R., and Joseph Logsdon. *Creole New Orleans: Race and Americanization* (1992).

Holli, Melvin G., and Peter d'A. Jones. *Biographical Dictionary of American Mayors, 1820–1980* (1981).

BRET A. WEBER

Morial, Marc (3 Jan. 1958–), politician and mayor of New Orleans, was born Marc Haydel Morial in New Orleans, Louisiana, as the second of five children to Sybil Haydel Morial, a teacher, and ERNEST N. "DUTCH" MORIAL, a lawyer and New Orleans's first African American mayor. Morial graduated from New Orleans's all-male Jesuit High School in 1976 and went on to complete a Bachelor's degree in Economics and African American Studies at the University of Pennsylvania in 1980. During this time he served as coordinator for his father's mayoral campaign. After receiving a Juris Doctor from Georgetown University in 1983, Morial worked for two years in a law firm in New Orleans before opening his own in 1985. During this time he served as board member for the Louisiana American Civil Liberties Union and received the Louisiana State Bar Association's Pro Bono Publico Award in 1988 for his legal service to the poor and disadvantaged.

Having started out in his father's campaign, Morial gained further political experience in JESSE JACKSON's 1988 presidential campaign and as delegate to the Democratic National Convention the same year. From 1987 to 1990 Morial served as adjunct professor of Constitutional and Business Law at Xavier University in New Orleans. After an unsuccessful run for Congress, he won a seat in the Louisiana State Senate in 1992, where he served for two years. During this time, he was named "Rookie of the Year," "Education Senator of the Year," and "Environmental Senator of the Year."

In the early 1990s New Orleans's high crime and murder rate attracted national media attention and started to undermine the city's profits from tourism, on which it heavily depended. Morial, thinking he could effect a change, entered the mayoral race in late 1993. Profiting from his father's popularity, he won 54 percent of the vote in a runoff election between him and his opponent Donald Mintz, a lawyer and civic activist. During his first one hundred days Morial concentrated on strengthening city-sponsored youth programs, remembering how these had kept him out of trouble, and instituted a curfew for juveniles. He reformed the police department, instating a new chief, and put more officers on the street. Within three months, the city's overall crime rate had dropped by 14 percent. In his second term Morial focused on preserving and reopening many of the city's recreational facilities, historic Canal Street, New Orleans's major thoroughfare, and expanding the convention center and airport. In 1995 *Ebony* magazine recognized him as one of the hundred most influential black Americans, and the following year New Orleans won the All-American City Award for the first time in fifty years. According to his own biography on the website of the National Urban League, violent crimes and murders dropped by 60 percent during his tenure, and the unemployment rate was cut in half. The city experienced its biggest economic growth in twenty years, being host of many sports and music events. Morial played a central role in successfully relocating the NBA's Hornets from Charlotte to New Orleans. In 1999 Morial married the journalist Michelle Miller. The couple has two children. Morial also has a daughter from an earlier relationship. In 2000 he was elected by his peers as president of the bipartisan U.S. Conference of Mayors for a period of two years. He served during a challenging period for urban governments, which faced increasingly complex security issues in the wake of the 11 September 2001 terrorist attacks on New York City. Toward the end of his term in office, Morial unsuccessfully sought to change the city charter allowing him to run for a third term. He left office with a 70 percent approval rating.

In 2003 Morial became the new president and CEO of the National Urban League, a civil rights organization founded in 1910. He was intent on changing people's understanding of the organization in a way that would emphasize its continuing importance. Focused on closing the economic gap between black and white citizens, Morial's efforts led to the creation of the Urban Youth Empowerment Program, which supports young adults in attaining sustainable jobs; the National Urban League Empowerment Fund, which invests into urban impact businesses; and Entrepreneurship Centers to help the growth of small businesses. In the aftermath of Hurricane Katrina, which devastated New Orleans in August 2005, Morial reprimanded divisive efforts at "whitening" the city's population and commended people of all backgrounds who came together to rebuild the city.

Additionally Morial served as an executive committee member of the Leadership Conference on Civil Rights, the Black Leadership Forum, and Leadership 18, a coalition of nonprofit CEOs. As board member he assisted the Muhammad Ali Center, a museum dedicated to the boxer MUHAMMAD ALI, as well as the New Jersey Performing Arts Center. He was awarded honorary degrees from both Xavier and Wilberforce universities, and the University of South Carolina Upstate, and was recognized by the *Nonprofit Times* as one of the top fifty nonprofit executives two years in a row in 2004 and 2005.

Morial continued as head of the Urban League through 2011. In that capacity he was a prominent spokesman on the growing economic problems facing African Americans in the wake of the 2008 financial crisis. He noted in an interview prior to the NUL's 101st conference in Boston in July 2011 that his organization served more people in the previous year than in any time in its history, because of the problems caused by unemployment, housing foreclosures, and debt in the black community. Morial worked closely with administration of BARACK OBAMA in 2009 and 2010 to ensure passage of health care insurance coverage of all Americans. He also urged the President to focus more attention on issues facing African Americans, specifically unemployment, which in the Fall of 2011 stood at 16 percent, double the rate for whites, and the highest it had been since the Reagan era.

FURTHER READING

Miller, Frederic P., Agnes F. Vandome, and John McBrewster. *Marc Morial* (2010).

Morial, Marc H. *Decisions of Courage: Moving New Orleans into the 21st Century: The Speeches of Mayor Marc H. Morial* (1998).

http://www.theroot.com/views/conversation-marc-morial 27 July, 2011.

GRETA KÖHLER

Morley-Ball, Joyce A. (12 Mar. 1953–), educator and popular therapist, was born in Dania, Florida, the youngest of fourteen children to parents Theophilus and Lucille Morley, vegetable farmers from the Eleuthera and Bahama Islands. Joyce spent her formative years in Dania until 1969, at which time she was sent by her mother to Rochester, New York, to live with her sister. Joyce's mother thought that her daughter might have access to a better educational system and decreased racial tensions in the North. Joyce graduated from Monroe Senior High School in Rochester, New York, two months following her seventeenth birthday. In 1973, she graduated cum laude from SUNY Geneseo with a B.S. in Elementary Education with a concentration in Psychology. While at Geneseo, Morley, along with her high school sweetheart, Bernard Watson, gave birth to their first daughter, Yolanda. In September 1973 Morley taught first, second, and third grades, beginning her career as an elementary school teacher at Nathaniel Hawthorne School Number 25, in Rochester, New York. However, the conditions under which she taught were trying—she taught the three grades in one overcrowded classroom for five years. She lobbied the Rochester school board and central office administration relentlessly for the reduction of class sizes in the public school as well as for the disaggregation of the multiple grades in classrooms. She then began to agitate for change through the parents of the students in her class. She continued to publicly decry the ill-treatment of students, particularly African American inner-city students, based on disproportionate class sizes. Eventually, she was successful and the Rochester City School District changed its policy to allow for singular groupings by grade in each classroom.

In 1975 Joyce and Bernard gave birth to their second daughter, Teknaya. The following year Joyce entered a master's program at SUNY Brockport and graduated with a master's degree in counseling in 1977. The next year, she became a public high school counselor in Rochester, New York, a position she held until 1981. In 1979 she married James Ball, a counselor with the New York State Department of Youth Services, with whom she had her third daughter, Natasha, in 1980. In 1983 she received her education specialist degree in educational administration from SUNY Brockport, and the following year received her second education specialist degree in counseling from the same institution.

In 1984 Morley-Ball opened a part-time, private psychotherapy practice specializing in group and individual counseling, as well as educational consulting. In 1986 she completed a one-year externship with the Marriage and Family Therapy Training Program of the University of Rochester's Department of Psychiatry, which allowed her to expand her practice to include marriage and family therapy. She was employed by this department as a marriage and family therapist for the next consecutive year. Over the course of the next several years, she would continue to serve in many administrative capacities within secondary and postsecondary educational institutions. In 1987 she entered the clinical doctoral program in Counseling, Family, and Worklife at the University of Rochester. Morley-Ball divorced her husband in 1989, and in 1990 relocated herself, her children, and her private practice to Atlanta, Georgia, in an effort to return to the region in which she was born and avail herself of the manifold professional opportunities she had heard were available for progressive African Americans. Once in Atlanta, she joined the faculty of Clark Atlanta University, in the department of Counseling and Human Development, as an assistant professor and supervisor of the Internship and Practicum program. In 1991 she graduated from the doctoral program at the University of Rochester—the first African American to receive the doctorate degree from this particular program (her two eldest daughters would later follow suit and obtain doctorate degrees as well, and her third daughter would get a master's degree).

In 1995 Morley-Ball began her service of two consecutive terms as president of the Atlanta Branch of the American Association of University Women—the first African American to serve in this position. She would continue to work at the postsecondary level as teacher and counselor at many Georgia institutions. She was honored by the former U.S. president William Jefferson Clinton in December 1996 for her facilitation of a roundtable discussion, sponsored by the White House, entitled "At the Table," which dealt with the inclusion of women's voices, roles, perspectives, and involvement in addressing issues that affect women's health, safety, and livelihood.

In 1999, Morley-Ball became the first African American to be elected president of the Athens, Georgia–based Jeannette Rankin Foundation Board, a nonprofit organization dedicated to raising funds for and awarding scholarships to low-income women, ages thirty-five and older. She held this leadership position for two consecutive terms. Morley-Ball was recognized as a national certified counselor by the American Counseling Association (ACA), a clinical member and approved supervisor by the American Association for Marriage and Family Therapy (AAMFT), and a certified criminal justice specialist by the National Association of Forensic Counselors (NAFC). She was a fully licensed psychotherapist in private practice and offered motivational speaking and training sessions at the national, state, and local levels. She spoke at Madison Square Garden as well as other major U.S. and international venues, and was recognized in *Who's Who in Medicine and Healthcare*, *Who's Who among Human Service Professionals*, and *The World's Who's Who among Women*.

Beginning in the late 1990s Morley-Ball gained local and national renown as "Doctor Joyce," the love and relationship doctor, and as such has served as an expert consultant, columnist, and relationship editor to many national magazines including *Essence, Ebony, Black Enterprise, Family Digest* and *Galz* magazines. From 1997 through 2000 she hosted the *Doctor Joyce Show*, a live, weekly, radio call-in talk show. From 2000 to 2003 she served as the relationship expert and cohost of the weekly *Love and Relationships* show on a top-rated CBS Radio affiliate in Atlanta. Her first book of poetry, *Weary but Not Worn: A Spiritual Reawakening*, was published in April 1999 and received critical acclaim. Another book, *Seeds for the Harvest of a Lifetime: Increasing Self-Awareness, Self-Esteem and Improving Relationships*, was published in 2005. A long way from the classroom, Doctor Joyce continued to be a highly sought-after public speaker, author, and psychotherapy expert for radio and television.

YOLANDA L. WATSON SPIVA

Morris, Elias Camp (7 May 1855–2 Sept. 1922), shoemaker, newspaper publisher, clergyperson, denominational leader and organizer, business leader, and political activist, was born the eighth of ten children to James and Cora Cornelia Morris near Spring Place in Murray County, Georgia, as a slave. On 24 November 1884 Morris married Fannie E. Austin of Alabama; they had five children. His father, James, came to Alabama from North Carolina in 1850. The father, relatively educated for the time, practiced a trade in town and visited the farm twice weekly, during which time he taught his family reading and writing in preparation for their eventual freedom. Elias augmented this home training by attending schools between 1864 and 1875 in Dalton, Georgia; Chattanooga, Tennessee; Stevenson, Alabama; and Nashville, Tennessee (the school that eventually became Roger Williams University). Converted in 1874, he was also licensed to preach by a Baptist church the same year. Upon his parents' death, he lived with a relative, the Reverend Robert Caver, who apprenticed him as a shoemaker; it was a

livelihood Morris continued until his ministerial obligations required his sole vocational attention.

While Morris's roots were in Georgia and Alabama; the bulk of his life's work came while he lived in Arkansas. In 1877, at the time of the Great Exodus of African Americans moving from the South to Kansas, for some reason Morris decided to settle in Helena, Arkansas. In 1879 he was ordained and called to pastor the Centennial Baptist Church in the city, a pastorate he retained until his death. He organized a local Baptist association and became secretary in 1880 and then president of the Arkansas Baptist State Convention in 1882. That same year Morris founded the *Baptist Vanguard* and served as its editor for the first two years of its existence. This newspaper became the major organ for Baptist news in Arkansas. Believing firmly in the necessity of education and Christianity, Morris established the Arkansas Baptist College in 1884.

Black Baptists during this time were continuing their efforts to form a successful national organization. An important move in that direction was the Baptist Foreign Mission Convention (BFMC), organized in 1880. Morris assumed the vice presidency of this group in 1892 and became president in 1894. Shortly thereafter, in 1895, two other Baptist groups united with the BFMC to form the National Baptist Convention, which immediately became the largest denominational body of black Christians. Morris headed that group until 1921. As president, he provided leadership for the establishment of boards and agencies for publishing, youth, ministerial benefits, home missions, and women's auxiliary. Perhaps his greatest struggle came when the National Baptist Convention split over the issue of the publishing board. RICHARD HENRY BOYD, founder of the National Baptist Convention of America in 1915, had incorporated the publishing board under his name and denied the claim of the original convention's supervision. With the loss to Boyd in the courts, the original body incorporated itself as the National Baptist Convention, USA, Inc., and founded a new publishing house. Morris was also active in moves among Baptists in North America and internationally to form cooperative organizations. He contributed greatly, for example, to the establishment of Baptist World Alliance. Beyond the Baptist denomination, Morris served as a vice president of the Federal Council of Churches, which was a forerunner of the National Council of Churches.

Like many other black religious leaders of the era, Morris also made important contributions in the areas of business and politics. Fostering the growth of African American businesses, Morris established the Helena Negro Business League in 1902 and became a member of the National Negro Business League, led by BOOKER T. WASHINGTON, with whom Morris established a close working relationship. Politically, Morris was active in the Republican Party at both the state and national levels. He served as a delegate to three national Republican conventions (1884, 1888, and 1904). For about forty years he served as delegate to the state party convention. Morris fought vigorously against the efforts of "lily white" Republicans to exclude blacks, but in 1920 he grew so disgusted with the challenges to the seating of some black delegates that he helped to organize a rival meeting. Although Morris was often a mediator between whites and blacks, he denounced lynching and Jim Crow segregation.

Later in life, Morris received two honorary degrees: a doctor of divinity from a state university in Louisville, Kentucky, in 1892, and a doctor of philosophy from Alabama State A&M in Normal, Alabama, in 1902.

Morris was a powerful example of black leadership in the late 1800s and early 1900s. Through his organizing efforts and devotion to religion, business, education, and politics, Morris sought to both Christianize and advance the condition of the entire African American populace. After a long illness, Morris died in 1922 at his son's home in Little Rock, Arkansas, and is buried in Magnolia Cemetery in Helena, Arkansas.

FURTHER READING

Hamilton, Green Polonius. *Beacon Lights of the Race* (1911).

SANDY DWAYNE MARTIN

Morris, Garrett (1 Feb. 1937–), comedian and actor, was born in New Orleans, Louisiana, to parents about whom little information is available. He was raised by his grandfather, a minister in a Baptist church and the guiding hand who would direct Morris into an early version of show business. Under his grandfather's watchful influence, Morris took up singing in the church choir and showed great flair for performance, even as a young boy. After high school, he attended Dillard University in New Orleans.

In 1958 Morris took part in a National Association of Negro Musicians singing competition, but on his way home to New Orleans, he stopped off in New York City and found a place with the Harlem YMCA Drama Club. The young man who wanted to be a singer had now been bitten by the theater bug. Not long after, Morris found work with the HARRY BELAFONTE Singers, with whom he sometimes soloed, but he also began to write plays and to look in earnest for acting work. In the meantime, he studied his craft at the Juilliard School in New York City and the Tanglewood music workshop in Lenox, Massachusetts. At Tanglewood he won an award as the best conductor in his class. Three years later, in 1960, he earned a part in *The Bible Salesman*, in a production at the Broadway Congregational Church. His career was just beginning to take shape when, in 1961, he was drafted by the army and spent nearly two years working as an X-ray technician. Upon his discharge, Morris returned to the Belafonte Singers (he stayed with them until 1968) and found more work as an actor.

Despite this early success, Morris found that his performances did not provide ample financial support. He took work as a high school teacher and later taught in a prison and a drug-rehabilitation center. During this time, Morris appeared in numerous plays and musicals, both on Broadway and off, among them *Hallelujah, Baby!* (1967–1968) and *Ain't Supposed to Die a Natural Death* (1971–1972). In 1972, his own play, *The Secret Place*, was produced at Playwrights Horizons theater in New York. It was at this time, too, that Morris made the move to television and film. He appeared in small roles in Carl Reiner's *Where's Poppa?* (1970) and Sidney Lumet's *The Anderson Tapes* (1971), as well as in a number of failed situation comedies and television pilots. In 1975, however, Morris did a well-regarded performance as a high school teacher in *Cooley High*. It was largely on the basis of this performance that, when he interviewed later that year for a spot as a writer on Lorne Michaels's new *Saturday Night Live* (SNL) sketch comedy show, Michaels instead hired Morris as a performer.

Morris's involvement with *SNL* was both a breakthrough and the beginning of an unhappy period for the young actor. Morris joined the first-season cast of the Not Ready for Primetime Players with Chevy Chase, John Belushi, Jane Curtin, and Gilda Radner, among others, but he was the only African American, and it at once became obvious that the writers were struggling to find an appropriate place for Morris among the cast. Much of the popular television and motion picture writing for black actors was still mired in worn stereotypes (Morris had opened his movie career as a mugger in *Where's Poppa?*), and so it was with *SNL*. Many of Morris's characters were stumblebums and smooth-talking grifters. Some of Morris's difficulties on the show have been attributed to his age—he was the oldest cast member by a decade (and so never really bonded with them)—others to his lack of experience as a short-form sketch performer. Unsure how to shape and use Morris's talents, *SNL* writers fell back on the kinds of stereotypes of African Americans that had plagued black actors for decades. On several occasions, they simply put him in a dress, first as TINA TURNER, later as a number of other black, female performers. Morris remained with the show for five seasons but was often criticized for his work there. He also struggled with an addiction to cocaine. In 1981 he married Freda Morris.

After leaving *SNL*, Morris again began to seek work as an actor. In 1982, his second produced play, *Daddy Picou and Marie Le Veau*, made its debut. Morris again found work on television with lesser or greater degrees of success. He appeared in the short-lived NBC sitcom *It's Your Move* (1984–1985), as a streetwise hustler on the cop show *Hunter* (1986–1989), and later in recurring roles in *Roc* (1991–1992), *Martin* (1992–1994), and *Cleghorne!* (1995). Morris also made numerous appearances in motion pictures, though again usually only in small roles. He appeared in *The Stuff* (1985), *Coneheads* (1993), *Twin Falls, Idaho* (1999), and *Jackpot* (2001), for which he was nominated for an Independent Spirit Award for Best Supporting Male. In 1994 Morris suffered a serious gunshot wound during what appeared to be an attempted robbery. The bullet injured Morris's spine, and the actor was left with lingering pain but otherwise made a full recovery.

Following his time on *SNL*, Morris became an outspoken critic of what he called the "White Adult Males Phenomenon," in which the major television networks either excluded African Americans altogether or else consigned them to small, supporting roles, and which refused to acknowledge the shifting realities of contemporary America's demographic makeup. Despite this, Morris has had a long and distinguished career on the stage and screen.

FURTHER READING
Shales, Tom, and James Andrew Miller. *Live from New York: An Uncensored History of Saturday Night Live, as Told by Its Stars, Writers, and Guests* (2002).
JASON PHILIP MILLER

Morris, Robert, Sr. (8 June 1823–12 Dec. 1882), probably the second black attorney to be admitted to practice law in the United States, was born in Salem, Massachusetts, to York Morris, a waiter, and Nancy Thomas. His grandfather, Cumons Morris, was brought to the United States from Africa while York Morris gained his freedom in 1781 and moved to Salem, working as a waiter. There he married Nancy Thomas, who gave birth to Robert and ten other children. Morris attended a private school in Salem and then became a waiter like his father. At age thirteen he moved to Boston under the patronage of the abolitionist attorney Ellis Gray Loring. Initially he was a servant in the Loring home; then he became a clerk in Loring's office, mostly copying documents. In 1844 he began reading law in Loring's office, and in 1847, shortly after his twenty-first birthday, he passed the Massachusetts bar. At the time, the only other black attorney in the nation was MACON ALLEN, who had been admitted to the bar in Maine and Massachusetts. The same year Morris was admitted to practice, Governor George N. Briggs appointed Allen as justice of the peace. Also that year Morris married Catherine Mason of Boston. They had one child, Robert Morris, Jr., who studied in Europe before becoming a lawyer in 1874.

In his first case Morris won a judgment for "services rendered" for a black plaintiff who had been denied proper compensation for his work. Although this was a simple legal action, this was also a case with civil rights overtones. For Morris, this was the beginning of a career in activism and social reform. Beginning in 1847, the decade before the U.S. Supreme Court decision in DRED SCOTT v. *Sandford*, Morris and Allen, joined by white activist attorneys, began the legal assault on the color barrier in American society and in American courtrooms. During this period Morris was active in the African Methodist Episcopalian church and served as a superintendent of the church's Sunday school. He was also a member of the mostly white Boston Lyceum, where mostly well-educated Bostonians met to hear lectures and readings by such luminaries as Caleb Cushing, Dr. Oliver Wendell Holmes Sr. and Edgar Allan Poe, presented their own research on various historical and literary topics, and discussed cultural and historical topics. The Lyceum also provided a library for members. Morris's membership in this organization underscores his high reputation, even among whites, and his keen intellect.

Morris's first major civil rights case involved a struggle to integrate Boston's schools. In 1840 both black and white abolitionists in Boston petitioned the school board to integrate the city's schools, but the board ignored them. Four years later, another abolitionist group petitioned the school board on this issue, but the board rejected their petition without written explanation. In 1846 this group again asked the board to end segregation in the schools. This time the board acknowledged the petitioners, only to reject their request, despite the dissents of two antislavery board members.

In the face of these failures, BENJAMIN F. ROBERTS, the father of five-year-old Sarah Roberts, decided to sue to make the board admit Sarah to the school nearest her home. Roberts filed the initial lawsuit in 1848. In 1849 the case—the nation's first challenging school segregation—went to the Massachusetts Supreme Judicial Court as *Roberts v. City of Boston*. Although he had initiated the case, Morris deferred in oral argument to his cocounsel: the more experienced, better trained, and politically connected Charles Sumner. Taking the case pro bono, Sumner made what turned out to be a prescient argument against segregation. In his brief, which was published and widely circulated as a pamphlet, Sumner outlined an argument against segregation that, with a few changes and some new social science data, would prevail nearly a century later in *Brown v. Board of Education*. Sumner even discussed the psychological damage of segregation.

Notwithstanding his brilliant argument, Sumner lost the case, as Chief Justice Lemuel Shaw ruled that separate but equal facilities were not inconsistent with the Massachusetts Constitution. Although the desegregation supporters in Boston lost the battle, they soon won the war. In 1855 the Massachusetts legislature prohibited segregation in the state's public schools.

Despite the negative outcome in *Roberts v. Boston*, Morris had made his mark as the first black attorney to appear before any state's highest court. Although there is no indication that he addressed the court, the official report of the case lists him as an attorney of record. In 1851 Morris almost broke the color line in the federal courts when he volunteered to help a fugitive slave named SHADRACH MINKINS. Ultimately, however, Morris wound up as a defendant, rather than as an attorney of record. In February of that year, federal marshals seized a black waiter known as Shadrach and brought him before U.S. Commissioner George T. Curtis under the Fugitive Slave Law of 1850. Several attorneys, including Morris, immediately offered to represent Shadrach Minkins. Morris was apparently the first lawyer to formally petition Commissioner Curtis for an extension of time so that Minkins could mount a defense. When the hearing on this petition began, four white abolitionist attorneys represented Minkins. However, spectators observed Morris sitting at the defense table and talking with the attorneys of record. If the hearing had continued, he probably would have become a formal part of the defense team, thus breaching the wall of segregation in at least one federal courtroom.

Although Morris never got the chance to defend Minkins in court, he was instrumental in obtaining Minkins's freedom. Commissioner Curtis granted the request for a delay, and the marshal ordered the courtroom cleared. At this point, someone—most likely Morris—opened the door to the courtroom, and a mob of blacks stormed in. They grabbed Minkins and whisked him from the scene before the startled and outnumbered court officers could act. Minkins quickly fled to Canada.

Federal authorities later sought treason indictments against Morris, alleging that he helped plan the rescue and opened the door to let Minkins escape. However, the federal grand jury in Boston only indicted him for a misdemeanor. After two trials, a jury acquitted Morris. By the end of the case, Morris had spent a great deal of time in federal court, but not as an attorney. In his own case, two white antislavery lawyers, Richard Henry Dana Jr., and U.S. Senator John P. Hale of New Hampshire, represented him. During this period, Morris continued to work against slavery as a member of Boston's racially integrated vigilance committee, which was organized to alert fugitive slaves and free blacks about the presence in Boston of slave catchers or suspicious southerners who might be hunting for fugitive slaves. The vigilance committee was organized in response to the Fugitive Slave Law of 1850. Within the black community some African American activists wanted to form their own committee, but Morris successfully argued for a joint, integrated committee. This position reflected his longtime commitment to interracial cooperation, racial equality, and integration.

In the early 1850s, shortly after the Minkins affair Morris became a justice of the peace in Massachusetts, and during the 1850s he sometimes served as a magistrate judge. He spoke at a meeting to celebrate the 1855 law banning school segregation in the state and publicly denounced the DRED SCOTT decision. During the Civil War he was an early advocate of enlisting black troops but insisted on black officers commanding them.

Morris's fight against discrimination was as personal as it was political and legal. A prosperous attorney, he faced hostile neighbors in the 1850s when he bought a house outside of Boston's traditional black neighborhoods. He was also sometimes forcibly removed from theaters and other places that he insisted on integrating. But he also successfully integrated some of these places when owners or managers changed their policies in the face of Morris's unyielding determination to end discrimination in the city that people often called "freedom's birthplace." In the 1850s Morris converted to Catholicism, which was unusual for Protestants at the time, but almost unheard of for blacks. His son, Robert Jr., studied at Harvard Law School and was admitted to the Massachusetts bar in 1874. Morris continued to practice law until his death in 1882 after a long illness. At the height of his career he was earning upward of $3,000 a year, providing legal service for both blacks and Irish immigrants.

FURTHER READING

Daniels, John. *In Freedom's Birthplace: A Study of Boston's Negroes* (1914).

Finkelman, Paul. "Not Only the Judges' Robes Were Black: African-American Lawyers as Social Engineers during and after Slavery," *Stanford Law Review* (1994).

Horton, James Oliver. *Free People of Color: Inside the African American Community* (1993).

Horton, James Oliver, and Lois E. Horton. *Black Bostonians: Family Life and Community Struggle in the Antebellum North* (1979).

Levy, Leonard W., and Douglas L. Jones, eds. *Jim Crow in Boston: The Origin of the Separate but Equal Doctrine* (1974).

Quarles, Benjamin. *Black Abolitionists* (1969).

Smith, J. Clay. *Emancipation: The Making of the Black Lawyer, 1844–1944* (1993).

PAUL FINKELMAN

Morris, Samuel (c. 1873–12 May 1893), student and Christian evangelist, was born Kaboo, son of a chieftain of the Kru tribe in the interior of West Africa, most likely in Liberia, Guinea, or the Ivory Coast. The details of his early life cannot be known with certainty, as there are conflicting accounts, but a general synthesis is possible. As the son of a chieftain, Prince Kaboo was twice held captive by tribal enemies to ensure the payment of war indemnities. He was treated brutally, but, in a series of events which he and his biographers viewed as miraculous, escaped and fled to the Liberian coast when he was fifteen or sixteen years of age.

Kaboo took work on a coffee plantation and learned to read and write rudimentary English. Conversations with a Miss Knolls and other missionaries influenced his decision to convert to Christianity. At his baptism Kaboo took the name Samuel Morris in honor of the Indiana lawyer who had supported Knolls financially in her preparation for the mission field. After working in the capital city of Monrovia for perhaps two years, Morris worked his way across the Atlantic. Already noted for his piety, he hoped to learn more about the Holy Ghost from a New York City Methodist minister and missionary leader named Stephen Merritt and acquire a biblical education before returning to Africa to work as a missionary.

After Morris had lived and ministered with Merritt for perhaps one month, Merritt and his colleagues, deeply impressed by Morris's piety and religious zeal, arranged for him to travel to Fort Wayne, Indiana, in late 1891 and begin studies at Taylor University. This small Methodist university was then in the midst of a financial crisis, and Morris's tuition was paid with contributions to a "Faith Fund" that was begun for his benefit and bears his name to this day. He was also supported by the Samuel Morris Missionary Society of New York City, a society that continued for many years and at one time had more than one thousand members.

Great interest was shown in Morris by local whites and African Americans during his student days at Taylor University, in part because of his African roots. Morris was the first black man to attend Taylor University. In the year that he began his studies, only 17 of 161 students were not from Indiana, and most of those students were from Ohio. By all surviving accounts Morris was well treated by the white students and faculty of Taylor, though local newspaper articles revealed traces of the racist beliefs then prevalent in Indiana and across the United States. Several local white women tutored Morris, who was reportedly a diligent student. He also seems to have been embraced by Fort Wayne's black religious community.

For many of Morris's acquaintances, the most remarkable thing about him was not his color or African origins but the fact that such an uneducated and "uncivilized" young man possessed such an intense and powerful spiritual life. His simple faith, fervency in prayer, and emphasis on the power of the Holy Spirit meshed well with the brand of holiness spirituality championed by Taylor University's new president, Thaddeus C. Reade. Morris's religious reputation created for him a somewhat liminal racial identity rare for that era. He became a member of the white Berry Street Methodist Episcopal Church and spoke at revival services held there during the winter of 1892–1893 even as he participated regularly in revival services held at a local African American church and preached there at least once.

Morris's life ended at a tragically early age. He contracted a severe cold in early 1893 and, after a lengthy illness, died from a condition diagnosed at the time as dropsy, though one modern physician has suggested that he suffered from pneumonia. He was probably around twenty years old. The white church to which Morris belonged was filled to overflowing for his funeral. Perhaps one thousand people viewed his remains. Local newspapers ran articles and stories about him, and hundreds of white and black mourners traveled to his burial site. Morris was buried in the "colored" section of Fort Wayne's Lindenwood Cemetery, though his grave was moved in 1928 to a prominent plot bridging the white and black sections.

While the degree of attention and respect accorded to this young African convert living in the midst of a deeply racist American society was remarkable, the power of his memory has been even more astonishing. This influence began shortly after Morris's death, when, at a university prayer meeting, three students volunteered to go to Africa as missionaries in his place. Morris's story has been used at Taylor University ever since as a rallying cry for foreign missions.

Even more influential were written accounts of Morris's life. While Morris was still alive, Thaddeus Reade built interest in him and the university by publishing notices in religious magazines. Stephen Merritt also wrote several articles about Morris. After Morris's death, Reade wrote a widely circulated biography. By 1924 it had sold more than two hundred thousand copies and been translated into several languages. In 1897 alone the book earned $1,200. Profits from the book funded scholarships for poor Taylor students. Reade and many subsequent observers credited the money and publicity generated by Morris's story with saving Taylor University from financial ruin and helping to shape the university's enduring religious character.

The story of Samuel Morris is still frequently told at Taylor University and in evangelical religious circles, and Morris is invoked as a symbol of simple faith, religious zeal, and racial reconciliation. Books about Morris have been written or translated into French, Spanish, New Guinea Pidgin, Hindi, and Chinese. Two biographies written in English for a popular audience are still in print. A 1954 film called *The Angel in Ebony* was widely viewed. Since 1894 Samuel Morris Hall has housed students on the campus of Taylor University, and in 1995 the university unveiled three statues of Morris by the sculptor Ken Ryden.

FURTHER READING

Information and documents about Samuel Morris are housed in the Sammy Morris Collection, Taylor University Archives, Upland, Indiana.

Baldwin, Lindley. *Samuel Morris* (1942).

Masa, Jorge O. *The Angel in Ebony* (1928).

Reade, Thaddeus C. *Samuel Morris (Prince Kaboo)* (1896).

ANDREW WITMER

Morrison, George (9 Sept. 1891–5 Nov. 1974), jazz violinist and orchestra leader, was born in Fayette, Missouri, one of fourteen children born to Clark and Alice Morrison, both talented musicians. Morrison's father held Missouri's title as a champion fiddler, and his mother played piano. Although Clark Morrison died when George was two, the boy wanted to play violin from an early age. When reprimanded for playing his father's violin, he made his own instrument from a hollowed-out cornstalk, a piece of wood, and some string. In 1900, when the family followed George's married sister to Boulder, Colorado, George learned to play guitar by ear, and by the time he was ten was playing mining camp saloons with his brothers. He worked as a bootblack to earn money for a violin and music lessons from the University of Colorado professor Dr. Harold Reynold. After graduating from Boulder High School he married Willa May of Denver on 28 August 1911, moved to Denver, and began studying with the violinist David Abramowitz and Dr. Horace Tureman, conductor of the Denver Civic Symphony Orchestra.

Though Morrison's dream of playing with a symphony orchestra could never be realized in the racial climate of the first half of the twentieth century, his desire to make a living in the music world did not die. Following his marriage he worked evenings in Denver's bordellos, supplementing that income with work as an elevator operator, deliveryman, and porter. The New England Conservatory offered him a scholarship, but Morrison did not want to move his family to the East Coast. They did move to Chicago, however, where he attended the Columbia Conservatory of Music, supporting his studies and his family by playing jazz at the Panama Cabaret and the Grand Theater.

Upon his return to Denver he formed George Morrison and His Orchestra, the group that caught the attention of the recording industry in 1920 with their melodic and danceable variety of jazz. During the decade that became known as the Jazz Age, the record industry sought black musicians to record for its so-called race records divisions, records it hoped to sell in the black community. Columbia Records invited Morrison and his eleven-piece group to New York, where they recorded under the name Morrison's Singing Jazz Orchestra. During that time the Victor Phonograph Company invited the group for a tone test. When Columbia Records learned of this invitation it hastened to inform Morrison that his contract with the company was exclusive. Victor asked Morrison if he could recommend another western jazz band, and he suggested Paul Whiteman, a white Denver bandleader whose career became legend. Columbia Records did not renew Morrison's contract, and the band returned to Denver—but not before Morrison caught the attention of the eminent classical violinist Fritz Kreisler. Kreisler heard him play at the Carleton Supper Club and was impressed enough to offer him six free lessons. In 1920 Morrison's orchestra toured Mexico, Canada, and England, where the group played a command performance for King George and Queen Mary.

Back in Denver Morrison signed with the Pantages Circuit, an agency that booked vaudeville houses in large western cities. Pantages gave the group top billing as a "symphonic jazz orchestra" that featured the singer-comedian HATTIE MCDANIEL, "the Female BERT WILLIAMS." As traditional theaters were refitted and became movie houses, however, vaudeville began to fade, and Morrison was forced to find other venues. He was just as happy to play closer to home at the Arena Ballroom at Sixth and Broadway and running the Casino, his own ballroom on Welton Street. Guests could roller skate or dance on alternate days—at the time a popular concept—and take lessons for either activity. During the 1930s and 1940s Morrison's orchestra played regularly at Lakeside Amusement Park's El Patio Ballroom as the Rigadooners, a catchy name chosen by Lakeside's general manager Joe Moore as a marketing ploy. Moore had decided to play on the word "Rigadoon," from a French word (rigaudon or rigodon) for a dance or music for a dance. Morrison's orchestra also became a favorite at Denver's country clubs, society parties, proms, and weddings.

As Morrison's children, Marion and George Jr., grew up, they had many opportunities to meet some of America's best jazz musicians, including FATS WALLER, LOUIS ARMSTRONG, COUNT BASIE, NAT "KING" COLE, DUKE ELLINGTON, Jimmie Lunceford, and LIONEL HAMPTON. Since these musicians could not stay in downtown hotels when they came to play in Denver, many of them stayed with the Morrison family. Although both children played musical instruments and Marion often accompanied her father and brother on the piano, neither of them was ever allowed to play jazz.

When Morrison died of cancer at age eighty he left memories of enjoyable times and good music, a solid reputation among professional musicians (Down Beat magazine named him "the Best Musician west of K.C." in 1940), and a legacy as a man actively committed to the affairs of his community. He had played his violin every Sunday for Shorter African Methodist Episcopal (AME) Sunday morning church services, helped establish and raise money for the Welton Street Branch of the YMCA, founded the Black Musicians Local #623 to help black musicians achieve fair wages and hours, tutored children in the public schools, and supported Denver's Cosmopolitan Club, whose motto was "Humanity Above Race, Nationality, or Creed." Everyone who knew him admired his honesty, pleasant manner, and genuine desire to help wherever he was able. On 18 February 1976, little more than a year after Morrison's death, Denver honored him with a park bearing his name at 32nd and Lafayette and High Streets in Five Points.

FURTHER READING
Various newspaper clippings collected by Morrison over the years, along with two or three of his song lyrics, a poem, and programs from various Denver clubs or organizations where he appeared are held in the manuscript collection, reference number M.S. ARL55, at the Blair-Caldwell Library in Denver, Colorado.
Reese, Joan. "Two Gentlemen of Note: George Morrison, Paul Whiteman, and Their Jazz," Colorado Heritage 2 (1986).

MOYA HANSEN

Morrison, Harry Lee (7 Oct. 1932–14 Jan. 2002), chemist, physicist, and educator, was born in Arlington, Virginia, the son of Charles Wilson Morrison, an automobile mechanic and inventor, and Ethel Elizabeth Moten. Gifted with the same high intelligence, technical curiosity, and drive that led his father to patent fourteen devices, Harry earned a bachelor's degree in chemistry in 1955 and a doctorate in chemistry in 1960 at the Catholic University of America. His Ph.D. dissertation was titled "Theoretical Investigation of the Excited States of Linear Triatomic Hydrogen." Morrison's first job was as a research chemist for the National Institutes of Health, a post that he held from 1955 to 1956. From 1960 to 1961 he was a National Research Council postdoctoral fellow at the National Bureau of Standards, where he was introduced to theoretical statistical mechanics, the field in which he later achieved renown.

Morrison's civilian career was put on hold when he was called to active military service in 1961. Reaching the rank of first lieutenant, he served as assistant professor of physics at the U.S. Air Force Academy from 1961 to 1964. Meanwhile he held a concurrent position at the Denver Research Institute as a theoretical physicist, and in 1963 he was awarded the Air Force Commendation Medal. Returning to civilian life, Morrison married Harriet Brock (the couple had one child, a daughter, Vanessa) just prior to accepting the position of research physicist at the Lawrence Radiation Laboratory in Berkeley, California, where he worked from 1964 until 1972, when he became associate director of the Lawrence Hall of Science, a museum established to encourage science education among elementary and high school students. In 1970 Morrison cofounded the highly successful Mathematics, Engineering, Science Achievement (MESA) outreach program to promote scientific and technical studies among minority and economically disadvantaged college students, a model that soon spread to campuses across the nation.

Morrison's research specialties were in quantum liquid theory and the foundations of quantum statistical physics. Intrigued by the interplay of mathematics and physics, he devoted much attention to the phenomenon of spontaneous symmetry breaking in superfluid helium, specifically the behavior of fluids when temperature dips and fluids are transformed into superfluids. Probably his most significant contribution to physics occurred in 1972 when, with the collaboration of Drs. John Garrison and Jack Wong, in a demonstration at the Lawrence Livermore National Laboratory he applied algebraic quantum field theory to the problem of physical systems and improved upon earlier analyses by establishing a mathematical basis for two-dimensional phase transitions. Several years later Morrison, with the aid of the graduate student James Lindesay, applied the theory of current algebra to the geometry of macroscopic quantum flows in superfluid helium, thus proving a-profound connection between microscopic and macroscopic physics.

In 1968 Morrison edited the book *Quantum Theory of Many-Particle Systems*, and in 1985 he wrote a chapter on the geometry of quantum flow for the book *Mathematical Analysis and Physical Systems*. His scholarly research was published in major scientific periodicals. Among other topics, he wrote on representations of the diffeomorphism group describing an infinite bose gas, long-range order in thin films, and Galilean relativity, locality, and quantum hydrodynamics in issues of the *Journal of Mathematical Physics;* the theory of superfluidity in two dimensions in the *Journal of Physics;* current algebra in liquid helium, the dynamics of quantum vortices, statistical mechanics in quantum physics, and Hodge decomposition and the vortex Hamiltonian in *Physical Review A;* symmetry breaking in the superfluid phase transition and the Kosterlitz-Thouless transition on compact Riemann surfaces in *Modern Physics Letters B;* and a version of the efficient linear L estimator in the *Journal of the American Statistical Association.* He maintained memberships in the American Mathematics Society and the International Society of Mathematical Physics, and he was elected to Sigma Xi, an honorary scientific research society.

Morrison was recruited to join the physics department at the University of California, Berkeley, in 1972 as associate professor. One of only a handful of black professors on campus at the time, he helped solidify the newly established blacks studies program. Recognizing the lack of course work acknowledging the role of African Americans in advancing science and technology, he co-created and taught a survey course called The African American Experience in Science and Technology, which included visits from Bay Area African Americans. In 1973 Morrison cofounded the National Society of Black Physicists (NSBP). He chaired the committee on minorities for the American Physical Society (APS) and served on that organization's executive council from 1971 to 1975. He was a fellow of both the NSBP and the APS. Also during the 1970s Morrison was a visiting professor at Howard University, Hampton University, the University of Colorado, and the Massachusetts Institute of Technology.

In 1975 he was promoted to full professor, followed ten years later by his appointment as assistant dean in the undergraduate advising office of the College of Letters and Science at Berkeley. A quiet, warm, and personable man, Morrison was sought after by students, particularly by African American students, for his kind and helpful counsel. Though he retired from teaching in the physics department in 1994, he continued in his position as a dean until 1996. An engaging conversationalist, he could discuss jazz and sports at length, and in his spare time he enjoyed reading books on the history of physics and mathematics. Morrison died of a heart attack at his home in Berkeley, California.

FURTHER READING

Jackson, Keith H. "Harry Lee Morrison," *Physics Today* 55 (Aug. 2002).

Kessler, James H., et al. *Distinguished African American Scientists of the 20th Century* (1996).

ROBERT FIKES JR.

Morrison, Toni (18 Feb. 1931–), novelist and Nobel laureate, was born Chloe Ardelia Wofford in Lorain, Ohio, a poor, ethnically diverse steel town. She was the second of four children of George Wofford, who worked, variously, as a welder in a steel mill and as a road construction and shipyard worker, and Ella Ramah Willis. Both of Morrison's parents had migrated north, seeking better opportunities and to escape racial and economic oppression in the South. Her maternal grandparents had come to Ohio from Alabama and Kentucky; her father was originally from Georgia. Like many African American migrants, her family eventually realized that the North was not free of racism and poverty. Yet Morrison's childhood in Lorain taught her to value a community in which people shared the limited resources available to them. She also learned to appreciate the value of storytelling at an early age.

Morrison converted to Catholicism when she was twelve years old. In honor of St. Anthony, she took Anthony as her baptismal name, which her friends shortened to Toni. A 1949 honors graduate of Lorain High School, she earned her B.A. in English at Howard University, in Washington, D.C., in 1953, where she joined the Howard University Players, a repertory troupe that performed for African American audiences in the South. After completing her thesis on William Faulkner and Virginia Woolf, in 1955 she received an M.A. in English from Cornell University. Early in her career she taught as an instructor of English, first at Texas Southern University, in Houston (1955–1957), and then at Howard (1957–1964). She married Harold Morrison,

Toni Morrison, listening to Mexico's Carlos Monsivais during the Julio Cortazar professorship conference at Guadalajara University, 25 November 2005. (AP Images.)

a Jamaican-born architect, in 1958, with whom she had two sons, Harold Ford and Slade Kevin. The couple divorced in 1964, and, pregnant with her younger son, Morrison took Ford and returned to Lorain.

Morrison has said that during the early years of the civil rights struggle, she was not especially interested in the movement to integrate institutions and public facilities. She had certainly seen firsthand the injustices of Jim Crow segregation, but she had been sustained by the power, wisdom, and imagination nurtured within black communities, and was concerned that integration would diminish the richness of African American culture. She doubted that integration alone would resolve the fundamental issues of racism and economic deprivation. Instead, like ZORA NEALE HURSTON, as well as many black teachers in southern schools, Morrison believed that African American children could thrive if schools in black communities received significant financial investment in faculty, buildings, and materials.

In 1965 Morrison was hired as a senior editor at Random House in its textbook subsidiary, L. W. Singer Publishing, in Syracuse, New York. She was promoted in 1967 to a senior editorship at Random House's New York City headquarters, where she worked for the next seventeen years. While at Random House Morrison built up an impressive client list of more than twenty authors, publishing thirty-five books. Projects for which she was responsible include LEON FORREST's *There Is a Tree More Ancient Than Eden* (1973) and *The Bloodworth Orphans* (1977); GEORGE JACKSON's *Blood in My Eye* (1972); Ivan van Sertima's *They Came before Columbus* (1976); fiction and essays of TONI CADE BAMBARA; GAYL JONES's first three novels; JUNE JORDAN's *Things That I Do in the Dark* (1977); Chinweizu's *The West and the Rest of Us* (1975); and ANGELA DAVIS's *An Autobiography* (1974).

During this period Morrison continued to teach at the university level. Appointed an associate professor of English at the State University of New York at Purchase in 1971–1972, she was also a visiting lecturer at Yale University in 1976–1977. From 1984 until 1989 she held the Albert Schweitzer Professorship of Humanities at the State University of New York, Albany, and was a visiting professor at Bard College from 1986 to 1988. She was appointed the Robert F. Goheen Professor of Humanities at Princeton University in 1989. In 1998 she was also named the A. D. White Professor at Large at Cornell University. Notwithstanding the considerable demands of her teaching and editorial work, she found time during these years to launch her own distinguished career as a writer.

Morrison produced *The Bluest Eye* (1970) during a period that saw the emergence of a new black aesthetic, and in the novel she explores the destructive impact of racist and elitist standards of beauty and value upon young black girls in particular and upon African American communities generally. *Sula* (1973), which was nominated for the National Book Award and received the Ohioana Book Award, appeared in the midst of the reinvigorated feminist movement and examines how the friendship between two women, as well as their relationships with men, are affected by the politics of labor, social mobility, and migration. *Song of Solomon* (1977) addresses the impact of post-Reconstruction migration and class politics on several generations of a wounded and haunted family; it was chosen as a main selection of the Book of the Month Club and received the National Book Critics Circle Award and the American Academy and Institute of Arts and Letters Award. With the publication of this book, Morrison began to see herself as a writer, rather than as an editor who also wrote.

Tar Baby (1981) is concerned with the impact of colonialism upon the relationships and conflicting cultures in a multiracial household. After it appeared, Morrison was appointed to the American Academy and Institute of the Arts and was featured on the cover of *Newsweek*. *Beloved* (1987) is a powerful novel that set a new standard for African American literature, and, indeed, a new benchmark in the history of American letters. Set during the era of Reconstruction, *Beloved* is based loosely on the true story of MARGARET GARNER, a fugitive slave who killed her own child rather than allow her to be sold into slavery. By means of powerfully lyrical, deeply suggestive language, the novel resurrects the dead baby and presents her insatiable desire for maternal love as well as the unfathomable depths of the mother's sense of loss. Moreover, it explores the profound impact of the traumatic memory of slavery upon black bodies, black communities, and, by extension, American culture. *Beloved* won Morrison numerous awards, most notably the Pulitzer Prize. It did not, however, win the National Book Award, for which it was nominated. In response to this perceived oversight, forty-eight African American writers and critics published a letter in the *New York Times* to express their outrage; in 1996 she received the National Book Award for Distinguished Contribution to American Letters. In 2006, after soliciting the opinion of 125 leading critics and authors, the *New York Times Book Review* announced that *Beloved* was "the single best work of American fiction published in the last 25 years."

Jazz, published in 1992, explores from an improvisational, captivating narrative perspective a set of passionate relationships in 1920s Harlem shaped by the experience of migration and the uncertainties of the urban context. The following year Morrison became the first African American to receive the Nobel Prize in Literature, and the Swedish Academy issued a stamp in her honor. She followed *Jazz* with the novels *Paradise* (1998), a powerful story of intimacy and violence set in an all-black community in Ruby, Oklahoma, and *Love* (2003), which explores both the passions several women feel for and project upon one man and that man's own complex emotional life.

Morrison is no doubt best known for her novels, which have earned her an extraordinary range of prizes and a wide readership. *Song of Solomon, Paradise, The Bluest Eye,* and *Sula* were all discussed on *The Oprah Winfrey Show,* and in 1998 a screen adaptation of *Beloved*, directed by Jonathan Demme and starring OPRAH WINFREY, DANNY GLOVER, and Thandie Newton, was released. Morrison's 2008 novel, *A Mercy*, about a slave child abandoned by her mother in 17th century New York, was selected as one of the year's ten best books by the *New York Times Book Review*. In 2011 she was awarded the Library of Congress National Book Festival Award for Creative Achievement. Her 10th novel, *Home,* set in the 1950s was published in 2012.

Morrison has, however, produced important work in a variety of other genres as well. Her name does not appear on it, but in 1974 she edited *The Black Book*, a collection of print artifacts that represent black lives as well as black cultural expression. The text, which contains newspaper clippings, photographs, songs, advertisements, slave bills of sale, Patent Office records, receipts, rent-party jingles, and other memorabilia, was the first of Morrison's critical forays into the production of historical memory. This concern has continued with two edited collections of essays on topical issues: *Race-ing Justice, Engendering Power: Essays on Anita Hill, Clarence Thomas, and the Construction of Social Reality* (1992) and, with Claudia Brodsky Lacour, *Birth of a Nation'hood: Gaze, Script, and Spectacle in the O. J. Simpson Case* (1997). In each collection, Morrison and other prominent literary and cultural critics and legal theorists tease out and rigorously analyze the implicit, repressed, and interlocking narratives of race, gender, and sexuality that underlie two pivotal

events in late-twentieth-century American life: the CLARENCE THOMAS Senate confirmation hearings and the O. J. SIMPSON criminal trial.

Her unpublished play, "Dreaming Emmett," concerned with the meanings of what is perhaps the most publicized lynching in U.S. history, that of EMMETT TILL in Mississippi in 1955, was produced in Albany, New York, in 1986. Her critical book, *Playing in the Dark: Whiteness and the Literary Imagination* (1992), is an influential and oft-cited analysis of ways in which preoccupations associated with writing by major authors such as Edgar Allan Poe, Herman Melville, and Willa Cather depend upon the construction of black figures who embody repressed fears and anxieties.

Morrison has participated in collaborative projects with other artists. For example, she wrote the lyrics to *Honey and Rue,* a song cycle set to music by the pianist, composer, and conductor Andre Previn and performed by KATHLEEN BATTLE, which premiered in Chicago in 1992. With MAX ROACH, the jazz percussionist and composer, and the dancer and choreographer BILL T. JONES, she wrote *Degga,* a dance, musical, and narrative piece that was performed at the Lincoln Center for the Performing Arts in New York City in 1995. In recent years she has written four children's books with her son Slade: *The Big Box* (1999), illustrated by Giselle Porter; *The Book of Mean People* (2002); and, in 2003, *Who's Got Game?: The Ant or the Grasshopper?* and *Who's Got Game?: The Lion or the Mouse?*, both illustrated by Pascal Lemaitre.

Toni Morrison has produced some of the most artistically, historically, and politically important work of the late twentieth and early twenty-first centuries, as well as some of the most formally precise and challenging prose of literature written in English. Her experiments with narrative perspective and chronology require readers to enter the worlds she creates on her terms, to relinquish the desire for certainty and closure, to accept the partial, competing truths of multiple points of view, and to acknowledge the mutually constitutive relationship between myriad ostensible polarities such as past and present, body and spirit, life and death. She ranks among the most highly regarded and widely read fiction writers and cultural critics in the history of U.S. literature. Her prose makes visible and articulate what is often unseen and unheard in African American culture as well as in American culture more broadly. From one perspective, her work would seem to have a timeless quality, since it appeals to such a broad audience, but it is always steeped in the realities of the political, social, economic, and historical constraints of African American culture.

Morrison has achieved an extraordinary visibility internationally as well as nationally—her novels have been translated into many languages, and her work has received attention from scholars, critics, and general readers all over the world. As a result, she has become a figure who challenges preexisting notions of what it means to be an American writer, a black writer, a woman writer, and a black intellectual. A novelist of the first rank, she is also a critic of her own work, a theorist of the presence of African Americans and their writings in U.S. literature more broadly, and a trenchant interpreter of the contemporary cultural and political scene.

FURTHER READING

Als, Hilton. "Ghosts in the House," *New Yorker* (27 Oct. 2003): 64–75.
Matus, Jill. *Toni Morrison* (1998).
Peach, Linden. *Toni Morrison* (2000).
Samuels, Wilfred D., and Clenora Hudson-Weems. *Toni Morrison* (1990).
Taylor-Guthrie, Danille. *Conversations with Toni Morrison* (1994).

VALERIE SMITH

Morrow, E. Frederic (20 Apr. 1909–19 July 1994), public servant and business executive, was born Everett Frederic Morrow in Hackensack, New Jersey, the son of John Eugene Morrow, a library custodian who was ordained as a Methodist minister in 1912, and Mary Anne Hayes, a former farmworker and maid. He was educated in public schools in Hackensack, where, he would later write in his second work of memoir, *Way Down South Up North* (1973), race relations were as treacherous as the situation in the Deep South. Morrow then attended Bowdoin College, to which he believed he won admission only because administrators assumed that he was a relative of Dwight Morrow, a leading politician, lawyer, and banker of the day. Having gained a B.A. degree during the depths of the Depression, Morrow secured a social work job sponsored by a New Deal agency and later worked as a bank messenger on Wall Street.

In 1935 Morrow joined the National Urban League as business manager of *Opportunity* magazine, and two years later he moved to the NAACP as a field secretary. At the NAACP, Morrow promoted the organization's grassroots development, traveling across the nation to foster the growth of membership and fund-raising. His military service during World War II was with the U.S. Army Field Artillery,

which he entered in 1942. Although at first he found access to officer training blocked on racial grounds, he eventually rose to the rank of major. On leaving the army in 1946, he attended the Rutgers University School of Law, from which he graduated with a J.D. degree in 1948. After a law clerkship in Englewood, New Jersey, Morrow returned briefly to active duty in the armed forces during the Korean War. In 1950 he joined the Columbia Broadcasting System (CBS) as a writer in its public affairs division.

A longtime Republican, Morrow began his full-time participation in politics when he joined Dwight Eisenhower's campaign train during the fall of 1952. At the end of the campaign, Morrow resigned from CBS after receiving an offer from Sherman Adams, Eisenhower's chief of staff, of a job in the administration. But Morrow did not then secure an appointment, and he later discovered that members of the White House staff had threatened to leave if Morrow joined them. In July 1953 he gained an assignment as adviser on business affairs in the Department of Commerce.

Morrow finally won appointment to the White House in July 1955, when he was named administrative officer for special projects. His duties in this capacity included support services for the work of two special assistants to Eisenhower, Harold E. Stassen on nuclear disarmament, and Nelson A. Rockefeller on psychological warfare. At the end of 1957 Morrow joined the staff of the White House speechwriter Arthur Larson, but within a few months he had returned to his former position. Although Morrow resisted special responsibility for African American affairs, preferring to be recognized as a member of the general staff, Adams assigned these duties to him in April 1958 when Maxwell Rabb, previously charged with liaison with minority groups, left the administration. In 1957 Morrow married Catherine Gordon.

The first African American member of a president's executive staff, Morrow was important to the White House as a symbol of racial progress. He accompanied Richard Nixon, the vice president, on a tour of African nations in 1957, and he gave speeches in support of the administration's record on civil rights. Yet Morrow's experiences tended to suggest that change was symbolic rather than substantive. He encountered both personal and professional humiliations in the White House. He was not, for example, officially sworn in as a member of the presidential staff until January 1959, and Eisenhower was unusually absent from the ceremony in order to avoid press attention to the delay. As the struggle for civil rights unfolded during the

1950s, senior figures rarely sought and even more rarely heeded the advice of Morrow, who occupied a marginal role in the administration, often being assigned duties of a mundane nature. Morrow felt "ridiculous standing on platforms all over the country, trying to defend the Administration's record on civil rights" (*Black Man in the White House*, 179). The work exposed him to criticism among some African Americans, and Morrow observed that he was perceived "as a symbol of disloyalty and a kind of benevolent traitor" (266). Among the initiatives on which Morrow disagreed with the administration's action was the Civil Rights Act of 1957; when Congress weakened the bill, he believed that Eisenhower should have vetoed it. During the Little Rock crisis of the same year, Morrow found himself excluded from decision-making circles, and he supported swifter and stronger action against Governor Orval Faubus's challenge to desegregation there.

Despite the gains made by Eisenhower among African Americans in 1956, especially in southern cities, Morrow believed that the Republican Party neglected an opportunity to boost its popularity among this group, preferring instead to seek votes in the white South. Leading Republicans, he discovered, were surprised that the gradualist progress under Eisenhower toward strengthening civil rights was not enough to challenge Democratic strength among African Americans. Morrow emphasized that economic factors ensured that many African Americans were wary about support for the Republican Party, but he told leading Republicans that expressions of concern about racial inequality and affirmative measures to include African Americans in party activities could transform this gloomy picture. "In most of the areas where I had been," he wrote of his travels during the 1958 midterm campaigns, "the Republican leadership was aloof, still looked upon Negroes as a lower class, and talked down to them rather than giving them any chance of equality" (*Black Man in the White House*, 261–262). Most Republicans did not respond positively to these suggestions, and Morrow discovered that the party overall was already viewing the African American community as a lost constituency. Morrow nevertheless joined the Nixon campaign during the fall of 1960, having developed a respect for the vice president as a politician with a commitment to equality. His hopes were disappointed, however, when he found himself excluded from the inner circle of a campaign that targeted gains in the white South rather than among African American voters.

In contrast to his white colleagues, Morrow found few opportunities in the private sector open to him at the end of the Eisenhower administration. In a *New York Times* interview, he spoke of "the jungle of racial barriers" that still affected his career, despite his position in the White House (23 Dec. 1960). Morrow wrote an account of his time in the Eisenhower administration, published as *Black Man in the White House* (1963). A significant text that testified to the difficulties and indignities suffered by Morrow and provided an insider account of the administration's approach to civil rights, the book sparked some controversy for its revelations of prejudice and discrimination within the White House. Although Morrow insisted that the president's intentions were good, his conclusion about Eisenhower's achievements in civil rights was ultimately a negative one. As he put it, "At no time had [Eisenhower] made any overt gestures that would encourage Negroes to believe that he sympathized with, or believed in, their crusade for complete and immediate citizenship" (300).

Morrow again broke racial barriers in 1964, when he joined the senior management of the Bank of America as an assistant vice president, becoming a vice president within three years and a division head within five. He encountered many frustrations similar to those that had blighted his earlier career, however, and concluded in his third work of autobiography, *Forty Years a Guinea Pig*, that "in the big corporations of America, Black executives, even senior ones, *can be in it but not of it*" (4). Morrow did not return to public life, turning down an invitation to join Nixon's 1968 presidential campaign. Retiring from the Bank of America as a senior vice president in 1975, he joined the Educational Testing Service in Princeton, New Jersey, as an executive associate.

Morrow died in New York City from complications following a stroke. Morrow's work in the White House made him significant during the 1950s as an African American pioneer at the highest levels of American government. That his work for the Eisenhower White House remained symbolic rather than substantial was a frustration to Morrow and a reminder of the limited nature of racial progress at this time.

FURTHER READING

There are collections of E. Frederic Morrow's papers at the Dwight D. Eisenhower Library, Abilene, Kansas, and at the Department of Special Collections, Mugar Memorial Library, Boston University.

Morrow, E. Frederic. *Black Man in the White House: A Diary of the Eisenhower Years by the*

Administrative Officer for Special Projects, the White House, 1955–1961 (1963).

Morrow, E. Frederic. *Forty Years a Guinea Pig* (1980).

Morrow, E. Frederic. *Way Down South Up North* (1973).

Burk, Robert Frederick. *The Eisenhower Administration and Black Civil Rights* (1984).

Katz, Milton S. "E. Frederick [*sic*] Morrow and Civil Rights in the Eisenhower Administration," *Phylon* 42.2 (1981).

Obituary: *New York Times*, 21 July 1994.

ROBERT MASON

Morrow, Willie Lee (9 Oct. 1939–), barber, entrepreneur, and inventor was born in Greene County, Alabama, the oldest of Holly and Olean (Jordan) Morrow's seven children. As a child, Willie worked on a farm planting corn and cotton. He worked in the fields before going to school, and he learned to cut hair by practicing on the children there. He became a barber at the age of seventeen when his mother took him to meet Jim Pierson, the owner of the Oak City Barber Shop in Tuscaloosa. Pierson employed him for three years and gave him a set of Oster clippers that replaced the rudimentary clippers he had used. Barbering became his lifelong vocation and would lead him into the beauty business—a world in which many African Americans had made their fortunes.

In 1959 Morrow took a train to San Diego, California, to work with his uncle, barber Spurgeon Morrow, and to attend barber school. His first job at Smitty's Barbershop paid twenty-six dollars a week, and ingenuity and frugality allowed Morrow to buy a car and a house within a year. He had mastered the skill of barbering and had built a respectable clientele. He saved his commissions and purchased the shop where he worked for $5,600 in 1960. In 1962 Morrow also studied theology at Linda Vista Bible College for three years and became a youth pastor. He was soon serving as an itinerant preacher to communities throughout Southern California. As the 1960s brought the nation's focus to black protest, Morrow was busy developing aesthetic manuals and implements to embrace the beauty of being black.

He began writing a textbook on barbering the hair of African Americans after he realized that barbering schools had overlooked the unique textures and methods required for styling black hair. This was the first of Morrow's many ventures, and he persuaded his customers to invest in the publishing project, guaranteeing them double on their investment. He raised ten thousand dollars to print *The Principles of Cutting and Styling Negro Hair*, which was published in 1966. The book was successful; he returned the investment at twenty-five cents on the dollar prior to the book being sold. He repaid all but one lender—one he could not locate. Morrow had begun the process of invention that would give him access to national markets. His mentor, Robert Mattox, a barber in Burbank, California, taught him the importance of creating a laboratory to experiment with techniques. Morrow followed this advice and created a cold-wave technique that became known as the Blow Out Kit. This kit was the first cream formula of hair relaxers for African Americans. It was sold all across the country and was even advertised in *Ebony* magazine. It would also serve as the forerunner of numerous innovations in black hair care. He then invented a comb derived from African styling principles that he called the Afro Pick. Morrow sent his inventions to civil rights workers and organizations to foster pride in their identity. The styles and products he created were soon featured on the pages of *Ebony* magazine. Furthermore, his book received attention from the military and led to a contract teaching barbering for black soldiers in the U.S. Army.

The Air Force was eager to see how he could improve the morale of African American enlistees, so he was flown to Texas to vie for a post as a trainer to its barbers. His insights and rapport with personnel quickly got him noticed by military officials such as David C. Jones, a four-star general who worried about racial tensions within the ranks; and by 1969 Morrow was earning three hundred dollars a day as a consultant on race relations among members of the armed forces. He was invited to lecture at West Point, and he traveled to bases in Germany, England, Italy, Turkey, and Spain, counseling the air force on a different kind of peace mission. In return, the military sent troops when Morrow requested assistance for testing a new product. The result was the Brush Shave, a product directed at black men to help manage the ingrown hairs they often incur after shaving.

In 1973 Morrow released a new book, *400 Years without a Comb*. It was based on the research he had conducted on African societies and the history of their styling systems. It presented theories and folklore of African American hair care adaptations during slavery and provided readers with an understanding of where some of the negative ideas toward black, kinky hair had originated. The book explored the difficulties of growing black hair without access to healthy, natural products or ingredients. It also examined the physical ailments that result from mismanagement. The book *400 Years without a Comb* was adapted to video in 1986, bringing to life the struggles African Americans have endured to maintain kinky hair.

Having established a reputation as one of the premier innovators in the black hair care business, in 1979 Morrow decided to purchase a two-million-dollar, thirty-eight-thousand-square-foot facility to house his styling enterprises. He paid cash for the block-long building in the heart of San Diego's black community on Market Street, but not without encountering some resistance from city leaders. He continued to expand his community development by purchasing a radio station (92.5 FM); he bought it in 1979 and owned it for the next ten years. He became affiliated with news agencies through advertising on the radio and in papers. As a result, he then established a local newspaper, *The San Diego Monitor News.* Trips to Africa also deepened areas of his knowledge and lifetime research in hairstyling. Upon attending a celebration with the ambassador of Dakar, Senegal, at the island of Gorée, in 1991, he discovered a museum there featuring exhibits that recognized that the history of black hair was unique and important. Morrow realized that there was nothing like it in the United States and that it was one of the best vehicles for telling the story of Africa's descendants. He opened the Hairitage Museum in 2003 and filled the building with artifacts that blacks used during slavery to straighten their hair. Displays included buckets of soap and lye used to create "the conk." The conk was short for Conkaleen, a product of the 1930s: the ingredients included lye, sodium hydroxides, a mixture of potatoes, butter, and lard. He pointed to the entertainers who popularized "conk" in the twentieth century who were known for having a "silky straight" haired look. Also displayed were some of the earliest forms of straightening combs, which were curling irons fashioned out of farming tools. The museum also featured prints of black hair pioneers such as MADAME C. J. WALKER and ANNIE TURNBO POPE MALONE along with products they developed. The museum chronicles shifts in hair styles through posters and photographs. It also contains the first barbering chair Morrow used in Tuscaloosa.

Morrow continued to reside in San Diego, California, with his wife, Gloria. They had two daughters, Cheryl and Angela, and a son, Todd.

FURTHER READING

Morrow, Willie L. *The Principles of Cutting and Styling Negro Hair* (1966).

Morrow, Willie L. *400 Years without a Comb: The Untold Story* (1973).

ISET ANUAKAN

Morton, Benny (31 Jan. 1907–28 Dec. 1985), jazz trombonist, was born Henry Sterling Morton in New York City. The names of his parents are unknown. As a child he was taught the trombone by Rohmie Jones, and he played with the Jenkins Orphanage Band. He began playing professionally as a teenager. In 1923 he was hired by Clarence Holiday's orchestra and was soon sitting in with the FLETCHER HENDERSON big band.

In 1926 Morton joined the Henderson band as a full-time trombonist and, at nineteen years old, was the group's youngest member. Despite his youth, Morton gained recognition with a sterling performance on a recording of "Jackass Blues" (1926) by the Henderson band. Morton's flawless technique and light, nimble style quickly earned him a reputation as one of the leading trombonist sidemen in the swing era of the 1920s and 1930s. He was also one of the first members of the Henderson band to employ the elaborate syncopation that became a hallmark of modern jazz. He stayed with the Henderson band until 1928, played with a variety of big bands in 1929, and in 1930 joined CHICK WEBB's big band. In 1931 Morton left Webb's band to play with DON REDMAN's orchestra, which was one of the leading African American big bands of the swing era. Morton stayed with the Redman band until 1937, when he joined the COUNT BASIE Orchestra. He performed with the Basie Orchestra for three years, then in 1940 was hired by TEDDY WILSON to play in a sextet. Morton played with the Wilson sextet until 1943, when he joined EDMOND HALL's band for a short time. In 1944 Morton formed his own group, which performed until the end of 1945.

From January 1946 through 1959 Morton worked in theater orchestras for Broadway musical productions, including *Guys and Dolls, Silk Stockings, St. Louis Woman,* and for several Radio City Music Hall productions in 1959. In the 1960s Morton returned to the jazz scene as a freelancer with various New York bands, including ones led by RED ALLEN in 1960, Ted Lewis in 1964, Wild Bill Davison in 1968, SY OLIVER in 1970 and 1971, and with the Saints and Sinners in 1967 and 1970. Morton joined the World's Greatest Jazz Band for a tour in 1973 and 1974, and in 1975 appeared on the

PBS television special *The World of John Hammond* with Benny Carter, Teddy Wilson, JO JONES, George Benson, and Red Norvo. He then continued playing on a freelance basis through the late 1970s and early 1980s. Morton died in New York City.

Though a sideman for nearly all of his career, Morton was nonetheless one of the most accomplished, innovative, and sophisticated trombonists of the swing era, and he can be considered a pioneer of modern jazz.

FURTHER READING
Dance, Stanley. *The World of Swing* (1974).
Schuller, Gunther. *Early Jazz: Its Roots and Musical Development* (1968).
Obituary: *Down Beat* 53 (Mar. 1986).
This entry is taken from the *American National Biography* and is published here with the permission of the American Council of Learned Societies.

THADDEUS RUSSELL

Morton, Ferdinand Quintin (9 Sept. 1881–8 Nov. 1949), attorney and political leader, was born in Macon, Mississippi, the son of Edward James Morton, a clerk in the U.S. Treasury Department, and Willie Mattie Shelton. Morton's parents were former slaves. His father accepted the position with the Treasury Department in 1890, when the family moved north to Washington, D.C. Morton attended school in Washington, then enrolled at Phillips Exeter Academy in New Hampshire. He graduated in 1902 and entered Harvard. He left Harvard after his junior year, in 1905, seemingly for financial reasons. Despite the fact that he was not a college graduate, he began studying at Boston University School of Law that fall. He remained there for only a year and a half, again leaving without a degree, probably because of monetary problems.

Morton next became involved in politics. In 1908 he moved to New York City and began working on the campaign of the Democratic presidential candidate William Jennings Bryan, giving speeches on his behalf. Bryan lost the presidency to the Republican William Howard Taft, but Morton retained his taste for Democratic Party politics. Still possessed with the desire to practice law, he worked as a law clerk for two years, then passed the New York State bar examination in 1910.

In addition to his work as a lawyer, Morton kept busy in the political arena. Shortly after his experiences with the Bryan campaign, he became a member of the United Colored Democracy, a political group established for the purpose of convincing New York's black population, made up traditionally of Republicans, to switch to the Democratic Party. The New York Democratic machine, known as Tammany Hall, was led by Charles F. Murphy, a man who admired Morton's speaking abilities and his intelligence. In 1915 Murphy secured Morton's nomination as leader of the United Colored Democracy in hopes of winning political backing from Harlem.

Balancing politics with his legal career, Morton practiced law for six years. In 1916 he was appointed assistant district attorney for New York County, and in 1921 he was placed in charge of the office's Indictment Bureau. Morton's tenure at that post was short-lived, however, because on 1 January 1922 he was appointed by Mayor John F. Hylan as the first black member of the New York Municipal Civil Service Commission. Morton's position on the commission helped guarantee an increase in the number of blacks employed by the city.

Blacks, however, were facing increased obstacles in other areas. In the 1920s white Democratic leaders tried to bring about the dissolution of the United Colored Democracy and instead incorporate its members into the more traditional Democratic political organizations. Morton refused to allow this to happen, believing that such a measure would do considerable damage to the political power of blacks as a whole, not to mention the harm it would inflict upon his own political clout. Morton eventually left his position with the United Colored Democracy in 1933, when the newly elected New York City mayor Fiorello LaGuardia threatened to remove him from the Civil Service Commission if he did not. Morton chose to remain on the commission, where his salary exceeded ten thousand dollars per year, placing him among the highest paid blacks employed by the city.

To fill the void left by his departure from politics, Morton in 1935 accepted the job of baseball commissioner of the Negro National League. He served as commissioner for four years, spanning the final two years that the National League was the sole black league and the first two years after the foundation of the rival Negro American League. In his role as commissioner, Morton was rarely called upon to do anything of consequence. His function was limited to appearances at league meetings. When in 1938 he attempted to call a league meeting on his own authority, GUS GREENLEE, the powerful owner of the Pittsburgh Crawfords, told the other owners not to bother to attend. The owners complied with Greenlee. Later that year the league abolished the office of commissioner.

On 16 July 1946 Morton was elected president of the Civil Service Commission. He continued as president until 10 January 1948, when the effects of Parkinson's disease forced him to retire. Morton, who never married, died in Washington, D.C., when the hospital bed in which he was receiving treatment caught fire from a lit cigarette.

FURTHER READING

Two brief studies of Morton in the Schomburg Center for Research in Black Culture of the New York Public Library provide details of his life: James Gardner, "Brief History of Ferdinand Q. Morton of N.Y.," and Samuel Michelson, "History of the Democratic Party in Harlem."

Peterson, Robert. *Only the Ball Was White* (1970).

Obituaries: *New York Times* and *New York Herald Tribune*, 9 Nov. 1949.

This entry is taken from the *American National Biography* and is published here with the permission of the American Council of Learned Societies.

FRANCESCO L. NEPA

Morton, Jelly Roll (20 Oct. 1890–10 July 1941), was born Ferdinand Lamothe (sometimes mistakenly given as Le Menthe) in New Orleans, the son of Edward Lamothe, who disappeared soon after his son was born, and Louise Monette, who was not legally married to his father. Monette then married William Mouton, who changed his name to Morton, and they had two daughters. There is some confusion over Morton's birth date, because he claimed that he was born in 1885. However, scholars have discovered church records that reveal the 1890 date. Gary Giddins, a jazz scholar and historian, speculates that one reason Morton gave 1885 as his birth date was that had he been born in 1890, he would have been only twelve years old in 1902, the year he claimed to have invented jazz.

Morton was a Creole of color, a member of the New Orleans black community rooted in French, Caribbean, and African culture that flourished when Louisiana was a French colony in the eighteenth century. Creoles of color were generally Catholic, spoke French, and often considered themselves the elite of the black community. Many were well educated, and music was an essential part of their recreational life. When Morton was born, New Orleans was a musical bouillabaisse, filled with the sounds and rhythms of street bands, Italian opera, French quadrilles, Latin tangos, military music, ragtime, popular music, the blues, and the "hot"

music from the night spots. Morton recalled that as a child he set out to "whip the word and conquer all [musical] instruments" (Lomax, 4). Even in his childhood his musical abilities were evident. By the time he was fifteen, Morton said he was considered "one of the best junior pianists in the city."

While still a teenager, Morton was offered a job playing the piano in the red-light district of New Orleans. When he told his grandmother what he was doing, Morton said she banished him from the family, telling him: "A musician is nothing but a bum and a scalawag. I don't want you around your sisters. I reckon you better move." Morton began to play in the "high class" bordellos in the tenderloin district. He became one of the kings of the piano, second only to Tony Jackson, who was considered the greatest piano player of his time. Morton claimed that before he invented jazz, most musicians played the blues or ragtime. "Ragtime," he said, "is a certain kind of syncopation … but jazz is a style that can be applied to any kind of tune. Jazz music came from New Orleans" (Lomax, 67).

Morton's music was shaped, in part, by the world of racial segregation. Segregation and disfranchisement had been relatively fluid and flexible in New Orleans in the decades following Reconstruction. By the 1890s, however, Louisiana—like the rest of the South—legalized segregation. In June 1892 HOMER PLESSY, a Creole of color from New Orleans, challenged Louisiana's law segregating public transportation. In 1896 the U.S. Supreme Court established the doctrine of "separate but equal," sanctioning segregation. Two years later the court unanimously approved laws designed to reduce black voting. In New Orleans, as in the rest of the South, blacks were not even allowed in the same houses with white prostitutes. Thus, Morton was required to sit behind a screen in the bordello where he worked to prevent him from looking at the white prostitutes when they danced for their customers. Morton said he got around the restriction by cutting a slit in the screen.

For Morton, music provided an escape from the world of Jim Crow, and it allowed him both creative freedom and the freedom to travel. By the end of the first decade of the twentieth century, he was touring the South. During this period he wrote some of his classic songs, including "Alabama Bound" and "King Porter Stomp." He performed with various vaudeville companies and minstrel shows as a musician, actor, and comic entertainer, and he worked as a gambler, pimp, and pool hustler when things were slow. Because of his association with prostitutes, he got a reputation as a lady's man and was given the nickname "Jelly Roll," a slang term for the female or male genitalia and for sexual intercourse.

Morton moved about from St. Louis and Chicago to New York and Kansas City, until he landed on the West Coast in 1917. After World War I, Chicago became the capital of "hot music." Many of New Orleans's greatest jazz musicians performed there, including LOUIS ARMSTRONG, KING OLIVER, and JOHNNY ST. CYR. Southern musicians had joined the massive migration of hundreds of thousands of blacks fleeing the Jim Crow South in search of a better way of life in the North. Jazz quickly crossed the northern color line as young whites flocked to listen, dance, and play the new music.

Jelly Roll Morton arrived in Chicago in 1923, at the height of his musical powers. He quickly became one of the biggest names in jazz, playing dance halls and clubs throughout the Midwest for both black and white audiences. He teamed up with the Melrose brothers, white music entrepreneurs who negotiated his record and sheet music contracts (and who allegedly skimmed much of the profits for themselves, as did many other white producers of black music). Morton put together the Red Hot Peppers, a recording band composed of top New Orleans musicians, including KID ORY, BARNEY BIGARD, JOHNNY DODDS, Johnny St. Cyr, and BABY DODDS, to record songs like "Black Bottom Stomp," "Sidewalk Blues," and "Turtle Twist." Alan Lomax, a music and folk historian, considered Morton's sessions with the Peppers, "the best recorded performances in jazz" of the period.

By the end of the 1920s Morton's career was booming. Money was rolling in, and everybody loved his music. He flashed diamonds wherever he went—on his watch, belt buckle, and tie clip—and he even sported a diamond tooth. Morton owned more than a hundred suits and dozens of pairs of shoes. His business cards read "Jelly Roll Morton—Inventor of Jazz." His critics called him a braggart and a fabricator, but Morton may not have been too far off the mark. For if he did not invent jazz, he was certainly one of its founding fathers and one of its greatest piano players, composers, and arrangers. As Giddins notes, Morton "did prove to be ... the catalyst who transfigured ragtime and minstrelsy into a new music that adroitly weighed the respective claims of the composer and the improviser—in a word—jazz" (Giddins, 70). Morton's style suitably impressed his fellow performer Mabel Bertrand, whom he met in 1927 and married the following year.

Morton's bragging earned him enemies among his fellow musicians as well as among whites who controlled his bookings and money. In the 1930s Morton's career all but disappeared. A new generation of musicians had emerged, and swing developed as a new form of jazz. Big bands like those led by DUKE ELLINGTON, FATS WALLER, FLETCHER HENDERSON, and Benny Goodman were all the rage. Younger musicians considered Morton a dinosaur, even while others continued to play his music with great success. For a while Morton played at the Red Apple in New York, a second-rate club in Harlem.

Morton left New York in 1935 and wound up at the Jungle Inn, an obscure club in Washington, D.C., tending bar and playing the piano. Down and out and in poor health, Morton seemed at the end of the line. But his glory days were not over. Young people started to come to hear him play music and talk about the glamorous days of New Orleans jazz. When he heard that W. C. HANDY had been introduced as the creator of jazz on a radio show, Morton exploded. He wrote an angry public letter stating that it was he, not Handy, who created jazz. The article made headlines and put Morton back in the limelight.

In 1938 Alan Lomax, a musicologist at the Archive of Folk Song at the Library of Congress, invited Morton to record his music for the Library of Congress. The session became not only a classic recording of Morton's jazz but also a unique historical portrait of the era. Mixing fact and legend, myth and reality, Morton narrated the musical life of New Orleans at the turn of the century. He played many of the songs he had written, some with ribald or frankly sexual lyrics. He brought the golden age of New Orleans to life again, resurrecting many of its legendary figures, from the trumpeter BUDDY BOLDEN and the pianist Tony Jackson to the blues singer Mamie Desdoumes and the rebel ROBERT CHARLES, whose legendary shoot-out with the police had made him a hero in the black community.

If the Library of Congress sessions secured Morton's fame for posterity, his financial condition was still anything but secure. In straitened circumstances and seriously ill, he tried desperately to collect back royalties from his publishers. Morton had attempted to join ASCAP, the musicians union, in 1934, because the union had the authority to collect some of the royalties due Morton. But ASCAP was slow to admit blacks as members, and it was not until 1939 that Morton was accepted. The union, however, did little to secure him his royalties.

In 1939 Morton's career had a brief resurgence. He recorded with SIDNEY BECHET for Victor Records and played many of his old songs. He continued to write music, most of which was not discovered until after his death. Ill and dying, his playing days over, Morton moved to Los Angeles in 1940. Too sick to perform or record, he remained confined to his bed until his death.

FURTHER READING

Giddins, Gary. *Visions of Jazz: The First Century* (1998).

Lomax, Alan. *Mr. Jelly Roll: The Fortunes of Jelly Roll Morton, New Orleans Creole and "Inventor of Jazz,"* with a new afterword by Lawrence Gushee (2001).

Reich, Howard, and William Gaines. *Jelly's Blues: The Life, Music, and Redemption of Jelly Roll Morton* (2003).

Obituary: *Down Beat* (1 Aug. 1941).

DISCOGRAPHY

Jelly Roll Morton: Jazz King of New Orleans (RCA/Bluebird 2002).

Jelly Roll Morton: The Library of Congress Recordings (Charly 1990).

Jelly Roll Morton: Pioneer of Jazz, 1923–1939 (Jazz Records 2003).

RICHARD WORMSER

Morton, Lena Beatrice (15 Jun. 1901–10 Jan. 1981), educator and author, was born in Flat Creek, Kentucky, the younger of two children of William Morton, a grocer and small truck-business owner, and Susie Anna Stewart Morton, a schoolteacher. Shortly after her birth, Morton's family relocated near Lexington, Kentucky. Her early childhood was defined by several moves between Lexington and various small towns in Kentucky; the family finally settled in Winchester, Kentucky, a community of approximately eight thousand people.

Morton's maternal grandfather, the Reverend H. A. Stewart, was the minister in the local Colored Methodist Episcopal Church. The Reverend Stewart, born enslaved in 1846, played a monumental role in guiding Morton's development, and he challenged her to think critically, independently, and to pursue all things with excellence. As a result, Morton excelled academically in the all-black schools of Winchester, including the high school, which lacked the resources to matriculate students or award diplomas. Morton's mother, who was educated at Berea College, and father sought a more promising educational landscape for Morton and her older brother Chester. In 1917 the family migrated to Cincinnati, Ohio, and there Morton

entered Woodward High as a bright and eager eleventh grader.

Morton found the bustling city of Cincinnati quite different from rural Kentucky, but she experienced a pleasant time of growth in the city's public schools, which had legalized integration in 1886. Morton graduated from the interracial Woodward High School in 1918 and immediately entered the University of Cincinnati in the fall, where she studied philosophy. In 1920 she and sixteen other female students chartered the Zeta chapter of Delta Sigma Theta Sorority, Inc., the first African American Greek letter organization on the campus. Morton graduated from the University of Cincinnati in 1922 with a bachelor's degree and a year later had obtained a graduate diploma in education. She immediately entered the University of Cincinnati's graduate program, from which she received a master's degree in 1925 while teaching in the public schools of Cincinnati.

Morton enrolled in evening graduate courses while teaching during the day, and the University of Cincinnati hired her as its cooperating teacher for ten years, from 1927 to 1935, then again from 1940 to 1942. As cooperating teacher, she was responsible for overseeing what would later be called student teaching assignments. In 1948, at a time when many smaller northern school districts began hiring their first African American teachers, Morton concluded her twenty-six year career as a public school teacher.

Throughout her teaching career, Morton never relinquished her aspiration of pursuing higher learning. The evening courses she pursued would eventually become part of her doctoral studies at Western Reserve University (now Case Western Reserve University). Known for its rigorous English program, Western Reserve University awarded Morton a Ph.D. in February 1947, making her the first African American to receive a degree in English from the university. Her dissertation focused on English poetry of the sea.

During the 1940s and 1950s, opportunities for teaching at schools other than predominantly black colleges were not readily available for African American scholars, so upon receiving her doctorate, Morton joined the faculty of historically black Langston University in Oklahoma, where she taught English for two years. At that time, her mother, with whom she was quite close, became ill. In order to live nearer to her family, Morton accepted a position as an English professor at Lane College in Jackson, Tennessee, in 1950. Morton quickly rose to the position of chair of the humanities division, then to the position of dean at a time when it was rare for women to fulfill administrative roles on college campuses. She remained at Lane College until 1955. Susie, Morton's mother, died the same year.

Morton's career was not limited to teaching only. An avid reader and writer, she penned several books and articles. Her first book, *Farewell to Public Schools—I'm Glad We Met: A Handbook for Teachers*, was published in 1952. In it, she reflected on her teaching career through a series of essays. Eight years later, she published her second major work, *Man under Stress* (1960).

In 1955 Morton joined the staff of Southern University in Baton Rouge, Louisiana, where she remained a professor of English until 1962, followed by a ten-year professorship and position as head of the humanities division at Texas College in Tyler, Texas. While at Texas College, which was affiliated with her religious denomination of Colored Methodist Episcopal, she authored her 1965 autobiography, *My First Sixty Years: Passion for Wisdom*. In it, she sketched the story of her life, including poems and thoughts on contemporary racial concerns. She also addressed her postdoctoral study at the University of London in 1956 and Harvard University in 1959.

Morton's fifty-year career in education concluded in 1972 when she completed a two-year visiting professorship at East Texas State University in Commerce, Texas. After the publication of her autobiography, her subsequent publications included *Patterns of Language Usage: A Study of Tyler's Negro Elementary Schools* in 1965, *The Development of Negro Poetry in America* in 1975 and *The Influence of the Sea on English Poetry from the Anglo-Saxon to the Victorian Period* in 1976. Morton contributed to various periodicals as well.

Outside her teaching duties, Morton was an active and cultured clubwoman. She taught music and piano, and she was a charter member of the UC Twelve, a group of African American women who supported African American youth and college students. Her other memberships included the Modern Language Association of America, Ohioana Library Association, Ohio Poetry Society, Conference of College Teachers of English in Texas, and the Texas Poetry Society. She was also an active member of her local chapter of Delta Sigma Theta Sorority, Inc.

After retiring from a career in education because of failing eyesight, Morton returned to Cincinnati, the bustling city that, some fifty years earlier, embraced a "timid, high school girl as green as the blue grass of Kentucky" (Morton, 20). In reflecting on her move to Cincinnati as a teenager, she continued, "I was reluctant to leave my old Kentucky home, for there I knew everyone and everyone knew me" (Morton, 20). Then, and throughout Morton's life, she adjusted quickly and successfully. Her lifelong passion for education and learning inspired a countless number of students, colleagues, and readers. In spite of the challenges posed against women and people of color in Jim Crow America, Morton achieved greatness, many times breaking unjust racial segregation laws. Morton died in 1981 in Cincinnati at age seventy nine.

FURTHER READING

Morton, Lena Beatrice. *My First Sixty Years: Passion for Wisdom* (1965).

"Dr. Lena Morton Inspired Young to Finish Education," *Cincinnati Post*, 14 January 1981.

Obituary: *Cincinnati Enquirer*, 14 Jan. 1981.

LANESHA NEGALE DEBARDELABEN

Morton, Paul Sylvester (30 July 1950–), bishop, denominational leader, and singer, was born in Windsor, Ontario, one of nine children of Matilda E. and Bishop Clarence Leslie Morton, a minister in the Church of God in Christ (COGIC). His father pastored in Windsor and Detroit, Michigan. Morton started singing at an early age and developed his musical gifts while working in his father's Detroit pastorate. By the time he reached his teen years his father had already left the COGIC to lead an independent movement. Morton graduated from the J. C. Patterson Collegiate Institute and attended St. Clair College in Windsor, where he studied music. He started preaching in 1967 and was influenced by his older brother, James, who had become pastor of True Faith Baptist Church in Detroit (1970–1984). Like James, Morton would later pastor a Baptist congregation.

In 1972 the young Morton was called to work as an assistant pastor to Rev. Percy Simpson at Greater St. Stephen Missionary Baptist Church in New Orleans. Greater St. Stephen was affiliated with the National Baptist Convention (NBC), the largest African American Protestant group. In 1975, after Simpson's death, Morton became the next pastor of Greater St. Stephen, which then reported a membership of six hundred. Morton furthered his theological studies at Union Baptist Seminary of Louisiana from which he graduated. He married Debra Brown, a member of Greater St. Stephen, in

1977. Three children were born from this union. Morton immersed himself in pastoral work and introduced healing and deliverance services, which transformed his Baptist pastorate into a congregation dependent on Pentecostal spirituality. His innovations paid off and soon he opened two satellite congregations in New Orleans, which made Greater St. Stephen one church in three locations. Continuous growth led Morton to build or acquire three sanctuaries of one thousand, two thousand, and three thousand seats each. He also organized a school of ministry, a Bible college, and an academy for babies and children through kindergarten. Pastor Morton preached widely in NBC circles, promoting free worship, faith healing, and the baptism of the Holy Spirit. He won over many black Baptists by telling them that the spiritual power manifested in the New Testament Book of Acts was available today and that they could be baptized in the Holy Spirit and receive healing through faith. Morton taught Baptists that they could practice Pentecostal spirituality and remain Baptist.

In 1992 Pastor Morton changed his church's name to Greater St. Stephen Full Gospel Baptist Church. Sensing a calling from God to serve as bridge between Baptists and Pentecostals on a large scale, Morton organized the Full Gospel Baptist Church Fellowship (FGBCF) that same year and in 1993 was consecrated Presiding Bishop of the FGBCF. In addition to Morton, the founding ministers of the new organization were Bishop Odis A. Floyd, Bishop Larry D. Trotter, Bishop Carlos L. Malone, Bishop J. D. Wiley, Bishop K. D. Johnson, Bishop Larry D. Leonard, Bishop Kenneth Robinson, Bishop Kenneth Ulmer, Bishop Fred Caldwell, Bishop Robert Blake, Bishop Eddie Long, and Bishop A. R. Williams. In 1993 Debra Morton was made co-pastor of Greater St. Stephen, which was against black Baptist polity, which usually reserves the ordained ministry to men. FGBCF was not founded as a new denomination but only as a forum for Baptists seeking a richer spirituality. The existence and growth of the FGBCF was an epochal event in African American religious history because it was the first time a Pentecostal minister was able to convince a large number of Baptists to adopt charismatic spirituality without denying their own religious roots. In doing so Morton accomplished among black Baptists what Bishop John Richard Bryant had been doing within the African Methodist Episcopal Church. In 1994 the FGBCF held its first annual conference, which was attended by more than twenty-five thousand people in New

Orleans. The next annual conference drew fifty thousand attendees. By then Greater St. Stephen reported eighteen thousand members drawn by an upbeat message of freedom from financial and spiritual bondage. The Mortons developed an extensive media ministry showcased on Dream Television Network, Black Entertainment Television, and Word Network. This accounted for the growth of FGBCF to an estimate of five thousand churches and one million members in thirty-five states by 1995. By then the NBC had found the full gospel message to be incompatible with Baptist teachings, which do not sanction speaking in tongues, women pastors, and free worship. The NBC under President Henry Lyons resolved that its churches could not be part of Morton's fellowship. In turn, many congregations left the NBC to remain in the FGBCF. Within a short period of time the FGBCF took the form of a denomination and has grown to become the second largest African American Pentecostal church group after the COGIC.

Morton's profile as a megachurch pastor and leader of a budding religious movement opened many doors for him. In early 1996 he attended a luncheon for two hundred black ministers hosted by the Democratic National Committee (DNC). During this gathering fifteen denominational leaders, including Bishop Morton, met with President Bill Clinton and Vice President Al Gore. DNC Chairman Donald L. Fowler encouraged the prominent ministers to work for the reelection of the Clinton—Gore ticket, stressing its interest in affirmation action. Although more interests claimed Bishop Morton's attention, he remained committed to the needs of the local community. Greater St. Stephen opened an affordable housing complex for seventy-five families, a Christian high school, and a senior citizen home. In 2004 Morton sounded a conservative voice when he joined a group of sixty African American ministers who went to lobby against gay marriage in Washington, D.C. These conservative ministers claimed that homosexual marriage threatened the stability of the family and advocated a constitutional amendment to limit marriage to one man and one woman.

Morton, a singer, was also a recording artist. His first solo album, "Crescent City Fire" (1999), was followed by five albums with the Greater St. Stephen Mass Choir. In January 2005 he won three Stellar awards in the following categories: Traditional Male Vocalist of the Year, Music Video of the Year for "Let It Rain," and Traditional Choir of the Year for "Bishop Morton & Full Gospel Baptist Church

Fellowship's Mass Choir." Bishop Morton served as chief executive officer of Tehillah Music Group. He authored several books including an autobiography, *Why Kingdoms Fall* (1999). Hurricane Katrina, which nearly destroyed New Orleans, damaged Morton's home and church in 2005. The bishop rebuilt his ministry and installed his wife as senior pastor at Greater St. Stephen. He moved to Atlanta, Georgia, and organized 222 former parishioners who had relocated there into the Changing a Generation Full Gospel Baptist Church (CAG) in 2006. Morton also moved the FGBCF headquarters to Decatur, Georgia. Morton served as the senior pastor of the Atlanta congregation while both he and his wife served as co-pastors of each other's churches. CAG grew to more than three thousand members. The FGBCF, a growing force in the black community, increased to more than twenty-five hundred congregations in forty-two states and twelve countries.

FURTHER READING

"Bishop Wins Three Stellar Awards," *The Atlanta Inquirer*, 29 Jan. 2005.

Harris, Hamil R., and Bill Broadway. "A Booming Voice; Maverick Bishop Paul Morton's Baptist Fellowship Gains National Following," *The Washington Post*, 16 May 1998.

Laiscell, Ed. "African American Religious Leaders Meet with DNC," *Washington Informer*, 17 April 1996.

Nolan, Bruce. "Full Gospel Thrives from N.O. Base," *Advocate*, 12 Aug. 1995.

Vara, Richard. "From the Ground, Up/To Survive, Pastor Says, New Orleans Must Rebuild Its Houses of Worship," *Houston Chronicle*, 22 Oct. 2005.

DAVID MICHEL

Morton, Theophilus B. (Jan. 1849–1910?), activist, was born into slavery in Virginia. The names of his parents are unknown. During the Civil War he escaped slavery and in 1864 aided the Eighth Illinois Cavalry Regiment in defense of Washington, D.C. In 1875 Morton migrated to California where he was active in Republican Party politics and rose to become one of the best-known African American activists in the west. In 1888 he married a Canadian, Clara, who had immigrated to the United States.

In 1890, when T. THOMAS FORTUNE founded the National Afro-American League—an organization for civil rights and uplift and early predecessor to groups like the National Association for the Advancement of Colored People—Morton was quick to recognize the league's potential. By 1891 he had organized a San Francisco branch of the Afro-American League, which attracted 150 prominent black Californians to its inaugural congress. Morton acted as president of the San Francisco Afro-American League for seven years and served as a secretary and prominent member thereafter. He and his wife, Clara, were leading members and speakers during California's state Afro-American League congresses. They advocated black support for the Republican Party, lobbied for secure federal jobs for black San Franciscans, and promoted business and commercial autonomy for African Americans in general.

During their fifth annual convention in 1895 the league could boast the modest successes of securing employment for mail carriers, messengers, clerks, porters, and election officers among other federal positions. Unsatisfied, Morton established and acted as treasurer of the Afro-American Cooperative and Investment Association, a short-lived organization fostering economic independence for black communities. These efforts paid dividends for Morton himself; when the Ninth Circuit Court of Appeals was formally established in January 1891, Morton was appointed messenger for the court, and in 1896 the National Republican Committee appointed him organizer of the African American vote in California. After only a few years as messenger Morton became the court's first black librarian. As a proponent of economic uplift, Morton was a great admirer and supporter of BOOKER T. WASHINGTON, and Washington and his agents considered him one of their most important allies in the west.

In addition to his work for the Afro-American League, Morton held positions of authority in the Third Baptist Church of San Francisco, Grand United Order of Odd Fellows, and Knights of Pythias; and although he and his wife had no children, Morton was an active promoter of philanthropic funding for the education of African American youth. Due to his extensive civic activism, Morton was a respected member of both white and African American communities. Nevertheless, he was well aware of the racism that barred most black Californians from profitable employment, and through his words and actions advocated for African American–run farms, fisheries, businesses, and industries, all the while denouncing lynchings, discriminatory state laws, the racist treatment of black soldiers in the Spanish-American War, and other abuses. Morton sought a future of racial justice in which "every American with pride can acknowledge the motherhood of earth, brotherhood of man, and the fatherhood of God" (*Los Angeles Times*, 12 Aug. 1896, 9).

It is unclear exactly when Morton died. He was active in the Afro-American League through 1906, but his name disappears from the historical record thereafter. He was deceased by the time DELILAH L. BEASLEY published her classic work, *Negro Trailblazers of California*, in 1919.

FURTHER READING

"Afro-Americans: First Session of the Annual Congress Held Yesterday," *Los Angeles Times*, Aug. 1896.

Broussard, Albert S. *Black San Francisco: The Struggle for Racial Equality in the West, 1900–1954* (1993).

Brown, Elsa Barkley, ed. *Delilah L. Beasley: The Negro Trail Blazers of California* (1919, reprinted 1998).

Wagner, Harr, ed. *Notable Speeches by Notable Speakers of the Greater West* (1902).

AMBER MOULTON-WISEMAN

Morton-Finney, John (25 June 1889–28 Jan. 1998), educator, lawyer, humanitarian, and World War I Buffalo Soldier, was born in Uniontown, Kentucky, one of seven children of George Morton-Finney and Mattie M. Gordon Morton-Finney. John grew up in a home where poetry readings and political debates were evening activities. His father was a former Kentucky slave and family lore had it that his ancestors migrated from Ethiopia to what is now Nigeria. At age fourteen his mother died so he and his siblings moved to their grandfather's farm in Missouri. His grandfather was one of the original settlers in Missouri when the government encouraged the westward movement in the mid-1800s. In 1911 John enlisted in the 24th U.S. Infantry regiment—known as the "Buffalo Soldiers." He rose to the rank of sergeant and applied for an officer's commission. His commander told him that although he had the intelligence and education, he was disqualified because of his race. Regardless of his rank, he received a citation from General John J. Pershing in 1914 for his service in the Philippines.

Morton-Finney earned his first bachelors degree from Lincoln College in Jefferson City, Missouri, in 1916. He was a teacher in a one room schoolhouse in Nelson, Missouri, but when the United States entered World War I he returned to duty in 1918 and served in France in the American Expeditionary Force. After being honorably discharged from the Army, Morton-Finney taught languages at Fisk University in Nashville and at his alma mater Lincoln College. He earned two

bachelor's degrees—one from Lincoln in 1920 and one from the State University of Iowa in 1922. During this time he met Pauline Ray who was a French teacher at Lincoln College. She was from Geneva, New York, and had earned her bachelor's degree from Cornell University. They were married in 1922, then relocated to Indianapolis, Indiana. With degrees in math, history, and French, he taught junior high math and social studies and served as the school's principal. In 1927, he was hired as the first teacher at the all-black Crispus Attucks High School where he became the head of the foreign language department and taught Greek, Latin, German, Spanish, and French. Students who entered his classroom learned life skills such as how to set goals, plan their future, and take responsibility for their actions. This school served as a model for the education of African American students and the foreign language department was the largest at any Indiana high school. His love for learning remained constant. Every summer and every semester he enrolled in a course. Morton-Finney completed two master's degrees at Indiana University—one in education in 1925 and one in French in 1933. In 1935, he earned his first law degree from Lincoln College.

During World War II he continued his patriotic duty and was cited for directing the rationing ticket program for African Americans in Indianapolis. In 1944 and 1946 he earned three law degrees from Indiana University. He regularly read three or four books at a time and would have twenty books stacked beside his bed with five sharpened pencils and the television turned to the news. In 1965 at the age of seventy-five, he earned another bachelor's degree from Butler University.

Morton-Finney was named Adeniran 1, Paramount Chief of Yoruba Descendants in Indiana in 1979. Members of the African Culture Resource Center of Indianapolis and Nigerian chiefs from Oyotunji Village performed the ancient coronation ceremony of the Yoruba tribe. His mother's ancestry goes back to Badadri, Nigeria—a shipping port for the slave trade—and his father's ancestors were from Mali, which was known as Melle until 1884. It has a French origin (Ferguson, 48).

Morton-Finney earned a trial advocacy diploma in 1987 and obtained barships with the Supreme Court of Indiana in 1935, the U.S. District Court of Southern Indiana in 1944, and the Supreme Court of the United States in 1971. In 1989 he received an honorary doctorate of letters (LittD) from Lincoln College and an honorary doctorate of humane letters

(LHD) from Butler University. Morton-Finney was inducted into the National Bar Association Hall of Fame in 1991 where he visited with President George H. W. Bush in the Rose Garden of the White House. In 1995 he received another honorary doctorate from Martin University in Indianapolis.

In an interview for his one-hundredth birthday, Morton-Finney said "I can get interested in so many things. There is so much to know in the world. And it is a pleasure for me to learn. Besides, a cultivated man would never say 'I finished my education' because he graduated from college. There is no ending to learning" (Terry, 10). In total, he earned twelve academic degrees including a Law degree from Indiana University School of Law, one diploma, and three honorary degrees and practiced law until he was 106 years old. He died in his sleep in 1998 at the age of 108 and received full military honors.

The Indianapolis Bar Association established the Dr. John Morton Finney Award for Excellence in Legal Education in 1998 to honor his memory. Recipients must be active in legal education projects, public education, and work within Indiana's law schools. In the same year Congresswoman Julia Carson made a tribute to him on the floor of the House of Representatives. The Indianapolis Public Schools Board honored his career that spanned forty-seven years as a teacher, department head, and administrator. In 2000 the Center for Educational Services near downtown Indianapolis was renamed to the Dr. John Morton Finney Center for Educational Services. The Dr. John Morton Finney Leadership program at Butler University awards tuition scholarships ranging from $2,000 to $12,000 based on leadership potential and academic strength. In 2003 the Indiana University Board of Trustees approved a residential house on the Indiana University Purdue University Indianapolis (IUPUI) campus to honor Dr. Morton-Finney. The residential facility opened in 2004 and is one of twenty-three houses that honors community leaders.

FURTHER READING

Few primary materials on John Morton-Finney have been discovered. A collection of private documents are available at The Buffalo Soldiers Research Museum http://www. buffalosoldiersresearchmuseum.org.

Ferguson, Blanche E. "The King Who Has No Country," *Indianapolis Star Parade Magazine* (26 Nov. 1983).

Hicks, G. III, and C. W. Hicks. *Our Journey with the Buffalo Soldiers* (2006).

Terry, Wallace. "It is Such a Pleasure to Learn," *Indianapolis Star Parade Magazine* (10 March 1990).

Obituary: *Indianapolis Star*, 29 Jan. 1998.

CARMON WEAVER HICKS

Morton Jones, Verina Harris (c. 1857–1943), physician, civil rights and women's suffrage activist, settlement worker, and clubwoman, was born Verina Harris in Ohio, one of five children of Charlotte (Kitty) Stanly, a schoolteacher, and the Reverend W. D. Harris, a minister of the African Methodist Episcopal (AME) Church. Her mother came from a family of North Carolina free blacks who had inherited slaves that they wished to emancipate in the North before the impending Civil War. Around 1850 the family moved to Ohio, where Kitty Stanly and her husband taught school. The year of Verina Harris's birth is given as 1865 in some sources, but most probably it was between 1853 and 1857. Little is known about her early life, but the family apparently moved south to Columbia, South Carolina, in 1870, while her father was serving in an AME ministry in various locations in South Carolina. More information is available about her great-grandfather, JOHN CARUTHERS STANLY (c. 1774–1846), a former slave who acquired great wealth, than has yet been uncovered about Verina Harris's early life. Her mother taught in the freedman schools in South Carolina. Harris probably attended the South Carolina Normal School in Columbia that had a brief existence between 1874 and 1877, and she taught school in Columbia for some years.

In 1884 Harris matriculated in the Women's Medical College of Pennsylvania (WMCP) in Philadelphia and attended for four years, graduating in 1888. The WMCP archives have her class photo as well as her thesis, entitled "Cholera Infanterum." During those years most medical schools had courses lasting only two years, and it was not until 1892 that WMCP required four years of attendance for its medical students. That Harris chose to attend for the four years probably gave her about the best medical education that one could attain in the country at that time.

Harris has frequently been credited with being the first woman physician of any race to practice medicine in the state of Mississippi, where she is reputed to have been the college physician at Rust College in Holly Springs, Mississippi. Unfortunately many archival materials at Rust were lost in a fire, so there is no record of her serving there, and recent research has found Florence L. Dickerson (1856 1929) to hold the honor of being the first woman physician to practice in Mississippi. At this time nothing has been found to absolutely dispute Verina Harris as having been in Mississippi. However, she was most likely the first woman physician to practice in the state of South Carolina. The South Carolina State Board of Health's Tenth Annual Report in 1889 and the Southern Medical Directories of 1890 and 1891 all list Verina M. Harris, MD, as practicing in Columbia, South Carolina.

Exactly what was happening to Verina Harris in the years between 1888 and 1890 is unclear, but by 1890 she was in the New York City area. Her sister Lotta and her sister's husband, T. McCants Stewart—a lawyer, minister, and community activist—would have been in New York at that time and could have helped with her transition to the city. On 15 August 1890 she married Walter A. Morton—an 1886 graduate of Bates College and an 1890 graduate of Dartmouth Medical School—in Brooklyn, New York, and had two children, Franklin Morton and Kitty. She registered to practice in the borough of Brooklyn in spring 1891. The young physician couple were quite successful in their respective practices and "made an attractive appearance," according to one source. In 1895 both her husband and her daughter passed away within weeks of one another. Some sources claim that she returned to Mississippi with her young son, but by 1901 she was back in Brooklyn to marry Emory Jones, a member of her church, Saint Augustine's Episcopal Church in Brooklyn.

From 1901 until 1927 when she left Brooklyn, Verina Morton Jones, MD, appears frequently in numerous published sources as a member of many groups devoted to racial uplift and to interracial amity and understanding. She was a member and leader within various groups like the Committee for the Improvement of the Condition of Colored Women and the National Association of Colored Women, both precursors of the NAACP. She was also a founding member of the Urban League in Brooklyn and owner of the building that housed it, the founder and head worker of the Lincoln Settlement House in Brooklyn, the president of the Brooklyn Equal Suffrage League, a speaker at the PHILLIS WHEATLEY branches of the YWCA on hygiene and health, a director of the Brooklyn Mothers' Club, a member of the interracial Cosmopolitan Club (a social and political group of New York City and Brooklyn reformers), and most frequently cited as "the first and only African

American woman to serve on the Executive Board of the National Association for the Advancement of Colored People," which she did from 1913 to 1923.

Though Morton Jones was clearly a club woman and tremendously energetic in working to bring about gender equality, racial justice, and uplift to literally generations of dispossessed, she remains, in spite of all the citations and references to her, a person about whom more questions are raised than answered. A study of her life requires much diligence in separating facts from repeated errors. A clearer and more personal picture of Morton Jones emerges, however, from a collection of her personal correspondence gathered along with that of her brother-in-law T. McCants Stewart and his family by Stewart's granddaughter, Kathleen Stewart Flippin. Morton Jones's grandson, Judge Franklin Morton II, still holds some family records as well.

She suffered tremendous personal loss during her adult life, beginning with her husband and daughter in 1895, her mother whom she cared for in her home in 1901, her sister Lotta in 1906, her adored nephew McCants very tragically by suicide in 1919, her other nephew Gilchrist in 1926, and her second husband in 1927. Yet throughout this time is when she appears again and again as a leader, an organizer, and a head of her various groups.

Even more remarkable, after the death of her husband in 1927, when Morton Jones was at least seventy years old, she did not retire but instead moved to Hempstead, Long Island, where in 1928 she helped establish the HARRIET TUBMAN Community Club, originally as a community social club, and directed its activities as a settlement house assisting young African American domestic workers arriving in New York from the South. She used her many years of experience in the settlement house movement in Brooklyn to continue the work in Hempstead. She did not retire from public service until 1939 when she returned to Brooklyn, where she was cared for by her daughter-in-law and friends until her death.

FURTHER READING

Some correspondence by Verina Harris Morton Jones can be found in the Stewart-Flippin collection at the Moorland-Spingarn Research Center, Howard University, Washington, D.C.

Cash, Floris Barnett. "Gender and Race Consciousness: Verina Morton Jones Inspires a Settlement House in Suburbia," in *Long Island Women: Activists and Innovators*, eds. Natalie A. Naylor and Maureen O. Murphy (1998).

Hine, Darlene Clark. "Co-Laborers in the Work of the Lord," in *"Send Us a Lady Physician": Women Doctors in America*, ed. Ruth Abrams (1985).

Schweninger, Loren. "John Carruthers Stanly and the Anomaly of Black Slaveholding," *North Carolina Historical Review* (Apr. 1990).

Scruggs, L.A. *Women of Distinction: Remarkable in Works and Invincible in Character* (1893).

SUSAN KNOKE RISHWORTH

Moseley Braun, Carol (16 Aug. 1947–), lawyer, activist, politician, and diplomat, was born Carol Elizabeth Moseley in Chicago, Illinois, the oldest of four children of Joseph J. Moseley, a police officer, and Edna A. Davie, a medical technician. She became involved in political activism at an early age; her first protest was a sit-in at a segregated restaurant while still at Parker High School in Chicago. At age sixteen, she marched with MARTIN LUTHER KING JR. to protest housing conditions in Chicago. Throughout her life, she sought to break down racial and gender barriers.

Moseley Braun earned a B.A. in Political Science from the University of Illinois in 1969. She graduated from the University of Chicago School of Law in 1972 and passed the Illinois State Bar in 1973. That same year, she married attorney Michael Braun, and the couple had one son, Matthew. They divorced in 1986. Following a short career in private practice, she worked on the staff of the assistant U.S. attorney of northern Illinois from 1973 until 1977. She became an Illinois state representative in 1979, and she stayed in this position until 1988, pursuing education reform, increased benefits for welfare recipients, and racial integration in public and private organizations. Following an unsuccessful bid for lieutenant governor in 1986, she served from 1988 to 1992 as recorder of deeds for Cook

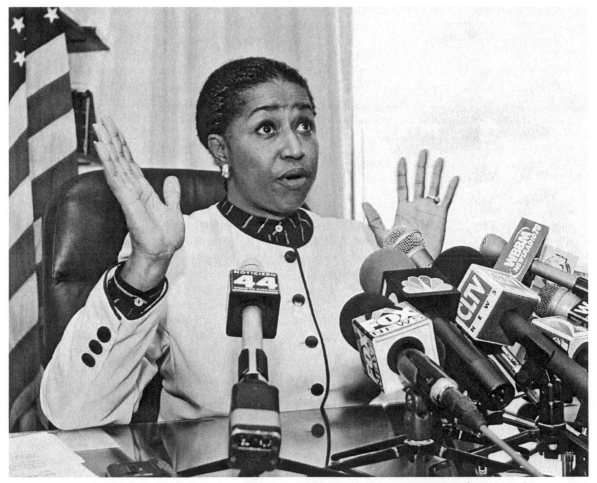

Carol Moseley-Braun, answering reporters at her office in Chicago, 20 August 1996. (AP Images.)

County, Illinois; she was the first African American elected to a Cook County executive position.

Infuriated over the spectacle of the CLARENCE THOMAS Supreme Court confirmation hearings in 1991, Moseley Braun became convinced that the predominantly white, male U.S. Senate needed to change. Illinois Senator Alan Dixon's vote to confirm Thomas following accusations of sexual harassment by Anita Hill motivated Moseley Braun to challenge Dixon, a two-term incumbent, in the next election. Few political observers thought she could defeat Dixon, but Moseley Braun sensed a growing anti-incumbent force. "By the time I got requests from white males in Republican counties," she said, "I knew something was up"(*New York Times*, 19 Mar. 1992). She won the primary election on 17 March 1992, and that November she defeated Republican candidate Richard Williamson with 53 percent of the vote. On 3 January 1993, Moseley Braun became the first female U.S. senator from Illinois and the first African American woman to serve in the U.S. Senate.

As one of only seven women senators in 1993, and the only African American, Moseley Braun faced intense public scrutiny and became burdened with a level of constituent demands rarely seen before. Within a week of her swearing-in, newspapers were declaring that Moseley Braun "still had a lot to learn" about politics and explained that when "expectations are enormous, missteps tend to be magnified" (*Chicago Tribune*, 10 Jan. 1993). Every misstep, real or perceived, dogged her for the next six years. Prominent among the accusations were misuse of campaign funds for personal items, a charge that resulted in a Federal Election Commission investigation; not reporting income from a sale of family land; and poor judgment when deciding to travel to Nigeria to attend the funeral of a family member of controversial Nigerian dictator, Sani Abacha. However, Moseley Braun was determined to work hard in the Senate and influence legislation. Her goals included lifting the ban on gays in the military, strengthening laws against discrimination, and promoting health care issues. She remained a strong advocate for civil rights legislation, and she sponsored a National Park Service initiative to fund preservation of the Underground Railroad sites. Among her legislative achievements was the Improving America's School Act, a bill she sponsored in 1994 to renovate public school facilities. She became one of the first three women to serve on the Senate Judiciary Committee, and she was the first woman on the Senate Finance Committee. Her maiden speech to the Senate, delivered 26 January 1993, was a eulogy to Supreme Court Justice THURGOOD MARSHALL.

Moseley Braun's Senate career will be remembered mostly for her confrontations with North Carolina Senator Jesse Helms. In May 1993 the Senate Judiciary Committee responded to Moseley Braun's request and denied the United Daughters of the Confederacy renewal of its ninety-five-year-old federal patent on an insignia that featured the Confederate flag. Two months later, she learned that Helms had introduced an amendment to reinstate the patent, so she issued an eloquent plea to stop the amendment. "Symbols are important," she told her colleagues. "Everyone knows what that insignia means"(Congressional Record, 22 July 1993). Mosley Braun won the argument—the Senate denied the patent with a 75-25 vote—but her battles with Helms continued. A few weeks later, she listened patiently in a Senate elevator as Helms sang several verses of "Dixie." When he vowed to continue singing until he made her cry, Moseley Braun retorted: "Senator Helms, your singing would make me cry if you sang 'Rock of Ages'" (*Washington Post*, 5 Aug. 1993).

Despite legislative successes and her high-profile confrontations with Helms, Moseley Braun faced a tough reelection campaign in 1998. Old charges of misconduct resurfaced, and she frequently found herself on the defensive, apologizing for old complaints that still lingered. Despite support from the Clinton administration, she was unable to build a strong coalition backed by sufficient funds to ward off a challenge from the wealthy Republican candidate Peter Fitzgerald, and she lost the election by less than four percentage points.

Moseley Braun then turned her attention to education, becoming a consultant for the Department of Education. On 9 October 1999 President Bill Clinton nominated her as ambassador to New Zealand and Samoa. During Senate confirmation hearings, Helms pledged to block the nomination, claiming that an "ethical cloud" hung over her Senate career (*Winston-Salem Journal*, 12 Nov. 1999, 18). Helms inadvertently allowed Moseley Braun to finally clear up lingering questions, as the Senate investigated charges prior to confirming her nomination. Consequently, results of the Federal Election Commission's five-year investigation into Moseley Braun's misuse of campaign funds were made public for the first time, and they showed a discrepancy of only $311, a far cry from the more than $200,000 in campaign funds that she was accused of diverting for personal use. When the Senate confirmed her nomination with a 96–2 vote on 10 November 1999, Moseley Braun claimed an end to "seven years of a smear campaign"(*Chicago Sun-Times*, 7 Nov. 1999, 24).

Moseley Braun remained ambassador to New Zealand and Samoa until 2001, after which she became a visiting professor at Morris Brown College, in Atlanta, and professor of business law at DePaul University in Chicago. In 2003 she returned to politics and entered the race for the Democratic presidential nomination in the 2004 election. Admitting that her candidacy was a long shot, she called herself a "peace dove and budget hawk" (Interview with NPR's *Morning Edition*, 6 May 2003) and vowed to bring more women and minorities into the democratic system. In January 2004, citing the difficulty of fund-raising, she dropped out of the race. Since ending her presidential bid, Moseley Braun has served as a business consultant and founded Good Food Organics, an organic foods company headquartered in Chicago, in 2005.

FURTHER READING

Carol Moseley Braun's senatorial papers are archived at the Chicago Historical Society. An oral history is-included in the "Explorations in Black Leadership" collection at the Institute for Public History, University of Virginia, http://www.virginia.edu/publichistory/bl/

Gill, LaVerne McCain. *African American Women in Congress: Forming and Transforming History* (1997).

Office of History and Preservation, Office of the Clerk, U.S. House of Representatives. *Women in Congress, 1917–2006* (2006).

BETTY K. KOED

Moses, Robert P. (23 Jan. 1935–), civil rights activist and math literacy advocate, was born Robert Parris Moses in New York City to Gregory Moses, a janitor, and Louise Parris. Bob Moses would later recall that his father's job was a good one during the Depression but that Gregory Moses, a hardworking, intelligent man, resented the lack of opportunities for African Americans in the 1930s. Determined that his sons would not face the same frustrations, Gregory Moses pushed them hard academically. Robert, a quiet and bookish child, won admission to the Stuyvesant High School for gifted students, where teachers encouraged his precocious interest in Chinese philosophy. He also captained the school baseball team and was elected senior class president. In 1952 Moses sought and won a scholarship to Hamilton College, a small, highly selective, and conservative school in Clinton, New York.

One of only a handful of black students at Hamilton, Moses found upstate New York to be a sharp contrast to Harlem, but he soon immersed himself in a range of college activities. At first he participated in a fundamentalist Christian study group and considered entering the ministry, but he was gradually drawn to the pacifist beliefs of several of his professors. They encouraged Moses to attend Quaker workshops and summer camps in Europe, where he helped to build low-income housing for the homeless, picked potatoes, and came to share his fellow volunteers' commitment to social justice. Following graduation in 1956, Moses traveled to Japan to explore his interest in Zen Buddhism. He had also become fascinated by the existential philosophy of Albert Camus, who argued that people should be driven by their individual consciences in confronting evil.

When Moses entered Harvard University's philosophy department in 1957, however, he focused not on Camus but on analytical philosophy, for which his interest in mathematics and questions of logic served him well. Soon after completing his MA, he returned to New York City in 1958 to be near his father, who had suffered a nervous breakdown following his wife's death from cancer. Moses found a job teaching math at the city's elite Horace Mann High School and became involved in civil rights activism with the veteran New York pacifist BAYARD RUSTIN.

Inspired by the wave of student sit-ins in early 1960, Moses traveled to Atlanta, Georgia, on Rustin's recommendation, to meet with ELLA BAKER. Baker, a veteran NAACP organizer in the South, was at that time executive secretary of the Southern Christian Leadership Conference (SCLC), founded by MARTIN LUTHER KING JR. in 1957. She was instrumental in promoting a new, youth-led organization, the Student Nonviolent Coordinating Committee (SNCC), that shared SCLC's goals of ending segregation through nonviolent protest, but which she hoped would be less reliant on charismatic leaders like King. Her philosophy of civil rights organizing appealed to Moses, since it was to all intents and purposes a practical expression of Camus's existentialism.

Baker and Moses believed that a racist society could be transformed only if those who suffered under it came to understand their oppression and then took a personal stand against their oppressors. Believing that SNCC had much to learn from local black leaders, Baker sent Moses to Cleveland, Mississippi, where the NAACP leader AMZIE

MOORE persuaded him to focus his efforts on voter registration, rather than try to replicate a sit-in of the type that had been effective in lunch counter demonstrations in Greensboro, North Carolina. In 1960 a mere 5 percent of black adults in Mississippi were registered to vote. Only with the power of the ballot, Moore argued, could African Americans overcome their own fear, and only then could they overcome segregation. Moses recognized that white resistance would be intense, but the Harvard philosophy student, known for his soft-spoken, sensitive demeanor, could barely conceal his euphoria about the prospect of battle. "Nobody starry-eyed," he wrote a fellow SNCC staffer, "these are nasty jobs but we're going to find some nasty people to do them, so put me down 'cause I'm not only getting mean I'm getting downright nasty" (quoted in Branch, 331).

Moses returned to Mississippi in the summer of 1961 to serve as SNCC's full-time field secretary. He began by opening a voter registration school in McComb, in the southwestern part of the state, to help would-be voters pass Mississippi's notorious literacy tests, which had been designed to keep blacks off the register. Working door-to-door, Moses and other SNCC volunteers persuaded forty locals to register, though by the end of the year only six black voters had been added to the electoral rolls. Such minimal gains came at a considerable cost. Practically every activist was intimidated, beaten, and jailed. Moses was arrested several times, and on one occasion a cousin of the local sheriff attacked him with the butt of a knife near the local courthouse. To the amazement of his colleagues, Moses continued, head bloodied, toward the courthouse, where he attempted to help a handful of residents register. Some who tried to register faced economic reprisals from white landlords and employers, and Herbert Lee, a farmer who had assisted SNCC, was shot and killed by E. H. Hurst, the county's representative in the Mississippi legislature. The McComb movement nonetheless emboldened Moses and others in SNCC, who came to understand the radical, indeed revolutionary, nature of their task. They also learned that revolutions do not happen overnight.

Throughout 1962 and 1963 Moses immersed himself in SNCC's day-to-day efforts to increase voter registration in Mississippi, and he also directed voter registration for the Council of Federated Organizations (COFO), an alliance of the state's civil rights groups. COFO targeted counties in the Mississippi Delta that had potential black electoral majorities but which were dominated by a tight oligarchy of white planters and businessmen. In May 1963 Moses testified before Congress about the failure of President Kennedy's administration to protect civil rights workers and Delta blacks who faced beatings and economic reprisals for attempting to vote.

Believing that the federal government would intervene only if SNCC and COFO provoked a direct confrontation with the white power structure in Mississippi, Moses encouraged more than a thousand student volunteers to come to the state in the summer of 1964 to aid in voter registration and literacy projects. Almost immediately, three of the "Freedom Summer" volunteers, JAMES CHANEY, who was black, and Andrew Goodman and Michael Schwerner, both white, went missing near Philadelphia, Mississippi, and were later found shot and beaten to death. The evidence was strong that members of the Ku Klux Klan had killed the three men, but the FBI's far-from-rigorous investigation of the murders did little to inspire Moses's faith in federal protection. The murders and the media coverage of Freedom Summer did, however, raise public awareness of the depth of white resistance to the rule of law in Mississippi.

The volunteers also helped Moses and local activists establish a new political organization, the Mississippi Freedom Democratic Party (MFDP), which drew eighty thousand members, almost all of them black, to rival the established state Democratic organization led by white supremacists like the U.S. senator James Eastland. Despite the efforts of Moses and FANNIE LOU HAMER, the MFDP failed to be seated at the 1964 Democratic National Convention in Atlantic City, New Jersey. Nonetheless, Hamer's televised testimony about the brutal beatings that she and other black registrants suffered in exercising their constitutional rights electrified the convention hall and convinced many Americans of the justice of the MFDP cause. Within a year Congress passed the Voting Rights Act, finally ensuring black voters the same constitutional protections enjoyed by all other citizens.

By 1965 Moses was becoming increasingly uneasy about his reputation as an inspirational, almost mystical, figure within SNCC. To many of his colleagues, especially whites, his name was no coincidence; they believed that the humble, soft-spoken Bob Moses would lead the civil rights movement to the promised land of equal justice and civil rights. Such thinking was at odds with Moses's enduring belief that the needs and desires of local leaders like Hamer should drive the movement. He changed his surname briefly to Parris and took a leave of absence from SNCC.

In 1966 Moses divorced Dona Richards, a fellow SNCC activist, after a brief marriage, and fled to Montreal, Canada, to avoid being drafted. At thirty-one years of age Moses was much older than the average soldier, and he believed that his vocal opposition to the Vietnam War had led the FBI to manipulate his induction. Physically and psychologically exhausted by the previous five years of struggle, he chose the anonymity of a series of laboring jobs in Canada before traveling to Tanzania in 1968 with his new wife, Janet Jemmott. Moses taught mathematics in a Tanzanian high school for eight years and returned to the United States in 1977, following President Jimmy Carter's amnesty for draft resisters. He settled in Cambridge, Massachusetts, with Jemmott and their four children, and planned to complete the Harvard philosophy doctorate he had begun two decades earlier.

Moses set aside his Ph.D. in 1982, however, when he received a MacArthur Foundation award to establish the Algebra Project, a campaign to increase mathematical knowledge among blacks and other racial minorities. Just as African Americans in the twentieth century had needed access to literacy and voting rights to ensure their full participation in society, Moses argued, so would blacks need access to the math and science skills essential to full participation in the technologically driven twenty-first century. By drawing on the lessons of the civil rights movement, particularly in trusting local people and communities to empower themselves, the Algebra Project has expanded to New York, Baltimore, the San Francisco Bay Area, and the Midwest and, most significantly, to many of the same counties in the Mississippi Delta where Moses and others campaigned for voting rights in the 1960s.

FURTHER READING

Moses, Bob. *Radical Equations: Math Literacy and Civil Rights* (2001).

Branch, Taylor. *Parting the Waters: America in the King Years, 1954–63* (1988).

Burner, Eric. *And Gently Shall He Lead Them: Robert Parris Moses and Civil Rights in Mississippi* (1994).

Carson, Clayborne. *In Struggle: SNCC and the Black Awakening of the 1960s* (1981).

STEVEN J. NIVEN

Moses, William Henry (20 Aug. 1901–19 Oct. 1991), architect and educator, was born in Cumberland County, Virginia, to Julia Trent and William Henry Moses Sr., a Baptist minister who moved the family of six children several times, living in Virginia; Washington, DC; South Carolina,; Tennessee; Texas; New York City; and finally Philadelphia. Moses Jr. attended public school in Philadelphia and graduated from Central High School in 1922, showing an inclination for drawing. After two years at Penn State, Moses withdrew when the family could not afford the costs. For the next seven years he worked in a variety of jobs in architecture, first for the noted African American architect Vertner Woodson Tandy and later as a draftsman for Louis E. Jallade.

In 1931 Moses returned to Penn State and graduated in 1933 with a bachelors of science in Architecture. He worked briefly for the Public Works Administration in New York before joining the faculty at Hampton Institute in Virginia in 1934. The first black educated as an architect to join the Hampton faculty, Moses pushed for a professional architecture curriculum and was the leader in developing the institution's architecture and construction program. He was appointed acting chair in architecture in 1945 and served as chair of the program from 1947 to 1965. Moses retired from full-time teaching in 1967 but continued as a part-time instructor until 1971. In 1969 Hampton's architecture program received accreditation, in large part due to the efforts of Moses.

During these years Moses was also a practicing architect. He collaborated with his fellow Hampton engineer Benson L. Dutton and the architect Charles Thaddeus Russell for years beginning in 1942. Moses was a deft hand at interior design as well as building design and was also a skilled landscape designer. The most rewarding and frustrating episode in Moses's career occurred in 1938, when he utilized his entire skill set in a competition to design Virginia's exhibit for the New York World's Fair. Although he received the rules for design just five days before deadline, Moses worked around the clock to complete the winning entry—a scale model of Colonial Williamsburg and a large photomontage map of Virginia. When the winner was announced and the Virginia Arts Commission learned Moses was black, a white William and Mary College professor was selected to design the state's exhibit, which ironically mimicked Moses's creation. William H. Moses was awarded the $350 entry prize but was not recorded as the competition's winner.

Much of his design reflects Moses's interest in housing, residential and communal. He designed numerous private residences in the Hampton Roads area as well as dormitories and public housing. As campus architect from 1956 until his retirement, his influence on Hampton is evident in the many campus buildings he designed. Although never registered as an architect, Moses enjoyed a highly successful career as an architect and educator. In 1980 he received a Distinguished Alumni Award from Penn State but is best known for fathering the professional architecture program at Hampton. The library at Hampton is named after him.

Moses was married in August 1937 to Julia Anne Mason and had two children. He died in 1991 and was buried in Hampton University Cemetery.

FURTHER READING

Howe, Mentor A. "Come to the Fair." *Phylon* 1 (1940): 314–322.

Spencer, John A. "William Henry Moses Jr. (1901–1991)." In *African- American Architects: A Biographical Dictionary, 1865–1945*, edited by Dreck S. Wilson, pp. 295–297 (2004).

BOYD CHILDRESS

Mosley, Walter (12 Jan. 1952–), author, was born in Los Angeles, California, the only child of Leroy Mosley, a school custodian, and Ella Mosley, a school administrator. Leroy Mosley, who rose from janitor to head custodian, provided inspiration for his son's best-known fictional characters, including Easy Rawlins and Socrates Fortlow, with his ethical approach to life and his stories from Louisiana and Texas. Ella Mosley, who introduced Walter to classic European writers such as Albert Camus, Charles Dickens, and Émile Zola, was born in the Bronx and descended from a Jewish family that fled Poland and Russia. Growing up in South Central Los Angeles, Mosley attended the Victory Baptist Day School, a private African American elementary school that offered courses in black history. When he was twelve years old his family moved to a working-class neighborhood in West Los Angeles, where Mosley attended Alexander Hamilton High School, whose students were largely black and Jewish, a combination reflected in Mosley's own heritage. After graduation Mosley moved to the East Coast to attend Goddard College in Vermont, but took some time off to hitchhike around the country, work as a potter and caterer, and finally to complete a B.A. in Political Science at Johnson State College in 1977. He began graduate studies in political science at the University of Massachusetts while working as a computer programmer, but decided not to pursue a degree. While living in Boston he met Joy Kellman, a dancer and choreographer. Together they moved to New York City in 1981. The couple married in 1987 but divorced in 2001.

While working as a programmer for Mobil Oil in New York, Mosley heard ALICE WALKER read and decided to try his hand at fiction. He enrolled in the Graduate Creative Writing Program at City College of New York and studied with Frederick Tuten, William Matthews, and Edna O'Brien. He was awarded the college's Du Jur Award and acquired an agent when Tuten, impressed with Mosley's fiction, showed it to his own agent. Mosley's initial vision was to write a sequence of novels about characters that, like his father Leroy, had migrated from the South to Los Angeles, inspired in part by Zola's *Rougon-Macquart* series. The first of these novels, *Gone Fishin'*, explored the coming of age of his now-famous characters Easy Rawlins and Mouse Alexander. However, the novel was turned down by fifteen publishers who liked the writing but who did not find his rural southern male subjects "marketable." This experience led Mosley to create a mystery environment for these characters. His first published novel, *Devil in a Blue Dress* (1990), initiated the highly successful Easy Rawlins

Walter Mosley, posing in his studio in New York on 11 June 2002. (AP Images.)

mysteries and launched Walter Mosley's reputation as a mystery writer. The novel was awarded a Shamus Prize, nominated for an Edgar Award for Best New Mystery, and made into a film starring DENZEL WASHINGTON (1995). It was followed by *A Red Death* (1991), nominated for a Golden Dagger Award, and *White Butterfly* (1992), which won the Golden Dagger. When President Bill Clinton named Mosley as one of his favorite authors in the early 1990s, Mosley's sales tripled. His subsequent books in the series, *Black Betty* (1994) and *A Little Yellow Dog* (1996), both made the New York Times Best-seller List.

Mosley is well known for creating memorable characters, as well as for addressing race, economics, and ethics through his fiction. The Easy Rawlins mysteries were also lauded for their evocation of a historically accurate black Los Angeles between World War II and the Vietnam War era. He was often compared to Raymond Chandler, whose hard-boiled detective novels are also set in Los Angeles, but Mosley's fiction was far more aware of class, race, and historical context. As Ron Charles wrote in the *Washington Post Book World*, "That's Mosley's genius: The entertainment takes place right in the cross hairs, while rich, complex issues dart by on the periphery." Once he became established as a popular writer, Mosley used his influence to become involved in black publishing and to advocate for black writers. In 1996 Mosley was named the first artist-in-residence at New York University's Africana Studies Institute, where he helped to found the Black Genius Lecture Series. These lectures were later published in a volume of the same title, to which Mosley contributed and which he also co-edited with his NYU colleagues Manthia Diawara and Clyde Taylor, and the University of Pennsylvania law professor Regina Austin. He was also instrumental in founding a publishing program at the City College of New York specifically for urban residents, the only one of its kind in the country. He chose Black Classic Press as the publisher for *Gone Fishin'* (1997), released as a prequel to the Easy Rawlins mysteries. Black Classic Press also published one of his three nonfiction monographs, *What Next?* (2003), a reflection on 11 September 2001, addressed primarily to African Americans, suggesting that they can play a leading role in the effort toward world peace.

In the midst of his popularity as a crime fiction writer, Mosley took a break from the Easy Rawlins mysteries and successfully tried his hand at other genres, including science fiction and literary fiction.

In *R.L.'s Dream* (1996) he explored a redemptive relationship between two social outcasts on New York's Lower East Side, a homeless African American blues musician named Soupspoon Wise and a white alcoholic woman, Kiki, who houses him in her apartment and obtains fraudulent insurance so his cancer can be treated and he can play music again. The novel was nominated for an NAACP Award in Fiction and won the Black Caucus of the American Library Association's Literary Award.

Mosley continued to explore literary fiction with his two Socrates Fortlow books, *Always Outnumbered, Always Outgunned* (1997) and *Walkin' the Dog* (1999). Set in contemporary Los Angeles and structured as a series of interlocking short stories, both books chronicle episodes in the life of the ex-convict Socrates Fortlow, who attempts to find meaning and moral compass in a life scarred by acts of violence. Like his philosopher namesake, Socrates leads others to a keener appreciation of the truth by asking them questions about their own lives and motives. These books earned Mosley further credibility as a serious literary writer. One of his Socrates Fortlow stories won an O'Henry Award and *Always Outnumbered, Always Outgunned* garnered him the Anisfield-Wolf Award. It was also made into an HBO movie, directed by Michael Apted and starring LAURENCE FISHBURNE (1998), for which Mosley wrote the teleplay. He also published three science fiction novels, including the best-selling *Blue Light* (1998), which elaborates on a concept of transcendence first introduced in *Always Outnumbered, Always Outgunned*; *Futureland: Nine Stories of an Imminent World* (2001); and *The Wave* (2006). Mosley was also at the forefront of experimenting in Internet self-publication; two of his works existed only as downloadable e-books. *The Greatest* (2000), is about a female boxer who is the product of an outlawed genetics experiment, and *Whispers in the Dark* (2000), about two boys living in the distant future. Science fiction enables readers to step outside the flawed world in which they live and to open their minds to the unquestioned assumptions that perpetuate injustice, Mosley suggests in *Life Out of Context*, his 2006 nonfiction monograph. "If we could create, in our minds, a wholly different world and then imagine how we would live in that world—then we could see the flaws in the way we live today," he wrote.

At the beginning of the twenty-first century Mosley returned to the crime genre and the L.A. setting with a new detective, Fearless Jones, and a new narrator, Paris Minton, owner of a used bookstore, in *Fearless Jones* (2001) and *Fear Itself* (2003). A widely published short story writer, he served as editor of *The Best American Short Stories 2003*. He introduced a series of nonfiction monographs on global issues; in addition to *What Next?*, he published *Workin' on the Chain Gang: Shaking Off the Dead Hand of History* (2000), a critique of the ways in which capitalism undermines democracy, and *Life Out of Context* (2006), a call to positive action for social change. Mosley returned to Easy Rawlins in *Bad Boy Brawley Brown* (2002), *Six Easy Pieces* (2003), *Little Scarlet* (2004), and *Cinnamon Kiss* (2005). *The Man in My Basement* (2004), a novel of ideas set in Long Island, continued his exploration of literary fiction, as did *Fortunate Son* (2006), which traces the fates of two adopted boys, one black and one white. In 2005 he published his first novel for young adults, *47*, which examines the legacy of slavery. The HBO movie based on *Little Scarlet* was optioned and scheduled for release in 2008, starring JEFFREY WRIGHT and Mos Def, with a screenplay by Mosley. In *The Long Fall* (2009), Mosley introduced a new character, Leonid McGill, an African American private investigator and ex-boxer, who also appeared in *Known to Evil* (2010) and *When the Thrill Is Gone* (2011). The *Los Angeles Times* praised Mosley's 2010 novel about a 91 year old in South Central LA, whose best friend is killed in a drive by shooting, noting that it "extends once again the boundaries of the hard-boiled suspense genre in which his best work always has been rooted." (http://articles.latimes.com/2010/nov/18/entertainment/la-et-rutten-20101118). In 2006 Mosley was honored by Robert Redford's Sundance Institute with a Risktaker Award for both his creative and activist efforts, and he was awarded an honorary doctorate by the City College of New York.

Mosley's aim was to write enthralling fiction that the average reader could readily understand. Rather than relying on strategies that have proved successful in the past, he used his solid reputation as a springboard for continual experimentation with various genres, including science fiction and public essays to advocate social change. As a social critic, Mosley did not espouse any one political party or philosophy, and he retained his independence even as he became a vocal public advocate for peace and positive social change, and an active resource for other writers, especially African American writers seeking a public audience for their imaginative creations. At the height of his prolific literary career he also became a public advocate for African American arts and cultural production and emerged as a visionary who aspired to contribute to the future direction of art and society.

FURTHER READING
Bryant, Jeffrey H. *Born in a Mighty Bad Land: The Violent Man in African American Folklore and Fiction* (2003).
Charles, Ron. "L.A. Confidential," *Washington Post Book World*, 18 Sept. 2005.
Cobbs, John L. "Walter Mosley," in *Dictionary of Literary Biography*, vol. 306: *American Mystery and Detective Writers*.
"Walter Mosley." *Contemporary Authors, New Revision Series* (2005).
Wilson, Charles E., Jr. *Walter Mosley: A Critical Companion* (2003).

ANN HOSTETLER

Moss, Annie Lee (9 Aug. 1905–15 Jan. 1996), a Pentagon employee who became a celebrated witness during Senator Joseph McCarthy's investigation of Communism in the government, was born in Chester, South Carolina. One of six children of Katie and Clemon Crawford, tenant farmers, she began picking cotton at the age of five. While in her teens, she moved with her parents to Salisbury, North Carolina, where she attended but did not graduate from high school. At twenty-one she married Ernest Moss, a worker at a tobacco factory in Durham, North Carolina. They had one son.

Moss moved to Washington, D.C., in 1941, where her husband took a construction job and she ironed at a laundry. In 1943 she became a dessert cook for the Welfare and Recreation Association, which assigned her to the Pentagon cafeteria. As a condition of employment, she joined the Washington Cafeteria Workers union, a local chapter of the United Federal Workers of America, which was later ejected from the Congress of Industrial Organizations (CIO) for having Communist leadership. In 1943 "Anna Lee Moss–cafeteria" (subsequently listed as "Annie Moss" and "Annie Lee Moss"), assigned card number 37269, appeared in the membership rolls of the Communist Party in Washington.

Seeking wartime housing, the Moss family lived for two weeks in a boardinghouse run by a woman later identified as a member of the Communist Party. After moving into their own home, copies of the Communist Party's newspaper, the *Daily Worker,* began arriving. When someone from the paper came to collect the subscription fee, Moss refused to pay, insisting that she had not subscribed. In October 1945 her name was dropped from the Communist Party's rolls. Seeking a less stressful, better-paying job, Moss became a clerk at the General Accounting Office in December. When security agents at the GAO asked in 1948 if she had a Communist Party membership card, she handed them her purse, which contained only a membership card for the YWCA. Moss was cleared by the GAO's loyalty board, but a postwar reduction in force terminated her job in 1949. She obtained a clerical position with the Army Signal Corps in 1950. The FBI provided the army with information about her name having appeared on Communist membership lists, but the army's loyalty board deemed it insufficient grounds for removal. At the Pentagon she operated a telegraph-typewriter that transmitted coded messages.

Moss came to public attention when the Senate Permanent Subcommittee on Investigations, chaired by McCarthy, looked into alleged Communist infiltration of the Signal Corps. In 1953 and 1954 McCarthy held hearings in which he made sensational charges about subversion and espionage, and he called hundreds of witnesses to testify. In November 1953 the subcommittee staff learned that army investigators had suspicions about Moss but lacked enough evidence to suspend her. The following February, when McCarthy came under fire for his rough treatment of Brigadier General Ralph Zwicker, he announced plans to expose a civilian employee at the Pentagon who was decoding top-secret messages despite being listed by the FBI as a Communist Party member. He claimed the case would prove that the army was placing "known Communists" in sensitive positions (*New York Times*, 23–24 February 1954).

On 23 February 1954 Mary Stalcup Markward, a white woman from Virginia who had joined the Communist Party as an undercover informant for the FBI, publicly revealed the name of Annie Lee Moss in testimony before McCarthy's subcommittee. Although Markward had been active in the Northeast Washington branch of the party that listed Moss as a card-carrying, dues-paying member, she could neither place Moss at any meetings nor identify her by sight. She knew only that Moss's address and employment records matched the information in the party's records. McCarthy insisted that the evidence showed Moss to be a Communist, and he said that if she denied it under oath, she would be subject to prosecution for perjury. "I am not interested in this woman as a person at all," he explained. "I am interested in knowing who in the military

kept her on and promoted her from a waitress to a decoding clerk" (*Army Signal Corps Hearings*, 333). Army officials responded that Moss transmitted only unintelligible coded messages, but they nevertheless transferred her to work in a supply room. She was then suspended but eventually reinstated and assigned to a position outside the Pentagon.

The House Committee on Un-American Activities questioned Moss in closed session in 1954. Finding no proof of disloyalty, it chose not to call her to testify in public. Illness prevented Moss from attending a preliminary executive session before McCarthy's Senate subcommittee, but she finally testified under oath at a public hearing on 11 March 1954. She denied having been a member of the Communist Party, having paid dues, or attended meetings. A small, frail widow, Moss appeared confused by the questioning. "Did you ever hear of Karl Marx?" a senator asked. "Who is that?" Moss answered, drawing laughter from the crowded hearing room (*Army Signal Corps Hearings*, 458).

Senator McCarthy left the hearing in the middle of her testimony. Moss's appearance represented a public relations disaster for his investigation, since the media portrayed her as a victim of circumstance. On 16 March 1954 Edward R. Murrow devoted his *See It Now* television show to her story. The program consisted mostly of video from the hearing, with little commentary, making it all the more convincing. The Moss case, followed shortly by the televised Army-McCarthy hearings, contributed to the erosion of McCarthy's credibility and to his censure by the Senate in December 1954.

Moss retreated into anonymity, living quietly with her son and grandchildren until her death in Washington at age ninety. In 1958 the defendant in another investigation sought to disqualify Mary Markward's testimony on the grounds that she had lied about Moss, but the Subversive Activities Control Board concluded that Markward had not been discredited as a witness since an Annie Lee Moss did appear on Communist Party rolls. The Board conducted no further investigation of Moss, however, leaving her political past unresolved. As with McCarthy, commentators across the ideological spectrum have shown less interest in Moss as a person than as a symbol. Rather than accept her word, some have speculated that she must have been shrewder and more politically savvy than she let on, wearing a mask of innocence to deceive her interrogators. The few reporters who interviewed Moss at her home described her as a deeply religious woman devoted to her family, church, and community. If she was a symbol, it was of a bewildering era when citizens were presumed guilty until they proved themselves innocent.

FURTHER READING

Annie Lee Moss's testimony was published in the Senate Permanent Subcommittee on Investigations hearings on the *Army Signal Corps–Subversion and Espionage* (1954); other material is contained in the files of the subcommittee at the National Archives and in the papers of her attorney, George E. H. Hayes, at the Historical Society of Washington, D.C. *Chicago Defender* reporter Ethel L. Payne discussed Moss in an oral history for the Women in Journalism Project of the Washington Press Club Foundation, National Press Club, Washington, D.C.

Doherty, Thomas Patrick. *Cold War, Cool Medium: Television, McCarthyism, and American Culture* (2003).

Oshinsky, David. *A Conspiracy So Immense: The World of Joe McCarthy* (1983).

Reeves, Thomas. *The Life and Times of Joe McCarthy: A Biography* (1982).

Rosteck, Thomas. *See It Now Confronts McCarthyism: Television Documentary and the Politics of Representation* (1994).

Obituary: *Washington Post*, 19 Jan. 1996.

DONALD A. RITCHIE

Moss, Carlton (14 Feb. 1909–10 Aug. 1997), filmmaker, producer, director, playwright, writer, and cultural critic, was born in Newark, New Jersey, but spent most of his childhood in North Carolina. Little is known about his family. After high school, Moss moved to Baltimore and attended Morgan State College, where he earned a bachelor's degree in 1929. He also attended Columbia University in New York City, where he formed a troupe of black actors called "Toward a Black Theater." The troupe toured around New York City and performed at various black colleges.

Moss was active in the theater and radio and acted in his first film, *The Phantom of Kenwood*, in 1933. The film was directed by OSCAR MICHEAUX, one of the more prolific early black filmmakers. Between 1932 and 1933 Moss wrote three dramas—"Careless Love," "Folks from Dixie," and "Noah"—for a radio series called *The Negro Hour*. Though the series only lasted a short time, the actors who participated in it formed the Lafayette Players, part of the legendary Lafayette Theatre in Harlem. In his role as assistant to John Houseman, who developed the Works Progress Administration's (WPA) Negro

Theater Project under President's Roosevelt's New Deal program, Moss was one of the principle members of the Lafayette Players. The Negro Theater's first production was an adaptation of Shakespeare's *Macbeth* (often referred to as "Voodoo Macbeth"), produced by John Houseman and Orson Welles in 1936. The production was a huge hit and enjoyed a long run in Harlem.

Moss was a prolific writer for the Negro Theater Project, which was under the WPA Federal Theater division, and he was chosen to teach drama for the WPA Negro Theater in Harlem. He became one of the chief consultants for the Federal Negro Theater Project, and a vibrant part of the Harlem arts community, writing numerous plays and radio shows, and eventually replacing Houseman as the director of the Harlem unit. For seven years Moss was the writer, creator, and actor for the radio talk show *Community Forum* for the NBC radio station WEVD. The Negro Theater Project also produced one of his plays, *Prelude to Swing* in 1939.

Moss was an active part of the Information and Education Division of the War Department, writing documentaries and directing theater performances for the military. In 1942 he wrote the play *Salute to Negro Troops*, which had its first run at the Apollo Theater in Harlem. In 1943 Frank Capra chose Moss to direct a film about black soldiers for the military's series of training films, entitled *Why We Fight*. The War Department hoped that such a film would counter Hollywood's racist portrayal of blacks and would help bolster the morale of black soldiers, raise African American enlistments, and foster patriotism within the black community. Moss was the director, technical adviser, and played the Preacher in his film *The Negro Soldier* (the official title was *OF-51*). Moss also wrote the script and, though Capra edited down certain sections that were more critical of American racism, the final result was a groundbreaking portrayal of the significant contributions of blacks to the history of the United States. The black community was well aware of its slave past, but many audience members were unaware of the tremendous social influence black Americans had on education, science, sports, and politics. The film's celebration of African American accomplishments was the first time many filmgoers, black or white, had ever seen positive portrayals of black Americans on film.

The Negro Soldier was a huge success, and in 1944 the army began showing the film to all orientation units. It also was required viewing for all soldiers at U.S. replacement centers until 1948 when

President Truman officially ordered the desegregation of the armed forces. In 1944, amid questions that the film was too supportive of racial tolerance for public release, *The Negro Soldier* was screened at the Pentagon for a group of black journalists, and that April it was released for public distribution. Though some critics felt Moss's film glossed over the painful realities of slavery and Jim Crow segregation, many felt the film was a landmark step in the fight for civil rights in the United States.

After finishing *The Negro Soldier*, Moss went to Europe and produced the documentary *Teamwork*. A sequel to *The Negro Soldier*, *Teamwork* highlighted the military contribution of black soldiers in a quartermaster unit called the "Redball Express." Both films were widely viewed for some time after the war and were seen as cinematic milestones in the fight against racial discrimination. Following the successes of *The Negro Soldier* and *Teamwork*, Moss moved to Hollywood where he focused his attention on industrial and school documentaries and training films. In 1950 he and co-author Helen Arstein wrote *In Person*, a biography of the singer LENA HORNE. Though Moss never achieved Hollywood acclaim, he continued his dedication to eradicating racism through his production company, Artisan Productions (cofounded with William Hurtz), which specialized in short industrial and educational films. For a number of years Moss also occasionally worked as a research assistant for the lyricist and writer E. Y. Harburg. He taught film at the University of California, Irvine, from 1970 to 1994 and wrote numerous articles for *Freedomways* and other journals, continuing his criticism of Hollywood's consistent negative stereotypes of blacks in film and television. Moss passed away at the age of eighty-nine in Los Angeles, California.

FURTHER READING

Cripps, Thomas. *Slow Fade to Black* (1986).
Cripps, Thomas, and David Culbert. "*The Negro Soldier* (1944): Film Propaganda in Black and White," *American Quarterly* 31.5 (1979): 267–275.
Smith, Jessie Carney. *Black Firsts* (1994).

DEBBIE CLARE OLSON

Moss, Thylias (27 Feb. 1954–), poet, playwright, memoirist, children's literature author, and educator, was born Thylias Brasier to Florida and Calvin Brasier in Cleveland, Ohio. Moss's father worked as a tire recapper and her mother as a maid; their working-class family life was stable. Moss experienced childhood in two highly dissimilar stages.

During her earliest years in the late 1950s, her family lived above a Jewish couple who showed Moss great warmth and affection. Her elementary school years, however, were filled with cruel treatment by a certain babysitter and by violent events in her neighborhood, such as children being killed in accidents or by violent acts. And when she moved to a mostly white school district at nine years old, she had additional traumatic experiences. However, during the most difficult years of her childhood, Moss found lifelines in church and poetry. In church, she was particularly drawn to the sermons as a vehicle to reach an audience.

Moss attended Syracuse University for two years, from 1971 to 1973, without getting a degree. Around this time, she also met her future husband, John Lewis Moss, and the two married on 6 July 1973. Moss returned to school and received a B.A. in Creative Writing from Oberlin in 1981, graduating first in her class with a grade point average of 4.11, and she earned an M.A. in English from the University of New Hampshire in 1983. Her prodigious spate of publications began immediately: Her initial collection of poetry, *Hosiery Seams on a Bowlegged Woman* (1983), was published upon completion of her master's degree, followed by two plays, *Talking to Myself* and *The Dolls in the Basement* (1984). Her first son, Dennis Moss, was born in 1986. Three more collections of her poetry were published from 1989 to 1991: *Pyramid of Bone* (1989), *At Redbones* (1990), and *Rainbow Remnants in Rock Bottom Ghetto Sky* (1991). From 1984 to 1992 Moss was on the faculty of Phillips Academy in Andover, Massachusetts—the same school the writer John Irving had attended and used as the setting for some of his novels. Her poetry began to attract notice, as she won a Pushcart Prize in 1990, the Witter Bynner Award for Poetry in 1991, and also a Whiting Award in 1991. Her work evidenced influence of the 1960s poetic inclination toward social commentary—also typical of the Black Arts Movement—combined with a profound sensitivity to everyday humanity. Her poems often featured a reflective and narrative style.

She served as a visiting professor at the University of New Hampshire in 1990 and 1991, and the Fannie Hurst Visiting Professor of Poetry at Brandeis University in 1992. In 1993 she published a volume of poetry entitled *Small Congregations: New and Selected Poems*. That same year, having achieved recognition for her poetry and with her substantial experience as a university professor, Moss was offered a tenured position at the University of

Michigan, in Ann Arbor. She accepted the offer and was later promoted to full professor in 1998. Her publications during this time included two works of children's literature, *I Want to Be* (1995) and *Someone Else Right Now* (1997), and her memoir, *Tale of a Sly-Blue Dress* (1998), which detailed the extensive abuse she suffered at the hands of her babysitter as a child. She was honored with a Guggenheim Fellowship in 1995 and a MacArthur Fellowship in 1996. She also published the poetry volumes *Last Chance for the Tarzan Holler* (1998), *Slave Moth: A Narrative in Verse* (2004), and *Tokyo Butter* (2006). Her work encompassed a range of mythologies, including religious symbolism, African American life, racism, and slavery.

Since 2004 Moss's poetry pursued an aesthetic she termed "Limited Fork Poetics" (LFP), which views poetry as "a complex adaptive system" that does not limit the poem to the page (*Tokyo Butter*). Instead, a "dynamic poem is event, occurs in time, and in its totality includes all versions" (*Tokyo Butter*). LFP recognizes and draws upon the visual, sonic, olfactory, and tactile dimensions of the poetic experience. *Tokyo Butter* (2006) was written in this aesthetic perspective.

Moss's youngest son, Ansted, was a pianist, composer, and image systems designer with whom she collaborated extensively using this LFP poetic methodology. She sought to create poems that hosted "interacting language systems" (*Tokyo Butter*) simultaneously; when the boundaries between these systems created new structures, Moss termed the product a "poam" (or, a product as the act of making) rather than a "poem" (http://tinetimes.blogspot.com). "Poams" are therefore not limited to literary products, but do include them. In this collection, the poams intersected via allusion with the history of painting, scientific principles, events in popular culture, the poetic canon; they interacted much like a hypertext as one reads. Furthermore, the volume refused conventional linearity by including, for example, a poem streaming along the bottom of the page below the ostensible main poems for twenty-two pages. The thematic structure of the text works much like fractals, repeated complex patterns from micro to macro scale found across multiple entities. Moss's LFP poams on the Internet included videos, music, and text and emphasized interaction with the reader, who became part of the poam.

FURTHER READING
Shapiro, Dan. "Interview with Thylias Moss," in *Lily: A Monthly Online Literary Review*. Available at http://freewebs.com/lilylitreview/1_7mossinterview.html. Accessed 4 Dec. 2006.

MALIN PEREIRA

Mossell, Aaron Albert, II (3 Nov. 1863–1 Feb. 1951), the first African American to graduate from the University of Pennsylvania Law School, sprang from a talented family with deep roots in the Methodist Episcopal and African Methodist Episcopal (AME) churches, free a generation before the Civil War. Mossell spent a good part of his adult life in Cardiff, Wales, after a sojourn in South Africa.

The youngest son of Aaron Albert Mossell and Eliza Bowers Mossell, Mossell was born in Canada, where his father owned a brickyard in Hamilton, Ontario. The family had moved there from Maryland due to limited educational opportunities and social restrictions on free people of African descent, although his grandmother, Mrs. Catherine Mossell, remained a life-long member of Baltimore's Sharp Street United Methodist Church until her death in 1891. Before Mossell's second birthday, the family moved again, to Lockport, New York, where he grew up.

Like his older brothers, CHARLES WESLEY MOSSELL and NATHAN FRANCIS MOSSELL, Aaron Albert Mossell went to Lincoln University in Pennsylvania, graduating in 1885. He graduated from University of Pennsylvania Law School in 1888, writing a paper during his final year challenging state antimiscegenation laws as contrary to the Fourteenth Amendment to the federal Constitution.

In 1890 he married Mary Louisa Tanner, sister of the artist HENRY OSSAWA TANNER and daughter of AME bishop BENJAMIN TUCKER TANNER, who conducted the wedding service. They had three children: Aaron Albert Mossell III (1893), Elizabeth Mossell (1894), and SADIE TANNER MOSSELL ALEXANDER (1898). During the early 1890s, he moved home to Lockport, where he was admitted to the federal district court 17 November 1892 (Smith, p. 154). Not until 1893 did he gain admission to the bar in Philadelphia (Smith, p. 172). He joined a law practice in Philadelphia with two other African American attorneys, including John Adams Sparks, later an assistant city solicitor. For a time he served as solicitor of the Frederick Douglass Clinic (later hospital) founded by his older brother (Lane, p. 182). Both brothers were featured on the platform for IDA B. WELLS's 1894 antilynching meeting at Association Hall (Lane, p. 204).

It was difficult for colored attorneys to find work in that era, because plaintiffs and defendants of any color sought "white" attorneys considered to have better connections to the power structure. Around 1900, Mossell separated from his wife and children, resulting in divorce, and left the area. Neither his nor his wife's family made any public disclosure as to the reason. His well-known daughter, Sadie Tanner Mossell Alexander, barely mentioned him, observing once that she was in eighth grade before she knew he wasn't dead. The 1900 census shows the family still living together at 713 15th Street, near Remberton, but it is possible Mossell was already gone, and his wife simply gave his name to the census taker as her husband.

There is even less record of the next quarter century of his life, though it appears he worked for a time in South Africa (Adi and Sherwood, p. 92). He arrived in Wales around 1905 (Johnson, p. 41, fn. 10), working at pit-head jobs in coal mining (Adi and Sherwood, p. 142), making his way to Cardiff by 1926, in time to help with the general strike that year. References to his stay in Cardiff sometimes describe him as an American communist (Bush, Barbara, *Imperialism, Race, and Resistance: African and Britain, 1919–1945*, p. 328, fn. 50), even though no communist party existed in the United States prior to 1919. There is no record of his return to North America between 1919 and 1926.

Cardiff, an industrial seaport for the coal industry, is the capital of Wales. A significant community of immigrant minority seamen developed in the early twentieth century, via the British merchant marine. Butetown (disparagingly known as Tiger Bay) was Cardiff's distinctively multiracial neighborhood near the docks, cut off from the rest of the city by canals on two sides and a railway. After World War I, unemployment on the docks, and objection among some who thought of themselves as "white" to the many marriages between men of African descent and women of Welsh and English descent, raised racial tensions. In June 1919 race riots rampaged through Liverpool, Cardiff, and other cities. Mobs set fire to black residences in Cardiff; at least three were killed, and troops were sent to quell violence. Articles in the local press demanded deportation of blacks.

In Cardiff, Mossell was instrumental in forming the United Committee of Coloured and Colonial Organizations in 1943, which he served as chair. The constituent organizations included the Moslem League, the Colonial Defense Association, the Youth League, the Sons of Africa, and the Islamic Society, sometimes considered the "Big Five" of Butetown (Johnson, p. 41). There is no record of

Mossell returning to the practice of law, although he was respected and esteemed by all classes, not only in the dock area but outside of it; he had for a time a Board of Trade certificate as a collier and seems to have supported himself by it (Johnson, p. 41, fn. 10).

The concept of black, dark, or mixed race was much more complex in Cardiff than in the nineteenth- and twentieth-century United States. Immigrant labor and seamen were recruited from Somalia, Yemen, West Africa, the West Indies, India, China, Scandinavia, Portugal, Egypt (*Race and Class*, Vol. 16, No. 2, Oct. 1974), Greece, and Malta (Tweedale, Iain, "From Tiger Bay to the Inner City: A Century of Black Settlement in Butetown," *Radical Wales*, 1987, p. 5). When the Butetown History and Arts Center was organized in 1988 (Gilroy et al., p. 167, fn. 4), the names of founders such as Glenn Jordan, Rita Hinds Delpeche, Marcia Brahim Berry, Olwen Blackman Watkins, Keith (Nino) Abdi, and Vera Roberts Johnson (Gilroy et al., p. 176) reflected a wide variety of family roots. Berry's father was a Muslim from Malaysia and her mother was a Roman Catholic born in Cardiff to a Nepalese father and a mother with both French and Welsh ancestors (Gilroy et al., p. 177, fn. 15). In 1950, shortly before Mossell died, about six thousand people, representing fifty-seven different nationalities, lived in Butetown (Lloyd, Bert, "Down the Bay," *Picture Post*, 22 April 1950).

The only known family connection during his years in Cardiff is that PAUL ROBESON visited Mossell frequently during the late 1920s and 1930s. Robeson's mother was Maria Louisa Bustill. Maria's sister, GERTRUDE BUSTILL MOSSELL was married to Aaron's older brother, Nathan Francis Mossell, known to Robeson as Uncle Frank. Robeson was deeply beloved by the South Wales Miners Union, often singing in Welsh male choirs, and many of the extras for the movie *Sanders of the River* starring Robeson came from Tiger Bay. During this period, Mossell lodged with the Jason family at 9 Loudon Square (Bourne, p. 37).

In December 1944 Mossell, age eighty-one, led opposition by Tiger Bay residents to a Cardiff Corporation Estates Committee proposal to build thirty-six houses, a youth center building, and a nursery school specifically for colored people in the district. Opposition from the United Committee emphasized that building homes "for the exclusive use of coloured people, would be the starting point in the creation of a coloured 'ghetto' in Cardiff." While welcoming any effort to improve deteriorated housing near the docks, Mossell and the organization he led emphasized that "It should be a general scheme, with no provisions to differentiate between white and coloured British citizens." Posters rapidly appeared on the walls around Tiger Bay, denouncing "any move suggestive of imposed segregation" (Johnson, p. 41).

Mossell served as a delegate to the 1945 Pan-African Congress in Manchester, representing the United Committee of Coloured and Colonial People's Associations, Cardiff, along with S. J. S. Andrew, J. Nurse, M. Hassan, and B. Roderick (Adi and Sherwood, p. 119). His initials are sometimes listed in the records as A. E. or A. S. rather than A. A. Mossell also served on the credentials committee and the platform committee (Adi and Sherwood, p. 120).

Records of the congress record that Mossell "pointed out the need for Africans to rise above their differences. In Cardiff, people of one tribe did not always mix freely with people of another, and that was also his experience when living in South Africa. Africans who had lived in other parts were often treated as foreigners. He himself was called a white black man. There was a clannishness it was difficult to get to the bottom of, and unless something was done to dig it out, it would hinder consolidation. In this consolidation Ethiopia and the Black Republics should have much to teach" (Adi and Sherwood, p. 92). He died in Cardiff six years later, at the age of eighty-seven.

FURTHER READING
Adi, Hakim, and Marika Sherwood. *The 1945 Manchester Pan-African Congress Revisited* (1995).
Gilroy, Paul, Lawrence Grossberg, Stuart Hall, and Angela McRobbie. *Without Guarantees: In Honour of Stuart Hall* (2000).
Johnson, Charles S., ed. "Storm over Tiger Bay." *Race Relations: A Monthly Summary of Events and Trends* 3 (1945–1946): 38–42. Fisk University Social Science Institute.
Lane, Roger. *William Dorsey's Philadelphia and Ours: On the Past and Future of the Black City in America* (1991).
Sinclair, Neil M. C. *The Tiger Bay Story* (1997).
Smith, Clay. *Emancipation: The Making of the Black Lawyer, 1844–1944* (1993).

CHARLES ROSENBERG

Mossell, C.W. (8 June 1849–Oct. 1915), minister of the African Methodist Episcopal (AME) Church, was born Charles Wesley Mossell in Baltimore, Maryland, the eldest son of Aaron Mossell and Eliza Bowers Mossell, free African American residents of that city. Aaron Mossell was a skilled brickmaker. Charles moved with his parents and oldest sister Mary to Canada in 1853, where he and Mary completed the lower grades of public school. Aaron Mossell established his own business in Hamilton, Ontario, where the family's most famous son, NATHAN FRANCIS MOSSELL, was born, as well as the youngest son, Aaron Jr. and younger daughter Alveretta. By 1865 the family had moved to Lockport, New York, where by 1870 Aaron Mossell owned $2,000 in real estate, including his brick-making business and the family home, and $300 in personal property.

Mossell graduated from Lincoln University in Pennsylvania in 1871. The same year, he assisted his younger siblings in securing admittance to the public schools of Lockport, thereby closing the separate one-room school for "colored" children. Aaron Mossell had secured a contract to provide bricks for the new High Street school, offering the lowest possible figure out of respect for civic improvement, and then instructed Nathan, Aaron, and Alveretta to attend the school, directly across from the family home. Teachers ignored their presence, but they persisted in coming, until a special Board of Education meeting was called. Charles, a graduate of Lockport High School, made a convincing presentation to the board.

Accepted in 1872 for study in Lincoln's theology department, in 1874 Mossell received a Bachelor of Divinity degree from Boston University School of Theology. On 29 October 1874 he married Mary Ella Forrester, a graduate of Baltimore Normal School and Lincoln University. Mossell's first pastoral assignment was in Georgetown, South Carolina, where he was also principal of Howard School, while his wife served the school as a teacher and was female superintendent of Sabbath School for the church. They moved to Columbia, South Carolina, in 1875, where MARY ELLA MOSSELL again was Sabbath school superintendent and taught in Sumner Public School. In April 1877 the family left for Haiti as missionaries on the S.S. *Alps*; the gathering of friends who saw them on their way included AME Bishop DANIEL ALEXANDER PAYNE. Before departure, Rev. Mossell found time to deliver a speech on "The supremacy of the Constitution and the sovereignty of the people" before a mass meeting of the citizens of Hagerstown, Maryland.

Boisrond Canal, president of Haiti when the family arrived, was overthrown in 1879. For the rest of their stay, the president was Lysius Felicite Salomon, who supported their work, offering warm praise in a public presentation in 1884. THEOPHILUS GOULD STEWARD, who preceded them in Haiti for a few months, wrote, "The country was solidly Catholic, the language French and Creole, the people far away in manner of thinking and in modes of life. My former experience among the freedmen of the South was of no value to me here. These people were not freedmen, but citizens of an independent country" (Steward, *Fifty Years in the Gospel Ministry*, p. 149).

Mossell first assumed pastoral duties at St. Peter's Haytien Union Methodist Episcopal Church, the result of missionary efforts forty to fifty years earlier, which insisted on its independence. Mossell, committed to the discipline of the AME church, then started St. Paul's AME.

Between May 1880 and May 1884 the Women's Parent Mite Missionary Society of the AME Church expended $2,075.98 in support of Mossell's mission, about four fifths of the regular collection, also taking up special collections of $261.42 to support Mary Ella Mossell's work developing a school, later named in her memory, and $353 for the Iron Church—which was constructed to provide St. Paul's with a fire-proof building. The entire family came down with yellow fever, which killed Alveretta Mossell, who had come in 1879 to join the mission.

The Mossell family nearly lost their lives in the Bazelais Revolution of September 1883, which destroyed ten acres of homes and shops in Port au Prince. Family recollections recorded by the Mossell's daughter, Mary M. Lee, describe those who forced their way into the home as rebels, but in 1884 Rev. Mossell filed a claim through the U.S. consulate in Haiti identifying his assailants as government soldiers. The Mossells were dragged through the streets, threatened by guns, swords, and knives, and with some assistance from friendly Haitians reached the American consulate. Mary was missing for four days. Mrs. Mossell gave birth prematurely, four days later, to a daughter who survived only eleven months. The family home was burned to the ground, with all furniture and other personal property.

During the mission, five young men were sent to Wilberforce University: John Guillcott, Emanuel Day, John Hurst, S. G. Dorce, and A. H. Meves. Dorce became Mossell's immediate successor in the mission at St. Paul's. Hurst was minister at St. Paul's from 1886 to 1887 and then superintendent of AME missions in Haiti from 1888 to 1889 and First Secretary, Haitian Legation in Washington, D.C., from 1889 to 1893. After pastoral assignments in Baltimore beginning in 1894 Hurst was chosen as a bishop of the AME church in 1912, where he served for eighteen years. By 1891 there were 10,204 Methodists in Haiti of a total population of 960,000.

After returning from Haiti in May 1885 Rev. Mossell enrolled at Johns Hopkins University in Baltimore for a course in semitic languages, listing his home as Lockport, New York. His wife, in poor health ever since the ordeal of September 1883 in Haiti, died in Baltimore on 29 June 1886 and was buried in Laurel Cemetery, with a memorial service some weeks later at Trinity AME Church, where John Mercer Langston, Minister Resident of the United States in Haiti, delivered the eulogy. Mossell did not remarry for thirteen years. Over the next twenty years, Rev. Mossell held pastoral appointments in Baltimore, Norfolk, Virginia, and Lockport, New York. After a period in Baltimore, by 1892 he was transferred to Lockport, where in 1896 he published *Toussaint Louverture, Hero of Santo Domingo*, drawing on manuscripts in the possession of the Louverture family, material compiled by Thomas Prosper Gragnon-Lacoste, and his own experience in Haiti. The following year, he served as a founding member of the American Negro Academy, along with W.E.B. DUBOIS, BOOKER T. WASHINGTON, AME Bishop BENJAMIN TUCKER TANNER, and several others. Rev. Mossell had a cordial correspondence with George Myers, who owned the Hollenden Barbershop in Cleveland, Ohio, and was active in Republican Party politics, connected to the Mark Hanna faction. In 1897 after a brutal lynching in Urbana, Ohio, Myers urged African American voters to stay with the Republican Party, taking sharp criticism from many who were disenchanted. Mossell intervened with THOMAS FORTUNE, publisher of the *New York Age*, to defend Myers.

On 21 December 1899 Mossell married Cornelia Hamilton, a native of Virginia, in Pittsburgh, Pennsylvania. After another period in Baltimore, in 1905 he was transferred to St. John's AME Church in Norfolk, Virginia, which had seceded from the Methodist Episcopal Church—South in 1863 because of "disloyalty of the pastor to the U.S. Government." The brick building constructed in 1887–1888 on East Bute Street is noted for its northern Italian, or Lombard, ecclesiastical style and a parsonage built in the Second French Empire style. His wife Cornelia died there in 1906. In May 1908 Rev. Mossell hosted the Twenty-Third General

Conference of the African Methodist Episcopal Church, which convened at St. John's.

Rev. Mossell's last years are obscure. The 1900 Census shows him living on Arundle Road in Bowie, Maryland, with his aging father, Aaron Mossell, and a stepmother, Mary Mossell, about C. W.'s own age, whom his father had married in 1885, several years after the death of Eliza Bowers Mossell. *The Crisis*, October 1915, announced "The Rev. C. W. Mossell, a prominent African M.E. Minister of Baltimore and brother of Dr. N. F. Mossell, is dead," but gave no date or cause of death.

He was survived by his brother, Nathan Francis, the first African American to obtain a medical degree from the University of Pennsylvania and founder of Frederick Douglass Memorial Hospital in Philadelphia; his brother, Aaron Mossell, the first African American to graduate from University of Pennsylvania Law School; his sister, Mary, who in 1883 married Professor A. Parker Denny, a teacher in the public schools of Princeton, New Jersey; and, among many nieces and nephews, SADIE TANNER MOSSELL ALEXANDER, the first African American woman to obtain a Ph.D. and a law degree. Dr. Mossell was "Uncle Frank" to the activist, lawyer, actor, singer, and athlete PAUL ROBESON, whose mother, Maria Louisa Bustill Robeson, was the sister of Dr. Mossell's wife, GERTRUDE BUSTILL MOSSELL, a published writer under the name Mrs. N. F. Mossell.

FURTHER READING
Mossell, C.W. "The Christian Religion in Haiti." *Toussaint Louverture, the Hero of Santo Domingo* (1896). [Chapter XLII, particularly starting at p. 395, "Protestantism," provides the only extant autobiographical account of the Mossells' mission to Haiti.]

Butt, Rev. Israel L., D.D. *History of African Methodism in Virginia, or Four Decades in the Old Dominion* (1908).

Handy, James A. *Scraps of African Methodist Episcopal History.* (1902).

Lee, Mary M. "Mary Ella Mossell." In *Homespun Heroines and Other Women of Distinction*. Hallie Q. Brown, ed. (1988).

Payne, Daniel Alexander. *History of the African Methodist Episcopal Church: 1811–1893*. Charles Spencer Smith, ed. (1891).

Smith, Charles Spencer. *A History of the African Methodist Episcopal Church, 1856 to 1922* (1922).

Wright, Richard R. *Centennial Encyclopaedia of the African Methodist Episcopal Church* (1916).

CHARLES ROSENBERG

Mossell, Gertrude Bustill (3 July 1855–21 Jan. 1948), writer, educator, and activist, was born the youngest of two girls to Charles Hicks Bustill and Emily Robinson Bustill in Philadelphia, Pennsylvania. Her father was a successful plasterer, was one of the grandsons of CYRUS BUSTILL, a prominent baker who served George Washington during the American Revolution, and was an early activist in Philadelphia's Free African Society. Among Cyrus Bustill's other descendents, GRACE BUSTILL DOUGLASS and SARAH MAPPS DOUGLASS were perhaps among the most prominent. Shaped by this family tradition of working for African American rights, Gertrude Bustill recognized early a call to serve—a call undoubtedly influenced by her family's ties to the Quakers (though family members later joined the Presbyterian Church).

Though her father's family gave her both economic stability and prominence, her childhood was, at times, difficult. Her mother died before Bustill turned five, and Bustill and her elder sister, Maria Louisa, seem to have moved between their father's home and the homes of various family members and friends. Both children attended Philadelphia's segregated schools; Bustill graduated from the Roberts Vaux Grammar School (which actually included secondary instruction) in June 1872. At the graduation exercises she presented an original essay, "Moral Courage," which the visiting bishop BENJAMIN TANNER TUCKER convinced her to submit to the *Christian Recorder* and which was published in the 6 July 1872 issue. Several of her poems and short essays appeared in the *Recorder* over the next decade.

She went on to teach in a range of schools in Pennsylvania, New Jersey, Delaware, and even Kentucky. At some point she met NATHAN FRANCIS MOSSELL, who was one year her junior. They married probably sometime around 1880. The son of Aaron Mossell, a Maryland free black brick maker, and his wife, Eliza, Nathan, like his three siblings, was born in Canada because his parents were unwilling to raise a family where slavery was permitted. The Mossell family's stance on black civil rights was not the only attraction that Nathan Mossell held. A graduate of Lincoln University in Pennsylvania, Mossell became the first African American graduate of the University of Pennsylvania Medical School in 1882, and in 1885 he became the first African American admitted to the Philadelphia Medical Society.

The couple settled in Philadelphia and had four children, though only two daughters, Mary

Campbell (Mazie) and Florence Alma, survived to adulthood. Though circumstances forced Gertrude Mossell from the classroom, she was able to turn again to writing. By 1890 her work had appeared in, among other publications, the *Philadelphia Times*, the *Philadelphia Independent*, *Our Women and Children*, the *A.M.E. Church Review*, *Ringwood's Magazine*, and the *Indianapolis Freeman*; later work would appear in publications like the *Colored American*. She also helped edit the *Lincoln Alumni Magazine* for her husband's alma mater. Her biweekly column in T.-THOMAS FORTUNE's *New York Freeman* (later the *New York Age*) appeared throughout the late 1880s. She also worked as the women's editor for the *Indianapolis World* and the *Philadelphia Echo*. This early writing took a forthright feminist approach, advocating both suffrage and education for women. On education her comments were especially rich, and she consistently argued that black women should be encouraged to pursue careers in journalism, medicine, and business. Like many early black feminists, Mossell saw her politics as completely consonant with her roles as wife and mother; she often wrote under the name "Mrs. N. F. Mossell."

The culmination of this work was the 1894 publication of *The Work of Afro-American Women*. Made up of a series of essays and poems, this small book is quite wide-ranging. The extended title essay catalogs African American women's accomplishments in education, literature, journalism, medicine, nursing, law, art, and a host of other fields; its consideration of black women educators has proven an especially valuable early record to historians. More focused essays on literature and journalism follow, including one of the earliest bibliographies of African American texts. Though these sections echo some of the material found in other African American biographical dictionaries of the period, the book's focus on women makes it fairly rare, and its feminist approach is almost unique.

Some critics have argued that the work that follows the biographical essays—including essays that focus on race and the World's Fair and on race in higher education, as well as a collection of Mossell's poems—does not clearly fit with the early sections. They thus treat *Work* as a miscellany. However, the later essays, which consider many of the pro-black and pro-women concerns raised in the more biographical sections, and the poems, which focus largely on Christian mothering and an almost Pan-Africanist sense of race, are logical extensions of the early parts of the book. Several of these writings were arguably ahead of their time, and their collection in *Work* suggests both that Mossell was developing a nascent womanist philosophy and that she had managed to create a supportive network: her preface thanks not only her husband and T. Thomas Fortune but also FRANCES E. WATKINS HARPER, and the book is dedicated to her two daughters, "praying that they may grow into a pure and noble womanhood."

Mossell's writing was more limited after 1900, though she never totally stopped such work. She wrote occasionally, for example, for the *Colored American Magazine* and produced a children's book, *Little Dansie's One Day at Sabbath School* (1902). A second edition of *The Work of Afro-American Women* was published in 1908.

Much of Mossell's later work focused on providing more direct aid to African Americans generally and black women in particular. She was instrumental, for example, in setting up Philadelphia's chapter of the National Afro-American Council. But the clear centerpiece of her efforts was also her husband's main focus: the establishment and ongoing support of Frederick Douglass Hospital. Gertrude Mossell was a major force in raising more than thirty thousand dollars to build a facility at Fifteenth and Lombard streets in 1895 to meet a deep need in Philadelphia's black community: a hospital that would admit them. Nathan Mossell became the hospital's first and most revolutionary director. In a demonstration of the Mossells' shared concern for women's education and employment, the hospital soon founded one of the nation's first black hospital schools for nurse training. Throughout the next five decades the Mossells raised funds, helped administer various components of the hospital, and worked in a range of other ways to provide aid; some of Gertrude Mossell's most notable service was as president of the hospital's social service auxiliary. Douglass Hospital merged with Mercy Hospital in 1948 and continued to offer medical care until 1973.

Mossell also continued to devote herself to her family, and Mary Campbell Mossell-Griffin followed briefly in her footsteps, writing a brief biographical dictionary, *Afro-American Men and Women Who Count*, in the early twentieth century. One of Mossell's nephews also rose to prominence: the actor and activist PAUL ROBESON was the son of William Drew Robeson and Mossell's sister Maria Louisa Bustill Robeson. Nathan Mossell died in 1946, and Mossell survived him for fifteen months before also dying in Philadelphia in the hospital they had worked so hard to build.

FURTHER READING

Mossell's papers remain uncollected, though some material on the Bustill family is included in the Bustill-Bowser-Asbury Papers at Howard University.

Lane, Roger. *William Dorsey's Philadelphia and Ours* (1991).

Streitmatter, Rodger. *Raising Her Voice: African American Women Journalists Who Changed History* (1994).

Obituary: *Philadelphia Tribune*, 24 Jan. 1948.

ERIC GARDNER

Mossell, Mary Ella (22 May 1853–29 June 1886), Haitian missionary, was born Mary Ella Forester in Baltimore, Maryland, the daughter of Perry Forrester, a local businessman, and an unknown mother. She graduated from the Baltimore Normal School with good knowledge of Latin, Greek, and German. She also studied voice, music theory, and the piano. In 1874 she married Charles W. Mossell, a minister of the African Methodist Episcopal Church (AME). When her husband was appointed to Haiti as a missionary in 1877, Mossell accompanied him to help a struggling mission outpost. In Haiti Mossell gave birth to a daughter, also named Mary.

In 1816 a group of prominent white Americans had founded the American Colonization Society to relocate free blacks to the continent of Africa. The Liberian scheme quickly lost its appeal to free northern blacks, particularly after they learned of the staggering death rates among the settlers. Although most African Americans rejected any colonization scheme as a repudiation of their right to American citizenship, some emigration attention turned toward Haiti, which became a symbol of black nationalism and a possible escape from American oppression. Some blacks found the idea of settling in Haiti, then facing a labor shortage, appealing. Jean-Pierre Boyer, the Haitian president, offered free transportation to potential emigrants. Thousands of blacks, including some members of the Philadelphia AME church, took the offer and settled in Haiti in 1824. Three years later the AME Church commissioned Scipio Beanes as its missionary to Haiti. Although African Methodists started at least three congregations in Haiti, they ministered mostly to their compatriots and did not develop an indigenous church. They also were severely handicapped by the fact they had no resident bishop or financial support from the mother church. Since only Methodist bishops could ordain clergy, a shortage of ministers ensued, and the mission dwindled.

Discouraged, the African Methodists in Haiti became independent in 1843. After the Civil War the AME Church gave more attention to its missions program, and church women created the Woman's Parent Mite Missionary Society (WPMMS) in 1874. The goal of this auxiliary was to raise funds for missions, and it sent the Mossells to Haiti.

The Mossells docked in the Haitian capital, Port-au-Prince, in April 1877. Mary Mossell's husband was welcomed to preach at St. Peters Haytian Union Methodist Episcopal Church, an independent congregation attended by former AME members. But he soon ran into problems with the church's leaders and left after nine months to plant a new mission, St. Paul AME, with forty members, in 1878. Like St. Peters, St. Paul at its founding was composed of African American families, not those indigenous peoples who tended toward Catholicism or African religions. Aware of the failures of the early AME missionary efforts, Mossell's husband worked hard to develop an indigenous ministry. He opened a French service and started celebrating the Eucharist in the French language. Mossell taught the girls' Sunday school class, instructing students ranging from five to eighteen years of age. According to her husband, "these girls without exception all professed salvation and united with the Church" (Mossell, 416). From his Haitian converts, Rev. Mossell chose five promising young men and sent them to study for the ministry at Wilberforce University in Ohio. In this latter project he was financially assisted by the Haitian president Lysius Salomon. Mossell also supported her husband's ministerial program and organized a concert to raise funds for the youths who were to study at Wilberforce. She also attended her husband's evangelistic campaigns outside Port-au-Prince. During a visit to Arcahaie, a town near the capital, Mossell sang French translations of several songs used in the Moody–Sankey campaigns. D. L. Moody was at the time the most prominent American evangelist, and Ira Sankey was his worship leader and musical director. Thus in Arcahaie, Mary Mossell was able to use both her language and musical skills.

The Mossells were concerned about more than saving souls; they also wanted to educate the children of the poor and so opened a day school. Indeed, the AME Church had been founded with a thorough dedication to black educational improvement. In the United States the AME Church was quickly becoming a middle-class institution in urban areas and already owned several colleges. A school was opened in Haiti under the direction of

Mary Mossell and was free, except for the music lessons. The curriculum was taught in both French and English. This educational endeavor drew about 130 students, and included a girls' department that taught needlework, sewing, and vocal and instrumental music. The AME Church much appreciated the work of their Haitian missionaries as evidenced by the support given them by the WPMMS. For the quadrennium 1880–1884, nearly $2,700—that is, more than 75 percent of monies raised by the WPMMS—was sent to support the Mossells, St. Paul, and the school.

Mossell also founded a Christian Musical Association composed of young men and women that performed from time to time at the National Theatre of Port-au-Prince. Her husband later reported, "That which charmed most on such occasions was the faultless rendering in French of hymns from the Moody and Sankey collection" (Mossell, 214). Though Haitian Creole was the indigenous language, French was Haiti's official tongue, and educated Haitians could only be impressed with foreigners who could speak it perfectly. Haitian president Salomon was impressed by Mossell's linguistic prowess and that she had deliberately sought to reach some of the Haitian elite through her French and music skills. Haiti was staunchly Catholic, owing to its status as a former French colony, and Haitian intellectuals were not enthusiastic about Methodism. Mossell, however, had much to offer and gained the attention of the island's educated class, among which she was "soon accepted in the homes of the cultured upon whom she drew for converts and for pupils" (Brown, 196). She composed French and Creole instrumental renditions, some of which were dedicated to Haitian dignitaries. *La Grande Marche* and *Le Bouquet* were dedicated to President Salomon and General Legitime, respectively. Mossell also made herself available to non-elites, something made easier by her fluency in the native patois, and native women in particular became interested in what she had to teach. Mossell collected some colored yarns and took pleasure in making them into patterns while she sat on her veranda. Native women passing by became interested in her craft and in this way were enticed to attend services. Several of these curious women later joined St. Paul.

Though she was enjoying her missionary endeavors, Mossell was forced to leave the country in 1885. On 23 September 1883 a violent revolution spread throughout Port-au-Prince that led a mob to burn her house. People who took refuge in St. Paul were murdered, and it was only through a miracle that Mossell's family was spared. Mossell, who was pregnant at the time of the evacuation, went into early labor and delivered another daughter who died shortly thereafter. In May 1885 the family returned to the United States, but Mossell never recovered from her ordeal and died a year later in Baltimore. A gifted and self-sacrificing missionary, Mossell dedicated her considerable talents and her life to assisting the women and children of Haiti.

FURTHER READING

Berry, L. L. *A Century of Missions of the African Methodist Episcopal Church* (1942).

Brown, Hallie Q. *Homespun Heroines and Other Women of Distinction* (1926; rpt. 1988).

Dixon, Chris. *African America and Haiti* (2000).

Mossell, Charles W. *Toussaint L'Ouverture* (1896).

Payne, Daniel A. *History of the African Methodist Episcopal Church* (1891).

DAVID MICHEL

Mossell, Nathan Francis (27 July 1856–27 Oct. 1946), physician and hospital founder and administrator, was born in Hamilton, Ontario, Canada, the son of Aaron Mossell, a brick manufacturer, and Eliza Bowers; both parents were free blacks from Baltimore, Maryland, who had moved to Canada to escape racial discrimination. When the Civil War ended and slavery was abolished, Aaron Mossell moved his family back to the United States. In 1865 they settled in Lockport, New York, a small town near Rochester.

In Lockport the Mossell children were assigned to a separate all-black school. Mossell's father successfully petitioned the Lockport Board of Education to close the all-black school, and Nathan and the other black children were allowed to attend integrated schools. The Mossell family's home life was highly religious: Aaron Mossell donated the bricks for the first African Methodist Episcopal (AME) Zion Church in Lockport.

After graduation from high school in Lockport in 1873, Nathan Mossell moved to Philadelphia, where he worked to acquire funds for college. He enrolled at Lincoln University in Lincoln, Pennsylvania, in 1875 and graduated in 1879 with a B.A. degree. During his four years at Lincoln University he taught Sunday school at the Bethel AME Zion Church in Wilmington, Delaware.

In 1879 Mossell gained admission to the Medical School of the University of Pennsylvania, from which he graduated with high honors in 1882. He was the first African American to apply to the university's medical program and the first to graduate. In the year before his medical school graduation he married Gertrude Bustill (GERTRUDE MOSSELL); they had two daughters.

After medical school Mossell worked in the outpatient clinic of the University Hospital. Because of racial attitudes, he was reluctantly given this position only through the influence of his former professors. Concurrently he completed a postgraduate course at the Philadelphia Polyclinic. He was refused membership, again because of his race, in the Philadelphia County Medical Society. After a bitter struggle and with letters of support from his former professors, he was accepted into the society in 1888, the first African American member.

In 1885 Mossell went to Europe for advanced medical training. He studied surgery at Guy's Hospital and St. Thomas Hospital in London, England. Back in Philadelphia, however, he was unable to gain a hospital staff appointment. Furthermore, he was disturbed that none of the more than twenty-four hospitals in the Philadelphia area would admit African American medical graduates to internships or African American women into their nurse training programs. Mossell was convinced of the necessity of better hospital care for African Americans and of training opportunities for black doctors and nurses. Several medical colleges in Philadelphia offered to assist him in establishing a hospital if he would agree that it would be segregated. Mossell and other black leaders refused this offensive condition.

Mossell was against hospitals exclusively for black people, which he thought were a wasteful duplication of effort and perpetuation of a caste system. However, the great needs of Philadelphia's African American community and discrimination at other hospitals forced him to act against his philosophy. In June 1895 Mossell convened other doctors to lay plans for establishing a hospital for patients of all races; it would provide a place for black physicians to treat their patients and to gain professional development and for African American interns and nurses to acquire training. With public fund-raising, church donations, and the work of African American women volunteers led by Gertrude Mossell, a three-story building was leased at 1512 Lombard Street and outfitted as a fifteen-bed facility. Frederick Douglass Memorial Hospital and Training School opened on 31 October 1895. Eighty-six percent of the funds needed to open the hospital and to operate it during the first year were raised in the African American community. Some blacks, however, criticized Mossell for conceding to race prejudice; some whites argued that there were already enough charitable hospitals.

Each year during its first decade Douglass Hospital's outpatient and inpatient censuses increased. Some of the first patients were veterans of the Spanish-American War. Beginning in 1905 annual state funding of six thousand dollars was gained in recognition of the number of poor patients being served. From the founding of Douglass Hospital until early 1931, Mossell served as both superintendent and medical director. The administrative and professional duties were separated in 1931, and he retained the post of medical director.

In early 1905 Mossell faced opposition from a segment of Douglass's professional staff. The board of directors requested his resignation. Some physicians had accused Mossell of retarding the professional growth of younger physicians by limiting their assignments to perform operations. Others faulted him for what they judged to be a turning of the hospital from a quasi-public institution to a more private one. Mossell overcame the attacks on him during 1905 with strong community support. In late 1905 a dissident group of doctors failed to get the board of managers to reorganize the hospital to free it from all appearances of being a private institution. They ended their affiliation with Douglass and established Mercy Hospital, which opened in 1907. The split between the supporters of Douglass and Mercy hospitals continued until the mid-1940s, when a merger was proposed. Mossell felt that a single hospital would better serve the growing African American population of Philadelphia and provided strong leadership toward the eventual merger forming Mercy-Douglass Hospital, which was not realized until two years after his death.

Mossell was a leading organizer of African American medical affairs and politics. In 1895 he was a founder of the National Medical Association (NMA), established by African American physicians because they were barred from the American Medical Association and its local chapters. In 1900 he helped establish the Philadelphia Academy of Medical and Allied Sciences, an NMA chapter. In 1907 he served as the eighth president of the NMA.

Medicine was not the only field in which Mossell combated racial discrimination and championed civil rights. In 1905 he joined the Niagara Movement, organized by W. E. B. DuBois, which called for immediate and full civil rights for African Americans. The Niagara Movement led to the founding of the NAACP in 1910. Mossell spearheaded protests in Philadelphia against the anti-black novel *The Clansman* and a Hollywood film, *The Birth of a Nation*, based on the novel. He led a fight in Philadelphia in 1944 to have African American youth admitted to Girard College, a privately funded but publicly administered institution.

Mossell died at his home in Philadelphia. For more than forty years he was a pioneering hospital developer and a forceful advocate for black-controlled hospitals, essential during a time when medical training and hospital practice for African American physicians and nurses were severely limited in the United States.

FURTHER READING

Cobb, William Montague. "Nathan Francis Mossell, 1856–1946," *Journal of the National Medical Association* 46 (Mar. 1954): 118–30.

Gamble, Vanessa Northington. *Making a Place for Ourselves: The Black Hospital Movement, 1920–1945* (1995).

Obituaries: *Philadelphia Inquirer* and *Philadelphia Evening Bulletin*, 28 Oct. 1946; *Pittsburgh Courier*, 2 Nov. 1946.

This entry is taken from the *American National Biography* and is published here with the permission of the American Council of Learned Societies.

ROBERT C. HAYDEN

Moten, Bennie (13 Nov. 1894–2 Apr. 1935), musician, composer, and bandleader, was born Benjamin Moten in Kansas City, Missouri. The names of his parents are unknown. His mother was a pianist. At age twelve he began performing as a baritone horn player in Lacy Blackburn's Juvenile Brass Band. As a teenager he switched to ragtime piano, studying with Charlie Watts and Scrap Harris, two of SCOTT JOPLIN's former pupils. By age twenty-four Moten was leading his own trio, B. B. and D., with Bailey Handcock on vocals and Duke Lankford on drums, which worked for over a year. In 1921 Moten formed a six-piece band consisting of Lamar Wright on cornet, Thamon Hayes on trombone, Woodie Walder on clarinet, Willie Hall on drums, George Tall on banjo, and himself on piano. The group worked at Kansas City clubs.

In 1923 Ralph Peer, talent scout and chief of A&R for the Okeh Record Company, an independent label that maintained a significant "race catalog," auditioned Moten's band and signed the group for its first recording session in September 1923 in St. Louis with the blues singers ADA BROWN and Mary Bradford. The Bennie Moten Orchestra recording was only part of an active year during which FREDDIE KEPPARD and Doc Cook's Gingersnaps, SIDNEY BECHET with CLARENCE WILLIAMS's Blue Five, and LOUIS ARMSTRONG with KING OLIVER's Creole Jazz Band also made recordings. Yet Moten's group managed to set itself apart from other bands.

In November 1924 Moten's orchestra, with the addition of Harry Cooper on trumpet, HARLAN LEONARD on alto saxophone, and Al "Abe" Bolar on tuba, recorded a second time for Okeh. Cooper's addition created a three-piece brass section, while Leonard's addition made for a complete reed section, the first in a Kansas City band. Bolar on tuba strengthened the 2/4 metric concept. Along with Thamon Hayes's composition of the parade-style chart "South," the November 1924 session began to lead the Moten orchestra away from New Orleans style toward a new type of swing based primarily on section riffs and fluid solo lines. The trend of doubling and tripling instrumentation fostered by Moten led toward simple improvised "head" arrangements. The remaining significant aspect of Kansas City swing, a strong 4/4 rhythm, was not realized until the acquisition of WALTER PAGE, string bassist and tubist, from the Blue Devils in the winter of 1931.

Moten recorded a final session for Okeh in May 1925 in Kansas City. The old mechanical recording techniques used in the previous sessions were replaced by electrical methods. Stronger performances of blues with significant interplay among brass and reeds were featured on the session. In 1926 Peer moved to Victor, taking Moten and most of Okeh's strongest talent with him. Moten was associated with Victor from 1926 to 1932. The Moten orchestra was the only Southwest band that held a record contract.

The status of Moten's band was quite high in Kansas City. The band had no serious hometown rival other than the GEORGE E. LEE Orchestra. The band also received acclaim along the Atlantic seaboard, where its 2/4 rhythms proved to be a novelty to audiences. Moten divided the earnings equally during this period, creating an appealing and stable atmosphere for the band. A recording session in Chicago on 13–14 December 1926 listed the following personnel: Lamar Wright on cornet; Thamon Hayes on trombone; Harlan Leonard, Woodie Walder, and LaForest Dent on reeds; Bennie Moten on piano; Sam Tall on banjo; Vernon Page on tuba; and Willie McWashington on drums.

Moten's success continued into 1928 with a renewed contract at Victor. Thamon Hayes's "South" became a runaway best-seller in September, ranked just below DUKE ELLINGTON on the lists. Ballrooms and theaters along the East Coast booked Moten's orchestra during its several Camden, New Jersey, recording sessions. However, because of its conspicuous absence in Kansas City, Moten's group was losing ground to other bands, such as the Blue Devils and Lee's band, which were viewed by local audiences as the unadulterated Kansas City style.

The band returned to Kansas City at the height of its national popularity. Moten increased efforts to recruit Blue Devils members COUNT BASIE, HOT LIPS PAGE, and EDDIE DURHAM. In the summer of 1929 Basie and Durham signed on. Durham's versatility on guitar and trombone, as well as his talent as a composer and arranger, along with Basie's energy and rhythmic vitality boosted the quality of the ensemble. Although he still played piano on a second piano alongside Basie, Moten turned his efforts toward management and direction of the band. His nephew Ira "Buster" Moten joined the group, playing both accordion and piano. The trumpeter Hot Lips Page and vocalist JIMMY RUSHING next left the Blue Devils to join Moten. With the brass section increased to five and Rushing ideal for the band, the next Victor session demonstrated advances in technical and musical cohesion.

In the winter of 1931 one of Moten's rivals finally capitulated. Walter Page, bassist and leader of the Blue Devils, joined the Moten orchestra, replacing Vernon Page. Walter's addition brought the final element central to the Kansas City style. Since he performed on both tuba and string bass, Walter Page was able on the bass to present a new rhythmic vitality in a 4/4 beat, while preserving the earlier two-beat style on tuba. With Walter on board, Moten's orchestra was in position to dominate jazz in the Southwest.

Musicians who subsequently joined Moten's ranks included the trombonist Dan Minor (formerly with ALPHONSO TRENT), the alto saxophonist Eddie Barefield (Eli Rice Cotton Pickers), Joe Keyes on trumpet (Johnson's Joymakers), and the young tenor saxophonist BEN WEBSTER (Coy's Black Aces). The windfall of talent afforded Moten one of the most spectacular bands in jazz history, yet a serious rift occurred among its members. The newcomers demonstrated contempt for what they perceived to be the limited performing abilities of the older members. The earlier members resented the fact that the band had grown away from its original Kansas City style; they also believed that Moten's change to a payroll system enabled him to siphon extra money for himself. Many of the older members left Moten and formed their own band to attempt to preserve the earlier style.

Nevertheless, Moten's group recorded in October 1931 and continued to gain momentum. By 13 December 1932, the band's last session for Victor, the ensemble was highly polished and turned out its best recordings ever. The twelve members of the 1932 band included Joe Keyes, Hot Lips Page, and Dee Stewart on trumpet; Dan Minor and Eddie Durham on trombone; Eddie Barefield, Ben Webster, and Jack Washington on reeds; and a rhythm section that featured Bill Basie, Leroy Berry, Walter Page, and Willie McWashington. Some of the works that resulted from this session were "Toby," "Moten's Swing," "Blue Room," "New Orleans," "Milenburg Joys," and "Prince of Wails."

Because of the flexibility of the rhythm section and the cohesiveness of the horn sections, many of the pieces in the Moten book were by this time either riff-based blues or head arrangements. With head arrangements, the basic tune of the piece was worked out in advance. Never written down, they would be played from memory, which allowed each performance to retain uniqueness and variety. In Moten's riff-based blues, a distinctly Kansas City specialty, usually short rhythmic and harmonic patterns were established and played over blues set up by the rhythm section. These works generated a sense of flow and allowed highly interactive exchanges among the reed, brass, and rhythm sections, balanced with rhythmically charged solos.

Moten's orchestra, even with no shortage of work, ran into other obstacles during the Depression. Venues sometimes closed down unexpectedly, leaving players stranded with no way home but riding the railcars. The band soon restricted its activity to Kansas City, where work was still available. Moten slowly reduced the band's numbers from an all-time high of fifteen in 1932 to six players by 1933. Nonetheless, players such as the tenor saxophonist LESTER YOUNG continued to play with the band.

In 1935 Moten sent the band ahead for a lengthy stint at the Rainbow Ballroom in Denver, remaining behind for a tonsillectomy. The surgeon was a personal friend of Moten's, and the evening before the surgery, both men spent the night on the town. The next morning, for whatever reason, the surgery went wrong, and Moten died on the operating table. Leadership of the band temporarily went to Buster Moten and Count Basie. The band eventually became the Count Basie Orchestra.

Moten was the pivotal figure in the development of jazz in Kansas City and the Southwest. He was responsible for developing the swing-era jazz orchestra or big band, with its reed, brass, and rhythm sections. The orchestra evolved the genres of riff-based blues and memorized head arrangements, and many members of the orchestra were outstanding musicians in their own right.

FURTHER READING

Driggs, Frank, and Chuck Haddix. *Kansas City Jazz: From Ragtime to Bebop* (2005).

Pearson, Nathan W., Jr. *Goin' to Kansas City* (1987).

Russell, Ross. *Jazz Style in Kansas City and the Southwest* (1997).

Schuller, Gunther. *Early Jazz: Its Roots and Musical Development* (1986).

This entry is taken from the *American National Biography* and is published here with the permission of the American Council of Learned Societies.

DAVID E. SPIES

Moten, Lucy Ellen (1851–24 Aug. 1933), educator, was born in Fauquier County, Virginia, near White Sulphur Springs, the daughter of Benjamin Moten, a U.S. Patent Office clerk, and Julia Withers. Taking advantage of their status as free blacks, the Motens moved to the District of Columbia when Lucy was only a child to secure the best possible education for their precocious daughter. Lucy attended Washington's pay schools until 1862, when she was admitted to the district's first public schools for African Americans. After attending the preparatory and normal departments of Howard University, Lucy Moten began teaching in the primary grades of the local public schools and taught there continually, except for a two-year interruption, from 1870 until 1883. In 1873 Moten moved to Salem, Massachusetts, to attend the State Normal School, from which she graduated in 1875.

In 1883 FREDERICK DOUGLASS recommended that Moten be appointed to fill the vacant principalship of the Miner Normal School, a public teacher training institution for black primary teachers in the District of Columbia. Although impressed with her experience and academic credentials, the members of the Board of Trustees of the Miner School were concerned that Moten's youth and physical attractiveness made her unsuited for such a responsible position. Only after she assured the

trustees that she would refrain from theatergoing, card playing, and dancing were they convinced that she was the right person for the job.

From 1883 to 1920 Moten ran the Miner Normal School with an iron hand. She was a strict taskmaster who demanded that her students maintain the highest personal and professional standards. She never challenged them, however, to do anything that she was unwilling to do herself and over time won their universal respect. Moten strongly urged the students with whom she worked to continue to educate themselves. She maintained a high standard in this regard by spending much of her spare time away from Miner furthering her own professional development. The same year she assumed the principalship at Miner, she graduated from the Spencerian Business College with honors. She worked closely with Alfred Townsend, a well-known elocution teacher, to sharpen her public speaking abilities.

Moten participated in countless professional conferences to increase her stock of pedagogical knowledge. She believed that all teachers should know something about health, physiology, and anatomy and attended medical school at Howard University to master these subjects, earning her MD in 1897. She employed the medical knowledge she had accumulated by initiating a series of lectures at Miner on health and hygiene. She spent many of her summers in the South teaching in vacation schools for veteran teachers and also found time to continue graduate work in education at New York University.

Moten's energy and enthusiasm for teaching were legendary and inspired at least two generations of African American educators in the District of Columbia. During the thirty-seven years that she was the principal of Miner Normal School, Moten took an active part in preparing most of the black primary teachers subsequently employed in the Washington Public Schools. She became so successful, in fact, in furnishing African American teachers for the District of Columbia that by 1890 the local school board was recommending that prospective teachers from around the country enroll at Miner to benefit from her outstanding leadership. To maintain the highest educational standards, Moten worked unceasingly for more rigorous admissions standards, smaller class sizes, and a larger, better-trained, and better-compensated faculty. Most of all she sought to make the Miner curriculum more demanding and relevant. In 1896 she successfully expanded the school's program from one to two years, and by the end of her tenure she had laid the foundation for extending the program to a full four years.

Moten probably worked hardest to ensure that the teachers with whom she worked were as committed to character development as they were to fostering academic success. This meant that she expected them to maintain habits of strict integrity and intellectual honesty, to be models of self-control and patience, to remain sympathetic and cheerful at all times, and to cultivate a refined aesthetic taste. To Moten, manners, morals, and intellect were equally important, especially for teachers preparing to instruct the very young. Her dignity, grace, and decency remained the moral standard by which her students proudly gauged their own contributions to the profession of teaching.

In 1914 Miner Normal School opened a new building modeled on a design suggested by Moten. An avid traveler and Anglophile, she had long admired the architecture of Christ's College at Cambridge University and urged the architects who planned the new Miner facility to base their design on this well-known English college. She also insisted, often over the objections of the board of education, which worried about the added expense, that the classrooms and hallways be well ventilated and well lighted and that in general the new building reflect the latest technology regarding the conditions most conducive to good education.

After Moten retired from Miner she lived most of the rest of her life in New York City and never married. She died tragically in 1933 when a taxicab struck her in New York's Times Square. Even in death her contributions to education continued. She left fifty-one thousand dollars to Howard University, requesting that the money be made available to students wishing to visit and study abroad. Finally, in recognition of Moten's important impact on primary education in the District of Columbia, a Washington elementary school was named for her in 1954.

FURTHER READING

Carothers, Thomasine. "Lucy Ellen Moten, 1851–1933," *Journal of Negro History* 19 (19 Jan. 1934).

Obituary: *Washington Post*, 8 Mar. 1934.

This entry is taken from the *American National Biography* and is published here with the permission of the American Council of Learned Societies.

STEPHEN PRESKILL

Moten, Pierce Sherman (28 July 1878–1 Feb. 1965), physician, was born in Winchester, Texas, the son of Pierce Moten, a farmer and businessman, and Amanda (maiden name unknown). His mother, who died when he was young, had planned for her sons to attend college. Moten studied in segregated public schools and pursued many interests, hoping to escape the sharecropper's life.

The *New York Age* editor T. THOMAS FORTUNE convinced Moten's father to send Moten to Tuskegee Institute, and Moten enrolled there in September 1896. Expressing an interest in medicine, he was employed in the doctor's office and drug room. After two years Moten was recommended for a position in a Tuskegee drugstore owned by a white physician. He learned to fill prescriptions and earned a prescription clerk certificate.

Moten continued to work in Tuskegee's drug room "with my heart and hopes set on the day I would become a doctor." In 1900 he graduated from Tuskegee. He directed Dr. C. L. Swain's Columbus, Georgia, drugstore for one month, but then he returned to Tuskegee when BOOKER T. WASHINGTON asked him to manage the school hospital's drug room. Moten also studied premedical courses with GEORGE WASHINGTON CARVER and ROSCOE CONKLING BRUCE, the Harvard-educated head teacher of Tuskegee's academic department.

By June 1902 Moten had moved to Montgomery, Alabama, where he was employed by Dr. Alfred C. Dungee in Dungee's office and drugstore. Dungee had worked with DR. CORNELIUS N. DORSETTE and kept Montgomery's primary black health center, the Hale Infirmary, operating after Dorsette's death. While working for Dungee, Moten received an emergency call to attend to a young boy who had been stabbed in his chest. The knife had penetrated the heart's chamber. Dungee ordered Moten to call Dr. Luther Leonidas Hill, a white physician. Moten held a kerosene lamp while Hill successfully sutured the wound in a pioneering procedure that was reported upon in international medical journals.

Moten resolved to become a physician. He enrolled in premedical courses at Walden University in Nashville and completed a medical degree at its affiliate, Meharry Medical College, in 1906. Moten financed his studies by spending his vacation time working in Chicago at the Armour Packing Company and at the Pullman Company. He was permitted to sit in on lectures at the College of Physicians and Surgeons at the University of Chicago. His pharmaceutical expertise, he learned, was of great benefit during his studies.

While waiting for the results of the Alabama state medical board examination Moten visited friends in Quincy, Florida, and passed that state's medical boards. He established a practice there and married Eula Lee Moore Young, whose adoptive father, the president of Florida A&M College, had taught at Tuskegee. The couple had four children. In 1912 Moten relocated to Birmingham, Alabama, where he established a medical practice the next year. After World War I the Courts of Calanthe of Alabama asked Moten to be medical director of that fraternal organization. Moten planned and managed a thirty-two-bed hospital for the group.

During the Depression Moten became acutely aware of the inferior medical facilities for the Birmingham black community. Most black women delivered infants at home because the county hospital was overcrowded, and white patients were given priority. Some women in labor who were turned away gave birth on the hospital's grounds. Moten observed one woman deliver her baby on the sidewalk outside the hospital. He was shocked that no one, himself included, had offered her or the baby assistance. Moten immediately contacted city leaders and determined to provide adequate delivery services for black women. He admitted that the "mental picture that I saw of myself and others made me determined to do my part to help correct this horrible situation." Because "the weakest link in our race 'chain' is the lack of concern and interest on the part of our men, for the welfare of Negro women and children" ("Dr. Pierce S. Moten," *Journal of the National Medical Association*), Moten gathered a group of doctors and citizens to create an "emergency station" for expectant mothers located at Thirty-second Street and Sixth Avenue, South.

The public embraced the Southside Clinic, and Moten planned for expansion as demand increased. He was encouraged by support from white politicians and from Rosenwald Foundation representatives who secured funds for modernization. By 1937 the new building, called the Slossfield Center, provided services in obstetrics, gynecology, and pediatrics. Moten directed obstetrics, developed postgraduate positions for black physicians, and secured accreditation for the hospital. He achieved reforms while battling political, social, and legal obstacles.

The Slossfield Center became a social center for the black community, hosting annual homecoming celebrations. Because no black schools were located nearby, Moten and his staff directed the construction of a playground and a school building for children. He petitioned the Birmingham Board of Education for supplies, and the school gradually grew to more than a thousand students and thirty-five teachers. Moten lauded, "A dream has become a reality, the community spirit is still moving."

In addition to serving the Slossfield Center Moten was general superintendent of the Tuggle Hospital in Birmingham and was on staff at Holy Family Hospital in Ensley, where he had helped draft the constitution and bylaws to gain accreditation. He also was vice president of the Alabama State Medical, Dental, and Pharmaceutical Association and participated in the National Medical Association. Moten was especially concerned with preserving the history of black medicine. Moten prepared an autobiographical account and was featured on the cover of the July 1961 *Journal of the National Medical Association*. The journal's editor advised readers, "May his story serve as an inspiration for those who still work with him and for those who must carry on."

Moten received honors from his community and peers. DR. FREDERICK D. PATTERSON, a former president of Tuskegee Institute, declared in a letter to Moten of 15 December 1960, "You have written a chapter in the history of medical aid to Negroes in Birmingham, Alabama, and the South, which is an outstanding contribution by any standards and worthy of preservation in the historical annals of medical education."

A civic and club leader, Moten belonged to the Elks and to the American Woodmen and was president of the Birmingham chapter of the Knights of Pythias. He devotedly attended the Sixth Avenue Baptist Church, South, and was an ordained minister of the gospel. After suffering for three weeks Moten died at the Holy Family Hospital in Birmingham.

The *Birmingham World*, an African American newspaper, eulogized Moten as "the family doctor, a collector of research in his profession, an investigator of facts surrounding maternity cases, organizer of clinics and builder of a hospital." The editor remarked that "To the end, Dr. Moten remained youthful in spirit, hopeful in outlook, and steadfast in his faith in the achieving potential of our group." Remembering him as "distinguished in looks, dignified in manners, and inquisitive in spirit," the newspaper summarized Moten's medical achievements: "Misunderstood at times, taunted by skeptics, shunned by the satisfied, challenged by the timid, and opposed by the selfish, he refused to take down nor give up on those projects and ideas he considered for the good of the community" (6 Feb. 1965).

FURTHER READING

Beardsley, E. H. "Making Separate, Equal: Black Physicians and the Problems of Medical Segregation in the Pre–World War II South," *Bulletin of the History of Medicine* 57 (Fall 1983).

Morais, Herbert M. *The History of the Afro-American in Medicine* (1976).

This entry is taken from the *American National Biography* and is published here with the permission of the American Council of Learned Societies.

ELIZABETH D. SCHAFER

Motley, Archibald J., Jr. (7 Oct. 1891–16 Jan. 1981), painter, was born in New Orleans, Louisiana, to Archibald John Motley Sr., a Pullman railway porter, and Mary F. Huff Motley, a schoolteacher. In 1892 the Motleys joined an early wave of African Americans by moving north and resettling in Chicago, Illinois, where they took their place among the city's middle class. During his early years, Motley attended area public schools, and the teachers there praised his artistic talents. After graduating from high school in 1914, he began his studies at the School of the Art Institute of Chicago. By the time he graduated with a bachelor's degree in Painting in 1918, he was well versed in the practices and philosophies manifested in the long tradition of Western artistic production.

The year after he graduated from the Art Institute was not an easy time for Motley. In 1919 he lost a job as a commercial designer to a less-qualified, white applicant. That same year, race riots broke out on Chicago's South Side. Though the neighborhood had been largely white when the Motleys settled there in the 1890s, following World War I large numbers of African Americans from the rural South moved to the city during a period known as the Great Migration, changing the makeup of the South Side. Though his style told of his formal training, his subject matter shifted away from that of the canonical Western paintings he studied while at the School of the Art Institute of Chicago.

In 1919 Motley began producing the portraits of African Americans that would initiate a new and more mature phase in his work. Painting portraits allowed Motley to combine his academic training with his goal of changing the way blacks were portrayed in most popular art. Through his work, Motley sought to move past black stereotypes in paintings, which often showed blacks in subservient or domestic roles, by representing a broader range of subjects from the African American community.

The first of Motley's paintings to be professionally exhibited was *Portrait of My Mother* (1919), which was shown to great acclaim at the Art Institute of Chicago's Annual Exhibition in 1921. The portrait shows his mother seated and facing the viewer, her eyes looking straight ahead. The warm, monochromatic palette of deep browns relieved only by a white collar and a large, red-jeweled pendant bring a sense of richness to this depiction of an attractive, prosperous woman. *Self Portrait* (1920) and *Portrait of the Artist's Father (Portrait of My Father)* (c. 1921) followed *Portrait of My Mother*. In 1924 Motley created his best-known painting from a series of family portraits. *Mending Socks* was a portrait of his paternal grandmother. As he did in the majority of his portraits, Motley placed his subject in a domestic setting surrounded by symbolic objects. In this case, Emily Motley sat with her attention focused downward on the sock she was holding in her lap. Above her was a crucifix and, to her side, was a table laden with books and sewing paraphernalia. Above the table there hung a portrait of a white woman. Motley based this portrait-within-a-portrait on an actual painting his grandmother had of the woman who had owned her as a slave.

During the early 1920s that Motley produced his family portraits, he also created portraits of women of mixed race. Following the same general pattern as in his family portraits, Motley depicted these women seated and surrounded by objects rife with symbolism. Motley made his interest in the women's ancestry explicit by titling their portraits using Creole terms for racial identity. The series included *Mulatress with Figurine and Dutch Seascape* (1920), *Octoroon* (1922), and *The Octoroon Girl* (1925). In these graceful portraits of fashionable women, Motley explored how viewers saw different types of blackness. The brief titles immediately alerted viewers to think about the categorizations created by society to describe race. Motley's use of Creole terms in the titles of these portraits harks back to his own family's Creole background and mixed-race ancestry. The light-skinned, middle-class Motley believed in a pseudo-scientific approach to racial identity, which correlated ancestry (and its outward signifier, skin color) and social class.

The success of these portraits enabled Motley to begin exhibiting both locally and nationally. By 14 February 1924 he felt financially secure enough to marry his longtime love, Edith Granzo, who was white.

In 1927 Motley had his first solo show in New York City. Following the success of this exhibition, Motley traveled through the South, visiting relatives and painting portraits and landscapes reflecting rural life. In 1929 Motley won a Guggenheim Foundation fellowship, which allowed Motley and his wife to spend the year in Paris. Motley used his year well, studying art at the Louvre, painting, and observing race relations in Europe. Perhaps his best known work, *Blues*, comes from this period. A closely cropped scene set inside a crowded club, *Blues* was packed with images of jazz musicians and energetic dancers. As in his earlier works, Motley wanted to explore the variety inherent in the black experience. Genre paintings such as these presented viewers with scenes from everyday life, and in *Blues* Motley gave the viewer access to jazz culture and the world of urban blacks.

By painting genre scenes, "Motley believed that he could alter negative attitudes toward black culture, thereby creating a market for depictions of the everyday experience of African Americans" (Mooney, 60). During his stay in Paris, Motley produced several paintings related to daily lives of black people, including *Senegalese Boy* (1929) and the nighttime scene *Jockey Club* (1929). Though he continued painting occasional portraits throughout his career, a definite shift occurred in Motley's artistic philosophy in Paris, and upon his return to Chicago he remained focused on creating genre scenes.

In 1933 the Public Works of Art Project, part of the Federal Art Project in Illinois and the Treasury Relief Art Project hired Motley as part of a program designed to bolster the economy and the national mood during the Depression. In this same year Motley's only son was born. For the next several years, Motley painted scenes of American life for public buildings around Illinois. At the same time, he continued painting and exhibiting his own work, using Chicago's black neighborhoods as the source of his subject matter. In the years after World War I, Chicago's African American population had soared, as poor Southern blacks moved north in a massive population shift known as the Great Migration. Chicago's growing and changing black community provided the inspiration for Motley's interior scenes such as *The Liar* (1936) and street scenes such as *Getting Religion* (1948).

The year 1948 marked the end of Motley's most productive and creative years. His wife died in December of that year. Throughout their marriage Edith had worked outside the home to help support the family. Following her death, Motley took a full-time job creating hand-painted shower curtains. He continued his painting outside of work, teaching, and exhibiting sporadically for the next several decades. In 1980 Motley received an honorary doctorate from the School of the Art Institute of Chicago and attended a White House reception honoring black artists.

FURTHER READING

Mooney, Amy M. *Archibald J. Motley Jr.* (2004).
Robinson, Jontyle Theresa, and Wendy Greenhouse. *The Art of Archibald J. Motley, Jr.* (1992).

ANGELA R. SIDMAN

Motley, Constance Baker (14 Sept. 1921–28 Sept. 2005), lawyer, jurist, New York state senator, and prominent civil rights advocate, was born Constance Baker in New Haven, Connecticut, the ninth of twelve children of Willoughby Alva Baker and Rachel Keziah Huggins, immigrants from the West Indian island of Nevis. Her father worked as a chef for Skull and Bones, a secret society at Yale, and owned a restaurant briefly in the 1930s, but the Depression caused the endeavor to fail. Her mother was a leader in the black community, particularly as a member of St. Luke's Church. One of the oldest African American Episcopal churches in the nation, the church served predominantly West Indian families.

Constance Baker was an excellent student and had published both a poem and a prize-winning essay on tuberculosis by the time she graduated from high school. At fifteen, Baker decided that she wanted to pursue a legal career. In her autobiography, *Equal Justice under Law* (1998), she writes, "My mother thought I should be a hairdresser; my father had no thoughts on the subject" (41). In spite of receiving little encouragement, Baker was determined to become an attorney. Her parents could not afford to send her to college, so after graduation Baker got a job with the New Deal's National Youth Administration, which entailed sewing hospital garments and refinishing old chairs for fifty dollars a month (the same salary, Baker once noted, that prisoners were receiving for the work).

In December 1940 Baker attended a meeting organized by Clarence Blakeslee, a local businessman and philanthropist, regarding the Dixwell Community House. Blakeslee had provided much of the money to create this youth center, which was designed to provide a space for community activities. It had not succcccdcd as he had hoped, however, so he organized a meeting to discuss possible solutions. As president of the New Haven Negro Youth Council, Baker caused a stir at the meeting by pointing out that the members of the community center's board of directors were all from Yale, and therefore the community itself had no real input or sense of ownership. Blakeslee was so impressed by Baker's independent nature and strong academic record that he volunteered to finance her education. Baker quickly applied to Fisk University in Nashville, Tennessee, and was off to college in February 1941.

As she made her way to Fisk, Baker experienced the Jim Crow South for the first time, and it made a deep impact on her. Indeed, she would dedicate much of her life to striking down discriminatory segregation laws. While attending Fisk, she was disappointed by how many of her fellow students cared more about their social lives than civil rights. When World War II began, many of the best faculty members at Fisk went on to government jobs. Worried that Fisk might lose its accreditation and therefore hurt her chances to be accepted to Columbia Law School, Baker transferred to New York University (NYU) and lived at the YWCA in Harlem. By attending Harlem community meetings and engaging in spirited conversations with her classmates, Baker broadened her political perspectives and actively began to debate civil rights, economics, and the war. She earned a B.A. in Economics from NYU in October 1943 and went on to Columbia Law School in February 1944. She was surprised to find many other women also pursuing legal careers, given the sexism present in the legal profession at the time.

In October 1945 Baker started working for the NAACP Legal and Educational Defense Fund (LDF), before completing law school. As a law

Constance Baker Motley, (right), talking with Martin Luther King, Jr. and his wife, Coretta Scott King, before the start of an Southern Christian Leadership Conference banquet in Birmingham, Alabama, on 9 August 1965. (AP Images.)

clerk for her mentor THURGOOD MARSHALL, Baker worked on several cases involving segregation in public education. An example of such is *Sweatt v. Painter* (1950), in which HEMAN MARION SWEATT challenged the University of Texas Law School's interpretation of the "separate but equal" ruling of *Plessy v. Ferguson*. The school had created a separate school for Sweatt, a black student, in an Austin basement. The result of this case was the admission of a black student to a white institution.

Baker passed the New York State bar examination in 1948, and the following year was appointed assistant counsel at the LDF. In her first solo effort, she argued against legal segregation in the public schools of Hempstead, New York, and emerged victorious. Also in 1949 she married Joel Motley, a real estate and insurance broker whom she had met in 1945 at the YMCA in Harlem when he was a student at NYU's Law School. The couple had one son.

As associate counsel, and later chief counsel, of the NAACP Legal Defense Fund, Constance Baker Motley wrote briefs for *Brown v. Board of Education* (1954) and would go on to argue many cases based on the egalitarian principles put forth in this landmark decision. She worked to desegregate not only public education but also the areas of housing, transportation, recreation, and public facilities. She argued the cases of CHARLAYNE HUNTER-GAULT and HAMILTON HOLMES to attend the University of Georgia (1959–1961), VIVIAN MALONE and JAMES HOOD to attend the University of Alabama (1963), and HARVEY GANTT to attend Clemson College (1963). Motley won nine of the ten cases she argued before the U.S. Supreme Court and represented such civil rights leaders as MARTIN LUTHER KING JR. and RALPH ABERNATHY. One of her most notable cases centered on JAMES MEREDITH's 1962 suit to attend the University of Mississippi. Although the suit was ultimately successful, it would take more than twenty thousand federal troops to restore order on the Ole Miss campus and to quell protests against Meredith's admission. The violent reaction to the Meredith case was extreme, but not unusual; during her twenty years with the NAACP Legal Defense Fund, Motley participated in almost every legal case related to the civil rights movement and often faced great personal danger while doing so.

While working for the NAACP, Motley also served on the New York State Advisory Council on Employment and Unemployment Insurance from 1958 to 1965. In 1963 she served out the remainder of JAMES WATSON's term as a New York state senator, and was then elected to the office in the following year, making her the first African American woman to serve in this capacity. While in this office, Motley lobbied to create low-income housing in New York's urban sectors. In 1965 Motley was elected as president of the borough of Manhattan, the first woman to be given this distinction, and she worked to revitalize Harlem. On 25 January 1966 President Lyndon B. Johnson nominated Motley to the Southern District Court of New York, the largest federal trial bench in the nation, making Motley the first African American woman to be named to a federal bench. After serving the court for sixteen years, Motley was named chief judge of the U.S. District Court for the Southern District of New York; she assumed senior status in 1986.

Motley received many accolades for her work, such as the New York State Bar Association's Gold Medal Award, Columbia University Law School's Medal of Excellence, the New York Women's Bar Association's Florence E. Allen Award, the Twentieth Anniversary Award from the Association of Black Women Attorneys, the NAACP Legal Defense and Educational Fund's Equal Justice Award, and, in 2003, the NAACP's Spingarn Medal for outstanding achievement by a black American. She was inducted into the National Women's Hall of Fame in 1993 and has received honorary degrees from more than thirty colleges, universities, and law schools. In 1998 Motley published her autobiography, *Equal Justice under Law*, a memoir of the legal battles Motley and the NAACP waged for civil rights. Baker died of congestive heart failure in New York City; she was eighty-four.

Constance Baker Motley once said, "Something which we think is impossible now, is not impossible in another decade." In a distinguished legal career spanning fifty years, Motley was instrumental in the struggle for civil rights. Her optimism for social change was founded not only in her own accomplishments, but also in the many lives those accomplishments changed for the better.

FURTHER READING

Constance Baker Motley's papers are held in the Sophia Smith Collection at Smith College in Northampton, Massachusetts.

Motley, Constance Baker. *Equal Justice under Law: An Autobiography* (1989).

Greenberg, Jack. *Crusaders in the Courts* (1994).

Taylor, Telford. *Perspectives on Justice: Telford Taylor, Constance Baker Motley, James K. Feibleman* (1975).

Obituary: *New York Times*, 29 Sept. 2005.

JENNIFER WOOD

Motley, Fannie (25 Jan. 1927–), educator, was born Fannie Ernestine Smith in Monroeville, Alabama, the eldest of five children of N. H. Smith Sr. and Lily Smith. She graduated with honors from Spring Hill College in Mobile on 29 May 1956, the first African American to graduate from a previously white college in Alabama. Her brother N. H. Smith Jr., with FRED L. SHUTTLESWORTH, founded the Alabama Christian Movement for Human Rights in Birmingham on 5 June 1956.

Motley's father, an itinerant Baptist pastor, served congregations in Monroeville and Moss Point, Mississippi. He did not allow his wife to take domestic work in the homes of whites. Thus Motley's upbringing in the church and in black schools insulated her from close contact with whites. Her parents stressed the importance of a college education, and all five siblings entered professions—the brothers as Baptist ministers, the sisters as teachers. She met D. L. Motley, a ministerial student, while attending Selma Baptist University, and they married shortly after she completed a two-year degree in 1946.

Spring Hill (SHC), a Catholic college founded in 1830, was Alabama's oldest college and had been run by Jesuit priests since 1847. By the time it was desegregated in September 1954 the Motleys had two young sons and were living in Plateau, north of Mobile, where D.L. pastored at Yorktown Baptist Church. D.L. insisted that Motley seize the opportunity to complete her college degree; however, the idea of taking classes with whites made her uncomfortable. Finally Motley registered for classes in February 1955 but balked at entering as a freshman. She negotiated a compromise with the academic dean, George Bergen, S.J., for provisional acceptance of her previous college credits.

Like all students at SHC she was required to take twenty-four semester hours in philosophy and theology. Since the college had only begun to admit white females in 1952 Motley was usually the only woman in her classes. She felt her segregated schooling prepared her well for the rigorous course work at SHC, and occasionally she already knew content that was unfamiliar to her fellow students. She recalled:

Several of my white classmates asked me not to be so studious, because I was showing them up. My reply to this was, "Your grades will not help or hinder me, nor mine yours." I think they were somewhat upset because one of the professors had said, "If Mrs. Motley can do all these assignments and get them in on time with a husband,

two small children, and a home to care for, the rest of you with no such responsibilities surely are expected to do so" (Padgett interview, 17 Jan. 1999).

Successful completion of her first semester's courses placed her not only on the dean's list but also on a path to graduation ahead of eight other black students who had enrolled the previous September.

Motley's most harrowing experience occurred when she and another African American student, Cecilia Mitchell, were invited to accompany their instructor, Albert Foley, S. J., to a sociology conference at Xavier University in New Orleans. The group of eight collegians departed the campus in two cars early on a Sunday morning. Near Biloxi, Mississippi, Foley decided to stop and "do an experiment." Motley remembered everyone in the restaurant stared as Foley steered the interracial group to a table. When the owner objected, Foley, in his black suit and Roman collar, insisted: "Well, you're going to serve them today. They're with me, so you're going to serve them." The owner relented and served the group, but Motley was unnerved: "I was nearly frightened to death, in Mississippi, in 1955, and the climate like it was. When we left there I kept looking back, because I felt that between there and New Orleans they were going to do something to us" (Padgett interview). Motley's fears were not unfounded, of course. The group's challenge to Jim Crow came only months before the murder in August 1955, in Money, Mississippi, of EMMETT TILL for allegedly flirting with a white woman and almost a decade before the Civil Rights Act guaranteed their right to eat together in public.

The peaceful and successful transition to desegregated education experienced by Motley and black students at Spring Hill College contrasted with that of AUTHERINE LUCY FOSTER, who faced eggs and epithets from rioters when she attempted to desegregate the University of Alabama in 1956. Motley reported cordial relationships with instructors and developed lasting friendships with several white classmates, including Theresa Ann Russell, an honors student and commuter, with whom she took metaphysics in the summer of 1955. Motley recalled that one of the professors told them, "You two exemplify what [desegregation] is all about." Motley's autograph book, an artifact unique in the desegregation of southern colleges, documents the esteem she held with teachers and classmates.

On one occasion Motley and Russell decided to defy social custom off-campus. Motley drove Russell downtown to catch her bus across Mobile Bay, and the friends spent a leisurely hour looking in windows and chatting socially along Dauphin Street in Mobile's shopping district. Motley recalled: "You wouldn't believe the storeowners and shop people who came out of their stores to see if we really were together. They couldn't believe that here was a black woman and a white woman walking down the street together socially. I guess they had no idea we were students from Spring Hill, and it didn't make any difference. That was just not done" (Padgett interview).

President Andrew C. Smith, S. J., had strictly controlled information about the college's integration, and Motley herself worried about reprisals from the Ku Klux Klan for her signal accomplishment. Nevertheless, in an outdoor commencement Smith shared the dais with high-profile invitees: John Sparkman, Alabama's New Deal senator; Joseph Langan, the mayor of Mobile; and Thomas J. Toolen, Mobile's Catholic bishop. In the graduation procession Motley was paired alphabetically with Walter Mullady, who had signed her autograph book and tried unsuccessfully to get the anxious celebrity to smile for photographers. Wire photos depicted Motley with head erect, eyes forward, gravely serious, while Mullady faced the same cameras beaming broadly, obviously delighted to share the spotlight. Motley's graduation was reported in Mobile's daily newspapers, the *New York Times*, *Jet*, *Time*, and other periodicals, but the only interview Motley granted occurred several days later with a family friend, Inez Baskin, of the *Montgomery Advertiser*.

Motley taught in public schools in Mobile and Cincinnati, Ohio, where her husband accepted a pastorate in 1962. Her closest brush with the leadership of the civil rights movement came when she and D.L. hosted a dinner in their home for MARTIN LUTHER KING JR., RALPH ABERNATHY, and local civil rights leaders. In 1969 she earned an M.A. in Guidance and Counseling from another Jesuit college, Xavier of Cincinnati. In 1977 she penned a brief memoir of her college experience that she sent to *Reader's Digest*; however, the editor rejected the piece as not relevant for those times when universities in the Deep South touted their dropping of racial barriers. Ironically, the college that graduated Motley and dozens of African Americans from 1956 to 1963 never publicized its desegregation nor summoned them back for recognition.

Finally, on 9 May 2004, in observance of the fiftieth anniversary of its desegregation, Spring Hill College conferred an honorary doctorate of humanities on Motley and announced the establishment of the Fannie Motley Endowed Scholarship to further diversity on its campus. In her remarks to the assembly Motley stated, "I did not enter Spring Hill for any other reason than to be able to go to school and finish my college training in the same town where my husband was pastoring."

Motley's achievement and her emergence from obscurity underscore that race is not a natural point of contention unless political, educational, and media institutions make it problematic. Motley and her Spring Hill classmates had other concerns, like studying, grades, teachers, socializing, work, family, and commuting, that equaled or superseded their concern with race.

FURTHER READING

Clark, E. C. *The Schoolhouse Door: Segregation's Last Stand at the University of Alabama* (1993).

Eskew, Glenn. *But for Birmingham: The Local and National Movements in the Civil Rights Struggle* (1997).

Padgett, Charles S. "Hidden from History, Shielded from Harm: Desegregation at Spring Hill College, 1954–1957," *Alabama Review* (Oct. 2003).

CHARLES S. PADGETT

Motley, Marion "Tank" (5 June 1920–27 June 1999), professional football player, was born Marion Motley in Leesburg, Georgia, to Shakeful and Blanche (Jones) Motley whose occupations are unknown. In 1924 Motley's family moved to Canton, Ohio, where his father worked as a foundry molder. Little else is known about Marion's background or life until he gained notice as a football player at Canton McKinley High School.

Motley was a standout, a three-sport star whose size advantage and dominance as a fullback helped usher in a new era of football. In 1937 he scored over sixty points only to best himself the following year with 113 points, which was unprecedented for a high school player. He earned All-Ohio honors and ranked eighth in all time McKinley rushers. Years later, in 1968, he would be enshrined into the school's Hall of Fame.

After graduating from high school in 1939, Marion went to South Carolina State and was recruited a year later by coach Jimmy Aiken from the University of Nevada, Reno. Aiken had seen Motley play at Canton McKinley High School when he was head coach at the nearby University of Akron and knew Marion, then a 220-pounder, was a bruising fullback and punishing linebacker who could help his team. The gifted fullback-linebacker, who was one of the few black players in college football during that era, also ran track, threw the javelin, and boxed, losing only one bout in the Reno Golden Gloves. But it was his true calling of football that propelled him to become an All-American at Nevada. Motley's contributions on and off the field became legendary. His friendliness made him well liked and accepted on campus and his records helped put the UNR Wolf Pack on the map. His statistics put him among the team's best in nine categories.

Marion played for the University of Nevada, Reno for three years before he injured his knee and was forced to leave college. He returned to his hometown of Canton, Ohio, where he worked as an ironworker for Republic Steel Corporation. That same year he married Eula Coleman. In 1944 Motley went to the Great Lakes Naval Training Station during World War II, where he played for

Marion Motley, running back for the Cleveland Browns, in 1948. (AP Images.)

the legendary coach Paul Brown. Brown made Motley his starting fullback over more-publicized college stars because of his sprinter's speed and the awesome power of his body. When the war was over in 1945, Marion, who was married with four sons, returned to his hometown of Canton to work again in the steel mill.

Upon hearing about the new All-America Football Conference (AAFC), Motley wrote to coach Brown, namesake of the Cleveland Browns, for a tryout. Motley knew this was his one big chance, but his request was denied by Brown, who said he had enough backs. Sometime later, he got a call and was asked to report to Bowling Green, Ohio, where the Browns were holding training camp. Motley never knew for sure but always believed during this time, when there were few African American pro football players, the invitation for a tryout came to help alleviate racial tension. Days before Marion reported to the team, Bill Willis, another African American, had signed on to play linebacker for the Browns and Marion believed the team contacted him because the Browns needed a roommate for Willis.

When Motley signed with the Browns he along with Willis, who integrated pro football, was one of the first African Americans to play professional football, breaking the unwritten color ban blacks had faced. He stood six feet one and weighed 240 pounds and was a tremendous blocker and receiving threat with great quickness and agility. Motley played linebacker his first two years in the AAFC, but being a straight-ahead power runner is how he made his mark. Marion's most dangerous play was what would come to be known as the draw; this is an offensive play in which the quarterback drops back as if to pass to "draw in" the defensive linemen, but then slips the ball to a running back who makes his way downfield. Opponents did not like to tackle him head on because he was a powerful force. It was this barreling type of play that earned him the nickname "Tank."

In the four-year history of the AAFC, Motley was the leading rusher, was an All-America choice three times, and helped lead the Browns to AAFC championships all four years the league existed. When the Browns entered the NFL in 1950, Motley was thirty years old with two bad knees, yet he still led the league in rushing. He was selected for the 1951 Pro Bowl and his Browns team won the NFL championship their first year in the league.

His success as a professional player did not lessen the racial hardships he faced throughout his career.

Motley endured bad treatment from opposing players. His hands were often bloody during a game because they were stomped on; he was gang tackled, elbowed, and called names while officials stood by silently. Motley made it a point not to mouth off, just to make it his business in the next play to run over his opponents and get even. Both he and Willis dealt with racism on and off the field and both believed that if they were hotheads and got into fights it would set race relations back ten years.

By 1953 Motley's career had slowed down due to knee injuries. He took the 1954 season off and attempted a comeback in 1955 with the Pittsburgh Steelers, but he retired after carrying the ball just two times. During his eight-year career, Motley averaged 5.7 yards per carry, a NFL record, gained 4,720 yards and caught 85 passes. In 1968 he became the second African American to be enshrined into the Pro Football Hall of Fame and in 1995 was named to the NFL's Seventy-fifth Anniversary All-Time Team. In 1973 the University of Nevada enshrined him into the Wolf Pack Hall of Fame as a charter member, the school retired his number forty-one jersey, the first such honor for a Pack athlete, and made him a member of its Team of the Century.

Marion Motley passed away in Cleveland, Ohio, after a lengthy battle with prostate cancer. He was admired for how he played the game and the dignity he displayed throughout his career. He is still looked upon as the standard of what a fullback should be. Motley was a quiet man who spoke loudly as a football player and who was without ego; he crossed the color line in professional sports before JACKIE ROBINSON, yet during his lifetime never got the same credit for his breakthrough. Only in death did he finally get his due.

FURTHER READING

Marion Motley's archives are housed in the Pro Football Hall of Fame, Canton, Ohio.

Keim, John. *Legends by the Lake: The Cleveland Browns at Municipal Stadium* (1999).

Porter, David. *African-American Sports Greats: A Biographical Dictionary* (1995).

Ross, Charles K. *Outside the Lines: African Americans and the Integration of the National Football League* (1999).

Smith, Thomas G. *Outside the Pale: The Exclusion of Blacks from the National Football League* (1934–1946).

Zimmerman, Paul. *Thinking Man's Guide to Pro Football* (1971).

PAMELA S. RIVERS

Motley, Willard Francis (14 July 1909–4 Mar. 1965), novelist, was born in Chicago, Illinois, the son of Florence Motley. He was reared by his maternal grandparents, Archibald Motley Sr., a Pullman porter, and Mary Huff. Motley grew up in a South Side Chicago neighborhood with few black families. He began his literary career precociously, writing a column for the *Chicago Defender*, a black weekly, under the pen name Bud Billiken. After his graduation from Englewood High School in 1929, however, he found it difficult to break into print and embarked on several cross-country trips—to the East Coast by bicycle and to the West Coast by automobile—in search of adventures to turn into fiction. For the same reason he left his grandparents' middle-class home for an apartment in a slum. At the end of the 1930s he began to publish in travel and outdoor magazines and in *Commonweal*, and while working for the Federal Writers' Project of the WPA in 1940, he began work on a naturalistic novel.

Knock On Any Door (1947) was based on Motley's experiences during the 1930s, including a thirty-day jail term in the Laramie County Jail in Wyoming for siphoning gas, a visit to a Colorado reform

Willard Francis Motley, photographed by Carl Van Vechten, 13 June 1947. (Library of Congress/Carl Van Vechten.)

school after he encountered one of the inmates staring wistfully through the fence and impulsively befriended him, his reporting for the writers' project, and informal research visits to Chicago-area courtrooms, prisons, and the execution chamber of the Cook County Jail. The protagonist of the novel, Nick Romano, is introduced as an innocent altar boy, but after his father loses his business in the Depression Nick begins an escalating conflict with the law. He graduates from petty theft to armed robbery to the murder of a policeman, from reform school to county jail to the electric chair—a victim of the twin environmental influences of poverty and harsh penal institutions.

The novel was Motley's greatest popular and critical success. It sold 350,000 copies during its first two years in print, was condensed by *Omnibook* and a King Features comic strip, was excerpted in an eleven-page picture story in *Look*, and was filmed by Columbia Pictures in 1949, with Humphrey Bogart in a major role. Favorable reviews appeared in large-circulation journals such as the *Saturday Review* and *Atlantic Monthly*. In *The Radical Novel in the United States* (1956), Walter Rideout called the book one of the top ten radical novels of the 1940s.

In 1951 Motley moved to Mexico, partly to escape the racism of his own country and partly to escape the notoriety that accompanied his early success as a writer; he eventually bought a house near Mexico City. Although he never married Motley had a family life there with his adopted son, Sergio López. His second novel, *We Fished All Night* (1951), was less successful than his first, partly because of its loose structure and partly because Motley attempted to treat too many themes, including Chicago politics, labor unions, the conflicts faced by racial and ethnic minorities, and the plight of veterans returning from World War II. Though more experimental in form than *Knock On Any Door*, the book was seen by most critics as a step backward for Motley.

With *Let No Man Write My Epitaph* (1958) Motley returned to the Romano family for a sequel about the lives of Nick Romano's former mistress Nellie Watkins, their illegitimate son Nick Jr., and Nick's younger brother Louie. Like Nick in the earlier novel, all three characters face problems with the law, but these problems are compounded by the growing menace of narcotics, as both Nellie and Nick Jr. become addicted to heroin.

In his earlier work Motley had been studiously color-blind, seeking to be identified as a novelist rather than as a black novelist. In *Epitaph*, however, he offered a limited view of the African American experience by treating the sensitive topic of interracial romance. Louie Romano falls in love with Judy, a black waitress, and each tries to introduce the other to his or her world, only to realize the enormousness of the gap between the two cultures. Besides Judy, who comes from a middle-class family much like Motley's own, Motley also creates an array of sympathetic lower-class black characters within the drug culture in which Nellie lives. Motley's views changed considerably over the years: in 1947 he had refused to allow his publishers to identify him as a "Negro" in publicity releases, but a decade later he was moving toward his final position, that it was necessary to "stand up and be counted."

Motley's third novel received mixed reviews. Perhaps the most thoughtful review, one by Granville Hicks, perceptively contrasted the "powerful directness" of *Knock On Any Door* with the distracting multiple plots of *Epitaph* and disapproved of Motley's graceless use of sociological statistics. Although *Epitaph* sold only modestly in its hardcover edition, it was reprinted in paperback in 1959 and was the basis for a film with an impressive cast, including James Darren, Shelley Winters, Burl Ives, ELLA FITZGERALD, and Ricardo Montalban.

In his final years Motley attempted to employ the insights that he had gained in Mexico. He wrote a nonfiction book, *My House Is Your House*, documenting both his love for his adopted country and his feeling of wonder at its cultural peculiarities, but he was unable to find a publisher. Instead of this good-humored book, Motley's literary exploitation of his Mexican experience became a posthumously published novel, *Let Noon Be Fair* (1966). As Motley's new publisher prodded him to produce a best-seller, he turned *Noon* into a sordid exposé of the deterioration of a charming Mexican village into a tourist trap where Mexican opportunists prey on amoral North American tourists who, in turn, come south to prey on a people they view as potential victims.

Motley's last years were unhappy, filled with rejections and poverty. After his American royalties fell prey to the Internal Revenue Service in 1963 for nonpayment of income taxes, he had to subsist on occasional sales of chapters from *My House Is Your House* to *Rogue*, a Chicago-based men's magazine, and on the European royalties from his first three books. Besides *My House Is Your House* Motley completed *Remember Me to Mama*, a novel for which he could not find a publisher; he also experimented with turning other short stories to screenplays. He died in a Mexico City hospital of intestinal gangrene brought on by poor nutrition and perhaps by alcohol abuse.

FURTHER READING

Most of Motley's manuscripts and a number of notes, letters, journals, and clippings are in the library of Northern Illinois University. A smaller number of manuscripts and a large number of notes, letters, and clippings are in the library of the University of Wisconsin.

Motley, Willard Francis. *The Diaries of Willard Motley*, ed. Jerome Klinkowitz (1979).

Fleming, Robert E. *Willard Motley* (1978).

Obituary: *New York Times*, 5 Mar. 1965.

This entry is taken from the *American National Biography* and is published here with the permission of the American Council of Learned Societies.

ROBERT E. FLEMING

Moton, Robert Russa (26 Aug. 1867–31 May 1940), educator and race leader, was born in Amelia County, Virginia, to Booker Moton, a field-hand supervisor, and Emily Brown, a domestic servant. Moton enjoyed a relatively pleasant childhood on the Samuel Vaughn plantation in Prince Edward County, where his parents moved to obtain work. At the age of thirteen, Moton went to Surry County, Virginia, where he worked as a laborer in a lumber camp. Seeking a formal education, Moton enrolled at Hampton Institute in 1885, where he remained until his junior year, when he withdrew to work and study law. After earning a license to practice law in Virginia, Moton resumed his education at Hampton in 1889, completed his senior year, and was appointed assistant commandant for the cadet corps of male students in 1890, becoming commandant in 1891 with the rank of major. Over the next twenty-five years Moton remained an ardent proponent of the institute's pedagogy, which stressed the acquisition of industrial skills and the cultivation of values centered on hygiene, grooming, and proper deportment, a combination thought by some to be the key to African American success in the years following Reconstruction.

Moton steeped himself in this educational ideology and emerged as a campus leader at Hampton Institute during the same period that his fellow Hampton alumnus BOOKER T. WASHINGTON stepped into the national spotlight as the principal of Tuskegee Institute and the heir apparent to FREDERICK DOUGLASS. As Washington continued to expand his political role and extend his influence, he increasingly sought out bright representatives and promising leaders in the black community to join his movement, establishing a network that some derisively described as "the Tuskegee Machine." The unassuming and genteel Moton was soon pulled into Washington's orbit.

Beginning in 1908 Moton traveled with Washington on major speaking tours, during which Washington would often use Moton as an example of the potential of the "full-blooded" black man of "pure African stock," and he encouraged Moton to lead choirs or audiences in the singing of African American spirituals. The musical role aside, Moton's dark skin and statuesque presence enabled Washington to make the point that excellence resides in every segment of the African American population, not only among those of mixed parentage. Because of his frequent appearances with Washington, Moton soon became recognized as a close associate and confidant. Moton's first wife, Elizabeth Hunt Harris, had died within a year of their marriage in 1905, and he and Jennie Dee Booth were married in 1908; they had five children.

Moton worked diligently in 1910 to effect a rapprochement between the Washington camp and the more strident leaders, white and black, of the newly founded National Association for the Advancement of Colored People. He had tried, unsuccessfully, as early as 1905 in the New York Conference to reconcile with Washington the so-called radicals led by the scholar W. E. B. DuBois, whom Washington himself had tried to draw to his side years before. With Washington's death in 1915, Moton led the field of his most likely successors, and aided by Theodore Roosevelt, a Tuskegee trustee, he became the second principal of Tuskegee Institute.

As the principal of Tuskegee, Moton continued the policies of his mentor and amassed an impressive record of achievement. Having previously served as an adviser to the presidents William Howard Taft and Woodrow Wilson, Moton maintained amicable relations with the White House under subsequent administrations, from Warren G. Harding to Franklin D. Roosevelt. During World War I, Moton was a leader in the campaign to have an all-black officers training camp established at Des Moines, Iowa. He persuaded the Wilson administration to appoint EMMETT JAY SCOTT as "special adviser on Negro Affairs" to Secretary of War Newton D. Baker, and after the war Moton traveled to France in 1919 as an emissary to black troops. He boosted their morale, but in the eyes of some, his pleas for patience and his aversion to agitation lowered the expectation that African American military participation in the war would translate into an abatement of racism on the home front.

In the early years of his tenure at Tuskegee, Moton experienced acute criticism from his rivals for failing to be more assertive in the fight for African American civil rights. It is likely that Moton's choice of tactics was not motivated by a lack of courage, but rather stemmed from his belief that, given the racial climate of the early twentieth century, economic development and self-help would produce more tangible results for his constituents than any amount of protest. To that end, in 1919 he assumed the chairmanship of the National League on Urban Conditions among Negroes, a predecessor to the National Urban League. In 1921 Moton was elected president of the National Negro Business League, a powerful organization of black entrepreneurs loyal to Washington.

In 1922 Moton was invited to speak for his race at the unveiling of the Lincoln Memorial. The speech he submitted was uncharacteristically bold and forthright, paraphrasing Lincoln and offering a rare indictment of American racism: "No more can the nation endure half privileged and half repressed; half educated and half uneducated; half protected and half unprotected; … half free and half yet in bondage" (Fairclough, 411). Taft ordered all such critical statements excised from Moton's speech. Those sentiments would not find expression at the Lincoln Memorial until MARTIN LUTHER KING JR. gave voice to them on that very spot forty-one years later.

Moton is credited with making Tuskegee Institute a college when, in 1925, the catalog announced a course of study leading to a B.S. in both Agriculture and Education. In his twenty years as principal of Tuskegee, Moton increased the institute's endowment from $2.3 million to $7.7 million. Drawing on his experiences as an educator in the Deep South, Moton attempted to provide insightful leadership as chairman of President Herbert Hoover's commission on educational problems in Haiti; had his recommendations been heeded more often, Haiti's schools would have been greatly improved. Moton went on to found the Negro Organization Society of Virginia, and dedicate himself to the improvement of the health of African Americans by, among other things, helping Booker T. Washington establish a national Negro Health Day.

In 1923 he secured the building of a Veterans Administration Hospital in Tuskegee, in part by donating three hundred acres of Tuskegee's campus to guarantee the project. Eventually, the facility came to comprise some forty-five buildings, making it one of the largest hospitals in the state and an important training ground for black doctors and nurses. Tragically, in 1931, shortly before Moton's retirement in 1935, the U.S. Public Health Service began a clandestine medical experiment at the hospital on 399 black men in the late stages of syphilis. Most of these men were illiterate sharecroppers from the poorest parts of Alabama, and neither they nor their wives were told what they were suffering from; rather they were told they were being treated for "bad blood," a folk term for a variety of ailments. In fact, the course of the disease in these men was merely being observed; effective treatment was withheld, even after penicillin became available in the 1940s.

This "experiment" continued until it was exposed in the *Washington Evening Star* in 1972, and though the survivors and their families were awarded $9 million in a class-action suit, it was not until May 1997 that a formal apology came from the government, when President Bill Clinton acknowledged: "What was done cannot be undone. But we can end the silence. We can stop turning our heads away. We can look you in the eye and finally say on behalf of the American people, what the United States government did was shameful, and I am sorry" (*Jet*, 2 June 1997, 6). Although it is unlikely that Moton had any knowledge of this experiment, and while Tuskegee was not directly involved, the reputation of the institute and those affiliated with it during those years was markedly damaged; in partial reparation President Clinton announced a grant for establishing the Tuskegee University National Center for Bioethics in Research and Health Care.

In 1920 Moton published his autobiography, *Finding a Way Out*, followed in 1928 by a political treatise, *What the Negro Thinks*, which was intended to bring attention to the ideas, issues, and problems affecting African Americans. He broadened his leadership activities in both white and black communities, serving as the chair of the Colored Advisory Commission to the American National Red Cross on the Mississippi Floods Disaster and as chair of the Campaign Committee Commission on Interracial Cooperation (1930), which was led by JOHN HOPE, president of Morehouse College and Atlanta University. Moton also became the president of Tuskegee Institute Savings Bank.

Among the many accolades he received were honorary degrees from Harvard University and Howard University, as well as the prestigious

Harmon Award and Spingarn Medal from the NAACP. In 1935 Moton's son-in-law, FREDERICK D. PATTERSON, succeeded him as the third president of the institute and largely continued the traditions that Washington and Moton had so firmly established. Moton's legacy is best appreciated for the role he played in establishing a strong foundation for historically black colleges during a time when Tuskegee was the flagship of black educational institutions. Although his politics may seem tepid compared with the stance of later generations of black leaders, many of those firebrands received their education from institutions like Tuskegee.

FURTHER READING

The main body of Moton's papers can be found at the Hampton University Archives, Collis P. Huntington Memorial Library; the Robert Russa Moton Papers, Hollis Burke Frissell Library, Tuskegee University; and the Moton Family Papers, Library of Congress, Washington, D.C.

Moton, Robert Russa. *Finding a Way Out* (1920).

Fairclough, Adam. "Civil Rights and the Lincoln Memorial: The Censored Speeches of Robert R. Moton (1922) and John Lewis (1963)," *Journal of Negro History* 82.4 (Autumn, 1997).

Hughes, William Hardin, ed. *Robert Russa Moton of Hampton and Tuskegee* (1956).

Jones, James H. *Bad Blood: The Tuskegee Syphilis Experiment* (1993).

Obituary: *New York Times*, 1 June 1940.

MACEO CRENSHAW DAILEY JR.

Mountain, Joseph (7 July 1758–20 Oct. 1790), outlaw, was born the slave of Samuel Mifflin of Philadelphia, father of the governor of Pennsylvania. He traveled to England when he was seventeen and devoted his life to crime, traveling in Britain and Europe, robbing individuals and coaches at gunpoint. On his return to America in 1790 he was executed for rape at New Haven.

Mountain's biography contains some of the usual elements of slave narratives, but the majority of his story consists of descriptions of the people he robbed, the places the robberies took place, and the value of the loot. The narrative was recorded in 1790 by David Daggett, the justice before whom Mountain was tried. The frontispiece states that Daggett "Has Directed That The Money Arising from the Sales Thereof Be Given to the ... Girl, Whose Life Is rendered Wretched by ... the Malefactor." This raises question of whether Mountain was coerced into making a detailed confession of his crimes or imagined that by giving a full confession he might save himself from execution. These possibilities call into question the reliability of his narrative. Was this narrative an attempt to justify an accusation of rape on the basis of a past life of crime rather than a genuine personal narrative? It also raises the question of whether his execution was an example of a "legal lynching."

Given these reasons to be skeptical of the text, Mountain's story is as follows. At the age of seventeen he boarded the ship *Chalkley*, which arrived in England on 20 May 1775. Mountain went to London, met Francis Hyde and Thomas Wilson "in an ale-house," (2) and together they traveled across London and the south of England with "a hand organ and various other musical instruments" (2) as a cover for "highway robbery" (3).

Money from their crimes was spent "in every species of debauchery" (5). Wanted in London they went to York and Newmarket to rob people and coaches. Returning to London, Mountain decided to stop being a criminal and boarded "the brig *Sally*, as cook." He sailed to Lisbon and back, then to Jamaica. Back in London he met two other criminals, Haynes and Jones, "joined them (and) resumed my former profession" (7). Mountain quit their company, believing it was their incompetence that caused a robbery upon a coach to go wrong, during which Jones was severely wounded. Mountain returned to highway robbery, traveling to Coventry, Newcastle, Warrington, Lancaster, and Liverpool. Then with another accomplice, Billy Coats, he went to Plymouth to rob naval officers.

In June 1780 Mountain joined an anti-Catholic mob that marched to the House of Commons, demanding the repeal of the Catholic Relief Act. The crowd of some 60,000 looted and burned Catholic churches and the homes of leading Catholics. These were the Gordon Riots, named for Lord Gordon, an extreme anti-Catholic and the leading public opponent of the act. Some 290 people were killed, Newgate prison was attacked, and prisoners escaped. The black writer Sancho, in his collected letters, described the events as an episode in which about a thousand mad men, armed with clubs set off for Newgate, to liberate their honest comrades.

Mountain states "I eagerly joined the sport, rejoicing in the opportunity ... (to) obtain considerable plunder in the general confusion" (12). Contemporary documents record that three "blacks" were involved in the riot, Benjamin Bowfey, John Glover, and Charlotte Gardiner, so Mountain's claim of being involved, even for reasons of criminal advantage, rings true. The details he gives of date, numbers involved, and geography are accurate.

While in England, in 1780 Mountain married Nancy Allingame, "a white girl aged 18" but the relationship only lasted three years during which time he, "exhausted all the property which came into my possession by the marriage" (13). Mountain then rejoined Hyde and Wilson. They travelled to Paris, and on to Madrid and Gibraltar, committing robberies. Then Mountain went to sea again and was involved in battles between the English and Spanish fleets in late 1782. Back in London, he met Hyde and Wilson. They journeyed to Amsterdam and robbed a bank of "two bags of gold, containing £1100 sterling" (15). In London again by spring 1784 they invested the money in property, but those involved in the Gordon Riots "were now daily arrested, tried and executed" (16) so he boarded a ship to Grenada as a sailor and worked in the slave trade, making two voyages from Guinea to Jamaica taking "cargoes of Negros" (16). After other voyages to Spain and St. Kitts, he returned to Boston on 2 May 1790.

Setting out for New York on foot, at East Hartford he stole five dollars from a boat on the Connecticut River. He was caught and whipped. On 26 May in the early afternoon, one mile from New Haven, he met "the unhappy girl" whom, he would say in his confession, "I have so wantonly injured." (17) Mountain seized her and "abused her in a most brutal and savage manner" (17). Mountain was captured and "was brought before Mr Justice Daggett" and "was ordered into immediate confinement" (18). The "Superior Court" (18) sentenced him to death. In his confession, he would claim that the court granted him "every indulgence" and his "trial was far more favourable than I expected." One Sunday he attended a meeting where the "address of the Rev. Dr. Dana awakened every feeling of my heart" for which he felt "gratitude … (for) such tender concern for my immortal interest" (19). He was executed on 26 October 1790.

There were many African Americans in Britain during the eighteenth and nineteenth century, most involved in the abolition movement and later the struggle for racial justice. Mountain, in contrast, is an example of a self-confessed criminal, a clear exception to the general trend of philanthropy and Christian probity. However, the nature of Mountain's narrative, whilst apparently accurate in some details, raises concerns that the classic accusation against black men of rape, followed by execution, was an early example of a "legal lynching,"

his narrative being composed by a third person as polemic against black men and as a justification for his execution.

FURTHER READING
Andrews, William L. *To Tell a Free Story: The First Century of Afro-American Autobiography, 1760–1865* (1986).
Cohen, Daniel A. "Social Injustice, Sexual Violence, Spiritual Transcendence: Constructions of Interracial Rape in Early American Crime Literature, 1767–1817," *The William and Mary Quarterly* (3 July 1999).
Daggett, David, ed. *Sketch of the Life of Joseph Mountain* (1790).
Sherwood, Marika. "Blacks in the Gordon Riots," *History Today* (Dec. 1997).

PAUL WALKER

Moutoussamy-Ashe, Jeanne (9 Jul. 1951–), photographer, was born Jeanne Marie Moutoussamy, in Chicago, Illinois. The name "Moutoussamy" is an English corruption of "Moutouswami," the surname of her East Indian paternal grandfather, who immigrated to the United States from the Caribbean island of Guadeloupe in the 1800s. Jeanne Moutoussamy is one of three children of John Moutoussamy Sr., an architect, and Elizabeth Hunt, an interior designer. Surrounded by creativity, she thrived artistically as a child and took classes at the Art Institute of Chicago until she graduated from high school. Influenced by the work of photographer Roy DeCarava, Moutoussamy studied photography at the Cooper Union School of Art in New York City. She received her BFA in 1975 and embarked upon a career as a photojournalist.

Moutoussamy prefers to work in black and white photography, and she has produced three books of photographic essays. The first, *Daufuskie Island: A Photographic Essay* (1982), focused on the Gullah culture of the Sea Islands off the South Carolina and Georgia coasts. Described as "haunting," the photographs are glimpses of African Americans who retain many of the cultural ways and some of the languages of their African ancestors. Her second book, *Viewfinders: Black Women Photographers* (1985), investigated the lives of influential African American female photographers. Moutoussamy's third book, *The African Flower—Singing of Angels* (2001) collected new and never-before-seen work.

Although she gained recognition for her photography, much of Moutoussamy's public life was defined by her marriage to tennis legend ARTHUR ASHE. In his memoirs, Ashe wrote:

"In the beginning, Jeanne was bothered by people who saw her as an appendage to a famous man. She detested being called Mrs. Arthur Ashe, as if she had no identity of her own and had brought nothing to our marriage. But I never intended to marry a nobody, and Jeanne was not that" (Ashe, 55).

The couple first met in October 1976 at a United Negro College Fund benefit at Madison Square Garden in New York City. At the time, Moutoussamy was a photographer working in the graphics department at NBC-TV, and she attended the event as a member of the press. Four months later, on 2 February 1977, Ashe and Moutoussamy were married by ANDREW YOUNG, who was then the U.S. ambassador to the United Nations. Their only child, a daughter, Camera Elizabeth Ashe, was born 21 December 1986.

Their marriage came to be characterized by a mutual understanding and support of each other's goals and ambitions in life, as well as a deep love. In an interview with *Ebony* magazine, Moutoussamy-Ashe said, "I was very independent. My father will tell you, 'Jeanne is going to follow her own mind no matter what anyone says.' I think those were the things Arthur loved about me. That I didn't just follow him. I followed him, yes. But there was a partnership. There was something for both of us to exchange" (Randolph, 32).

In 1988, Ashe was diagnosed with AIDS, the result of a tainted blood transfusion during one of his two open-heart surgeries. Moutoussamy-Ashe supported him as he announced his disease to the world in April 1992. When he became overcome with emotion during the press conference, it was Moutoussamy-Ashe who completed the statement for him. In 1993 Moutoussamy-Ashe wrote *Daddy and Me: A Photo Story of Arthur Ashe and His Daughter, Camera*. Written from the viewpoint of their daughter and illustrated by Moutoussamy-Ashe's photographs, the book, she said, would "help other children understand you can live with illness and help people who are sick." After Ashe's death on 6 February 1993 from AIDS-related pneumonia and complications, Moutoussamy-Ashe served as the chairperson of the Arthur Ashe Foundation for the Defeat of AIDS, Inc. She held this post until 1995.

Moutoussamy-Ashe's work has been exhibited in the United States as well as in Paris, Florence, and London. Her work can also be found in the collections of the National Gallery of Art, the Schomburg Center for Research in Black Culture, and the Studio Museum of Harlem. Moutoussamy-Ashe holds two honorary doctorates, and in 1995 she was named an alternate representative to the fiftieth session of the General Assembly of the United Nations.

Jeanne Moutoussamy-Ashe, with her husband-to-be Arthur Ashe in his apartment in New York City, 17 February 1977. (AP Images.)

FURTHER READING

Ashe, Arthur, and Arnold Rampersad. *Days of Grace* (1993).

Randolph, Laura. "Jeanne Moutoussamy-Ashe: On Love, Loss and Life after Arthur," *Ebony* (October 1993).

Sakaia, Neela. Interview with Bookwire.com (9 Jan. 2002).

Wilson, Judith. "A Look at Three Contemporary Artists," *Essence* (May 1986).

LAWANA HOLLAND-MOORE

Mr. Imagination (30 Mar. 1948–), self-taught artist, was born Gregory Warmack in Chicago, Illinois, to Margaret Warmack. Raised on Chicago's South and West Sides, he was the third of nine children in a religious, financially impoverished family. His mother encouraged him to develop his burgeoning artistic talents. As a small child he spontaneously composed his own sculptures, collages, paintings, and other artworks out of discarded items, such as cardboard boxes. His church gave him his first commissions. By his teens he had produced so much art that his work took up all the space in his room, and he had to sleep under the kitchen table. Throughout his teens and twenties he worked odd jobs while crafting canes, hats, tree-bark carvings, and jewelry from castoff materials and selling them on the street and in neighborhood restaurants and bars.

In 1978 Warmack had a life-changing experience. One evening a man he recognized as a neighbor mugged him and discovered he had only forty cents in his pocket. The assailant then fired two bullets into Warmack's stomach at point-blank range and left him on the street to die. Warmack spent six weeks in a coma, unable to speak. Yet he perceived himself traveling out of his body into an encounter with a bright light that held black artists from the past. Warmack described their ancient African civilizations while seeing himself as royalty.

Warmack returned from his near-death experience with a deepened sense of purpose and reverence for the supposedly ordinary and especially for the discarded. He decided to rethink his artwork as a sort of playful ministry. In a vacant lot he discovered chunks of sandstone and discards from steel manufacturing and began sculpting them, sometimes into furniture. He collected large quantities of bottle caps and fashioned them into clothing. He eventually donned a bottle cap–encrusted cowboy hat as his signature headgear. He experimented with West African–style masks, images of Egyptian royalty, and thrones that evoked elements of the Afrocentric, post–Black Power style. In sum, he sought to depict the revelations he experienced during his comatose state. Although Warmack did not abandon his given name entirely, he adopted the new name Mr. Imagination, or "Mr. I" for short. He later explained his hope that the name Mr. Imagination would help awaken the creative powers that all people had in them. His choice of a name marked his passage from personal and racial trauma into survival and life-giving spiritual transformation. Warmack's newfound identity and philosophical transformation, outwardly symbolized by a name change, resonated with similar examples in African American biographies, especially those of the emancipated slave and orator SOJOURNER TRUTH (born Isabella Baumfree) and the boxer MUHAMMAD ALI (born Cassius Clay).

During the 1980s so-called outsider art rose in popularity with art-establishment dealers, galleries, museums, and their constituents. Many artists identified as "outsiders" were creative people without formal training in art schools or workshops; some had disabilities or came from marginalized racial, ethnic, or socioeconomic groups, just as Mr. Imagination did. Although such artists belonged to an ever-growing niche of the Western art market, the description "outsider" only compounded their sense of alienation. Mr. Imagination himself disliked the label, even as he appreciated the opportunities that opened up for self-taught artists such as himself.

In 1983 Chicago's Carl Hammer Gallery invited Mr. Imagination to exhibit his work, which was the first of nearly a dozen shows he had with the gallery. By 2000 Mr. Imagination had participated in several solo and group shows around the United States and abroad, including his 1996 Recycle Reuse Recreate African tour. He was commissioned to fashion public artworks for the House of Blues chain, Disney World, community centers, playgrounds, and other spaces. These public works ranged from a meditative grotto at the Elliot Donnelly Youth Center in Chicago to the whimsical eleven-foot Coca-Cola bottle he constructed out of bottle caps for the 1996 Atlanta Olympics.

Throughout his travels, Mr. Imagination enjoyed performing public workshops, especially for children. With his humor, gentleness, and charisma, he quickly engaged the participants in making their own art, such as the act of transforming discarded paintbrushes into lively human figures. The founder and president of the Children's Defense Fund, MARIAN WRIGHT EDELMAN, personally gave Mr. Imagination his Children's Defense Fund Award in 1995, and the Folk Art Society of America named him an artist of distinction in 1997.

In 2001 Mr. Imagination moved from Chicago to Bethlehem, Pennsylvania, hoping, along with other artist-residents, to beautify and revive the depressed former steel town. He sought space to grow a garden with two-story morning glories and enough quiet and with solitude to refresh his creativity. The biblical names of the town and its neighbors Nazareth and Emmaus also appealed to him. Mr. Imagination built a community of friends among local artists, musicians, and restaurant owners. He continued to make smaller-scale and public artworks in long-familiar veins, such as his bottle-cap installation at a local bus shelter. Yet over his first five years in Bethlehem he ventured into computer graphics and holograms and returned to past favorite approaches, such as wood carving and drawing on paper. At Lehigh University he helped a friend on the faculty, Norman Girardot, teach a course on African and African American art and religion. Starting in 2003 Girardot invited Mr. Imagination and several other artists to help teach the course by involving students in actual artistic projects on campus. On one project Mr. Imagination involved the students in work on a concrete arch originally begun on the campus to mark the millennium.

In 2006 Mr. Imagination opened his first show in Bethlehem and took part in Home and Beast, a group exhibit that included Christina Sefolosha, Loring Cornish, and crafters of Ghanaian art coffins at Baltimore's American Visionary Art Museum. In early 2007 the Goggle Works Factory in Reading, Pennsylvania, presented Art/Life/Spirit, a major Mr. Imagination retrospective. His work is in the collections of museums such as the Smithsonian Museum of American Art in Washington, D.C., and the Museum of American Folk Art in New York City.

FURTHER READING

Gehman, Geoff. "Bottle Cap Artist Bubbles with Inspiration," *Allentown (Pa.) Morning Call*, 14 Sept. 2006.

Patterson, Tom. *Reclamation and Transformation: Three Self-Taught Chicago Artists; David Philpott, Mr. Imagination, and Kevin Orth* (1994).

Shaw, Kurt. "Mr. Imagination Shows Off His Odd Collection of Throwaway Objects—Now Art," *Pittsburgh Tribune-Review*, 22 Nov. 2002.

Thomas, Mary. "Artist Creates a Magical World with Playful yet Serious Sculptures," *Pittsburgh Post-Gazette*, 14 Nov. 2002.

MARY KRANE DERR

Mr. T (21 May 1952–), actor, performer, and minister, was born Laurence Tureaud in the rough and tumble Robert Taylor housing projects in Chicago, Illinois. He was the youngest of twelve children. His father, Nathaniel, a minister, abandoned the family when Laurence was five years old, leaving the young boy's mother to raise her large family on a meager welfare check. Tureaud attended Dunbar Vocational School and won a football scholarship to Prairie View A&M in Texas. He matriculated in 1971 but was expelled after just a year (presumably for academic indifference, though the official reasons are unclear).

His academic career apparently at an end, Tureaud enlisted in the U.S. Army, where he served as a military policeman, but that too turned out to be a brief association. In 1971 he married Phyllis Clark. The couple would have three children but later divorced. Two years later he tried out for the Green Bay Packers football team, but a knee injury ended that ambition, and he returned to Chicago to find work. Not long after, Tureaud began taking jobs as a bouncer at nightclubs around the city, including the fashionable Chazzo20, and later, as his reputation grew, as a bodyguard for a number of celebrity clients, including Steve McQueen, DIANA ROSS, and MUHAMMAD ALI. An attention-seeker and something of a showman, he began to create the Mr. T character that would become familiar to his fans. He displayed virtual mountains of gold chains and jewelry, originally baubles he had picked from the lost-and-found boxes of the clubs where he worked. After he saw a photograph of an African Mandikan warrior in an issue of *National Geographic*, he shaved his hair into a mohawk. His alias carried the constant honorific, Tureaud later said, so that people would have to address him with respect. At the height of his success as a professional bodyguard, he was earning $3,000 a night.

In 1980 Tureaud was invited to take part in an "America's Toughest Bouncer" contest on the National Broadcast Company network (NBC). That episode brought him to the attention of the actor, director, and producer Sylvester Stallone, whose smash-hit *Rocky* movie franchise was casting for its third installment. Tureaud was originally slated for a small part, but his role soon grew into that of *Rocky III*'s main villain, Clubber Lang. It was during the filming of *Rocky III* that Tureaud coined the line "I pity the fool" (spoken in reference to Stallone's Rocky Balboa character) that would become his television and movie catchphrase. With the success of *Rocky III*, Tureaud became something of an instant celebrity. His immediately recognizable appearance and style of dress, broad (if gently self-mocking) performance style, and repeatable one-liners made him an easy addition to a large family of early-eighties public personalities. In 1983 he played a cabbie named Samson in the Joel Schumacher–helmed comedy *D.C. Cab* (and was featured prominently in the movie's promotional posters), itself a box office hit. That same year, Nancy Reagan, then First Lady of the United States, asked Tureaud to attend the White House Christmas party. She requested that he dress as Santa Claus (which he did, complete with gold chains) and the photographs of the first lady sitting on Mr. T's lap and kissing his forehead were widely published.

In 1983, Tureaud was given his own cartoon on NBC's Saturday morning lineup. In it, he voiced a character named Mr. T, the coach for a traveling group of crime-solving gymnasts. The show highlighted what would become Mr. T's abiding concern for the well-being, health, and educations of young people. That year also saw the premier of *The A-Team*, a primetime NBC series about a band of military special forces vets on the run for a crime they did not commit. The show, which also starred George Peppard and Dirk Benedict, became an instant success and ran for five seasons. Tureaud's character—the gruff-but-lovable, airplane-fearing engineer Sergeant B. A. ("Bad Attitude," of course) Baracus—fit perfectly with the show's bloodless cartoon violence, formula-driven plots, and refusal to take itself too seriously. In 1984 he produced a motivational video, *Be Somebody... or Be Somebody's Fool*. In 1985 he appeared with the professional wrestler Hulk Hogan in *Wrestlemania* doing battle against a number of "bad guy" wrestling teams. After *The A-Team* ended its run, Tureaud played a private eye in the syndicated series *T. and T.* The show premiered in 1987 and ran for three seasons. By now, Mr. T had become virtually a household name.

By the end of *The A-Team*'s run, however, Tureaud's fame had begun to dim somewhat. His health began to flag, and he receded from the public eye. In 1995 he was diagnosed with T-cell lymphoma; his recovery from the disease turned him toward born-again Christianity and increased his role as motivational speaker and frequent guest on various Christian Broadcasting Network (CBN) programs. He began again appearing in movies and on television shows (perhaps most notably *Late Nite with Conan O'Brien*, where he poked gentle fun at his gruff onscreen demeanor), but mostly in cameo spots. He also appeared in a number of commercials, including spots for the *World of Warcraft* online fantasy video game. In 2006 he was featured in a reality television show, *I Pity the Fool*, but the TV Land show only lasted a few episodes before being canceled. In 2009 he was offered, but turned down, a chance to make a cameo appearance in the movie adaptation of *The A-Team*. Also in 2009 he supplied a voice for the animated

Mr. T, with singer Boy George, during the filming of television show *The A-Team* in 1986. (AP Images.)

children's film *Cloudy with a Chance of Meatballs*. His Mohawk Productions produces video games and graphic novels about the exploits of the sometimes fictional persona.

FURTHER READING
Mr. T. *The Man with the Gold: An Autobiography of Mr. T* (1985).
Ross, Dena. "Words of Wisdom from Mr. T." http://www.beliefnet.com/Entertainment/Celebrities/Words-Of-Wisdom-From-Mr-T.aspx

JASON PHILIP MILLER

Muddy Waters. *See* Waters, Muddy.

Muhammad, Clara (2 Nov. 1899–12 Aug. 1972), religious leader, activist educator, and social reformer, was born Clara Belle Evans in Wenona, Georgia, the youngest of four children (one was a-half-sister) of Quartus Evans and Mary Lou Thomas, sharecroppers. Evans grew up in an impoverished but devout Christian family. She and her family were members of an African Methodist Episcopal (AME) church, and she sang in the choir. Although formally educated through the seventh or eighth grade—a feat for a black child in the post-Reconstruction rural South—her informal training as an activist educator came in the early 1930s from Master Wallace D. Fard (or W. Fard Muhammad), cofounder of the Nation of Islam (NOI). In 1919 she married Elijah Poole (later ELIJAH MUHAMMAD), the son of a Baptist minister. They had six boys and two girls.

The Red Summer of 1919 intensified the racial tensions in Georgia during the Pooles' first years of marriage. In 1923 they moved from Macon, Georgia, to Detroit, Michigan, to seek refuge from the racial and economic depression of the Deep South like nearly a million of their southern black compatriots who migrated northward during this period. Much to their dismay, they soon discovered that racism and poverty thrived even in their newfound promised land. By 1926 they were so mired in abject poverty that they often went without food, water, heat, or even appropriate clothing. According to some accounts, an overwhelmed Elijah Poole began drinking. His wife was not only forced to look for work as a domestic in the homes of whites but also at times she had to search for her drunken husband and allegedly carry him home on her back. The arrival of the Great Depression in 1929 served only to worsen the family's already deteriorating condition.

At the same time Detroit was a mecca of black religious and political activity, and Elijah Poole reportedly became involved with MARCUS GARVEY's Universal Negro Improvement Association and NOBLE DREW ALI's Moorish Science Temple of America, both of which he believed would provide a solution to the troubles of their race. But it was Clara Poole who in 1930 discovered the goods peddler Fard, a man of-many aliases and disputed ethnic origins. He preached a proto-Islamic liberation theology of socioeconomic, spiritual, and physical uplift based on Islamic and Christian scriptures interspersed with a philosophy that elevated the black race to a supreme status and required adherence to strict dress, moral, and dietary codes. Clara Poole immediately saw in Fard's message an opportunity to help her husband, and her vision led to Elijah becoming Fard's dedicated protégé and later chief minister.

In 1932, under Fard's guidance, Clara Poole, with her then six children around the dining room table as her first students, became the cofounder and first instructor of the University of Islam, the first black primary through secondary school in the United States with an anti-Eurocentric curriculum. The core curriculum of racial pride, higher mathematics, and higher sciences was taught through the movement's lenses of self-knowledge, self-reliance, and self-discipline. Clara also co-developed, under Fard's directive, the Muslim Girls' Training (MGT) and General Civilization Class (GCC) that oriented Muslim women and girls in military instruction, security, self-defense, modesty, diet, domestic skills, business skills, and conduct, stressing the importance of the black woman's role as a supportive wife in the black man's success.

Around 1933 Fard gave the Pooles the surname Muhammad. Because homeschooling at the time was illegal in Detroit, Elijah was arrested in 1934 for supporting the movement's flourishing public school alternative, now fully staffed in a larger facility. When police later tried to arrest Clara at her home, she responded, "I will die as dead as this doorknob before I allow my children to attend public school!" (Ross).

When Fard disappeared around 1934, Elijah Muhammad succeeded him but not without challengers from among the membership and increasing pressure from police suspicious of the separatist movement. This forced Elijah to flee for his life, on and off for nearly ten years. During this time he entrusted his wife with both the children's care and the survival of the movement, which she managed under his directives, freeing him to establish temples and schools in the places where his flights had taken him.

In 1942 Clara Muhammad arrived in Washington, D.C., with $5,000 packed in a suitcase for her husband's bail after he was arrested there on charges of draft evasion. By this time FBI surveillance had officially targeted her as a leader of the movement. When Elijah began to serve his sentence as a conscientious objector in 1943, he appointed Clara supreme secretary of the Nation of Islam, giving an official title to her informal, nearly decade-long, leadership. Now living in Chicago, the location of the NOI headquarters, she continued raising her then eight children, endured constant harassment from the Chicago authorities and the FBI, and represented Elijah publicly and among the membership. By the 1950s Elijah had become the undisputed leader of the NOI and maintained a constant presence in Chicago. Clara continued to stand in for him as needed, such as on those occasions when he went to Phoenix, Arizona, to get relief from his chronic respiratory illness.

Up until the last few years of her life, Clara Muhammad skillfully used her power and influence as the "mother" of the NOI to improve the lives of thousands of poor men, women, and children through continued involvement with the MGT and the GCC, whose goals she exemplified in her sacrifices as a mother and wife and through devotion to the now nationwide NOI schools' success. She never gave up on Fard's vision of opening a school wherever there was a temple, and so her presence at graduations, sometimes as commencement speaker, and other events ensured financial support, supplies, media attention, and increased student morale.

By the time of Clara Muhammad's death, the NOI had become an internationally respected religious and political movement with more than 100,000 members and over $50 million in assets. While both Clara and Elijah are responsible for the establishment of the NOI that evolved out of Fard's initial guidance and teachings, Clara humbly considered herself Elijah's follower. Even publicized allegations by their once surrogate son MALCOLM X of Elijah's infidelity and illegitimate children did not keep her from standing behind her husband's leadership until her death. In "An Invitation to 22 Million Black Americans," published in a 1967 edition of the NOI's weekly paper *Muhammad Speaks*, she pleaded with black people in America to "get behind the Honorable Elijah Muhammad"

because she truly believed that his Islamic teachings were "the only way out of this hell" for her "poor people."

Known in the early twenty-first century as "Sister Clara" and "Mother Clara," Muhammad, through her initial foresight about Fard's teachings and her critical role in keeping the NOI alive during its most formative years, led to the evolution of a movement that not only produced five of America's most influential and internationally respected African American and Muslim leaders—Elijah Muhammad, WARITH (WALLACE) DEEN MOHAMMED (her son and Elijah's successor who transitioned the NOI to traditional Islam), El-Hajj Malik El-Shabazz (Malcolm X), MUHAMMAD ALI, and LOUIS FARRAKHAN—but also forever changed the American religious and educational landscape. Islam is either the second- or, after Judaism, the third-largest religion in the United States—no consensus had emerged in the early twenty-first century as to the precise number of its adherents—with its most populous ethnic group being African Americans, the majority of whom are Muslim, by birth or conversion, as a direct result of the proto-Islamic legacy of Muhammad's husband that evolved into the traditional Islamic leadership of her son. More than forty independent Sister Clara Mohammed (Muhammad) Schools, renamed in her honor from the University of Islam by Warith Deen Mohammed in the late 1970s and incorporating a traditional Islamic-based curriculum as opposed to race-based, existed nationwide and in Bermuda in the early twenty-first century. These schools paved the way for black nationalists and Afrocentric schools and programs that came later and clearly established Clara Muhammad as a pioneer in the development of Afrocentric and Islamic education in the United States.

FURTHER READING

Evanzz, Karl. *The Messenger: The Rise and Fall of Elijah Muhammad* (1999).

Rahman, Ajile A. "She Stood by His Side and at Times in His Stead: The Life and Legacy of Sister Clara Muhammad, First Lady of the Nation of Islam," Ph.D. diss., Clark-Atlanta University (1999).

Rashid, Hakim M., and Zakiyyah Muhammad. "The Sister Clara Muhammad Schools: Pioneers in the Development of Islamic Education in America," *Journal of Negro Education* 61, no. 2 (1992): 178–185.

Ross, Rosetta E. *Witnessing and Testifying: Black Women, Religion, and Civil Rights* (2003).

PRECIOUS RASHEEDA MUHAMMAD

Muhammad, Elijah (10 Oct. 1897–25 Feb. 1975), leader of the Nation of Islam, was born Robert Poole in Sandersville, Georgia, the son of William Poole, an itinerant Baptist preacher and sharecropper, and Mariah Hall, a domestic for local white families. In 1900 the family moved to Cordele, Georgia, where Muhammad went to public school until the fourth grade, when he dropped out to supplement his family's income as a laborer in sawmills and with the Cherokee Brick Company. In 1919 he married CLARA EVANS [MUHAMMAD] of Cordele, and they had two daughters and six sons.

With thousands of other African Americans from the rural South, Muhammad migrated to Detroit, Michigan, in the early 1920s. A depressed southern agricultural economy, hampered by boll weevil infestation of cotton crops and increasing mechanization of farm labor, forced many small farmers to join the Great Migration to the booming industrial cities of the North. Muhammad and some of his brothers found work in the automobile plants of Detroit. In 1931 he met Master Wallace Fard (or Wali Farad), a peddler of sundry goods in Detroit's ghettos, who claimed that he had a message of redemption for the "Asiatic black man."

Elijah Muhammad, leader of the Black Muslim Nation of Islam. (AP Images.)

Using the Bible and the Koran, the Muslim scripture, Fard began proselytizing among poor people in July 1930, starting with meetings in houses until he had enough members to rent a storefront, which he called Temple of Islam No. 1. Through his hard work, disciplined devotion, and intelligence, Robert Poole was chosen by Fard to be his chief aide. Fard made him a "minister of Islam" and changed his name to Elijah Muhammad.

Fard mysteriously disappeared in 1934, claiming that he was going back to Mecca. With no traces of its leader, the Nation of Islam split into several contending factions, and violent squabbles erupted. Fearing for their lives, Muhammad led his followers to several midwestern cities before finally settling in Chicago in 1936. Temple of Islam No. 2 was established in Chicago as the main headquarters for the fledgling Nation of Islam. With only thirteen members at the beginning, the Nation of Islam experienced its growth spurt only after Muhammad's incarceration from 1943 to 1946 for refusing the draft during World War II. His imprisonment demonstrated his faith and contributed to his emergence as a confident leader. In 1950 at a Savior's Day rally, several hundred members attended. Muhammad also instituted the worship of Master Fard as Allah, a black man as god, and stated that he himself was Allah's messenger or prophet. As the main leader of the Nation of Islam, he was always addressed with the honorific "the Honorable." Muhammad built on the teachings of Fard and combined aspects of Islam and Christianity with the black nationalism of MARCUS GARVEY into a "proto-Islam," where aspects of Islamic teachings and practices were used to coat a message of black nationalism that had a strong racial slant. Muhammad also installed the ritual of celebrating Master Fard's birthdate, 26 February, as Savior's Day, a special time for gathering the members of the Nation in Chicago.

In the racial mythology of the Nation of Islam, the black man was the "original man." Whites were created as a hybrid race by a black mad scientist named Yacub, and they were to rule for a period of six thousand years through deceit and "tricknology." At the end of that period, a battle of Armageddon will occur, and black people will emerge victorious and resume their rightful place as rulers of the earth. In this mythology the usual color valences of the English language are reversed: white is associated with evil and death, and black with goodness and life. Whites are also viewed as "devils." In the lives of many poor black people, this mythology functioned as a theodicy, an explanation of the injustices, pain, and suffering that they were experiencing in a deeply segregated American society.

Muhammad's message of racial separation focused on the recognition of the true black identity and stressed economic independence. "Knowledge of Self" and "Do for Self" became the rallying cries in Muhammad's sermons and writings, *The Supreme Wisdom: Solution to the So-Called Negroes' Problems* (1957) and *Message to the Black Man* (1965). Muhammad stressed that black people had lost the knowledge of their true selves, so that they were viewed by the wider society as "Negroes" or as "coloreds" and not as the "original black man." Moreover, he understood the vulnerability of the black psyche, and he hammered away at the slave mentality that had encumbered the demeanor and lifestyle of African Americans. As a means of getting black people to find a new identity, he had them drop their surnames, which most of them had inherited from their slave masters, and replace them with an *X*. *X* meant an unknown quantity; it also meant ex-slave, ex-Christian, ex-smoker, and ex-alcoholic. By reforming the mental attitudes and the behavior of his followers, he set about creating a new nation of black people.

In a similar manner, Muhammad placed priority on economic independence for members of the Nation of Islam. They could not be on welfare and had to work. It was best if they owned their own businesses. So members of the Nation set up hundreds of small businesses, such as bakeries, grocery stores, restaurants, and outlets for fish and bean pies. The men of the movement were required to sell a weekly quota of the Nation's newspaper, *Muhammad Speaks*, which became the main financial support for the movement. The Nation had also established its own educational system in 1932; although it was called the University of Islam, the focus was on the years from elementary to high school. Members of the Nation also followed Muhammad's strict dietary rules outlined in his book *How to Eat to Live* (1972), which enjoined one meal per day and complete abstention from pork, drugs, tobacco, and alcohol. He also instituted a Ramadan fast of one week during the month of December, mainly to counter the pervasive influence of the Christmas celebration of Christians in African American communities.

In *Message to the Black Man*, Muhammad taught that black people were not Americans, that they owed no allegiance to the American flag, and that they should not join the military. Muhammad spent four years in a federal prison for encouraging draft refusal during World War II and for refusing the draft himself. Several of his sons also spent time in prison for refusing the draft during the Korean War. The eventual goal of the movement was to create a separate black nation, a homeland for black people. The actual place or territory of this black nation—whether it would be in the United States, Africa, or elsewhere—was never specified.

Two internal organizations within the Nation of Islam were created for men and women. The Muslim Girls Training (MGT) provided classes for training young women in the domestic arts, housekeeping, cooking, and raising children. The private sphere of the home was the realm for women. Women could not go out alone at night; they had to be escorted by a Muslim male. The Fruit of Islam was set up as the security arm of the Nation. Trained in the martial arts, security techniques, and military drill, they guarded the ministers and leaders of the Nation. Everyone entering a Muslim temple or attending a national meeting was subject to body searches by the Fruit or the MGT. At national meetings, drill competitions were held for Fruit of Islam groups from different cities. Muhammad's brother-in-law, Raymond Sharieff, was the chief commander of the national Fruit of Islam.

The Nation of Islam reached its peak years through the efforts of Minister MALCOLM X, with whom Elijah Muhammad had corresponded when Malcolm was in prison. After his release in 1952, Malcolm became an indefatigable organizer and proselytizer for the Nation. He founded many temples of Islam on the East Coast, throughout the South, and on the West Coast. Malcolm was a favorite visitor in Muhammad's home, and he was regarded as his seventh son. As a charismatic speaker, Malcolm encouraged the rapid spread of the Nation of Islam in the 1950s and early 1960s. He also started *Muhammad Speaks* in May 1960 in the basement of his home. Muhammad appointed Malcolm as the minister of Temple No. 7 in Harlem, the most important temple outside Chicago, and in 1962 he named Malcolm his national representative. However, in December 1963, after President John F. Kennedy was assassinated in Dallas, Muhammad ordered a three-month period of public silence for Malcolm as a result of Malcolm's comment that the assassination was an expression of the violence inherent in the culture of white America. His ill-spoken words inflamed the American public. As the period of silence was extended beyond three months, Malcolm eventually resigned from the Nation of Islam and began his own organizations. He also publicly accused Muhammad of fathering a number of illegitimate children with several of his secretaries. Malcolm was assassinated on 21 February 1965 at the Audubon Ballroom in Harlem. Muhammad and the leadership of the Nation denied any involvement in Malcolm's death.

Muhammad appointed one of Malcolm's protégés, Minister LOUIS FARRAKHAN from Boston, to become the national representative and minister of Temple No. 7 in Harlem. During its peak years in the 1960s, the Nation of Islam had close to five hundred thousand devoted followers, influencing millions more particularly during the period of increased cultural awareness among blacks from 1967 to 1975. It also accumulated an economic empire worth more than $80 million, which included farms in Georgia and Alabama, a modern printing press operation for its newspaper, a bank, and plans for establishing a Muslim hospital and university. As a person suffering from respiratory illnesses, Muhammad also had a large house in Phoenix, Arizona, where he often spent the winters.

Although he had only a third-grade education, Muhammad became the leader of the most enduring black militant movement in the United States. He was a shrewd judge of character and was able to control and contain a number of fiery, charismatic personalities in his movement. He died in Chicago and was succeeded by the fifth of his six sons, WARITH DEEN MUHAMMAD (born Wallace D. Muhammad). After Warith disbanded the Nation of Islam and led many of its members into the fold of Sunni Islam, or orthodox Islam, Farrakhan resurrected the Nation of Islam in 1978, using the teachings of Elijah Muhammad as its primary vehicle. Farrakhan also instituted a second Savior's Day celebration in his Nation, honoring the birth date of Elijah Muhammad.

FURTHER READING

Clegg, Claude Andrew, III. *An Original Man: The Life and Times of Elijah Muhammad* (1997).

Essien-Udom, E. U. *Black Nationalism* (1962).

Evanzz, Karl. *Messenger: The Rise & Fall of Elijah Muhammad* (1999).

Lincoln, C. Eric. *The Black Muslims in America* (1961).

This entry is taken from the *American National Biography* and is published here with the permission of the American Council of Learned Societies.

LAWRENCE H. MAMIYA

Muhammad, Warith Deen (30 Oct. 1933–9 Sept. 2008), or Wallace D. Muhammad, clergyperson and Islamic leader and organizer, was one of eight children born to Elijah Poole (later ELIJAH MUHAMMAD) and Clara Poole (later CLARA MUHAMMAD) in Detroit, Michigan. Muhammad was born less than a year before his father, Elijah Muhammad, assumed leadership of the Nation of Islam (NOI) upon the disappearance of its founder, Fard Muhammad. The Nation of Islam, while claiming to be Islamic and teaching high standards of personal behavior and ethics, was clearly at odds with traditional Islam, Sunni or Shiite. Its teachings included that Fard Muhammad was God or Allah, who was corporeal rather than spiritual in nature; Elijah Muhammad was the Messenger of Allah whose divine appointment involved the resurrection of blacks from ignorance of their true selves; blacks or "the so-called Negroes" were the Original People from whom an evil scientist or devil had extracted an inferior, evil white race whose millennia of rule was about to end; and racial separation and self-sufficiency were encouraged while racial integration and intermarriage were rejected, though segregation as government policy was not approved.

From 31 October 1961 to 10 January 1963 Wallace Deen Muhammad was imprisoned because of his refusal to accept a military draft or a substitute appointment in a hospital (claiming the status of religious objector). During this time he had opportunity to think more deeply about the differences between the teachings of the NOI and traditional Islam. He was also impressed with MALCOLM X, the human rights leader and Black Nationalist, who in the middle of the 1960s was also making his own spiritual journey to more orthodox Islam. The relationship between Muhammad and the elder Muhammad's NOI was rocky between 1964 and 1974. During this period he was expelled from the group at least three times and evidently sought unsuccessfully to establish alternative Islamic organizations. In 1974 he was finally reconciled with his father and to the surprise of many assumed leadership of the group upon Elijah Muhammad's death in 1975.

Within a few years, Muhammad succeeded in converting the heterodox Nation of Islam into a traditional, Sunni membership. In assuming leadership of the 100,000 member group with at least seventy worship houses across the country, Muhammad rapidly instituted major changes. In 1975 he opened membership to whites and eliminated the Fruit of Islam, a paramilitary group within the organization. He altered the name of the group to World Community of Al-Islam in the

West (1975), then to American Muslim Mission (1980), and later to the Muslim American Society. He renounced the doctrine of racial separation and corollary ideas of innate moral superiority of blacks over whites; emphasized that God was spiritual being, non-racial, and that Islam was for all peoples; changed the name of the major news organ from *Muhammad Speaks* to the *Bilalian News* and later to the *Muslim Journal*; decentralized the organization, stepping aside as its leader and encouraging (with eventual success) that the national board replacing his leadership dissolve itself; and taught the necessity of the Five Pillars of Religious Duty in accordance with worldwide Islamic practice. Smoothing this radical shift from the former Nation of Islam to this more mainstream, inclusive form of Islam, Muhammad explained that the former program of the Nation was a means by which Islam was introduced to a people so oppressed that they needed such extraordinary teachings to prepare them for authentic Islam.

Muhammad also moved to interact more with those outside the movement, Muslims and non-Muslims. He took concrete measures to connect with other Muslims, in the United States and abroad. As early as 1978 he became a consultant to Persian states regarding the distribution of monies in the Western hemisphere and later gained a seat on the influential Supreme Council of Masjid of the Muslim World League. In the United States he made purchases and secured governmental contracts for his movement and in 1992 became the first Muslim to offer prayer as the United States Senate opened its session.

Many of these moves toward orthodox Islam met with resistance. As of the first decade of the 2000s there were still Muslim groups among African Americans whose theologies remained close to those of Elijah Muhammad. In the late 1970s LOUIS ABDUL FARRAKHAN sought to resurrect the original Nation of Islam and became the most prominent and powerful opponent of Muhammad's mainstreaming attempts. Forming a separate group, Farrakhan was never able to match the membership size of Muhammad's movement but in many ways exercised a more influential public presence than Muhammad, who generally shied away from such personal exposure. Many blacks, including non-Muslims, were pleased with Farrakhan's public denunciation of continued racial injustice and in equality, his appeals to racial pride, and his public stances such as supporting the Reverend JESSE L. JACKSON SR.'s presidential bids in the 1980s and

the Million Man Marches of the 1990s. By the early 1990s, however, the chasm between the two leaders had narrowed. As Farrakhan struggled with life-threatening health problems, Muhammad expressed sympathy and compassion. Farrakhan himself showed signs of moving closer to orthodox Islam, even stating in 2000 in a joint appearance with his erstwhile opponent that Elijah Muhammad would approve of his son's changes. An enduring problem facing African American Muslims in the twenty-first century was the sometimes tense and uneasy relationship, or lack thereof, between even orthodox black practitioners and the "immigrant" Muslim community. Seemingly, this rift was often fueled by racial prejudice of immigrants, mutual cultural misunderstanding, and both parties' ethnic-cultural identities.

On 9 September 2008 Warith Deen Muhammad died from heart disease and diabetes. His lasting legacy is his success in strengthening the presence of Islam in American society.

FURTHER READING

Aaseng, Nathan. *African-American Religious Leaders* (2003).

Henderson, Ashyia N., ed. *Contemporary Black Biography: Profiles from the International Black Community* (2001).

McMickle, Marvin A. *An Encyclopedia of African American Christian Heritage* (2002).

Murphy, Larry G., J. Gordon Melton, and Gary L. Ward. *Encyclopedia of African American Religions* (1993).

Williams, Michael W., and R. Kent Rasmussen, eds. *The African American Encyclopedia* (2001).

SANDY DWAYNE MARTIN

Mullen, Harryette (1953–), poet, critic, and essayist, was born in Florence, Alabama, to James Otis, a social worker and administrator, and Avis Ann Mullen, a teacher. Her parents, originally from Pennsylvania, met at Talledega College in Alabama. When Mullen was three her family moved to Fort Worth, Texas, where she grew up in a religious Baptist household that valued reading and family. Her grandfather and great-grandfather were Baptist ministers. When she was eleven years old, her family moved into a white neighborhood in a still-segregated Fort Worth and experienced the extreme reactions of the neighbors. In an interview with Calvin Bedient, Mullen commented on the multiple cultures and discourses that intersected in her daily life and the ways in which that multiplicity shaped her poetry: "My text is deliberately a multi-voiced text, a text that tries to express the actual diversity of my own experience living here, exposed to different cultures. 'Mongrel' comes from 'among.' Among others. We are among; we are not alone. We are all mongrels."

Mullen began writing in childhood to entertain her family and friends. She was influenced by folklore such as jump-rope rhymes and games, the Spanish she heard in her neighborhood, and the language of sermons and hymns, as well as the literary texts she studied. When she was in high school her teacher entered a poem that Mullen had written for an English assignment in a contest; the poem won and was published in the local paper. When she began to attend poetry readings, Mullen became inspired to participate in the poetry community and began publishing and performing her own poetry.

After high school Mullen went to the University of Texas at Austin and received a B.A. in English in 1975. From 1978 to 1981 she worked with the Artists in Schools Program, sponsored by the Texas Commission on the Arts, as a visiting writer and workshop leader. Her first book of poetry, *Tall Tree Woman* (1981), draws on images of family and community and is written in a style conversant with the Black Arts Movement. As she continued the study of literature in graduate school at the University of California at Santa Cruz, from which she received both an M.A. (1987) and a Ph.D. in English (1990), Mullen also continued to write poetry, along with literary criticism and essays.

The interplay of poetry and theory was productive and mutually enriching for Mullen's oeuvre. Her scholarly writing on slave narratives revolved around her argument for the importance of including writerly texts (as well as oral sources) in the African American canon, mirroring her attempt to integrate written and oral dimensions in her poetry. "Any theory of African-American literature that privileges a speech based poetics, or the trope of orality, to the exclusion of more writerly texts will cost us some impoverishment of the tradition," she argued in "African Signs and Spirit Writing" (*Callaloo* 19 [1996]), a work of criticism based on her dissertation research.

Mullen began teaching at Cornell University in 1988. She continued teaching at Cornell as an assistant professor from 1990 to 1995, at which time she moved to UCLA, where she became a professor of English. While teaching at Cornell she introduced her creative writing students to OULIPO,

the French experimentalist school whose exercises for poetry influenced the language movement, an avant-garde movement associated with postmodernism, and Mullen's own work. At UCLA she was active in the vital cutting-edge poetry scene in Los Angeles. Her poem "Wipe That Smile off Your Aphasia" appeared on city buses as part of the Poetry in Motion program.

Mullen's poetry bridges many different styles while it asks her readers to think about identity and its relationship to language in new ways. Her work was inspired both by performance poetry and the avant-garde; it brings together phrases from the oral culture of her southern African American upbringing with fragments from media culture, feminism, and poetic discourse. The critic and poet Aldon Nielsen said that Mullen "posed important critical and historical questions more forthrightly than most recent writers attempting to reconfigure our understanding of African-American cultural productions" (*Black Chant*, 36).

The theoretical turn of Mullen's poetry is evident in all of her subsequent volumes of poetry. Her second poetry collection, *Trimmings* (1991), is a black feminist response to Gertrude Stein's *Tender Buttons*, engaging its racial subtext in the Steinian spirit of wordplay and punning. Mullen's use of fragments, her awareness of writing for both ear and eye, and her open-ended form in this book set the direction for her subsequent work. Mullen's connection to the language poetry movement was established when her next two books were selected by Gil Ott for publication by Singing Horse Press: *S*Perm*K*T* (1992) and *Muse and Drudge* (1995).

S*Perm*K*T (Supermarket/Spermkit) is a book of poetry that investigates the supermarket and makes liberal use of puns and wordplay, beginning with the title. Mullen noticed that while her first book had attracted black audiences, her readings from her next two books attracted largely white audiences. *Muse and Drudge* attempts to bridge these audiences, to continue radical linguistic experimentation while engaging a vocabulary that invokes both Sappho and SAPPHIRE, the lyric and the blues, and while exploring images and stereotypes of women, in particular African American women. The open-ended quatrains and associative structure of this work invites readers to make their own associations and interpretations. The "muse" and "drudge" of the title refer to the ways in which women have often been constructed by culture, and the poem invites readers to dismantle the binary structure of that representation. In its use of the quatrain to form a long poem through parataxis, Mullen also brings together the short lyric and the long poem.

Mullen's ability to reach a variety of audiences with her experimental poetry was confirmed by the publication of *Sleeping with the Dictionary* (2002), which was nominated for the National Book Critics' Circle Award and was a finalist for both the National Book Award and the Los Angeles Times Book Prize. That same year Mullen's early uncollected poems as well as poems from *Tree Tall Woman* were collected in *Blues Baby: Early Poems* (2002). In the fall of 2006 her seminal and now rare experimental collections—*Trimmings*, *S*Perm*K*T*, and *Muse and Drudge*—were republished together under the title *Recyclopedia*. Mullen has clearly become one of the leading experimental poets in the United States.

FURTHER READING

Bedient, Calvin. "The Solo Mysterioso Blues: An Interview with Harryette Mullen," *Callaloo* 19.3 (Summer 1996).

Frost, Elisabeth A. "An Interview with Harryette Mullen," *Contemporary Literature* 41.3 (Autumn 2000).

Nielsen, Aldon. *Black Chant: Languages of African American Post-Modernism* (1997).

Williams, Emily Allen. "Harryette Mullen, 'The Queen of Hip Hyperbole': An Interview," *African American Review* 34.4 (Winter 2000).

ANN HOSTETLER

Mulzac, Hugh Nathaniel (26 Mar. 1886–1971), sailor, was born on Union Island, St. Vincent, British West Indies, the son of a shipbuilder. As a child he attended St. Vincent Grammar School because his father wanted him to be an engineer. Mulzac himself wanted to be a sailor, a desire that became a passion when his father took him to visit HMS *Good Hope* in Kingston, Jamaica.

On completing grammar school Mulzac sailed as a seaman on the schooner *Sunbeam*, captained by his brother John. He subsequently sailed on a Norwegian ship from Barbados through the Caribbean and the Atlantic, again as a seaman. When the ship's captain invited Mulzac to church with him in Wilmington, North Carolina, Mulzac encountered his first taste of segregation when the sexton directed him to the black church some blocks away.

Mulzac received his training at Swansea Nautical College in South Wales and in New York City. He became an American citizen in 1918. He earned his rating as captain in 1920 but found no command

because of the racism of his times. When offered command of an all-black crew, he refused, sailing instead as a mate. Later he served as chief cook on various commercial vessels throughout the 1920s and 1930s.

Mulzac traveled the world and observed international affairs. He rejected the view that African Americans should support Japanese aggression because the Japanese and black Americans were equally discriminated against by the white world. He countered that Japan had held Korea in slavery since 1905 and was busy taking control of large sections of China. He disapproved of the sale of American scrap metal and iron to Japan and supported the West Coast embargo by seamen and longshoremen in 1939. "The bombs that rained over Pearl Harbor on December 7, 1941, were, in a very real way, our own steel chickens coming home to roost," he argued in his autobiography. Mulzac also objected to the American exploitation of Cuba, and he backed the idea of the double V: victory abroad against tyranny, victory at home against racism.

For twenty-four years he waited to be treated fairly in his profession. Then the United States entered World War II, and Mulzac lobbied President Franklin Roosevelt, successfully, for a command. Even though he won his command, he had not won his fight. When the merchant marine expanded at the outset of World War II, the old guard persisted in refusing to allow blacks to command whites. In anticipation of a need for more transport capability, Roosevelt ordered the building of stripped-down cargo vessels, which were called Liberty ships. Instead of their construction taking many months, as was the case with traditional ships, Liberty ships were built in an average of six weeks. The merchant marine, which sailed these ships, was integrated. Roughly a tenth of the merchant marine—twenty-four thousand people—during the war were African Americans. Mulzac insisted on an integrated command. "Under no circumstances will I command a Jim Crow ship," Mulzac told the maritime commission. He wrote in his autobiography: "If there was ever a moment when the real meaning of democracy could and had to be demonstrated to the peoples of the world, the moment was now! And what was America's answer in this hour of need? A Jim Crow ship! Named for a Negro, christened by a Negro, captained by a Negro, and no doubt manned by Negroes!"

Fourteen Liberty ships were named for noted African Americans, four were named for dead black sailors, and four were named for black colleges. The

10,500-ton BOOKER T. WASHINGTON was one of the new vessels. Other Liberty ships were named for ROBERT S. ABBOTT, Robert J. Banks, GEORGE WASHINGTON CARVER, William Cox, FREDERICK DOUGLASS, PAUL LAURENCE DUNBAR, JOHN HOPE, JAMES WELDON JOHNSON, George A. Lawson, JOHN MERRICK, JOHN H. MURPHY, Edward A. Savoy, HARRIET TUBMAN, ROBERT L. VANN, James K. Walker, and BERT WILLIAMS. MARIAN ANDERSON, the Metropolitan Opera contralto who three years earlier had been kept from performing at Constitution Hall in Washington, D.C., by the Daughters of the American Revolution, christened the *Washington*. When the *Washington* was launched, Mulzac recalled:

> Everything I ever was, stood for, fought for, dreamed of, came into focus that day. The concrete evidence of the achievement gives one's strivings legitimacy, proves that the ambitions were valid, the struggle worthwhile. Being prevented for those twenty-four years from doing the work for which I was trained had robbed life of its most essential meaning. Now at last I could use my training and capabilities fully. It was like being born anew.

Mulzac commanded SS *Booker T. Washington* for twenty-two round-trip voyages over five years. During that time his ship transported more than eighteen thousand troops to Asia and Europe. He captained a crew that included eighteen different nationalities. Mulzac never lost a man despite sailing through waters infested with enemy submarines. His crew even shot down two enemy aircraft. During World War II four African Americans captained Liberty ships. They were Adrian T. Richardson, JOHN GODFREY, CLIFTON LASTICS, and Mulzac, who was the first African American to become an officer in the American Merchant Marine. He was the first to command an integrated crew, something he fought for his entire career.

After the war the *Washington* hauled coal for a time. Then in 1947 the *Washington* was released from federal service and returned to the merchant marine. Mulzac never again had a command. In 1950 he refused to testify before the House Un-American Activities Committee (HUAC) about his 1930s involvement with the union movement. The HUAC blacklisted him, and he got another maritime job only in 1960. Retired to the reserve fleet, the *Washington* became scrap at Portland, Oregon, in 1969. Because Mulzac was in the merchant marine rather than the navy, his wartime service did not qualify him as a veteran. Veteran status for the merchant marine's first African American captain of an integrated crew came posthumously in 1988, after a long court battle.

FURTHER READING
Mulzac, Hugh. *A Star to Steer By* (1963).

JOHN H. BARNHILL

Mundy, Jimmy (28 June 1907–24 Apr. 1983), jazz composer, arranger, and saxophonist, was born James Mundy in Cincinnati, Ohio, to parents whose names are unknown. His father was a singer and multi-instrumentalist; his uncle, James Ahlyn Mundy, was a successful vocal chorus director. Little is known about Mundy's childhood, except that he studied classical violin extensively and by around 1919 was performing with the touring evangelical band of Gene Becton. It was with this group that he switched to tenor saxophone, doubling clarinet and soprano saxophone. After leaving Becton, Mundy took sideman work with the Chicago-based bands of CARROLL DICKERSON and ERSKINE TATE before moving to Washington, D.C., where he joined the White Brothers Orchestra around 1926.

Being a thoroughly trained musician with exceptional reading skills, Mundy soon found work with other Washington bands. By 1931 he had joined the orchestra of the drummer Tommy Myles (who had previously taken over the White Brothers' group). Although Mundy had been writing music since his Cincinnati days, it was with the White-Myles group that he took up band arranging in earnest. During a performance at the Crystal Caverns his work was noticed by the visiting Chicago pianist EARL "FATHA" HINES. As Mundy later recalled, "Earl heard a thing called 'Cavernism' that I had written, and he flipped over it. He asked me to join his outfit ... that was my ticket to Chicago at the beginning of 1933" (Dance, 197).

The next three years with the Hines orchestra gave Mundy the opportunity to build his arranging skills, orchestrating for the floor shows at the Grand Terrace nightclub where the band held residency. The writer's reputation grew as well: Mundy arrangements recorded by Hines in this period included "Cavernism," "Copenhagen," "Rock and Rye," "Fat Babes," and "Bubbling Over." Mundy's style was marked by an up-to-date harmonic concept combining a direct melodic presentation with more complex supporting riff or response material, soon to typify the best of swing-era ensemble writing. Additionally, Mundy was being regularly featured as a tenor saxophonist on songs like

"Copenhagen," and he developed some reputation as a soloist.

In 1935—still with Hines—Mundy began writing for the Benny Goodman Orchestra, then being featured on nationwide radio broadcasts from Chicago. During Goodman's weekly *Let's Dance* broadcast series, Mundy served as one of Goodman's staff arrangers, writing five scores a week for the band. He quickly found favor with Goodman, who went on to record more than forty of Mundy's arrangements through the late 1930s. Mundy's contributions, hailed as some of the Goodman orchestra's greatest recordings, included "Madhouse," "Swingtime in the Rockies," "House Hop," "There's a Small Hotel," and "In a Sentimental Mood." The definitive swing-era hit that climaxed Goodman's historic Carnegie Hall concert of 16 January 1938—Louis Prima's "Sing, Sing, Sing"—was an extended head arrangement adapted from Mundy's original chart for the band.

In 1937, after leaving Hines, Mundy led and arranged a small group recording session that included the Hines sideman and legendary drummer CHICK WEBB. Mundy also made an attempt at leading his own working big band in 1939, taking a residency at the Onyx Club on Fifty-second Street and recording four sides for the Variety label. But this group—including the future jazz stars Jimmy Hamilton and Bill Doggett—was short-lived, folding in early 1940.

Returning to freelance arranging, Mundy continued to write for Hines and Goodman, including writing the guitarist CHARLIE CHRISTIAN's feature, "Solo Flight," as well as producing landmark charts for COUNT BASIE ("Super Chief," "Feather Merchant," "Fiesta in Blue"), Gene Krupa ("Bolero at the Savoy," "Murdy Purdy"), Artie Shaw ("Tea for Two"), and Tommy Dorsey ("A Lover Is Blue"). After working in another staff arranger role for the Krupa band, Mundy moved to California in 1941, writing for the Paul Whiteman Orchestra on the Gracie Allen radio show until beginning his military service in 1943.

After his discharge from the army in 1945, Mundy led various Hollywood studio big bands, recording V-Discs and performing for Armed Forces Radio broadcasts in 1945 and 1946, on occasion with future jazz stars such as the trumpeter ART FARMER and the drummer Chico Hamilton. Mundy also turned increasingly to stage-musical and film-score work, and he sought to improve his orchestration by studying with Dr. Ernest Toch. Mundy looked back on his lessons favorably: "I lacked confidence in my own ability, and I wanted to improve my knowledge.... I've profited by the studying I did" (quoted in Dance, 200).

In 1948 Mundy returned to New York, freelancing in a number of fields: radio; film, most notably as arranger for the Academy Award–winning *The Man on the Eiffel Tower* in 1949; and Broadway musicals, including *The Vamp* in 1955, for which he served as composer, arranger, and orchestrator. With his broad stylistic background, Mundy was able to branch out into other fields when jazz went into popular decline. "They don't really like you to write jazz out there in Hollywood," he observed (quoted in Dance, 200).

But Mundy did continue his association with jazz bands, including two albums recorded under his own name for the Epic label, *On a Mundy Flight* in 1958 and *Playing the Numbers* in 1959. Other jazz work included collaborations with the saxophone stars GENE AMMONS in 1957, ILLINOIS JACQUET in 1962 and 1969, and SONNY STITT in 1962, as well as with the vocalists Chet Baker in 1964, JOHNNY HARTMAN in 1949, Al Hibbler in 1951, CARMEN MCRAE in 1956, and JIMMY RUSHING in 1946. Mundy even found big band work again, writing for the Harry James Orchestra from 1955 to 1958. During the period 1959–1960 Mundy worked in France as musical director of the Barclay record label.

After returning to the United States, Mundy managed to maintain his career when few in his occupation were able to do so. Though never achieving the great popularity of the performers he wrote for, Mundy—who was married to Brucie (maiden name unknown), with one son, Jamie—continued to freelance in New York until his death at the age of seventy-five.

FURTHER READING

Dance, Stanley. *The World of Earl Hines* (1977).
"The Man behind the Band: Jimmy Mundy," *Tempo* (1937).

DISCOGRAPHY

Jimmy Mundy: Playing the Numbers (Epic 3557).

JOHN WRIGGLE

Mungin, Lawrence (19 Nov. 1957–), lawyer and plaintiff, was born Lawrence Dwayne Mungin in Harlem, New York, the second of three children born to Lawrence Lucas Mungin Jr. and Helen (Dicks) Mungin. Mungin later described his father as the type of man "black people call 'no good'" and he spent a lifetime trying to distinguish himself from his father. His parents separated for the final time when their children were in elementary school. Dwayne, as he was known by his family, grew up in the Bedford-Stuyvesant section of Brooklyn but was bused with his sister and brother to a predominantly white school in Queens at the behest of his mother, whose high expectations for her children rested on an unequivocal faith in the power of education and integration. Helen was the key figure in her son's life, and she encouraged him to succeed even as she herself struggled with depression and alcoholism.

In 1966 Mungin's mother moved her family into an integrated housing project in Woodside, Queens, which was made available to her through her job as a secretary for the New York Housing Authority. A bit of a loner and one of the few black students at Bryant High School, Mungin nonetheless rose to the top of his class, becoming senior class president, a key member of the debate team, and a French language prize winner. Surpassing even his mother's hopes, Mungin entered Harvard College in 1975. Following his sophomore year he took a four-year hiatus from Harvard to work for U.S. Navy intelligence. This deliberate effort to set himself apart from his well-heeled and politically liberal classmates succeeded and Mungin returned to Harvard in 1981 with renewed self-confidence and focus.

After graduation in 1983 he entered Harvard Law School, where, as in elementary, high school, and college, he associated mostly with whites, eschewing African American political, professional, and social organizations. In 1986 with "double Harvard" credentials, Mungin chose a job with a law firm in Houston, Texas, where he could shine as a big fish in a small pond. Within a year he had moved to the Houston office of Weil, Gotshal & Manges, a large, New York–based firm. Three years later he moved to Atlanta and joined the firm of Powell, Goldstein, Frazer & Murphy, which soon transferred him to its Washington, D.C., office. When the firm froze wage hikes, however, Mungin started looking for a new job.

In April 1992 Mungin took a job in the Washington, D.C., office of Katten Muchin & Zavis, a large Chicago-based firm. Offered a higher rate than his current salary and hoping to be considered for partnership after one year, Mungin took the job despite Katten Muchin's limited bankruptcy practice, which was Mungin's specialty. Within a year Mungin was convinced he had made a mistake. When its only bankruptcy partner left the firm, effectively stanching assignments in his area

of expertise, the firm did not reevaluate Mungin's role. Instead, he became a catchall for lower-level work more appropriate for a first- or second-year associate. Instead of challenging—and career-advancing—assignments, his work now included filing clients' proofs of claim, collecting outstanding firm receivables, and acting as liaison for a computer overhaul. Frustrated, he petitioned to correct the situation only to be ignored by the firm's partners and administrators. Excluded from the firm's more sophisticated and revenue-producing projects, Mungin's hourly billing rate was reduced by more than 30 percent. He was rarely invited to department meetings and had little contact with either the firm's partners or clients. After a year and a half with Katten Muchin, Mungin had received an initial pay increase but had never been reviewed, even though it was the firm's practice to review associates twice a year. When he forced a performance evaluation, he received noncommittal reviews because none of the partners had worked closely with him. Although he did receive a second annual raise, Mungin was told that his name never even came up for partnership consideration and that he had "fallen through the cracks." By this point Mungin had concluded that the firm's pattern of mistreatment was the result of his race. At the time he was the only African American lawyer in the firm's Washington, D.C., office of fifty attorneys, a statistic even more dismal than the city's startling inequity with regard to minority hiring (the D.C. Bar Conference on Opportunities for Minorities in the Legal Profession reported that in 1993 minorities made up les than 6 percent of the 3,700 lawyers working in Washington's thirty-six largest firms).

In October 1994 Mungin sued Katten Muchin & Zavis and four of its partners for racial discrimination. In February, after dismissing much of the case, the judge allowed it to go to trial. As Mungin's attorney explained in her opening statement in March 1996, "This is a case where you are not going to hear blatant racial slurs, cruel jokes. It's not direct. It has to be inferred." Mungin charged that despite repeated attempts to redress the situation, the firm failed to give him work commensurate with his experience or provide him with proper mentoring, evaluation, or appropriate access to partners and clients, all of which derailed him from consideration for partnership. He also charged that he was paid less than white associates. In its defense, Katten Muchin admitted to poor management but denied that it was motivated by race discrimination, explaining that Mungin's experiences were typical of associates at big firms, especially at satellite offices. Further complicating the case was the fact that Katten Muchin acknowledged that it considered Mungin's race in both hiring him and choosing not to lay him off (during restructuring, a number of associates were laid off), which they claimed showed he actually received preferential treatment because of his race. In her closing statement Mungin's lawyer set out the central issue of the case: "We know at this point in time that Larry wasn't treated right. The question is whether you believe he wasn't treated right because of his race."

After four days of testimony and only an hour-and-a-half of deliberation, the mostly black, working-class jury of eight Washington, D.C., residents returned a unanimous verdict in favor of Mungin, awarding him a record-breaking $2.5 million in damages. With headlines like the *Washington Post*'s "Discrimination Award Shakes Up the Big Firms," both popular and legal news venues reported on the unexpected verdict and award. In a second surprising ruling sixteen months later, the U.S. Court of Appeals for the D.C. Circuit overturned the verdict, ruling that no "reasonable jury" could have discerned any discrimination. The majority opinion was issued by two white male judges, both Republican presidential nominees, one of whom asked, apropos of nothing, how Mungin had done at Harvard and whether he had been fired from his previous firm. Concurring in part but dissenting from the court's decision to throw out the jury verdict, was HARRY THOMAS EDWARDS, the panel's sole African American judge.

In 1993, despite repeated discussions concerning the hiring and retention of minority lawyers, Katten Muchin had only six African American associates and one black partner in a firm of 400 lawyers. By May 1996 the firm had improved its numbers slightly: of its 242 lawyers, twenty-two associates and six partners were African American. The Mungin case, however, sought to confront policies beyond hiring goals by challenging the effects of tokenism, neglect, and exclusion from the social and internal relationships, factors that necessarily lead to partnership and opportunities for rewarding work.

Mungin's case would have faded away if not for a book on the subject by Paul Barrett. A white legal affairs reporter for the *Wall Street Journal* and Mungin's former Harvard Law School roommate, Barrett saw in Mungin's experiences a portrait of the complexities and gray areas of race relations in the late twentieth century. In *The Good Black: A*

True Story of Race in America Barrett argued, "His story reflects the experiences of countless other blacks who do not sue—people who overcome obstacles, work hard, achieve some success, yet still fell thwarted" (Barrett, 5). From his unique perspective, Barrett also chronicled his friend's shifting attitudes with regard to his own racial identity. "I decided to write a book," Barrett wrote in the *Washington Post* (7 Feb. 1999), "about how a person who seemed to me to have spent his whole life preparing to leap the race line could end up plunging into racial combat." "From childhood on," Barrett explained, "[Mungin] had swallowed his anger over indignities big and small, even as he amassed the emblems of American success … he did so as part of a bargain he felt he'd made: Larry would follow the rules, work hard and never make an issue of race; in turn, he expected his bosses would treat him fairly. When the law firm, in his eyes, broke the bargain, his impulse to launch a legal assault was fueled by pent-up fury."

Published in 1999, *The Good Black* received considerable media coverage on National Public Radio, *The Today Show*, and CNN, in legal and national news magazines, and in most major dailies, bringing the slippery issues of white-collar race discrimination to the fore. Many African Americans saw themselves in Mungin's story. Some whites, while sympathetic, remained unconvinced that race was the motivating factor in Mungin's mistreatment at the hands of "callous fat cats." The *New York Law Journal* responded with a call for professional self-discipline and better treatment of all law firm associates. Despite the fact that Katten Muchin never complained about the quality of Mungin's work, Barrett found that many people immediately leapt to that opinion. "In an unusually candid summary of the attitude among many white lawyers toward black associates," Barrett reported, "one ex–Katten Muchin partner told me, 'Anyone who spends any time in the profession would know there are lots of minorities, African Americans especially, who are running around with Harvard and Yale degrees who are not qualified in any sense'" (Barrett, 55). Mungin's case soon became fodder for anti–affirmative action pundits, as illustrated by the comments of Linda Chavez, president of the Center for Equal Opportunity, in her weekly syndicated column of 2 February 1999: "If ever there was a case study in the destructive possibilities of affirmative action, it is a new book by *Wall Street Journal* reporter Paul Barrett…. Don't tell me affirmative action doesn't carry a stigma. And all the well intentioned motives of liberals in promoting it can't makeup for the very real damage it inflicts on the Lawrence Mungins of the world."

Mungin's case against Katten Muchin was tried five months after the announcement of the verdict in the O. J. SIMPSON trial and as was the case in Simpson's trial, reactions of whites and blacks to the Mungin jury verdict and the subsequent appellate reversal refracted broader, more complicated attitudes about race in America. At least within the legal profession, Mungin's case will continue to be discussed. At Harvard Law School, Mungin's case is studied as an example of "mounting evidence of widespread management problems in law firms."

FURTHER READING

Barker, Emily. "Invisible Man," in *The American Lawyer* (May 1996).

Barrett, Paul. "Black, White and True: Can I See What He Saw?" *Washington Post*, 7 Feb. 1999.

Barrett, Paul. *The Good Black: A True Story of Race in America* (1999).

LISA E. RIVO

Murphy, Calvin (9 May 1948–), basketball player, was born in Norwalk, Connecticut. Although Murphy was undersized by his sport's standards at five feet nine inches, his basketball career at Norwalk High School was legendary. He was named to the all-state team three times and was named a high school All-American twice. After receiving hundreds of scholarship offers, he eventually settled on Niagara University, where in addition to basketball duties he would perform as a baton twirler during halftime of the nearby Buffalo Bills football games.

In 1966, as Murphy entered college, the National Collegiate Athletic Association (NCAA) had a rule in place barring freshmen from playing varsity basketball. While playing for the freshman team, he averaged forty-nine points and nine rebounds a game, attracting nationwide attention. There was some speculation that he might transfer after he voiced concern over being one of the few blacks and non-Catholics at the school, but he remained at Niagara. The following year, as racial tensions escalated in Buffalo, Murphy was asked to join baseball icon and activist JACKIE ROBINSON at a meeting aimed to keep the Niagara Falls community from similar unrest.

As a sophomore on the varsity, Murphy was named second-team All-American, and finished second in the country in points scored behind Louisiana State University's "Pistol" Pete Maravich.

Though Murphy achieved incredible individual success, his team struggled.

In 1969, after his junior season, he was named first team all-American, along with future NBA greats Lew Alcindor (KAREEM ABDUL-JABBAR), Spencer Haywood, and Maravich. That same year, Robert Miller—Murphy's brother, who also starred at Norwalk High School—joined the Niagara team. Although pressured by the American Basketball Association (ABA) to leave college early and join the professional ranks, Murphy stayed for his senior year.

While opponents devised increasingly complex tactics to contain his scoring, Murphy showed off his all-around game, especially his passing and defensive skills. Finally, as a senior, his team made the NCAA tournament, and he was again named a first-team all-American. As his collegiate career came to a close, Niagara retired his number twenty-three jersey. That same year Murphy married a fellow student at Niagara, Vernetta Sykes, with whom he had three children.

Despite his dominance at the college level, some doubted that a player his size could excel as a professional, and in the NBA draft, he was chosen after every one of his All-American peers. He was eventually taken by the San Diego Rockets, a team that had only been around since 1967. He accepted a contract with the Rockets, again spurning the ABA and also rejecting an offer from the Harlem Magicians, a Harlem Globetrotters spin-off. Proving his detractors wrong, Murphy finished his first season as a member of the NBA's All-Rookie team. The Rockets then moved to Houston, Texas, where Murphy would play out the remainder of his career.

Murphy was recognized there as a fierce, relentless competitor, and with his help the Rockets began to develop a formidable franchise. In 1979 he was named to the NBA All-Star team for the first and only time. He later became known for his prowess as a foul shooter and in 1981 broke the record for most consecutive foul shots made (seventy-eight), and for highest free-throw percentage in a season (95.8). In 1981 the Rockets, led by Murphy and Hall-of-Fame center Moses Malone, made it to the NBA Finals before losing to the Boston Celtics. In total, Murphy played thirteen seasons with a career 17.9 points per game average.

Upon his retirement in 1983, he remained active with the Houston Rockets, working in the front office and as a broadcaster. Meanwhile, praise for his playing career kept coming. The State of

Calvin Murphy, reacting outside the courthouse in Houston, Texas, after receiving a not guilty verdict in his trial on 6 December 2004. (AP Images.)

Connecticut declared 23 May 1984 Calvin Murphy Day. In his hometown of Norwalk, he received the keys to the city and had a street named after him. In 1993 he received his profession's greatest honor: he was inducted into the Naismith Memorial Basketball Hall of Fame in Springfield, Massachusetts. Two years later, his son, Calvin Murphy Jr., joined the Niagara University basketball team that his father had helped put on the collegiate map.

In 2005 Murphy was inducted into the Jackie Robinson Professional Wing of the Coastal Fairfield County Sports Commission's Hall of Fame. It was a fitting tribute for a man who had stood with Robinson during the 1960s, and who, much like Robinson, exemplified how inspirational and socially influential sports figures can be. Calvin Murphy never bowed to the expectations of his detractors, and he refused to let his size sideline his basketball dreams.

FURTHER READING

Abdul-Jabbar, Kareem. "Murphy: A David and the N.B.A. Goliaths," *New York Times* (Dec. 1976).

Anonymous. "Baton Twirler Lifts Hoop Hopes," *New York Times*, Nov. 1967.

Hartmann, Douglass. *Race, Culture, and the Revolt of the Black Athlete: The 1968 Olympic Protests and Their Aftermath* (2004).

GERARD SLOAN

Murphy, Carl (17 Jan. 1889–25 Feb. 1967), journalist, editor, publisher, and civil rights leader, was born in Baltimore, Maryland, to JOHN HENRY MURPHY SR. and Martha Elizabeth Murphy. John Murphy Sr., a former slave and Civil War veteran, is best known as the owner and publisher of the Baltimore *Afro American* newspaper. His mother, Martha Elizabeth Murphy, was one of the founders of Baltimore's first "Colored" YWCA and served as its president for fifteen years. She was also active in a number of religious and civic organizations. Carl grew up under the limitations of de jure segregation. Although African Americans in Maryland possessed the right to vote, racial customs and legal barriers determined where they would live, the schools they attended, and often their life occupations. Murphy's circumstances were mitigated by his father's successful career as a newspaper owner. In 1907 he graduated from Baltimore's

Colored High School (later FREDERICK DOUGLASS High School) and then went to Howard University, where he completed his undergraduate degree in German in 1911.

Initially deciding on a path quite different from his father's, Murphy attended Harvard University, receiving a master's degree in German in 1913. During the following year he studied at the University of Jena in Berlin, returning to the United States shortly after the start of World War I. Murphy embarked on a career as a professor and head of the German department at his alma mater, Howard University, where he stayed until 1918. In addition to his professorial duties, Murphy joined the family business as an associate editor of the newspaper in 1916. While teaching he met his future wife, a student at Howard named Vashti Turley, one of the founding members of the Delta Sigma Theta sorority. After her graduation in 1914, they married in 1916; the couple eventually had five daughters.

In 1918 Murphy left Howard University to work with the *Afro American* full time, and on the death of his father in 1922, Murphy became the driving force and dominant voice of the newspaper. As president and publisher, he assumed an important role in the black community as the leader of one of the most visible and well-functioning activist institutions in the civil rights struggle, whose influence equaled traditional organizations such as the Baltimore NAACP, established in 1914, and the Baltimore Urban League, founded in 1924. Under his guidance, the *Afro American* became even more confrontational in the fight to end racial discrimination. In addition to its civil rights work, during Murphy's forty-five year reign, from 1922 until 1967, the paper also grew as a financial institution. Along with the Baltimore edition, the company published weeklies in New Jersey, Philadelphia, Richmond, and Washington, D.C., as well as a national edition.

Along with covering national and international news, the newspaper served as a partner in Baltimore's black community, not only as an employer but also by publicizing and participating in events like the annual "Business Men's Exhibit." The newspaper also played an active role in social aspects of community life, creating a Clean Block Campaign in 1935, and holding forums on economic, social, and political issues. It supported its readers by highlighting local accomplishments, academic, and athletic achievements, as well as cultural, artistic, and political endeavors. The newspaper repeatedly encouraged citizens to get involved in the political and social life of their community through initiating its own voter registration drives, cooking schools, and education classes. The *Afro American* also included weekly reports of the social activities of local clubs and fraternal organizations along with notices of the births, deaths, and marriages of prominent local socialites.

Under Murphy's leadership the Afro American Company, which included the newspaper and several related businesses, promoted entrepreneurial growth in the black community, including purchasing stock as an investment in a short-lived department store located in Northwest Baltimore, on Pennsylvania Avenue, the central shopping local in the black community. Most importantly, the *Afro* reporters stood as representatives of the community, engaging in investigative journalism that put them on the front lines. Taking their cues from their employer, journalists like Ralph Matthews and Clarence Mitchell Jr. adopted an active role in challenging elected officials, local law enforcement, and business owners on issues of racial discrimination. And in the absence of an active NAACP in the early 1930s Murphy directed his reporters to give special attention to the City-Wide Young People's Forum, led by the dynamic youth leader Juanita Jackson.

Carl Murphy, as president and editor of one of the largest black newspapers in the country, commanded local and national attention. It was not uncommon for Murphy to initiate conversations with elected officials and civil rights leaders and for them to seek him out for advice on appointments. The *Afro American* featured stories by national African Americans leaders like KELLY MILLER, JOEL A. ROGERS, and NANNIE HELEN BURROUGHS, and Murphy was in regular conversation with NAACP leaders like Robert Bagnall, CHARLES H. HOUSTON, and WALTER WHITE, along with Maryland's top elected officials. In anticipation of the civil rights campaigns of the 1930s, Murphy and the *Afro American* launched several major investigative campaigns in areas such as unequal teachers' salaries, the barring of black students from the University of Maryland, and the discriminatory practices of department stores. During the 1930s and 1940s Murphy and the *Afro American* advocated for the hiring of blacks on the police force and in the fire department, black representation on the city, county, and state boards of education, and on the boards of state institutions with black residents, the inclusions of blacks in labor unions, equal salaries for black teachers, and a state-supported university and an agricultural college for African Americans.

In 1935 the newspaper devoted substantial attention to the *Murray v. University of Maryland* case and the legal efforts of THURGOOD MARSHALL to desegregate the state law school, going so far as to take the unusual step of publishing portions of the court transcripts.

As one of the leading figures in black Baltimore, Murphy was crucial in the reformation of the local branch of the NAACP in 1935. Although he declined the position of president for himself, he staunchly supported his Colored High School classmate, LILLIE M. JACKSON, throughout her tenure as head of the Baltimore NAACP. Murphy provided Jackson with editorial support and news coverage, served as a member of her executive board and chair of the Legal Redress Committee, and he generously contributed to the branch's campaigns. As partners in the struggle for racial justice, Jackson's ability to mobilize the community was buttressed by Murphy's ability to command the attention of the state's political apparatus. Unlike his compatriot, ROSCOE DUNJEE, the publisher of Oklahoma's *Black Dispatch* who served as president of the state conference of NAACP branches, Murphy seemed to prefer a supportive rather than leading role in civil rights organizations. His part, however, was no less crucial to developing a civil rights movement in Baltimore and throughout Maryland.

In 1944 the *Afro American* newspaper published *This Is Our War*, a collection of essays written by black reporters, including Murphy's own daughter, Elizabeth Murphy Philips, the first African American female international war correspondent. In the 1950s Murphy was active in the campaign to desegregate public education, wrote directly to the attorney general to integrate the Maryland National Guard, and continued to press for the dismantling of both customary and legal Jim Crow in the state. Along with his work with the Baltimore branch of the NAACP, Murphy was a longtime member of the board of directors of the national NAACP, and served as chairman of the Board of Trustees of Morgan College. In the 1950s Murphy received a number of awards honoring his work as both a newspaperman and a civil rights leader. In 1953 he was elected president of the National Newspaper Publishers Association and in 1954 he received the American Teamwork Award from the National Urban League, which celebrated the civil rights work of the press. Finally, in 1955 he received the NAACP's most prestigious award, the Spingarn Medal, which honors individuals for exemplary service in the struggle for racial equality.

By the time of his death in 1967, most of the barriers to integration in Maryland had been removed. African Americans could attend integrated schools from the elementary to the postsecondary levels, utilize any public accommodations, try on clothes at any department store, and sit at any lunch counter. Although the Fair Housing Act had yet to be passed, the *Afro American* newspaper, along with local civil rights activists, continued the struggle for housing and jobs. In his forty-five years at the helm of the *Afro American*, Murphy used the pages of the newspaper, in conjunction with his personal influence, to press for an end to racial injustice.

FURTHER READING
The papers of the *Afro American* newspaper are housed at Moreland-Spingarn Archives at Howard University.
Farrar, Hayward. *The Baltimore Afro-American, 1892–1950* (1998).
Rollo, Vera. *The Black Experience in Maryland* (1980).
Obituaries: *New York Times*, 26 Feb. 1967; Baltimore *Afro American*, 28 Feb. 1967.
                    PRUDENCE CUMBERBATCH

Murphy, Eddie (3 Apr. 1961–), film actor, comedian, director, and producer, was born in the Bushwick section of Brooklyn, New York, the second of three sons of Charles Lee Murphy, a transit policeman, and Lillian Murphy, a telephone company employee. Murphy's parents divorced when he was three. A few years later his mother married Vernon Lynch, a former boxer who worked as a factory foreman. In 1969 Murphy's biological father was murdered by a girlfriend, an event that some would later say marked the young man for life, particularly in regard to his relationships with women. When Murphy was eleven the family moved to the all-black suburb of Roosevelt, Long Island. As a child Murphy spent hours perfecting impressions of actors such as Bruce Lee, singers such as Elvis Presley, and cartoon characters. Though he was never a diligent student, Murphy's sense of humor and sharp wit made him popular with his classmates at Roosevelt Junior-Senior High School. By the time he was fifteen he was performing his own routines at school, youth centers, and, though he was underage, local bars and clubs.

Soon Murphy came to the attention of Robert Wachs and Richard Tienken, co-owners of the Comic Strip, a Manhattan comedy club, who asked if they could manage his career. After graduating from high school in 1979, Murphy briefly attended

Nassau Community College in Garden City, New York, but concentrated most of his energies on his performances. In 1980, at nineteen, he landed a spot as a featured player on NBC's long-running *Saturday Night Live* (*SNL*). In his second season with *SNL* he was given more screen time and the artistic freedom to create some of the show's most memorable characters: Velvet Jones, an entrepreneurial pimp; Mr. Robinson, the inner-city avatar of the children's television star Mr. Rogers; and the disgruntled Gumby. One of the most controversial characters he created during his time at *SNL* was a parody of the character Buckwheat (originally played by WILLIAM THOMAS JR.) from *The Little Rascals*, which some felt revived early cinematic stereotypes of African Americans.

In 1982 Murphy recorded his first comedy album, *Eddie Murphy*, and he made his feature-film debut opposite Nick Nolte in the interracial buddy film *48 Hrs.* His portrayal of the wisecracking convict Reggie Hammond led to a co-starring role with Dan Aykroyd in *Trading Places* (1983). Murphy received Golden Globe nominations for both performances. Chafing at the restrictions of television, he abandoned *Saturday Night Live* in the spring of 1984 to devote himself full-time to stand-up comedy and film. He disappointed fans and critics with his first film after leaving *SNL*, *Best Defense*, but earned his third Golden Globe nomination for his portrayal of Axel Foley in the highly successful *Beverly Hills Cop*. His performance in the latter film sealed his popularity with white and black fans alike. Black audiences responded to his character's irreverent attitude toward the white establishment and his successful navigation of white dominated spaces and situations. Also in 1984 he released his second album, *Eddie Murphy: Comedian*, which, like the first, was successful and earned him a Grammy Award for the Best Comedy Album category. Murphy next starred in *The Golden Child* (1986) and *Beverly Hills Cop II* (1987), both popular but neither as successful as the original *Beverly Hills Cop*.

In the 1980s Murphy's films earned nearly $700 million for Paramount Pictures, which had signed the star to an exclusive contract. He hosted the first MTV Video Music Awards in 1984 and continued to perform stand-up comedy in front of sold-out crowds. Murphy's raunchy comedy—he was well known for his use of expletives—in the style of RICHARD PRYOR contrasted with the affable if naughty characters he played on the screen. Murphy considered himself an heir to both white and black comedic traditions, drawing on each to create his own style. What is more, the foul-mouthed comedian made a point of emphasizing the fact that he did not smoke, drink, or do drugs.

Eddie Murphy: Delirious (1983), his first concert film, established homophobia as an essential part of his act. His follow-up show, *Eddie Murphy: Raw*, put an angry, misogynistic Murphy on public view. Though fans loved both shows, Murphy made women and homosexuals the target of his biting humor. He was criticized by gay rights groups for his homophobic remarks, a response that was echoed in 2007 when the film *Norbit*, which featured Murphy in the roles of both the title character and his overweight, overbearing wife, rankled African American women's groups with its promotion of what they considered stereotypical images of black women.

In 1988 Murphy departed from the biracial "buddy" film convention with *Coming to America*, a comedy in which he portrayed an African prince who comes to New York to find a bride, and one which featured a primarily black cast. The success of the film motivated Murphy to undertake another project with a predominantly black cast. He starred in and made his directorial debut with *Harlem Nights* in 1989, a film about the famous Cotton Club in the 1920s. After the film failed to resonate with either audiences or critics, Murphy starred in the romantic farce *Boomerang* (1992), which was sandwiched between the franchise sequels *Another 48 Hrs* (1990) and *Beverly Hills Cop III* (1994). Though *Boomerang* failed to please some critics, Murphy himself considered its portrayal of the black professional class, a portrayal largely absent from Hollywood films, important.

Murphy's career cooled until he starred in the 1996 remake of *The Nutty Professor*. The film, in which, aided by layers of latex and makeup, he played seven different characters of all ages and both genders, showcased Murphy's talent for physical humor and was a popular and critical success. He reprised the entire set of characters in the *Nutty Professor II: The Klumps* (2000). Murphy also began making more family-friendly films. He starred in a remake of *Dr. Dolittle* (1998), *Dr. Dolittle 2* (2001), *The Adventures of Pluto Nash* (2002), and *The Haunted Mansion* (2003). He also provided the voices for the dragon Mushu in Disney's animated feature *Mulan* (1998), Donkey in the animated films *Shrek* (2001) and *Shrek 2* (2004), and

Thurgoode Orenthal Stubbs in the animated television show *The PJs*, which was also co-produced by Eddie Murphy Productions.

In 2006 Murphy again won critical and popular acclaim for his portrayal of a soul singer in the film version of the hit Broadway musical *Dreamgirls*. For his efforts he earned a Golden Globe Award and an Oscar nomination for Best Supporting Actor.

Murphy's personal life was sometimes fodder for the tabloids. He married the actress Nicole Mitchell in 1993 and they had five children before they divorced in 2006. Murphy also had a son with the actress Tamara Hood and another with Paulette McNeely. In 2007 he had a daughter with the Spice Girl Melanie Brown.

Though he was without a doubt one of the most popular comedic actors of all time, Murphy's career was sometimes the object of criticism. He was taken to task by the comedian BILL COSBY, who urged him to clean up his act in the 1980s. A phone call from Cosby to Murphy became the subject of a segment in Murphy's concert film *Raw*. He was also rebuked by the director SPIKE LEE for not using his position in the entertainment industry to help other black actors. The film studies scholar Ed Guerrero argued that Murphy's films offer white audiences palatable representations of black men as buffoons, and observed that the biracial buddy films that put Murphy in white environments generate "mega hits," while those, up until *Dreamgirls*, that put him in a black environment surrounded by a primarily black supporting cast have been box office and critical failures (Guerrero, 129). Indeed, the success of Murphy's films and their appeal to a mass interracial audience often hinged on the tensions of race and class in America while stopping short of offering a critique of them.

FURTHER READING

Guerrero, Ed. *Framing Blackness: The African American Image in Film* (1993).

Parish, James Robert, and George H. Hill. *Black Action Films: Plots, Critiques, Casts and Credits for 235 Theatrical and Made-for-Television Releases* (1989).

Sanello, Frank. *Eddie Murphy: The Life and Times of a Comic on the Edge* (1997).

LAURA ISABEL SERNA

Murphy, Isaac (16 Apr. 1861–12 Feb. 1896), jockey, was born Isaac Burns on a farm near Frankfort, Kentucky, the son of James Burns, a bricklayer, and a mother (name unknown) who worked as a laundrywoman. During the Civil War, his father, a free black, joined the Union army and died in a Confederate prisoner-of-war camp. Upon the death of his father, his widowed mother moved with her family to Lexington, Kentucky, to live with her father, Green Murphy, a bell ringer and auction crier. Accompanying his mother to work at the Richard and Owings Racing Stable, the diminutive Isaac was noticed by the black trainer Eli Jordan, who had him suited up for his first race at age fourteen. His first winning race was aboard the two-year-old filly Glentina on 15 September 1875 at the Lexington Crab Orchard. Standing five feet tall and weighing only seventy-four pounds, Murphy had by the end of 1876 ridden eleven horses to victory at Lexington's Kentucky Association track.

Since colonial times, African Americans had been involved in the care and training of horses, particularly on antebellum and post–Civil War farms and plantations in the South. They had also ridden them as jockeys, an occupation once considered beneath the dignity of white men. At the inaugural Kentucky Derby in 1875, fourteen of the fifteen jockeys were black. Blacks triumphed in fifteen of the first twenty-eight derbies. In his first

Isaac Murphy in his jockey uniform, c. 1895.

Kentucky Derby in 1877, Murphy (who had adopted his grandfather's surname as a tribute) placed fourth aboard Vera Cruz. He later rode the same horse to victory in another major-stakes race and tallied nineteen first-place finishes that year. Two years later, Murphy signed with J. W. Hunt Reynolds and came in second in the Kentucky Derby with the moneymaker Falsetto. Among Murphy's numerous victories between 1879 and 1884 (the year he signed with Ed Corrigan of New York) were the Clark Handicap in Louisville, Kentucky; the Distillers Stakes in Lexington, Kentucky; the Saratoga Cup in New York; the Brewers Cup in St. Louis, Missouri; and the first American Derby in Chicago, Illinois. Incredibly, he posted wins in forty-nine of the fifty-one races he entered at Saratoga in 1882. His first Kentucky Derby win at Churchill Downs, on 27 May 1884 aboard Modesty, was clocked at 2 minutes 40.25 seconds, two lengths ahead of his nearest rival. It was the first of three such conquests there; the other two occurred successively in 1890 and 1891, with the mounts Riley and Kingman, respectively.

Renowned for his adept manipulation of his mounts via intuitive, precise pacing, Murphy rarely employed stirrups or the whip except to please the crowd, and his trademark come-from-behind finishes became known as "Murfinshes." It was his habit to lay on the horse's neck to coax it to the finish line. At a time when jockeys customarily wagered on the outcome of races, Murphy, a devout Baptist, enjoyed a reputation for scrupulous honesty and integrity. A mild-mannered, gracious man who never swore, he married Lucy Osborn in 1882; they had no children. Murphy and his wife resided in a mansion at 143 North Eastern Avenue in Lexington, overlooking the backstretch of a nearby racetrack. At the peak of his career, his yearly salary ranged from ten thousand to twenty thousand dollars excluding bonuses, making him the highest-paid jockey in the nation. His income befitted a man who rode nearly every premier horse of the era to victory at all the major racing events except the Futurity. It is believed that Murphy was the first black American to own a racehorse—he owned several, in fact—and he invested his winnings in racehorses and real estate. He spent extravagantly on clothes and soirees at his home and was attended at the track by his personal valet.

Several writers have asserted that Murphy's most memorable and exciting race was that which occurred at Sheepshead Bay in New York on 25 June 1890. It matched him against the heralded white jockey Ed "Snapper" Garrison and attempted to settle the long-standing debate as to who was the better professional. The event had pronounced racial overtones that in certain respects prefigured the JACK JOHNSON versus Jim Jeffries boxing match twenty years later. Murphy, riding Salvador, edged out Garrison, aboard Tenny, by half a head in one of the most publicized races of the century.

Ironically, just two months later Murphy's popularity was tarnished and his career began to unravel when he fell off of his mount at the end of the running of the Monmouth Handicap. He maintained that he suffered from chronic dieting and that he may even have been drugged. Nonetheless, he was charged with drunkenness and suspended. The press, including the *New York Times* (27 Aug. 1890), was quite baffled by such uncharacteristic behavior from the gentlemanly Murphy and roundly chastised him. Although he continued to rack up victories at the track the following year (1891), his penchant for champagne and the struggle to hold down his weight, which had risen to 140 pounds, eventually took their toll. In 1892 he won six races, the next year four races, and in 1894, the year he was suspended for a second time for being drunk at the track, he failed to win a race. Retirement was forced upon him in November 1895. Within three months Murphy died in Lexington, the ravages of alcohol and dieting having weakened his resistance to pneumonia. He left thirty thousand dollars to his wife, but this sum was hardly enough to satisfy his creditors, and she died a pauper.

Murphy, arguably the most influential and widely respected African American athlete of the nineteenth century, was curiously ignored for many years by historians and journalists. A half century after his death, an article filled with anecdotes and quotations pertaining to his career appeared in the *Negro Digest* (Nov. 1950). Its title bemoaned, "No Memorial for Isaac Murphy." In 1967, through the efforts of the Lexington sportswriter Frank Borries Jr., Murphy's remains were transported from their ignominious location in the city's decrepit No. 2 Cemetery and reinterred in Man o' War Park. In 1977 the remains of both the jockey and the famed thoroughbred (whom Murphy never rode) were moved to hallowed ground near one another at the Kentucky Horse Park outside of Lexington. In 1955 he was the first jockey inducted into the National Museum of Racing Hall of Fame, and in 1956 he was also enshrined in the National Jockey's Hall of Fame at Pimlico, Maryland.

Murphy's three Kentucky Derby wins were later exceeded by Eddie Arcaro (five), Bill Hartack (five), and Bill Shoemaker (four); his back-to-back Kentucky Derby wins were later equaled by the African American JIMMY WINKFIELD (1901 and 1902), Ron Tucotte (1972 and 1973), and Eddie Delahoussaye (1982 and 1983). To his recollection, he was victorious in 44 percent of his contests, winning 628 of 1,412 mounts; but according to other sources, Murphy's winning percentage was closer to 33 percent. In any event, 33 percent represented the best winning record of any jockey in American turf history. The annual Isaac Murphy Award was established in 1993 by the National Turf Writers' Association to honor the jockey with the best win-loss record. The Isaac Murphy Stakes (formerly the American Derby, which Murphy won on four occasions) was initiated in 1997 at Chicago's Arlington International Racecourse.

FURTHER READING

Ashe, Arthur R. *A Hard Road to Glory: A History of the African American Athlete, 1619–1918* (1988).

Bolus, Jim. "Honest Isaac's Legacy," *Sports Illustrated* (29 Apr. 1996).

Borries, Betty. *Isaac Murphy: Kentucky's Record Jockey* (1988).

Cushing, Rick. "Isaac Murphy: A Pioneer Who's Had Few Followers," *Louisville Courier-Journal*, 30 Apr. 1990.

Phelps, Frank T. "The Nearest Perfect Jockey," *Thoroughbred Record* (13 May 1967): 1245–1248.

Savage, Stephen P. "Isaac Murphy: Black Hero in Nineteenth Century American Sport, 1861–1896," *Canadian Journal of History and Physical Education* 10 (1979): 15–32.

Tarelton, L. P. "A Memorial," *Thoroughbred Record* (21 Mar. 1896): 136.

This entry is taken from the *American National Biography* and is published here with the permission of the American Council of Learned Societies.

ROBERT FIKES

Murphy, John Henry, Sr. (25 Dec. 1840–5 Apr. 1922), newspaper publisher, was born in Baltimore, Maryland, the only son of Benjamin Murphy Jr., a whitewasher, and Susan Coby. John Henry Murphy was born a slave, and the *Baltimore Afro-American*, the newspaper that he guided to prominence during the first two decades of the twentieth century, described Murphy's educational attainment as "limited." A short man, he walked with a limp, the result of a childhood horseback riding incident that left one leg longer than the other. Freedom for the

Murphys came through the Maryland Emancipation Act of 1863.

Despite his limp Murphy answered Abraham Lincoln's call for troops and joined the Union army during the Civil War. He enlisted as a private in Company G of the mostly black Thirtieth Regiment of the Maryland Volunteers—an infantry unit—on 18 March 1864. During his twenty-one months in uniform he served under General Ulysses S. Grant in Virginia and under General William T. Sherman in North Carolina. He left the army in December 1865 as a sergeant.

After his discharge Murphy returned to Baltimore. On his first day back home he met Martha Elizabeth Howard, daughter of a well-to-do Montgomery County, Maryland, farmer. Howard's family had been born slaves, but her father, Enoch George Howard, had purchased his own freedom and later that of his wife and children, and he eventually even bought his former master's property. It took two years for Murphy to convince Martha Elizabeth's father that he was sincere about marriage. The couple wed in 1868; they had eleven children.

To support his growing clan Murphy worked at various jobs over the next twenty years. He followed his father as a whitewasher for a time, until the use of wallpaper became widespread. Murphy later used his veteran's status to get a political patronage job with the U.S. post office, but he lost that when the Democrats came to power with the 1884 election of Grover Cleveland as president. Subsequent jobs included being a porter, a janitor, and a feed store manager. Neither Murphy nor others who have written about him cite dates or lengths of time that he stayed at his various jobs.

Murphy was in his forties when he decided to become a printer, as he described himself. Active in local organizations, particularly the African Methodist Episcopal (AME) Church, in the 1880s Murphy became superintendent of Sunday schools for the Hagerstown, Maryland, AME Church District. For years Murphy had wanted to structure black church schools into some type of organization, and he saw a newspaper as a means of achieving this goal. His initial publication, designed to generate more community interest in Sunday school work, was the *Sunday School Helper*, which he began in the late 1880s in the basement of his home. Murphy's competition came from publications started by other local black church groups. The *Afro-American*, which under the leadership of the Reverend William Alexander carried a combination of church and community news, was the Baptists' publication. The *Ledger*, edited by the Reverend GEORGE F. BRAGG, was allied with the Episcopal Church. Initial publication dates have yet to be established for any of these weekly publications.

The *Afro-American*'s parent company was the Northwestern Family Supply Company, an enterprise of the Reverend Alexander's that operated a dry goods store. When in 1896 Alexander's larger business failed and was auctioned off, Murphy acquired—with two hundred dollars borrowed from his wife—the *Afro-American*, then a one-page weekly with a circulation of 250. Murphy merged his two publications and dropped the *Sunday School Helper* name but retained the church and community news content. As time passed, Murphy brought his children into the enterprise by assigning them various editorial, printing, and circulation tasks. Between 1900 and 1901 the *Afro-American* merged with the *Ledger* and was known for a time as the *Afro-American Ledger* (1901–1916), when it was published semiweekly. Under this arrangement Murphy became the publisher and Bragg became the editor. Murphy eventually obtained total control and returned the newspaper to its former—and current—name, the *Afro-American*. During the last three decades of his life Murphy guided the operation as it became one of the premier black newspapers of all time. In the process, not only did he achieve success, fame, and financial reward but he also laid the foundation for a venerable publishing concern that would be headed by generations of Murphys for nearly a century.

Murphy said that he wanted to publish a newspaper that would "render service to the whole community." Like many of his contemporary black newspaper executives, he was a Republican, but he vowed not to let the *Afro-American* be a newspaper "tied to the apron strings of any political party, fraternal organization or religious denomination." Murphy established the paper's motto of "Independent in All Things, Neutral in Nothing." Murphy credited two characteristics for his success: faith and industry. He said that he had "faith in the ability of the black man to succeed in this civilization, faith in myself and faith in God. Then, too, I believe in just plain, everyday, hard work."

Murphy had hoped to live to be one hundred years old, and on his eightieth birthday he wrote a letter to be opened on Christmas Day 1940. A reflection on his life and a statement of the philosophy that made him one of the most respected "race" men of his time, the letter reads in part:

I measure a newspaper not in buildings, equipment and employees—those are trimmings. A newspaper succeeds because its management believes in itself, in God and in the present generation. It must always ask itself whether it has kept faith with the common people; whether it has no other goal except to see that their liberties are preserved and their future assured; whether it is fighting to get rid of slums, to provide jobs for everybody; whether it stays out of politics except to expose corruption and condemn injustice, race prejudice or the cowardice of compromise.... [The *Afro-American*] has always had a loyal constituency who believed it honest, decent and progressive. It is that kind of newspaper now and I hope it never changes.

Murphy remained active until shortly before his death in Baltimore. Tributes poured in. The one from the Negro (later National) Newspaper Publishers Association (NNPA), the black newspaper publishers' trade organization, was a fitting epitaph. To his peers, it said, Murphy was "a noble Roman of the fourth estate and ... an inspiration to future generations of black men."

By the time he died Murphy had managed to establish a newspaper with an extensive readership outside the city that was once called "the graveyard of black newspapers." The *Afro-American*'s circulation of fourteen thousand at the time of his death made it one of the ten largest black newspapers in the United States. As the number of black newspapers grew along with the migration of blacks to the North, the *Afro-American* became one of the "Big Five" black newspapers of the first half of the twentieth century. Although Murphy did not start the *Afro-American* he was the driving force that transformed the publication from a local newspaper into one of the most significant and influential black journals in the nation. John Henry Murphy was a man of perseverance and vision, and his life indicates that one is never too old to succeed.

FURTHER READING

The *Afro-American* Archives are located at Bowie State College, Bowie, Maryland.
"John Henry Murphy," *Afro-American*, 7 Apr. 1922.
Wolseley, Roland E. *The Black Press, U.S.A.*, 2d ed. (1990).

This entry is taken from the *American National Biography* and is published here with the permission of the American Council of Learned Societies.

JAMES PHILLIP JETER

Murray, Albert (12 May 1916–), writer and critic, was born in Nokomis, Alabama, the son of Sudie Graham, a Tuskegee Institute student, and John Young, a businessman. Soon after his birth Mattie Murray, a housewife, and her husband, Hugh, a laborer and timber worker, adopted him. Murray, who later enjoyed a close relationship with Graham and Young, joked of his adoption by less-wealthy parents, "It's just like the prince left among the paupers" (Gates, 30). He learned about the folkways of segregation in Magazine Point, a community on the outskirts of Mobile, Alabama, where his family had moved during World War I. "We didn't dislike white people," he recalled. "We saw too many bony-butt poor white crackers. We were going to feel inferior to them?" (Maguire, 139). Murray's rejection of any notion of black inferiority was further strengthened by exposure to Mobile's baseball legend SATCHEL PAIGE and to teachers at the intellectually rigorous Mobile County Training School. A studious youth interested in drama, Murray was also quarterback on the school football team and captain of the basketball squad. Voted the school's best all-around student in 1935, he received a scholarship to Tuskegee Institute.

Tuskegee's well-stocked libraries suited Murray's voracious appetite for literature. Although he was aware of the black writers associated with the Harlem Renaissance, he was drawn instead to the white Southern Renascence novelists Robert Penn Warren and William Faulkner and to the modernist fiction writers Ernest Hemingway and Thomas Mann. This passion, along with jazz, he shared with his older Tuskegee contemporary, RALPH ELLISON. But unlike Ellison, who left for New York in 1936, Murray followed an intellectual and critical development that was rooted in his native South. He graduated from Tuskegee in 1939 and, after briefly studying at the University of Michigan, returned to his alma mater to teach literature and composition a year later. In 1941 he married Mozelle Menefee, a Tuskegee student, and two years later enlisted in the army air forces, serving until 1946.

During World War II, easy access to air travel gave Murray the opportunity to fly to New York City and scavenge the Gotham Book Mart, and he returned to Manhattan in 1947 to study for a master's degree at New York University. He also reacquainted himself with Ellison, who was then on the verge of literary stardom with the publication of *Invisible Man* (1952),

Albert Murray at his home in Harlem, New York, 15 June 1998. (AP Images.)

and spent as much time as possible in the city's jazz clubs. There he developed friendships with DUKE ELLINGTON and COUNT BASIE and began to conceptualize jazz not only as a metaphor for African American and American society but also, with its riffs and breaks, its sudden changes and bursts of creativity, as a means of understanding life itself. After returning to Tuskegee to teach in 1948, Murray was called back to the air force in 1951 and remained there for the next eleven years.

Murray later recalled that long periods of inactivity in the armed forces gave him plenty of time to read, think, and travel to Morocco, Greece, and Italy. However, military service also delayed his grand ambition to be "the JOE LOUIS of literature" (Maguire, 107). His career as a published writer began to take shape in the early 1960s, however, when he retired from the air force with the rank of major and settled in Harlem with his wife and their only child, Michelle. Murray quickly immersed himself in the New York literary scene and found common intellectual spirits in Ellison, the writer JAMES BALDWIN, and the artist ROMARE BEARDEN. Although he taught at Columbia University's School of Journalism in 1968, Murray devoted most of his time to writing essays for small but influential journals like the *New Leader*.

Several of these essays later appeared in his first full-length work, *The Omni-Americans* (1970), an iconoclastic manifesto that celebrated the "incontestably mulatto" culture of America at a time when the nationalistic Black Arts Movement of LARRY NEAL and AMIRI BARAKA was in vogue. In this volume Murray dismissed what he saw as the posturing of the Black Power movement and lambasted its guru, ELDRIDGE CLEAVER, for adopting the "pseudo-existential *esthetique du nastiness* of Norman Mailer" (178).

Murray also criticized social theorists like Kenneth B. Clark and Daniel Patrick Moynihan, whose studies depicted the cultural deprivation of inner-city blacks. A culture that had produced Ellington, MA RAINEY, and JACK JOHNSON, Murray argued, could in no way be seen as deprived or inferior. Although White Anglo-Saxon Protestants might dominate America's economic and legal power structure, he contended that the nation's culture "even in its most rigidly segregated precincts is patently and irrevocably composite." Black nationalists and white liberals alike, in Murray's view, were misguided in suggesting that African Americans lived outside the mainstream. Blacks—or, as he insisted, Negroes—*were* the mainstream, and their "blues idiom," the African American cultural forms of spirituals, jazz, and the blues, defined what was

truly distinctive about the United States. Moreover, he concluded, "When the Negro musician or dancer swings the blues, he is fulfilling the same fundamental existential requirement that determines the mission of the poet, the priest and the medicine man" (*The Omni-Americans*, 58).

Although *The Omni-Americans* did not enjoy popular success, it received mainly favorable reviews and established the broad contours of Murray's later work: his disparagement of "social workers, liberals, and other do-gooders" who contributed to the "fakelore of black pathology"; his use of a rich southern black vernacular; and his concept of a blues idiom that spoke to the beauty, pain, and complexity of the human condition. Over the next three decades he employed a variety of literary genres to elaborate on these themes: travelogue in *South to a Very Old Place* (1971), published lecture in *The Hero and the Blues* (1973), semiautobiographical fiction in *Train Whistle Guitar* (1974) and *The Spyglass Tree* (1991), biography in *Good Morning Blues: The Autobiography of Count Basie as Told to Albert Murray*, literary correspondence in *Trading Twelves: The Selected Letters of Ralph Ellison and Albert Murray* (2001), and poetry in *Conjugations and Reiteration* (2001).

Most critics regard *Stomping the Blues* (1976) as Murray's finest work, a labor of love that capitalizes on his encyclopedic knowledge of the jazz world and showcases his talent for making words swing as ebulliently as a LOUIS ARMSTRONG solo. The blues, Murray argued, speaks to our fundamental ability to improvise and persevere in the face of adversity and to transcend that hardship with creativity, not to give in to the blues, but to shake them off. As he stated on PBS's *MacNeil/Lehrer NewsHour* in March 1996: "Life is rough. So are you going to cut your throat, or are you gonna get yourself together and stomp at the Savoy by 9:30 that night?" That philosophy proved highly influential not only to cultural critics such as STANLEY CROUCH but also to jazz musicians, notably the trumpeter and composer WYNTON MARSALIS. In the 1990s both Marsalis and Murray served on the board of New York City's prestigious Jazz at Lincoln Center program and influenced the center's preference for revivals of stomping "old masters," such as Basie and Ellington, over newer or more experimental jazz artists.

Three decades after the publication of *The Omni-Americans*, Albert Murray's view of the nation as a cultural hybrid seemed far less dissonant than it had in 1970. If Bill Clinton, a saxophone-playing white southerner, can be praised as America's "first black President" and inducted into the Arkansas Black Hall of Fame, then Murray's description of the "incontestably mulatto" culture of the United States seems particularly apt. Indeed, if Murray has a failing as a cultural critic, it may be that his vision has been too narrow. By focusing so exclusively on early twentieth-century African American culture, he ignores the even greater global resonance of later black musical forms, notably soul—which he dismisses in *Stomping the Blues* as "sentimental"—and hip-hop, which has developed its own idiomatic style in communities as diverse as Toledo, Tangiers, and Tokyo.

On 23 April 2007 it was announced that Murray would receive the W. E. B. DuBois Medal from the W. E. B. DuBois Institute for African and African American Research. The Institute's director, HENRY LOUIS GATES JR., said the award was "to let him know that his life's work is not only valued, but also recognized as vital and central to our intellectual and artistic tradition."

FURTHER READING

The Albert Murray Papers are housed at the Houghton Library, Harvard University, Cambridge, Massachusetts.

Gates, Henry Louis, Jr. *Thirteen Ways of Looking at a Black Man* (1997).

Maguire, Roberta S., ed. *Conversations with Albert Murray* (1997).

STEVEN J. NIVEN

Murray, Daniel Alexander Payne (3 Mar. 1852–31 Dec. 1925), librarian, bibliographical researcher, and political figure, was born in Baltimore, Maryland, the youngest son of George Murray, a free black who worked as a timber inspector, and Eliza (Wilson) Murray, a woman of mixed African and American Indian ancestry. Daniel Murray, who was named after his father's close friend, the African Methodist Episcopal (AME) Church bishop DANIEL ALEXANDER PAYNE, began school at the age of five at a small primary school in his neighborhood. He continued to study in Baltimore public schools and entered a Unitarian seminary, graduating in 1869. On 19 April 1861 he witnessed the attack on the Sixth Massachusetts Regiment in Baltimore. An early account of Murray's life in *Colored American Magazine* reported that as a young boy he supplied Union soldiers with water during an attack in Baltimore and earned accolades for spying a rebel soldier trying to poison the water supply.

After spending several summers in Washington, D.C., he moved there and worked at the United States Senate restaurant managed by his brother. Murray began his career in 1871 when Ainsworth R. Spofford, a librarian with the Library of Congress, hired the nineteen-year-old as his personal assistant. While working for Spofford, Murray acquired extensive historical and literary knowledge, honed his research skills, and studied modern languages. In 1879 he married Anna Evans, a native of Oberlin, Ohio, a graduate of Oberlin College, and an advocate of kindergarten education. Together they had seven children. Murray remained Spofford's assistant until 1897, having been made an assistant librarian in 1881, a post that he held until he retired in 1922. For a few months in 1897 he served as chief of the periodical division.

In addition to his job at the Library of Congress, Murray was heavily involved in the civil affairs of Washington, D.C. Politically, Murray held a combination of conservative and radical views. He supported BOOKER T. WASHINGTON and argued for blacks to align with industrialists rather than with organized labor. He advocated industrial training, although he maintained that all black education, whether technical or traditional, should be of the highest quality. In one instance he opposed Washington's support of ROSCOE C. BRUCE, the assistant superintendent for colored schools in the District of Columbia, who allowed teachers to instruct classes outside of their respective subject areas. An optimist, Murray strongly believed that racist violence would end once businessmen and politicians appreciated the necessity of black labor to southern industry and society. He maintained that African Americans should not compromise on the issue of liberty, and although he encouraged workers to organize and boycott to fight injustice, he did not advise them to form unions.

Murray also worked in real estate and construction, and he served on numerous committees. He built several homes and directed the remodeling of St. Luke's Church. He was the first African American elected to the Board of Trade, Washington, D.C.'s major business association. In 1894, while collecting data for a presentation to a U.S. congressional committee, Murray drafted a proposal for a taxation law that was later implemented. In 1899 he was appointed to a special committee to escort Admiral George Dewey from New York City to Washington, D.C. He chaired the Sub-Committee on Public Comfort, the group in charge of African American visitors to four presidential inaugurations. In 1908 and 1920 he was elected delegate for Washington, D.C., to the Republican National Convention. Murray was a director of the National Afro-American Council, a chairman of the Committee on Racial Literature, a founder of St. Luke's Protestant Episcopal Church, an executive committee member of the National Sociological Society, and a member of the National Geographic, Washington Historical, and Oldest Inhabitants societies.

Because of his extensive knowledge of African American history and politics, Murray was called upon to speak and write about the race problem, often testifying before Congress. For example, in 1902 he testified before the United States House Committee on Interstate and Foreign Commerce in an effort to lift segregation laws on train cars. That same year he appeared before the House Committee on Labor to discuss Afro-American migration. He also received numerous requests from groups interested in black literature and history. The *Voice of the Negro*, one of the most prominent black newspapers, frequently published his work.

Murray began the research for which he is best known in 1899 when Herbert Putnam, Spofford's successor at the Library of Congress, asked him to prepare an exhibit of books and pamphlets by "colored authors" for display in the American exhibit at the 1900 Paris Exposition. Murray's preliminary list, which he prepared in two weeks, featured 270 titles. It was published in January 1899 with a request for information on all extant books and pamphlets authored by African Americans. Murray's final list included 1,100 titles. The exhibit, presented in Paris in-1900 as well as at the Pan-American Exposition in Buffalo, New York, and the American and West Indian Exposition in Charleston, South Carolina, the following year, included five hundred volumes. The books were assembled at the Library of Congress, where they formed the basis of Murray's encyclopedia project.

By 1904 Murray had doubled his list for the Paris Exposition, and by 1907 he had compiled five thousand titles of books and pamphlets by African Americans for the Jamestown, Virginia, Tercentenary. As his research expanded, Murray became increasingly critical of his research methods. In particular he was troubled by his reliance on photographs to determine an author's ancestry. This led him to conduct more extensive research into the lives of authors, which inspired his *Bibliographia-Africana*, a text that included both the titles of black literary works and biographical information on the authors. In this collection he aimed to demonstrate the intellectual accomplishments of blacks, and featured works spanning various disciplines, from history and literature to the sciences.

The amount of material that Murray amassed also motivated him to propose another project, and in 1912 he announced his *Historical and Bibliographical Encyclopedia of the Colored Race throughout the World*. The prospectus for this ambitious project proposed six volumes documenting the accomplishments of black individuals as well as the progress of the race as a whole. It envisioned 25,000 biographies, 6,000 titles of books and pamphlets, a list of fiction by white authors who dealt with race, and a list of 5,000 musical compositions by composers of African descent. For this project Murray assembled some of the nation's most prominent and well-educated blacks to contribute as assistant editors, including JOHN EDWARD BRUCE, ARTHUR ALFONSO SCHOMBURG, JOHN WESLEY CROMWELL, L.-M. Hershaw, Bishop J. Albert Johnson, WILLIAM S. SCARBOROUGH, and Richard Robert Wright Jr., as well as scholars from Africa and the Caribbean.

Despite his efforts, Murray was unable to raise enough financial support to secure a publisher. Publication was also hindered by the emergence of similar anthologies and encyclopedias, although none of them approached the scope of Murray's proposed work. Nevertheless he persisted, even working after his retirement in 1922. On 31 December 1925, exactly three years after his retirement, Daniel Murray died of natural causes in his home in Washington, D.C. Anna Murray continued with the project for almost two decades after her husband's death.

In 1966 the Murray family donated most of the accrued material to the State Historical Society of Wisconsin in Madison. Although Murray's encyclopedic work was never published, it is preserved within the archives and rare books division of the Library of Congress and the State Historical Society of Wisconsin. As a pioneer of black history, Daniel Murray should be remembered not only as a determined and enthusiastic researcher but also as a visionary whose dream of a comprehensive black encyclopedia far exceeded the expectations of his contemporaries and peers.

FURTHER READING
Murray's papers are in the Library of Congress Archives, Washington, D.C.
Harris, Robert L. "Daniel Murray and the Encyclopedia of the Colored Race," *Phylon* 37, no. 3 (1976).

Hodges, Leonard. "Daniel Alexander Payne Murray: Bibliographer and Political Activist, 1871–1925," *Journal of the Afro-American Historical and Genealogical Society* 6, no. 4 (1985).

Josey, E. J., and Ann Allen Shockley. *Handbook of Black Librarianship* (1977).

Lee, Edwin A. "Daniel Murray: Bibliographer of Afro-American Literature in the Library of Congress," *Colored American Magazine* 5, no. 6 (1902).

Sinnette, Elinor Des Verney, W. Paul Coates, and Thomas C. Battle, eds. *Black Bibliophiles and Collectors* (1990).

ELIZABETH SIMONEAU

Murray, Eddie (24 Feb. 1956–), baseball player, was born Eddie Clarence Murray in Los Angeles to Charles Murray, a rug company mechanic, and Carrie Murray. The eighth of twelve children, Eddie was raised in the poverty-stricken neighborhood of Watts, but was closely watched by his parents, who readily dispensed chores and discipline. Playing baseball in the backyard, he and his siblings used broomstick handles to hit tin foil balls and swerving Crisco can lids. Though he also played basketball at Locke High, Eddie was the star first baseman and pitcher on the diamond, where he played with the future Hall of Famer OZZIE SMITH. Scoring admirably on a psychological exam given to amateur players, the results of the exam showed that he had "tremendous emotional control. He had a lot of drive, but it was masked by his emotional control," according to former Orioles scout Dave Ritterpusch (Christensen, "The Payoff," *Baseball Digest*, June 2003). Eddie was selected by the Baltimore Orioles in the third round of the 1973 draft. Murray was seventeen years old when he graduated high school in 1973. Murray joined three brothers, and eventually a fourth, in professional baseball. After five weeks of negotiations between his mother and the Orioles, Eddie signed with Baltimore.

Along with three All-Star appearances in the minor leagues, Murray learned to hit left-handed at the end of his third season. Becoming a switch-hitter increased his versatility as a player, and on Opening Day 1977 he made his debut as the Orioles' designated hitter, stroking his first major-league hit off Bert Blyleven. Murray went on to play 160 games in his first year, hitting twenty-seven home runs with a .283 batting average—a level of consistency he would maintain throughout his career, earning the nickname "Steady Eddie." At the end of the season, he won the American League Rookie of the Year. He took over first base duties the following season, and in 1979 was named to the first of his eight All-Star teams, helping Baltimore reach the World Series.

Murray became a full-fledged star in 1980, posting his first .300 batting average, and leading the team in home runs and RBIs. Murray's popularity in Baltimore (supported by the fans' rhythmic shout of "Ed-die!") seemed to be cemented with the arrival of Cal Ripken Jr. and the team's 1983 World Series championship. Though he hadn't put together an MVP season (he finished second in 1982 and 1983), Murray had respect from his colleagues, who considered him one of the best in the game. His two home runs in the fifth game of the 1983 series helped clinch the championship.

Murray seemed to carry a relaxed approach to the game, earning him the additional sobriquet "Easy Eddie." Though he had always been reluctant to deal with the media, he was affable and mischievous during his early days with the Orioles. Throughout his career, he remained popular in the clubhouse and adopted a leadership role on each of his teams.

Arguably the most popular Oriole between Brooks Robinson and Ripken, Murray saw his relationship

Eddie Murray of the Baltimore Orioles, after hitting a home run out of Oriole Park at Camden Yards in Baltimore, 14 August 1996. (AP Images.)

with the fans and press sour after he was named the franchise's captain in early 1986. As the Orioles endured their first losing season in twenty years, Murray went on the disabled list for the first time in his career and became a scapegoat for Baltimore's tailspin. Hampered by a pulled hamstring and sore hand, Murray suffered a poor season, even though he made the All-Star team for the seventh time and led the team in batting average and RBIs. His reluctance to train in the offseason and his increase in weight left the front office displeased; owner Edward Bennett Williams publicly took Murray to task for the team's failure. In response, Murray repeatedly aired his desire to leave Baltimore, and cut himself off from the press entirely.

Despite his frosty relationship with the media, Murray was a consistent—but relatively unpublicized—benefactor to charities, spending time with inner-city children and donating to large organizations like the Red Cross. Murray gave $500,000 from his 1985 contract extension with the Orioles to start a new Outward Bound camp, which he named for his mother who had passed away the year before.

The Orioles traded Murray to the Los Angeles Dodgers in December 1988. He spent three seasons there, posting his best numbers in 1991, when he hit a career-best .330. Murray joined the New York Mets as a free agent, and amidst a poor relationship with the press, drove in 193 runs over his two years for an embattled team that finished fifth and seventh in their division. On 23 January 1993, he married his wife, Janice, with whom he would have two daughters, Jessica and Jordan.

Murray signed with the Cleveland Indians in December 1993, and as the DH (designated hitter) on one of the most potent lineups of the decade, helped secure a World Series appearance in 1995, the same year he notched his three-thousandth hit. Murray was traded back to the Orioles the following year, where lingering resentment between him and the city was put aside. In his first game in a Baltimore uniform since 1988, Murray hit a home run. His veteran presence in the clubhouse helped the Orioles gain their first postseason appearance since 1983.

Murray spent parts of the following season with the Anaheim Angels and the Dodgers before rejoining the Orioles as a bench coach for 1998. Though Baltimore had retired his number after trading him, they conducted another ceremony in his honor. Murray spent two years on the bench and two as the team's first-base coach before becoming the Indians' hitting instructor from 2001 to 2005.

Despite never hitting more than forty home runs in a season or winning the MVP award, "Steady Eddie" brought reliability to his game. When he retired, he joined HANK AARON and WILLIE MAYS as the only players with three thousand hits and five hundred home runs. Upon breaking Lou Gehrig's consecutive games streak, Cal Ripken Jr. extended specific thanks to Murray, saying, "Eddie taught me the importance of being in the lineup every day" (Geffner, 11).

Murray was elected to the Hall of Fame on his first attempt in January 2003. At the induction ceremony with media favorite Gary Carter six months later, Murray was serenaded with the familiar "Ed-die!" chant as he gave an uncharacteristically long speech, offering thanks to numerous teammates and friends, including his wife Janice.

Murray also extended his work beyond the baseball field, donating money to help revitalize Baltimore's poorer areas, serving as a patron of many charities. Through a large donation from Murray in the late 1980s, Baltimore established a nature center named after his mother, Carrie Murray; and the Eddie Murray Fund helps with the prevention and treatment of kidney ailments. During his career, Murray was also a finalist for the ROBERTO CLEMENTE Award.

FURTHER READING

Geffner, Michael P. "Great Big Stick," *Sporting News*, 3 July 1995.

Justice, Richard. "Dodger Blue Drives out Oriole Blues," *Washington Post*, 12 Mar. 1989.

Justice, Richard. "More than Ever, Orioles Are Eddie's," *Washington Post*, 23 Feb. 1986.

ADAM W. GREEN

Murray, George Washington (22 Sept. 1853–21 Apr. 1926), organizer and lecturer for the Colored Farmers Alliance, farmer and author, owner of eight patents for agricultural implements, and U.S. congressman from South Carolina (1893–1897), was born in Sumter County, South Carolina, to enslaved parents whose names have never been established and who died before 1865. Murray took up farming during his teen years after the Civil War and by 1880 had acquired his own land: forty-nine acres tilled and fifteen acres of woodland, worth about $1500 including buildings and improvements, producing income of around $650 a year.

He made several attempts to obtain an education. Applying to a local school in 1871, he was instead appointed teacher. Classes were held three to four months a year. Even when school was in session, he worked his fields in the morning and evenings. In 1874 he entered the University of South Carolina—temporarily filled with students of African descent, because when the first arrived in 1873, teachers and students who continued to think of themselves as "white" departed. Most new faculty were northern Methodists, with one Harvard-trained African American professor. Murray and his entire class were expelled in 1877, after the former confederate general Wade Hampton was elected governor and began to dismantle Reconstruction in the state.

Returning to his relatively prosperous farm, Murray married Ella Reynolds. Their first son was born in December 1879 and a daughter in 1881. Another daughter died in infancy. He was able to hire one hand to help with the five acres of corn, twenty-one acres of cotton, the horse, mule, cow, and ox, and four pigs, eight cherry trees, eight peach trees, and four apple trees on his land. In April 1880, he was elected as a delegate to the state Republican Party convention and obtained work as an enumerator for the U.S. Census.

He rose slowly in the ranks of the Republican Party, which was split by many shifting factions. In 1886, after again serving as a delegate to the state Republican convention, Murray wrote a fifteen-page letter to President-Elect Benjamin Harrison, opposing the appointment of non-Republicans to federal office. Many in the national party were looking for ways to appeal to southern white voters, which included the appointment of "independent" people to government posts, playing to antiblack code words like "moral worth and intellectual fitness" (i.e., white). Murray emerged as a public speaker that year at a barbecue sponsored by the Colored Alliance, with some leading members of the white Farmers Alliance attending, in Sumter County. He emphasized self-help, morality, education, obedience to law, and economic improvement.

Farmers' Alliances were soon to become the base of the People's Party, sometimes known as Populists, leading western farmers and southern African Americans temporarily from Republican loyalties, while many impoverished southern Democrats briefly abandoned "the white man's party." In South Carolina, this potential alliance died stillborn. Benjamin F. Tillman, although a substantial landowner himself, ran for governor in 1890, representing himself as champion of the small farmer. He neither advocated nor implemented the populist economic program.

Murray had little cause to give up his Republican affiliation. A local Colored Alliance in Shiloh, in the spirit of interracial cooperation, endorsed Tillman, but white Alliance members, taunted by the conservative Democratic establishment, denied they either sought or desired colored support. Tillman became a pioneer of black disfranchisement, foreshadowing the increasingly virulent forms of racism that followed the collapse of populism across the South after 1896. Murray, therefore, was cast into the forefront of efforts to stop disfranchisement of African Americans, while the Colored Alliance disappeared from South Carolina by 1892.

It was during this trying period that he was elected twice to the U.S. House of Representatives. His first race, in 1892, was in the Seventh District, which was created with a black supermajority so that all six other districts in South Carolina would have an effective white majority. Voters of African descent had been so effectively kept away from the polls that the race was close and depended on how a Tillman-appointed election board ruled on disputes. Murray was declared the winner by 4995–4955, over a conservative Democrat, E. W. Moise, opposed to the Tillman faction.

By 1894, Tillman's administration had rearranged the districts, punishing their conservative rivals in Charleston by combining substantial black-majority areas with part of Charleston, while drawing lines that might, with fewer dark-skinned citizens registered to vote, elect "white" representatives from all seven districts. Murray ran in the new First District, losing in the votes counted to the Democrat William Elliot, 5650–3913; poll watchers certified massive exclusion of voters based on color. In April 1896, the House Election Committee certified Murray as the winner, and he was seated 5 June 1896.

Murray was, along with the Civil War hero and congressman ROBERT SMALLS and the former judge WILLIAM J. WHIPPER, one of seven black delegates to the state constitutional convention of 1895, but their numbers were too few to block the residency laws, poll taxes, and property and literacy tests that disfranchised nearly all black citizens. In the 1896 election, with the Republican vote split between Murray and a white railway mail clerk, Cecil Cohen, Elliott was elected. This time, an increasingly indifferent congressional Republican majority took no action.

Between 1888 and 1901, Murray had engaged in a series of land purchases and sales, heavily mortgaged, with the intention to settle as many black farmers as possible on land they would eventually own, meeting the requirement in the state constitution that a voter must own $300 in property. He sometimes had as many as two hundred tenant families on his land, making rent and purchase payments, which covered his mortgage and provided him a profit on the transaction. In 1903 a civil case over one of these leases was used to frame a forgery charge against Murray. After conviction by an all-white jury, he was sentenced to a $250 fine and three years on the county chain gang or state penitentiary. There was little possibility a man his age would survive either.

By the time his appeal was rejected by the South Carolina Supreme Court, Murray had placed his property in trust, with instructions for paying his debts, and left the state, forfeiting $2500 bail. He settled primarily in Chicago, where he was involved in a short-lived department store venture, worked as a red cap on the Central Illinois railroad, served as president of the Chicago *Conservator*, and joined the Chicago Colored Men's Business League. His wife refused to leave South Carolina; he married Cornelia Martin in Chicago in 1908. In September 1909, an attempt was made to extradite him, but the matter was dropped; some substantial (white) citizens back home still respected him, others didn't want to make a martyr of him, and all were satisfied that he had been driven from South Carolina politics. There is speculation that President William Howard Taft may have brokered a deal between the governors of South Carolina and Illinois during a boat trip on the Mississippi River in October.

Murray spent the next ten years traveling, visiting thirty states by 1917, staying no more than a few months in any one place. He published a pamphlet entitled *Race Ideals*, which went through four printings (1910–1914). Settling again in Chicago, he and his wife were foster parents in the 1920s until his death from cancer in 1926.

FURTHER READING

Fordham, Damon L. *True Stories of Black South Carolina* (2008).

Marszalek, John F. *A Black Congressman in the Age of Jim Crow: South Carolina's George Washington Murray* (2006).

Middleton, Stephen. *Black Congressmen during Reconstruction: A Documentary Sourcebook* (2002).

Ragsdale, Bruce A., and Joel D. Treese. *Black Americans in Congress, 1870–1989* (1990).

CHARLES ROSENBERG

Murray, Pauli (20 Nov. 1910–1 July 1985), lawyer, writer, and minister, was born Anna Pauline Murray in Baltimore, Maryland, the daughter of William Henry Murray, a public school teacher, and Agnes Fitzgerald, a nurse. She had African, European, and Native American ancestry. Her parents both died when she was a child (her mother had a cerebral hemorrhage in March 1914; her father was murdered in a state hospital in June 1923), and she grew up from age three in North Carolina with her maternal grandparents and her mother's oldest sister, Pauline Fitzgerald Dame, a public school teacher who adopted her.

Murray graduated in 1926 from Hillside High School (which went only through grade eleven) in Durham, North Carolina, and then lived with relatives in New York City and graduated in 1927 from Richmond Hill High School. After working for a year in Durham for a black newspaper and a black insurance company, she returned to New York and entered Hunter College in 1928. She changed her

Pauli Murray, the first black woman ordained as a priest of the Episcopal Church, at her ordination at the Washington Cathedral in Washington, D.C., on 8 January 1977. (AP Images.)

name to Pauli, and, after time out for work and for what proved only a brief marriage (1930; later annulled), earned a B.A. in English in 1933. She spent a year as field representative for *Opportunity* magazine, the voice of the National Urban League. She worked for four years (1935–1939) with the Works Progress Administration as a remedial reading teacher and then with the Workers' Education Project. Wishing to return home, she applied in 1938 for graduate study at the University of North Carolina, where her white-great grandfather had studied and his father had been a trustee, but that school rejected her because of her race.

Murray was active in civil rights in the 1940s. The first time was unintended, when she found herself arrested for "disorderly conduct" in March 1940 in Petersburg, Virginia, while taking a bus south to visit her family in North Carolina. Determined to implement what she understood of Gandhi's *Satyagraha* (nonviolent direct action)—despite what she later termed her "urge toward kamikaze defiance of Jim Crow"—she challenged the constitutionality of segregating interstate bus passengers. She courteously demanded fair treatment in jail while awaiting trial, returning to jail rather than paying the fine when she was convicted. As a result of this experience, she learned that "creative nonviolent resistance could be a powerful weapon in the struggle for human dignity." From 1940 to 1942 she worked with the Workers Defense League in a coast-to-coast campaign for a new trial for ODELL WALLER, a black sharecropper who, convicted by an all-white jury of men who had paid their poll taxes, was eventually executed for the murder of his landlord in Pittsylvania County in Virginia.

Murray's involvement in the Waller case led to her decision to attend law school, and she entered Howard University in 1941 "with the single-minded intention of destroying Jim Crow." During her time at Howard, she planned and participated in student sit-ins from 1943 to 1944 designed to achieve the desegregation of drugstores and cafeterias in the nation's capital. She earned a law degree at Howard University in 1944, graduating cum laude and first in her class.

Deciding to obtain a graduate degree so that she could return to teach law at Howard, she applied to Harvard Law School, but that school rejected her because of her gender. She went instead to Boalt Hall Law School at the University of California at Berkeley, where she earned an LLM in 1945 with a thesis titled "The Right to Equal Opportunity in Employment." Years later, she attended Yale University Law School, where she earned a JDS in 1965 with a dissertation titled "Roots of the Racial Crisis: Prologue to Policy." She abandoned her plans to teach at Howard when her mentor there, LEON A. RANSOM, was bypassed in 1946 for the deanship. Between her studies at Berkeley and Yale, she worked briefly as deputy attorney general in California and for the American Jewish Congress's Commission on Law and Social Action in New York, passed the bar exams in California and New York, ran as a Liberal Party candidate for a seat on the city council from Brooklyn in 1949, and from 1946 to 1960 spent much of her time in private practice in New York, eventually (1956–1960) in the law firm of Paul, Weiss, Rifkind, Wharton, and Garrison.

Race, Murray had learned, was not the only major obstacle to a black woman's educational and professional advancement. She contributed to the constitutional theory of litigation against racial and sexual discrimination, and later put that theory into practice when she served on President John F. Kennedy's Commission on the Status of Women (1962–1963). That commission helped to ensure that the 1964 Civil Rights Act included a ban on sex, as well as race, discrimination in employment. In 1966 she was a founding member of the National Organization for Women, established as a feminist counterpart to the NAACP. And she conceived her last major work, *Song in a Weary Throat: An American Pilgrimage* (1987), as "an autobiographical book on Jim Crow and Jane Crow" alike, on the costs of and struggles against segregation and discrimination by gender as well as by race.

Recent scholarship by the historian Doreen Drury suggests that Murray also struggled mightily in her personal life to come to terms with her transgendered sexuality. Drury argues that Murray was sexually attracted to women, but did not view herself as a lesbian. Instead, Drury posits, Murray viewed herself as a latent heterosexual male. In 1957 Murray met Irene Barlow and maintained a loving, spiritual, and emotional relationship with her until Barlow's death in 1973.

As she made her political and spiritual pilgrimage through the twentieth century, Murray changed professions from time to time. Leaving her position with the New York law firm, she taught in West Africa at the Ghana Law School in Accra (1960–1961) and coauthored *The Constitution and Government of Ghana* (1961). After her studies at Yale, she served as vice president at Benedict College, a black school in South Carolina (1967–1968). In 1968 she accepted a temporary position at Brandeis University. Five years later she relinquished a tenured position there as the Louis Stulberg Professor of Law and Politics in the American studies department, for she felt called to the Episcopal ministry, and in 1976 she earned an MDiv from the General Theological Seminary in New York City. That year the Episcopal Church changed its policy to permit the ordination of women priests, and in January 1977 at the National Cathedral in Washington, D.C., she was ordained and consecrated one of the church's first female priests and the first who was black. From 1977 to 1984 she served churches in Washington, D.C., and Baltimore, Maryland.

An accomplished writer as well as lawyer, educator, and minister, Murray also attempted to achieve social change by writing letters to newspapers and public officials, an activity she called "confrontation by typewriter." She published essays and articles in progressive magazines and in law and theology journals, and authored *States' Laws on Race and Color* (1951). That volume, the first to comprehensively catalog the pervasiveness of racial segregation laws in almost every state in the nation, proved invaluable to the NAACP's Legal Defense Fund and others seeking to overcome Jim Crow. She wrote an account of her North Carolina family and childhood, *Proud Shoes: The Story of an American Family* (1956), a volume of poetry, *Dark Testament and Other Poems* (1970), and her posthumously published, award-winning *Song in a Weary Throat*, which was republished as *Pauli Murray: The Autobiography of a Black Activist, Feminist, Lawyer, Priest, and Poet* (1989).

At the forefront of social change in the United States from the 1940s to the 1980s, Murray achieved prominence as a lawyer, poet, educator, and minister. She worked to promote the rights of workers during the New Deal, of African Americans, notably in the 1940s, and of women, especially in the 1960s, as she demonstrated her commitment to "consciousness combined with action" and "reconciliation as well as liberation." By the 1970s she could note with some pleasure that, though she routinely lost her legal challenges in the 1930s and 1940s, the Supreme Court eventually decided cases the way she had hoped, and she had "lived to see my lost causes found." And yet she looked in vain for "a truly integrated society," and she entered the ministry in part because, she realized, "we had reached a point where law could not give us the answers." In an afterword to her autobiography, a friend, the historian Caroline F. Ware, wrote of "the tremendous energy that drove her to achieve excellence in everything she undertook." The recipient of honorary degrees and other awards, Murray retired in 1984 and died in Pittsburgh, Pennsylvania.

FURTHER READING
The Pauli Murray Papers are in the Schlesinger Library, Radcliffe College, Cambridge, Massachusetts.
Murray, Pauli. *Pauli Murray: The Autobiography of a Black Activist, Feminist, Lawyer, Priest, and Poet* (1989).
Diamonstein, Barbaralee, ed. *Open Secrets: Ninety-four Women in Touch with Our Time* (1972).
Obituaries: *Washington Post* and *New York Times*, 4 July 1985; *Jet* (22 July 1985).
This entry is taken from the *American National Biography* and is published here with the permission of the American Council of Learned Societies.

PETER WALLENSTEIN

Murray, Peter Marshall (9 June 1888–19 Dec. 1969), physician, was born in Houma, Louisiana, the son of John L. Murray, a longshoreman, and Louvinia Smith, a laundress and practical nurse. Murray received his B.A. from Dillard University in 1910. His medical degree, awarded by Howard University in 1914, was one early sign of his drive and talent, bolstered by solid preparation. Like many Howard students, he financed his medical education by working a full-time government job, in his case a clerical post in the census bureau. But his responsibilities went beyond his own wants. His ailing mother in Louisiana also needed help, so he took a second job, a night watchman position; its sole advantage was that it gave him some time for study. After receiving his degree he remained in Washington, first as an intern at Freedmen's Hospital and then as a Howard instructor in surgery. In 1917 he married Charlotte Wallace, the daughter of a Colored Methodist Episcopal minister; the couple had one child.

By 1920, his preparation over, Murray was ready to make his own way. The path he took was that of hundreds of talented young blacks. Their destination was New York City and Harlem, and the influence Murray would exert—in the 1920s and until his death there a half century later—in opening medicine and surgery to blacks made him as much a part of the Harlem Renaissance as JEAN TOOMER or LANGSTON HUGHES. By the mid-1920s he had performed surgery and won staff privileges in a number of New York and New Jersey hospitals, whose staffs were previously all white, including in 1928 the prestigious Harlem Hospital (where Murray was the second black physician admitted to practice and where he served until his retirement in 1953). In 1930 he was the first black physician to be board certified in gynecology. In 1949, as a member of the Medical Society of the County of New York, the nation's largest affiliate of the American Medical Association, Murray became the first black to gain a seat in the AMA House of Delegates. From that position he pushed the AMA to officially repudiate the segregation practices of southern medical societies. Though the AMA took no action that year, Murray sensed a growing readiness, and in 1950, aided by pressure from the NAACP and from the National Medical Association editor WILLIAM MONTAGUE COBB (who like Murray had been battling AMA exclusion for years), Murray won the passage of an AMA resolution urging segregated affiliates to eliminate racial restrictions. Leaving the pace of change up to the southern societies, the AMA appeal brought no immediate change, but it did put segregation under a cloud. By the mid-1950s, owing to pushing by black doctors at the local level, every southern state organization but two had integrated. Now, the way lay open for black doctors not just to mingle professionally with white physicians but also—and more important—to gain staff privileges at southern hospitals. In addition they were able to become part of the medical referral system and win appointment to state and local boards of health—all relevant to professional success and all contingent on membership in local AMA affiliates. In 1954, in recognition of Murray's achievements, his New York medical society elected him its first black president.

Murray's success in breaching white barriers was draped in irony, however. He built it not by militantly challenging white discrimination but by going along with medical segregation, to the extent of publicly acknowledging white medical superiority and black professional dependence. Had BOOKER T. WASHINGTON been alive in the pre–World War II era, he surely would have applauded Murray's strategy, for it seemed to bear out his own faith that the route to black inclusion in white society lay in hard work and accommodation to segregation.

One memorial to Murray's racial conservatism was his long campaign as leader of the all-black National Medical Association (which he served as president-elect in 1931, president in 1932, and chairman of its publications committee from 1943 to 1957) to improve black hospitals—a crusade that aimed to improve opportunities for black physicians

and patients alike. That campaign also exposed the sharp division within the black medical community between those who, like Murray, supported accommodation and a minority that insisted on integration as the only moral course.

In 1932, for example, spokesmen for the latter strategy—a group led by a combative New York doctor, LOUIS TOMPKINS WRIGHT—strongly opposed the creation of a new, all-black Veterans Administration hospital in the city on the ground that it would transplant segregation to a region where it had not yet taken root. To Murray, who favored the VA facility, Wright's position was not only misguided but also demagogic. Admittedly, he told the National Medical Association in his 1932 presidential address, demanding "our full rights" instead of half a loaf "might send a thrill down your spines." But when the issues were the welfare of thousands of black veterans and the professional needs of hundreds of black doctors, Murray felt, as did one professional correspondent, that "we must look to practical results rather than resort to cowardly cant." Discrimination was objectionable, but "we must not be so everlastingly afraid of so-called segregation that we rule ourselves out of … opportunities. It is not the ideal America that we are dealing with…. It is a prejudiced America."

Although the VA hospital project collapsed, Murray persevered in what he saw as the more realistic approach to "prejudiced America." One critical need of black Americans was better hospital care. Not only were available facilities shockingly deficient, but also their physicians were poorly prepared and professionally torpid. To Murray the surest way to address those problems was by improving black hospitals. Usually that meant providing white directors; blacks, he lamented in 1932, simply were not capable of running their own facilities.

But black physicians would ultimately benefit. One defect of black medical education was a lack of accredited internships (a shortfall of about twenty per year). Although 1,400 approved posts went unfilled in white hospitals each year, Murray's preferred solution was not to try to open any of them to blacks but to create accredited internships by making black hospitals better. Although his foes protested, Murray's segregationist strategy usually prevailed in the councils of white foundations (such as the Duke Endowment and the Rosenwald Fund) because they found it philosophically preferable to integration. Probably Murray owed his own rise in establishment medicine to the same cause: whites liked him because he was safe, a man unlikely to make an issue of segregation.

To his credit, however, once he was inside white gates, Murray tried to push them open to other blacks—witness his effort against AMA segregation. Moreover, where black professional gains clearly depended on forcing open the doors of white institutions, Murray did not hang back. Thus, early on he lined up the NMA behind the desegregation of health department staffs, medical schools, and internships in tax-supported hospitals. Integrationists like Louis Tompkins Wright might have finally won the day, but until desegregation occurred, conservative realists like Murray pushed black medicine steadily ahead via the segregated road.

In the annals of African American history, the career of Peter Marshall Murray is in a way comparable to those of PHILLIS WHEATLEY, MATTHEW HENSON, JULIAN BOND, and EDWARD BROOKE. Just as those individuals registered important firsts— the first black published poet, polar explorer, major party vice presidential nominee, and modern U.S. senator—Murray, too, was a breaker of color bars, in medicine and public health. He died in New York City.

FURTHER READING

Murray's papers are in the Moorland-Spingarn Research Collection at Howard University.

Beardsley, E. H. *A History of Neglect: Health Care for Blacks and Mill Workers in the Twentieth-Century South* (1987).

Logan, Rayford W. *Howard University: The First 100 Years, 1867–1967* (1969).

Murray, Peter. "Presidential Address," *Journal of the National Medical Association* 24 (Nov. 1932): 1–8.

Obituary: *New York Times,* 21 Dec. 1969.

This entry is taken from the *American National Biography* and is published here with the permission of the American Council of Learned Societies.

E. H. BEARDSLEY

Murray, Robert Fulton, Jr. (19 Oct. 1931–), geneticist and physician, was born in Newburgh, New York, the son of Robert Fulton and Henrietta Frances (Judd) Murray. Murray stayed close to home for most of his education, completing a B.S. with a pre-med concentration from Union College in Schenectady, New York, in 1953, before proceeding to the University of Rochester School of Medicine for his MD in 1958. Murray married Isobel Ann Parks on 26 August 1956, while still in medical

school. Their marriage produced four children: Colin Charles, Robert Fulton III, Suzanne Frances, and Dianne Akwe.

After completing medical school, Murray and his wife moved to Denver, Colorado, where he began a long career in clinical medicine. He completed an internship at Denver General Hospital (1958–1959) before moving on to the University of Colorado Medical Center for a residency in internal medicine (1959–1962). For the next three years (1962–1965) Murray served as a senior surgeon for the U.S. Public Health Service, assigned to the National Institute of Arthritis and Metabolic Diseases (NIAMD), a division of the National Institutes of Health (NIH). It was at the NIAMD that Murray undertook his first major study of genetic disorders, a passion he would continue to explore by completing a fellowship in medical genetics and an M.S. in Genetics at the University of Washington (1965–1967).

Murray's research interests at this time concerned diseases related to polymorphic proteins, molecules that carry out most of the biological processes within the cell. The structure of a protein is determined by its sequence of amino acids, which in turn is specified by the DNA sequence that codes for the specific protein. Because proteins' functions are tied so closely to their structure, a single point change in the DNA sequence (a mutation) can have a dramatic effect on cellular function. In many proteins mutations cause problems so severe that only the correct sequence produces a working molecule, but others, known as polymorphous proteins, may have several functional structures. Sickle cell anemia is one of the best-known conditions caused by a single point mutation. Hemoglobin produced by the sickle cell gene is less effective at carrying oxygen than normal hemoglobin, but the gene is thought to have survived because it provides some resistance to malaria.

The 1950s and 1960s, when Murray was just undertaking his research, were dramatic times for genetics and genetic medicine. James Watson and Francis Crick's announcement of the structure of DNA in 1953 opened the doors to understanding how genetic material was transmitted and reproduced; in the mid-1960s, Marshall Nirenberg and H. Gobind Khorana led teams that mapped the relationship between DNA sequence and protein expression—the so-called "genetic code." In the response to these developments, a growing number of geneticists and physicians were coming to believe that any number of inheritable diseases could be prevented or possibly even cured through genetic screening and treatment programs. As genetic screening tests became available for diseases such as sickle cell anemia, PKU, Tay-Sachs, some states began making these tests mandatory for marriage and admission to public schools. Although many physicians, including Murray, were enthusiastic about the possibilities of this research for human health, some in the black community pointed a skeptical finger at genetics' long association with scientific racism and eugenics. In the late 1970s, for example, the Du Pont Company required genetic screening as a preemployment test and refused to hire workers with sickle cell.

Murray, who had joined the faculty of Howard University as an assistant professor of pediatrics and medicine in 1967, soon became a leading advocate for an ethical and socially responsible approach to genetic medicine. In 1972 he was named chair of the National Research Council's Committee for the Study of Inborn Errors of Metabolism and the ad hoc Committee on S-hemoglobinopathies; that same year he also joined the scientific advisory board of the National Sickle Cell Anemia Foundation. In 1982 he served on the Office of Technology Assessment's Advisory Panel on Occupational Genetic Testing. Along with James E. Bowman, a professor of medicine and pathology at the University of Chicago, he authored what has become the standard textbook on genetic issues in persons of African heritage. Meanwhile Murray's career continued to advance at Howard, where he held a number of academic and administrative appointments, including Chief of the Medial Genetics Unit (1968–1972 and 1975–), Chairman of the Department of Genetics and Human Genetics (1976–), and professorships in pediatrics, medicine, and oncology.

Murray was a fellow of the American College of Physicians, the American Association for the Advancement of Science, and member of the Institute of Medicine at the National Academy of Sciences. He served on the board of directors of the Hastings Center, a leading bioethics research institution, since 1972. Murray's professional memberships included the American Medical Association, the American Society of Human Genetics, the Environmental Mutagen Society, the Genetics Society of America, and Sigma Xi.

FURTHER READING

Bowman, James E., and Robert F. Murray Jr. *Genetic Variation in Peoples of African Origin* (1990).

Harris, Ron. "Tampering with Genes: A New Threat to Blacks?" *Ebony* (Sept. 1980).

Lindee, M. Susan. *Moments of Truth in Genetic Medicine* (2005).

Who's Who in America, 46th ed. (1990–1991).

AUDRA J. WOLFE

Muse, Clarence E. (7 Oct. 1889–13 Oct. 1979), actor, producer, and writer of plays and films, was born in Baltimore, Maryland, the son of Alexander Muse and Mary Sales. He was educated at Dickinson College in Carlisle, Pennsylvania, where he became interested in music and participated in choral groups; although he graduated with a bachelor's degree in International Law in 1911, he immediately embarked on a musical and theatrical career. In 1907 he married Frieda Belle Moore; the marriage was apparently dissolved soon after the birth of their son in 1910.

Muse sang with a hotel employees' quartet in Palm Beach, Florida, for one season. In 1912 he helped organize the Freeman-Harper-Muse Stock Company at the Globe Theater in Jacksonville, in partnership with comedian George Freeman and choreographer Leonard Harper. The company toured in *Stranded in Africa* in 1912, starring Muse in the role of King Gazu.

By 1914 Muse was married to and performed in vaudeville on the East Coast with Ophelia (maiden name unknown), billed as the team of Muse and Muse. They had two children before their marriage ended. They settled in Harlem, New York, where they established the Muse and Pugh Stock Company (in partnership with another vaudevillian) at the Franklin Theatre. They soon moved their company to the Crescent Theatre, where they produced several plays during their brief residence, including *Another Man's Wife*, starring the two Muses. The company moved again to a better venue, the Lincoln Theatre, where it merged with the Lincoln Players, a newly formed stock company already in residence. In mid-1916 the group joined the Lafayette Players, who were just beginning to establish a name for themselves at the Lafayette Theatre.

Muse soon became the leading dramatic actor of the Lafayette Players. For the next six years he was featured in a variety of plays, such as *The Master Mind*, *A Servant in the House*, and *Dr. Jekyll and Mr. Hyde*; in the last he played in whiteface makeup, creating a sensation. The Muses' last performance together was in 1922.

In 1920 Muse became one of the founding directors of the Delsarte Film Corporation in New York City, a black independent film company, for which he wrote, produced, and starred in several films (1920–1921), including *Toussaint L'Ouverture* and *The Sport of Gods*, based on a story by PAUL LAURENCE DUNBAR. He was supported in these films by members of the Lafayette Players.

After this film venture Muse moved to Chicago, where he became associated with the Royal Gardens Theatre, owned by an African American businessman. There he produced and directed shows such as *Hoola Boola* (1922), *Rambling Around* (1923), *The Charleston Dandies* (1926, 1927), *The Chicago Plantation Revue* (1927), and *Miss Bandana* (1927). These shows toured the South on the newly organized black Theater Owners' Booking Association (TOBA) circuit. He also directed and supervised the production of the opera *Thais*, which was performed in Chicago and St. Louis with a cast of nearly two hundred singers and actors.

In 1929 Muse went to Hollywood, at the invitation of the Fox Film Corporation, to portray the ninety-year-old leading character, Uncle Napus, in an all-black musical of plantation life, *Hearts in Dixie* (1929), under a twelve-month contract at a reported salary of $1,250 per week. Muse remained in Hollywood for the rest of his career. He became the protégé of white director Frank Capra, who used him in several films; the most notable was *Broadway Bill* (1934), a horse-racing film in which Muse played the black companion and alter ego of Warner Baxter, the white star, while observing the distance in rank and station that the color barriers of the time required. Although Muse played a subservient domestic in this and most of his other Hollywood films, he managed to maintain a dignity in his carriage and manner that was unusual for black house servants in these early films. Capra treated him with great sensitivity and respect, and when he remade *Broadway Bill* with Bing Crosby, as *Riding High* (1950), Muse reprised his original role.

Other notable films that Muse made in his fifty-year stay in Hollywood were *Huckleberry Finn* (as Jim, 1931); *The Count of Monte Cristo* (as a deaf-mute, 1934); *So Red the Rose* (as Cato, a rebellious slave, 1935); *Show Boat* (1936); *Spirit of Youth* (1937); *Way Down South*, for which he cowrote the story,

Clarence Muse, in a half-length portrait, with porcelain statue. (Library of Congress.)

screenplay, and songs with LANGSTON HUGHES and played the part of Uncle Caton (1939); *Broken Strings*, an independent black film in which he starred as a concert violinist, his finest screen role (1940); *Porgy and Bess* (1959); *Buck and the Preacher* (1972); *The World's Greatest Athlete* (1973); *Car Wash* (1976); and *The Black Stallion*, his last film (1979).

While making films, Muse also starred in *Porgy* and in a new production of *Dr. Jekyll and Mr. Hyde* presented by the Lafayette Players, who were transplanted to the Lincoln Theatre in Los Angeles after they left New York in 1928. He also directed the WPA's Federal Theatre production of HALL JOHNSON's *Run, Little Chillun*, presented in Los Angeles and Hollywood in 1938–1939. He is credited as cowriter of a number of songs, including "When It's Sleepy Time Down South."

At some point Muse married Willabella Marchbanks, with whom he had one child before they divorced in 1949. His final marriage, in 1954, was to Irene Claire Kellman.

Muse was elected to the Black Filmmakers Hall of Fame in 1973. He died on his ranch in Perris, California, a week after his ninetieth birthday.

FURTHER READING

Documents relating to Muse are in the Schomburg Center for Research in Black Culture at the New York Public Library. Muse's publications include *Way Down South* (1932), written with David Arlen, and *The Dilemma of the Negro Actor* (1934).

Bogle, Donald. *Blacks in American Films and Television: An Illustrated Encyclopedia* (1988).

Leab, Daniel J. *From Sambo to Superspade: The Black Experience in Motion Pictures* (1988).

Peterson, Bernard L., Jr. *A Century of Musicals in Black and White: An Encyclopedia of Musical Stage Works by, about, or Involving Black Americans* (1993).

This entry is taken from the *American National Biography* and is published here with the permission of the American Council of Learned Societies.

BERNARD L. PETERSON

Myers, George A. (5 Mar. 1859–17 Jan. 1930), influential barber and longtime Republican Party leader in Ohio, was born in Baltimore, Maryland. He was the oldest of three children of Isaac Myers, a prominent shipyard owner and labor activist in Baltimore, and his first wife, Emma Virginia Myers, who died when George was nine. Educated initially in the preparatory division of Pennsylvania's Lincoln University, George returned home to complete his education in Baltimore's public schools after his father married Sarah Elizabeth Deaver.

Barred from attending the racially segregated Baltimore City College High School, and unwilling to study medicine elsewhere, as his father wished, George Myers first moved briefly to Washington, DC, to work as a housepainter. He soon returned to Baltimore to undergo training as a barber, and in 1879, moved to Cleveland, Ohio.

George Myers was married twice. In 1884 he married Annie E. Deans, a Baltimore schoolteacher, and they had one son, Herbert Deaver Myers, born in 1885 and named in honor of his stepmother. His second wife was Maude E. Stewart of Cleveland, whom he married in April 1896. They had one daughter, Dorothy Virginia Myers (Grantham), a longtime Cleveland schoolteacher.

In Cleveland, Myers first worked as a foreman in the well-known Waddell House Barber Shop. In 1888, having cultivated a large personal clientele, Myers opened his own barbershop at the city's new Hollenden Hotel, which he ran for the next four decades. A shrewd, perceptive businessman with an appealing personality, Myers gradually transformed his operation into Ohio's most famous stop for politicians, including governors and as many as eight U.S. presidents among those who frequented the Hollenden shop.

By 1892 Myers had also built his own strong political name, becoming a valued confidant to the kingmaker Marcus A. Hanna, and was named an alternate delegate from Cleveland to the Republican national convention in Minneapolis. A thoughtful conservative on most political and economic matters, Myers became one of the party's most trusted political references, and few African American office-seekers from Ohio could advance without his recommendation. Yet he remained a determinedly backstage operative, refusing offers of personal appointment.

Myers served as a prudent lieutenant in Hanna's 1896 operation, carefully marshaling black delegates from Ohio and key southern states on William McKinley's behalf. After McKinley's inauguration in 1897, Myers served as a key White House advisor on issues of patronage among Midwestern African Americans. In 1897 and 1898, Myers represented Hanna on the influential Republican State Executive Committee, and Myers's voluminous correspondence includes letters from influential Republican players of both races, seeking his advice or his blessing. After serving three terms on that committee, he retired from active politics in 1904.

In 1900 Myers served as an alternate delegate at large from Ohio to the Republican national convention in Philadelphia, and played a key role in preserving the strength of southern party delegations. But he lost interest in politics after the 1901 assassination of President McKinley and the 1904 death of Hanna, his friend and mentor. Myers refused a 1912 offer from the Republican National Committee, one brokered by Booker T. Washington, to manage the party's national campaign activities among black voters, the first time a black man had been asked to handle the party's entire national effort.

A relentless defender of the political and civil rights of African Americans, Myers successfully demanded that Cleveland newspapers stop using offensive racial terms, and opposed creating a "Jim Crow" YMCA branch for the city in 1911 (*The Booker T. Washington Papers*, 10:578). He once took the noted white American historian James Ford Rhodes to task for neglecting African American participants in historical writings about the Reconstruction period, even though Rhodes was a close personal friend. Their decade-long correspondence provides a unique perspective on matters of both race and history.

Despite poor health, Myers continued to operate his Hollenden Hotel barbershop until his death, after the hotel management informed him of their plans to replace his entire staff—some thirty barbers, manicurists, and others—with white employees once he retired. While preparing for a vacation in Hot Springs, Arkansas, Myers died of a heart attack in the ticket office at the Union Trust Building in Cleveland, Ohio.

His collected papers and correspondence, housed at the Ohio Historical Society, offer a rich, comprehensive inside view of Republican politics of the period, particularly during the 1890s and early 1900s.

FURTHER READING

Garraty, John A., ed. *The Barber and the Historian: The Correspondence of George A. Myers and James Ford Rhodes, 1910–1923* (1956).

Harland, Louis R., ed. *The Booker T. Washington Papers*, vol. 10 (1987).

James, Felix, "George A. Myers." In *Dictionary of American Negro Biography* (1982).

BENJAMIN R. JUSTESEN

Myers, Isaac (13 Jan. 1835–26 Jan. 1891), labor leader, was born in Baltimore, Maryland, the son of free parents whose names and occupations are unknown. Myers was barred from public education, but he did attend a private day school run by a local clergyman. Leaving school at age sixteen he served an apprenticeship with a leading black ship caulker and then entered the trade himself, becoming by the age of twenty a supervisor, responsible for caulking some of Baltimore's largest clipper ships. During this period he married Emma V., though neither the precise year of the marriage nor her full maiden name is known. They had three children, the first born in 1859.

Myers worked as a porter and shipping clerk for a wholesale grocer from 1860 to 1864, ran his own store for a year, and then went back to ship caulking. Soon after he returned to this trade, however, the city's white caulkers went on strike, demanding that all black caulkers be fired. By the efforts of the city government and the police, more than a thousand black workers were driven from their jobs. In response Myers proposed that the ousted men establish their own shipyard. Canvassing the local black churches he managed to raise $10,000 in $5 shares. With another $30,000 borrowed from a ship captain, the group bought a shipyard and railway and in the winter of 1866 established the Chesapeake Marine Railway and Dry Dock Company. Within six months the firm was providing work for more than 250 African Americans. The business grew rapidly, virtually dominating the local shipbuilding industry and winning a major government contract against the bids of shipbuilders in several cities. Soon whites, too, joined the workforce, while the mortgage—scheduled to run six years—was paid off in five.

Myers's first wife died in 1868, and he married Sarah E. Deaver; they had no children. The following year Myers helped organize a statewide union of "colored mechanics," with representatives from every trade. At about the same time he was elected head of Baltimore's Colored Caulkers' Trades Union Society. Segregation was still the rule in the labor movement, but the relatively harmonious cooperation between these black unions and their white counterparts led Myers to think that it might be possible to achieve the same kind of relationship on a larger scale—a national union of African Americans working in tandem with the leading white labor organizations.

White leaders were having similar thoughts, and in August 1869 the National Labor Union (NLU) for the first time opened its convention to African Americans and to women. Myers, who attended with nine other blacks (four from Maryland), galvanized the convention with a speech hailing biracial-cooperation. "Silent, but powerful and far-reaching," he said, "is the revolution inaugurated by your act in taking the colored laborer by the hand and telling him that his interest is common with yours." The speech was warmly received, and although little integration occurred within individual unions, the convention did agree to admit black unions as affiliates.

At their own national labor convention that December, 214 African American delegates from eighteen states established the Colored National Labor Union (CNLU), with Myers as president. A few months later he set out on a nationwide tour promoting the CNLU gospel of public education, apprentice training, unionism, and cooperative business ventures. Speaking to audiences of both black and white workers Myers reiterated that they must work together, but he stressed that black unity was the necessary first step. Unions and cooperative associations, he explained, were the key to black prosperity.

By this time Myers had left the shipyard to become a messenger to the collector of customs in Baltimore, a position that made him only the second African American in Maryland history to receive a federal appointment. In 1870, with support from both white and black Republicans, Myers became a special agent of the Post Office Department. Returning to the NLU that summer—now as one of five black delegates—Myers found his political loyalties put to the test because many of those present had decided that labor should abandon the Republicans and form a new party dedicated to labor reform. The black delegates strongly disagreed. Though acknowledging the Republicans' flaws, they felt that it would be foolish to abandon the party that had emancipated their race for an untested alliance with white workers who had so often excluded them in the past. When Myers urged the convention to stick with the Republicans he aroused such intense hostility that he was almost assaulted. The Labor Reform Party was endorsed in a landslide vote, and black delegates attended no more NLU conventions.

Five months later Myers ended his presidential term at the Colored National Labor Union. Progress had been made in organizing black workers, he reported, but not as much as had been hoped, and the union faced severe financial difficulties. Calling for the creation of more black unions Myers urged members to avoid politics and concentrate on "the business interests of the people." He closed by stressing again the need for solidarity among black workers as a necessary prelude to cooperation among workers of all races. The CNLU survived only one more year, disbanding soon after its third and final convention in 1871.

Myers worked as a detective in the Post Office Department from 1872 until his retirement in 1879, after which he operated a coal yard in Baltimore and then held another federal appointment as a gauger from 1882 to 1887. He organized and directed the Maryland Colored State Industrial Fair Association in 1888, founded the Colored Business Men's Association of Baltimore and the Colored Building and Loan Association, and was an active member of the African Methodist Episcopal (AME) Church. He died from paralysis at his home in Baltimore.

"If American citizenship means anything at all," Myers told the NLU convention in 1869, "it means the freedom of labor, as broad and universal as the freedom of the ballot." While the larger institutions with which Myers worked—the white labor movement and the Republican Party—proved less staunch than he had hoped in defending those two freedoms, he held to his conviction that black workers could, by their own energy and talent, achieve the status they sought. Although he suffered many disappointments in pursuing that vision, Myers's career represents an important milestone in the history of the African American labor movement.

FURTHER READING

Foner, Philip S. *History of the Labor Movement in the United States*, vol. 1 (1947).

Foner, Philip S. *Organized Labor and the Black Worker, 1679–1973* (1974).

Foner, Philip S., and Ronald L. Lewis. *The Black Worker: A Documentary History*, vol. 1 (1978).

Laurie, Bruce. *Artisans into Workers: Labor in Nineteenth-Century America* (1989).

Montgomery, David. "William H. Sylvis and the Search for Working-Class Citizenship," in *Labor Leaders in America*, ed. Melvyn Dubofsky and Warren Van Tine (1987).

This entry is taken from the *American National Biography* and is published here with the permission of the American Council of Learned Societies.

SANDRA OPDYCKE

Myers, Stephen A. (1800–13 Feb. 1870), who called himself "Agent and Superintendent of the Underground Railroad," and had also worked as a steamboat steward, was born in Hoosick, Rensselaer

County, New York, legally defined at birth as the property of Dr. Johnathan Eights, a doctor who established a practice in Albany in 1810.

New York's 1799 law for the gradual abolition of slavery provided that Myers should be emancipated at the age of twenty-eight, but he was freed earlier, when he was eighteen. He then worked as a grocer before getting a job as steward on the *Armenia*, one of the faster steamboats on the Hudson River, making the trip from New York City to Albany entirely in daylight.

Myers married in the late 1830s—there is no published record of Harriet Myers's maiden name. Their children, at least those who survived infancy and were still alive in 1860, were Stephen Jr., born around 1840; Abram, one year younger; Catherine, born around 1846; and Harriett, born around 1849.

By the early 1840s, both Stephen and Harriet Myers had begun assisting fugitive slaves from points further south, where no gradual emancipation had been legislated, to either settle in New York or move on to Canada. Their station served a route running from New York City up the eastern side of the Hudson River, sustained by towns with either Quaker meetings or settlements of free African Americans, through Poughkeepsie to Albany. One route then ran west along the Erie Canal, crossing into Canada at Buffalo. Myers's Albany Committee of Vigilance was praised by his fellow abolitionist DAVID RUGGLES as "the most efficient organization in the State of New York in the business of aiding the way-worn and weather-beaten refugee from slavery's shambles" (Hodges, p. 181).

Among the Underground Railroad operators they were connected with were WILLIAM STILL in Philadelphia, JERMAIN W. LOGUEN in Syracuse, and people as far away as Delaware and Maryland, as well as in Canada. HARRIET TUBMAN, one of the railroad's most famous conductors, frequently relied on the Myers as a stop on trips from the south to Auburn, where she lived, or Canada. From 1851 to 1855 they were assisted by WILLIAM H. JOHNSON, a man of African descent born to free parents in Alexandria, Virginia, in 1833; Johnson later had some familiarity with the preparation for John Brown's attempted insurrection in Harper's Ferry.

Myers founded the Northern Star Association, publisher of the *Northern Star and Freeman's Advocate*, 1842–1843. Over the course of ten months (1855–1856) Myers assisted 287 fugitives, paying $542.36 for transportation and $76.60 to feed them. Over six months during late 1857 and early 1858, they assisted another 118. He finally had to make a semipublic appeal for funds, because "The hundreds of fugitives that have fallen in my care during the last twelve years have required a great deal of labor and expense to make them comfortable. They are sent to me by the Underground Railroad, south of Albany, and in many cases they come poorly clad and are greatly in want of clothes, such as coats, pants, and under garments, both males and females" (Christianson, p. 68).

Moving several times during the 1850s around the Arbor Hill neighborhood in Albany, the Myers settled at 194 Livingston Avenue, which is still standing. A renovation project began in 2007 to preserve it as a museum. Myers established the Florence Farming and Lumber Association in 1848, promoting settlement of a black farming community on land in Oneida County, New York, donated by Gerrit Smith, a real estate promoter who acknowledged that, of the eighteen thousand acres he had once owned in the town of Florence, the few hundred remaining were of very moderate fertility. The association eventually dissolved.

Most of the funds for Myers's operation came from members of the newly formed Republican Party, including Thurlow Weed, publisher of the *Albany Evening Journal*. Myers eventually depended on the railroad for his income, retiring from work on the steamboat to devote himself full-time to the cause, living on about 10 percent of each dollar he received. He aided many to obtain work with local farmers, or other job openings, considering placement in the countryside safe and enabling them to earn some money. One of Myers's higher-profile passengers was Charles Nole, or Nalle, who had settled for a time in rural Sand Lake, where be was betrayed and apprehended. This set off a widely publicized campaign to prevent his reenslavement, including a dramatic physical rescue on 27 April 1860 by a large crowd of local abolitionists, led by Harriet Tubman.

After the Civil War, Myers returned to working as a steward, at the Delavan House and the Fort William Henry Hotel, and as janitor to the postmaster in New York City. He also edited the *Pioneer*, and the *Telegraph and Temperance Journal*.

Myers died in 1870 due to a diseased kidney. Funeral services were held at the African Methodist Episcopal Church on Hamilton Street, where the Myers had been members. At least one child, Stephen Jr., had married by then; his wife Julia and their children Abraham L., 5, and Elizabeth, 8, were among the surviving family members. The Stephen and Harriet Myers Middle School, constructed in 2005 in Albany, is named in honor of the couple's work.

FURTHER READING

Christianson, Scott. *Freeing Charles: The Struggle to Free a Slave on the Eve of the Civil War* (2010).

Hodges, Graham Russell. *David Ruggles: A Radical Black Abolitionist and the Underground Railroad in New York City* (2010).

Ripley, C. Peter. *The Black Abolitionist Papers: The United States, 1830–1846* (1991).

Obituary: *Albany Evening Times*, 14 Feb. 1870.

CHARLES ROSENBERG

Myers, Walter Dean (12 Aug. 1937–), author, was born Walter Milton Myers in Martinsburg, West Virginia, to George Ambrose and Mary Green. When he was three years old, his mother died while giving birth to another son. Myers's father decided he could not raise Walter, and gave him to Florence Dean, a friend of Myers's mother who was of German and American Indian descent, and her husband Herbert, an African American. The adoption was an informal arrangement. The family soon relocated to Harlem, New York, where Herbert took work as a factory worker and janitor. Florence taught reading in high school, and was herself self-taught. In the late 1960s, following the publication of his first children's book, Walter changed his middle name to Dean, after the people who became his parents.

Myers attended local schools, including Stuyvesant High, one of New York's most selective public high schools. Florence encouraged him to read. Like many young boys, Myers favored comic books. One day at school, however, a teacher discovered him reading a comic and took it from him, destroying it. Myers was aghast until the teacher replaced the comic with a number of prose books from the school's library; Myers later recalled this as a seminal event in the development of his love of language and writing.

Myers's school environment was difficult. He had a speech impairment that made class presentations and readings difficult and embarrassing, and his fellow students made fun of him. He fought with students who made fun of him, and soon earned a reputation for his bad behavior. His teachers appear to have been supportive. One of them thought that he might have an easier time pronouncing words he himself had chosen, and encouraged him to

Walter Dean Myers tours his old Harlem neighborhood in 2010. (AP Images.)

write. Myers was a good student, and his grades were strong, but on his seventeenth birthday he dropped out and joined the U.S. Army.

Myers served for three years, until 1957, at which poiMyers, Walter Deannt he returned to New York and took on whatever work he could find, including postal and factory jobs. Meanwhile, he wrote. He began submitting short stories for publication, though at first with limited success. He was briefly a stringer for the *National Enquirer*. In 1968 he submitted a story to a competition held by the Council on Interracial Books for Children (CIBC). His story, *Where Does the Day Go?* won first place. The book—a children's story about a walk in the park and a conversation about life's various unexplained mysteries, such as that of the title—was accepted for publication by Parents Magazine Press and published in 1969. Myers's career as an author of children's and young people's books was under way. It was around this time, too, that he married Constance Brendel, who was herself a writer and who helped Myers to bring his works of fiction to life. Together they would have three children.

Myers was a prolific writer, and he soon became a popular and widely respected one. Among his early well-known work was *The Dragon Takes a Wife* (1972), *Fly, Jimmy, Fly!* (1974), and *The World of Work: A Guide to Choosing a Career* (1975). His first novel-length work for young adults, *Fast Sam, Cool Clyde, and Stuff* (1975), came about through a misunderstanding with an editor over a short story. The editor mistakenly believed that the story was one section of a larger work in progress. When she later bumped into Myers at a social gathering, she asked how his novel was coming along. Myers improvised the plot of his nonexistent novel and was offered a book contract.

Myers's work for young adults became standard reading in school libraries and in high school reading programs. In 1979 *The Young Landlords* won the coveted Coretta Scott King Award, given to works of fiction of particular interest or edification to young African American readers. Myers would win two more such awards during his long and successful career.

His books often tackled difficult or complex social themes, such as violence, poverty, and the toll exacted on young men by war. His novel *Fallen Angels* (1988) recounts the story of a young man killed during his first firefight in Vietnam and is based on the life and death of Myers's own brother, Sonny. The book was controversial for both its language and the honesty of its violence. *Scorpions* (1988) is about the problem of guns in black neighborhoods and in the hands of young people. His novel *Somewhere in the Darkness* (1993) recounts the way that violence and crime shape the relationships between fathers and their sons.

Perhaps Myers's most respected and well-known work, *Monster,* appeared in 1999. The book recounts what happens after a young man is bullied by some of the kids in his neighborhood into taking part in a robbery and murder. *Monster* won both the Coretta Scott King Award and the American Library Association's first Michael L. Printz Award. Among Myers's more recent work is *Malcolm X: A Fire Burning Brightly* (2000), *The Greatest: The Life of Muhammad Ali* (2000), *Bad Boy: A Memoir* (2001), *Patrol: An American Soldier in Vietnam* (2002), *The Hellfighters: When Pride Met Courage* (2006), *Jazz* (2006), and *Ida B. Wells: Let the Truth Be Told* (2008), among many, many others. By 2011, Myers, who was living in New Jersey, had published some eighty books. *Lockdown* (2010) was a National Book Award finalist in the Young People's Literature category.

FURTHER READING
McElmeel, Sharron. "A Profile: Walter Dean Myers." In *Book Report* (2001).
"Myers, Walter Dean." In *Encyclopedia of World Biography*. http://www.notablebiographies.com/news/Li-Ou/Myers-Walter-Dean.html
Rand, Donna, Toni Trent Parker, and Sheila Foster.*Black Books Galore! Guide to Great AfricanAmerican Children's Books* (1998).

JASON PHILIP MILLER

Nabrit, James Madison, Jr. (4 Sept. 1900–27 Dec. 1997), civil rights attorney and educator, was born in Atlanta, Georgia, the oldest of eight children born to James Madison Nabrit Sr., a Baptist pastor, and Augusta Gertrude Nabrit. As a child in the Jim Crow South, Nabrit was exposed to racial violence at an early age. He was just ten years old when he saw an African American man lynched and burned for celebrating the victory of the black boxer Jack Johnson over his white opponent Jim Jeffries. Nabrit attended Morehouse College High School and went on to Morehouse College, where he was captain of the debate team. Nabrit received a B.A. with honors in 1923 and enrolled at Northwestern University School of Law in Chicago. While in law school, Nabrit supported himself by working as a baggage handler at a train station, and he also taught English and political science at Leland College in Baker, Louisiana, from 1925 to 1927. On 30 December 1924, he married Norma Clarke in Aiken, South Carolina. They had one son, James Madison III, born in 1932. Nabrit graduated from Northwestern with honors in 1927 but did not receive any job offers, although his white classmates quickly found employment.

After serving as dean of Arkansas State College in Pine Bluff, Arkansas, from 1928 to 1929, Nabrit moved to Houston, Texas, and established the firm of Nabrit, Atkins, and Wesley. Between 1930 and 1936, Nabrit worked on several civil rights cases, many of which focused on ensuring African Americans' ability to vote in primary elections. In 1936 Nabrit became associate professor of law at Howard University in Washington, D.C. Two years later, he assembled over two thousand case studies to establish what is considered the first civil rights course in an American law school. Nabrit assisted with some of the civil rights cases that helped lead to the desegregation of public schools. The case for which he is perhaps best known, *Bolling v. Sharpe*, was filed in 1951 by Nabrit and fellow attorney George E. C. Hayes to overturn racial segregation in the Washington, D.C., public schools. Though Nabrit and Hayes were defeated at the initial trial, they were invited by the Supreme Court to argue their case along with four other school desegregation cases from Virginia, Delaware, South Carolina, and Kansas that had made their way to the Court by 1952. Nabrit and Hayes argued *Bolling v. Sharpe* in December 1953 and pursued a strategy that differed from those used in the four state cases, now called *Brown v. Board of Education*. The *Brown v. Board of Education* cases used the Fourteenth Amendment and its equal protection provision to argue the inherent unconstitutionality of segregation. Because *Bolling v. Sharpe* dealt with Washington, D.C., a federal territory, and the Fourteenth Amendment applied directly to states, Nabrit and Hayes instead argued the principle of strict scrutiny. This principle required a clear justification for laws that sanctioned differential treatment of racial groups, and Nabrit and Hayes countered that in the instance of school segregation, there was none. The Supreme Court agreed, and on 17 May 1954, it issued rulings in *Brown v. Board of Education* and *Bolling v. Sharpe* declaring segregated public schools unconstitutional.

In 1960, Nabrit succeeded Mordecai Johnson to become the second African American president of Howard University. As Nabrit stated in a press conference that July, his aim was for Howard "to become a great university" (Logan, 464), and his administration witnessed an expansion in the university's enrollment, faculty, and physical plant. Nabrit also directed more research funds to the humanities and social sciences, fields often slighted in favor of economics and natural science, and established a College of Fine Arts. In 1961 Nabrit engineered the transfer of the Freedmen's Hospital to the university; the hospital, established in 1862, was one of the only places to which black doctors had regular access. The facility served as a teaching hospital for Howard students and eventually became Howard University Hospital in 1975. Nabrit took a brief leave from Howard between 1965 and 1967 when President Lyndon Johnson appointed him to the U.S. delegation to the United Nations. In 1966 Nabrit became the first African American to serve as deputy to the chief delegate, the second-highest position in the delegation.

Nabrit's presidency coincided with the surge of student activism sweeping college campuses across the country in the 1960s, as civil rights agitation was joined by protest against the war in Vietnam. Nabrit himself was hesitant to associate the two causes, telling a 1966 White House Conference on Civil Rights, "I don't want to put that albatross around the neck of the Civil Rights Movement" (Logan, 461). After thirty students prevented a speech by Selective Service System Director General Lewis B. Hershey in March 1967, the university issued a policy statement permitting campus demonstrations so long as they did not interrupt scheduled activities. The attempt to reconcile free speech and orderly operations was not enough to appease some student activists, who boycotted classes on 10 May. Nabrit came under fire from the American Association of University Professors for expelling eighteen students and firing five professors for their participation in disorderly demonstrations in 1967. Nabrit retired in 1969 but maintained that student unrest had not motivated that decision.

An avid golfer, a widely published legal scholar, and a recipient of fifteen honorary degrees, Nabrit died at age ninety-seven in Washington, D.C. Though the challenge of ensuring integrated education continued, Nabrit played an indispensable role in dismantling one of the most debilitating structures of segregation. Although Nabrit assumed a cautious stance toward the student activism of the 1960s, he helped establish the legal civil rights framework that encouraged further agitation not only among African Americans but also among women, gays and lesbians, Latinos, and Native Americans in later decades. His commitment to civil rights was carried on by his son, who was an attorney with the NAACP Legal Defense and Education Fund from 1959 to 1989.

FURTHER READING

Cottrol, Robert J., Raymond T. Diamond, and Leland B. Ware. *Brown v. Board of Education: Caste, Culture, and the Constitution* (2003).

King, Colbert I. "James Nabrit: A Lawyer's Gallantry," *Washington Post*, 3 Jan. 1998.

Logan, Rayford W. *Howard University: The First Hundred Years, 1867–1967* (1969).

Obituary: *New York Times*, 30 Dec. 1997.

FRANCESCA GAMBER

Nabrit, Samuel Milton (21 Feb. 1905–2003), biologist, university administrator, and public policy maker, was born in Macon, Georgia, the son of James Madison Nabrit, a Baptist minister and educator, and Augusta Gertrude West. The elder Nabrit, who taught at Central City College and later at Walker Baptist Institute, encouraged his son to prepare for a career in higher education by studying Latin, Greek, and physics. Samuel rounded out his education by playing football and baseball, and honed his managerial and journalistic skills working on his high school (and later college) student newspaper. He entered Morehouse College in Atlanta in 1921, and after receiving a traditional liberal arts education, was awarded a B.S. in 1925. Samuel's brother, JAMES MADISON NABRIT JR., was an important aide in the NAACP's legal team during the 1950s. Working closely with THURGOOD MARSHALL in his unsuccessful attempts to begin the desegregation of graduate and professional schools in Texas and Oklahoma, James Nabrit later served as president of Howard University.

The precocious Nabrit's college career was so successful that he gained the attention of Morehouse president JOHN HOPE, who recruited Nabrit to teach zoology. Beginning in 1925 Nabrit taught biology while he also worked on and earned an M.S. at the University of Chicago. He then pursued a doctorate at Brown University in Rhode Island under the tutelage of the distinguished zoologist J. W. Wilson, and during the summers between 1927 and 1932 he conducted research on the regeneration of fish embryos at the famed Marine Biological Laboratory at Woods Hole, Massachusetts. Despite his academic achievements, Nabrit was snubbed by the renowned African American zoologist ERNEST EVERETT JUST at Woods Hole, who believed that African Americans in the sciences had to prove themselves superior to their white peers in order to deserve recognition.

Nabrit was awarded his doctorate from Brown in 1932, making him the first African American to receive a Ph.D. from that prestigious Ivy League institution. Furthermore, his research on regeneration was published in the renowned *Biological Bulletin*, and citations of his work appeared in such important scientific publications as the *Anatomical Record*, the *Journal of Experimental Zoology*, and the *Journal of Parasitology*. Indicative of the significance of his research, his groundbreaking contributions were still being cited as late as 1980.

After receiving his doctorate, Nabrit served in two administrative posts at Atlanta University for the next twenty-three years, first as chair of the department of biology, and then after 1947 as dean of the graduate school of arts and sciences. Nabrit's most significant administrative contribution during his years as dean was his nurturing of the National Institute of Science, an organization founded in 1943 for the purpose of resolving research and teaching problems peculiar to African American scientists, most of whom were teaching at historically black colleges and universities. Nabrit also wrote articles and book reviews for journals, including *Phylon, Science Education*, and the *Negro History Bulletin*, in order to broaden the perspectives, opportunities, and expectations of African American scientists and mathematicians.

The capstone of Nabrit's administrative career came in 1955, when he was appointed president of the fledgling, all-black Texas Southern University in Houston. Serving for more than a decade, Nabrit was also appointed to key national educational association committees. Moreover, his services were welcomed by federal officials in the U.S. Department of State and the U.S. Department of Health and Human Services. Nabrit was appointed to the National Science Board by President Dwight D. Eisenhower in 1956. A decade later, President Lyndon B. Johnson appointed Nabrit to the highly controversial Atomic Energy Commission. Nabrit's long and illustrious career ended in 1981, after a fifteen-year tenure as the director of the Southern Fellowship Fund.

Despite his numerous achievements, Nabrit experienced some disappointing moments. When Allan Shivers, the arch-segregationist governor of Texas, spoke at Texas Southern University in 1956, the integrationist NAACP protested during the ceremony. As the president of a state-supported all-black college dependent on people like Shivers for funding, Nabrit was inhibited from challenging the system of segregation or offering support to such demonstrations. Although Nabrit had supported Texas Southern students in their protest against the kidnapping and torture of Felton Turner in March 1960, he created a stir among African American activists when he warned Eldrewey Stearns, a prominent Houston reformer, about the use of college students as picketers at the Loew's Theater in downtown Houston in 1961.

Nabrit, with his gradualist style of reform (an orientation similar to that of JAMES E. SHEPARD, the president of the North Carolina College for Negroes), will be remembered for his concrete efforts to bring African Americans into the mainstream of American scientific and technical education.

FURTHER READING

Cole, Thomas R. *No Color Is My Kind: The Life of Eldrewey Stearns and the Integration of Houston* (1997).

Manning, Kenneth R. *Black Apollo of Science: The Life of Ernest Everett Just* (1983).

VERNON J. WILLIAMS JR.

Nagin, C. Ray (11 June 1956–), businessman, politician, mayor of New Orleans during Hurricane Katrina (2005), was born Clarence Ray Nagin in New Orleans's Charity Hospital to Clarence Ray Nagin Sr., who worked as a fabric cutter by day, and a janitor at New Orleans City Hall at night, and Theresa, who worked at the lunch counter in a local New Orleans Kmart store. Clarence Ray Jr. and his two sisters grew up in the historic Seventh Ward section of New Orleans, home to many Creole, Roman Catholic families. He attended O. Perry Walker High School in New Orleans, where he excelled in baseball and basketball. In 1978, after having played on a baseball scholarship, Nagin graduated from Tuskegee University in Alabama with a degree in accounting. In 1982 Nagin married Seletha Smith, with whom he had three children, Jeremy, Jarin, and Tianna.

After short stints with General Motors in the late 1970s and the Associates Corporation in Dallas, Texas, in the early 1980s, Nagin became controller of Cox New Orleans, a local cable company. He climbed up the ranks to become the vice president and general manager of Cox Communications. After successfully turning around Cox's poorest-performing cable television operations into a moneymaker, Nagin turned to politics. Running on a platform of anticorruption and economic development, in 2002 C. Ray Nagin Jr. was elected mayor of New Orleans, succeeding Marc Morial. Shortly after taking office, Mayor Nagin launched an anticorruption operation within city government, ending systematic corruption within the Taxicab Bureau, Utilities Department, and the vehicle inspection process. Outspoken about unfairness or what many viewed as a historical preferential political treatment, Mayor Nagin allowed for his own cousin to be arrested in conjunction with the Taxicab Bureau corruption. However, Nagin's most infamous public feud occurred in the days after Hurricane Katrina, a powerful Category 5 storm, devastated New Orleans and left more than 80 percent of the city under water. After having ordered a mandatory evacuation, the first in the city's history, Nagin was faced with tens of thousands of residents who were unable to leave the city and who needed aid and evacuation in the days after the storm. Mayor Nagin publicly and bluntly criticized the delays in aid to the city, and expressed anger with what he saw as the slow federal and state response.

In the first months after the storm, Mayor Nagin was burdened with many questions, including how to rebuild and repopulate the mostly devastated and evacuated city. When many residents were concerned about future demographics in New Orleans, as the city pre-Katrina was majority African American, Mayor Nagin assured the city's displaced residents that New Orleans would remain a "Chocolate City." His remarks were viewed as polarizing, which caused him to lose his appeal with white voters in the 2006 election. While he originally captured 85 percent of white voters, the 2006 election represented a dramatic shift with Nagin winning only 20 percent of white voters and 80 percent of the black electorate.

In his second term as mayor of New Orleans, Nagin undertook an unprecedented level of capital improvement—street and landscape enhancement projects to rebuild New Orleans to prestorm conditions. Mayor Nagin successfully lobbied the federal government to secure $6 billion to rebuild and improve the city's levee protection system. During his administration, the city secured $10.4 billion for housing and infrastructure development. The Nagin administration was also key in securing $8.8 billion in tax incentives, credits, and relief through the Gulf Opportunity Zone legislation. He restored the city's population to more than 75 percent of its pre-Katrina numbers, surpassing many experts' repopulation projections by more than 100,000 residents.

Nagin was the past president of 100 Black Men of Metro New Orleans. He has sat on the boards of the United Way and Covenant House. He has been a member of the Orleans and Jefferson Parish Business Councils and the Greater New Orleans Education Foundation. In 1993, he earned a Masters in Business Administration from the Freeman School of Business at Tulane University. In 1994 he was given the Distinguished Business Partner Award by the Louisiana State Board of Education. In 1995 he earned a Young Leadership Council Diversity and Role Model Award. In 1998 the *Gambit Weekly* named him New Orleanian of the Year.

Despite Nagin's effort to maintain the city's black foothold in politics, in 2010 C. Ray Nagin, term-limited, was replaced by his former rival Mitch Landrieu, who became the city's first white mayor in over thirty years.

In 2011 Nagin's self-published memoir, *Katrina's Secrets: Storms After the Storm* was released. In it Nagin defended his actions during Hurricane Katrina, and also highlighted his role in helping the city recover in the years that followed. Some reviews of the book questioned the veracity of Nagin's claim that he feared the CIA might assassinate him because of his criticism of President Bush's inaction during Katrina.

FURTHER READING

Firestone, David. "TV Executive Defeats Police Chief to Become Mayor of New Orleans." *New York Times*, 3 Mar. 2002.

Miester, Mark. "Ray Nagin." *Tulanian* (2003).

Stevens, Andrew. "Despite Controversy, Mayor Ray Nagin Remains the Champion of New Orleans." *City Mayors*, 28 May 2006.

ALEXANDER J. CHENAULT

Nail, John E. (22 Aug. 1883–6 Mar. 1947), real estate entrepreneur, was born in New London, Connecticut, the son of John Bennett Nail, a businessman, and Elizabeth (maiden name unknown). Nail was raised in New York City and graduated from a New York City public high school. His father was the role model on which he based his own business career. The elder Nail was an entrepreneur who prospered from the growth of Harlem and its inflated real estate market. He was one of several blacks who prior to the turn of the century recognized the potential of Harlem's housing market. The younger Nail, known to friends and family as Jack, worked for a time in his father's business, where he first entered into the real estate profession in the 1900s. After a brief stint as a self-employed real estate agent in his own Bronx office, Nail accepted employment with PHILIP A. PAYTON JR., whose Afro-American Realty Company was one of the most successful black-owned real estate firms in New York at the time.

Payton, a real estate trailblazer like Nail's father, had also seized the opportunity to invest in the Harlem real estate market. Between 1890 and 1914 southern blacks flooded into New York City in pursuit of social and economic betterment. Many gravitated to Harlem, where a sizable black settlement had taken shape as a result of earlier migration. By 1910 there were 91,709 blacks living in New York City, 60,534 of whom were born in the South. This mass migration of blacks placed an unforeseen pressure on the city. Racial antagonism and violence intensified, as did social and residential segregation. Areas formerly open to blacks became restricted, and blacks found themselves relegated to an increasingly crowded Harlem. Nail saw his opportunity in this evolving situation. Following Payton's example he educated himself on the intricacies of New York City's segregated housing market. In 1907, when Payton's company suffered financial setbacks (it went bankrupt in 1908), Nail and a colleague, Henry C. Parker, resigned their sales positions and founded the real estate firm of Nail & Parker, Inc. In 1910 Nail married Grace Fairfax; they had no children.

Nail was the moving force in Nail & Parker. He served as president, and Parker served as secretary-treasurer. From modest beginnings the firm, with the implementation of an aggressive advertising campaign, developed into a full-service company that offered mortgages to blacks, collected rents, and bought, sold, managed, and appraised properties. Nail recognized the need for black property ownership as a way to counter the discriminatory real estate practices of white lending institutions and white landlords. He urged blacks to invest in Harlem property to secure the future of the black community there. The firm engineered a significant coup when it successfully broke the deeply entrenched unwritten covenant that maintained that certain Harlem blocks were to remain white; blacks could neither own nor rent property in these areas. Furthermore, the covenant established restrictions in an attempt to prevent black real estate agents from controlling the Harlem housing market. It was a difficult battle, but ultimately Nail & Parker were victorious in their efforts to dismantle the system.

In 1911 Nail & Parker, Inc., negotiated a million-dollar deal. Working as agents for St. Philip's Episcopal Church, of which Nail was a member, the real estate firm figured prominently in the transaction in which the church purchased several properties in Harlem for $1,070,000. The annual rents collected on these investments amounted to twenty-five thousand dollars. The church, the real estate agents, and the black community all benefited from this transaction. Nail & Parker aggressively pursued other Harlem properties not only to increase the company's revenues but also to provide housing and stability for the community. The firm also sold a property for two hundred thousand dollars to MADAME C. J. WALKER, who had amassed a fortune developing hair-care products. In 1929 the firm was granted management responsibilities of the largest and finest apartment building in Harlem, which was owned by the Metropolitan Life Insurance Company. As their client list expanded and their transactions multiplied, Parker and Nail established respectable reputations both for themselves and for their business. Nail in particular earned respect from members of the white and black communities alike, and he emerged as an authority on property condemnation. Even the city of New York sought his expertise.

Despite Nail's status, black tenants claimed that he was an exploitive landlord who overcharged his tenants. The threat of a mass exodus from Harlem during the 1920s and early 1930s in response to exceedingly high prices for rentals was quelled when the company reluctantly reduced some rents. In his own defense Nail cited the high prices for rentals elsewhere in the city. Nail's philosophy reflected that of BOOKER T. WASHINGTON, who emphasized the importance of establishing an economic foundation on which blacks could build a stronger and more stable community and compete more directly with the white power structure.

Although Nail & Parker temporarily weathered the Depression, the firm collapsed in 1933, at which time Parker and Nail took forty-five shares of the company apiece, and the remaining ten shares went to Isador D. Brokow, their silent white partner. Parker and Nail parted ways, and that same year Nail established a new real estate venture, the John E. Nail Company, Inc., with Nail as president and David B. Peskin, a white real estate agent, as secretary and treasurer. The firm was active in several large real estate transactions, including as broker in a deal whereby the St. Philip's Church leased to Louis B. Lipman ten six-story apartment houses for an aggregate rental price of $1 million.

Nail's reputation earned him a place as the first black member of the Real Estate Board of New York, and he became the only black member of the Housing Committee of New York; he was also a member of the Harlem Board of Commerce. News of Nail's accomplishments extended beyond New York's boundaries; he acted as consultant for President Herbert Hoover's Committee on Housing during the Depression.

Nail's interests were not confined to housing. He and an influential coterie, among them ROBERT ABBOTT, publisher of the *Chicago Defender*, and HARRY PACE, a respected entrepreneur, engineered a campaign to discredit the race leader MARCUS GARVEY. Garvey's rise to prominence threatened their elite group, and they accused Garvey and his black nationalism philosophy of inciting hatred between the races. Nail and a self-styled Committee of Eight had nurtured a careful relationship with the white community, and they believed that Garvey's rhetoric undermined their efforts to stabilize race relations. The battle between Garvey, who charged his attackers with being "Uncle Tom Negroes," and the members of the committee represented a broader split between an elite group of blacks and the masses of lower-income blacks who supported Garvey's celebration of African culture and his philosophy of self-help. Ironically, the two opposing factions shared a belief in the importance of economic development.

Nail's deep commitment to the black community is reflected in his role in the development of the Colored Merchants' Association (CMA), created to advance race solidarity and economic stability. Unfortunately the first Harlem CMA cooperative, established in 1930, failed to attract black consumers, who complained of high prices during a time when people were just trying to survive. Nail was also concerned with the overall plight of urban blacks and for a time held the position of vice president of the New York Urban League. He was chair of the Finance Committee of the 135th Street Branch of the YMCA, which was located in the heart of Harlem, and was involved with the NAACP. Nail died in New York City.

FURTHER READING

Ingham, John N., and Lynne B. Feldman. *African-American Business Leaders: A Biographical Dictionary* (1994).

Osofsky, Gilbert. *Harlem, the Making of a Ghetto: Negro New York, 1890–1930* (1966).

This entry is taken from the *American National Biography* and is published here with the permission of the American Council of Learned Societies.

LYNNE B. FELDMAN

Nance, Ethel Ray (13 Apr. 1899–19 July 1992), secretary and administrative assistant, civil rights worker, researcher, and writer, was born Ethel Ray in Duluth, Minnesota, the youngest of four children of a racially mixed couple, William Henry Ray, a black man from North Carolina, and Inga Nordquist, a Swedish immigrant. Inga and William met and married in Minneapolis in the 1880s, settling in segregated Duluth in 1889 in an immigrant neighborhood. In a city with less than two hundred African American residents, the Rays faced hostility from their white neighbors, prompting resistance from the defiant and proud William Henry Ray, who kept his hunting rifle loaded for self-defense. William fortified Ethel and her siblings against racism with stark tales of racial oppression and heroic resistance he had witnessed in Raleigh, where his parents and their neighbors took up guns to protect northern teachers who had come South to educate blacks after the Civil War. The family's isolation generated Ethel's childhood desire to leave Duluth, yearnings that were later intensified by stories of the excitement of big cities and tales of college life relayed by students from Howard, Fisk, and other historically black universities, who worked at Minnesota resorts during summer vacations.

Ethel was educated in public schools in Duluth, graduating from high school in June 1917, having mastered secretarial skills rarely possessed in the black world at that time. That training later made her an invaluable resource to a long line of grateful executives that would include W.E.B. DuBois and CHARLES S. JOHNSON. She also received a parallel education in racial politics from her autodidact father who had his own library and subscribed to the *Messenger*, the *Guardian*, and *The Crisis*. Nance often read aloud the articles on racial struggle and uplift. Rounding out her youthful education in racial reality, in 1919 Nance was taken on an intensive four-month trip by her father. With his birth city, Raleigh, as the ultimate destination, the two made stops in Chicago, Philadelphia, Detroit, New York, and other major cities, where Nance was introduced to leading personalities in the African American world, including WILLIAM MONROE TROTTER and A. PHILIP RANDOLPH. In the South, she bore witness to the harsh segregation governing the lives of their southern relatives.

Financially unable to attend college, Nance began work in 1918, eventually landing a stenographer's position after a frustrating job quest prolonged by racial discrimination in Duluth. This first post came only when massive forest fires in northern Minnesota in 1918 created a high demand for workers. The Minnesota Forest Fires Relief Commission hired Nance first in Duluth, and then later in nearby Moose Lake, itself rampant with discrimination. The brutal and highly publicized lynching of three African American men near the family residence in Duluth in 1920 brought her back home. A personal and community turning point, this atrocity not only gave Ethel new awareness of the dangers of her hometown but it also galvanized Duluth's small black community and paved the way for the city's first NAACP branch, organized by Nance's ever-vigilant father.

Nance's participation in what would become a lifetime commitment to the NAACP and to W. E. B. DuBois began in 1921 when she introduced DuBois to members of the fledgling branch. Following DuBois's visit, she ardently embraced his call to work for the passage of the Dyer antilynching bill. Her lobbying of Minnesotans so impressed WALTER WHITE that he wrote her a personal letter of thanks and praise. This political work gave her some insight into the legislative process and resulted in a move to St. Paul, where, in what would be a stream of "racial firsts," Nance broke the secretarial color bar in the state legislature, becoming its first African American stenographer. Publicized in the local and national press, Nance's boundary-breaking activity brought letters of praise from women's and civil rights organizations and job offers from across the country. She accepted a position with the Kansas City Urban League, where she met Charles S. Johnson, editor of *Opportunity* magazine and director of research for the New York Urban League. Moving in the spring of 1924 to become Johnson's secretary and editorial assistant, Nance eagerly joined the ranks of other "New Negro" women seeking meaning and adventure in New York.

Nance's stay in New York was both brief and brilliant, and was the high point of her long career. Lasting under two years, the intense New York sojourn took place during the critical cultural coming-of-age period for black America and for the generation that gave birth to the Harlem Renaissance. New York provided the opportunity for Nance's stellar administrative and organizational skills to flourish. In addition to serving as Johnson's secretary, she sought new talent in college publications, helped edit *Opportunity*, and undertook research projects. She helped organize the first *Opportunity Awards Dinner* held in 1925 and participated in the ensuing compilation of *Survey Graphics's* groundbreaking "Negro" number, which gave birth to *The New Negro*. An extension of the *Opportunity* office, "Dream Haven," the apartment she shared at 580 St. Nicholas with REGINA ANDERSON ANDREWS, nurtured members of the younger generation, including LANGSTON HUGHES, COUNTÉE CULLEN, ZORA NEALE HURSTON, AARON DOUGLASS, and other "New Negroes," who wined, dined, and discoursed with Carl Van Vechten and other members of the older generation. W. E. B. DuBois regarded her as a valuable liaison to the younger generation and deeply regretted Nance's reluctant return to Duluth in 1926 to attend her ailing mother.

From 1926 until a short but exciting position at the founding of the United Nations in San Francisco in 1945, Nance worked in various positions, none of which fully utilized her talents and ambitions. Outside the office she enjoyed a fulfilling life. She sponsored literary discussions (using books lists from DuBois), participated in civil rights organizations, and followed national and international currents in letters with DuBois and others. Nance took another brief secretarial position in the state legislature in St. Paul in 1926, leaving to become associate head resident at the Phyllis Wheatley Settlement House in Minneapolis (1926–1928). Not heeding her father's advice that she run for political office, she became Minneapolis's first policewoman of color, working from 1928 to 1932; then became secretary to the Commissioner of Education in St. Paul from 1937 to 1940. In 1929 she married Leroy Williams and between 1932 and 1934 gave birth to their two sons, Thatcher and Glenn Ray. From 1940 to 1943 she was an administrative assistant at Hampton Institute, moving to Seattle, Washington, in 1943 to be with her second husband, Clarence Nance. Spending four exhilarating months in San Francisco in 1945, she was DuBois's assistant when he became NAACP special consultant during the founding meeting of the United Nations. Nance was invigorated by her contact with delegates from all over the world and regarded this four-month assignment as the second high point in her career.

From 1945 to 1953, Nance was an administrative assistant in the NAACP's San Francisco office, helping the organization establish its West Coast regional site, while finding time to do research, act as sales agent, and provide other assistance to DuBois. In 1953 she once again accepted a position with Charles S. Johnson, when he became the first black president of Fisk University. Her return to San Francisco in 1954 was marked by intense volunteer activities in civil rights and women's organizations, while employed in secretarial positions at the Veterans Administration, from 1954 to 1956; the San Francisco school district, 1956 to 1964; and the U.S.

Post Office, from 1964 to 1969. Helping to found the San Francisco Historical and Cultural Society in 1959, Nance was delighted to serve as program director and research assistant from 1970 to 1977. As renewed interest in the Harlem Renaissance emerged, she enjoyed sharing her reflections with scholars while working on DuBois's memoirs; she would remain in contact with him up to his death in 1963. In the early 1970s she assisted Regina Andrews in compiling "A Chronology of African Americans in New York," which, while unpublished during their lives, served as source for the Schomburg's successful millennium exhibition and book *The Black New Yorkers: The Schomburg Illustrated Chronology* (2000). At the age of seventy-eight in 1977 she received her B.A. from the University of San Francisco, becoming its oldest graduate. Upon Nance's death in 1992 the San Francisco Board of Supervisors adjourned in honor of her distinguished service to the community.

FURTHER READING

Two oral histories that Nance undertook in the 1970s contain source material for her life and work. The one completed by Ann Shockley is part of the Black Oral History Collection at Fisk University and is accessible online at http://www.fisk.edu. Part of the Black Minnesotan's project sponsored by the Minnesota Historical Society, David Vassar Taylor's interview, which includes Nance's reaction to the Duluth lynchings, is available at www.collection.mnhs. The Bancroft Special Collections Library at the University of California, Berkeley, holds 170 letters between Nance and W.E.B. DuBois.

Lewis, David Levering. *When Harlem Was in Vogue* (1979).

Lewis, David Levering. *W. E. B. DuBois: The Fight for Equality and the American Century* (2000).

Smith, Jesse Carney, ed. *Notable Black American Women* (1992).

Wintz, Cary. *Encyclopedia of the Harlem Renaissance* (2005).

Obituary: *San Francisco Examiner*, 19 July 1992.

ONITA ESTES-HICKS

Nance, Lee (dates unknown), political writer and activist, was born in Newberry, South Carolina, the son of a storekeeper, politician, and former slave named Lee A. Nance. Little else is known of Nance's early years. The elder Nance, however, served as delegate to the South Carolina Constitutional Convention from 14 January 1868 to 18 March 1868. He was president of his local Union League and in 1868 was elected to

the South Carolina House of Representatives, but he was assassinated on 19 October 1868 by whites (three other representatives and one senator also were killed that year) before he could take his seat. One source points to the Ku Klux Klan as being behind the killing, while a Works Progress Administration narrative by Jane Wilson more specifically blames a white man named Murtishaw for the murder. The older Nance's death was part of a grisly pattern of political violence during the Reconstruction period that shaped his son's views. Southern whites angered by the upheaval caused by the defeat of the Confederacy and the emancipation of slaves viciously intimidated and killed black voters and officeholders in a campaign to strip African Americans of their political rights and return control of the South to white supremacists.

By 1880, if not earlier, Nance was lecturing around the North, advocating black rights. In Chester, Pennsylvania, for instance, he delivered public remarks demanding that "We want no more than a white man's chance; we want no less. It is one of their liberties to have opinions; to think them; to speak them to others, and to act in accordance with those opinions. It is one of ours, too, and we demand that it be recognized (*Christian Recorder*, 16 Dec. 1880). By November 1882 he was working in the office of the Controller of Currency in Washington, D.C., and becoming influential. He read a paper at the home of General William Starke Rosecrans for several congressmen that appeared as a pamphlet in 1884. *The Industrial or Material Status of the Colored Race* criticized politics as a path of progress and bitterly mentioned the death of his father, along with other black politicians, as an example of the empty promises of Republicans. He also demanded that Congress create a commission to investigate the true condition of African Americans to see if they were in need of government help. Ending with a grim warning that if America did not do justice to African Americans grave dangers awaited the nation, Nance vividly conveyed the sense of urgency in this fragile period after the death of Reconstruction.

Nance's convictions earned him some renown in black leadership circles, and the editor of the AME Church's *Christian Recorder* had "no hesitation in ranking him with the thoughtful men of the day; indeed, with the really able men" (27 Sept. 1883). But the *Recorder* was uneasy about the radical opinions that Nance had printed in a letter to the paper:

It is my deep conviction that a great fight is to occur upon our land during your and my day. It will be between the people and the powerful moneyed monopolies. The latter are at present seeking to control the whole political and business interests and judicial affairs of the Republic—all in behalf of interests which clash with the people's. The people, though now slumbering as to such a matter, will yet become aroused and indignantly demand the oppressive monopolies to hold; let alone the interests and affairs of the government. This the monopolists will not do; the fight will begin; it is inevitable. Aside from this there is ahead, fast approaching us as a people, great danger (27 Sept. 1883).

In 1886 even the *New York Times* took note of Lee Nance "of Washington," mentioning that he had become involved in a political protest against a white Republican district leader and storeowner who refused to sell to black customers.

By 1893 Nance had moved again, this time to Chicago. He wrote *Pen Picture of the World's Columbian Exposition*, a pamphlet extolling the majesty of the Chicago World's Fair that purportedly sold over a million copies and brought him some fame and fortune. The next year he wrote his most scathing criticism of U.S. race relations in his pamphlet *A Republic or Despotism, Which?* Nance again voiced his conviction that political parties did not serve black voters and outlined how much of the wealth of America was built by descendents of Africa. Most emphatically, he warned that rising racial discrimination had the potential to corrupt American political values and turn the nation from republicanism to despotism. The pamphlet was dedicated to the victims of mob violence, and the subject of lynching received special focus as the most glaring example of American injustice. Along with IDA BELL WELLS-BARNETT and a few others, Nance was one of the early voices calling attention to the issue of lynching. He emphasized the sin of lynching and offered many detailed descriptions of the gruesome deaths black Americans suffered at the hands of white mobs. By emphasizing the cruelty of torture, Nance impressed upon his readers the importance of staying focused on the main issue: no matter what the crime committed by an African American, lynching was morally wrong and had no place in a republic.

Although responsible for only a few pamphlets, Lee Nance is an important voice in the black freedom struggle of the late nineteenth century. During the chaos of the post-Reconstruction period, his voice represented a continuation of the quest for black freedom born in the antislavery movement and affirmed after the Civil War. His writings identified many themes that would grow in importance in the next century: distrust of automatic black support for the Republican Party; a focus on lynching as a primary roadblock to black advancement; celebration of black contributions to the nation; and the belief that segregation and racism violated America's political promise.

FURTHER READING
"Distinction for a Colored Man," *New York Times*, 27 Aug. 1893.
Foner, Eric. *Freedom's Lawmakers: A Directory of Black Officeholders during Reconstruction*, rev. ed. (1996).
Holt, Thomas. *Black Over White: Negro Political Leadership in South Carolina during Reconstruction* (1977).
McPherson, James M. *The Abolitionist Legacy: From Reconstruction to the NAACP* (1975).
Moore, Jacqueline M. *Leading the Race: The Transformation of the Black Elite in the Nation's Capital, 1880–1920* (1999).

MICHELLE KUHL

Nance, Ray (10 Dec. 1913–28 Jan. 1976), jazz musician, was born Ray Willis Nance in Chicago, Illinois. His parents' names and occupations are unknown. Nance displayed musical ability early. At age six he took piano lessons from his mother, and at nine he began five years of violin study with a private teacher. By his fourteenth birthday Nance was accepted at the Chicago College of Music. At first his study of the violin was meant to please his mother, he said, "but after a time, I got to like it." He continued instruction with Max Fischel, the college's best teacher, for seven more years while he attended public school.

Nance's high school, Wendell Phillips, had an excellent music program. There he learned to play trumpet, mainly on his own. He played in the school band and also learned to twirl the baton, becoming, he claimed, "the shortest drum major anyone ever saw." His full adult height was five feet four inches. In addition he played violin with the school's symphony, although he was not yet a match for an older student, Milt Hinton, who went on to become a leading jazz bassist.

After graduating around 1930 Nance attended Lane College in Jackson, Tennessee, intending to start his own band. Instead he was expelled after a single semester for a firecracker prank. After returning to Chicago he formed a sextet, which soon became a staple at Dave's Cafe on the South Side, playing for dancing, performing novelty vocal numbers, and improvising enough for Nance to develop jazz skills.

Nance's chief influence was the trumpeter LOUIS ARMSTRONG, although some of his early recorded solos also show the influence of Harry James (though without James's characteristic vibrato). Nance also listened to the best jazz violinists of the era: Joe Venuti, whose technique he "appreciated"; STUFF SMITH, who aroused Nance's greatest enthusiasm; and the classically trained Eddie South, whose playing was closest to Nance's own later style.

After several years at Dave's Cafe, Nance's sextet moved to the Midnite Club in 1935 for an extended stay. In February 1937, by which time the group had split up, Nance was ready to join the EARL HINES Orchestra at Chicago's Grand Terrace Ballroom. With Hines he played trumpet, not violin. He remained with the band for almost two years, gaining "a world of experience" during engagements in California and New York City. Nance recorded his first novelty vocal while with Hines, the precursor of many more recordings.

Information is sketchy, but Nance probably married Gloria (maiden name unknown) at some point in the later 1930s. When the Hines band prepared for another road trip Nance stayed behind and joined HORACE W. HENDERSON's band at Swingland in January 1939. Nance and Emmett Berry were the band's trumpet soloists, and Nance resumed playing violin. He recorded one of his best string solos with Henderson, two thirty-two-bar choruses of "Kitty on Toast," which the composer-critic Gunther Schuller describes as displaying "a level of skill ... beyond most 'jazz' violinists of the period."

When Henderson made travel plans in March 1940, Nance again chose to remain in Chicago. Working as a single at a musical variety club, he added tap and acrobatic dancing to his repertoire. In recognition of his diverse talents a bandmate nicknamed him "Floorshow."

In November 1940, when the veteran trumpeter COOTIE WILLIAMS left the Duke Ellington band to join Benny Goodman, Ellington surprised many by hiring Nance to replace Williams. Nance proved equal to the challenge. He learned the "growl" technique, an Ellington trademark initiated by Bubber Miley and closely identified with Williams. The style was more than "just a matter of blowing with the mute," Nance explained. "You've got to concentrate to produce a certain sound.... It has great descriptive quality."

In the pianist-composer BILLY STRAYHORN's "Take the 'A' Train," Nance's first recorded Ellington feature, in February 1941, Nance played what was quickly recognized as a classic trumpet solo. With mute, then open horn, he created subtly inflected phrases memorable in themselves yet naturally coalescing. Ellington soon made full use of Nance's violin as well. In June 1941 Nance recorded his initial string solo with the band, "Bakiff," and seven months later he recorded one of his most celebrated violin solos in "Moon Mist."

In 1944 Nance took a leave of absence from the band for nine months of work-a-night jobs. By early 1945 he was happy to come back to the Ellington fold. Ellington immediately featured Nance's violin in recordings of "Prelude to a Kiss," "Caravan," and "Black Beauty." Nance continued as a band regular for the next eighteen years.

Some of Nance's best work on Ellington recordings includes his solos in various versions of some of the longer Ellington compositions and collaborations with Strayhorn, among them the symphonic suites *Black, Brown, and Beige* (1943) and *Liberian Suite* (1947) and the songs "Perfume Suite" (1945) and "Suite Thursday" (1960). Also noteworthy are Nance's contributions to such albums as *Historically Speaking—The Duke* (1956), *Blues in Orbit* (1959), *Anatomy of a Murder* (1959), *Afro-Bossa* (1963), and *Duke Ellington's Jazz Violin Session* (1964).

An incident in February 1961 stunned Ellington's public. During a Las Vegas engagement Nance, the tenor saxophonist Paul Gonsalves, and two other band members were arrested on charges of marijuana possession. At trial Gonsalves was acquitted, but Nance was discovered to have been convicted on drug charges in New York five years earlier; he received a sixty-day jail sentence.

Ellington accepted Nance back with the band upon his release, and by all accounts Nance's conduct as a performer was untainted over the next two years. Then during a government-sponsored tour of the Near East in September 1963 Nance and the recently returned Cootie Williams became involved in a mounting dispute. At a concert in Amman, Jordan, Nance refused to stand during national anthem ceremonies. A minor diplomatic scandal may have been headed off because senior band members persuaded Ellington that Nance's erratic behavior made him unfit to remain with the orchestra, and Ellington fired him.

Although Nance was heard in Ellington recordings from 1965 until 1971, he never officially rejoined the band. He led his own group in 1964, worked with a studio orchestra at the New York World's Fair in the mid-1960s, was with the clarinetist Sol

Yaged's group for six years until 1971, played with the pianist Brooks Kerr in 1973, and took part in Chris Barber's tour of England in 1974. He made albums under his own name and with Gonsalves. He died in New York City.

Ellington in his characteristically formal way once said that, musically, "Raymond has perfect taste." Whether or not that was actually the case, Nance was an important and affecting jazz soloist and was an integral part of the Ellington orchestra for many years. He seldom reached the heights of the great jazz soloists, but he left an indelible personal mark on the music's history.

FURTHER READING
Dance, Stanley. *The World of Duke Ellington* (1970).
Ellington, Duke. *Music Is My Mistress* (1973).
Hasse, John Edward. *Beyond Category: The Life and Genius of Duke Ellington* (1993).
Lawrence, A. H. *Duke Ellington and His World* (2001).
Tucker, Mark, ed. *The Duke Ellington Reader* (1993).
Obituary: *New York Times*, 30 Jan. 1976.
This entry is taken from the *American National Biography* and is published here with the permission of the American Council of Learned Societies.

ROBERT MIRANDON

Nanton, Joe (1 Feb. 1904–20 July 1946), jazz trombonist, was born Joseph N. Irish in New York City of West Indian parents whose names are not known. Joe, who came to be called Tricky Sam Nanton, first worked professionally in the early 1920s with the pianist Cliff Jackson. He held obscure jobs in Harlem, playing at Leroy's Club with the pianist Fat Smitty and the drummer Crip and then for about two years at another club with the pianist Earl Frazier, the banjoist Seminole, and Crip. In 1925 he rejoined Jackson's group, then called the Westerners, at the Nest Club.

In 1926 Nanton joined DUKE ELLINGTON's Big Band at the Kentucky Club. To this point he had been known as Joe Nanton. Fellow Ellington alto saxophonist Otto Hardwick explained, "I nicknamed Tricky Sam, too. He could always do with one hand what someone else did with two. Anything to save himself trouble" (Dance, 61). Nanton immediately became one of Ellington's featured soloists. He remained with the band throughout its years in residency at the Cotton Club, from 1927 to 1931, and then toured with the band except for a period in October 1937 when he had pneumonia. Late in 1945 he suffered a stroke. He was fit enough to resume touring with Ellington around May 1946 but died

soon afterward while in San Francisco with the band. Nanton was survived by his wife Marion; her maiden name and details of the marriage are unknown.

Nothing more is known of Nanton's life, but his colleague in Ellington's band, the cornetist REX STEWART, gave a sense of his personality:

> Before he got the nickname Tricky Sam, Joe was sometimes called the Professor, because he knew something about almost everything.... He was well acquainted with such erudite and diverse subjects as astronomy, how to make home brew, and how to use a slide rule. He could recite poetry by ancient poets that most of us never knew existed, and he knew Shakespeare.... [He was] a fierce nationalist and devoted follower of Marcus Garvey back in the thirties (when political awareness was unheard of in a musician).

Nanton was one of the most distinctive soloists in jazz. Emulating Ellington's trumpeter BUBBER MILEY he adapted Miley's "growl and plunger" technique to the trombone, combining vocalizing with a muted sound to achieve an almost human and conversational instrumental sound. A famous and characteristic solo may be heard on "Ko-Ko" (1940): focusing on a little two-note motif, Nanton effectively "speaks" the syllables "ya-ya" through his trombone over and over again, each time altering fine details of the motif's rhythm and pitch; instrumental jazz is often alleged to "tell a story," and here it almost does. Hundreds of excellent recorded examples survive, including several versions each of "East St. Louis Toodle-Oo" (1926–1927) and "Black and Tan Fantasy" (1927); "The Blues I Love to Sing" (1927); several versions of "Jubilee Stomp" (1928); "Yellow Dog Blues" (1928); "Harlem Flat Blues" (1929); "Hot Feet" (1929); "Stevedore Stomp" (1929), on which Ellington uncharacteristically featured Nanton playing open rather than muted trombone; several versions each of "Old Man Blues" and "Ring Dem Bells" (both 1930); "Mood Indigo" (1930); "It Don't Mean a Thing (If It Ain't Got That Swing)" (1932); "Slap Happy" (1938); "Blue Serge" (1941); "Just A-Settin' and A-Rockin'" (1941); and "Main Stem" (1942). In addition Nanton appears in the Amos 'n Andy movie *Check and Double Check* (1930) and Ellington's film shorts *Black and Tan* (1929), *Symphony in Black* (1934), and *Duke Ellington and His Orchestra* (1943).

FURTHER READING
Dance, Stanley. *The World of Duke Ellington* (1970, 1981).
Stewart, Rex. *Jazz Masters of the Thirties* (1972, 1982).

Obituary: *Down Beat*, 12 Aug. 1946.
This entry is taken from the *American National Biography* and is published here with the permission of the American Council of Learned Societies.

BARRY KERNFELD

Napier, James Carroll (9 June 1845–21 Apr. 1940), politician, attorney, and businessman, was born on the western outskirts of Nashville, Tennessee. His parents, William C. Napier and Jane E. (maiden name unknown), were slaves at the time of his birth but were freed in 1848. After manumission and a brief residency in Ohio William Napier moved his family to Nashville, where he established a livery stable business. James attended the black elementary and secondary schools of Nashville before entering Wilberforce University (1864–1866) and Oberlin College (1866–1868), both in Ohio.

James Napier began his career as a race leader and politician during the Reconstruction era in Tennessee as Davidson County commissioner of refugees and abandoned lands in the Freedmen's Bureau. In 1870 he led a delegation of black Tennesseans to petition President Ulysses S. Grant and Congress for relief from politically motivated violence aimed at nullifying black voting strength, for removal of the state's conservative government, and for rejection of the state's 1870 constitution. Unsuccessful in this effort Napier and his delegation urged the president and Congress to establish a national school system and to enforce the Fifteenth Amendment in their home state.

Napier subsequently received a position as a Treasury Department clerk in Washington, D.C., possibly the first African American to hold such a post. Under the tutelage of JOHN MERCER LANGSTON, the prominent black politician and acting president of Howard University, Napier entered Howard's law school in the District of Columbia. After obtaining a law degree in 1872 he returned to Nashville to begin a practice and in 1878 married Langston's only surviving daughter, Nettie Langston. Theirs was a childless union that lasted sixty years.

Under presidents Rutherford B. Hayes, James A. Garfield, and Chester A. Arthur, Napier held patronage appointments in the Nashville offices of the Internal Revenue Service, serving as a gauger (1879–1881), clerk (1883–1884), and deputy collector (1885). Owing to his business, legal, and political acumen Napier emerged as the ranking African American politician in Tennessee in the two decades after the Civil War. He served on the Nashville City Council from 1878 to 1889 and on the state Republican Party executive committee, was a delegate to six Republican National Conventions, and made an unsuccessful bid for election to the Fifth District congressional seat in 1898. As a city councilman Napier led successful efforts to hire the first African American schoolteachers in Nashville, to establish the city's first modern schools (including high school training) for African Americans, and to employ the city's first African American firefighters. In the 1890s, however, the rise to power of the "lily whites," dedicated to the removal of blacks from political participation in the South, and the emergence of more outspoken, younger African American leaders such as ROBERT R. CHURCH JR. of Memphis curtailed Napier's influence in state and local politics.

Napier remained a force to be reckoned with, however, because of his dignified manner, political connections, and behind-the-scenes approach to getting things done. His friendship and alliance with the educator BOOKER T. WASHINGTON in 1891 kept Napier in the inner circles of federal politics. He became a member of the so-called black cabinet that advised Republican presidents. Offered positions as consul to Bahia, Brazil, in 1906 and as consul general for Liberia in 1910, Napier refused both appointments. A recommendation from Washington led to Napier's appointment in 1911 as register of the U.S. Treasury, the most prestigious and highest federal position then available to an African American. Napier acquitted himself well in this position. Presiding over a staff of seventy-three, in addition to his official duties accounting for the receipt and expenditure of all public money, Napier found time to press for the continued development of the African American community. He testified before Congress in 1912 for passage of the Page Bill for equitable distribution of funds (set aside in the Morrill Acts of 1863 and 1890) for African American land-grant colleges in the South. Napier's efforts were to no avail. He resigned from his post two years later to protest President Woodrow Wilson's sanctioning of segregation in federal office facilities. After 1913 Napier retreated from involvement in national politics to focus exclusively on economic self-help in the black community.

Napier used his influence as lawyer, lecturer, businessman, head of the Nashville Board of Trade, and organizer of a branch of the National Negro Business League (NNBL) to promote economic and educational development among African Americans. Aware of the collapse of the Freedmen's Bank and the resulting economic

James C. Napier, register of the U.S. Treasury, 1911–1913. (Library of Congress.)

dislocation in the African American community during Reconstruction, Napier entered the banking business to provide saving, credit, and investment opportunities to blacks and to demonstrate the advantages, both personal and collective, of entrepreneurial endeavors. He used his own estate as collateral for funds to underwrite the first year's operation of the Nashville One-Cent Savings Bank in 1903. He went without salary as the cashier of the bank to ensure its success and development. He and RICHARD HENRY BOYD, the founding president of the enterprise (later renamed the Citizens Savings Bank), steered it toward ultraconservative fiscal policies in lending and investment to guarantee the bank's financial success so that it might serve as a model for other black businessmen and bankers. The bank was founded to inspire "systematic saving among our people," according to Napier. From its opening on 6 January 1904 (with deposits of $6,392 from 145 individuals), deposits of the

Citizens Savings Bank reached a high of $209,942 within 35 years.

Napier supported larger cooperative black capitalist endeavors by joining Booker T. Washington's NNBL, which first convened in Boston in 1900. This organization was designed to bring black businessmen from around the nation to annual meetings to discuss entrepreneurship as a means to individual and collective uplift in the black community. The 1903 annual NNBL meeting was held in Nashville, under the aegis of Napier, one of the vice presidents of the organization. Napier inherited the NNBL presidential mantle after Washington's death in 1915, serving until 1919. He attended the upstate New York Amenia Conference of 1916 and was one of the ranking Bookerites to effect a successful but short-lived modus vivendi between the Washington and the W. E. B. DuBois–NAACP factions vying for leadership of the black community.

Napier continued to promote the idea of industrial development and training as an economic strategy to provide jobs and entrepreneurial opportunities for blacks as one of the founders of Nashville's Tennessee Agricultural and Industrial State Normal School for Negroes (later Tennessee State University). Serving as a trustee of Meharry Medical College, Fisk College, and Howard University, Napier also took a keen interest in higher education and publicly extolled the virtues of both higher and industrial education in preparing African Americans for "all the duties and responsibilities of life." As trustee of the Anna T. Jeanes Fund, which supported educational opportunities for black southerners, Napier was instrumental in obtaining more than $75,965 between 1909 and 1926 for Tennessee and in establishing the organization's presence in twenty-eight counties in the state. Napier lectured frequently on medical jurisprudence at Meharry. In the 1920s he served as a member of the southern regional Commission on Interracial Cooperation, established to prevent violence and conflict between blacks and whites. Two years before his death in Nashville, Napier was appointed to the city's housing authority at age ninety-three. He was reported shortly after 1900 to have amassed personal wealth of more than one hundred thousand dollars; the value of his real estate was assessed at $43,016 at the time of his death.

FURTHER READING

A collection of Napier's papers is at Fisk University.

Clark, Herbert L. "James Carroll Napier: National Negro Leader," *Tennessee Historical Quarterly* 49 (1990).

Obituaries: *Nashville Banner*, 23 Apr. 1940; *Journal of Negro History* 25 (July 1940).

This entry is taken from the *American National Biography* and is published here with the permission of the American Council of Learned Societies.

MACEO CRENSHAW DAILEY

Nash, Charles Edmund (23 May 1844–21 June 1913), Reconstruction politician and U.S. congressman, was born in Opelousas, Louisiana, the son of free blacks Richard Nash and Masie Cecile. He received little public school education and as a young man worked as a bricklayer in New Orleans.

In 1863 nineteen-year-old Nash joined the Tenth Regiment of the Corps d'Afrique, later renamed the Eighty-second U.S. Colored Infantry. He joined the army as a private but was soon promoted to the rank of sergeant major. Nash's regiment fought at the Battle of Port Hudson, Louisiana, and was involved in the last infantry battle of the Civil War, the Battle of Fort Blakely, Alabama, in April 1865. While storming Fort Blakely, Nash received wounds that cost him most of his right leg and earned him an honorable discharge. Apparently, about ten days before his discharge, he received promotion to first lieutenant, but the promotion was not approved. His leg wounds pained him for many years, and he may have been adjusting to life during the years 1865 to 1869, when there is little information about him.

In 1869 Nash returned to Louisiana, where his military record and his political affiliations with the Republican Party earned him a position as a night inspector in the politically influential New Orleans Custom House. In 1874 this association allowed him a triumphant nomination as the Republican candidate from the Sixth Congressional District in Louisiana. Nash won the election and took his seat in 1875, assigned to the Committee of Education and Labor. Nash's tenure in Congress was short, and the only bill that he introduced, a bayou survey in his district, was swiftly quashed. Sometime after his election to Congress, he married Martha Ann Wycoff. They had no children.

As a freshman congressman, Nash found it difficult to get the floor to speak. Finally, on 7 June 1876, he made a significant address on political affairs in his state. Nash consistently supported the Fourteenth Amendment while pleading for racial peace and criticizing the efforts of white southern Democrats to suppress native Republicans. He urged national reconciliation on the part of all Americans, pledged his loyalty to the Republican Party, pleaded for decency in the treatment of southern blacks, and emphasized

Charles Edmund Nash, Civil War veteran, Reconstruction politician, and Republican representative from Louisiana, c. 1870. (Library of Congress/Brady-Handy Photograph Collection.)

the importance of education for black and white Americans. In his speech Nash warned of the perils of unfair election practices and inadequate education, citing "the ignorance of the masses" as Louisiana's gravest danger and most injurious obstacle to harmony. "The race issue is the issue of ignorance," he argued. In his prescription for a healthy southern society, Nash explained that "education dispels narrow prejudices as the sun dispels the noxious vapors of the night. The South needs more and better schools." Furthermore, he insisted on the importance of "equal rights before the law, and … participation in the elective franchise" for all male citizens. Nash concluded with a call to northerners and southerners, and black and white Americans, to strive for these goals together. Referring to the ending of the Civil War, he exhorted: "The battle-cry is no longer sounded; war's thunder-clouds have rolled muttering away, and the skies are bright after the storm. The heroes of one side are sleeping side by side with those whom they withstood in battle. … [T]his country is our joint inheritance, this flag has always been our joint banner. The glories of our past belong to both of us…. Let there be peace between us, that these swords which we have learned to use so well, may if used again strike only at a common foe."

Nash received the Republican nomination for a second term in the House of Representatives, but his bid for reelection was defeated in 1876 when he lost to a white Democrat opposed to Reconstruction reforms. Nash's impassioned speech had gone over well on the floor of Congress, but not so well in his home state. The election of 1876, commonly cited as the end of Reconstruction, marked the end of Nash's political career. He returned to Louisiana in March 1877. In 1882 he served briefly as the postmaster of the coastal town of Washington, Louisiana, before moving back to Opelousas, where his first wife died two years later. Nash then moved to New Orleans, where he took a job making cigars and married a French woman named Julia Lacy Montplaisir in February 1905. Nash died in New Orleans.

In many ways Nash typifies the experiences of politically active African Americans during the Civil War and Reconstruction. He supported the Union during the war and espoused patriotism, reconciliation, and political involvement after the war. During Reconstruction he gained access to the government that would have been impossible before the Civil War. A by-product of the New Orleans Custom House political "machine," Nash never distinguished himself as a congressman. His incredibly brief tenure did not encourage his independence in Congress, and he never made a notable political impact.

FURTHER READING

Ficklen, John R. *History of Reconstruction in Louisiana* (2001).
Foner, Eric. *Freedom's Lawmakers: A Directory of Black Officeholders during Reconstruction* (1996).
Hepworth, George H. *The Whip, Hoe, and Sword, or the Gulf Department in '63* (1864, 1979).
Pipkin, J. J. *The Story of a Rising Race* (1902, 1970).
Taylor, Joe Gray. *Louisiana Reconstructed 1863–1877* (1974).

This entry is taken from the *American National Biography* and is published here with the permission of the American Council of Learned Societies.

CHANDRA MILLER

Nash, Diane Judith Bevel (15 May 1938–), civil rights activist, was born in Chicago, Illinois, the only child of Leon Nash, a dentist, and Dorothy Bolton Nash, a keypunch operator, recording information on war bonds. Soon after Diane turned a year old, her parents divorced. Nash was reared as a Catholic on Chicago's South Side. With her mother working outside the home, Nash's maternal grandmother, Carrie Bolton, cared for her during the first seven years of her life. After the end of the World War II, Dorothy B. Nash went on to marry John Baker, a Pullman car waiter, after which the family enjoyed a comfortable lifestyle among Chicago's black middle class.

After graduating from St. Anselm Roman Catholic Elementary School in 1952 Nash attended Park High School, graduating in 1956. She began her college career at Howard University in Washington, D.C., as an English major with an education minor. In 1959 she transferred to Fisk University in Nashville, Tennessee, where she soon joined the African American freedom struggle. In Nashville she came to face to face with southern-style racial segregation and ultimately became one of the leading catalysts of societal change.

On a date to the Tennessee State Fair, Nash first encountered the pervasive "White" and "Colored" signs that marked the Jim Crow South. In response to this indignity Nash began attending nonviolent workshops conducted by the REVEREND JAMES LAWSON, under the alliance of the Nashville Christian Leadership Council (NCLC), an affiliate of DR. MARTIN LUTHER KING's Southern Christian Leadership Council (SCLC).

In November and December of 1959 Nash was among those who "tested" Nashville's policy of segregated lunch counters. Elected chair of the Student Central Committee she played a pivotal role in Nashville's student movement. However, before the Nashville students could stage their first full-scale sit-in, four male North Carolina Agriculture and Technical College students, with no plan or formal preparation, staged a sit-in on 1 February 1960 in Greensboro, North Carolina.

Twelve days later, on 13 February, 124 students from the city's four predominantly black institutions of higher education entered Kress's, McClellan's, and Woolworth's in downtown Nashville. Student protesters in Nashville conducted numerous sit-ins during the first four months of demonstrations. As the sit-ins continued, the poised and articulate Nash emerged as their spokesperson, a role that often made her the target of white mob violence. Holding to the precepts of nonviolence, which became her way of life, she found the inner strength to endure the threat and reality of physical violence.

Nash was among the first student activists to advocate the "jail, no bail" strategy. Among the students arrested on 27 February 1960, her dedication to the constructs of civil disobedience and direct nonviolent protest and command of the situation manifested themselves, when as reported by the 2 March edition of the Nashville *Tennessean* she stated to John I. Harris, the presiding special judge of the Nashville City Court, "We feel that if we pay these fines we would be contributing to and supporting the injustice and immoral practices that have been performed in the arrest and convictions of the defendants." The attorney and city councilman Z. Alexander Looby, who had litigated civil rights cases across Tennessee and served as one of the Nashville students' attorneys, became the target of violence. On 19 April 1960, after the bombing of his home, incensed demonstrators organized a mass march to city hall and sent a telegram to then mayor Ben West, asking him to meet them.

After the Reverend C. T. Vivian read a statement, the mayor attempted to recite all that had been done for the African American community. According to the 20 April 1960 edition of the Nashville *Tennessean*, Nash boldly interrupted, "Mayor West, do you feel it is wrong to discriminate against a person solely on the basis of their race or color?" Stunned by the young woman's question, West responded with a simple, unguarded, "yes." What had been a silent multitude broke into jubilant applause. On 10 May 1960 Nashville became the first major city in the South to begin desegregating its downtown lunch counters. Other counters around the city remained segregated as their owners continued to fight against desegregation. Sit-ins would continue in Nashville.

Over the Easter weekend, 16–18 April 1960, Nash was among those college students who met with SCLC acting director ELLA BAKER in Raleigh, North Carolina, at Shaw University. There they established the Student Nonviolent Coordinating Committee (SNCC). Although Nash was considered a favorite, MARION BARRY, her fellow Fiskite, was instead elected to lead the organization.

The following February Nash was among a group of SNCC students, including Ruby Doris Smith, who participated in the Rock Hill, South Carolina, protest for desegregation. Again arrested, Nash and the other students refused to pay bail and "jail, no bail" became the movement's resonating motto. Sentenced to thirty days in the York County jail, Nash reaffirmed her commitment to the tenets of nonviolence. In an 8 March 1961 letter from jail, which was published in the Rock Hill *Herald*, Nash wrote, "We are trying to help focus attention on a moral question ... the principle of racial inferiority has been challenged ... let us truly love one another, and under God, move toward a 'redeemed community.'"

Soon after her release from jail the leader of Nashville's student movement decided to leave Fisk to work in the movement full-time. Earning approximately twenty-five dollars a week working for both SNCC and SCLC, she rented a room at the Nashville YWCA. Firmly committed to the precepts of nonviolent direct action, Nash prepared herself for her life's work. When asked by *Jet* magazine about her plans, she responded, "I'll be doing this for the rest of my life." As one of the chief architects of the Nashville stand-in movement, which assaulted the city's segregated movie theaters, Nash moved from the Nashville's student movement to a position of leadership in the Freedom Rides, an effort to force bus stations throughout the South to comply with federal desegregation rules, and finally into a full-time civil rights work with the Student Nonviolent Coordinating Committee.

Although not the progenitor of the Freedom Rides of the 1960s, Nash became its leading light. On 4 May 1961 the Congress of Racial Equality (CORE) sent two buses with thirteen interracial freedom riders on what was supposed to be a two-week trip from Washington, D.C., to New Orleans to test desegregation in southern bus stations. The interracial group encountered only a few problems during its first week of travel, but upon reaching Anniston, Alabama, on 14 May it met a vicious horde of more than one hundred angry whites. After the FBI passed on the Freedom Riders' schedule to the Alabama police, who in turn gave the information to the Ku Klux Klan, a mob toting iron pipes and other implements of destruction greeted the riders in Birmingham, where they were battered, knocked unconscious, and hospitalized.

Although the violence attracted national and international attention to the Freedom Riders' cause, CORE leader JAMES FARMER decided to terminate the ride. Diane Nash and the Nashville student contingent moved into action. Questioning CORE's decision to allow "violence to vanquish nonviolence" Nash and her fellow activists felt that the Freedom Rides testing the U.S. Supreme Court's *Boynton v. Virginia* decision must continue for the sake of the movement. Both Farmer and the Reverend FRED SHUTTLESWORTH, an activist minister from Birmingham, warned her that a bloodbath was probable. "Well, we realize that," she retorted, "We're not stupid. But we can't let them stop us with violence. If we do that, the movement is dead. Every time we start something, they'll just answer with violence" (Olson, 184). On 17 May Nash's recruits left Nashville for Birmingham, Alabama. Holding steadfastly to her belief and commitment to the Freedom Ride struggle Nash never relented, not even to the Kennedy administration, which ordered her to call off the Freedom Rides. As the U.S. Justice Department official John Seigenthaler, dispatched as an observer by the Kennedy administration, stated, "She never listened to a word" (Olson, 185).

The Freedom Rides continued for the next four months. Nash and other activists met with Attorney General Robert F. Kennedy and on 22 September 1961, under pressure from the Kennedy administration, the Interstate Commerce Commission crafted regulations to prohibit racial segregation in train and bus terminals.

A tested civil rights veteran, Nash became chair of SNCC's direct action division. In the fall of 1961 Nash married fellow activist JAMES BEVEL (from whom she was divorced in 1969) and moved to Jackson, Mississippi. There she helped to organize the Ruleville meeting at which FANNIE LOU HAMER joined the movement. She was instrumental in teaching nonviolent direct action to high school students in Mississippi, for which she was arrested in May of 1962 for contributing to the delinquency of minors. Pregnant with her first child, Nash elected to serve a two-year prison sentence. "This will be a black baby born in Mississippi, whether I am in jail or not, he will be in prison. I believe that if I go to jail now it may help hasten the day when my child and all children will be free—not only on the day of their birth but for all of their lives" (Ross, 182). Fearing that jailing a pregnant woman would turn her into a martyr, Judge Russell Moore refused to execute his earlier ruling and instead sentenced Nash to ten days—for failure to move from the "white side" of the courtroom. On 5 August 1962 Nash gave birth to her first child, Sherrilynn. Two years later, on 15 May, she gave birth to a son, Douglass.

An astute tactician as well as a courageous and innovative leader of the student civil rights movement, Nash's ideas were instrumental in initiating the 1963 March on Washington. She and her husband conceptualized and planned the initial strategy for the Selma Right-to-Vote movement that helped bring about the Voting Rights Act of 1965. One of six women honored with an award at the 28 August 1963 March on Washington, Nash participated in the Vietnam Peace Movement. Believing that women should have the same equal political, social, and economic rights as men, she also participated in the feminist movement and supported the freedom struggles for the liberation of southern Africa.

Residing in Chicago and the grandmother of two, Diane Judith Nash worked in real estate and educated people in the philosophy and strategy of nonviolence. She believed that, regardless of people's interests and issues, by empowering them with the tenets of nonviolence, they will be able to bring to fruition the social change they desire.

FURTHER READING

Some of the information in this article is from an interview with its subject, conducted on 10 Jan. 2005.

Nash, Diane. "Inside the Sit-ins and Freedom Rides: Testimony of a Southern Student," in *The New Negro*, ed. Mathew H. Ahmann (1969).

Halberstam, David. *The Children* (1998).

Lewis, John, with Michael D'Orso. *Walking with the Wind: A Memoir of the Movement* (1998).

Olson, Lynn. *Freedom's Daughters: The Unsung Heroines of the Civil Rights Movement from 1830 to 1970* (2001).

Powledge, Fred. *Free at Last?: The Civil Rights Movement and the People Who Made It* (1998).

Ross, Rosetta E. *Witnessing and Testifying: Black Women, Religion, and Civil Rights* (2003).

Wynn, Linda T. "The Dawning of a New Day: The Nashville Sit-Ins, February 13, 1960–May 10, 1960," *Tennessee Historical Quarterly* (Spring 1991).

LINDA T. WYNN

Nash, Helen Elizabeth (8 Aug. 1921–), physician, educator, and community advocate, was born in Atlanta, Georgia, third among the six children of Marie Graves, a homemaker, and Homer E. Nash, a doctor. Helen and her brother Homer E. Nash Jr. were both inspired to enter medicine by their father's example. A 1910 Meharry graduate, their father ran a private practice on Atlanta's Auburn Avenue, working up to his death at age ninety-four in 1981. Helen also grew up quite aware of a much-admired black woman physician, Georgia Dwelle, who founded and directed Atlanta's first successful, black-run private and maternity hospital, the Dwelle Infirmary, where Nash was in fact born.

A family tragedy shaped Nash's choice to specialize in pediatrics. Her firstborn sibling, a girl, died at twenty-two months from a gastrointestinal illness that caused severe diarrhea and dehydration. Well into the twentieth century, diarrhea-related dehydration was a major cause of child mortality throughout the country, as it is still is in the Two-Thirds World (sometimes called the Third World or "developing" world). Inexpensive, easily prepared, yet lifesaving intravenous and oral rehydration therapies came far too late for Nash's sister.

Helen Nash graduated from Spelman College in 1942. Her father initially opposed her plan to attend Meharry in Nashville, Tennessee. Then her maternal grandfather, Antoine Graves, gave his blessing from his deathbed and asked for the sale of family property to fund her medical education. Nash's mother advised her to insist on equal treatment with her overwhelmingly male classmates. Nash made the honor roll her first semester at Meharry and graduated in 1945, one of only four women in her class. She undertook a one-year rotating internship and three-year pediatrics residency at Homer G. Phillips Hospital, St. Louis, Missouri. This segregated, city-run hospital was unusual in offering black physicians advanced training. Atlanta's enclave of relatively prosperous blacks and then Meharry had largely protected Nash from the worst daily indignities of racism and sexism. In St. Louis, however, no buffer stood between her and Jim Crow, and she constantly encountered the stereotype of women doctors as incompetent. Nash soon proved herself skillful in turning such prejudices upside down. An encouraging mentor helped her become chief resident. She used her authority to challenge the horrific mortality rate—80 percent among premature infants—from infectious diarrhea and other largely preventable causes on the pediatric ward. She insisted on simple, common sense infection control procedures that had been neglected. Nash successfully agitated for her patients to receive the same treatment as the children at the white municipal hospital: nourishing, potassium-rich bananas, and electric fans and ice cream in hot weather. Sometimes, however, Nash felt that no else cared about her patients. Once she insisted to a male surgeon that a baby had appendicitis. He contemptuously replied that a woman doctor was incapable of making that judgment. The child was dead by morning.

In 1949 Nash opened a private practice with her own savings and support from her father. She did so despite repeated warnings that a woman doctor could not attract enough patients. Her practice boomed. It began at 1048A Vandeventer in the black business district, then moved over a nearby drugstore at Sarah and Finney streets. By the late 1960s or early 1970s, Nash and her husband, James B. Abernathy Sr. (who had died by the early 1990s), purchased land and built spacious, comfortable offices at 1441 North Grand Boulevard. Until retiring from her practice in 1994, Nash saw thousands of mostly poor patients. Many were drawn by her reputation for openness with difficult matters that many doctors had traditionally avoided, such as death and sexuality. Long before doctors were educated about sensitivity to grief, she visited and talked with the family of any child who died, sent flowers, and attended the funeral. Nash set aside a practice room, nicknamed "the Sex Room," for instructing sexually active but uninformed teens and sometimes their families in basic anatomy, self-respect, responsibility, birth control choices, and parenting skills.

The year 1949 was a decisive one for Nash's medical career in two other important ways. She was the only woman in the group of four black doctors, and the first black woman ever appointed to the faculty of Washington University Medical School. Nash taught clinical pediatrics there until 1993, then served as dean of minority affairs (1994–1996). In 1949 Nash also became the first African American pediatrician ever hired on staff at St. Louis Children's Hospital. One of her mentors there, Dr. Alexis Hartmann, invented Ringer's lactate, an early IV treatment for diarrhea-related dehydration. Nash also returned for a time to Homer G. Phillips as pediatric supervisor and associate director (1950–1964). Nash served on numerous committees at St. Louis Children's Hospital (1949–1979), where she was also attending staff association president (1977–1979). She joined the American Academy of Pediatrics in 1953 and was named to offices on the Health and Welfare Council of Metropolitan St. Louis and the Committee of the State Welfare Department of Missouri. She advocated for public health through the Children's Bureau and helped to desegregate the regional school for deaf youth. She was awarded honorary lifetime memberships in the St. Louis Medical Society (1975) and the Medical Woman's Society (1991). In 1994 the NAACP magazine *Crisis* gave her its Women's Medal of Honor. During the early 2000s Nash continued her longtime trustee board and philanthropy work with the St. Louis Symphony Orchestra, Missouri Botanical Garden, and other nonprofit organizations.

Starting in 1996 the Washington University School of Medicine has annually granted a Dr. Helen E. Nash Academic Achievement Award to an exceptional student. Through her clinical work, teaching, and advocacy, Nash served three generations of mostly poor children and their families, black and white alike. Nash's legacy also includes her pointed reflections concerning "three generations of young lives ruined by ignorance about sexuality" while "three generations of public school officials bob and weave on the subject of sex education" and "the public health system that once supported young mothers and newborns rot[s] away, when it is needed now more than ever" (Bertelson).

FURTHER READING

The Archives and Rare Book Department, Bernard Becker Medical Library, Washington University, St. Louis, displays some of its holdings on Helen E. Nash online at beckerexhibits.wustl.edu, especially in the "Oral History Project" and "We've Come a Long Way, Maybe" exhibits.

Bertelson, Christine. "Dr. Helen E. Nash Is Retiring, Angry about Teens, Sex," *St. Louis Post-Dispatch*, 27 Nov. 1993.

Harrison, Leticia. "Woman Lauded for 40 Years in Medicine," *St. Louis Post-Dispatch*, 17 June 1989.

Robinson, Melanie. "Girls Need Better Role Models, Family Support, Doctor Says," *St. Louis Post-Dispatch*, 10 Nov. 1994.

MARY KRANE DERR

Nash, William Beverly (1822–19 Jan. 1888), slave, businessman, and politician, was born in Virginia to slave parents whose names are unknown. When William was thirteen he was either sold or brought by his owner to Columbia, South Carolina, where he served his apprenticeship as a barber. Many barbershops in antebellum Columbia were owned by blacks who had purchased their freedom, and Nash, an enterprising young man, may have harbored ambitions to do likewise. He does not appear to have succeeded in doing so prior to the end of the Civil War, but he was able to save some money he earned from tips for his labors as a bootblack, porter, and waiter at Hunt's Hotel in Columbia. It was while working at this hotel that Nash learned to read and write, assisted by his master, W. C. Preston, a local politician who fired his slave's interest in political debate. According to Preston's granddaughter, Bevelina Pearson, who was interviewed by the Works Progress Administration in the 1930s, Nash would read, write, and cipher for more than two hours every night of the week.

Nash's literacy, savings, and intimate knowledge of Columbia's white and black political elites would serve him well in freedom. In November 1865 he served as a delegate from Columbia to a black political convention called to protest the postwar enactment of the black codes by the South Carolina legislature, which sought to restore African Americans to a state of de facto slavery. Nash's actions at the convention—as in much of his later career—may be viewed as both radical and conservative. In one speech he passionately demanded equal suffrage for black men and asked that African Americans be equally represented on juries. Since blacks formed the majority of the population in South Carolina, the eventual enactment of Nash's desire for full political equality would later result in a radical transformation in the state's political culture. Nash, however, was adamantly opposed to the practice of confiscating lands from rebel planters to redistribute among the freedmen. At the convention he initiated a motion to postpone any discussion of the land distribution question.

Nash's vigorous defense of property rights was most likely the consequence of his own postwar entrepreneurial success. Within five years of emancipation he owned five thousand dollars in real estate and two thousand dollars in personal property, which placed him among the wealthiest of South Carolina blacks, on a par with his fellow barber JOSEPH RAINEY and the lawyer ROBERT BROWN ELLIOTT, both of whom were later elected to the U.S. Congress. Nash built his fortune—still modest compared to that of most white South Carolina businessmen and landowners—from several businesses, including a grocery, a brick manufactory, and a coal yard; he also invested in railroads and banks.

In March 1867 Nash was the most prominent and vocal of the black delegates to a biracial gathering called by Columbia's Universal Union Brotherhood. Like Nash, most of his fellow black delegates were small businessmen who had been urban slave artisans. The white delegates to this forum included a former U.S. senator, a former mayor of Columbia, and Wade Hampton III, one of the largest and wealthiest slaveholders in the nation before the Civil War, all of whom were at that time disenfranchised as former Confederate officers. In a well-received speech Nash repeated his belief in full suffrage, at least for all men: "I want to see everybody vote, except the women," he told the convention (Saville, 155). Nash also expressed the view that the best hope for the freedmen gaining suffrage lay with former white Confederates of Hampton's ability, and not with antebellum southern Unionists who were at that time attempting to form a South Carolina Republican Party along with members of the free black elite and northern Radical Republicans. Nash was on occasion contemptuous of the self-appointed free black elite, many of whom were of mixed racial background, though he couched his class resentment in racial terms. He declared his pride in ancestors who "trod the burning sands of Africa," but dismissed as "mongrels" the freeborn blacks "in whose veins runs a preponderance of white blood" (Holt, 60).

Because of Nash's insistence on full male suffrage without any restrictions on education or property ownership, he eventually gravitated toward the Republican Party, which emerged as the most likely guarantor of political equality. In 1868 he represented Richland County at South Carolina's Constitutional Convention, at which political equality was finally assured. Elected to the South Carolina state senate that same year, Nash continued to oppose any notion of land confiscation and to support the rights of capital and property owners. He was also a forceful advocate of state-financed, integrated schools, and he gradually emerged as one of the leading African American members of the state legislature. As blacks came to play an increasing (though never dominant) role in Reconstruction politics between 1872 and 1875, Nash chaired three of the senate's most important economic committees: Finance, Claims, and Contingent Accounts.

Historians have largely deflated the widely held canard that South Carolina's Reconstruction legislature was uncommonly corrupt, but there is substantial evidence of good, old-fashioned, American graft by members of both races, Nash included. In 1869, for example, he bribed a member of the state land commission so he would resign and be replaced by an African American appointee. In 1872 Nash accepted a five-thousand-dollar bribe from railroad interests and voted according to their wishes. Nash later justified his actions by arguing that since he already intended to vote in support of the railroad's goals, "I merely took the money because I thought I might as well have it" (Foner, *Freedom's Lawmakers*, 159). During Reconstruction Nash also held a series of appointive posts, among them magistrate for Columbia (1867–1868), trial justice (1870–1874), president of the board of regents of South Carolina's lunatic asylum, and director of the state penitentiary. In that latter capacity Nash also used his political office for personal financial gain in 1873 by persuading his fellow legislators to build a new prison with materials purchased from his brickyards.

Under investigation for fraud in 1877, Nash resigned from the state legislature and later repaid the state for the money he had embezzled. He never returned to political prominence, though largely because of the diminished opportunities for African Americans following the end of Reconstruction. Information about Nash's personal life is scarce. The name of his wife is unknown, but it appears that the couple had several children, some of whom died in infancy, but at least one of whom, a daughter named Doreas, survived into adulthood and provided Nash with grandchildren.

William Beverly Nash, who died in Columbia, was among the more successful of the second tier of black Reconstruction politicians. Conservative on matters of land and property, he was among the most radical proponents of universal male suffrage and integrated public education. His political service was, however, compromised by his dishonest, though by no means atypical, abuse of his elected and appointed offices.

FURTHER READING
Holt, Thomas. *Black over White: Negro Political Leadership in South Carolina during Reconstruction* (1977).
Saville, Julie. *The Work of Reconstruction: From Slave to Wage Laborer in South Carolina, 1860–1870* (1994).
Williamson, Joel. *After Slavery: The Negro in South Carolina during Reconstruction* (1965).

STEVEN J. NIVEN

Navarro, Fats (24 Sept. 1923–7 July 1950), jazz trumpeter, was born Theodore Navarro Jr. in Key West, Florida, to Theodore Navarro Sr. and Miriam Williams. It is believed that his father was a barber and that he was of Cuban, African American, and Chinese ancestry. As a child, he had piano lessons, but then he switched to trumpet and tenor saxophone. While still in high school in Key West he began to play professionally on the tenor saxophone, before switching definitively to trumpet. On his graduation in 1941, he joined Sol Allbright's band on the road, traveling north to Cincinnati, Ohio, where he took some formal lessons on trumpet. Later that year he joined Snookum Russell's band in Indianapolis, with whom he traveled around the Midwest for almost two years. His main influences on trumpet until that time had been his third cousin CHARLIE SHAVERS and then, more significantly, ROY ELDRIDGE, the harmonic link between LOUIS ARMSTRONG and the beboppers of the 1940s.

In late 1943 Navarro joined ANDY KIRK's band, and the presence of HOWARD MCGHEE in the trumpet section brought a bebop influence to his playing. His first recordings were with Kirk, but they

Fats Navarro, jazz trumpeter, New York City, c. 1947. (© William P. Gottlieb; www.jazzphotos.com.)

included no solos of note. In 1944, while the Kirk band was in New York, Navarro sat in at Minton's (sometimes referred to as "the bebop laboratory") and was noted by at least one critic (Leonard Feather) for his solo work with the band at the Apollo Theater. In January 1945 he replaced DIZZY GILLESPIE, who was by then a significant influence on him, in BILLY ECKSTINE's band, the most modern and influential big band of the time, having had several notable members besides Gillespie, including CHARLIE PARKER, DEXTER GORDON, and ART BLAKEY. In June 1946 Navarro left Eckstine, choosing to spend the remainder of his brief career in small groups (except for a brief stint with LIONEL HAMPTON in 1948) primarily in the New York area. He acquired the nickname "Fats" or "Fat Girl" because of his weight, cherubic face, and high voice. Navarro married Rena Clark sometime in the late 1940s and they had one daughter. He died in New York City of tuberculosis complicated by heroin addiction.

A few recorded solos with the Eckstine band exist, but most of Navarro's work is in the small-band format favored by the beboppers. He made more than one hundred recordings, primarily as a sideman with groups led by BUD POWELL, Parker, TAD DAMERON, KENNY CLARKE, COLEMAN HAWKINS, and Gordon, among others. A small number of these recordings are compositions by Navarro himself. Navarro can be heard to good advantage on *The Fabulous Fats Navarro* (1947–1949); "Wail," with the Bud Powell Quintet (1949); "Lady Bird," with the Tad Dameron Septet (1948); *One Night in Birdland* (1950); and "Street Beat" (1950), recorded live with Parker.

Navarro had a highly individual style and was, along with Gillespie, one of the leading bebop trumpeters of the 1940s. He had a big, beautiful sound, quite different from Gillespie's, and though he had a wide range (concert Fs above high C appear regularly in his solos), he exploited the upper register less than Gillespie. Very long, clearly articulated phrases and a strong sense of swing characterize his style. In these respects and in his general fluency Navarro was a significant influence on, most importantly, CLIFFORD BROWN, among many others. According to Gillespie, who was quoted in an obituary by George Simon in *Metronome*, Navarro was "the best all-around trumpeter of them all. He had everything a trumpeter should have: tone, ideas, execution, and reading ability."

FURTHER READING
Gitler, I. *Jazz Masters of the Forties* (1966).
Obituary: *Metronome* (Oct. 1950).
This entry is taken from the *American National Biography* and is published here with the permission of the American Council of Learned Societies.

HOWARD BROFSKY

Naylor, Gloria (25 Jan. 1950–), writer and educator, was born in New York City to Roosevelt Naylor and Alberta McAlpin, who migrated north from their native Mississippi shortly before her birth. She was conceived in the Deep South in Robinsonville, Mississippi, where her parents labored as sharecroppers, and she considered her writer's heart to have been conceived there also, given how deeply she was influenced by the region's language and culture. The family moved throughout the city during her childhood, from a housing project in the upper Bronx to a Harlem apartment building, and eventually, to Queens. Her father worked as a master framer in a custom frame shop and as a transit worker after being discharged from the armed forces in 1952. Though her mother, a telephone operator, received little formal education, she loved to read and had a great impact on the young Naylor's own developing interest in literature.

When she was young, Naylor's mother would work extra hours in the fields in order to save up enough money to purchase books that were unavailable to her in Mississippi's segregated libraries, so she encouraged Naylor and her two sisters, Fanny Bernice and Carolyn, to visit the libraries in New York once they were old enough to write their names on their library cards. Reading became a refuge for the shy Naylor, who seldom spoke. When her mother presented her with her first diary at age twelve, she was able to write about feelings she had difficulty vocalizing. While remaining an avid reader of nearly all the books that she could obtain, including English classics that she was introduced to in school, Naylor soon began to write vignettes, poems, and short stories of her own.

A strong student academically, Naylor graduated from high school in 1968 during a time of great social upheaval in the United States. The Reverend MARTIN LUTHER KING JR. had been assassinated on 4 April in Memphis, Tennessee, that same year, and she found herself searching for how she might use her own life to better the conditions of the world. Her mother was baptized as a Jehovah's Witness when Naylor was thirteen, and at age eighteen Naylor decided to follow a similar path. She traveled through New York and the South evangelizing from 1968 to 1975, and she saw preaching about a hoped-for theocratic government as a way to respond to the problems enveloping society. She was drawn to the sense of community, the appreciation for language, and the opportunities for travel that being a missionary provided, but the seven years that she spent witnessing were also quite isolating and left her feeling disconnected from mainstream social relations. She had almost no exposure to the rapidly growing literary production of African Americans during this time, and she was increasingly concerned about her own lack of marketable skills, the restrictions and oppressive aspects of the religion, and her few opportunities to progress professionally. In 1975, after supporting herself while a missionary by working in fast-food restaurants and for various hotels as a switchboard operator, she decided to leave the faith and return to school back in New York City.

Naylor first studied nursing at Medgar Evers College upon her return before transferring to Brooklyn College, part of the City University of New York, to major in English. It is important to note that she still had never read a novel by a black woman at this time. That all changed, however, in a creative writing class in 1977 when she encountered TONI MORRISON's *The Bluest Eye*—a text that spurred her own thoughts about writing and greatly influenced her ability to envision herself as a writer with a story to tell. As Naylor became exposed to other African

Gloria Naylor, whose novels include *The Women of Brewster Place* (1982) and *Linden Hills* (1985), won a Guggenheim Fellowship in 1988. (Austin/Thompson Collection.)

American women writers, such as NIKKI GIOVANNI, PAULE MARSHALL, and ALICE WALKER, her own confidence and voice began to take hold. By age twenty-eight she decided that she would become a writer, and in 1979 she submitted a story to *Essence* magazine, whose editor offered her great encouragement. The story was published in 1980, the same year she entered into a short-lived marriage.

After receiving her bachelor of arts degree from Brooklyn College in 1981, Naylor began graduate work in African American Studies at Yale University. In 1982 she arrived on the literary scene with her successful debut novel *The Women of Brewster Place*, a text centering on seven women who find themselves on a dead-end street, literally and otherwise, and must seek sanctuary in one another. The novel was met with wide acclaim and earned Naylor an important place in the African American literary canon. Its exploration of female community, family life, and the threats posed to women's emotional, spiritual, and physical wholeness in a divided society make it a particularly compelling investigation into the impact of class, gender, race, and sexual oppression on

African American women's lives. The novel was later filmed as a made-for-television movie starring such celebrated actors as OPRAH WINFREY, CICELY TYSON, and Robin Givens, and it aired as a two-part miniseries in 1989. It also brought Naylor a National Book Award (then called the American Book Awards) in 1983 for the year's best first novel, the same year that she received her master of arts degree from Yale University.

Although Naylor had originally planned to obtain a Ph.D. in American Studies so that she could get a tenured position, she decided that she did not want to delay her writing for as long as that would take. It was a decision many of her readers were grateful that she made. Naylor followed *The Women of Brewster Place* with her second novel *Linden Hills* in 1985, which was originally her master's thesis at Yale. Centered on a middle-class African American neighborhood and influenced by the circular geography of Dante's hell in *The Inferno*, the text explores themes of materialism, social divisions, the nature of integration, and the sacrifices individuals and families make to their community, consciousness, and history when faulty notions of success and achievement take center stage in one's life. That same year Naylor received a National Endowment for the Arts Fellowship and served as a cultural exchange lecturer in India for the United States Information Agency.

Naylor's efforts to capture openly and honestly the varied dimensions of the black community resulted in her conceiving of a quartet of novels representing distinct aspects of African American life. This in itself was one of her most important interventions as an author, since representations of a singular black experience had long been insisted upon by many readers and a larger public reluctant to embrace the diversity of the African American community. Her third novel, *Mama Day*, testifies again to her range and depth as an author. Published in 1988, the novel is alternately set in New York City and Willow Springs, a mystical sea island off the coasts of Georgia and South Carolina. As with much of her work, scholars often point to how the book exists in dialogue with other texts, reverberating with aspects of Shakespeare's *The Tempest*. *Mama Day* was followed by *Bailey's Café* in 1992, which was later produced as a play directed by Novella Nelson. Naylor returned to Brewster in her fifth novel, 1998's *The Men of Brewster Place*, a book she wrote for her father who, like many of her lead characters, worked hard all his life to preserve home and family amidst difficult circumstances.

Naylor's carefully crafted and insightful work has garnered her many of the nation's top accolades and fellowships, including the Mid-Atlantic Writers Association Distinguished Writer Award (1983), the Candace Award from the National Coalition of One Hundred Black Women (1986), a Guggenheim Fellowship (1988), a Lillian Smith Award (1989), a New York Foundation for the Arts Fellowship (1991), a Brooklyn College President's Medal (1993), and the American Book Award (1999). In addition to teaching at the University of Kent, Princeton University, George Washington University, New York University, and Boston University as a visiting professor and lecturer, she was also scholar in residence at the University of Pennsylvania and was named senior fellow in the Society for the Humanities at Cornell University. Her novels have been translated into more than twelve languages.

Although Naylor is best known as one of America's most celebrated African American novelists, her interests and talents are wide ranging. She edited the collection *Children of the Night: The Best Short Stories by Black Writers, 1967 to the Present* (1995), became active in a literacy project in the Bronx, and in 1990 established her own multimedia production company called One Way Production, an independent film company aimed at presenting positive images of the black community. Inherent in her body of work is the value that lies in preserving and maintaining an African American identity and African American culture in the face of cultural and social injustice. Always, it seems, she reminds her readers that the black experience is as various as it is rich in history, diversity, depth, and strength.

FURTHER READING

Gates, Henry Louis, Jr., and Kwame Anthony Appiah. *Gloria Naylor: Critical Perspectives Past and Present* (1993).

Montgomery, Maxine Lavon. *Conversations with Gloria Naylor* (2004).

Whitt, Margaret Earley. *Understanding Gloria Naylor* (1999).

Wilson, Charles. *Gloria Naylor: A Critical Companion* (2001).

AMANDA J. DAVIS

Neal, Larry (5 Sept. 1937–6 Jan. 1981), critic, theorist, poet, dramatist, essayist, editor, and folklorist, was born Lawrence Paul Neal in Atlanta, Georgia. Soon afterward, his parents, Woodie, a railroad worker, and Maggie Neal, a domestic, moved Larry and his four brothers to Philadelphia, Pennsylvania, where they spent their formative years. Neal graduated from the city's Roman Catholic High School in 1956 and went on to pursue a degree in history and English at Lincoln University, a predominantly black university near Philadelphia. After completing his formal education with a master's degree from the University of Pennsylvania in 1963 and teaching briefly at the Drexel Institute of Technology (later Drexel University), Neal moved to New York City, where he married Evelyn Rogers. They settled in the Sugar Hill section of Harlem and later adopted a son, Avatar. Though Neal lived in Washington, D.C., and other cities throughout his life, teaching at Wesleyan (1969–1970) and Yale (1970–1975), and lecturing at Case-Western and Howard universities, it was in New York City that he launched his distinguished and varied career. From Harlem, Neal would establish himself as a key presence in a burgeoning revolutionary movement of the national black arts community.

After working briefly as a copywriter for John Wiley and Sons in 1963, Neal soon became a prominent figure in the Black Arts Movement, a group of black writers fast gaining a foothold in the Harlem arts community. As one of its central theorists and practitioners Neal helped to articulate the philosophy of the movement in critical pieces published in several influential black publications such as *Journal of Black Poetry*, *Black Dialogue*, *Negro Digest* (later *Black World*), and *Liberator*, a journal for which he would become arts editor. Working with other young writers such as Askia Muhammad Touré, A. B. SPELLMAN, and AMIRI BARAKA (LeRoi Jones), Neal sought to advance a theory of black expression that would liberate black artists from the stifling constraints of Western cultural modes and form the groundwork for a radical resistance to American racial apartheid. The establishment of the Black Arts Repertory Theatre in 1964 by Baraka, Neal, and others helped to solidify the movement by giving it a physical home base in Harlem. Though short-lived, "BARTs," as it was called, became the staging ground for a campaign designed to articulate a completely distinct "black aesthetic," and to work specifically for the liberation of black people in America. To this end, the collective sponsored seminars and classes, and also produced plays, poetry readings, and concerts intended to infuse arts into the community landscape. As a radical counterforce to mainstream arts and politics in New York, Neal and his comrades at times faced a public hostile to their efforts, and in 1965, while leaving the Schomburg Center of the New York Public Library, Neal was shot and wounded by an assailant who found his views objectionable.

In 1968 Neal and Baraka co-edited the most important work of the movement, *Black Fire*. This groundbreaking anthology included criticism, poetry, and drama by a number of leading black writers including ED BULLINS, SONIA SANCHEZ, HOYT FULLER, and STOKELY CARMICHAEL. Neal's conclusion to the collection, "And Shine Swam On," most thoughtfully articulated the book's objective. In it Neal explains that the book should be "read as a rejection of anything that we feel is detrimental to our people." He goes further to argue for the intellectual integrity of identifying a black aesthetic—that by rejecting western "political, social, and artistic values," black people would be able to "liberate ourselves, destroy the double consciousness." During that same period, Neal published another vitally important essay in the *Drama Review*. "The Black Arts Movement," an essay often thought of as the artistic and political manifesto of the movement, further articulated the idea of a black aesthetic, arguing that a black approach to art was needed to replace a weak and crumbling Western aesthetic. Claiming that black intellectuals had failed to reject Western artistic forms, Neal questioned the potency of those forms, denying their usefulness to black people. He argued forcefully that it was the duty of the black artist to use distinctly black forms in creating art that struggles for the liberation of black peoples, emphasizing the movement's staunch belief that for black artists, "your ethics and your aesthetics are one."

Neal demonstrated the ideas he discussed in his essays in his creative work, publishing two books of poetry, *Black Boogaloo* in 1969 and *Hoodoo Hollerin Bebop Ghosts* in 1971. Both collections drew on Neal's committed belief in the central role of black music and folk culture as sources of artistic sensibility, providing the new "symbolism" and "mythology" of the Black Arts Movement. Neal also wrote two plays, *The Glorious Monster in the Bell of the Horn* in 1976, and *In an Upstate Motel*, which was produced in 1981. He continued to write critical pieces during the 1970s and 1980s, all the while reconsidering his previous positions. He produced a number of essays during that time addressing politics and culture as well as music and literature. Before his death he was working toward collecting some of these under the title, "New Space: Critical Essays on American Culture." Those essays, along with additional poems, a play, and commentary by

Baraka, Jayne Cortez, Charles Fuller, and Stanley Crouch, were eventually collected and published posthumously as *Visions of a Liberated Future: Black Arts Movement Writings* in 1989.

Though Larry Neal died tragically and prematurely at the age of forty-three, his influence can still be felt in his work with the Black Arts Movement. While Baraka is often thought of as the fiery soul of the movement, Neal was its reasoned voice, describing its theoretical shape as it took form. It was his careful and thoughtful articulation of the movement's beliefs that would stand as its intellectual legacy. From his critical writing to his screen and teleplays to his service as executive director of the Washington, D.C., Commission on the Arts and Humanities, Larry Neal's career made a lasting impression on an entire generation of artists and activists. His depth of thought and uncompromising dedication to intellectual integrity mark him as one of the defining figures of African American letters.

FURTHER READING

Larry Neal's papers, 1961–1985, are housed in the Schomburg Center for Research in Black Culture, New York City.

Benston, Kimberly, ed. "Larry Neal: A Special Issue," *Callaloo* 23 (Winter 1985).

Spady, James G. *Larry Neal: Liberated Black Philly Poet with a Blues Streak of Mellow Wisdom* (1989).

Obituary: *New York Times*, 9 Jan. 1981.

DAVID TODD LAWRENCE

Neely, Barbara (1941–), mystery novelist and short story writer, was born in Lebanon, Pennsylvania, the oldest of three children of Bernard and Ann Neely. Lebanon was a small Dutch community, and not only was Neely the only African American student to attend her elementary and high school but she was also the only child in her elementary school class to speak fluent English.

Neely moved to Pittsburgh in 1971, where she received her master's degree in Urban and Regional Planning at the University of Pittsburgh. Three years after taking her degree, Neely designed and founded a community-based home for formerly incarcerated women in a Pittsburgh suburb. Despite protests from local residents and pressure to move the project to the inner city, Neely successfully fought to keep the home in place, a fight that would secure her reputation as a community and women's activist.

In addition to her activism, Neely had written several short stories, but it was not until a 1978 incident that she received the inspiration she needed to pursue a writing career. According to *Voices from the Gaps*, "After watching an old woman in San Francisco dance in front of a band, Neely was convinced to take her work to the next level. Neely recalls, 'She [the dancing woman] started pointing to people, and when she turned and pointed to me, it seemed to me that she was saying, 'Do it today, because today is all you have.'" Three years later Neely published her first short story, "Passing the Word," in *Essence* magazine (1981). Her short fiction later appeared in many anthologies, including *Test Tube Women* (1984), *Things That Divide Us* (1985), *Angels of Power* (1986), and *Breaking Ice: An Anthology of Contemporary African American Fiction* (1990).

In 1981 Neely moved from Pittsburgh to North Carolina, where she wrote for *Southern Exposure* and produced radio shows for the African News Service. Neely served as a branch director for the YWCA; the head of a consulting firm for nonprofit organizations; a visiting researcher at the Institute for Social Research; and the executive director of Women for Economic Justice.

Despite her extensive involvement in community activism and service, Neely was best known as a mystery writer, and more specifically as the creator of the Blanche White mystery series. Neely's first novel in the series, *Blanche on the Lam* (1992), introduced readers to the proud character of Blanche, a middle-aged, heavy-set, dark-skinned woman, who uses her job as a domestic worker to observe various power players in the white dominated world she works in. When Blanche finds herself the prime suspect in a murder at the summer home of the wealthy family she works for, she must rely on her intelligence, her intuition, her powers of deduction, and most importantly her close network of fellow domestics to prove her innocence. Neely explores the problems of color and class discrimination in the second novel in the series, *Blanche among the Talented Tenth* (1994), where Blanche accompanies her children on an excursion to the exclusive, all-black resort of Amber Cove in Maine. Though Blanche's job and dark skin make her an object of scorn in the wealthy, light-skinned community, she volunteers her services to investigate the suspicious death of one of the other guests. In the third novel in the series, *Blanche Cleans Up* (1998), just when Blanche thinks her life is settling down, she again finds herself enmeshed in scandal, intrigue, and murder in the house of powerful Boston Brahmin politicians, all while trying to raise her niece and nephew. In the last book in the series, *Blanche Passes Go* (2000), we find Blanche back in her hometown of Farleigh, North Carolina, ready to retire from domestic service; instead of finding peace, however, Blanche must confront the ugly memory of David Palmer, the man who raped her eight years before and who shows up as a guest at the first catering event hosted by Blanche's best friend, Ardell.

What is most significant about Neely's mystery novels is that they move beyond stereotypical associations with the genre and seek to explore the important albeit difficult themes of racism, classism, sexism, ageism, and assumptions about beauty, in terms of both color and body type. By presenting these stories to us through the voice of Blanche White, Neely places importance on the narrative of the African American domestic worker, a voice all too often ignored in contemporary society. Dorothea Fischer-Hornung and Monika Mueller claim that in the character of Blanche White, Neely "wants to counteract the once brutally forced acculturation of African Americans by having [Blanche] … reclaim her African cultural roots by worshipping in front of an ancestor altar and by developing an increasingly black separatist stance as the Blanche White series progresses" (13).

Through Blanche White, Neely was able to address many of the social and political issues she was concerned with in her own activism. According to *Voices from the Gap*, "Neely uses Blanche not only to entertain, but also as a medium to discuss serious societal issues. In effect, Blanche is Neely's political voice that will reach the mainstream through the genre of feminist mystery writing." Neely received several awards for her activism, including the Community Works Social Action Award for Leadership and Activism for Women's Rights and Economic Justice, and the Fighting for Women's Voices Award from the Coalition for Basic Human Needs. In 2001 she became the host of *Commonwealth Journal*, a radio program in Massachusetts also broadcast online at http://www.wumb.org/commonwealthjournal/.

FURTHER READING

Collette, Ann. "Damn, She Done It," *Ms.* (June/July 2000).

Fischer-Hornung, Dorothea, and Monika Mueller. *Sleuthing Ethnicity: The Detective in Multiethnic Crime Fiction* (2003).

MALINDA WILLIAMS

Nehemiah, Renaldo (24 Mar. 1959–), track-and-field athlete, professional football player, and sports agent, was born in Newark, New Jersey, the eldest of three children of Harriet and Earl Nehemiah, the latter a bookbinder (his mother's occupation is not known). A wide receiver on his high school football team, Earl Nehemiah instilled in his sons an interest in athletics. At a young age, Renaldo "Skeets" Nehemiah and his younger brother Dion participated in wrestling, boxing, basketball, and karate. Nehemiah's nickname of "Skeets," a family reference to his scampering around the house as a child, would accompany him throughout his life. In 1973 his mother died of cancer; as the eldest child, he assisted his father in taking care of the house and his two siblings. He ran hurdles in junior high school and later at Scotch Plains-Fanwood High School from 1973 to 1977. His track coach, Jean Poquette, assisted Nehemiah in developing a training style and philosophy that would make him a dominating hurdler and successful athlete in general. As a senior in 1977, his athletic abilities and academic record won him recognition as the *Track and Field News* High School Athlete of the Year. He set national high school records with times of 12.9 seconds in the 120-yard high hurdles and 13.5 seconds in the 110-meter high hurdles.

Nehemiah began attending the University of Maryland, College Park in 1977, where he had received a full scholarship. The university had won over twenty consecutive ACC titles, and under Coach Frank Costello, Nehemiah won the 1978 NCAA sixty-yard indoor high hurdles with a time of 7.16 seconds. During the 1979 track season, Nehemiah stunned the world with his NCAA record-breaking times of 6.90 seconds in the indoor sixty-yard hurdles and 13.16 seconds in the 110-meter hurdles, breaking the world record of 13.21 set by Cuban Alejandro Casanas in 1977. Nehemiah later ran against Casanas and Gregory Foster at the UCLA invitational and lowered his own world-record time to 13.00 seconds. At the Penn Relays in Philadelphia, Pennsylvania, in April 1979 Nehemiah demonstrated proficient teamwork by aiding his team's victory in the two-hundred- and four-hundred-meter relays. He successfully defended his NCAA outdoor 110-meter hurdle title with a record time of 12.91 seconds. That same year, he achieved victories in the Pan-American Games in San Juan, Puerto Rico, and at the World Cup in Montreal. To the disappointment of Coach Costello, Nehemiah decided to accept financial reimbursement from Puma, his shoe-company sponsor. By accepting payment, Nehemiah lost his college eligibility in 1980, but was able to maintain his amateur status.

He forfeited his full scholarship, and Puma footed the bill for his remaining two years of college. He continued his studies at the University of Maryland and graduated in 1981 with a B.A. in Arts and Humanities.

After his disqualification from collegiate competition, Nehemiah spent his days gearing up for the 1980 Olympic Games. World politics would keep him from realizing his Olympic dream, however, after the USSR's invasion and occupation of Afghanistan, and President Jimmy Carter's boycott of the 1980 Games in Moscow. Even after his Olympic disappointment, Nehemiah continued to run in international competitions. In August 1981 he ran his official personal best at the Weltklasse track meet in Zurich, Switzerland; he broke his own world record with a time of 12.93 seconds in the 110-meter high hurdles and became the first athlete to officially break the thirteen-second barrier in this event.

In 1982 the National Football League's San Francisco 49ers offered Nehemiah a contract to play as a wide receiver, and he decided to make the switch to professional football. The 26 April 1982 issue of *Sports Illustrated* featured Nehemiah on the cover as a hurdler dressed in a football uniform. The next year, however, he suffered a serious concussion and lower back injury during a game. As a member of the 49ers, Nehemiah caught only forty-three passes and scored four touchdowns. Although he could not compete in the 1984 Olympics in Los Angeles, Nehemiah attended as a sports commentator for the ABC television network. The back injury he sustained in 1983 ultimately led to his early retirement from football in 1985.

After a long legal battle to retain his amateur status, the International Amateur Athletic Federation reinstated Nehemiah and he returned to track and field in July of 1986. In an international track meet in Italy, he ran for a time of 13.48 seconds in his first 110-meter high hurdles race since his last competition in 1981. Although he achieved several world rankings from 1988 to 1991, Nehemiah retired from track-and-field in 1994 without winning either an Olympic or world-championship medal. With his track and field days behind him, he continued to pursue his interest in athletics by hosting a cable network children's exercise show and then becoming assistant track-and-field coach at George Mason University. In 1997 Renaldo "Skeets" Nehemiah was inducted into the Track-and-Field Hall of Fame. In 2006 he joined the sports marketing company, Octagon, as the director of track and field. As a world record–breaking track star, Nehemiah not only paved the way for other athletes to make a living in track and field but also helped raise national and international awareness about the sport.

FURTHER READING
Amdur, Neil. "Meticulous is the Word for Cool Nehemiah," *Baltimore Evening Sun* (June 1979).
Barry, John M. *Power Plays: Politics, Football, and Other Blood Sports* (2001).
Kovalakides, Nicholas. *Men's Track and Field at the University of Maryland: Its First 101 Years, 1894–1994* (1994).
Oden, Bev. "Renaldo Nehemiah, Would-Be Football Star," *Sports Illustrated* (1998).

ELIZABETH A. MCALLISTER

Nell, William Cooper (20 Dec. 1816–25 May 1874), abolitionist and historian, was born in Boston, Massachusetts, the son of William Guion Nell, a tailor, and Louisa (maiden name unknown). His father, a prominent figure in the small but influential African American community in Boston's West End during the 1820s, was a next-door neighbor and close associate of the controversial black abolitionist DAVID WALKER. Nell studied at the all-black Smith School, which met in the basement of Boston's African Meeting House. Although he was an excellent student, in 1829 he was denied honors given to outstanding pupils by the local school board because of his race. This and similar humiliations prompted him to dedicate his life to eliminating racial barriers. To better accomplish that task, Nell read law in the office of the local abolitionist William I. Bowditch in the early 1830s. Although he never practiced, his legal skills and knowledge proved valuable in the antislavery and civil rights struggles of his era.

Nell naturally gravitated toward the emerging abolitionist crusade. In 1831 he became an errand boy for the *Liberator*, the leading antislavery journal, beginning a long and close relationship with its editor, William Lloyd Garrison. His talents were quickly recognized, and he was soon made a printer's apprentice, then a clerk in the paper's operations. In the latter position, which he assumed in 1840, he wrote articles, supervised the paper's Negro Employment Office, arranged meetings, corresponded with other abolitionists, and represented Garrison at various antislavery functions. The pay was low, so he was forced to supplement his income by advertising his services as a bookkeeper and copyist. But he remained one of Garrison's most ardent supporters, even as the Boston abolitionist grew increasingly controversial because of his singular devotion to moral rather than political means and his embrace of a wide variety of reforms.

After the antislavery movement divided into two hostile camps in 1840 over questions of appropriate tactics and women's roles, Nell vehemently criticized those black abolitionists who parted company with Garrison. He moved to Rochester, New York, in 1848 and helped FREDERICK DOUGLASS publish the *North Star*. But when growing conflict between Garrison and Douglass forced him to choose sides, he returned to Boston and the *Liberator*. In 1856 Nell traveled through lower Canada West (later Ontario) and the Midwest, visiting black communities, attending antislavery meetings, and submitting regular reports to the *Liberator*. His accounts of this journey are a useful record of African American life in those areas at the time.

Nell was perhaps the most outspoken and consistent advocate of racial integration in the antebellum United States. He worked closely with white reformers and regularly pressed other blacks to abandon "all separate action, and becom[e] part and parcel of the general community" (Smith, 184). Nell participated in a statewide campaign to end segregated Jim Crow cars on Massachusetts railroads in the early 1840s. He used the antislavery press as a vehicle to attack black exclusion from or segregation in churches, schools and colleges, restaurants, hotels, militia units, theaters, and other places of entertainment.

From 1840 to 1855 Nell led a successful petition campaign to integrate the public schools of Boston, which ended when the Massachusetts legislature outlawed racially separate education in the state. He even opposed the existence of voluntary separatism among African Americans. In 1843 he represented Boston at the National Convention of Colored Citizens in Buffalo, New York, and used that forum as a vehicle to speak out against exclusive black gatherings and activism. An outspoken critic of the black churches, he often attended the predominantly white Memorial Meeting House in West Roxbury.

But Nell supported separate black organizations when they met needs not performed by integrated ones. For example, in 1842 he helped establish the Freedom Association, a local black group founded to aid and protect fugitive slaves. He remained active in this group for four years until the interracial Boston Vigilance Committee was founded for the same purpose. Although he established numerous cultural and literary societies—most notably the Adelphi Union and the Boston Young Men's Literary Society—for Boston blacks after 1830, these were always open to individuals of every race and class.

Nell tempered his opposition to politics and exclusive black activism in the early 1850s. He was nominated by the Free-Soil Party for the Massachusetts legislature in 1850. After the Fugitive Slave Act of 1850 was passed, he stepped up his role in local Underground Railroad activities until illness forced his temporary retirement from the antislavery stage.

About this time Nell began extensive research on the African American experience in the United States. He perceived that black history and memory would help shape the identity of his race and advance the struggle against slavery and racial prejudice. His research resulted in the publication of *Services of Colored Americans in the Wars of 1776 and 1812* (1851), *Colored Patriots of the American Revolution* (1855), and dozens of articles and pamphlets. The careful scholarship and innovative use of oral sources in Nell's works, which were far broader than their titles suggest, made them the most useful and important histories of African Americans written in the Civil War era.

Nell's historical activism also took a more popular turn. In 1858 he organized the first of seven annual CRISPUS ATTUCKS Day celebrations in Boston to honor African American heroes of the American Revolution. Held the fifth day of every March in Faneuil Hall, the festivities consisted of speeches, martial music, displays of Revolutionary War relics, and the recollections of aged black veterans. These gatherings symbolically rejected the decision of the U.S. Supreme Court in *Dred Scott v. Sanford* (1857), which unequivocally denied black claims to American citizenship. Nell also petitioned the Massachusetts state legislature on numerous occasions for an Attucks monument in Boston.

When the Civil War came, Nell embraced the Union cause, anticipating the end of slavery and racial inequality in American life. His hopes were buoyed in 1861, when he was employed as a postal clerk in the Boston post office. This made him the first African American appointed to a position in the U.S. government, and he held the job until his death. He was further encouraged by the Emancipation Proclamation and the decision to enlist black troops in the Union army.

The end of the war brought a series of personal changes for Nell. When the *Liberator* ceased operations in December 1865, it marked the denouement of Nell's lengthy career in reform journalism. But it did not mean the abandonment of activism; during the late 1860s he waged a successful campaign to end racial discrimination in theaters and other public places in Boston. Nell married Frances A. Amers of New Hampshire in 1869; they had two sons. He spent the remainder of his life completing a study of African American troops in the Civil War. It was apparently unfinished when he died in Boston of "paralysis of the brain."

FURTHER READING

Nell's published letters and editorials are available in the microfilm edition of *The Black Abolitionist Papers*, C. Peter Ripley, ed.

Horton, James O. "Generations of Protest: Black Families and Social Reform in Ante-Bellum Boston," *New England Quarterly* 94 (1976): 242–256.

Horton, James O., and Lois E. Horton. *Black Bostonians: Family Life and Community Struggle in the Antebellum North* (1979).

Smith, Robert P. "William Cooper Nell: Crusading Black Abolitionist," *Journal of Negro History* 55 (1970): 182–199.

Wesley, Dorothy Porter. "Integration versus Separatism: William Cooper Nell's Role in the Struggle for Equality," in *Courage and Conscience: Black and White Abolitionists in Boston*, ed. Donald M. Jacobs (1993).

Obituary: *Pacific Appeal* (San Francisco), 18 July 1874.

This entry is taken from the *American National Biography* and is published here with the permission of the American Council of Learned Societies.

ROY E. FINKENBINE

Nelson, Jill (14 June 1952–), writer, novelist, journalist, was born and raised in Harlem, New York. She was the third of four children raised in a privileged family in the 1950s; her father, Stanley Earl Nelson, was a prosperous dentist. His wife, A'Lelia Ransom Nelson, worked as a librarian. (A'Lelia was named for MADAME C. J. WALKER's daughter, A'LELIA WALKER; her father worked as a general manager at Walker's company.) Stanley Nelson left the family when he divorced A'Lelia, whom everyone called Leil, when Jill Nelson was fifteen.

Nelson majored in journalism at the City College of City University of New York and graduated in 1977. She later earned a master's degree at the Columbia University School of Journalism in 1980 and began freelancing for publications like the *Village Voice*, a well-known alternative weekly newspaper in New York City that has been a training ground for black journalists for decades; *Essence*; and *Ms.* for more than a decade. She became an adjunct lecturer at her alma mater in 1982 and in 1983, she worked in the same capacity at Hunter College.

As Nelson penned works of international scope about issues affecting black women in America, she was interviewed and subsequently hired at the *Washington Post* to write for its new weekly magazine in 1986. During her tenure there, in the early days of the magazine, Nelson won the Washington, D.C., Journalist of the Year award.

Her experience at the paper, however, was marked by the discrimination she faced as a middle-class woman of color in a large white-owned and white-run corporation. Shortly after she was reassigned from her job at the magazine to work with a team of reporters assigned to cover the cocaine possession and perjury trial of the former D.C. mayor MARION BARRY, she resigned from her position in 1990. Nelson was apparently frustrated by her demotion from writing longer, more high-profile pieces to covering "the black story." Fueled by her frustration, Nelson went on to write a popular memoir about her experience, *Volunteer Slavery: My Authentic Negro Experience* (1993). The memoir was lauded by many and one reviewer at the San Francisco *Chronicle* even called it "one of the most provocative and illuminating newspaper memoirs on record." Nelson's memoir is probably the sole autobiography of its kind written by a black female reporter in the twentieth century and one of the first to explore black womanhood in the context of a white corporate environment. It won the American Book Award the same year it was published. The most frequent comment about the book was that it not only revealed the struggles of one different voice in a corporate world, which holds universal truths for anyone who doesn't fit neatly into a box, but *Volunteer Slavery* is also as entertaining a read as it is sharp and sad.

Between 1998 and 2003, Nelson was a journalism professor at City College and she continued to write books. Her second memoir, *Straight No Chaser: How I Became a Grown-up Black Woman* (1997), was actually a book of essays. She has said it was written for her daughter, Misu, and the collection explored the difficulty black women have speaking up for themselves. Nelson maintained that it was written out of love, not to silence black men. Her first foray into fiction, *Sexual Healing* (2003), was a best seller among *Essence* readers. She published a follow-up to the steamy book, *Let's Get It On* (2009), which was also a hit.

Nelson blended her talent for reporting and writing in the nonfiction book, *Finding Martha's Vineyard: African Americans at Home on an Island* (2005). The book weaves memoir, with her retelling of her summers spent at the twelve-room family home on the island known for attracting upper- and middle-class blacks looking for respite and refuge among other African Americans. The memoir talks not only of Nelson rubbing elbows with prominent black artists like the author BEBE MOORE CAMPBELL and filmmaker SPIKE LEE, but it also tells the tale of how a family goes on without its matriarch—Nelson's mother died in 2001.

Her other creative works include numerous documentary screenplays including *Mandela* (1985) and *Police Brutality: An Anthology* (2000). Twenty years after she began her foray into print journalism, Nelson was still going strong and producing work for the digital age. She was widely consulted after her essay "The Audacity of Whiteness," about the dearth of black reporters covering politics in the age of BARACK OBAMA, was published on NiaOnline.com and TheHuffingtonPost.com. A frequent lecturer who resided in Harlem after her national success, Nelson also contributed to MSNBC.com and *USA Today*.

FURTHER READING

"Not for Men Only," *Ebony* 58 (Aug. 2003): 30–32.

JOSHUNDA SANDERS

Nelson, Juanita Morrow (1923–), civil rights activist and war tax resister, was born Juanita Morrow in Cleveland, Ohio. The names and occupations of her parents are not known. When she was sixteen she engaged in her first act of resistance to injustice when traveling by train with her mother. Rather than sit in the dilapidated "colored" coach car Morrow moved to a white coach car. In 1942 Morrow entered Howard University. While there she worked with a group of African American women, including the civil rights activist PAULI MURRAY, to organize the Civil Rights Committee and open public accommodations in the nation's capital to blacks, using tactics of nonviolent resistance.

After graduating, Morrow moved back to Cleveland, Ohio, where she founded a local chapter of the Congress of Racial Equality (CORE). In 1946 Morrow spearheaded an effort to desegregate Cleveland's large amusement park, Euclid

Beach, using nonviolent tactics. While working as a journalist for the black newspaper, *The Call and Post*, she interviewed WALLACE NELSON, an African American conscientious objector who was conducting a hunger strike in prison. Nelson and Morrow stayed in close touch until his release in 1946, when they married. Morrow (now Nelson) supported her husband's decision to join the 1947 Journey of Reconciliation to test the 1946 U.S. Supreme Court decision, *Morgan v. Virginia*, which found segregation in interstate public transportation to be unconstitutional.

In 1948 Juanita Morrow Nelson and Wallace Nelson became founding members of the Peacemakers, a radical pacifist organization dedicated to nonviolent direct action and war resistance. Beginning in 1948 the Nelsons became tax resisters, living below the taxable income so as not to support any federal expenditure for war. Together the couple moved just outside of Cincinnati, Ohio, where they took their deep belief in pacifism and interracialism to the level of everyday life. They bought a home with a white couple who were also Peacemakers, Ernest and Marion Bromley, in Gano, Ohio, in 1950. There they lived communally, raised the Bromley's children, engaged in wage work to bring in funds for the household, and refused to pay taxes as part of their continued commitment to pacifism.

The Gano Peacemakers, as they became known, founded the Cincinnati affiliate of CORE, the Citizen's Committee for Human Rights (CCHR). The CCHR successfully desegregated two local music schools, and picketed downtown restaurants and theaters that refused to serve blacks. Their biggest campaign, however, was an effort to desegregate Coney Island amusement park. Nelson's experience protesting Euclid Beach Park's segregation in Cleveland proved invaluable in this campaign. Several summers of nonviolent activism at the park, including total noncooperation upon arrest, persuaded the management to open the park grounds and rides to African Americans in 1955. However, the park's lavish swimming pool and dance hall remained closed as private clubs.

Following the Coney Island campaign, Nelson continued her education at Ohio State, while remaining active with the Peacemakers movement. Her return to school in 1956 followed significant turmoil in CORE, as more moderate New York activists sought to purge the organization of communists and refused to commit to radical nonviolence. In 1954 Wallace Nelson lost his position as a field organizer in CORE, and Juanita, who had served as secretary, resigned in disgust. In 1957 the Nelsons spent four months at Koinonia Farms, an interracial pacifist community in Americus, Georgia. After finishing her degree, Nelson moved to Philadelphia with her husband. In 1959 she was arrested for her continued war tax resistance. The police took her in while she was wearing her bathrobe, and she appeared in court, defiant, in the same robe. Despite this experience, Nelson continued to pay no federal taxes and remained an active member of Peacemakers.

In addition to her commitment to pacifism, Nelson carried on her civil rights activism. In 1961, after hearing of the indignities suffered by African diplomats on the highway connecting Washington, D.C., to New York City, Nelson and her husband staged a restaurant sit-in in northeastern Maryland. As they had done in Cincinnati during the Coney Island campaign, the Nelsons practiced total noncooperation when arrested during the sit-in, including carrying out a hunger strike while in jail. This act of conscience sparked CORE to launch the Route 40 Freedom Ride project to desegregate all public accommodations along the highway.

After a decade in Philadelphia, Nelson and her husband moved to Ojo Caliente, New Mexico, in 1970. There they homesteaded for four years before moving to Woolman Hill in Deerfield, Massachusetts. In Deerfield the Nelsons built their own home from salvaged wood, started an organic farm, and continued their work as tax refusers. In 1975 they founded the Pioneer Valley War Tax Resisters. In 1988 Nelson published a collection of articles and recollections, *A Matter of Freedom and Other Writings*. Her commitment to racial equality and pacifism continued into the new century.

FURTHER READING

Information about Juanita Morrow Nelson's peace activism can be found in the Marion Bromley and Ernest Bromley Papers, 1920–1997, and the Peacemakers Papers, both in the Swarthmore College Peace Collection, Swarthmore, Pennsylvania.

Nelson, Juanita Morrow. *A Matter of Freedom and Other Writings* (1988).

Brown, Flora Bryant. "NAACP Sponsored Sit-Ins by Howard University Students in Washington, DC 1943–44" *Journal of Negro History* 85, no. 4 (Autumn 2000) 274–286.

Meier, August, and Elliott Rudwick. *CORE: A Study in the Civil Rights Movement* (1975).

Mollin, Marian. *Radical Pacifism in Modern America: Egalitarianism and Protest* (2006).

Murray, Pauli. *Song in a Weary Throat: An American Pilgrimage* (1987).

VICTORIA W. WOLCOTT

Nelson, Marilyn (26 Apr. 1946–), poet and translator, was born in Cleveland, Ohio, the daughter of Melvin M. Nelson, a Tuskegee Airman and serviceman in the U.S. Air Force, and Johnnie Mitchell, a teacher. Moving frequently because of her father's career, she attended school in several states and began composing poetry while still in grade school. After earning a B.A. in English in 1968 from the University of California, Davis, she earned an M.A. in English from the University of Pennsylvania in 1970, serving as a lay associate at Cornell University's Lutheran Campus Ministry between 1969 and 1970. Also in 1970 Nelson married Erdmann F. Waniek and subsequently began teaching English in Oregon at Lane Community College and at Reed College. The next year she taught at Nørre Nissum Seminarium in Denmark, and in 1973 she became an assistant professor of English at St. Olaf College in Minnesota. In 1978 she earned a Ph.D. in English from the University of Minnesota, submitting a dissertation titled, "The Schizoid Nature of the Implied Author in Twentieth-Century American Ethnic Novels."

Upon completing her doctorate, Nelson joined the faculty at the University of Connecticut at Storrs and published her first collection of poetry, *For the Body* (1978). The title suggested the central metaphors driving the text: a celebration of the human body as well as the encompassing bodies of family and community. In 1979 she divorced Waniek and married Roger B. Wilkenfeld, also a professor at the University of Connecticut; however, she continued to publish as Marilyn Nelson Waniek until 1995. With Wilkenfeld she had a son and a daughter. The couple divorced in 1996.

In 1982 Nelson published, with Pamela Espeland, a translation of comic poems by the Danish writer Halfdan Rasmussen, *Hundreds of Hens and Other Poems for Children*. At this time Nelson was awarded a grant from the National Endowment for the Arts (NEA). Working again with Espeland, Nelson published another lighthearted collection, *The Cat Walked through the Casserole and Other Poems for Children* (1984). Her next volume of poetry for adult readers, *Mama's Promises* (1985), further considered the body as grounds of female spirituality as she would later detail in an autobiographical essay for the *Contemporary Authors Autobiography Series* (Vol. 23, 1996).

In 1990 Nelson won a Connecticut Arts Award and earned a second grant from the National Endowment for the Arts. This same year she published *The Homeplace*, a collection of poems spanning her family history and juxtaposing sketches of her maternal ancestors with narrative glimpses of her father's experiences with the Tuskegee Airmen. A major publication in Nelson's career, this lyric fusion of historical and personal subjects was a finalist for several awards, including the 1991 National Book Award, and won the 1992 Annisfield-Wolf Award. Her 1994 collection *Magnificat* had a similarly complex scope, in which personally based lyrics explore the tensions between the erotic and the spiritual. In 1995 Nelson was awarded a Fulbright Fellowship to teach in France.

Nelson's next compilation, *The Fields of Praise: New and Selected Poems* (1997), was a finalist for the 1997 National Book Award and won several prizes, including the 1998 Poets' Prize. In 1998 Nelson's version of Euripides' play *Hecuba* was published in the Penn Greek Drama Series and premiered with the African Continuum Theatre Company of Washington, D.C. In 2000 she received a Contemplative Practices Fellowship from the American Council of Learned Societies. Over this span of years, from 1996 until 2002, Nelson also worked in a visiting capacity in writing programs at the William Joiner Center at the University of Massachusetts, Boston; at West Chester University in Pennsylvania; and at the Vermont Studio Center.

In 2001 Nelson produced a young adult's volume that further conjoined the biographical and the lyric, in this case to revere a historical figure, GEORGE WASHINGTON CARVER. *Carver: A Life in Poems* (2001) was named a Newbery Honor Book and a Coretta Scott King Honor Book, and became a finalist for the 2001 National Book Award in Young Adult Literature. *Carver* also earned the Boston Globe–Horn Book Award and the Flora Steiglitz Straus Award from the Bank Street College of Education that year. Also in 2001 Nelson won a Guggenheim Fellowship to work on *The Cachoiera Tales*, published in 2005, a long poem depicting African American tourists in Brazil on a pilgrimage suggesting Chaucer's *Canterbury Tales*. In addition, in 2001 she published two poetry chapbooks, *Triolets for Triolet* and *She-Devil Circus*. During this period she held visiting positions at Vanderbilt University (1999) and the U.S. Military Academy at West Point (2000). At West Point she edited

Marilyn Nelson, poet and professor emeritus of English at the University of Connecticut, in Storrs, Connecticut, 2001. (AP Images.)

Rumors of Troy (2001), a collection of poems based on *The Iliad* that the academy commissioned to use in introductory English courses.

In 2002 Nelson became part of the Cave Canem community of African American writers founded by TOI DERRICOTTE and Cornelius Eady. She retired from the University of Connecticut and taught briefly at the University of Delaware from 2002 to 2004 before returning to the University of Connecticut part time. A conversation at this juncture between Nelson and poet Dana Gioia, director of the National Endowment for the Arts, led to Operation Homecoming, an initiative supported by the NEA that offered writing workshops to military personnel who had served in Afghanistan and Iraq and their families. This project culminated in the publication of *Operation Homecoming: Iraq, Afghanistan, and the Home Front, in the Words of U.S. Troops and Their Families* (2006). Also in 2003 Nelson founded Soul Mountain, a writers' retreat in East Haddam, Connecticut, supported in part by the University of Connecticut.

Thereafter Nelson published two other major works of poetry with historical overtones. The first, *Fortune's Bones: The Manumission Requiem* (2004), another book for young adults, celebrated the life of a slave in eighteenth-century Connecticut whose skeleton is in the Mattatuck Museum in Waterbury; this work was adapted for choral and orchestral performance by Ysaye Barnwell of the musical group Sweet Honey in the Rock. In the second work, *A Wreath for Emmett Till* (2005), Nelson developed a cycle of sonnets to lament the brutal lynching in Mississippi in 1955 of a black teenager from Chicago.

From 2001 to 2006 Nelson served as poet laureate of Connecticut, undertaking a range of projects that included writing four books based on historic events in Connecticut as well as an essay for the Academy of American Poets Web site on the state's literary history; placing donations of poetry books in Connecticut hospitals and doctors' offices; maintaining a "Dial-A-Poem" telephone line; and organizing a group reading and poetry celebration in the state capital. Nelson also published two other translations, *The Thirteenth Month* (2005), poems by Inge Pedersen, and *The Ladder* (2006), a verse narrative by Rasmussen.

FURTHER READING

The Thomas J. Dodd Research Center at the University of Connecticut houses a selection Nelson's papers.

KATHARINE RODIER

Nelson, Rachel West (c. 1955–), civil rights activist, was born Rachel West, the eighth of eleven children to Lonzy West and Alice Mactin West. West grew up surrounded by activists in the civil rights movement. Her parents, civil rights activists themselves, raised their family in a modest apartment in the George Washington Carver Homes development in Selma, Alabama. Her mother worked in a child development center that she helped found and became a licensed home day-care provider certified in early childhood development. As a child, Rachel West attended St. Elizabeth Mission School. Her best friend and neighbor, Krisandra Sheyann Webb, attended the local public school, Clark School, and the two often walked to school together. It was this friendship and these walks that brought West and Webb to the frontlines of civil rights protests in Selma in 1965.

Rachel West was nine years old in 1965 when her family welcomed several aides of DR. MARTIN LUTHER KING JR. into their home to live while they planned voting rights rallies and marches. Alice and Lonzy West were among the earliest Selma residents to agree to participate in these events. Though Rachel knew of her houseguests' plans, she did not intend to take part in the movement until a meeting at Brown Chapel AME Church attracted Sheyann Webb's attention as the two walked to school. Webb skipped school to attend the meeting that day and continued to do so throughout the early planning stages. After a short while, West joined her. The girls were charged with leading the attendees in song. They sang Negro spirituals about freedom and songs about standing up to the power holders of the time, like Alabama governor George Wallace.

Brown Chapel AME Church served as the site of many meetings where Selma residents, including teachers, clergy, and visiting civil rights workers, gathered to strategize and plan marches and to comfort and motivate one another in 1965. It was also the place where Rachel West first met Martin Luther King Jr. There King encouraged West and Webb to seek freedom. He grew fond of the girls, encouraged their singing, and regularly spoke with them on his visits to Selma.

The Southern Christian Leadership Conference (SCLC) and the Student Nonviolent Coordinating Committee (SNCC) spearheaded the movement that compelled Selma residents, including the Wests, to march in a nonviolent effort to win the right to vote. Members of these organizations and Selma residents conducted several peaceful marches to the Dallas County courthouse in early 1965 to attempt to register residents to vote. They were regularly confronted by Dallas County sheriff James Clark, who was determined to prevent black residents from registering to vote. Sheriff Clark grew increasingly frustrated with the demonstrators as the protests continued, especially since Selma's black residents and civil rights workers ignored an injunction prohibiting mass meetings. While West was afraid of what the sheriff might do to her and the other demonstrators, she continued to march alongside adults in the movement. The work of the Selma marchers compelled others in Alabama's Black Belt to march for the right to vote as well. Their marches also included the historic march from Selma to the State Capitol in Montgomery from 21 to 25 March 1965, to protest Alabama's voting restrictions on black residents and the violence against peaceful voting rights demonstrators.

In February 1965, the West family opened their home to Jonathan Daniels, a white seminary school student from Keene, New Hampshire, who traveled to Selma to help the people of Dallas County and the surrounding areas fight for the right to vote. The Wests welcomed others, but few endeared themselves to the West family and to Rachel West as did Daniels. West considered him to be her friend. In August 1965, Daniels traveled to Lowdnes County, Alabama, to help with voter registration after President Lyndon Johnson signed the Voting Rights Act of 1965 into law. While there, he joined a protest march and was jailed for six days with other marchers. Daniels was shot and killed shortly after his release as he protected a fellow protester at whom a part-time sherif's deputy had pointed his gun. The child development center where West's mother worked was later renamed in Daniels's honor.

West saw her march for the right to vote as a march for freedom. Even as a child she understood that her fight was not born of hatred for the white Selma residents who opposed voting rights initiatives, and to prove it she publicly sent get well wishes and prayers to Sheriff Clark upon his hospitalization for chest pain. Sheriff Clark would live until June 2007; throughout his life, he believed that he was right to oppose Selma's protesters. During the time of the voting rights protests in Selma, West saw violence against protesters, including the aftermath of "Bloody Sunday," 7 March 1965, when Alabama state troopers and local deputies attacked peaceful demonstrators attempting to cross the Edmund Pettus Bridge. She also met several people who would die in the movement. Still, she would later note that things had to happen in Selma the way that they did in 1965 or she would not have been able to vote as an adult. Rachel West Milhouse would go on to work for the state of Alabama and to live in Selma.

FURTHER READING

Webb, Sheyann, et al. *Selma, Lord, Selma: Childhood Memories of the Civil-Rights Days* (1997).

NZINGA HILL

Nelson, Wallace Floyd (27 Mar. 1909–23 May 2002), civil rights activist and war tax resister, was born in Altheimer, Arkansas, the youngest son of Lydia (Durand) and Duncan Nelson, a Methodist minister and sharecropper. He spent much of his childhood in Little Rock, Arkansas, and finished high school living with his older brother in Ohio. Nelson graduated from Ohio Wesleyan, where he became active in the YMCA and Student Christian movement. During the 1930s Nelson was a member of the Methodist Youth Movement and read works by Gandhi, Tolstoy, and Thoreau. Influenced by these authors and active in the growing pacifist movement, in 1934 Nelson made a pledge to resist any war of aggression.

This pacifist pledge was tested during World War II, when Nelson registered as a conscientious objector. He initially served in a Civil Public Service Camp, Camp Coshocton in Ohio. However, Nelson walked away from the camp because of its policy of segregation and his increasing unease with making any contribution to the war effort. He lived in a Detroit Co-operative house for seven months before the authorities located and imprisoned him for a sentence of six years. After two years in prison Nelson, frustrated with the conditions and racist policies, went on a hunger strike. While in prison he was interviewed by an African American journalist, JUANITA MORROW. When Nelson was released early he married Morrow, who was leading Cleveland's Congress of Racial Equality (CORE) chapter and was a fellow pacifist.

After his release from prison in 1946 Nelson went on a six-month speaking tour with fellow conscientious objectors and pacifists. In 1947 he joined sixteen activists, associated with the Fellowship of Reconciliation (FOR) and CORE, to carry out the Journey of Reconciliation. This first freedom ride tested the 1946 Supreme Court ruling, *Morgan v. Virginia*, which ruled interstate travel could not be segregated. While participating in the Journey of Reconciliation, Nelson befriended a fellow pacifist, Ernest Bromley, a white minister and FOR member. Bromley invited Nelson and his wife to join his family in a pacifist community just outside of Cincinnati. In 1948 the Bromleys and the Nelsons helped to organize the Peacemakers, a group of war resisters dedicated to the use of nonviolence to achieve peace and racial equality.

In the early 1950s Nelson became the first national field organizer for CORE. In Cincinnati's local chapter he helped organize a series of dramatic protests against the segregated amusement park, Coney Island. During these protests Nelson engaged in passive resistance, going limp when arrested, and total noncooperation with the authorities. He taught others these tactics when directing CORE's summer workshops in Washington, D.C., in 1951 and 1952. The workshop members, under Nelson's leadership, successfully integrated two public playgrounds in the nation's capital. Nelson's promotion of radical nonviolence, however, created conflict within CORE, as more conservative members became concerned about the red scare and felt that pacifism would alienate supporters. In 1955 this faction forced Nelson out of his leadership position in CORE, and the following year he left Cincinnati to accompany his wife to Columbus, Ohio, where she was attending graduate school.

Nelson had engaged in war tax refusal as a member of the Peacemakers since 1948. Although he left the communal household he had formed with the Bromleys, he continued to be active in Peacemakers throughout his life. In 1957, for example, he and Juanita spent four months at Koinonia Farms, a Christian interracial pacifist community in Americus, Georgia. Nelson then moved to Philadelphia, where he headed the Tax Refusal Committee of the Peacemakers and continued to engage in civil rights activism. Along with his wife, Nelson helped desegregate public accommodations along the highway from Washington, D.C., to New York City in 1961. As they had done in the Coney Island campaign, the Nelsons practiced total noncooperation when arrested. Their work pushed CORE into organizing the Route 40 Freedom Ride project to desegregate all public accommodations along the highway. In 1968 Nelson fasted for twenty-one days in support of Caesar Chavez's United Farm Workers campaign.

In 1970 Nelson moved with his wife to Ojo Caliente, New Mexico, where they lived on a small plot of land, growing their own food and living independently. Four years later they relocated for a final time to Woolman Hill in Deerfield, Massachusetts. There the Nelsons built their own home from salvaged materials, grew an extensive garden of organic vegetables, and founded the Pioneer Valley War Tax Resisters.

The Nelsons often lived on less than $5000 a year, below the level that required them to pay federal income taxes. There was a debate among the Tax Refusal Committee of the Peacemakers about local taxes, often called "school taxes," because these taxes did not go to the military; most members did pay them, including the Nelsons. At the time of his death Nelson had not paid federal taxes for fifty-four years.

FURTHER READING

Information about Nelson's peace activism can be found in the Marion Bromley and Ernest Bromley Papers, 1920–1997, and the Peacemakers Papers, both in the Swarthmore College Peace Collection, Swarthmore, Pennsylvania.

Meier, August, and Elliott Rudwick. *CORE: A Study in the Civil Rights Movement* (1975).

Mollin, Marian. *Radical Pacifism in Modern America: Egalitarianism and Protest* (2006).

Tracy, James. *Direct Action: Radical Pacifism from the Union Eight to the Chicago Seven* (1996).

Wittner, Lawrence S. *Rebels against War: The American Peace Movement, 1941–60* (1969).

VICTORIA W. WOLCOTT

Neville Brothers The Arthur "Art" Lannon Neville Jr. (17 Dec. 1937–); Aaron Joseph Neville (24 Jan. 1941–); Charles Barrow Neville (28 Dec. 1938–); and Cyril Garrett Neville (10 Oct. 1948–), singers and musicians, were born in New Orleans, Louisiana, to a spirited, musical family that included their influential and beloved uncle, the pianist and dancer George "Chief Jolly" Landry.

The brothers were educated at a combination of Catholic and secular schools, all of them segregated. Keyboardist Art started his first band, the Hawketts, landing a hit in 1954 with "Mardi Gras Mambo." Charles picked up the saxophone, quitting school at age fifteen to tour with Gene Franklin and the House Rockers. Inspired by their father and uncle's adventurous tales of foreign countries, Art and Charles later joined the navy hoping for a brighter educational future. Dismayed by the overt racism of the military, however, both returned to music and Charles eventually studied music theory at Southern University. Aaron, whose strongest influences came from brother Art, gospel, doo-wop, and the plaintive cries of cowboys in old western movies, sang with the Avalons, his high school music teacher's group. And Cyril, percussionist and vocalist, gained most of his musical training by listening to his brothers and sitting at the feet of masters such as the keyboard legend PROFESSOR LONGHAIR. There was little other formal training. However, the importance of New Orleans' funeral marches and second line traditions cannot be overstated, serving the brothers as their primary, if somewhat disjointed, music teacher. For many New Orleanians these traditions provided a significant cultural environment. For the Neville brothers, the brassy, rhythmic quality of the second line music and the bits and pieces of the Mardi Gras Indians' shouted mantras would inform their own music decades later. The Nevilles' funk owed a tremendous debt to the street parade musical sensibility; the second line would get its due when funk's history emerged.

The Neville Brothers, a singing group from New Orleans, during a visit to New York City, 2 March 1989. From left: Cyril, Art, Charles, and Aaron. (AP Images.)

Charles and Art took to the road early on, influenced by doo-wop, bebop jazz, R&B, and the perennial sounds of second line parades. Aaron had a hit in 1966 with "Tell It Like It Is" and toured many months supporting the ballad. By the age of seventeen Cyril, influenced by numerous genres and styles, including those of STEVIE WONDER and CHARLES MINGUS, added songwriting to his drumming skills. Unfortunately, during this time and for decades to come, most of the brothers' battles with drug and alcohol addiction truncated their individual and group success.

Though the Neville brothers played in many and varied bands—including the profoundly influential Meters and the Wild Tchoupitoulas—their unified musical gestation was long and circuitous. Since their beginning, band personnel crossed over and intersected; the Meters and Wild Tchoupitoulas, even the Soul Machine, were no different. It is one of the reasons perhaps that a number of the Neville Brothers's songs were played and reshaped, retooled to fit the band they were in. The Neville Brothers finally formed in 1977. The group was born at the Bijou Theater in Dallas, upon the breakup of the Meters. Finally, the Neville Brothers—all of them—came together as one musical family.

During the 1970s the Nevilles' most arduous and prevalent enemy was disco music. Despite their natural tendency toward combining many sounds, disco wasn't one of them. Standing firmly against the tide of the wildly popular dance music, they recorded their first, eponymous album for Capitol in 1978. Unfortunately, sales were commensurate with the lack of label promotion. However, the follow-up for A&M in 1981, *Fiyo On The Bayou*, featuring Aaron's luminescent vocals on the standard "Mona Lisa" and covers "Iko Iko" and "Brother John" provided a break in the monotony of hard luck. Despite receiving favorable critiques from fellow musicians, the album did not sell well and the group had no record deal from 1981 until 1987. Despite this, their concerts eventually sparked fiery live records, *Neville-ization* and *Live at Tipitina's*. Then in 1989 the Neville Brothers, with their producer Daniel Lanois on the boards, recorded what was considered one of their finest efforts, *Yellow Moon*. Finally, the charts and a Grammy nomination reflected their musical success. In the 1990s, after a tremendously long road to recognition, the Nevilles' popularity grew to international proportions. In 2004 *Walkin' In The Shadow of Life* marked a return to the spare, funky quality and the spiritual lyricism of the earlier records.

If the Nevilles' musical influences were vast and deep, their contributions were equally so. Funk bands and hip-hop artists paid some of their greatest dues to both the Nevilles and the Meters. The Nevilles were known for bringing their family into the mix, and Ivan Joseph Neville (son of Aaron) was a full-time member of the band. Often seen on stage was Ian Arthur Neville (son of Art) and at any time a handful of Neville progeny could be seen at live shows, adding even greater blend to the Nevilles' remarkable legacy.

FURTHER READING

Ritz, David, with the Neville Brothers. *The Brothers Neville* (2000).

Gothard, Jody. "New Spirit for the Neville Brothers," *Lagniappe* (Arts and Entertainment Section, New Orleans *Times Picayune*) (4 Nov. 1988).

Kent, Joan. "It's About Time! Nevilles Hope New Album Spells Permanent End to Chitlin Circuit," New Orleans *Times Picayune* (May 1981).

Palmer, Don. "The Neville Brothers: R&B Dynasty," *Down Beat* (Mar. 1985).

Palmer, Robert. "New Orleans Inspires the Neville Brothers," *New York Times* (28 June 1981).

Sinclair, John. "The Nevilles Come Home," *Wavelength* (May 1989).

Spera, Keith. "Band of Brothers," *Lagniappe* (Arts and Entertainment Section, New Orleans *Times Picayune*) (22 Oct. 2004).

WENDI BERMAN

Newborn, Phineas (14 Dec. 1931–26 May 1989), jazz pianist, was born Phineas Newborn Jr. in Whiteville, Tennessee, the son of Phineas Newborn Sr., a drummer, and Rosie Lee Murphy. While Newborn Sr. led a band at the Flamingo Club on Beale Street in Memphis, the six-year-old Phineas began jazz and classical studies with Georgia Woodruff, his first-grade teacher. He later studied arrangement with Onzie Horne and learned to play trumpet, baritone horn, French horn, and tuba in high school. He began his professional career in 1945 as a pianist. Prodigiously gifted, he was inspired by the great jazz pianists of the 1930s, above all the virtuoso ART TATUM. Yet he also spent years accompanying rhythm and blues and urban blues musicians, with whom he toured the South during school vacations. Newborn began playing with his father's band by the age of fifteen and was a regular member from 1948 to 1950. He also joined the band of the electric guitarist and singer Saunders King in 1947,

and he was on the electric guitarist and singer B. B. KING's first recordings in 1949. These experiences gave Newborn's style an earthy lyricism generally lacking in Tatum's work.

After graduating from high school Newborn taught himself to play vibraphone. While majoring in music at Tennessee Agricultural and Industrial State University in Nashville from 1950 to 1951, he learned to play still more instruments: alto, tenor, and baritone saxophone. He left Tennessee A&I in 1952 when his father refused to let him transfer to the Juilliard School in Manhattan. Newborn also studied at Lemoyne College in Memphis from 1952 to 1953. He worked with the vibraphonist LIONEL HAMPTON's band in 1950 and 1952, and he was a member of the rhythm and blues tenor saxophonist Willis Jackson's band in 1953. Also in the early 1950s he toured with B. B. King and Jackie Brenston and did session work in Memphis.

After serving in the army from 1953 to 1955 Newborn spent ten months as a sideman in his father's group; he also worked with his brother, the guitarist Calvin Newborn. Phineas then formed his own quartet, including Calvin. The Willard Alexander Agency convinced the quartet to leave Tennessee and come north, initially to perform in Philadelphia at Pep's nightclub late in 1955. Following the advice of COUNT BASIE, who had heard Newborn play in Memphis in 1952, the writers and promoters John Hammond and Leonard Feather went to hear Newborn in Philadelphia and were deeply impressed. Hammond secured jobs for the quartet in New York. With Calvin, fellow Memphis bassist Jamil Nasser (known at that time as George Joyner), and the drummer KENNY CLARKE, Newborn debuted at the Basin Street club and began recording in the spring of 1956. OSCAR PETTIFORD replaced Joyner for Newborn's first recording session, and several drummers, including PHILLY JOE JONES, DENZIL BEST, and ROY HAYNES, played with Newborn in his first years of international exposure.

In February 1958 Newborn performed with the poet LANGSTON HUGHES and the bassist CHARLES MINGUS at the Village Vanguard. He then worked with Mingus on the soundtrack of John Cassavetes's film *Shadows* (1959). In 1958 he recorded the albums *Fabulous Phineas* and *We Three*, worked with the drummer Roy Haynes at Birdland in New York, toured Europe with a Jazz from Carnegie Hall package in October, and performed with Haynes at the Five Spot club in New York toward year's end. He briefly toured Italy in April 1959.

Hammond and Feather had touted Newborn as the next major jazz sensation, but even while admiring his technical facility, other critics disparaged his musical content as shallow and accused him of overplaying. Touring proved grueling for Newborn, and he suffered personal and health problems. He temporarily stopped performing but reemerged in 1961 in Los Angeles, where he recorded with the tenor saxophonist Teddy Edwards and the trumpeter HOWARD MCGHEE. He also made two outstanding albums of his own, *A World of Piano!* and *The Great Jazz Piano of Phineas Newborn* for Contemporary. In October 1962 Newborn's trio performed on television in the *Jazz Scene* series, but he remained in California, declining the tours that would have followed the success of his albums.

In the late 1950s Newborn married Dorothy Stewart, and they had two daughters. The failure of this marriage (which ended in divorce), business problems, the death of his father, as well as Newborn's difficulty in handling responsibility, led to a nervous breakdown sometime around 1960. Newborn was intermittently confined to Camarillo State Hospital, and he restricted his performances to local clubs in Southern California. He made only a few additional recordings, including the albums *The Newborn Touch* (1964) and *Please Send Me Someone to Love* (1969). He later fathered a son with another woman.

Newborn returned to Memphis in 1971 to live with his mother. Further episodes of mental instability plagued him. In 1974 he recorded the album *Solo Piano*. At this time he was mugged and badly beaten; although several of his fingers were broken he recovered and resumed playing. He recorded *Solo* (1975); *Back Home* (1976), with Ray Brown and Elvin Jones; and *Look Out ... Phineas Is Back!* (1976), with Brown and Jimmy Smith. A tour of solo concerts began in 1975 at the Shrine Auditorium in Los Angeles. That year he also performed at the Keystone Korner nightclub in San Francisco, and he made the first of several Japanese tours, during one of which he recorded *Phineas Is Genius* (1977) with a trio in concert. In 1978 he was again in Japan, and he returned to New York for the first time, performing at the Village Gate. In July 1979 Newborn starred at the Montreux Jazz Festival in piano duets with JAY MCSHANN, Hank Jones, and JOHN LEWIS, in a piano trio with HERBIE HANCOCK and Chick Corea, and in a trio with Ray Brown and the drummer DANNIE RICHMOND. Throughout the 1980s he occasionally made brief annual performances in New York City, usually at the Sweet Basil club. In the 1980s he frequently played in Memphis clubs. Newborn died in Memphis; the cause of his death was not disclosed, but his agent Irvin Salky reported that X-rays had recently revealed a growth on one lung.

Newborn's most personal signature was the perfectly coordinated doubling of swift melodies in the right and left hands, separated by two octaves. He articulated fast bop melodies in a hard, cutting, precise manner, but he also ranged into more lyrical areas of jazz, presenting blues-tinged pop themes, inserting passages of harmonized melody in two-handed block chords and passages of old-fashioned "oom-pah" striding in the left hand, and replacing the general restlessness of bop with a willingness to repeat ideas.

FURTHER READING

Booth, Stanley. *Rhythm Oil: A Journey through the Music of the American South* (1992).

Hunt, David C. "Phineas Newborn, Jr.: Problems of a Virtuoso," *Jazz & Pop* 9 (June 1970).

Obituaries: *New York Times*, 28 and 29 May 1989; *Jazz Journal International* 42 (July 1989).

This entry is taken from the *American National Biography* and is published here with the permission of the American Council of Learned Societies.

BARRY KERNFELD

Newby, Dangerfield (1820?–17 Oct. 1859), one of the first African American raiders killed in John Brown's raid on Harpers Ferry in 1859, was born to Elsey Newby, a slave, and Henry Newby, who was white. Henry Newby freed Dangerfield's mother and his siblings in 1858, and Dangerfield was freed at the same time. Henry Newby was a somewhat typical Virginia landowner whose motives concerning manumission are unknown. That he freed family members does not necessarily distinguish him from slave owners who kept their children or other relations in bondage. The Newbys lived in Culpeper County, near the Old Dominion's Blue Ridge Mountains. For some years Henry Newby was a typical white slaveholder. In 1840 he held nine slaves, including a male who was most likely Dangerfield, and a female, probably Elsey Newby. Ten years later, in 1850, he possessed seventeen slaves. By 1860, however, they had all disappeared from Culpeper. A white, seventy-seven-year-old farmer, Henry Newby now lived in Bridgeport, Ohio, across the Ohio River from Wheeling, along with twenty-one other people designated as "mulattos." Ohio offered the Newbys some sanctuary. Henry Newby's 1858 move was fortunate not only because Ohio laws and a recent state court judicial decision favored freed African Americans but also because he moved there just three years prior to his December 1861 death. Elsey Newby, Dangerfield's mother, who had been born an enslaved African American in Fauquier County, Virginia, about 1799, died a free Ohio resident in 1884. Several of Henry Newby's black children also lived for some time in Ohio.

Dangerfield Newby was born probably sometime around 1820, and therefore was approximately thirty-nine when he died. A craftsman, he had been a blacksmith and had worked, perhaps as a hireling, on the Rappahannock River Canal. That he was able to form a family with an enslaved woman who lived in Warrenton (Fauquier County) and later in Brentsville (Prince William County) is but one indication of the mobility an enslaved craftsman could enjoy. One contemporary said Newby was "a tall, well-built mulatto, … with a pleasing face" (Joseph Barry, *Annals of Harpers Ferry*, 1872, 52). A relative declared Newby to be "a quiet man, upright, quick-tempered and devoted to his family," who "never talked much about slavery and kept his intention of joining John Brown, whom he had met in Oberlin, to himself." To Annie Brown, John Brown's daughter, Newby was "a smart and good man for an ignorant one" (quoted in BENJAMIN QUARLES, *Allies for Freedom: Blacks on John Brown*, 1974, 87). A photograph reveals an intense man in his late thirties or early forties.

Like his father, Dangerfield Newby tried to free his wife and children in 1858 and 1859. Newby followed the lead of other African Americans who solicited funds for their freedom or that of others. Newby traveled through northern Ohio to solicit money for his wife's (and perhaps his children's) expected sale price. His skills may have helped him earn some purchase money as well. He began to collect funds soon after the Newby family's move to Bridgeport earlier in the fall of 1858. He bought bank certificates of deposit three times, the last time in spring or summer 1859. The Dangerfield Newby estate papers confirm that he had raised nearly $742 in three certificates.

Newby's wife and children lived in Brentsville, Prince William County, Virginia, north of the present-day Quantico Marine Reservation. He and his wife, Harriet, were devoted to each other. Harriet wrote at least three moving letters to "husband," during 1859. "Come this fall with out fail monny or no monney I want to see you so much," she pleaded; later she looked her precarious position in the face: "I want you to buy me as soon as possable

for if you do not get me somebody else will." She went on to inform Newby that "it is said Master is in want of monney[;] if so I know not what time he may sell me an[d] then all my bright hops of the futer are blasted."

The Newbys had several (perhaps six) children whom they hoped to free. "The children are all well," Harriet informed her husband in early April 1859, adding that she was, "looking forward to the promest time of your coming" and that "nothing would give me more pleasure than to see you." In August the message was the same. Harriet Newby was, like her husband, nearly desperate. A house slave, she had to care for Mrs. Jennings, her owner's wife, who had recently given birth. By August 1859 her domestic situation had worsened because the "servents are very disagreeable; they do all thay can to set my mistress against me." The main problem, the source of greatest anxiety, was naturally the chance that her master might sell her for want of money before Newby could buy her.

Harriet's owner, who strongly influenced the chain of events that led to Dangerfield Newby's joining John Brown, was probably Dr. Lewis Augustine Jennings, a physician of Warrenton and Brentsville, Virginia. There is circumstantial evidence that he was facing financial troubles. Jennings reportedly had agreed to a price of one thousand dollars to free at least Harriet. However, Dangerfield's fund-raising campaign bore no fruit. Either Newby was unable to make the required purchase offer or Dr. Jennings turned it down. Dangerfield Newby now looked for other means of freeing Harriet and all of their children. If Newby were not already enraged that he had to raise the money to make a protective purchase of his own wife, he certainly must have been after his offer was refused.

Newby decided to join the planning for the Harpers Ferry raid of 1859. About sixty miles by road from Harriet in Brentsville, Newby selected Harpers Ferry as the base camp for an attempt to rescue his family. His desire and love of family were stronger than his strategic and tactical experience, however, so he failed to see the fatal flaws in Brown's plan. Instead he was killed very early in the raid. Some Harpers Ferry residents even beat Newby's body with sticks, then shoved those sticks into the appalling and deadly wounds Newby had suffered. His remains were interred in a secret location and stayed there until the 1890s, when a Washington, D.C., physician and others disinterred them and removed them to the John Brown Farm, now a New York State Historical Site in North Elba, New York.

Newby made the supreme sacrifice in the raid of October 1859, unaware of the consequences for his family. His wife and (perhaps) his children were sold away. Newby's death may have sealed the fate of Harriet and their children; however, the exact nature of that fate is obscure. Reports that Harriet Newby and the children were sold to Louisiana are vivid reminders of one of the most feared experiences of bondage, being "sold down the river." Harriet's master died of cancer in April 1860, about half a year after her husband's death. This death probably put Harriet as well as Jennings's other slaves in an even more precarious position. Even the disposition of Dangerfield Newby's estate, which consisted of the money he'd raised to free his family, emphasizes Harriet's and their children's circumstance. Newby's brothers and sisters forced the issue judicially, suing Harriet and her children for the money. The defendants obviously could not appear, so the court ordered an official to distribute the remainder of the estate to his brothers and sisters.

What ultimately happened to Harriet and her children, whom sale condemned to uprooting and perhaps a new kind of enslavement? One author asserted in 1894 that Harriet was "found in Louisiana," having been "made free by the civil war"; another declared in 1910 that "it is said" that Harriet had come back to Ohio. She in fact remarried as Harriet Robinson and moved to Fairfax County, Virginia. Her daughter Agnes Newby Proctor, whom Harriet mentioned in her letters to Dangerfield, married and named her firstborn son after her father. Besides Newby relatives in Ohio, Gabriel Newby, another child of Dangerfield and Harriet Newby, resided in Kansas City in 1900, and in St. Louis until his 1919 death.

John Brown and Dangerfield Newby may have brought on the end of slavery indirectly. But Newby's brother William directly contributed to emancipation: as a private in Company C of the Fifth Regiment, U.S. Colored Troops, he made the supreme sacrifice in the 1864 siege of Petersburg, which a year later forced Confederate troops to surrender at Appomattox. The successful Civil War emancipation measures and the Thirteenth Amendment finally guaranteed Harriet Newby and her children the freedom that Dangerfield Newby had been unable to gain for them in 1858 and 1859.

FURTHER READING
Genealogical information on Newby and his descendants can be found in the U.S. Census, 1880,

Virginia, 288C [Mount Vernon District, Fairfax County, Virginia.]; 361A and 382B [Alexandria, Virginia]. His estate papers can be found in the Belmont County, Ohio, Court of Probate, Inventories, H (1860–1862): 18–19, 545–556, Belmont County Courthouse, St. Clairsville, Ohio.
Schwarz, Philip J. *Migrants against Slavery: Virginians and the Nation* (2001).

PHILIP J. SCHWARZ

Newby, William H. (1828–24 Mar. 1859), writer and activist, was born in Virginia to parents whose names remain unknown. Newby's enslaved father died in his youth. His free mother moved the family to Philadelphia in the early 1830s. She may have been the laundress Maria Newby listed in the 1850 Federal Census of Philadelphia, though the surname is not uncommon (p. 362). A 20 June 1863 *Pacific Appeal* article on Newby by journalist PHILIP ALEXANDER BELL referred to him as largely "self-educated" but did note his attendance at the city's segregated public schools. Working first as a barber and then as a daguerreotypist, Newby seems to have stood at least at the fringes of the city's Black society; Bell remembered him as a member of the Philadelphia Library Company of Colored Persons and a "skillful debater."

Probably in response to the limitations imposed by Northern racism and the hope of the Gold Rush, Newby made his way to California in 1851. He settled in San Francisco and quickly became active in that city's small but lively black community. He engaged in both Masonic activities and agitation against California's recently passed black laws (especially those prohibiting black testimony), and, in 1853, with local activists JONAS H. TOWNSEND, MIFFLIN WISTAR GIBBS, and a group of other area African Americans, founded the San Francisco Athenaeum, a literary and debating society modeled after those in Philadelphia and New York City.

In August 1854, under the playful pseudonym "Nubia," Newby wrote to *Frederick Douglass's Paper* offering to be its San Francisco correspondent. That letter, which was published in the 22 September issue of FREDERICK DOUGLASS's Rochester-based weekly, turned out to be the first of several. In addition to providing an important record of one segment of California's nascent black community, Newby's letters considered a range of national issues and are still striking for their wit and determination.

Newby also continued his local activism. He led calls for the 1855 California Convention of African

Americans, and, when that body met in Sacramento in November 1855, he chaired the Committee on Resolutions. The convention focused heavily on continuing to combat California's legal strictures on blacks. Newby attempted to introduce measures designed to create a black newspaper, but these were thwarted. However, through both a smaller August 1856 meeting of San Francisco blacks—including Townsend, future AME Zion Bishop JOHN JAMISON MOORE, and future *Pacific Appeal* founder PETER ANDERSON—and the later 1856 state convention, Newby and Townsend were able to create support for California's first black newspaper, *The Mirror of the Times*. According to Bell, Newby was involved with the *Mirror* until the fall of 1857—often writing, sometimes editing, and sometimes serving as the paper's traveling agent. Most copies of the *Mirror*, though, remain lost, and so scholars do not yet have a full sense of the paper's content or Newby's contributions.

During this period, Newby befriended Guillaume Patrice Dillon, who had been representing French interests as the consul to California since 1850. Dillon was reassigned to Haiti by a decree of 1 March 1856 and turned his San Francisco office over to his successor at the end of the year. Prior to leaving, Dillon asked Newby to follow him to Port-au-Prince and become his personal secretary. Newby, now suffering from consumption, accepted in part because he hoped that his failing health would rebound in Haiti and in part because he had grown more and more emigrationist out of frustration with U.S. policies. A San Francisco meeting of prominent blacks chaired by Peter Anderson presented Newby with a gold pen in celebration of his community-centered literary efforts, and he traveled to New York at the end of 1857.

In New York, Newby studied French, moved in black activist circles, met and befriended both Bell and abolitionist JAMES MCCUNE SMITH, and may have begun persuading Bell to move to California. However, Newby did not know that Dillon, too, had been ailing—and had actually returned to France in late 1857 and died in Paris that October. When Newby arrived in Haiti in early 1858, he found no job waiting for him and so decided to return to California. However, by the time Newby resettled in San Francisco, the *Mirror* was dead and the Athenaeum, dying. He formed a new literary society—the Dillon Literary Association, named for his French friend—but he was too ill to make it flower.

Bell described him as "a close reasoner and a shrewd debater; more of a controversialist than a logician ... of lymphatic nervous temperament; in person, tall, well-shaped but delicate; his complexion ... pure black ... in temper ... irritable and nervous, arising from his organization, but not violent; his friendships were not easily formed, but they were lasting." A pioneering black Western writer and activist, he died in San Francisco.

FURTHER READING

Lapp. Rudolph. *Blacks in Gold Rush California* (1977).

Ripley, C. Peter, et. al., eds. *The Black Abolitionist Papers*. Vol. 4, *The United States, 1847–1858* (1991).

ERIC GARDNER

Newcombe, Donald (14 June 1926–), baseball player, baseball executive, and advocate for alcohol abuse education, was born Donald Newcombe in Madison, New Jersey, one of four sons born to Sadie Sayers and Ronald Newcombe, a chauffeur. When Newcombe was five years old, Ronald Newcombe's employer moved to Union, New Jersey, and the family relocated to Elizabeth, New Jersey.

Newcombe's father introduced him to alcohol at age eight and Newcombe continued to drink into adulthood. As a boy, he played sandlot baseball and occasionally attended professional baseball games in Newark, New Jersey, with his father and brothers, observing the Newark Eagles of the Negro National League and International League Newark Bears, a farm club of the New York Yankees. An older brother briefly managed a semiprofessional baseball team and occasionally allowed his younger brother to practice with the team. Newcombe's older next door neighbor, John Grier, took an interest in the young man and taught him how to pitch and play other sports. Newcombe played football and baseball in junior high school, but his high school, Jefferson High, did not have a baseball team.

In 1942, Newcombe joined the U.S. Army but was released for being underage. He joined the Navy in August of 1943 but was discharged a month later, again because of his age. Newcombe dropped out of high school with the vague intention of becoming a truck driver. An acquaintance arranged for Newcombe to meet Mrs. Effa Manley, owner of the Newark Eagles, and in the spring of 1944 Newcombe was invited to try out for the team during spring training in Virginia. He made the squad and pitched for the Eagles in 1944 and 1945.

In October 1945, Brooklyn Dodger scout Clyde Sukeforth signed Newcombe to a contract to play for the Brooklyn Brown Dodgers, a new African American team that was being created by Brooklyn

Dodger owner Branch Rickey to play in Brooklyn's Ebbets Field when the Dodgers were on the road. A few days later, on 23 October 1945, the Dodgers and the Montreal Royals announced that JACKIE ROBINSON had been signed to a contract to play for the Royals, integrating professional baseball. One day later, Newcombe received a call and was asked to meet Dodger owner Branch Rickey and Sukeforth in Brooklyn. They terminated Newcombe's contract with the Brown Dodgers and signed Newcombe to a contract to play in the Dodger farm system.

In 1946, Newcombe and one other African American, catcher ROY CAMPANELLA, played for Nashua, New Hampshire, in the New England League. Newcombe won fourteen games in 1946 and nineteen games in 1947. In 1948, he pitched for Montreal in the International League and won seventeen games. In 1949, after making five more appearances for Montreal, he was promoted to the Brooklyn Dodgers and on 20 May 1949 became the fifth African American to appear in the major leagues.

Newcombe, who stood six feet four and weighed 225 pounds, featured a good fastball and a hard, breaking curve ball and was considered one of the best hitting pitchers of his era.

He was an immediate success and became the first great African American pitcher to appear in the major leagues, making the National League All-Star team in each of his first three seasons. In 1949, he won seventeen games and was named the National League Rookie of the Year. In 1951, he won twenty games, the first African American to do so in the major leagues. After the 1951 season, he was drafted into the U.S. Army and served two years before returning to the Dodgers in 1954. In 1956, his twenty-seven victories led the major leagues. He was named the National League Most Valuable Player and the inaugural winner of the Cy Young Award, given to baseball's most outstanding pitcher, making him the only player in major league history to be named both Rookie of the Year and Most Valuable Player and also win a Cy Young award.

Although Newcombe was successful on the field, he was also an alcoholic. Partly because of his abuse of alcohol, his pitching career began to decline in 1957. In 1958, he was traded to the Cincinnati Reds and was then traded by the Reds in 1960 to the Cleveland Indians. He was released at the end of the season, finishing his major league career with a record of 149–90. In 1962, Newcombe became the second American and the first African American to play professionally in Japan when he played one

season with the Chunichi Dragons, pitching and playing first base.

Upon his return to the United States, Newcombe purchased a nightclub and his alcoholism led to personal problems and financial trouble. In 1966, Newcombe stopped drinking after his wife threatened to leave him. In the late 1960s, he was employed by the Opportunities Industrialization Center in the Watts neighborhood of Los Angeles.

In 1970, Newcombe approached the Los Angeles Dodgers and proposed the creation of a community relations department. The Dodgers accepted his proposal, becoming the first team in baseball to create such a department, and named Newcombe Director of Community Affairs.

In 1978, Newcombe convinced the Dodgers to establish an alcohol-abuse assistance program. While continuing his role with the Dodgers, he became a spokesperson for the National Clearing House for Alcohol Information developed by the National Institute on Alcohol Abuse and Alcoholism of the U.S. Department of Health.

In 2009, after thirty-nine years as Director of Community Relations, Newcombe was named special advisor to Frank McCourt, the Dodger's Chairman of the Board. Newcombe was married three times, first to Freddie Cross, with whom he adopted two children, and then to Billie Roberts, with whom he had three children. His third marriage was to Karen Kroner.

FURTHER READING

Golenbock, Peter. *Bums: An Oral History of the Brooklyn Dodgers* (1984).

Painter, Jill. "True Blue Ambassador Newcombe Proud to be a Dodger Since '49," *Los Angeles Daily News*, November 14, 2006.

Stout, Glenn, and Richard Johnson. *The Dodgers: 120 Years of Dodgers Baseball* (2004).

Tygiel, Jules. *Baseball's Great Experiment: Jackie Robinson and His Legacy* (1983).

Waters, Sean. "Former Ace Delivers a Timely Pitch," *Los Angeles Times*, February 6, 1994.

GLENN STOUT

Newman, Isaiah DeQuincey (17 Apr. 1911–21 Oct. 1985), minister, civil rights activist, and state senator, was born in Darlington County, South Carolina. He was the youngest child of Charlotte Morris, a schoolteacher, and Milton C. Newman, an itinerant minister. Newman, who had three older sisters, was raised in the home of his paternal grandmother in Hartsville, South Carolina, after his mother died when he was six years old. His father's second wife, Serena, a member of the Hamilton family of Charleston, South Carolina, was also a teacher. Eleven children were born to this union. Newman's white paternal grandmother and his biracial paternal grandfather owned a mill and two plantations in Hartsville, South Carolina. Unlike many other less privileged rural black families, the Newmans held a vision of hope and progress and tenaciously clung to the goal of attaining higher education. As a youngster, Newman attended public school in Williamsburg County and completed high school at Claflin College in 1930 (later Claflin University). Claflin, in Orangeburg, South Carolina, served as a high school for blacks because black schools, especially in the rural areas, only offered a third- or fourth-grade education. Newman then enrolled at Clark Atlanta College (later Clark University) in Atlanta, Georgia, graduating in 1934 with a B.A. in English Literature. He continued his studies at Gammon School of Theology (later Gammon Theological Seminary), from which he graduated in 1937 with a bachelor of divinity degree and the ability to read and write in six foreign languages, including Hebrew, German, and Latin. Three events shaped Newman's life and guided his career choices. The first was a deathbed promise to his mother that he would become a minister. The second event occurred three years later when he witnessed the death of an African American convict who was burned to death by the Ku Klux Klan near the family's home. The third incident occurred while he was a student pastor in Red Oak, Georgia. He interceded on behalf of a sick sharecropper on a plantation, and was ordered at gunpoint by the plantation owner to leave the property.

One month prior to graduating from Gammon, Newman married Anne Pauline Hinton of Covington, Georgia, on 27 April 1937. Newman's wife was a seventeen-year-old high school graduate, the blue-eyed daughter of Oscar Cornelius, a white man and a biracial mother, Sarah Elizabeth Hendricks. A daughter, Emily Morris DeQuincey, was born to this union in 1947. As a Methodist minister, ordained in 1929, Newman held pastoral appointments in Georgia and South Carolina and also served as superintendent of Sumter District of South Carolina Conferences and General Conferences of the church. Newman retired from full-time ministry in 1973, but continued to work as a supply minister until 1982.

Newman assumed a leadership role in the NAACP and in 1943 helped organize the

Orangeburg, South Carolina, branch and became its president. A few years later he became active in the executive committee of the NAACP in Sumter and in 1948 became the vice president of the state's NAACP conference. In 1958 he was elected president of the NAACP conference and went on to become state field director of the NAACP in 1960. He believed that nonviolent protest was the most effective means to bring about social change, but also believed in the organization's direct action methods. He was arrested approximately twelve times and was nearly lynched by an angry mob when he led a "wade-in" at Myrtle Beach State Park in 1961.

A low point in Newman's leadership resulted from the tension and resistance on the part of the white establishment to desegregate Orangeburg, South Carolina. The tension eventually erupted into what later was described as the "Orangeburg Massacre." The violence that ensued resulted in the death of a seventeen-year-old high school student from the local black high school and two eighteen-year-old students from South Carolina State College (later South Carolina State University). The students were killed by law enforcement agents and members of the National Guard. Although there were some agreements on the actual events resulting in the death of the students, most interpretations of what happened are conflicting.

Newman retired in 1969 as the field director of the NAACP, and from 1972 to 1974 he assumed the position of special assistant to the Commissioner of the South Carolina Department of Social Services. From 1970 to 1973 he served on the State Advisory Council for Comprehensive Health Planning and the state's Study Committee on Aging. From 1971 to 1974 he was Commissioner of the State Housing Authority and a member of that agency from 1974 to 1980. From 1975 to 1980 he was secretary of the State Board of Health and Environmental Control and until 1981 director of the governor's Office of Rural Development.

Newman had belonged to the Republican Party, but in 1958 switched his political allegiance. He served as a delegate in the National Democratic Convention in 1968, 1972, and 1988, and was president of the Columbia Ward 19 Democratic Club and chairman of the State Black Caucus. In 1978 he was President Jimmy Carter's personal representative to the Solomon Islands' independence celebrations. He served as director for Richland Memorial Hospital from 1982 to 1983, founded and directed the Society for the Preservation of Black History,

Art, and Folklore. He was a member of South Carolina Historical Society, and the Shriners, and he belonged to the Omega Psi Phi fraternity. He owned radio station WDPM-FM in Columbia, South Carolina, and in 1979 was awarded the Order of the Palmetto, the highest civilian award in the state given to individuals who worked to transform nonproductive systems in the state.

Although Newman was elected in a special election to the South Carolina State Senate on 25 October 1983—the first black to serve in that legislative body since Reconstruction—and was reelected in 1985, he resigned on 31 July 1985 because of ill health. Newman received four honorary doctorate degrees for his humanitarian contributions. In 1994 the College of Social Work at the University of South Carolina established the I. DeQuincey Newman Endowed Chair and Professorship in recognition of his tireless effort to promote equal opportunity in the state and the nation. Newman died of lung cancer and emphysema at the age of seventy-two.

FURTHER READING

Bailey, N. L., M. L. Morgan, and C. R.Taylor, eds. *Biographical Directory of South Carolina Senate, 1776–1985* (1985).

Brinson, C. S. "The Reverend Mr. Newman: A Long Way from Police-lined Streets to Golden Anniversary Celebration," Columbia, SC, *State Newspaper*, June 1979.

Woolley, D. "Newman Provided a Cool Head when Tempers Ran Hot." Columbia, SC, *State Newspaper*, 22 Oct. 1985.

SADYE L. LOGAN

Newsome, Joseph Thomas (2 June 1869–8 Mar. 1942), lawyer and editor, was born in Sussex County, Virginia, the son of Joseph Newsom and Ann (maiden name unknown), former slaves. He graduated from Virginia Normal and Collegiate Institute (later Virginia State University) in 1894 and, after teaching for a time in Sussex County, graduated from Howard University School of Law in Washington, D.C., in 1899. Newsome joined the Virginia bar in 1899, moved to Phoebus (near Hampton), and then settled in Newport News. He married Mary B. Winfield, an 1892 graduate of Virginia Normal, in 1900; they had one daughter.

Newsome—or "Lawyer Newsome," as he was known—practiced for four decades in the Newport News area. Active in politics, he served as the assistant sergeant at arms at the 1920 Republican National Convention in Chicago. Yet, bridling at the "lily-white" practices of his party, he ran in 1921 for the office of attorney general on a state ticket that the Lily Black Party mounted that year. In the 1928 presidential campaign, as some leading black Virginians contemplated breaking with the Republican Party to back Democrat Al Smith, Newsome brokered a compromise agreement that the leaders would not pledge collectively to support either candidate but rather would decide for themselves individually. He helped found and lead the Warwick County Colored Voters League, which lobbied for schools, community improvement, and voter registration. Newsome's efforts led to the establishment during World War I of Huntington High School for black residents of Newport News. In 1931 he was one of two black attorneys who made a successful appeal to the state supreme court in *Davis v. Allen*, a case that originated in Hampton, alleging that black residents were routinely rebuffed in their efforts to register to vote.

Newsome and the black church were important to each other throughout his life. He taught Sunday school for many years, first in Sussex County and then in the Trinity Baptist Church in Newport News until 1923. He also served Trinity Baptist as a Sunday school superintendent, a member of the board of trustees, a choir member, and an usher. Afterward he-served at Carver Memorial Presbyterian Church. He spoke of his commitment to "the Cause," which he associated with the religious concerns of his fellow black Virginians. Newsome could have—and may have—applied the term as readily to the civic improvement and political empowerment of black Virginians in the Tidewater area. His home was a community center from the time he purchased it in 1906 until his death, and BOOKER T. WASHINGTON met there on occasion with local leaders.

Newsome edited the *Newport News Star*, a black newspaper, from the late 1920s after its founder, Natt N. Lewis, died. He stepped down as editor after the newspaper was taken over in the late 1930s by the *Journal and Guide*, the black voice of neighboring Norfolk. That newspaper subsequently issued a Peninsula edition that for a time was called the *Norfolk Journal and Guide and Newport News Star*. During the last few years of his life, Newsome contributed a column titled "In the Drift of the Current" to the *Journal and Guide*.

A noted criminal lawyer, Newsome was involved in some famous cases in eastern Virginia. In 1939, for example, when Newsome defended June Clark against the charge that she had murdered her stepson in her home, he convinced the jury to acquit her on the grounds of self-defense. Similarly, in 1941 Lindsay Smith went on trial on the charge that he had murdered a white soldier stationed at Fort Eustis. The soldier had invaded Smith's home after an argument that originated with the white soldier's refusal to stop harassing young black women. Newsome convinced the jury that Smith had the right to protect his home, by force if necessary, if convinced that his life was in danger.

Even in his seventies, Newsome remained an active participant in public affairs. Early in World War II, Governor James H. Price appointed Newsome to the Hampton Roads Regional Defense Council, and Newport News mayor T. Parker Host named him to a local committee for the organization of a civilian defense police force. In 1940 Judge Herbert G. Smith of the Newport News Corporation Court appointed Newsome as a commissioner of chancery. At the time of his death, Newsome was serving as the president of the Old Dominion Bar Association, recently established as a black counterpart to the Virginia State Bar Association.

Newsome died at his home in Newport News. Appropriations in the late 1980s of $125,000 from the Newport News City Council and $150,000 from the Virginia legislature made it possible for his home to be restored and converted into a black history museum and community center, called Newsome House.

FURTHER READING

Newsome's papers are at the Newsome House, Newport News, Virginia.

Buni, Andrew. *The Negro in Virginia Politics, 1902–1965* (1967).

Obituaries: *Norfolk Journal and Guide* and *Richmond (Virginia) Afro American*, 14 Mar. 1942.

This entry is taken from the *American National Biography* and is published here with the permission of the American Council of Learned Societies.

PETER WALLENSTEIN

Newsome, Mary Effie Lee (18 Jan. 1885–12 May 1979), author, editor, and illustrator, was born Mary Effie Lee in Philadelphia, Pennsylvania, one of five children of Mary Elizabeth Lee and Benjamin Franklin Lee, Wilberforce University professor and president, bishop of the African Methodist Episcopal (AME) Church, and chief editor of its official publication, *Christian Recorder*. Newsome learned to appreciate literature at an early age from her parents. She loved the nature stories she heard from her mother, who also taught her children how to draw pictures of birds, insects, and flowers. Her well-read father also shared an appreciation for art and literature and encouraged Newsome's artistic and literary expression. When she moved to Waco, Texas, at the age of seven, when her father was elected an AME bishop, Newsome continued to explore nature through verse and sketches and attempted to publish her work. Four years later her family established its permanent home in Xenia, Ohio. At age sixteen she began her extensive training in the liberal and fine arts, first at Wilberforce University (1901–1904), where both her parents were educated, and later at Oberlin College (1904–1905); the Philadelphia Academy of Fine Art (1907–1908); and the University of Pennsylvania (1911–1914).

Mary Effie Lee first began publishing in 1915 in *Crisis*, where more than one hundred of her poems were printed over the next nineteen years. She found another publishing outlet when *Crisis* editor W. E. B. DuBois established a magazine in 1920 devoted to African American children, ages six to sixteen, called the *Brownies' Book*. The monthly publication was meant to "make colored children realize that being 'colored' is a normal, beautiful thing" and "to make them familiar with the history and achievements of the Negro race" (*Crisis*, Oct. 1919). Newsome saw eleven of her poems in the *Brownies' Book*, which lasted only two years.

In 1920 Mary Effie Lee changed her name to Effie Lee Newsome after marrying the African Methodist Episcopal Church Reverend Henry Nesby Newsome, who taught at Wilberforce. They moved to Birmingham, Alabama, where her husband was assigned an AME congregation. Newsome organized the Boys of Birmingham Club and became an elementary school teacher and children's librarian. She and her husband soon moved back to Wilberforce, where she took a job as a librarian at Central State College.

In 1924 DuBois transferred his effort in the *Brownies' Book* to a column in *Crisis*, recruiting Newsome to edit and write "The Little Page," which featured poems, illustrations, and short prose writing. Newsome produced nature poetry, drawings, nonsense verse, and parables relating to African American youth facing racial discrimination. These prose pieces aimed to instill pride in black youth by emphasizing the history of Africa and its descendants.

Newsome also appeared in other major publications such as *Opportunity*, from 1925 to 1927, and *Phylon*, another journal edited by DuBois, from 1940 until 1944. Though she published nonfiction and short stories, Newsome's reputation rests mostly on her poetry. In 1940 she published her only book, a collection of poems. *Gladiola Garden: Poems of Outdoors and Indoors for Second Graders* is a testimony to her devotion to the wonders of nature. Mary Hastings Bradley, in the foreword, described Newsome's book as possessing charm and significance beyond what children would value. "The spirit of kindness, of gentle insight, and of quiet understanding underlies even the gayest of her fantasies." Newsome dedicated the book to her sister for "keeping the garden of hope alive," revealing her own optimism, which Bradley claims captures the attitude of their time. The editors of the *Negro History Bulletin* (Feb. 1947) depicted her encouraging spirit well when they said that Newsome's "aim is not only to help children to appreciate the good and the beautiful but to express themselves accordingly."

Newsome received some critical notice for her adult poems, especially "Morning Light: The Dew-Drier." The poem is perhaps Newsome's most enduring legacy, anthologized in COUNTÉE CULLEN's *Caroling Dusk* (1927); ARNA BONTEMPS's *American Negro Poetry* (1963); LANGSTON HUGHES's and Bontemps's *Poetry of the Negro: 1746–1970* (1970); and Arnold Adoff's *Poetry of Black America* (1973). Published in 1918 in *Crisis*, "Morning Light" describes the role of "dew-driers," African boys who bushwhacked paths for white explorers and safari hunters. Leading the way, these boys absorbed the wet grasses and faced serious dangers, a role Newsome foretells for black people in the era following the World War I: "May not his race, even as the Dew Boy leads / Bear onward the world to a time / When tolerance, forbearance, / Such as reigned in the heart of ONE / Whose heart was gold / Shall shape the world for that fresh dawning / After the dews of blood?"

Newsome's "Morning Light" contributed to the early momentum of the Harlem Renaissance, which began at the end of World War I, by bringing attention to the value of African American heritage. Her work also reflected the spirit of the Harlem Renaissance through the African and African American images that she drew to accompany her poems. However, she was not known for the social and political activism associated with the Harlem Renaissance. Instead, Newsome was appreciated for her mastery of "the difficult art of writing verses for children that keep a sense of literary values and do not offend by too much of a juvenile air" (230), as she is described in *The Negro Genius* (1937). Venetria K. Patton and Maureen Honey's effort to redress the historical emphasis on male writers from the Harlem Renaissance included several of Newsome's poems in *Double-Take: A Revisionist Harlem Renaissance Anthology* (2001) on the strength of her writings for children. Her reputation as a gifted children's writer also lives on among early childhood educators. Rudine Sims Bishop, who wrote the introduction to *Wonders: The Best Children's Poems of Effie Lee Newsome* (1999), applauded Newsome for her timeless gift of capturing the way a child views the world. Newsome stopped publishing in 1944. She retired from her work as a librarian at Wilberforce University in 1963 and lived in Wilberforce until her death.

FURTHER READING

The only surviving paper of Effie Lee Newsome is a biographical sketch that she wrote for Arna Bontemps, kept in the Harold Jackman Collection, Atlanta University Center Library, Atlanta, Georgia.

MacCann, Donnarae. "Effie Lee Newsome: African American Poet of the 1920s," *Children's Literature Association Quarterly* 13 (1988): 60–65.

Rollins, Charlemae Hill. *Famous American Negro Poets* (1965).

CALEB A. CORKERY

Newton, Alexander Herritage (5 Nov. 1837–29 Apr. 1921), abolitionist, Civil War veteran, African Methodist Episcopal (AME) minister, and doctor of divinity, was born in New Bern, North Carolina. He was one of several children born to an enslaved father and a free black woman. Although Newton inherited his mother's legal status as a free person, he nonetheless developed a hatred of the slave system. While still a teenager he aided an acquaintance, Henry Bryan, in a daring escape from bondage. Newton first disguised Bryan in female clothing and led him to a hiding place in the attic of a local slaveholder; this plan was of course implemented with the help of the enslaved people of the household. Offers of a reward for the capture and return of Bryan yielded nothing, and with Newton's further help he safely left the attic hideaway and made his way to freedom in the North. Newton recounted this incident in his autobiography published in 1910, an indication that his early involvement with the Underground Railroad had a powerful, lasting effect on his developing consciousness.

Newton learned the bricklayer's trade when he entered service as an apprentice to Jacob Gooding in 1852. In 1857 Newton traveled to Beaufort, North Carolina, where he found work as a cook aboard a schooner bound for New York City. Once there he was reunited with his mother, who had probably left North Carolina to settle in Brooklyn shortly before Newton began his apprenticeship to Gooding. Newton discovered that his mother had been collecting money to purchase the freedom of her husband Thaddeus, still enslaved in New Bern. She received assistance in this endeavor from some notable New York abolitionists, including Theodore Tilton and the Reverends Henry Ward Beecher and Henry Highland Garnet. While in New York, Newton was able to acquire some schooling while working as a bricklayer. He also performed other jobs such as whitewashing houses and working on the New York City docks chopping tea and weighing cotton. The black abolitionist leader ROBERT HAMILTON befriended the young Newton and assisted him in finding employment—a providential circumstance, for Newton later married Hamilton's eldest daughter, Olivia Augusta, in Brooklyn in 1859. Three children were born to the couple: Ada Augusta, William Alexander, and Mary Hamilton. In New York, Newton also heard the preaching of the African Methodist Episcopal ministers James Morris Williams and George A. Rue, and met the AME bishops Daniel Alexander Payne and William Paul Quinn. These encounters made a deep impression on Newton and the remainder of his adult life, following his military service during the Civil War, was devoted to furthering the growth and prosperity of the AME Church.

After the firing on Fort Sumter and President Abraham Lincoln's call for 75,000 volunteers to put down the rebellion, Newton joined the Thirteenth, a white regiment organized in Brooklyn. It is unclear under what circumstances he was able to do this or under what terms and conditions he served. President Lincoln's call galvanized Northern black communities, and black men eagerly offered their services. These offers were repeatedly rejected, however, and the general consensus among white Northerners was that the Union would be defended by white men, and that black men were neither needed nor wanted as soldiers. Despite the racist prohibition Newton apparently served in the Thirteenth. Indeed, a small minority of black men served in white Union regiments as soldiers and sometimes as personal servants to white officers. After January 1863 Northern black men had the opportunity to enlist in large numbers with the creation of the famed Fifty-fourth Regiment of Massachusetts Volunteer Infantry. In the fall of 1862 other African American Union regiments had been organized in South Carolina, Kansas, and Louisiana. In May 1863 the War Department established the Bureau of Colored Troops, and other Northern states quickly followed the example of Massachusetts in creating black units to fill state quotas for enlistees, albeit in segregated regiments.

By 1863 Newton had moved his family—wife, children, and both parents—to New Haven, Connecticut. On 18 December 1863 he enlisted in the Twenty-ninth Regiment (Company E) Connecticut Volunteers—the state's lone black unit—under the command of Colonel W. B. Wooster. The men of the Twenty-ninth left New Haven in March 1864 for Annapolis, Maryland, and from there were ordered to Hilton Head and Beaufort, South Carolina. By August 1864 the regiment was in Virginia, and Newton saw his first action at Malvern Hill. The Twenty-ninth was heavily engaged in the campaigns against Petersburg and Richmond throughout the remainder of 1864 and spring of 1865, and in April the Twenty-ninth was the first infantry unit to march into the conquered city of Richmond. Newton witnessed the triumphal entry of President Lincoln, and he was still in Richmond when he received news of the President's assassination. From Virginia, the Twenty-ninth was ordered to Texas for garrison duty. After enduring many battles and hardships Newton was mustered out of the Union army on 25 October 1865 and honorably discharged at Hartford, Connecticut, on 25 November 1865. He had served with honor and attained the rank of commissary sergeant. Newton did not suffer physical injury but he suffered nonetheless with the loss of many comrades in arms. This anguish was intensified by the death of his brother Steven, a member of the Fourteenth Rhode Island Battery, who was killed at Fort Pillow.

Back at home Newton endured more personal tragedy with the deaths of his daughter Mary Hamilton and his wife Olivia; the latter died in 1868. A widower with two young children to support, Newton resolved to devote himself to the ministry and the AME Church, feeling that God had spared his life during the war for this purpose. He received his AME Exhorters' License and preached his first sermon in 1871; shortly thereafter he received his first appointment and took charge of the church at Pennington, New Jersey. As an AME minister, Newton was sent all over the country by the church leadership. He assumed the direction of various congregations and took on many responsibilities in each locale, including building church membership and fund-raising—often for the construction of a new church building. At the annual AME conference in Nashville in 1874, Newton was ordained a deacon. Two years later he was ordained an elder and assigned to the Bethel AME Church at Little Rock, Arkansas. There he met Lulu Campbell, secretary of the Sunday school, and the two were married on 1 June 1876. Newton continued his ministry, nurturing his new family along the way. From Little Rock he was assigned to Louisiana, where a daughter, Ella, was born in 1878; Garfield, the second and last child of the marriage, was born in Pennsylvania in 1881. Soon after his son's birth, Newton was able to settle somewhat in New Jersey, where he directed a number of churches during the 1880s, including those in Morristown, Madison, and Camden. During this period Newton was also able to purchase a house at 332 Washington Street in Camden, which became the family home.

Newton recorded in his autobiography that the years 1899 to 1904 were painful and difficult to bear. His daughter died in 1899; Garfield and Ella died in 1902 and 1905, respectively. The loss of his mother was yet another cause for grief; she died at the age of ninety-two in 1904. However, adversity never dampened Newton's spirit for very long, nor stifled his ambition. While attending the annual AME conference in 1907, held at Orange, New Jersey, Newton heard the Reverend Samuel G. Miller speak on the necessity of an educated ministry. Discussions with Miller convinced Newton that he should continue his education, and at the age of seventy he entered the Bible College of Philadelphia. After completing a three-year course of study which included Hebrew and New Testament Greek, Newton was awarded a doctor of divinity degree in 1910, the same year he published his autobiography. This accomplishment, achieved so late in his life, was a testament to Newton's quest for self-improvement through continuing education. Throughout his career he was a strong advocate of an educated ministry, and often had occasion to lament his own lack of an advanced degree. In 1910 Newton realized one of his most cherished dreams. Alexander Herritage Newton died at the age of eighty-four of chronic heart disease at his home in Camden, New Jersey. He was survived by his wife Lulu L. Campbell Newton.

FURTHER READING

Newton, Alexander Herritage. *Out of the Briars: An Autobiography and Sketch of the Twenty-ninth Regiment Connecticut Volunteers* (1910, repr. 1969).

Angell, Stephen W., and Anthony B. Pinn, eds. *Social Protest Thought in the African Methodist Episcopal Church, 1862–1939* (2000).

Berlin, Ira, Joseph P. Reidy, and Leslie S. Rowland, eds. *Freedom: A Documentary History of Emancipation 1861–1867*, series II: *The Black Military Experience* (1982).

Glatthaar, Joseph T. *Forged in Battle: The Civil War Alliance of Soldiers and White Officers* (1990).

Morgan, Joseph H. *Morgan's History of the New Jersey Conference of the A.M.E. Church from 1872 to 1887* (1887).

Redkey, Edwin S., ed. *A Grand Army of Black Men: Letters from African-American Soldiers in the Union Army, 1861–1865* (1992).

DEBRA JACKSON

Newton, Frankie (4 Jan. 1906–11 Mar. 1954), jazz trumpeter, was born William Frank Newton in Emory, Virginia. Nothing is known of his parents, childhood, or musical training, but his first professional work was with the Cincinnati-based band of Clarence Paige, with whom he began playing several years before 1926. In early 1927 while in Lexington, Kentucky, he joined Lloyd Scott's Symphonic Syncopators, then on tour. When Lloyd and his brother Cecil Scott returned home to work in Ohio, Newton settled in Harlem, where he played trumpet during the summer of 1927 in ELMER SNOWDEN's band at the Nest Club. In the fall he went on another tour with the Scotts, and in December the band took up residency at the Savoy Ballroom in Harlem.

Newton remained at the Savoy through the next two years, making his first records with Cecil Scott's Bright Boys in November 1929. After their return to the Savoy following a June 1930 tour the Bright Boys quit en masse after a falling-out over unpaid back earnings. Now freelancing and based in Harlem, from mid-1930 through 1931 Newton played with CHICK WEBB at the Savoy, Charlie Johnson at Small's Paradise, Snowden at the Nest Club, Bobby Neal at the Strand Ballroom, and FATS WALLER at Connie's Inn. In 1932 he played briefly with the pianist Garland Wilson on the radio station WEVD and then joined the SAM WOODING Orchestra for residencies at the Arcadia Ballroom and the Pelham Heath Inn.

In September 1933 Newton returned to the Johnson band, and in November he accompanied BESSIE SMITH on her last recording date. In late 1935 he left Johnson for medical reasons but returned to the band briefly in early 1936. Starting in the spring of 1936 he spent a year in Teddy Hill's band, leaving in May 1937 when he suffered from complications following a tonsillectomy. He had also appeared on records by TEDDY WILSON, Art Karle, and Mezz Mezzrow in 1936 and by Teddy Hill in 1936 and 1937. From July through September 1937 Newton worked at the Onyx Club in New York City with BUSTER BAILEY, Pete Brown, Don Frye, and JOHN KIRBY, who was soon appointed leader of the group. In August, Newton and Kirby recorded a session with Charlie Barnet's otherwise all-white band, while in the surrounding months the nucleus of the Kirby group participated in recording dates led by Bailey, WILLIE "THE LION" SMITH, and the singers Jerry Kruger, MAXINE SULLIVAN, and Midge Williams. Using essentially the same men, but with the addition of Cecil Scott and with EDMOND HALL in place of Bailey, Newton also recorded sessions under his own name in March, April, and July 1937. In November and December 1937 Newton played in Mezzrow's short-lived 14 Disciples of Swing at both the Harlem Uproar House on Fifty-second Street and at the Savoy, but the public proved unwilling to accept the racially mixed group, and Mezzrow soon dissolved the band. From December 1937 through February 1938 Newton worked with the Mills Blue Rhythm Band, under the leadership of LUCKY MILLINDER.

Starting in December 1938 Newton led his own octet at Café Society Downtown, and except for an absence in February because of illness he remained there through 1939, recording sessions with that band in April and August. A few days before the first of these dates he recorded some of his best blues work in a group called the Port of Harlem Jazzmen, and later that month he provided the muted trumpet on Billie Holiday's famous recording of "Strange Fruit" for Commodore. The following June the Port of Harlem group returned to the Blue Note studios, this time with the addition of SIDNEY BECHET. In February 1940 Newton took a racially mixed band, including the tenor saxophonist Joe "Flip" Phillips, into Kelly's Stable in New York, and the group remained there through the summer. He played later engagements at various vacation resorts in the spring of 1941 and at Harlem's Mimo Club in the fall, and he returned to Kelly's Stable that winter. In a revealing departure from his usual working environs Newton spent the summer of 1941 in Bechet's quintet at the leftist-oriented Camp Unity in Wingdale, New York.

From November 1942 through February 1943 Newton led a sextet in Boston. In April he took this group, with the trombonist VIC DICKENSON, into Café Society. In June 1944 Newton worked at George's in New York, and from August through December he was at the Pied Piper in Greenwich Village with JAMES P. JOHNSON, the celebrated stride pianist with whom he had recorded an exceptional session the previous June. During the next two years he led his own group at several locations in Boston and New York City and made a number of recordings with MARY LOU WILLIAMS, Buck Ram, Miss Rhapsody, Hank D'Amico, JOE TURNER, and Stella Brooks, on whose date he was once again reunited with Bechet. The Brooks session was Newton's last studio effort.

In early 1947 Newton worked at Fifty-second Street's Downbeat Club in SID CATLETT's quartet, but from the spring through the fall he was inactive because of illness. In late 1947 he worked with Ted Goddard's band at the Savoy in Boston, but in the summer of 1948 he lost his home and trumpet in a fire. By early 1949 he was freelancing in Boston and that summer played in several concerts and appeared with Edmond Hall's band. In May 1950 he again had his own band at the Savoy, but by 1951 his playing was limited to occasional Friday night appearances at the Stuyvesant Casino in lower Manhattan. By this time Newton had settled in Greenwich Village, where he devoted himself primarily to politics, social work, and painting. His decision to stop playing may have been prompted by failing health and by resentment toward the lack of opportunities for jazz performers of his generation to work in the bop-dominated scene of the day. A long-standing spokesman for racial and economic equality, in the 1930s Newton had become attracted to Marxist philosophy and left-wing causes, an interest that he shared with the equally literate and politically conscious Edmond Hall. Newton died, reportedly of acute gastritis, in New York City. On 26 April 1954 a memorial concert was held on his behalf at New York's Basin Street, featuring the bands of Eddie Condon, RED ALLEN, Jimmy McPartland, and Bob Wilber, as well as soloists Pee Wee Russell, Flip Phillips, Willie "The Lion" Smith, BUCK CLAYTON, and Pete Brown.

Though not as influential as Red Allen, REX STEWART, ROY ELDRIDGE, Bunny Berigan, COOTIE WILLIAMS, or Buck Clayton, Frankie Newton was nevertheless one of the better trumpet players of the swing era. Obviously inspired by LOUIS ARMSTRONG, he had a full, broad tone that was equally compelling with or without a mute, and he could improvise with great originality. Apart from his playing on many of the records under his own name, as well as on most of those by the Port of Harlem groups, his better solos are found on Cecil Scott's "In a Corner," Art Karle's "Lights Out," Mezz Mezzrow's "The Panic Is On," Teddy Wilson's "All My Life," Teddy Hill's "Blue Rhythm Fantasy" and "China Boy," Charlie Barnet's "Emperor Jones," Jerry Kruger's "So You Won't Sing," Buster Bailey's "Dizzy Debutante" and "Chained to a Dream," and Midge Williams's "An Old Flame" and "The One Rose." Of the few records that Newton made in the 1940s sessions with James P. Johnson and Joe Turner, Miss Rhapsody's "Sweet Man" and Hank D'Amico's "Gone at Dawn" serve as prime examples of Newton's inventiveness.

FURTHER READING

Chilton, John. *Sidney Bechet: The Wizard of Jazz* (1987).
Coleman, Bill. *Trumpet Story* (1990).
McCarthy, Albert. *Big Band Jazz* (1974).
Wells, Dicky, with Stanley Dance. *The Night People: The Jazz Life of Dicky Wells* (1991).

DISCOGRAPHY

Bruyninckx, Walter. *Swing Discography, 1920–1988* (13 vols.).
Bruyninckx, Walter. *Traditional Jazz Discography, 1897–1988* (5 vols.).
Rust, Brian. *Jazz Records, 1897–1942* (1982).
Selchow, Manfred. *Profoundly Blue: A Bio-Discographical Scrapbook on Edmond Hall* (1988).

This entry is taken from the *American National Biography* and is published here with the permission of the American Council of Learned Societies.

JACK SOHMER

Newton, Huey P. (17 Feb. 1942–22 Aug. 1989), leader of the Black Panther Party, was born Huey Percy Newton in Monroe, Louisiana, the son of Amelia Johnson Newton and Walter Newton, a sharecropper and Baptist preacher. Walter Newton so admired Louisiana's populist governor Huey P. Long that he named his seventh and youngest son after him. A proud, powerful man, Newton defied the regional convention that forced most black women into domestic service and never allowed his wife to work outside the home. He always juggled several jobs to support his large family. Like thousands of black southerners drawn to employment in the war industries, the Newtons migrated to California during the 1940s. Settling in Oakland, the close-knit family struggled to shelter young Huey but could

Huey Newton, Black Panther Party minister of defense, speaks at a press conference in New York City, 22 August 1970. (AP Images.)

not stop the mores of the ghetto from shaping his life. Years later, those same ghetto neighborhoods became the springboard of the Black Panther Party that thrust Newton into national prominence.

While attending Oakland's Merritt College, Newton met BOBBY SEALE, a married student recently discharged from the army, when they became involved in developing a black studies curriculum. Discovering that they both felt impatient with student activism in the face of blatant discrimination and police violence, the two formed a new organization in October 1966. Adopting the symbol of the all-black political party in Lowndes County, Alabama, that the Black Power spokesman STOKELY CARMICHAEL had helped organize, they named their organization the Black Panther Party for Self-Defense.

Seale and Newton wrote out a ten-point platform and program for the group, demanding as its first point "power to determine the destiny of our black community." The program outlined aspirations for better housing, education, and employment opportunities and called for an end to police brutality. It insisted that blacks be tried by juries of their peers, that all black prisoners be released because none had received fair trials, and that blacks be exempted from military service. It concluded with a quotation from the Declaration of Independence asserting the right to revolution.

Initiating patrols to prevent abusive behavior by local police, the disciplined, uniformly dressed young Panthers immediately attracted attention. Wearing black leather jackets and black berets, the men and women openly carried weapons on their patrols. These acts were legal under the gun laws then in force, but the California legislature swiftly acted to prohibit the patrols in July 1967.

The Black Panthers were buoyed along by the current of dissent and protest surging through black communities. As in other urban areas, Oakland's black families felt a deep sense of injustice at the treatment meted out by the police, and the Black Panther Party continued to attract members. In October 1967 Newton was wounded following a late-night traffic stop in which the Oakland police officer John Frey was killed. Upon his arrest, the startling news that the minister of defense of the Black Panther Party was accused of killing a white policeman was broadcast nationally. Police killings of black youths had triggered numerous riots and urban uprisings, but in all the previous incidents no policemen had been killed. Newton's indictment for murdering Frey threw a spotlight over Oakland's Black Panther Party. Soon, Charles R. Garry, a prominent San Francisco trial attorney, took up Newton's legal defense, and the Black Panther's minister of information, ELDRIDGE CLEAVER, initiated the "Free Huey" movement that made Newton internationally famous.

Newton's case became the centerpiece of a massive mobilization campaign advocating the Black Panther Party program. Membership soared. During the murder trial in the summer of 1968, a fateful year marked by the assassinations of the Reverend MARTIN LUTHER KING JR. and the U.S. senator and presidential candidate Robert Kennedy, thousands of supporters flocked to rallies outside the Oakland courthouse. The international effort in defense of Newton succeeded in blocking his conviction (and execution) for murder, but the jury found him guilty of manslaughter.

Newton openly advocated revolutionary changes in the relationship between poor blacks and the larger white society and concentrated on the untapped potential of what he called the urban "lumpen proletariat" to forge a vanguard party. The "Free Huey" movement galvanized blacks, resulting in phenomenal growth and the development of a national Black Panther Party buoyed by the rallying cry "All Power to the People!" The Panthers advocated self-determination to replace the racist, economic subjugation of blacks they viewed as "colonialism." By the time Newton was released following a successful appeal in 1970, the Black Panther Party had offices in more than thirty cities, including New York, Philadelphia, Chicago, and Los Angeles. It had established an international section in Algeria and inspired the creation of similar organizations in Israel, the West Indies, and India.

As were numerous leaders and members of the Black Panther Party, Newton was subjected to nearly constant surveillance, police harassment, frequent arrests, and a barrage of politically inspired invasions of privacy. He faced two retrials on the manslaughter charge but was never again convicted of killing Frey (both trials ended in hung juries). In the meantime, Panther leaders in Los Angeles and Chicago were shot to death in 1969 under circumstances in which special police units worked secretly with federal intelligence agents—many of the criminal charges brought against Panthers resulted from clandestine police-FBI collaborations engineered by COINTELPRO (the U.S. government's counterintelligence program). Between 1968 and 1973, thousands of Panthers were arrested, hundreds were tried and imprisoned, while thirty-four were killed in police raids, shoot-outs, or internal conflicts.

Newton's symbolic appeal to young blacks was powerful, especially because of the defiant resistance to police authority he represented. Such conduct had never been so central to any previous black leader, and it shocked many who were accustomed to a more restrained demeanor. Newton, who often expressed the belief that it was crucial "to capture the peoples' imagination" in order to build a successful revolutionary movement, was more effective as a catalyst than as a traditional leader. Newton was not an especially captivating speaker or skilled political organizer; rather, his talent lay in inspiring a small group of exceptionally talented individuals, directing their energies, and eliciting a loyalty so profound that they were willing to risk their lives building the revolutionary organization he founded.

The unique way the Black Panther Party fused conflicting elements within one organization paid tribute to Newton's vision. Free breakfasts for schoolchildren and other programs provided community service, but unlike other reformers, the Panthers also simultaneously engaged in electoral politics and challenged the imperialist domination of blacks—all with a flamboyant bravado. While the traditional civil rights organizations sought "first-class citizenship," the Panthers viewed the legacy of slavery, segregation, and racism as a form of colonialism in which blacks were subjects, not citizens, of the United States; instead of seeking integration, the Panthers identified with the struggles of other colonized Africans and Asians and sought black liberation.

The Black Panthers were not ideologically consistent over time; the party moved from a nationalism inspired by MALCOLM X to a Marxist anti-imperialism influenced by Frantz Fanon, Che Guevara, and Mao Tse Tung and finally into a synthesis that Newton called "intercommunalism," which he claimed was required by the collapse of the nation-state within the global economy. Although the Black Panthers remained an all-black organization, it forged coalitions with other radical groups involving whites, Asians, and Latinos. The volatile mixture of external repression, internal dissension, and an escalating use of purges led to several highly publicized expulsions that divided the governing central committee.

Precipitated by Newton's denunciation and expulsion of Eldridge Cleaver and the entire International Section in February 1971, the Black Panther Party broke into rival factions, a division the press named the "Newton-Cleaver split." The factions were loosely defined by ideological differences. Whereas the Newton-controlled portion of the party abruptly backtracked and began to advocate moderate solutions to black oppression—and ceased to attract new members—those opposing Newton escalated their devotion to revolutionary tactics and coalesced around a network of freedom fighters who eventually formed the underground Black Liberation Army.

An increasingly paranoid Newton took bold steps to consolidate his personal supremacy over the volatile organization, and as chapters dwindled or were closed, he introduced the "survival pending revolution" program. While the Panthers publicly engaged in conventional political and economic activities, Newton, who had become heavily addicted to cocaine, led the organization into subterranean criminal activities. Following indictments brought against him for assaulting several Oakland residents, including a prostitute who later died, Newton fled to Cuba in 1974. He left behind an organization virtually in shambles, saddled with an Internal Revenue Service investigation into its finances, and dwindling numbers of supporters. Even the party chairman Bobby Seale repudiated the unsavory developments and left the organization.

En route to Cuba, Newton married his secretary, Gwen Fontaine. Following his return in 1976, Newton was tried on assault and murder charges but was not convicted. He then enrolled in the History of Consciousness program on the Santa Cruz campus of the University of California. He received his Ph.D. from that program in 1980, by which time the Black Panther Party had virtually disbanded. Although a small retinue of supporters continued to be drawn to Newton's strong personal magnetism, he ceased to function as the leader of a revolutionary movement. By 1982 his marriage had ended in divorce and the last vestige of the Black Panther Party, its Youth Institute, had closed for lack of funds.

Newton married Frederika Slaughter of Oakland in 1984. His repeated efforts to overcome alcohol and cocaine addiction were not successful, and he briefly spent time in prison in 1987 for a probation violation. Early on the morning of 22 August 1989 Newton was shot and killed in Oakland by a twenty-five-year-old crack dealer whom he had insisted give him drugs free because of who he was. Newton's flamboyance, vision, and passion came to symbolize an entire era, yet in the end, the same demons that ravaged the community he had sought to transform destroyed him as well.

FURTHER READING

Huey P. Newton's papers, which include a significant amount of legal material, are housed at the Department of Special Collections, Stanford University Library.

Newton, Huey P. *Revolutionary Suicide* (1973, repr. 1995).

Hilliard, David, and Don Weise, eds. *The Huey P. Newton Reader* (2002).

Jeffries, Judson L. *Huey P. Newton: The Radical Theorist* (2002).

Keating, Edward M. *Free Huey* (1970).

Van Peebles, Mario, with Ula Y. Taylor and J. Tarika Lewis. *Panther* (1995).

Obituary: *New York Times*, 23 Aug. 1989.

This entry is taken from the *American National Biography* and is published here with the permission of the American Council of Learned Societies.

KATHLEEN N. CLEAVER

Nicholas, Albert (27 May 1900–3 Sept. 1973), jazz clarinetist and saxophonist, also known as "Nick," was born in New Orleans, Louisiana. Although his parents' names and occupations are unknown, it is known that Nicholas was the nephew of the New Orleans clarinetist and trumpeter Wooden Joe Nicholas, from whom he received his first training on the clarinet in 1910. At age thirteen he began studying with the famed soloist and teacher LORENZO TIO JR. By age fifteen Albert was playing with the cornetists MANUEL PEREZ, KING OLIVER, and Buddy Petit, as well as working with Oak Gaspard's Maple Leaf Orchestra. In November 1916 he enlisted in the navy, and while based in Cuba and Gibraltar aboard the convoy ship USS *Olympia* he played clarinet in the ship's otherwise all-white band.

Shortly after his discharge in December 1919 Nicholas resumed his professional career in New Orleans by joining first Petit and then Gaspard's orchestra. By September 1921 he was playing at the Cadillac Club with DuPas's band, which at that time included the young Panamanian pianist LUIS RUSSELL. The following spring Nicholas worked with Perez's quartet at the Oasis and later that year began a lengthy engagement at Tom Anderson's cabaret leading a six-piece band comprising among others Russell, the saxophonist BARNEY BIGARD, and the drummer PAUL BARBARIN. In May 1924 Nicholas turned the group over to Russell so that he could take BUSTER BAILEY's place in King Oliver's Creole Jazz Band for a week at Chicago's Grand Theater and on a six-week tour of one-night stands in Pennsylvania, Illinois, and Indiana. Nicholas was back in New Orleans by the summer and resumed leadership of his band until December 1924, after which he returned to Chicago to play in Oliver's newly formed Dixie Syncopators at the Plantation Cafe. After appearing on several exceptional recordings with Oliver and fellow New Orleanian Richard M. Jones, Nicholas left the Syncopators in August 1926 for a prestigious job at the Plaza Hotel in Shanghai, China, with the drummer Jack Carter, whose band also included the pianist Teddy Weatherford and the trumpeter and singer VALAIDA SNOW.

Nicholas left Carter in October 1927 and with the banjoist Frank Ethridge traveled widely throughout Asia with stops at Hong Kong, Manila, Singapore (where they played at the famed Raffles Hotel), Sumatra, Java, and India. In December they moved on to Egypt, where they were asked to add their talents to the local dance bands at Cairo's Fantasio and at Alexandria's plush Casino San Stefano. After a brief stopover in Paris, where he reunited with his old friend SIDNEY BECHET, Nicholas returned home in October 1928. A short time later he joined Russell's new band in New York City at Club Harlem, followed by back-to-back bookings at the Savoy Ballroom, the Roseland, the Saratoga Club, and Connie's Inn. During 1929 and 1930 he and other Russell bandsmen used their layoff time to work and record with JELLY ROLL MORTON, an experience that Nicholas repeated in 1939 and 1940. After his departure from the Russell band in December 1933 he played at the Savoy with CHICK WEBB's band, at the Cotton Club in Philadelphia with SAM WOODING, and on radio in New York with a novelty group called the Blue Chips. In December 1934 he joined the guitarist Bernard Addison's jazz group at Adrian's Tap Room, a midtown Manhattan club run by the famed jazzman Adrian Rollini, and stayed on when the bassist JOHN KIRBY assumed leadership of the band for the duration of the job.

In the spring of 1937 Nicholas rejoined the Russell band, now serving as background to the star trumpeter and singer LOUIS ARMSTRONG, but because of minimal opportunities for creative expression he left Armstrong after two years to join the drummer ZUTTY SINGLETON's trio, with the pianist Clyde Hart, at Nick's Tavern in Greenwich Village. They opened in December 1939, and from February to May 1940 they alternated sets with Bechet's quintet. Nicholas remained at this venue until June, when the trio, now with the pianist Eddie Heywood and then with Don Frye, moved into the neighboring Village Vanguard. Nicholas's career took a downward turn shortly after the termination of the Vanguard job in October 1940. He worked in the white trumpeter Bobby Burnet's all-black sextet at Café Society between February and March 1941, occasionally substituted for Bailey in John Kirby's popular sextet, and continued participating in the Sunday jam sessions at Jimmy Ryan's on Fifty-second Street, but by the summer of 1941 he felt compelled to find regular employment outside of music.

Nicholas first took a job as a subway guard on New York's Eighth Avenue line, and then for the duration of World War II he worked for the government in Washington, D.C. In late 1945, however, the pianist Art Hodes hired him for the group he was bringing into New York's Stuyvesant Casino, Nicholas's first steady job as a musician in five years. He started recording again as a featured soloist with Bechet, BABY DODDS, MUTT CAREY, and Wild Bill Davison, as well as with his own quartet in June 1947, the first time that he had led a recording session in more than two decades as an artist. He also appeared with BUNK JOHNSON in concert around this time, worked with KID ORY in Los Angeles in February 1946, led his own group at Jimmy Ryan's the following September, and from January through August 1947 was heard regularly on the historic *This Is Jazz* radio series. He left the show after a dispute with the producer and host Rudi Blesh.

In 1948 Nicholas played at the Barrel in St. Louis in a trio with the pianist Ralph Sutton and the drummer Art Trappier. Between 1949 and 1953 he led his own groups in and around Los Angeles and San Francisco, recorded with Bob Scobey's Frisco Band in 1950, and appeared at several prestigious jazz concerts. Around June 1953 he worked with the cornetist REX STEWART's band at Boston's Savoy Café and also recorded with them. Acting on Bechet's suggestion he moved to Paris in October 1953, and with the exception of a few American sojourns between 1959 and 1970 he remained in Europe until his death in Basel, Switzerland. During his 1959 visit he recorded with the Minneapolis cornetist Doc Evans and with Art Hodes's Chicago-based All-Star Stompers. Now at the peak of his musical powers, Nicholas saw his concert appearances and recording activities skyrocket as never before, and he was the object of adulation all over the continent, second only to his lifetime friend Bechet. He spent the last twenty years of his life delighting in his hard-won fame.

As did most clarinetists of his generation Nicholas started out playing the older Albert-system clarinet, but while in Egypt he purchased a Boehm-system clarinet to facilitate his mastery of the difficult classical parts that he sometimes had to play. Indeed, all of his best records beginning with the 1929 sessions with Russell and Morton were performed on this technically improved model. Nicholas's warm and woody tone, a characteristic shared by other Tio students, is linked directly to the delicacy and grace of the French approach to classical clarinet playing, a heritage indigenous to the New Orleans–born Creoles. But there was more to Nicholas than his tone. He was also a highly imaginative and thrilling improviser, a masterful technician, and an ensemble player of the greatest sensitivity. He could handle his instrument with flawless control even at the fastest tempos, yet he was also capable of playing slow blues with passion and conviction. There is no question that as a consummate jazz clarinetist his place among the pantheon of the giants is rightfully deserved.

FURTHER READING

Charters, Samuel, and Leonard Kunstadt. *Jazz: A History of the New York Scene* (1962).

Jones, Max. *Talking Jazz* (1988).

Rose, Al, and Edmond Souchon. *New Orleans Jazz: A Family Album* (1978).

Shaw, Arnold. *52nd Street: The Street of Jazz* (1971).

This entry is taken from the *American National Biography* and is published here with the permission of the American Council of Learned Societies.

JACK SOHMER

Nicholas, Fayard, and Harold Nicholas (28 Oct. 1914–24 Jan. 2006) and (27 Mar. 1921–3 Jul. 2000), dancers and performers who together made up the Nicholas Brothers dance duo, were born Fayard Antonio Nicholas, in Mobile, Alabama, and Harold Lloyd Nicholas, in Winston-Salem, North Carolina, to Ulysses Nicholas, a jazz drummer, and Viola Harden, a jazz pianist. In 1926 the Nicholas family moved to Philadelphia, Pennsylvania, where Ulysses and Viola led a pit orchestra. Fayard and Harold performed in Philadelphia vaudeville theaters and radio stations from 1929 to 1931 as part of the Nicholas Kids (a sister, Dorothy Nicholas, was briefly in the act). In 1932 the Nicholas Brothers appeared with EUBIE BLAKE and NINA MAE McKINNEY in the short film *Pie, Pie, Blackbird*. That same year the Nicholas Brothers debuted at the Cotton Club, where they were so well received that they became known as "The Show Stoppers." Also, because they were children, they were allowed to mingle with the white audience after the show.

In 1933 Harold appeared with PAUL ROBESON in *The Emperor Jones*, and in the following year the Nicholas Brothers appeared together in their first feature-length Hollywood film, *Kid Millions*. In the 1930s the Nicholas Brothers performed in films such as *The Big Broadcast of 1936* (1935), *The Black Network* (1936), and *Calling All Stars* (1937). They made their Broadway debut in *The Ziegfeld Follies of 1936*, appeared in the West End of London in Lew Leslie's *Blackbirds of 1936*, and were invited by George Balanchine to perform their own number in Rodger and Hart's *Babes in Arms* (1937). Their song, "All Dark People Is Light on Their Feet," is commonly dropped from revivals of the play. Their acrobatic, full-bodied tap style contributed to their reputation as two of the premiere "flash" or "specialty" dancers of their time; their signature moves included jumping into a split and then rising upright without using their hands.

In 1940 the Nicholas Brothers began a series of six films for Twentieth Century–Fox that contain their most notable performances: *Down Argentine Way* (1940), *Tin Pan Alley* (1940), *Sun Valley Serenade* (1941), *The Great American Broadcast* (1941), *Orchestra Wives* (1942), *Stormy Weather* (1943), and *Take It or Leave It* (1944). In these films, their collaboration with the choreographer Nick Castle (born Nicholas John Casaccio) led to some

Harold Nicholas looks up after performing the song "Blue Skies" during a Tribute to Fred Astaire, 5 December 1999, at the Getty Center in Los Angeles. (AP Images.)

Fayard Nicholas strikes a pose at his residence in Woodland Hills, California, 28 June 1999. In their prime, Fayard and his brother Harold performed as a song-and-dance team on Broadway, in Las Vegas and in the movies. (AP Images.)

spectacular innovations. In *Orchestra Wives* (1942), Harold takes two vertical steps up a wall and then executes a backward flip into a split. In *Stormy Weather* (1943, starring LENA HORNE and BILL ROBINSON), they appear with CAB CALLOWAY and his orchestra in "Jumpin' Jive," a routine in which the Nicholas Brothers keep the rhythm with their feet while leaping and dancing over and on top of the orchestra (they dance on round pedestals made to look like the tops of drums). The end of the routine features a sequence in which Harold and Fayard descend a flight of stairs by leap-frogging over each other and landing into splits. Fred Astaire called "Jumpin' Jive" the greatest musical number he ever saw on film. The brothers later remarked that they performed the number in one take and that they had not rehearsed it beforehand.

Despite the virtuosity of the Nicholas Brothers, racial segregation limited their film roles. Most of their numbers were short and not integrated into the plots of the films so that the sequences could easily be removed when the films were exhibited for white audiences in the South. Moreover, as the brothers aged they could no longer be seen as precocious children devoid of sexuality. In most of their films they had no scenes or dialogue with the female leads; the only woman with whom they danced on film was DOROTHY DANDRIDGE, who later married Harold Nicholas, in the "Chattanooga Choo Choo" number in *Sun Valley Serenade* (1941). The Nicholas Brothers did not dance with a white star on film until they performed with Gene Kelly in their last Hollywood film, *The Pirate* (1948).

Disillusioned by racial tension in the United States, in the 1950s Harold elected to stay in France following a European tour with his brother. "The way we were treated there was a revelation," he said (Tom Vallance, "Obituary: Harold Nicholas," *Independent* [London] 5 July 2000). Based in Paris, Harold appeared with JOSEPHINE BAKER at the Olympia, and also toured European and North African nightclubs. While in Europe, Harold made occasional films both with and without Fayard, including *Botta e Risposta* (Italy, 1949) and *L'Empire de la Nuit* (France, 1963). In 1964 Harold and Fayard reunited for three *Hollywood Palace* television specials and other cabaret performances. In subsequent years Harold often performed as a singer. Other films in which Harold appeared include the SIDNEY POITIER comedy *Uptown Saturday Night* (1974), the Nick Castle film *Tap* (1989), and ROBERT TOWNSEND's *The Five Heartbeats* (1991).

In 1970 Fayard appeared in a dramatic role in the William Wyler film *The Liberation of L. B. Jones*. By 1975 he was suffering from severe arthritis in both hips; in 1985 he underwent hip replacement surgery. During this period, though he occasionally performed as a soloist and with Harold, Fayard devoted more time to teaching and choreography. In 1989 Fayard received a Tony Award as one of four co-choreographers for the Broadway musical *Black and Blue*. In 1991 both Nicholas Brothers received Kennedy Center Honors. In 1992 the Nicholas Brothers were the subject of a documentary feature directed by Chris Boulder, *Nicholas Brothers: We Sing and We Dance*.

Fayard's first marriage, to Geraldine Pate, which produced two sons, ended in divorce in 1955. He was married a second time to Lee Barton. He was married a third time, to Barbara January, in 1967, and a fourth time, in 2000, to Katherine Hopkins. Harold married the actress Dorothy Dandridge in 1942. Their daughter, Harolyn, born in 1943 with severe brain damage, was eventually institutionalized. Nicholas and Dandridge divorced in 1949. His

second marriage, to Elyanne Patronne, with whom he had a son, Melih, also ended in divorce. He was married a third time to Rigmor Newman.

In the Broadway musical *Bring in 'Da Noise, Bring in 'Da Funk* (1996), GEORGE C. WOLFE and SAVION GLOVER (who appeared with Harold in *Tap*) satirized the Nicholas Brothers as "Grin and Flash," smiling Uncle Toms who sacrificed their heritage for financial gain. Fayard's response: "He was saying the studios used us.... Why bring us down? We are the ones who made it possible for them to be where they are today" (Caroline Palmer, "Amazing Feet: The Nicholas Brothers," *City Pages* [Minneapolis/St. Paul] 18 Aug. 1999).

Fayard Nicholas died in 2006 in Los Angeles. The cause was pneumonia and other complications of a stroke he suffered in November 2005. Harold died in 2000 in New York City, from heart failure following surgery at New York Hospital.

FURTHER READING
Frank, Rusty E. *Tap!: The Greatest Tap Dance Stars and Their Stories, 1900–1955* (1990).
Hill, Constance Valis. *Brotherhood in Rhythm: The Jazz Tap Dancing of the Nicholas Brothers* (2000).
Obituaries: *New York Times*, 26 Jan. 2006 (Fayard Nicholas); *New York Times*, 4 Jul. 2000 (Harold Nicholas).

MATTHEW SEWELL

Nichols, Barbara Ware (19 June 1938–), health industry executive, nurse, and educator, was born Barbara Lauraine Ware in Waterville, Kennebec County, Maine, the daughter of Lloyd Russell Ware and Mildred Murray. An only child, she and her mother moved to Portland, Maine, during World War II, where she graduated from Portland High School in 1956.

After receiving her nursing diploma from Massachusetts Memorial Hospital School of Nursing in Boston in 1959, Nichols joined the U.S. Navy, serving as head nurse at the naval hospital in St. Albans, New York. After her three-year military stint, she earned a bachelor's degree in nursing and social psychology from Case-Western Reserve University in 1966 and a master's of science degree in behavioral disabilities and counseling from the University of Wisconsin in Madison in 1973.

Nichols became a professor at the University of Wisconsin and director of St. Mary's Hospital Medical Center, a position that in 1978 led to her becoming the first African American to be elected president of the American Nurses' Association.

After serving as executive director of the California Nurses Association, Nichols became the chief executive officer (CEO) of the Commission on Graduates of Foreign Nursing Schools in 1998. As CEO of the Philadelphia-based not-for-profit organization, Nichols traveled widely. Responsible for the implementation of policy, programs, and services, she led the program that provided national and international certification for nurses around the world, credential evaluation, and immigration screening programs and services.

Her work in the medical field, in teaching, and as an executive has resulted in several honorary degrees, including doctorate of science from the University of Wisconsin–Milwaukee in 1979 for leadership and widespread influence in the field of education and delivery of health care in urban settings.

In 1982, she was awarded a doctorate of humane letters, honoris causa, from the University of Lowell in Lowell, Massachusetts, for accomplishments and services as a professional nurse, teacher, scholar, advocate, and fellow citizen.

Rhode Island College in Providence awarded Nichols an honorary doctorate of pedagogy in 1983 for contribution and leadership in the nursing profession, and Miami University in Oxford, Ohio, bestowed upon Nichols an honorary doctorate of science degree in 1986 for leadership and contribution to the health care of others.

Active from the beginning of her career, Nichols developed and taught courses at the University of Wisconsin at Madison School of Nursing while simultaneously holding the director's job at St. Mary Hospital Medical Center. She also represented the School of Nursing on the Center for Health Sciences Commission on Women and was a member of the school's Graduate Division Minority Recruitment Committee.

Nichols continued at St. Mary's while serving as chief elected officer of the American Nurses' Association, where she was spokesperson for the 200,000-member professional association of registered nurses in the United States. Nichols also served as liaison to international, national, and governmental health agencies and associations during her four-year stint as CEO.

In January 1983, Nichols was named secretary of the Department of Regulation and Licensing in Wisconsin, filling an unexpired term. In June 1985, she was reappointed to the post, where she exercised direct statutory authority in the licensing of private detectives, registration of charitable organizations, and regulation of boxing clubs and exhibitions, bingo, and real estate. As secretary, she managed a biennial budget of $10 million.

When she is not traveling the world, Nichols' home is in Madison, Wisconsin, with her husband and three children, a daughter and twin sons.

FURTHER READING

http://www.cgfns.org/sections/about/exec.shtml
http://www.minoritynurse.com/minority-nurse-leaders/eyes-prize
http://www.nsna.org/pubs/imprint/febmar06/impfeb_BTN.pdf
http://www.nytimes.com/1981/02/22/magazine/where-have-all-the-nurses-gone.html?sec=health&spon=&pagewanted=5

BOB GREENE

Nichols, Charles H. (6 July 1919–14 Jan. 2007), university professor, was born in Brooklyn, New York, the last of seven children born to Charles F. Nichols and Julia E. King, who were Plymouth Church of the Brethren missionary immigrants from Christ Church, Barbados. Reared in a tradition of rigorous and Calvinistic Bible study, his gift for learning became obvious during childhood. His father, anticipating future job discrimination, enrolled him in a vocational school to learn the printing trade. Soon after, he was accepted at the prestigious Boys High School, where he excelled and was the salutatorian of the 1938 class. Nichols attended Brooklyn College on a State of New York university scholarship and a Rachel Herstein scholarship administered by the NAACP. He was a member of the debate team and the glee club, and graduated cum laude in 1942 with a B.A. in English.

Except for unskilled jobs in the garment district Nichols was unable to find employment in New York. He moved south to become a teaching assistant in the English department at Hampton Institute (later Hampton University), where he also coached a winning debate team. With a University Scholarship and a Julius Rosenwald Fellowship, Nichols began a Ph.D. program in English and American literature at Brown University in Providence, Rhode Island, in 1945. There Nichols became attracted by the pacifism and antislavery legacy of the Quakers and joined a Quaker meeting. His dissertation, "A Study of the Slave Narrative" (1948), was a pioneering analysis of the history of slavery as written by former slaves between 1830 and 1865, an assessment of the former slaves' psychological reaction to their enslavement, and a critique of the literary merits of the narratives. Academic appointments followed at Morgan College (later Morgan State University) in Baltimore, Maryland (1948–1949), and at Hampton Institute in Hampton, Virginia (1949–1959). It was at Hampton that he met Mildred Elizabeth Thompson, who would later become, among other things, the executive director of the Rhode Island State Occupational Information Coordinating Committee. They married on 19 August 1950 and had three sons, David, Keith, and Brian. In 1954 and 1955 Nichols was a Fulbright professor at Aarhus University in Aarhus, Denmark. While there he lectured at many European universities on American writers and on the American higher education system. In 1959 he joined the German higher education system as a tenured professor of North American language and literature at the John F. Kennedy Institute for American Studies at the Free University in West Berlin, Germany (1959–1969). Nichols returned to Brown University (1969–1989) as professor of English and to lead the development of an interdepartmental program in Afro-American studies. He worked with other universities to help them establish similar programs.

Nichols was a prolific writer and a highly regarded teacher, mentor, and lecturer. For more than forty years he published scholarly articles that examined the issues of race, American character, and the human condition through the works of Herman Melville, Mark Twain, Dorothy Parker, Henry David Thoreau, LANGSTON HUGHES, RICHARD WRIGHT, JAMES BALDWIN, RALPH ELLISON, and others. His books include *"Many Thousand Gone— The Ex-Slaves' Account of Their Bondage and Their Freedom* (1963); *Black Men in Chains* (1972); and *Arna Bontemps—Langston Hughes Letters: 1925–1967* (1980). He served on the advisory editorial boards of *African American Review, Black Literature Forum*, and *die Lexikon der Philosphie*. He always taught African American literature as an integral part of American literature. He supervised the theses and dissertations of dozens of graduate students who went on to become professors at universities in the United States, Germany, Japan, and other nations. He helped lay the foundation for the development of departments of Africana/African American studies. In 1990 an anonymous donor endowed the Professor Charles H. Nichols National Scholarship at Brown University. Nichols died in Providence.

FURTHER READING

Beckham, Barry. "The Modest Professor," *Brown Alumni Monthly* (Mar./Apr. 2007).

Dunbar, Earnest. *The Black Expatriates, A Study of American Negroes in Exile* (1968)

MILDRED T. NICHOLS

Nichols, Herbie (3 Dec. 1919–12 Apr. 1963), composer and musician, was born Herbert Horatio Nichols in New York City, the son of Joel Nichols, a building supervisor, and Ida (maiden name unknown). His parents, originally from Trinidad and St. Kitts, had moved to New York in 1910. Nichols first lived at Sixty-first Street and Eleventh Avenue, in the area known at the time as San Juan Hill. The family moved to Harlem when Nichols was seven. When he was not practicing or winning at chess, checkers, or marbles, the young Nichols spent much time in the public library. From age seven to age fourteen he took lessons in classical piano and general music instruction with Charles L. Beck. An intelligent and motivated youngster, Nichols attended DeWitt Clinton High School and began study at City College of New York at age fifteen.

While still in high school Nichols, who was introduced to jazz piano by Roy Testamark, formed an impressive small combo. In 1937 he joined the Royal Baron Orchestra, led by Freddie Williams, which included noted musicians such as the bassist George Duvivier, the drummer Rip Harewood, and the arranger Billy Moore Jr. Nichols wrote several arrangements for the group so challenging that he himself was afraid to sight-read them. In 1938 he became the house pianist at Monroe's Uptown House for the rhythm and blues alto saxophonist Floyd "Horsecollar" Williams. There in the late 1930s Nichols participated in the jam sessions that were instrumental in the evolution of an emerging style called bop, playing with LESTER YOUNG, KENNY KERSEY, and DIZZY GILLESPIE.

Drafted into the army in September 1941 Nichols went overseas with the Twenty-fourth Infantry Regiment of the Ninety-second Division on standby in the Pacific. During this time he read widely, wrote more than fifty poems, and composed a number of tunes. Later in his tour of duty he was assigned to an army band, first playing drums and then piano. Nichols maintained a strong fondness for the drum. He valued its acoustical properties and African heritage and scored for drums melodically as well as rhythmically.

After his discharge in August 1943 Nichols returned to New York City and attempted to create a forum for his own music, but he had little success. He landed meager work accompanying dancers and singers, and he learned to play multiple styles during this period, a skill that allowed him to remain a viable working musician for the rest of his life. In 1945 he worked for six months in Harlem with a bop combo featuring the alto and baritone saxophonist Sahib Shihab. He recorded with DANNY BARKER for Apollo Records (c. 1946) and worked with the swing leader Hal Singer in Brooklyn and with the Dixieland drummer Freddie Moore at the Village Vanguard. During this time Nichols discovered THELONIOUS MONK, who had not yet recorded for Blue Note. The two pianists became colleagues, sharing each other's philosophies and insights, and in 1946 Nichols wrote an article for *Music Dial*, one of the earliest known writings about Monk, in which he recognized Monk's unique style and touted his innovative approach.

Nichols traveled the eastern and midwestern dance circuit during late 1946 and early 1947 with a relatively advanced swing band that included the noted trombonist J. J. JOHNSON, the tenor saxophonist ILLINOIS JACQUET, and Jacquet's brother Russell Jacquet on trumpet and vocals. In an unsuccessful attempt to promote his own style Nichols worked in New York as a freelance pianist and leader later in 1947. He procured several dance jobs in New York City as a leader in 1948. He also worked with the blues drummer Johnny Felton and supplemented his income by teaching piano privately. At the end of the 1940s he toured the Midwest with JOHN KIRBY's band.

Although Nichols was unable to obtain work playing his music in 1950, he recorded as a sideman in swing and rhythm and blues styles for the Mercury, Decca, and Abbey labels. The composer and bandleader Edgar Sampson hired Nichols as a sideman at Club 845 in the Bronx, and during that time he became versed in Latin music styles, particularly the mambo. He also worked with the saxophonist Lucky Thompson. For a short time Nichols pursued commercial musical avenues with limited success, writing arrangements for vaudeville acts.

Thelonious Monk introduced Nichols's music to the composer and pianist MARY LOU WILLIAMS in 1951. Nichols played from his songbook for Williams, who admired Nichols's style. Williams recorded several of his songs, including "The Bebop Waltz" (as "Mary's Waltz"), "Stennel" (as "Opus 2"), and "At Da Function" on her Atlantic recording, *Mary Lou Williams Trio*. This break for Nichols sparked some interest in his music among audiences previously unfamiliar with his work, and during 1952 in New York he recorded for the first time as a leader with his own quartet for Hi-Lo. An

unrehearsed, impromptu effort, the 78 included "S'Wonderful" on one side and Nichols's "Whose Blues" on the other. Although the album received a favorable review in *Down Beat*, the only work that he landed for the rest of the year was as a sideman performing Dixieland and blues along the East Coast.

Little changed for Nichols during the next three years. Traveling throughout the East he worked mostly as a sideman, performing music that diverged from his own style. However, he occasionally had rewarding performance opportunities with musicians such as SONNY STITT, REX STEWART, Arnett Cobb, Big Nick Nicholas, and WILBUR DE PARIS. While he continued to promote his own music to record companies and clubs, Nichols studied classical music, jazz, and music from both Africa and the Caribbean.

Nichols's persistence paid off in 1955 when Al Lion of Blue Note Records, persuaded by CHARLES MINGUS and Teddy Kotick, signed Nichols to record his own original trio compositions. The four dates between May 1955 and April 1956 included the drummers ART BLAKEY and MAX ROACH and the bassists Al McKibbon and Teddy Kotick. The sessions, originally slated for twenty-four compositions, yielded twenty-nine original titles, many of which were distributed over two ten-inch albums titled *The Prophetic Herbie Nichols, Volumes 1 and 2*, released in 1955. Though critically acclaimed upon their release, the recordings made little money. Regardless, Blue Note released additional titles on the twelve-inch album *The Herbie Nichols Trio* the next year.

Nichols continued to perform his own music occasionally in New York City from 1955 to 1958; in November 1955 he performed solo piano sets, sandwiched between sets of Blakey's Jazz Messengers, at the Cafe Bohemia. In 1957 he performed at Basin Street South with a trio including Billy Phillips and G. T. Wilson. Nichols played in the house band at Page 3, accompanying performers such as the singer Sheila Jordan. Nichols's colleagues, including Thelonious Monk, Randy Weston, and CECIL TAYLOR, regularly heard him at the club and recognized the distinction of his style. Nichols also recorded his last sessions as a leader for Bethlehem. Seven of these twelve titles were released first in 1957 as *Love, Gloom, Cash, Love*, later titled *The Bethlehem Sessions*.

However, Nichols continued to work more with Dixieland, blues, and swing musicians for his remaining years. During his later years his most regular job was with a revivalist Dixieland band at the Riviera in Greenwich Village, a trendy hangout for Ivy Leaguers. The creative outlets for Nichols's own music were limited to concerts on cruise ships, in concert halls, and at universities. Many of these performances served as apprentice opportunities for younger musicians. Steve Swallow played alongside Nichols during a shortened tour on a cruise ship in the spring of 1960. Buell Neidlinger first performed with Nichols during one of many Dixieland appearances that Nichols made at Jimmy Ryan's. Roswell Rudd performed alongside Nichols and the saxophonist Tina Brooks in the fall of 1960 during a jam at a college party at Yale University. Rudd and Neidlinger, both students at Yale, studied with Nichols during this period. Nichols returned to Yale in the spring of 1961 along with Rudd and BILLY HIGGINS as part of an NAACP benefit concert featuring JOHN LEE HOOKER, Paul Bley, and Cecil Taylor.

Nichols's final documented performance of contemporary jazz was a loft concert in 1962 with the hard-bop and avant-garde saxophonist ARCHIE SHEPP and the hard-bop bassist Ahmad Abdul Malik. Nichols briefly toured Scandinavia during 1962 with a mixed group of Dixieland and apprentice musicians; though he mostly accompanied the larger group, he also had the opportunity to lecture on his own music and to play some trio selections. One of his final appearances was in 1963 in Harlem accompanying the rhythm and blues tenor saxophonist Hal "Cornbread" Singer, one of the first musicians ever to employ Nichols. Four months after returning to New York City from a lengthy gig during the fall of 1962 at a Newfoundland air force base, Nichols checked into Kingsbridge VA Hospital, where he was diagnosed with acute myelocytic leukemia. He died several days later. He never married.

Nichols was an intellectual and serious composer who read widely and wrote more than fifty poems. His sources of musical inspiration included painting, sculpture, architecture, literature, boxing, and dancing. He was an ardent student of both classical and jazz composers, equally fascinated with works by Béla Bartók, Igor Stravinsky, Johann Sebastian Bach, Ludwig van Beethoven, Frédéric Chopin, Heitor Villa-Lobos, JELLY ROLL MORTON, DUKE ELLINGTON, JOHN LEWIS, and ART TATUM. He was also influenced by contemporary musicians and composers like the conductor Dimitri Mitropoulos and the composers Paul Hindemith, Dmitri Shostakovitch, and Walter Piston. A

particular focus upon orchestral literature reflected Nichols's vision of a larger medium for his works that went beyond his trios, including larger sections of winds and brass.

Nichols maintained a detailed personal catalog of his own works, dating from 1939 to 1961. It included approximately 170 titles, twenty-nine recorded by Blue Note and twelve recorded by Bethlehem. Mary Lou Williams recorded four of his titles on Atlantic, and "Lady Sings the Blues" was written for and recorded by BILLIE HOLIDAY in June 1956. More than half the listed titles included lyrics, and a wide variety of styles were indicated throughout, including ballad, march, stomp, shuffle, blues, waltz, calypso, mambo, tango, swing, and rag.

In addition to Western European classical music Nichols's efforts emphasized constant study of African music and culture. His emphasis on these areas in his music anticipated the contributions of the Association for the Advancement of Creative Musicians and many other musicians of the middle to late 1960s. Nichols commented on the beauty of African village singing and attributed special significance to the drum as a melodic instrument in jazz, with its specific tuning in fifths as a highly desirable quality. His compositions often featured drum parts integrated in a way that was critical to their success. Nichols observed how drummers for bop musicians such as Dizzy Gillespie and CHARLIE PARKER would "drop bombs" at critical points in the structure of a chart, and he stated in an interview with A. B. Spellman, "Each 'bomb' created a newly rich and wholly unexpected series of overtones, beginning in the lower registers. These rich syncopations were fitting accompaniments to the supplemental overtones played by the horns in the higher registers. That is why the pianists became so percussive with their left hands" (175). Specific jazz drummers influencing Nichols were Art Blakey, DENZIL BEST, and SONNY GREER.

Nichols's advanced level of education created a rift between himself and other musicians that was perceived by jazz audiences at large. He felt incompatible with the competitive jazz scene, which he saw as laden with Uncle Toms and drug addicts. His strong, highly personal philosophy about his own compositions and performance was original to jazz musicians of his time. Versed in vastly differing musical idioms, Nichols developed an amalgamated musical style that, although meagerly acknowledged, was unique among his contemporaries.

Roswell Rudd and Buell Neidlinger both recorded Nichols tribute albums, most notably Rudd's 1983 *Regeneration* album for Soul Note. Another tribute from Soul Note, *Change of Season*, appeared in 1985.

FURTHER READING

Giddins, Gary. *Rhythm-a-ning* (1985).

Litweiler, John. *The Freedom Principle: Jazz after 1958* (1984).

Spellman, A. B. *Four Lives in the Bebop Business* (1966, 1970).

DISCOGRAPHY

The Complete Blue Note Recordings of Herbie Nichols (Mosaic).

This entry is taken from the *American National Biography* and is published here with the permission of the American Council of Learned Societies.

DAVID E. SPIES

Nichols, Nichelle (28 Dec. 1933–), dancer, actress, and writer, was born Graciella Nichols in Robbins, Illinois, the eldest daughter of Samuel G. Nichols, a chemist, town magistrate, and eventually mayor of the predominantly African American town of Robbins, and Lishia Mae Parks, known as Lydia. Nichols's early talent was as a ballet dancer. At age seven her parents enrolled her in ballet classes. At fourteen she discovered Afro-Cuban dance by chance when she practiced her ballet moves at a dance studio owned by Carmencita Romero. During the day she studied ballet, and at night she learned the moves of Afro-Cuban choreography.

Noticing her gift for dance, Romero arranged an audition for her with the Sherman House Hotel. Nichols won a role and danced as part of the College Inn troupe. While she danced there, the dancer and choreographer KATHERINE DUNHAM saw her performance and invited Nichols to join her troupe. Because of her age, however, her parents refused to allow her, but she continued to win accolades at the College Inn and met several famous African American performers, including LENA HORNE, SARAH VAUGHAN, JOSEPHINE BAKER, and DUKE ELLINGTON. She decided to leave the College Inn and become a full-time performer, and it was then that she changed her name from Graciella to Nichelle, which was chosen by her mother.

Nichols married her first husband, Foster Johnson, who was also a performer, after her eighteenth birthday in 1951. She and her husband performed together as a song-and-dance duo for a while with DUKE ELLINGTON's Orchestra. On 14 August 1951 Nichols gave birth to her only child, a son named Kyle. She and Johnson separated and divorced only four months after they were wed. After her divorce and while touring the country as a performer, Nichols had to decide whether to continue pursuing her dreams in show business or find steady employment so that she could support herself and her son. She became a file clerk at the Goldenrod Ice Cream Company. The company wanted to send her to business school, but after agonizing over whether to stay with Goldenrod, Nichols resigned and enrolled in Cosmopolitan Law School, where she took some courses. During this period she began studying dance with Jimmy Payne and became a headliner in his critically acclaimed revue, *Calypso Carnival*.

In 1963 Nichols was cast in an episode of Gene Roddenberry's *The Lieutenant*, in which she portrayed the fiancée of a black marine played by Don Marshall. Nichols and Roddenberry developed a close professional relationship, and when she appeared on the lot where *The Lieutenant* was filming, she would stop by his office to exchange greetings. Roddenberry was instrumental in bringing Nichols to the attention of MGM executives, who proposed a contract of seven years at $750 a week with an option for renewal. Nichols was one of the few African American actresses to receive a contract from a major studio. However, when one of the executives demanded that she sleep with him and she refused, Nichols lost the contract.

After *The Lieutenant* was cancelled, Roddenberry began work on another series that would become known as *Star Trek*, with a part for Nichols that was groundbreaking for portraying an African American woman as a member of a team of highly trained professionals. Initially Roddenberry was met with resistance when it became clear that Nichols's role as Lieutenant Uhura (the name is a slight misspelling of the Swahili word *uhuru*, which means "freedom") would be substantial and her lines would go well beyond, "Yes, Captain!" Roddenberry found a way around the network by using Nichols as a day player, which allowed him to use her more than if she had been under contract. During the first year of *Star Trek*, Nichols also appeared as a nurse on *Peyton Place*. Each year, *Star Trek* was in danger of cancellation because of low ratings, but the cast, and Nichols in particular, received a large amount of fan mail, some of which was hidden from her by studio employees. Discovering this, Nichols contemplated leaving the show, but she was convinced to stay by DR. MARTIN LUTHER KING JR., who met Nichols at an NAACP event. He told her, "You have the first non-stereotypical roles on television, male or female. 'You have broken ground" (Nichols, 164).

During the filming of the second season of *Star Trek*, Nichols was offered a new role as Peggy Fair, a secretary for a private eye named Joe Mannix, portrayed by Mike Connors on the television show *Mannix*. Roddenberry refused to allow Nichols out of her contract, and she lost the role to Gail Fischer. Ironically, *Mannix* lasted several years, while *Star Trek* was cancelled the next year. In 1968 she and William Shatner made television history by sharing the first interracial kiss, during an episode titled "Plato's Stepchildren."

After *Star Trek* ended, Nichols found it difficult to obtain roles. She appeared in a blaxploitation movie titled *Truck Turner* (1973) with ISAAC HAYES, and she performed voiceover narration for a cartoon version of *Star Trek* from 1973 to 1974, but her acting career remained stagnant until she returned to the screen with the first *Star Trek* movie in 1979. She appeared in six *Star Trek* movies and traveled around the country speaking on behalf of NASA, encouraging young African Americans to consider science and space as viable occupations. As Lieutenant Uhura, Nichols inspired many young African Americans through her portrayal of a strong character who was more multi-dimensional than previous television depictions of African American women. Nichols was the first African American actress to appear as a professional and gained critical acclaim from critics and fans alike for her portrayal of an officer on a starship. The former astronaut DR. MAE JEMISON, who herself broke ground as one of the first African American women astronauts, has said that Nichols inspired her career choice.

FURTHER READING
Nichols, Nichelle. *Beyond Uhura: Star Trek and Other Memories* (1994).

YVONNE D. SIMS

Nickens, Armistead Stokalas, Jr. (1836–27 Apr. 1907), farmer, miller, the first elected public official of African American descent in the state of Virginia, and the first and only African American representative to the House of Delegates for Lancaster County. Nickens was born in Lancaster County, Virginia, the youngest child of Armistead Stokalas Nickens Sr. and Polly Weaver Nickens.

Armistead Sr. and Polly were wed on 21 January 1819 in Lancaster County, Virginia, and had two other children, Robert V. Nickens and Judith A. Nickens. The Nickens family had been free since the late seventeenth century, and several members of that family served in the American Revolution. Armistead's maternal grandfather, Elijah Weaver, was also a seaman during the Revolution.

Home schooled as a youth, Nickens was taught to read and write by his father, and went on to further self-study with books he purchased on his own. Armistead lost his father as a young teenager. His mother Polly is listed alone in the 1850 Census with the two young men, thirteen-year-old Armistead and sixteen-year-old John. John supported the family as a laborer. The 1850 Census shows them owning no real estate, or personal property; however, they were not destitute enough to be classified as paupers. Ten years later, in 1860, Polly had a small personal estate.

Armistead was married twice, first to the former Sophronia Wood, of Heathsville in neighboring Northumberland County, Virginia, on 20 November 1862. Sophronia was the daughter of Reverend Holland and Sally Wood. Reverend Wood was a miller as well as an ordained Methodist Episcopal minister. To their union were born two children, Holland Armistead and Sarah Elizabeth Nickens. Sophronia died between 1869 and 1870. By 1870 Armistead and the children lived alone with his mother Polly. Armistead owned some real estate, as well as a larger personal estate. On 16 November 1871 he married Violet Jones Watkins, his childhood neighbor, daughter of Mahala Jones, and widow of Holland Watkins. Violet brought two children from her first marriage, Louise and Mary Watkins, and with Nickens had three additional children. They had a set of twins, Joseph and Josephine Nickens, as well as another daughter, Sophronia Nickens. When Armistead and Violet opened an account at the Freedman's Bank in Richmond in 1872, Armistead reported having seven children.

As a gentleman farmer, Armistead owned and operated a 135-acre truck farm, which produced oats, corn, and wheat, as well as timber, and sold cordwood to produce additional income for his family. Sharing her father's work ethic, his eldest daughter, Sarah, worked in a tomato factory at age sixteen and went on to become the first African American midwife in Lancaster County. He became a founding member of Calvary Baptist Church in Kilmarnock; and, along with his youngest daughter, Sophronia, he helped lay bricks for the church's foundation. Beyond that, Armistead helped other local men haul logs needed for lumber to build the church building in 1892. After the formal dedication of the church on 11 June 1892, Armistead was officially ordained as a deacon.

Aware of the need for education among the youth of his community, in 1870 Nickens is said to have donated land for and built a school. The structure was the first public school for African Americans in Lancaster County. However, no records have been found to substantiate this transaction.

On 6 December 1871 Armistead became the Honorable Mr. Armistead Nickens when he took the oath of office to become a delegate to the Virginia House of Delegates, representing Lancaster County. He turned out to be the first and only African American to hold that office in Lancaster County as late as 2007. By so doing, he made history as the first elected official of African American descent in that state. This was just two years after the ratification of the Fourteenth and Fifteenth Amendments to the U.S. Constitution and he served in the House of Delegates until March 1875. The Fourteenth Amendment made the newly freed slaves citizens of both the United States and their individual states. The Fifteenth Amendment prohibited denying men the right to vote. With the passage of the Reconstruction Acts of 1867, many African American men could vote while many former Confederates could not. This fact enabled African Americans in areas where they were the majority to elect their own to public office. Nickens was one of eighty-seven African American legislators in the Virginia General Assembly during Reconstruction.

He served on two committees: one being Militia and Police, and the other was Agriculture and Mining. He also aspired to relieve the isolation of the Northern Neck peninsula and introduced legislation for the construction of a bridge over the Rappahannock River from Warsaw, Richmond County, Northern Neck to Tappahannock, Essex County, Middle Peninsula. Prior to this the only transportation was a private boat or the public ferry. Nickens's bill failed, and the bridge did not come to fruition until 16 February 1927, after the bill was reintroduced by State Senator Thomas N. Downing for whom the bridge is named. The first bridge opened twenty-one years after Nickens's death, and was commemorated in 2002 on the seventy-fifth anniversary of the bridge opening. Unfortunately, Nickens's name was not included in the resolution to commemorate that structure.

Armistead spent his final days in the loving care of his family. He is buried in the family cemetery in Kilmarnock, off Good Luck Road, near Kamps and Carter's Millponds. Armistead Nickens's descendants continued his legacy of firsts. Whereas Sarah was the first African American midwife, bringing lives into the world, her son, (his grandson) Quentin DePernell Campbell became the first native-born African American embalmer on the Northern Neck, laying people to rest when their work in this life was over. Quentin's daughter (Armistead's great granddaughter), Brenda Elizabeth Campbell, followed her father into the mortuary profession, becoming the first licensed female embalmer on the Northern Neck—white or black. In 2007 the Campbell Funeral Home was still in operation in Kilmarnock, Virginia, down the street from the church her great-grandfather helped found. Many members of the family still attended Calvary Baptist Church in 2007, and Brenda's sons assisted her with funerals.

FURTHER READING

Jackson, Luther Porter. *Negro Office Holders in Virginia 1865–1895* (1945).

Jett, Carolyn H. *Lancaster County, Virginia: Where the River Meets the Bay* (2003).

KAREN E. SUTTON

Nickens, James (c. 1737–1825), free black veteran of the American Revolution, was born in Lancaster County, Virginia, to Elizabeth Nicken, a free woman, and an unnamed father. Early in life James indentured himself to Edward Ingram until his thirty-first birthday (1768). In 1776 James Nickens may have moved in with his cousin, John Nickens, to establish himself. He was finally on his own when he decided to join the war effort.

Nickens served first as a seaman in the Virginia state navy. Since African Americans dominated the water professions, it was natural that many, including Nickens, chose to serve on the water during the war. Perhaps he heard about hostile British ships entering the Chesapeake Bay and threatening Virginia waters in January 1777. Enlisting in the navy on 19 July 1777, Nickens served three years on board the *Revenge* and the *Hero*. There he helped perform the state navy's chief function to guard Virginia's coastline and prevent the enemy from establishing themselves or utilizing the waterways. His duties may have included pilot, fisherman, housekeeper, and laborer. The *Revenge*, a schooner, operated from 1776 to 1777. The *Hero* was a long row galley, the most common ship. It was heavily armed and used to defend Virginia's rivers and shoreline. Nickens was one of a crew of fifty seamen and marines aboard that vessel. With him on the *Hero* was another free black neighbor, James Sorrell, a gunner's mate from Northumberland County.

In 1781 Nickens enlisted in the First Virginia Regiment of the State Line (army) from Lancaster Courthouse for the duration of the war as a substitute. Perhaps he substituted for his former master Ingram or some member of Ingram's family. From there Nickens marched to Cumberland Courthouse to join the artillery of the army. At Cumberland, Nickens was assigned to accompany his commander, Captain Drury Ragsdale, to South Carolina. On the way to South Carolina, Ragsdale became ill and remained behind. Nickens's regiment was present at the battle of Eutaw Springs, South Carolina. During that campaign he was stationed at the rear for "baggage Negro" duty to guard Captain Gaines and John T. Brooke's luggage.

Eutaw Springs, South Carolina, became headquarters for the British colonel Alexander Stewart on 22 August 1781. Stewart was there to obtain food for his men. They fought the actual battle on 8 September 1781. On that day, about 4:00 a.m., General Nathanael Greene's forces began to advance. Continental troops from North Carolina, Virginia, and Maryland formed the second line of defense. They caught the enemy unawares, digging sweet potatoes. The British troops did this every day around daybreak. Unfortunately, that morning the rooting party (a British term) traveled outside the protection of their regiment and fell into enemy hands.

Not long afterward Ragsdale recovered and rejoined the regiment. News of the British general Charles Cornwallis's surrender at Yorktown (19 Oct. 1781) reached the Eutaw Springs troops on 8 November 1781. Nickens stayed with Ragsdale and the southern army until the end of the war. When the Americans proclaimed peace, Ragsdale and Nickens returned to Virginia together. After the war Nickens remained in Virginia, having served in the army for two or three years.

On 28 July 1787 Nickens received a certificate for the balance of his full pay, which he promptly delivered to Captain James Saunders. Nickens also received a pension as a reward for his service. He testified on 18 March 1818 to apply for his pension. According to law, Nickens swore that he was a U.S. citizen and that he had not sold, given away, or otherwise disposed of any property that would make him in eligible for the Pension Act for Revolutionary Veterans passed on 18 March 1818. Nickens testified that his only property, as certified by the court, was an old table (except bedding and wearing clothes), one horse (bought with his pension pay), two sheep, and one chair, all valued at $23. He was self-employed as a farmer, lived alone, and was in good health. Further, since then he had not sold, given away, or otherwise disposed of any property that would make him ineligible for the pension. Finally, he testified that no one held any property for him.

Nickens's son Hezekiah was a seaman in the Virginia state navy as well and served onboard the *Gloucester*. Hezekiah may have died a prisoner of war, as he received a Bounty Land Warrant posthumously. A Bounty Land Warrant was a certificate for land in Ohio, a reward for services rendered in the state army or navy. A sailor, seaman, or soldier received one hundred acres of land. A captain received 3,000 to 4,666 acres, and a major general (the highest ranking officer) received 15,000 to 17,500 acres as a reward for his service. Because Hezekiah died childless, his brothers and sisters received the certificate.

Nickens married Sally, and they had four children. Their daughters were Elizabeth Nickens and Judy Watkins, and the other son was James Nickens Jr. They received a pension for both their father and their brother. The younger James was born in 1775 in Lancaster County, and on 17 July 1793 he married Mary Peggy Berden in Culpeper County, Virginia. By 1800 James Jr. and Mary had moved to Fauquier County and owned a horse. In 1810 both James Nickens Sr. and James Nickens Jr. were in Fauquier County. The younger had four free blacks at home, and the elder was head of household of eight.

Nickens's naval service entitled him to bounty land for being a substitute for the war. His surviving children, all in Frederick County, Virginia, testified before the justice of the peace that Nickens was their father. On 9 January 1832 William Selden awarded Nickens's family a 100-acre Bounty Land Warrant for his three years of service as a sailor in the Virginia state navy. In 1835 the family sold the land. Nickens excelled above all the fighting, serving on land and at sea, and the United States fulfilled the promise of freedom that he fought to ensure. Surely the money from the sale of the bounty land enhanced their financial and social positions. Many of his descendants lived in the northern Virginia and the Washington, D.C., area in the early twenty-first century and worked in the medical and dental professions.

FURTHER READING

Brown, Kathleen M. *Good Wives, Nasty Wenches, and Anxious Patriarchs: Gender, Race, and Power in Colonial Virginia* (1996).

Jackson, Luther Porter. "Virginia Negro Soldiers and Sailors in the American Revolution," *Journal of Negro History* 27 (July 1943): 133–287.

Kulikoff, Alan. *Tobacco and Slaves: The Development of Southern Cultures in the Chesapeake, 1680–1800* (1986).

Ludlow, Susie Nickens. *Carry Me Back: A Family and National History of Slavery and Freedom* (2000).

Sutton, Karen. *The Nickens Family, Non-Slave African American Patriots* (1994).

KAREN E. SUTTON

Nigger Add (1845?–24 Mar. 1926), cowboy, roper, and bronc rider, also known as Negro Add or Old Add, was born Addison Jones, reportedly in Gonzales County, Texas; his father and mother are unknown. The early life of Add is clouded in conjecture. He may have been a slave on the George W. Littlefield plantation in Panola County, Mississippi, and relocated with the Littlefields when they settled in Gonzales County, Texas, in 1850. It is also possible that he was born in Gonzales County and was purchased by the Littlefields after they arrived. There is no record of his youth and early adulthood.

There are many stories about Add in cowboy memoirs and biographies, but the only name given is Nigger Add or Old Negro Add. It apparently seemed of little consequence in cowboy country that Add had a last name. (Addison Jones's full name was revealed in print for the first time by Connie Brooks in 1993.) Contemporaries who spoke or wrote about Add agreed, however, that he was an outstanding cowboy and bronc buster. Vivian H. Whitlock, who cowboyed with Add for several years on the LFD ranch in Texas and eastern New Mexico, called him "the most famous Negro cowpuncher of the Old West." J. Evetts Haley, the biographer of George W. Littlefield, called him "the most noted Negro cowboy that ever 'topped off' a horse."

Add's reputation with horses was due to his ability, as he used to say, "to look a horse square in the eye and almost tell what it was thinking" and to ride every horse he saddled, with one exception. Add is reported to have been thrown only by a bronc named Whistling Bullet. In typical cowboy fashion Add tried Whistling Bullet again, and according to Pat Boone, a district judge in Littlefield, Texas, he was the only man to ride him.

While the work of "taking the first pitch out of a bronc" often fell to black cowboys, Add performed this task with a special skill, daring, and raw nerve. Several cowboys commented that they saw Add perform this feat on various occasions. According to Haley:

> He would tie a rope hard and fast around his hips, hem a horse up in the corner of a corral or in the open pasture, rope him around the neck as he went past at full speed, and where another man would have been dragged to death, Add would, by sheer skill and power on the end of a rope, invariably flatten the horse out on the ground (184).

Cowboys from neighboring ranches often worked roundups together, and Add, who was known and respected by ranchers and cowboys of eastern New Mexico and west Texas, was a familiar sight. N. Howard "Jack" Thorp, the noted cowboy song collector and songwriter, spoke of camping with Add and a group of black cowhands from south Texas in March 1889 at the beginning of his first song-hunting trek. Later Thorp helped to ensure Add's place in history by writing a cowboy song titled "Whose Old Cow?" that in a humorous fashion recognized Add's ability to identify earmarks and brands.

As cowboys gained experience in the cattle business, they rose from the rank of tenderfoot to top hand or even range boss or foreman. Thorp, in fact, referred to Add as the LFD outfit's range boss. West Texas black cowboys, however, had little chance to pass cowboy status, as was suggested by Whitlock: "He [Add] was a good cowhand, but because of the custom in those days, never became what was known as a 'top' hand." There also was a certain unwritten yet generally understood deference black cowboys were expected to extend to their white counterparts. This situation was the legacy of slavery, which crossed the frontier with the settlers, ranchers, and cowboys. A black cowboy who challenged those traditions did so at his peril.

Add at various times came up to that line and sometimes crossed it. One white cowboy, Mat Jones, said that Add was "a privileged character" (*Fiddlefooted* [1966]). This may have referred to the fact that he was well liked or even protected by LFD officials. Jones told a story that became legend on the LFD about Cliff Robertson, a white cowboy who came from a neighboring ranch as a "rep," or representative. Ranches often sent reps who were seasoned cowboys to other ranches during roundups to make sure that their stock was identified, properly branded, and returned to their home ranch. Add rode up to change his horse and said to Robertson, "What horse do you want, lint?" The term "lint" was a derisive one that referred to a young, inexperienced cowboy from east Texas with cotton lint still in his hair. Robertson tried to catch his own horse and threw a lasso and missed. Add then threw his rope and caught the horse and began to drag it out. Robertson, feeling insulted and embarrassed, came after Add with his rope doubled, or, as some cowboys said, with a knife to cut the rope. At this point Bud Wilkerson, the LFD's range wagon boss, rode between them and said to Add, "Drag the horse out, and I will tend to the lint." Robertson was so angered by the experience that he cut out his horses and went back to his home ranch.

Add, like many cowboys, traveled to other ranches where he could not depend on the protection and goodwill of the LFD. Jones related another story when Add was the LFD rep at the Hat ranch and breached the proper etiquette for a black cowboy. Add went to drink from a water bucket and, finding it empty, followed a standard cowboy procedure that he apparently used on the LFD without thought. He began to siphon water through a hose attached to a large water tank. To get the water started, Add used a method referred to as "sucking the gut." As Add was in the process of starting the water, a white cowboy named Tom Ogles picked up a neck yoke and hit him on the back of the neck, knocking him out. When he regained consciousness, Add, who was reported to have knocked out a black man from a neighboring town with one punch and was described by everyone as stocky, short, and very powerfully built, did nothing. He waited for the remuda to arrive, got his horse, and rode home. This incident provided ample evidence that Add recognized the limitations that society had placed on him.

Add's reputation as a roper also gained him respect and renown. He was able, according to some of his fellow cowboys, to go into a corral and rope any horse with uncanny accuracy. One roping story told by Whitlock attests to Add's roping talents as well as his sense of cowboy humor. One day Add was sitting on his horse in front of the Grand Central Hotel in Roswell, New Mexico, when a runaway team of horses pulling a milk wagon came racing down the street. He made a big loop in his lariat, rode alongside the team, threw it around the horses' heads, and allowed the slack to drape over the wagon. He then turned his horse off in a steer-roping style and caused the wagon, horses, and milk bottles to crash and scatter all over the street. After Add retrieved his rope, he was reported to have said, "Them hosses sure would've torn things up if I hadn't caught them."

Addison Jones was more fortunate than many black cowboys west of the Pecos in that he found someone locally to marry. It was not uncommon for black men in west Texas either to travel back to east Texas to find a wife or to remain single. In 1899 Add and Rosa Haskins were married by the Reverend George W. Read. Add gave his age as fifty-four, while his bride was listed as thirty-six. Haskins, who was a cook and domestic for a number of prominent Roswell families, came to New Mexico from Texas sixteen years before she married Add. There is very little to indicate whether the couple enjoyed marital bliss, but according to Thorp, the announcement of the wedding to a few friends prompted ranchers throughout the Pecos valley to send wedding gifts to Old Add. The lack of a wedding registry and communications may have been the reason that Add and Rosa found nineteen cookstoves at the freight office in Roswell when they came to pick up their wedding presents.

Add's life was lived and ended, according to former Texas and New Mexico sheriff Bob Beverly, the way an old cowboy's life should be:

> Add … realized his work was over. He had ridden the most dangerous trails and had conquered the wildest horses. He had always been thoroughly loyal to the Littlefields and the Whites. He was at the end of his road and he laid down and died knowing full well that his efforts had been recognized and appreciated by the really great cowmen of Texas and New Mexico (Bonney, 141).

Addison Jones died in Roswell and, according to Elvis Fleming, suffered a final double indignity of having his name misspelled and the improper birth data carved into his tombstone. The name on Add's grave is Allison Jones, with a birth date of 24 March 1856, rather than 1845. Old Add lived an ordinary yet extraordinary life as a black cowboy in West Texas and New Mexico. He succeeded in living a life worth remembering, which was something few cowboys, black or white, were able to achieve.

FURTHER READING

Bonney, Cecil. *Looking over My Shoulder: Seventy-five Years in the Pecos Valley* (1971).

Brooks, Connie. *The Last Cowboys: Closing the Open Range in Southeastern New Mexico, 1890s-1920s* (1993).

Fleming, Elvis E. "Addison Jones, Famous Black Cowboy of the Old West," in *Treasures of History III*, Historical Society for Southeast New Mexico (1995): 34–46.

Haley, J. Evetts. *George W. Littlefield, Texan* (1943).

Whitlock, Vivian H. *Cowboy Life on the Llano Estacado* (1970).

This entry is taken from the *American National Biography* and is published here with the permission of the American Council of Learned Societies.

MICHAEL N. SEARLES

Nighthawk, Robert (30 Nov. 1909–5 Nov. 1967), blues musician, was born Robert Lee McCullum (or McCollum) in Helena, Arkansas. Almost nothing is known of his parents except that his father's surname was McCullum, that his mother's maiden name was McCoy, and that they were sharecroppers. When still in his teens Robert left home to travel and work. He began his musical career as a harmonica player but switched to guitar around 1930 when he and a cousin, Houston Stackhouse, were working on a farm in Murphy's Bayou, Mississippi. Stackhouse, who had traveled with and learned from the Delta blues legend TOMMY JOHNSON, recalled that he taught McCullum to play guitar, passing along much of the Johnson repertoire. At the same time McCullum taught his brother Percy to play harmonica, and the three began playing locally, eventually branching out to such Mississippi venues as Crystal Springs and Jackson.

After a mid-1930s altercation—one that supposedly involved a shooting—McCullum left Mississippi and settled in St. Louis, then the urban blues capital of the country. Through a connection with Walter Davis, a St. Louis pianist and part-time talent scout, McCullum was brought to the attention of Bluebird Records. On 5 May 1937 he was one of five St. Louis artists who participated in a marathon recording session for Bluebird in Aurora, Illinois. McCullum played as a duo with BIG JOE WILLIAMS and as a trio with Williams on guitar and SONNY

BOY WILLIAMSON on harmonica, an early foreshadowing of the 1950s Chicago band sound. At that session McCullum waxed six sides as a featured artist, among them "Prowling Nighthawk," the inspiration for the name by which he later became best known. On these first recordings, though, he used his mother's maiden name, calling himself Robert Lee McCoy, possibly still fearing repercussions from the earlier trouble in Mississippi.

Proving himself competent on both guitar and harmonica McCullum worked as a house musician for Bluebird from 1937 to 1940, the most prolific recording period of his career. A 1938 session with Williamson and Speckled Red yielded eight sides, this time issued under the name "Rambling Bob." A switch to the Decca label in 1940 found McCullum using the alias "Peetie's Boy" in deference to the Decca star PEETIE WHEATSTRAW. That same year McCullum married the washboard player Anne (or Amanda) Sortier.

By 1942 McCullum had switched to electric guitar, transforming techniques that he had picked up from the guitarist TAMPA RED into an exciting slide style that eventually influenced such artists as EARL HOOKER, MUDDY WATERS, and ELMORE JAMES. Now playing as Robert Nighthawk he began using radio to promote his band, create a reputation, and acquaint countless aspiring blues artists with his distinctive instrumental sound. Beginning with station KFFA in his birthplace, he gained fame, if not fortune, on the airwaves, ensuring attendance at his band's many regional appearances.

Although leading the life of a musical celebrity in the South, Nighthawk traveled to Chicago sporadically. In 1948 Muddy Waters, at whose wedding reception Nighthawk had played in 1932, brought Nighthawk to the attention of the Chess brothers, Leonard and Phil, owners of the Chess record label. A 1949 session for Chess resulted in a two-sided classic, "Black Angel Blues" and "Annie Lee Blues," two electric-slide blues drawn from the repertoire of Tampa Red. Nevertheless Chess appeared to lose interest in Nighthawk after 1950.

Sessions for the United label in 1951 and for its subsidiary label States in 1953 produced other classics in the Delta blues tradition, among them "The Moon Is Rising" and Tommy Johnson's "Maggie Campbell." The recordings were poorly distributed and promoted, however, and did little to further Nighthawk's career.

Nighthawk returned south to play around Helena and nearby Friar's Point, Mississippi. He visited Chicago in 1960 to work with Kansas City Red and visited again in 1964 to work with a band called the Flames of Rhythm that played in the Maxwell Street market district, a magnet for blues artists. Also in 1964 he recorded several cuts for a British album, recorded an album for the Testament label, and appeared at the Chicago Folk Festival. After this brief flirtation with the mushrooming folk and blues revival audience, Nighthawk once again returned south to play clubs in Jackson and Lula, Mississippi. In 1965 he took over KFFA's *King Biscuit Time* after the death of the show's longtime star, SONNY BOY WILLIAMSON II.

By 1967 Nighthawk, his own health failing, had reunited with his cousin and first teacher, Stackhouse, for a final Testament recording. Nighthawk died of congestive heart failure at Helena Hospital.

Nighthawk's limited recording activity in the 1950s and early 1960s, the heyday of his peers, led later critics to label him "overlooked" and "underappreciated." Described as introverted by those who knew him, he went little noticed during the blues revival. Instead he remained true to his roots, returning again and again to the audiences that had supported him throughout his life. Nighthawk's significant albums include *Lake Michigan Blues 1934–1941*, *Robert Nighthawk: Bricks in My Pillow*, and *Robert Nighthawk and His Flames of Rhythm: Live on Maxwell Street*.

Remembered by history as a 1930s recording artist and influential guitar stylist, Nighthawk actually made his deepest impression through radio and live performances, which were warmly recalled by the southern black audiences whose culture and traditions he embraced. Unlike artists who moved to Chicago, Nighthawk preferred his familiar southern venues. His southern audiences likewise appreciated his art, as did his fellow blues musicians. As the guitarist and mandolinist Johnny Young put it, "Nighthawk was a hell of a good musician.... He was so good he almost made me cry." Robert Nighthawk was inducted into the Blues Foundation Hall of Fame in 1983.

FURTHER READING

Harris, Sheldon. *Blues Who's Who: A Biographical Dictionary of Blues Singers* (1979, 1989).
O'Neal, Jim. "Living Blues Interview: Houston Stackhouse," *Living Blues*, no. 17 (Summer 1974).
This entry is taken from the *American National Biography* and is published here with the permission of the American Council of Learned Societies.

BARRY LEE PEARSON AND
BILL MCCULLOCH

Nix, Robert (9 Aug. 1898–22 June 1987), congressman, was born Robert Nelson Cornelius Nix in Orangeburg, South Carolina. He was the son of Nelson and Silvia Nix. His father was the dean of arts and sciences at the historically black Southern Carolina State University, and his mother was a homemaker. Robert Nix attended Townsend Harris Hall High School, a distinguished private school in New York, and graduated in 1921. Shortly thereafter Nix was motivated to attend Lincoln University in Oxford, Pennsylvania, and earn a bachelor of arts degree in 1921. Nix chose to continue his education at the University of Pennsylvania Law School, where he earned his law degree in 1924.

After becoming a resident of Philadelphia, Nix sought to be active in local politics. In 1932 he joined the Democratic Party and quickly became a key figure in the Democratic politics of Philadelphia's Fourth Ward. From 1934 to 1938 he served as both the special deputy attorney general of the Pennsylvania State Department of Revenue and the special assistant deputy attorney general of the Commonwealth of Pennsylvania.

From 1938 to 1956 Nix practiced law in Philadelphia. He and his wife, Ethel Lanier, raised a son, Robert N. C. Nix Jr., born in 1928. In 1956 Nix Sr. once again turned his attention to politics when he was named a delegate to the Democratic National Convention.

Because of a vacancy created by the early resignation of U.S. Representative Earl Chudoff in 1958, Nix won a special election as a Democrat to the Eighty-fifth Congress. Historically this appointment made Nix the first African American from Pennsylvania to hold a seat in Congress. Nix would hold this position for ten consecutive terms for a total of twenty years in office. During this period Nix served on the Committee on Veterans' Affairs, the Foreign Affairs Committee, and the Committee on Merchant Marine and Fisheries.

Nix held his office during a period of intense civil rights debate and was instrumental in putting together much of the legislation. When ADAM CLAYTON POWELL was being considered for exclusion from the Ninetieth Congress, Nix privately sought to prevent this action. His efforts proved meaningless when, in 1967, Congress stripped Powell of his seniority because of his constant absenteeism, his numerous trips abroad at the expense of taxpayers, and his refusal to pay slander judgment. Powell was eventually reelected when the U.S. Supreme Court ruled the judgment of the Congress unconstitutional in June 1969.

In 1975 Nix introduced legislation mandating that the Defense Department must provide to Congress information on identities and fees received by the agents who negotiate the terms of international arms sales for U.S. firms, hoping to make the process less clandestine. In 1976 Nix ran for reelection against an ambitious young African American named WILLIAM GRAY III. Nix was able to beat his challenger, and he served his tenth term until 1978, when Gray once again challenged him. This time Gray was able to garner enough support to defeat Nix in the primary election. Following his defeat Robert Nix retired from politics. He died at the age of eighty-nine.

FURTHER READING

A collection of Nix's papers is available at the African American Museum in Philadelphia.

Barker, Lucius J., and Jesse J. McCorry Jr. *Black Americans and the Political System* (1976).

Boast, Thomas. *Robert N. C. Nix, Democratic Representative from Pennsylvania (Citizens Look at Congress/ Ralph Nader Congress Project)* (1972).

Christopher, Maurine. *America's Black Congressmen* (1971).

Smith, Jessie Carney, ed. *Notable Black American Men* (1999).

ARTHUR HOLST

Nixon, Edgar Daniel (12 July 1899–25 Feb. 1987), Alabama civil rights leader, was born in Robinson Springs, Alabama, near Montgomery, the son of Wesley Nixon, a tenant farmer and, in later years, a Primitive Baptist preacher, and Susan Chappell. Nixon's mother died when he was nine, and thereafter he was reared in Montgomery by a paternal aunt, Winnie Bates, a laundress. Nixon attained only an elementary education, and at thirteen began full-time work, first in a meatpacking plant, then on construction crews, and in 1918 as a baggage handler at the Montgomery railway station. As a result of friendships that he made in this last job, he managed in 1923 to become a Pullman car porter, a position he would hold until his retirement in 1964. In 1927 he was married to Alleas Curry, a schoolteacher. The couple soon separated, but they had Nixon's only child. In 1934 he married Arlet Campbell.

Exposed by his railroad travels to the world beyond Montgomery, Nixon grew increasingly to hate racial segregation. He became a devoted follower of A. PHILIP RANDOLPH, who was attempting in the late 1920s and early 1930s to unionize the all-black Pullman porters. In 1938 Nixon was chosen as president of the new union's Montgomery local. In 1943 he organized the Alabama Voters League to support a campaign to obtain voter registration for Montgomery's blacks. The effort produced a vigorous white counterattack, but Nixon himself was registered in 1945.

Montgomery's blacks were sharply divided between a middle-class professional community centered around the campus of Alabama State College for Negroes and the working-class blacks who lived on the city's west side. The Montgomery branch of the National Association for the Advancement of Colored People (NAACP) was dominated by college-area professionals and failed to support Nixon's voter registration drive actively. Nixon therefore began organizing the poorer blacks of west Montgomery, where he resided, to attempt a takeover of the branch. He was defeated for branch president in 1944 but was elected in 1945 and reelected in 1946 in bitterly contentious races. In 1947 he was elected president of the Alabama Conference of NAACP Branches, ousting the incumbent, the Birmingham newspaper editor EMORY O. JACKSON. But national NAACP officials, who were hostile to his lack of education, quietly arranged for Nixon's defeat for reelection to the state post in 1949. In 1950 he also lost the presidency of the Montgomery branch to the same man he had beaten in 1945. Nevertheless, in 1952 he won election as president of the Montgomery chapter of the Progressive Democratic Association, an organization of Alabama's black Democrats. And in 1954 he created consternation among Montgomery's whites by becoming a candidate to represent his precinct on the county Democratic Executive Committee. Though he was unsuccessful, he thus became the first black to seek public office in the city in the twentieth century.

During his years with the NAACP, Nixon had become a friend of ROSA PARKS, the branch secretary during much of this period. When Parks was arrested on the afternoon of 1 December 1955 for violating Montgomery's ordinance requiring racially segregated seating on buses, she called Nixon for help. After he bailed her out of jail, he began telephoning other black leaders to suggest a boycott of the buses on the day of Parks's trial, 5 December, to demonstrate support for her. The proposal was one that black leaders had frequently

Edgar Daniel Nixon, standing with Adam Clayton Powell (right) in front of a cheering crowd after delivering a speech in New York City, 1956. (New York World-Telegram and the Sun Newspaper Photograph Collection/Library of Congress.)

discussed in the past, and it was greeted enthusiastically by many of them. The black Women's Political Council circulated leaflets urging the action, and a meeting of black ministers gave it their approval. The boycott on 5 December was so complete that black leaders decided to continue it until the city and the bus company agreed to adopt the plan of seating segregation in use in Mobile, under which passengers already seated could not be unseated. The Montgomery Improvement Association was formed to run this extended boycott, and Nixon became its treasurer. Nixon, however, became increasingly antagonistic toward the association's president, the Reverend MARTIN LUTHER KING JR. Nixon viewed King as an ally of the Alabama State College professionals, and he believed that King's growing fame was depriving him, and the poorer blacks whom he represented, of due credit for the boycott's success. After King moved to Atlanta in 1960, Nixon engaged in a protracted struggle

for leadership of Montgomery's blacks with the funeral director Rufus A. Lewis, the most prominent figure among his rivals in the middle-class Alabama State community. The contest culminated in the 1968 presidential election, when Nixon and Lewis served on alternative slates of electors, each of which was pledged to Hubert H. Humphrey. The Lewis slate defeated the Nixon slate handily in Montgomery. Nixon thereafter slipped into a deeply embittered obscurity. He accepted a job organizing recreational activities for young people in one of Montgomery's poorest public housing projects, a position he held until just before his death in Montgomery.

FURTHER READING

The Library of Alabama State University, Montgomery, holds several scrapbooks of clippings and other material related to Nixon. Transcripts of oral history interviews with Nixon are held at Alabama

State University; the Martin Luther King Center, Atlanta; and Howard University, Washington, D.C. See also the Montgomery NAACP Branch Correspondence, NAACP Papers, Library of Congress.

Baldwin, Lewis V., and Aprille V. Woodson. *Freedom Is Never Free: A Biographical Portrait of Edgar Daniel Nixon, Sr.* (1992).

Garrow, David J. *Bearing the Cross: Martin Luther King Jr. and the Southern Christian Leadership Conference* (1986).

Thornton, J. Mills, III. *Dividing Lines: Municipal Politics and the Struggle for Civil Rights in Montgomery, Birmingham, and Selma* (2002).

Obituary: *New York Times*, 27 Feb. 1987.

This entry is taken from the *American National Biography* and is published here with the permission of the American Council of Learned Societies.

J. MILLS THORNTON

Nixon, Lawrence Aaron (9 Feb. 1883–6 Mar. 1966), physician and civil rights activist, was born in Marshall, Texas, the son of Charles Nixon, chief steward of a private railroad car owned by the general manager of what was then the Texas and Pacific Railroad. When the private car was moved in 1886, the Nixon family followed it to New Orleans, where Charles Nixon was able to send his four children to private school, providing them with a better education than was available in the substandard public schools reserved for black children. When the family returned to Marshall in 1892, Lawrence's schooling continued through Wiley College, the oldest historically black college west of the Mississippi River, where he completed his undergraduate education.

Nixon worked at various jobs while obtaining his education, but began to fulfill his true professional dreams in 1902 when he entered Meharry Medical College in Nashville, Tennessee. Earning his medical degree in 1906, he moved to Cameron, Texas, in 1907 to set up a practice. He also married his childhood sweetheart, Esther Calvin, and their son Lawrence Joseph Nixon was born in 1909.

During his first year in Cameron, Nixon witnessed the public killing of a black man by a white mob. In a nearby building other whites sat on the balcony to better witness the event and listen to the cries of the dying man as he was burned at the stake, according to Nixon, who was behind locked doors. Such sights were not uncommon in the United States during that time, and an increase in the number of lynchings in and around Cameron led Nixon to seek a safer place to live. It was then that he remembered El Paso, Texas.

In 1894 Lawrence had accompanied his mother to El Paso to visit her brother, the memory of which led him to hope that life there might be better. Thus, on the last day of 1909, Dr. Nixon and friend LeRoy White set out for El Paso, sharing a freight car with the doctor's furniture and his horse and buggy. Despite segregation and racial restrictions, Nixon was able to establish a thriving medical practice in El Paso serving blacks and Latinos. Unfortunately, in 1918 his wife Esther succumbed to the deadly influenza epidemic that claimed thousands of lives that year.

El Paso's small black community—then only 3 percent of the population—was of little consequence in local politics. Yet the black residents were politically astute and active, voting in all elections. In the early 1900s in Texas, only the Democratic Party was strong enough to even make a showing at the polls, so that city, county, and state elections usually pitted one Democratic faction against another. As Nixon pointed out, those who thought it their duty to vote had no choice but to vote with the Democrats (Bryson, 75). Then, in 1923, Texas enacted the white primary statute, prohibiting black participation in primary elections.

When the National Association for the Advancement of Colored People (NAACP) looked for someone to go to the polls in defiance of the white primary order, Nixon (who had helped organize the El Paso branch) volunteered. This was no small matter. At a time when Jim Crow laws and open intimidation served to curtail meaningful black political participation, and when Ku Klux Klan hate activities raged unbridled throughout the South and elsewhere, it was much more than mere civic mindedness that Nixon displayed. It was deep conviction and courage. In some ways, though, El Paso was a relatively safe venue in which to challenge the statute. It was more western than southern and, although active, the Klan was never able to gain a real foothold there. On 26 July 1924 Dr. Nixon took his poll tax receipt to the local precinct and requested a ballot to vote in the Democratic primary election. He was denied. Citing the state law, election judges refused his request. Nixon faced similar scenarios repeatedly over the years.

Nixon's action marked the beginning of a twenty-year legal battle against the "lily-white"

Democratic primary that flourished in the American South, helping set the stage for the civil rights movement. Ironically, while the primary had been conceived as a basis for white solidarity, "the process of fighting to overturn it led to the unity of blacks" (Hine, 251). With the financial and moral backing of the NAACP and the local black community, Nixon continued to challenge the exclusionary Texas law, resulting in two major cases that went all the way to the United States Supreme Court (*Nixon v. Herndon*, 1927; *Nixon v. Condon*, 1932). The Supreme Court decisions, while ostensibly in Nixon's favor, left gaping loopholes by which states could still circumvent black voting rights. These cases took a heavy toll on NAACP resources, resulting, on the one hand, in little immediate effect on the political status of blacks. Yet on the other hand, these cases were touted as strategic victories and they created precedents for challenging the unconstitutionality of the Texas statute. Joined by other cases brought by Texas blacks, the Nixon cases finally resulted in the casting of a ballot in 1934. However, only two El Paso blacks—Nixon and his business associate—were allowed to vote, and even then only as something of a "trick." Wanting to avoid further court action, white officials gave Nixon a "special" ballot marked "colored," signaling to vote counters that the ballot—while seemingly in compliance with the law—was to be ignored. In general Supreme Court decisions reflected fundamental agreement with prevailing white sentiments supporting black disenfranchisement.

Meanwhile in 1929 Nixon met Drusilla Tandy Porter who came to El Paso for health reasons. In 1930 she returned to her parents' home in Toledo, Ohio, but Nixon and she maintained a correspondence, and married in November 1935. With his son Lawrence Joseph and her daughter Dorothy from a previous marriage, their family also expanded with the births of their daughters Edna and Drusilla Ann (Annie). When Dr. Nixon filed his first suit, his children could attend only one school in El Paso, he could live only in restricted areas, he would be denied service at first class hotels and restaurants, and, although a fully qualified physician, he could not join the local medical society nor could he send patients to hospitals unless sponsored by a white doctor.

Finally in 1944, after subsequent rulings on the fundamental issues raised in the Nixon cases, the Supreme Court took an uncompromised position, rejecting previous decisions in support of black

disenfranchisement. On 22 July 1944 in El Paso where the battle had begun twenty years earlier, Dr. Lawrence A. Nixon and his wife walked to the polls and voted in the Texas Democratic primary. By 1955 school desegregation in El Paso was well underway, commercial access began opening, and, although not without contention, the Texas State Medical Association and the El Paso County Medical Society abolished their white membership requirement.

Lawrence Nixon died at the age of eighty-two. A crusader for justice, a visionary, and a remarkable humanist, he is remembered in El Paso with a road, Nixon Way, and a school, Lawrence A. Nixon Elementary, both named in his honor.

FURTHER READING

Bryson, Conrey. *Dr. Lawrence A. Nixon and the White Primary* (1992).

Hine, Darlene Clark. *Black Victory: The Rise and Fall of the White Primary in Texas* (2003).

Renteria, Ramon. "Civil Rights Pioneer Left Legacy of Love, Learning, and Understanding," *El Paso Times*, 24 Oct. 1999.

CONNIE L. MCNEELY

Noble, Jeanne L. (18 July 1926–17 Oct. 2002), educator, leader, and writer, was born Jeanne Laveta Noble in Albany, Georgia (although some reports suggest she was born in Palm Beach, Florida), to Aurelia and Floyd Noble. She was reared primarily by her grandmother, Maggie Brown, who was a first grade teacher and owned a florist shop. Her mother was young and her father left the family before Noble reached five years of age. Noble, the eldest child with three younger brothers, took her grandmother's advice to pursue a career and an education in order to secure her economic independence. Noble, like many children in the Jim Crow South, had a rude awakening to the contradictions of American society. She was sent home from a visit to a church-affiliated camp for presuming that she could engage in church activities alongside white children. As a result, Noble refused to associate with the church until adulthood exposed her to a broader world.

In pursuit of her degree at Howard University, a historically black university, Noble sought out the most challenging and dynamic African American scholars on the faculty, among them E. FRANKLIN FRAZIER, ALAIN LOCKE, and STERLING BROWN. Noble, who avoided enrolling in courses taught by white professors, changed her attitude after taking a humanities course with a professor who was white and a Quaker. In 1946, at age nineteen, she was awarded her degree.

Noble went on to earn both a master's degree in 1948 and a Ph.D. in Educational Psychology and Counseling in 1955 from Columbia University. She also studied in England at the University of Birmingham. Her career as an educator began in historically black institutions (or HBCUs— historically black colleges and universities), first as a teacher at Albany State College in Georgia in 1948 and then as dean of women at Langston University in Oklahoma from 1950 until 1952. She accepted the position at Langston reluctantly, expecting her primary role to be that of disciplinarian. To her surprise she enjoyed the work a great deal and served on the administrative council. She later taught at New York University, where she became the first African American woman to move through the ranks and earn tenure at a majority university. In her later years Noble retired as professor emeritus from the guidance and counseling graduate faculty of Brooklyn College–City University of New York. She also sat on trustee boards at Marymount Manhattan College and Lincoln University, which was an HBCU in Pennsylvania.

In 1960 Noble authored her first scholarly publication on education: *College Education as Personal Development* (1960), a text for college freshman orientation. In 1965 she won the Bethune-Roosevelt Award for service in education. For her publication *The Negro Woman College Graduate* (1970), she received the Pi Lambda Theta Research Award. She produced a recording for Delta Sigma Theta Sorority, Inc., *Roses and Revolutions* (1973) and collaborated with OSSIE DAVIS and RUBY DEE on *75 Years of Retrospect*, a drug abuse public service announcement. She also wrote *Beautiful, Also, Are the Souls of My Black Sisters* (1976). Serving as a professor on the weekly educational program *The Learning Experience*, this TV show enjoyed a five-year run and won a regional Emmy Award in 1977. Her television credits also include cohosting *Straight Talk* (1979), a weekly talk show.

Noble consulted on numerous government, public, and private educational organizations, from school systems and university programs to national foundations and corporations. She represented the United States as a delegate to the World Assembly in Denmark. Noble's expertise earned her appointments on multiple government commissions by three U.S. presidents: Lyndon B. Johnson, Richard Nixon, and Gerald Ford. Among other posts, she was appointed to the Advisory Panel on Essentials for Effective Minority Programming, the Bicentennial Commission, the Corporation for Public Broadcasting, the Defense Advisory Committee on Women in the Service, the Department of Agriculture, the Peace Corps, and UNESCO.

Additionally, Noble served on the boards of the Urban League of Greater New York, the Haryou Act, Girl Scouts of America, International Center for Integrative Studies, Governors of Common Cause, and the Alvin Ailey Dance Foundation. She was national vice president of the National Council of Negro Women and helped initiate the National Arts and Letters Commission as the youngest elected president of Delta Sigma Theta Sorority, Inc.

A short list of Noble's accolades in the 1980s and 1990s include the National Association of Black Women in Higher Education Lifetime Achievement Award (1989), the Bennett College honorary Doctor of Humane Letters (1991), and the Consortium of Doctors Award of Perseverance (1993). Noble died of congestive heart failure in 2002.

FURTHER READING

Collins, Grace E. "Jeanne Noble," in *Notable Black American Women, Book 2* (1996).

Troup, Cornelius V. *Distinguished Negro Georgians* (1962).

MARCELLA L. MCCOY

Noil, Joseph (1841–?), seaman in the U.S. Navy and Medal of Honor recipient, was born in Nova Scotia, Canada. Nothing certain is known of his early life or his family background, though it may be speculated that, based on his origin in one of Canada's maritime provinces, he may have been a sailor in the merchant trade and that, if so, his activities in this area likely facilitated his arrival in the United States.

Joseph Noil's arrival in the United States is also undocumented, but by 1872 at the latest he had enlisted in the U.S. Navy at New York. While serving aboard the sidewheel steam frigate *U.S.S. Powhatan* at Norfolk, Virginia, he earned the Congressional Medal of Honor when he saved a fellow crewman, Boatswain J. C. Walton, from drowning on 26 December 1872. Noil was undoubtedly an experienced sailor; this is not only indicated by his action that earned him the Medal of Honor, but also by his rating as a seaman. Below the position of seaman in the naval rating system at the time were the positions of ordinary seaman and landsman, both held by men with little or no seafaring experience. The *U.S.S. Powhatan*, manned by a crew of about three hundred officers and enlisted men, was part of the Navy's Home Squadron based at Norfolk during the time when Noil performed his feat of heroism, and though the ship by this time was near the end of its active service, the posting was a good one for Noil and his fellow crewmen as the *Powhatan* was seldom at sea for very long!

Joseph Noil is an important figure not just for his Medal of Honor status, but also for several other reasons. Not only is he the only Canadian of color to receive this most prestigious of all U.S. military decorations, but he is also representative of a small and largely forgotten group of men, including ROBERT SWEENEY, WILLIAM JOHNSON, and ALFONSE GIRANDY, that earned the medal in the interim period prior to World War I, when it was awarded not just for actions during wartime, but also for peacetime acts of heroism. Most of these interim Medal of Honor recipients were members of the U.S. Navy who earned the award by saving a fellow shipmate while at sea. By World War I the requirements needed to qualify as a Medal of Honor recipient had changed and peacetime actions no longer qualified for the medal. Despite this change, the actions of these peacetime Medal of Honor recipients are still worthy of remembrance, as each recipient, men like Joseph Noil, went above and beyond, going into action without hesitation and without regard for their own personal safety to help a fellow crewman in immediate peril.

Following his award of the Medal of Honor, Joseph Noil vanishes from history; nothing is known of his subsequent naval service, residence, or even time and place of death.

FURTHER READING

An artist' conception of Joseph Noil in period naval uniform may be viewed at: http://www.history.navy. mil/photos/pers-us/uspers-n/j-noil.htm.

Hanna, Charles W. *African American Recipients of the Medal of Honor* (2002).

GLENN ALLEN KNOBLOCK

Noll, Malinda (1820–?), one of the first slaves to enter the Kansas Territory, was born in Madison County, Kentucky. In her narrative dictated to the

Scottish American abolitionist James Redpath in 1858, Noll does not name her parents but notes that she, like her mother, a cook, was owned by William Campbell, a prominent landowner, while her father was owned by a man named Barrett, who lived three miles away. Among the other slaves owned by Campbell were LEWIS GARRARD CLARKE and John Milton Clarke, who both later escaped slavery and became prominent abolitionists in Boston in the 1850s. As of 1858 Noll incorrectly believed that Lewis Clarke, upon whom Harriet Beecher Stowe modeled the character George Harris in *Uncle Tom's Cabin* (1851), had been caught and returned to slavery in Kentucky.

When Noll was fourteen her master moved to Clay County, Missouri, bringing with him Noll's mother and all of her siblings except for one brother, Millar, whom William Campbell sold to a cousin in Kentucky, and who was later sold again to a plantation in the Deep South. In her narrative, Noll recalled that one of her sisters died on the arduous journey to Missouri, and that her mother grieved for that loss and for her separation from her husband. In an act that explains Noll's view of her owner as "a kind master; one of the best there was," William Campbell left his son-in-law in charge of his slaves in Indiana and returned to Kentucky to purchase Noll's father, who was later reunited with his family in Missouri (Redpath, 258). Noll also recalled that Campbell owned between six hundred and seven hundred acres of land, was wealthy, and did not push his slaves and hired hands as some owners did. Within a few years, however, she would learn that her master's benevolence took second place to a slave owner's right to property.

In 1835, when Malinda was fifteen, she married a man named Nathaniel Noll, a slave who lived on a nearby plantation and who was half-brother to his master, who owned his mother. She recalled that in Missouri, as in Kentucky, it was the custom for all the neighbors, both black and white, to attend the wedding ceremony when a "respectable colored girl gets married," and that around three hundred people attended hers, which was held at her master's home. Perhaps wrapped up in the moment of the ceremony, she paid little heed to the words of her master, which followed the blessing by a local minister: "You join these people together; *that is, till I choose to make a separation*" (Redpath, 259). After the wedding Noll remained working as a cook for her master, who treated her husband "pretty well," she recalled, allowing him to stay with her on Saturday nights as long as he left before daybreak on Monday mornings. The Nolls had three children in four years.

As Malinda Noll's siblings reached adulthood and as William Campbell's own children grew older, married, and established farms of their own, he began parceling out his slaves to them. In 1843 Campbell gave Noll and her two youngest children, Georgy and Julia, to his daughter, Margaret Jane and her husband, Levi Hinkle, a forage master who worked at Fort Leavenworth in the Kansas Territory. Other than federal troops and employees at Fort Leavenworth, there were at that time few white settlers in Kansas, and there were almost no African Americans. Under the terms of the 1820 Missouri Compromise, the Kansas Territory was to be closed to slavery once statehood was achieved. The Nolls' eldest son, Miller, remained with William Campbell, while Nathaniel Noll also remained with his master in Kentucky. Malinda Noll's brothers and sisters were also separated from their spouses and children, a fate that led to their mother's nervous breakdown. Noll recalled, "You could hear her screaming every night as she was dreaming about them. No sooner was she beginning to get sort-of reconciled to one child being gone, then another was taken and sold away from her. My poor old mother! It was awful to see her" (Redpath, 262).

Although Nathaniel Noll's owner allowed him to visit his wife and children twice during her first year in Kansas, he was forbidden to leave the state again after that point, no doubt because his master feared he would not return. Malinda Noll later learned that her husband remarried and had children with his second wife. Her own life in Kansas became increasingly difficult. In addition to being separated from her siblings, husband, and eldest son, she suffered the death of her only daughter, Julia, after only two years at Fort Leavenworth. Noll recalled that her new owners fed and clothed her well at first, but that her mistress, whom she had lived with since childhood, became increasingly jealous of the attention her husband paid her, and to his frequent praise of Noll's work as a cook and domestic. Fearing that a sexual relationship would develop if she left Noll alone with her husband, Margaret Jane Campbell brought her slave with her on frequent trips home to Missouri, where she struck Noll over the head with a broom. When Campbell attempted to do so again when they returned to Kansas, Noll resisted her and forced her to back off. Campbell told her husband, however, who punished his slave by stripping her clothes off and whipping her, Noll recalled, "till the blood rained off my back and arms. Then he put handcuffs on me and threatened to sell me South" (Redpath, 263). Noll's defiant request that he do precisely that almost paid dividends when a Missouri slave owner offered to purchase her, but Hinkle refused his offer upon learning that the Missourian intended to take her to California to free her after two years' service.

Subsequently, eight years after arriving in Fort Leavenworth, Hinkle sold Noll to Major Ogden, an army officer for whom she worked for five years, and who brought her, still a slave, to Connecticut. She recalled that she "had more work to do than ever in my life before" but also had privileges and was treated well (Redpath, 264). Although now living in a free state, she did not try to run away, though she would have done so, she insisted, had Ogden been transferred to a slave state. Having served her contract with the officer's family, Noll earned her freedom and began saving money to purchase the freedom of her son Miller, who remained a slave in Parkville, Missouri. The growth of abolitionist sentiment in the North by the mid-1850s, particularly after the passage of the Fugitive Slave Act, the Kansas-Nebraska Act, and the U.S. Supreme Court's DRED SCOTT decision, greatly aided Noll's efforts. Traveling throughout the North she received small and large donations from various benefactors, though her son's owner raised his price to twelve hundred dollars upon hearing how much money she had raised. On 11 November 1858 Malinda Noll successfully purchased her son and was at last reunited with him. At that point she disappears from the historical record, and it is unknown whether she was ever reunited with her other surviving son, Georgy, who was at that time still a slave in Kansas.

FURTHER READING

Redpath, James. *The Roving Editor, or Talks with Slaves in the Southern States*, ed. John R. McKivigan (1996).

STEVEN J. NIVEN

Norman, Jessye (15 Sept. 1945–), opera singer, was born in Augusta, Georgia, to Silas Norman, an insurance salesman who also sang in the church choir, and Janie King, a secretary and accomplished amateur pianist. The Normans made certain that their five children studied piano, and they encouraged Jessye to sing in church and community programs at a very early age. A 78 rpm recording of Brahms's *Alto Rhapsody*, sung by MARIAN ANDERSON, was one of Jessye's most powerful inspirations. At age ten, she recounts, "I heard her voice and I listened.... And I wept, not knowing anything about what it meant" (Gurewitsch, 96).

After graduating with honors from Augusta's Lucy Craft Laney High School in 1963, Norman went on to study voice with Carolyn Grant at Howard University in Washington, D.C. During the summer after her graduation in 1967, she attended the Peabody Conservatory in Baltimore, Maryland, after which she studied voice with Pierre Bernac and Elizabeth Mannion at the University of Michigan, receiving a master of music degree in 1968.

Norman's professional career began overseas in 1968 after she won first prize in an international music competition sponsored by Bavarian Radio in Munich, Germany. The following year she signed a three-year contract with Deutsche Oper Berlin, and made her triumphant operatic debut on 12 December 1969 as Elisabeth in Richard Wagner's *Tannhäuser*—a demanding role for a twenty-four-year-old. In 1972 she made her professional American debut in Verdi's *Aïda* at the Hollywood Bowl in Los Angeles, with James Levine conducting. Throughout the 1970s Norman's opulent voice and extraordinary intelligence continued to draw rave reviews, and she was booked in concerts and festivals worldwide. In 2006 Norman received the Grammy Lifetime Achievement Award.

Norman's debut with the Metropolitan Opera in New York City in September 1983 propelled her to new heights of popularity, especially with American audiences. The Met featured Norman as the tormented prophetess Cassandra in Berlioz's epic *Les Troyens*, a role she had sung in 1972 at Covent Garden in London. At subsequent performances, Norman changed roles from the dark-hued mezzo-soprano of Cassandra to the rich, searing soprano of Dido. Because of her gifts in character portrayal, she was able to interpret and delineate each role with authority and a profound sense of tragedy.

Norman's other performances with the Met included twenty-two performances as the Prima Donna/Ariadne in Richard Strauss's *Ariadne auf Naxos* and the Wagner roles of Elisabeth in

Jessye Norman performs during a 100th Birthday Tribute for Marian Anderson at New York's Carnegie Hall, 27 February 1997. (AP Images.)

Tannhäuser, Kundry in *Parsifal*, and Sieglinde in *Die Walküre*. Norman lent her hypnotic, expressive, and robust voice to modern work as well. Critics called her richly dramatic interpretation of Schoenberg's *Erwartung* a tour de force and praised her performances in Bartók's *Bluebeard's Castle*, Poulenc's *Dialogues of the Carmelites*, and Stravinsky's *Oedipus Rex*.

Primary among Norman's unique talents was her wide vocal range. She moved with grace and sensitivity from a sparkling high C-sharp to a voluptuous middle range to a rich low G. Her ability to draw expressive power and color from her roles encouraged diversity within her repertoire as well. She maintained, "I don't allow myself to be cast in a particular repertoire—or *only* in a particular repertoire—because I like to sing what I'm able to sing" (Gurewitsch, 99). Her curiosity also drew her to the less standard works, such as those of Monteverdi, Rameau, Purcell, Stravinsky, Schoenberg, and Philip Glass, which challenged her passions as well as her intellect. She opened Lyric Opera of Chicago's 1990–1991 season in Robert Wilson's innovative production of Gluck's *Alceste*. To understand the intense emotions of

Phèdre in Rameau's opera *Hipployte et Aricie*, she read Racine. Norman strived to know her characters completely, visualizing the minutest details of every scene.

Performing under such distinguished conductors as Claudio Abbado, Riccardo Muti, Colin Davis, Daniel Barenboim, and Seiji Ozawa in orchestras around the world, Norman honed a signature style and repertoire, which includes Isolde's impassioned "Liebestod" from Wagner's *Tristan und Isolde*, which she sang with the New York Philharmonic in 1989. Norman was also famous for her stunning interpretations of Mahler's *Das Lied von der Erde* and Richard Strauss's *Four Last Songs*, about which the music critic Robert C. Marsh wrote, "If we must die, let us go with Jessye Norman singing" (*Chicago Sun-Times*, 21 Oct. 1986). In August 2002 she sang Alban Berg's romantic *Seven Early Songs* with the Metropolitan Opera Orchestra in Baden Baden, Germany.

Recitals with piano, which allowed her to explore the art song repertoire, as well as spirituals and popular music, especially appealed to the singer. In any language she always knew the meaning behind every word, each of which was lovingly caressed through her singing. "Time and again she found just the right inflection or color to illuminate the text," explains Derrick Henry (*Atlanta Journal-Constitution*, 11 Mar. 1989).

In 2000 Norman premiered Judith Wier's song cycle, *woman.life.song*. Based on texts by TONI MORRISON, MAYA ANGELOU, and Clarissa Pinkola Estes, the work was commissioned for Norman by Carnegie Hall. Norman's collaborations with other African American artists includes performing the sacred music of DUKE ELLINGTON and theatrical partnerships with the ALVIN AILEY Repertory Dance Ensemble, and the choreographer BILL T. JONES.

Jessye Norman's brilliant career is reflected in the numerous awards and honors she has received. Her recordings—from Purcell and Beethoven to Cole Porter and jazz—number more than seventy, among them her 2003 recording of Mahler's *Kindertotenlieder* commemorating the 150th anniversary of the Vienna Philharmonic. She won four Grammy Awards, a *Grand Prix National du Disque*, a Gramophone Award, and an Edison Prize. A special favorite in France, she received the title *Commandeur de l'Ordre des Arts et des Lettres* in 1984 and the *Legion d'Honneur* from President François Mitterrand in 1989. She holds more than thirty honorary doctoral degrees from universities, including Brandeis, Harvard, the University of Michigan, and Howard. In 1997 she became the youngest recipient of a Kennedy Center Honors award, and in 1999 President Clinton invited her to sing at the White House for the fiftieth anniversary celebration of the North Atlantic Treaty Organization.

In 1990 Jessye Norman was appointed an honorary United Nations ambassador. She also served on the board of directors of numerous organizations, including the Lupus Foundation, the New York Public Library, the New York Botanical Garden, the Dance Theatre of Harlem, the National Music Foundation, and the Elton John AIDS Foundation. The amphitheater and plaza overlooking the Savannah River in Norman's hometown of Augusta have been named for her.

With all her glories, however, Norman managed to retain her unpretentious demeanor, described as having a quick wit and a smile that "hits the eyes like the sudden opening of Venetian blinds on a sunny day" (*Current Biography Yearbook* [1976], 295). A tall woman (five feet ten inches) with a large, imposing frame, she had a ready answer to a friend who asked how she managed to get up after falling in Dido's suicide scene. With a wink, she said, "I choreographed every muscle beforehand." Norman was active in community affairs, especially in helping to promote historically black educational institutions. A dignified artist with elegance, poise, and grace, Jessye Norman brought joy and wisdom to both her art and her audiences.

FURTHER READING
The Metropolitan Opera Archives, New York, contains press clippings, reviews, cast lists, and other production information relating to Norman's career.
Gurewitsch, Matthew. "The Norman Conquests," *Connoisseur* (Jan. 1987): 96–101.
Mayer, Martin. "Double Header," *Opera News*, 18 Feb. 1984, 9–11.
Story, Rosalyn M. *And So I Sing: African-American Divas of Opera and Concert* (1990).
ELISE K. KIRK

Norris, J. Austin (1893–Mar. 1976), lawyer, journalist, civil rights activist, and political leader, was born to working-class parents in the small, rural Pennsylvania town of Chambersburg. His mother crafted artistic hairpieces and his father was a barber. At the age of four, the family relocated to Pittsburgh.

Norris attended a Pittsburgh Methodist college prep high school. Upon graduating in 1908, he enrolled in historically black Lincoln University in Oxford, Pennsylvania, where he engaged in a classical education curriculum, studying Latin, Greek, and philosophy. He also played on the university's basketball team. He credited his time at Lincoln University for teaching him about self-worth and personal discipline. After his graduation in 1912, Norris began his legal education at Yale University. He financed his legal education first as a dishwasher and then as a waiter, where he believed his charisma would bolster his wages through tips. Yale not only provided a traditional legal education but also introduced him to elite organizations and secret societies.

Norris finished his education at Yale Law in 1917. Despite the prestige and opportunity that usually accompanied an Ivy League legal education, Norris faced a formidable foe in the form of a segregated society. Upon graduating from law school, Norris joined a segregated unit of the U.S. Army in the midst of World War I. He was stationed at Camp Lee in Petersburg, Virginia. Drawing from his training at Yale Law, Norris organized letters of protest against the treatment of black soldiers. In November 1917, he was transferred to Maryland's Camp Meade, where he roomed with future noteworthy leaders such as CHARLES HAMILTON HOUSTON, JOSEPH L. JOHNSON, RAYFORD W. LOGAN, AND JOHN ROBINSON.

His advocacy against the unequal treatment of black soldiers earned him a hard-fought opportunity to take the qualification exam to become an artillery officer. Norris became part of a select group of black Army officers to serve in France during World War I. By the end of his military tenure, he had gained a personal education in the evils of racism and developed a disgust for it that would guide his life's work. Upon his honorable discharge from the Army, Norris sat for the Pennsylvania Bar Exam and relocated from his long-time home in Pittsburgh to Philadelphia. Consistent with widespread discrimination across the country, the opportunities for a Yale Law-trained black attorney were sparse.

When Norris joined the Philadelphia bar, he was one of only six black practicing attorneys in the city. Criminal law, real estate work, and domestic relations were the predominant sources of employment for Philadelphia's black attorneys. The heart of the city's black professionals was Lombard Street, which was located in the seventh ward. Norris spent his initial years working there and in 1919 founded the *Philadelphia American*, a weekly publication. Within a year, the paper boasted a circulation of eight thousand readers but Norris sold it after the debts exceeded the profits. The sale proceeds were used by Norris to open a seventh ward law office.

As Norris's professional career grew, so did his community involvement. After serving as counsel for the Philadelphia branch of MARCUS GARVEY'S Universal Negro Improvement Association (UNIA), Norris was elected as a member. The relationship, however, was brief. Norris's affiliation with the UNIA became strained after the death of James Eason, an African Methodist Episcopal Zion minister. Eason was the first UNIA chaplain general in 1919 and went on to serve as central leader at the 1920 UNIA convention. One week prior to his scheduled appearance as a government witness in Garvey's mail fraud trial, Eason was fatally shot. Norris aided the Federal Bureau of Investigation in locating information about Eason's murder.

Norris's fractured relationship with the UNIA did not deter him from fostering more civic and professional networks within the black community. His ability to develop networks across racial boundaries jump-started his political career. Norris's political aspirations dated back to his initial arrival in Philadelphia. In 1924, he turned down an offer to serve as a candidate for the state legislature because of the paltry $1,500 salary. While continuing his seventh ward legal practice, he became a supporter of the Postal Cards—a group of white postal workers who focused on increasing black support of the Republican Party. After growing increasingly frustrated with the lack of voice given to blacks within the Republican Party, he switched his political affiliation to the Democratic Party in 1931. As a Democrat, Norris worked on garnering the black vote for presidential nominee Franklin D. Roosevelt. His work with the Democratic Party broadened his networks and in 1932 he was elected seventh ward leader by a diverse committee that included members of Irish, Jewish, and Italian descent.

Norris's legal practice flourished alongside his political ascension. In 1931, Norris took on University of Pennsylvania Law School graduate Walter A. Gay Jr. as a law partner. Drawing from his networks in the community, in black churches, and with various civic organizations, Norris expanded the firm's client base. Norris and Gay remained partners until 1937. In 1937, Norris set out to expand his civil practice—an area in which black lawyers were sparsely represented. He also publicized Roosevelt's New Deal programs using newspapers such as the *Philadelphia Independent* to generate political support in the black community. As city editor of the paper, he was able to utilize it as a tool to bolster political activism among blacks. He wrote editorials in support of President Roosevelt's re-election bid, endorsed the gubernatorial campaign of George H. Earle—Pennsylvania's first Democratic governor in the twentieth century—and wrote about various issues affecting the black community such as housing inequality, public accommodation, and civil rights.

On 9 March 1935, Norris became Special Deputy Attorney General—a position he accepted only after he was offered the same salary as his white counterparts. His primary role was to oversee the foreclosure of banks and other businesses closing as a result of the Great Depression. His tenure in the Attorney General's office led several influential Democrats to recommend him for a Court of Common Pleas judgeship in 1937. He declined the offer because as a judge he would have been precluded from political activities. Well recognized by the late 1930s as one of the leading black democrats in the city, Norris sought an appointment on the Board of Revision of Taxes. Up until that point, the influential board had been Republican controlled. Members of the board assessed residential and commercial properties, determined which properties were tax exempt, and set the market value for taxable or tax exempt property. Viewed as someone who valued issues above politics, Norris was supported by both Republicans and Democrats in his campaign. On 16 July 1937, he stepped down from his position as Deputy Attorney General and became not only the first but also the only black member of the Board of Revision Taxes. His tenure lasted thirty years. His understanding of eminent domain law made Norris a central policy maker on the board.

A successful law practice, thriving political career, and acknowledgment as a large influence over the black vote positioned Norris at the apex of Philadelphia's black leadership. In 1942, he became editor of the Philadelphia edition of the *Pittsburgh Courier*. The paper was one of the largest circulating black newspapers in the country. Norris used his position at the *Courier* to share news about blacks in other major cities with Philadelphia residents and to continue to opine on civil rights issues such as housing, employment, politics, and economics. Norris used his political capital not only to enlighten others about the plight of discrimination, but also to fight for key appointments of other black leaders within the Commonwealth, such as the state parole board, city council, school board, zoning board, and Commission on Human Relations.

Norris developed a number of notable relationships as a result of his work. In particular, he became very close with FATHER DIVINE and the Peace Mission Movement after about ten years of contact during his time on the tax review board. In 1952, Norris became the attorney for Father Divine and his movement.

In 1955, Norris joined the first major African American law firm, which became Norris, Schmidt, Green, Harris & Higginbotham upon his joining. The firm produced four federal judges—A. LEON HIGGINBOTHAM, CLIFFORD SCOTT GREEN, Herbert Hutton, and William Hall, who was the first African American appointed as a federal magistrate judge. Judge Higginbotham would go on to be Chief Judge of the Court of Appeals for the Third Circuit. Two other members, Doris Harris and Harvey Schmidt, were elected judges of the Philadelphia Court of Common Pleas and President Nixon appointed another firm member—William Brown—to chair the Equal Employment Opportunity Commission. The firm practiced both criminal and civil work and Norris enjoyed a national reputation for his expertise on eminent domain law.

By 1971, the firm operated as Norris and Brown because Higginbotham, Green, and Harris had all moved on to become judges. Norris continued to rely upon his political influence to mobilize the community and sustain the firm's business. Despite his commitment to expanding the firm's business, Norris also welcomed a large number of pro bono clients. Equally important was his commitment to fostering mentorships with young attorneys by offering them employment at his firm and ensuring they received rigorous training.

Norris passed away in 1976. As demonstrated by the number of free clients and legions of lawyers with whom he worked who moved on to prestigious legal opportunities, he left a legacy of steadfast commitment to his community and to the legal profession. Speaking about his former colleague, the Honorable A. Leon Higginbotham said:

When the High Court of History decides the great American lawyers, it will choose not merely those who informed the Supreme Court of the right direction to go; it will also choose those who gave backbone to later generations to go forward. [J.] Austin Norris used to say—and I don't mean to be disrespectful—"I don't give a damn about the big firms. We'll whip' em and we'll be as good as they are, even though we'll have only four or five lawyers." Norris had the capacity to take young men and force them to recognize that if you persevere, you'll make it. I've always said that he was a true and great hero (Higginbotham).

FURTHER READING

Higginbotham, Hon. A. Leon. *"The Dream with Its Back against the Wall."* Speech given at the 1989 Yale Law School Alumni Weekend.

Porter, Aaron C. *The Career of a Professional Institution: A Study of Norris, Schmidt, Green, Harris, Higginbotham, and Associates* (unpublished dissertation, University of Pennsylvania, 1993).

JOCELYN L. WOMACK

Northup, Solomon (July 1808–1863?), author, was born in Minerva, New York, the son of Mintus Northup, a former slave from Rhode Island who had moved to New York with his master early in the 1800s and subsequently been manumitted. Though Solomon lived with both his parents and wrote fondly of both, he does not mention his mother's name or provide any details regarding her background, except to comment that she was a quadroon. She died during Northup's captivity (1841–1853), whereas Mintus died on 22 November 1829, just as his son reached manhood. Mintus was manumitted upon the death of his master, and shortly thereafter he moved from Minerva to Granville in Washington County. There he and his wife raised Northup and his brother Joseph, and for the rest of his life Mintus remained in that vicinity, working as an agricultural laborer in Sandy Hill and other villages. He acquired sufficient property to be registered as a voter—a notable accomplishment in those days for a former slave.

As a youth Northup did farm labor alongside his father. Only a month after the death of Mintus, Northup was married to Anne Hampton, and he soon began to do other kinds of work as well. He worked on repairing the Champlain Canal and was employed for several years as a raftsman on the waterways of upstate New York. During these years, 1830 to 1834, the Northups lived in Fort Edward and Kingsbury. In addition to his previous labors, Northup began farming, and he also developed a substantial reputation as a fiddler, much in demand for dances. Anne,

meanwhile, became well known as a cook in local taverns. They moved to Saratoga Springs in 1834, continuing in the same professions. They maintained their household there, which soon included three children, until 1841, when what had been a quite normal life took a dramatic turn for the worse.

In March of that year Solomon Northup met a pair of strangers in Saratoga who called themselves Merrill Brown and Abram Hamilton. Claiming to be members of a circus company, they persuaded him to accompany them for a series of performances until they rejoined their circus. As their terms seemed lucrative and Northup needed money, he agreed to join them as a fiddler. These con men, to secure Northup's trust, told him that he should obtain free papers before leaving New York, since they would be entering the slave territories of Maryland and Washington, D.C. They further lulled him by paying him a large sum of money. In Washington, however, Northup was drugged, chained, robbed, and sold to a notorious slave trader named James H. Burch.

Thus began Northup's twelve years as a slave. His narrative, *Twelve Years a Slave: Narrative of Solomon Northup*, far more than just a personal memoir, provides a detailed and fascinating portrait of the people, circumstances, and social practices he encountered. His account of the slave market, his fellow captives, and how they were all treated is especially vivid. Burch's confederate, Theophilus Freeman, transported Northup and the others by ship to New Orleans, where they were sold in a slave market. Northup was purchased by William Ford, a planter in the Red River region, and though Ford was only his first of several masters, Northup spent his entire period of captivity in this section of Louisiana.

Despite the heinous injustice of Northup's kidnapping and enslavement, he speaks quite favorably of the man who becomes his master: "In my opinion, there never was a more kind, noble, candid, Christian man than William Ford. The influences and associations that had always surrounded him, blinded him to the inherent wrong at the bottom of the system of Slavery" (*Puttin' on Old Massa*, ed. Osofsky, 270). This passage, distinguishing between Ford's personal character and environmental influences, reflects Northup's extraordinary fair-mindedness, a trait that makes his text especially compelling and persuasive. Nonetheless, Northup's respect for Ford did not reconcile him to accept his plight as a slave. Northup, called "Platt" while enslaved, made attempts as opportunities arose to escape and to notify his friends and family in New York of his situation. As his narrative shows, however, the constant surveillance and severe punishments of the slave system stifled such efforts. Even to obtain a few sheets of writing paper required waiting nine years. He feared to reveal his identity as a freeman, lest he suffer extreme reprisals.

Northup's skills as a rafter brought him distinction along the Red River, but financial difficulties forced Ford to sell him in the winter of 1842 to John M. Tibeats, a crude, brutal, and violent neighbor. The choleric Tibeats compulsively worked, whipped, and abused his slaves. Eventually he attacked Northup with an ax, and in self-defense Northup drubbed him mercilessly, then fled to the swamps. Luckily, by a legal technicality, Ford retained partial ownership of Northup, and when the fugitive arrived back on Ford's plantation after several days of struggling through the swamps, Ford was able to shield him from Tibeats's wrath. New arrangements were made, which contracted Northup out to work for Edwin Epps, an alcoholic plantation owner in Bayou Boef, who remained Northup's master for the next decade. Northup's skills as a carpenter, a sugarcane cutter, and especially as a fiddler kept his services in demand, making him perhaps the most famous slave in the region—but, ironically, known by the false name Platt.

Northup's fortunes took a turn for the better in 1852 when a Canadian carpenter named Bass came to work on Epps's new house. A genial but passionate man, Bass was regarded as an eccentric in the community because of his outspoken antislavery views. Hearing him debate Epps on the topic, Northup decided that Bass was a white man worth trusting. The two became friends, and Bass promised to mail a letter for Northup. At Northup's direction, Bass composed a letter to William Perry and Cephas Parker of Saratoga, New York, informing them of Northup's situation. When these men received the letter, they consulted Henry B. Northup, the son of Mintus Northup's former master. He, in turn, initiated a complicated series of arrangements that led to his being appointed by the governor of New York as a special agent charged to secure the rescue of Solomon Northup from slavery in Louisiana. Fortunately New York had enacted in 1840 a law designed to address cases like Northup's, where New York citizens were kidnapped into slavery. The process, however, required obtaining proofs of citizenship and residence and various affidavits. Consequently it was the end of November before Henry Northup was empowered to act on behalf of the governor. Solomon Northup, meanwhile, grew deeply depressed, having no way of knowing whether the letter had been delivered.

Nevertheless, Henry Northup acted with dispatch and arrived in Marksville on 1 January 1853 to seek out and liberate Solomon Northup. Unfortunately, though the local officials cooperated with his mission, no one knew a slave named Solomon Northup. A lucky inference by the local judge produced an encounter between Henry Northup and Bass, who revealed his authorship, the slave name, and the location of Solomon Northup. Henry and the sheriff journeyed to the Epps plantation and laid claim to Northup before the furious Epps could avoid a large financial loss by sending him away. After a brief formal proceeding, Northup regained his freedom and returned northward with Henry.

They decided to stop in Washington and bring kidnapping charges against James Burch, which they filed on 17 January 1853. Due to various technicalities, Burch evaded conviction, but the case did serve the important purpose of bringing many facts into the public record, thereby confirming Solomon Northup's own account. He arrived in Sandy Hill, New York, on 20 January and proceeded to Glens Falls, where he was reunited with his wife and children, who had grown to adulthood in his absence. The narrative ends at this point, and little is known of Northup's subsequent life, except that he contracted with David Wilson, a local lawyer and legislator, to write this memoir, which was published later in 1853. It sold quite well and resulted in the identification and arrest of Northup's kidnappers, whose real names were Alexander Merrill and Joseph Russell. Their trial opened 4 October 1854 and dragged on for nearly two years, snarled by technicalities over jurisdiction, which finally received a ruling by the state supreme court that returned the case to the lower courts, who in turn simply dropped it. Northup never received legal recompense for the crimes committed against him. The sale of his book earned him three thousand dollars, which he used to purchase some property, and he returned to work as a carpenter. Nothing is known of his ensuing years. He apparently died in 1863, but scholars have not been able to confirm this. His narrative remains, however, one of the most detailed and realistic portraits of slave life.

FURTHER READING

Northup, Solomon. *Twelve Years a Slave*, eds. Sue L. Eakins and Joseph Logsdon (1853, repr. 1968).

Blassingame, John. *The Slave Community* (1972).

Phillips, Ulrich Bonnell. *American Negro Slavery* (1918, 1966).

Stampp, Kenneth. *The Peculiar Institution* (1956).

This entry is taken from the *American National Biography* and is published here with the permission of the American Council of Learned Societies.

DAVID LIONEL SMITH

Norton, Eleanor Holmes (13 June 1937–), women's and civil rights activist and congresswoman, was born Eleanor Katherine Holmes, the eldest of three daughters of Coleman Sterling Holmes, a public health and housing inspector, and Vela Lynch Holmes, a teacher, in segregated Washington, D.C. Oral history dates the family's residence in Washington to the early 1850s, when her paternal great-grandfather walked off a Virginia plantation to freedom in the District of Columbia. Holmes's father attended Syracuse University in upstate

Eleanor Holmes Norton reads over a proposal in her office in the House Rayburn building in Washington, 9 April 2007. (AP Images.)

New York and worked his way through law school, though he never took the bar exam and never practiced law. Holmes's mother, born on a family farm in North Carolina, completed normal school in New York, where she earned a teaching certificate. After she married and moved to Washington, she earned a bachelor's degree from Howard University and passed the district's teacher certification exam, becoming the financial stronghold of her family.

As a child, Holmes grew up admiring the educator and social activist MARY CHURCH TERRELL and was influenced deeply by her paternal grandmother, Nellie Holmes, who taught her "the assertiveness she was expected to show in public" (Steinham, 33). Her father reinforced the prospect of command and responsibility especially expected of the eldest daughter. Throughout her childhood her father taught Holmes to strive for the best and to insist on respect. At home and at school she consistently received messages advocating equality among the races. Holmes's leadership began early in school and community activities. Quite popular among her age group, she was junior high school class president, leader of a community service club for teens, a debater, and a debutante during her senior year. She also excelled in her work from elementary through secondary school. In 1955, a year after the U.S. Supreme Court's *Brown v. Board of Education* school desegregation decision, Holmes graduated as one of the top students from Washington's prestigious Paul Laurence Dunbar High School in its last segregated class.

During the fall of 1955, as the civil rights movement was gathering momentum, Holmes entered Antioch College in Ohio. Although she selected Antioch in large measure because of the work-study plan that would enable her to earn money for tuition, the very liberal atmosphere at the college shaped her emerging progressive political views. At Antioch, Holmes's concern for racial justice matured and expanded to include broader questions of equality and social action. Ever a leader among her peers, Holmes eventually chaired both the campus Socialist Discussion Club and the campus NAACP chapter, the latter of which sent a "sizeable contribution" (Steinham, 65) to support the Montgomery bus boycott. In early 1960, during her last semester, when a wave of student-led sit-ins against segregated facilities spread across the South, Holmes organized similar protests in towns near the Antioch campus. She graduated from Antioch in June 1960, ranked twentieth among 165 graduates.

That fall, in a class with few women of any race and not many African Americans, she entered Yale Law School, along with MARIAN WRIGHT EDELMAN. In New Haven, Holmes continued her civil rights activism. She helped found and coordinate a chapter of the Congress on Racial Equality (CORE), and during the summer of 1963 she worked with the Student Nonviolent Coordinating Committee (SNCC) in Mississippi. Her presence in Mississippi proved to be pivotal, since she was able to initiate crucial outside contact with FANNIE LOU HAMER, Lawrence Guyot, and several others who had been arrested and beaten and were being held in Winona, Mississippi. Guyot, also a SNCC worker, had received the same treatment as Hamer and others when he went to investigate their disappearance. Later that summer Holmes represented U.S. students on a European tour and worked at the New York headquarters of the March on Washington. In the fall she returned for her final year at Yale. She completed a four-year dual program in the spring, taking degrees in law and American studies and earning honors in the latter subject.

Having anticipated a career in civil rights law, Holmes headed for work with SNCC in Mississippi in 1964, immediately upon completion of her degree at Yale. That was the summer of the historic Mississippi Freedom Democratic Party (MFDP) challenge at the Democratic Party's Atlantic City convention. Holmes was assigned to her hometown delegation, Washington, D.C., where she joined the civil rights and labor attorney Joseph L. Rauh Jr. in writing a brief arguing the MFDP's case to the Democratic Party credentials committee. In Atlantic City, Holmes directed MFDP lobbying, including activities as varied as preparing and placing MFDP representatives to speak with credentials committee members and coordinating demonstrations outside the convention center. Yet despite the efforts of Rauh, Norton, BOB MOSES, and Fannie Lou Hamer, the MFDP failed to achieve its goal of supplanting the regular, whites-only, Mississippi delegation at the convention with an integrated slate of delegates.

Continuing her preparation for civil rights work, she took a post in the fall as clerk for the newly appointed U.S. District Court judge, A. LEON HIGGINBOTHAM (a fellow graduate of Antioch), in Philadelphia, Pennsylvania. A year later, on 9 October 1965, Eleanor Holmes married Edward Norton, whom she had met four months earlier at the home of a longtime friend. The couple moved to Manhattan, where Edward Norton was finishing law school at Columbia University, and where Eleanor Holmes Norton took a position with the American Civil Liberties Union (ACLU). The Nortons, who separated after twenty-five years of marriage, had two children, Katherine and John.

At the ACLU, Norton's reputation as a First Amendment expert emerged through the notoriety of her amicus curiae brief supporting JULIAN BOND's efforts to be seated in the Georgia state legislature, and her successful defense of George Wallace, the segregationist governor of Alabama, and of the National States Rights Party, a white supremacy group. Norton also filed and won what was likely the first class-action suit involving gender when she challenged *Newsweek* magazine's practice of barring women from jobs as reporters. In 1970 Norton was named head of New York City's Human Rights Commission, where she implemented new civil rights laws and pioneered antidiscrimination policies and programs. Her significant accomplishments at this time included diversifying the city's definition of civil rights constituencies and conducting a complete review and reordering of the city's public school staffing that made way for a more diverse workforce in school classrooms and administration. Within a year the Human Rights Commission post expanded to include a role as the mayor's executive assistant. During this time Norton taught a course in women and the law at New York University School of Law and coauthored the groundbreaking book *Sex Discrimination and the Law: Causes and Remedies* (1975). Norton continued to work as New York's human rights commissioner for seven years until, in 1977, President Jimmy Carter appointed her the first woman to chair the Federal Equal Employment Opportunity Commission (EEOC).

When Norton took over as EEOC director, the agency had a massive backlog of complaints and a slow-moving bureaucracy. She engineered the agency's reorganization, which resulted in streamlined and speedy claims processing and near complete handling of backlogged cases. She also led the EEOC's broad-scale approach to employment discrimination by going after corporate and industrial "patterns and practices" instead of focusing solely on single cases. This resulted in closing prominent agreements with major corporations, including AT&T and the Ford Motor Company. Norton also initiated new EEOC procedures on fair employment and established pioneering guidelines to deal with the problem of sexual harassment in the workplace. Both of these initiatives have had a long-term influence on fair employment and sexual harassment policy. In January 1981 Norton resigned the post as the administration of Ronald Reagan took office. One of Norton's successors at the EEOC was CLARENCE THOMAS.

After a brief time recuperating from the grueling schedule of the EEOC, Norton took a post as professor at the Georgetown University Law Center. She taught constitutional law and cofounded the Women's Law and Policy Fellowship Program. She also kept a busy speaking schedule, continuing to advocate civil rights improvements despite the country's turn away from advances of the era. While a professor at Georgetown, Norton joined RANDALL ROBINSON, WALTER FAUNTROY, and MARY FRANCES BERRY in a 1984 protest at the South African Embassy in Washington, D.C., that highlighted growing American opposition to the South Africa's apartheid regime. In 1990 she was elected to the 102d Congress, succeeding Walter Fauntroy as the district's nonvoting representative. Taking office at a difficult time in D.C.'s history, Norton was successful in helping to restore credibility and resources to the beleaguered District of Columbia. She also attempted to make the issue of voting representation in Congress for District of Columbia residents a national civil rights issue. Norton combined eye-catching publicity campaigns, such as having D.C. license plates read "taxation without representation," with political pragmatism. Realizing many Republicans would oppose voting rights for overwhelmingly Democratic D.C., Norton worked with those pushing for an additional Congressional district for the state of Utah.

Known as tenacious, sharp, and focused in all her work, Norton's career of public service reflects her ongoing evolution as an advocate of equal rights for all Americans. Norton has received numerous honorary degrees and in 1982 was elected to the Yale University Corporation. She later was selected to serve on boards of several Fortune 500 corporations, including Pitney Bowes, Metropolitan Life Insurance, and Stanley Works.

Among Norton's signature achievements in Congress has been her ability to secure jobs for the District, notably in relocating 6,000 jobs to the Washington Navy Yard, and in ensuring that the Department of Homeland Security headquarters compound—the largest federal construction project in the country in 2011—was located in Anacostia, a historically African American and mainly poor neighborhood. By 2011, Norton had served eleven terms as the Congresswoman for the District of Columbia. In the minority after the Democrats lost the House to the Republicans in 2010, in the 112th Congress Norton was the ranking member of the House Subcommittee on Economic Development, Public Buildings, and Emergency Management, and served on the Committee on Oversight and Government Reform and the Committee on Transportation and Infrastructure. While MAXINE WATERS and some members of the Congressional Black Caucus openly criticized the administration of BARACK OBAMA for compromising too much with the right wing of the Republican Party, Norton argued that the problem lay as much with the black community at large as with the President. She noted in her blog that "African Americans spent the first two years of the Obama administration so infatuated with our own success in electing the first African American president and so in love with the President's celebrity, that we gave little attention to what it would take to keep him there. Meanwhile, the Tea Party, which detested the idea of Obama as much as we loved it, lost no time in going for old-fashioned remedies—grassroots organizing and getting their people elected." (Norton, 2011). Norton, however, joined with several of the House's more liberal members to question the constitutionality of Obama's support for the NATO led bombing of Libya in the spring and summer of 2011.

FURTHER READING

Lester, Joan Steinau. *Fire in My Soul: the Life of Eleanor Holmes Norton* (2003).

Norton, Eleanor Holmes. "Tough Talk Tonic," , 1 10. 2011. http://www.norton.house.gov/index. php?option=com_content&view=article&id=3001:t ough-talk-tonic&catid=68:blog.

ROSETTA E. ROSS

Norton, Kenneth (Ken) Howard (9 Aug. 1943–), professional boxer and actor, was born in Jacksonville, Illinois, to George Florence, a World War II veteran, and Ruth Norton, an activities director at a hospital, who would later marry John Norton, a fireman and police dispatcher. From an early age Norton excelled in sports, which he claimed protected him from much of the racism that pervaded his hometown. In high school, Norton became a star in football, baseball, and track and field. Although gifted intellectually, Norton did only the work required of him and as a result did not do well in school. However, his athletic achievements led

Ken Norton, world heavyweight champion, with Muhammad Ali during a news conference in New York City, 3 May 1973. Ali points to where Norton broke his jaw in their bout earlier that year. Although Ali said his upset loss to Norton was "a humbling experience," he predicted that in his next bout with Norton, "I'll win easy." (AP Images.)

to scholarship offers from over ninety institutions. Fearful of venturing too far from home, Norton accepted a football scholarship from Northeast Missouri State University (later Truman State University), a teacher's college where he played basketball and football. During his sophomore year, Norton got into an argument with one of his coaches and left the school. His adoptive father John Norton was disappointed, and offered his son three choices: go back to school, start working full time, or join the service. Norton chose the third, enlisting in the U.S. Marine Corps in 1964.

After boot camp, Norton was assigned to communications school for basic training and was then transferred to Camp Lejeune in North Carolina. Looking for a way to earn special privileges such as better food and a later wakeup time, Norton joined the base football team, but quit following an on-field conflict with a white officer who he felt was racist. Norton was then introduced to Pappy Dawson, who ran the marine corps boxing team. Norton accepted Dawson's invitation to join the squad and began a successful amateur career, winning the All-Marine Championship three years in a row. In 1966 Norton married Jeanette Brinson; they had met six months earlier in the nightclub near the base her father owned, and on 29 September 1966 she gave birth to Ken Norton Jr., who later became a professional football player. Norton was transferred to Camp Pendleton in San Diego that year, where he completed his four-and-a-half years in the marines as a radio technician. His marriage dissolved less than a year later, in no small part because of his infidelity. Norton was planning to return to Jacksonville to become a police officer when two businessmen offered him $100 a week and a share of his purses to remain in Southern California and become a professional boxer. Norton accepted the offer and began training at the Hoover Street Gym in Los Angeles. To supplement his income, he also took a job at the Ford Motor Company.

Norton began his boxing career with a victory in November 1967. After his third professional fight, his trainer Henry Davis left for Germany to instruct another fighter. This would turn out to be one of the most fortuitous events of Norton's life because it led to his being trained by the legendary Eddie Futch, one of the greatest minds the sport has ever known.

Norton reeled off sixteen straight victories before he was upset by Jose Luis Garcia in Los Angeles on 2 July 1970. Norton rebounded by winning seventeen fights in a row before being matched with MUHAMMAD ALI at the San Diego Sports Arena in Norton's adopted hometown on 21 March 1973.

Norton, whose last fight had taken place in front of seven hundred spectators and earned him a $700 purse, was a heavy underdog. It was Ali's first bout shown live on free TV since 1967, and the huge viewing audience witnessed the sport's biggest upset in years. Guided by the masterful Futch, Norton pressured Ali relentlessly, countering his jab and breaking the former champion's jaw with a right hand. With the fight tied going into the last round, Norton stepped up his attack and earned a split-decision victory that vaulted him into title contention and seemed to spell the end of Ali's career. Some observers, citing Norton's military background and Ali's refusal to be drafted into Vietnam War service, tried to impress political symbolism onto the bout, but neither Norton nor Ali acknowledged such interpretations. Six months later, Ali won a razor-thin split decision victory over Norton in their rematch. Once again, however, Norton impressed observers with his ability to hold his own against the great Ali. Promoters then matched Norton for a title bout in Caracas, Venezuela, on 26 March 1974 with the heavyweight champion GEORGE FOREMAN, who exposed Norton's greatest weakness as a fighter, his inability to ward off devastating punchers. Foreman easily penetrated Norton's defenses, knocked him down, and scored a technical knockout victory in the second round. Although Norton was paid $200,000 for the bout, it was a devastating loss. Norton rebounded with several strong victories, including a stoppage of contender Jerry Quarry and a knockout over former conqueror Jose Luis Garcia. These victories led to a third fight with Ali, who had regained the championship from Foreman. In this bout, held on 28 September 1976, Ali escaped with a unanimous decision, but hordes of observers believed that Norton won the fight. Two years later, Norton took on Larry Holmes for a portion of the heavyweight title that was stripped from Ali. In a classic match, Norton was outfought in the final round to lose an extremely close decision. Norton boxed for a few more years, but first-round knockout losses to the hard punchers Earnie Shavers and Gerry Cooney convinced him to quit the sport with his health intact in 1981.

Norton's victory over Ali, combined with his good looks, Herculean physique, and articulateness, turned him into a celebrity during the mid-1970s. He was cast in the feature film *Mandingo*, which sparked controversy over its portrayals of slavery and interracial sex, and he made a number of television appearances as an actor and broadcaster. Norton was also cast to play Apollo Creed in *Rocky*, but backed out and was replaced by Carl Weathers. In 1983 Norton became a sports agent and formed the Ken Norton Personal Management Co. This successful venture was derailed when, on 23 February 1986, Norton was involved in a horrific one-car accident that resulted in devastating injuries. For two years he was wheelchair-bound, but rehabilitated himself significantly and regained almost all of his speech and motor skills. In the early 1990s Norton was involved in a highly publicized misunderstanding with his son Ken, after the younger man took offense to his father's suggestion that he sign a prenuptial agreement before marrying his fiancée, which led to their not speaking for two-and-a-half years. The two later reconciled. In 1999 he opened Ken Norton's Restaurant & Nightclub in Irvine, California, near his home. Beginning in 2000 Norton began working as an advisor for boxers, a broadcaster for the Showtime cable-television network, and did public relations work for a number of businesses.

FURTHER READING

Norton, Ken, with Marshall Terrill and Mike Fitzgerald. *Going the Distance* (2000).

Ashe, Arthur. *A Hard Road to Glory: The African-American Athlete in Boxing* (1993).

Sammons, Jeffrey. *Beyond the Ring: The Role of Boxing in American Society* (1990).

MICHAEL EZRA

Notorious B. I. G. (Christopher Wallace) (21 May 1972–9 Mar. 1997), rapper, was born Christopher George Latore Wallace in the Clinton Hill neighborhood of Brooklyn, New York, the only child of Voletta Wallace, a preschool teacher, and George Letore. The child of Jamaican immigrants, he was raised in a home that placed a strong emphasis on education. He attended Catholic schools in Brooklyn during his youth and was an honor roll student with particular strengths in math, science, and art. He also was noticed for an early lyrical style that set him apart from other children his age. Taking a cue from the nursery rhymes of his childhood, he would create lyrics in a similar style and commit them to memory, unlike other lyricists who relied on paper. Often larger in stature than his colleagues from elementary school on, Wallace accepted the nickname of "Big" and was well respected and looked to as a leader in school as well as in his community. He participated in a youth mentoring program and worked in a local grocery as a bag boy during his teenage years. He left this job to earn more money as a petty hustler, selling small quantities of marijuana from a corner near his home. His notoriety in the neighborhood grew during this period, and he began to look forward to a better life financially. In spite of his mother's protests, Wallace dropped out of high school at the age of seventeen, determined to make his fortune in music, his ambitions paid for by his drug dealing. His fortune was not immediate, however; in 1989, he was arrested in North Carolina for selling crack cocaine. After a nine-month jail term Wallace returned to New York determined to focus on his music.

After leaving school, Wallace, now self-named Quest, began working collaboratively with local artists. He began to MC with his good friend and neighbor Chico Delvico, his only resources being two Technics turntables and a room in the back of Delvico's house. Beyond Brooklyn another critical influence in Wallace's development as an artist was the rising popularity of gangsta rap. Widely recognized as a West Coast style, it is defined in large part by its lyrical content. Earlier lyrics discussing cars and girls now took a more aggressive tone through graphic tales of violence and lyrics that described women as "whores" and celebrated gunplay and weaponry such as MAC-10 machine guns. Wallace altered his lyrical style to reflect this new turn in the music, and through mixing his eclectic musical and cultural influences—his Jamaican heritage and location in Brooklyn—his stamp on hip-hop matured. By the time of his nineteenth birthday the work had paid off; he had a demo tape circulating and was now receiving recognition beyond his neighborhood. His friend and collaborator 50 Grand also became a fan of Wallace's style and passed his tape on to Mister Cee, who worked with rap icon Big Daddy Kane. After hearing the tape, Cee was instrumental in Wallace's being profiled in the March 1992 "Unsigned Hype" column of the urban magazine the Source. This became Wallace's first public notice.

That same year brought the collaboration that would change Wallace's life. Around the time of the Source publication Mister Cee received a phone call from a young A&R executive at Uptown Records, SEAN "PUFFY" COMBS, who asked Cee for information on new talent. Cee pointed him toward Wallace, and the two men met. After discussing business plans, Combs signed Wallace to Uptown Records. Wallace dropped his performance name of Quest and adopted Biggie Smalls, a name taken from the SIDNEY POITIER and BILL COSBY film Let's Do It Again.

In 1993 Wallace had a daughter named T'Yanna with his girlfriend Jan Jackson, and he took a professional leap forward as a guest MC on Mary J. Blige's album What's the 411?. This recognition propelled him toward his first single, "Party and Bullshit." All of this momentum was put in jeopardy in 1991 when Combs was fired from Uptown. Wallace was ousted along with Combs, yet this was an opportunity in disguise for both men; after gaining seed money from a major label, Arista Records, Combs started his own label, Bad Boy Entertainment, with Biggie as his star. News of a California artist also using the name Biggie Smalls compelled Wallace to change his name yet again. For the launch of his first album, Ready to Die, released in 1994, he became the Notorious B. I. G. His private life changed as well; in 1995 Wallace married Bad Boy Entertainment's newest artist, R&B singer Faith Evans. A son, Christopher Jr., arrived in 1996. The relationship was rocky early on and was ultimately short-lived. His self-fashioned notorious identity as a playboy and thug, along with two number 1 singles, "Big Poppa" (1994) and "One More Chance" (1995), moved Wallace into the celebrity mainstream as the East Coast gangsta don.

His venture into the mainstream made Wallace aware of the positive and negative aspects of stardom. He was able to go back to his Brooklyn neighborhood and hire some of the youth to be part of his crew—including those who made up the Bad Boy rap group Junior M.A.F.I.A.—offering them professional and financial opportunities that he did not have growing up. He also had the money that he lamented the absence of in his song "Juicy." But his fame also brought to light the dark side of the entertainment industry. In the mid-1990s, a rivalry developed between the East Coast artists and those of the West Coast. Gang violence, media hype, and ego fed the growing antagonisms between artists. As the battle narrowed, Wallace and Bad Boy Entertainment became the icons of the East, and Wallace's former friend, TUPAC SHAKUR, and Shakur's new label, Death Row Records, became the icon of the West. Wallace and

Shakur began their friendship early in Wallace's career with Shakur serving as a mentor figure for the young MC, but the relationship ended in 1994 when Shakur accused Bad Boy of being involved in a robbery in which he was shot five times. Shakur's track "Hit 'Em Up" (1996), in which he claims to have had an affair with Wallace's wife, Faith Evans, solidified the division between the two men and deepened the resentment felt by those involved in the enmity.

The repercussions of the rivalry became deadly on 7 September 1996 when Shakur was gunned down in Las Vegas following a boxing match. He was pronounced dead six days later. Given his very public battle with Wallace, it was not surprising that many pointed the finger of responsibility in the direction of the Bad Boy crew. No arrests were made and no charges were filed in the case, and many wondered if this major casualty would cool the flames raging within the industry. Approximately six months later, in March 1997, the animosity was still felt in Los Angeles. Wallace was in town to put the finishing touches on his forthcoming album. He had been there a number of weeks by the time the *Soul Train Awards* were filmed on 8 March. Wallace presented the Best Female R&B/Soul Album award at the show, and as he walked onstage, he was immediately and unrelentingly booed. Taking it in stride, he and Combs left the awards show for a night on the town. As he sat at a traffic light between parties, a car approached on the passenger side of his SUV—where he was seated—and opened fire. Wallace was hit with four shots to the chest and was pronounced dead on arrival at Cedars-Sinai Medical Center on Sunday, 9 March 1997. As in Shakur's case, no arrests were made and no charges filed. The 18 March funeral procession in Brooklyn drew a crowd of thousands. His album, *Life after Death*, was posthumously released one week later and entered the *Billboard* 200 at number 1.

FURTHER READING

Marriott, Michel. "The Short Life of a Rap Star, Shadowed by Many Troubles," *New York Times*, 17 Mar. 1997.

Scott, Cathy. *The Murder of Biggie Smalls* (2000).

Wallace, Voletta, with Tremell McKenzie. *Biggie: Voletta Wallace Remembers Her Son, Christopher Wallace, AKA Notorious BIG* (2005).

SHANA L. REDMOND

Nunez, Elizabeth (18 Feb. 1944?–), author and educator, was one of eleven children born in Cocorite, Trinidad and Tobago, to Waldo Nunez, an oil company executive and labor commissioner for the government, and Una Nunez. When she was about nine years old Elizabeth Nunez submitted a short story, unbeknownst to her parents, to a children's writing competition in the *Trinidad Guardian*. She won the contest, launching a lifelong writing career and acquiring the first of many accolades.

Raised in the Catholic faith, Nunez attended Tranquility Elementary School until winning an exhibition that secured her a place at St. Joseph's Convent in Port-of-Spain. Her family relocated to the city of Diego Martin when she was sixteen. After completing her tenure at St. Joseph's, Nunez was employed briefly with Shell Oil Company before being recruited by a priest to attend a small Catholic women's college in Fond du Lac, Wisconsin. Nunez, joined by a fellow Trinidadian and two Haitian students, enrolled as a student at Marian College in 1963. Her immigration to the United States came at a pivotal moment in African American history. Her first year of college was punctuated by the Birmingham, Alabama, church bombing in September 1963, which killed CAROLE ROBERTSON, ADDIE MAE COLLINS, CAROL DENISE McNAIR, and CYNTHIA WESLEY, and ended in June 1964, coinciding with the discovery of the slain bodies of civil rights advocates Michael Schwerner, Andrew Goodman, and JAMES EARL CHANEY. Nunez's tenure at Marian College was marked by the same unabashed racism, ignorance, and hostility that led to those deaths.

Nunez combated the stereotypes and misconceptions about people from the Caribbean that she encountered in the American Midwest by excelling in her academic work while working part time to pay for her room and board—a condition not mentioned in-her scholarship. Her name appeared on the dean's list every year, and she held the position of student body president—an office no one actually expected her to win. Despite the election, however, the yearbook staff left her photograph out of its annual publication. As a graduating student, Nunez brought her luggage with her to her final exam location in anticipation of leaving the unwelcoming campus immediately following the exam period. Nunez graduated from Marian College in 1967 with a B.A. in English and returned eagerly to her native Trinidad.

After six grueling months of submitting applications for a teaching position and getting rejected, Nunez challenged the Trinidadian Ministry of Education, making clear her distaste for the department's bias in favor of hiring Canadian teachers. To quell her outspoken protest the ministry finally granted Nunez an assignment to Woodbrook Secondary School but did not pay her the salary commensurate with the skills and expertise of a degree-holding professional. Humiliated and fed up with what she perceived to be her country's political agenda concerning education, Nunez decided to return to the United States to pursue opportunities as a professional and a writer. Rather than returning to the Midwest, she sought the cosmopolitanism of New York City, where she entered graduate school at New York University in the fall of 1968. She was awarded an M.A. in English in 1971 after struggling to cover her living and education expenses by working odd jobs and rooming with a group of Iranian students. Nunez accepted a position in 1972 at the newly opened Medgar Evers College, a unit of the City University of New York (CUNY). Completing her doctoral degree in English from NYU in 1977, Nunez served as the chair of the department of humanities at Medgar Evers College and is credited with developing many of the first major academic programs at the college.

Nunez married and gave birth to two sons before publishing her first novel, *When Rocks Dance* (1986), as Elizabeth Nunez-Harrell. Nunez's first novel is the story of Emilia, a Trinidadian woman living at the opening of the twentieth century, who must negotiate between the worlds of her own culture and that of the colonizer. Her English lover desires an heir from Emilia, who in turn desires land and prosperity. After giving birth to three sets of stillborn male twins, in a ritual sacrifice she allows the fourth set of male twins, born alive, to die in order for a ninth child to survive. The ninth child, Marina, is an omen, and the community is uncertain whether this is a positive or negative sign.

The author JOHN OLIVER KILLENS, a friend of Nunez-Harrell, worked largely as her mentor, reading the manuscript of her first novel. With their creative energies working so well together, Killens and Nunez-Harrell founded the National Black Writers Conference in 1986 with a sponsorship from the National Endowment for the Humanities. Nunez served as director from 1986 to 2000. In 1998 Nunez-Harrell released her second novel, *Beyond the Limbo Silence*, loosely based on her experience at Marian College with her Caribbean companions. The novel reconstructs many of the events of the civil rights era, including the murders of Chaney, Schwerner, and Goodman, and conveys the reality of immigrating to a new land and adjusting to a new culture.

Nunez wrote four other novels, published under her maiden name following the dissolution of her marriage. *Bruised Hibiscus* (2000), a story recalled from a real-life incident her mother witnessed as a child, won the 2001 American Book Award. *Discretion* (2002) and *Grace* (2003) both interweave the cultures and locations of the black Atlantic world into the storyline via complicated love triangles. *Discretion* explores the life of an African man, Oufoula, who harbors a deep infatuation for Marguerite, a Jamaican, though he is married. The novel is told from a man's perspective, which was a new approach for the author. Similarly, *Grace* is told from the perspective of the male protagonist, Justin Peters, who, as a Caribbean immigrant to the United States, must adjust his cultural perspective to assist with his wife's recovery from witnessing as a child the traumatic murder of her father by the Ku Klux Klan. Her 2006 novel, *Prospero's Daughter*, recaptures the magic of Shakespeare's *The Tempest* through a Caribbean writer's pen. Nunez coedited an anthology, *Defining Ourselves: Black Writers in the 90s*, in 1999, with Brenda M. Greene, and edited *Blue Latitudes: Caribbean Women Writers at Home and Abroad*, a collection of short stories, in 2005. In addition to her novels and anthologies, Nunez published numerous articles, interviews, book reviews, and critical essays in several scholarly journals.

In the latter portion of her career Nunez was named CUNY Distinguished Professor of English at Medgar Evers College. She also served as executive producer for the series *Black Writers in America* for CUNY-TV, hosted by the actor OSSIE DAVIS, which was nominated in 2004 for the New York Emmy Award for Best Television Series in the historical/cultural category. She chaired the board for the Center for Black Literature as well as the PEN American Center's Open Book Program. Marian College awarded her an honorary doctorate in humane letters for her dedication to the arts and education. Elizabeth Nunez continues to bring the culture of the Caribbean to life through her fiction, activism, and teaching, both celebrating and solidifying a shared heritage across the African diaspora.

FURTHER READING
Lewis, Barbara. "Negotiating Multiple Worlds: A Public Interview with Elizabeth Nunez," *Black Renaissance/Renaissance Noire* (Summer/Fall 2002).

KAMEELAH L. MARTIN

Nutter, Corinthian (10 Dec. 1906–11 Feb. 2004), Kansas elementary school teacher and principal who successfully campaigned to desegregate schools in Merriam, Kansas, 1948–1949, was born Corinthian Ricks in Forney, Texas, the third of Robert R. Ricks and Roxie Anna Ford Ricks's five children.

Robert Ricks was a railroad laborer in 1910; the family lived in Dewson City, Grayson County. By 1920 the family worked a farm in Smith County on Robert Ricks's "own account," as did most of their neighbors, listed in the census as a mix of "black," "mulatto," and "white" families. Corinthian Ricks was briefly married at fourteen, and when that marriage fell apart, she moved to Kansas City in 1922, where she played the organ for silent movies and piano for visiting entertainers, initially living at the YMCA. Later, she boarded at the home of Willie Mack Washington—a drummer in Bennie Moton's orchestra, who introduced her to a piano player named Willie (Count) Basie. Living with Washington's wife and mother had benefits: "I got to go to all the dances because I was with them," she recalled years later (Hoskins). When she had her own residence, she said, "my house became a party house and everyone would come to my house."

She completed her high school diploma at Western University in Quindaro, Kansas, in 1936, then a two-year junior college program, earning a teaching certificate. Her first teaching job, in 1938, was at a school in Shawnee Kansas, designated for students considered to be "colored," with one other teacher. For the next twelve years, she spent summers at Emporia State Teachers College, earning a bachelor's degree in 1950, and later a master's degree. Ricks married Austin Kline Nutter on 2 June 1941, in Kansas City, Missouri. In 1943 she moved to Walker Elementary School in Merriam. Walker was the only school for children designated as "black" or "colored" in the 1940s. The building was old, poorly maintained, had no indoor plumbing, and was supplied with books and other materials that had been discarded by other schools in the district.

Johnson County School District No. 90 had been integrated for decades after it was organized on 24 May 1888. County historians reference that "The 1900 census lists 250 residents, including four 'negro' families. Early school records described a one-room schoolhouse built in 1888 for the 'colored and white children who lived in the area'" (Davis et al., p. 333). When a new school was built in 1912, it was designated as for "white" children only, while the old one-room school was renamed for Madame C. J. Walker, a well-known businesswoman of African descent, and designated for "colored" children. This school, with few improvements, was the building Corinthian Nutter came to teach at three decades later.

The spark that launched a battle to integrate was the construction of South Park Elementary School in 1947, with eight modern classrooms, a multipurpose auditorium, a lunchroom, and a playground, still reserved for "white" students only. Walker had eight grades taught in two classrooms with two teachers, only one certified. Initially, parents of the excluded children sought a commitment to make vast improvements in Walker elementary, but the school board said it had no funds to do that. Esther Brown, who employed the mother of a Walker student as a domestic worker, suggested filing a lawsuit. After forming a local NAACP chapter, the parents did so, and thirty-nine out of forty-one students boycotted the school for a year.

Nutter and fellow teacher Hazel McCray Weddington taught students in the homes of local residents. Parents organized fundraisers to pay them. Parents, and Brown, were threatened with murder, mayhem, and arson. In the case that became *Webb v. Board of Education of School District 90*, NAACP attorneys argued that state law prohibited towns with a population under fifteen thousand from segregating students by race. The school board blandly told the court that racial segregation was not its objective in drawing the school zones for South Park and Walker schools.

A key witness in the case, Nutter later summarized, "I just told them the truth. The school was dilapidated, we had no modern conveniences, had to go outside to go to the toilet. And if they were going to build a new school and the parents were paying taxes like everybody else, why couldn't their children go? Schools shouldn't be for a color. They should be for children" (Buller).

In June 1949 the Supreme Court of Kansas ruled that the school board's policy was arbitrary and unreasonable, and ordered the board to rebuild the Walker school to comparable standards—with a zoning plan so children of any color could attend either school. Meantime, the board was ordered to admit students of African descent to the only school available, South Park, the following September. Walker was never rebuilt.

After completing her bachelor's degree in 1950, Nutter began teaching sixth grade at Lincoln school in Olathe, Kansas—at that time specifically for "colored" children. When racial distinctions were dropped from school assignments a few years later, she became principal at the West View Elementary School, where for a time she was the only "person of color" in the school. She returned to teaching fifth and sixth grade for a few years before retiring in 1972.

A member of the Paseo Baptist Church, Nutter became a life member of the NAACP, and in the course of her education, a member of Alpha Kappa Alpha sorority, and the American Association of University Women. Austin Nutter died in 1998. Five years later, Corinthian Nutter was inducted into the Mid America Education Hall of Fame on 1 November 2003. She died a few months later, at the age of ninety-seven, survived by nephews Robert Ricks Jr., Austin Clay Petty, Tyler Austin Irving, and Austin Cline Irving, and godson Howard C. Petty Jr.

FURTHER READING

Davis, Donna M., Jennifer Friend, and Loyce Caruthers. "The Fear of Color: *Webb v. School District No. 90* in Johnson County, Kansas, 1949." *American Educational History Journal* 37, no. 2 (2010): 331–345.

Hoskins, Alan. "Civil Rights Leader Corinthian Nutter into Education Hall of Fame. *Kansas City Call,* 17 Oct. 2003.

Obituary: *Kansas City Star,* 12 Feb. 2004.

CHARLES ROSENBERG

Nutter, Michael A. (29 June 1957–), mayor of Philadelphia, was born Michael Anthony Nutter in Philadelphia, Pennsylvania, the son of Basil, a drug company sales representative and part-time plumber and Catalina Bargas Nutter, a worker at Bell Telephone. He grew up in West Philadelphia and attended St. Joseph's Preparatory School in North Philadelphia. His prep experience imbued Nutter with an intellectual curiosity about life, work, politics, and race. He studied the work and writings of MALCOLM X and Dr. MARTIN LUTHER KING JR. and joined the school's Black Culture Club. Even at an early age Nutter was concerned with social justice for those he believed were dispossessed, repressed, or otherwise exploited by the mainstream society. At the same time, he developed an interest in music and the post–civil rights movement of black culture and politics. Nutter was a strong student and earned a B.A. in Business in 1979 from the prestigious Wharton School of Business at the University of Pennsylvania. In 1991 Nutter married Lisa Johnson and the couple have a daughter, Olivia.

Following college, Nutter went to work at Xerox and later as an investment banker. But he had been active in politics since his formative days in the 1970s, where he was attracted to Reverend Bill Gray's Northwest Alliance. Gray, a high-ranking U.S. congressman and later head of the United Negro College Fund, was one of the most influential politicians in Philadelphia. Gray had long been active in efforts to assert African American control of the predominately black wards of the city. And Nutter would benefit from these changes. He was active in various elections as early as 1983. And by 1987, he was a candidate for the city council in Philadelphia. Although he lost the race, in 1991, won election as the representative of the 4th district. Over the next fifteen years, Nutter impressed observers as an intelligent, capable, and ambitious politician. He also served as the Democratic Ward Leader for the 52nd Ward since 1990.

As a ward leader, city councilman, and local politician, Nutter developed a reputation for advocating clean living standards and antismoking ordinances as well as economic development for Philadelphia, generally, and the city's poor, specifically. In a city with a long history of political corruption and dysfunctional government, Nutter managed to keep his nose clean while also developing a political persona that was representative of his generation: inclusive, positive, ambitious, and professional. Like his contemporaries BARACK OBAMA, KENDRICK MEEK, KEITH ELLISON, and CORY BOOKER, Nutter's politics marked a distinct shift from the politics of protest that so epitomized the '60's generation.

While on the City Council, Nutter was put in charge of the Police Advisory Commission. He also took on the controversial issue of gay rights during the late 1990s. Nutter had promised to support same-sex benefits in 1993 but effectively reneged. Instead, Nutter shepherded a similar bill in 1997–98 in one of the most difficult periods in recent memory. No bid contracting, always a scourge of government watchdog groups, was ended, in large part, because of Nutter's actions on the City Council. Due to his successful tenure on the City Council, as well as his growing ambition, Nutter announced his campaign for mayor of Philadelphia in 2006.

Instantly, Nutter was a serious candidate to replace the aging John Street. His campaign emphasized better government, open government, economic development, busting crime, and reform. His toughness and embrace of the Gray machine, while also presenting himself as an outsider, served him well. In the May 2007 primary, Nutter won with nearly 40 percent of the vote, twelve percentage points ahead of his closest opponent. In November 2007, Michael Nutter won election of mayor of Philadelphia handily. Although Mayor John Street was prevented from seeking another term by term-limits, it was considered a direct challenge to the scandal-plagued Street administration. Nutter's tenure, however, has not been without its difficulties. Coming into office at the same time as the U.S. economy entered a severe recession, Nutter has had to contend with declining tax revenue, increasing violent crime, and a housing crisis. As the mayor of a major American city and as a African American, Nutter is a major figure in the Democratic Party.

Mayor Nutter, like many established African Americans politicians, supported Senator Hillary Rodham Clinton (D-NY) in the 2008 Democratic presidential primaries against Senator Barack Obama (D-IL). Believing that Clinton was the strongest Democrat in the race, Nutter campaigned for her in Philadelphia, incurring the wrath of younger, and often African American, voters, who saw Clinton as too minimal a departure from the outgoing administration of George W. Bush. Obama won Philadelphia over Clinton with 65 percent of the vote. Like most of Clinton's African American supporters, he enthusiastically supported Senator Obama after Obama clinched his party's nomination in June 2008, putting his political muscle behind Obama in Philadelphia, and Pennsylvania generally. Considered a rising star in the Democratic Party and generally popular in Philadelphia, most pundits predicted his easy reelection as mayor in 2011.

FURTHER READING

Fagone, Jason. "Michael Nutter's Dilemma: Is This Man Too Much of a Reformer to Be Mayor? Or so Hungry to Be Mayor That He Can't be a Real Reformer?" *Philadelphia Magazine*, 29 Dec. 2006.

Portnoy, Jenna. "Michael Nutter Is Not as Boring as You Think: Which Is a Good Thing, Considering He Wants to Be Your Next Mayor," *Philadelphia City Paper*, 8–14 Sept. 2005.

Taussig, Doron. "Michael Nutter for Mayor: The City Paper Endorsement," *Philadelphia City Paper*, 2 May 2007.

DARYL A. CARTER

Nutter, Thomas Gillis (15 June 1876–June 1959), attorney, West Virginia state legislator, business owner, founder and president of the West Virginia conference of NAACP branches, sometimes known in public as T. Gillis Nutter, was born in Princess Anne, Somerset County, Maryland, the son of William Nutter and Emma Henry Nutter.

He was educated in public schools in Maryland, and awarded the L.L.B. degree from Howard University Law School on 28 May 1898. For two years afterward he taught school and was a principal in Fairmount, Maryland. Nutter was admitted to the bar in Marion County, Indiana, in 1900, and moved to Charleston, West Virginia, in 1903. He established his reputation as a defense lawyer by convincing a jury in the "Grice murder case" to convict a black man charged with killing a white man of voluntary manslaughter rather than murder; then, in the case of Campbell Clark, charged with raping a white woman, Nutter secured a conviction for attempted assault. In 1908 he attended the national Republican convention, which nominated William Howard Taft for president. In 1913 he was appointed a clerk in the land department, office of the auditor-general for the state of West Virginia, holding the position for the next six years.

Nutter was a founder, secretary, and treasurer of the Mutual Savings and Loan Company in Charleston, "the only bank owned and operated by Colored people in West Virginia" (Caldwell, p. 179). He served from 1913 to 1916 as Grand Exalted Ruler of Elks of the World, and in 1916 was elected secretary of the Mountain State Bar Association, organized by lawyers of African descent earlier that year. In 1918 he was elected Grand Chancellor of the Grand Lodge of Colored Knights of Pythias of West Virginia, serving for three years. He was later president of the Pythian Mutual Investment Association. That year he worked with MORDECAI JOHNSON, later president of Howard University, to found the Charleston Branch of the National Association for the Advancement of Colored People (NAACP), in 1921 succeeding Johnson as president, a position he held for the rest of his life.

Nutter was elected in 1919 to the West Virginia legislature, with a large majority in a district where about 10 percent of the voters were of known African descent. On 18 December 1920, he married Sarah (Sadie) Meriwether, a graduate of Howard University and Miner Teacher's College, previously a teacher at Dunbar High School in Washington, DC, and at Howard, and a founder of Alpha Kappa Alpha sorority. Both as Sarah M. Nutter and as

Mrs. T. G. Nutter, she was repeatedly recognized for her own contributions to the local NAACP branch over the next three decades.

Beginning his second term in the House of Delegates, Nutter was assigned to the Judiciary Committee in 1921, as well as the committees on federal relations, and arts, sciences and general improvements. Working with Harry J. Capehart, in 1921 he secured passage of an antilynching bill, described in *The Crisis* as "one of the strongest of its kind any where in the United States" (vol. 22, no. 2, June 1921, p. 67). After the first conviction under the law in 1931, the state's supreme court upheld the statute's constitutionality, and the convictions. On a later occasion, Nutter represented relatives of a lynching victim in securing $5,000 compensation under another provision of the law.

Nutter provoked a firestorm after persuading the socialist-leaning *Messenger* to print an article reporting that black miners who once lived in crude shacks now enjoyed "comfortable houses of four, five and eight rooms, that have modern conveniences." E. FRANKLIN FRAZIER, a young Morehouse College sociologist, responded that four-fifths of West Virginia's miners lived in company owned housing, more than two-thirds with tar paper roofs, only 7 percent having running water, only 3 percent having bathtubs or inside toilets (Lewis, Ronald L., *Black Coal Miners in America: Race, Class, and Community Conflict, 1780–1980*, 1987, p. 149).

After completing two terms in the legislature, Nutter traveled outside the state in support of antilynching legislation. At a mass meeting in the Second Baptist Church of Kansas City, Missouri, featuring Representative L. C. Dyer, who had introduced an antilynching law in the U.S. Congress, Nutter said, "The day has passed when the Negro can expect somebody else to fight his battles." Although a life-long Republican, he added, "So far as I am concerned the Republican Party does not mean a thing to me. I never intend to vote for any man who does not stand foursquare on the race question .... If I found a man like Mr. Dyer in the Democratic Party I would vote for him" (*The Crisis*, Nov. 1923, 25–26).

In 1928 Nutter joined the National Legal Committee of the NAACP. The following year, he was admitted to the American Bar Association, the ABA's first African American from West Virginia. It is not known whether the West Virginia branch of the ABA explicitly identified Nutter by race when submitting his name for membership. A resolution adopted by the ABA in 1912, after objections were raised to three "persons of the colored race" having been accepted as members, resolved that "it has never been contemplated that members of the colored race should become members of this Association," and directed local councils recommending "a person of the colored race" for membership to include "a statement of the fact that he is of such race." (Smith, p. 543).

One way or another, Nutter was eventually accepted as a member; he also retained membership in the National Bar Association. In 1929 he received the Madame C. J. Walker Gold Medal (*The Crisis*, Feb. 1930, p. 58), presented annually to the person who has contributed most to the work of the NAACP each year. He was recognized for two legal victories, one preventing public libraries of West Virginia from excluding citizens identified as Negroes, and the other nullifying covenants restricting real estate sales by the race of the buyer.

In 1932 Nutter was instrumental in keeping most African American voters in West Virginia loyal to the Republican ticket, supporting Herbert Hoover over Franklin D. Roosevelt. He reported to the NAACP after the election "we hardly knew there were any Negro Democrats on election day, as they were so few in number and were rather quiet" (Thomas, Jerry Bruce, *An Appalachian New Deal: West Virginia in the Great Depression*, 1998, p. 202). By 1936 Roosevelt attracted a majority of black voters in the state.

Nutter was nominated for the NAACP national board of directors in 1935—a position he held until his death. In 1938 he was hired in a twelve-million-dollar land dispute to represent a set of clients who thought of themselves as "white," and were generally recognized as such by law. Historians have speculated that Nutter may have been hired because most local attorneys who were also considered "white" had conflicts of interest in the case.

Wendell Wilkie, the Republican candidate for president in 1940, appointed Nutter to the Republican Campaign Advisory Committee. At the second annual student conference of the NAACP the same year, 1–3 November, at West Virginia State College, Nutter delivered a presentation on "Supreme Court Decisions as Qualifying Decisions in Negro Citizenship."

Four African American residents of Montgomery, West Virginia, retained Nutter 1946–1947 to secure access to a municipal swimming pool, which had been leased to a private Parks Association in an effort to avoid a state civil rights law. Nutter chose to sue in federal court, writing to NAACP attorney THURGOOD MARSHALL that local courts in Fayette County had been unresponsive to any suit by black plaintiffs against local officials. The federal judge Ben Moore was, at the time, still bound by the U.S. Supreme Court precedent of *Plessy v. Ferguson*, but issued an injunction restraining the city "from again denying plaintiff the right to use the swimming pool at any time when the pool is open for public use, unless there be provided by the City other and equal swimming facilities available to persons of the Negro race" (Wiltse, Jeff. *Contested Waters: A Social History of Swimming Pools in America*, 2007, p. 165). City officials kept the pool closed until 1961.

Sarah Nutter died in 1950, nine years before her husband, who was elected the following year as an NAACP national vice president. In 1954 he led a successful court case to desegregate the public schools of Greenbrier County, then an investigation into racial incidents perpetrated in the county by Bryant W. Bowles, organizer of the National Association for the Advancement of White People. Nutter died of a heart condition in St. Francis Hospital, Charleston, West Virginia, at the age of eighty-three. His funeral was held Friday 26 June at the First Baptist Church in Charleston. The state NAACP conference presents the annual T. G. Nutter award to the West Virginian who has made significant contributions to the causes of equality and justice.

FURTHER READING
Caldwell, Arthur Bunyan. *History of the American Negro and His Institutions* (1923).
The Crisis, published by the NAACP, contains over twenty issues with reference to details of Nutter's career, many of which are documented nowhere else. Most of them can be found by a search using Google Books.
Smith, J. Clay, Jr. *Emancipation: The Making of the Black Lawyer, 1844–1944* (1999).
Obituary: *The Crisis*, Aug.–Sept. 1959, p. 439.

CHARLES ROSENBERG

Obadele, Imari (2 May 1930–18 Jan. 2010), educator and activist, was born to parents Walter and Vera Henry in Philadelphia, Pennsylvania, as Richard Bullock Henry. Known later as Imari Obadele, he became one of the most recognized organizers of the reparations movement in the United States.

An important influence in Obadele's decision to become an activist was his older brother Milton Henry (1919–2006), who joined the military around the time Richard joined the Boy Scouts at age eleven. Milton eventually achieved the rank of second lieutenant, but against the harsh waves of Jim Crow segregation he surfaced as one of the leading opponents of the rigid forms of discrimination then endured by black officers. Because of his dissent he eventually was court-martialed and dishonorably discharged. Nevertheless, even without the benefits of the GI Bill, he went on to graduate from Lincoln University and, after being denied admission to Temple University, attended Yale Law School, where he graduated in 1947. Milton's heroic struggles were chronicled nationally by black newspapers such as the *Pittsburgh Courier* and *Afro-American* in Baltimore. His celebrity and continued activism once home from the military inspired the younger Richard to commit himself to the African American freedom struggle. With Milton as a mentor, the younger Richard embarked on a radical path of social activism that spanned six decades and made significant impacts in two regions of the United States.

Obadele graduated from Philadelphia's Central High School in 1946 as one of six African Americans in his class. While in Philadelphia, Richard and Milton helped to form a civil rights organization that led in a boycott campaign to desegregate the armed forces. This local thrust was part of a larger, national movement that most likely impacted President Harry S. Truman's decision to integrate military units at the beginning of the Korean War in 1950. The group was also responsible for inviting W. E. B. DuBois to Philadelphia to give a speech. Having passed the Michigan Bar, Milton eventually relocated to Detroit, and Richard followed.

In Detroit, Richard, Milton, and other local activists formed an economic and civil rights organization called GOAL (The Group on Advanced Leadership), founded in 1961. Participants in the group included the Marxist theorists Jimmy and Grace Lee Boggs, and the Shrine of the Black Madonna founder Reverend ALBERT CLEAGE Jr. (Jaramogi Abebe Agyeman). Through GOAL, Richard engaged a politically diverse constellation of radical activists who would leave an indelible imprint on his growing political awareness. Married with four children, working at an auto plant, and studying at Wayne State University, Richard was also introduced to the social activist MALCOLM X by Milton, who had become one of Malcolm's closest political allies in the Detroit area. Malcolm and other civil rights leaders had visited Detroit at the invitation of GOAL, and it was during this visit that Malcolm X delivered his now famous speech, "Message to the Grassroots." Malcolm's shifting political philosophy in his last days was influenced by his interaction with GOAL members, most notably its most radical tendency spearheaded by the Henry brothers.

Soon after Malcolm X's assassination in 1965, Richard and Milton helped found the Malcolm X Society, an organization committed to spreading the political ideals (i.e., self-defense, community control, etc.) he advanced after his break with the Nation of Islam. In 1968 Richard adopted the name "Imari Obadele" (Milton adopted the name "Gaidi Obadele") and the society issued a call for a Black Government Conference in Detroit. More than two hundred individuals from across the United States attended the conference to discuss the formation of a sovereign nation, and on 31 March 1968, four days before Dr. MARTIN LUTHER KING JR. was assassinated in Memphis, Tennessee, one hundred individuals signed a Declaration of Independence for the Republic of New Africa (RNA). Robert F. Williams (1925–1996), then exiled in China, was named the first president. Milton was named first vice president, and BETTY SHABAZZ, the widow of Malcolm X, was named second vice president. Imari Obadele was named minister of information.

The organization's ability to implement its program was severely hampered by COINTELPRO, a covert counterintelligence program run by the Federal Bureau of Investigation. Shortly after its founding, the RNA was targeted by as many as fourteen policing and intelligence agencies within the United States. The repression, which resulted in raids, gun battles, and mass arrests, continued until 1973, when the organization was effectively neutralized in Detroit. A gun battle between the organization's paramilitary wing, the Black Legion, erupted in March of 1969; one police officer was killed. A year later, in 1970, the organization suffered a split when Milton Henry publicly rejected its use of violence. With Imari Obadele as its newly elected president and de facto leader, the RNA relocated its headquarters to Jackson, Mississippi, where they attempted to purchase eighteen acres of farmland. But this endeavor was interrupted by the FBI. On 18 August 1971 a raid aimed primarily at Obadele, who was now COINTELPRO's central target, was conducted at the group's headquarters in Jackson and, again, one policeman was killed. Although Obadele was found to be ten blocks away, he was later convicted in related proceedings of conspiracy to assault a federal agent and given a twelve-year sentence. He served five years.

In 1980 Obadele began to combine his activism with scholarship. He earned a Ph.D. in political science from Temple University in 1985. While writing extensively on reparations and the RNA he taught at Prairie View A&M, a historically black college located outside Houston, Texas. His primary attention turned toward reparations, and on 21 August 1987 he called for a meeting of more than twenty-five organizations to meet in Washington, D.C., to discuss the issue. A year later, 1988, the National Coalition of Blacks for Reparations in America was founded.

Among civil rights and black power activists Obadele was most widely known as the provisional president of the RNA, an organization dedicated to the idea of establishing a sovereign nation within the U.S. South controlled by citizens of African descent. As a political prisoner, he was one of the first American citizens designated as such by Amnesty International.

FURTHER READING

Information on the RNA and Imari Obadele can be found on the Brown-Tougaloo Archives website: http://www.stg.brown.edu/projects/FreedomNow/archive.html

Davenport, Christian. "Understanding Covert Repressive Action: The Case of the U.S. Government against the Republic of New Afrika," *Journal of Conflict Resolution* 49, no. 1 (Feb. 2005): 120–140.

Kelley, Robin, D. G. *Freedom Dreams: The Black Radical Imagination* (2002).

Young, Jasmine A. "Detroit's Red: Black Radical Detroit and the Political Development of Malcolm X," *Souls* 12, no. 1 (Jan.–Mar. 2010): 14–31.

LARVESTER GAITHER

Obama, Barack (4 Aug. 1961–), lawyer, writer, US Senator, and President of the United States, was born Barack Hussein Obama Jr. in Honolulu, Hawaii, the only child of Barack Obama, a government official in Kenya, and Stanley Anne Dunham, an educator. His mother was a white American originally from Kansas, and his father was a black Kenyan. The couple met while studying at the University of Hawaii at Manoa, and separated when their son was two years old. Obama Sr. left Hawaii to study at Harvard University and later returned to Africa to work as an economic planner for the Kenyan government. After the couple divorced, Anne Dunham married Lolo Soertoro, an Indonesian businessman, with whom she had a daughter, Maya.

Hawaii was the primary site of Barack's childhood and adolescence, although from the age of six to ten he lived in Jakarta, Indonesia, in the household of his stepfather. For his secondary schooling

Barack Obama, Democratic senator from Illinois, speaks at a charity event in New York, 4 December 2006. (AP Images.)

Obama attended the elite Punahou School in Honolulu, Hawaii, graduating in 1979. He attended Occidental College in Los Angeles for two years before transferring to Columbia University in New York City, where he received a B.A. in political science in 1983. He then worked for several years as a community organizer in Chicago, Illinois, before entering Harvard Law School in 1988. It was at Harvard that influential observers first glimpsed the intellectual power, political dexterity, and personal magnetism that have subsequently become widely appreciated. Obama earned a position as an editor of the *Harvard Law Review,* the most prestigious forum in legal academia, and then in 1990 proceeded to be elected as its president, the first African American to ascend to that post.

After graduating magna cum laude from Harvard Law School in 1991, Obama returned to Chicago where he reconnected with community organizing and married a fellow lawyer, Michelle Robinson (*see* OBAMA, MICHELLE), in 1992. The couple had two daughters, Malia and Natasha (known as Sasha). After working on Project Vote,

a voter registration effort in 1992 that helped win Illinois for the Democratic presidential candidate Bill Clinton and the Democratic U.S. Senate candidate CAROL MOSELEY BRAUN, he began work as an associate attorney with the law firm of Miner, Barnhill, and Galland in 1993. Obama also taught constitutional law at the University of Chicago Law School from 1993 to 2004, but it became increasingly apparent that Obama had decided on a career in politics rather than academia. In 1994 he won election to the Illinois State Senate and twice won reelection, representing a district in Chicago's South Side. In 2000 he made a bid for a seat in the U.S. House of Representatives, challenging the incumbent, BOBBY RUSH, who soundly defeated him in the Democratic primary election. In 1995 Obama published *Dreams from My Father: A Story of Race and Inheritance.* In this memoir, he ruminates on the complexities of his upbringing, particularly the haunting absence of his father, and reveals indiscretions as a teenager involving the use of drugs.

Because of his parentage and upbringing, several commentators have raised questions about his racial status. The journalist Debra. J. Dickerson asserts, for example, that Obama should not be designated as black; she writes that "by virtue of his white American mom and his Kenyan dad ... [Obama] is an American of African immigrant extraction." Obama himself is quite clear about the matter, describing himself as an African American (or black) largely on the basis of ascription. "If you look African American in this society," he remarked, "you're treated as an African American." In 1940 W. E. B. DuBois quipped that "the black man is a person who must ride 'Jim Crow' in Georgia." Obama updates that view, noting that when he tries to catch taxis in Manhattan, drivers are quite clear about his race; they all too often refuse to pick him up for obvious racially discriminatory reasons, just as they all too often willfully ignore other black men seeking rides.

In 2003 Obama sought election to the U.S. Senate. Initially his chances of winning seemed slim as he faced Democratic Party competitors who were more experienced or had superior access to funding. Obama, however, prevailed handily in the 2004 primary. In the general election, scandal helped Obama as his Republican opponent quit the race in light of revelations stemming from an acrimonious divorce. In desperation the Illinois Republican Party recruited ALAN KEYES, a conservative black former diplomat and media commentator from Maryland, to run against Obama. But that gambit failed miserably as Obama swept to a landslide victory—winning about 70 percent of the popular vote—to become the junior Senator from Illinois. Obama was only the fifth black Senator in the history of the United States, following Republicans HIRAM RHOADES REVELS of Mississippi, BLANCHE K. BRUCE of Mississippi, EDWARD W. BROOKE of Massachusetts, and Democrat Carol Mosley Braun of Illinois.

In the middle of his senatorial campaign, Obama delivered an address at the 2004 Democratic National Convention that made him a celebrity. In his speech "The Audacity of Hope," beyond urging the election of Massachusetts Senator John Kerry (a plea that the electorate rejected by a slim margin), Obama sounded a rousing call for national unity that resonated far beyond the base of supporters that rapturously cheered him:

> There is not a liberal America and a conservative America—there's the United States of America. There is not a black America and white America and Latino America and Asian America—there's the United States of America.… The pundits like to slice and dice our country into Red States and Blue States: Red States for Republicans, Blue States for Democrats. But I've got news for them, too. We worship an awesome God in the Blue States, and we don't like federal agents poking around in our libraries in the Red States. We coach Little League in the Blue States and yes, we've got some gay friends in the Red States … We are one people, all of us pledging allegiance to the Stars and Stripes, all of us defending the United States of America.

The meteoric trajectory of Obama's career following his much-cited DNC speech and senatorial victory was astounding. Popular fascination and admiration gave rise to a new phenomenon—"Obamamania." *Time* has named him one of "the world's most influential people" and "one of the most admired politicians in America." Observers compared him to John F. Kennedy, who had been the first Catholic and last incumbent Senator to win the presidency.

Obama's second best-selling book, *The Audacity of Hope: Thoughts on Reclaiming the American Dream* (2006), helped feed the growing public curiosity about Obama's political philosophy. A declaration of his ambitious desire to reform a broken American political system, the book offered a lucid dissection of Obama's views on economic opportunity, politics, faith, race, and family. The fact that the book sold over 180,000 copies in its first three weeks of publication was testament to his skills as a stylist. Indeed, a review of the book in the *New York Times* suggested that Obama was "that

rare politician who can actually write—and write movingly and genuinely about himself" (Kakutani, "Obama's Foursquare Politics, With a Dab of Dijon," *New York Times*, 17 Oct. 2006).

Having struggled as a youngster with the issue of his racially mixed background, Obama as a mature adult openly embraced the various traditions and influences to which he was an heir. In an October 2006 interview on the *Oprah Winfrey Show*, Obama quipped that when his extended family gets together for holidays "it's like the minifamily United Nations. I've got relatives who look like Bernie Mac, and I've got relatives who look like Margaret Thatcher. We've got it all." He unequivocally describes himself as black, yet insists that that designation place no limits on either his own imagination or his image in the minds of others. "I am rooted in the black community," he has declared, "but I am not limited to it."

The Democratic Party's recapture of Congress in the 2006 midterm elections further boosted speculation that Obama might launch a bid for the presidency in 2008, even though he had not yet completed a full term in the Senate. The issue of Obama's lack of experience seemed of less concern to many voters, however, in the light of growing concerns about the American military presence in Iraq. While many of the leading Democratic candidates for 2008, notably New York Senator Hillary Clinton, had supported President George W. Bush's invasion of Iraq in 2003, Obama, then still in the Illinois Senate, had opposed the war.

On 10 February 2007 Obama announced his candidacy for president of the United States. In the first quarter of 2007 alone he had raised $25 million, an indication of his likely viability as a candidate in 2008. Whether Obama would become the first black to win the presidency was unclear. What was clear, however, was that his candidacy constituted a serious effort, as opposed to a merely symbolic one, as was largely the case of the presidential candidacies of SHIRLEY CHISHOLM, AL SHARPTON, and even JESSE JACKSON. That hard-boiled professional politicians believed that Barack Obama had a chance to win the highest public office in the United States was itself a historic landmark. By January 2008, Obama's campaign had raised an additional $115 million and his fundraising had overtaken even Hillary Clinton, the junior senator from New York and favorite for the nomination. Obama won the Iowa caucus but then lost the New Hampshire primary to Clinton, a foreshadowing of the rest of the nomination race, during which the Clinton team worked their every advantage, including the issue of Obama's relative lack of executive experience and the idea that white Americans were ultimately incapable of rallying behind a black candidate.

In fact, though race was a factor throughout the nomination process, it never became as great an issue as feared (or hoped for, depending on the person) by many around the country. Much of the race-focused attention and debate centered on Obama's pastor, the Reverend Jeremiah Wright, with whom Obama had a long-term and close relationship stretching back twenty years. Many people were offended by remarks made by Wright after the September 11, 2001, terrorist attacks, which were taken to be anti-American. This led to heightened scrutiny of Wright's sermons, which were construed especially by conservative commentators and the mainstream media in particular to be not only anti-American, but also racist and anti government—regardless of the original context in which such statements and sermons were made, and ignoring similar statements from white evangelicals.

In an attempt to quell the criticism over Wright, Obama delivered his "More Perfect Union" speech at the Constitution Center in Philadelphia on 18 March 2008. In it Obama discussed his relationship with Wright and repudiated many of Wright's more inflammatory statements. Obama then went on to more broadly discuss the history of race and class relations in America, his own history as a person of mixed race, and his hopes for a future in which the problems of race moved beyond the simple dichotomy of whites versus minorities in America, where the march toward a "more perfect union" had reached a "racial stalemate," in which blacks and whites harbored resentments that they had no means of expressing, instead letting them fester, which led to further divisiveness. Though lauded by people all over the country, liberals and conservatives alike, the speech failed to end the controversy, especially after Wright took it upon himself to go around the country to defend and justify himself, which only added fuel to the fire. As a result, Obama was forced to publicly break with Wright and to leave Trinity Church, which effectively stifled the furor and largely refocused public attention away from race and back to issues like the war in Iraq, the economy, and health care.

Throughout the rest of the nomination contest, Obama and Clinton raised unprecedented amounts of money and stayed very close in the delegate count, trading victories in primaries and caucuses. Obama did best in caucuses and primaries in the upper Midwest, west of the Mississippi, and in the states that had made up the Confederacy, where African Americans constituted as much as half of Democratic voters. Clinton outperformed Obama in primary states in the East, in California, and in Texas, where Hispanics voters overwhelmingly preferred her over Obama. In nearly all states, white women and voters over sixty-five years old strongly preferred Clinton. However, despite an especially strong showing by Clinton in the latter part of the nomination race, by the end of the primaries, it was clear that Obama would be the first African American to secure the nomination of any major national party for the office of President of the United States. On 7 June 2008 Senator Clinton ended her run for the nomination and endorsed Obama's candidacy.

Obama quickly moved to unify the party and to begin campaigning against the Republican candidate, John McCain, a Vietnam veteran and ex-prisoner of war and long-time senator from Arizona. Obama chose Senator Joe Biden as his running mate, while McCain's running mate was the governor of Alaska, Sarah Palin, a little known and politically inexperienced conservative evangelical. Though the race for president appeared close at various times throughout the campaign, most commentators and serious students of American politics predicted a victory for Obama. A number of factors contributed to Obama's victory. The discipline of Obama's campaign in terms of message, unity of effort, and personal discipline showed Obama to be "presidential material" despite his relative lack of executive experience. Added to the strength and discipline of his campaign staff and supporters, by mid-October 2008 Obama had raised a record $640 million, at least half of which came from individuals giving less than $200. These record amounts gave Obama a great advantage over the McCain campaign in advertising and state-by-state efforts to "get out the vote." Perhaps most importantly, voters clearly wanted the change that Obama represented: in foreign policy and the war in Iraq, in health insurance and access to healthcare, and especially with the economy, particularly in the wake of the banking and stock market crises that broke in the campaign's final weeks. Finally, a great many people around the country who early on leaned toward supporting McCain were severely put off by his selection of Sarah Palin as his running mate. The ill-prepared and inexperienced Palin was viewed by many as a cynical pick, chosen more as a way to shore up the archconservative base of the

Republican party than as a serious choice of someone capable of taking over the presidency if such a need arose.

In the end, Obama's victory was decisive. He won the electoral college by 365 to 173. His margin of victory in the popular vote was the largest ever for a nonincumbent presidential candidate and his popular vote percentage of 53 percent was the highest for a Democrat since 1964, when Lyndon Johnson was elected to a full term in his own right. It was the highest overall percentage of votes since George H. W. Bush won in 1988. Indeed, Obama received more votes than any presidential candidate in American history, beating George W. Bush's record total of just over 62 million in 2004.

Obama's inauguration on 20 January 2009 was attended by an estimated 1.8 million people, far more than had attended any previous inaugural. The *Rasmussen* daily tracking presidential opinion poll registered approval of 65 percent of Americans for the new president. Hundreds of millions watched the ceremonies live across the globe, and, indeed the expectations for Obama's presidency may have been even higher abroad than in the United States itself. The consensus among wordsmiths was that, compared to several of his more notable speeches, Obama's 2009 Inaugural was "prose, not poetry." But this was his intent. The straightforward, somber tone of the speech deliberately matched the severity of the crises at hand. It more closely resembled Franklin Delano Roosevelt's first inaugural address in 1933, also given at a time of global tension and economic crisis, than John F. Kennedy's inspirational 1961 address, which captured the rising expectations of domestic postwar prosperity and decolonization abroad. Obama blamed the economic crisis not only on "the greed and irresponsibility" on Wall Street, but on a "collective failure to make hard choices and prepare the nation for a new age." Americans, he insisted, would have to "put away childish things" and begin to make the hard choices necessary to restructure the economy, notably in terms of energy efficiency, education and job retraining, and health care. "The question we ask today," he stated. "is not whether our government is too big or too small, but whether it works, whether it helps families find jobs at a decent wage, care they can afford, a retirement that is dignified."

In terms of foreign policy, Obama's address offered both continuity and change. In words that echoed George W. Bush, he vowed, "We will not apologize for our way of life nor will we waver in its defense." To Al Qaeda and others "who seek to advance their aims by inducing terror and slaughtering innocents," Obama was unyielding: "Our spirit is stronger and cannot be broken. You cannot outlast us, and we will defeat you." Significantly, however, he also rejected as "false the choice between our safety and our ideals," a stinging rebuke of the Bush administration's restrictions on civil liberties and use of torture, and a clear indication of his plans to close the Guantanamo Bay detention center. Obama's direct appeal to the Muslim world that he would "seek a new way forward, based on mutual interest and mutual respect," marked a sharp break with his predecessor. It also reflected a clearheaded assessment that such a rapprochement was necessary for America to "responsibly leave Iraq to its people and forge a hard-earned peace in Afghanistan."

An analysis of Obama's success or failure in meeting the goals set out in that address must necessarily be tentative, from the vantage point of his first four years in office. In terms of the economy, Obama presided over an era in which unemployment has remained at levels significantly higher than in any decade since World War II. As Obama entered office in January 2009 the official rate stood at 7.8 percent, a dramatic increase from only 12 months earlier, when the rate had been only 4.6 percent. In October 2009 unemployment rose to near record postwar levels, reaching 10.1 percent, dipping back below 9 percent a year later, and remaining around 9 percent for most of 2011. Joblessness was particularly pronounced in California, Michigan, Florida, and North Carolina, all electorally rich states that had voted for Obama in 2008. While agreeing that the unemployment rate remained too high, the Obama administration reminded Americans of the undoubted global economic crisis it inherited, and that the proposals offered by Republicans in Congress—to drastically cut spending Social Security, Medicare, and Education, and ending Obama's health care reforms—would have increased unemployment, weakened the economy, and impoverished many millions of American. Critics on Obama's left suggested that Obama had naively sought compromise with a Republican Party that had no intention of meeting Obama halfway, notably on health care reform and reining in the excesses of Wall Street. Such criticism gained force following the midterm Congressional elections of 2010, when Democrats lost control of the House of Representatives and maintained only a slender advantage in the Senate that was often overcome by conservative Democrats voting with Republicans. Obama declared the defeat a "whupping," while Republicans declared it a national vote of no confidence in Obama's approach to the economy, and especially his health care proposals, which expanded insurance coverage to 30 million Americans, and had narrowly been approved by Congress earlier that year. While Congressional Republicans lacked the numbers to overturn "Obamacare" other opponents of the 2010 Patient Protection and Affordable Care Act looked to the courts to reject the Act as unconstitutional. Although Obama was able to make two appointments to the Supreme Court—Sonia Sotomayor, the nation's first Hispanic Justice, and Elena Kagan—he did not radically shift the Court by doing so, since they replaced two of the more liberal Justices.

While no major Democratic politician officially opposed Obama's policies in the way that Senator Edward Kennedy had attacked incumbent President Jimmy Carter in the 1970s, the president was not without critics on his left. Nobel Laureate economist Paul Krugman, for example, argued that a more expansive, traditionally Keynesian stimulus to the economy was necessary to revitalize a broken economic system. Obama maintained very strong support among African Americans throughout the first two years of his presidency, but that began to decline by the summer of 2011, as African American unemployment levels reached 16 percent—the highest since the era of Reaganomics. A Washington Post-ABC poll in September 2011 found that, while 86 percent of black Americans had a favorable view of the President, the number who were "strongly" favorable towards his performance had declined to 56 percent, from 83 percent five months earlier. Among Obama's more vocal opponents within the African American community have been the public intellectual CORNEL WEST, talk show host TAVIS SMILEY, and Congresswoman MAXINE WATERS, who have criticized him for doing more to bail out Wall Street than to help poor and working-class Americans, and for failing to highlight the specific problems faced by people of color. Along with the Occupy Wall Street protests that began in the Fall of 2011, such criticism sought to move Obama to the left, as a corrective to the rise of the right wing Tea Party movement which in 2009–2011 shifted an already conservative Republican Party even farther to the right.

Compared to his economic record, opposition to Obama's foreign policy has been more muted, both in Congress and the country at large. Many—Obama included—expressed surprise when he was awarded the 2009 Nobel Peace Prize, having been in office for less than a year. Nonetheless, by adopting a more internationalist, less didactic tone than his predecessor, notably in a well-received speech on America's relations with Islam in Cairo in 2009, Obama continued to enjoy a strong degree of support abroad. Obama's failure to close the Guantanamo Bay detention center drew some criticsm at home and abroad. While many Republicans in Congress attacked Obama for "betraying" Israel, the consensus of opinion in most nations—Israel and a few western European nations aside—was that Obama had been insufficiently critical of Israel's settlement programs and military actions in Gaza. Most observers at home and abroad credited the Obama administration with three solid foreign policy achievements: limiting and then definitively ending the American military presence in Iraq by the end of 2011; capturing or killing many Al Qaeda leaders, most notably Osama Bin Laden in May 2011; and working through NATO to assist the Libyan resistance movement that toppled the regime of Moamar al-Qadaffi in October 2011. To be sure, some criticized Obama's use of drone technology to eliminate targets in Pakistan, Afghanistan, and the Horn of Africa, but the tactic has proved popular. Domestically, Obama faced some opposition for his intervention in Libya from isolationists (of both left and right) who saw it as an intervention too far and some Senate Republicans like John McCain who had wanted greater and earlier American involvement. Overall, military budgets increased under Obama from 2009 to 2011, and were projected to remain high through 2012, despite the broad efforts by both political parties to cut overall government spending.

While there was some debate as to whether an actual "Obama Doctrine" in foreign policy could be determined, his administration's pragmatic approach to the "Arab Spring" of 2011 is instructive. In the cases of the mass movements to overthrow autocratic regimes in Tunisia and Egypt, Obama's response was to encourage reform, place diplomatic pressure on the old leaders to step aside, and to take a relatively hands off approach to the reform process once the *ancien regimes* had been toppled. In Libya, pressure from NATO allies resulted in the U.S. committing weaponry and logistical support to the rebels, while limiting American boots on the ground. Obama also called for autocratic Syrian leader Bashar al-Assad to step down as a result of his brutal repression of dissent, and imposed stringent economic sanctions when it did not. Obama stopped short, however, from seeking a military solution in Syria, however, aware that, unlike Qadaffi, who had lost any influence he once had over African and Middle Eastern allies, Syria's Assad continued to enjoy the support of both Iran and Iraq.

On the two most important foreign policy issues facing his presidency—Iran and Afghanistan—it remained unclear what Obama's legacy would be. On Iran, Obama's initial approach was more conciliatory than his predecessor, but continued to pursue sanctions and to urge Iranian abandonment of its nuclear weapons program. That program appears to have been delayed by sanctions and by the Stuxnet computer virus—perhaps released by Israel—which degraded Iran's uranium enrichment capacity. An alleged ploy by Iran to assassinate the Saudi Arabian ambassador to the U.S. in Washington prompted Obama to propose even tougher sanctions against Iran. As he had promised, Obama did draw back forces from what he viewed as a "war of choice" in Iraq in order to focus on the "war of necessity" in Afghanistan. In 2009 Obama agreed to an increase of 33,000 extra personnel to Afghanistan, to remain until 2012. Two years later, that surge—a compromise between the more hawkish and dovish members of his administration—had made little headway. Despite the elimination of many Taliban leaders, large swathes of the nation remained hostile to the occupation or to the Hamid Karzai regime, while Karzai himself became increasingly hostile to the American presence. October 2011 marked the tenth anniversary of the American military presence in Afghanistan, a period longer than the U.S. involvement in World War I, World War II and Korea, combined.

Obama's 2012 re-election campaign against Republican Mitt Romney focused largely on economic matters. Romney promised to repeal Obamacare (a term the president came to embrace) and attacked Obama for failing to cut the unemployment rate. While factually correct—unemployment was 7.8% on inauguration day and 7.9% on election day—most voters endorsed Obama for turning around the economic catastrophe delivered by his predecessor, for creating 5.4 million new private sector jobs, and for his bailout of the auto industry. They also backed his plan to restore Clinton-era tax rates on incomes over $250,000. On November 6, 2012, Obama won re-election with 332 electoral votes, losing only Indiana and North Carolina from 2008. His diverse 2008 coalition remained largely intact—increased African American and Hispanic turnout offset Obama's losses among whites—and on election day secured Obama 3.5 million more votes than Romney. Obama thus became the first Democrat since FDR to twice win more than 50 percent of the popular vote.

FURTHER READING

Kennedy, Randall. *The Persistence of the Color Line: Politics and the Obama Presidency* (2011).

Kloppenberg, James T. *Reading Obama: Dreams, Hope, and the American Political Tradition* (2010).

Obama, Barack. *The Audacity of Hope: Thoughts on Reclaiming the American Dream* (2006).

Obama, Barack. *Dreams from My Father: A Story of Race and Inheritance* (2007).

Remnick, David. *The Bridge: The Life and Rise of Barack Obama* (2010).

RANDALL KENNEDY AND
STEVEN J. NIVEN

Obama, Michelle (17 Jan. 1964–), First Lady of the United States of America, lawyer, and health-care executive was born Michelle LaVaughn Robinson in Chicago's South Side to working-class parents. Her father, Fraser Robinson III, was a city employee, who worked tending boilers at a water-filtration plant in the city until his death due to complications from multiple sclerosis. Her mother, Marian Shields Robinson, worked as a secretary for the Spiegel catalogue store before becoming a-stay-at-home mother. Michelle's older brother, Craig, born in 1962, would, like his sister, graduate from Princeton University. He later became the head basketball coach at Oregon State University.

As BARACK OBAMA noted in his March 2008 speech on race at the National Constitution Center in Philadelphia, his wife "carries within her the blood of slaves and slave owners." And, indeed, genealogical research has revealed that Michelle Obama's earliest known paternal ancestor, her great-great grandfather, Jim Robinson, was born a slave in 1850, on a rice plantation in the South Carolina low country. While information regarding her earliest ancestors remains sketchy, fragments about her paternal grandparents reveal that her grandfather, Fraser Robinson Jr. (b. 1912), and his wife, LaVaughn, were part of the Great Migration generation. LaVaughn's origins were in Mississippi, while Robinson moved from Georgetown County, South Carolina, to South Side Chicago. There he landed a job with the post office. One of his sisters migrated to Princeton, New Jersey, where she worked as a maid and was there when both Craig and Michelle attended Princeton University. About her family history, Michelle has declared, "You've got to be able to acknowledge and

First Lady Michelle Obama talks with medical personnel before visiting wounded soldiers at Landstuhl Regional Medical Center in Germany, 11 Nov. 2010. LRMC is the largest American hospital outside of the United States and one of only two active trauma centers in the Department of Defense. (Official White House Photo by Chuck Kennedy.)

understand the past and move on from it. You have to understand it, and I think a lot of us just don't have an opportunity to understand it—but it is there" (Murray). She has also noted the linked fate of black and white Americans: "Somewhere there was a slave owner—or a white family in my great-grandfather's time that gave him a place, a home that helped him build a life—that again led to me. So who were those people? I would argue they're just as much a part of my history as my great-grandfather" (Murray).

An honor student, Michelle Robinson graduated from Chicago's first magnet school for the academically gifted, Whitney Young High School, in 1981, where, among her classmates was Santita Jackson, the daughter of the Reverend JESSE JACKSON. After graduating in 1985 from Princeton University with a major in sociology and a minor in African American studies, she continued her professional education at Harvard Law School and earned her degree in 1988. She got by on student loans combined with income from her work at Harvard Legal Aid Bureau. In that position, she assisted people on low incomes with housing and child custody problems in the greater Cambridge area. Armed with a law degree she returned to Chicago to work as an associate at the Sidley & Austin law firm, specializing in copyright and trademark law. In June

1989, Michelle met, and began dating, BARACK OBAMA, a Harvard Law School student who was a summer associate at the firm. They married on 3 October 1992 in the Trinity United Church of Christ, pastored by the Reverend Jeremiah Wright. The Obamas had two children, Malia Ann, born in 1998, and Natasha (Sasha), born in 2001.

Commitment to family and community, and the problems of balancing those values with work has been central to Michelle Obama's private and professional life. The importance of family to Obama's intellectual development, her commitment to personal professional achievement, and her interest in improving the lives of working-class blacks can be seen in her 1985 undergraduate senior year thesis, "Princeton-Educated Blacks and the Black Community." She dedicated the thesis to her mother, father, and special friends and expressed gratitude to them for "loving me and always making me feel good about myself." The dedication hints at the forces that the young Michelle Robinson viewed as a threat to her sense of worth and belonging, and that challenge the self-esteem of other young black women in her situation. The dedication becomes more poignant when she describes her feelings of alienation at Princeton. She wrote, "No matter how liberal and open-minded some of my

White professors and classmates try to be toward me, I sometimes feel like a visitor on campus, as if I really don't belong." She continued, "Regardless of the circumstances under which I interact with Whites at Princeton, it often seems as if, to them, I will always be Black first and a student second" (Robinson, 2). Based upon a survey of graduates of Princeton University, young Michelle arrived at a jarring conclusion in her thesis. She found that "more respondents tended to identify," with working-class blacks during their time at Princeton "in every measured respect." However, after graduating from Princeton, as they became engrossed in building careers and moved away from their communities of origin, black Princeton graduates registered decreased levels of identification with or feelings of responsibility toward "lower class" blacks and their communities (Robinson, 53). To be sure, she carefully noted, "There are other Blacks who, in being integrated have not lost touch. They have maintained an awareness of and a sincere appreciation for the uniqueness of the Black culture" (Robinson, 54). In her professional career, Michelle Robinson Obama would be one of those black Princeton graduates determined not to lose touch with the community values that formed her and to maintain contact with the community, family, and friends who nurtured her.

After three years working in corporate law, Obama decided that it did not offer her sufficient fulfillment. She pursued and secured a job in public service. Valerie Jarrett, then deputy chief of staff to Chicago mayor Richard M. Daley, hired her as an assistant commissioner of planning and development and as a member of the mayor's staff. Valerie subsequently became a close friend of the Obamas and accompanied them to the White House in January 2009. About Michelle, Jarrett explained to *Vanity Fair*, "She just knew the private practice of law was not sufficiently satisfying, and she was willing to walk away from a huge salary potential and all the trappings of power that go along with it" (Bennetts).

Her next job would connect her even closer to the poor black communities she desired to serve. In 1992 Barack Obama had been instrumental in founding the board of directors of Public Allies. He resigned shortly before Michelle became the founding executive director of the Chicago office of Public Allies in early 1993. Through this agency she provided leadership training for young adults. Three years later, in 1996, she accepted a position as associate dean of student services at the University of Chicago. In 2002 she joined the administration of the University of Chicago Hospitals as executive director of community affairs and was promoted to vice president, shortly thereafter. In 2007 she reduced her work hours and then took a leave in order to work three days a week on her husband's campaign for the presidency of the United States. She loved him, believed in him, and decided to help make his dream—and the dream of millions of African Americans—a reality.

On 10 February 2007 Michelle stood by her husband on the steps of the Old State Capitol building in Springfield, Illinois, as he announced his candidacy for president of the United States in the 2008 election. For twenty-one months she played an invaluable role in humanizing, normalizing, and explaining her husband to a skeptical public that often questioned his ethnicity, citizenship, religion, experience, and vision, and challenged her pride in her country. Indeed, since Barack Obama's first major political race—his failed bid to oust Congressman BOBBY RUSH in 2000—it was Michelle who most eloquently challenged those who questioned whether he was "black enough." Responding to a reporter who raised the issue during that election, Michelle stated, with clear anger, "I've grown up in this community. I'm as black as it gets. I put my blackness up against anybody's blackness in this state. And Barack is a black man. And he's done more in terms of meeting his commitments and sticking his neck out for the community than many people who criticize him…. And I can say that, cause I'm black" (Mundy, 135).

However, one group of citizens stood firm in their commitment to Michelle and by extension to her husband. African American studies scholar and biographer Paula Giddings of Smith College confided, "many of us [meaning black women] began to take him (Barack Obama) seriously only after we saw and heard Michelle." She continued, "that Barack Obama would choose for his life partner a nearly six-foot-tall, incredibly smart, loquacious lioness of a woman told us virtually all we needed to know about his fundamental character—and the way he felt about us." Giddings concluded by affirming and claiming Michelle as being, "[O]ur first lady who makes us feel that we are supposed to be here" (Giddings, 76, 79).

Barack Obama's successful bid for the nation's highest office made possible the first black first lady. But he would not have acquired the presidency had it not been for her. And not only because she has had "veto power" over his decisions to run, first for the U.S. Senate in 2004, and then for the presidency.

Their fates were inextricably interlinked. It is well to put Michelle's position of first lady into a broader context of black women's long struggle for elective office in the federal government. In 1968 SHIRLEY CHISHOLM (D-NY) became the first black woman elected to the U.S. House of Representatives. In 1972 she made a serious bid for the Democratic Party's nomination, establishing the plausibility of an African American candidacy for president. BARBARA JORDAN (D-TX) became the first African American woman from the South to win a seat in the U.S. House of Representatives and in 1976 she became the first African American keynote speaker at a Democratic National Convention. The major gains for black women in politics came even later. In 1992—assisted by Project Vote organizer Barack Obama—CAROL MOSELEY BRAUN (D-IL) was the first black woman elected to the United States Senate. In 2001 CONDOLEEZZA RICE became the first African American woman to serve as National Security Adviser, and in 2005 was the first black, female U.S. Secretary of State. During Obama's presidential bid, black women including OPRAH WINFREY and Atlanta mayor Shirley Franklin endorsed Obama's candidacy and galvanized millions of others. This was important during the Democratic Primary inasmuch as the majority of prominent African American leaders and politicians, including black Congresswomen Maxine Waters (D-CA) and Stephanie Tubbs Jones (D-OH) were aligned in support of New York senator Hillary Rodham Clinton. Black women voters were less divided. In recent elections, black women have been 60 percent of the black vote, and in the 2008 primaries, the vast majority supported Obama over Clinton—arguably providing his margin of victory in terms of the popular vote. In the 2008 general election, over 95 percent of the African American vote went to Barack Obama, and the figure for black women was even higher. One exit poll from North Carolina suggested that 100 percent of black women in that state supported Obama.

As she began her term as first lady, Obama stated that her primary responsibility would be to be "Mom-in-Chief," that is, to make sure that their daughters are taken care of and that they make a smooth transition to their new life and new school. Toward this end her mother, Marian Robinson, decided to join the family in the White House to provide a degree of continuity for her grandchildren at a time of extraordinary change in their lives. In so doing, the Obamas and Robinsons are relying on the traditional kin networks that have always sustained black families.

In her official capacity as first lady, Michelle Obama has focused attention on the needs of military families. With the United States involved in two major wars in Afghanistan and Iraq, and with many personnel forced to serve several successive tours of duty, military families, like the military itself, have been overstretched. The *New York Times* has noted that, as a result of such strains, nearly one in five service members returning from Iraq and Afghanistan have symptoms of post-traumatic stress disorder or major depression. In addition to this signature issue, First Lady Obama has also shown an interest in helping communities improve public education and in addressing women's frustration about achieving a manageable work–family balance. She has also been a powerful advocate in the public heath campaign against childhood obesity. In 2010, Obama launched her "Let's Move" campaign to promote outdoor exercise and healthy eating habits by young Americans, noting that "the physical and emotional health of an entire generation and the economic health and security of our nation is at stake."

Ultimately, Michelle Obama has been a powerful role model for African American girls and women who see in her the possibility to reverse, if not completely to destroy the negative stereotypical images of black women. As the youngest first lady since Jacqueline Kennedy, she shares with that predecessor an interest in fitness and style, and although she refers to herself as "the little black girl from the South Side of Chicago," she is an important agent of change in the larger society's perception of black women (Samuels). She represents the millions of professional women juggling demands of career and family. Moreover, as one woman declared, "Michelle is not only African American, but brown. Real brown…. It's nice to see a brown girl get some attention and be called beautiful by the world" (Samuels). Through the power of her example, Obama helps young black women see themselves and their possibilities in an entirely new light.

FURTHER READING

A PDF file of Michelle L. Robinson's Princeton senior thesis, "Princeton-Educated Blacks and the Black Community" can be found online at http://www.suntimes.com/news/1307497,CST-NWS-mobama01.article.

Bennetts, Leslie. "First Lady in Waiting," *Vanity Fair* Online, 27 Dec. 2007 (www.vanityfair.com/politics).

Giddings, Paula J. "The Woman Beside Him," *Essence,* Jan. 2009.

Herrmann, Andrew. "How Princeton shaped Michelle Obama's views," *Chicago Sun Times*, 1 Dec. 2008.

Mundy, Liza. *Michelle: A Biography* (2008).

Murray, Shailagh. "A Family Tree Rooted In American Soil: Michelle Obama Learns About Her Slave Ancestors, Herself and Her Country," *Washington Post*, 2 Oct. 2008.

Samuels, Allison. "What Michelle Means to Us," *Newsweek*, 1 Dec. 2008.

Summers, Carrie E. "Our First Lady: Michelle Obama," *Today's Black Woman*, Mar. 2009.

DARLENE CLARK HINE

O'Dell, Jack (11 Aug. 1923–), civil rights, peace, and social justice organizer, and writer, was born Hunter Pitts O'Dell on the west side of Detroit, Michigan. Jack's parents were George Edwin O'Dell and Emily (Pitts) O'Dell. His father was a hotel and restaurant worker in Detroit who later owned a restaurant in Miami, Florida. His mother had studied music at Howard University and became an adult education teacher, a classical and jazz pianist, and an organist for Bethel AME Church in Detroit. His grandfather, John H. O'Dell, was a janitor in the Detroit Public Library system and a member of the Nacirema Club, which was a club for prominent African American Detroiters. Jack O'Dell later took his grandfather's signature, "J.H. O'Dell" as his nom de plume when he became a writer.

Raised by his paternal grandparents, O'Dell grew up during the Great Depression and witnessed the sit-down strikes and marches that highlighted the civil rights unionism and antipoverty movements of the 1930s. From an early age he was imbued with a profound affinity toward America's laboring classes.

Jack O'Dell attended Wingert Elementary, McMichael Intermediate, and Northwestern High School in Detroit. In 1941, at the age of eighteen, O'Dell left his hometown to study at the School of Pharmacy at Xavier University in New Orleans, Louisiana, at that time one of only three traditionally black colleges that had professional schools in either medicine or pharmacy. That same year, the United States entered World War II and many African Americans enlisted to fight for "Double-Victory" against fascism abroad and racism at home. O'Dell's friend Jesse Gray, a merchant marine, told him about a progressive, desegregated, "left-led" union for seamen called the National Maritime Union (NMU), a CIO affiliate.

O'Dell decided to forego his studies to enlist in the merchant marine and assist in the fight against fascism—a decision that would bring him into contact with leftist shipmates who lent him books by W. E. B. DuBois and Karl Marx. It was on ships carrying cargo around the world that he received his real education and learned "the great lesson of his life": that ordinary working people could create social change. He was elected by his shipmates to attend an NMU Labor Organizers School and was a steward for the union at sea. He also volunteered for the CIO-organized "Operation Dixie" union drive in the southern states and helped organize Local 209 of the Hotel and Restaurant Workers Union in Miami Beach in 1946–1947. O'Dell also had two family members—his father George O'Dell and Dr. Elmer Ward, a pharmacist—who were among the eight black plaintiffs in a suit against the city of Miami that won the rights for African Americans to use the municipal golf course in the late 1940s. In 1948 in New Orleans, O'Dell was part of "Seamen for Wallace," a campaign supporting Progressive Party presidential candidate Henry Wallace.

In the labor movement O'Dell became more fully acquainted with Marxism and the Communist Party (CP). At the height of McCarthyism, which was particularly rampant in the southern states, he narrowly escaped expulsion from his union in 1948 when he supported the incumbency of progressive black union leader FERDINAND CHRISTOPHER SMITH in the union leadership elections. But he was eventually removed from the union in 1950, brought up on charges by a top NMU official from Galveston, Texas, named Tex George. As he stated in an interview with this author in 2003, O'Dell was subsequently "red-baited" out of the NMU for circulating an anti–Cold War petition promoting jobs and international trade that allegedly brought the union "into ill-repute." After his expulsion from the NMU he joined the waterfront section of the Communist Party in 1950 and became one of the party's most effective southern organizers.

Plagued throughout the 1950s by FBI harassment and the House Un-American Activities Committee (HUAC) hearings for his work in the CP throughout the 1950s, O'Dell was chased from jobs he held as a waiter in New Orleans and as an insurance agent in Birmingham, Alabama. By the late 1950s he had become involved with the nonviolent civil rights struggles to desegregate the South and decided to leave the CP because he saw the civil rights movement emerging and knew that the United States was not, as he said, a "normal" country where "Communists could run in elections" (Rocksborough-Smith, 14). He joined the Alabama

Christian Movement for Human Rights, led by FRED SHUTTLESWORTH, and later moved to New York to assist his old NMU comrade Jesse Gray in the struggle for tenants' rights and public housing—work that led in 1960 to an invitation to organize a get-out-the-vote campaign for "Bronx Citizens for Kennedy" in a black and Latino area. In October of 1959, O'Dell volunteered to be the southern organizer for the March on Washington and petition campaign for integrated schools as mandated by the Supreme Court five years earlier. O'Dell helped organize this march with such eminent civil rights and union activists as A. PHILIP RANDOLPH, MARTIN LUTHER KING JR., JACKIE ROBINSON, and lifelong pacifist and civil rights intellectual BAYARD RUSTIN. O'Dell, alongside Rustin and Randolph, represented an impressive cast of leftists still working together for social change over ten years after McCarthyite red-baiting had begun.

The march had brought a petition to Congress to implement the 1954 Supreme Court decision and prevent another Little Rock School crisis—it had also brought 25,000 people to Washington. Through Bayard Rustin, O'Dell was introduced to civil rights lawyer Stanley Levison, who asked him to promote a fund-raiser for the Southern Christian Leadership Conference (SCLC) at New York's Carnegie Hall in 1961. The concert featured the entertainers SAMMY DAVIS JR., Frank Sinatra, and other members of the famous "Rat Pack"—and raised $35,000. O'Dell was soon put in charge of SCLC's direct-mail fundraising office in New York, and owing to his experiences as an activist in the southern states, was put in charge of southern voter registration with already cited SCLC. Thus, when O'Dell first met Martin Luther King Jr., King was, as Taylor Branch put it, "a colleague rather than a celebrity" (Branch, 574).

In 1963, before SCLC's well-known Birmingham campaign, O'Dell attended a strategy session of King's closest advisers and staff members. O'Dell had all the necessary facts and figures on voter registration he had been overseeing in various southern cities, as well as the fund-raising reports. This data enabled SCLC's leaders to assess the position of the movement and to decide whether it was indeed the right time to move on Birmingham.

At this time O'Dell was caught up in the FBI's efforts to vilify, discredit, and red-bait the civil rights movement. As the FBI wiretapped SCLC's offices and targeted O'Dell and Stanley Levison for "Communist espionage," publicly and privately John F. Kennedy was negotiating with King around the passage of the Civil Rights Act. After J. Edgar Hoover

and the FBI claimed through the press that O'Dell was "the number-five Communist in the country" (Branch, 837), President Kennedy made O'Dell the subject of a White House walk in the Rose Garden with King in June 1963 and told King to "get rid of" O'Dell and Levison. O'Dell was always open about his communist leanings and never made any secret about the fact that he had friends in the party even though at this time he was no longer a member. But when the U.S. government targeted SCLC in such a way, he was forced to resign. Although King did not want O'Dell to leave, they agreed that it was for the good of the movement. O'Dell did not want to give the government an excuse for backing out of the civil rights legislation, so he resigned his post. As former SCLC leader ANDREW YOUNG put it, he was "like a good soldier making his sacrifice for the greater good." O'Dell was outraged by the FBI's interference in the civil rights movement, but not with King and SCLC for losing his job. According to Young, King "had many second thoughts about Jack's resignation" and that he "felt bad about asking Jack to resign" (Young, 264–269).

After O'Dell left the SCLC he became an associate editor of *Freedomways*, an influential organ that covered the international black freedom struggle and for which he continued to write articles and editorials for the next twenty-three years. Among the many essays O'Dell penned for the magazine was the first editorial opposing the Vietnam War to appear in a black periodical (April 1965). He also worked in New York and California on Eugene McCarthy's 1968 campaign for the Democratic presidential nomination and as an instructor in economic history at the Antioch Graduate School in Washington, D.C., from 1969 until 1973 (when it closed). Beginning in 1972, he worked closely with JESSE JACKSON in Operation PUSH (People United to Serve Humanity) and then in the National Rainbow Coalition as director of international affairs, beginning in 1985.

In the late twentieth century O'Dell served in numerous other leadership roles. He was volunteer national board chair of Pacifica Radio from 1977 to 1997, one of the five central coordinators for the 12 June 1982 mobilization for disarmament that brought one million marchers into the streets of New York, a senior foreign policy adviser to the first "Jesse Jackson for President" campaign in 1984, and part of the leadership that led the National Campaign for Peace in the Middle East, which organized major demonstrations on both coasts against the 1991 Gulf War. O'Dell also traveled extensively throughout the Middle East and South Africa during this period.

In 1994 O'Dell moved to Vancouver, British Columbia, with his wife, Jane Power. In the early twenty-first century he was a mentor to a group of students and adults associated with the Institute for Community Leadership (ICL). This organization does nonviolent–social change education in public schools and, among other honors, has been awarded the Martin Luther King prize by the Seattle, Washington, Public School system.

For over fifty years O'Dell organized movements for social change throughout North America. As a veteran of the industrial unionism of the 1940s as well as the civil rights movements of the 1950s, 1960s, and 1970s, O'Dell's lifetime of activism connected the major periods of the twentieth-century African American struggle for social justice.

FURTHER READING
Branch, Taylor. *Parting the Waters: America in the King Years—1954–1963* (1988).
McWhorter, Diane. *Carry Me Home: Birmingham, Alabama—The Climactic Battle of the Civil Rights Revolution* (2002).
Rocksborough-Smith, Ian. "'That's a Hell of a Dialectic, Man': Jack O'Dell and the Influence of Left-Wing Radicals in the Postwar Civil Rights Movement," in Michael Zweig, ed. *Jack O'Dell: The Fierce Urgency of Now* (2005).
Young, Andrew. *An Easy Burden: The Civil Rights Movement and the Transformation of America* (1996).

IAN ROCKSBOROUGH-SMITH

Odetta (31 Dec. 1930–2 Dec. 2008), folk singer and musician, was born Odetta Holmes Felious Gordon to Rueben and Flora Holmes in Birmingham, Alabama (her parents' occupations are unknown). Rueben Holmes died when Odetta was a young girl, and Flora remarried shortly after, giving her children their stepfather's last name, Felious. In 1936 the family left the economically depressed South and migrated to Los Angeles, California, where Odetta spent her adolescent years.

At age ten, Odetta's teachers discovered her vocal abilities and encouraged her to pursue her interest in music. When Odetta was thirteen, her mother enrolled her in classical voice lessons. Odetta made remarkable progress and developed her coloratura soprano voice; however, her training was interrupted when her mother could no longer afford the lessons. Felious, who worked at the Turnabout Theatre in Beverly Hills, introduced Odetta to the puppeteer Harry Burnette. He was impressed with the young singer's abilities and agreed to sponsor Odetta's voice lessons until she graduated from high school. After graduation, she assumed the cost of her musical education, and enrolled at the Los Angeles City College to study classical music and voice.

Though classical music was Odetta's first passion, her exposure to folk music in San Francisco's North Beach community altered her career path and her perspective on musical genres. In 1949–1950, she toured with the Los Angeles production of *Finian's Rainbow*. While playing dates in San Francisco, Odetta frequented North Beach, where she reconnected with junior high school friend and aspiring folk artist Jo Mapes. Mapes taught Odetta about folk music's long history as a socially conscious art form and its potential to mobilize a generation of young Americans. Odetta began spending her days off at North Beach where she fully immersed herself in folk music culture, learning how to play acoustic guitar and studying the bluesy chords of the musician Sonny Terry's harmonica. She and Mapes frequented the Vesuvios Bar and performed with the folk duo Wilson and Nan Fowler.

In the fall of 1950 Odetta returned to Los Angeles where she worked as a housekeeper and honed her skills as a guitarist and vocalist. Discouraged by the racial barriers standing in the way of a black woman hoping to enjoy a lucrative career in opera, Odetta committed herself to developing a folk repertoire that showcased her eclectic musical taste. She cultivated her signature sound, which synthesized elements of blues and gospel with operatic techniques. Odetta began to experiment with her voice, singing notes from coloratura soprano to baritone. Her music was as varied as the artists from whom she drew inspiration—MARIAN ANDERSON, Pete Seeger, HARRY BELAFONTE, PAUL ROBESON, and MAHALIA JACKSON. She appropriated prison work songs and spirituals to articulate her anger and frustration with racism and prejudice in the United States.

Her dedication to folk music proved fruitful as she performed regularly in the early fifties. She was featured at several Los Angeles venues and was once billed with her personal hero Paul Robeson. Returning to San Francisco, Odetta gained visibility performing at the city's most popular folk music dive, the hungry i. Odetta garnered the attention of the legendary folk singers Pete Seeger and Harry Belafonte, who promoted her career, securing her shows at folk clubs and introducing her to record label executives.

Odetta traveled to New York City and performed briefly in Greenwich Village at the Blue Angel. She soon returned to San Francisco and played at the Tin Angel, where she met wide acclaim. Her performances at the Tin Angel were recorded and released on her first album, *Tin Angel* (1954) with Fantasy Records. In 1959 she played at the first annual Newport Folk Festival, a weekend-long concert that showcased the vast range of aesthetic styling within folk music—from Odetta's bluesy folk to the commercial sound of the Kingston Trio.

The 1960s were a prolific period for the rising star as folk music became a premiere American music form. Odetta yielded sixteen albums, including the critically acclaimed *Christmas Spirituals* (1960), *Folk Songs* (1963), which became one of the best-selling folk albums of the year, and *Odetta Plays Dylan* (1965), making Odetta one of the most popular and highly paid folk artists. Like other folk singers, Odetta had a particularly strong fan base among the U.S. counterculture milieu, including leftist college students, bohemians, intellectuals, and activists. In 1960 *Time* magazine named Odetta, along with Seeger, Baez, the Weavers, and a handful of others, the most lucrative folk performers in America.

Odetta was one of few folk musicians who could transgress the color line while maintaining the respect and admiration of both the black and white communities. Folk artists did not have a large African American fan base, yet Odetta had a significant black audience. Her commitment to black liberation was evident even on songs that were not explicitly political. She performed at the 1963 March on Washington concert and she participated in the Selma to Montgomery March in 1965. DR. MARTIN LUTHER KING JR. heralded Odetta as the "Queen of American Folk Music" (Blothcher, "Oh, Our Odetta," *Chronogram*, 30 Apr. 2007, 1).

After her monumental success in the 1960s, Odetta's rigorous recording and performing schedule slowed dramatically, producing only two albums between 1970 and 1990. However, a new generation of fans in the 1990s rediscovered her music, and several of her albums were rereleased. In 1999 she recorded *Blues Everywhere I Go*, her first studio album in over a decade. *Blues* was nominated for a Grammy in 2000. President Bill Clinton honored Odetta with the National Endowment for the Arts Medal for the Arts in 1999. In 2006 she headlined a tour of the United States, Canada, Latvia, and Scotland.

Odetta made an indelible mark in the world of music. Her anomalous hybrid of classical music and black folk music traditions influenced artists such as Joan Baez, Bob Dylan, Janis Joplin, and Tracy Chapman. She redefined images of black womanhood and transgressed America's deeply entrenched color line, making her an icon for generations of African Americans. Odetta died of heart disease in New York City, aged 77.

FURTHER READING
Barnwell, Ysaye. *Odetta: Exploring Life, Music, and Song* (1999).
Bielawski, Toby. "Folk Diva: The Wisdom and Music of Odetta," *Radiance* (Winter 1999).
Cohen, Ronald. *Rainbow Quest: The Folk Music Revival and American Society, 1940–1970* (2002).
Obituary: *New York Times*, 2 Dec. 2008.

TANISHA C. FORD

Odrick, Alfred (1812–1894), a former slave who helped facilitate the establishment of the first African American school in Virginia, which allowed for the formation of a thriving African American community bearing his name. Odrick was born into slavery and owned by the Coleman family of Dranesville, a district of Fairfax County located in northern Virginia. Little was documented about his life as a slave. However, it is known that immediately following his post–Civil War emancipation, Odrick moved to Chicago, Illinois. While in Chicago, Odrick employed his abilities as a carpenter, a trade he mastered during his enslavement. After his time in Chicago, Odrick returned to Virginia.

Once in Virginia, Odrick married "Maria" Annie Marie Riddle, who had also been born into slavery and had belonged to the Todd family of Difficult Run in northern Virginia. With Maria, Odrick started a family beginning with John, his eldest son, followed by Frank, Thadeus, Lewis, Anna Marie, and Sarah. In the 1880 census, Odrick listed his occupation as a "farmer." However, Odrick was also recognized in his local community as a skilled carpenter and homebuilder. In the winter of 1872 he acquired thirty acres of land for 450 dollars from George West Gunnell, a McLean resident who was related to the Coleman family by marriage. Odrick replaced the existing log house with a two-story, two-chimney house he built himself. At the time, the house was renowned as one of the most luxurious homes in the area. A personal property tax report in 1880 showed that his household had all the characteristics commonly associated with fairly prosperous landowners. The report stated that Odrick owned a horse, five cattle, and two carriages or wagons, as well as a clock. After he had owned the land for only three years, the recorded monetary value of Odrick's construction improvements on the land was listed at 150 dollars. In the five years thereafter, the value of the land continued to increase to 350 dollars.

In 1879 Odrick found further use for his land by donating it to be the foundation for the first African American school in Virginia. He used his skills as a carpenter to help build the one-room school house that caused the literacy rates of the surrounding African American community to increase. Even though both Odrick and his wife were illiterate, their children were not, most likely due to the Freedman's Bureau that had existed in northern Virginia since 1865. Odrick's school was also one of the first in the entire area to have a bus, which ran until 1952. Before the construction of the Shiloh Baptist Church in 1887, the school was used for church services. The church created an African American family for locals.

Oral history consistently links Odrick with community institutions such as the first Shiloh Baptist Church, which would become one of the oldest black churches in the area. He was said to have donated the land on which the church was built and to have helped in the institution's construction. The 1870s marked a decade of great African American population increase in the area surrounding Odrick's School and the Shiloh Baptist Church. Alfred Odrick passed away in 1894 and was buried on the land he had once purchased as a recently freed slave. The Coleman family, Odrick's former owners, was rumored to have been among the mourners at Odrick's funeral procession. The appearance of the Coleman family was greatly appreciated by several of the African Americans who attended the funeral, conveying the rarity of such an occurrence. Some accounts credit Odrick with reducing tensions between the African Americans and the whites in the area of McLean who knew him as "Uncle Alfred," a term of endearment in the greater white community. African Americans, however, often viewed such terms as "uncle" and "aunt" as paternalistic at best. Even after Odrick's death, the community that had developed around his school continued to grow and prosper.

The African American community would later bear the name of its creator and be known as Odrick's Corner. In the late 1950s the Odrick's Corner community created its own organization to further integration, known as Neighbors for a Better Community. Agnes Sallenberger and Harold L. Lawson, members of the Odrick's Corner community, also teamed up to advocate for and eventually form an integrated Girl Scout troop. Sallenberger further promoted integration, with help from her Odrick's Corner's neighbors. Sallenberger gained permission from white McLean families who had swimming pools to allow African American children to take swimming lessons. In the 1950s, Neighbors for a Better Community also drove black children to swimming pools, museums, and other cultural institutions in Washington, DC, since such facilities remained segregated in Virginia until the early 1960s.

Odrick's school and the original Shiloh Baptist Church, which Odrick was connected to, no longer exist. In 1926 the Shiloh Baptist Church burned down, and the congregation had to hold services in Odrick's school until 1929, when the congregation began construction on a new church. Shortly after in the 1950s Odrick's school was closed. In 1984 the thirty acres that Odrick once owned was converted into the Dulles toll road entrance, and the area once recognized as Odrick's Corner was transformed into the modern Tyson's Corner. To commemorate Odrick's contribution to the African American community, a plaque dedicated to his services to his community stands at the place where Odrick's school once stood.

Odrick was one of the early African Americans who was born into slavery and was later able to not only support his own family but also establish a thriving African American community. Though most of Odrick's tangible contributions to Odrick's Corner have been destroyed, the community that grew around it has continued to prosper, with an average household income of $149,431 in 2010.

FURTHER READING

Crawford, Beverly. "Odrick's Corner Recognized after 130 Years," *Great Falls Connection* (2004).

Herrick, Carole L. *Yesterday: 100 Recollections of McLean and Great Falls.* Vol. 1. (2007).

Johnson, Joseph R. "Northern Teacher to the Freedmen's Bureau Commissioner." *Land and Labor, 1865: Freedmen and Southern Society Project* (2008).

Seaberry, Jane. "Looking Back at Black Life," *Washington Post* (1992).

LEANDI VENTER, HANNAH HEILE, AND MICAELA GINNERTY

Offley, Greensbury Washington (18 Dec. 1808– c. 1895), minister and author, was born in the area around Centerville, Queen Anne's County,

Maryland. He was one of three children born to an enslaved woman from Virginia and a free black man from Maryland whose names are unknown. Offley's mother was freed by her master's will, and that document also ordered Offley and his sister freed at age twenty-five. Apparently, a codicil to the will required that Offley's younger brother be similarly freed at twenty-five, but Offley's mistress destroyed it before probate.

This complex, but not uncommon, arrangement—a mix of free and enslaved people within a family—could well have led to significant problems. First, it was likely that Offley's mistress and her children, having already destroyed part of the will (and so enslaving his brother for life), might have attempted to sell off Offley and his sister. Second, Maryland, like several states with strict black codes, had provisions about freeing black children and about free blacks' residences. Offley's father thus attempted to buy all three children to keep them safe by owning them. Offley's master's children objected. In his 1859 narrative, Offley recounted, in language that must have reminded readers of MARGARET GARNER, how his mother "told them they might buy them and welcome, but you had better throw your money in the fire, for if you buy one of my children I will cut all three of their throats while they are asleep, and your money will do you no good" (4).

Offley's father successfully purchased the children. But as the Offleys had more children—eventually, a total of eight—the financial hardship grew. Almost immediately, Offley's father hired the three older children out, and from youth Offley was involved in a range of work—making brooms, baskets, and the like, and, when older, chopping wood. He worked for his father until he was twenty-one. He did not learn to read until his late teens, when an itinerant black minister stayed briefly with the family. He also learned to wrestle and box during this time, and eventually would give pointers on fighting to other young men in exchange for help with his struggle toward literacy. In his twenties, he gradually moved north, working for both railroads and hotels along the way.

Offley settled in Hartford, Connecticut, on 15 November 1835, and he notes that "good white friends" helped him with his education. On 21 February 1836 he had a conversion experience and was called to preach; by 1850 he was an established Methodist Episcopal minister in the black community. It is likely he interacted closely with JAMES W. C. PENNINGTON, who was also preaching in Hartford during this period, and ANN PLATO, as for more than a decade, Offley lived close to the extended family of Henry and Deborah Plato. At some point he married a woman named Ann who was two years his junior, though no record of this relationship beyond census data has yet been found. She apparently died in the 1850s, as in the 1860 census he was listed with a wife named Elizabeth who was more than a decade younger. No record of children with either wife has been found. What seems to be a namesake nephew (also George Washington Offley) was raised in Hartford, taught for a time in Reconstruction-era South Carolina, and became a minister of some prominence in Philadelphia, Pennsylvania, in the 1880s and 1890s.

Offley's narrative was published locally by an unknown Hartford printer in 1859. A brief twenty-four-page chapbook, it emphasizes his youth in Maryland and the nature of his theology (centering on good works and focused on aiding African Americans of like mind) and contains two brief hymns. Like many slave narratives, it includes authenticating apparatus; in Offley's specific case, such was made up of a testimonial signed by several white New England ministers, including prominent local figures like Horace Bushnell. It seems intended more for a regional audience than a national one, and was clearly a production of the clergy rather than the agents of organized abolition. While it shares the harrowing story of his initial purchase by his father, its tone is generally quite conciliatory. Given this, its size, and its sometimes rough prose, it has generally been seen as a relatively minor slave narrative; still, the narrative was expanded and published in a new edition in 1860 and was reprinted in the late twentieth century.

After the publication of his narrative, Offley becomes more difficult to trace. He seems to have left the ministry after 1860, and is absent from the public record in the 1870s. It seems likely that he stayed in touch with his extended family, though, which had roots in Hartford, New Bedford, Massachusetts, and Baltimore during this period. He resurfaces in 1880, still married to Elizabeth, as the owner of a farm in New Bedford. He is listed there in New Bedford directories with some regularity until 1894, although the date and circumstances of his death and burial remain unknown.

FURTHER READING

Offley, Greensbury Washington. "A Narrative of the Life and Labors of the Rev. G. W. Offley, a Colored Man, Local Preacher and Missionary," in *Five Black Lives*, ed. Arna Bontemps (1971).

ERIC GARDNER

Ogbu, John Uzo (1939–20 Aug. 2003), professor of educational anthropology at the University of California, Berkeley, was a prolific scholar and researcher in the areas of minority achievement in education and cultural identity. Ogbu is well known for his theories on collective identity among minorities. Born in Umuezikwu Village, Ebonyi State, Nigeria, and raised in a Nigerian Presbyterian mission school, Ogbu was led to the United States by his educational pursuits. In 1965 he earned his B.A. in anthropology from the University of California, Berkeley, where he also pursued graduate work and received his Ph.D. in anthropology in 1971.

Ogbu's career flourished at Berkeley, where he received tenure in 1976 with a promotion to full professor in 1980. His work brought him many distinctions, including an election to the International Academy of Education in 1997, an appointment as the chancellor's professor at Berkeley in 1997, and the meritorious American Educational Research Association's Research Contribution to Education Award in 1998.

Ogbu's work reflected his dedication to understanding the differences that exist among minority cultures. In a span of more than three decades at Berkeley, Ogbu dedicated his research to conceptualizing minority educational achievement. Very early in his career he refuted the notion that gaps in academic achievement among ethnic groups was genetically based. His study of six societies, considering minority and majority cultures, found that academic achievement was not based on hereditary, but rather was a factor of how students respond to their surroundings.

The dynamics of Ogbu's work involved understanding the systems that guide minority behavior in shaping its culture. He explored these systems from many different perspectives. His perspective differentiated immigrants who chose to come to the United States from those colonized in America. He made a further distinction between cultural development within schools and within the community. Using his own experience as an immigrant in the United States, Ogbu found a fundamental difference among minorities and the way they responded to societal pressures. For example, his research denoted a typology indicating that "voluntary minorities" are those who choose to leave their homelands to pursue a better life by improving their educational opportunities in a host country. "Involuntary minorities" are those who were enslaved and colonized against their will. Ogbu found this difference between these minorities to be key in understanding the interpretations that minorities have about society and educational achievement.

Ogbu also looked to the use of language in minority educational achievement. In 1986 he examined how blacks and Chicanos refused to speak standard English for fear of being associated with the white culture. The term "acting white" was often used by Ogbu to describe the behavior that these minority groups ascribed to the use of standard English. Although the findings of this study are often viewed as controversial, Ogbu maintained that this type of behavior was directly linked to the educational success of minority students.

His groundbreaking work in cultural identity among minority groups sought to make connections between the study of anthropology and the study of education. In fact he is often referred to as a cultural ecologist whose work focused on the systems (both institutional and community) that influence patterns of behavior among minority students. His work in this area was the foundation for what is generally known as the cultural-ecological theory of minority student performance, or CE.

The four basic principles of this theory are (1) the general idea that students' academic success is impacted by community forces and system forces, and that not enough attention has been paid to the ways in which community forces contribute to involuntary minority student failure; (2) the distinction among voluntary, involuntary, and autonomous minorities; (3) the recognition of universal primary and secondary discontinuities between students and the school they attend; and (4) the idea that involuntary minorities have developed survival strategies. This theory suggests that minorities within the United States interpret academic success very differently. Their interpretations guide behavior and ultimately affect their academic achievement.

One of Ogbu's more controversial studies examined the influence of community forces on student achievement. The site for this study was Shaker Heights, Ohio. There Ogbu looked to the systems within the community that fostered educational achievement among minorities and found that adults played an integral part in the educational development of students. Moreover, he found that the leadership forces within a community operated based on an "allocation of responsibility." He wrote extensively on this issue, which is also referred to as the system force–community force dichotomy.

Ogbu discovered three problematic areas: educational policies, teacher expectations and assessments, and societal rewards for educational achievement. In addition, he asserted that black parents should play a more active role in educating their children. Although his evaluation of community and school participation was not welcomed by many in the community, many of his recommendations for improving school/community culture were implemented. The efforts for this Shaker Heights study ultimately culminated in his last publication, *Black American Student in an Affluent Suburb: A Study of Academic Disengagement* (2003).

Ogbu's work continues to provide theoretical guidance in the building of educational and anthropological applications. His contributions to the study of minority educational achievement were well researched and have served to foster the ongoing dialogue on racial dynamics and relations. His work is highly regarded and continues to be a source of school and community improvement. Even though most of Ogbu's work focused on the educational achievement of students in the United States, his legacy contributes to student achievement abroad in his homeland of Nigeria, where there is an ongoing effort for the development of educational support. Ogbu was survived by wife, Marcellina, and their five children: Grace, Christina, Cecelia, Elizabeth, and Nnanna.

FURTHER READING

Berube, Maurice R. *Eminent Educators: Studies in Intellectual Influence* (2000).

PAMELA FELDER THOMPSON

O'Grady, Lorraine (1940–), cultural critic, historian, performance and installation artist, photographer, writer, and activist, was born in Boston, Massachusetts. Her mother, Lena, emigrated from Jamaica to Boston in the 1920s. She earned a B.A. from Wellesley College in Spanish and economics and an MFA in fiction writing from the University of Iowa, studying in its renowned Writers' Workshop. From Iowa, she moved to New York City and began writing for the *Village Voice* and *Rolling Stone* as a rock critic. She changed her career course with her first performance pieces in the 1980s and her critical writings about art and its effect on students and peers.

O'Grady's first performed as Mlle. Bourgeoise Noire, loosely translated into Ms. Black Middle Class; her alter ego was a rowdy uninvited guest to numerous high-profile art exhibitions. *Mlle.*

Bourgeoise Noire Goes to JAM (1980), *Mlle. Bourgeoise Noire Goes to the New Museum* (1981), and *Art Is/Fly By Night* (1983) at the Franklin Furnace were unexpected, uninvited protests where O'Grady drew attention to herself by shouting poetry and wielding a bullwhip. Usually dressed in a tiara, a dress made entirely of white gloves, and a sash proclaiming her identity as Mlle. Bourgeoise Noire, O'Grady parodied the exclusionary club of artists, gallerists, and collectors that dominated New York City's elite art scene. She performed this character in political settings, too, including the Afro-American Day parade in Harlem in 1983. Mlle. Bourgeoise Noire was a feminist spectacle, created to challenge societal norms, constricting gender roles, and taboos that governed the body.

O'Grady's performances took on personal and historical themes, often merging the two through images and phrases in the early 1980s. *Nefertiti/Devonia Evangeline* was her first commissioned piece, performed at the Just Above Midtown Gallery in New York in 1980 and the Allen Memorial Art Museum in Oberlin, Ohio, in 1982. Unlike the political persona of Mlle. Bourgeoise Noire's, Nefertiti/Devonia Evangeline fused ancient Egyptian history with O'Grady's memories of her younger sister Devonia, who had died two years earlier in 1978. O'Grady traveled to Egypt and researched the Amarna period of ancient Egypt and Nefertiti's rule. *Nefertiti/Devonia* was a spoken word performance that linked O'Grady and Devonia to Nefertiti and her younger sister Mutnedjmet, drawing analogies between the physical and emotional similarities in the sisters' relationships.

O'Grady officially retired Nefertiti in 1989 but pulled some of the images into a visual installation, *Miscegenated Family Album*, a work that interrogates notions of racial purity. Moving from performance to mixed-media installation she created several more pieces that were included in group shows at the Dia Center for the Arts in New York in 1993 and the Institute of Contemporary Art in Boston in 1996. Her work gained wide recognition and accolades, and she received fellowships from the National Endowment for the Arts, Harvard University, and the New School in New York. Solo exhibitions followed at the Hartford Atheneum in Connecticut in 1993 and the Thomas Erben Gallery in New York in 1993 and 1998.

O'Grady's groundbreaking essay, "Olympia's Maid: Reclaiming Black Female Subjectivity" (1994), examined racial and gender representation in art and appeared in various anthologies. She also contributed articles and essays to *Artforum, Afterimage, Art Journal, High Performance*, and *Heresies*. She continued to work on studies for "Flowers of Evil and Good," a project begun in 2000 that explored the relationship between the nineteenth-century French poet Charles Baudelaire and his Haitian common-law wife of more than twenty years, Jeanne Duval. O'Grady's series of digital cibachrome diptychs combine images of Baudelaire and Duval with text, sketches, and ephemera in large-scale mixed-media portraits. This series was about rewriting Baudelaire's history through uncovering Duval's presence to his life, since she was largely forgotten by his biographers because of her race.

O'Grady went on to serve as assistant professor of fine arts and African American studies at the University of California, Irvine, retiring in 2005. However, she continued to lecture and perform, in March 2007 participating in the exhibit *WACK! Art and the Feminist Revolution* at the Geffen Contemporary at MOCA (Los Angeles).

FURTHER READING

Exhibition Catalog, Institute for Contemporary Art, Boston.

Feucht-Haviar, Thomas. "Lorraine O'Grady's 'Olympia's Maid': Reclaiming Black Female Subjectivity" http://prod-images.exhibit-e.com/www_alexandergray_com/0258675b.pdf.

Higonnet, Anne. "*Hypocrite Lecteur, Mon Semblable, Mon Frere*! Hybrid Viewer, My Difference, Lorraine O'Grady!" in *New Histories*, eds. Lia Gangitano and Steven Nelson (1996).

Powell, Richard J. *Black Art and Culture in the 20th Century* (1997).

Wilson, Judith. *Lorraine O'Grady: Photomontages* (1991).

JENNIFER LYNN HEADLEY

O'Hara, James Edward (26 Feb. 1844–15 Sept. 1905), lawyer and politician, was born in New York City, the son of an Irish merchant and a West Indian woman, who were not married. Little is known of his early life, most of which he spent in the Danish West Indies. He returned to the United States as a teenager, visiting Union-occupied eastern North Carolina for the first time in 1862. At nineteen he became a teacher and operated freedmen's primary schools in the eastern North Carolina towns of New Bern and Goldsboro. He married Ann Marie Harris in 1864, but they separated in 1866, when he accepted the teaching post in Goldsboro. They later divorced.

With the advent of congressional Reconstruction, O'Hara began to participate in politics, serving as engrossing clerk at the state constitutional convention of 1868 and the subsequent session of the legislature. In 1869 he married Elizabeth Eleanor Harris; they had one son. O'Hara had earlier fathered a son out of wedlock. O'Hara spent about two years in Washington, D.C., working as a clerk in the U.S. Treasury Department and studying at Howard University. Upon his return to North Carolina, he secured a license to practice law in 1873 and assumed a leading role in Republican politics. Hostile Democratic journalists soon noticed O'Hara, calling him "a bright mulatto, with cheek a plenty" and a man with "more than ordinary intelligence."

The young lawyer settled in Halifax County, one of the state's most important cotton-growing counties and the most populous county in the Second Congressional District, which had a strong black (and Republican) majority. Speaking at the Second District Republican Convention in 1874, O'Hara insisted to applause that "colored aspirants" should not be ruled out "on account of their color."

Though not nominated for Congress in 1874, O'Hara was elected to the Halifax County Board of Commissioners and served for the next four years as chairman of this powerful arm of local government. He was elected to the state constitutional convention in 1875. Nominated as a presidential elector in 1876, he withdrew after Democrats attempted to make an issue of his race.

It is difficult to assess O'Hara's tenure as county commissioner, especially in light of repeated Democratic accusations that the board was corrupt and extravagant. The Republican commissioners were indeed indicted for malfeasance in office, although O'Hara claimed that the charges were politically motivated. The results of these court cases were inconclusive, and the state prosecutor dropped all charges after O'Hara and one associate pleaded nolo contendere and agreed to pay costs.

For five consecutive elections O'Hara pursued the Republican congressional nomination in the "Black Second." When he was first nominated to Congress in 1878, a host of enemies within the Republican Party accused him of corruption and asserted that O'Hara, who had divorced his first wife a decade earlier, was actually guilty of bigamy. Three weeks before Election Day, Republican leaders convened a new nominating convention and chose another candidate. Refusing to withdraw, O'Hara was victorious in the three-way general election until canvassing boards in three counties rejected hundreds of votes on flimsy technicalities and gave the victory to the Democratic nominee, William H. Kitchin. O'Hara contested the election but was unsuccessful.

O'Hara held no elective office between 1878 and 1883, though he was a significant leader in the statewide antiprohibition campaign of 1881, in the Liberal coalition between Republicans and dissident Democrats in 1882, and in organized black protests against Republican patronage policy. At another disorderly district convention in 1882 he claimed the Republican nomination for Congress and, after several months of conflict, secured the withdrawal of a competing Republican candidate, incumbent representative Orlando Hubbs. O'Hara easily won election and, backed by an unusually united party, won a second term two years later. He was then at the zenith of his political career, not only dominating his district but wielding considerable influence in the state and national party.

In 1886, however, O'Hara faced renewed opposition, as a divided Republican convention once again produced two "nominees." O'Hara received three-quarters of the Republican votes, despite complaints that he had grown distant from his constituents, protests about the way he distributed patronage, and even negative comments about his complexion from an opponent proud to be "of unmixed African blood." But the election was lost to the youthful Democratic candidate, Furnifold Simmons.

During his four years in Congress, with the Republican Party in the minority, O'Hara found it difficult to shape significant legislation or influence debate. He proposed a constitutional amendment to fill the void left by the Supreme Court's nullification of the Civil Rights Act of 1875, advocated reimbursement for depositors in the failed Freedman's Savings and Trust Company, and sought federal aid for education, but these bills were ignored by the Democratic majority. His only success was securing the passage of seven private pensions, or relief bills. He made no lengthy speeches on the floor of the House, preferring instead to offer brief comments.

O'Hara's only significant national attention came in December 1884, when he offered a controversial amendment to the Reagan Interstate Commerce Bill providing that all railway passengers should "receive the same treatment and be afforded equal facilities ... as are furnished all other persons holding tickets of the same class without discrimination." Supported by racially moderate northern Democrats, the amendment passed, although, after considerable debate, southern Democrats succeeded in tacking on another amendment making the point that "equal" could be separate.

O'Hara never held public office again after 1887, though he remained active in the Republican Party into the twentieth century. He practiced law and briefly published a weekly newspaper, the Enfield *Progress*. He moved to New Bern, North Carolina, in 1890 and spent the last fifteen years of his life there.

Throughout his career O'Hara served as a convenient symbol for both friends and foes. For Republicans, this talented "carpetbagger" represented the aspirations of a small but increasing group of black professionals who demanded a greater voice in the party's awkward biracial alliance. For black voters, even impoverished landless laborers, he symbolized the hope that former slaves could participate in American democracy. For Democrats, especially the generation that ultimately chose to disenfranchise blacks, O'Hara was a symbol of dangerous black assertiveness, though time and again they paid grudging compliments to his skill and resourcefulness.

FURTHER READING
Anderson, Eric. *Race and Politics in North Carolina, 1872–1901: The Black Second* (1981).
This entry is taken from the *American National Biography* and is published here with the permission of the American Council of Learned Societies.

ERIC ANDERSON

O'Kelly, Berry (c. 1860–14 Mar. 1931), businessman, was born in Chapel Hill, North Carolina, the son of slave parents. His father's name is unknown. His mother, Frances Stroud, died when O'Kelly was very young, and he was raised by members of her family. After emancipation, he attended local schools in Orange and Wake counties, North Carolina, and subsequently worked as a railroad freight and ticket agent. Frugal and hardworking, O'Kelly saved the wages he earned working as a store clerk in the all black town of Mason Village, near Raleigh, North Carolina, and eventually bought a share of the business. By 1889 he was the sole owner of the general store, serving both Mason Village and Raleigh customers. Described as optimistic, genial, warm, and sympathetic, he was also a hard-nosed businessman and real estate investor. In 1890 Mason Village was renamed Method, and O'Kelly became the town's postmaster, a position he held for more than twenty-five years. He married Chanie Ligon, who died childless in 1902.

By the early twentieth century O'Kelly had branched out into construction and brick manufacturing and invested in a Raleigh shoe store. The R. G. Dun and Company mercantile agency reference firm estimated his "pecuniary strength" in 1905 as among the best in Raleigh. In 1915 and 1918 O'Kelly was listed as owning a general store and a brick manufacturing enterprise, Dun and Company placing his pecuniary strength at between thirty-five thousand and fifty thousand dollars and listing his credit rating as "high." In the 1920s he bought a brick building in Raleigh and leased commercial space to black businesses, headed both the Acme Realty Company and the Eagle Life Insurance Company, and invested in a black newspaper, the *Raleigh Independent*. He later served as an officer of the Raleigh branch of the Mechanics and Farmers Bank. His wealth and business achievements were remarkable in their day, equaled by only a small number of black southerners.

In the town of Method, O'Kelly was, according to one account, "general director of community affairs." Active in the African Methodist Episcopal (AME) Church, he also served as chair of Method's primary school committee. In the 1910s and 1920s he helped develop the school into a much larger normal school and industrial education institution, the Berry O'Kelly Training School.

O'Kelly's success was aided by supportive black institutions, such as the Durham-based North Carolina Mutual Life Insurance Company, from which he borrowed money when he needed ready cash. He was a member of the National Negro Business League, founded in 1900 by BOOKER T. WASHINGTON to promote black enterprise. By the time of his death in Wake County, amid the Great Depression and despite a severe drop in land values, O'Kelly owned fifty-five tracts of land there, including thirty-seven in Raleigh, and several thousand acres of farmland in Virginia. An inventory of his holdings, excluding the Virginia land, which was heavily mortgaged, calculated the worth of his estate at between $145,000 and $156,000, making O'Kelly one of the wealthiest African Americans in North Carolina. He was survived by Marguerite Bell, whom he had married in 1923, and an infant daughter.

Despite his remarkable economic success, O'Kelly did not become a national black leader. Like other prosperous African Americans of his day, he devoted most of his energies to his business pursuits. Though active in local bond, road, and school elections, he remained aloof from party politics. His leadership qualities, however, were apparent, not only in his material success but also in his active participation in every aspect of community building in the African American town of Method, North Carolina.

FURTHER READING

Powell, William S., ed. *Dictionary of North Carolina Biography*, vol. 4 (1991).

Richardson, Clement, ed. *The National Cyclopedia of the Colored Race* (1919–).

Obituary: *Raleigh News and Observer*, 26 Mar. 1931.

This entry is taken from the *American National Biography* and is published here with the permission of the American Council of Learned Societies.

LOREN SCHWENINGER

O'Leary, Hazel R. (17 May 1937–), U.S. secretary of energy, was born Hazel Reid in Newport News, Virginia, the youngest of two daughters of Dr. Russell E. Reid, and a mother about whom little is known, except that she was also a physician. Hazel and her sister, Edna, were raised in Newport News by their father and stepmother, Hazel Palleman Reid, in a loving and supportive environment that encouraged a solid education, independence, and compassion for others. Hazel's grandmother, founder of Newport News's only black public library, kept a box of clean and neatly packed clothes on her back porch for neighbors to take as needed.

O'Leary's life lessons began in the Reid household and continued with her elementary and middle school teachers at the segregated public schools in Newport News, where she was a star pupil. Although the Reid sisters led sheltered childhoods, their parents also encouraged their independence and intellect. O'Leary was an exceedingly bright and competitive child with an abundance of self-confidence. Visionary when it came to their children's futures, the Reids sacrificed both emotionally and financially to send their daughters "up north" to complete their education. From eighth grade through high school, Hazel and Edna lived under the care of an aunt who resided in Essex County, New Jersey. O'Leary studied voice and alto horn at the Arts High School for artistically talented youth and graduated with honors in 1956. She moved to Nashville, Tennessee, that year to attend Fisk University and received a B.A. degree cum laude from Fisk in 1959.

Hazel O'Leary, energy secretary, at a news conference in Berkeley, California, 4 June 1996. She holds up a beaker of water purified by UV Waterworks, a small simple device that uses ultraviolet light to cheaply disinfect water of bacteria that cause deadly diseases. (AP Images.)

In 1960, just a year after graduating from Fisk, Hazel Reid married Dr. Carl Rollins. During her early years of marriage, she put her education on hold while she perfected her role as housewife. After the birth of a child, Carl G. Rollins, in 1963, however, she resumed her education, enrolling in Rutgers University School of Law. She graduated in 1966 with a J.D. degree. Over the next twenty-five years, Hazel Reid Rollins's intellect, ambition, and self-confidence would serve her well, propelling her into increasingly prominent roles in state and federal government. In 1967 she was appointed assistant prosecutor in Essex County, New Jersey, and was subsequently appointed assistant attorney general in that state. Carl and Hazel Rollins's marriage dissolved shortly before her next career move—to Washington, D.C. Upon moving there with her son, she joined the prominent accounting firm of Coopers and Lybrand as one of the first African American partners and one of a few female partners at that time.

In 1974 O'Leary left the accounting firm and resumed her career in public service. Over the next twenty-five years she served under three presidents, Gerald Ford, Jimmy Carter, and Bill Clinton. In all three administrations her keen understanding of energy and energy conservation policy would be tapped. In 1974, during Ford's tenure, O'Leary joined the Federal Energy Administration (FEA) as director of the Office of Consumer Affairs/Special Impact—managing a number of the antipoverty programs initiated during the Great Society years of the 1960s. Despite her Rollins's appearance of privilege, she was known in some Washington circles as an advocate for the poor. In the Carter administration she served, from 1976 to 1977, as general counsel for the Community Services Administration; as assistant administrator for conservation and environment with the FEA; and, in 1978, as chief of the Department of Energy's (DOE) Economic Regulatory Administration.

O'Leary has been described as a lightning rod—attracting controversy wherever she happened to work and garnering either hot or cold reactions from friends and foes. As a regulator and an administrator, she received both praise and criticism over the years. Described as a fair administrator, however, she gained respect even from environmentalists and energy executives, who lauded her conservation initiatives—including underwriting the cost of insulating homes for low-income families.

During her tenure with the Carter administration, she met and worked with John F. O'Leary, deputy secretary for the DOE. Their friendship probably was ignited by a shared interest in and passion for the world of energy and conservation. In 1980 they married and, shortly thereafter, founded an international energy, economics, and strategic planning firm. Hazel O'Leary resigned her post at DOE to run the firm. John O'Leary passed away in 1987, leaving the responsibility of running O'Leary and Associates to his wife. In 1989 O'Leary closed the doors of the firm and, over the next three years, reestablished working relationships with other energy entities. These companies included Applied Energy Services, an independent power producer; NRG Energy, the major unregulated subsidiary of Northern States Power Company; and, later, its parent company, Minneapolis-based Northern States Power Company—an energy supplier to five contiguous states in the northern Midwest.

In November 1992 President-elect Bill Clinton made history when he appointed four African Americans to his cabinet: O'Leary, RON BROWN, JOYCELYN ELDERS, and MIKE ESPY. Despite her past controversy among environmentalists, O'Leary was confirmed unanimously as secretary of energy just one day after Bill Clinton's inauguration, and she was sworn into office in a White House ceremony one day later. O'Leary, only the seventh secretary of energy, was the first racial minority and the first woman to control one of the most unwieldy departments in the federal government. Early in her tenure O'Leary was dubbed one of the bright stars of the Clinton cabinet, bringing what one reporter described as a savvy respect for the consumer market, grassroots politics, and environmental concerns. Over time, however, it was these very attributes that would be used against her.

O'Leary viewed her mission at the department as that of shepherding the organization into the twenty-first century—and, to a large extent, she accomplished that mission. She boldly undertook initiatives that greatly influenced the lives of the American people and opened public debate within the DOE, the national laboratory system, and the national security community on nuclear weapons and their associated cleanup program and on nuclear testing. She is also credited with influencing President Clinton's decision to end nuclear testing in the United States and with spearheading a more accessible DOE.

Yet it was O'Leary's "outside the box" approach to government and her nontraditional leadership style that can be credited with her rocky tenure in the Clinton administration. Her last year was fraught with public and legal crises, including congressional criticism and investigations into her trade missions to foreign countries and her trip expense reports. O'Leary submitted her resignation to President Clinton in December 1996. In an exit interview with the *New York Times* in January 1997, an obviously weary O'Leary described her four years in office as "exhausting" and despaired that probably no secretary of energy taking office after her would undertake the important trade missions she had, given the scrutiny she had undergone.

Upon leaving the Clinton administration in January 1997, O'Leary gravitated again to the private sector. She signed on as CEO for Blaylock & Partners LP, a New York–based full-service investment firm whose major client focus is on energy, transportation, telecommunications and technology, and consumer products. O'Leary's role includes support of the firm's expanding mergers and acquisitions interests, particularly in energy-related businesses. In July 2004 O'Leary was appointed president of her alma mater, Fisk University.

Hazel O'Leary's uncharacteristic courage and sense of fair play in a bureaucratic environment is part of her legacy. At the DOE she was a leader who took bold steps to reform an out of control bureaucracy and make government a place that worked for all people. In doing so, she raised the bar for those coming after her. As a business leader and world-renowned public figure, O'Leary has become a role model for young people, women, and minorities, who understand the difficulties of success against the odds. As she travels the world, this confident and determined woman remains a sterling example of her parents' teachings: reverence, honor, and a good education transcend any obstacle.

FURTHER READING

Healey, Jan. "Hazel R. O'Leary: A Profile," *Congressional Quarterly* 177 (23 Jan. 1993).

Lippman, Thomas W. "An Energetic Networker to Take Over Energy," *Washington Post*, 19 Jan. 1993.

Thompson, Garland L. "Four Black Cabinet Secretaries—Will It Make the Difference?," *Washington Times*, 4 Feb. 1993.

Wald, Matthew. "Interview with Secretary Hazel O'Leary," *New York Times*, 20 Jan. 1997.

JANIS F. KEARNEY

Olive, Milton Lee, III (7 Nov. 1946–22 Oct. 1965), Vietnam War soldier and Medal of Honor recipient, was born in Chicago, Illinois, the son of Milton Olive Jr. and his wife Clair Lee Olive. His mother died within hours of giving birth, but his father would remarry in 1952 to Antoinette Mainor, who subsequently helped raise young Milton as her own. The Olive family roots were originally in Holmes County, Mississippi, near Lexington, and as a young man Milton spent much time living with his grandparents, including Milton Sr., and later attended high school in the area. When in Chicago, young Milton, nicknamed "Skipper" from an early age, was doted on by his parents, and even partnered with his dad, who was called "Big Milton," in a modest local photography business they operated when he was just twelve years old. Though young Milton was a skinny kid and not even six feet tall, there was something about him that seemed to leave a deep impression on those who knew him. He continued to live in Mississippi until his father and grandmother, upon discovering that he was helping civil rights workers register blacks to vote in Lexington, feared for his safety and sent him back north (Terry). When he dropped out of high school at the age of seventeen to enlist in the army, his father thought it "would be good for his son, make a man of him … no one had heard of Vietnam," at least not yet (Terry).

Milton Olive III attended Saints Junior College High School in Chicago and left during his junior year, enlisting in the army on 17 August 1964. Little is known about his early assignments after completing basic training, but in June 1965 he was sent for duty in the Republic of Vietnam, and in July was assigned to Company B, 2nd Battalion (Airborne), 503rd Infantry, 173rd Airborne Brigade as a replacement soldier. He soon had six paratrooper jumps under his belt and shortly after joining his new unit earned the Purple Heart Medal when he was wounded in a firefight. This unlikely looking soldier was well liked by the members of his unit; though "he was kind of clean cut" and "wasn't one of those street-smart kind of cats" according to fellow soldier John Foster, "he wasn't a square, either" (Terry).

The service of African Americans during the Vietnam War, men like Milton Olive, DWIGHT JOHNSON, and GARFIELD LANGHORN, was important in many ways. The Vietnam War was the first American conflict since the American Revolution where black servicemen served in entirely integrated circumstances from start to finish and, more importantly, their capabilities as combat soldiers at all levels, from enlisted man to officer, were no longer in question. As a consequence, African American soldiers serving in Vietnam were also the first such men since the Civil War to receive equal consideration with white servicemen when it came to the awarding of combat decorations, including our nation's highest award for valor, the Medal of Honor. While no African American servicemen were awarded the Medal of Honor during World War I and World War II, and only two men were so decorated during the Korean War, twenty African Americans were awarded the medal for their service in Vietnam. While it is true that the times had changed, that is not to say that racial integration solved all of America's race problems in regard to its military service branches; racism still abounded when it came to housing and other base facilities, while tensions between black and white soldiers in general would take a generation to solve.

Private First Class Milton Olive III became the first African American to be awarded the Medal of Honor during the Vietnam War when he was killed in action while on patrol with 3rd Platoon, Company B at Phu Cuong, Vietnam on 22 October 1965. While operating in the jungle pursuing Viet Cong insurgents, Olive's unit, led by Lieutenant James Sanford and platoon Sergeant Vince Yrineo, came under heavy attack and a grenade was thrown in their midst. Private Olive shouted out a warning to his lieutenant then grabbed the grenade and fell on it, absorbing the full blast, which killed him instantly. His brave action saved the lives of his fellow platoon soldiers, including Sanford, Yrineo, Private John Foster, and Private Lionel Hubbard. For over four decades thereafter, Sergeant Yrineo has carried a fragment of Milton Olive's shattered dog-tag as a reminder of the man that saved his life (Terry). The Medal of Honor was subsequently presented to Milton Olive III's family on 26 April 1966 at a White House ceremony. Among those in attendance were Sanford and Foster, as well as Chicago Mayor Richard Daly. Milton Olive III was buried at the West Grove Methodist Baptist Cemetery, Lexington, Mississippi, where a headstone with his picture and an engraving of the Medal of Honor marks his final resting place. In 1999 the Milton L. Olive III Park in Chicago was dedicated in his honor.

FURTHER READING

Hanna, Charles W. *African American Recipients of the Medal of Honor* (2002).

Terry, Don. "The Men of Olive Company; Four Soldiers Survived Vietnam Because Milton Olive Didn't." *Chicago Tribune*, 12 May 2002.

GLENN ALLEN KNOBLOCK

Oliver, King (11 May 1885–8 Apr. 1938), cornetist and bandleader, was born Joseph Oliver in or near New Orleans, Louisiana, the son of Jessie Jones, a cook; his father's identity is unknown. After completing elementary school, Oliver probably had a variety of menial jobs, and he worked as a yardman for a well-to-do clothing merchant. He appears to have begun playing cornet relatively late, perhaps around 1905. For the next ten years he played in a variety of brass bands and large and small dance bands, coming to prominence about 1915. Between 1916 and 1918 Oliver was the cornetist of trombonist EDWARD "KID" ORY's orchestra, which was one of the most highly regarded African American dance orchestras in New Orleans. Early in 1919 Oliver moved to Chicago and soon became one of the most sought-after bandleaders in the cabarets of the South Side black entertainment district.

In early 1921 Oliver accepted an engagement in a taxi-dance hall on Market Street in San Francisco, and he also played in Oakland with his old friend Ory and perhaps in local vaudeville as well. After a stop in Los Angeles, he returned to Chicago in June 1922, beginning a two-year engagement at the Lincoln Gardens. After a few weeks, Oliver sent to New Orleans for his young protégé LOUIS ARMSTRONG, who had been Oliver's regular substitute in the Ory band some five years earlier. With two cornets (Oliver and Armstrong), the trombonist HONORE DUTREY, the clarinetist JOHNNY DODDS, the string bassist William Manuel Johnson, the drummer WARREN "BABY" DODDS, and the pianist Lillian Hardin (LIL ARMSTRONG), King Oliver's Creole Jazz Band made a series of recordings for the Gennett, Okeh, Columbia, and Paramount labels (some thirty-seven issued titles), which are regarded as supreme achievements of early recorded jazz. (Other musicians substitute for the regulars on a few of these recordings.) There is ample evidence that a great many musicians, black and white, made special and repeated efforts to hear the band perform live.

By early 1925 Oliver was leading a larger and more up-to-date orchestra with entirely new personnel. This group was the house band at the flashy Plantation Cafe (also on the South Side) and as the Dixie Syncopators made a series of successful recordings for the Vocalion label. Oliver took his band to the East Coast in May 1927, but after little more than a month, it dispersed. For the next four years Oliver lived in New York City, touring occasionally and making records for the Victor Company at the head of a variety of ad hoc orchestras; these are widely considered inferior to his earlier work.

His popularity waning and his playing suffering because of his chronic gum disease, Oliver spent an unprosperous six years between 1931 and 1937 incessantly touring the Midwest and the upper South. Savannah, Georgia, became his headquarters for the last year of his life; he stopped playing in September 1937 and supported himself subsequently by a variety of odd jobs. He died in Savannah of a cerebral hemorrhage; he was buried in Woodlawn Cemetery in New York City. The REVEREND ADAM CLAYTON POWELL JR. officiated, and Louis Armstrong performed at the funeral service. He was survived by his wife, Stella (maiden name unknown), and two daughters.

Oliver is the most widely and favorably recorded of the earliest generation of New Orleans ragtime/jazz cornetists, most influential perhaps in his use of straight and plunger mutes; aspects of Louis Armstrong's style clearly derive from Oliver. Oliver's best-known contributions as a soloist are his three choruses on "Dipper Mouth Blues," copied hundreds of times by a wide variety of instrumentalists on recordings made during the next twenty years. His major achievement, however, remains the highly expressive and rhythmically driving style of his band as recorded in 1923–1924. While the band owed its distinctiveness and energy, like all early New Orleans jazz, to the idiosyncratic musical talents of the individual musicians, its greatness was undoubtedly the result of Oliver's painstaking rehearsals and tonal concept.

FURTHER READING

Gushee, Lawrence. "Oliver, 'King,'" in *New Grove Dictionary of Jazz*, ed. Barry Kernfeld (1988).
Wright, Laurie. *"King" Oliver* (1987).
Obituary: *Chicago Defender*, 16 Apr. 1938.
This entry is taken from the *American National Biography* and is published here with the permission of the American Council of Learned Societies.

LAWRENCE GUSHEE

Oliver, Sy (17 Dec. 1910–27 May 1988), jazz arranger, composer, and trumpeter, was born Melvin James Oliver in Battle Creek, Michigan, the son of Melvin Clarence Oliver, a music teacher, concert singer, and choir director. His mother (name unknown) was a music teacher and a church organist. Oliver studied piano from age six but without any special interest in it. Raised in Zanesville, Ohio, from age ten he decided to play trumpet. He bought a cheap cornet and learned so quickly that he was soon performing with local bands. He switched from cornet to its close cousin the trumpet early on. His father had a stroke, and Oliver in his sophomore year in high school began playing professionally with Cliff Barnett's Club Royal Serenaders to help support himself.

Upon graduating from high school Oliver joined Zack Whyte's Chocolate Beau Brummels in 1927 (or perhaps early in 1928). While with Whyte he acquired his nickname, "Psychology," which he later said was given to him simply because it sounded ridiculous. Oliver also explained that he began writing arrangements out of frustration with the band members' inability to memorize what was supposed to be played. Despite these frustrations he praised the band's musical talent highly, and he remained with Whyte until late in 1930, when he spent a few months, extending into 1931, helping ALPHONSO TRENT reconstruct a big band library after Trent lost his music in a nightclub fire in Cleveland. In 1931 Oliver returned to Whyte but also played briefly in the drummer Speed Webb's big band. During this period his home base was Columbus, Ohio, where he worked as a teacher and a freelance arranger while making further intermittent returns to Whyte's band.

In 1933 Oliver married Lillian Clark Farnsworth; they had two children. That same year he joined JIMMIE LUNCEFORD's orchestra. Oliver intended merely to travel with Lunceford to New York, where he would enroll in school, but the orchestra was such a sensation in New York that Oliver stayed on, becoming for many listeners Lunceford's most significant musician. Oliver sang with the band, and he played many trumpet solos, as heard and seen in the film short *Jimmie Lunceford and His Dance Orchestra* (1936), but his performances were far less significant than his writing was.

Throughout his early career Oliver had a reputation as an impossibly impatient, tactless, and ill-tempered man, but Lunceford recognized that this contentiousness was in part a result of Oliver's quick and creative musicality. Under Lunceford's direction, which was disciplinary and inspirational rather than directly musical, Oliver's creativity reached its peak. Among his best arrangements are his own compositions "Stomp It Off" (1934), "For Dancers Only" (1937), and "Le Jazz Hot" (1939); his versions of the popular songs "My Blue Heaven" (1935), "Margie" (1938), and "'Tain't What You Do (It's the Way That You Do It)" (1939); and above all his reworking of "Organ Grinder's Swing" (1936). In "Organ Grinder's Swing" the arrangement of a childlike folk tune—familiar from the lyrics "I like coffee, I like tea"—is merely the launching point for a creative exploration of stark and unusual instrumental groupings and contrasts, inspired in part by DUKE ELLINGTON's "Mood Indigo" and all presented within the context of a lilting rhythmic bounce and politely bluesy harmonies.

Weary of the rigors of the traveling musician's life Oliver left Lunceford in mid-1939, again with the intention of going to school in New York, but instead he immediately joined Tommy Dorsey's orchestra as an arranger when Dorsey made a spectacular offer of a raise in salary of five thousand dollars and no obligation to tour with the band. Oliver's arrangements of "On the Sunny Side of the Street" and his own "Opus No. 1" were perhaps the finest swing tunes that Dorsey's big band

performed. These were probably written in 1943, but owing to the musicians union's recording ban then in force Dorsey did not cut studio versions of these titles until late the following year, by which time Oliver was in his second year as an army bandleader, in which capacity he resumed playing trumpet from 1943 to 1945.

After leading his own band in New York in 1946, Oliver worked for record companies as a music director and supervisor, initially in a decade-long association with Decca. He wrote and conducted arrangements for such notables as LIONEL HAMPTON, BILLIE HOLIDAY, LOUIS ARMSTRONG, ELLA FITZGERALD, SAMMY DAVIS JR., Jackie Gleason, PEARL BAILEY, Gene Kelly, Judy Garland, Frank Sinatra, and Danny Kaye.

In December 1967 Oliver traveled to Paris, where he became musical director at the Olympia Theatre (1968–1969). Back in New York he resumed playing trumpet to lead a nonet that debuted at the Downbeat in April 1969 and then held residencies at the Riverboat, the Rainbow Grill, and the Americana. Oliver reorchestrated his well-known big band arrangements and also arranged many other popular songs for the nonet, as heard on the album *Yes, Indeed!* recorded in Paris in 1973. In 1974 Oliver returned to Europe with the memorial Tommy Dorsey band under the trombonist Warren Covington's direction. From 1974 to 1984 Oliver's nonet held a residency at the Rainbow Room on top of the RCA building in New York. The group also performed at jazz festivals. In the mid-1970s Oliver was one of four musical directors of the short-lived New York Jazz Repertory Orchestra, pioneering an effort to keep jazz masterpieces alive long before the formation of the Lincoln Center Jazz Orchestra. He retired in 1984. Oliver died in New York City.

One of the best arrangers of the swing era, Oliver exhibited in his finest pieces an interest in drawing novel sound combinations from a conventional big band and had the talent of doing so without sacrificing a sense of orchestral balance and relaxed swing.

FURTHER READING

A large collection of scores, parts, and memorabilia is held at the New York Public Library for the Performing Arts, Lincoln Center.

Garrod, Charles. *Sy Oliver and His Orchestra* (1993).

McCarthy, Albert. *Big Band Jazz* (1974).

Schuller, Gunther. *The Swing Era: The Development of Jazz, 1930–1945* (1989).

Travis, Dempsey J. *An Autobiography of Black Jazz* (1983).

Obituary: *New York Times*, 28 May 1988.

This entry is taken from the *American National Biography* and is published here with the permission of the American Council of Learned Societies.

BARRY KERNFELD

O'Neal, Frederick Douglass (27 Aug. 1905–25 Aug. 1992), actor, activist, arts leader, and union organizer, was born in Brooksville, Mississippi, to Minnie Bell Thompson, a former teacher, and Ransome James O'Neal Jr., a teacher who later joined the family business, RJ O'Neal and Son, a general store started by his father, Ransome Sr. Named after the famed abolitionist FREDERICK DOUGLASS, O'Neal was the sixth of eight children. He developed an interest in the theater at an early age and at age eight gave a recitation in grade school that proved to be a formative moment in his decision to pursue acting as a career. His father constructed a little hall next to the family store, where O'Neal, at age ten and eleven, put on small shows. After his father died unexpectedly when O'Neal was fourteen, his mother sold the store and moved her family to St. Louis, Missouri, in 1920. O'Neal, who had attended public school in Brooksville, finished elementary school at Waring School in St. Louis. In 1922 he entered Sumner High School. Soon after, he began to work as a file clerk at the Meyer Brothers Drug Company, a job that necessitated his move to night school. O'Neal also worked the graveyard shift as a post office clerk, further interfering with his desire to become an actor.

During the 1920s and 1930s O'Neal grew even more determined to become an actor. He joined the St. Louis branch of the Urban League in 1920 in order to perform in their annual plays, which included the 1926 production of Shakespeare's *As You Like It*, in which he starred. In 1927, with assistance from the Urban League's director, John Clark, and the entrepreneur ANNIE TURNBO MALONE, O'Neal founded the St. Louis Aldridge Players. Named after the actor IRA ALDRIDGE (and later renamed the Negro Little Theatre of St. Louis), the troupe produced three plays per year and remained in operation until 1940. Dedicated to community service and to the encouragement of black playwrights, the Aldridge Players performed at the St. Louis YMCA, at local high schools, and at Annie Turnbo Malone's Poro Beauty College.

In 1936, on the advice of ZORA NEALE HURSTON, O'Neal left St. Louis for New York to further his acting career. With his previous experience at Meyer Drug Store, he landed a day job working as a laboratory assistant. At night he studied voice, movement, and acting at the New Theatre School and the American Theatre Wing. He also received a scholarship for private lessons. This training provided a solid foundation for his future work in theater and film. And while he had hoped to work with the New York Negro Unit of the Federal Theatre Project before it was disbanded in 1939, he joined the ROSE McCLENDON Players in 1938, remaining with the company until it folded a year later.

Following the dissolution of the Rose McClendon Players, O'Neal and the playwright ABRAM HILL founded the American Negro Theater (ANT) to provide opportunities for black theater artists, writers, and designers. O'Neal served as company manager. Modeled after its insect namesake the "ant," the American Negro Theatre proclaimed itself to be a communal effort eschewing the conventional star system in favor of working diligently and collectively for the good of the whole. ANT's first production, *On Strivers Row*, a satire of the black middle class written by Hill, ran for five months on weekends in the basement theater of the Harlem branch of the public library. *Row* was followed by the folk opera *Natural Man*, a play by THEODORE BROWNE that featured O'Neal in the role of the preacher. In 1944 ANT mounted its most successful production, an adaptation of Philip Yordan's play about a Polish working-class family in a Pennsylvania industrial town, *Anna Lucasta*. The play, costarring O'Neal as Frank, garnered critical acclaim and soon moved to Broadway, where it ran for 956 performances and won O'Neal both the Clarence Derwent Award and the New York Critics Award.

While working with the ANT in 1941, O'Neal met Charlotte Talbot Hainey at a YMCA dance. The couple married on 18 April 1942; they had no children. In October, O'Neal was drafted into the army and stationed at Fort Dix, New Jersey, after which he was transferred to Fort Huachuca, Arizona, where he served until his honorable discharge in 1943. Free from the service, O'Neal returned to his wife and to his career in the theater in New York City.

From the 1940s through the 1960s O'Neal enjoyed a successful movie and stage career. His first film appearance was in the 1949 feature *Pinky*, the Elia Kazan drama about passing, starring Jeanne Crain, ETHEL WATERS, and Ethel Barrymore. O'Neal was cast in a number of lesser film productions, playing a variety of "jungle roles," including King Burlam in *Tarzan's Peril* (1951), a Mau-Mau leader in *Something of Value* (1957), and Buderga in *The Sins of Rachel Cade* (1961). On Broadway, O'Neal costarred as Lem Scott in the 1953 play *Take a Giant Step*. Six years later he recreated the role in the film version, which starred RUBY DEE and the singer Johnny Nash. O'Neal also reprieved the role of Frank in the 1958 film version of *Anna Lucasta* costarring EARTHA KITT and SAMMY DAVIS JR. In 1959 he portrayed Moses in the Hall of Fame production of *The Green Pastures*. In the theater, he appeared in *The Winner* in 1954, as Houngan in *House of Flowers* in 1954, and as the preacher in *God's Trombones* in 1960.

As O'Neal furthered his leadership and activism in the arts, he also performed on television. He was a regular on the television sitcom *Car 54, Where Are You?* in the 1960s. He played in Jack Smight's *Strategy of Terror* (1959); *Free, White and 21* (1963); and OSSIE DAVIS's *Cotton Comes to Harlem* (1970).

At the same time as he found success in his own career, O'Neal fought passionately for the rights of all black actors. Recognizing the unequal treatment of black performers, O'Neal in the 1950s published articles in *Crisis* and *Equity News*, the newsletter of the professional actors' union, Actor's Equity Association (AEA), calling for producers to cast black actors in roles that were not racially specific. He also gave speeches on the need for "nontraditional casting" before groups such as the Catholic Interracial Council. The council, along with the NAACP, organized protests in 1953 against racial representation on network television. As a result of his activism, O'Neal found himself blacklisted by several television networks. This experience led him to become increasingly active in the struggle for the rights of actors and ultimately resulted in his being elected as the first black president of AEA in 1964.

O'Neal's service as president of AEA marked a continuation of his institutional agitation for the equal treatment of black actors. In 1944, as chair of AEA's Hotel Accommodations Committee, he had worked to change the discriminatory housing practices faced by black traveling performers. In 1961, a time when he also functioned as first vice president of the AEA, O'Neal had served as president of the Negro Actors Guild, a branch of AEA dedicated to advocating for the rights of black performers. As AEA president from 1964 through 1973, O'Neal forthrightly advanced the concerns of minority actors. He also lobbied for the establishment of the National Foundation for the Arts and Humanities, which was signed into law by President Lyndon B. Johnson in September 1965. One of the final acts of O'Neal's terms as president was the establishment of the AEA Paul Robeson Citation Award. PAUL ROBESON himself was the first recipient in 1974. That same year, O'Neal assumed the presidency of Associate Actors and Artists of America, the international governing union of actors, and he held this post for eighteen years.

Later in life O'Neal received many accolades. He won the Negro Trade Union Leadership Council Humanitarian Award in 1974, the Frederick Douglass Award in 1975, and the NAACP Man of the Year Award in 1979. The AEA presented him with the 1985 Paul Robeson Citation Award, the award he had helped found. In 1990 he received the Black Filmmakers Hall of Fame Award and was also named an American Theatre Fellow by the John F. Kennedy Center. After a prolonged battle with cancer, he died in his Manhattan home, only four months after he and his wife had celebrated their fiftieth wedding anniversary and two days before his eighty-sixth birthday. On 15 September 1992 friends and family gathered at the Shubert Theater in New York City for a final tribute to Fredrick Douglass O'Neal, a pioneer and leader in the American theater.

FURTHER READING

"Actors' New Boss: Frederick O'Neal Heads Actors' Equity Assn," *Ebony* 19 (June 1964).

Simmons, Renee. *Frederick Douglass O'Neal: Pioneer of the Actor's Equity Association* (1996).

Obituary: *Jet* (14 Sept. 1992).

HARRY ELAM

O'Neal, Ron (1 Sept. 1937–14 Jan. 2004), actor, director, and screenwriter, was born in Utica, New York, and reared in a working-class African American neighborhood in Cleveland, Ohio. His father was a factory worker and his mother was a homemaker. O'Neal was sixteen years old when his father died; he then learned that his father had been a jazz musician in the 1920s and had even played in the pit orchestra for Flournoy Miller's Blackbirds. He believed that hard labor caused his father an untimely death and swore not to be worked to death. Even more, the young O'Neal was driven by the discovery of a clarinet and saxophone his father had kept hidden in the attic for so many years; he saw these musical instruments as symbols for his own vision of a better life. Six months after his father passed, his brother, a truck driver, died in an accident. O'Neal's mother found employment at a hospital to support the family. O'Neal graduated from Glenville High School, then attended Ohio State University in Columbus, Ohio. His tenure at Ohio State lasted only a semester because he was more interested in playing bridge and chess than in studying.

O'Neal had poor grades in college; so at age nineteen he returned home and began painting houses for income. He went with a friend to see *Finian's Rainbow* at Karamu House, an interracial theater in Cleveland dating back to 1913. O'Neal was amazed by the production and within months had joined the ensemble at Karamu and began performing in their productions of Tennessee Williams's *A Street Car Named Desire* and LORRAINE HANSBERRY's *A Raisin in the Sun*, among others. He was not paid for his performances but considered Karamu a good learning opportunity. After eight years with Karamu, O'Neal was offered a job with the Harlem Youth Arts Program and relocated to New York. He auditioned for off-Broadway productions while he taught, and was continually rejected because of his appearance—with a light skin complexion and long straight hair, he failed to meet standard expectations for African American men in theater.

In 1970 he went to an audition for *Ceremonies in Dark Old Men*; when rejected by the producer, he returned wearing an Afro wig and won the part. Simultaneously he was offered a role with the small Joseph Papp Public Theater, playing a bar owner and part-time pimp up against the local mob. Although *Ceremonies* paid $112 per week, O'Neal stopped teaching and chose to go with Papp and the untested production of Charles Gordone's, *No Place to Be Somebody*. Papp loved the production and signed the cast to contracts before the play began a long run at the American National Theater Academy. Gordone became the first African American to win a Pulitzer Prize in drama for the play, and O'Neal was awarded several honors; among them, the Clarence Derwent, Obie, and Drama Desk awards. He took a role in the 1970 film *Move*, with Elliot Gould, and then returned to perform in the three-week Broadway run of *No Place to Be Somebody*. Papp offered him a part in his Shakespeare Summer Series but the new director did not believe that blacks should perform Shakespeare; O'Neal appreciated his honesty and moved on.

In 1971 O'Neal landed a role in a film with SIDNEY POITIER, *The Organization*. He also joined the Negro Ensemble Company for the Los Angeles and New York run of *The Dream on Monkey Mountain*. The year 1971 ushered in the era of blaxploitation films with two releases in particular, *Shaft* by GORDON PARKS SR., and MELVIN VAN PEEBLES's action film, *Sweet Sweetback's Baad Asssss Song*. O'Neal and his good friend Phillip Fenty, who ran a successful advertising agency, hoped soon to be a part of the blaxploitation trend. Despite his current profession, Fenty was writing a screenplay with O'Neal in mind to portray the lead character. Ultimately, Gordon Parks Jr. was enlisted as director of Fenty's screenplay, *Superfly*, released in 1972. As promised, O'Neal portrayed Youngblood Priest, a Harlem cocaine dealer who had grown tired of street life and designed a plan to amount a small fortune before leaving the business. Corrupt law enforcers and lethal mobsters threaten his freedom and life; yet, Priest escapes unscathed with his fortune intact, a hero. Warner Brothers studio had feared negative publicity behind cries from the NAACP against negative images in *Superfly*; however, O'Neal maintained that Priest was trying to escape the lifestyle, not glorify it. The film owed much of its publicity to word of mouth and a stellar soundtrack produced by musical genius, Curtis Mayfield. It was an instant success for O'Neal and was immediately hailed as a blaxploitation classic. O'Neal directed the 1973 sequel *Superfly TNT*; and again portrayed Priest; now living in Europe, Priest misses his former lifestyle and gets involved in illegal operations inspired by African rebels. The film received poor reviews, and soon Blaxploitation would become the object of cult fans.

O'Neal was typecast by his portrayal of Youngblood Priest and found difficulty winning solid roles. He primarily appeared in action films and as supporting character; *Billy Jack* (1975), *A Force of One* (1979), *When a Stranger Calls* (1979), *Brave New World* (1980), *The Final Countdown* (1980), *St. Helens* (1981), and *Red Dawn* (1984). His first television role came opposite MUHAMMAD ALI in *Freedom Road* (1979). Other television roles followed, with O'Neal portraying a featured character on *Hill Street Blues, Living Single, A Different World, Frank's Place*, and the Civil War miniseries *North and South*. In 1991 he directed *Up against the Wall* featuring the actors Marla Gibbs and Stoney Jackson, and the newcomer Catero Colbert. In 1996 O'Neal was cast in the film *Original Gangstas*, featuring many stars from the blaxploitation genre together for the first time; including RICHARD ROUNDTREE, PAM GRIER, and JIM BROWN.

On 10 November 1973 O'Neal married Carol Tillery Banks; they divorced in 1980. Later he married Audrey Poole. O'Neal was diagnosed with pancreatic cancer in 2000; he died on 14 January 2004 at Cedars-Sinai Medical Center in Los Angeles, California.

FURTHER READING

Briggs, John Bob. *Turning Points in Film History* (2004).

Howard, Josiah. *Blaxploitation Cinema: The Essential Reference Guide* (2008).

Walker, David, Christopher Watson, and Andrew J. Rausch. *Reflections on Blaxploitation: Actors and Directors Speak* (2009).

SAFIYA DALILAH HOSKINS

O'Neal, Shaquille Rashaun (6 Mar. 1972–), basketball player, actor, and rapper, was born in Newark, New Jersey, to Lucille O'Neal and Joseph Tooney. Within six months of O'Neal's birth, Tooney left Lucille O'Neal. Shaquille and his three half-siblings were raised by Lucille and army sergeant Philip Harrison. O'Neal grew up as an "army brat," relocating with his family to military bases in New Jersey, Georgia, Germany, and San Antonio, Texas. By the time he was thirteen, O'Neal had already grown to six-feet-five. His lack of coordination and recurring status as the "new kid" led him to feel like an outcast without many close friends.

O'Neal's life changed dramatically once he began to participate in sports. Although athletic success did not come immediately (he failed to make his high school basketball team as a freshman), O'Neal eventually became a dominant athlete, leading San Antonio's Robert G. Cole Senior High School to a 68-1 record during his two years there, including a 36-0 record his senior year, when he was named High School Player of the Year and helped his school to capture the state championship. After he graduated from Cole in 1989, he accepted a basketball scholarship from Louisiana State University (LSU). By the time he enrolled in college, O'Neal and then-LSU coach Dale Brown had already enjoyed a long relationship. Brown first met O'Neal at a basketball camp on the U.S. Army base in Wildflecken, West Germany, when O'Neal was thirteen. During his three years at LSU, O'Neal was twice named First Team All-American and the Southeastern Conference (SEC) Player of the Year. He was named NCAA Men's Basketball Player of the Year in 1991.

Shaquille O'Neal hangs onto the rim after a slam dunk in the final moments of the first half against the University of Connecticut in the NCAA Midwest Regionals in Minneapolis, Minnesota, 14 March 1991. (AP Images.)

After his junior season, O'Neal entered the 1992 NBA Draft and was selected by the Orlando Magic as the first overall pick. Immediately, O'Neal's power and quickness troubled opposing defenses, who often were forced to choose between fouling O'Neal or trying to defend him with two or three players. O'Neal's best move was his explosive drop step, which O'Neal nicknamed the "Black Tornado." O'Neal won the 1993 Rookie of the Year Award, averaging over twenty-three points and nearly fourteen rebounds per game. Between his first and second seasons, O'Neal starred as a top college basketball recruit in the film *Blue Chips*, with Nick Nolte. O'Neal would appear in two other films over the next few years: *Kazaam* (1994) (as a three-thousand-year-old genie), and *Steel* (1997), as John Henry Irons, whose alter ego is a superhero named "Steel" who is committed to fighting street gangs. Although critics panned O'Neal's films, many audience members—particularly children—loved them. O'Neal also made cameo appearances in a number of feature films, including *Scary Movie 4* (2006), *Freddy Got Fingered* (2001), and *He Got Game* (1998).

Also between his first two seasons, O'Neal recorded his first rap album, *Shaq Diesel* (1993). Though not critically acclaimed, O'Neal's musical career was nevertheless financially successful. *Shaq Diesel*, driven by the hit single "I Know I Got Skillz," was certified platinum within a year of its release, and his 1994 release, *Shaq-Fu: Da Return*, was certified gold in January 1995. O'Neal went on to release *The Best of Shaquille O'Neal* (1996), *You Can't Stop the Reign* (1996), *Respect* (1998), and *Shaq O'Neal Presents His Superfriends, Vol. 1* (2001).

O'Neal followed his successful rookie season by leading the Magic into the playoffs for the first time in franchise history, averaging over twenty-nine points per game and leading the NBA by hitting 60 percent of his field goals. After the season, he helped the United States win the 1994 FIBA World Championship. He led the NBA in scoring his third season as he led his team to the NBA Finals in 1995, where the Houston Rockets, led by the veteran center Hakeem Olajuwon, swept the Magic in four games. Olajuwon, whom O'Neal often called the best center he ever faced, dominated O'Neal in the series but was nonetheless impressed by O'Neal's ability to control the flow of a game, particularly at the offensive end.

Following the 1995–1996 season, in which he missed twenty-eight games due to injury, O'Neal became a free agent. He eventually signed a $121 million, seven-year contract with the Los Angeles Lakers. The summer before his first season with the Lakers, O'Neal helped the United States win the gold medal in men's basketball at the 1996 Olympics in Atlanta. At the 1997 NBA All-Star Game, despite his relatively short tenure in the league, O'Neal was named one of the Fifty Greatest Players in NBA History.

For his first three seasons with the Lakers, O'Neal struggled with injuries that caused him to miss a significant number of games. Meanwhile, Lakers' GM Jerry West struggled to find the right mix of players, as well as the best coach, to put the Lakers' in a situation to compete for the NBA championship. In addition to playing basketball, O'Neal worked on completing his coursework at LSU, and on 15 December 2000 he earned a B.A. in General Studies with a political science minor. (He went on to earn an MBA from the University of Phoenix on 26 June 2005). Also, O'Neal began to explore his longtime interest in law enforcement. He attended the Police Academy in Los Angeles and became a reserve officer with the L.A. Port Police.

By the start of the 1999–2000 season, West had assembled a team of able role players around O'Neal and the teenage prodigy Kobe Bryant. In addition, West hired Phil Jackson, who had coached the Chicago Bulls to six titles, as the team's new head coach. O'Neal and Bryant thrived in the "triangle offense" designed by Jackson and Assistant Coach Tex Winter, and they went on to lead the Lakers to NBA titles in 2000, 2001, and 2002. Along the way, the two formed a symbiotic relationship, with O'Neal serving as a mentor for Bryant, to whom O'Neal often referred as his little brother. O'Neal won the 1999–2000 Most Valuable Player Award as he finished first in scoring, second in rebounds, and third in blocked shots. Following the run of championships, O'Neal and the Lakers struggled through two straight playoff losses, which led to major roster changes and eventually to the Lakers shifting the focus of the team from O'Neal to the younger and healthier Kobe Bryant, whose relationship with O'Neal had cooled significantly by the 2002–2003 season. Even after the Lakers offered him a contract extension in February 2004, O'Neal felt slighted by the team, declining the extension, and demanding a trade.

O'Neal wedded Shaunie Nelson, an entertainment and sports reporter, in 2002. The couple had four children together (two sons, Shareef and Shaqir, and two daughters, Amirah and Me'arah). Nelson's son, Myles, and O'Neal's daughter, Taahirah—both were children from previous relationships—gave the couple a total of six children. On 14 July 2004 O'Neal was traded to the Miami Heat for Lamar Odom, Caron Butler, Brian Grant, and a future first-round draft choice. In Miami, O'Neal quickly formed a relationship with the dynamic guard Dwayne Wade similar to the one he once had with Kobe Bryant, serving as a mentor for the younger player on and off the court. To celebrate the trade, the city of Miami held a parade, at which O'Neal promised to bring a championship to Miami. In his second season with the Heat, as the team's second offensive option behind Wade, O'Neal did just that, helping Miami defeat the Dallas Mavericks for its first NBA Championship. In addition to continuing his basketball career in Miami, O'Neal also continued his career in law enforcement. On 2 March 2005 he became an honorary U.S. Deputy Marshal and the spokesman for the Safe Surfin' Foundation, which pursues sexual predators who attempt to lure children over the Internet. On 8 December 2005 O'Neal was sworn in as a Miami Beach reserve officer.

A fifteen-time All Star, one-time NBA MVP, four-time NBA champion, three-time NBA Finals MVP, and fourteen-time member of the All-NBA First Team, Shaquille O'Neal was one of the most dominant centers in NBA history. He was the only player to average at least twenty points and ten rebounds per game in a season for thirteen consecutive seasons. In addition, he was one of only seven players to score twenty-five thousand points and collect ten thousand rebounds in his career, one of only four to win NBA Finals MVP three times, and was one of only two to win the award in three consecutive seasons.

O'Neal also held the dubious honor of being one of the worst free throw shooters in NBA history. At the end of his career in 2011, he had a career percentage of 52.7. Don Nelson was the first of many opposing coaches to invoke the "Hack-a-Shaq" strategy, fouling O'Neal late in games because his performance at the free-throw line suggested he would miss. This one glaring weakness in his game was not lost on O'Neal, as evidenced in his remarks on 26 February 2007, when he became the fourteenth player in NBA history to score twenty-five thousand career points: "I am kind of disappointed in myself," he told the Associated Press, "because if I make free throws I'd be at thirty thousand rather than twenty-five thousand."

O'Neal left the Heat for the Phoenix Suns in the 2007-2008 season, helping them to the 2008 playoffs, but failing to make the postseason for the first and only time in his career in 2008-2009. He then joined the Cleveland Cavaliers, and, in a supporting role to LeBron James helped the Cavs to finish as the best team in the regular 2009-2010 season. He failed, however, to "win a ring for the king [James]" when the Boston Celtics defeated the Cavaliers in the Eastern Conference semifinals. O'Neal's last season was with the Celtics, again making the playoffs, although his minutes were greatly restricted by injuries. O'Neal retired after nineteen seasons in June 2011. He averaged 23.7 points and 10.9 rebounds throughout his career and was expected by most observers to make the NBA Hall of Fame at his first attempt.

FURTHER READING

O'Neal, Shaquille. *Shaq Talks Back* (2001).
Jackson, Phil, with Michael Arkush. *The Last Season: A Team in Search of Its Soul* (2004).
Nelson, Murry R. *Shaquille O'Neal: A Biography* (2006).

DANIEL DONAGHY

O'Neal, Stanley (7 Oct. 1951–), corporate executive, was born Earnest Stanley O'Neal in Roanoke, Alabama, the oldest of four children of Earnest O'Neal, a farmer, and Ann Scales, a domestic. The family lived in a small farming town called Wedowee, but because its hospital would not admit African Americans, he was born in the neighboring town of Roanoke. The grandson of a former slave, O'Neal lived with his family in poverty. Although his house had no indoor plumbing, it was inhabited by a loving extended family of aunts, uncles, and cousins. With a population less than eight hundred, Wedowee offered scarce resources. O'Neal was educated in a one-room schoolhouse heated with a wooden stove and with one teacher to instruct all the grades. Outside the classroom, he and his siblings spent hours picking cotton on their grandfather's fields. Very early on, O'Neal's father told him that he was not the farming type and advised him to explore other options for his future.

These options increased when the family moved to Atlanta, Georgia, in the 1960s. When they arrived, the O'Neals moved into a federal housing project, which Stanley welcomed because "it was 'ten stories higher' than anything he had ever known" (*Fortune*, 28 Apr. 1997). O'Neal attended West Fulton High School, where he was one of the first black students. In addition to his schoolwork, he took on various odd jobs to help his family. His father got a job on the General Motors (GM) assembly line in Doraville, Georgia, just as the factory was being integrated. After high school graduation, O'Neal reached a turning point in his life when GM offered him the chance to study at the General Motors Institute (now Kettering University). He studied in six-week stints, alternating between work in a factory and his education in the classroom. He graduated with a B.S. in industrial administration in 1974, the first in his family to graduate from college. He was ranked in the top 20 percent of his class and accepted an offer to become a supervisor at the very factory where his father worked. After some time working there, GM gave him a scholarship to study at Harvard Business School. He graduated in 1978 and set off for New York City to work in one of the most dynamic business environments in the world.

Awaiting him in New York City was a job as an analyst for GM. O'Neal moved up the corporate ladder quickly, his rise fueled by his strong command of numbers and a work ethic that had him sitting in his office till 10:00 P.M. on a regular basis. After two years he became a director, and in

Stanley O'Neal, Merrill Lynch chief financial officer rides an escalator into the company's World Financial Headquarters in New York, 27 March 2002. (AP Images.)

1982 he moved to Spain to become treasurer of the company's Spanish division. In 1984 he returned to New York as GM's assistant treasurer. In the treasury office he worked with his future wife, Nancy Garvey, an economist. The two married in 1983 and had twins, a son and a daughter.

Another turning point in O'Neal's life came in 1986, when he decided that he was ready for new challenges and a new industry. Having clearly demonstrated that he understood the language of numbers at GM, he decided to go to Wall Street to join the financial services firm Merrill Lynch. O'Neal first made a name for himself in the company's corporate finance division, a lucrative area that he understood, because he had had to deal with many investment bankers at GM. Within five years he was chosen to head Merrill Lynch's high-yield department.

O'Neal came to this position at a time when high-yield bonds, more commonly known as "junk bonds," were distrusted because of a scandal involving Drexel Burnham Lambert, another Wall Street firm. Despite the tough market, Merrill Lynch rose to the top of this field, acting as lead manager of deals worth $3.9 billion. For the rest of O'Neal's tenure as head of the group, the firm remained at or near the top of the industry, resulting in O'Neal's selection as head of Merrill's entire capital markets division in 1996. After he left, the high-yield department dropped to eighth place in industry rankings.

In 1998 O'Neal moved to the top management level at Merrill Lynch when he was named chief financial officer, his first administrative job. This signaled to Wall Street insiders that he was in the running to be the firm's chief executive officer. It provided another chance for O'Neal to prove his leadership qualities, because in the fall of that year a Russian financial crisis and the collapse of a powerful hedge fund named Long-Term Capital Management sent the bond markets into a free fall. Merrill Lynch found itself stuck with bonds dropping in value, and O'Neal took charge of navigating the firm through the tough time.

From there, O'Neal's ascent was meteoric. In February 2000 he was named the head of the firm's private client group, a significant position, because Merrill Lynch has the largest brokerage on Wall Street. He was the first person to run the fifteen thousand brokers who himself had never been a broker. In the summer of 2001 O'Neal was named president and chief operating officer, and in December 2002 he took over as chief executive officer. He was the first African American to head a major firm on Wall Street.

As O'Neal stepped into his new historic position, he also inherited a number of challenges. One problem came from the moribund economic climate that had emerged after the boom years of the 1990s. Fewer companies were going public, stock prices had declined dramatically, and the drop in activity had shrunk profits on Wall Street. In addition to these inauspicious market conditions, Merrill Lynch was trying to escape scandal. Months before O'Neal took over as CEO, the firm had agreed to a $100 million fine to settle a probe issued by the New York State's attorney general's office that charged Merrill research analysts with issuing false praise of corporations to win investment-banking business.

Taking the helm at Merrill Lynch, O'Neal's vision was to "build a 'new kind of financial-services firm' that redefines Wall Street by offering a far greater range of services" (*BusinessWeek*, 5 May 2003). In order to do so he embarked on a ruthless process of cutting costs and shredding staff. Within three years of his becoming CEO, twenty thousand jobs were cut and hundreds of offices deemed superfluous were closed. O'Neal was determined to replace the old boys' club atmosphere of Merrill with a meritocracy. His restructuring of Merrill bore fruit.

Profits soared and Merrill once again had margins to rival its major competitors. Described as cool and calm and willing to make tough decisions, it appeared that O'Neal had once again demonstrated an ability to help get his team out of complicated financial problems.

Certainly, O'Neal's rapid rise drew such great attention that in 2002 *Fortune* named him the "Most Powerful Black Executive in America." By 2007, however, the culture of risky investment he fostered—notably in subprime mortgage bonds—caused Merrill Lynch to lose $8 billion in its third quarter, as subprime mortgage defaults led to a housing market crash. It was the company's largest quarterly loss in its history. The Merrill Lynch board further criticized O'Neal for claiming as late as July 2007 that the subprime crisis had been contained, and for seeking to negotiate a merger with Wachovia Bank without the Board's permission. On 30 October, under strong pressure from the board, O'Neal stepped down as chairman and CEO of the company he had worked for for twenty-one years. Many commentators were highly critical of his severance package of $161.5 million.

FURTHER READING

Bell, Gregory S. *In the Black: A History of African Americans on Wall Street* (2001).

Cassidy, John. "Subprime Suspect: The Rise and Fall of Wall Street's First Black CEO," *The New Yorker* (31 Mar. 2008: 78-91).

Clarke, Robin D. "Running with the Bulls," *Black Enterprise* (Sept. 2000).

Thornton, Emily. "The New Merrill Lynch," *Business Week* (5 May 2003).

GREGORY S. BELL

O'Neil, Buck (13 Nov. 1911–6 Oct. 2006), Negro League baseball player, coach, and manager, was born John Jordan O'Neil Jr. to John Jordan O'Neil Sr., a farm and sawmill laborer and small-business owner, and Luella O'Neil, a homemaker and cook, in Carrabelle, Florida. O'Neil realized early on that his baseball talents could earn him a ticket out of the area's celery fields, and he began playing semipro ball at the age of twelve. He received his nickname through a case of mistaken identity in his twenties. A bootlegger named "Buck" O'Neal owned the all-black Miami Giants. When O'Neil left Florida to play on national barnstorming teams he was billed as "Buck"—perhaps as a result of innocent confusion, but more likely in an effort to

capitalize on O'Neal's name recognition—and the moniker stuck.

O'Neil attended segregated public schools in Sarasota, Florida, and Edward Waters College in Jacksonville. He left college before earning his degree to join the Tampa Black Smokers, his first truly professional team, and he soon signed on with the more established Miami Giants. Professional baseball was almost totally segregated during O'Neil's era. Black ballplayers had to scuffle to make a living; they jumped from team to team often, and their brand of baseball was geared as much toward pure entertainment as it was toward competition. O'Neil, for instance, left Florida and played for a time with the Zulu Cannibal Giants, a gimmicky barnstorming team whose players "painted their faces, put rings in their noses, and played in straw dresses." In retrospect, O'Neil wrote, "the idea of playing with the Cannibal Giants was demeaning"(O'Neil et al., 70). He and other Negro Leaguers insisted in later years, however, that even if their brand of baseball had been separate, their best players had been equal to—if not better than—the best white players of their day.

O'Neil played on a succession of teams that traveled throughout the United States, Canada, and Mexico during the depths of the Great Depression. As a native southerner, he was initially taken aback by the fair treatment he received in places such as Dunseith, North Dakota: "You'd think it might be just the opposite," he wrote, "but it was some kind of compensation or something.... They didn't have all these Jim Crow rules because the issue hardly ever came up" (O'Neil et al., 64–65).

O'Neil reached the pinnacle of his profession in 1937 when he signed with the Kansas City Monarchs of the Negro American League, arguably the most elite franchise in all of black baseball. Between 1937 and 1947 O'Neil won two individual batting titles and the Monarchs won seven pennants and a Negro World Series championship behind SATCHEL PAIGE, their Bunyanesque pitcher, and O'Neil, the team's first baseman. In 1948 O'Neil became the club's manager, though he continued to play in the field. He led the team to another four Negro American League pennants in his seven seasons at the helm. O'Neil played in three East-West All-Star Classics, the Negro Leagues' all-star games that filled Southside Chicago's Comiskey Park with enthusiastic spectators, and managed the West team on four occasions. His teams won all four games. As a member of the barnstorming Satchel

Paige All-Stars, O'Neil won six of thirteen games during the 1946 off-season against a team of top white major leaguers, the Bob Feller All-Stars. O'Neil married Ora Lee Owens in 1946; the couple would have no children.

Buck O'Neil positively loved being a *black* baseball player. He relished his celebrity and rubbed shoulders with jazz greats in luxurious black hotels across the United States. BILL "COUNT" BASIE and LIONEL HAMPTON, among many other jazz artists, became his close friends (O'Neil considered jazz and black baseball the two most important cultural forms created by African Americans in the twentieth century). His playing career was interrupted in 1945 when he was drafted into the U. S. Navy. He served for two years in a stevedore battalion in the Marianas and the Philippines and chafed under the segregated conditions. "What made it worse," he later wrote, "was that our own government, which was putting our lives on the line for freedom, was the one telling us to sit at the back of the bus" (O'Neil et al., 159). O'Neil joined the NAACP while in the service, and he remained active in the organization throughout his life.

After JACKIE ROBINSON, a former Monarchs shortstop, broke the color barrier of Major League Baseball with the Brooklyn Dodgers in 1947, the Negro Leagues became something of a farm system for the majors. Seventeen Monarchs would eventually play for major league teams, and for a time the team stayed in business only by selling players' contracts to teams in the previously all-white leagues. The desegregation of the major leagues killed the institution of black baseball little by little. By 1954 O'Neil and the Monarchs had resorted to playing a female second baseman as a publicity stunt, and after the 1955 season the Monarchs franchise, one of the last four remaining in the Negro American League, was sold to a Michigan promoter and all but disbanded. O'Neil went to work as a scout for the Chicago Cubs.

The first player O'Neil signed for the Cubs was his young shortstop from the Monarchs, ERNIE BANKS. Banks, who would become the very face of the Cubs franchise, hit 512 home runs in a Hall of Fame career. O'Neil became a coach for the Cubs in 1962, making him the first African American coach in the majors, but he never had a chance to assume on-field duties for the team because of lingering prejudice in Major League Baseball. He called that "one of the few disappointments I've had in over sixty years in baseball" (O'Neil et al., 230).

O'Neil returned to scouting, first for the Cubs and later for the Kansas City Royals, in 1964. In addition to Banks and many others, O'Neil would sign such future African American superstars as LOU BROCK, another member of the Hall of Fame; Lee Smith, the game's all-time saves leader; and Joe Carter, hero of the 1993 World Series. O'Neil claimed to have a "tremendous advantage" in scouting and signing black players. "A white man watching a game between Savannah State and Morris Brown might as well hang a sign around his neck saying, 'Major League Scout,'" he wrote. "On the other hand … coaches and managers told me things they would never tell a white scout" (O'Neil et al., 219).

Buck O'Neil became an overnight national celebrity in 1994 at the age of eighty-three with the screening of Ken Burns's multipart documentary film *Baseball* on American public television. The film introduced O'Neil and his infectious thousand-watt smile to a much larger audience and generated a widespread interest in the history of Negro League baseball. O'Neil used his newfound celebrity shrewdly, publicizing the Negro Leagues Baseball Museum in Kansas City, Missouri, whose board of directors he chaired.

A member of the Veterans Committee of the National Baseball Hall of Fame in Cooperstown, New York, O'Neil was instrumental in the elevation of several Negro Leaguers to the sport's pantheon. He was also active with Reviving Baseball in Inner Cities, a program sponsored by Major League Baseball to promote the game among minority youth, and the Baseball Assistance Team (BAT), which provided former ballplayers—and Negro Leaguers in particular—with financial and medical assistance.

O'Neil promoted the immensely colorful folklore of the Negro Leaguers, but he also applied empirical methods to recognize their greatness. An anecdote from his memoirs illustrated this proclivity. He repeated the oft-told tale of JAMES T. "COOL PAPA" BELL, the outfielder who, it was said, was so swift that "he could turn out the light and get in bed before the room turned dark." O'Neil then explained that Bell had once noticed that the light switch in a hotel room he shared with Satchel Paige had a short in it. Bell wagered Paige that he could turn off the switch and jump in bed before the room turned dark. Because the short caused a delay, he won the bet. By reporting the literal truth of this claim, O'Neil somehow made Bell seem even faster (and more clever) than the tall tale did, and the legend lived on. In any case, more than any other individual, O'Neil was responsible for seeing that Negro Leaguers received their due. As he said in a eulogy at Paige's 1982 funeral, "People say it's a shame that Satchel Paige never got to pitch against the best. But who's to say he didn't?"(O'Neil et al., 240)

Baseball would disappoint O'Neil one last time in 2006, when the Baseball Hall of Fame Veterans Committee he had once served on inexplicably failed to select O'Neil for inclusion at Cooperstown. He died at a Kansas City hospital on 6 October 2006. On December 7 of that year he was posthumously awarded the Presidential Medal of Freedom, the United States' highest civilian honor.

FURTHER READING

O'Neil, Buck, with Steve Wulf and David Conrads.
    I Was Right on Time: My Journey from the Negro Leagues to the Majors (1996).
Obituary: *New York Times*, 8 Oct. 2006.

J. TODD MOYE

Onesimus (fl. 1706–1717), slave and medical pioneer, was born in the late seventeenth century, probably in Africa, although the precise date and place of his birth are unknown. He first appears in the historical record in the diary of Cotton Mather, a prominent New England theologian and minister of Boston's Old North Church. The Reverend Mather notes in a diary entry for 13 December 1706 that members of his congregation purchased for him "a very likely *Slave*; a young Man who is a *Negro* of a promising aspect of temper" (Mather, vol. 1, 579). Mather named him Onesimus, after a biblical slave who escaped from his master, an early Christian named Philemon.

This biblical Onesimus fled from his home in Colossae (in present-day Turkey) to the apostle Paul, who was imprisoned in nearby Ephesus. Paul converted Onesimus to Christianity and sent him back to Philemon with a letter, which appears in the New Testament as Paul's Epistle to Philemon. In that letter Paul asks Philemon to accept Onesimus "not now as a servant, but above a servant, a brother beloved" (Philemon 1:16). Mather similarly hoped to make his new slave "a Servant of Christ," and in a tract, *The Negro Christianized* (1706), encouraged other slave owners to do likewise, believing that Christianity "wonderfully Dulcifies, and Mollifies, and moderates the Circumstances" of bondage (Silverman, 264).

Onesimus was one of about a thousand persons of African descent living in the Massachusetts colony in the early 1700s, one-third of them in Boston. Many were indentured servants with rights comparable to those of white servants, though an increasing number of blacks—and blacks only—were classified as chattel and bound as slaves for life. Moreover, after 1700, white fears of burglary and insurrection by blacks and Indians prompted the Massachusetts assembly to impose tighter restrictions on the movements of people of color, whether slave, servant, or free. Cotton Mather was similarly concerned in 1711 about keeping a "strict Eye" on Onesimus, "especially with regard unto his Company," and he also hoped that his slave would repent for "some Actions of a thievish aspect" (Mather, vol. 2, 139). Mather believed, moreover, that he could improve Onesimus's behavior by employing the "Principles of Reason, agreeably offered unto him" and by teaching him to read, write, and learn the Christian catechism (Mather, vol. 2, 222).

What Onesimus thought of Mather's opinions the historical record does not say, nor do we know much about his family life other than that he was married and had a son, Onesimulus, who died in 1714. Two years later Onesimus gave the clearest indication of his attitude toward his bondage by attempting to purchase his release from Mather. To do so, he gave his master money toward the purchase of another black youth, Obadiah, to serve in his place. Mather probably welcomed the suggestion, since he reports in his diary for 31 August 1716 that Onesimus "proves wicked, and grows useless, Froward [ungovernable] and Immorigerous [rebellious]." Around that time Mather signed a document releasing Onesimus from his service "that he may Enjoy and Employ his whole Time for his own purposes and as he pleases" (Mather, vol. 2, 363). However, the document makes clear that Onesimus's freedom was conditional on performing chores for the Mather family when needed, including shoveling snow, piling firewood, fetching water, and carrying corn to the mill. This contingent freedom was also dependent upon his returning a sum of five pounds allegedly stolen from Mather.

Little is known of Onesimus after he purchased his freedom, but in 1721 Cotton Mather used information he had learned five years earlier from his former slave to combat a devastating smallpox epidemic that was then sweeping Boston. In a 1716 letter to the Royal Society of London, Mather proposed "ye Method of Inoculation" as the best means of curing smallpox and noted that he had learned of this process from "my Negro-Man *Onesimus*, who is a pretty Intelligent Fellow" (Winslow, 33). Onesimus explained that he had

> undergone an Operation, which had given him something of ye Small-Pox, and would forever preserve him from it, adding, That it was often used among [Africans] and whoever had ye Courage to use it, was forever free from the Fear of ye Contagion. He described ye Operation to me, and showed me in his Arm ye Scar (Winslow, 33).

Reports of similar practices in Turkey further persuaded Mather to mount a public inoculation campaign. Most white doctors rejected this process of deliberately infecting a person with smallpox—now called variolation—in part because of their misgivings about African medical knowledge. Public and medical opinion in Boston was strongly against both Mather and Dr. Zabdiel Boylston, the only doctor in town willing to perform inoculations; one opponent even threw a grenade into Mather's home. A survey of the nearly six thousand people who contracted smallpox between 1721 and 1723 found, however, that Onesimus, Mather, and Boylston had been right. Only 2 percent of the six hundred Bostonians inoculated against smallpox died, while 14 percent of those who caught the disease but were not inoculated succumbed to the illness.

It is unclear when or how Onesimus died, but his legacy is unambiguous. His knowledge of variolation gives the lie to one justification for enslaving Africans, namely, white Europeans' alleged superiority in medicine, science, and technology. This bias made the smallpox epidemic of 1721 more deadly than it need have been. Bostonians and other Americans nonetheless adopted the African practice of inoculation in future smallpox outbreaks, and variolation remained the most effective means of treating the disease until the development of vaccination by Edward Jenner in 1796.

FURTHER READING

Herbert, Eugenia W. "Smallpox Inoculation in Africa," *Journal of African History* 16 (1975).

Mather, Cotton. *Diary* (1912).

Silverman, Kenneth. *The Life and Times of Cotton Mather* (1984).

Winslow, Ola. *A Destroying Angel: The Conquest of Smallpox in Colonial Boston* (1974).

STEVEN J. NIVEN

O'Ree, Willie (15 Oct. 1935–), hockey player, was born William Eldon O'Ree in Fredricton, New

Willie O'Ree, the first black player of the National Hockey League, warms up in his Boston Bruins uniform before the game with the New York Rangers at New York's Madison Square Garden, 23 November 1960. (AP Images.)

Brunswick, Canada, to Harry Douglas O'Ree, a civil servant, and Rosebud Wright. The youngest of thirteen children, O'Ree took to the ice almost as soon as he could walk. In the frigid Maritime Provinces of Canada, it was common for the streets to be covered in ice for months during the long winters; he often found skating easier than walking. The O'Rees, one of only two black families in town, were well respected. His childhood was largely absent of racial discrimination, although there remained places in Fredricton that were off-limits to blacks.

O'Ree played hockey for the first time at five years of age and proved to be innately talented. By the time he was fifteen he had won a spot with the local amateur club, the Fredricton Junior Capitals. A left-handed shooter with outstanding speed, he excelled at the left wing position. But his career nearly came to a premature end while playing for the Kitchener-Waterloo Junior Canucks in 1955. As a teammate fired a shot, he rushed to the goal hoping for a rebound. He collided with another player, fell to the ice, and was hit in the face by the puck. The incident left O'Ree 95 percent blind in his right eye. Doctors recommended he quit hockey, but with his left eye undamaged he had a better solution:

switch to the right wing position. Concealing the injury, he was signed out of juniors by the Quebec Aces in 1956. His first professional contract paid him the handsome sum of $4,000.

Although O'Ree was not the first black hockey player, Canada's small black population made him stand out. During some games he would be the only black person in the entire arena. No black players had made it to the apex of the sport—the National Hockey League. The league was composed exclusively of Canadian players at the time, and blacks made up less than 0.25 percent of the population. With only six teams and 120 players in the entire league, the absence of black players was more a matter of statistical probability than discrimination. But discrimination existed. In the 1930s perhaps the finest hockey player in Canada was Herb Carnegie, a three-time MVP of the elite Quebec League. Toronto Maple Leafs' founder Conn Smythe was amazed by Carnegie, but instead of offering him an NHL contract he announced that he would "give $10,000 to (anyone) who can turn Herbie Carnegie white" (O'Ree and McKinley, 48). Playing in the Quebec League was O'Ree's first significant exposure to widespread racism. He had not heard his first racial insult until the age of twelve, but playing hockey as an adult provided enough slurs to last a lifetime. Fights, both on the ice and in the stands, were common for him, but he continued to play hard. He felt that the NHL was within his reach.

After two stellar seasons with the Aces, the Boston Bruins of the NHL invited him to try out in 1957. He was cut, but his disappointment was short-lived. The Bruins phoned O'Ree during the winter of 1958 to inform him that he was being called up. On 18 January 1958 Willie O'Ree became the JACKIE ROBINSON of hockey when he stepped on the ice of the Montreal Forum in a contest between the Bruins and the Montreal Canadiens. He was sent back to the Aces after just two games, but he returned to the Bruins in 1960. He played in forty-three games, scoring four goals, but the season was marred by an incident during a game against the Black Hawks in Chicago.

Chicago's Eric Nesterenko approached him, shouted a racial slur, and hit him with his stick, breaking his nose and knocking out two teeth. O'Ree opened a large cut on Nesterenko's head in response. Racial tensions in the United States were much higher than in Canada, and the media insinuated that O'Ree was the aggressor in the fight. Fans escalated the racial abuse he received during every road game. It is unclear whether the incident influenced the Bruins' decision to trade him after the season, but he was sent to Montreal. The Canadiens were by far the league's best team, and O'Ree knew he could not crack their roster. They sent him to the minor leagues and he never returned to the NHL. In 1962 he married Bernardine Plummer; the couple would have two sons.

His professional career did not end when he left Boston. He was traded to the Los Angeles Blades of the Western Hockey League (WHL), where he won the league scoring title in 1964. His travel schedule was strenuous, though, and his long absences contributed to his divorce from Plummer in 1966. He moved on to play for the San Diego Gulls, winning another scoring title in 1968. In that year he also had a chance encounter with a young Indian immigrant sportswriter in Victoria, British Columbia. O'Ree happened to meet the man's sister, Deljeet, after the interview and in less than a year, on 6 November 1969, they were married; they would have a daughter.

When the WHL folded in 1974, an aging O'Ree hung up his skates. He briefly returned in 1978 to play for the new San Diego Hawks, but the impending birth of his daughter made his second retirement permanent. O'Ree and his family continued living in San Diego, where he worked for a security firm. In 1998 he joined the NHL Diversity Task Force, a position in which he continued to be active in the early twenty-first century.

Willie O'Ree's career defied the odds. He broke the NHL color barrier while playing blind in one eye. His stay in the NHL was brief, but the significance of his career is not measured by the number of goals he scored. He inspired a new generation of black players who hoped to follow in his footsteps. Upon being the first black player inducted into the Hockey Hall of Fame in 2003, GRANT FUHR's acceptance speech began with the phrase "I'd like to thank Willie O'Ree."

FURTHER READING

O'Ree, Willie, and Michael McKinley. *The Autobiography of Willie O'Ree, Hockey's Black Pioneer* (2000).
Harris, Cecil. *Breaking the Ice: The Black Experience in Professional Hockey* (2004).

EDWARD M. BURMILA

Organ, Claude H., Jr. (16 Oct. 1928–18 June 2005), surgeon and medical educator, was born Claude Harold Organ Jr. in Marshall, Texas, the second of three children born to Claude Harold Organ Sr., a postal worker, and Ottolena Pemberton, a school-teacher. At age sixteen Claude Jr. graduated as valedictorian from Terrell High School in Denison, Texas, and followed his sister to Xavier University, a historically black Catholic school in New Orleans, from which he graduated cum laude in 1948.

Inspired by the achievements of the celebrated physician-inventor CHARLES RICHARD DREW and encouraged by two maternal uncles, Organ chose to study medicine. He was not allowed to enroll at the University of Texas because of his race. His application to Creighton University in Omaha, Nebraska, however, was accepted, and he became only the second African American to be admitted into its medical school. A focused, hard-driven student with a gift for public speaking, Organ was one of the first blacks to be initiated into the national medical fraternity Phi Rho Sigma. In 1953 during his surgical internship he married Elizabeth Lucille "Betty" Mays, whom he had earlier met at Xavier; they had seven children, three of whom became doctors.

After finishing his medical degree in 1952 Organ published his first of more than 250 scientific papers, a study of acute appendicitis in infants and children that was featured in the *American Journal of Surgery*. His 1957 master's thesis on the acid-reducing mechanisms of the duodenum, researched while he was a resident at Creighton University Affiliated Hospitals, generated three peer-reviewed publications. Upon completion of his residency in 1957 Organ entered the U.S. Navy Medical Corps. After serving aboard USS *Hornet* he spent the balance of his two-year military stint as lieutenant commander and director of dependent surgery services at the U.S. Naval Hospital at Camp Pendleton in Southern California.

Organ returned to the Creighton University School of Medicine in 1960 as an instructor of surgery and by 1971 had become a full professor and head of the department of surgery. As chairman he recruited twenty-one faculty members, initiated a surgical honors program and visiting professorships in his department, steered residents toward biomedical research, and had success in persuading many to consider careers in academic surgery.

In 1982 Organ was named professor of surgery at the University of Oklahoma Health Sciences Center in Oklahoma City. During his first three decades in the medical profession he achieved a number of milestones for an African American physician: he was the first to be chair of a surgery department at a predominantly white medical school; the first to chair the Southwestern Surgical

Congress (1984); the second to be elected president of the California Medical Association (1985) and of the American College of Surgeons (2003); the first to head the American Board of Surgery (1984); and the first to serve as editor of the prestigious *Archives of Surgery* (1988–2003), the largest surgical journal printed in English. Other medical groups that Organ led included the Alpha Omega Alpha Honor Medical Society (1979–1989), the Western Surgical Association (2002), and the Society of Black Academic Surgeons. His international stature as a medical educator and researcher was enhanced by his participation in foreign medical groups like the Royal Association of Surgeons of Great Britain and Ireland, lectureships at medical schools in eleven countries, escorting several delegations of surgeons to the Federal Republic of Nigeria, and receiving an honorary doctorate at the University of Athens.

A willingness to advance the careers of those around him gained Organ loyal colleagues and endeared him to graduate students. Alongside his professional and academic activities Organ displayed a commitment to social justice and community improvement throughout his career. Having experienced racial segregation in Texas and Louisiana, he remained committed to eliminating racial discrimination in the medical establishment. In the early 1960s he was active in the Urban League of Nebraska, and by the mid-1970s he served on the board of Father Flanagan's Boys Town, as a member of the National Catholic Conference for Human Justice, as chairman of the executive committee of Nebraska's regional support group of the United Negro College Fund, and as president of the Nebraska Urban League's Urban Housing Foundation. From 1976 to 1978 he chaired the board of trustees of Xavier University, where he and his wife established the Claude and Elizabeth Organ endowed professorship in biology. Organ also served as a trustee of Howard University in Washington, D.C., of Meharry Medical College in Nashville, Tennessee, and of Fontbonne College in St. Louis, Missouri. In addition, he sat on the boards of directors of Northwestern Bell Telephone Company and the St. Paul Companies.

In 1989 Organ relocated to Oakland, California, to found the University of California's East Bay Department of Surgery, which he chaired for four years. Twice allowed the honor of delivering the opening address of the Clinical Congress of the American College of Surgeons, in 1999 he was given the Distinguished Service Award, the highest honor given by the surgeons' group. Widely known for his extraordinary efforts to expand opportunities for underrepresented minority groups and females, Organ reflected on the history of the nation's African American surgeons in *A Century of Black Surgeons: The U.S.A. Experience* (1987), which he coedited, and chronicled their record of scientific inquiry in *Noteworthy Publications by African-American Surgeons* (1995). A specialist in endocrine surgery, Organ wrote two books that reflected his medical research: *Gasless Laparoscopy with Conventional Instruments* (1993) and *Abdominal Access in Open and Laparoscopic Surgery* (1996). In 1995 the Southwestern Surgical Congress established the Claude H. Organ Jr. Basic Science Lecture, and in 2001 his colleagues founded the Claude H. Organ Jr. Surgical Society. In 2003 Organ retired to his home in Oakland, where he died two years later from a heart condition.

FURTHER READING

DeFao, Janine. "Claude Organ—Surgeon, Medical Educator," *San Francisco Chronicle*, 26 June 2005.

Leffall, LaSalle D. "Claude H. Organ, Jr., M.D., F.A.C.S.," in *A Century of Black Surgeons: The U.S.A. Experience*, eds. Claude H. Organ Jr. and Margaret M. Kosiba (1987).

Webster, Raymond B. *African American Firsts in Science and Technology* (1999).

ROBERT FIKES JR.

Ormes, Jackie (1 Aug. 1911–26 Dec. 1985), cartoonist, was born Zelda Mavin Jackson in Pittsburgh, Pennsylvania, the younger daughter of Mary Brown Jackson, homemaker, and William Winfield Jackson, printer and printing business owner. "Jackie," the name she would be known for, came from Jackson, her maiden name. Jackie Ormes was the first African American woman cartoonist. She created four different cartoon series, all in African American weekly newspapers, mostly in the late 1940s and early 1950s: *Torchy Brown in "Dixie to Harlem"* from 1 May 1937 to 30 April 1938 in the *Pittsburgh Courier; Candy* from 24 March 1945 to 21 July 1945 in the *Chicago Defender; Patty-Jo 'n' Ginger* from 1 September 1945 to 22 September 1956 in the *Pittsburgh Courier; Torchy in Heartbeats* from 19 August 1950 to 18 September 1954 in the *Pittsburgh Courier*. Ormes grew up in a middle-class, mixed race neighborhood in Monongahela, Pennsylvania, where, she once said, she taught herself to draw by copying comics out of the newspaper. After high school graduation in 1930 she became an assistant proofreader for the *Courier*. In Pittsburgh she

met and married Earl Clark Ormes, a banker. Earl and Jackie's daughter died at age three and though they had no more children, they did have a happy forty-five-year marriage. It is thought that Jackie Ormes later created her little girl cartoon character, Patty-Jo, partly as a way to have a joyful relationship with a child who was always in the pink of health.

Torchy Brown in "Dixie to Harlem," her first comic strip, was a Depression era rags-to-riches caper about teen Torchy running away from her Mississippi farm and finding stardom in Harlem's Cotton Club. There are visual references to black celebrities: movie star BILL "BOJANGLES" ROBINSON dances with Torchy, she sings with bandleader CAB CALLOWAY, and in the last strip, dancer JOSEPHINE BAKER claims Torchy as "My baby!" Along with entertainment, Ormes created a poignant allegory of the Great Migration of African Americans who moved from the South to the North. Such multilayered comics would become Ormes's forté, blending together humor, collective understanding, racial uplift, and strategies for success.

In 1938 the Ormses lived in Salem, Ohio, and four years later they moved to Chicago where the *Chicago Defender* assigned Ormes a few reporting stints. Soon single panel *Candy* briefly appeared on the editorial page of the *Defender*. Set at the home front of World War II, *Candy* featured an attractive, clever housemaid given to wisecracking about her employer's unpatriotic hoarding while appropriating beautiful clothes from her closet. Mainly a self-taught cartoonist, at this time Ormes took some drawing classes at the School of the Art Institute, Chicago.

Her longest running cartoon, *Patty-Jo 'n' Ginger*, was a little sister/big sister set up with gags about domestic life and satirical comments on society and politics. Drawn in Ormes's characteristic clean, elegant style, the panels have ample white space with crisp, black outlined figures and carefully detailed hair, clothing, and shoes. Precocious child Patty-Jo does all the talking, commenting on topics straight from the late 1940s headlines, like taxes, labor strikes, the HUAC and McCarthyism, U.S. foreign policy, free speech, education, housing, and jobs. Ginger's role was to look beautiful and wear the latest fashions—or very little in occasional unabashed pin-up mode. At a time when mammy dolls and Topsy-types dominated the black doll market, Ormes transformed her Patty-Jo character into a realistic, high quality Patty-Jo doll, manufactured from 1947–1949 by the Terri Lee Company.

She promoted the doll in cartoons, and once had Patty-Jo holding a coupon with Jackie Ormes's home address on it, and saying "All I ask for my birthday is a DOLL that won't out-talk ME!"

The 1950s full color strip *Torchy in Heartbeats* chronicled the adventures of Torchy, now a mature, independent woman who sought true love. In one episode Torchy challenged racism and called for environmental justice, a comic strip theme that was ahead of its time. Violence against women was unheard of in comic strips, but several times Ormes showed Torchy defending herself. Accompanying the strip were Ormes's *Torchy Togs* paper doll cut-outs with elaborate, gorgeous wardrobes. People who knew her have said that Ormes looked and dressed a lot like her cartoon characters.

The Ormses lived in various hotels that Earl Ormes managed, the most notable being the upscale Sutherland Hotel where many famous black entertainers would stay while in Chicago. Her connections, her cartoons, and the doll boosted Ormes to celebrity status in South Side Chicago where she was also known for her volunteer work producing fund-raiser fashion shows for the Urban League, the NAACP, the Chicago Negro Chamber of Commerce, theater groups, and housing projects. Though she was never prosecuted, the FBI put Ormes under surveillance during the Cold War era because she participated in groups they believed to be subversive, such as the South Side Community Art Center, the Artists' Guild, the Cultural Club, and the DuBois Theater Guild. For decades Ormes promoted the March of Dimes in her cartoons, and she also organized door-to-door collection campaigns. After her cartooning days ended she was on the founding board of the DuSable Museum of African American History, Chicago. Ormes enjoyed fine art drawing and painting, and made landscapes and portraits on commission. She collected antique and modern dolls and was a member of the United Federation of Doll Clubs. Her later years were troubled by rheumatoid arthritis, especially in her hands, possibly exacerbated by years of drawing and erasing.

Jackie Ormes presented elegant, well-dressed, and well-spoken black cartoon characters in contrast to the mainstream press's black characters that were stereotypes and caricatures. She was the only black woman cartoonist in a male dominated industry until Barbara Brandon's strip *Where I'm Coming From* in 1989. Most of Ormes's cartoons and comics were not syndicated, but rather almost all ran in the fourteen different city and regional editions of the *Pittsburgh Courier*, the largest African American newspaper serving over a million readers from coast to coast. Other notable black newspaper cartoonists of Ormes's time include E. SIMMS CAMPBELL, Chester Commodore, OLIVER HARRINGTON, Wilbert Holloway, Jay Jackson, and Samuel Milai.

FURTHER READING

Brunner, Edward. "'Shuh! Ain't Nothin' to It!': The Dynamics of Success in Jackie Ormes's Torchy Brown," *MELUS* 32, no. 3 (Fall 2007): 23–49.

Goldstein, Nancy. *Jackie Ormes: The First African American Woman Cartoonist* (2008).

Jackson, Tim. *Pioneering Cartoonists of Color* (2007). http://web.mac.com/tim_jackson

NANCY GOLDSTEIN

Ory, Kid (25 Dec. 1890–23 c. Jan. 1973), jazz trombonist, bandleader, and composer, was born Edward Ory in La Place, Louisiana, of Creole French, Spanish, African American, and Native American heritage. His father was a landowner; the names and other details of his parents are unknown. Ory first spoke French. The family made weekend visits to New Orleans, thirty miles away, where Ory had many opportunities to hear musicians. He built several instruments before acquiring a banjo at age ten, shortly before his mother died.

His father having become an invalid, Ory took over the support of his younger sisters and then, after the younger ones went to live with relatives, an older sister. He apprenticed as a bricklayer, caught and sold crawfish, and worked as a water boy for field hands. At age thirteen he began performing in public with his own band. He started to play trombone—first a valved instrument and then a slide trombone—at around age fourteen. Not long afterward the legendary cornetist BUDDY BOLDEN asked Ory to join his band, but Ory was too young to accept the offer.

Ory fulfilled a promise to his parents that he would take care of the older sister until he was twenty-one, and on that birthday (c. 1911) he moved to New Orleans. He married Elizabeth "Dort" (maiden name unknown) in 1911; they had no children. From about 1912 to 1919 he led what was widely regarded as the best band in New Orleans. His sidemen included MUTT CAREY on trumpet, KING OLIVER or LOUIS ARMSTRONG on cornet, JOHNNY DODDS, SIDNEY BECHET, Big Eye Louis Nelson, or Jimmie Noone on clarinet, and Ed Garland on string bass.

Having asked his wife if she would rather live in Chicago or California, Ory went west in October 1919. Carey and Garland joined his new band, which worked mainly in Los Angeles and San Francisco as Kid Ory's Brownskinned Babies and Kid Ory's Original Creole Jazz Band, the latter also known as the Sunshine Orchestra. In Los Angeles in June 1922, as Spikes' Seven Pods of Pepper, this group recorded "Ory's Creole Trombone" and "Society Blues." Ory's trombone solo is crude and unswinging, but the performances nonetheless have historical significance as some of the first instrumentals made by an African American jazz band.

Around late October 1925 Ory traveled to Chicago to record with Armstrong and to join Oliver at the Plantation Cafe. He initially worked as an alto saxophonist until trombonist George Filhe finished out his six-week notice to Oliver. Over the next two years he was involved in many of the greatest early jazz sessions. With Armstrong, Ory recorded his own composition "Muskrat Ramble" (1926), which was titled "Muskat Ramble" on original issues by the producer and publisher Walter Melrose, who thought "muskrat" offensive. "Muskrat Ramble" became a staple of the traditional jazz repertory. Ory also recorded "Drop That Sack" (1926) with Louis Armstrong and his wife, the pianist LIL ARMSTRONG, who led the session; with the pianist JELLY ROLL MORTON's Red Hot Peppers, "Dead Man Blues," "Doctor Jazz," and "Smokehouse Blues" (all 1926); with the New Orleans Wanderers, "Perdido Street Blues" and "Gate Mouth" (also 1926); with Louis Armstrong, "Potato Head Blues," "S.O.L. Blues," and an updated rendition of "Ory's Creole Trombone" (all 1927); and with Oliver's Dixie Syncopators, "Every Tub" (1927).

Ory started on Oliver's tour to New York City in May 1927, but he returned to Chicago by early June. He joined DAVE PEYTON's orchestra and then transferred to Clarence Black's group at the Savoy Ballroom, at which point he composed "Savoy Blues," recorded with Armstrong in December. Ory left Black in 1928 to become a member of the Chicago Vagabonds at the Sunset Cafe. He remained into 1929. He returned to Los Angeles in 1930. His last job was with Leon René's band in the show "Lucky Day" in San Francisco in the early 1930s.

Leaving music, Ory sorted mail at the Santa Fe Railroad post office, ran a chicken ranch in Los Angeles, worked as a cook, and served as a custodian at the city morgue. He resumed playing in 1942 as a member of the clarinetist BARNEY BIGARD's

group in Los Angeles. Bigard categorically denied a fairly unimportant but nonetheless oft-told story, that Ory initially played string bass in the group, but the clarinetist Joe Darensbourg remembered that Ory played bass pretty well.

In any event, Ory was soon back on trombone. He gave concerts with the cornetist BUNK JOHNSON in San Francisco in 1943. In February 1944 he broadcast on Orson Welles's show as a member of a cooperative seven-piece traditional jazz group that included Carey, Noone, Garland, and the drummer ZUTTY SINGLETON. Welles's show was a great success, and the group returned weekly for many months. Noone died in April, and Bigard was among several new band members. The band became Ory's, and he recorded under his name, with the clarinetist OMER SIMEON for Bigard on "Get Out of Here" and "Blues for Jimmie" (both 1944) and Darnell Howard taking Simeon's place for "Maryland, My Maryland," "Down Home Rag," and "Maple Leaf Rag" (all 1945). These disks are among the central recordings of the New Orleans jazz revival.

Ory's band held extended runs at the Jade Room on Hollywood Boulevard in Hollywood, beginning in April 1945, and at the Beverly Cavern in Los Angeles from 1949 to 1953. Among his sidemen were Howard, Darensbourg or Bigard, and the drummer Minor Hall. In rather bitter remembrances of Ory, Bigard reported that he helped the trombonist secure royalties for "Muskat Ramble." Ory received eight thousand dollars immediately, followed by quarterly checks for several hundred dollars. Bigard said that Ory bought a house and changed for the worse, leaving his wife in an underhanded manner, remarrying, and treating his sidemen badly. Ory married Barbara (maiden name unknown) around 1952; they had one daughter.

Ory recorded the album *Kid Ory's Creole Jazz Band, 1954*, and from 1954 to 1961 ran his own club, On the Levee, in San Francisco. He also had a role in the movie *The Benny Goodman Story* (1955), and he toured Europe in 1956 and England in 1959. In July 1961 he moved back to Los Angeles and resumed band leading at the Beverly Cavern. From 1964 onward he reduced his activities to performances on the riverboat at Disneyland, and in 1966 he retired to Hawaii. Ory suffered a serious bout of pneumonia in 1969. Four years later he died in Honolulu, Hawaii.

The writer Martin Williams supplied a remembrance: "Ory was stiff or standoffish with everyone, but if you had a pretty girl with you, a kind of Creole graciousness would come out.... He was always a frugal man, you know. He always saved money and lived well. And he usually did his own business management and booking. Ory has the mentality of a French peasant, with all the charm that that implies, and all the shrewdness and stinginess and caginess too."

In the mid-1920s Ory was a shaky, awkward, coarse soloist by comparison with his frequent companions Armstrong and Dodds, but he excelled in collective improvisations, offering definitive examples of the raucous, sliding technique known as "tailgate trombone" within the New Orleans jazz style. He played the instrument open and muted, mainly using a cup mute. During his second career, he sometimes sang; his manner was entertaining but utterly unremarkable, save for the occasional use of Creole patois rather than English. While retaining his formidable ensemble skills, he became a smoother trombone soloist, and he expanded his collection of mutes to achieve a variety of timbres.

FURTHER READING

Charters, Samuel Barclay, IV. *Jazz: New Orleans, 1885–1963: An Index to the Negro Musicians of New Orleans* (1963; rev. ed. 1983).

Williams, Martin T. *Jazz Masters of New Orleans* (1967; repr. 1979).

Obituary: *New York Times*, 24 Jan. 1973.

This entry is taken from the *American National Biography* and is published here with the permission of the American Council of Learned Societies.

BARRY KERNFELD

Osbey, Brenda Marie (12 Dec. 1957–), poet and essayist, was born in New Orleans, Louisiana, to Lawrence C. Osbey, a boxer, and Lois Emelda Hamilton, a teaching assistant, writer, and homemaker. Osbey identified her mother and grandparents as writers and storytellers who sparked her initial interest in writing, an interest that she developed through high school.

As an undergraduate at Dillard University in New Orleans, Osbey developed her interests in languages and literature. She studied abroad for a year as a Council for the Development of French in Louisiana scholar and studied an additional year at the Université Paul Valéry at Montpélliér, France. After graduating from Dillard she taught French and English there, and then she worked in the foreign-language acquisition and Afro-Louisiana history divisions of the New Orleans Public Library. In 1980 she won the Academy of American Poets Loring-Williams Prize. She later continued her education at the University of Kentucky, where she earned her M.A. in English and Afro-American Literature.

Osbey went to the University of Kentucky to study with the editor, critic, and educator Charles H. Rowell, under whose tutelage Osbey wrote the series of poems from which were selected those that make up her first book, *Ceremony for Minneconjoux* (1983). This book introduced the use of female narrative voices and the vital presence of New Orleans that are prominent features of Osbey's work. Of her women, Osbey says that they are "bound and determined," "take no shit," are caught up in "madness," and are "beautiful. But they live in a world that just *can not* accept their vision, their reality" (Bryan, 29–30).

After her graduate work Osbey attained positions that allowed her to concentrate on and develop her poetry. In the mid-1980s she directed public and community relations for the Arts Council of New Orleans. She resumed teaching as resident scholar in creative writing at Currier House, at Radcliffe College, Harvard University. She was selected as a Bunting fellow at the Mary Ingraham Bunting Institute for 1985–1986, was a fellow at the Millay Colony for the Arts in Austerlitz, New York, in 1986, and was a fellow at the Fine Arts Work Center in Provincetown, Massachusetts, in 1987–1988.

In 1988 Osbey returned to Dillard University to teach, and subsequently taught at UCLA, Loyola University in New Orleans, Tulane University, Southern University, Dillard University again, and Louisiana State University. As a teacher Osbey encouraged writing students to plumb their environments, particularly in the South, for those biographies that have yet to be told. She encourages students to tackle the tough topics of race, racism, and living in the South and to embrace those writers whose work can be seen as controversial when confronting the harshness of slavery and its legacies.

The productivity of the workshops and writing posts led to Osbey's second book, *In the Houses* (1988). Included were poems that Osbey had originally prepared for inclusion in *Ceremony*. "Madwomen" live on in *Houses*—identified by Osbey as "madhouses" in and of themselves—oddly sane in their madness, sure in purpose as they redefine for themselves the world around them in their New Orleans homes, "transformed," Osbey says, "into a higher form of genius" (Bryan, 45).

Unlike the first two collections, with their varied narrative voices, Osbey's next work, *Desperate Circumstances, Dangerous Woman* (1991), is the story of one woman, Marie Crying Eagle. The Vodun (voodoo or hoodoo) of New Orleans is central to this work, as are the themes of love, memory, family, spirituality, and place.

In her next work, *All Saints* (1997), Osbey expanded upon the techniques and themes of the first three books. She said that she sought to pull together a number of aspects of New Orleans life not heavily examined by her earlier works, such as music and slave heritage, while continuing to feature those traits of New Orleans and its people that characterize the earlier works, especially women and religion. Connections to the past are vital in Osbey's work. She said on different occasions that most of her work is set before 1949. She reminds us that we are to honor the dead, the elderly, our parents, ourselves, and our commitments. Part I of *All Saints* is a collection of elegies for those who have died. Part II is an homage to the past, gleaning from French and Spanish documents, maps, ledgers, photo collections, and more, to recreate the past of the Faubourg Treme, a New Orleans neighborhood settled by free blacks in the early 1700s.

In honor of her poetic accomplishments, Osbey was named poet laureate of Louisiana in 2005. However, her poetry seems only a part of that designation; for what has nourished Osbey's poetry for so long has been her emphatic and seemingly tireless commitment to the preservation of Louisiana's heritage, particularly that of New Orleans. Her work has been that of not only the academic but also the historian, archivist, translator, essayist, and more. All that makes up New Orleans—its varied past, traditions, neighborhoods, food, music, religion, people, the living, the dead—culminated in Osbey's poetry. However, her role as state advocate did not limit itself to poetry; her essays appear in the New Orleans magazine *Gambit Weekly*, the *New Orleans Tribune*, the *Georgia Review*, *Creative Non-fiction*, and elsewhere.

Since the face of New Orleans was changed by Hurricane Katrina in August and September 2005, Osbey's literary treatment and advocacy of New Orleans took a somewhat new direction. Not only did she continue to write poetry of past experience, but she also expanded her role as speaker and ambassador, stressing publicly the need to rebuild New Orleans after its destruction by floodwaters. In an interview with Ed Gordon on National Public Radio, Osbey reminded listeners that New Orleans and its people have given and taught much about music, food, and history, but that it "will now teach people [how] not merely to survive and endure a devastating cataclysmic event like this, but how to rebuild and how once again, to welcome the world back to us" ("News and Notes," 16 Sept. 2005). The stories she told through her narrative poetry were always rooted in her Creole and New Orleans heritage. She calls New Orleans "the true spiritual core of everything I do" (Lowe, 101).

FURTHER READING

Bryan, Violet Harrington. "An Interview with Brenda Marie Osbey," *Mississippi Quarterly* 40 (Winter 1986–1987).

Lowe, John. "An Interview with Brenda Marie Osbey," in *The Future of Southern Letters*, eds. Jefferson Humphreys and John Lowe (1996).

CATHERINE E. LEWIS

Osborne, Estelle Massey Riddle (3 May 1901–12 Dec. 1981), nursing leader, was born Estelle Massey in Palestine, Texas, the daughter of Hall Massey and Bettye Estelle (maiden name unknown). At the time of her birth, many black Americans lived in conditions of poverty and sickness that were comparable to those during slavery. Because black doctors were scarce, black nurses provided the bulk of health care for their communities. Thus for working-class and poor black women, nursing offered an appealing way to embark on a profession, to enter the middle class and gain prestige, and to help others of their race at a time when segregation was common and racism virulent.

As a young woman, Osborne considered becoming a dentist like her brother. He dissuaded her, however, arguing that she did not have enough money for dental training and that in any case, nursing was a more suitable job for a woman. At the time, the profession was racially segregated across much of the nation. In 1920, after briefly attending Prairie View College in Prairie View, Texas, Osborne enrolled at the nursing school based at the racially segregated Homer G. Phillips Hospital in St. Louis, Missouri; she graduated in 1923 and later scored 93.3 percent on the Missouri state nursing exam. Named head nurse of a large ward at the hospital, she became the first black administrator there.

In 1927 Osborne moved to New York City, where she enrolled in Teachers College at Columbia University. Three years later she earned a bachelor of science degree in nursing education. In 1931, supported by a grant from the Julius Rosenwald Fund, she obtained a master's degree in nursing education—the first black American nurse to do so. She became an instructor at Harlem Hospital and later served as educational director at Freedmen's Hospital in Washington, D.C. In the mid-1930s she returned to St. Louis and became the first black nursing director at Homer G. Phillips Hospital. She also participated in a Rosenwald-funded study of health and welfare in the rural South.

At that time, white-run southern nursing schools and colleges rejected black students, while most northern schools set a quota on the number of black applicants that were admitted. The professional societies were no less segregated. Black nurses were denied membership in seventeen state affiliates of the American Nurses Association and in the National League of Nursing Education. In addition, salaries for black nurses were markedly lower than those for whites. The National Association of Colored Graduate Nurses (NACGN), founded in 1908, tried to defend the rights of black nurses but was hampered by its tiny membership—only 175 members in 1933. The following year, Osborne was elected president.

MABEL KEATON STAUPERS was Osborne's choice as NACGN's first executive secretary. Their energetic collaboration would do much to rejuvenate the organization and thereby mobilize the NACGN toward the goal of opening up the profession to black nurses. As women, Osborne and Staupers had much in common. Both had been married to black doctors, then divorced, then remarried; neither had any children. An associate described both women as "flamboyant"; Osborne was "tall, had a high sense of fashion, wore exquisite jewelry, was noted for her hats, and her sense of grooming and dress" and would have appeared "perfectly at home in *Vogue* or *Harper's Bazaar*" (Hine, 121). Together the two women toured the eastern and midwestern states, where they met with black nurses and observed their working situations. As Hine has recorded, they encountered "dozens of moribund state affiliates, disillusioned nurses, and a generally uninformed public…. The overwhelming majority of black nurses neither belonged to nor apparently identified with the NACGN" (121).

Throughout her five-year tenure as NACGN president, Osborne wrote articles decrying the serious shortage of black nurses, particularly in the South. "Hundreds of miles of rural areas are untouched by Negro nurses in both the North and the South," she reported in the *Journal of Negro Education* in 1937. "If a county has money to employ but one or two nurses the preference is given to the white nurse, irrespective of the size of the Negro population." In addition, many black nurses received poor training. Osborne charged that of the more than one hundred "so-called training schools for Negro nurses" then in operation, only twenty-six were accredited by the National League of Nursing Education.

During World War II, Osborne served on the NACGN Special Defense Committee, which fought racial discrimination in the hiring of military nurses. She also became consultant to the National Nursing Council for War Service. In 1943 her friend and congresswoman Frances Payne Bolton of Ohio pushed through the bill authorizing the creation of the U.S. Cadet Nurses Corps as an arm of the U.S. Public Health Service. The bill's antidiscrimination clause marked a major step forward for black nurses. However, although the war effort had afforded blacks greater economic opportunities, the battle for fair treatment of black nurses was far from won. In August 1945, the last month of the war, Osborne pointed out (with coauthor Josephine Nelson) in the *American Journal of Nursing* that there were only eight thousand registered black nurses in the United States—2.9 percent of the total number—even though blacks made up 10 percent of the population.

In 1946 Osborne became the first black member of the nursing faculty at the New York University School of Education, a post she held until 1952. Also in 1946 she received the MARY MAHONEY Award from the NACGN, named for the first black registered nurse trained in the United States, and became associate general director of the National League for Nursing; she held that post until 1967. Having gained a national reputation, Osborne served as secretary of the New York State committee supporting Progressive Party candidate Henry A. Wallace's 1948 presidential campaign. That same year she became the first black member elected to the board of directors of the American Nurses Association (ANA), a position she held for four years. In 1949 she was an ANA delegate to the International Congress of Nurses held in Stockholm, Sweden. In 1952 she was elected first vice president of the National Council of Negro Women, which she had helped to found in 1935 and which she had served previously as second vice president.

In the late 1940s and early 1950s, with the emergence of the civil rights movement, opportunities for black nurses improved dramatically. By

1949, as Osborne reported in the *Journal of Negro Education*, 354 U.S. nursing schools had adopted a nondiscrimination policy, compared to only twenty-nine in 1941; and over the same eight-year period, the number of southern nursing associations that refused to accept black nurses as members had been cut almost in half. These gains were seemingly so significant that in 1951 NACGN officials voted to disband the organization because they believed it had achieved its primary goals. At the group's final meeting, however, Osborne cautioned her colleagues about continuing inequalities in preliminary education and the problem of segregated and inadequately supported nursing schools, about salary differentials on the basis of race, and about fewer job opportunities and resistant barriers to advancement. "Frequently there is merely token or no representation of Negro nurses in the policy-making areas at the highest levels of participation," Osborne said, linking the NACGN's unfinished work with the "unfinished business of democracy" (Carnegie, 100).

In 1959 New York University honored Osborne by presenting her its Nurse of the Year award. In 1978 she became the first black nurse to be recognized as an honorary fellow by the American Academy of Nursing. That same year—another sign of how much American nursing had changed since her youth—the American Nurses Association elected its first black president, Barbara Nichols. Osborne died in Oakland, California. In 1984 the American Nurses Association inducted her into its Hall of Fame.

FURTHER READING
An oral history interview conducted by Patricia Sloan is filed in the M. Elizabeth Carnegie Nursing History Archive at Hampton University School of Nursing, Hampton, Virginia.
Carnegie, Mary Elizabeth. *The Path We Tread: Blacks in Nursing, 1854–1984* (1986).
Hine, Darlene Clark. *Black Women in White* (1989).
Staupers, Mabel Keaton. *No Time for Prejudice* (1961).
Obituary: *New York Times*, 17 Dec. 1981.
This entry is taken from the *American National Biography* and is published here with the permission of the American Council of Learned Societies.

KEAY DAVIDSON

Osborne, William T. (1854–1932), pastor and educator, was born in slavery at Burnt Corn, near Monroeville, Monroe County, Alabama, one of twelve children born of John (surname unknown), a Native American (probably Creek), and Rachel (surname unknown), a Virginia-born mixed-race slave of the Tait family. In the late spring of 1865, Osborne, an eleven-year-old attracted by uniforms and drums, followed the soldiers of the 117th Illinois Infantry as they marched through Monroeville for points beyond. He made himself useful in practical ways to the officers and men, and he won the sympathy of Lt. Col. Jonathan Merriam (whose horse became Osborne's special responsibility). When Merriam was mustered out of the army on 5 August 1865, Osborne accompanied him to Merriam's farm near Atlanta, Logan County, Illinois. Merriam was a prosperous farmer who was active in Illinois politics and was an ardent Protestant, and he promised the illiterate Osborne a home and an education. The Merriam family prepared Osborne for the local school by teaching him to read and write. In the fall of 1866 he began attending public school in Atlanta, Illinois. Despite his academic progress, racism thwarted him at every turn. In 1867 the district refused to allow him to return to school, and Osborne's benefactors began to look for educational opportunities elsewhere. In November 1867 they addressed an inquiry to Jonathan Blanchard, president of Wheaton College in Wheaton, Illinois, thirty miles west of Chicago. Blanchard agreed to welcome Osborne, and the teenager moved to Wheaton, Illinois, and boarded with a local family.

Blanchard had a long history of involvement in social reform movements. A convert to abolitionism during his student days in New England, he moved in Illinois circles populated by those committed to racial justice. Wheaton College had been established in 1853 as the Illinois Institute by staunch abolitionist members of the Wesleyan Church, a small Northern denomination that split from the Methodist Episcopal Church, in part over the slavery question. Blanchard, meanwhile, drew his spiritual inspiration from the Congregationalist Lyman Beecher, father of several famous antislavery activists. Therefore, when Blanchard assumed the presidency of the Illinois Institute in 1859, which he renamed Wheaton College, he began to make it the hub for his lifelong reformist agenda. He advertised equal access to education for blacks and whites, railed against the liquor trade, and denounced secret societies, all the while working to publicize and expand Wheaton College.

The school's first African American student, a young woman born in slavery, had arrived from far southern Illinois before Blanchard took his position at the college. The second, a male student of mixed race who was born in slavery in Mississippi took the collegiate course during the Civil War and with Blanchard's help went on to seminary in Massachusetts. William Osborne, then, was the third African American student to enroll at Wheaton, and he was the only black student during his years at the school. He lived in its men's dormitory. Because he needed to complete his basic education before attempting a college course, Osborne enrolled first in the college's academy, a department of the school that prepared young people for a collegiate course or for work in various professions. By 1872 he had completed the preparatory course. He already had a reputation as an able speaker and debater, skills he continued to hone in college debates during the next four years. Wheaton College awarded him a bachelor's degree in 1876.

After graduating, Osborne moved to Monroe City in northern Missouri and began to teach school. The area had more than one thousand African American children. Osborne struggled to make ends meet, but he managed to continue his own studies as well as to find satisfaction in his work. In 1879, he received a master's degree from Wheaton College for work done through a small Wesleyan seminary in Missouri. The 1880 census reveals his marriage to Parthena Butler, the Missouri-born daughter of former slaves. The couple had two children, a son and a daughter.

In northern Missouri, Osborne became active in the African Methodist Episcopal Church (AME), a denomination that expanded rapidly in the post–Civil War era. In 1883, Osborne left teaching to affiliate with the North Missouri Conference of the AME Church. In 1884 he was ordained a deacon. He became an elder in 1888 and during the next eighteen years served as a pastor with various congregations with distinction, among them churches in the northern Missouri cities of Huntsville, Louisiana, Palmyra, St. Charles, Columbia, and Macon. Short in stature but powerful in speech, Osborne came to be known as the "little giant." He showed the ability to organize and grow congregations and improve sanctuaries while also maintaining involvement in the larger black community of the cities he served. During Osborne's ministry in Missouri, his wife died. He remarried in 1903. His second wife, Pinkie Jackson Osborne, was a Macon, Missouri, public school teacher who had taken advantage of the post–Civil War creation of opportunities for black education. She was a graduate of Walden University in Tennessee, a school established in Nashville by northern Methodists in 1865 to educate free blacks, and she had also studied at Western University in Macon, Missouri, and at Dixon College in Dixon, Illinois. She devoted herself to helping her husband realize his vision for his ministry, which mainly focused on improving the lives of African Americans.

In 1906 Osborne transferred to the Colorado Conference of the AME Church and was appointed to St. James AME Church in Helena, Montana (a state encompassed by the Colorado Conference). There he gained a reputation for eloquence and made his church the hub for literary societies, social outreach, and educational opportunities for African Americans. A reporter for the *Montana Plain Dealer* wrote in 1907 that he was worried that Osborne's obvious abilities might mean that larger opportunities would soon beckon. They did, and Osborne moved on to Seattle, where he oversaw the construction of a large church (now closed). From 1912 to 1917 Osborne served St. John AME Church in Omaha, the oldest black church in Nebraska. There as elsewhere church records noted the creative energy Osborne's wife brought to her husband's pastorates. In 1917 Osborne accepted a call to Ebenezer AME Church in Kansas City, Missouri, where he served from 1918 until 1924. He also served that city's Trinity AME Church, and from 1924 he was presiding elder of the denomination's Kansas City jurisdiction and its Nebraska Conference. From 1912 to 1928 he was a general conference delegate. For several years he was the Northern Missouri Conference delegate to the board of Wilberforce University.

During his busy life, Osborne remained apart from his family of origin in Alabama. In 1912 he returned to Monroe County to reconnect with his siblings and rediscover his home state. Although he was not estranged from his family, they had no real place in his life, and he returned North without them.

Osborne died in Kansas City, Missouri, on 20 January 1932. His funeral was a lavish display of AME respect for this son of Alabama who invested his life in church-centered outreach to African Americans. Members of the AME congregation called him "gospel preacher," and he inspired them with a gospel animated by hope for this life and confidence about the next.

Osborne's life has become an important part of the collective memory that sustains Wheaton College. He was the school's most successful early

African American graduate, and the college named a scholarship for minority students in his honor. The school takes pride in the accomplishments that followed Osborne's commitment to the school's motto: "For Christ and his kingdom." Osborne's life in the North—and the way he wandered off from his family and was adopted by another—offers a lens on African American experience in Illinois in the decade immediately following the Civil War. But though his association with Wheaton College prepared Osborne in formal ways for his future, he found his niche in a very different world from that of his Illinois benefactors. Osborne played a role in the dramatic expansion of the African Methodist Episcopal Church. That denomination provided the arena in which his oratorical skills and entrepreneurial instincts catapulted him to prominence. His life is a case study in lived religion and grassroots denominational growth. Conscientious concern for the well-being of African American people drove his community-centered focus. So the son of a slave and a Native American, torn from his native soil and imported north, came to have importance for both the ethos of an Illinois evangelical college and the story of African American Christianity.

FURTHER READING

The best single source of information on William T. Osborne is his file in the Archives and Special Collections, Buswell Library, Wheaton College, Wheaton, Illinois.

EDITH L. BLUMHOFER

Otabenga (c. 1883–20 Mar. 1916), elephant hunter, Bronx Zoo exhibit, and tobacco worker, was born in the rain forest near the Kasai River in what is now the Democratic Republic of Congo. The historical record is mute on the precise name of his tribe, but they were a band of forest-dwelling pygmies— averaging less than fifty-nine inches in height— who had a reciprocal relationship with villagers of the Congolese Luba tribe. Otabenga and his fellow pygmies hunted elephants by playing a long horn known as a *molimo* to replicate the sound of an elephant bleat. Once they had roused the animal from the forest, they killed it with poisoned spears and traded the elephant hide and flesh to the Luba villagers in exchange for fruits, vegetables, and grains. Very little is known about Otabenga's family life, other than that he was married with two children by the age of twenty.

Around that time, while Otabenga was on an elephant hunt, his wife, children, and fellow members of his band were killed by Congolese agents of the Belgian colonial Force Publique, who had raided their community in search of ivory. When he returned, the Force Publique whipped him and forced him to march for several days, leaving him as a slave in a village inhabited by the warlike Baschilele. It was there, in March 1904, that the Reverend Samuel Phillips Verner, a white South Carolinian missionary, anthropologist, and pursuer of get-rich-quick schemes, secured Otabenga's release from the Baschilele for the sum of a pound of salt and a bolt of cloth. Verner had first traveled to the Congo in the 1890s, and his stay with the missionary WILLIAM H. SHEPPARD enabled him to learn the topography and many languages of the Congo. In 1904 he returned to find pygmies for an exhibit of native peoples to be held at the St. Louis World's Fair. In doing so, Verner and the fair organizers were guided by the scientific racism that pervaded American and European thought at that time. Eminent scholars at Harvard and other leading colleges believed that a racial hierarchy existed among the different peoples of the world and that northern European humans represented the highest stage of evolutionary development. Display and rigorous scientific study of allegedly "primitive" groups like the Congolese pygmies and North American Apaches, the fair's organizers believed, would educate the eighteen million visitors to St. Louis about the evolutionary process.

Few of the fair's visitors were interested in such science—or pseudoscience. Most gawked at Otabenga and the Batwa pygmies whom Verner had also found in the Congo. Others took intrusive photographs and, on occasion, poked and prodded them. One newspaper described him as a "dwarfy black specimen of sad-eyed humanity" (Bradford and Blume, 256). The inhumanity of his hosts, on the other hand, was little commented upon. Press reports did, however, note the public's fascination with Otabenga's teeth, which he had filed into sharp triangles, a practice erroneously cited as evidence of his cannibalism. Displaying a keener understanding of his hosts' values and culture than those hosts showed for his own, Otabenga charged fairgoers a fee of a nickel or a dime before he would display his two rows of sharpened incisors.

When the fair ended in December 1905, Verner returned with the pygmies to Africa. There Otabenga married his second wife, a Batwa woman who died from a snakebite soon afterward. The Batwa blamed Otabenga for her death and shunned him. That decision appears to have strengthened his relationship with Verner, also an outsider, who had remained in the Congo to collect artifacts and native animals for sale to American museums and zoos. To that end, the two traveled throughout the Congo for several months, and, according to a biography of Otabenga drawn chiefly from Verner's reminiscences, their relationship evolved into one of great mutual regard. In August 1906 they returned to America, where Verner left Otabenga in the care of the Museum of Natural History in New York City and then in the hands of William Hornaday, president of the Bronx Zoological Gardens.

Otabenga initially had free rein to wander the zoo, occasionally assisting the keepers and observing both animals and New Yorkers at close quarters. Hornaday then encouraged Otabenga to sleep in the monkey house and placed a sign on his cage informing spectators that it contained "The African Pygmy" and listing his name, age, height, and weight. Otabenga's biographers write that, inspired by a combination of "Barnumism, Darwinism, and racism," Hornaday scattered bones around the cage to highlight the pygmy's alleged savagery and introduced into his enclosure an orangutan. Otabenga would play with the orangutan to the fascination of the thousands of spectators who flocked to the zoo. The spectacle prompted a flurry of articles in the *New York Times*, but only a few criticized the pygmy's treatment. The Reverend James Gordon, the head of an African American orphanage, did, however, protest Hornaday's presumption that Africans provided an evolutionary "missing link" to apes. Gordon did this mainly out of respect for Otabenga's humanity but also because he opposed Darwinism. Hornaday ignored such protests, but he did respond when Otabenga brandished a knife at a zookeeper who had provoked and forcibly restrained him. With Verner's permission, and with Otabenga's own seeming approval, the African was then placed in the Reverend Gordon's care.

Thereafter the press and the public showed little interest in Otabenga, though his later years serve in some ways as a rebuke to those who had placed him in a cage and doubted his humanity. He learned to read and write at the orphanage and later studied for a semester at a Baptist school in Lynchburg, Virginia, where he converted to Christianity. After working for several years as a farm laborer on property owned by the Reverend Gordon on Long Island, New York, Otabenga returned to Lynchburg. He found the climate of the Blue Ridge foothills more amenable than New York's and also better for hunting, although wild turkey had replaced elephants as his game. Much to his delight, he discovered marijuana plants in the woods near Lynchburg, enabling him to smoke the seeds that he had known as *bangi* in his homeland. Although he was able, like most immigrants, to replicate some aspects of his native culture, Otabenga also adapted to American ways. He changed his name to Otto Bingo, wore overalls like those of his fellow tobacco factory workers during the week, and at week's end put on his Sunday best, in the manner of his fellow Baptists. He even capped his sharpened teeth. As a friend of the noted Lynchburg poet ANNE SPENCER, Otabenga also met African American leaders, including W. E. B. DuBois and Booker T. Washington.

Such a life of relative normality may have failed to compensate for the personal tragedies Otabenga endured: the death of two wives and two children, the slaughter of his band of pygmies, his capture and near execution by the Force Publique, his exile in the United States, and his humiliations in St. Louis and the Bronx. Such explanations offer clues, but, of course, they can never fully explain the reasons for his suicide on 20 March 1916.

Otabenga lived in the era described by the historian RAYFORD W. LOGAN as the nadir of American race relations. During the thirty or so years of Otabenga's life, four thousand Americans were lynched, the vast majority of them black southerners. Hundreds of black Americans also died in white-instigated race riots in those years—in Wilmington, North Carolina, in 1898; in New Orleans in 1900; and in Atlanta, Georgia, and Bronzeville, Texas, both in 1906. In addition to this wave of physical violence, southern Democrats led white-supremacy campaigns in those same decades that systematically disfranchised black voters and institutionalized the concept of separate and unequal facilities. The federal government either ignored or, as in the case of *Plessy v. Ferguson* (1896), endorsed these efforts to erode the Constitution's promise of equal protection under the law. That historical context suggests, tragically, that Otabenga's life story is much less extraordinary, and perhaps much more representative, than at first appears.

FURTHER READING

Bradford, Phillips Verner, and Harvey Blume. *Ota Benga: The Pygmy in the Zoo* (1992).
Kennedy, Pagan. *Black Livingstone: A True Tale of Adventure in the Nineteenth-Century Congo* (2002).
Turnbull, Colin. *The Forest People* (1961).

STEVEN J. NIVEN

Ottley, Roi (2 Aug. 1906–1 Oct. 1960), journalist, was born Vincent Lushington Ottley in New York City, the son of Jerome Peter Ottley, a real estate broker in Harlem, and Beatrice Brisbane. His parents were both immigrants from the West Indies. Ottley grew up in Harlem in the 1920s. As a young person, Ottley witnessed the great expansion of black participation in cultural and intellectual activities as well as in politics and entertainment. He watched the parades held by the black nationalist MARCUS GARVEY and his supporters in the Universal Negro Improvement Association. He also attended the largest black church in the United States, the Abyssinian Baptist Church in Harlem, where ADAM CLAYTON POWELL SR. was the minister.

Ottley attended public schools in New York City; a city sprinting championship in 1926 won him a track scholarship to St. Bonaventure College in Olean, New York. He began his career in journalism at St. Bonaventure, drawing cartoons and illustrations for the student newspaper. In 1928 he studied journalism at the University of Michigan. Although he never earned an undergraduate degree, Ottley briefly studied law at St. John's Law School in Brooklyn and writing at Columbia University, City College of New York, and New York University.

Ottley sought employment as a newspaper writer during the Great Depression. In 1932 he began writing for the *Amsterdam News*, a black newspaper published in New York City. At the same time he worked for the New York Welfare Department and in the Abyssinian Baptist Church relief program providing free meals. He was fired from his job as editor of the sports and theater pages of the *Amsterdam News* in 1937, ostensibly for his support of a new labor union, the New York Newspaper Guild. Ottley then began working for the Federal Writers' Project, a Works Progress Administration program under the New Deal. The program provided work for unemployed writers during the Great Depression. Ottley became one of the supervisors of a project that researched and wrote a history of the experience of black people in New York. The result of this project, *The Negro in New York*, edited by Ottley and William J. Weatherby, was not published until 1967, after Ottley's death, by the New York Public Library from the Federal Writers' Project research collection that had been deposited by Ottley in the Schomburg Collection.

Ottley used the material from the Federal Writers' Project as the basis for his first book, *"New World A-Coming": Inside Black America* (1943). This history of black people in New York City covers the period from the first appearance of eleven black slaves in 1626 to a discussion of African American opinion concerning America's entrance into World War II. The book was published in the middle of World War II, as race riots erupted in Detroit and Harlem and black Americans demanded that the United States practice democracy at home by ending racial discrimination. More than a history, the book attempted to explain the condition of black people in contemporary society and to explain their demands as well. Ottley warned that the black American's "rumblings for equality in every phase of American life will reverberate into a mighty roar in the days to come. For the Negro feels that the day for talking quietly has passed" (344). *"New World A-Coming"* won the Life in America Prize, the Ainsworth Award, and the Peabody Award.

After the Federal Writers' Project ended in 1940, Ottley began freelance writing for several periodicals and newspapers. During World War II he was a war correspondent in Europe and North Africa for the New York newspaper *PM*, for *Liberty* magazine, and for the *Pittsburgh Courier*. When he returned to New York after the war, he continued freelance writing, contributing articles to African American publications, including the *Negro Digest*, *Jet*, and *Ebony*.

In 1948 Ottley's second book, *Black Odyssey*, a history of African Americans in the United States, was published. Both *Black Odyssey* and *"New World A-Coming"* were noteworthy because they attempted to present the experiences of black people from their own perspective using original documents and interviews. In *Black Odyssey* Ottley presented the position that the United States must extend full civil rights to all of its citizens. His history stressed the international implications of American racial discrimination in the post–World War II climate, in which the United States sought to maintain its position as a model for democracy around the world. A third book, *No Green Pastures* (1951), based on Ottley's experience as a war correspondent, was primarily a record of his observations and feelings as he traveled in Europe, Egypt, and Israel from 1944 through 1946. The thesis of *No Green Pastures* was that black Americans should not delude themselves into thinking that they would find less racial discrimination in Europe.

In 1950 Ottley moved to Chicago and began writing for the black weekly newspaper the *Chicago Defender*. After his previous marriages, to Mildred M. Peyton and to Gladys Tarr had ended in divorce, Ottley in 1951 married Alice Dungey, a librarian at the *Defender*; the couple had one child. In 1953 he began writing regular bylined articles for the *Chicago Tribune* on issues that concerned African Americans. During this period Ottley also hosted a radio interview program. In 1955 he published *The Lonely Warrior*, his biography of ROBERT S. ABBOTT, the founder of the *Chicago Defender*, whom Ottley described as one of the greatest influences on African American thought in his position as the founding editor of one of the nation's most widely read black newspapers.

At the time of his death in Chicago, Ottley had nearly finished his first book of fiction about an interracial marriage, *White Marble Lady*. His wife edited and published the book in 1965.

FURTHER READING

Material collected during the Federal Writers' Project under Ottley's supervision is in the Schomburg Collection at the New York Public Library in Harlem.

"Ottley Sees New World A'Coming," *New York Post*, 7 Apr. 1944.

Obituaries: *Amsterdam News*, *New York Times*, and *Chicago Tribune*, 2 Oct. 1960; *Chicago Defender*, 8 Oct. 1960.

This entry is taken .from the *American National Biography* and is published here with the permission of the American Council of Learned Societies.

JENIFER W. GILBERT

Outlaw, Wyatt (1820–26 Feb. 1870), slave, entrepreneur, civic leader, and murder victim, probably was born in Alamance County, North Carolina. His mother gave her name as Jemima Phillips; she may have been a member of a free African American family named Phillips who lived in Caswell County, North Carolina, in the early nineteenth century. His father is unknown. Some of Outlaw's contemporaries thought he was the son of Chesley Farrar Faucett, a merchant with agricultural and tanning operations in northern Alamance County who served in the state legislature from 1844 to 1847 and from 1864 to 1865.

The judge and writer Albion Tourgée knew both Outlaw and Faucett and characterized them fictionally in *Bricks without Straw* (1880). Tourgée depicted Faucett sympathetically as an aged justice of the peace known for kindness as a slaveholder, quiet wartime unionism, and cooperation with the Union League during Reconstruction. Outlaw is glimpsed in two composite characters, both of whom were slaves owned by the Faucett figure.

One was an educated and frail preacher of African and European ancestry, a pensive strategist who supported himself as a shoemaker. By contrast, the other man was a strong, dark-skinned, assertive, and successful tobacco farmer.

Young Wyatt lived much of his prewar life on the farm of George Outlaw and Nancy Outlaw, neighbors of Faucett. George Outlaw's 1854 will indicated a special status for "my man Wyatt": he was not to be sold, and it appears that Wyatt was to receive the money from his annual hire. Likely Wyatt Outlaw was a cabinetmaker or furniture maker, the occupation he pursued following the Civil War. The 1860 census suggests he also grew tobacco with or for Nancy Outlaw and her daughter. The farm produced 3,500 pounds of tobacco that year. Nancy Outlaw was 69, and the only other adults on the farm were her 35-year-old daughter and a 40-year-old enslaved man of mixed ancestry, presumably Wyatt Outlaw.

Outlaw served in Company B of the Second Regiment U.S. Colored Cavalry in Virginia and Texas from 1864 until February 1866. He was back in Alamance County by April. He bought a lot with a four-room house on Main Street in Graham, the county seat, where he opened a woodworking shop. He also repaired wagons and sold liquor at the shop, which became a gathering place for blacks and for white and black working people. A black Baptist church and an African Methodist Episcopal (AME) church organized in the shop. Outlaw served as marriage bondsman for at least six men during 1866 and 1867. William A. Albright, a white magistrate and a Republican, did the paperwork for most of Outlaw's bonds. Albright's courthouse office as clerk of superior court was convenient to Outlaw's shop, and they were friends.

In 1866 Outlaw attended the Freedmen's Convention in Raleigh and was elected to the five-man board. With seven other officers, they were to coordinate statewide "agents" and "lecturers." Delegates were urged to promote the organization of "auxiliary leagues" of "colored people" throughout their counties for the purpose of reporting "cruelties" and "outrages" to the state organization and the newspapers. At the convention Outlaw probably met William Woods Holden, provisional governor of North Carolina, who would be elected governor in 1868. Holden was one of a handful of white dignitaries who accepted the convention's invitation to attend. The governor urged education for black children and stressed his view that "the colored people were entitled to all their civil rights, and would have them. The common government would see to that, if necessary" (*Minutes of the Freedmen's Convention*, 26).

Soon Outlaw organized the Alamance County Loyal Republican League, which consisted of black and white workingmen. Later a member recalled that "Mr. Outlaw" had organized the league with the purpose of building a church and a school in Graham. Another member described the organization as helping voters resist intimidation. In July 1867 Outlaw accepted a Union League commission from Holden, who encouraged various Republican forces in North Carolina to unite. Outlaw was to organize local councils of the league and supervise them. A year later, as the newly elected Republican governor, Holden appointed Outlaw as a town commissioner for Graham, and later Outlaw was elected town commissioner. This body organized an armed night patrol of five men, black and white, in response to Ku Klux Klan attacks in the town. Outlaw was part of a police patrol that dispersed a party of night riders.

Outlaw's success as a leader and spokesperson for full political rights for black men and for previously powerless white men was an obstacle to any return to the social, political, and economic statu quo ante bellum of his county. In addition, local features heightened the tensions and lent credibility to challenges to the old order. The area had not presented a proslavery front before the Civil War, and prewar leaders enforced the appearance of a pro-Confederate consensus with difficulty during the war. After the war their key concern was cheap labor: blacks for agriculture and whites for textiles. The North Carolina Railroad crossed Alamance County and had established its company shops near the center. Cooperation and conflict among black and white railway workers focused some of the tension and connected it with state and regional railway and political interests.

Testimonies gathered in the wake of Outlaw's death and also for the Holden impeachment indicate that the company shops camp of the Ku Klux Klan made the decision to kill Outlaw and assigned the execution to a camp in the Hawfield community east of Graham, where slavery and the pro-Confederate consensus had been stronger than in most other sections of the county. Seizing Outlaw in his home shop, the attackers bludgeoned him down Main Street to the center of Graham and hanged him from an elm tree facing the courthouse. The following morning, a Sunday, the body was taken into the courthouse. Eighteen men were indicted for Outlaw's murder. By the time the cases came to trial in March 1874, the state legislature had followed a federal precedent in indemnifying persons accused of crimes as members of "secret societies," so the charges were dropped.

The murders of Outlaw and John Walter Stephens, a white political ally in Caswell County, attracted national notoriety to Ku Klux Klan violence in the area. Holden ordered the state militia to put down insurrection in the two counties. Soon the governor's political enemies demanded his impeachment, charging that his militia had used unlawful and cruel methods in rounding up persons suspected of Ku Klux Klan activity. Further, Holden's attackers secured the influence of the newspaperman Josiah Turner Jr. Turner blamed black–white political alliances typified by Outlaw and Holden for alleged black-on-white crime. Turner's accounts of Reconstruction events later formed the basis for Joseph Grégoire de Roulhac Hamilton's seminal *Reconstruction in North Carolina* (1914), originally a 1904 dissertation written under William A. Dunning (1857–1922). Thus Outlaw's life and death came to transcend his locale.

Cohabitation bonds for Alamance County did not survive Reconstruction, and thus the name of Outlaw's wife is not known. The lack of a postwar reference to her suggests that she died or moved prior to his 1866 return. Apparently they had three sons. Two months after Outlaw's death, his mother moved the children from Graham. The 1870 census listed Julius Outlaw, 10; Wyatt Outlaw, 8; and Oscar Outlaw, 6; as living with her a few miles west of Chesley Faucett's store. By 1880 both Outlaw's mother and Faucett had died, and two of the boys were living in Graham. Young Wyatt lived with a white merchant who had served with his father on the Graham town council. Julius lived nearby with a veteran of the Second Regiment U.S. Colored Cavalry and his family.

FURTHER READING

Alexander, Roberta Sue. *North Carolina Faces the Freedmen: Race Relations during Presidential Reconstruction, 1865–67* (1985).

Nelson, Scott Reynolds. *Iron Confederacies: Southern Railways, Klan Violence, and Reconstruction* (1999).

Raper, Horace W., and Thornton W. Mitchell, eds. *The Papers of William Woods Holden, 1841–1868* (2000).

Trelease, Allen W. *White Terror: The Ku Klux Klan Conspiracy and Southern Reconstruction* (1971).

Troxler, Carole Watterson. "'To look more closely at the man': Wyatt Outlaw, a Nexus of National, Local, and Personal History," *North Carolina Historical Review* 77 (Oct. 2000).

This entry is taken from the *American National Biography* and is published here with the permission of the American Council of Learned Societies.

CAROLE WATTERSON TROXLER

Outterbridge, John (12 Mar. 1933–), artist and arts administrator, was born in Greenville, North Carolina, the son of John Ivery Outterbridge, a self-employed truck hauler, and Olivia Outterbridge, a homemaker whom her son imaginatively describes as a "poet of family life." John Outterbridge's decades of artistic accomplishments, including paintings, sculptures, and mixed media assemblages, influenced and inspired younger artists of all backgrounds throughout southern California and the nation. His artwork, reflecting his profound dedication to recapturing the African and African American past, made him a legendary figure in African American art. Throughout his career, moreover, he combined administrative leadership in Los Angeles–area community art programs with a prolific record of studio production.

Each step of his life informed his artistic perspective. Discovering his creativity in early childhood, he drew and painted with his parents' active encouragement. He experienced both the slights and insults of the Jim Crow era as well as the influence of a supportive black community. Following his high school graduation in 1951, he enrolled at the North Carolina Agricultural and Technical University in Greensboro, North Carolina. After studying engineering there for an academic year, Outterbridge enlisted in the U.S. Army, having been rejected from flight school on racial grounds.

Stationed in Germany, he had the opportunity to paint and sketch, becoming the unofficial artist of his army division. He also took advantage of efficient European rail transportation, visiting great art museums in Paris and elsewhere and viewing other expressions of continental culture. This galvanized his desire to seek advanced artistic training and pursue an artistic career.

Discharged from the army in 1955, Outterbridge went to Chicago to commence formal artistic study at the American Academy of Art. Soon thereafter, he became a bus driver for the Chicago Transit Authority, a job he held for several years. His eight years in Chicago became his third significant life phase, providing the foundation for his future success as a highly visible Los Angeles artist. Complementing his formal study, he encountered some of the key figures of African American art in Chicago, especially Archibald Motley and MARGARET BURROUGHS. He visited the Art Institute regularly and also performed in a jazz singing group, adding a musical dimension to his overall creative vision.

His 1960 marriage to Beverly Marie McKissick, ended in divorce in 1990. The couple had one daughter, Tami, born in 1966. In 1963 Outterbridge and his wife relocated to Los Angeles. There he found various art-related jobs and began creating the artworks that would soon propel him to strong critical acclaim and high visibility. He experimented with three-dimensional elements, salvaging materials from the streets and junkyards, and focusing primarily on the assemblage form for which he is recognized as an artistic pioneer.

The early and middle sixties, a time of great political, social, and cultural ferment in Los Angeles, profoundly impacted his life and his work. The civil rights movement and the shift toward black power and nationalism affected African American artists throughout the United States. The explosive impact of the 1965 Watts rebellion similarly informed Outterbridge's consciousness, resulting in decades of socially conscious art. With Los Angeles–area artistic friends and collaborators, he helped to formulate strategies to use art as a tool for racial consciousness and social change. Outterbridge joined Noah Purifoy, BETYE SAAR, John Riddle, David Hammons, and many others in forming the vanguard of an African American sculptural renaissance.

The social and cultural ferment of the era encouraged many black artists to seek positions in arts administration in order to assist their fellow artist seeking to transcend their marginalization in the mainstream art world. Outterbridge responded to this development by embarking on yet another key phase in his creative evolution. From 1967 to 1992 he worked at the Pasadena Art Museum, co-founded the Communicative Arts Academy in Compton, and, in his most visible administrative position, directed the Watts Towers Art Center for the Los Angeles Municipal Art Department. In the latter role, he was responsible for every aspect of the center's multifaceted operations: art exhibitions, jazz festivals, youth classes, and others.

Despite the tension and time conflicts of his demanding administrative responsibilities, John

Outterbridge maintained an active program of artistic production. Over his career, he created a new black voice through his innovative use of materials for his sculptural efforts. Comfortable with discarded objects since childhood, he became a "visual archeologist," whose "trash" and "junk" discoveries became the raw material for his artwork. Adding yams and other organic material, he expanded his commitment to infuse African elements into his art, joining many other modern African American artists in seeking to express ancestral themes. The works in this vein resisted the dominant society's educational and media institutions that were responsible, in his view, for African Americans' ignorance of their African roots. Many of his sculptural works encouraged black audiences to reverse this destructive process, instead restoring the dignity and vibrancy of African creative achievement.

Outterbridge produced several thematically coherent series of sculptural works during his decades of living in Los Angeles. Among others, his *Containment Series, Rag Man Series,* and *Ethnic Heritage Group* became icons of African American art. He also joined other prominent African American artists like FAITH RINGGOLD, David Hammons, Dana Chandler, and others who transformed the U.S. flag into a symbol of oppression rather than liberty during the 1960s and 1970s protest era, adding powerful dimensions to the broader tradition of American visual political criticism.

Retirement from his work as an arts administrator provided time to expand his artistic expression. Throughout the 1990s and the early years of the new century, Outterbridge expanded his visual expression of family and racial history and social commentary. His 1993 three-dimensional artistic tributes to his mother, *First Poet, Olivia,* and to his father, *John Ivery's Truck: Hauling Away Traps and Keeping Yams,* are classics of artistic family tributes. Both works reinforce a view of loving African American family life, constituting an artistic counter to ubiquitous racist stereotypes to the contrary.

Among many other social themes, Outterbridge's art focused on the growing dangers of drug use in black communities, the welfare of children, and the continuing struggles against bigotry and racism. In his senior years, he began achieving substantial national and international critical recognition. In 1993–1994, he had a major retrospective of his career at the California African American Museum in Los Angeles, featuring fifty of his mixed media assemblages. His works were also shown in Brazil and South Africa later in that decade. In his seventies, Outterbridge observed that he was still developing his body of work, enabling him to add further luster to the long tradition of African American visual excellence.

FURTHER READING
Collins, Lizetta Lefalle. "John Outterbridge," in *St. James Guide to Black Artists*, vol. 1, ed. Thomas Riggs (rev. ed. 1976).
Lewis, Samella. *African American Art and Artists* (2003).
Lewis, Samella, and Ruth Waddy. *Black Artists on Art*, vol. 1 (rev. ed. 1976).
Selz, Peter. *Art of Engagement: Visual Politics in California and Beyond* (2006).
Von Blum, Paul. *Resistance, Dignity, and Pride: African American Artists in Los Angeles* (2004).
PAUL VON BLUM

Overstreet, Joe (20 June 1933–), painter and cofounder of New York City's Kenkeleba House, was born in Conehatta, Mississippi, to Cleo Huddleston, an entrepreneur and author, and Joe Overstreet, a mason. He was the second of three children. His oldest sibling, La Verda O. Allen, owned a construction management firm, and the youngest, Harry, was an architect. Between 1941 and 1946 the Overstreet family moved five times before finally settling in Berkeley, California. Joe graduated from Oakland Technical High School in 1951 and then joined the merchant marine and worked part-time in this capacity from 1951 through 1958. At the same time he also worked as an animator at the Walt Disney Studios.

Overstreet began his art studies in 1951 at Contra Costa College. He established a studio on Grant Avenue in San Francisco, near SARGENT CLAUDE JOHNSON's studio. Mentored by the artists Johnson and Raymond Howell, Overstreet also trained at the California School of Fine Arts from 1953 to 1954. He became part of the Beat era in San Francisco's North Beach neighborhood and published a journal, *Beatitudes Magazine*, in his studio. During the early 1950s Overstreet exhibited in galleries, teahouses, and jazz clubs like Cousin Jimbo's Bop City. His co-exhibitors included the Bay Area artists JAMES WEEKS, Nathan Olivera, and Richard Diebenkorn.

In 1958, attracted by the lure of the New York School of abstract expressionists, Overstreet moved to the city with his friend, the poet Bob

Kaufman, and set up a studio on West Eighty-fifth Street. Overstreet exhibited his work in solo shows at Gallery International, Spanierman Gallery A, and the Hugo Gallery. His relationships with established artists such as ROMARE BEARDEN, Willem de Kooning, Franz Kline, Larry Rivers, and HALE A. WOODRUFF, according to Overstreet, represented his "real art education." In 1962 he moved downtown and set up his studio on Jefferson Street in a loft building where the jazz musician ERIC DOLPHY lived. Overstreet moved again in 1963 and spent the following fifteen years living on Bowery Street in lower Manhattan, where his sons Jahn and Jamahl were born. Overstreet also fathered a daughter, Veronica, in 1954 and a son, Dominic, in 1960.

First inspired to study African art by his San Francisco mentor Johnson and further influenced by Woodruff, Overstreet considered the status of African art in history and its importance for African Americans. Both Johnson and Woodruff had been Harmon Foundation prizewinners and Federal Arts Project workers in the Depression era. Both also studied many different styles of art, including African, Central and South American, and European. Johnson, who produced wood, enamel, and ceramic sculpture, painting, and graphic art, explained his goal: "I am producing strictly a Negro Art.... It is the pure American Negro I am concerned with, aiming to show the natural beauty and dignity" (Lewis, 77). Johnson was an important model for Overstreet, who admired his work ethic, intellectual tenacity, and commitment to a black aesthetic. Woodruff reinforced ALAIN LOCKE's encouragement in the use of African elements, and this enabled Overstreet to reconcile his desire to fuse a European painting tradition with his search for a black aesthetic and used African geometric elements in his early work.

As did many other African American artists in the 1960s, Overstreet participated in the civil rights movement. He organized exhibitions and other projects that created opportunities for black artists. Overstreet worked with AMIRI BARAKA (LeRoi Jones), the founder of the Black Arts Repertory Theatre and School, as art director and developed movable stages that became the model for the Jazzmobile, a citywide traveling program that presented jazz performances to the New York City public. He experimented with technology, creating oil and water light projections for Al Grant at the Electric Circus, and he worked as an art preparator (someone who prepares art for exhibition, shipping, or storage) for the *Engineering,*

Art, and Technology (EAT) exhibition at the New York Armory.

Overstreet had been involved with theater productions in California in the 1950s and continued this activity in New York, designing sets for Baraka's *The Dutchman* and *Psychedelic Burlesque.* In 1968 Overstreet received a Menil Foundation commission to produce a large-scale version of his 1963 painting *The New Jemima.* In this provocative rendering, Overstreet undermined the image of the servile black by presenting the racially iconic figure with a machine gun.

Overstreet participated in many group exhibitions relating to the civil rights movement, including the traveling exhibit *New Black Artists; Lamp Black* at the Boston Museum of Fine Arts; *Afro American Artists:* New York and Boston at the National Museum of Afro-American Artists; *Black Artists: Two Generations* at the Newark Museum; and *Black Images* at the Crockett Museum in Sacramento and at the San Francisco Museum of Modern Art. By 1968 Overstreet's shaped canvases had given way to sewn, shaped canvas constructions suspended by ropes. These works, which can be "viewed either as tents of nomadic peoples or refugee shelters," were presented in solo exhibitions in California and New York, including the Ankrum Gallery, the Berkeley Rotary Gallery, the Dorsky Gallery, and the Oakland Museum of California (McEvilley, 30). Overstreet also showed in group exhibits at the Bellamy Galley, the Martha Jackson Gallery, the Perls Gallery, the Allan Stone Gallery, and the Tenth Street Aegis Gallery.

From 1970 through 1973 Overstreet taught studio art courses at the University of California, Hayward. Upon his return to New York he met Corrine Jennings, an instructor in the English department at Queens College, CUNY and the daughter of Wilmer Jennings, a painter and printmaker. By 1974 Overstreet, Jennings, and the writer Samuel C. Floyd had established Kenkeleba House, an all-purpose, multidisciplinary space for exhibitions, performance, dance, and literature. The name Kenkeleba is the Malinke word for a plant that possesses healing properties and has spiritual and nutritional value. In one of Overstreet's Bowery studios they produced experimental and interdisciplinary work and developed a "pilot project," which was a "total cultural concept of cultural immersion" (Overstreet, interview). In 1976 the New York State Department of Education contracted with the Kenkeleba House to feed five thousand children for the summer at various sites throughout the city, at churches, parks, and other community places. At these sites Kenkeleba provided programs in painting, dance, sculpture, music, and literature, and also hired storytellers and a nutritionist to plan menus to improve the children's health.

In 1979, when Overstreet and Jennings moved their studio to East Second Street, they began the Summer Arts program, teaching children painting, sculpture, printmaking, and environmental art. The program ended in 1982 because drug trafficking in the neighborhood made it too dangerous for all involved. At this time Overstreet painted *Pressure Point*, a painting that clearly represented the daily violence on the Lower East Side of Manhattan. The painting's title refers to Operation Pressure Point, the New York City Tactical Police effort to eliminate the Lower East Side drug trade.

Overstreet's art production continued unabated; his search for new materials led him to paint on wire cloth applied to canvas after a visit to Barbados. His work was exhibited in *Aspects of the 1970s: Spiral* at the National Center for Afro-American Art in Boston; in *Artists: New York/Taiwan,* in the Hatch–Billops collection at the American Institute in Taiwan; in *Jus, Jass: Correlations of Painting and Afro-American Classical Music,* at the Kenkeleba Gallery at the University of Massachusetts; in the traveling exhibition *Since the Harlem Renaissance: 50 Years of Afro-American Art;* and in *Tradition and Conflict: Images of a Turbulent Decade, 1963–1973,* at the Studio Museum in Harlem. A solo *Storyville Series* was shown at the Kenkeleba Gallery at the Vaughn Cultural Center in St. Louis, Missouri, and at Montclair College, New Jersey. In 1982 Overstreet won a commission to produce a seventy-five-panel work of neon and Cor-Ten steel for tunnels A and C at the San Francisco International Airport.

Overstreet produced *Gay Head* after he and Jennings visited Martha's Vineyard during 1984 and met the Wampanoag Indians (Black Indians) at their reservation in Gay Head. Overstreet easily moved between his stylistic roots that were Native American and African American. From the early 1960s he was able to combine those graphical and stylistic elements with his modernist abstractionism and concern for materials. At the same time, when he deemed it necessary, he could move from abstraction to figuration. His *Storyville Series* (1988) exemplifies his use of narrative combined with an excellent sense of color and illustrates his personal connection to music and to jazz in particular.

Overstreet and Jennings traveled to Granada, Spain, to visit the Alhambra and other historic Moorish sites on the Iberian Peninsula in 1984. This excursion resulted in paintings such as *Savilla,* whose title references Seville, the city from which Columbus set sail. Between 1989 and 1992 Overstreet produced *Tensions,* a series of works in which he constructed layers of canvas.

In 1991 Overstreet visited his birthplace, Conehatta. Conehatta is a small town concealed by a large swamp. Overstreet's African ancestor escaped from a slave ship docked in New Orleans, Louisiana, and eventually arrived in Conehatta. The town's population was and remained entirely Native American and African American; there were three buildings when Overstreet's family left in 1941 and three buildings when he returned in 1991. Jennings and Overstreet also visited the Tuskegee Institute, where they viewed paintings by GEORGE WASHINGTON CARVER. Overstreet considered Carver to be a shaman because of Carver's mixture of art and science. On Overstreet's return to his studio he commemorated Carver with his painting *Sound in Sight.* Overstreet visited Japan in 1992 with the *Dream Singers* and *Storytellers* exhibitions, and he visited Santiago, Chile, for a group exhibition at the Museo Nacional des Bellas Artes. Also in 1992 Overstreet exhibited in the Dakar Biennale and visited the slave trade center at Goree Island, Senegal. Upon his return to New York, Overstreet produced a series of ten-by-twelve-foot abstract paintings in the *Door of No Return* series, which was exhibited at the Kenkeleba Gallery and in *(Re)call and Response* at the Everson Museum in Syracuse, New York, in 1993. In 1996 a retrospective exhibition was held at the New Jersey State Museum in Trenton, and Overstreet's watercolors were shown at the Aljira Center for Contemporary Art in Newark, New Jersey.

In 1999 Overstreet's solo exhibition at Dartmouth College displayed paintings rich with surface texture. These works led to *Silver Screens,* exhibited in 2001, an exploration of transparency and chiaroscuro that brought him back to painting on steel wire cloth. Overstreet continued using the steel wire cloth and returned to abstraction, exhibiting *Meridian Fields* in 2003, which brings together the past and the future and was named in part for his father's place of birth.

After 2003 Overstreet was involved in many important survey and traveling group exhibitions, including *Something to Look Forward To,* at Franklin and Marshall College in Lancaster,

Pennsylvania, and *When the Spirit Moves: African American Arts Inspired by Dance,* at the National Afro-American Museum and Cultural Center, Ohio. Overstreet exhibited his work nationally and internationally. He organized exhibitions to bring attention to overlooked master artists, promising midcareer artists, and emerging artists. His dedication to art, artists, and the community at large is manifest through his contributions of his own work and through the opportunities that Kenkeleba House and the Wilmer Jennings Gallery (named for Jennings's artist-father) have provided for artists of color.

FURTHER READING

Gibson, Ann. "Strange Fruit: Texture and Text in the Work of Joe Overstreet," in *Joe Overstreet: Works From 1957 to 1993* (1996).

Lewis, Samella. *African American Art and Artists* (1990).

Piche, Thomas, Jr. *Joe Overstreet: (Re)call and Response* (1996).

Sandler, Irving. *The New York School: The Painters and Sculptors of the Fifties* (1978).

CYNTHIA HAWKINS

Owen, Chandler (5 Apr. 1889–2 Nov. 1967), journalist and politician, was born in Warrenton, North Carolina; his parents' names and occupations are unknown. He graduated in 1913 from Virginia Union University in Richmond, a school that taught its students to think of themselves as men, not as black men or as former slaves. Migrating to the North, where he lived for the remainder of his life, Owen enrolled in Columbia University and the New York School of Philanthropy, receiving one of the National Urban League's first social work fellowships. In 1915 he met another southern transplant, A. PHILIP RANDOLPH, with whom he formed a lifelong friendship. The pair studied sociology and Marx, listened to street corner orators, and joined the Socialist Party, working for Morris Hillquit's campaign for mayor of New York City in 1917. Concerned about the exploitation of black workers, Owen and Randolph opened a short-lived employment agency and edited a newsletter for hotel workers, which was the predecessor for their later Marxist-oriented monthly magazine, the *Messenger,* which they edited from 1917 to 1928.

World War I and the postwar red scare propelled Owen into the most significant years of his life. During this period he had his most significant influence on black affairs and was at his most influential in attracting white attention to black issues. He and Randolph believed that capitalists had caused the war and that the working masses of all nations, including African Americans, were being sacrificed for purposes that would bring them no benefit. They admired the Russian Revolution and therefore exempted Russia from censure. The first issue of the *Messenger* in 1917 expressed these themes and the view, shared by many blacks, that World War I was a "white man's war." Subsequent articles argued that blacks could hardly be expected to support a war to "make the world safe for democracy" when they suffered lynching and discrimination. An article in the July 1918 *Messenger* entitled "Pro Germanism among Negroes" prompted the Post Office Department to cancel the magazine's second-class mailing permit, and for the remainder of the war Owen and Randolph printed their most radical essays in pamphlet form. Both men declared themselves conscientious objectors. Randolph escaped military service because he was married, but Owen was inducted in late 1918 and served to the end of the war.

Chandler Owen, coeditor of the socialist magazine *The Messenger* and, later, Republican Party activist. (Library of Congress.)

The Department of Justice and army intelligence watched Owen and Randolph closely. They were charged with treason in the summer of 1918 for allegedly impeding the war effort, but the judge dismissed the charges, refusing to believe the two young African Americans were capable of writing the socialist and antiwar essays offered as evidence. During the rest of the war and throughout the red scare, the Justice Department's Bureau of Investigation (later renamed the Federal Bureau of Investigation) monitored Owen and Randolph's activities and writings, burglarized their offices, and unsuccessfully sought their prosecution. J. Edgar Hoover, head of the Justice Department's antiradical campaign, charged that Owen and Randolph's *Messenger* was "the most dangerous Negro magazine" and the worst example of black radicalism. Hoover and other guardians of the racial status quo objected particularly to its admiration for Russian Bolshevism, enthusiasm for the Industrial Workers of the World, legitimization of armed self-defense against lynchers and rioters, and demand for social equality between the races. Hoover hoped to prosecute Owen and Randolph in 1919, using the wartime Espionage Act, but was thwarted when federal attorneys argued that a jury was unlikely to convict them.

Surveillance of Owen and Randolph by infiltrators and the bureau's first black agents continued into the 1920s. The pair coined the term "New Crowd Negroes" to describe their own generation, which rejected not only the racial accommodationism once promoted by BOOKER T. WASHINGTON but also the leadership of W. E. B. DuBois, whom they considered to be insufficiently militant. They continued to promote the Socialist Party, Owen running unsuccessfully for the New York State Assembly in 1920. The post office refused to restore the magazine's second-class rate until 1921, when the *Messenger* resumed full publication, devoting much of its energy to the campaign against the West Indian Pan Africanist MARCUS GARVEY. Owen and Randolph were completely opposed to Garvey's rejection of a future in the United States for blacks; they believed that integration and full civil rights should be the goals for all American blacks. In January 1923 Owen wrote a controversial public letter to Attorney General Harry M. Daugherty, signed by seven other prominent blacks, urging the government to speed up its prosecution of Garvey, charging him with worsening race relations and encouraging violence against his opponents.

After the red scare of 1919 and 1920 Owen became disillusioned with socialism, moved to Chicago in 1923, and for a time was managing editor of the *Chicago Bee*, a black newspaper that supported Randolph's efforts to organize a Pullman porter's union. Changing his political course, Owen joined the Republican Party and ran unsuccessfully for the House of Representatives in 1928. For the rest of his life he worked in journalism and public relations, for a number of years writing a column for the *Chicago Daily News*. During World War II Owen wrote a patriotic government pamphlet, *Negroes and the War* (1942) five million copies of which were distributed to civilians and soldiers. He wrote speeches for the presidential candidates Wendell Willkie and Thomas Dewey and campaigned for Dwight Eisenhower in 1952. Owen's long-standing Republicanism was only interrupted in 1964, when he felt he could not support Barry Goldwater and instead backed Lyndon Johnson. He died in Chicago.

FURTHER READING
Kornweibel, Theodore, Jr. *No Crystal Stair: Black Life and the Messenger, 1917–1928* (1975).
This entry is taken from the *American National Biography* and is published here with the permission of the American Council of Learned Societies.

THEODORE KORNWEIBEL

Owens, Carl (29 Aug. 1929–11 Dec. 2002), portrait artist and illustrator, was born in Detroit, Michigan, and grew up in the predominantly black west side of the city. He was the second of three children born to Carl Frank Owens, a bus driver, and Ada Mae Lightfoot Owens. As early as when he was four years old, Owens became well known in his neighborhood for his ubiquitous sketchpad and his ability to make likenesses of his family and playmates. His early formal education included attendance at Sampson Elementary, McMichael Middle School, and Northwestern High School, from which he graduated in 1949.

Although Owens's parents were supportive of his choice to make a career as an artist, they also encouraged him to pursue teaching. In 1952 he earned a bachelor of science degree in art education from Wayne State University. That same year Owens landed his first professional job, teaching art in the Detroit public schools, but three weeks after he started, he was drafted into the army for a tour of service in Korea. He was stationed at

Fort Leonard Wood in Missouri, where his commanding officers were so impressed by a mural he painted for the mess hall that they gave him new duties: to design posters and training manuals for the army, thereby escaping any combat whatsoever. In 1954 he was honorably discharged and resumed his work as an art teacher. Two years later he married the music teacher Katherine Frisby, who gave birth to their first child, Brian Ray Owens, in 1958. A second son, Duane Frank Owens, was born in 1960. Carl and Katherine divorced in 1968.

Wanting to spend more time as an artist, Owens in 1959 convinced the Detroit board of education to create the position of staff artist for him. In this capacity he created all of the maps, charts, and historical figures for the school system's textbooks, filmstrips, and teaching handbooks. Despite many of the new freedoms he experienced as a full-time artist, directives given to Owens by the administration regarding how he could depict ethnic images disturbed him. One institutional policy that posed professional constraints for Owens was the Detroit public school system's practice of basing textbook content and distribution on the city's socially stratified ethnic enclaves. For example, illustrations of black historical figures appeared only in textbooks intended for distribution in African American neighborhood schools, illustrations of notable Italians appeared only in textbooks intended for Italian neighborhood schools, and so on. Owens felt increasingly limited by the board's restrictive policies and left the Detroit educational system in 1968 to become a freelancer. In that same year he produced a charcoal and ink poster entitled *Picture History of the American Negro*, which was subsequently bought by the publishers Rand-McNally for national distribution for schools throughout the United States.

Owens's work was beginning to enjoy wide recognition by this stage of his career, especially in the black press, which often referred to him as the Black Man's Norman Rockwell. However, unlike many African American artists who did not want to be "pigeonholed" by their ethnicity, Owens did not concern himself with racial distinctions because he believed they might limit his professional stature. Actually, he was pleased to be recognized for his service to the African American community. Essentially, the images that Owens created for Rand-McNally and other corporations rendered the dominant visual iconography of African American history, especially in the several decades following the civil rights movement. His work has contributed to shaping the popular imagination of the thousands of Americans who have come into contact with his illustrations and has influenced the way subsequent generations of African Americans have to come to view themselves and to be seen by the larger society. His contributions were honored by both mainstream and black artist illustration societies, including the New York Society of Illustrators and the National Conference of Artists. In 1969 he exhibited in the Detroit Institute of Art, the Whitney Museum of American Art, the Art Institute of Chicago, and the Smithsonian Institution. In addition, the governments of Egypt, Grenada, Zambia, and Zimbabwe added Owens's work to their national collections. In keeping with his commitment to black American nationalism, however, Owens operated largely outside the elite art world, marketing his work highlighting "black and proud" images to middle-class African American art consumers.

In 1976 Owens visited Lagos, Nigeria, where he was honored at the African International Art Festival. That year he unveiled *Affonso I* and *King Khama* for the Great Kings of Africa poster series for the Anheuser-Busch corporate campaign. This was a controversial contract for Owens as well as the other African American artists who participated in the campaign, because the poster series prominently displayed the beer company's logo. Because the posters were designed for cultural outreach and circulated throughout American inner-city schools, they drew criticism for targeting underage (and black) drinkers. The Great Kings campaign sparked a debate that continues to this day about how corporations appropriate African American images for marketing.

Other corporations that commissioned Owens's work include McDonald's, Pepsi-Cola, Georgia Power, Time Warner, Ford Motor Company, Aetna Life, and Encyclopedia Britannica. Throughout the 1970s Owens designed numerous album covers for the Motown recording company for artists such as DIANA ROSS, MARVIN GAYE, and the Jackson Five, as well as several cover designs for Motown's educational and cultural spoken-word label featuring speeches by MARTIN LUTHER KING JR., STOKELY CARMICHAEL, LANGSTON HUGHES, and many more. However, Owens's choice to bypass traditional artistic avenues did not mean that he was giving up on high art. A 1979 article published in the *Detroit Free Press* quotes Owens as saying, "I guess you could say I don't exactly fit into either the commercial or fine arts mold right now. But I'm moving more toward fine arts painting for myself and away from commercial work."

During the 1980s and 1990s Owens produced many of the works for which he is best known, such as *Little Flower*, *The Quest*, *The Mask*, *Duality*, and *Legacy*. These acrylic oil paintings were converted to commercially successful prints as they incorporated popular colors in fashion and interior design to attract consumer demand. Common themes of his work involve stylized binary juxtapositions of idealized black manhood and womanhood, as well as depictions of little black boys and girls smiling and playing. Many of his paintings incorporate Afrocentric themes. Throughout this period, Owens traveled quite extensively, dividing his time between homes in Detroit and Oaxaca, Mexico. In 1986 Owens married Habiba Harrell, a fellow artist known for her collage work. Owens's distinction as a foremost chronicler of African American portraiture was acknowledged in 1987 when he was commissioned by Detroit's Museum of African American History to render a life-size painting of ROSA PARKS in honor of her seventy-fifth birthday.

In 1988 Owens was diagnosed with prostate cancer, which went into remission after a year of radiation therapy. Owens divorced his second wife in 1994, although they remained very close friends. His art was popularized on the sets of sitcoms like *The Cosby Show*, *Living Single*, and *The Steve Harvey Show*. As a result of their appearing on these hit television shows, inexpensive prints of Owens's work continue to decorate the working- and middle-class homes of African people all over the United States.

In 1996 Owens moved to Atlanta, Georgia, where he took on a mentoring role for the many aspiring artists in that city. In 2000 he developed a partnership with the Atlanta Studioplex and Spelman College, where he organized weekly figure-drawing classes that continued until his death in 2002 from cancer. The career of Carl Owens serves as a case study of how racial imagery depicting African Americans in a positive light is central to modern notions of American multiculturalism, and continues to influence the popular imagination of African American culture.

FURTHER READING

McClure, Sandy. "Mayor Young Done in Oils: Artful Politics," in *Detroit Free Press* (11 February 1979).

NICOLE MCFARLANE

Owens, Jesse (12 Sept. 1913–31 Mar. 1980), Olympic track champion, was born James Cleveland Owens in Oakville, Alabama, the son of Henry Owens and Mary Emma Fitzgerald, sharecroppers. Around 1920 the family moved to Cleveland, Ohio, where the nickname "Jesse" originated when a schoolteacher mispronounced his drawled "J. C." A junior high school teacher of physical education, Charles Riley, trained Owens in manners as well as athletics, preparing him to set several interscholastic track records in high school. In 1932 the eighteen-year-old Owens narrowly missed winning a place on the U.S. Olympic team. Enrolling in 1933 at Ohio State University, Owens soared to national prominence under the tutelage of the coach Larry Snyder. As a sophomore at the Big Ten championships, held on the Ann Arbor campus of the University of Michigan, on 25 May 1935 he broke world records in the 220-yard sprint, the 220-yard hurdles, and the long jump, and equaled the world record in the 100-yard dash.

Scarcely did the success come easily. As one of a handful of black college students at white institutions in the 1930s, Owens suffered slurs on campus, in the town of Columbus, and on the athletic circuit. Personal problems also intruded. Just over a month after his astounding athletic success at Ann Arbor, Owens was pressured to marry his high school sweetheart, Minnie Ruth Solomon, with whom he had fathered a child three years earlier. Academic difficulties added to his ordeal. Coming from a home and high school bare of intellectual aspirations, Owens found it impossible to perform well academically while striving for athletic stardom. For two years at Ohio State he stayed on academic probation; low grades made him ineligible for the indoor track season during the winter quarter of 1936.

Allowed again to compete during the spring quarter outdoor track season, Owens set his sights on winning a place on the 1936 Olympic team. His great obstacle was a less-heralded but strong Temple University athlete, Eulace Peacock. A varsity football running back, Peacock had already beaten Owens in five of their previous six head-to-head sprints and long jumps. At the Penn Relays in late April, however, the heavily muscled Peacock snapped a hamstring that kept him limping through the Olympic trials.

Eighteen African American athletes represented the United States in the 1936 Olympics in Berlin, dominating the popular track-and-field events and winning fourteen medals, nearly one-fourth of the

Jesse Owens at the start of his record-breaking 200 meter race in the 1936 Olympics. (Library of Congress.)

fifty-six medals awarded the U.S. team in all events. Owens tied the world record in the 100-meter sprint and broke world records in the 200-meter sprint, the long jump, and the 4-by-100-meter relay to win four gold medals. On the streets, in the Olympic village, and at the stadium, his humble demeanor and ready smile mesmerized foes and friends alike. As part of its concerted propaganda efforts, the Nazi regime commissioned the German filmmaker Leni Riefenstahl to make a film of the games. The resulting film, *Olympia*, released in 1938, featured Owens prominently. The German chancellor Adolf Hitler ceremoniously attended the games to cheer for German athletes. In the most enduring of all sports myths, Hitler supposedly "snubbed" Owens, refusing to shake his hand after his victories; Hitler allegedly stormed out of the stadium, enraged that Owens's athleticism refuted the Nazi dogma of Aryan superiority. This morally satisfying, endearingly simple yarn has no basis in fact. Spread by the *Baltimore Afro-American* (8 Aug. 1936) and other American newspapers, the story quickly became enshrined as one of the great moral minidramas of the time.

After the Berlin Games, Owens incurred the wrath of Olympic and Amateur Athletic Union (AAU) officials when he returned home to capitalize on various commercial offers rather than complete an exhibition tour of several European cities; the tour had been arranged to help pay the expenses of the U.S. team. He left the tour in London, provoking the AAU to ban him from future amateur athletic competition. Supported in his decision by his Ohio State coach Snyder, Owens returned to the United States to cash in on numerous endorsement offers. Most of the offers proved bogus, however, but from the Republican presidential candidate Alf Landon he received a goodly sum to campaign for black votes. Shortly after Landon's defeat, Owens was selected as the Associated Press Athlete of the Year, and on Christmas Day 1936 he won a well-paid, highly publicized race against a horse in Havana, Cuba. Various other fees for appearances and endorsements brought his earnings during the four months following the Berlin Olympics to about twenty thousand dollars.

For the next two years he barnstormed with several athletic groups, supervised playground activities in Cleveland, and ran exhibition races at baseball games. In 1938 he opened a dry cleaning business in Cleveland, but within the year it went bankrupt. Now with three daughters and a wife to support, he nevertheless returned to Ohio State hoping to finish his baccalaureate degree. He gave up that dream just a few days after Pearl Harbor, and during World War II he held several short-term government assignments before landing a job supervising black workers in the Ford Motor Company in Detroit.

With the onset of the cold war, in the late 1940s Owens enjoyed a rebirth of fame. In 1950 he was honored by the Associated Press as the greatest track athlete of the past half century. Moving to Chicago, he served briefly as the director of the South Side Boys' Club, the Illinois State Athletic Commission, and the Illinois Youth Commission, and emerged as an effective public speaker extolling patriotism and athleticism to youth groups, churches, and civic clubs. In 1955 the U.S. State Department tapped him for a junket to India, Malaya, and the Philippines to conduct athletic clinics and make speeches in praise of the American way of life. At government expense, in 1956 he went as a goodwill ambassador to the Melbourne Olympics, then served for a time in President Dwight D. Eisenhower's People-to-People Program. Republican to the marrow, Owens largely ignored the civil rights movement.

Deprived of White House patronage when the Democrats returned to power in 1960, he linked his name to a new public relations firm, Owens-West & Associates, in Chicago. While his partner managed the business, Owens stayed constantly on the road addressing business and athletic groups. For several years he carelessly neglected to report his extra income and in 1965 was indicted for tax evasion. He pleaded no contest and was found guilty as charged by a Chicago federal judge. At the sentencing, however, the judge lauded Owens for supporting the American flag and "our way of life" while others were "aiding and abetting the enemy openly" by protesting the Vietnam War. To his great relief, Owens was required merely to pay his back taxes and a nominal fine.

At the Mexico City Olympics in 1968, the politically conservative Owens reacted in horror to the demonstrative black power salutes of the track medalists TOMMIE SMITH and John Carlos. He demanded of them an apology; they dismissed him as an Uncle Tom. Two years later, in a book ghostwritten by Paul Neimark, *Blackthink: My Life as Black Man and White Man* (1970), Owens savagely attacked Smith, Carlos, and others of their ilk as bigots in reverse. Laziness, not racial prejudice, condemned American blacks to failure, Owens insisted. "If the Negro doesn't succeed in today's America, it is because he has chosen to fail" (84). In response to hostile reactions from black readers and reviewers, Owens again collaborated with Neimark to rephrase his principles in more moderate terms published in *I Have Changed* (1972). Two more Neimark-Owens potboilers, *The Jesse Owens Story* (1970) and *Jesse: A Spiritual Autobiography* (1978), blended reminiscences with prescriptions of the work ethic, patriotism, and religious piety as means to success.

Owens's own success in the 1970s came largely from contracts with major corporations. Atlantic Richfield Company (ARCO) owned his name for exclusive commercial use and sponsored annual ARCO Jesse Owens Games for boys and girls. At business conventions and in advertisements, Owens also regularly represented Sears, United Fruit, United States Rubber, Johnson & Johnson, Schieffelin, Ford Motor Company, and American Express. His name was made all the more useful by a bevy of public awards. In 1972 he finally received a degree from Ohio State, an honorary doctorate of athletic arts. In 1974 he was enshrined in the Track and Field Hall of Fame and honored with a Theodore Roosevelt Award from the National Collegiate Athletic Association for distinguished achievement since retirement from athletic competition.

To his black critics, the aging Owens was an embarrassment, a throwback to the servile posture of BOOKER T. WASHINGTON; to his admirers, his youthful athleticism and enduring fame made him an inspiration. On balance, his inspirational achievements transcended race and even politics. In 1976 he received the Presidential Medal of Freedom from the Republican president Gerald Ford for serving as "a source of inspiration" for all Americans; in 1979 the Democratic president Jimmy Carter presented Owens a Living Legends award for inspiring others "to reach for greatness." Within the next year, Owens died in Tucson, Arizona.

FURTHER READING
Barbara Moro's transcript of interviews with Jesse Owens and Ruth Owens in 1961 is in the Illinois State Historical Library, Springfield.
Bachrach, Susan D. *The Nazi Olympics: Berlin 1936* (2000).
Baker, William J. *Jesse Owens: An American Life* (1986).
Hart-Davis, Duff. *Hitler's Games: The 1936 Olympics* (1986).
Johnson, William O., Jr. *All That Glitters Is Not Gold: The Olympic Game* (1972).
Mandell, Richard D. *The Nazi Olympics* (1971).
Obituary: *New York Times*, 1 Apr. 1980.
This entry is taken from the *American National Biography* and is published here with the permission of the American Council of Learned Societies.

WILLIAM J. BAKER

Owens, Joan Murrell (30 June 1933–25 May 2011), English teacher and marine biologist, was born Joan Murrell in Miami, Florida. Her father, William, was a dentist, and her mother, Leola, was a homemaker. Her family lived close to the ocean, and she spent much of her childhood exploring the shoreline. This experience instilled in her a desire to become a marine biologist, the subject she naively planned to major in at Fisk University in Nashville, Tennessee. Much to her surprise, she discovered that Fisk offered no such major; nor, for that matter, did any historically black college or university offer such a program since careers in marine biology were simply off-limits to African Americans at that time. Forced to surrender, at least temporarily, her childhood dream, she majored in fine art and received a BFA from Fisk in 1954. She spent the next two years studying commercial art and guidance counseling at the University of Michigan, and after receiving an M.S. in guidance counseling from Michigan in 1956, she took a job teaching English to emotionally disturbed children at the Children's Psychiatric Hospital in Ann Arbor, Michigan. In 1958 she accepted a position at Howard University teaching remedial English to college freshmen. Six years later, she joined the staff at the Institute for Services to Education (ISE) in Newton, Massachusetts, where she developed programs for teaching English to educationally disadvantaged high school students. These programs were so successful that they served as a model for the Upward Bound program, a U.S. Department of Education initiative to prepare outstanding high school students whose parents had never been to college for a successful undergraduate career.

In 1970 Owens transferred from Newton to ISE's offices in Washington, D.C. Having never entirely lost her dream of becoming a scientist, that same year she entered George Washington University's geology program. She received a B.S. in geology in 1973, the same year she married Frank Owens. She received an M.S. in geology in 1976. Following completion of her master's thesis, she returned to Howard to teach geology while she continued her graduate work. In 1984 she became the first African American woman to receive a Ph.D. in geology from an American university.

While Owens was pursuing her degrees in geology, she was also taking a number of zoology courses, enough to qualify her to conduct research in marine biology. Thus, shortly after she had rejoined the Howard faculty, the Smithsonian Institution invited her to study a large assortment of corals, sea creatures with stony skeletons that a British expedition had collected in 1880. This project led her to become interested in button corals, deep-sea corals that are about the size and shape of a button. At the time, button corals were rather mysterious because they are considerably different from the more common reef corals; they live so deep in the ocean that they never come in contact with sunlight, they live individually rather than in colonies, and their skeletons are internal rather than external. After completing a study of button coral skeletons, she felt that the existing classification system of button corals left much to be desired, so she undertook to reclassify all the known button corals. In 1986, during the course of her reclassification, she discovered a new genus, or group of related species, of button coral, which she named *Rhombopsammia*, as well as the two species that make up the genus, *R. niphada* and *R. squiresi*. She also discovered a new species in the genus known as *Letepsammia*, which she named *L. franki*, in honor of her husband.

In 1992 Howard closed its geology department, so Owens transferred to the biology department. The closing proved to be serendipitous, because it allowed her to pursue her childhood dream of working with marine biology. Although she retired from Howard in 1995, having spent only three years as an "official" marine biologist, she continued to conduct research in marine biology for a number of years thereafter. She died in 2011.

FURTHER READING

Kessler, James H., et al. *Distinguished African American Scientists of the 20th Century* (1996).

Spangenburg, Ray, and Kit Moser. *African Americans in Science, Math, and Invention* (2003).

Warren, Wini. *Black Women Scientists in the United States* (1999).

CHARLES W. CAREY JR.

Owens, Major Robert Odell (28 June 1936–), librarian, civil rights activist, state senator, and congressman, was born in Collierville, Tennessee, one of the eight children of Ezekiel Owens and Hannah Owens. During Owens's childhood his family moved to Memphis, where Owens graduated from Hamilton High School in 1952 at the age of sixteen. After graduation and upon the receipt of a Ford Foundation scholarship, Owens attended Morehouse College in Atlanta, where he majored in mathematics, earning his bachelor's degree in 1956. In 1957 Owens earned a master's degree in library science from Atlanta University.

After earning his master's degree Owens married Ethel Werfel, whom he met at Morehouse College, and moved to New York City. Employed in the Brooklyn Public Library system, Owens also became active in politics and civil rights in the early to mid-1960s. In 1964 he was named community coordinator for a federal program to encourage library use, served as chairman of the Brooklyn chapter of the Congress of Racial Equality (CORE), and headed the Brooklyn Rent Strike Coordinating Committee.

As a leading community activist in Brooklyn, Owens led CORE in staging a successful uprising against New York City's Democratic leadership. Calling themselves the Brooklyn Freedom Democratic Party (BFDP), the insurgents dedicated themselves to giving African Americans an equal voice in the New York Democratic Party. Though Owens was the BFDP's unsuccessful candidate for city council, he and CORE helped foil Robert Wagner's bid for a fourth consecutive term as mayor of New York. Claiming that Wagner had "complete apathy [and] disregard for the Negro and Puerto Rican communities," Owens led CORE's fight to unseat the mayor.

In 1965 Owens helped create and lead the Brownsville Community Council. Under Owens's leadership the council founded a credit union, ran a Head Start center, and operated a jobs-training program. By the mid-1960s Brownsville, a thickly settled section of eastern Brooklyn that was predominantly populated by African Americans and Latinos, was a locus of antipoverty and civil rights activism. For Owens, Brownsville had become and was to remain his political base.

As a leader in an increasingly radicalized civil rights movement, Owens became known as "the quiet man from Brooklyn." By 1968 Owens's brand of dignified activism caught the attention of New York's mayor, John Lindsay, who appointed him commissioner of the city's Community Development Agency (CDA). As commissioner Owens challenged city hall to treat Brownsville and other ghettos like undeveloped nations and be "as generous [with aid] as the United States" is with foreign nations. Though many Latinos claimed that Owens's antipoverty programs were dominated by a "black clique," Lindsay supported his commissioner's approach.

Despite Lindsay's rhetorical support, Owens saw the dismantling of the city's antipoverty programs when budgets were slashed each year. Frustrated by the political backlash against antipoverty programs in 1974, Owens left the Lindsay administration for electoral politics. After winning a New York state senate seat representing Brownsville, the professorial and reserved Owens was an effective legislator. After eight years in the state senate, in 1982 Owens ran for the United States Congress to replace SHIRLEY CHISHOLM, who was retiring. The contest over New York's Twelfth Congressional District pitted Owens against his fellow African American state senator Vander Beatty.

Though on the surface the two men were similar, they were polar opposites. Beatty, who was endorsed by Chisholm, was as flamboyant and unpredictable as Owens was steady. Infamous for his ill-fated drives to recall New York mayor Edward Koch and even unseat Chisholm, Beatty was also involved in numerous voting fraud scandals. At a distinct financial disadvantage and with Chisholm's and the party's active opposition to his candidacy, Owens was the clear underdog.

Surprising most observers, Owens beat Beatty by 3,000 votes (out of 34,000 cast). In reaction, Beatty charged the Owens campaign with fraud and demanded a new election. However, it was Beatty who orchestrated a massive campaign of fraud, as he and his underlings forged hundreds of registration cards on which they based their charges of voting irregularities. Ironically, Owens's margin of victory in New York's most predominantly black congressional district came from white voters who were attracted to his record as a racial conciliator and ethical politician.

Once in Congress Owens became a member of the Education and Workforce and the Government Reform committees, as well as the Congressional Black Caucus (CBC). As chairman of the CBC's task force on Haiti, he helped pressure President Bill Clinton to restore Jean-Bertrand Aristide to the presidency.

In the 1980s Owens was at the center of New York City's broiling race relations. On a number of occasions tensions among African Americans, Jews, and whites had exploded in violence and murder. Though Congressman Owens led the charge against racially motivated violence, he was also a moderating influence within the black community. A frequent critic of AL SHARPTON and LOUIS FARRAKHAN, Owens has always maintained his belief in racial comity and healing.

In 1985 Owens's first marriage, which produced three children, ended in divorce. In 1991 he married Maria Cuprill. Though Owens founded his career on being an advocate for civil rights and racial healing, his congressional career was very nearly upended by ethnic tensions within Brooklyn's black community. In 2000 a one-time protégée and woman of Afro-Caribbean heritage, Una Clarke, challenged Owens for his seat. Charging that Owens was anti-immigrant and ineffectual, Clarke drew on the tensions that existed between Brooklyn's African Americans and its increasing Afro-Caribbean population. Owens won the very bitter and divisive primary battle and won reelection in 2000. Owens was reelected in 2002 and 2004 but chose not to run in 2006.

FURTHER READING

Hicks, Jonathan. "Bitter Primary Contest Hits Ethnic Nerve among Blacks," *New York Times*, 31 Aug. 2000.

Kihiss, Peter. "Brooklyn Negro Leader Named Head of a City Poverty Agency," *New York Times*, 13 Mar. 1968.

Smothers, Ronald. "Two Ex-State Senators Vie for Rep. Chisholm's Job," *New York Times*, 16 Sept. 1982.

JEFF BLOODWORTH

P. Diddy. *See* Combs, Sean.

Pacalé, Yves (Yves *dit* Pacalé, Pacale) (c. 1730–18 Dec. 1818), slave, freeman, and successful agriculturalist, was either born in Natchitoches, Louisiana, or arrived in the French colony as an enslaved young adult. He may have been born in Africa, as Pacalé is not a Catholic name, while the name Yves would have been given at his baptism. In some records he is called Yves *dit* Pacalé—Yves known as Pacalé. He was baptized on 2 January 1736 as the son of Jean Baptiste and Marie, black slaves of the white French Derbanne family. Little is known of Pacalé's years as a slave. The period of the mid- to late eighteenth century was one of great change in Louisiana; the state was a French colony that in 1763 became Spanish, making Natchitoches's role as a frontier post with Spanish Texas redundant. The area's economy transformed from defense and trade to plantation agriculture, focusing on the growth of tobacco. Pacalé therefore probably had a variety of jobs during his time as a slave. We know that in 1765 he was supplied with six other slaves to a Jacques Rachal to work on some land growing corn, beans, potatoes, citrus fruits, and tobacco. At the death of Madame Pierre Derbanne in 1798, her four heirs finally liberated Pacalé. He was already sixty years old. Although by this time he was only worth the small amount of $100, liberation, even of an elderly person who was considered a "burden" on slave owners, was not routine, and Pacalé must have petitioned hard to be freed.

In 1800 Pacalé began the process of buying an enslaved woman called Marie Louise from the Derbanne family. Marie Louise was almost certainly a relative as the document makes it clear that she was bought to be emancipated. Pacalé bought another relative, a woman named Eteroux, who was possibly his wife, on 1 January 1806. Eteroux is probably a French spelling of an African name, and like Pacalé she would have been considered old at sixty-five, although her price of $250 suggests her owners still considered her of some use, meaning she probably worked in the house or kitchen rather than the fields.

After five years as a freeman, Pacalé on 16 April 1803 bought a long and narrow tract of land south of Natchitoches on the Cane River from the white Frenchman Paul Poissot. The land had little water frontage on the Cane River but went deep into the cypress forest behind. The rather unpromising piece of land, which had neither been improved nor built upon, was sold for the relatively cheap price of $180 in cash. On buying the land, Pacalé ensured that it was surveyed in his name, an action that stood him in good stead later when an attempt was made by the Poissot family to claim the land back for themselves. Eteroux and Marie Louise may have helped him work the plantation, although only one of them was living with him in 1810 according to the U.S. Census. In this same year Pacalé made a will leaving all his possessions to Marie Jeanne, a free black woman. Marie Jeanne might be the French name for Eteroux.

Their main help on the plantation came from a Congolese slave called François, whom Pacalé bought around 1810. François was in his early twenties and must have been an expensive purchase as young men had the highest value of all slaves. Around this time Pacalé began to run into financial difficulties, which can be traced to his 1812 purchase of another slave, his daughter Thérèse, age forty, for

$800. She was immediately liberated "for the paternal affection that he has for the said Thérèse," as the manumission paper states (Natchitoches Parish Courthouse Archive, Conveyance Book 37 record 4059). He had paid a high price for Thérèse, who at forty was quite old; this suggests both that Pacalé was determined to buy her and that her owner may have been reluctant to sell her. To pull off the sale, Pacalé had to mortgage his land and François to AUGUSTIN METOYER, a free person of color, for $800. However, Pacalé was evidently unable to keep up the repayments, and on 27 May 1813 François was sold to Metoyer for $600 ($200 being waived). Two days later Pacalé's land was sold to Auguste Langlois for 300 piastres with the provision that Pacalé was able to continue to cultivate it. Pacalé's determination to buy Thérèse meant that he lost the plantation he had owned and worked on, but he was able to give his daughter her freedom. Shortly after her liberation, Pacalé changed his will in her favor, leaving all his property to her. At some point, Pacalé constructed a small cabin to live in, which oral history identifies as a building called the "Roque House." That house has been moved up the Cane River and now stands in the center of Natchitoches. The cabin is of a distinctive vernacular shape and is constructed of a timber frame filled in with *bousillage*, a mixture of mud, moss, and fur.

Pacalé died on 18 December 1818 from fever. Catholic church records state that he was about eighty. His life stands as testament to the many emancipated slaves who left little record of their achievements in the historic documents. He was determined to be free and devoted his later years to freeing his own family members. The name of Pacalé has been spoken across generations, linking this man with the Roque House, which stands as a marker of the hard work and determination of free blacks to create and enjoy their own lives and spread their good fortune to others.

FURTHER READING

Surviving materials related to Pacalé and his family are at the Natchitoches Parish Courthouse, Natchitoches, Louisiana, and the Cammie G. Henry Research Center, Northwestern State University, Natchitoches.

Gould, P., R. Seale, R. Deblieux, and H. M. Guidry *Natchitoches and Louisiana's Timeless Cane River* (2002).

Mills, E. S., and G. Mills. *Tales of Old Natchitoches* (1978).

FIONA J. L. HANDLEY

Pace, Harry Herbert (6 Jan. 1884–26 July 1943), entrepreneur, was born in Covington, Georgia, the son of Charles Pace, a blacksmith, and Nancy Francis. Pace's father died when he was an infant, but Pace was nonetheless able to secure a good education. He finished elementary school in Covington by the time he was twelve, and seven years later he graduated as valedictorian of his class at Atlanta University.

Pace learned the trade of printer's devil as a youth and worked in the Atlanta University printing office. After graduation he took a job in a new firm established by a group of prominent blacks in Atlanta. Pace served as foreman and shop manager, but the venture was unsuccessful and soon closed. In 1904 Pace became an instructor at the Haines Institute in Augusta, Georgia, where he remained for only a year before W. E. B. DuBois, who had been one of his teachers at Atlanta University, persuaded Pace to join him in launching the *Moon Illustrated Weekly*, a magazine for blacks to be published in Memphis, Tennessee. DuBois was editor of the journal, which commenced publication in December 1905, and Pace was its manager. Although the venture was relatively short-lived, it was one of the earliest efforts at a weekly magazine for blacks and provided Pace with a favorable introduction to the rising African American business community of Memphis.

When the *Moon* folded in July 1906, Pace was offered a position as professor of Latin and Greek at Lincoln University in Jefferson City, Missouri, where he remained for a year. In 1907 ROBERT R. CHURCH SR., president of Solvent Savings Bank in Memphis, asked the young man to join the bank as cashier. Pace proved himself an excellent businessman. Within four years he had increased the bank's assets from fifty thousand dollars to six hundred thousand dollars, turning it into an exceedingly profitable venture.

In 1912 HEMAN PERRY, the owner of Standard Life Insurance Company of Atlanta, offered Pace the position of secretary of the firm, which was just being organized. Perry and Pace made Herculean efforts for the company, and in 1913 Standard Life became the first black insurance company organized solely for the purpose of selling ordinary life insurance and the third black insurance company to achieve legal reserve status. Standard Life grew rapidly over its first ten years. Pace installed rigorous business systems at Standard, but these exacting regulations did not suit the entrepreneurial personality of Perry, causing the two men to clash often over Perry's cavalier attitude. Nonetheless, Pace managed to work with Perry until the summer of 1917, when petty friction while Pace was on his honeymoon with Ethlynde Bibb, with whom he had two children, finally exploded into a confrontation that ended with Pace leaving Standard Life.

Pace headed for New York City, where in 1918 he joined W. C. HANDY, the great composer and compiler of the blues, in establishing Pace and Handy Music, a sheet-music publishing company. The two had worked with each other since 1907 in Memphis, where Pace had often written lyrics to accompany music written by Handy. Pace and Handy Music was a dynamic and successful business in New York for a number of years. Pace, who served as its first president, stayed with the company until 1921. Handy continued to run the company as Handy Brothers Music Company until the 1950s.

Pace and Handy's greatest success was with "St. Louis Blues," written earlier by Handy, which became a huge hit. But Pace was frustrated. White-owned record companies would buy their songs and then record them using white artists. In March 1921 Pace started his own record firm, Black Swan Records—the first record firm in the United States to be owned by blacks. Pace did not have an easy time getting the firm established because white-owned companies set up obstacles, preventing him for a time, for instance, from purchasing a record-pressing plant. Ultimately, however, he set up recording studios and a pressing laboratory, and he obtained other supplies necessary to produce records. The future for Black Swan Records seemed bright in 1922–1923, but the advent of radio as a popular, and much cheaper, means of transmitting music destroyed the prospects of the company and threatened to send even white record firms into bankruptcy. As a result Pace decided to sell his firm to Paramount Records in 1925. Although many of Pace's artists, such as ETHEL WATERS, continued to be recorded, much of the authenticity of the firm's earlier black music was lost. Most importantly, blacks were largely shut out of the management side of the record business.

In 1925 Pace moved back into the insurance industry, participating in the organization of Northeastern Life Insurance Company in Newark, New Jersey, and serving as its president. Although the firm struggled in its first few years, Pace operated it fairly successfully until 1929, when he began talking with Truman K. Gibson Sr. about the possibility of merging Northeastern with Supreme Life and Casualty of Columbus, Ohio. Supreme Life had large holdings of industrial insurance, with salesmen trained to sell it, while Pace's Northeastern had an excellent investment portfolio and first-rate management. Neither firm, however, had been profitable in 1928, so they began seeking another company that had larger cash reserves. They merged with Liberty Life Insurance of Chicago, one of the largest and most successful black companies in the country. The new firm, called Supreme Liberty Life Insurance, had combined capital of $400,000, insurance in force of $25 million, total assets of more than $1.4 million, and 1,090 employees. Pace was named president and chief executive officer of the new company.

The early years of Supreme Liberty Life were ones of struggle. Just after the merger in 1929, the devastating Great Depression struck. The situation for Supreme Liberty was more desperate than it was for many insurance firms because the company relied more heavily on the ordinary life insurance market. These policies were expensive, so poor blacks, who suffered greatly from the Depression, were more likely to allow the policies to lapse. To deal with these crushing problems Pace focused the firm more on the industrial insurance market. This was successful, and Supreme Liberty became increasingly profitable in the late 1930s. This recovery was based largely on a system called "mass production" in which largely untrained agents were sent out to write as many policies as they could without requiring any financial settlement at the time of signing. After the policy had been processed and issued the agent would then try to get the client to sign it, stressing the small weekly premiums to be paid. This technique allowed a rapid expansion of Supreme Liberty's industrial holdings, even if the expansion was itself quite expensive. Supreme Liberty's lapse rate was the highest among black firms, and the expense of collecting premiums on policies in force was also high. Although this did little to enhance the reputation of Supreme Liberty, the total insurance in force increased from $16.6 million in 1930 to $83.1 million by 1944.

After the American entrance into World War II, with black employment and wages rising rapidly, Supreme Liberty began to sell the more profitable ordinary life insurance. But this new era was faced by Gibson after Pace's death in Chicago. Pace was a member of the National Negro Insurance Association, serving as its president in 1928–1929. Partially because of this position, he became an influential writer on insurance issues among blacks and wrote a number of articles for the African

American insurance industry that appeared in major African American publications.

Pace was the founder or cofounder of an impressive number of important African American companies, at times introducing blacks into industries where they previously had no standing. He networked with most of the prominent African Americans of the time to the extent that he operated at the very apex of the status and power pyramids in the black communities of Memphis, Atlanta, New York City, and Chicago at various points in his life.

FURTHER READING

At least two letters from Pace to BOOKER T. WASHINGTON are in the Booker T. Washington Papers at the Library of Congress. A number of letters between Pace and ROBERT L. VANN concerning Black Swan Records are in the Percival L. Prattis Collection at the Moorland-Spingarn Research Center at Howard University.

Partington, Paul G. "The *Moon Illustrated Weekly*—the Precursor of *The Crisis*," *Journal of Negro History* (July 1963).

Puth, Robert C. "Supreme Life: The History of a Negro Life Insurance Company," *Business History Review* (Spring 1969).

Obituaries: *Chicago Defender* and *Amsterdam News*, 31 July 1943.

This entry is taken from the *American National Biography* and is published here with the permission of the American Council of Learned Societies.

JOHN N. INGHAM

Padmore, George (1903?–23 Sept. 1959), writer and Pan-Africanist, was born Malcolm Ivan Meredith Nurse in Arouca, Trinidad, the son of James Hubert Alfonso Nurse, a teacher, and Anna Susanna Symister of Antigua. In Port-of-Spain he attended Tranquillity School and St. Mary's College of the Immaculate Conception before graduating from Pamphylian High School in 1918. As a reporter of shipping news for the *Weekly Guardian*, he saw in the arrogant treatment the white editor meted out to a black assistant editor the future that lay in store for him. In 1924 he traveled to the United States with the declared intention of studying medicine. His wife, Julia Semper, joined him later, leaving behind their daughter, Blyden.

In the United States, Nurse evolved quickly into a political leader. While a student at Fisk University in Nashville, Tennessee, he wrote to Nnamdi ("Ben") Azikiwe, a Nigerian studying at Storer College in West Virginia, proposing an organization of "foreign Negro students in American colleges and universities…. to foster racial consciousness and a spirit of nationalism aiming at the protection of the sovereignty of Liberia" (Azikiwe, 138). Although the organization did not apparently materialize, later, when both Nurse and Azikiwe had moved on to Howard University Law School in Washington, D.C., Nurse organized a demonstration against the British ambassador, who was visiting the campus, and Azikiwe participated. A personal network of African liberationists was taking shape, and already Nurse was playing a key role in creating it.

By 1928 Nurse had associated himself with the Workers (Communist) Party and had taken the political name George Padmore. Dividing his life between Washington, D.C., and New York City, Padmore gave speeches at Communist gatherings, wrote for the *Daily Worker*, and in Harlem worked alongside his fellow West Indians CYRIL BRIGGS and RICHARD B. MOORE at the *Negro Champion*, a paper published by the American Negro Labor Congress.

In 1929, before Padmore had completed any American degrees, he attended a League Against Imperialism conference in Frankfurt, Germany. Just a few months later, leaving his wife behind in the United States, Padmore traveled to Moscow. However, upon his return he was barred from reentering the country by American authorities, and would never return.

Recognizing Padmore's talent as a writer, speaker, and organizer, the Communist International named him head of the International Trade Union Committee of Negro Workers. He moved in high circles in Moscow and traveled in Africa and Europe to recruit potential leaders for conferences or study in the Soviet Union. He wrote for the ITUC-NW's magazine, the *Negro Worker*, and became its editor with the October–November 1931 issue. Several Harlem writers contributed to the magazine, among them Cyril Briggs and LANGSTON HUGHES. Via sailors leaving Hamburg, Germany, his headquarters, Padmore sent copies of the *Negro Worker* to ports around the world. Considered seditious by colonial governments, the magazine was sometimes banned and its copies confiscated. Then in February 1933, not long before the Reichstag fire, the Nazis arrested Padmore and closed the *Negro Worker* office. After a brief time in prison, Padmore was deported to England. He published three more issues of the *Negro Worker*, using Copenhagen, Denmark, as a publishing address. But the Soviet Union was no longer eager to anger Britain and France, which were potential allies against Germany and major targets of the *Negro Worker*'s anti-imperialist rhetoric. Padmore learned in August 1933 that the ITUC-NW was being shut down. He resigned from his positions there and was subsequently expelled from the Communist International in 1934.

Relocating to Paris, Padmore wrote an exposé of life in the British African colonies, *How Britain Rules Africa*. He had difficulty finding a publisher, but Wishart Books, a press in London, brought the book out in 1936. By that time Padmore had moved to London. There he reconnected with his boyhood friend C. L. R. JAMES, who had become a Trotskyist writer and agitator. An organization that James had started in order to oppose Italian aggression against Ethiopia evolved in 1937 into a new organization, the International African Service Bureau, of which Padmore became chair. Other IASB leaders included men Padmore had known in his Communist International days, Kenya's Jomo Kenyatta and Sierra Leone's I. T. A. Wallace Johnson. Operating with meager resources and observed by British intelligence, the IASB published pamphlets and short-lived periodicals that were sometimes seized in the African colonies.

Still a staunch socialist despite his break with the Communists, Padmore became a regular contributor to the British Independent Labour Party publication, the *New Leader*. He often recycled his *New Leader* articles in *The Crisis*, the NAACP's magazine in the United States. A new publisher on the British scene, Secker & Warburg, published books by several leading members of the Padmore circle, including Padmore's *Africa and World Peace* (1937).

For twenty-two years Padmore would use London as a base for a far-flung political operation dedicated to ending the British Empire. He lived on a low income earned by his writing and the secretarial work of Dorothy Pizer, the Englishwoman who became known as his wife (although he was never divorced from Julia). Their flat became a crossroads for African nationalists visiting or studying in London. When the South African Peter Abrahams arrived in London after the beginning of World War II, he found Padmore pounding out dispatches on a worn office typewriter. The copies he mailed to little magazines and newspapers around the world bore the request: "Please pass on to other periodicals" (Abrahams, 38). Running his

one-man press service, Padmore sent articles to newspapers and magazines in Africa, the United States, the Caribbean, and Asia.

During the war, Padmore wrote a short book, *The White Man's Duty: An Analysis of the Colonial Question in the Light of the Atlantic Charter* (1942), with Nancy Cunard, the editor of an anthology, *Negro (1934)*, to which Padmore had contributed. In collaboration with Dorothy Pizer, he also wrote another book, *How Russia Transformed Her Colonial Empire*, but wartime publishing difficulties delayed its appearance until 1946. At the end of the war, Padmore organized the Fifth Pan-African Congress, held at Manchester in 1945. Presided over by W. E. B DuBois, the conference ushered in the postwar anti-imperialist movement. After the conference, one of the organizers, Kwame Nkrumah, returned to the Gold Coast (now Ghana) to build the independence movement there, while Kenyatta, another political colleague, returned to Kenya, where he eventually became prime minister and then president. To provide ammunition for this more vigorous postwar effort to end the empire in Africa, Padmore wrote *Africa: Britain's Third Empire* (1949), which was banned in several colonies.

As Nkrumah's star rose in the Gold Coast, Padmore increasingly focused his efforts on that West African country. He traveled there in 1951, ostensibly to write about political developments for the African American press, but touring the country as Nkrumah's guest, he spoke to sizable audiences. Returning to London to write *The Gold Coast Revolution: The Struggle of an African People from Slavery to Freedom* (1953), he encouraged his American friend RICHARD WRIGHT, another writer disillusioned with Stalinism, to write his own book about the Gold Coast, and Wright produced *Black Power: A Record of Reactions in a Land of Pathos* (1954). Meanwhile, Padmore acted as Nkrumah's representative in London, meeting with European companies to discuss contracts to build housing, conferring with sympathetic members of Parliament, and writing front-page articles for the *Accra Evening News* (renamed the *Ghana Evening News* in 1953). In his most influential book, *Pan-Africanism or Communism?: The Coming Struggle for Africa*, published in 1956, Padmore presented a united, socialist Africa as an alternative to communism. In his foreword to the book, Wright called Padmore "the greatest living authority on the fervent nationalist movements sweeping Black Africa today" (11). That same year Peter Abrahams, a former London ally, pilloried Padmore in a roman à clef, *A Wreath for Udomo* (1956), as a theorist out of touch with African reality.

After Ghana's independence in 1957, Padmore accepted Nkrumah's invitation to move to Accra, Ghana, as an adviser on African affairs. He accompanied Nkrumah on state visits to other countries and organized the 1958 All African Peoples' Conference in Accra. But resentment by others in the Nkrumah government made his position uncomfortable, and a year after he came, he told Nkrumah he wanted to leave. Nkrumah persuaded him to stay, but just a few months later Padmore died at a London hospital of a hemorrhage precipitated by cirrhosis of the liver. His ashes were taken to Ghana for burial at Christiansborg Castle. On Ghana Radio, Nkrumah predicted that "one day the whole of Africa will surely be free and united and when the final tale is told the significance of George Padmore's work will be revealed" (Hooker, 140).

FURTHER READING
Correspondence to, from, and about Padmore is scattered across collections on several continents, for example in the papers of RICHARD WRIGHT, Beinecke Library, Yale; ST. CLAIR DRAKE and Cyril Ollivierre, Schomburg Center for Research in Black Culture, New York Public Library; Nancy Cunard, University of Texas, Austin; Kwame Nkrumah, Moorland-Spingarn Research Center, Howard University; C. L. R. James, University of West Indies, St. Augustine; and Daniel Guerin, University of Paris-Nanterre, France.

Abrahams, Peter. *The Black Experience in the 20th Century: An Autobiography and Meditation* (2001).

Adi, Hakim, and Marika Sherwood. *The 1945 Manchester Pan-African Congress Revisited* (1995).

Azikiwe, Nnamdi. *My Odyssey: An Autobiography* (1970).

Hooker, James R. *Black Revolutionary: George Padmore's Path from Communism to Pan-Africanism* (1967).

Makonnen, Ras. *Pan-Africanism from Within; As Recorded and Edited by Kenneth King* (1973).

CAROL POLSGROVE

Page, Alan Cedric (7 Aug. 1945–), associate justice of the Minnesota Supreme Court, defensive lineman, and NFL star football player for the Minnesota Vikings and Chicago Bears, was born in Canton, Ohio, the youngest of four children of Howard Page, a nightclub owner, and Georgianna Page, a country club locker-room attendant. Like most black families in Canton, the Pages lived on the town's Southeast side. His parents' salaries provided for a standard of living that others in the heart of Canton's black community considered well-to-do. Page described his family's social status as "upper lower class" in an interview with journalist Larry Batson.

Regardless of status, the Page children, Marvel, Twila, Howard Jr., and Alan, suffered the same indignities and lack of opportunity as many postwar African American families. The children attended Canton City Schools. When Page was a fifth grader at South Market Elementary School, Howard Page decided to move his family from urban Canton into rural Osnaburg Township as a result of an incident involving his oldest daughter, Marvel, and two friends. The girls were drenched by a bucket of water thrown from an upstairs window at Canton's McKinley High School. The family believed a white teacher threw water on the girls.

Instead of finding the educational "promised land," Howard and Georgianna soon learned that they and the Powells were the only African American families in the entire Osnaburg school district. Ironically, both families gained national attention through their chosen sport, Page in football and the Powells in golf. Bill Powell was the only black man in America to design, build, and own a golf course. Clearview Golf Course celebrated its fiftieth anniversary in 1998 and was still operated by and the Powell children, following the death of Powell in 2010. His daughter, Renee Powell, who attended school with Alan, became the second African American woman to play professional golf on the LPGA circuit. Both the Page and the Powell children were subjected to overt acts of racism. The final straw for the Pages came during a school band and choir concert. Page's sister Twila remembers walking up to the stage and removing Page, a tuba player in the school band, from the stage when the all-white choir began singing a selection from "Old Man River," which included the derogative term "niggers."

The thought of Page having to listen to those lyrics through week after week of practice incensed his family. Page's sisters, who began attending a Catholic Church while visiting a cousin in Indianapolis, were baptized into the Catholic Church. They were transferred to Canton Central Catholic High School, although his parents were not Catholic. Page's mother attended a Baptist church and his father was a Christian Scientist. The boys, like their older sisters, chose to become Catholic. Howard Jr. and then Page were enrolled into the parochial high school where girls and boys attended separated classes. The Page boys were a welcome sight to Central Catholic's head football coach, John McVay. Although Page had not played football in the midget leagues like many young black boys in this football town, he began playing as a high school freshman ostensibly because his brother liked the game and loved to play.

Page regrets that his mother never saw him play football because of her untimely death. A trip to the Cleveland Clinic to have a biopsy on a lymph node in the neck led to the unexpected death of Page's mother when he was only fourteen. Compounding the emotional loss, the family faced threats of removal and separation. Embraced by extended family members, the Page children were able to remain at home with their father and continue their education.

Only Page attended Central Catholic for his entire secondary schooling. None of the children had scholarships, so the family paid tuition. Unfortunately, Howard Jr. never received his diploma because of unpaid fees. Saved by an unknown benefactor, who paid Pages's fees, Page graduated in 1963.

Alan had the combination that most coaches dream about—size and quickness. Weighing in at more than 230 pounds and standing six feet four inches, Page was an imposing figure on the high school football field. It was no surprise to Canton's football fans that Page was highly recruited by colleges and universities. He chose Notre Dame University, continuing his education in the Catholic tradition and leading the Fighting Irish to the 1966 national championship. He graduated in 1966 with a B.A. in Political Science.

In December of 1966 Page married Lorraine Johnson in Washington, D.C. They had two children, Nina and Georgianna, both of whom Alan raised after their divorce. The Minnesota Vikings drafted him as a first-round pick in 1967. Often dubbed "the indestructible Page" by sportswriters, Page started in every game for the next fifteen years, a total of 236 consecutive kickoffs. He recorded 173 sacks, blocked 28 kicks, and recovered 23 fumbles. He was selected to play in the Pro Bowl nine times, was a four-time NFC Defensive Player of the Year, and achieved the National Football League's Most Valuable Player in 1971, retiring from the game as a member of the Chicago Bears in 1981. Page was named NFC's Defensive Player of the Year four times, the first defensive player to earn the NFL's MVP award.

In 1973 Page married Diane Sims and had two more children, Khamie in 1974, and Justin in 1976. At his wife's urging, he began long-distance running, finishing a 26-mile marathon while actively playing professional football. He is believed to be the first NFL player to do so. The Vikings' head office, however, warned Page to stop running because of the resulting weight loss; defensive players needed to be big. When he refused and continued to run competitively, the Vikings waived him. Within two days of placing Page on waivers, the Vikings reassigned his locker to another player and accepted $100 from the Chicago Bears for his contract. Page continued as a starter and played for the Bears until his retirement in 1981.

Although he gained fame and fortune playing professional football, his real passion was for education, particularly the education of minority students. Projecting his characteristic independence, Page chose Willarene Beasley, principal of North Community High School in Minnesota, to present him at his 1988 induction into the Pro Football Hall of Fame in his hometown of Canton, Ohio. In his acceptance speech, Page said: "We are doing no favors to the young men…if we let them believe that a game shall set them free. At the very best, athletic achievement might open a door that discrimination once held shut."

Page's stunning football career led to many other honors and awards including honorary doctorates from, among others, St. John's University (1994); Winston-Salem State University, (2000); Gustavus Adolphus College, (2003) and both a Doctorate of Laws (1993) and Doctorate of Letters (2004) from his alma mater, Notre Dame. In 2005 he received the National Football Foundation Distinguished American Award.

But his own grit, family values, and belief in education also lead to his success in a second career as a lawyer. In 1978 he earned a law degree from the University of Minnesota, while still playing professional football. After working with a Minneapolis Law Firm from 1979 to 1985, he was appointed a state's Assistant Attorney General, before being elected in 1992 as the first African American associate justice on the Minnesota Supreme Court. Page was reelected to that position in 1998 and 2004. In 1988 he founded the Page Education Foundation to mentor and provide aid to disadvantaged minority students.

FURTHER READING

Batson, Larry. *An Interview with Alan Page* (1977).

Information on Page's football career can be found in the Pro Football Hall of Fame's Archives and Information Center in Canton, Ohio.

Plaut, David. *Black Star Risen: The Alan Page Story.* Documentary for NFL Films broadcast on ESPN (2002).

NADINE MCILWAIN-MASSEY

Page, Clarence (2 June 1947–), journalist and columnist, was born Clarence Eugene Page Jr. at Miami Valley Hospital in Dayton, Ohio, the son of Clarence Hannibal Page, a factory worker and custodian, and Maggie Williams, owner of a catering service. Clarence attended Middletown High School in Middletown, Ohio, where he was feature editor of the school's biweekly newspaper during his senior year. He also won an award from the Southeast Ohio High School Newspaper Association for the year's best feature article. At age seventeen, while still in high school, Page became a freelance writer and photographer for both the *Middletown Journal* and the *Cincinnati Enquirer.* After graduating from high school in 1965, Page attended Ohio University in Athens, where he worked on the university's campus newspaper the *Post.* By the time he graduated in 1969 with a B.S. in Journalism, Page had served for one year as an intern reporter for Dayton's *Journal-Herald.*

It was in college that Page read Jimmy Breslin and Tom Wolfe, practitioners of the New Journalism, an unconventional style of news writing and journalism of the 1960s and 1970s. Page called Breslin and Wolfe his "initial role models" (Bigelow, 188). He was also influenced by the struggles of "both the militant and pacifist elements" of the civil rights movement, as represented by MARTIN LUTHER KING JR. and MALCOLM X (Bigelow, 188).

Immediately after graduating from college, Page moved to Chicago to work as a reporter for the *Chicago Tribune.* Six months later he was drafted into the U.S. Army, where he served as a journalist in the press office of the 212th Artillery at Fort Lewis, Washington. He returned to the *Tribune* in the fall of 1971 and was employed as a reporter whose beats included police, religious, and neighborhood news. In 1972 he shared a Pulitzer Prize as a member of a task force team reporting on vote fraud in Chicago. In 1974 he married LEANITA MCCLAIN; the couple had one son. Page became a foreign correspondent in Africa in 1976, winning the Edward Scott Beck Award for a series on the changing politics of southern Africa. Upon his return to Chicago in 1979, he became an assistant city editor for the *Tribune.* In 1980 he was awarded the Illinois UPI Award for community service.

In 1980, seeking to broaden his career interests, Page joined WBBM-TV, a CBS-owned station in Chicago. In 1981 he and his wife divorced. For two years he was director of the Community Affairs Department and an on-air reporter, and from August 1982 to July 1984 he was a News Department reporter and planning editor.

On 28 May 1984 Page's ex-wife, a columnist for the *Chicago Tribune* and the first black member of the paper's editorial board, committed suicide at the age of thirty-two. Two months after her death, in July 1984, Page returned to the *Tribune* as a columnist and member of the editorial board. In 1986 he edited and wrote the introduction for *A Foot in Each World: Essays and Articles by Leanita McClain.* The following year his twice-weekly columns for the *Tribune's* op-ed page were syndicated by the Tribune Media Services and began to run in more than two hundred newspapers. Page was called a voice of thoughtful moderation, and the topics in his columns ranged from economics to presidential politics to racism to housing, covering both domestic and international issues. He frequently wrote about the behavior of black leaders, middle-class black society and values, and leadership at all levels.

On 3 May 1987 Page married the Chicagoan Lisa Johnson. A son was born from the union on 3 June 1989, the same year that Page won the Pulitzer Prize for commentary. He was the first black journalist to be so honored. Also that year he received the American Civil Liberties Union James P. McGuinn Award for his columns on constitutional rights. In 1990 he taught political science at Chicago's Roosevelt University, where he held the Harold Washington Chair in Political Science.

In May 1991 Page moved to the Washington, D.C., bureau of the *Tribune.* The following year he was inducted into the Chicago Journalism Hall of Fame. In a departure from his writing career, Page played himself as a talk show panel member in the film *Rising Sun* (1993). He published *Showing My Color: Impolite Essays on Race and Identity* in 1996, a series of fourteen essays that describe and question the nature of race and race relations since the 1960s. One essay, "Survivor's Guilt," addresses the life and death of his ex-wife. In 1999 he wrote the introduction to *What Killed Leanita McClain? Essays on Living in Both Black and White Worlds.*

Page became a regular news analyst and commentator for ABC's *This Week* and a frequent guest panelist on such programs as *The McLaughlin Group*, PBS's *The News Hour with Jim Lehrer*, and National Public Radio's *Weekend Edition Sunday*. Beginning in the 1980s he wrote freelance articles for a number of publications, including the *Chicago Magazine, New York Newsday*, the *Wall Street Journal, Washington Monthly*, and the *New Republic*. He also did twice-weekly commentary on WGN-TV in Chicago.

Page received honorary doctorates from Columbia College in Chicago, Lake Forest (Illinois) College, Nazareth College in Rochester, the Chicago Theological Seminary, and his alma mater Ohio University (where he had been the commencement speaker in 1993 and 2001). He was a member of the Chicago Association of Black Journalists and the Chicago Academy of Television Arts and Sciences.

FURTHER READING

Bigelow, Barbara Carlisle, ed. *Contemporary Black Biography* (1993).

Edgar, Kathleen J., ed. *Contemporary Authors* (1995).

Riley, Sam G. *Biographical Dictionary of American Newspaper Columnists* (1995).

GARY KERLEY

Page, Hot Lips (27 Jan. 1908–5 Nov. 1954), jazz trumpeter and singer, was born Oran Thaddeus Page in Dallas, Texas. His parents' names are unknown. His father, who worked in the moving business, died in 1916. His mother taught school and gave Page his first music lessons. He played piano, clarinet, and saxophone before taking up trumpet when he was twelve.

Page played in adolescent bands locally before touring in carnival and minstrel shows during the summer after he turned fifteen. At some point he toured on the Theater Owners' Booking Association circuit, accompanying the blues singers BESSIE SMITH and IDA COX. By one account Page attended high school in Corsicana, Texas, but dropped out to work in a Texas oil field; by another, he organized bands while attending a college in Texas. Accompanying the blues singer MA RAINEY, he went on tour to New York for performances at the Lincoln Theater in Harlem.

By the late 1920s Page had become one of the first trumpeters to make a career of patterning his playing and singing after LOUIS ARMSTRONG. From early 1928 to 1930 he was a member of the bassist WALTER PAGE's southwestern band, the Blue

Hot Lips Page, warming up at the Apollo Theatre, New York City, c. October 1946. (© William P. Gottlieb; www.jazzphotos.com.)

Devils, with whom he recorded solos on "Blue Devil Blues" and "Squabblin'" in November 1929. Along with other musicians from the Blue Devils, Page had transferred into the Kansas City–based big band of BENNIE MOTEN by October 1930, when he made his first recordings under Moten, including "That Too, Do." Page was unquestionably the finest soloist in Moten's band, as heard for example on "The Blue Room" and "Milenberg Joys," from a magnificent recording session of December 1932 that the group made in the midst of an otherwise disastrous trip east.

As work for Moten declined in 1933, Page found work with Moten's former pianist COUNT BASIE, playing in Basie's Cherry Blossom Orchestra in Little Rock, Arkansas, and in the Southwest from 1933 into 1934. The group gradually dissolved. Page returned to Kansas City in 1934. After Moten's death in April 1935, Page formed a quintet that included the tenor saxophonist Herschel Evans and the pianist PETE JOHNSON. He also worked as a freelancer with Basie's new band, of which he became a member while they were at the Reno Club in Kansas City in 1936. At this now legendary venue, Page participated in broadcasts on WXBY that led to Basie's discovery and subsequent fame. In what has been deemed one of the worst career moves in the history of jazz, Page excluded himself from this success in the summer of 1936 when he was persuaded by Armstrong's manager, Joe Glaser, to leave Basie and to work instead as a soloist. Page led an assortment of bands in New York from 1937 on, but often he just participated in jam sessions for lack of steady work. Many have speculated that Glaser made this move to undermine Page, thus protecting Armstrong from one of his most direct competitors.

Before organizing his own band in New York, Page joined the trumpeter Louis Metcalf's big band in the autumn of 1936 for performances at the Renaissance Casino in Manhattan and the Bedford Ballroom in Brooklyn. Page's first big band performed in August 1937 at Small's Paradise in Harlem and in May 1938 at the Plantation Club, a whites-only venue, but it broke up a month later. He then formed a group at the Brick Club, which became in effect a venue for out-of-work musicians, playing for whatever they could take in at the door; this did not last, either.

Page recorded "Skull Duggery" as a leader in 1938, participated in the Spirituals to Swing concert at Carnegie Hall on 23 December, and in June 1939 recorded "Cherry Red" with the pianist Pete Johnson and His Boogie Woogie Boys, featuring the singer BIG JOE TURNER. Later that year he led another band at Kelly's Stable and the Golden Gate Ballroom in New York. In January 1940 he recorded "Gone with the Gin." He toured as the featured soloist with the tenor saxophonist Bud Freeman's big band in July 1940, joined the clarinetist Joe Marsala in October, and then formed another short-lived big band for a stand at the West End Theater Club in November, in which month he recorded "Piney Brown Blues" with Turner and "Lafayette" and "South" under his own name.

Page returned to Kelly's Stable as the leader of a septet from May 1941 into the summer. He then joined the clarinetist Artie Shaw's big band in August 1941 and soon made a hit with his singing and trumpeting on "Blues in the Night" and "St. James Infirmary." Like others of his era, including the singer BILLIE HOLIDAY and the trumpeter ROY ELDRIDGE, Page suffered from racist taunts as the African American star in a white band. In any event, the association was short-lived, as Shaw broke up the band in January 1942 to enlist in the navy.

Page once again led an unsuccessful big band. Writer Greg Murphy reports, "The pattern of Lips' life now reflected the increasing frustration with big bands that seemed accident prone, compensated by large intakes of alcohol and throwing himself into the jam session without restraint." From the summer of 1943, he usually led small groups, while forming big bands for special occasions. His playing and singing are featured on "Uncle Sam Blues," made with Eddie Condon (March 1944), and "I Keep Rollin' On" (June 1944), the latter session as a leader also including one of his finest instrumentals, "Pagin' Mr. Page." He participated in several of Condon's weekly concerts at Town Hall in New York in May and June 1944. At year's end he recorded "The Sheik of Araby" under his own name.

Page performed with DON REDMAN at the Apollo Theater in the summer of 1945, and that July he recorded under the pseudonym Papa Snow White with the reed player SIDNEY BECHET. In the spring of 1946 he accompanied ETHEL WATERS in New York. That year Page's first wife died; her name and details of the marriage are unknown.

This period of Page's career was recalled by the record store owner and producer Milt Gabler, who ran a swing-style session at Jimmy Ryan's on Fifty-second Street in competition with a concurrent bebop session: "There was only one musician who played both jams: Hot Lips Page. He would play one set in our place and run across the street and play theirs."

Page continued to lead a small band. Between March and August 1949 he performed occasionally on Condon's television program *Floor Show*, and early in May he went to Paris to participate in the first Festival International de Jazz. That same year Page and the singer PEARL BAILEY recorded a hit record, pairing together "The Hucklebuck" and "Baby, It's Cold Outside" (1949), but its success did much more for her career than for his. Page married Elizabeth (maiden name unknown) around 1950. Whether his son was from the first or second marriage is unknown.

Page worked mainly as a freelance soloist during the 1950s. He toured Europe from July to October 1951 and again in the summer of 1952, and he held a residency at the downtown location of Café Society in New York from May to June 1953. By this time his health was failing. He suffered a heart attack late in 1953 and another in October 1954, shortly before his death in New York City.

Perhaps Page's most devoted fan was jazz writer Dan Morgenstern, who well captured his essential qualities:

Hot Lips Page was one of the most powerful trumpeters in jazz history. When he wanted to, he could make walls shake. But he could also play softly and tenderly, and everywhere in between. His tone was broad and brilliant, with a wide but pleasing vibrato. He was a master of the growl and of the plunger mute—only trombonist Tricky Sam [Joe] Nanton could approximate the depth of feeling evoked by Page on a minor blues....Yet he could also make swinging, stinging sounds with a Harmon mute, or make a romantic ballad bloom the way an Armstrong or a Coleman Hawkins can.

As a singer, Page excelled at the blues. According to Morgenstern, "He had a marvelous sense of humor....He could also be savage and scathing.... And in the wee hours of the morning, when most of the blowing was done, Page could sit and sing the blues, happy and sad at once, making up new verses or remembering some good old ones, in a way that no witness will ever forget" (*Music '65*, 84).

FURTHER READING

Chilton, John. *Who's Who of Jazz: Storyville to Swing Street*, 4th ed. (1985).

Russell, Ross. *Jazz Style in Kansas City and the Southwest* (1971).

Schuller, Gunther. *Early Jazz: Its Roots and Musical Development* (1968).

Obituary: *New York Times*, 7 Nov. 1954.

This entry is taken from the *American National Biography* and is published here with the permission of the American Council of Learned Societies.

BARRY KERNFELD

Page, Inman Edward (29 Dec. 1853–25 Dec. 1935), educator, was born a slave in Warrenton, Virginia, to Horace Page and Elizabeth Page. His father was able to purchase freedom for himself and his family, and in 1862 to move to Washington, D.C. There Inman attended the private school of GEORGE F. T. COOK for three years. When financial problems forced Inman to leave the school, however, he was hired out to help his family. He also attended a night school taught by GEORGE B. VASHON, and acquired a knowledge of Latin. After the opening of Howard University he resolved to enroll there, so took a job as an ordinary laborer at fifteen cents per hour, grading the university's grounds. That enabled him to attend Howard University, and he was employed as a clerk for General O. O. Howard, the commissioner of the Freedmen's Bureau.

In 1873 Inman Page and George W. Milford became the first black students to enter Brown University in Providence, Rhode Island. At first Page faced a great deal of prejudice, which he over-

came by winning a prize in a school oratorical contest. He was unanimously picked later to give the oration at the graduation exercise of the senior class. In 1877, with B.A. degree in hand, Page began teaching at the Natchez Seminary in Natchez, Mississippi. After the school year he returned to Providence to marry Zelia R. Ball, who had graduated in 1875 from Wilberforce University. They had three children: Zelia, Mary, and Inman E. Page Jr., who died at age seven.

Page went to Jefferson City, Missouri, in 1878 to teach at Lincoln Institute as professor of ethics and to serve as assistant principal. In 1880 officials put him in charge of the school and of the institute's high school. Page served as president of Lincoln Institute for eighteen years. In 1880 Brown University awarded him a master of arts degree. Wilberforce and Howard universities awarded him honorary degrees of doctor of laws.

Upon assuming the presidency Page saw success in greatly increased enrollments and new support from the state legislature. Under Page's leadership Lincoln Institute continued to grow and develop. In 1887 college work was added to the curriculum, and in 1891 the school was designated as a land-grant institution. The state also appropriated ten thousand dollars for an industrial arts building and an additional nine thousand dollars for tools, machinery, and apparatuses. In addition the legislature provided one thousand dollars to build a residence for the president on the campus. In 1895 Memorial Hall, dedicated to the school's founders, was built with forty thousand dollars from the state.

In 1898 state political leaders forced Page out as president of Lincoln Institute. He then became the first president of the Colored Agricultural and Normal University at Langston, in Oklahoma Territory. Page instituted the same curriculum and building program for the new Langston University and the black citizens of Oklahoma as he had done for Lincoln Institute over the previous eighteen years. During his seventeen-year tenure at Langston he was elected head of the Oklahoma Association of Negro Teachers. With the coming of statehood for Oklahoma, though, Page, a lifelong Republican, was forced out of the presidency because of partisan policies.

From 1916 to 1918 Page served as president of the Colored Baptist College of Macon, Missouri. Later Page went to Nashville, Tennessee, where he served as president of a larger Baptist institution, Roger Williams University. However, his health failed, and he returned to Oklahoma City in 1920. From 1921 to 1922 Page was supervising principal of the city's black elementary school and principal of Douglass High School. In 1922 he was recalled to Lincoln Institute (later Lincoln University), but in August 1923, on leave from the Oklahoma City Schools, he tendered his resignation and resumed his duties at Douglass High School.

Page spent his remaining twelve years as an administrator in Oklahoma City's public schools. In June 1935 he retired and was given the title principal emeritus and his full salary for life. Six months later he died at the age of eighty-one in the home of his daughter Zelia in Oklahoma City. He was buried on the campus of Langston University. Four buildings in Oklahoma were named in Page's honor. In 1950 and again in 1996 Lincoln University named its library in memory of Inman E. Page.

FURTHER READING

Holland, Antonio F., Timothy R. Roberts, and Dennis White. *The Soldiers' Dream Continued: A Pictorial History of Lincoln University of Missouri* (1991).

Marshall, Albert P. *Soldiers' Dream: A Centennial History of Lincoln University* (1966).

Patterson, Zella J. Black. *Langston University: A History* (1979).

Savage, W. Sherman. *History of Lincoln University* (1939).

ANTONIO F. HOLLAND

Page, Lawanda (19 Oct. 1920–14 Sept. 2002), comedian and actress, was born Alberta Peal in Cleveland, Ohio; however, she referred to St. Louis, Missouri, as her home. There is little public information available about Page's early life, except that at the tender age of fifteen she began a professional dance career as a chorus girl and stripper in local venues. Known as "The Bronze Goddess of Fire" she focused on her ability to light cigarettes with her fingers, swallow fire, and touch torches to various places on her body. At the age of seventeen, she gave birth to a daughter, Clara, who later became an Evangelist, and also survived her in death.

In the early 1940s, Page became a stand-up comic, a career move that acted as the springboard for her future fame. She signed with Laff Records, an independent record label dedicated to adult comedy recordings, and produced several live comedy albums in the 1960s and 1970s. Around the same time, one of Page's childhood friends, REDD FOXX, recruited her to audition for a part in a new situation comedy series, *Sanford & Son*. Initially, she did not think Foxx was serious when he offered her the job, but his enthusiasm

and teasing threats convinced her that the offer was legitimate. Page was cast in the role of Fred Sanford's (played by Foxx) ultra-religious sister-in-law, "Aunt Esther" Anderson in 1973. Her character's signature line, "Watch it, Sucker!" became not only a household phrase but also the title of one of Page's subsequent comedy albums. As a revival of and tribute to her bawdier days, she reprised a tamer version of her "Bronze Goddess" character as part of an episode in which Sanford hosted a circus in his yard.

After the popular comedy series ended in 1977, Page continued in her role as Esther in two of the show's sequels, *The Sanford Arms* (1977) and *Sanford* (1981). Following the lackluster performance of these spin-offs, she appeared as a guest on the *Redd Foxx Comedy Hour* and, in later years, on other predominantly African American comedy series, such as *Amen* with SHERMAN HEMSLEY (1991), and *Martin* with Martin Lawrence (1992–1993). During this time she also supported herself with work in TV commercials, most notably for the Church's Chicken chain based out of Atlanta, Georgia.

In the late 1980s through the 1990s, Page made appearances in a number of feature films, including *Zapped!* (1982), *My Blue Heaven* (1990), *Friday* (1995), and *Don't Be a Menace in South Central While Drinking Your Juice in the Hood* (1996). She also returned to the stage in the plays *The Inquest of Sam Cooke* (Jerry Jones, 2002) and *Take It to the Lord...Or Else* (Don B. Welch, 1999).

In 1996 Page suffered a stroke from which she never recovered fully. She died in Los Angeles, California, of complications from diabetes.

FURTHER READING

Broadcasting & Cable, 30 Sep. 2002.

Obituaries: *Jet*, 7 Oct. 2002; *Entertainment Weekly*, 3 Jan. 2003.

SIBYL COLLINS WILSON

Page, Walter (9 Feb. 1900–20 Dec. 1957), jazz bassist and bandleader, was born Walter Sylvester Page in Gallatin, Missouri, to parents about whom little information is known. In 1917 Walter graduated from Lincoln High School in Kansas City with a sound musical education gained primarily from the teaching of Major N. Clark Smith, a man responsible for training a number of jazz musicians of the era. Page attended Kansas State Teacher's College from 1917 to 1920 but did not complete a degree in music education. From there he entered the free-wheeling Kansas City jazz scene.

Page's first professional gig came in 1918 with the BENNIE MOTEN Orchestra, playing rhythm tuba, the popular dance-band predecessor to string bass. He also played the bass and baritone saxophone, as well as the sousaphone. Some bandleaders preferred the sousaphone for dance numbers because it could be heard more clearly than a string bass. Page stayed with Moten until 1923.

During the mid-1920s Page traveled throughout Oklahoma and Texas, playing in a number of small bands with names like the Jeter-Pillars Club Plantation Orchestra. It was a hectic life, and in 1927 he returned to Kansas City and the relative stability of Moten's band, where he now played bass, his instrument of choice. This second round with Moten lasted until 1929, when he broke away and formed his own band, Walter Page's Blue Devils.

The Blue Devils were destined to become an important and influential band in the history of jazz. Page enlisted COUNT BASIE as his pianist, the altoist Buster Smith, the tenor sax player LESTER YOUNG, the trombonist and arranger EDDIE DURHAM, the trombonist Dan Minor, the drummer Alvin Burroughs, the vocalist JIMMY RUSHING, and the trumpeter HOT LIPS PAGE, who claimed to be Walter Page's younger half brother (though some disagreement exists as to their actual relationship, if any). Himself a formally trained musician Page was able to teach many of his musicians to read and to play in a disciplined band setting. In their heyday, from 1929 to 1931, the Blue Devils were considered the finest band in the Southwest. As was the custom at the time, bands frequently "battled" one another in contests designed to demonstrate a group's skills and ability to play virtually any arrangement. The Blue Devils took on all comers, including such unlikely contestants as the bands of Lawrence Welk and Vincent Lopez. More often than not, Page's group was victorious. Unhappily, however, and though the Blue Devils were recorded in 1929, when the best members were still present (some scholars, however, argue that Basie was not the pianist in these sessions but that instead Willie Lewis was), the recording quality is such that Page can barely be heard.

In 1929 Moten successfully hired away some of the leading players from the group and employed them in his own orchestra. When Page could not effectively replace them he turned the band over to James Simpson in 1931 and rejoined Moten for a third time, staying until 1935. After Moten died early in 1935 as a result of a botched tonsillectomy, Page and others struggled unsuccessfully to keep the aggregation together. In 1934 Count Basie had formed his own band, and Walter Page became its bassist in late 1935 or early 1936. He remained with Basie until the fall of 1942, with another stint from 1946 to 1948. It was with the Basie band that Page achieved his greatest fame and influence. Nevertheless, he also toured or recorded with SIDNEY BECHET, Jimmy Rushing, Jimmy McPartland, Eddie Condon, Harry James, Benny Goodman, and many others from the late 1930s until his death.

Although Page was initially influenced by the bassist WELLMAN BRAUD, whom he first heard in 1917, he quickly moved beyond Braud's traditional style and became an important innovator on the instrument. Probably the major contribution of Page and the Blue Devils, along with Moten's band (and, later, Basie's), was the introduction of Kansas City swing, a loose, riff-based dance music. (A riff is a musical phrase of just a few notes repeated in varying tones by different sections of the band, sometimes as a background to a soloist or vocalist and sometimes as foreground material in its own right, as exemplified by a number of Basie arrangements.)

Working with the Basie drummer Jo Jones, Page discovered that the bass could lead a band and that the drums (particularly cymbals) could complement that lead. Jones, Page, Basie, and the guitarist Freddie Green experimented with ever greater simplification. Page's bass counted off the beats but did little else, and yet there was a sense of the rhythm, a shading of the notes, along with unexpected emphases. Before their experiments, standard jazz rhythm was usually a 2/4 that was driven by the drummer; Page introduced a more flowing 4/4 that was led by the string bass. That rhythmic smoothness, coupled with repeated riffs, became the trademark of the Kansas City sound. In addition, Page pioneered the "walking" or "strolling" bass, what was to become a standard fixture in many jazz aggregations. The result was a forward-driving propulsion that could carry an entire band.

During his lifetime Page was nicknamed "the Big One" (or "Big 'Un") and "Horse" because of his size and strength with the unwieldy bass. He was also called "Big Four" for his powerful walking 4/4 bass line. It is said that he could drive a band without drums, although, unfortunately, there is not much evidence of this on record. He felt that the rhythm section should be a team and that the bass player should constantly push the band. He built on a simplification, or a paring down, of previous styles, and he demonstrated that swinging jazz need not be played loudly for the swing to be felt or sensed. His numerous recordings with the Count Basie orchestra, wherein "the All-American Rhythm Section" of Basie, Jones, Green, and Page propelled the band, give the best examples of his prowess. He rarely soloed, but he was a great influence on the evolution of the string bass in jazz. Page died in New York City.

FURTHER READING

Brown, Kenneth T. *Kansas City…And All That's Jazz* (1999).

Dance, Stanley. *The World of Count Basie* (1980, 1985).

Pearson, Nathan W., Jr. *Goin' to Kansas City* (1988).

Schuller, Gunther. *The Swing Era: The Development of Jazz, 1930–1945* (1989).

This entry is taken from the *American National Biography* and is published here with the permission of the American Council of Learned Societies.

WILLIAM H. YOUNG

Paige, Richard G. L. (31 May 1846–21 Sept. 1904), lawyer, assistant postmaster, businessman, and state legislator, was born in Norfolk, Virginia, to a slave father and a prominent white woman.

Sources suggest that Paige escaped from Norfolk by way of the Underground Railroad at the age of nine or ten, hiding in a vessel leaving the port. The waters of the Chesapeake and its tributaries were often used as passageways to the North. Paige then traveled to Boston, where he made contact with the family of Judge George Ruffin, who had also moved from Virginia. Paige was educated in Boston, trained to be a machinist, and later returned to Virginia after the Civil War.

Considered to be one of the wealthiest African Americans in postwar Virginia, Paige owned property in both Norfolk County and Norfolk City, and had established an extensive law practice that included both black and white clients. He served in the Virginia House of Delegates from 1871 to 1875 representing Norfolk County. He studied law at Howard University and secured admission to the bar in 1879. He operated a successful law practice in Norfolk before serving again in the Virginia House of Delegates, from 1879 to 1883.

Paige, a Republican, was viewed as one of the principal leaders of the House by all of his colleagues and was well noted for his oratorical skills. One of his most notable accomplishments as a legislator was his ability to influence black voters to support the Readjuster Movement. The continuous promotion of social injustice caused many black activists to support the local popular movement. The Readjuster Movement began in 1879 with the establishment of the biracial Readjuster Party, led by William Mahone, a former Confederate general. The movement was dedicated to the readjustment of Virginia's antebellum debt from $45,000,000 to $21,000,000 in an effort to fulfill campaign promises benefiting poor black and white communities. The Readjusters also increased spending on education for both races, hired more black teachers in black schools, and built a state hospital for mentally ill African Americans. Most importantly, the Readjusters encouraged black political participation, and urged abolition of the poll tax.

Believing that African Americans in Virginia would be better served by the Readjusters than the Republican Party, in February 1880 Paige joined William Roane, Cornelius Harris, Martin Woolridge, and other veteran activists to devise a strategy to unseat the established leadership of the Republican Party. This plan entailed the promotion of popular politics and mass organizing in black communities. Paige and Roane, also a lawyer, even began to challenge segregation in restaurants and theaters, an issue opposed by white Readjusters, but supported by many blacks.

At the height of Readjuster control, from 1879 to 1883, blacks made up 27 percent of Virginia's employees in the Treasury Department, 11 percent in the Pensions Bureau, 54 percent in the Secretary's Office, 38 percent in the Post Office, and 28 percent in the Interior Department. The visibility of blacks in government constituted a radical change in the distribution of political power and was seen by many whites as a threat to white political rule in Virginia.

Conservative whites in Virginia worked hard to reestablish their power. The rise of the Ku Klux Klan and racially motivated assaults and killings by white supremacists went unchecked by the authorities. In response Paige initiated antilynching legislation in 1880. Unfortunately, the proposed antilynching legislation did not receive the support of whites and was buried in committee by a vote of 69 to 12. Even though the antilynching legislation failed, many African Americans viewed it as an important precedent for defeating mob violence through political activism and government intervention.

In 1895, however, the Readjuster Party lost control of the governor's mansion, and black representation and political power began to dwindle. Paige came to realize that a lawyer's license was no guarantee of financial success due to the stagnant Virginia economy that limited the demand for legal services. Because few whites would hire them, and few blacks could afford to hire them, most black lawyers in the state of Virginia had great difficulty earning a living from their profession. The prospect of limited income meant that many black lawyers had to support themselves through other means of employment. Although Paige was one of the most successful lawyers in the state of Virginia, in 1887 he found it advantageous to supplement his income by working as an assistant postmaster in the Norfolk City Post Office.

Paige served two terms on the Board of Curators for Hampton Normal and Agricultural Institute, 1882 to 1886 and 1886 to 1890. He was elected secretary to the board in 1882.

Paige was married to Lillian Ruffin of Massachusetts. Some sources state that they had eight children, and others suggest six children: Warren Clifton; Florence (Boulding); Lewis; Joseph; Emma (Crocker); and Richard G. L. II. Richard G. L. Paige died 21 September 1904. The cause of his death is unknown. A granddaughter, DOROTHY BOULDING FEREBEE would be a prominent physician and women's rights activist in the twentieth century.

FURTHER READING

Brundage, W. F. *Lynching in the New South* (1993).
Hylton, Joseph G. *The Black Lawyer, The First Generation: Virginia as a Case Study* (1994).
Moore, James T. "Black Militancy in Readjuster Virginia, 1879–1883," *The Journal of Southern History* 41, no. 2 (1975).
Rachleff, Peter. *Black Labor in Richmond, 1865–1890* (1989).

CRYSTAL L. JOSEPH

Paige, Rod (17 June 1933–), educator and U.S. secretary of education, was born Roderick Raynor Paige in Monticello, Mississippi, the son of Raynor C. Paige, a school principal, and Sophia Paige, a librarian. When he graduated from Lawrence County Training High School in Monticello, Mississippi, the surrounding institutions of higher education in Mississippi, Tennessee, and Kentucky did not admit black students. Thus Paige chose Mississippi's Jackson State College, the closest historically black college available to him. After receiving his B.A. in Physical Education from Jackson State in 1951, he enrolled in a physical education master's degree

program at Indiana University, Bloomington, eventually earning his degree in 1964.

In July 1956, Paige married Gloria Gene Crawford. They were married for twenty-three years, had one son, and divorced in 1982. After graduating from Indiana in 1969 with a doctorate in Physical Education, Paige left Indiana to become an assistant football coach at the University of Cincinnati. The late 1950s and early 1960s marked the first years of the hiring of black coaches by white universities, a period that also found the first black athletes entering into competition against whites in many sports. Paige left Cincinnati in 1984 to become head football coach and athletic director at Texas Southern University, one of the first college football coaches to hold a doctorate. He insisted that in addition to the athletic appointment his contract also grant him faculty rank at Texas Southern since he wanted to teach descriptive statistics, which is the formal research method used to describe data analysis. When the dean of the College of Education left midyear, Paige was chosen as the acting dean because of his exemplary leadership skills. As acting dean, he established the Center for Excellence in Urban Education to research issues relating to instruction and management in urban school systems; he was later named dean.

Paige served as the deacon and superintendent of the Sunday school at Brentwood Baptist Church in Houston, Texas, and was president of a civic club. He helped organize a protest against a landfill controlled by Browning Ferris Industries, a case that eventually went to the Texas Supreme Court. Paige never imagined or desired involvement in elective politics, but in 1988, after Congressman Mickey Leland died in a plane crash over Ethiopia, a member of the board of education of the Houston Independent School District resigned to run for the vacant congressional seat. Seeing the newly created school board vacancy, leading ministers in the community approached Paige to run for the position. With support from his pastor, Paige ran for school board and was elected in 1989. In 1990, while an officer of the board of education, he co-wrote "A Declaration of Beliefs and Visions," a statement for the district on decentralization, accountability, and a core curriculum that became a pattern for the rest of the country. In 1994 Paige left Texas Southern to become superintendent of the Houston Independent School District (the seventh-largest school district in the country), a position he approached with the research strategies he had developed as an academic. He became known for tying principals' jobs and salaries to school performance and ending the tradition of social promotion, that is, passing failing students because of their age. Paige refused to believe that successful reform of an urban public education system could not happen or that reform was impossible when working with poor black students. During his tenure as school superintendent, the district's black and Latino populations' tests scores rose to some of the highest in the state.

Applying organization theory and development, Paige established reform goals that included partnership and efficiency as a path toward student achievement. One such innovation was the Peer Evaluation, Examination, and Redesign Program, where he was able to solicit nearly twenty committees of local experts in business, finance, and transportation to offer pro bono advice to the school board for school and student programs. Paige was one of the few superintendents of his day to champion a voucher program in his own school district at a time when many districts were highly suspicious of and adversarial toward such programs. He also created the Community Education Partners, a system of alternative education for students who committed school-related felonies. Paige's educational successes in Houston became known as part of the larger "Texas miracle" of increased test scores and decreased dropout rates. The validity of these gains compared with national scores was later questioned by major newspapers and watchdogs, including the *New York Times* and the Texas Education Agency; the Texas Education Agency audited Houston's dropout records and found instances of falsification and missing data. Lawsuits were filed and eventually three school board members resigned, including the then-superintendent Kay Stripling.

Paige was nominated for Outstanding Urban Educator of 1999 and National Superintendent of the Year in 2000, and his popularity did not go unnoticed by then Texas governor George W. Bush. Paige was attracted to Bush's desire to close the achievement gap, the gap in educational outcomes between the races, particularly between black and white students. The same theme would later undergird the Bush administration's efforts with the No Child Left Behind Act, whose main principles included accountability for results—through tying state and district funding to performance and compliance, offering more choices to parents (including free tutoring vouchers and the ability to transfer their children out of low performing schools), and emphasizing research-based approaches to education instruction and reform. On 21 July 2001 President Bush nominated Rod Paige as the seventeenth secretary of the U.S. Department of Education—the first African American appointed to this position. Paige's main priority was implementing the sweeping changes in the new education law. For Paige, that meant closing the achievement gap through "accountability, visibility and choice."

After an active tenure and with a somewhat divided legacy, Paige submitted his resignation on 5 November 2004, the longest-serving secretary of education under a Republican president.

On 23 February 2004, while speaking to the a gathering of the nation's governors, Paige called the National Education Association (NEA) a "terrorist organization." Paige's statement against the largest teachers' union in the country and a major political player made headlines across the country, resulting in many calls for his resignation and later Paige's own acknowledgement of his "poor choice of words." Paige would echo these same sentiments three years later in his first book, *The War against Hope: How Teachers' Unions Hurt Children, Hinder Teachers, and Endanger Public Education*, writing that "no special interest is more destructive than the teachers' unions, as they oppose nearly every meaningful reform." Paige acknowledged that No Child Left Behind was a work in progress but remained committed to the philosophy that the greatest impact one can make in an imperfect system is to develop a culture of change.

FURTHER READING

Paige, Roderick Raynor. *The War against Hope: How Teachers' Unions Hurt Children, Hinder Teachers, and Endanger Public Education*. (2007).

McAdams, Donald R. *Fighting to Save Our Urban Schools...and Winning! Lessons from Houston*. (2000).

RYAN REID BOWERS

Paige, Satchel (7 July 1906–8 June 1982), Negro League baseball pitcher and Hall of Famer, was born Leroy Robert Paige in Mobile, Alabama, the son of John Paige, a gardener, and Lulu (maiden name unknown), a washerwoman. Paige acquired his nickname as a youth after rigging a sling for toting satchels for travelers from the Mobile train station. He joined his first organized team, at the W. H. Council School, at age ten and soon developed a reputation as one of Mobile's best schoolboy players. But he also gained notoriety with the truant officer for frequently playing hooky and getting into gang fights. When he was twelve, Paige was committed to the Industrial School for Negro Children at Mount Meigs, Alabama, after he stole a handful of toy rings from a store. Paige later reflected that the five and a half years he spent at Mount Meigs "did something for me—they made a man out of me…and gave me a chance to polish up my baseball game."

The slender, six-foot three-and-one-half-inch Paige joined the semipro Mobile Tigers for the 1924 season. By his own account, he won thirty games and lost only one that year. Two years later, the peripatetic Paige jumped to the Chattanooga Black Lookouts of the Negro Southern League. Sold to the Birmingham Black Barons of the Negro National League in 1927, he moved on to the Nashville Elite Giants of the Negro Southern League in 1931. The team left Nashville for Cleveland that year, but the Depression hurt attendance, and the club folded before season's end.

That left Paige a free agent, of which he took advantage by selling his services to Gus Greenlee's Pittsburgh Crawfords. Greenlee, who ran the numbers in Pittsburgh's Hill District from his Crawford Grill, had taken on a black sandlot club the year before and was intent on remaking them into the top black club in the country.

Greenlee recruited some of the best players in the nation, including future Hall of Famers JOSH GIBSON, COOL PAPA BELL, JUDY JOHNSON, and OSCAR CHARLESTON. He built Greenlee Field, the finest black-owned stadium in the country, for the Crawfords to play in, and he resurrected the Negro National League, which had collapsed in 1931. With Gibson and Paige, the Crawfords had not only black baseball's best battery, but its two most marketable and highly paid players. Paige, who had filled out to 180 pounds, pitched for the Crawfords and also hired himself out on a freelance basis to semipro teams through the 1933 season. (It was not uncommon for a black pro club to add a semipro player, usually a pitcher, when playing an unusually heavy schedule of games. Negro League players also sold their services on an ad hoc basis.) After a contract dispute with Greenlee, Paige left the Crawfords for a white semipro club in Bismarck, North Dakota, in 1935, returning for the 1936 season.

He did not stay for long. During spring training in New Orleans the following year, he was seduced by a lucrative offer to pitch for Ciudad Trujillo, a club in Santo Domingo associated with the Dominican Republic dictator Rafael Trujillo. Paige said in his autobiography that he was offered thirty thousand dollars for his services and for recruiting eight other players, with the division of the money up to him. Gibson, Bell, and a half dozen other Crawfords joined him, decimating the Crawfords but winning the island championship for Ciudad Trujillo.

Branded an outlaw by the Negro National League, Paige barnstormed with the Trujillo All-Stars on his return to the United States. Barnstorming meant traveling from town to town, usually living on buses, playing against teams of white major leaguers or local semipros, and splitting the proceeds at the gate. Greenlee then sold Paige's contract to the Newark Eagles, but he refused to report. Instead, he pitched in the Mexican League during the 1938 season, until a sore arm caused him to return to the United States.

Paige's career seemed over, and most black teams declined to bid for his services. Finally, Kansas City Monarchs' owner J. L. Wilkinson signed him to play for the Monarchs' second team, which barnstormed through the Northwest and Canada. Still a draw at the gate, Paige was advertised to pitch every game. Relying more on guile than his once-famous fastball, he would pitch for three innings before retiring to the bench. But as the summer wore on, his arm came back, and he reported to spring training with the Monarchs' regular club for the 1940 season.

For the next nine seasons, with Paige as their ace, the Monarchs challenged the Homestead Grays as black baseball's best team. A regular at the Negro League East–West All-Star game, Paige was known for his "bee ball" (you could hear it but not see it), pinpoint accuracy, and hesitation pitch. During the 1942 Negro League World Series, he won three of the Monarchs' four victories over the Grays.

In 1948, Paige made his long-awaited debut in the major leagues. Cleveland Indians' owner Bill Veeck signed him during the 1948 pennant drive, and the forty-two-year-old "rookie" responded with six victories and only one defeat. Some 201,000 fans attended his first three starts, as the Indians set night-game attendance records at home and in Chicago. Paige pitched for the Indians through the 1949 season, but he lost his spot on the roster after Veeck sold the team. His record that year was 4–7, with a 3.04 ERA and five saves. Paige returned to the long bus rides through the night that characterized independent baseball, pitching for the Philadelphia Stars and for remnants of the Kansas City Monarchs.

He returned to the majors in 1951, reunited with Veeck, by then the owner of the St. Louis

Browns. Paige won twelve games in 1952 for the hapless Browns and was selected to the American League All-Star team. After the 1953 season, Paige once again returned to barnstorming, but he was soon back in the minors, with stays at Miami in the International League (1956–1958) and Portland of the Pacific Coast League (1961). His last major league appearance came with the Kansas City Athletics in 1965. The Athletics' owner, Charles O. Finley, who signed Paige to help him qualify for a major-league pension, put a rocking chair in the bullpen for the fifty-nine-year-old pitcher, who hurled three shutout innings against the Boston Red Sox. He is thought to be the oldest player to appear in a major-league game.

Paige ended his career in 1967, riding the bus with black baseball's last team, the Indianapolis Clowns. He coached for the Atlanta Braves the following season. His major-league statistics of 28 wins, 31 losses, 476 innings pitched, and a 3.29 ERA were only a belated addition to the numbers he put up during five decades on the mound.

Negro League and independent baseball records are incomplete, but, by his own account, Paige threw an estimated 55 no-hitters and won more than 2,000 of the 2,500 games in which he pitched. Many of the games were against semipro opposition. "I had that suit on every day, pretty near 365 days out of the year," he said. Paige told his biographer that he reckoned he had pitched before about 10 million fans. Given his constant travels and ability to pitch virtually every day, it is likely that more fans personally witnessed Paige play than any other ballplayer.

Paige is perhaps most popularly remembered for the all-star aggregations of Negro Leaguers he led in exhibition games against teams of major-league stars during the 1930s and 1940s. In these encounters, which sometimes matched Paige versus Dizzy Dean or another Hall of Fame pitching opponent, the Negro Leaguers more than held their own. His feats in such games became part of baseball mythology. Many a fan recounts a story about a game in which Paige intentionally walked the bases loaded with major leaguers, told his fielders to sit down, and then struck out the side.

Paige married Janet Howard in 1934, but they divorced in 1943. He later married Lahoma Brown in 1974 and had six children with her.

Paige, who toured with the Harlem Globetrotters and appeared in a motion picture, *The Wonderful Country*, which starred Robert Mitchum, offered six rules as his guide to longevity:

1. Avoid fried meals, which angry up the blood.
2. If your stomach disputes you, lie down and pacify it with cool thoughts.
3. Keep the juices flowing by jangling around gently as you move.
4. Go very light on the vices, such as carrying on in society. The social rumble ain't restful.
5. Avoid running at all times.
6. Don't look back. Something might be gaining on you.

Satchel Paige embodied life in baseball's Negro Leagues. Black baseball's best-known performer, the lanky right-hander barnstormed his way across the United States, Canada, and into the Caribbean basin in a career that spanned half a century. By combining showmanship and incredible durability with magnificent talent, Paige became one of baseball's most enduring legends. In 1971 he was the first Negro League player elected to baseball's Hall of Fame. "To tell you the truth," Paige said in 1981, "all over Cuba, Santo Domingo, Puerto Rico, South America, everywhere I played, I had bouquets on my shoulder …I just could pitch. The Master just give me an arm….You couldn't hardly beat me." He died in Kansas City, Missouri.

FURTHER READING

Paige, Leroy (Satchel), with David Lipman. *Maybe I'll Pitch Forever* (1962).

Holway, John B. *Josh and Satch: The Life and Times of Josh Gibson and Satchel Paige* (1991).

Ribowsky, Mark. *Don't Look Back: Satchel Paige in the Shadows of Baseball* (1994).

This entry is taken from the *American National Biography* and is published here with the permission of the American Council of Learned Societies.

ROB RUCK

Painter, Nell Irvin (2 Aug. 1942–), historian, academic, and writer, was born Nell Elizabeth Irvin in Houston, Texas, to Frank Edward Irvin, a chemist and chemistry administrator at the University of California at Berkeley, and Dona Lolita McGruder, a homemaker and personnel officer for the Oakland Public Schools. Her older brother Frank Jr. died during a tonsillectomy at age five in 1943. When Nell was just an infant, her parents moved to Oakland, California, seeking better work opportunities and living conditions. She attended public schools, including Oakland Technical High School, and she was an active youth member of Downs Methodist Church.

Nell Irvin Painter during a visit to Wesleyan University in Middletown, Conn., on 3 Feb. 2005. (AP Images.)

Nell Irvin enrolled in the University of California at Berkeley in 1960 and decided on an anthropology major after spending the summer of 1962 in Kano, Nigeria. A student participant in Operations Crossroads Africa, she helped build a local school and experienced the country from a grassroots level. As a result, she deepened her long-standing interest in African and African Diaspora studies. She spent her junior year in France studying at the University of Bordeaux before returning to Berkeley where she graduated in 1964. Returning to Africa with her parents in 1965, she taught French for a year then did postbaccalaureate study at the Institute of African Studies at the University of Ghana. At the Institute, she was exposed to scholarly literature, research and discussion of imperialism and political issues related to race, class, and economics. Also in 1965, Nell Irvin married Colin Painter, a professor of linguistics at the University of Ghana. The marriage ended in divorce a year later.

She returned from France and Ghana with a commitment to history. Painter earned a master's degree in African history at the University of California in Los Angeles in 1967 and continued graduate study at Harvard University, shifting from a concentration in African to American history. At Harvard, she was a teaching fellow in Afro-American studies (1969–1970) and history (1972–1974). She received the CORETTA SCOTT KING Award from the American Association of University Women in 1970 and a Ford Foundation Fellowship that facilitated her completion of the research and writing of her dissertation on the migration of former slaves from the South to settlements in Kansas.

After receiving the Ph.D. in 1974 Painter became assistant professor (1974–1977) of history at the University of Pennsylvania during which time her first book, *Exodusters: Black Migration to Kansas After Reconstruction*, was published (1976). A promising scholar early in her professional career, she was a Fellow of the American Council of Learned Societies, Charles Warren Center for Studies in American History, and the Radcliffe/Bunting Institute between 1976 and 1977. She became a tenured associate professor in 1977; she left the university shortly thereafter and in 1980 she became professor of history at the University of North Carolina at Chapel Hill. Opportunities for research continued, with her being chosen as a W. E. B. DuBois Institute (Harvard University) Research Associate (1977–1978), National Humanities Center in North Carolina Fellow (1978–1979), and a John Simon Guggenheim Foundation Fellow (1982–1983). For the academic year 1985–1986, she was Russell Sage Visiting Professor of History at Hunter College of the City University of New York. In addition, she was presented the Candace Award in 1986 by the National Coalition of One Hundred Black Women.

While a Fellow at the National Humanities Center in North Carolina, she published *The Narrative of Hosea Hudson: His Life as a Negro Communist in the South* (1979), an oral history derived account of a semiliterate steelworker, union organizer, and Communist Party operative in Alabama from the 1930s to 1950s. Her next book considered the effect of industrialization on Americans over a forty-year time span. *Standing at Armageddon: The United States, 1877–1919* was published in 1987 and won the Letitia Brown Memorial Publication Prize.

After an eight-year affiliation with the University of North Carolina, she accepted the position of professor of history at Princeton University in 1988. That same year she became a Fellow at the Center for Advanced Study in the Behavioral Sciences. On 14 October 1989 Nell Irvin Painter married Glen R. Shafer, who was then the Ronald G. Harper Distinguished Professor in the Business School at the University of Kansas, and subsequently became the Board of Governors' Distinguished Professor at the Rutgers University Business School. With the union, Painter became stepmother to Richard and Dennis Shafer.

Painter distinguished herself as clearly among the nation's preeminent scholars in the research, interpretation and instruction of American history during her tenure at Princeton. As acting director of the Program in Afro-American Studies (1990–1991), Edwards Professor of American History (1991–2005) and director of the Program in African American Studies (1997–2000), she received the Kate B. and Hall J. Peterson Fellowship from the American Antiquarian Society in 1991 followed by a National Endowment for the Humanities Fellowship from 1992 to 1993.

Her historical depictions of African Americans, women and working class people, particularly during the Progressive and Reconstruction eras, propelled her to the forefront of the discipline. Exhibiting a consistency for commitment to exhaustive research, attention to the smallest detail, and consideration of the full implications of race, gender, class, sexuality, and culture when framing the study of American history, she trained a generation of historians to unify rather than compartmentalize history by example as well as instruction.

Her critically acclaimed book, SOJOURNER TRUTH: *A Life, A Symbol* (1997), exposed her abilities as a meticulous researcher, as she carefully explored the complex life of the nineteenth-century abolitionist and women's rights advocate. The book won the Black Caucus of American Library Association nonfiction award. Additional writings included editing two Penguin Classic volumes—*Narrative of Sojourner Truth* (1998) and *Incidents in the Life of a Slave Girl* (2000), and countless articles addressing issues pertinent to the history of the southern region. In 2002 she converged discussions of the histories of the South, women, and African Americans in *Southern History Across the Color Line*, a study that candidly considered relationships among men and women of different races in the region. She subsequently authored *Creating Black Americans: African American History and Its Meanings, 1618 to the Present* (2006), a textbook and cross study of imaging, the historical and cultural tracking of the African American presence from the perspectives of African Americans.

Appearances on public television programs, participation on several radio broadcasts, and her role as a reviewer of literature by other writers representing various disciplines enhanced the fame Painter already enjoyed as one of the nation's leading historians.

She held honorary degrees from Wesleyan University, Dartmouth College, SUNY-New Paltz, and Yale University; and she served on a number of editorial boards of academic presses, the University of North Carolina Press, University of South Carolina Press, and the Encyclopedia of American Cultural and Intellectual History, to name but a few. An executive board member of the American Academy of Political and Social Science, she served in the same capacity for the Organization of American Historians and Society of American Historians, and Southern Regional Council. She also chaired the Society of American Historians Francis Parkman Prize Committee, the Organization of American Historians Avery O. Craven Award, and the Schomburg Center for Research in Black Culture Scholars-in-Residence Program.

Nell Irvin Painter retired from teaching in 2005, three years after receiving the Nancy Lyman Roelker Mentorship Award from the American Historical Association for graduate teaching. Princeton University hosted a two-day conference in celebration of her contributions to history titled "Constructing the Past, Creating the Future: The Legacy of Nell Irvin Painter."

Selected president of the Southern Historical Society for 2007 and the Organization of American Historians, 2007–2008, the largest learned society devoted to the study of American history, she studied painting at Rutgers University. In 2011 Painter earned an MFA in painting from the Rhode Island School of Design. That year she also released a paperback edition of *The History of White People*, which was published by W.W. Norton to critical and popular acclaim in 2010.

AMALIA K. AMAKI

Pajaud, William (3 Aug. 1925–), artist and curator, was born in New Orleans, the son of William Etienne Pajaud Sr., a trumpet player and bandleader, and Audrey Du Conge, a college professor of social work. For well over half a century, his prolific body of paintings, drawings, and prints established him as a renowned figure in modern African American art. His watercolors, oils, acrylics, and prints celebrate the triumphs and beauty of his people, focusing on the New Orleans jazz, Christian and Jewish religious figures, landscapes, women, and many other themes. In addition, Pajaud worked for thirty years as art and public relations director at black-owned Golden State Mutual Life Insurance Company in Los Angeles. There he developed one of the most outstanding private collections of African American art in the United States.

As a child in New Orleans, he experienced the vitality of African American life and culture, especially its vibrant musical tradition and legacy, which informed his subsequent artistic career. At Xavier University, he earned a B.A. in fine arts in 1946, with a minor in romance languages. After completing his studies, he moved to Chicago and worked as a sign artist and a freelance designer. He married Hariette Craft in 1946, and the couple had three sons before they divorced in 1953.

In 1949 Pajaud moved to Los Angeles. While working as a postal clerk from 1953 to 1957, he pursued further training at Chouinard Art Institute, where he earned a certificate in advertising and design in 1955. He was the only full-time African American student at Chouinard and stated that he endured racist comments and directives from the Institute's staff. Pajaud's experiences were typical in postwar Los Angeles, where racism was subtly expressed, and in that way, differed from the Jim Crow discrimination and terror in the South. Racism spurred Pajaud to action for he considered his art a tool for social justice.

In 1957 Pajaud joined Golden State and continued to paint and draw in the evenings and on the weekends. He also developed close friendships with black artists in Los Angeles and elsewhere. His relationships, especially his extremely close forty-year friendship with painter and muralist JOHN BIGGERS of Houston, influenced his artistic efforts throughout his life. Pajaud was briefly married to Seda Coycault, from 1957 to 1959.

His most enduring contribution there was his development of the Golden State art collection. With profound vision and a minuscule budget, Pajaud used his personal knowledge and contacts to purchase first-rate African American art. At times, he traded his own paintings for works of distinguished colleagues throughout the nation. His curatorial efforts enabled the company to acquire paintings, drawings, photographs, and sculptures by Biggers, HENRY OSSAWA TANNER, CHARLES

ALSTON, James Van Der Zee, Hughie Lee-Smith, Romare Bearden, Jacob Lawrence, Charles White, Elizabeth Catlett, Samella Lewis, Betye Saar, John Riddle, Varnette Honeywood, Richard Wyatt, and CHARLES DICKSON. This Golden State collection is a veritable Who's Who of twentieth-century African American art. Hung in the lobby, hallways, and private offices of the company building, the company's art is a premier cultural and art historical resource in southern California and the United States. It educates, inspires, and empowers its local, national, and international viewers. In 2007, however, the company, facing economic hardship, sold many of the most prominent works through Swann Galleries in New York.

Pajaud exhibited his art in Los Angeles in black Protestant churches and other places of worship, community centers, and at the Heritage Art Gallery, which defied the racially exclusionary practices of mainstream area art institutions in the early 1960s. He also exhibited at the black-owned Brockman Gallery in 1966. Over the years, his paintings, drawings, and prints combined outstanding technique, vibrant color, and engaging black subject matter. His watercolor skills garnered him substantial recognition, establishing him as one of the finest practitioners of this medium in American art history. He served as president of the National Watercolor Society in 1974.

Pajaud was briefly married to Shirley Frazier (c. 1969–1970). His subsequent 1970 marriage to Donlaply Wang Charoensuk produced two daughters and ended in divorce in 1994.

Pajaud's recollections of New Orleans jazz, and of his father's performances at funerals and other functions, inform his art. His jazz images are a loving tribute to African American contributions to American expressive culture. Likewise, his artistic treatment of women honors millions of anonymous black women whose collective efforts ensured the survival of the race throughout America, the Caribbean, and elsewhere. His striking portraits reflect a deep appreciation of black women's beauty, dignity, and moral stature. They provide a compelling antidote to the destructive racist caricatures like Aunt Jemima and others that pervaded American popular culture.

Retired from Golden State in 1987, Pajaud continued a vigorous record of visual production. After living in Las Vegas from 1991 to 1994, he returned to Los Angeles, exhibiting widely in museums and galleries throughout the nation. He married June White in 1996 and added dramatic new features to his artistic vision. In 2006 he presented an exhibition of more than forty watercolors and mixed media works at the M. Hanks Gallery in Santa Monica, California, addressing the tragedy of Hurricane Katrina in New Orleans in 2005. These powerful yet disturbing images combined Pajuad's usual vibrant colors with figurative tributes to African tribes and religious icons. Above all, the exhibition revealed his continuing concern with his birth city and the welfare of its black residents.

FURTHER READING

Driskell, David. *The Other Side of Color* (2001).

Hanks, Eric, ed. *The Artwork of William Pajaud* (2003).

Lewis, Samella. *African American Art and Artists* (2003).

Pajaud, William. *The Sights and Sounds of My New Orleans* (1999).

Von Blum, Paul. *Resistance, Dignity, and Pride: African American Artists in Los Angeles* (2004).

Von Blum, Paul. "William Pajaud," in *St. James Guide to Black Artists*, ed. Thomas Riggs (1997).

PAUL VON BLUM

Palmer, Earl (25 Oct. 1924–19 Sept. 2008), drummer, grew up next to the French Quarter in the predominantly African American Treme District in New Orleans. Palmer's mother, Thelma, was a dancer, who at one point became a member of a traveling vaudeville show called IDA COX's "Darktown Scoundrels." Palmer never knew his father. As a child, he was told that his father was once a cook on a whaling ship that sailed out of Newfoundland when he was killed in an accident. Palmer grew up learning to tap, while also learning to play the drums. He felt his tap dancing background was advantageous in developing his drumming style.

In 1943 Palmer joined the racially segregated U.S. Army. He attained the rank of staff sergeant in the 642nd Ordnance Ammunition Company, but he was later reduced in rank for arming himself and other African American infantrymen with live ammunition. Palmer was then shipped to the coastal artillery in Salinas where he plotted shell trajectories for the artillery group. In the summer of 1944 Palmer was shipped to Europe, landing in Liverpool, England. Following the footsteps of the Allied invasion, Palmer's unit later embarked from Southampton, England, across the English Channel and landed at Omaha Beach in France. On 1 November 1944 Palmer's unit crossed into the city of Herleen in Holland where he befriended a member of the Dutch underground named Johann

Dohmen. Palmer was smitten by Johann and his Dutch family, often visiting and eating dinner with them. Palmer also helped supply his surrogate Dutch family with rations during his stay in Holland.

In December 1944 Palmer's unit was under fire in a foxhole near Malmedy, where he contracted tetanus and a case of frostbite. Palmer was ultimately moved to Marseille, France, where he served for the remainder of his military career as a military policeman. While in France, Palmer visited a local club and witnessed a duet performing. Not realizing who they were, Palmer approached the musicians to tell them how much he liked their performance. Much later Palmer realized he had congratulated the legendary guitar player Django Reinhardt and the violinist Stephane Grappelli. When World War II ended, he returned to his hometown. Even though Palmer was already considered an accomplished drummer by local jazz musicians, he decided to attend New Orleans's Grunewald School of Music on the G.I. Bill. The Grunewald School was segregated, but African American and white jazz musicians broke the color line and socialized in the stairwells between the floors of the school.

Palmer was first married in 1947 to Catherine Roy. They had four children: Earl Cyril Palmer Jr., Donald Alfred Palmer, Ronald Raymond Palmer, and Patricia Ann Palmer. In 1947 Palmer secured his first job with DAVID BARTHOLOMEW's jazz band. Palmer supplied the backbeat for Bartholomew's protégés FATS DOMINO and LITTLE RICHARD. Little Richard's forceful style compelled Palmer to develop drum set beats that were as dynamic as Little Richard's piano playing. His drumming legacy is his creation of the rim shot–laden backbeat, now considered standard in popular music performance. He recorded extensively with various New Orleans artists at Cosimo Matassa's J&M Studio. Palmer's knowledge of New Orleans's second-line shuffles made him a much-in-demand percussionist in his hometown. The second-line shuffle was associated with onlookers watching a traditional New Orleans jazz funeral procession, who were considered to be the first line. The jazz music played by musicians in the funeral motivated members of the second line to dance back home after the funeral was over.

In the late 1940s and early 1950s, Palmer played drums on what many consider the best-recorded drum tracks in rock and roll and R&B recording history. In 1949 Palmer recorded on Fats Domino's

"The Fat Man." In 1952 he played on Lloyd Price's hit "Lawdy Miss Clawdy," and SMILEY LEWIS's "I Hear You Knocking." In 1953 Palmer recorded on Little Richard's "Kansas City," followed by "Tutti Frutti" in 1955. The following year he provided the drumbeats on Little Richard's recordings of "Long Tall Sally" and "Slippin' and Slidin'." In 1957 Palmer played on Little Richard's recording "Lucille" and SAM COOKE's "You Send Me."

In 1957 Palmer left the New Orleans music scene and moved to Hollywood, California, to become a first-call recording artist. During the late 1950s, Palmer played drums on recordings of Eddie Cochran's "Summertime Blues," NAT KING COLE's "Ramblin' Rose," Ritchie Valens's "La Bamba," and Little Richard's "Good Golly Miss Molly." Palmer also played drums for Sheb Wooley's popular novelty song "The Purple People Eater." In 1959 Palmer played on another hit novelty record, "Farmer John" by Don and Dewey. In the same year, he also played on Jan and Dean's "Baby Talk" and Connie Stevens's "Sixteen Reasons."

By the 1960s Palmer was considered by many Los Angeles musicians to be the most creative drum recording artist in popular music. Palmer's drumming in the 1960s included Bobby Bare's "The Book Of Love" and Bobby Vee's number-one hit "Take Good Care of My Baby." In 1961 Palmer played drums to a variety of pop hits on his first solo album, *Drumsville*, on the Liberty label; one year later recorded another solo album titled *Percolator Twist*. In the same year, he provided drum accompaniment on the number-1 RAY CHARLES hit "I Can't Stop Lovin' You." In 1963 Palmer drummed for Jan and Dean's "Drag City" and "Surf City." In the same year Nino Tempo and April Stevens used Palmer's playing for their recording "Deep Purple." In the mid 1960s Palmer again recorded with Jan and Dean on "Dead Man's Curve," and "The Little Old Lady from Pasadena," as well as the Righteous Brothers' "You've Lost That Lovin' Feeling" and "Unchained Melody." He also played drums on Sonny and Cher's debut album as well as on Beach Boys and Supremes LPs. In 1966 Palmer played drums on IKE and TINA TURNER's record "River Deep Mountain High." Additionally, he crossed over into television soundtrack drumming, where he played drums on theme songs for several popular TV series, including *Batman*, *Mission Impossible*, *77 Sunset Strip*, and *Hawaiian Eye*. Palmer also recorded what he considered some of his most difficult recording performances for a variety of popular TV cartoons. According

to Palmer, cartoon music scores were difficult to play because of the complexity of the syncopated drumbeats.

Palmer continued to record in the popular music genre with a diverse range of artists, including Herb Albert, DINAH WASHINGTON, Glen Campbell, the Monkeys, Bobby Darin, LOU RAWLS, the Beach Boys, ELLA FITZGERALD, the Jackson Five, GLADYS KNIGHT and the Pips, DIANA ROSS, Frank Sinatra, the Temptations, SCREAMIN' JAY HAWKINS, Willie Nelson, Neil Young, TAJ MAHAL, Henry Mancini, and Elvis Costello.

Earl Palmer's contribution to the American music recording industry represents an astounding career that tore down many racial covenants. Palmer's drumming legacy remains unmatched as he is regarded by many to be the greatest rock-and-roll drummer in history. He was inducted into the Rock and Roll Hall of Fame at the fifteenth annual induction dinner in March of 2001. At his induction, Palmer reminded the audience that he was often forced into recording songs in a manner that fit into a timed jukebox format, ultimately changing the true nature of the recordings. To accomplish this, Palmer cleverly sped up particular rhythms so the songs would be within this time frame. Palmer also questioned the ethics of American and English bands who recorded covers of R&B songs, many of them originally written by African American musicians from New Orleans who got little money or credit for their efforts. He also noted how little he was paid for a multitude of recording sessions that eventually sold millions of copies. Earl Palmer continued to record and demonstrate his drum technique for drumming students and music professionals. In 2008 Palmer died at his home in Los Angeles after a lengthy illness.

FURTHER READING

Flans, Robyn. "Earl Palmer: Rock 'N' Roll Studio Legend," *Modern Drummer* (Mar. 2005).
Scherman, Tony. *Backbeat: Earl Palmer's Story* (1999).

DAN SHOPE

Pandit, Korla (16 Sept. 1921–2 Oct. 1998), entertainer, pianist, organist, lecturer, television and radio personality, was born John Roland Redd in St. Louis, Missouri, to Doshia O'Nina Johnson and Ernest Samuel Redd, a minister. His ancestry is both black and white, the white lineage through his maternal grandmother, Frances Maria Lankford-Johnson, stemming from Langfords who first came to Virginia from England in 1645.

Pandit's family is unusually rich in musical and creative talent. Pandit's great-uncle Philip Benjamin "PB" Lankford taught jazz to numerous musicians who went on to careers in orchestras led by LOUIS ARMSTRONG, DUKE ELLINGTON, Singleton Palmer, FATE MARABLE, Charles Creath, Dewey Jackson, and CAB CALLOWAY. Another great-uncle, John Anderson Lankford, was known as "the Dean of African American Architects," and others in the family—Arthur Edward Lankford, Robert Bumbary Sr., and Robert Bumbary Jr.—also became notable architects. Pandit's brother Speck was a successful jazz pianist and music teacher in Des Moines, Iowa, and had his own radio show. Pandit's nephew Adrian Pepo was lead singer for The Amazing Platters and Zola Taylor's Platters. Another nephew, Gary Bass, performed for years with singer Janet Jackson.

Shortly after Pandit's birth the family relocated to Hannibal, Missouri, where his father, a Baptist minister, worked at the Eighth & Center Streets Baptist Church. The family again relocated in 1930 to Columbia, Missouri, where his father presided over the Broadway Baptist Church. At the time Pandit graduated from high school in 1937, he was living with his older brother Ernest Redd Jr. (also known as Speck Redd), in Omaha, Nebraska. The following year he played piano in jazz bands in Des Moines and Ottumwa, Iowa, with his brothers Harry and Speck.

Pandit moved to Los Angeles in 1939, following his sister Frances Redd (also known as Frances Pepo), who had moved there to work with the African American director and producer George Randol on *Midnight Shadow*, her first and only Hollywood film. The jeweled turban that was to become Pandit's trademark is said to have been inspired by a character in the film played by John Criner. Frances's work as a hair and makeup artist led to Pandit's acquaintance with her friend and his future wife, Beryl June DeBeeson, who was working for Disney Studios and was the daughter of George DeBeeson, who provided the storyboards and animation for Disney's *Pinocchio*. The two were married in Tijuana, Mexico, on 21 July 1944. They had two sons, Shari and John.

In 1943 Pandit was an organist for Los Angeles radio station KMPC, as well as staff organist and music clearance agent for NBC in Hollywood. He was then going by the name Juan Rolando and became one of the first to make 16-inch radio transcription discs for Capitol Records' Radio Transcription Division. He was first heard, again as

Juan Rolando, on the Jubilee radio show in 1946. This station was created for black servicemen in World War II and featured black entertainers. Pandit was already becoming well known for being able to play the piano and Hammond B-3 organ simultaneously.

In 1948 Pandit became the music director for the revival of the radio show *Chandu the Magician*, and he transformed his persona, becoming the India-born Korla Pandit, supposedly with a French mother and Indian father. As music director, he was then playing five days a week when television pioneer Klaus Landsberg offered Pandit his own daily fifteen-minute television show, *Adventures in Music*, on Los Angeles station KTLA. Part of the arrangement was that Pandit would provide the music for another of Landsberg's television shows, *Time for Beany*. This show eventually became the cartoon *Beany & Cecil*, while Korla Pandit's *Adventures in Music* made television history. Both shows were broadcast live five days a week, and the latter gained a national audience and ran for more than nine hundred episodes. When Pandit left *Adventures in Music* in the 1950s, a younger musician was brought in to replace him; this young man was Liberace, and the show launched his career. In 1955 Pandit revived his version of the show as *Korla Pandit—Adventures in Music*, first on Channel 7, KGO, and then on Channel 11, KNTV. By 1951 Pandit was an innovator on radio and television and the first to venture into syndication with the world's first music videos.

Pandit made his first of three movie appearances in 1952 with *Something to Live For*, appearing at the piano and organ in Hindu dress and, as was to be the pattern with his roles, having no speaking lines. He was later in *Which Way Is Up?* (1977) and *Ed Wood* (1994).

Pandit made his first national recordings as part of Roy Rogers's Sons of the Pioneers in the early 1950s, with RCA Victor. He also recorded on Vita Records, until he established his own label, India Records, in 1954. On India he released his first LP, *The Universal Language of Music*. Because of its success, he signed with Fantasy Records in 1958. During this period he teamed with a real estate developer named Louis D. Snader and made what were then called telescriptions. These were ten- to fifteen-minute segments on 16-mm film that showcased his musical talents and were used as fillers in the daily programming of television stations around the country. They proved so popular that they were eventually used by such artists as NAT KING COLE and Peggy Lee.

Throughout the 1960s Pandit's recording and concert career expanded. By the 1970s, however, the public lost interest in him, and he could be seen playing in local restaurants, bowling alleys, and drive-ins. However, he never lost his dignity and professionalism. He added to his portfolio by scoring several movies, including the restored version of Lon Chaney's *Phantom of the Opera* and *Spectres of the Spectrum* (1989; re-released in 1999). Pandit's close friend and promoter Michael Copner helped him embark on a highly successful comeback in the 1980s, and he ultimately became known as The Godfather of Exotica.

Pandit's health failed in the 1990s and he passed away at the Petaluma Valley Hospital on 2 October 1998. Throughout his life, many had tried to expose Korla Pandit as a fake and fraud who had nothing to do with France or India, believing he was simply trying to pass as white. He was an African American of white (British) and slave descent who, like so many before and after, had successfully morphed himself into a popular and saleable performer.

FURTHER READING

Boston Globe (13 Oct. 2002).
Des Moines Tribune (29 Aug. 1974).
Indiana Evening Gazette (20 Jan. 1977).
Los Angeles Examiner (13 Feb. 1931).
New York Press (vol. 12, no. 40, 2004).

DAVID DE CLUE

Parish, Robert L. (30 Aug. 1953–), basketball player, born in Shreveport, Louisiana, to Robert and Ada Parish, who worked for a local manufacturer and the school district, respectively. As a youngster, Parish was unskilled and uninterested in basketball, but with practice and encouragement, he flourished. While dealing with the turbulence of a newly integrated high school, Parish led his team to the state championship and was chosen Louisiana's Basketball Player of the Year in 1972.

The dominating center drew interest from elite college programs. However, he was ineligible because his high school grades and ACT scores predicted he would not achieve at least a 1.6 GPA. Only Centenary College, in Louisiana, offered Parish a scholarship. When the NCAA learned that the college had manipulated his and others' scores, it placed the school on probation. Out of loyalty to Centenary, Parish stayed on the team (graduating in 1976) even though the NCAA did not recognize any of his statistics after 1973.

Parish's prospects were not diminished. He won a gold medal with the United States national team at the 1975 Pan Am games. In 1976, the 7'1" center was drafted by the Golden State Warriors but languished in that system. The Boston Celtics acquired Parish and the draftee Kevin McHale in 1980. With Larry Bird, they formed the famed "Big Three" who energized professional basketball by rekindling the Celtics-Lakers rivalry. Parish melded with his new team, earning the nickname "the Chief" after the quiet, yet imposing, character in the novel and movie, *One Flew Over the Cuckoo's Nest*. Parish's reserve turned to resolve when dealing with aggressive opponents or racial inequities.

The Celtics have a prominent place in the discussion of race and professional basketball. They were the first team to draft a black player (Chuck Cooper in 1950), start five black players (1963), and hire a black coach (BILL RUSSELL in 1966). Still, black Celtics experienced racial profiling and harassment in the community, causing some media, opponents, and fans to hype the Larry Bird–MAGIC JOHNSON rivalry as the "white" Celtics vs. the "black" Lakers. None of this was lost on Parish, who demanded and received contract extensions and salary increases comparable to his white teammates. Parish knew it was the combined talent of the Celtics that won championships. Coaches and teammates agree that Parish, the ideal team player, focused on winning.

The official NBA statistics rank Parish among the league's top players. As a Celtic, he played in fourteen consecutive post-seasons, nine All-Star games, and scored over twenty thousand points. The team won championships in 1981, 1984, and 1986. After Bird and McHale retired, Parish signed with the Charlotte Hornets in 1994. In 1996 he amassed the most games played in NBA history. That year he joined the Chicago Bulls, was named one of the fifty greatest players in NBA history, and won his fourth championship. When Parish retired in 1997 with 23,334 points in 1,611 games, he was among the greatest rebounders (14,715). The Celtics retired Parish's number, "00," in 1998, and he was inducted into the Naismith Basketball Hall of Fame in 2003.

FURTHER READING

Lane, Jeffrey. *Under the Boards: The Cultural Revolution in Basketball* (2007).
May, Peter. *The Big Three* (1994).
May, Peter. *The Last Banner* (1996).

AMY E. CARREIRO

Parker, Allen (May or June 1838–18 June 1906), businessman and author of a slave narrative, was born to Jeff Elliott (also known as Jeff Ellick), a slave of William Elliott, and Millie, a slave of Peter Parker, in Chowan County, North Carolina. Parker died while Allen was a young child, and ownership of both Millie and her children passed to Parker's young daughter Annie. Annie Parker's guardians hired Millie out to a series of poor white masters, ranging from "good" masters to some who were quite violent. Allen generally lived with her at least until he was ten. After he reached that age, when slaves usually began to have to work in the field, his time too was being hired out, again to a series of masters of varying temperament. There is some possibility that Parker married another slave in his youth, though definitive documentation is lacking.

The beginning of the Civil War changed Parker's life in many ways: his mother died early in the war, his mistress was married (in April 1862 to Robert Winborne), he witnessed several slaves run for Union lines, and, though he claimed that the Parker family had always been "kind" to him, he began to have a "very strong yearning for freedom" (Parker 85). In late 1862, along with three slaves from a neighboring farm, Parker escaped and found refuge aboard a Union gunboat that was patrolling the James River. Parker worked for the Union navy for a time before finally enlisting on 1 September 1863 at New Bern, North Carolina. His enlistment papers erroneously list his age as twenty and note that he was 5'4", a laborer, and a "contraband" (that is, a fugitive slave seeking refuge with the Union forces). Though his muster record lists his vessel as the *Albemarle*, a captured Southern schooner, in his narrative, Parker notes the "Knockum," which scholars have speculated was actually the *Knockern*, a ship deployed to the area with the *Albemarle* in 1863. Parker served in the U.S. Navy until 13 December 1864.

He then worked at a sawmill and as a ship's steward, but he soon traveled to New Haven, where he lived with a cousin—probably Lucretia Veney, who filed a deposition in support of Parker's pension application—and eventually met his wife, Sarah Maria Coates. The Maryland-born Coates seems to have been married previously, inasmuch as her son Charles Coates lived with the couple at various points over the next three decades. Parker and Coates married on 28 June 1877 and had four children, none of whom lived to adulthood. Parker's health was uneven, and the family's existence was peripatetic; records show they spent time in Meriden, Connecticut, as well as Saugus, Westfield, Lynn, Springfield, Northampton, Chelsea, and Worcester, Massachusetts, over the next decade. They eventually settled in Worcester. Though he was a member of Worcester's Pleasant Street Baptist Church, Parker often attended the Belmont Street African Methodist Episcopal Zion Church, and he was active in the local chapter of the Grand Army of the Republic and the United Order of Galilean Fishermen, a church organization.

Sarah worked as a laundress, and Allen worked as a laborer, carpet cleaner, ice cream dealer, and, finally, as a confectioner who made and sold popcorn and candy. A generation of Worcester children came to know him as "Pop" Parker, and this popularity may have been one factor in Parker's decision to compose his short autobiography, which was published in 1895 under the title *Recollections of Slavery Times*. *Recollections* actually says much less about Parker's own life, though, than it does about facets of rural slavery—from the complexities of the hiring-out process to practices surrounding raccoon and opossum hunting. Still, his book addresses both Parker's escape and Civil War service.

Parker's health continued to vary for the rest of his life. He filed for a military pension in 1898, and some of the supporting documents suggest that he suffered from a variety of ailments, including rheumatism and kidney disease. The pension was not granted until 1903. His financial condition also seems to have varied. Though some sources place him as working class, both extant obituaries note that he traveled to Europe in 1904. He died in Worcester.

While Parker has been little-studied, his narrative offers an important look at slave life in rural North Carolina, and his life offers a fascinating demonstration of one former slave's entry into the fabric of the Northeast.

FURTHER READING

Parker, Allen. *Recollections of Slavery Times* (1895).

Cecelski, David, ed. "The Allen Parker Slave Narrative." Available at http://core.ecu.edu/hist/cecelskid/

Obituaries: *Worcester Daily Telegram*, 19 June 1906; *Worcester Evening Post*, 20 June 1906.

ERIC GARDNER

Parker, Charlie (29 Aug. 1920–12 Mar. 1955), jazz alto saxophonist, known as "Bird," "Yardbird," or "Yard," was born Charles Parker Jr. in Kansas City, Kansas. He was the only child of Charles Parker Sr., a chef on the Pullman Line who was a former dancer and singer, and Addie Boxley, a charwoman for Western Union who also cleaned houses, did laundry, and rented to boarders. Parker had an older half brother, John "Ikey," who was his father's son from a previous relationship. The Parkers, without the often absent Charles Sr., moved to Kansas City, Missouri, in 1927. Parker attended Penn School in Westport and during that time began to play the alto saxophone. He enrolled at Lincoln High School in 1932 and joined the school marching band, where he played the alto horn and later the baritone horn. During this time Parker started playing alto saxophone with the pianist Lawrence Keyes and spent his nights on Twelfth Street listening to professional musicians, including the orchestra of COUNT BASIE and the tenor saxophonist LESTER YOUNG. Parker was able to experience the Kansas City nightlife because his mother worked at night, and this lifestyle probably contributed to his dropping out of high school.

Charlie "Bird" Parker, alto saxophonist and jazz composer, plays at Carnegie Hall in New York City, c. 1947. (© William P. Gottlieb; www.jazzphotos.com.)

During these years Parker participated in after-hours jam sessions to test himself against more experienced musicians. Two well-known jam sessions were failures—his performances were considered unacceptable. The first took place at the High Hat Club; after that he "did not play again for three months" (Russell, 64–65). After Parker's second failure in 1936 at the Reno Club, he left the club humiliated. He did not give up easily, however, and continued to seek instruction from more advanced musicians.

On 10 April 1934 the Ruffin family, including their daughter, Rebecca Ellen, moved into the Parkers' house as boarders. On 25 July 1936 Parker and Rebecca were married. Addie Parker had to give her consent because both of them were underage. Parker and Rebecca had a son, Francis Leon, born 10 January 1938. After his wedding Parker began working with Ernest Daniels in the Ozarks. En route to an engagement, he was in a serious car accident; during his recuperation he began using drugs. After his recovery, Parker started working with Tommy Douglas, a well-educated musician who taught Parker the fundamentals of his art, instructing him about reeds and proper embouchure (the formation of the mouth and lips while playing). Douglas may also have been the first to teach Parker about the use of "passing chords," whereby a musician superimposes additional chords over a given chord progression while improvising.

In the summer of 1937 Parker took a job with GEORGE E. LEE in the Ozarks. When the band was not performing, Parker received instruction in the cycle of fifths and passing chords from fellow band members, the guitarist Efferge Ware and the pianist Carrie Powell. Parker also transcribed and memorized several improvised solos of the tenor saxophonist Lester Young from recordings of Count Basie. When Parker returned to Kansas City in the fall of 1937, he participated in another jam session at the Reno Club, this time to the approval of the other musicians. Later that fall, Buster "Prof" Smith hired Parker to play in his band, which included Jesse Price and JAY MCSHANN. Smith taught Parker how to adjust reeds and became Parker's musical mentor. In 1938 Smith moved to New York, and the band broke up.

During this time the Kansas City Pendergast political machine was overturned, and, as a result, many nightclubs were closed. Parker left Kansas City for Chicago in the fall of 1938. In Chicago, he sat in with the King Kolax band, and the musicians in attendance were astounded at his virtuosity. In a few weeks Parker was on a bus to New York to locate his teacher and mentor Buster Smith. Smith and his wife took Parker into their home for a short time. To support himself, Parker took a dishwashing job at Jimmy's Chicken Shack, where he heard and was probably influenced by the pianist ART TATUM. In New York, too, Parker befriended the guitarist Bill "Biddy" Fleet, who gave him advice about harmony. Parker was soon performing around the city and in jam sessions at Clark Monroe's Uptown House and Dan Wall's Chili House.

In 1940 Parker received a telegram telling him that his father had died, and he returned to Kansas City for the funeral. He remained in Kansas City, where he befriended the pianist and arranger TAD DAMERON, who taught him the practical applications of music theory. Later in 1940 Parker joined the Jay McShann Orchestra, where he "rehearsed the reed section, played many solos, and kept everyone in good spirits" (Giddins, 58). Parker can be heard playing as a soloist on several recordings of the McShann band on Decca Records and on several bootleg recordings dating to this time. His first recorded solos were innovative improvisations that were studied and memorized by many jazz musicians. After numerous tours and recordings, Parker left McShann in December of 1942.

Parker returned to New York City and joined the EARL HINES band on the recommendation of George "Scoops" Carey, who had heard Parker in Chicago a few years earlier. Parker played tenor saxophone in the Hines band, which included DIZZY GILLESPIE, with whom Parker would establish a strong musical friendship. Hines did not record during Parker's tenure with the band because of the American Federation of Musicians' ban on recording during this period. However, several jam session recordings that feature Parker from that time are now available.

On 10 April 1943 Parker married Geraldine Scott in Washington, D.C., but the marriage was not considered legal, because he was still married to Rebecca at the time. The relationship with Geraldine probably ended sometime in 1944. Parker left the Hines band after May 1943 and returned to Kansas City, his drug problem worsening. He worked for a short time around Kansas City before he was hired by BILLY ECKSTINE to join his new big band, which included Dizzy Gillespie. Parker left Eckstine's band in 1944, and there are no extant recordings of that particular group. At about that time, Rebecca officially divorced Parker, and she retained custody of their son.

Parker returned to New York City, where he performed and recorded with LLOYD "TINY" GRIMES and Dizzy Gillespie and with his own groups. The recordings with Gillespie from 1945 are considered to be prototypical of the new bebop style. During this time Parker was living with Doris Sydnor. In December 1945 Parker went to Los Angeles with Dizzy Gillespie and his group. When the L.A. engagement ended the following February, Parker stayed on, and his drug addiction reached extreme levels. His drug problem and declining health finally led to a physical breakdown and his arrest. He was hospitalized at Camarillo State Hospital, where Doris Sydnor visited him often. In January 1947 he was released from Camarillo and continued performing in the Los Angeles area and recording for Ross Russell's Dial Records. Parker and Doris Sydnor returned to New York in April 1947 and were married on 20 November 1948.

In 1947 Parker formed his own band, including MILES DAVIS, Duke Jordan, Tommy Potter, and MAX ROACH. The group recorded for Dial, Savoy, and Clef, and they performed extensively. In 1948 Parker began an almost exclusive recording relationship with Norman Granz that included recordings with "conventional and Latin big bands, a string section, a big band and string combination, a vocal and wind ensemble, an all-star jam session, a reunion with Dizzy Gillespie and THELONIOUS MONK, and several one-time small groups" (Woideck, 46). Granz was able to get wide distribution for Parker's records, and it was not long before Parker was regularly winning magazine polls. In 1949 Parker's new quintet, including Kenny Dorham, Al Haig, Tommy Potter, and ROY HAYNES, traveled to Paris, where they were well received. Upon returning to the United States, Parker replaced Kenny Dorham with the trumpeter Red Rodney. Also in 1949 the nightclub Birdland, a celebration of Parker's nickname "Bird," opened in New York.

When Parker's marriage to Sydnor ended in 1950, he began living with Chan Richardson. Although Parker and Richardson were never legally married, she took his name, and Parker adopted Richardson's daughter Kim. Parker and Richardson also had a daughter, Pree, born 17 July 1951 and a son, Baird, born 10 August 1952. In 1950 Parker's regular quintet gradually broke up as agents found it easier and more profitable to book Parker as a solo act. During the same year Parker was hospitalized for a stomach ulcer caused by his heavy drinking. In July 1951 his cabaret card was revoked because of his drug arrest, and his ability to earn a living was severely limited. He had to travel outside New York, usually as a solo performer, to gain employment. He performed with Granz's Jazz at the Philharmonic tours and continued to record for Granz, even though he was apparently unhappy with the situation. In 1953 Parker's cabaret card was reinstated after the authorities heard his plea to work because of his daughter's health problems.

Pree Parker died on 6 March 1954 while Parker was performing in Los Angeles. This emotional blow contributed to Parker's increased drinking and drug abuse. When he returned to New York, he was hospitalized twice at Bellevue after apparent suicide attempts. In December 1954 Parker and Richardson separated, and Parker recorded for Granz for the last time. Parker died on 12 March 1955, probably in the apartment of the jazz patron Pannonica de Koenigswarter in the Stanhope Hotel in Manhattan. His death was attributed to "stomach ulcers and pneumonia, with a contributing condition of advanced cirrhosis and the possibility of a heart attack" (Russell, 358). Parker's funeral took place in New York, and he was buried in Lincoln Cemetery in Kansas City, Missouri.

Parker, who acquired his musical education through the African American oral and aural traditions, made numerous important contributions to jazz and remains one of the most important jazz musicians in history. He was a major innovator of the bebop style, influencing jazz performers on every instrument during his life and since. Parker was a primary influence on such jazz innovators as Dizzy Gillespie, BUD POWELL, Miles Davis, JOHN COLTRANE, PAUL CHAMBERS, and CANNONBALL ADDERLEY. Parker's improvisations were innovative in their use of syncopation, accents, asymmetric phrasing, melodic invention, ornamentation, and harmonic substitution. He was also adept at musical quotations of jazz musicians who inspired him, including Lester Young, COLEMAN HAWKINS, and ROY ELDRIDGE, as well as musical quotations of classical themes and popular songs of the day. His improvisations revolutionized jazz to the extent that nearly every jazz musician since has absorbed his musical vocabulary.

Parker contributed numerous compositions to the jazz repertoire, most of which were based on the chord progressions of the twelve-bar blues or standard repertoire of the day. Some of his best-known compositions include "Billie's Bounce," based on the twelve-bar blues; "Anthropology," based on "I Got Rhythm" by George and Ira Gershwin; "Ornithology," based on "How High the Moon" by Nancy Hamilton and Morgan Lewis; and "Donna Lee," based on "Back Home Again in Indiana" by Ballard McDonald and James F. Hanley. Parker's practice of composing new melodies on existing chord progressions crystallized his melodic vocabulary, and many of his compositions have become standards of the jazz repertoire.

FURTHER READING
Giddins, Gary. *Celebrating Bird: The Triumph of Charlie Parker* (1987).
Reisner, Robert G. *Bird: The Legend of Charlie Parker* (1962).
Russell, Ross. *Bird Lives!: The High Life and Hard Times of Charlie (Yardbird) Parker* (1973).
Woideck, Carl. *Charlie Parker: His Music and Life* (1996).
Obituary: *New York Times*, 15 Mar. 1955.

DISCOGRAPHY
Bregman, Robert M., Leonard Bukowski, and Norman Saks. *The Charlie Parker Discography* (1993).

KENT J. ENGELHARDT

Parker, Jim (3 Apr. 1934–18 July 2005), professional football player, was born James Thomas Parker in Macon, Georgia, where he worked on his family's farm. His parents' names and occupations are unknown. There is also little information about his early childhood and upbringing. He spent his senior year at Scott High School in Toledo, Ohio, graduating in 1953. He was then recruited to play tackle at Ohio State University under legendary coach Woody Hayes.

During his freshman year in 1953 Parker lived off-campus with the often cranky Hayes because so few blacks lived on the Ohio State campus. Both Hayes and Parker shared a mutual admiration for one another. Hayes saw commitment and intelligence in Parker, and in turn, Parker saw Hayes as a father figure whose frequent mood fluctuations, going from compassion to anger and back, matched his own. Parker was named to all-America teams twice and in 1956 won the Outland Trophy as college football's most outstanding lineman, the second African American to have won the award. He graduated from Ohio State in 1957 with a bachelor's degree in physical education.

Parker was selected by the Baltimore Colts in the first round of the 1957 National Football League (NFL) draft as the eighth overall pick. He was signed to a two-year contract that would pay him $12,500 a year, a high salary for the time, especially for an unproven lineman. He also received a $1,500 signing bonus, paid in $1 bills by General Manager Don Kellett to stress the generous amount of the payment. Because Ohio State quarterbacks threw few passes, Hayes thought Parker would become a defensive tackle, but Weeb Ewbank, the Colts' coach, believed that the massive rookie would provide superb protection for star quarterback Johnny Unitas. At a time before weight training, when most linemen weighed 230 to 250 pounds, Parker stood six feet three inches and weighed 275 pounds. Despite his size, he had quick feet, enabling him to be a superb blocker on both running and passing plays. Eugene "Big Daddy" Lipscomb, the Colts' great defensive tackle, became Parker's tutor, teaching him how to counter the techniques of specific defensive linemen. Parker has been called the prototype of the modern offensive lineman, becoming, along with the New York Giants' Roosevelt Brown (also an African American), one of the first players to escape the anonymity that often came with being an offensive lineman.

The Colts' greatest strength during Parker's NFL career (1957 to 1967) was the passing of quarterback Unitas. Because Unitas was not mobile, giving him enough time to find his receivers was imperative. Parker was told by Ewbank that he would be the most unpopular player on the team if the quarterback ever got hurt. Unitas would later praise the immense pride Parker took in his work. Another teammate, Pro Football Hall-of-Fame running back Lenny Moore, also credited Parker with contributing to his success. More significantly, Parker was one of the first African Americans in the NFL to become a team leader both on the field and in the locker room. In the pre–Super Bowl years, Parker helped the Colts win NFL championships in 1958 and 1959, beating the New York Giants both times. The 1958 championship game was the first overtime game in National Football League history, as Parker dominated Giant defensive end Andy Robustelli, arguably the best pass rusher of the era. The Colts' 23–17 victory over the Giants has often been called the greatest game in professional football history. The excitement it generated helped propel the NFL into greater public prominence, with professional football soon surpassing baseball as America's favorite spectator sport. The Colts won the 1959 championship game more handily, 31–16.

Parker played left tackle until switching to left guard midway through the 1962 season. He was named to the NFL All-Pro team and was selected to play in the Pro Bowl eight consecutive seasons. He also did not miss a game during his first ten seasons, playing in 139 consecutive games. Hobbled by arthritic knees, Parker chose to retire in 1967 rather than weaken his team's chances of winning. Coach Don Shula called this gesture the most unselfish act in sports history. Considered by many to be the greatest lineman in NFL history, he was elected to the Pro Football Hall of Fame in 1973 in his first year of eligibility. Parker was also selected to the Ohio State, Baltimore Colts, college football, and the state of Georgia halls of fame. He was a unanimous choice for the NFL's Seventy-fifth Anniversary team. A *New York Daily News* poll of the fifty greatest professional football players of the twentieth century ranked him twentieth on the list.

In 1994 Parker told *Sports Illustrated* that playing offensive tackle was the only job he had ever been able to master. He said that his first marriage broke up because he spent so much time in his basement watching films of opposing players. He lived in Columbia, Maryland, a Baltimore suburb, and operated a liquor store in the Liberty-Garrison neighborhood of Baltimore for thirty-five years until 1999, when he closed the store because of his ill health. Suffering from diabetes, he had a stroke in 1993 and spent three months in a hospital. He died of congestive heart failure and kidney disease in a Columbia nursing home on 18 July 2005. At the time of his death, he was married to his third wife, Esther Mae. He was survived by his wife and eight children.

FURTHER READING

Bagli, Vince, and Norman L. Macht. *Sundays at 2:00 with the Baltimore Colts* (1995).

Harrington, Denis J. *The Pro Football Hall of Fame: Players, Coaches, Team Owners and League Officials, 1963–1991* (1991).

Zimmerman, Paul. "Total Package," *Sports Illustrated* (Sept. 1994).

Obituary: *New York Times*, 21 July 2005.

MICHAEL ADAMS

Parker, John P. (1827–30 Jan. 1900), abolitionist and entrepreneur, was born in Norfolk, Virginia, the son of a slave mother and a white father whose names are unknown. At the age of eight, Parker was sold as a slave to an agent in Richmond, where he in turn was purchased by a physician from Mobile, Alabama. While employed as a house servant for the physician, Parker learned to read and write. In Mobile he was apprenticed to work in furnaces and iron manufactures as well as for a plasterer. Beaten by the plasterer, Parker attempted to escape, only to be captured aboard a northbound riverboat.

From 1843 to 1845 Parker was hired out as an iron molder and stevedore in the Mobile area. He proved to be an extraordinarily skilled molder, which enabled him to earn enough money to purchase his freedom for $1,800 at the end of the two-year period. Obtaining a pass for Indiana, Parker moved to the Cincinnati area after a freeman requested his assistance in aiding escaped slaves from Kentucky. Thus began his career as a "conductor" on the Underground Railroad.

In 1848 Parker married Miranda Boulden, a Cincinnati native. They had eight children, a number of whom became teachers. Also in 1848 he left Cincinnati, where he had worked as a molder, to open a general store at Beechwood Factory, Ohio. In 1850 Parker moved to Ripley, Ohio, on the Ohio River across from Mason County, Kentucky, which was the home of the Reverend John Rankin, a Presbyterian clergyman who was also an abolitionist and operator on the Underground Railroad. Parker worked separately from Rankin, believing it not proper "to ask white men how to abduct slaves from Kentucky," and held that the organized church was not sympathetic to the plight of the slave. He assisted fugitives by sending associates to meet them by night and conduct them on rowboats across the Ohio River. Once in Ohio the runaways were escorted by guides to safe havens. During the decade before the Emancipation Proclamation, Parker reputedly helped more than one thousand slaves escape to freedom.

Concurrent with his abolitionist activities, Parker established a small foundry in 1854 that produced special and general castings. His employees included white Kentuckians such as James Shrofe, whose family owned slaves whom Parker hid and sent north to Canada.

During the Civil War, Parker recruited volunteers for the Twenty-seventh Regiment, U.S. Colored Troops, one of two such Ohio units. He was largely responsible for recruiting Kentuckians to the regiment. Meanwhile, his foundry furnished castings for the Union cause.

Parker's entrepreneurial and inventive skills blossomed after the Civil War. His firm, which came to be known as the Ripley Foundry and Machine Company, manufactured slide-valve engines and reapers. At its peak in the 1880s the company employed twenty-five men. A century later the company was still in operation although no longer under family ownership. As the operator of a company of that size, Parker was a wealthy African American by the standards of his day. Perhaps Parker's greatest claim to recognition was as an inventor. He was one the few African Americans who obtained patents before 1900. He patented a screw for tobacco presses in September 1884 and one for a similar device the following year. He is credited with the invention of the "Parker Pulverizer," a type of harrow.

In his later years Parker recounted his life story to Frank M. Gregg, an Ohio newspaperman and the author of several historical studies. The historian Louis Weeks's evaluation best captures Parker's contributions, naming him "an important, yet unheralded, participant in the Underground Railroad...a successful inventor and businessman...and...an independent, militant black man in an essentially white power structure." Parker's significance has been obscured by the tendency of most standard works on the Underground Railroad to emphasize the role of white abolitionists and overlook African American involvement and also because he often worked independently from white abolitionists and received less recognition in the abolitionist press. Parker died in Ripley.

FURTHER READING
The "Autobiography of a Slave, John Parker, Brown County, Ohio, Circa 1800" is a typescript in the Flowers Collection of Southern Americana at the Duke University Library, Durham, North Carolina.
Baker, Henry E. *The Colored Inventor: A Record of Fifty Years* (1913).
Weeks, Louis. "John P. Parker: Black Abolitionist Entrepreneur, 1827–1900," *Ohio History* (Spring, 1971).
This entry is taken from the *American National Biography* and is published here with the permission of the American Council of Learned Societies.
FRANK R. LEVSTIK

Parker, Junior (27 May 1932–18 Nov. 1971), blues musician, was born Herman Parker Jr. in either Clarksdale, Mississippi, or West Memphis, Arkansas. As with the exact place of his birth, few details about his early life or upbringing are known. He sang in his church choir as a young boy, and was noted for his smooth, soft delivery. The Memphis blues scene was alive and jumping, and Parker fell under the influence of the blues great SONNY BOY WILLIAMSON, who taught him to blow harmonica. In 1949 he learned under the tutelage of no other than HOWLIN' WOLF.

In 1951 he started a band—the Beale Streeters—with B. B. KING, among other notables. In 1952 he started another, the Blue Flames, and this group soon came to the attention of IKE TURNER, who signed Parker and the others (including the guitarist Pat Hare) to the Modern Records label. The affiliation there was short. The Blue Flames produced one single before being whisked away by Sun Records in 1953. That year saw a trio of blues hits: "Feelin' Good," "Love My Baby," and "Mystery Train." "Feelin' Good" hit number five on the R&B charts. "Mystery Train" was later recorded by Elvis Presley. The success led Parker to sign with the Houston-based Duke label. In 1957 he turned in a hit with "Next Time You See Me." His 1961 cover of the ROOSEVELT SYKES number "Driving Wheel" was an even bigger hit.

More hits followed under the Duke label: "In the Dark" made a splash in 1961, followed by "Annie Get Your Yo-Yo" a year later. He covered Guitar Slim's "The Things That I Used to Do" in 1963 and hit with Harold Burrage's "Crying for My Baby" in 1965.

Despite his success at Duke, Parker moved on a year later, signing with the Mercury label. It was, however, the end of his successful period. He recorded no hits, though listeners and fans continued to consider him a blues great, even as national listening tastes were changing. In a nod to the times, Parker even resorted to recording Beatles covers. After leaving Mercury, he signed on for brief stints with a number of other labels, including Capitol, though without much success.

In 1971 Parker was diagnosed with a brain tumor. He was admitted into a hospital in Blue Island, Illinois, for surgery but died during the procedure. He was just thirty-nine. In 2001 he was admitted posthumously into the Blues Hall of Fame.

FURTHER READING

Cohn, Lawrence, ed. *Nothing but the Blues: The Music and the Musicians* (1997).

Wilcock, Donald E., with Buddy Guy. *Damn Right I've Got the Blues* (1993).

JASON PHILIP MILLER

Parker, Lawrence. *See* KRS-One.

Parker, Mack Charles (1937?–24 Apr. 1959), lynching victim, was born near Tylertown, Mississippi, the eldest of four children born to Liza Parker (maiden name unknown). The name of his father is unknown, as is the family's means of making a living, but it is known that they were very poor—perhaps among the most poverty-stricken of families living in the nation's most economically deprived state. Sometime around 1942 the Parkers moved to Lamar County in the Piney Woods section of southern Mississippi, where the family of six crowded into three small rooms in a shack in the town of Lumberton. Parker, or M.C., as he came to be known, attended Lamar County's segregated public schools, but, like many African Americans in Mississippi—a state which spent far more to educate its white students than its black students—he dropped out before graduating from high school.

Faced with meager job opportunities in Lumberton, Parker enlisted in the U.S. Army when he was eighteen. His service record was unremarkable, but he appeared in military court twice; first, in 1956, during his basic training at Camp Gordon, Georgia, and again in 1957, while he was stationed at Fort Crowder, Missouri. On both occasions he was found guilty of theft of government property. Parker's second conviction resulted in a general discharge from the military. Back in Lumberton in 1957 he was unemployed for a short period, but after his father died, he found a job as a truck driver for a pulpwood firm. His younger brother Elmo had enlisted in the military, and thus Parker served as the primary breadwinner for the family, working long hours to look after his mother, his youngest brother, Charles, who was only four, his sister Dolores, and her son, Peanut. Not long after returning to Lumberton, Parker had married Mattie Pearl Ott, a childhood acquaintance, but the marriage lasted only a year or so. In spite of his trouble in the military, Parker had never been arrested in his native Mississippi, and he managed to avoid any run-ins with the law. A neighbor of the Parkers, Ruby Lee, described him as "a decent sort. He did his work and came home at night" (Smead, 19).

Parker did, however, run with a gang described by one neighbor as a "hard-drinking crew"—David Alfred, Rainbow Malachy, Curt Underwood, and Tommy Lee Grant, all in their early twenties, who "did what came to their mind" (Smead, 19). On the evening of Monday, 23 February 1959, the five friends set off drinking in Elmo Parker's Chevy. It was cold and blustery, but Monday was payday in the lumber industry, and they began by purchasing a half gallon of moonshine, which they quickly consumed. With Parker at the wheel—having drunk as much as his passengers—the five spent the next few hours drinking, playing cards, and, as one of them put it, "just joe-jacking around" the juke joints and bars on the road between Lumberton and Poplarville, in nearby Pearl River County (Smead, 5).

Sometime around midnight, Parker parked the Chevy behind a broken-down Dodge on a quiet stretch of Highway 11, near where Lamar and Pearl River counties meet. After telling his friends that he might steal the car's tires, Parker jumped out and shone his flashlight into the Dodge, before returning to his own car. Three of Parker's companions, including his sister Dolores's ex-husband, Curt Underwood, later told police that Parker told them that there was a white woman in the car and that he had suggested, "Why don't we stop and get some of that white stuff?" (Smead, 5). Shortly afterward Parker drove past a white man attempting to hitch a ride and identified him as the woman's husband, seeking help for his broken-down car. Again Parker boasted that he would "git back down there before [the woman's husband]," but to the relief of his friends he kept on driving into Lumberton, where he dropped his friends at their respective homes, telling at least one of them that he had only been joking about the white woman (Smead, 5). Heavily drunk by the time he arrived home around 1:00 A.M., Parker fell and cut his hand; he bandaged it roughly, and, in spite of his mother's pleas, he drove off again, alone.

The next morning police officers dragged Mack Charles Parker from his bed, where he lay asleep and hung over, took him out to the nearby woods, and beat him severely. Despite the beating, Parker refused to confess to the charge laid against him: the rape, earlier that morning, of a white woman, June Walters, on Highway 11, just inside the Pearl River County line. Walters, who was two months' pregnant, had been waiting with her four-year-old daughter Debbie in the family's broken-down Dodge while her husband, Jimmy, had set off for help. June Walters told police officers that a middle-aged man with a bandaged hand had approached the locked car, smashed a window with the butt of his gun, and threatened to kill both Walters and her daughter. The man, who claimed to be an escaped convict who had killed five people, then forced the woman and girl into his car and drove a mile away to a narrow dirt track road, where he forced Debbie out of the car. The man then raped June Walters inside the car.

The police had rounded up thirty black men that night as possible suspects, but were convinced that M. C. Parker was their man. David Alfred had told his father of Parker's boast that he would return to have sex with the woman in the broken-down car, and Alfred's father had told the police. The three other young men confirmed the story, though it later emerged that some of them had been beaten by police officers before doing so, and that others were threatened with beatings. The police also believed they had compelling circumstantial evidence that indicated Parker's guilt: June Walters had mentioned her attacker's badly cut hand and gave a description of the interior of her assailant's car that closely matched Parker's beat-up Chevy; tire tracks left at the scene of the crime also matched.

R. Jess Brown, the Vicksburg attorney hired by Liza Parker to defend her son, believed, however, that Parker, who insisted on his innocence and had passed several lie-detector tests, had a case. Though Brown accepted that the confessions of Parker's friends were problematic, he began assembling a case that questioned the validity of June Walters's testimony. Her identification of Parker as her assailant was uncertain; she had stated that the rapist was large and aged thirty-nine to forty, while Parker was slight and either twenty-two or twenty-three years old. Brown also intended to challenge the proposed venue for Parker's trial, the Pearl River County Court, on the grounds that African Americans were unconstitutionally excluded from jury lists in that county. Brown was unable to raise these points on Parker's behalf, however, because a white mob of eight to ten men abducted M.-C. Parker from his Pearl River County jail cell on the evening of 24 April 1959. The hooded mob beat Parker, dragged him from the jail, and shot him several times. Parker's body was found ten days later in the Pearl River.

Coming only four years after the EMMETT TILL lynching, the Mack Parker case again focused national and international attention on Mississippi's disregard for the rule of law. Civil rights activists and others charged that the sheriff of Pearl River County and his deputies had assisted the white mob and shared the mob's view that it would be an outrage for a black attorney to question a white female rape victim in court. An extensive FBI investigation of the case also found a prevailing white belief that the federal courts would release Parker on the grounds raised by Jess Brown, namely that Pearl River

County's all-white jury pool was unconstitutional. The FBI's investigation established the identity of several members of the lynch mob—who were also known to local law enforcement agencies—but an all-white grand jury refused to return indictments against the men. No one has ever been convicted for his or her role in lynching M. C. Parker.

The Mack Parker lynching was in one respect a rather traditional lynching. During the nadir in southern race relations at the turn of the twentieth century it was not at all unusual for white mobs to break into jails to lynch African American prisoners. By 1959, however, such flagrant disregard for the rule of law came as a surprise, even to hardened civil rights leaders. Upon hearing of the case, Mississippi's MEDGAR EVERS was so angered that he told his wife that he'd "like to get a gun and just start shooting" (Dittmer, 85). The North Carolinian activist ROBERT F. WILLIAMS likewise cited the Parker lynching as justification for his call for African Americans to arm themselves. Williams noted that "non-violence never saved George Lee [shot dead by white supremacists in 1955] in Belzoni, Miss., or Emmett Till, nor Mack Parker" (Tyson, 154). Most African Americans did not share Williams's view that the Parker lynching justified an armed response, but it proved to be one of several prominent cases in the late 1950s that stiffened the resolve of young civil rights activists and spurred the more militant and more successful campaigns in the 1960s to overcome racism, especially in Mississippi.

Though he was never a member of the NAACP and never went on a civil rights march, Mack Charles Parker has subsequently been regarded as a civil rights martyr. His name is one of forty listed on a Montgomery, Alabama, civil rights memorial, which honors those killed during the black freedom struggle in the South between 1955 and 1968.

FURTHER READING

Dittmer, John. *Local People: The Struggle for Civil Rights in Mississippi* (1995).

Smead, Howard. *Blood Justice: The Lynching of Mack Charles Parker* (1986).

Tyson, Timothy B. *Radio Free Dixie: Robert F. Williams and the Roots of Black Power* (1999).

STEVEN J. NIVEN

Parker, Noah B. (1845 or 1846–Dec. 1875), farm laborer and justice of the peace, was born a slave in Alabama to parents whose names have not been recorded. It is not known when Parker arrived in Rolling Fork in Issaquena County in the Yazoo-Mississippi Delta, or why he left Alabama. It is possible that Parker, like many former slaves after emancipation, embarked on a perilous journey of several hundred miles to rejoin family members who had been sold to southwest Mississippi. Or he could have made that journey in the late 1860s when thousands of black freedmen and their families began flocking to the Delta in search of their own land. More likely he was himself one of thousands of African American slaves brought to the Delta in the decade before the outbreak of the Civil War by owners seeking the vast fortunes to be made from that region's dark, rich, alluvial soil.

Such fortunes could be made by white planters like Stephen Duncan, who owned seven hundred slaves, and whose Issaquena plantations were valued at more than $1.3 million in 1860. On the eve of the Civil War, Issaquena was the second-wealthiest county in the nation. Almost all of that wealth was shared by the county's 587 white residents, but it was produced by the 7,244 slaves who labored from sunup to sundown to clear a wilderness of swamps, forests, and canebrakes to make way for fields that yielded nearly twice as much cotton per acre as in counties outside of the Delta. The slaves also constructed the levees needed to control the destructive annual flooding of the Mississippi River and to maintain those vast profits for the region's wealthiest planters.

The 1870 federal census reveals that Parker was in that year a twenty-four-year-old farm laborer, residing in a cabin on Deer Creek, near Rolling Fork in Issaquena County. He was married to Rebecca Foreman, also a twenty-four-year-old farm laborer, with whom he had a one-year-old daughter, Aguilla, who had been born in Mississippi. The census states that Parker was literate and had recently attended a school, probably one established by the Freedman's Bureau or by visiting northern missionaries. His ability to read and write was at that time rare among the black citizens of Issaquena County, and it was probably a key factor in his prominence in local Republican Party politics and in his ability to secure election as justice of the peace for Issaquena County in 1871. Blacks outnumbered whites by more than 10 to 1 in Issaquena—and by 50 to 1 in Deer Creek. With the passage in 1869 of a new constitution that gave all adult males the right to vote in Mississippi, Issaquena was one of several black-majority counties that elected African Americans to a wide range of local offices, including the sheriff and the local Board of Supervisors. Prior to Reconstruction all of these offices had been in the hands of whites. Parker, then, was in the vanguard of a revolution in local politics in the Delta, a revolution supported, at least from 1870 to 1873, by a significant number of Delta whites.

Parker's jurisdiction as justice of the peace included Rolling Fork, the swampy, least-developed part of Issaquena County, which in 1875 was established as Sharkey County. In such dangerous frontier conditions, he represented law and order as best he could. In March 1873 he investigated a suspicious fire at a country store at Rolling Fork Landing that had resulted in the death of five people asleep in the building. All five, including the owner, were white. Whites in Issaquena County were convinced that a marauding band of black outlaws had torched the building. Blacks believed that the building's occupants—white northern carpetbaggers—had been targeted because of their support for Reconstruction and had been killed by some of the landless and desperate Confederate veterans who were also known to roam the Delta backcountry. Parker interviewed suspects of both races, but he was unable to secure a conviction due to a lack of evidence.

In the spring of 1875 Parker was tried, convicted of embezzlement, and forced to step down from his position as justice of the peace. The trial judge concluded that Parker himself had not appropriated the monies from various fines and fees that it was his duty to collect from Rolling Fork's residents. Parker was nonetheless found guilty, since he had deputized a constable, Bowie Foreman, to collect those fees, and Foreman, who had a reputation as a heavy drinker, had apparently kept the money. That a prominent white Democratic lawyer defended Parker at his trial is perhaps suggestive of his ability to cooperate with his political opponents.

In the wake of Mississippi's elections in November 1875, however, it became apparent that several white Democrats in Issaquena County were unwilling to cooperate with Parker. Although Parker was no longer a candidate, he had remained a Republican activist and ensured that his party once again secured a significant majority in Issaquena in that year's election. Most of the county's elected officials were still African American. Statewide, however, the Democrats had secured a majority in both houses of the Mississippi legislature and were determined to put an end to Reconstruction. The Democrats in the legislature immediately prepared to impeach Adelbert Ames, the state's Maine-born Republican governor, as well as his deputy,

ALEXANDER K. DAVIS, whose terms were not due to expire until 1877.

In Issaquena a self-selected group of white Democrats achieved the same goal in December 1875 by forcing recently elected black members of the county's Board of Supervisors to resign, having made it clear that they would be killed if they refused. The mood in the county was tense, and made worse by a fight at a county store, which resulted in a black man being stabbed and a white man beaten. Rumors spread among the white minority that Governor Ames had supplied a large number of African Americans with arms, and that they had threatened to burn down the planters' valuable gin houses and cotton stores and to kill whites. Noah B. Parker was rumored to be the leader of this planned insurrection. He was, according to one white Democrat, a "bad character…likely to lead the innocent, inoffensive colored people in the county into a trouble that would have resulted in a terrible loss of life" (*Mississippi in 1875*, 708). In a preemptive strike, a white posse rounded up six of the alleged leaders of this insurrection, including Parker and another black justice of the peace. The six men were shot dead in an open field near Parker's home in Deer Creek. Although Bowie Foreman and others testified about the killings before a U.S. Senate investigation in 1876, no one was ever tried or convicted for these murders.

The execution of Noah Parker signaled the end of Reconstruction in the Mississippi Delta. African Americans would continue to vote and even be elected to minor political offices in the region until 1890, but only as long as they accepted the realities of white supremacy. The fate of Noah Parker and of the state senator CHARLES CALDWELL, murdered a few weeks after the Deer Creek executions, served as a warning to the post-1875 generation of black politicians in Mississippi of what could happen if they did not accept those realities.

FURTHER READING

For information on Reconstruction in Issaquena County and the murder of Noah B. Parker at Rolling Fork, see *Mississippi in 1875: Report of the Select Committee to Inquire into the Mississippi Election of 1875*. United States Congress, 1875, 589–755.

Coletta, John Philip. *Only a Few Bones: A True Account of the Rolling Fork Tragedy and Its Aftermath* (2000).

Harris, William C. *Day of the Carpetbagger: Republican Reconstruction in Mississippi* (1979).

STEVEN J. NIVEN

Parker, Toni Trent (10 July 1947–15 September 2005), publisher and author, was born in Winston-Salem, North Carolina, the daughter of William J. Jr., an executive director of the United Negro College Fund, and Viola Scales, a homemaker. The youngest of three daughters, she grew up in New York City. She graduated from Oberlin College in 1970 with a degree in history, later doing graduate work in African American history at the University of California at Berkeley.

After her graduate studies, Parker worked for the Phelps-Stokes Fund in New York, compiling an annotated bibliography of books, reports, and papers sponsored by the Phelps-Stokes Fund that was published in 1976. She married Barrington D. Parker, Jr., a federal judge, and moved to Stamford, Connecticut, where the couple started their family. As a mother, she became concerned about the limited number of books available for young readers that featured positive images of African Americans. To address this problem, she, along with Sheila Foster, a friend and fellow member of the Stamford playgroup that their children belonged to, cofounded Black Books Galore!, being joined later by a third partner, Donna Rand. The company, which eventually came under Parker's sole ownership, published four bibliographies of African American children's literature that have become standards in the industry: *Black Books Galore's Guide to Great African American Children's Literature* (1991), *Great African American Books About Girls* (2001), *More Great African American Children's Books* (2001), and *Great African American Children's Books About Boys* (2001). These bibliographies are among the first fully annotated guides to selecting the most positive, well written, and widely acclaimed children's books featuring African American characters. For ease of use, they are organized by age level and indexed by title, topic, author, and illustrator; portraits of selected authors and illustrators; and listings of award winners and Reading Rainbow Books.

In 1996 Parker, in collaboration with the Kennedy Center, began the Kennedy Center Multicultural Book Festival, featuring authors from a wide array of cultures and experiences. In 1998 Kids Cultural Books was started by Parker as a nonprofit enterprise associated with the book company with the goal of organizing book fairs around the country to give the public the chance to meet the authors of children's books as well as to encourage reading and promote literacy.

Beginning in 2002 and continuing until her death in 2005, Parker wrote a number of illustrated children's books, all featuring black children. Her last book, published in the year of her death, is titled *Sienna's Scrapbook* and portrays a young African American girl and her family as they visit black cultural and historical sites around the country. This character is modeled after her own children when they were young. The books are illustrated with photographs by Earl Anderson and narrated with simply-worded lyrics: *Painted Eggs and Chocolate Bunnies* (about Easter), *Hugs and Hearts* (about Valentine's Day), *Sweets and Treats* (about Halloween), and *Snowflake Kisses and Gingerbread Smiles* (about Christmas), are considered by reviewers to be delightful additions to any child's bookshelves.

Parker received much recognition for her efforts to bring a wider array of children's books to the public's attention. These include several citations from *Parenting* Magazine, acknowledgments from the NAACP, recognition from the board of the John F. Kennedy Center for the Performing Arts, and honors and awards from many other organizations and individuals.

HER CHILDREN'S BOOKS INCLUDE:

- *Hugs and Hearts*, photographs by Earl Anderson, Scholastic (New York, NY), 2002.
- *Painted Eggs and Chocolate Bunnies*, photographs by Earl Anderson, Scholastic (New York, NY), 2002.
- *Sweets and Treats*, photographs by Earl Anderson, Scholastic (New York, NY), 2002.
- *Snowflake Kisses and Gingerbread Smiles*, photographs by Earl Anderson, Scholastic (New York, NY), 2002.
- *Being Me: A Keepsake Scrapbook for African-American Girls*, illustrated by Meryl Treatner, Scholastic (New York, NY), 2002.
- *Sienna's Scrapbook: Our African-American Heritage Trip*, illustrated by Janell Genovese, Chronicle Books (San Francisco, CA), 2005.

HER OTHER PUBLICATIONS INCLUDE:

- (Compiler) *Annotated Bibliography of Books, Reports, and Papers Published, Written, or Sponsored by the Phelps-Stokes Fund*, Phelps-Stokes Fund (New York, NY), 1976.
- (With Donna Rand and Sheila Foster) *Black Books Galore! Guide to Great African-American Children's Books*, John Wiley & Sons (New York, NY), 1998.

- (With Donna Rand) *Black Books Galore! Guide to Great African-American Children's Books about Boys*, John Wiley & Sons (New York, NY), 2001.
- (With Donna Rand) *Black Books Galore! Guide to Great African-American Children's Books about Girls*, John Wiley & Sons (New York, NY), 2001.
- (With Donna Rand) *Black Books Galore! Guide to More Great African-American Children's Books*, John Wiley & Sons (New York, NY), 2001.

FURTHER READING

Black Enterprise, February, 1999, Sonja Brown Stokely, review of *Black Books Galore! Guide to Great African-American Children's Books* p. 211.

Black Issues Book Review, July, 2001, Khafre K. Abif, review of *Black Books Galore! Guide to Great African-American Children's Books about Girls* and *Black Books Galore! Guide to Great African-American Children's Books about Boys*, p. 73.

Booklist, December 15, 2000, Hazel Rochman, review of *Black Books Galore! Guide to Great African-American Children's Books about Girls*, p. 830.

Ebony, April, 2001, review of *Black Books Galore! Guide to Great African-American Children's Books about Girls* and *Black Books Galore! Guide to Great African-American Children's Books about Boys*, p. 16.

Feminist Collections, winter, 2002, Phyllis Holman Weisbard, review of *Black Books Galore! Guide to Great African-American Children's Books about Girls*, p. 24.

Living in Stamford, November–December, 2000, Abby West, "Black Books Galore! Works to Expand Children's Literary Horizons One Book at a Time," pp. 81–82.

Philadelphia Inquirer, February 27, 2002, Lucia Herndon, "Mothers Created a Special Book Fair."

Publishers Weekly, January 1, 2001, review of *Black Books Galore! Guide to Great African-American Children's Books about Girls* and *Black Books Galore! Guide to Great African-American Children's Books about Boys*, p. 94;

December 3, 2001, review of *Hugs and Hearts*, p. 62;

December 24, 2001, review of *Painted Eggs and Chocolate Bunnies*, p. 66.

School Library Journal, September, 1999, Marie Wright, review of *Black Books Galore! Guide to Great African-American Children's Books*, p. 249;

March, 2001, Eunice Weech, review of *Black Books Galore! Guide to Great African-American Children's Books about Boys*, p. 289;

May, 2002, Mary Lankford, review of *Black Books Galore! Guide to More Great African-American Children's Books*, p. 183;

September, 2002, Be Astengo, review of *Sweets and Treats*, p. 204; October.

GEORGE P. WEICK

Parker, William (1822?–?), slave narrative author and resistance leader, was born a slave to Louisa Simms in Anne Arundel County, Maryland, at Rowdown, a plantation with approximately seventy slaves, mostly field hands. What we know about William Parker is drawn from his own account published in 1866. His mother died early in his life, and Parker was raised by his grandmother, who was a cook in the plantation's main house.

Upon the death of Rowdown's owner, Major William Brogdon, the plantation was divided between his sons, William and David. Parker, along with many other slaves, including his brother and his uncle, was sent to live with David, who had built a house called Nearo on the southwestern portion of the farm. According to Parker's narrative, neither of the young masters abused his slaves, and he and the other slaves "were as contented as it is possible for slaves to be" (154). Slave sales, however, were another matter altogether. "No punishment was so much dreaded by the refractory slave as selling," Parker wrote (155). After Parker's friend Levi was deceived and sent by his owner to deliver a letter to a family acquaintance, a man to whom he had secretly been sold, Parker began to consider escape seriously. He estimates that he was sixteen or seventeen at the time.

After a confrontation with his owner, Parker and his brother, Charles, escaped via Baltimore, Maryland, and York, Pennsylvania, to a farm area about five miles east of Lancaster, Pennsylvania. After working there for three months, Parker visited his brother, who had settled in Bart Township, near Smyrna, fifteen miles to the east. Parker remained with him for thirteen months before getting work with a physician named Dr. Dengy.

Through Quaker influence, the region, located in the southeastern portion of Pennsylvania, had long been a focal point of antislavery activity and an important stop on the Underground Railroad. The tensions between slave catchers and abolitionists were intensified by the 1850 Fugitive Slave Law, which required free states to return escaped slaves to their southern owners or face federal penalties. Lancaster County was particularly dangerous for black Americans because of the Gap Gang, a roving group that patrolled the region looking for escaped slaves, who could be returned for bounty, and for free blacks, who could be captured and sold into slavery. The violence of these patrols increased after a series of altercations, including one clash that left three slave catchers dead following their attempt to return an escaped slave girl to Maryland.

While living with Dr. Dengy, Parker attended an antislavery meeting at which FREDERICK DOUGLASS—with whom he had been acquainted when they were both slaves in Maryland—and William Lloyd Garrison spoke. Parker joined with Douglass and other African Americans in opposing the Fugitive Slave Law by forming a self-protection society to defend African Americans against slave catchers and northern white vigilantes. By then Parker had married a woman named Eliza Ann Elizabeth Howard, who was also an escaped slave from Maryland. Howard's mother, brother, and sisters had also escaped and were living in the Lancaster area. Howard, who married Parker when she was about sixteen years old, was twenty-one and the mother of their three children when Parker began his abolitionist work.

Parker reports in his narrative that on 9 September 1851 Edward Gorsuch, accompanied by a small group of men, arrived in Philadelphia, Pennsylvania, from rural Baltimore County, Maryland, with the intention of traveling to Christiana, Pennsylvania, to capture four former slaves who in November 1849 had stolen five bushels of Gorsuch's wheat. The four escaped slaves had been directed to Parker, who had developed a reputation in his community for assisting fugitive slaves. Gorsuch had learned that the men he sought resided with Parker, and he intended to reclaim them. Gorsuch and his six men, however, encountered more than Parker and the fugitives. Seventy-five to one hundred armed neighbors—both black and white—had responded to a horn blown by Parker's wife. The armed confrontation quickly escalated, leaving Gorsuch dead and his son, his nephew, and others wounded. The incident came to be known as the Christiana Resistance.

Newspapers widely circulated accounts of the resistance, and Parker quickly became a marked man. To avoid arrest, Parker, sending his wife separately, journeyed to Canada via the Underground Railroad. He traveled north through Rochester, New York, where he briefly stopped at Frederick Douglass's home before departing for Toronto, Ontario, arriving in Canada in September 1851. There, Parker learned that Pennsylvania's governor,

William Johnston, was seeking his return to the state under the terms of the Extradition Treaty. Parker's wife arrived two months after Parker's arrival in Toronto, having narrowly escaped capture on several occasions. With the help of supporters, Parker was eventually able to purchase land and build a house. Little is known of his life in Canada, and the date and circumstances of his death are unknown.

Parker's narrative, "The Freedman's Story. In Two Parts," first published in 1866 in the *Atlantic Monthly*, illuminates a number of aspects of slavery, including, to some extent, the workings of the Underground Railroad. The account chronicles the experiences of African Americans in antebellum Lancaster County, Pennsylvania, and makes clear that African American resistance was organized around an intricate network of warnings, plans, and armed defense. The narrative is significant as well for its first-person account of the Christiana Resistance. The veracity of Parker's narrative, however, remains in doubt. Because Parker was most likely illiterate, his narrative was edited by someone identified only as "E.K.," who writes in the introduction, "The manuscript of the following pages has been handed to me with the request that I would revise it for publication, or weave its facts into a story which should show the fitness of the Southern black for the exercise of the right of suffrage." The narrative, published fifteen years after the Christiana Resistance, clearly has an agenda that reaches beyond the particulars of Parker's life. According to Parker's account, for example, he was a primary participant during the resistance. Contemporaneous accounts, however, indicate that he was only one of many resistance leaders.

Although potentially compromised, Parker's narrative provides the only account of the incident from a combatant who was inside the house. And even though the centrality and extent of Parker's involvement may be questioned, the strength of his beliefs should not. Parker's involvement in the Christiana Resistance represents the larger dissatisfaction that many felt with the Compromise of 1850 and the Fugitive Slave Law.

FURTHER READING
Parker, William. "The Freedman's Story. In Two Parts," *Atlantic Monthly: A Magazine of Literature, Science, Art and Politics* 17 (Feb. and Mar. 1866).
STERLING LECATER BLAND JR.

Parker, William (10 Jan. 1952–), jazz bassist, was born in the Bronx, New York. William Parker's father, Thomas Parker, repaired furniture while his mother, Mary Louise Jefferson Parker, was a school aide. Growing up in New York City, Parker's family were passionate music lovers and engaged in nightly dance contests at home listening to DUKE ELLINGTON's *Live at Newport 1957*. Parker's musicianship developed in his teens, as he played the trumpet and trombone, and later at fifteen he took up the cello. He also played baseball and football in the Buddy Young Football league. Parker started his study of bass in his early twenties from the 1960s bass luminaries Richard Davis, Jimmy Garrison, and WILBUR WARE. Along with eschewing classical music education, Parker also studied the music of JOHN COLTRANE rather than the earlier bebop music of THELONIOUS MONK and CHARLIE PARKER. This unorthodox approach allowed a more experimental sound to emerge, fitting well with the playing style of free jazz musicians he worked with early in his career. In 1973 Parker helped form the Music Ensemble, a collective of younger free-jazz musicians including the violinist Billy Bang, the trumpeter Malik Baraka, the reed player Daniel Carter, and the drummer Roger Baird. The following year saw the cofounding of Centering Music/Dance Ensemble with his wife, the choreographer Patricia Nicholson, whom he married in 1975. The mid-1970s also saw the beginning of Parker's association with CECIL TAYLOR in both big and small band formats. Parker performed with Cecil Taylor's big band at Carnegie Hall, instituting a working relationship that culminated in Parker joining the Cecil Taylor Unit, a small ensemble, in 1980. By the end of the 1970s Parker had worked with DON CHERRY, David S. Ware, and Dennis Charles. In 1979 Parker finally released his first record as a leader on his own label (Centering Records), *Through the Acceptance of the Mystery Peace*, with the violinist Billy Bang and the saxophonists Charles Brackeen and Jemeel Moondoc.

After joining the Cecil Taylor Unit at the turn of the decade, Parker accompanied the group on a successful European tour. The 1980s also saw Parker's art reflect more of the political realities of the time, as he named compositions "Peace Suite," composed and performed an opera for the opening of UN Second Special Session for Disarmament (June 1982), and wrote ballets ("Vision Peace and Battle Cries"). As the decade progressed, Parker produced more compositions and expanded his work from jazz into other areas of art, including dance, poetry, and the aforementioned operas.

Moreover, Parker expanded his attention to children's workshops and became active organizing festivals with other free jazz musicians such as Roy Campbell, Daniel Carter, Raphe Malik, Jemeel Moondoc, and Charles Tyler. In the late 1980s Parker received a Fellowship grant from the New York Foundation for the Arts.

William Parker approached the 1990s as a New York jazz community catalyst, leaving the Cecil Taylor Unit and founding his Little Huey Creative Music Orchestra. He performed in his quartet ("In Order to Survive"); continued to write pieces for music, dance, and poetry; co-organized music festivals; and commenced teaching at university-level schools around the world, including the New England Conservatory of Music and the Music Conservatory in Rotterdam, the Netherlands. His growing reputation drew praise from the *Village Voice*, which in 1995 labeled Parker "the most consistently brilliant free jazz bassist of all time." The same year he released *Flowers Grow in My Room* on his Centering label, the first recording of the Little Huey Creative Music Orchestra. Its popularity registered in the *College Music Journal*, reaching the number-1 position on its charts. This success illustrated the popularity of free jazz in the college and independent music community as well as showed the latent possibilities of a wider listenership if given the exposure of the mainstream bop revivalists. The 1990s also saw Parker cement a relationship with the drummer Hamid Drake. Their work with the European free-jazz pioneer Peter Brötzmann gained the pair's rhythm section recognition as "one of the most potent, and shockingly groove-oriented, rhythm sections in free jazz" (Freeman, 74). Moreover, Parker remained in high demand as a bass player among musicians such as Roy Campbell, David S. Ware, Matthew Shipp, and Rob Brown.

In 2000 Parker received a commission from Arts for Art (funded by the New York State Council on the Arts) for his composition "Kaleidoscope," as well as releasing three of his own albums: *Mayor of Punkville*, *Painter's Spring*, and *O'Neal's Porch*. Between 2001 and 2007 Parker released at least two records a year. Ever expanding his musical reach, Parker teamed up with DJ Spooky for a 2003 festival in Berlin and worked with the young Olmec Group (2006)—an album that serves to connect West Africa with Olmecs (Mexico, 1300–400 b.c.e.). In 2006 he collaborated with Hamid Drake, Dave Burrell, AMIRI BARAKA and others for a festival performance and album based on the songs of

CURTIS MAYFIELD. Through such projects, William Parker remained one of the most influential and prolific artists of the jazz avant-garde well into the twenty-first century.

FURTHER READING
Freeman, Phil. *New York Is Now: The New Wave of Free Jazz* (2001).
Stewart, Jesse. "Freedom Music: Jazz and Human Rights," in *Rebel Musics: Human Rights, Resistant Sounds, and the Politics of Music Making* (2003).
Such, David G. *Avant-Garde Jazz Musicians Performing 'Out There'* (1993).

DANIEL ROBERT MCCLURE

Parks, Gordon, Jr. (7 Dec. 1934–3 Apr. 1979), filmmaker, was born in Minneapolis, Minnesota, the eldest son of Sally Alvis and GORDON PARKS SR., the latter an award-winning photojournalist, author, composer, and filmmaker. Born less than a year into his parents' marriage, Gordon Jr. was nicknamed Butch as a newborn by his maternal grandfather, Joe Alvis. "There was not too much I could give my first three children being a waiter on a railway," recalled Gordon Parks Sr. in the 2001 film documentary *Half Past Autumn*. In 1940 the Parks family moved to Chicago. There Gordon Jr. spent much of his childhood while his father forged his career. Parks developed a passion for riding horses, which became a lifelong interest.

When he was sixteen Parks moved to Paris, where his father had been assigned for two years by *Life* magazine. In Europe he developed a keen interest in the fine arts, also cultivating a desire to travel that greatly influenced his later career as a filmmaker. He attended the American School in Paris, where he learned French as a second language, and accompanied his father to concerts, museums, and weekend and summer jaunts to St. Tropez and Cannes. While in school he took up painting and began to direct student plays.

After moving back to New York, Parks watched as his parents' marriage crumble. Estranged from his mother, Parks and his siblings, Toni and David, went to live with his father. In 1952 he graduated from high school in White Plains, New York. In an attempt to distance himself from the career path of his famous father, Parks worked for a time in the garment district of New York City, moving clothing racks. When he was photographing a story for *Life* magazine, however, Gordon Sr. offered his son the opportunity to spend a weekend hanging out with the infamous gang leader Red Jackson. The

opportunity presumably had an effect on the inner-city realism that Parks later brought to his first feature film, *Superfly*.

In 1957 Parks was drafted into the U.S. Army. While stationed in Desert Rock, Nevada, his convoy truck broke down and he narrowly missed radiation exposure from a nearby atomic test. After six months of close observation, he was discharged from the army and returned to New York City. During the early 1960s Parks played guitar and sang folk music in bars and coffeehouses in New York City's Greenwich Village.

Much of Parks's professional life, however, was spent in the shadow of his father. Because their names are so much alike, many of Parks's accomplishments have been mistakenly credited to his father. Commenting on their father-son relationship, Parks's stepmother, Genevieve, noted in the film documentary *Half Past Autumn* that there was always a "certain air of competitiveness between the two." Like his father, Parks developed a professional interest in photography, using the name Gordon Rogers for several years to distance himself from his birth name. In 1969 he was hired as a still photographer for the Marlon Brando film *Burn!* and performed the same role on a more famous Brando film in 1972—*The Godfather*. Parks also worked as a cameraman on his father's 1969 debut film, *The Learning Tree*. From these experiences, Parks learned much about making films. "I love movies, I've spent hours at movies, our generation is all movies," he said in an interview. "I've lived with film all my life" (*Oakland Post*, 3 Aug. 1972).

In 1972 Parks capitalized on his passion for movies by directing the action-thriller *Superfly*. The story of Priest, a drug pusher attempting to better his life, *Superfly* became noted for its gritty realism and its ability to elicit audience sympathy for its criminal antihero. Released on the heels of his father's landmark 1971 detective drama *Shaft*, the film was largely produced by black businessmen, using a black crew, on a shoestring budget of five hundred thousand dollars. Widely considered the zenith of the so-called blaxploitation films of the early 1970s, *Superfly* went on to gross tens of millions of dollars. The film sparked a huge commercial boom in black-themed films and catapulted the careers of a number of black directors. Critics have credited Parks with some of the film's more interesting touches, including its steamy, risqué sex scene, the photographic black-and-white stills that appear toward the middle of the narrative, and the decision to foreground the film's now-classic musical score composed by CURTIS MAYFIELD. *Superfly*, however, unleashed a maelstrom of controversy about the moral direction of black films in Hollywood. While some critics saw it as a harsh and invigorating depiction of black urban life, others criticized the film for its romanticization of machismo, drug use, and crime.

Having moved to his horse ranch in the California Valley, Parks continued to direct films. In 1974 he helmed the lumbering *Thomasine and Bushrod*, starring Max Julien and Vonetta McGee. A black *Bonnie and Clyde* set at the turn of the twentieth century, the film recounts the story of Oklahoma thieves who steal from rich whites to give to poor people of color. His next film, *Three the Hard Way* (1974), starred the action heroes JIM BROWN, FRED WILLIAMSON, and Jim Kelly as a trio out to save the United States from a white-supremacist plot to taint the national water supply. In 1975 he directed *Aaron Loves Angela*, an inner-city update of the *Romeo and Juliet* story transformed into a black and Puerto Rican conflict, which was released just months before his father's *Leadbelly*. Each of Parks's releases faded into obscurity, either because of studio neglect or audience disinterest, and many critics felt that Parks had lost his artistic footing after *Superfly*.

In 1979 tragedy struck. Parks had just started an independent production company, African International Productions/Panther Film Company, and planned to make the first of three films on the African continent. On 3 April 1979 he died in Kenya when his plane crashed in an aborted takeoff on the runway of the Nairobi airport. After his cremation, some of his ashes were left in Africa and the rest brought back to New York City, where services were held at the United Nations' Chapel. At the time of Parks's death, his wife, Leslie, was pregnant with his first child, Gordon III.

Even in death, newspaper and radio reports mistakenly announced that Gordon Parks Sr. had been killed, and bibliographical accounts still often confuse the two men.

FURTHER READING

Bogle, Donald. *Toms, Coons, Mulattoes, Mammies, and Bucks: An Interpretive History of Blacks in American Films* (1989).

Kovel, Mikel J. *Blaxploitation Films* (2001).

Parks, Gordon, Sr. *Half Past Autumn: A Retrospective* (1997).

Parks, Gordon, Sr. *Voices in the Mirror: An Autobiography* (1990).

Obituary: *Jet* (19 Apr. 1979).

JASON KING

Parks, Gordon, Sr. (20 Nov. 1912–7 March 2006), photographer, filmmaker, author, and composer, was born Gordon Roger Alexander Buchanan Parks in the small prairie town of Fort Scott, Kansas, to Andrew Jackson Parks, a dirt farmer, and Sarah Ross, a maid. Gordon was the youngest of fifteen children, the first five of which, he later discovered, were really half siblings, born to his father and a woman other than his mother. Parks's poor Kansas childhood, and his memories of its unbridled racism, feature prominently in his later work, especially his books "thick with those memories." The first phase of Parks's life ended with the death of his mother in 1928. "Before the flowers on my mother's grave had wilted," Parks remembered, "my father had me on a train to my sister in Minnesota. I ran into some hell there" (Russell, 145). Within a month of his arrival in-Minneapolis–St. Paul, Gordon's brother-in-law kicked him out of the house, forcing him to survive the winter by riding the light-rail cars at night and hanging out in pool halls during the day. High school was merely a place to stay out of the cold, and Parks soon dropped out. Years later Parks dedicated one of his forty-six honorary degrees to his high school teacher who counseled her black students, "Don't bother to go to college and spend your mother's and father's money, because you're gonna be porters and maids" (Russell, 145).

For a while, at least, that teacher was right. Parks worked as a waiter and busboy, first at the Minnesota Club and later at the Hotel Lowry, where he catered to white patrons and met musicians in the big bands. Having taught himself to play by ear, Parks began composing songs and landed a job playing piano in a St. Paul brothel. Invited to join a touring orchestra, Parks arrived in Harlem in March 1933. The group, however, disbanded almost immediately, and he was stranded without a job. After making a few deliveries for a dope dealer, he joined the newly established Civilian Conservation Corps (CCC), planting trees and clearing camping grounds and beaches until July 1934.

While in the CCC, Parks met and married Sally Alvis. The couple moved back to Minneapolis and had three children, GORDON PARKS JR., Toni, and David. Parks returned to playing piano and waiting tables until 1935, when he was hired by the North Coast Limited railroad. A discarded

Gordon Parks Sr. directing a scene of the film "The Learning Tree" in December 1968. (AP Images.)

magazine featuring the work of Farm Security Administration (FSA) photographers such as Walker Evans, Dorothea Lange, Ben Shahn, and Arthur Rothstein captured Parks's attention. After visiting the Art Institute of Chicago on a layover and watching a newsreel of the 1937 sinking of USS *Panay* taken by photojournalist Norman Alley, who was present at the screening, Parks bought his first camera, a Voightlander Brilliant, at a Seattle pawnshop.

After Parks was fired following a racial incident provoked by a white steward, he played for a season as a semiprofessional basketball player with the House of David team before being hired by the Chicago and Northwestern Railway. Parks photographed while on the road and regularly contributed to the *Minneapolis Spokesman* and the *St. Paul Recorder*, and in February 1938 he had his first exhibition in the window of a Minneapolis Eastman Kodak store. Parks's personal charisma and his eye for beauty—in women and line—led him to fashion photography. At the urging of Marva Louis, JOE LOUIS's wife, Parks moved his family to Chicago, where he photographed fashions and did portrait work for both black and white clients. In what would

become a lifelong pattern, he divided his time between these glamorous subjects and photojournalism. In Chicago he documented the devastating effects of poverty, accompanied the FSA photographer Jack Delano on several assignments, and shadowed Edwin Rosskam during preparation for the book *12 Million Black Voices*, for which RICHARD WRIGHT wrote the text. The book proved a powerful influence on Parks's work, especially in shaping his approach to the relationship of word and image and the sequencing and juxtaposing of images.

When Parks won a Julius Rosenwald Fellowship in 1941, the first ever awarded in photography, he arranged for an apprenticeship at the FSA in Washington, D.C., under Roy Emerson Stryker. Parks and his family were not prepared for the racism they encountered upon their arrival in the nation's capital. "You have to get at the source of their bigotry, and that's not easy," Stryker counseled Parks. "The camera becomes a powerful weapon" (Parks, 1997, 32). Stryker sent Parks to research the FSA photo files and suggested that he talk with ELLA WATSON, an African American cleaning woman who worked in the building. Among the series of photos Parks took of Watson and her family was a posed image of Watson standing in front of an American flag with a mop in one hand and a broom in the other. The photo, later dubbed "American Gothic," referencing Grant Wood's 1930 painting of the same name, was Parks's first official FSA photo, and it became one of photography's iconic images.

Stryker sent Parks on assignment in New England, upstate New York, and Washington, D.C, and, in August 1943, to photograph Richard Wright in Harlem. When the FSA was disbanded in 1943, Parks went with Stryker to the Office of War Information (OWI), for which he photographed the military's first black fighter pilots under the command of Lieutenant Colonel BENJAMIN O. DAVIS JR. In 1944 Parks resigned and moved to Harlem, looking for work in fashion photography. Through Edward Steichen, he was hired by *Glamour* and then *Vogue*. From 1944 to 1948 he also worked for Stryker at Standard Oil of New Jersey, which had launched a photography project established to document American life.

Parks's photographic style—unsentimental, confident, and graphically strong—was already established, and in 1947 he published his first book, a how-to volume entitled *Flash Photography*. The next year he followed with *Camera Portraits: Techniques and Principles of Documentary Portraiture*, which included, among others, portraits of ADAM CLAYTON POWELL JR. and RALPH ELLISON.

In 1948 Parks talked his way into a job at *Life* magazine, the nation's most popular and influential general interest magazine. *Life*'s first black staff photographer, Parks remained with the magazine for over twenty years, completing more than three hundred assignments and fifteen magazine covers. His first assignments, balancing the disparate worlds of fashion and a photo essay centering on the sixteen-year-old Harlem gang leader Red Jackson, were illustrative of the range of his *Life* career. After eighteen months Parks was assigned to *Life*'s Paris bureau for two years. Over the years, Parks photographed cowboys and priests, movie stars and royalty, Broadway shows and the emerging world of television, international events and political campaigns, fashion shows and the daily lives of Americans. "Tyrants, dictators, dethroned kings, beggars, queens, harlots, priests, the uplifting and the despoilers," recalled Parks, "all stared into my camera with eyes that were unveiled. The camera revealed them as they were—human beings imprisoned inside themselves" (Parks, 1997, 13). Lauded for his portraits, Parks photographed such leading personalities as ALTHEA GIBSON, SUGAR RAY ROBINSON, SIDNEY BECHET, EARTHA KITT, LOUIS ARMSTRONG, DUKE ELLINGTON, Leonard Bernstein, Barbra Streisand, Marcel Duchamp, Alberto Giacometti, Alexander Calder, and Dwight D. Eisenhower.

Meanwhile, Parks was producing photo essays on social issues, and by the 1960s he had become one of the country's most respected and influential photojournalists. In 1956 Parks documented the effects of segregation on one family in the photo essay "Segregation in the Deep South, Choctaw County, Alabama." Over the next few years, he continued to tackle America's underbelly with "Segregation in the North," "Crime across America," and "Unemployment in Philadelphia." "Freedom's Fearful Foe: Poverty," published in the 16 June 1961 issue of *Life* and arguably Parks's most influential photo essay, was originally slated for only one photo. The stark photos of an ailing and malnourished Brazilian boy, Flavio de Silva of Rio de Janeiro, prompted a spontaneous response from American readers, who sent in thirty thousand dollars. Several years later when *Life*'s editor Phil Kunhardt asked, "Why are black people rioting in the middle of America," Parks

responded by moving in with the Fontenelle family in Harlem for one week. The result was "Poverty in Harlem," a groundbreaking photo essay published in 1968.

"*Life* magazine was very good about not assigning me 'black stories,'" Parks always maintained. He did, however, cover—in word and image—the significant figures and events of the civil rights and Black Power movements, joining CHARLIE MOORE, MONETA SLEET, Robert Haggins, Jonathan Eubanks, Jack T. Franklin, and ERNEST WITHERS as one of the most significant documentarians of the period. In 1963 he published major stories on the March on Washington and on black Muslims. Following MALCOLM X's assassination two years later, Parks published the photo essay "Death of Malcolm X," after which, on the recommendation of the FBI, who took seriously threats from the Nation of Islam, the Parks family was sent overseas for a short time. As the decade progressed, Parks photographed STOKELY CARMICHAEL, KATHLEEN CLEAVER and ELDRIDGE CLEAVER, and MUHAMMAD ALI, covered the funeral of MARTIN LUTHER KING JR., and spent three weeks with the Black Panthers in Berkeley, California.

Unpretentious, spare, and straightforward, Parks's photographs belie the formal rigor of their construction. Parks's careful attention to the strategic possibilities of space and light, and his decisive use of objects and signs, both literal and poetic, produced a lifetime of rich images. As his photographic career progressed, Parks became increasingly interested in color and abstraction, and by the 1980s he was exhibiting paintings and works in other media as well as color photographs.

In 1963, encouraged by his friend and *Life* photographer Carl Mydans, who chided, "Man you've got a novel in you," Parks published *The Learning Tree*, a novel based on his Kansas childhood. The book became a best-seller, and *Life* commissioned a series of photographs that it published alongside Parks's essay "How It Feels to Be Black." With help from the filmmaker John Cassavetes, Parks wrote, directed, and scored a Hollywood film based on the book in 1969. Thirty years later the film was among the twenty-five films placed on the National Film Registry of the Library of Congress. Parks's first films, documentaries made in the mid- to late 1960s, had grown out of *Life* stories: *Flavio* (1964), *Diary of a Harlem Family* (1968), and *The World of* PIRI THOMAS (1968). After the success of *The Learning Tree*, he entered the arena of popular fiction film with *Shaft* (1971), starring RICHARD ROUNDTREE.

Shaft's Big Score! (1972) and *The Super Cops* (1974) followed. Parks returned to documentary filmmaking with *Leadbelly* (1976) and SOLOMON NORTHUP'S *Odyssey* (1984).

Parks published three full-length autobiographies, in 1966, 1979, and 1990. He was one of the founders of *Essence* magazine, serving as editorial director from 1970 to 1973, during which time he published *Born Black* (1971), a collection of essays. *The Weapons of Gordon Parks*, a television adaptation of his earliest memoir, was presented on network television in 1969. Parks combined photographs and poetry in *A Poet and His Camera* (1968), *Whispers of Intimate Things* (1971), *In Love* (1971), *Moments without Proper Names* (1975), *Aries in Silence* (1994), and *Glimpses toward Infinity* (1996). Other publications included two historical novels, *Shannon* (1981), set in New York during World War I, and *The Sun Stalkers* (2003), based on the life of the painter Joseph M. W. Turner. Parks also produced an autobiographical film, *Gordon Parks: Moments without Proper Names*, which aired in 1988.

In addition to his photographic, film, and literary work, Parks continued playing and composing music, including several classical compositions. Beginning with *The Learning Tree*, he wrote several film scores, some of which were released as independent albums. In 1989 he wrote the libretto and music for *Martin*, a ballet based on the life of Martin Luther King Jr., which he later put on film.

In 1961 Parks and Sally Alvis divorced. Two years later he married Elizabeth Campbell, daughter of the pioneering black cartoonist ELMER "E. SIMMS" CAMPBELL. The couple had a daughter, Leslie, and divorced in 1973. The same year he married Genevieve Young, his editor at Harper and Row. The couple divorced in 1979, the same year that his son, Gordon Parks Jr., director of the film *Superfly*, was killed in a plane crash at the age of forty-four.

Parks was awarded the NAACP's highest honor, the Spingarn Medal, in 1972, and a National Medal of Arts in 1988. In 1997 the Corcoran Gallery of Art in Washington, D.C., organized Half Past Autumn, the first major museum retrospective of Parks's work. Described by Parks as a "a tone-poem," the exhibition, which traveled through 2003 to ten major cities, included more than two hundred photographs, as well as films, novels, poetry, and music. A companion documentary of the same name, coproduced by DENZEL WASHINGTON, aired on HBO in 2000. Parks wrote the exhibition's accompanying book, dedicating it "For Momma and Poppa I stay drenched in the showers of their love." Parks died in his home in Manhattan on 7 March 2006. He was ninety-three.

FURTHER READING

Parks's papers, photographs, films, and music are held by the Library of Congress.

Parks, Gordon. *A Choice of Weapons* (1966).

Parks, Gordon. *Half Past Autumn: A Retrospective* (1997).

Parks, Gordon. *To Smile in Autumn* (1979).

Parks, Gordon. *Voices in the Mirror: An Autobiography* (1990).

Bush, Martin. *The Photographs of Gordon Parks* (1983).

Russell, Dick. *Black Genius* (1998).

LISA E. RIVO

Parks, Henry Green, Jr. (29 Sept. 1916–24 Apr. 1989), business executive, entrepreneur, and civic leader, was born in Atlanta, Georgia, the son of Henry Green Parks Sr. His mother's name is unknown, but both of his parents at one time worked as domestic laborers. Seeking a better life the family moved to Dayton, Ohio, when Henry Jr. was six months old. There his father found work as a hotel bartender and later as a wine steward in a private club. Because both of Parks's parents worked long hours the family did not spend much time together. Henry spent most of his time with his paternal grandmother, whom he described as "very religious." The example that Parks's father set for him was one of diligence, perseverance, risk-taking, and making hard choices, attributes that would be evident throughout Parks's life.

Parks graduated from the public schools of Dayton, Ohio. Had he chosen to follow the prevailing wisdom of the time he would have applied to attend a historically black college or university. One of his first hard choices, however, was to apply to Ohio State University, the premier university in the state. He believed that although he would face prejudice he could advance further with a degree from Ohio State. While attending the university he roomed with the future Olympic gold medal winner JESSE OWENS. They both encountered racism but strove to rise above it.

Parks started out as an accounting major but soon switched to marketing when it became apparent that he had a flair for salesmanship. He worked his way through college, graduating with honors in 1939. The only black student in his class, he was advised by a counselor that if he really wanted to succeed in business he should to go to

South America, acquire a Spanish accent, change his name, and return to the United States under an assumed identity.

Parks chose not to follow the advice. After several months he found a job with the National Youth Administration in Cincinnati. While he was in college Parks had met DR. MARY MCLEOD BETHUNE, an educator and the founder of Bethune-Cookman College, who had encouraged him to be productive and an achiever wherever he was. Bethune became Parks's mentor and subsequently helped him get a job with the Resident War Production Training Center in Wilberforce, Ohio, where he had his first business management experience. With a staff of fifty, Parks trained several hundred young people for jobs in industry. During his stay at Wilberforce he met JOE LOUIS, the world champion boxer, and they later became partners in several business ventures. Parks was the road manager for the singer Marva Louis, Joe Louis's wife, and he headed a soft-drink company that produced Joe Louis Punch. The soft-drink company was not particularly successful, but through it Parks did manage to gain additional management experience.

From 1940 until 1942 Parks worked for Pabst Brewing Company as a beer salesman, becoming a national sales representative. During this time he devised a plan to market Pabst to blacks, employing popular black recording artists such as LENA HORNE, DUKE ELLINGTON, and CAB CALLOWAY to appeal to black customers while at the same time not offending white customers. He also designed a strategy to displace Budweiser as the exclusive supplier for the nation's railroads, enlisting the help and cooperation of railroad porters, dining car attendants, and waiters to increase sales of his product. Parks far exceeded the company's expectations in both efforts. In 1942 Parks and a coworker, W. B. Graham, resigned from Pabst and formed W. B. Graham and Associates, a public relations and advertising business. Although this business was moderately successful, Parks wanted more. He became part owner and salesman for Crayton Southern Sausage in Cleveland in 1949. Within two years the business had expanded so quickly that Parks's partners wanted to slow down. The ambitious Parks objected and allowed himself to be bought out.

While on a train to Boston in 1948 Parks met a powerful Baltimore businessman, William "Little Willie" Adams. Adams was impressed with Parks—it was unusual for a black person to have a degree in business—and suggested that he might have some business ventures that could be profitable for the two of them. This led Parks to relocate to Baltimore, Maryland, where he initially worked in Adams's real estate firm. Next Parks managed a drugstore, and later he owned a business that produced cement blocks. Finding a bank willing to finance another business proved to be impossible; however, with the backing of Adams and with his profits from the sale of his part in the Crayton operation, Parks began a new venture in Baltimore.

In 1951 Parks Sausage Company opened in an abandoned dairy at North and Pennsylvania avenues. With the help of two employees Parks made the sausage one day and sold it the next. The business struggled. Parks sold his house and borrowed against his life insurance to purchase reconditioned equipment and a few delivery trucks. Recalling his success at Pabst he began a whirlwind marketing campaign aimed at the city's black community and subsequently expanded the effort to include white-owned businesses. He was one of the first to give cooking demonstrations and taste tests in supermarkets. The company symbol, Parky the Pig, gave gifts to children, and the Parks salesmen conducted a "Customer of the Day" program.

About a year later Parks began to distribute his products to a grocery chain in Washington, D.C., and he received a letter of appreciation from First Lady Mamie Eisenhower. The business prospered, developing a national reputation for high quality control—Parks sampled the product personally every day for nearly twenty years—and a unique marketing strategy, including the famous slogan "More Parks sausages, Mom!" The combination of a quality product and a well-executed marketing plan formed the backdrop for Parks's success. The company's shares were traded on the NASDAQ stock exchange from 1969 until 1977, at which time the company was taken over by private investors. Parks and Adams also made a tidy profit in real estate. In the mid-1970s Parks began to suffer from Parkinson's disease, and in 1977 he and Adams sold their interests in the company to the Miami-based Norin Corporation. At the time each held 158,000 shares valued at approximately $1.58 million. In 1979 the giant Canadian Pacific Corporation acquired Norin. After Parks sales fell dramatically the conglomerate planned to liquidate it, until a group led by Raymond V. Haysbert Sr., who became chief executive officer, bought the company in 1980.

Parks believed in the American dream, and he made it a reality for himself. He was fond of saying, "Blacks in America have nothing to run from, just a lot to run toward." He also believed that he was his brother's keeper and provided business exposure for many novice black businesspeople, among them EARL GRAVES, the owner of *Black Enterprises* magazine. Parks's personal life suffered a blow when his marriage ended in divorce, though he maintained a close relationship with his two daughters.

Parks also had a short but brilliant political career in Baltimore. Many thought that he might eventually become mayor of Baltimore, and at one point he was courted to run for lieutenant governor of the state of Maryland. Significantly, Parks defeated James H. "Jack" Pollack's political machine, which benefited other politicians, too, such as William Donald Shaefer, future mayor of Baltimore and future governor of Maryland, and Marvin Mandel, also a future governor of Maryland. Moreover, Parks's 1963 election to the city council helped increase black influence in city politics.

Believing that it was his duty to share his influence, time, business skills, and financial support, Parks served on numerous boards, including those of W. R. Grace & Co., Magnavox, Warner Lambert, and First Pennsylvania Corporation. He was the first black appointed president of the Baltimore Board of Fire Commissioners (1981) and was vice president of the Chamber of Commerce of Metropolitan Baltimore. Recipients of Parks's fund-raising efforts included the United Negro College Fund, the NAACP, and the National Urban League. Parks served on the National Citizens Committee for Human Relations and the National Public Advisory Committee on Regional Economic Development. In 1983 the Greater Baltimore Committee presented him with the J. Jefferson Miller Award.

Parks proved that with the right education, experience, expert advice, and a plan, minority business success can happen, and not just by concentrating on ethnic patrons. From humble beginnings he created H. G. Parks Incorporated, the first black company to go public. At its height the company had annual sales exceeding $30 million and distributed sausage and scrapple, made from an old family recipe, along the East Coast in some twelve thousand retail stores. Parks died in Towson, Maryland.

FURTHER READING

Parks's papers are in the Henry Parks file in the Maryland Room at the Enoch Pratt Free Library, Baltimore.

Obituaries: *Baltimore Evening Sun*, 25 Apr. 1989; *Afro-American*, 29 Apr. 1989.

This entry is taken from the *American National Biography* and is published here with the permission of the American Council of Learned Societies.

MARSEILLE M. PRIDE

Parks, Lillian Rogers (1 Feb. 1897–6 Nov. 1997), White House seamstress and author, was born Lillian Adele Rogers, the daughter of Emmett E. Rogers Sr., a waiter, and Margaret "Maggie" Williams. Source information is sketchy regarding her early years, but her godchild, Peggy Holly, believed that Lillian Parks was born in the District of Columbia and as a child spent summers with relatives in Virginia. Her father—by Parks's account an alcoholic unable to hold a job—left his family when she was a child. In 1909 her mother took a job at the White House at the beginning of William Howard Taft's presidency and often found it necessary to take her daughter along with her when she went to work. A victim of polio at the age of six, Parks used crutches for the rest of her life. She attended St. Ann's Catholic School and Stephens Elementary School in the District of Columbia. As she got older, she enjoyed listening to her mother's accounts of the day's events at the White House. After dropping out of Phelps Business School because of ill health, she began taking in sewing jobs and accompanied her mother to the White House on Sunday nights to turn down the bedcovers for the first family. She also worked as a cashier in a movie theater, as a doctor's receptionist, and as a seamstress in a dress shop. In 1935 Lillian Rogers married Carlton Parks; there were no children, and the couple quietly divorced in 1946.

In the fall of 1929 the current first lady, Lou Henry Hoover, a fastidious woman who took pride in her appearance and knew the value of good tailoring, brought Parks to the White House as a seamstress and maid. In 1948 Parks expected to be transferred to the U.S. Department of the Treasury when the White House was closed for structural restoration, but instead she went with the Trumans to Blair House, the temporary presidential residence, where she maintained a sewing room on the top floor. Parks returned to the White House in 1952 when the renovation was completed and remained there until her retirement in 1959.

After reading a book that Frances Spatz Leighton cowrote with a former chef in the Eisenhower White House, Parks realized that she had many memories of her White House years that would be interesting to others. In 1961 she published *My Thirty*

Years Backstairs at the White House, written with Leighton, as a series of personal vignettes of first ladies and their families as seen from the servants' viewpoint, beginning with the Tafts in 1909. The book contained the notes and recollections of both Parks and her mother, Maggie Rogers, who rose to the position of top White House maid before retiring in 1939. The memoirs constituted an inside view of life in the White House over fifty years. Parks admitted that she left out much of what she might have reported because she did not want to embarrass the eight first families she and her mother had worked for. The book received much attention, remaining on the *New York Times* best-seller list for more than six months, creating a certain notoriety for its author, and prompting First Lady Jacqueline Bouvier Kennedy to request that all White House domestic employees pledge to refrain from writing about the private lives of their first families. Many years later, in 1979, Parks's book was the basis of a television miniseries.

In spite of the concerns voiced in some circles, the book's anecdotal "revelations" were positive and benign. In general, Parks was complimentary to all of the first families she or her mother served, but Bess Truman—of whom she said, "Bess is best"—was clearly a favorite of hers. Parks always felt comfortable with Mrs. Truman because the first lady put on no fancy airs and knew who she was at all times: a midwestern matron in a happy marriage who appreciated the staff for their worth as human beings and for the work they did for her family. She respected them as equals and saw to it that they were well treated, often sending the maids home early on Sunday afternoons, assuring them, over their protests, that she was perfectly capable of turning down beds by herself. Parks and Bess Truman continued to correspond with Christmas and birthday cards long after both had left the White House.

More evidence of how well Parks was treated in the White House is an incident she related in her book. During World War II, when White House domestic staff members were not allowed to use the elevator (to leave it free for the disabled president, Franklin D. Roosevelt, in case of an emergency), the handicapped Parks, who was only four feet ten inches tall, was given an exemption and allowed to use the elevator. Parks's recollection of her treatment by Roosevelt indicates that the polio they both had suffered from created a special bond between them, since no one else in the White House knew what it was like to walk with crutches and endure the hardships of living with such a condition. Although she respected and admired Eleanor Roosevelt, Parks felt free to voice criticisms in her next book, *The Roosevelts: A Family in Turmoil* (1981). She may have tried to set the record straight about the Roosevelts' long stay at 1600 Pennsylvania Avenue, but few of her apparent revelations were really new because books by two of the Roosevelts' children and by close friends of the family had brought to light more telling and personal details. Reviews of the book reflected this, generally praising the intimate tone but criticizing the lack of a more insightful view that her position as a White House insider presumably afforded her. Her third publication, *It Was Fun Working at the White House* (1969), was a children's book that contained much material from *My Thirty Years Backstairs at the White House.*

After her retirement, Parks lived in Takoma Park, Maryland, just outside Washington, D.C., in a home decorated with presidential mementos. She appeared on several radio and television talk shows to reminisce about her White House years and was active in Neighbors Inc. (a community organization in the Washington ward where Parks had resided), the National Association of Negro Business and Professional Women's Clubs, and Don't Tear It Down (a preservation society in the District of Columbia). On her eighty-fifth birthday, the Washington City Council bestowed the honor of declaring it Lillian Rogers Parks Day.

In the summer of 1992 Parks was one of several former White House employees who appeared at the Smithsonian Institution's annual American Folklife Festival on the Washington Mall to discuss her experiences at the White House. In 1994 the Smithsonian's Center for Folklife Programs and Cultural Studies, in cooperation with the White House Historical Association and the National Archives, mounted the exhibit Workers at the White House at the Charles Sumner School Museum and Archives in Washington; reproductions of scrapbooks maintained by Parks were displayed there. She died of a heart attack in Washington at Sibley Memorial Hospital.

In her retirement, Parks never expressed bitterness about the clearly defined "upstairs–downstairs" atmosphere that existed in the White House during her years there. She considered it a remarkable stroke of good fortune to have worked at 1600 Pennsylvania Avenue at a time when minorities in Washington, D.C., had few opportunities to advance. Whatever their failings, her books provided the first behind-the-scenes accounts of the domestic lives of presidential families from the Tafts to the Eisenhowers; as such, they remain valuable documents.

FURTHER READING
The records of the White House Office (Record Group 130), which contain material on housekeeping activities with reference to Parks, are in the National Archives, College Park, Maryland. The Washingtonia Collection, Martin Luther King Public Library, Washington, D.C., has a clippings file on Parks. The Smithsonian Institution produced a video of the 1994 exhibit at the Sumner School, *Workers at the White House*, which includes an interview with Parks. A transcript of an oral history is in the Moorland-Spingarn Research Center, Howard University, Washington, D.C.
Parks, Lillian Rogers, with Frances Spatz Leighton. *My Thirty Years Backstairs at the White House* (1961).
Parks, Lillian Rogers, with Frances Spatz Leighton. *The Roosevelts: A Family in Turmoil* (1981).
Obituaries: *New York Times* and *Washington Post*, 12 Nov. 1997.

This entry is taken from the *American National Biography* and is published here with the permission of the American Council of Learned Societies.

MARTIN J. MANNING

Rosa Parks This booking photo was taken on 22 Feb. 1956. after she was arrested for refusing to give up her seat on a bus for a white passenger on 1 Dec. 1955 in Montgomery, Alabama. (AP Images.)

Parks, Rosa (14 Feb. 1913–24 Oct. 2005), was born Rosa Louise McCauley in Tuskegee, Alabama, the daughter of James McCauley, a carpenter, and Leona Edwards, a teacher. Her father migrated north when Rosa was two years old, and her mother schooled her at home until, at age eleven, she enrolled in the Montgomery Industrial School for Girls. She attended Alabama State Teacher's High School, but left before graduation to care for her mother. On 18 December 1932 Rosa Louise McCauley married Raymond Parks, a barber from Wedowee in Randolph County, Alabama. With her husband's encouragement, Parks completed her high school education in 1934. A member of the St. Paul AME Church, she was responsible for preparing Holy Communion.

From the beginning of their marriage Raymond and Rosa Parks embraced social activism, working, for example, to secure the release of the SCOTTSBORO BOYS, nine black youths accused of raping two white girls. During the 1940s Rosa Parks joined the Montgomery chapter of the NAACP, and as secretary of the branch from 1943 until 1956 she often hosted the organization's dynamic field secretary,

ELLA BAKER, when she visited Montgomery. E. D. NIXON, organizer of the Black Brotherhood of Sleeping Car Porters Union in Montgomery and head of the Progressive Democrats, was president of the local NAACP chapter.

Rosa Parks proved adept at working with young people. She helped train a group of NAACP youths to protest segregation in the Montgomery Public Library, and she participated in voter registration drives. Indeed, in 1945 Parks became one of just a few African Americans who were registered to vote in Montgomery. The registrar had failed her the first two times she took the literacy text. The same determination displayed in her pursuit of the vote surfaced when Parks chose to be arrested rather than to abide segregation on Montgomery's buses. It is important to underscore the extent to which Parks was anchored to the organizational and institutional infrastructure of the Montgomery black community. This is essential to understanding why she was able to inspire the modern civil rights movement.

Weary of the daily humiliations of second-class citizenship and the indignity of Jim Crow racial subordination, on 1 December 1955, the bespectacled and composed Rosa Parks refused to comply with the bus driver James F. Blake's order that she give the bus seat she occupied in the first row of the black section to a white male passenger. Three other African Americans vacated their seats, but Parks refused to move. The city's complex segregation laws dictated that African Americans pay their fares, exit the bus, and reenter through the rear door. Whites enjoyed the privilege of sitting in the front of the bus, and blacks occupied reserved seats in the rear. If the white section filled up and more white passengers boarded the bus, the black passengers were required to move.

Parks had not planned to disobey the law on that fateful day, but her thirty-year commitment to social justice prepared her to do so. Indeed, in June 1955 Parks had attended a summer workshop at the Highlander Folk School founded by Myles Horton in Monteagle, Tennessee, which had long been a training ground for labor organizers and social activists. In 1959 the State of Tennessee would label the Highlander Folk School a subversive organization. Still, at Highlander, Parks, like her fellow activists Ella Baker and SEPTIMA CLARK, acquired a deeper appreciation of and skills for community organizing, use of direct-action tactics, and administration of citizenship schools. Their preparation and long involvement in community affairs placed black women at the center of the civil rights movement.

For her defiance of the segregation ordinance, the Montgomery police hauled Parks off to jail. Montgomery's police lieutenant, Drue Lackey (who served as police chief from 1965 to 1970), took her fingerprints. Responding to a call from Nixon, the white attorney Clifford Durr took her case, but Nixon posted her bail. The court found Parks guilty of disorderly conduct and fined her ten dollars and another four dollars in court costs. Rosa Parks was not the first black woman to have suffered arrest for refusal to countenance bus segregation. In 1941 an angry mob beat Hannah Cofield before she was arrested for refusing to yield her seat to a white passenger. In 1944 Viola White met a similar fate. In March 1955, a few months before Parks's arrest, Claudette Colvin, an unmarried, pregnant fifteen-year-old girl, had objected to vacating her seat and was jailed.

The local black leadership had long debated challenging bus segregation, but decided to wait for an incident involving someone who embodied the politics of respectability and whose private life could withstand relentless scrutiny. Thus, although Cofield, White, Colvin, and later, Mary Louise Smith, protested bus segregation, their resistance failed to ignite a larger social protest movement. Propitiously, in July 1955, the U.S. Court of Appeals in Richmond, Virginia, declared in *Flemming v. South Carolina Electric and Gas Company* that bus segregation, even on buses that operated within one state, was unconstitutional.

When the police arrested Rosa Parks, diverse factions within the Montgomery black community swung into nonviolent direct action. On 2 December 1955 the Women's Political Council (WPC), under the leadership of JO ANN ROBINSON, an English professor at Alabama State College, mimeographed and, with two hundred volunteers, distributed more than thirty thousand handbills imploring black citizens to stay off the buses. The flyer declared: "Another Negro woman has been arrested and thrown into jail, because she refused to get up out of her seat on the bus for a white person to sit down....Negroes have rights, too, for if Negroes did not ride the buses, they could not operate....The next time it may be you, or your daughter, or mother" (Robinson, 45–46).

Actually, the WPC had long prepared to declare a boycott. Black leaders called a mass meeting at Holt Street Baptist Church and voted to continue the boycott under the aegis of the newly formed Montgomery Improvement Association (MIA). A number of women served on the MIA executive committee, including Robinson and Parks and Erna Dungee Allen, who served as financial secretary. A young minister of Dexter Avenue Baptist Church, the Reverend MARTIN LUTHER KING JR., accepted the presidency of the MIA and led the discussions and negotiations with white authorities. Parks's arrest sparked the bus boycott movement that began on 5 December 1955 and lasted 381 days, ending on 20 December 1956. The black attorney FRED D. GRAY, on behalf of the MIA, filed a lawsuit against segregation in federal court on 1 February 1956. On 2 June 1956 in a 2 to 1 decision, the federal court found the Montgomery bus segregation ordinances to be unconstitutional. On appeal, on 13 November 1956, the U.S. Supreme Court concurred with the federal court, ruling that racial segregation on public transportation in Montgomery and throughout the South was unconstitutional.

Parks's successful challenge to racial segregation attracted threats of violence and harassment and resulted in the loss of her job as a seamstress at Montgomery Fair Department Store. In 1957

Raymond and Rosa Parks and Rosa's mother joined her younger brother, Sylvester, in Detroit to seek jobs and personal security. For several years Rosa Parks worked as a seamstress. In 1965 she accepted a special assistant position on the staff in the Detroit office of Representative JOHN CONYERS JR. She remained in his employ for nearly twenty years, during which time she assisted Conyers in his efforts to make Martin Luther King Jr.'s birthday a national holiday. In 1977 Parks's husband and brother died. Ten years later she and a friend, Elaine Eason Steele, founded a nonprofit organization, the Raymond and Rosa Parks Institute for Self-Development, to honor her husband's memory and commitment to the struggle for social justice and human rights.

In the last decades of the century Parks received national recognition for her role in the civil rights movement. The NAACP gave her its highest honor, the Spingarn Award, in 1977. She also received the Presidential Medal of Freedom, the nation's highest civilian honor. On 15 June 1999 Parks was awarded the Congressional Gold Medal. In introducing the bill authorizing the award, Representative JULIA CARSON of Indiana declared: "Rosa Parks is the Mother of America's Civil Rights Movement. Her quiet courage that day in Montgomery, Alabama, launched a new American revolution that opened new doors of opportunity and brought equality for all Americans close to a reality" ("Carson Calls for Cosponsors for Bill to Award Congressional Gold Medal to Rosa Park," 24 Feb. 1999). On 24 October 2005 Parks died of natural causes at her home; she was ninety-two. After lying in honor in the Capitol Rotunda (the first woman to be so honored), Parks was laid to rest in Detroit, Michigan. Her funeral was attended by more than four thousand mourners.

FURTHER READING

Parks, Rosa. "Rosa Louise Parks Biographical Sketch," from the Rosa and Raymond Parks Institute for Self- Development, Detroit, Michigan (2003).
Parks, Rosa, with Jim Haskins. *My Story* (1999).
Brinkley, Douglas. *Rosa Parks* (2000).
King, Martin Luther, Jr. *Stride toward Freedom: The Montgomery Story* (1958).
Robinson, Jo Ann Gibson. *The Montgomery Bus Boycott and the Women Who Started It: The Memoir of Jo Ann Gibson Robinson* (1984).
Thornton, J. Mills, III. *Dividing Lines: Municipal Politics and the Struggle for Civil Rights in Montgomery, Birmingham, and Selma* (2002).
United States House of Representatives Press Release, "Carson Calls for Cosponsors for Bill to Award Congressional Gold Medal to Rosa Parks," 24 Feb. 1999.

DARLENE CLARK HINE

Parks, Suzan-Lori (10 May 1964–) playwright, was born at Fort Knox, Kentucky, to Francis McMillan, an educator, and Donald Parks, an army officer and, later, professor. From her parents Parks gained cultural exposure, a love for literature, and an understanding of the value in education. Her ability as a writer surfaced early on, and she began writing stories at age five. With her father in the army, Parks spent her childhood years in a variety of different locales, including six American states and West Germany. Rather than the traditional American schools attended by the children of most servicemen, Parks attended a German high school.

Parks then entered Mount Holyoke College in South Hadley, Massachusetts, graduating cum laude and Phi Beta Kappa in 1985 with a B.A. in English and German. While at Mount Holyoke, she studied creative writing with the celebrated writer JAMES BALDWIN. Impressed with her ability as well as her dexterity with dialogue, Baldwin recommended that she try her skills at playwriting. After graduating from college, Parks studied acting at the Drama Studio in London in 1986.

Parks exploded onto the American theater scene on her return to the United States from London. Beginning in 1986, sections of her play *Imperceptible Mutabilities in the Third Kingdom* premiered at the Brooklyn Arts Council Association Downtown (BACA) and the Brooklyn Fringe Festival, both in New York. Parks's work attracted so much attention that in 1989 the BACA mounted the entire four parts of the play. Directed by Parks's longtime associate Liz Diamond, the play won the 1990 Obie Award for Best Off-Broadway Play. *Imperceptible Mutabilities*, abstract in both form and language, explores in five playlets the legacy of African American experiences under the hegemony of a racist white world. Parks uses symbolism, metaphor, humor, and irony to probe the relationship between the African American historical past and the construction of contemporary African American identity. In one particularly striking section, titled "Emancipation Day," black actors performed in whiteface at the BACA.

Her next work, *Betting on the Dust Commander*, premiered at the Gas Station in New York in 1987. The following year, her play *Pickling* was

Suzan-Lori Parks celebrates in front of the Ambassador Theater in New York City after learning her play "Topdog/Underdog" won the 2002 Pulitzer Prize for drama. (AP Images.)

produced at the BACA Downtown and broadcast on New American Radio in 1990. Parks's critically acclaimed *Death of the Last Black Man in the Whole Entire World* was first produced in New York at the St. Mark's Poets Theatre in 1988 and then at the BACA Downtown in 1990. Two years later it was reproduced under the direction of Liz Diamond at Yale Repertory Theatre in New Haven. In the play Parks confronts historical events, questions stereotypes, and debunks cultural myths through the story of a husband and wife in crisis. The wife, Black Woman with Fried Drumstick, struggles with the return of her husband, Black Man with Watermelon, whom she believed to be dead.

Parks's plays are extremely experimental. She crafts both hyperrealistic dramas and nonrepresentational expressionistic plays. Even as her style has changed, Parks has remained profoundly interested in questions of African American identity and history. American history, she argues, has too often excluded African American experiences, and so she seeks to "make some history up" (Pearce, 26). She is particularly interested in language and celebrates the elasticity, power, and poetry of black dialect.

The America Play, one of Parks's most intellectually provocative and stylistically challenging works, premiered at the Public Theater in New York City in 1994, under the direction of Liz Diamond. Parks set the first act of the play, a monologue delivered by an African American character called the Foundling Father—who resembles Abraham Lincoln—in what she calls "A great hole. In the middle of nowhere. The hole is an exact replica of the Great Hole of History" (*The America Play*, 159). In the second act wife Lucy and son Brazil search for the now deceased father, the Lincoln character. The play interrogates the relationship of African

American history to the myth of Lincoln's freeing the slaves, the perpetuation of which has created real scars for African Americans.

Parks won her second Obie Award for Best Off-Broadway Play in 1996 for *Venus*. Written with the assistance of grants from the Kennedy Center Fund for New American Plays and the W. Alton Jones Foundation, *Venus* was first staged at the Yale Repertory Theatre under the direction of Liz Diamond in 1996 and remounted at the Public Theater under the direction of the famed avant-garde theater artist Richard Foreman. With *Venus* Parks revisits the story of Saartjie Baartman, the South African !Kung, or KhoiKhoi, tribeswoman who was brought to London in 1810 by the British trader Hendrik Cezar for display as the "Venus Hottentot" in a sideshow. In thirty-one scenes, the play chronicles the path of Baartman's life in reverse, beginning with her death in Paris and moving back to her capture from South Africa. The play ends as it begins, with Baartman's death.

Venus marked a turning point in Parks's theatrical career. *In the Blood*, which opened in 1999 at the Public Theater under the direction of David Esbjornson, was the first of two plays—*The Red Letter Plays*—which adapt and explore the story of Hester Prynne, the doomed sinner in Nathaniel Hawthorne's book *The Scarlet Letter*. Like her namesake Hester Prynne, Parks's Hester La Negrita, a homeless woman with a brood of illegitimate children living beneath a bridge, has been ostracized from society because of her sexual transgression. The play was nominated for the Pulitzer Prize.

Parks directed the first production of her second *Red Letter Play*, *Fucking A*, for Infernal Bridegroom Productions in Houston, Texas, in February 2000. The play opened at the Public Theater in New York under the direction of Michael Greif in 2003. Different in style from *In the Blood* and her earlier works, *Fucking A* employs an invented language, or "Talk," that the characters occasionally speak. The play's central figure, Hester, who performs illegal abortions, wears an "A" on her chest as a symbol of her profession.

In 2002 Parks became the first African American woman to win the Pulitzer Prize for Drama with *Topdog/Underdog*. The play, which opened at the Public Theater under the direction of GEORGE C. WOLFE, moved to Broadway soon after. It continued earlier themes of legacy, identity, and history through its two characters, brothers whose conflict uncovers painful family secrets and long-festering fraternal jealousies. Their names—Lincoln and Booth—represent the source of their conflict and evidence of their destinies.

Parks married the blues musician Paul Oscher in 2001. She has received a Ford Foundation Grant, a Whiting Foundation Writers Award, a Lila Wallace-Reader's Digest Award, and a CalArts/Alpert Award in the Arts. In 2001 she was awarded a Guggenheim Foundation Fellowship and, the following year, a MacArthur Foundation Award. In addition to her work as a playwright and novelist, Parks has also authored numerous screenplays for major artists. These include an adaptation of TONI MORRISON's novel *Paradise* for OPRAH WINFREY Productions and the screenplay for SPIKE LEE's film *Girl 6* (1996). Parks also produced her own film, *Anemone Me*, in 1990. Parks's first novel, *Getting Mother's Body*, was published in 2003. In part a paean to William Faulkner's *As I Lay Dying*, the novel examined the disintegration of family relationships catalyzed by the death of a mother. Beginning in 2006, Parks embarked on her most ambitious project, *365 Days/365 Plays*. A one-year-long play cycle, *365 Days/365 Plays* featured one piece by Parks every day for a year in theaters all across the world. All performances were free to the public, and grassroots theater companies were encouraged to put on productions.

FURTHER READING

Als, Hilton. "The Snow Woman," *New Yorker* (30 Oct. 2006).

Bryant, Aaron. "Broadway, Her Way: African American Playwright Suzan-Lori Parks," *New Crisis* 109.2 (Mar.–Apr. 2002).

Garrett, Shawn Marie. "The Possession of Suzan-Lori Parks," *American Theatre* 17.8 (2000).

Jiggetts, Shelby. "Interview with Suzan-Lori Parks," *Callaloo* 19.2 (1996).

Pearce, Michele. "Alien Nation: An Interview with the Playwright," *American Theatre* 11.3 (Mar. 1994).

Smith, Dinita. "Tough-Minded Playwright Chooses a Title Tough to Ignore," *New York Times* (16 Mar. 2003).

Solomon, Alisa. "Signifying on the Signifyin': The Plays of Suzan-Lori Parks," *Theater* 21.3 (1990).

Zoglin, Richard. "Moving Marginal Characters to Center Stage," *Time* (19 Feb. 2001).

HARRY ELAM

Parris, Pedro Tovookan (c. 1833–1860), slave, artist, and public speaker, is believed to have been born on the east coast of Africa, near the River Juba in present-day Somalia. Twice a slave, Pedro's life is documented both by his own narrative paintings and a brief but detailed chronicle penned by his boyhood friend Percival J. Parris. Although Parris was only eleven when Pedro died, his vivid reminiscences allow deeply personal glimpses as well as an historic view of the young man.

Pedro "remembered that he lived near the sea and that he had seen hippopotami in the water," writes Parris. "His people lived in huts made with poles and used mats for doors and to sleep on." The tribe was agricultural, "each took to himself such lands as he chose to cultivate…by marking out as much as he needed," and "fowls were kept for their eggs" (Parris, p. 61). Men were permitted two or more wives, but Pedro recalled his father having only one wife, Pedro's mother.

When he was about ten, Pedro's family was attacked in the middle of the night by a neighboring tribe. His father was killed and the family scattered in the dark, attempting to escape. As Pedro was rushed away by the slave-hunting tribe, he caught his last view of his home: his grandmother screaming from on top of a rock where she had sought refuge.

The slaves marched all that night and the next morning Pedro found that his three brothers had also been captured. Continuing a grueling forced march for several weeks, over hundreds of miles, they finally reached the island of Zanzibar in Mozambique Channel (a strait in the Indian Ocean on the east coast of Africa). Here Pedro was sold to a Portuguese slave dealer named Sebastian. A harsh man, Sebastian subjected the young boy, whom he dubbed "Pedro," to numerous beatings in an effort to get him to learn Portuguese, thereby making him more saleable. Tovookan, the name given him by his family, means "to run away." Pedro told Parris he was called this because of his passive nature. Much to his father's dismay, he refused to engage in conflict, even when other children taunted him.

Pedro was next purchased in Zanzibar by a Captain Paulo who was more kindly and kept him as his personal servant. In December 1845 Paulo bought a full cargo of slaves and set sail for Rio de Janeiro with Pedro by his side, aboard an American vessel, the *Porpoise*, captained by Cyrus Libby of Scarborough, Maine. Although such a cargo was illegal, a great number of merchant seaman at the time shipping out from New England ports engaged in what was known as the "Triangle Trade," of molasses, slaves, and rum.

The sailors who were working on the *Porpoise*, however, had not signed on as slavers and were appalled on discovering the nature of their cargo. One of the crew wrote a note about the illegal business, tied it to a rock and tossed it onto a boat belonging to the U.S. Consul at Rio, George William Gordon.

Gordon arrested Libby on arrival at Rio, sending him and the *Porpoise* to Boston under escort of an American warship, the *Raritan*, on the charge of slaving. Pedro and two other boys were taken to act as witnesses. Libby's legal proceedings continued for close to a year in Portland, Maine, where Pedro was, ironically, kept in prison until the trial. Eventually the charges against Libby were dropped, but the ship's seizure was upheld, a fact that embittered Libby for the rest of his life. Pedro, released from both prison and slavery, was then officially adopted into the family of the U.S. marshal from Maine, Virgil D. Parris, who had come to know him well while visiting him in prison, and was taken to live in the family mansion on Paris Hill, fifty miles from Portland.

Pedro was sent to school with the Parris children, learning to read and write and mastering "the first four principals of arithmetic." Developing an interest in public speaking, Pedro participated in the school debating society where, although his "forensic ability was somewhat limited," wrote Percival Parris many years later, "his use of the English language (was) odd enough to be a source of delight to the small boys" (Parris, p. 63).

Pedro's hard won oratorical skills found a national purpose during the presidential campaign of 1856 when the Whig and American Know-Nothing parties united in nominating George Gordon as candidate for governor in Massachusetts. The party, in attempting to keep the abolitionists from joining the Republican camp, employed Pedro, whose rescue from slavery was attributable to Gordon, to stump for him. (It has been suggested that Pedro, with his speeches against slavery, might have had some influence on Hannibal Hamlin, whose own home in Maine was within yards of that of the Parris family. Hamlin, as vice president to Lincoln in his first term, was a radical antislavery advocate.)

Restless upon returning to his home in Paris after weeks on the campaign trail, Pedro began to seek self-expression in a number of ways, including teaching his adoptive brother Percival native songs recalled from his youth. These they performed together, theatrically, in various settings on Paris Hill. "He longed to be a showman," wrote Parris, and, "when by himself was often making strange noises in his efforts to become a ventriloquist" (Parris, p. 64).

Pedro also began painting. One piece, a watercolor consisting of three large sections on a roll of glazed linen, depicts an emotional account of his journey from Brazil to Maine. The first view shows troops marching in front of a church in Rio de Janeiro, the second a strikingly detailed rendering of the *Raritan* sailing from Rio to Boston, and the third, a view of Beacon Hill alongside Paris, Maine, including a large drawing of his stepmother, Columbia Parris, at the gates of the Parris home.

During the harsh winter of 1859–1860 Pedro caught pneumonia, which led to his death, surrounded by his adoptive family in his home, in April of that year. His funeral was "one of the most fully attended that had been held in the village," writes Parris, and an obituary states, "few have gone from our midst, whose loss is more generally or sincerely mourned." Pedro rests in the Parris family cemetery near his friend Percival, and, "a decent stone marks his grave." (Parris, p. 65)

FURTHER READING

Pedro Tovookan Parris's watercolors and an ambrotype of Pedro Tovookan Parris are in the Historic New England collection in Boston.

Parris, Percival J. "Pedro Tovookan Parris," in *Old-Time New England*, January–March 1973.

Obituary: *The Oxford Democrat*, 13 Apr. 1860.

DIANE HUDSON

Parrish, Mary E. Jones (29 Feb. 1892–Aug. 1972?), teacher and writer, was born in New York State. She chronicled the Tulsa Riots of 1921 in her book *Events of the Tulsa Disaster*, which was privately printed shortly after the riot. Little is known about Parrish's life or her family either before or after the riot. She first came from Rochester, New York, to Tulsa in 1918 to visit a brother, who had lived there for some time. Then she returned to New York to care for her ailing mother. Upon her mother's death, she moved to the African American section of Tulsa (known as Greenwood) around 1919 and worked as a teacher. Her gifts with language and her desire to tell the story of the riot makes *Events of the Tulsa Disaster* the most reliable and complete contemporary account of the incident. When used in conjunction with testimony in the court cases filed by J. B. STRADFORD in Chicago, *Stradford v. American Central Insurance Company*, and William Redfearn in Tulsa, *Redfearn v. American Central Insurance Company* (1926), a comprehensive picture of the events of 1921 emerges.

Parrish's book emerged from her work as a reporter for the Tulsa Inter-Racial Commission, a group of both black and white leaders organized shortly after the riot to assist with rebuilding. She was hired to interview survivors and to record the causes and consequences of the riot. The book's preface emphasizes opposition to lynching and the pursuit of equality, central concerns of African American intellectuals at the time. Her cry against the nation's criminal conduct toward African Americans spoke for many: "Oh America! Thou Land of the Free and Home of the Brave! The country that gives its choicest blood and bravest hearts to make the world safe for democracy! How long will you let mob violence reign supreme?" (Parrish, 11). She also urged support for Congressman L. C. Dyer's Anti-Lynching Bill, which passed the House in 1922 but then quickly died in the Senate (the Senate apologized in June 2005 for its failure to pass Dyer's Bill and other antilynching legislation). Parrish also wrote about the goals of the United States in World War I, such as the preservation of democracy and the black community's antilynching campaign. She also discussed the local community's self-help programs and its economic advancement. Through those themes, Parrish located herself at the center of African American intellectuals who urged self-help, economic progress, and demands for equality. *Events of the Tulsa Disaster* emerges as an important intellectual statement and as a glimpse of the grand ideas circulating on the prairie in the 1920s; and it also contains important information about the riot available nowhere else. It is "the first book published about the riot, and a pioneering work of journalism by an African American woman" (Franklin and Ellsworth, 28).

Parrish provides a brief account of her involvement in the Tulsa riot, which destroyed the thriving African American section of Tulsa, known as Greenwood, on the evening of 31 May and the morning of 1 June 1921. Approximately 8,000 people lived in the community at the time of the riot, where most of Tulsa's African Americans lived. Greenwood had two weekly newspapers and two movie theaters, along with schools, hotels, and restaurants. Parrish was one of the participants in Greenwood's vibrant community. She was teaching typing on the evening of 31 May 1921. After her class ended around 9 p.m., she was reading a book while her young daughter was playing. Her daughter called out when she saw men gathered on the street outside their apartment with guns. Parrish went out into the street to investigate and learned about the threatened lynching of

Dick Rowland, who was accused of attempting to assault a young white woman the day before (the accusation was false). People such as J. B. Stradford, a successful Greenwood businessman, and A. J. Smitherman, editor of the *Tulsa Star*, were hoping to stop the lynching. As the evening wore on, several dozen Greenwood men armed themselves and went to the jail where Rowland was being held. A confrontation ensued at the courthouse, when the Greenwood men tried to make sure that Rowland was safe; a white man (perhaps a police officer) tried to disarm the leader, and shooting began on both sides. The riot immediately followed. Parrish witnessed the fighting, including buildings burning throughout the early morning hours of 1 June. In what seemed like a strange microcosmic twist on the Civil War, she wrote of Greenwood men who fought "like Stonewall Jackson of old...offsetting each and every attempt to burn Greenwood and the immediate vicinity" (Parrish, 19). Around dawn she and her daughter fled, at first on foot, then a truck came by and offered them a ride farther out of town. As they drove from Tulsa, they passed an airfield, where Parrish saw men with high-powered rifles getting into the airplanes. Some witnesses told her that men from those planes fired at Greenwood residents. Parrish thus provided an important clue to a mystery that circulated at the time concerning airplanes that had flown over Greenwood during the riot. A number of black newspapers, including the *Oklahoma City Black Dispatch* and the *Chicago Defender*, reported that airplanes had dropped bombs on Greenwood. Other reports circulated of airplanes shooting at Greenwood residents. The white newspapers of Tulsa reported that the airplanes were used for reconnaissance only, especially to spot people fleeing from Greenwood. "The aeroplanes continued to watch over the fleeing people like great birds of prey watching for a victim" (Parrish, 23). She believed, though, the planes only fired on people in Greenwood. This is, of course, a major question concerning the riot, and the interpretations differed at the time along racial lines: reports in the black community consistently emphasized that the planes had attacked Greenwood with deadly force; those in the white community contended that the planes were used merely for surveillance.

For several days, Parrish and her daughter stayed on a farm, some thirteen miles from Tulsa. Even at that distance, she saw smoke from the fires that had destroyed most of her community and left thousands homeless (Parrish, 23). Greenwood residents who had stayed behind had been rounded up by the Tulsa police and taken to detention centers around the city. Then some of those policemen and their deputies, along with a mob, looted and burned most of what remained of the community. After a few days, a Red Cross flatbed truck carried Parrish, her daughter, and other fugitives through the white community to a Red Cross camp in Greenwood. "Dear reader," Parrish asked, "can you imagine the humiliation of coming in [to Tulsa] like that, with many doors thrown open watching you pass, some with pity and others with a smile?" (Parrish, 24) The humiliation was compounded by the cards that Tulsa officials required Greenwood residents to wear in the aftermath of the riot. The green cards, labeled "Police Protection," had the names of the white employers who vouched for the wearers. Because Parrish had not worked for a white person before the riot, she had trouble obtaining a tag.

The second part of *Events* includes short statements from a number of survivors. They attributed the riot to such underlying factors as black prosperity and the hostility that became prevalent in the white community, the lynching culture, the failure of the "better class" of white and black people to cooperate, corruption in city politics, and few job opportunities. In short, Parrish's study offers a broad range of theorizing on the causes of racial violence. The final section of the volume, "Aftermath," includes excerpts from a *Literary Digest* article on the riot and brief sketches of A. J. Smitherman, Madame George W. Hunt, a beautician, and the law firm of the Spears, Franklin, and Chappelle, as well as a lengthy but still partial list of property losses. The volume stood as an important collection of thought and opinions from the Greenwood community, as it struggled to rebuild and continue on the mission of post-riot progress. Parrish is believed to have died in Tulsa in 1972.

FURTHER READING

Parrish, Mary Jones. *Events of the Tulsa Disaster* (1922, reprinted 1998).

Brophy, Alfred L. *Reconstructing the Dreamland: The Tulsa Riot of 1921—Race, Reparations, Reconciliation* (2002).

Brophy, Alfred L. "The Tulsa Race Riot of 1921 in the Oklahoma Supreme Court," *Oklahoma Law Review* 54: 67–148 (2001).

Franklin, John Hope, and Scott Ellsworth. "History Knows No Fences," in *Tulsa Race Riot: A Report by the Oklahoma Commission to Study the Tulsa Race Riot of 1921* (2001).

ALFRED L. BROPHY

Parsons, Lucy (1853?–7 Mar. 1942), labor activist and writer, was born in north-central Texas. Information about her parentage is inconclusive, though she may have been the daughter of Pedro Díaz González and Marie (maiden name unknown); her ancestry was in part African American. At the time she met her future husband in the early 1870s she was living with Oliver Gathings, a former slave. After using many maiden names, Lucy finally settled on González when she married in an attempt to establish a Mexican ancestry that would appear more acceptable to dominant whites in that part of Texas.

In the late nineteenth century the Ku Klux Klan rose to power in several southern states and successfully ended Reconstruction's all-too-brief experiment in biracial democracy. During the period in which the Klan and others violently reasserted "white supremacy," Lucy witnessed atrocities that affected her deeply. Around 1870 she met Albert Parsons, and reportedly they wed on 10 June 1871, although it is uncertain whether Lucy and Albert Parsons ever officially married. Laws against miscegenation may have prevented their marriage in Texas. The couple had two children. Parsons's husband was hired as a journalist in Philadelphia, Pennsylvania, and after she joined him they traveled in 1873 to Chicago, where there is no record that they wed in that city.

Settling in a poor working-class German neighborhood that housed basement sweatshops, Lucy Parsons was exposed to unemployment, poor working conditions, and workers' protests. After Albert joined the Social Democratic Party of North America, members often met in the Parsonses' home and through them Lucy Parsons came in contact with the works of Karl Marx and other socialist thinkers. She also found acceptance among her socialist friends who never questioned her racial background.

At that time in industrializing America, tensions between workers and owners ran at a fever pitch, and rumors of revolution escalated the fears of industrialists while giving hope to the poor. In 1877 a strike by railroad workers erupted on the eastern seaboard and gathered strength as it moved across the country to Chicago. After Albert spoke before striking railroad workers, he was fired from his job as a typesetter, and Lucy took over the support of the family, working as a seamstress and opening her own dress and suit shop.

Parsons, no less radical than her husband, opposed the capitalist system and the way that American workers were treated. Following the 1877 strikes, which ended in failure and the death of many workers, both Parsons and her husband realized that they needed to move to the forefront of the labor movement. Joining the Chicago Working Women's Union in 1879 and hoping to add fuel to the fight for equal pay for equal work, Parsons supported the call for a woman's suffrage plank in the Socialist Labor platform. She believed that the conflict between workers and owners had come to an impasse and saw revolution as the only solution.

Parsons expressed her opinions in the *Alarm*, the weekly newspaper of the International Working People's Association (IWPA), as well as in the *Socialist*, the *Denver Labor Enquirer*, and the *Labor Defender*. Her well-known article, "To Tramps," published in the first issue of the *Alarm* in 1884, was reprinted and widely distributed by the IWPA. In the article Parsons advised tramps who were thinking of committing suicide because of their suffering in the economic depression of 1883–1884 not to die alone but to take with them a few rich people and to "learn the use of explosives."

In 1885–1886 Parsons joined in organizing seamstresses to demand an eight-hour day. Strikes and protests heightened in May 1886 when during a meeting at Haymarket Square in Chicago, an unknown person threw a bomb, which, when followed by police gunfire, resulted in the death of seven policemen and injured at least sixty bystanders. Although at the time she and her husband were walking away from the crowds, Albert was arrested with seven other men, convicted, and sentenced to hang. Arrested and released herself, Parsons was placed under surveillance by the authorities and was assailed by rumors about her past and racial origins. At her husband's trial Lucy wore black to proclaim the death of free speech and spent the next year and a half fighting to have the death sentences commuted for Albert and the others. Parsons took her message to the American people in Ohio, New Jersey, and Connecticut, hoping they might secure her husband's release. She did not soften her message, however, but explained why she believed that anarchism would rectify the evils of the country's capitalist system.

After her husband was hanged in November 1887, Parsons spent more than fifty years speaking to audiences about freedom, equality, and justice for the downtrodden. Two years after her husband's execution she published *The Life of Albert R. Parsons, with Brief History of the Labor Movement in America* and in 1891 coedited *Freedom, A*

Revolutionary Anarchist-Communist Monthly. In 1905 and 1906, the years she edited the *Liberator*, she helped unionist Big Bill Haywood found the Industrial Workers of the World (IWW), also known as the Wobblies. The IWW, a coalition of socialist, anarchist, and labor union activists, sought to challenge untrammeled corporate power, most notably in the mining regions of the Far West. Parsons joined with the IWW in a series of strikes in 1913 in San Francisco and was arrested the following year in Chicago, where she was campaigning against hunger and led a group of striking workers. Perhaps her most significant contribution to the African American working-class cause lay in helping to found the International Labor Defense in 1925, a radical organization that aided workers and political dissidents, including the Atlanta Communist ANGELO HERNDON and the wrongly convicted SCOTTSBORO BOYS in the 1930s. Parsons finally broke with her anarchist past in the 1930s and joined the Communist Party, which she saw as the only solution to the problems of the working class, in 1939. She remained active until 1942, when a fire engulfed her home in Chicago, taking her life.

Police removed the personal writings of Lucy Parsons from her home, but her words echoed in the memory of many. A woman of warmth and conviction, she held to no middle ground but loved and hated with intensity. Many remembered her only as the defender of her husband's name, but her concerns were far-reaching. She argued that workingwomen were "slaves of slaves" and that they were "exploited more ruthlessly than men." Her stand extended beyond women's rights to equal pay. She also advocated their right to divorce, to practice birth control, and to be free from rape. Her radical spirit gave her the voice to continually keep the issues of human rights alive.

FURTHER READING

Ashbaugh, Carolyn. *Lucy Parsons: American Revolutionary* (1976).

Foner, Philip S. *History of the Labor Movement in the United States*, vol. 2 (1947).

Foner, Philip S. *Women and the American Labor Movement: From Colonial Times to the Eve of World War I* (1979).

Obituaries: *Chicago Tribune*, 8 and 9 1942.

This entry is taken from the *American National Biography* and is published here with the permission of the American Council of Learned Societies.

MARILYN ELIZABETH PERRY

Parsons, Richard Dean (4 Apr. 1948–), corporate executive and lawyer, was born in Brooklyn, New York, the second of five children of Lorenzo Parsons, a technician, and Isabelle Judd. When Richard was five years old, the family moved to a middle-class neighborhood in Queens. He later recalled his father as "intellectual and gentle" and his mother as "full of steely determination and grit" (Clarke, 153). In his childhood, academic excellence was far from Richard's top priority, and at John Adams High School he did well but always with as little effort as possible. Still, his talents propelled him to graduate early, at the age of sixteen. In 1964 he applied to the University of Hawaii primarily because he had been attracted to his Hawaiian-born high school physics lab partner, who had constantly told him stories about the exotic state.

Parsons worked at various odd jobs, including at a parking garage and gas company, to support himself while at the University of Hawaii. He became social chairman of his fraternity and made the varsity basketball team but remained unenthusiastic about academics. On occasion, he showed up for final exams after skipping a class for an entire semester. He later described his college experience as "fun filled but academically disastrous" (*Los Angeles Times*, 4 Dec. 1994).

The real turning point in his life came when Parsons married his college sweetheart, Laura Ann Bush, a child psychologist, after graduation in 1968. After earning a scholarship to Union University's Albany Law School, Parsons graduated as class valedictorian in 1971 and earned the highest score among the 3,600 people taking the New York State bar exam. Upon the recommendation of his law professor, Parsons interviewed for a position in the office of New York's governor, Nelson Rockefeller. In 1971, at the age of twenty-three, Parsons became an assistant counsel to the governor.

Although he was much younger than the other lawyers on staff, Parsons quickly became an important part of the office. Rockefeller, in turn, became an important mentor to the young lawyer, and Parsons later described himself as a "Rockefeller Republican," socially liberal and fiscally conservative. Within two years Parsons was promoted to first assistant counsel, a job that necessitated representing the governor in Albany and at sundry gatherings. Because it was rare to find an African American in these circles, Parsons often disrupted people's expectations. On one occasion, after sitting down for a meeting at the Metropolitan Museum of Art, he was met with silence. "We are waiting for

Richard Dean Parsons, co-chief operating officer and CEO-designate of AOL Time Warner, during a panel discussion on corporate citizenship at the World Economic Forum in New York City on 4 Feb. 2002. (AP Images.)

Governor Rockefeller's counsel" one of the other men said. "I hate to tell you," Parsons replied, "but I am already here" (*New York Times*, 10 June 1988).

When Rockefeller became vice president under Gerald Ford in 1974, Parsons followed him to Washington, D.C., and became a White House deputy counsel and, soon after, associate director of domestic counsel. The following year, when Ford lost to Jimmy Carter, Parsons moved back to New York. Upon his return, Judge Harold Tyler Jr., a colleague from the Washington deputy attorney general's office, invited him to join his law office, the powerful firm of Patterson, Belknap, Webb, and Tyler. Parsons worked there for more than a decade and eventually became one of two black partners. In 1988 Harry Albright, chief executive officer of one of the firm's clients, Dime Savings Bank of New York, was looking for someone to groom as his successor. In July of that year he chose Parsons, who joined Dime Savings as president.

Parsons immersed himself in this new challenge, which enabled him to work in the growing and increasingly important financial services sector. By 1990 he was promoted to chief executive officer, becoming the first African American to head a major banking institution. After the New York real estate crash in the early 1990s left Dime stuck with nonperforming loans, Parsons won universal praise for leading the company away from the brink of bankruptcy. He demonstrated his leadership by ridding the bank of $1 billion of bad debt, cutting costs, and negotiating with regulators. In 1994, after restoring Dime's fiscal health, Parsons oversaw its merger with Anchor Savings Bank, a move that created the fourth-largest thrift in the nation.

Parsons ruffled some feathers when he supported the Italian American Rudolph Giuliani's mayoral bid over DAVID DINKINS in 1993. Giuliani, who had befriended Parsons when they were both young attorneys at Patterson, Belknap, Webb, and Tyler, rewarded Parsons's support by naming him head of his transition team and offering him the job of deputy mayor for economic development. Parsons turned down the offer but agreed to serve as chair of New York's Economic Development Commission. With Dime's turnaround complete, Parsons decided to move on to another challenge, and in February 1995, after three years on the board of directors, he became president of Time Warner Inc. Parsons, who quickly won over many in top management with his warm demeanor, became the company's problem solver by bringing opposing parties to common ground and making them feel good about their compromises. As president, he oversaw the company's filmed entertainment and music businesses and all corporate staff functions, including financial activities, legal affairs, public affairs, and administration.

Arguably his greatest challenge came after Time Warner merged with the Internet company America Online (AOL) in January 2000. At the time of the merger, the combined company was valued at $284 billion. More than two years later, after the Internet bubble burst, it was valued at approximately $60 billion. Eventually, the two architects behind the deal—Time Warner's Gerald Levin and AOL's Steve Case—both stepped down from their leadership positions. By 1999 Parsons had been elevated to co-chief operating officer, overseeing the company's content businesses, Warner Brothers, New Line Cinema, Warner Music Group, and AOL Time Warner Book Group, in addition to its human resources and legal departments. Parsons took over as CEO in May 2002 and chairman of the board in May 2003, becoming, along with KENNETH CHENAULT at American Express and FRANKLIN DELANO RAINES at Fannie Mae, one of a handful of black executives to lead a Fortune 500 company. Some business observers have suggested that Parsons is ideally suited to the job of restoring Time Warner's reputation and profits. His famously congenial manner may also calm the reported culture clashes between the two companies. *BusinessWeek* reported on 19 May 2003, for example, that "Parsons inspires extravagant admiration among close colleagues past and present."

Parsons has been active in other initiatives. From 1995 to 2001 he was chair of Upper Manhattan Zone, an organization that aims to bring economic development to Harlem, and his revitalization efforts earned praise from the veteran Democratic congressman CHARLES RANGEL, among others. In 2001 Parsons served as cochair of President George W. Bush's commission on Social Security reform. Parsons, who sat on the board of directors of Citigroup, Fannie Mae, and Estée Lauder, was named chair of the Apollo Theater Foundation and has served on the boards of the Colonial Williamsburg Foundation, the Museum of Modern Art, Lincoln Center, and Howard University. Since its inception in 1986, Parsons has been a consultant to the Executive Leadership Council, a nonprofit organization for African American senior executives. In 2002 Fortune ranked him the third most powerful black executive in the country behind STANLEY O'NEAL and Kenneth Chenault.

Parsons stepped down as Time Warner CEO in 2007, and as the company's Chairman in late 2008. Most Wall Street observers concurred that Parsons had ended the internecine warfare at Time Warner and had steered a steady, if unspectacular course as CEO, but criticized him for allowing the company's stock price to stagnate.

In 2008 Michael Bloomberg encouraged Parsons to run to succeed him as Mayor of New York, but Parsons declined, prompting Bloomberg to run for a third term. In January 2009, after serving as an economic advisory board member of BARACK OBAMA's presidential transition team, Parsons was appointed chair of Citigroup, which was the world's largest banking group prior to the 2008 world banking crisis. Citi had suffered billions of dollars of losses during that crisis, and shortly after Parsons took office, the U.S. federal government took a 36% equity stake in Citigroup to prevent its collapse and bankruptcy, which would have had global repercussions. The federal government injected $20 billion cash into the company, guaranteed losses on over $300 billion of the company's assets, and placed restrictions on the company's operations until the federal loans were repaid. By December 2010, Citigroup had paid back the government assistance and returned to profitability.

In an age when the power of media lies in the hands of only a few individuals, Richard Dean Parsons has become one of the most important executives in the world.

FURTHER READING

Bianco, Anthony, and Tom Lowry. "Can Dick Parsons Rescue AOL Time Warner?" *BusinessWeek* (19 May 2003).

Clarke, Caroline V. *Take a Lesson: Today's Black Achievers on How They Made It and What They Learned along the Way* (2001).

Margolick, David. "At the Bar," *New York Times*, 10 June 1988.

Wollenberg, Skip. "New Time Warner President Taking on His Biggest Job Yet," *Los Angeles Times*, 4 Dec. 1994.

GREGORY S. BELL

Patience, C. Edgar (27 Aug. 1906–7 June 1972), coal sculptor, was born Charles Edgar Patience in West Pittston, Pennsylvania, the son of Harry B. Patience, a coal carver, and Elsie Miller Patience. They resided in a small borough where a few African Americans had migrated from the South to work for wealthy white families. However, when the next generation of African Americans came of age, most of them emigrated in the 1940s to work in cities such as New York, Philadelphia, and Washington, D.C., the black community dwindling to only the Patience family. C. Edgar's father, Harry, was the son of a runaway North Carolina slave who had joined the Union army. After his discharge he settled in the Wyoming Valley, Pennsylvania. Harry had learned to carve coal as a boy during his time working at a colliery and had later, following an injury that took him off the job, opened a coal novelty business.

Harry trained his six sons as coal carvers while insisting they complete high school. After C. Edgar graduated in 1924 he continued working for his father until Harry's sudden demise. Patience remained in the business while his brothers found other employment. He could not, however, compete with coal carvers who possessed machinery for mass production. Besides, his dream was to be a sculptor, not merely the producer of coal novelties.

C. Edgar Patience got his first sculpting exposure in 1939 when he and his youngest brother, Harold, constructed a model of New York World's Fair theme, Trylon and Perisphere. The model measured two feet from its base to the top of an obelisk that was formed from a single chunk of anthracite. Cut from a sixty-pound chunk, the polished circular base measured twenty inches in diameter and three inches deep. Six inches in diameter, the round Perisphere held a circular ramp extending thirty-one inches. The most difficult feat was fashioning the ramp from a single piece of coal. The replica of the Trylon and Perisphere was one of the main items of interest in the anthracite exhibit. In 1948 Patience married Alice Patterson; they had no children.

Not until the 1950s was Patience able to fulfill his dream of making a living as a sculptor. He was commissioned to create a four thousand-pound, seven-by-three-foot altar for the King's College Chapel in Wilkes-Barre, Pennsylvania. The front and side surfaces are a series of jewel-like jutting mounds with a cross, while the smooth-surfaced centerpiece is engraved with two inscriptions on the front of the coal block: "CONGREGATIO A SANCTA CRUCE" and "SPES UNICA."

Another monolith on which Patience worked was a three-and-one-half-ton chunk of anthracite, one of the largest ever removed from any mine. The reflective upper surface was hand-buffed and polished by Patience before the piece was shipped to Washington, D.C., in 1960 for placement in the new Arts and Manufacturers Building, where it was to sit just inside the door of the Mining and Industries Hall of Coal. However, since the plans for the Arts and Manufacturers Building never reached fruition, the monolith instead sits in a Smithsonian storage facility in Suitland, Maryland.

A second altar created by Patience in 1961 was placed in the chancel of St. Peter's Lutheran Church in Hanover Township, Pennsylvania. A fourteen-foot, 600-pound carving of "Christ in Blessing" is suspended in midair above an altar faced with twenty-four blocks of anthracite coal.

When dignitaries visited the Wyoming Valley, Congressman Daniel J. Flood regularly called upon Patience to create special gifts for them. Patience made each piece unique, sculpting a vacuum cleaner for the Hoover archives in Canton, Ohio, and the bulldog mascot for the Mack Truck executive offices in Allentown, Pennsylvania. When Lady Bird Johnson visited Wilkes College to dedicate a new science building in 1964, she was presented with an anthracite clock.

During the 1960s Patience's work became known outside the United States. At the 1967 Expo in Montreal he exhibited an anthracite bust of President John F. Kennedy. The 101st Airborne Division presented Queen Juliana of the Netherlands with an anthracite clock and a graduated coal "pearl" necklace to celebrate the twenty-fifth anniversary of Holland's liberation from German occupation in World War II. Another of his works was the seal of Barbados, commissioned for the prime minister Errol Walton Barrow of that island nation in 1966.

One of Patience's greatest challenges occurred in 1970 when he agreed to sculpt a likeness of the Pennsylvania secretary of mines and minerals industries, H. Beecher Charmbury. Because the bust was intended to be a surprise, the sculptor worked from photographs, as he had on previous occasions.

A number of Patience's works are in the collection of the Anthracite Heritage Museum in

Scranton, Pennsylvania. *Coaltown*, including busts of George Washington and "Amalarice," an African woman, first exhibited in 1981 at the Afro-American Historical and Cultural Museum in Philadelphia.

Following a television interview in Pittsburgh on 3 June 1972, Patience developed pneumonia and died in Wilkes-Barre as a result of the damage his lungs had sustained from years of inhaling coal dust from his work as a coal carver. Although he had read the March 1970 *Ebony* article about his work, sadly, he did not live to see his name listed in the 1972 publication of *Who's Who in America*. Much of his remaining work was sold at an exhibition at Kings College on 12 March 1973. Until August 2007, the Patience family would retain a collection of his work, including a small bust of Abraham Lincoln and a pair of African masks. Now they, too, are at the Anthracite Heritage Museum in Scranton. In addition, *Anthracite*, a sculpture of gleaming stippled coal in its natural, unpolished state, was purchased from his widow, Alice Patterson Patience, in 1977 for presentation to President Jimmy Carter when he signed one of the first surface mining laws.

FURTHER READING

Blockson, Charles. *Pennsylvania's Black History* (1975).

DuBose, Carolyn. "Coal-Black Art," *Ebony* (Mar. 1970).

Moss, Emerson I. *African Americans in the Wyoming Valley 1778–1990* (1992).

Moss, Juanita Patience. *Anthracite Coal Art by Charles Edgar Patience* (2006).

Patience, Alice Patterson. *Bittersweet Memories of Home* (1999).

JUANITA PATIENCE MOSS

Patience, Crowder (25 Dec. 1846–29 Jan. 1930), slave, Union soldier, and farmer, was born to unknown parents in Chowan County, North Carolina, possibly on the Briols farm, located three miles from Edenton. Crowder was illiterate, and on his military records his surname is spelled Pacien. Some years after the Civil War, when his children entered school, their teachers spelled it Patience. When he applied for a government pension after the war, a member of the Fifth Massachusetts Colored Calvary by the name of Thomas Patience also gave his birthplace as that the Briols farm. Since the name of Patience is relatively uncommon, it is likely that they were brothers. Unfortunately, no records exist to verify the supposition.

When the Union army penetrated the South, many slaves fled in search of the freedom promised to them if they could reach the Yankees. Crowder

Patience was one of these slaves. At the age of eighteen he enlisted at Plymouth, North Carolina, in the 103rd Pennsylvania Volunteers Regiment. After enlisting in the army he was sent to Roanoke Island, North Carolina, with Company C of the 103d Pennsylvania Volunteers. At the time, one company from each regiment garrisoned at Plymouth spent six months on Roanoke Island, at the mouth of the Albemarle Sound, to maintain the blockade so that the Confederacy could not exchange cotton and tobacco for European guns and ammunition.

Patience was most fortunate to avoid the Battle of Plymouth, which was fought from 17 to 20 April, some three months after his enlistment. The Union forces were defeated, with all either killed or captured and transported to Andersonville Prison in Georgia, including Private JOHN ROLAC, the only known escaped slave to be buried at Andersonville. When the battle erupted there were thirteen black cooks, all ranked as privates, serving in four of the eight white regiments. Military records indicate that they were either captured and returned to slavery or listed as "whereabouts unknown." Private Patience, also a cook, fortunately, was safe on Roanoke Island.

After the war ended, the black soldiers at the Battle of Plymouth were forgotten. Contemporary historians are not aware of them because their service was not well documented. Other blacks who served in white regiments have similarly been forgotten. Because of Patience, whose military papers were preserved by his descendants, those soldiers finally are being remembered. Patience left behind no war stories. Perhaps there were none to tell since boredom was the bane of the Yankees garrisoned on Roanoke Island. They had joined the army to see action. Little did they realize how lucky they were until they learned the disastrous news about the Battle of Plymouth.

When the war was over Patience was mustered out of the army in New Bern, North Carolina, but in order to receive his last pay, he had to travel by train with the 103d to Harrisburg, Pennsylvania. The names of those mustered out on 13 July 1865 on the steps of the Pennsylvania state capitol are included in Luther Dickey's *History of the 103rd Regiment* (1910). Crowder Pacien was listed with the members of Company C; however, no racial identification appears next to his name, and so a reader would have no idea that the Pennsylvania soldiers had taken an African American man back home with them.

Excellent with horses, Patience worked several jobs, such as delivering horses from a breeder to the new owners, before settling in the Wyoming Valley, Pennsylvania, in 1880 with his wife, Elsie Veden, and several children. Three years later he was in the employ of the Carpenter family, original settlers in the area. They were prosperous farmers, and one of Patience's jobs was to plow the land. In addition, for forty-five years he faithfully tended the furnaces for Carpenter's greenhouses and took care of the teams of horses used for delivering produce from the farm to restaurants in nearby cities. The Carpenters thought much of Patience and wanted him to remain in their employ, so they built a brand-new house in the borough of West Pittston for him and his growing family to replace the small cabin in which they had been living.

A soft-spoken gentleman, Patience earned the respect of the citizenry of West Pittston, where he and his wife reared their children surrounded by a tapestry of European cultures. Immigrants had flocked to the Wyoming Valley to work in the anthracite coal mines. At the turn of the twentieth century the Patience family was one of just a few African American families who worked for wealthy whites. Soon, however, they were the only black family in the area, as the older generation died and the younger one moved away to seek better employment.

Well known in the town, Patience would march proudly in the annual Decoration Day (later Memorial Day) parade with his white comrades, all members of the GAR (Grand Army of the Republic). After he was no longer able to march, he rode in an automobile with other veterans until the year before his death at age eighty-three.

Patience was known for his kindness and generosity. A loving husband, father, grandfather, and great-grandfather, he was just like many other men. He deserves recognition, however, not because he accomplished any great thing, but because the story of Private Crowder Patience of the 103d Pennsylvania Volunteer Regiment represents all of the black soldiers who served in white regiments and who had been forgotten for 140 years.

FURTHER READING

Dickey, Luther S. *History of the 103rd Regiment, Pennsylvania Veteran Volunteer Infantry, 1861–1865* (1910).

Jordan, Weymouth, and Gerald Thomas. "Massacre at Plymouth," *The North Carolina Historical Review* (Apr. 1995).

Moss, Emerson. *African Americans in Wyoming Valley 1778–1990* (1992).

Moss, Juanita Patience. *Battle of Plymouth, N.C., April 17–20, 1864: The Last Confederate Victory* (2003).

Moss, Juanita Patience. *Created to Be Free: A Historical Novel about One American Family* (2001).

Moss, Juanita Patience. *The Forgotten Black Soldiers in White Regiments During the Civil War* (2004).

JUANITA PATIENCE MOSS

Patrick, Deval (31 July 1956–), governor of the Commonwealth of Massachusetts, was born in Chicago, Illinois, the only son of Emily Wintersmith Patrick and Laurdine (Pat) Patrick, a musician. Reared on the south side of Chicago by his mother, since his parents separated when he was four, and with his sister, Rhonda Patrick-Sigh, he attended Chicago Public Schools. Challenged by poverty and always seeking educational opportunities, his mother supported his application to *A Better Chance*, an organization dedicated to securing positions in independent and public schools for children of color. In 1970 Milton Academy in Massachusetts became the springboard for his stellar academic career. He graduated from Harvard University in 1978 cum laude with an AB in English and American Literature, becoming the first member of his family to receive a college degree, and Harvard Law School in 1982. During the intervening year between college and law school, he worked with a United Nations program in the Darfur region of the Sudan and traveled in Africa.

Deval Laurdine Patrick's first professional position was as a law clerk for the U.S. Court of Appeals for the Ninth Circuit in Los Angeles, California, where he met his wife, Diane Bemus. A native of New York City, she graduated from Loyola Law School in Los Angeles and specialized in labor and employment law. Following his fiancée's career in 1983, the couple moved to New York City, where he secured a position as a staff attorney with the National Association for the Advancement of Colored People (NAACP) Legal Defense Fund. In a voting rights case, Patrick sued the State of Arkansas under the leadership of Governor William Clinton.

The Patricks were married in Brooklyn on 5 May 1984, and by 1986 the family had declared Massachusetts their home. They soon purchased a house in Milton, situated on Patrick's old high school paper route, residing there with their two daughters, Sarah and Katherine. Patrick continued his legal career as a partner in Boston firm Hill & Barlow, handling commercial and civil rights litigation.

Having continued communications with Patrick since his tenure with the NAACP Legal Defense Fund, in 1994 President Clinton nominated him for the position of assistant attorney general in the Civil Rights Division of the U.S. Department of Justice. After his Senate confirmation, Patrick took over the agency primarily responsible for enforcing federal laws that prohibit discrimination on the basis of race, ethnicity, gender, and disability, reporting to Attorney General Janet Reno. By 1996, alarmed by a growing number of suspicious fires at predominantly black churches in the South, Patrick was at the center of a Justice Department investigation into arsonist activities with potential civil rights violations.

The Patrick family returned to Boston in 1997 and, for the next two years, the seasoned litigator practiced as a partner with Day, Berry & Howard. Corporate America's Fortune 50 energy company, Texaco sought his services to address the company's tarnished record and reputation burdened by an unprecedented settlement of $115 million in an employment race discrimination class action suit. Patrick took the reins as vice president and general counsel responsible for global legal affairs. In 2001 he moved to the multinational soft drink giant, Coca-Cola Company, where he served as executive vice president, general counsel, and secretary.

Patrick's plans to seriously explore a run for the highest office in the Commonwealth of Massachusetts coincided with the 2004 Democratic National Convention held in Boston. He consulted first with family and friends to discuss his ambitions and plans and then visited with a broad cross-section of leaders. The Democratic Party had already selected its candidate and asked the newcomer to state politics to wait his turn. Undeterred, Patrick sought the support of the many disengaged citizens. Crisscrossing the state, he met with residents in their homes, community centers, restaurants, businesses, and anywhere groups gathered to hear his message.

Patrick's campaign of civic engagement ignited a disinterested electorate resulting in a powerfully organized show of support at party caucuses held in February 2006. Those delegates elected at the caucuses gathered at the Democratic State Convention in June, casting their votes and displaying overwhelming support for Patrick when he took the podium as the favored winner. After his resounding success at the convention, two opposing Democratic candidates, better funded and better known, attempted to gain ground. Patrick's campaign continued to recruit volunteers and to raise dollars using the Internet, decisively capturing 50 percent of the vote in the Democratic Primary in September. The primary won, there were three opposing candidates in the general election. The most viable was Republican Lieutenant Governor Kerry Healey, leaving Massachusetts to elect either the first woman or African American chief executive officer.

On 7 November 2006 Patrick's inspired campaign for the governorship increased voter turnout, causing some polling places to run out of ballots. With 40,000 contributors and volunteers waging a grassroots strategic organizing campaign that spanned the Commonwealth of Massachusetts, Patrick emerged as the first Democratic governor in sixteen years, since Michael Dukakis returned to private life in 1991. Patrick was the only African American governor elected in 2006 and only the second in the nation's history.

Patrick took his oath of office on 4 January 2007 with his hand placed upon the *Mendi Bible*, given to President John Quincy Adams for his successful defense before the U.S. Supreme Court of the kidnapped Africans in the *Amistad* decision of 1841. The inauguration ceremony was held before a joint session of the Massachusetts legislature on the steps of the state capitol before a massive crowd of devoted supporters.

Patrick was re-elected Governor of Massachusetts in November 2010. While his share of the vote dropped from 56 percent to 48 percent, many pundits had predicted his defeat, in part because of the significant national opposition to the Democratic Party, which had resulted in a Republican victory in the state's U. S. Senate race to replace Ted Kennedy earlier that year, and which delivered the House to the GOP in the 2010 midterm elections. Patrick nonetheless overcame his frosty relations with the Democratic leaders of the state house and senate (notably over plans to allow casinos in the state); his increase of the state sales tax; and an increase in state unemployment, to defeat his opponent by 150,000 votes.

FURTHER READING

Jacobs, Sally. "Patrick Shaped by Father's Absence," *Boston Globe*, 25 Mar. 2007.

Kinnon, Joy Bennett. "The New Black Power: The Search for 'One Black Leader' May Be Over as a

New Wave of Political Candidates Takes the Stage," *Ebony* (Nov. 2006).

Mooney, Brian C. "Patrick sparks a Democratic resurgence in cities across state," *Boston Globe*, 9 Nov. 2006.

Phillips, Frank. "Bay State win makes history," *Boston Globe*, 8 Nov. 2006.

BEVERLY MORGAN-WELCH

Patrick, Jennie R. (1 Jan. 1949–), chemical engineer, activist, and the first African American woman to receive a Ph.D. in Chemical Engineering, was born in Gadsden, Alabama, the fourth of five children of James and Elizabeth Patrick. Her parents had little formal education beyond the sixth grade; her father worked as a janitor and her mother was a maid. They wanted their children to be educated and successful. They talked repeatedly about using the mind as a way out of poverty. As a child, Jennie loved to read and enjoyed encyclopedias because they stretched her imagination and opened her world. During her early childhood years, she attended the segregated elementary and junior high schools in her home town. When she was of high school age in 1964, she was able to attend an integrated high school because the full effect of the *Brown v. Board of Education* decision had been implemented. She preferred the newly integrated Gadsden High School because she was now interested in pursuing a career in science and because Gadsden High possessed well-equipped laboratories. She had to survive this high school academically, emotionally, psychologically, and physically (there was always the threat of violence and harassment from the white students), which created a great challenge for her. Neither the teachers nor the students wanted her to succeed. She managed to overcome these obstacles by learning to respect herself so that her attitude forced them to respect her. She chose a technical college preparatory curriculum in spite of discouragement from her teachers and counselors. She graduated from Gadsden High in 1967 with honors.

She received an offer to attend the University of California at Berkeley on a scholarship, but her mother wanted her to stay close to home, so she chose Tuskegee University and majored in chemistry. When Tuskegee started a chemical engineering department, she was the first to sign up for that major, although she had little familiarity with the subject. The chemical engineering program soon closed, so she left Tuskegee in order to continue her studies at the University of California, Berkeley.

Berkeley did not provide scholarships for transfer students, so she had to work odd jobs for a year in order to earn the funds to attend. She only had enough money to survive for two thirds of the year, but she managed to struggle through to get a B.S. in Chemical Engineering in 1973, despite the fact that she experienced racism at Berkeley.

She worked at two summer jobs while at Berkeley, as an assistant engineer for Dow Chemical (1972) and an assistant engineer for Stouffer Chemical Company (1973). She decided to pursue a Ph.D. in chemical engineering and chose the Massachusetts Institute of Technology (MIT) because it was one of the best engineering schools in the nation and the climate for black students in science and engineering was purportedly good. She had a position as a research associate at MIT from 1973 to 1979. She enjoyed the intellectual challenge at MIT and succeeded in spite of the racism she endured. In one case, a professor refused to acknowledge her as a student in his class until she managed to get a good grade on her first test. She graduated in 1979 with a Ph.D. in Chemical Engineering, the first black woman to do so. Her dissertation was entitled "Superheat-Limit Temperature for Nonideal-Liquid Mixtures and Pure Components." She also worked during the summer as a Chevron research engineer and an Arthur D. Little engineer in between semesters at MIT.

Upon graduation, she obtained a position at General Electric Research Institute in Schenectady, New York. She became an expert in the field of supercritical fluid extracting technology and as such was a pioneer in this new field. Choosing to leave for career advancement reasons in 1983, she next worked at the Phillip Morris research facility in Richmond, Virginia, where she headed the supercritical fluid extraction program and designed a state of the art pilot plant. In 1985 she moved again to Rohm and Hass Company Research Laboratory Research Labs in Bristol, Pennsylvania. There she became research manager of the company's first fundamental research engineering group. So she was able to combine technical expertise with managerial and administrative expertise. While there, her group helped to develop improved products, improved processes, and devised more cost-efficient processes. She also worked as an adjunct professor at two universities, Rensselaer Polytechnic Institute (1980–1983) and Georgia Institute of Technology (1983–1987). Her next corporate move was to Southern Company Services as assistant to the executive vice president, a position she held from 1990 until 1993. In that latter year she became 3M Eminent Scholar and Professor of Chemical Engineering at Tuskegee University. This was an endowed chair by the 3M Company and the state of Alabama in which she taught students and did research in material science. At Tuskegee she was able to share her experiences with students and make a difference in their lives.

Patrick was a victim of an industrial accident which exposed her to hazardous and toxic chemicals. She became a victim of a debilitating environmental illness known as "multiple chemical sensitivity." She managed to teach and work in spite of this illness, and she set about to tell the African American community that they should be aware of the environmental hazards of normal household cleaning products and personal hygiene products. She devoted much of her time and energies to talking to young black students to motivate them to study math and science and to remind them that they can succeed in spite of all odds, using her own life as an example. Patrick also strove to make young scientists aware of the possible health hazards of working in the chemical industry so that they took all precautions to work safely.

During her time at MIT, Patrick was recognized by the American Institute of Engineers as Outstanding Research Associate. In 1980 she received the National Organization for the Professional Advancement of Black Chemists and Chemical Engineers (NOBCChE) Outstanding Women in Science and Engineering Award, and in 1983 she was featured by the CIBA-GEIGY Corporation in its Exceptional Black Scientists Poster series. Patrick was a member of the American Institute of Chemical Engineers, Sigma Xi, and NOBCChE. Patrick was married but had no children. She lived in the Atlanta area, where she worked as an education consultant and motivational speaker.

FURTHER READING

Jordan, Diann. *Sisters in Science* (2006).
Sammons, Vivian Ovelton. *Blacks in Science and Medicine* (1990).
Smith, Jessie Carney, ed. *Notable Black American Women, Book II* (1996).
Warren, Wini. *Black Women Scientists in the United States* (1999).

JEANNETTE ELIZABETH BROWN

Patterson, Floyd (4 Jan. 1935–11 May 2006), two-time heavyweight boxing champion of the world, was born into poverty near Waco, North Carolina, the third of eleven children born to Thomas Patterson, a laborer for the Seaboard Railway and later a sanitation worker and truck helper at a fish market, and Anna Belle Patterson, a maid and bottling-plant worker. Shortly after his first birthday, Patterson's family moved to the Bedford-Stuyvesant section of Brooklyn, New York, where they lived in a series of cold-water, four-room railroad flats. As a boy, Patterson felt that he was a burden to his family, and he would often leave the apartment for days at a time, stealing fruit and milk to feed himself and sleeping in the basement of his elementary school or in subway stations. Patterson's truancy and his family's constant moving led him in and out of several public schools. Following a series of brushes with the law for petty crimes, he was sent to the Wiltwyck School for Boys in Esopus, New York, a reformatory where he discovered boxing and began to turn his life around. In 1947 Patterson was released to P.S. 614, an experimental vocational public high school in New York City. He then attended Alexander Hamilton Vocational High School for a year before deciding to devote himself full-time to boxing in hopes of one day turning professional.

Following a successful amateur career in which he won the Inter-City Golden Gloves tournament and a gold medal in the 1952 Olympics in Helsinki, Finland, Patterson turned professional under the tutelage of the trainer Cus D'Amato. Four years later, on 30 November 1956, after thirty victories in thirty-one fights, Patterson was matched with ARCHIE MOORE for the heavyweight championship vacated by Rocky Marciano. He defeated Moore by fifth-round knockout to become the youngest man ever to win the heavyweight title. Earlier in the year Patterson had married his high school sweetheart, Sandra Elizabeth Hicks, in a civil ceremony. She introduced Patterson to Catholicism, and the two were again married in a religious ceremony the following July. Under D'Amato's guidance, Patterson defended the championship four times over the next three years. On 26 June 1960 Patterson lost the title when he was floored seven times by Sweden's Ingemar Johansson and knocked out in the third round. A year later Patterson avenged the loss by knocking out Johansson to become the first fighter to regain the heavyweight championship. He then successfully defended the title twice more before taking on CHARLES "SONNY" LISTON.

The fight between Patterson and Liston, held on 25 September 1962, took on great symbolic importance because of the contrast in what the two fighters were believed to represent. In the midst of the civil rights movement, many blacks and whites felt that Patterson was a good role model and representative of his race. They also considered Liston, who was often surly to the press and public and was a convicted felon whose managers had ties to organized crime, someone who would somehow set back race relations. When President John F. Kennedy invited Patterson to the White House before the bout, he told the fighter, "Make sure you keep that championship" (Ashe, 53). The United Nations diplomat and Nobel Peace Prize winner RALPH BUNCHE similarly advised Patterson of the importance of defeating Liston. The fight generated nearly $5 million in revenues, then an all-time record, and was one of the most heavily publicized contests in boxing history. The bout, however, was no contest, as the bigger, stronger, and more skilled Liston knocked Patterson out in the first round. Patterson fared no better in the rematch a year later, again falling to Liston in the opening round. Patterson would never again hold the championship.

On 22 November 1965 Patterson challenged MUHAMMAD ALI, who had previously defeated Liston, for the heavyweight title. As with his first bout against Liston, the fight against Ali was injected with extra-athletic meaning by the press, the public, and perhaps most of all Patterson. In a series of articles for *Sports Illustrated*, Patterson told readers that he was a better person and a better champion for America than the militant and defiant Ali and likened the bout to a moral crusade. He refused to call Ali by his chosen name, instead repeatedly calling the champion by his birth name, Cassius Clay. Patterson also disparaged the Nation of Islam, of which Ali was a member. While this may have pleased large portions of black and white America, it also stirred resentment among many people and served to infuriate and motivate Ali, who vowed to punish Patterson when they met. In his classic book *Soul on Ice*, ELDRIDGE CLEAVER referred to Patterson as a white hope and claimed that blacks wanted "to see Uncle Tom defeated, to be given symbolic proof of the victory of the autonomous Negro over the subordinate Negro" (91). Ali dominated the fight, winning nearly every round. Many observers felt that he carried Patterson in order to inflict as much damage on the challenger as possible. The referee stopped the contest in the twelfth round.

Patterson fought on for seven more years, and he had some impressive performances against good boxers, although he would never again seriously challenge for the undisputed heavyweight championship. His career ended in 1972, and he retired financially secure and in relatively good health. Patterson remained close to the sport and in 1995 was named chairman of the New York State Athletic Commission. He held the position for three years before being forced to resign because of memory-loss problems stemming from his long career in the ring. He was diagnosed shortly thereafter with Alzheimer's disease, which led to his death in May 2006.

FURTHER READING

Patterson, Floyd, with Milton Gross. *Victory Over Myself* (1962).

Ashe, Arthur R., Jr. *A Hard Road to Glory: The African-American Athlete in Boxing* (1988).

Cleaver, Eldridge. *Soul on Ice* (1968).

MICHAEL EZRA

Patterson, Frederick Douglass (10 Oct. 1901–26 Apr. 1988), educator, was born in Washington, D.C., the youngest of six children of William Ross Patterson and Mamie Brooks Patterson, educators. Like countless other African Americans, the couple had migrated North in search of an improved educational, cultural, social, and racial climate for their children. Patterson's birthplace was within three blocks of the home of FREDERICK DOUGLASS, for whom he was named. Patterson was only two when his parents died of tuberculosis. In a detailed will, each child was assigned to a relative or family friend. Although the will stipulated that Patterson was to be raised by "Aunt" Julia Dorsey, he was moved several times and ultimately his oldest sister, Wilhemina, assumed responsibility for him. From her meager earnings as a schoolteacher, she financed his tuition and room and board at the elementary school operated by what is now Huston-Tillotson College in Austin, Texas. In the eighth grade he lived with Wilhelmina. Perhaps the many changes in his living arrangement had a negative effect; in high school he was, at best, a mediocre student. After enrolling at his parents' alma mater, Prairie View State Normal and Industrial Institute and with his sister's constant encouragement, he became more dedicated to his studies and developed an interest in veterinary medicine.

After completing Prairie View's two-year program, Patterson found summer employment in Des Moines, Iowa, and earned tuition for college. With Wilhelmina financially subsidizing his part-time earnings as a waiter, he enrolled at Iowa State, where he was one of the few African American students and the only one in the veterinary medicine department. He started a rug and clothes cleaning business, a short-lived venture which interfered with his studies. Following graduation in 1923, Patterson taught for two years at Virginia State College. With a fellowship from the Rockefeller-funded General Education Board, he returned to Iowa State, earning a master's degree in 1927.

In 1928 Patterson was hired to head the veterinary division at Tuskegee Institute and subsequently served as the director of its School of Agriculture. As his level of education increased so did his responsibility. Patterson earned a doctorate of veterinary medicine from Iowa State and a Ph.D. in Bacteriology from Cornell University. In 1935 he was named the third president of Tuskegee, a position he held until 1953.

Under Patterson's leadership many progressive programs were instituted at Tuskegee. He founded the Commercial Dietetics program, enabling domestic science students to broaden their career opportunities to include catering and restaurant work. The school began to offer graduate courses and in 1944 the School of Veterinary Medicine was started. More than three-quarters of the nation's African American veterinarians were Tuskegee graduates. Patterson convinced the federal government to establish an air base at Tuskegee; nearly 1,000 African Americans received training there as combat pilots. Some distinguished themselves as the Tuskegee Airmen during World War II. As a result of their skills and service, the desegregation of the armed forces was hastened. Viewing education as a mechanism for improving the quality of life for all people, Patterson created and implemented a program for constructing durable, low cost housing from concrete blocks manufactured at Tuskegee. This program was replicated throughout the country and internationally.

While Tuskegee's board of directors consisted of black and white northerners and southerners who met together without bowing to southern customs of racial separation, white trustees who stayed overnight were housed in the campus guest house while the African Americans slept in student dormitories. At mealtime, the white trustees dined in the guest house and the African Americans ate in the faculty dining room. Patterson successfully, and without fanfare, integrated the dining facilities. He worked to increase African American participation in Red Cross projects and was instrumental in improving racial interaction in the organization.

He further demonstrated his ability to successfully negotiate racial barriers by convincing the Alabama Legislature to raise Tuskegee's annual appropriation from $2,500 to $110,000. This led to increased funding from northern philanthropists including John Rockefeller and Andrew Carnegie who were willing to make substantial donations to African American schools.

Having obtained his education as a result of great struggle and personal sacrifice, Patterson was committed to providing increased educational opportunities for others of modest means. He devised and established the first collaborative effort to raise funds for college scholarships, the United Negro College Fund. Annually this fund supports approximately 65,000 students at 950 schools. As of March 2006, the fund had net assets in excess of $234 million. Additionally, Patterson developed the College Endowment Funding Plan and convinced insurance companies to lend funds to black colleges at lower than market rates.

In honor of ROBERT RUSSA MOTON, his predecessor at Tuskegee, Patterson established the Moton Memorial Institute to recruit and retain qualified African American students at historically black colleges and universities. As director of the Phelps-Stokes Educational Fund, he worked to improve education for Native Americans, Africans, and low-income whites as well as African American students. Through service on President Truman's Education Commission, he helped develop the nation's community college system.

Patterson married the former Catherine Moton, daughter of Tuskegee's president in June 1935.

Patterson died of a heart attack in New Rochelle, New York, after which his cremated remains were housed at Tuskegee. Prior to his death, his contributions to the United States were recognized when he received the nation's highest civilian honor, the Presidential Medal of Freedom.

FURTHER READING

Patterson, Frederick D. *Chronicles of Faith, The Autobiography of Frederick D. Patterson* (1991).

Patterson, Frederick D. *The College Endowment Funding Plan* (1976).

Obituary: *Washington Post*, 27 Apr. 1988.

DONNA TYLER HOLLIE

Patterson, Gilbert Earl (22 Sept. 1939–20 Mar. 2007), pastor and church leader, was born in Humboldt, Tennessee, the youngest son of Mary Louise Williams and William Archie Patterson, a pastor in the Church of God in Christ (COGIC). The family later moved to Memphis, where Patterson attended Lincoln Elementary School. In 1951 he was saved during a revival at Holy Temple, the church pastored by his father. In 1952 the Pattersons moved to Detroit, where Elder William A. Patterson became the pastor of New Jerusalem Church of God in Christ. The younger Patterson attended and graduated from Hutchins Intermediate School and Central High School. He also sang with the youth group of his father's church. He received a divine call to the ministry, was licensed by his father in 1957, and entered Detroit Bible College. In 1958 he was ordained and three years later returned to Memphis to serve as co-pastor at Holy Temple, where his father had remained the senior pastor. Patterson also enrolled at LeMoyne—Owen College in Memphis. Until the mid-1990s Patterson's church contacts were within his own ethnic community because white churches were slow to welcome African Americans.

For three years Holy Temple, which had eighty adult members, experienced no growth, which led Patterson to ask the congregation to enter a fast of three days and three nights. Subsequently he sponsored a thirty-day tent revival that won fifty-five converts to the congregation. In 1964 the young pastor established the G. E. Patterson Evangelistic Crusade and a radio ministry. By 1965 he became known as "God's Young Apostle" because of his ability to draw large crowds and to win large numbers of converts. In 1967 he married Mary Louise Dowdy, a salesperson at a department store in Memphis. She worked for many years as his secretary and became a strong supporter of his ministry. No children were born from this union. Patterson and his wife established Bountiful Blessings, an umbrella organization for their growing ministry.

In 1968 local sanitation workers called a strike seeking better pay, better equipment, and the right to organize a labor union. Patterson was the only COGIC minister to support the strike from the beginning, partly because some of the strikers were his parishioners. Because most of the strikers were black, the National Association for the Advancement of Colored People (NAACP) got involved and the strike took the character of a fight for civil rights. When labor organizers were legally prohibited from leading the strike, local ministers moved to the forefront, called and supported marches and boycotts, raised funds, shared announcements on their radio broadcasts, and offered their churches for rallies. In addition to the NAACP, the National Urban League and the Southern Christian Leadership Conference supported the sanitation workers. Patterson shared strike updates on his radio broadcasts, attended rallies, and provided spiritual support to the workers. He later joined the nine-member strategy committee that invited Dr. MARTIN LUTHER KING JR. to Memphis. On 3 April 1968, the day before his assassination, King spoke in Mason Temple, a COGIC auditorium that seated five thousand. Patterson and many members of the COGIC were in Mason Temple when King gave the "I've Been to the Mountain Top" speech. On 12 April 1968 the strike ended when the city granted the sanitation employees a pay increase and the right to join the American Federation of State, County, and Municipal Employees (AFSCME). Local 1733 of the AFSCME, which represented the sanitation workers, became the first union to represent employees of the municipality of Memphis. It opened the door for other city employees to unionize. Thus Patterson's participation in the strike contributed to the future unionization of city employees.

In 1975 Patterson resigned from Holy Temple, left the COGIC, and opened Bountiful Blessings Deliverance Church. At its first service Bountiful Blessings welcomed more than four hundred members. Within two years the membership grew to two thousand and a twelve-hundred-seat edifice costing $1.2 million was built in 1978. Patterson planted seven churches and in 1986 he returned to the COGIC on the condition that he be made a bishop. He changed his church's name to Temple of Deliverance Cathedral of Bountiful Blessings Church of God in Christ. Two years later his uncle, Presiding Bishop JAMES OGLETHORPE PATTERSON appointed him bishop over Tennessee's Fourth Jurisdiction. Bishop Gilbert E. Patterson sold videotapes of his sermons when local television stations refused to sell air time to blacks and reached a larger audience with the publication of a magazine from 1988 onward.

The 1990s were productive years for Bountiful Ministries. Patterson became the first COGIC minister to host regular shows on the Black Entertainment Network and Trinity Broadcasting Network and acquired a gospel radio station. In 1992 COGIC delegates, noting Patterson's progressive ministry, elected him to the General Board, the ruling body of the denomination. Two years later Patterson and Samuel Middlebrook, the white pastor of Raleigh Assembly of God, co-chaired the local committee for a Memphis meeting of the Pentecostal Fellowship of North America (PFNA). This meeting saw the disbanding of the white PFNA and its reorganization into the inter-racial Pentecostal and Charismatic Churches of North America (PCCNA). Founded in 1948, the PFNA declined to receive black members for more than forty years. In 1994 COGIC became one of the few black groups to join the PCCNA, which voted COGIC Bishop Ithiel C. Clemmons as chairman and Bishop Bernard E. Underwood of the International Pentecostal Holiness Church as co-chairman. In politics Patterson and the COGIC supported Democrat Bill Clinton's presidential campaigns in 1992 and 1996. Patterson ran for Presiding Bishop in 1996 and lost the elections by one vote to Bishop Chandler Owens. In 1998 he founded Podium Records, which released several important projects. In 1999 he inaugurated a new five-thousand-seat church built at the cost of $13 million. During his lifetime Temple of Deliverance grew to more than eighteen thousand members.

The first decade of the twenty-first century witnessed the crowning of Patterson's ministry. In 2000 he was elected COGIC Presiding Bishop for a four-year term. This victory was historic because it was the first time that a COGIC presiding bishop was unseated. Patterson chose Bishop Charles Blake of Los Angeles as First Assistant Presiding Bishop and according to Blake, Patterson brought "an air of efficiency and organization and administration to the life of the denomination" (Flores, *Newsweek*, 5 Sept. 2005). Patterson contributed to the internal growth of the denomination through organizing the following agencies or programs: All Saints Bible College; Church Growth and Development; Office of Ecumenical Relations and Urban Affairs; acquisition of new property for the COGIC Publishing House; and redevelopment of church property in downtown Memphis. The new presiding bishop also worked hard to increase the visibility of the COGIC in the public square. In July 2001 Patterson endorsed President George W. Bush's Faith-Based Initiative and founded COGIC Charities the following year. In May 2002 he preached "The God Loves New York Revival Crusade" in Madison Square Garden in an attempt to bring spiritual healing to the people of New York after the infamous terrorist act of 11 September 2001. In January 2003 Patterson, on behalf of the COGIC, sent a letter to President Bush questioning the undefined goals of the proposed Iraq War and the claim of a moral justification for preemptive strike. In doing so Patterson distanced himself from the majority of white evangelicals who supported military action against Iraq. That same month, the COGIC leadership criticized the Justice Department's negative stand on affirmative action in a Supreme Court case involving the University of Michigan. In March 2003 Patterson forwarded a letter to Saddam Hussein asking him to comply with Resolution 1441, which called for United Nations inspection of Iraqi facilities and for Iraq to prove that it had no existing weapons of mass destruction. In 2004 COGIC released a statement against homosexuality and civil union of same-sex couples. Later that year, COGIC delegates showed their approval of their presiding bishop by reelecting him to a second four-year term. President Bush honored Bishop Patterson by having him deliver the invocation at the presidential inaugural service in 2005.

The founding of COGIC Charities allowed the COGIC to donate $1 million to the victims of Hurricane Katrina (2005) and to assist East African countries affected by a major tsunami and neglected by most international relief efforts. In 2005 COGIC donated $150,000 and $100,000 to the United Nations Food and Agriculture Organization and the Horn of Africa Relief and Development Organization, respectively, for rebuilding the infrastructure of East Africa. Patterson, always a singer, won the 2007 Stellar Award for Traditional Male Vocalist for the record "Bishop GE Patterson and Congregation—Singing the Old Time Way, Volume 2." Patterson's extensive media ministry widely publicized the image of a progressive COGIC in America and overseas. He died from heart failure in Memphis. His nephew, Elder Milton Hawkins, replaced him as pastor; Bishop Blake moved up as Presiding Bishop; and his wife, Mary D. Patterson, took over Bountiful Blessings, the corporation they had founded together.

FURTHER READING

Campo-Flores, Arian. "A Passionate Voice and a Moral Vision," *Newsweek*, 5 Sept. 2005.

Dries, Bill. "'Pursue Peace,' COGIC Head Urges Hussein," *The Commercial Appeal*, 1 Mar. 2003.

Jackson, Hattie Elie. *65 Dark Days in '68: Reflections, Memphis Sanitation Strike* (2004).

Robeck, C.M. Jr. "Clemmons, Ithiel Conrad" in *The New International Dictionary of Pentecostal and Charismatic Movements* (2002).

Obituary: *Los Angeles Times*, 22 Mar. 2007.

DAVID MICHEL